D0222875

CONSTITUTIONAL LAW

CONSTITUTIONAL LAW

13th Edition

Jacqueline R. Kanovitz

AMSTERDAM • BOSTON • HEIDELBERG • LONDON
NEW YORK • OXFORD • PARIS • SAN DIEGO
SAN FRANCISCO • SINGAPORE • SYDNEY • TOKYO

Anderson Publishing is an imprint of Elsevier

ELSEVIER

Acquiring Editor: Shirley Decker-Lucke
Development Editor: Greg Chalson
Project Manager: Jessica Vaughan
Designer: Kristen Davis

Anderson Publishing is an imprint of Elsevier
225 Wyman Street, Waltham, MA 02451, USA

© 2012 Elsevier, Inc. All rights reserved.

No part of this publication may be reproduced or transmitted in any form or by any means, electronic or mechanical, including photocopying, recording, or any information storage and retrieval system, without permission in writing from the publisher. Details on how to seek permission, further information about the Publisher's permissions policies and our arrangements with organizations such as the Copyright Clearance Center and the Copyright Licensing Agency, can be found at our website: www.elsevier.com/permissions.

This book and the individual contributions contained in it are protected under copyright by the Publisher (other than as may be noted herein).

Notices
Knowledge and best practice in this field are constantly changing. As new research and experience broaden our understanding, changes in research methods or professional practices, may become necessary. Practitioners and researchers must always rely on their own experience and knowledge in evaluating and using any information or methods described herein. In using such information or methods they should be mindful of their own safety and the safety of others, including parties for whom they have a professional responsibility.

To the fullest extent of the law, neither the Publisher nor the authors, contributors, or editors, assume any liability for any injury and/or damage to persons or property as a matter of products liability, negligence or otherwise, or from any use or operation of any methods, products, instructions, or ideas contained in the material herein.

Library of Congress Cataloging-in-Publication Data
Kanovitz, Jacqueline R.
    Constitutional law / Jacqueline R. Kanovitz. – Thirteenth edition.
        pages cm
    Includes bibliographical references and index.
    ISBN 978-1-4557-3007-0
    1. Criminal investigation–United States. 2. Constitutional law–United States. I. Title.
    KF9625.K36 2012
    342.73–dc23

                                                                                    2011046254

British Library Cataloguing-in-Publication Data
A catalogue record for this book is available from the British Library.

ISBN: 978-1-4557-3007-0

Printed in the United States of America
12 13 14 15 16   10 9 8 7 6 5 4 3 2 1

Working together to grow
libraries in developing countries

www.elsevier.com | www.bookaid.org | www.sabre.org

ELSEVIER   BOOK AID International   Sabre Foundation

For information on all Anderson publications visit our website at www.andersonpublishing.com

Table of Contents

Chapter 3
Authority to Detain and Arrest; Use of Force 87

Section

Chapter 4
Search and Seizure   163

Chapter 5
Laws Governing Police Surveillance   261

Chapter 8
Right to Counsel   395

Chapter 9
Trial and Punishment   421

Chapter 10
Constitutional Rights and Liabilities in the Workplace   473

PART II

Preface

Extensive footnotes are among this title's chief strengths. Instructors can read the full text of most cases cited in the footnotes, free of charge, at the following sources.

Lexisone (http://www.lexisone.com/caselaw/freecaselaw) contains a searchable database containing the full text of all Supreme Court cases from 1781 to the present and all lower federal court and state court cases decided during the last 10 years.

Findlaw (http://www.findlaw.com/casecode) is another valuable resource. It contains links for all Supreme Court decisions and federal statutes, more recent federal court decisions, and select state materials, plus additional legal resources, such as the Supreme Court's current docket and briefs and transcripts of oral arguments. For cases decided since September 2000, Findlaw offers readers a choice between the full text or an opinion summary, plus access to other secondary materials

For more in-depth research, the reader can go to http://scholar.google.com/, type in the name of a Supreme Court cases, check the box entitled "articles," and have access to numerous law review articles, books, abstracts of court opinions, and references to other online repositories, universities, and Web sites that contain relevant information.

About the Author

Jacqueline Kanovitz is an Emeritus Professor of the Brandeis School of Law where she taught for thirty years and served as Associate Dean for Student Affairs. She also taught at other law schools. She holds a J.D. (summa cum laude) from the University of Louisville School of Law. She is the recipient of numerous awards for teaching and writing excellence and has been a co-author of this textbook since the first edition in 1968.

Case Citation Guide

The following list provides an explanation of case citations used in *Constitutional Law*, Thirteenth Edition, for readers who may be unfamiliar with how court decisions are cited.

U.S.
United States Reports. Published by the United States government, this is the official source of United States Supreme Court decisions. It reports only United States Supreme Court decisions.

S. Ct.
Supreme Court Reporter. Published by West Publishing Company, this publication reports United States Supreme Court decisions.

L. Ed./L. Ed. 2d
United States Reports, Lawyers' Edition, First Series/Second Series. Published by Lawyers Cooperative Publishing Company, this publication reports United States Supreme Court decisions.

F.2d/F.3d
Federal Reports, Second Series/Third Series. Published by West Publishing Company, it reports decisions of the Federal Courts of Appeals.

F. Supp.
Federal Supplement. Published by West Publishing Company, this reports decisions of the Federal District Courts.

Sample Case Citations

Gideon v. Wainwright, 372 U.S. 335 (1963). This case is located in volume 372 of the United States Reports, beginning on page 335. It was decided in 1963.

Gideon v. Wainwright, 83 S. Ct. 792 (1963). Gideon v. Wainwright is published in volume 83 of the Supreme Court Reporter, beginning on page 792.

Gideon v. Wainwright, 9 L. Ed. 2d 799 (1963). Gideon v. Wainwright is also published in volume 9 of Supreme Court Reports, Lawyers' Edition, Second Series, beginning on page 799.

Phillips v. Perry, 106 F.3d 1420 (9th Cir. 1997). This case is located in volume 106 of Federal Reports, Third Series, beginning on page 1420. It was decided by the Ninth Circuit Court of Appeals in 1997.

Brockway v. Shepherd, 942 F. Supp. 1012 (M.D. Pa. 1997). This case is located in volume 942 of Federal Supplement, beginning on page 1012. It was decided in 1997 by the Federal District Court for the Middle District of Pennsylvania.

Table of Cases

PART I

History, Structure, and Content of the United States Constitution

1

We the People of the United States, in Order to form a more perfect Union, establish Justice, insure domestic Tranquility, provide for the common defence, promote the general Welfare, and secure the Blessings of Liberty to ourselves and our Posterity, do ordain and establish this Constitution for the United States of America.

Preamble to the United States Constitution

Chapter Outline

§ 1.1   History of the United States Constitution

The men who met in Philadelphia in 1787 had ample precedent for the notion of a written constitution. Americans had been living under colonial charters for more than 100 years. After declaring their independence, the 13 former colonies immediately began working on constitutions to prepare for statehood. New Hampshire was the first to complete this process.[1] By 1779, all 13 former colonies had constitutions in place. The governments established by the early state constitutions were patterned after the English parliamentary system. Nearly all provided for a bicameral legislature that was responsible for selecting the governor.

§ 1.2   — Early Steps Toward National Unity

The federal union established by the Constitution of 1789 was not the first attempt at alliance. In 1643, the colonies of Massachusetts, New Plymouth, Connecticut, and New Haven formed a coalition, known as the New England Confederacy, for mutual defense against the Dutch and Indians. The New England Confederacy was a loose association whose chief function was to provide protection against external threats. The member colonies maintained exclusive control over their internal affairs.

The Revolutionary War provided the first major impetus for unification. Coordinating the war effort required something more than 13 independent nations fighting separately toward a common goal. All colonies except Georgia sent delegates to the First Continental Congress, which assembled in Philadelphia in 1774.[2] Our colonial forefathers were apprehensive about establishing a strong central government with sovereign authority over them. Preparing to wrest power from one sovereign, they were in no hurry to turn it over to another. Consequently, they gave the Continental Congress only powers that were strictly necessary for carrying on the war. The Continental Congress functioned as an agent of the states, with the states retaining sovereignty.

§ 1.3   — Articles of Confederation

It soon became apparent that greater centralization was needed. In 1776, a committee was appointed to study this problem. This committee wrote the Articles of Confederation, which went into effect in March of 1781. While the Articles of Confederation set up a national government, the government's powers over domestic affairs were so limited that the government was doomed to fail before it began. Distrustful of a strong central government, the states refused to delegate the vital power to levy taxes, regulate commerce, or pass laws affecting domestic affairs.[3] The Union

---

[1]   Eriksson, American Constitutional History, ch. 7 (1933).
[2]   Evans, Cases on Constitutional Law, ch. 1 (1933).
[3]   Eriksson, *supra* note 1.

established under the Articles of Confederation was little more than a loosely joined league of sovereign and independent states. The chief function of the national government was to represent the league of states in foreign affairs.

After the War of Independence was won, the American people were confronted with the realization that the government they had hastily thrown together for the purpose of carrying on the war was too weak to protect their common interests in peacetime. Fortunately, the leaders of this period were reasonable people and were able to solve this problem without the power struggles and bloodshed that so often follow a revolution.

§ 1.4   — Drafting the United States Constitution

In February of 1787, the Congress established under the Articles of Confederation adopted a resolution calling for a convention to consider revision. Three months later, 55 delegates, representing every state except Rhode Island, assembled in Philadelphia and selected George Washington as their unanimous choice to preside over the Convention. The session lasted nearly four months.

The most immediate question facing the Convention was whether the Articles of Confederation could be salvaged or whether it was necessary to begin anew. James Madison recommended salvaging the best feature of the Articles of Confederation — the idea of separating the powers of the national government into three branches — and building a new constitution around it. After heated debate and compromise on such issues as the amount and kinds of powers to delegate to the national government, the basis for representation in the national legislature, and the relation between the nation and the states, the Convention ended with a constitution that bore little resemblance to the document the delegates had been assembled to revise. The proposed Constitution conferred broad powers on the federal government.

§ 1.5   — Ratification by the States

Although drafting the Constitution was a monumental task, an even greater one remained. Public sentiment was divided about the wisdom of conferring broad powers on the national government. James Madison, Alexander Hamilton, and John Jay undertook the task of selling the Constitution to the people. In their historic Federalist Papers, they argued that a strong central government was necessary to ensure political stability and national security. Their opponents countered that:

1.   Granting the federal government the power to tax was dangerous.
2.   The Constitution lacked a Bill of Rights and the assurance of a fair trial.
3.   Concentrating so much power in the federal government threatened the sovereignty of the states.

The ratification process moved forward in the face of heated debate. On June 21, 1788, New Hampshire became the ninth state to ratify the Constitution. Although ratification by nine states was sufficient to make the Constitution operative in the states that had ratified it, New York and Virginia had to be won over in order to ensure the political future of the new government. On June 25, 1788, Virginia ratified the Constitution by a narrow margin. On July 2, 1788, the Constitution was declared to have been duly ratified. New York ratified the Constitution less than a month later. North Carolina and Rhode Island remained outside the Union, watching from the sidelines for many months. The passage by Congress of a tariff on foreign imports, including goods imported from North Carolina and Rhode Island, drove them into the union. North Carolina and Rhode Island ratified the Constitution on November 21, 1789, and May 29, 1790, respectively.[4]

On September 13, 1788, the Continental Congress passed a resolution putting the new Constitution into effect. On April 30, 1789, George Washington was inaugurated as the first president of the United States. Within a span of 25 years, the 13 former colonies accomplished two major victories: they won the War of Independence and established a firm and stable government that has endured for more than 200 years.

§ 1.6   Structure and Content of the Constitution

The United States Constitution is divided into seven parts, called articles. The content of each article is summarized below.[5]

ARTICLE I.   Article I establishes the legislative branch of government. It provides that the legislative powers of the United States shall be vested in Congress, which shall consist of two chambers — the Senate and the House of Representatives. Sections 2 through 7 provide for the number and qualifications of the representatives in each chamber, the method of selecting them, the procedures to be followed in enacting legislation, and the manner of impeachment. Section 8 outlines the powers of Congress in domestic and foreign affairs; sections 9 and 10 impose various limitations on the powers of Congress and of the states.

---

[4]   The dates that the individual states ratified the Constitution are as follows: Delaware — December 7, 1787; Pennsylvania — December 11, 1787; New Jersey — December 18, 1787; Georgia — January 2, 1788; Connecticut — January 9, 1788; Massachusetts — February 6, 1788; Maryland — April 26, 1788; South Carolina — May 23, 1788; New Hampshire — June 21, 1788; Virginia — June 25, 1788; New York — July 26, 1788; North Carolina — November 21, 1789; Rhode Island — May 29, 1790.

[5]   The Constitution is reprinted in the Appendix. You are encouraged to read the full text now and reread the individual sections when they are discussed in later chapters.

ARTICLE II.   Article II establishes the executive branch of government. It provides that the executive powers of the United States shall be vested in the President and outlines the President's powers and duties. The remainder of this article deals with the qualifications of the President and Vice President, the manner of election, oath of office, and the method and grounds for removal.

ARTICLE III.   Article III establishes the judicial branch of government. The Supreme Court is the only court expressly created by the Constitution. Article III vests the judicial power of the United States in the Supreme Court and in such inferior courts as Congress should see fit to establish. It goes on to outline the jurisdiction of the Supreme Court and the lower federal courts. Article III also defines the crime of treason and the proof necessary for a conviction.

ARTICLE IV.   Article IV establishes the duties states owe one another. These duties include the duty to extend full faith and credit to the laws of sister states, to grant the citizens of sister states equal privileges and immunities, and to surrender fleeing felons for interstate extradition. Article IV also provides for the admission of new states, grants Congress plenary power to govern territorial possessions of the United States, and assures each state a republican form of government. Finally, it guarantees the states federal protection against external invasions and internal insurrections.

ARTICLE V.   Article V establishes procedures for amending the Constitution. Constitutional amendments can be proposed in one of two ways: either by a two-thirds vote in both houses of Congress or through a recommendation endorsed by two-thirds of the state legislatures. Once proposed, the amendment must be ratified by the legislatures of three-fourths of the states, or by conventions in three-fourths of the states, in order to become part of the Constitution.

ARTICLE VI.   Article VI contains the "supremacy clause. The supremacy clause provides that the Constitution, laws, and treaties of the United States shall be the supreme law of the land and shall bind state judges, displacing contrary provisions in state constitutions and statutes. Federal and state officials are required to take an oath of office to support the Constitution.

ARTICLE VII.   Article VII has historic importance only. It provides that the Constitution shall go into effect once it is ratified by nine states and shall be operative in the states that ratified it.

§ 1.7   — Separation of the Powers of the National Government

The Framers were apprehensive of concentrated power. They believed that liberty would be more secure if the national government's powers were divided into three branches — a bicameral legislature with the power to make laws, an executive with the power to enforce them, and a judiciary with the power to interpret the laws and apply them in individual cases.[6] They accomplished this in the first three articles. These articles distribute the powers of the national government among three branches — Congress, the Presidency, and the Judiciary — and describe the powers allocated to each. This allocation is fixed. The Constitution prohibits one branch from encroaching on the powers delegated to another branch and from turning its powers over to another branch.

Figure 1.1
Separation of Powers

Our Constitution divides the powers of the national government among three branches —a bicameral legislature with the power to make laws, an executive with the power to enforce them, and a judiciary with the power to interpret and apply them in individual cases.

A. Encroachment on Powers Delegated to a Coordinate Branch

While Congress has the power to enact laws, it may not exercise this power in ways that encroach upon the powers of the President or the judiciary. Congress, for example, cannot overturn the Supreme Court's constitutional rulings by statute. This is because the power to interpret the Constitution belongs to the courts. The Supreme Court is the ultimate expositor on what the Constitution means. When the Supreme Court hands down a ruling interpreting the Constitution, the decision become embedded in the Constitution the same as if it were written there. A constitutional amendment is the only action that can eradicate it.[7] Amending the Constitution is a cumbersome process that has been undertaken successfully only 27 times in American history.

The Supreme Court's statutory interpretations stand on a different footing.[8] Because Congress has the power to enact laws, Congress can change them if it does not like the way they are interpreted. The amended statute will govern the decisions of courts in future cases. However, Congress cannot change the outcome of cases that

---

[6] The Federalist No. 47, at 241 (J. Madison) (J. Gideon ed. 1831).
[7] Dickerson v. United States, 530 U.S. 28, 120 S. Ct. 2326, 147 L. Ed. 2d 405 (2000) (invalidating a federal statute that attempted to overturn the *Miranda* rule).
[8] Engel v. Vitale, 370 U.S. 421, 82 S. Ct. 1261, 8 L. Ed. 2d 601 (1962).

were previously decided under the statute because the judicial power includes the power to render binding decisions, subject to reversal solely by a higher court.[9]

B. *Delegation of Power to Coordinate Branch*

The doctrine of separation of powers also prohibits one branch from turning its powers over to another branch. Congress, for example, cannot delegate responsibility for enacting laws to the executive or judicial branches. The nondelegation doctrine stems from the language of Article I, Section 1, which declares that "[a]ll legislative powers herein granted shall be vested in a Congress of the United States." However, the Constitution does not prohibit Congress from asking coordinate branches for assistance. The volume of regulations needed to run the nation is so mammoth that Congress could not function unless able to legislate in broad terms, leaving discretion to fill in the details to others. Under settled interpretation, Congress does not violate the constitutional separation of powers by delegating rule-making authority to agencies within the executive branch, provided it lays down clear standards to guide the agencies in exercising their delegated authority. When Congress enacted the Controlled Substances Act, for example, it delegated authority to the Attorney General to update the controlled substance schedules by adding new drugs found to meet certain statutory criteria. The addition of new drugs automatically made their manufacture, possession, and distribution a federal criminal offense. The Supreme Court, nevertheless, upheld the delegation because the Controlled Substances Act contained adequate criteria to guide the Attorney General's exercise of the delegated authority.[10]

Regulations adopted by federal agencies to implement the statutes that Congress enacts are published in the Code of Federal Regulations, which is one of today's most important bodies of law.

§ 1.8 — Division of Power between the National Government and the States

The Constitution also divides power between the national government and the states. Understanding the vertical division of power calls for a brief review of history. With the signing of the Declaration of Independence, the colonies renounced their allegiance to England and Parliament's authority over them, and assumed the status of separate sovereign entities. Each state had its own constitution and functioned autonomously. The states retained their sovereignty and independence under the Articles of Confederation. However, they were forced to yield a portion of it to form a federal union. There was no historical precedent for the dual (federal-state) system of government established by the Framers. It remained for the subsequent course of history to

---

[9]   Plaut v. Spendthrift Farms, Inc., 514 U.S. 211, 115 S. Ct. 1447, 131 L. Ed. 2d 328 (1995).

[10]   Touby v. United States, 500 U.S. 160, 111 S. Ct. 1752, 114 L. Ed. 2d 219 (1991).

define and redefine the precise nature of the federal union and the relationship between the nation and the states.

The division of power between the federal government and the states is accomplished through a combination of three sections. The Constitution begins by listing the powers delegated to the federal government. This is accomplished in Article I, Section 8. Article I, Section 10 then withdraws certain powers from the states by prohibiting the states from exercising them. The implication from this scheme is that all powers that have not been delegated to the federal government and that the states are not forbidden to exercise remain in the states, from whence the power originated. This implication was made explicit with the adoption of the Tenth Amendment in 1791, which reads: The powers not delegated to the United States by the Constitution, nor prohibited by it to the States, are reserved to the States respectively, or to the people.

There are three things to keep in mind about the division of power between the federal government and the states. First, the federal government is a government of enumerated and limited powers. It can exercise only those powers that have been delegated. These powers are found primarily in Article I, Section 8, which is the focus of the next section. Second, while the federal government is a government of enumerated and limited powers, it is supreme within its sphere of operation. When Congress enacts a law within the scope of its delegated powers, the federal law supersedes and annuls conflicting state laws. This results from the supremacy clause of Article VI, which declares that [t]his Constitution, and Laws of the United States which shall be made in Pursuance thereof, ... shall be the supreme Law of the Land, ... any Thing in the Constitution or Laws of any state to the Contrary notwithstanding. For example, should Congress decided to pass a law reducing the maximum speed on federal highways to 50 miles per hour, this law would supersede and annul state laws permitting a higher speed. Third, all powers that have not been delegated to the federal government and that the states are not prohibited from exercising belong to the states.

The Civil War put to the test whether a state, having once joined the union and surrendered a portion of its sovereignty, could withdraw from the union by a unilateral act of secession. The indestructible nature of the federal union was decided on the battlefield. The union was permanent.

Figure 1.2
Division of Power Between the Federal Government and the States

> The Constitution divides power between the federal government and the states by: (1) enumerating the powers delegated to the federal government, (2) prohibiting states from exercising certain powers, and (3) providing that [t]he powers not delegated to the United States by the Constitution, nor prohibited by it to the States, are reserved to the States ..." The federal government, though a government of enumerated and limited powers, is supreme in its sphere of operation. When Congress enacts legislation within the scope of its delegated powers, its laws prevail over contrary state laws.

§ 1.9 — Powers Granted to the Federal Government

Brevity is a striking feature of the Constitution. The Framers did not clutter the Constitution with unnecessary details that might have rendered it obsolete within a generation or two. Instead, they laid out a broad framework, having faith that courts would interpret the language wisely and in accordance with the evolving needs of society.

Every law enacted by Congress must be based on one or more of its enumerated powers. The powers granted to the federal government are found primarily in Article I, Section 8. The following section provides an overview of the federal government's powers, emphasizing those that are most important.

A. The Power to Levy Taxes and Make Expenditures for the National Defense and General Welfare

The federal government has the power to tax. This power is essential because no government can survive without a source of revenue. The lack of taxing power was a major weakness of the government established by the Articles of Confederation. Congress occasionally uses the taxing power for purposes other than raising revenue.[11] The Harrison Anti-Narcotics Act[12] is an example. Congress imposed an occupational tax on drug dealers and required them to register with the Internal Revenue Service. The tax was small and Congress' main reason for imposing it was to force drug dealers to register and identify themselves or face federal prosecution for tax evasion. The Harrison Act was, nevertheless, upheld as a constitutionally valid exercise of the taxing power.[13]

B. The Power to Borrow Money on the Credit of the United States

The federal government also has the power to borrow money. This power provides an auxiliary source of revenue when taxes are insufficient to cover the government's operating expenses.

C. The Power to Regulate Interstate and Foreign Commerce

Congress has the power to "regulate Commerce with foreign Nations, and among the several States." This is one of the most important powers granted to the federal government. It gives Congress authority to regulate: (1) the channels and instrumentalities

---

[11] United States v. Doremus, 249 U.S. 86, 39 S. Ct. 214, 63 L. Ed. 493 (1919); Sonzinsky v. United States, 300 U.S. 506, 57 S. Ct. 554, 81 L. Ed. 772 (1937).

[12] 26 U.S.C. § 4701 et seq. (1989).

[13] Minor v. United States, 396 U.S. 87, 90 S. Ct. 284, 24 L. Ed. 2d 283 (1969).

used in interstate commerce; (2) persons and articles that move in interstate commerce; and (3) any commercial activity that substantially affects interstate commerce.[14]

Figure 1.3
Commerce Clause Powers.

> The commerce clause gives Congress regulatory authority over three areas: (1) instrumentalities and channels used in interstate commerce, (2) persons and articles that move in interstate commerce, and (3) commercial activities that substantially affect interstate commerce.

The first category — channels and instrumentalities used in interstate commerce — gives Congress authority to regulate highways, navigable waters, bridges, tunnels, canals, airlines, railroads, trucking concerns, telecommunications networks, and similar mediums. Congress has plenary power to regulate anything that has to do with them, including preventing criminal activity on, involving, or against them, and prohibiting their use for harmful or immoral purposes.

The second category — persons and articles that move in interstate commerce — permits Congress to regulate persons, products, transactions, activities, and services that extend across state lines. This category has provided the basis for a large body of federal criminal statutes, such as the Mann Act, which makes it a federal crime to take an individual across state lines for the purpose of engaging in illegal sexual activity; the National Motor Vehicle Theft Act, which makes it a crime to transport stolen vehicles in interstate commerce; and the Federal Kidnapping Act, which makes it a crime to kidnap persons and take them across state lines.[15] It also provided

---

[14]   *See, generally*, United States v. Darby, 312 U.S. 100, 61 S. Ct. 451, 85 L. Ed. 609 (1941) (upholding Fair Labor Standards Act prohibiting the shipment in interstate commerce of goods produced by employees whose wages and hours of employment did not conform to requirements of the Act); United States v. Wrightwood Dairy Co., 315 U.S. 110, 62 S. Ct. 523, 86 L. Ed. 726 (1942) (stating that the commerce power extends to those *intra*state activities "which so affect *inter*state commerce or the exertion of the power of Congress over it as to make regulation of them an appropriate means to the attainment of a legitimate end, the effective execution of the granted power to regulate interstate commerce execution"); Wickard v. Filburn, 317 U.S. 111, 63 S. Ct. 82, 87 L. Ed. 122 (1942) (holding that Congress could regulate a farmer's cultivation of wheat to feed his own livestock, even though none was sold on the market, because homegrown wheat satisfies needs that otherwise have to be met through purchases, thus affecting market supply, demand, and prices); Gonzales v. Raich, 545 U.S, 1, 125 S. Ct. 2195, 162 L. Ed. 2d 1 (2005) (upholding authority to regulate cultivation of marijuana for personal medical use); **United States v. Lopez, 514 U.S. 549, 115 S. Ct. 1624, 131 L. Ed. 2d (1995)** (noting that there are three categories of permissible commerce clause regulation: (1) channels and instrumentalities of interstate commerce, (2) goods and people who move in interstate commerce, and (3) commercial activities that substantially affect interstate commerce); United States v. Morrison, 529 U.S. 598, 120 S. Ct. 1740, 146 L. Ed. 2d 658 (2000) (same).

[15]   These statutes are contained in 18 U.S.C. § 2423, 18 U.S.C. § 2312, and 18 U.S.C. § 1201.

the constitutional basis for the Public Accommodations Act of 1964 and the Fair Housing Law.[16]

The third category is the broadest. It empowers Congress to regulate any commercial activity that substantially affects interstate commerce, even though it takes place entirely within the confines of a single state. Congress has used the third category to enact minimum wage and hour laws, safety standards in industry, crop restriction programs, antitrust laws, and numerous other measures. The regulatory reach of the third category is limited to commercial activity. Congress cannot regulate *intra*state noncommercial activity, like domestic relations, and child welfare.[17] The power to regulate purely local noncommercial activity belongs to the states and cannot be regulated by Congress under the commerce clause.[18]

D. *The Power to Establish National Rules Regarding Immigration, Naturalization, and Bankruptcy*

The federal government alone can regulate immigration and naturalization. The states are forbidden to legislate on this subject. The federal government also has exclusive legislative control over bankruptcy laws and the establishment of bankruptcy courts. States, nevertheless, remain free to enact laws dealing with the legal rights of debtors and creditors, so long as they do not conflict with federal bankruptcy laws.[19]

E. *The Power to Coin Money, Regulate Currency, and Punish Counterfeiting*

Congress has the exclusive power to regulate currency. This includes the power to coin money, designate the medium of exchange, forbid melting, defacing, and counterfeiting, and establish agencies to enforce the currency laws.

---

[16] *See, e.g.*, Katzenbach v. McClung, 379 U.S. 294, 85 S. Ct. 377, 13 L. Ed. 2d 290 (1964) (upholding congressional power to ban racial discrimination in restaurants that serve food, a substantial portion of which has moved in interstate commerce); Heart of Atlanta Motel, Inc. v. United States, 379 U.S. 241, 85 S. Ct. 348, 13 L. Ed. 2d 258 (1964) (upholding congressional power to prohibit hotels from discriminating based on race because discrimination has a disruptive effect on interstate commerce and travel).

[17] *See, e.g.*, **United States v. Lopez**, *supra* note 14 (holding that enactment of the Gun-Free School Zones Act which made it a federal crime to possess a firearm in a school zone exceeded the powers of Congress under the commerce clause); United States v. Morrison, *supra* note 14 (holding that Congress lacked power to enact the Violence Against Women Act which created a federal civil remedy for victims of gender-motivated violence).

[18] *See* sources *supra* note 17.

[19] Kesler v. Department of Public Safety, 369 U.S. 153, 82 S. Ct. 807, 7 L. Ed. 2d 641 (1962).

F. *The Power to Establish Post Offices and Post Roads*

Congress also has the power to establish post offices and post roads. This power enables Congress to regulate what can be placed in the mail, to make theft from the mails and use of the mails for illegal purposes federal crimes, and to establish federal agencies to enforce the postal laws.

G. *The Power to Secure for Authors and Inventors the Exclusive Right to Writings and Discoveries for a Limited Period of Time*

The Constitution grants Congress the power to secure for authors and inventors the exclusive rights to the fruits of their labors. This provision supplies the constitutional basis for federal patent and copyright laws.

H. *The Power to Establish Judicial Tribunals Inferior to the Supreme Court*

The Supreme Court is the only court expressly created by the Constitution; however, Congress was given the power to establish judicial tribunals inferior to the Supreme Court. In 1789, Congress exercised this power. The Judiciary Act of 1789 provided for the establishment of 13 district and three circuit courts. While the number of lower federal courts has grown, the basic pattern remains the same today. The federal court system has three tiers. Federal district courts are at the bottom: they function as federal trial courts. Federal criminal trials are held in federal district courts. Federal circuit courts are above them. Federal circuit courts are appellate courts rather than trial courts: they hear appeals from federal district courts. The Supreme Court is the highest court of the land. Very few appeals ever reach the Supreme Court.

I. *The Power to Make and Enforce Laws Related to Piracies and Felonies Committed on the High Seas and Offenses against the Laws of Nations*

Congress has the power to regulate criminal activity committed on the high seas on or against United States vessels.

J. *The Power to Declare War*

Congress alone has the power to declare war. The domestic powers of Congress are expanded during wartime, allowing Congress to impose some controls that would be unconstitutional in peacetime.[20] The Constitution, nevertheless, makes the President Commander-in-Chief of the armed forces. This division of authority has given rise to a peculiar state of affairs. In modern times, successive presidents have claimed

---

[20]   Johnson v. Maryland, 254 U.S. 51, 41 S. Ct. 16, 65 L. Ed. 2d 126 (1920).

authority, as Commander-in-Chief, to send American troops into combat abroad without waiting for Congress to declare war. Congress has declared war only five times; American troops have been deployed in combat operations abroad over a 100 times.[21] Because Congress has never called the President to the task for initiating military operations without congressional approval, the Supreme Court has never had to decide whether the President as Commander-in-Chief has the inherent power to deploy American troops in military actions without consulting Congress.

K. The Power to Raise and Support an Army and Navy and Provide for their Regulation

Congress has the authority to enact draft laws, acquire land for military installations, establish military regulations, and set up military courts. The Uniform Code of Military Justice derives from this power.

L. The Power to Organize a Militia and Call the Militia into the Service of the United States When Necessary to Execute Federal Law, Suppress Insurrections, and Repel Invasions

"Militia" refers to the organization today known as the National Guard. The Constitution divides control of the militia between the federal government and the states. Congress is responsible for organizing and equipping the militia and has the authority to call the militia into federal service when needed to suppress insurrections, repel invasions, and execute the laws of the United States. The states are responsible for training the militia according to standards prescribed by Congress. Enlistment in the state National Guard simultaneously results in enlistment in the Army National Guard. Enlistees retain their status as state Guard members until ordered into active federal duty and again revert to state status when they are relieved from federal service.[22]

M. The Power to Govern the District of Columbia and All Federal Enclaves and Establishments

Congress has exclusive legislative control and oversight of the District of Columbia and federal installations such as military posts, national parks, and federal buildings, even though they are located inside a state.

---

[21]   John Yoo, *The Continuation of Politics by Other Means: The Original Understanding of War Powers*, 84 Cal. L. Rev. 167, (1996).

[22]   Perprich v. Department of Defense, 496 U.S. 334, 110 S. Ct. 2418, 110 L. Ed. 2d 312 (1990).

N. *The Power to Enact All Laws Necessary and Proper for Carrying into Execution the Specifically Enumerated Powers*

The final clause of Article I, Section 8 grants Congress the power to enact "all Laws which shall be necessary and proper for carrying into execution . . . all other Powers vested by this Constitution in the Government of the United States, or in any Department or Officer thereof . . ." This clause is known as the necessary and proper clause. It grants Congress broad discretion as to the choice of means for executing its constitutionally delegated powers.[23] In 1819, a controversy arose about whether Congress had the power to establish a national bank.[24] The Supreme Court ruled that Congress had this power, even though no specific language in the Constitution mentioned it; the power existed under the necessary and proper clause. Chief Justice Marshall, who wrote the Court's opinion, proclaimed:

> Let the end be legitimate, let it be within the scope of the Constitution, and all means which are appropriate, which are plainly adapted to that end, which are not prohibited, but consistent with the letter and spirit of the Constitution, are constitutional.

The ends the federal government can pursue are circumscribed by its delegated powers. However, if the ends are constitutional, the federal government can select any means that are appropriate. Because Congress had the power to lay and collect taxes and to borrow money, Congress could establish means for safeguarding federal revenues pending their expenditure. Incorporating a bank was, therefore, appropriate. Marshall's interpretation of the necessary and proper clause forms the basis of the implied powers doctrine. The federal government has the implied power to adopt any measures, not prohibited by the Constitution, that are appropriate for carrying its delegated powers into effect.

§ 1.10   —Powers the States Are Forbidden to Exercise

Article I, Section 10 expressly forbids the states from doing five things.[25] States may not:

1. Enter into treaties, alliances, or confederations.
2. Coin money, emit bills of credit, or make anything besides gold or silver coin legal tender in payment of debts.
3. Lay duties on imports or exports without the consent of Congress.

---

[23] **United States v. Comstock, 560 U.S. -, 130 S. Ct. 1949, 176 L .Ed. 2d 878 (2010)** (the necessary and proper clause empowered Congress to enact a statute providing for civil commitment of sexually dangerous federal prisoners beyond the date they would otherwise be released).
[24] McCulloch v. Maryland, 17 U.S. (4 Wheat.) 316, 4 L. Ed. 579 (1918).
[25] U.S. Const., art. I, § 10.

4.   Keep troops or ships of war in times of peace.
5.   Pass bills of attainder, *ex post facto* laws, or laws impairing the obligations of contract.

The federal government has the exclusive power to make treaties, establish currency, regulate foreign commerce, and declare war; the states are prohibited from exercising legislative authority in these areas. These four restrictions have a common thread. They involve matters in which a uniform national policy is necessary.

The fifth restriction outlaws three arbitrary practices. States are forbidden to enact bills of attainder, ex post facto laws, or to impair the obligations of contract. A bill of attainder is a legislative act that brands a person a criminal without a trial.[26] Legislatures cannot declare individuals criminals and impose sanctions on them. Only a court can do this.

States are also forbidden to enact ex post facto laws. Ex post facto means "after the fact." This clause protects an accused from being disadvantaged by changes made in the law after his/her crime was committed. Laws that (1) change the elements of a crime or make conduct, innocent when done, criminal,[27] (2) increase the punishment,[28] or (3) reduce the evidence needed to convict cannot be applied to crimes completed before they were enacted.[29] The same holds true for laws that change sentencing guidelines and credit for good behavior.[30] However, the accused enjoys no ex post facto protection against mere changes in procedural rules, even when they work to his/her disadvantage. In *California Department of Corrections v. Morales,*[31] the Supreme Court rejected an *ex post facto* challenge to a prison regulation decreasing the frequency of parole hearings because the change was procedural and presented little risk of prolonging the duration of a prisoner's confinement.

The restrictions discussed above are found in the text of the Constitution. Certain other restrictions are implicit from the nature of federalism. The principle that a state may not tax an agency of the federal government is an example. Permitting the states to tax an agency of the federal government runs counter to federalism because it permits the states to exert control over the operations of the federal government.

---

[26]   Landgraf v. USI Film Products, 511 U.S. 244, 114 S. Ct. 1483, 128 L. Ed. 2d 229 (1994).

[27]   Calder v. Bull, 3 Dall. 386, 390, 1 L. Ed. 648 (1798). Article I, Section 9, Paragraph 1 contains an identical *ex post facto* clause applicable to the federal government.

[28]   California Department of Corrections v. Morales, 514 U.S. 499, 115 S. Ct. 1597, 131 L. Ed. 2d 588 (1995); Johnson v. United States, 529 U.S. 695, 120 S. Ct. 1795, 146 L. Ed. 2d 727 (2000); Wilkinson v. Austin, 545 U.S 209, 125 S. Ct. 2384, 162 L. Ed. 2d 174 (2005).

[29]   Carmell v. Texas, 529 U.S. 513, 120 S. Ct. 1620, 146 L. Ed. 2d 577 (2000) (retroactive application of statute authorizing conviction for certain sexual offenses on the victim's testimony alone, where corroborating evidence was previously required, violated the *ex post facto* clause); Stogner v. California, 539 U.S. 607, 123 S. Ct. 2446, 156 L. Ed. 2d 544 (2003) (statute authorizing criminal prosecutions after prior limitations period for the offense had expired violated *ex post facto* clause).

[30]   Lynce v. Mathis, 519 U.S. 433, 117 S. Ct. 891, 137 L. Ed. 2d 63 (1997); Miller v. Florida, 482 U.S. 423, 107 S. Ct. 2446, 96 L. Ed. 2d 351 (1987).

[31]   *Supra* note 28.

However, the most far-reaching restrictions on state power did not become part of the Constitution until after the Civil War. These restrictions are contained in the Fourteenth Amendment and are discussed in 1.15 and 1.16 of this chapter.

§ 1.11   — Sovereign Powers Retained by the States

Believing that diffusion of powers increases protection for liberty, the Framers of our Constitution delegated specific powers to the federal government and provided that all powers not so delegated would be reserved to the governments of the states and the American people. The powers retained by the states are called police powers. These powers are ascertained through constitutional mathematics. Before the adoption of the Constitution, sovereignty resided in the states. The states surrendered a portion of their sovereignty when they formed a federal union. The powers retained by the states are determined by subtracting from their original sovereignty, the powers they delegated to the federal government (Art. 1, § 8) and the powers the Constitution forbids them to exercise (Art. 1, § 10). This method of fixing the boundaries of federal and state power is set forth in the Tenth Amendment, which reads: "The powers not delegated to the United States by the Constitution, nor prohibited by it to the States, are reserved to the States respectively, and to the people."

In making this division of power, the Framers assumed that the powers retained by the states would be greater than those delegated to the federal government. James Madison made this point in the Federalist Papers where he described the balance of power as follows:

> The powers delegated by the proposed Constitution to the Federal Government, are few and defined. Those which are to remain in the State Governments are numerous and indefinite. The former will be exercised principally on external objects, as war, peace, negotiation, and foreign commerce .... The powers reserved to the several States will extend to all the objects, which, in the ordinary course of affairs, concern the lives, liberties and properties of the people; and the internal order, improvement, and prosperity of the State.[32]

This description, though accurate in 1798, is no longer true today. A shift occurred in the federal/state balance during the New Deal era. Article 1, Section 8 describes the powers delegated to the federal government in broad, general language. The elasticity of the language allows it to be stretched. Since the states hold the residual of power (i.e., all powers that have not been delegated to the federal government), the powers retained by the states pivot on the interpretation of the delegated powers. Expansive interpretations placed by the Supreme Court on the scope of the commerce clause during the New Deal era caused a corresponding constriction of the powers retained by the states. However, the constitutional tide has now turned. Beginning in the mid-1990s, the Supreme

---

[32]   THE FEDERALIST No. 45, at 313 (J. Cooke ed. 1961).

Court issued a series of decisions limiting the power of Congress to regulate noncommercial activities that are local in nature. The Court stated that the commerce power must be interpreted in light of our nation's dual system of government which requires a distinction "between what is truly national and what is truly local." The power to regulate noncommercial activities that are local in nature falls within the regulatory domain of the states and cannot be regulated by Congress under the commerce clause.[33]

While the federal government has vast regulatory powers, its powers are mainly over the American people, not the states. Principles of federalism prevent the federal government from using its Article I powers to regulate the actions of the states in ways that infringe on their sovereignty.[34] The federal government, for example, may not use its Article I powers to force state governments enact particular laws,[35] administer federal programs,[36] or compensate private parties for violating the rights under federal statutes enacted under Article I.[37] In *Printz v. United States*,[38] the Supreme Court struck down a provision of the Brady Handgun Violence Prevention Act that required state law enforcement officers to conduct criminal background checks before issuing handgun permits. The Court stated that requiring state law enforcement officers to administer federal programs is "fundamentally incompatible with our constitutional system of dual sovereignty."

The reader should not infer that the federal government is powerless to regulate the actions of state governments. The Fourteenth Amendment, which was adopted immediately after the Civil War, placed certain restrictions on state governments and authorized the federal government to enforce the restrictions by appropriate legislation. The states were forbidden to discriminate on the basis of race, religion, gender,

---

[33] *See, e.g.,* **United States v. Lopez,** *supra* **note** 14 (holding that Congress exceeded the scope of its authority under the commerce clause in making it a federal crime to possess a gun on school property); United States v. Morrison, *supra* note 14 (holding that Congress exceeded the scope of its authority under the commerce clause in creating a federal civil remedy for domestic violence).

[34] *See, e.g.,* New York v. United States, 505 U.S. 144, 112 S. Ct. 2408, 120 L. Ed. 2d 120 (1992) (holding that Congress overstepped the boundaries of federal power in directing the States to provide for disposal of radioactive waste generated within their borders); **Printz v. United States, 521 U.S. 98, 117 S. Ct. 2365, 138 L. Ed. 2d 914 (1997)** (holding that Congress lacked power to require local law enforcement officials to perform criminal background checks on gun purchasers); Alden v. Maine, 527 U.S. 706, 119 S. Ct. 2240, 144 L. Ed. 2d 636 (1999) (holding that Congress cannot require state courts to enforce private claims against the state governments for violating federal statutes enacted under Article I); Kimel v. Florida Board of Regents, 528 U.S. 62, 120 S. Ct 631, 145 L. Ed. 2d 522 (2000) (same).

[35] New York v. United States, *supra* note 34.

[36] **Printz v. United States,** *supra* note 34.

[37] Alden v. Maine, *supra* note 34 (Congress may not require state courts to enforce private claims against the state governments for violating federal statutes enacted under Article I); Kimel v. Florida Board of Regents, *supra* note 34 (same).

[38] *Supra* note 34.

or national origin or to deprive persons of their life, liberty, or property without due process of law.[39] These restrictions are discussed later in this chapter.

§ 1.12   The Bill of Rights

During the ratification debates, there was a strong push for a bill of rights. Delegates to the state conventions wanted assurance that the liberty of the people would be secure.[40] The Federalists originally disputed the need for a bill of rights, but eventually capitulated and agreed to make the framing of a bill of rights the first order of business when the new Congress met. During the first session of Congress, James Madison introduced 20 amendments culled from the hundreds that had been proposed. Of these, 12 were approved by Congress and 10 were ratified by the states. The first 10 amendments went into effect in November of 1791.

The first 10 Amendments to the Constitution, or more appropriately, the first eight, are called the Bill of Rights. Before discussing the contents of the Bill of Rights, two observations are in order. First, the Bill of Rights is not a declaration of the rights that the American people have against each other. It is a declaration of their rights against the government. Second, the government against which these rights are held is the federal government. This is apparent from the wording. The First Amendment begins "Congress shall make no law respecting the establishment of religion . . ." In an early case, the Supreme Court ruled that the rights protected by the Bill of Rights could not be asserted against state governments.[41]

Figure 1.4 shows the rights protected by the first eight amendments. Review the text of the Bill of Rights in the Appendix and carefully study the material below.

The most important safeguards are found in the First, Fourth, Fifth, Sixth, and Eighth Amendments. The First Amendment protects freedom of speech. The Fourth, Fifth, Sixth, and Eighth Amendments limit the government's authority to arrest, search, and interrogate persons suspected of crimes and establish procedural safeguards that apply during criminal trials. Because these Amendments are given in-depth treatment in later chapters, they will not be discussed here.

---

[39]   *See, e.g.*, Title VII of the Civil Rights Act of 1964, 42 U.S.C. § 2000e *et seq.*, covered in § 10.7 *infra*, making it an unlawful employment practice to discriminate based on race, color, religion, gender, or national origin; 42 U.S.C. § 1983, covered in § 10.9 *infra*, creating a federal civil cause of action against persons who act under color of state law in depriving citizens of their federal constitutional and statutory rights. *See* also Nevada Department of Human Resources, et al. v. Hibbs, 538 U.S. 721, 123 S. Ct. 1972, 155 L. Ed. 2d 953 (2003) (holding that state employees may recover damages against their government employer for violating their rights under federal laws enacted under the Fourteenth Amendment).

[40]   Eriksson, *supra* note 1, at 220.

[41]   Barron v. Mayor and City Council of Baltimore, 32 U.S. (7 Pet.) 243, 8 L. Ed. 672 (1833).

Figure 1.4
Content of the Bill of Rights

Amendment	Rights Protected
First Amendment	**Freedom of speech**[42] **Freedom of the press**[43] **Right to assemble**[44] **Right to petition Congress for a redress of grievances**[45]
Second Amendment	**Right to keep and bear arms**[46]
Third Amendment	*Protection against involuntary quartering of soldiers in private homes*
Fourth Amendment	**Protection against unreasonable searches and seizures**[47] **Protection against the issuance of warrants without probable cause, supported by an oath or affirmation, particularly describing the place to be searched or the persons or things to be seized**[48]
Fifth Amendment	Right to be indicted by a grand jury before being tried for a capital or otherwise infamous crime[49] **Protection against double jeopardy (i.e., against being tried more than once for the same offense)**[50] **Protection against compulsory self-incrimination**[51] Protection against deprivation of life, liberty, or property without due process of law[52] **Right to just compensation when private property is taken for a public use**[53]
Sixth Amendment	**Right to a speedy criminal trial**[54] **Right to a public criminal trial**[55] **Right to a jury trial in criminal cases**[56] **Right to be informed of the nature and grounds of a criminal accusation** **Right to confront and cross-examine prosecution witnesses**[57] **Right to compulsory legal process to compel attendance of defense witness**[58] **Right to the assistance of counsel in criminal cases**[59]
Seventh Amendment	Right to a jury trial in civil cases when the amount in controversy exceeds $20[60]
Eighth Amendment	**Protection against excessive bail**[61] **Protection against excessive fines**[62] **Protection against cruel and unusual punishment**[63]

Boldface type means that this protection has been incorporated into the Fourteenth Amendment and applies to the states.
Regular type means that this protection does not apply to the states.
Italicized print means that the Supreme Court has not decided this question.

The Second Amendment reads that "[a] well-regulated Militia, being necessary to the security of a free state, the right of the people to keep and bear arms, shall not be infringed." This language establishes an individual right to possess firearms for personal use, and not simply a collective right that applies to state-regulated militias.[64] The Second Amendment, nevertheless, does not guarantee "a right to keep and carry any weapon whatsoever in any manner whatsoever and for whatever purpose." The government can impose reasonable restrictions on gun ownership and use. However, it cannot make it a crime for law-abiding citizens to keep a loaded handgun in their home for self-defense.[65] This protection goes to the core of the Second Amendment and cannot be denied.

The Ninth and Tenth Amendments, technically speaking, are not part of the Bill of Rights because they do not establish individual rights. The Ninth Amendment states:

---

[42]   Gitlow v. New York, 268 U.S. 652, 666, 45 S. Ct. 625, 630, 69 L. Ed. 1138 (1925); Stromberg v. California, 283 U.S. 359, 51 S. Ct. 532, 75 L. Ed. 1117 (1931).

[43]   Near v. Minnesota, 283 U.S. 697, 701, 51 S. Ct. 625, 626, 75 L. Ed. 1357 (1931).

[44]   DeJonge v. Oregon, 299 U.S. 353, 57 S. Ct. 255, 81 L. Ed. 278 (1937).

[45]   Id.

[46]   McDonald v. City of Chicago, ____ U.S. ____, 130 S. Ct. 3020, 177 L. Ed. 2d 894 (2010).

[47]   Mapp v. Ohio, 367 U.S. 643, 81 S. Ct. 1684, 6 L. Ed. 2d 1081 (1961).

[48]   Id.

[49]   Hurtado v. California, 110 U.S. 516, 4 S. Ct. 292, 28 L. Ed. 1903 (1947).

[50]   Benton v. Maryland, 395 U.S. 784, 89 S. Ct. 2056, 23 L. Ed. 2d 707 (1969).

[51]   Malloy v. Hogan, 378 U.S. 1, 84 S. Ct. 1489, 12 L. Ed. 2d 653 (1964).

[52]   This provision applied, and continues to apply, only to the federal government. However, this fact ceased to be consequential with the passage of the Fourteenth Amendment which contains an identical limitation on state governments. The Fifth and Fourteenth Amendment due process clauses have received the same interpretation. The meaning of the due process clause is discussed in §1.14 - §1.15 infra.

[53]   Chicago, B. & Q. R. Co. v. Chicago, 166 U.S. 226, 17 S. Ct. 581, 41 L. Ed. 979 (1897).

[54]   Klopfer v. North Carolina, 386 U.S. 213, 87 S. Ct. 988, 18 L. Ed. 2d 1 (1967).

[55]   In re Oliver, 333 U.S. 257, 68 S. Ct. 499, 92 L. Ed. 682 (1948).

[56]   Duncan v. Louisiana, 391 U.S. 145, 149, 88 S. Ct. 1444, 1447, 20 L. Ed. 2d 491 (1968).

[57]   Pointer v. Texas, 380 U.S. 400, 85 S. Ct. 1065, 13 L. Ed. 2d 923 (1965).

[58]   Washington v. Texas, 388 U.S. 14, 87 S. Ct. 120, 13 L. Ed. 2d 923 (1965).

[59]   Gideon v. Wainwright, 372 U.S. 335, 83 S. Ct. 792, 9 L. Ed. 2d 799 (1963).

[60]   Minneapolis & St. Louis R. Co. v. Bombolis, 241 U.S. 211, 36 S. Ct. 595, 60 L. Ed. 961 (1916).

[61]   Schilb v. Kuebel, 404 U.S. 357, 365, 92 S. Ct. 479, 30 L. Ed. 2d 502 (1971) (stating that the Eighth Amendment proscription of excessive bail "is assumed to have application to the states through the Fourteenth Amendment").

[62]   Cooper Industries, Inc. v. Leatherman Tool Group, Inc. 532 U.S. 424, 121 S. Ct. 1,678, 149 L. Ed. 2d 674 (2001).

[63]   Louisiana ex rel. Francis v. Resweber, 329 U.S. 459, 67 S. Ct. 374, 91 L. Ed. 422 (1947); Furman v. Georgia, 408 U.S. 238, 257, 92 S. Ct. 2726, 2736, 33 L. Ed. 2d 346, 360 (1972).

[64]   **District of Columbia v. Heller, 554 U.S. 570, 171 L. Ed. 2d 637 (2008);** McDonald v. City of Chicago, *supra* note 46.

[65]   Id.

"The enumeration of the Constitution, of certain rights, shall not be construed to deny or disparage others retained by the people." What this language means remains a constitutional mystery. The argument is occasionally made that the Ninth Amendment authorizes the Supreme Court to recognize constitutional rights beyond those mentioned in the Bill of Rights. The Supreme Court has been uncomfortable with this interpretation and has never accepted it. Authorizing courts to recognize constitutional rights that lack textual support would open up a Pandora's box. For this reason, the Supreme Court has never relied on the Ninth Amendment as the sole basis for any constitutional decision.

The Tenth Amendment deals with federalism and was discussed in § 1.11.

§ 1.13 — Applying the Bill of Rights to the States Through the Fourteenth Amendment

The Bill of Rights constituted a declaration of rights that the American people had against the federal government. Americans had no protection against arbitrary acts of state governments until almost a century later. The Fourteenth Amendment, ratified in 1868, contained a mechanism that was used to impose the Bill of Rights guarantees on the states. That mechanism was the *due process clause*.

The Fourteenth Amendment forbids the states to "deprive any person of life, liberty or property without *due process of law*." The phrase *without due process of law* means "without the process that is due under the law."[66] Restated, the Fourteenth Amendment forbids the states from depriving people of life, liberty, or property without affording them the process due them under the law. Where did the Supreme Court look to determine what process was due? You guessed it — the Bill of Rights.

The central guarantees contained in the Bill of Rights have gradually been absorbed into the Fourteenth Amendment due process clause and made binding on state governments through an approach known as *selective incorporation*. Under this approach, rights deemed fundamental to the American system of justice are regarded as components of the due process that states are forbidden to deny.[67] Most provisions found in the Bill of Rights have been incorporated. The standard used to decide whether to incorporate a particular right is whether the right is fundamental to the American justice system.[68] Figure 1.5 shows the current incorporation status of each of the rights guaranteed by the Bill of Rights. Notice that all but four rights have been incorporated.

Incorporation into the Fourteenth Amendment means that states must provide at least as much protection as the United States Constitution requires. Federal standards become the constitutionally minimum protection, but states remain free to impose a higher standard under their own constitutions.[69]

---

[66] In re *Winship*, 379 U.S. 358, 90 S. Ct. 1068, 25 L. Ed. 2d 368 (1979).

[67] Duncan v. Louisiana, 391 U.S. 145, 88 S. Ct. 1444, 20 L. Ed. 2d 491 (1968).

[68] *Id.*

[69] Cooper v. California, 386 U.S. 58, 87 S. Ct. 788, 17 L. Ed. 2d 730 (1967).

Figure 1.5
Overview of the Fourteenth Amendment

> The Fourteenth Amendment: (1) makes most of the Bill of Rights applicable to the states; (2) prevents the states from depriving people of life, liberty, or property without procedural and substantive due process; (3) prohibits the states from treating people differently because of race, gender, or national origin except under extraordinary circumstances; and (4) gives Congress power to pass legislation enforcing these restrictions.

§ 1.14   The Fourteenth Amendment as a Limitation on State Power

The Civil War altered the relationship between the national government, the states, and the American people. Before the Civil War, the American people viewed the states as the watchdogs of their liberty and feared the federal government. The fact that the Bill of Rights was directed at the federal government alone shows this. The Civil War changed things. After the Civil War, the states were viewed as the threat and the federal government the protector. Demand for federal protection against oppressive acts of state governments led to the passage of the Fourteenth Amendment.

The Fourteenth Amendment reads:

> No State shall make or enforce any law which shall abridge the privileges or immunities of citizens of the United States; nor shall any State deprive any person of life, liberty, or property, without due process of law; nor deny to any person within its jurisdiction the equal protection of the laws.

We previously saw how the Fourteenth Amendment served as the vehicle for imposing the central guarantees of the Bill of Rights on the states. However, the importance of the Fourteenth Amendment goes far beyond this. Before delving into its contents, there are two things you need to keep in mind. Both stem from the first three words. The Fourteenth Amendment begins "[n]o state shall . . . ." First, the Fourteenth Amendment is addressed to the states. It regulates the conduct of states; it does not regulate the conduct of the federal government or private citizens. Second, the Fourteenth Amendment is phrased in the negative. It forbids the states to take arbitrary action; it does not require them to take helpful action. This point was made tragically clear in *DeShaney v. Winnebago County Department of Social Services*.[70] The plaintiff, Joshua DeShaney, was a four-year-old boy who suffered permanent brain damage due to his father's beatings. The defendants were social workers, employed by the state, who allegedly knew that Joshua was being abused, but took no steps to remove him from his father's home. Joshua claimed that their failure to protect him from his father's

---

[70]   489 U.S. 189, 109 S. Ct. 998, 103 L. Ed. 2d 249 (1989).

violence deprived him of liberty without due process in violation of the Fourteenth Amendment. The Supreme Court disagreed, ruling that:

> ...[N]othing in the language of the Due Process Clause itself requires the State to protect the life, liberty, and property of its citizens against invasion by private actors. The Clause is phrased as a limitation on the State's power to act, not as a guarantee of certain minimal levels of safety and security. It forbids the State itself to deprive individuals of life, liberty, or property without "due process of law," but its language cannot fairly be extended to impose an affirmative obligation on the State to ensure that those interests do not come to harm through other means.

DeShaney's message, though disturbing, is a correct interpretation of the Fourteenth Amendment. The Fourteenth Amendment forbids the states from engaging in oppressive action; it does not require them to take helpful action.

§ 1.15   — Due Process of Law

The Fourteenth Amendment due process clause reads "[n]o State shall ... deprive any person of life, liberty, or property, without due process of law ...."[71] This clause provides two kinds of protection — one procedural and the other substantive. *Procedural due process* requires states to use fair procedures in reaching decisions that deprive a person of life, liberty, or property. *Substantive due process* requires them to have an adequate justification or, in other words, a good enough reason for the deprivation. Procedural and substantive due process work together to prevent arbitrary deprivations of life, liberty, and property. Suppose that a state child welfare agency wants to remove a child from a parent's home. Since the right to the care and custody of one's children is part of the liberty protected by the due process clause,[72] the state cannot take this right away without establishing an adequate justification (substantive due process) and providing notice and a hearing (procedural due process). The strength of the justification required to satisfy the demands of substantive due process varies with the importance of the rights at stake. The state cannot interfere with rights that qualify as "fundamental rights", such as the right of parents to raise their children, without establishing a "compelling reason."

> *Procedural due process* requires states to use fair procedures in reaching decisions that deprive a person of life, liberty, or property. *Substantive due process* requires them to have an adequate justification or, in other words, a good enough reason for the deprivation. Procedural and substantive due process work together to prevent arbitrary deprivations of life, liberty, and property.

---

[71] The Fifth Amendment contains an identical clause that is binding on the federal government and is interpreted in the same way. Consequently, federal and state officers are subject to identical constitutional limitation on their authority.

[72] Troxel v. Granville, 530 U.S. 57, 120 S. Ct. 2054, 147 L. Ed. 2d 49 (2000); Stanley v. Illinois, 405 U. S. 645, 92 S. Ct. 1208, 31 L. Ed. 2d 551 (1972).

A. Procedural Due Process

Suppose when you go home tonight, you discover that your furniture and possessions are gone and you are informed that a judge awarded them to your landlord for nonpayment of rent. How would you feel? You would probably feel that this was unfair. You should have been notified that legal proceedings affecting your property were taking place and allowed to appear and present your side of the story. Your sense of injustice is due to a lack of procedural due process.

Procedural due process requires the government to give notice and a hearing before depriving a person of life, liberty, or property. This requirement is not limited to criminal proceedings. It applies whenever the government takes any action that deprives a person of life, liberty, or property. Procedural due process, for example, is required before the government can suspend a student from public school, revoke an offender's probation,[73] or fire a tenured government employee[74] because each of these actions deprive the person affected of liberty or property.

The procedures necessary to satisfy due process vary with (1) the importance of the right at stake; (2) the extent to which the additional safeguards would reduce the risk of an erroneous decision; and (3) the increased fiscal or administrative burden on the government of providing them.[75] Maximum procedural protection is required at criminal trials because the stakes are at their highest. When the government accuses a person of a crime and threatens to take away his life or liberty, the Constitution insists on a broad array of procedural safeguards. These safeguards include the right to notice of the charges[76]; to be tried before an impartial tribunal[77]; to cross-examine prosecution witnesses[78]; to testify and compel attendance of defense witnesses[79]; to be represented by counsel of his choice[80] or an attorney furnished by the government if he cannot afford representation[81]; to be assisted by experts, such as psychiatrists[82]; and to be set free unless the government proves guilt beyond a reasonable doubt.[83]

---

[73]   Young v. Harper, 520 U.S. 143, 117 S. Ct. 1148, 137 L. Ed. 2d 270 (1997); Morissey v. Brewer, 408 U.S. 71, 92 S. Ct. 2593, 33 L. Ed. 2d 484 (1972).

[74]   Gilbert v. Homar, 520 U.S. 924, 117 S. Ct. 1807, 138 L. Ed. 2d 120 (1997); Cleveland Bd. of Education v. Loudermill, 470 U.S. 532, 105 S. Ct. 1487, 84 L. Ed. 2d 494 (1985).

[75]   Cafeteria & Restaurant Workers Union v. McElroy, 367 U.S. 886, 895, 81 S. Ct. 1743, 1748, 6 L. Ed. 2d 1230 (1961).

[76]   U.S. Const., amend. VI.

[77]   Id.

[78]   Id.

[79]   Id.

[80]   Id.

[81]   Gideon v. Wainwright, 372 U.S. 335, 83 S. Ct. 792, 9 L. Ed. 2d 799 (1963).

[82]   Ake v. Oklahoma, 470 U.S. 68, 105 S. Ct. 1087, 84 L. Ed. 2d 53 (1985).

[83]   In re *Winship*, 397 U.S. 358, 90 S. Ct. 1068, 25 L. Ed. 2d 368 (1970).

B. *Substantive Due Process*

The due process clause does more than guarantee fair procedures. It also has a substantive component.[84] The concept of substantive due process is rooted in the term "liberty" found in the due process clause. Although the Fourteenth Amendment confers broad protection on individual liberty, the Constitution nowhere defined this term. This is the role of substantive due process. The two main areas where courts use the concept of substantive due process are (1) to protect "fundamental rights"[85] and (2) to hold government officials accountable for egregious misconduct that is not otherwise prohibited by the Constitution.[86]

1. Protection of Fundamental Rights

Some rights are so fundamental to the liberty of free citizens that they cannot be denied without a compelling reason. These rights are called "fundamental rights." Once a right is labeled as fundamental, it is placed largely beyond the government's control. The label of a fundamental right has been reserved for important choices that are central to an individual's self-concept, dignity, and autonomy. Rights that have been recognized as fundamental include the right to marry,[87] to have children,[88] to direct their upbringing and education,[89] to enjoy privacy,[90] to practice birth control,[91] to terminate

---

[84] Planned Parenthood of Southeastern Pennsylvania v. Casey, 505 U.S. 833, 112 S. Ct. 2791, 120 L. Ed. 2d 674 (1992). For a discussion of substantive due process, *see, generally*, Erwin Chemerinsky, Substantive Due Process, 15 TOURO L. REV. 1501 (1999); Rosalie Berger Levinson, Protection against Government Abuse of Power: Has the Court Taken the Substance Out of Substantive Due Process? 16 U. DAYTON L. REV. 313 (1991).

[85] *See* authorities cited in notes 87 - 97 *infra*.

[86] County of Sacramento v. Lewis, 523 U.S. 833, 118 S. Ct. 1708, 140 L. Ed. 2d 1043 (1998) (holding that police conduct must "shock the conscience" to state a claim for denial of substantive due process).

[87] *See, e.g.*, Loving v. Virginia, 388 U.S. 1, 87 S. Ct. 1817, 18 L. Ed. 2d 1010 (1967) (invalidating law prohibiting marriage between persons of different races); Cleveland Board of Education v. LaFleur, 414 U.S. 632, 639-640, 94 S. Ct. 791, 39 L. Ed. 2d 52 (1974). ("This Court has long recognized that freedom of personal choice in matters of marriage and family life is one of the liberties protected by the Due Process Clause of the Fourteenth Amendment.")

[88] *See, e.g.*, Skinner v. Oklahoma ex rel. Williamson, 316 U.S. 535, 62 S. Ct. 1110, 86 L. Ed. 1655 (1942) (invalidating law requiring sterilization of felons after third conviction of an offense involving "moral turpitude").

[89] *See, e.g.*, Troxel v. Granville, *supra* note 72 (overturning court order granting visiting rights to grandparent as a violation of a parent's fundamental rights "to make decisions concerning the care, custody, and control of their children"); Meyer v. Nebraska, 262 U.S. 390, 43 S. Ct. 625, 67 L. Ed. 1042 (1923) (invalidating law prohibiting teaching of foreign language to students below the eighth grade as undue interference with fundamental right of parents to make decisions about the education of their children); Pierce v. Society of Sisters, 268 U.S. 510, 45 S. Ct. 571, 69 L. Ed. 1070 (1925) (invalidating law requiring parents to educate their children in public schools as undue interference with the fundamental right of parents to make decisions about the education of their children).

[90] *See, e.g.*, Griswold v. Connecticut, 381 U.S. 479, 85 S. Ct. 1678, 14 L. Ed. 2d 510 (1965) (recognizing the right of married couples to privacy in use of contraception).

[91] *See, e.g.*, *Id.*; Eisenstadt v. Baird, 268 U.S. 510, 92 S. Ct. 1029, 31 L. Ed. 2d 349 (1972) (invalidating law prohibiting sale of contraceptives to unmarried persons).

unwanted pregnancies,[92] to make health-care decisions,[93] and to forego life-sustaining treatment.[94] The Supreme Court has explained that " '[a]t the heart of liberty is the right to define one's own concept of existence, of meaning, of the universe, and of the mystery of human life. Beliefs about these matters could not define the attributes of personhood were they formed under compulsion of the State.' "[95]

Having said this, the Supreme Court, nevertheless, declined for many years to recognize the right to be a practicing homosexual as a fundamental right. In *Bowers v. Hardwick*,[96] the Court upheld a state statute making sodomy a crime. Four Justices dissented, arguing:

> Only the most willful blindness could obscure the fact that sexual intimacy is "a sensitive, key relationship of human existence, central to family life, community welfare, and the development of human personality". The fact that individuals define themselves in a significant way through their intimate sexual relationships with others suggests, in a Nation as diverse as ours, that there may be many "right" ways of conducting those relationships, and that much of the richness of a relationship will come from the freedom an individual has to choose the form and nature of these intensely personal bonds.[97]

Bowers v. Hardwick was later overruled in *Lawrence v. Texas*.[98] Police, responding to a hoax call that a weapons disturbance was taking place in John Lawrence's apartment, burst into the apartment and found Lawrence having consensual sex with another adult male. They arrested him for engaging in "deviant sexual intercourse," a crime defined under Texas law as having "anal or oral sex with a member of the same sex."[99]

---

[92]   *See, e.g.*, Roe v. Wade, 410 U.S. 113, 93 S. Ct. 705, 35 L. Ed. 2d 147 (1973) (upholding the right of women to terminate an unwanted pregnancy); Carey v. Population Services International, 431 U.S. 678, 97 S. Ct. 2010, 52 L. Ed. 2d 675 (1977). (" [T]he Constitution protects individual decisions in matters of childbearing from unjustified intrusion by the State.")

[93]   *See, e.g.*, Washington v. Harper, 494 U.S. 210, 110 S. Ct. 1028, 108 L. Ed. 2d 178 (1990) (recognizing a substantive due process right to avoid unwanted administration of antipsychotic drugs). Substantive due process also protects the right to bodily security and integrity. *See, e.g.*, Rochin v. California, 342 U.S. 165, 72 S. Ct. 205, 96 L. Ed. 183 (1952) (holding that government may not pump a suspect's stomach to retrieve evidence).

[94]   *See, e.g.*, Cruzan v. Director, Mo. Dept. of Health, 497 U.S. 261, 278, 110 S. Ct. 2841, 2851, 111 L. Ed. 2d 224 (1990) (recognizing right of competent adults to refuse unwanted lifesaving medical treatment). *But see* Washington v. Glucksberg, 521 U.S. 702, 117 S. Ct. 2258, 138 L. Ed. 2d 772 (1997) (right to assistance in committing suicide is not a fundamental right).

[95]   Planned Parenthood of Southeastern Pennsylvania v. Casey, *supra* note 84.

[96]   478 U.S. 186, 106 S. Ct. 2841, 92 L. Ed. 2d 140 (1986) (substantive due process does not protect the right to engage in homosexual sodomy).

[97]   *Id*. at 478 U.S. at 205, 106 S. Ct. at 2851.

[98]   539 U.S. 558, 156 L. Ed. 2d 508, 123 S. Ct. 2472 (2003).

[99]   Before 1960, all 50 states outlawed sodomy. Lawrence v. Texas, *supra* note 98. At the time of Bowers v. Hardwick, more than half the states had repealed their sodomy laws. *Id*. By 2003, when Lawrence v. Texas was decided, only 13 states —Alabama, Florida, Idaho, Kansas, Louisiana, Mississippi, Missouri, Oklahoma, North Carolina, South Carolina, Texas, Utah, and Virginia —made sodomy a crime. *Id*. Of these, only four states —Texas, Kansas, Oklahoma, and Missouri —criminalized sodomy only when both partners were of the same sex. *Id*.

The Supreme Court set the conviction aside, holding that there are certain spheres of life "where the government should not be a dominant presence." Private sexual conduct behind closed doors is one of them. This case did not involve sex with a minor, public conduct, prostitution, or "whether the government must give formal recognition to any relationship that homosexual persons seek to enter." Rather, it involved private sexual conduct between two consenting adult homosexuals. "The State," the Court declared, "cannot demean their existence or control their destiny by making their private sexual conduct a crime. Their right to liberty under the Due Process Clause gives them the full right to engage in their conduct without intervention of the government."[100]

Lawrence v. Texas is constitutionally important, not only because it invalidates sodomy laws, but also because it undercuts the most powerful argument justifying discrimination against gays and lesbians, namely that their behavior is immoral and illegal.[101] Although the Court could have overturned the Texas statute on equal protection grounds because it made sodomy a crime only when both partners were of the same sex, the Court went further than expected and seized the occasion to deliver a strong statement that moral disapproval of homosexual conduct does not justify legal intolerance.[102] *Lawrence v. Texas* has been hailed as the *Brown v. Board of Education* of the gay community. It has already had far-reaching effects and is likely to have ever greater effect in the future.

2. Egregious Misconduct by Public Officials

Substantive due process also provides a theory for holding government officials accountable for egregious misconduct that is not addressed elsewhere in the Constitution.[103] Courts, for example, have held that police have a substantive due process duty to obtain necessary medical treatment for prisoners taken into custody.[104]

---

[100] *Id*. 123 S. Ct. at 2484.

[101] *Id*. 123 S. Ct. at 2482. ("When homosexual conduct is made criminal by the law of the State, that declaration in and of itself is an invitation to subject homosexual persons to discrimination both in the public and in the private spheres.")

[102] *Id*. 123 S. Ct. at 2484. ("The petitioners are entitled to respect for their private lives. The State cannot demean their existence or control their destiny by making their private sexual conduct a crime. Their right to liberty under the Due Process Clause gives them the full right to engage in their conduct without intervention of the government. 'It is a promise of the Constitution that there is a realm of personal liberty which the government may not enter.' The Texas statute furthers no legitimate state interest which can justify its intrusion into the personal and private life of the individual.")

[103] County of Sacramento v. Lewis, *supra* note 86. If the underlying behavior is already addressed by another, more specific provision of the Constitution, the claim must be analyzed under that provision, rather than substantive due process. *See, e.g.*, Graham v. Connor, 523 U.S. 833, 118 S. Ct. 1708, 140 L. Ed. 2d 1043 (1998).

[104] *See, e.g.*, Estelle v. Gamble, 429 U.S. 97, 97 S. Ct. 285, 50 L. Ed. 2d 251 (1976) (state has the duty to provide adequate medical care to incarcerated prisoners); Watkins v. City of Battle Creek, 273 F.3d 682 (6th Cir. 2001); Carr v. Tatangelo, 338 F.3d 1259 (11th Cir. 2003); Haywood v. Ball, 586 F.2d 996 (4th Cir. 1978); El-Uri v. City of Chicago, 186 F. Supp. 2d 844 (N.D. Ill. 2002); Tagstrom v. Pottebaum, 668 F. Supp. 1269 (N.D. Iowa 1987).

However, substantive due process only reaches conduct at the extreme end of the fault spectrum. In the language of the Supreme Court, the conduct must be so egregious that it "shocks the conscience."[105] In the case of failure to obtain necessary medical treatment, this standard is satisfied only if the failure of the police reflects *deliberate indifference* to a prisoner's known, serious medical needs.[106] Thus, while substantive due process expands the constitutional accountability of police officers, it does so only in situations when they are guilty of extreme misconduct.[107]

§ 1.16   — Equal Protection of the Laws

The Fourteenth Amendment contains another equally important safeguard — the equal protection clause. This clause forbids a state to "deny any person within its jurisdiction the equal protection of the laws."[108] The equal protection clause was included to protect former slaves against unfair treatment at the hands of state governments, a purpose that was not fully realized until almost a century later. In 1896, the Supreme Court handed down *Plessy v. Ferguson*,[109] in which it held that state-mandated racial segregation satisfied the equal protection clause, provided that equal facilities were available to members of both races. *Plessy* established the doctrine of

---

[105]   County of Sacramento v. Lewis, *supra* note 86 (establishing this standard and holding that where police act in an emergency with no time to deliberate, such as in the context of a high-speed chase, only an actual intent to inflict harm can satisfy this standard).

[106]   *See* cases *supra* note 104; Wesson v. Oglesby, 910 F.2d 278, 284 (5th Cir. 1990) (holding that an inmate's swollen and bleeding wrists from handcuffing did not constitute serious medical need); Martin v. Gentile, 849 F.2d 863, 871 (4th Cir. 1988) (cut over one eye, bruises on shoulders and elbows, and a quarter-inch piece of glass did not constitute serious medical conditions); Davis v. Jones, 936 F.2d 971 (7th Cir. 1991) (scraped elbow and shallow one-inch cut in temple sustained during arrest were not serious medical conditions).

[107]   For cases finding that the misconduct alleged in the plaintiff's complaint stated a claim for denial of substantive due process, *see* United States v. Lanier, 520 U.S. 259, 117 S. Ct. 1219, 137 L. Ed. 2d 432 (1997) (judge sexually assaulted women in his chamber); Rogers v. City of Little Rock, Ark., 152 F.3d 790 (8th Cir. 1998) (police officer intimidated motorist into having sex); Wood v. Ostrander, 879 F.2d 583 (9th Cir. 1989), cert. denied, 498 U.S. 938, 111 S. Ct. 341, 112 L. Ed. 2d 305 (1990) (police left female passenger stranded in dangerous neighborhood late at night after arresting driver; woman was subsequently raped by unknown man with whom she accepted ride); Reed v. Gardner, 986 F.2d 1122, 1127 (7th Cir.), cert. denied, 510 U.S. 947, 114 S. Ct. 389, 126 L. Ed. 2d 337 (1993) (police arrested sober driver and left a drunken passenger to drive home on his own; drunken passenger later struck and killed a pedestrian).

[108]   The Fourteenth Amendment equal protection clause applies only to state governments. However, the Fifth Amendment due process clause has been interpreted as imposing an identical limitation on the federal government. *See, e.g.*, Adarand Constructors, Inc. v. Pena, 515 U.S. 200, 11 S. Ct. 2097, 132 L. Ed. 2d 158 (1995); Bolling v. Sharpe, 347 U.S. 497, 74 S. Ct. 693, 98 L. Ed. 884 (1954).

[109]   163 U.S. 537, 16 S. Ct. 1138, 41 L. Ed. 256 (1896).

"separate but equal." After this, segregation codes flourished, infesting every avenue of American life, from restrooms, drinking fountains, telephone booths, hospitals, and prisons, to the books used by children in segregated public schools.[110] Justice Harlan alone dissented in *Plessy*, sounding what would become the Supreme Court's position in 1954. Justice Harlan wrote:

> . . .[I]n view of the Constitution, in the eye of the law, there is in this country no superior, dominant, ruling class of citizens. There is no caste here. Our Constitution is color-blind, and neither knows nor tolerates classes among citizens. In respect of civil rights, all citizens are equal before the law. The humblest is the peer of the most powerful. The law regards man as man and takes no account of his surroundings or his color when his civil rights as guaranteed by the supreme law of the land are involved.

The national conscience was reawakened in 1954, when the Supreme Court handed down the landmark decision of *Brown v. Board of Education*,[111] in which it announced that the "separate but equal" doctrine no longer satisfied the Constitution in the field of public education. It soon became apparent that *Brown v. Board of Education* was not limited to public education. *Brown v. Board of Education* ended the era of government-imposed barriers to racial equality.

Protection against unequal treatment at the hands of the government is a right that all Americans enjoy, not just racial minorities. The meaning of the equal protection clause can be summarized in one sentence. *The government must treat all persons who are similarly situated alike*. This does not mean that the government is barred from making distinctions. Drawing lines and making distinctions is an inescapable part of legislating. Welfare programs, for example, cannot operate without income eligibility requirements. Income eligibility requirements result in persons with different incomes being treated differently. Differences in legal treatment offend the equal protection clause only when the distinctions made are *arbitrary*.

A law restricting welfare benefits to persons who have brown eyes is an example of an arbitrary distinction. The distinction is arbitrary because it serves no purpose. Fortunately, regulations like this are rare because legislatures generally have some reason for drawing the line where they drew it. Whether the distinction can survive an equal protection challenge depends on the standard used to test its constitutionality. Courts use three different review standards, called *levels of scrutiny*: *low*, *intermediate*, and *strict scrutiny*.

Statutory classifications that do not involve race, color, nationality, religion, or gender are tested by the lowest standard, called rational relationship review. Deference is given to the legislature's judgment that the distinction is necessary. The distinction is presumed constitutional and the court is required to uphold it unless the challenger proves that the distinction has *no rational relationship to any legitimate government*

---

[110]   WOODWARD, THE STRANGE CAREER OF JIM CROW 83-86 (1965).
[111]   347 U.S. 483, 74 S. Ct. 686, 98 L. Ed. 873 (1954).

purpose.[112] This is usually hard to do. As a result, statutory classifications reviewed under the lowest standard are generally upheld.

Classifications based on gender are subject to intermediate-level scrutiny. Courts examine the legislature's reason for making the distinction more closely. For a gender-based distinction to survive intermediate-level scrutiny, the government must provide *an exceedingly persuasive justification* for treating men and women differently. Virginia Military Institute's (VMI) all-male admissions policy, for example, was struck down years ago because VMI was unable to do this.[113] The policy could have withstood rational relationship review because VMI advanced many legitimate reasons for why the school should remain all-male. However, gender-based distinctions require a stronger justification. The all-male admissions policy was declared unconstitutional because VMI was unable to come up with any exceedingly persuasive reason for refusing to admit qualified women into its program.

Race, color, religion, and nationality are known as *suspect classes*. Differences in treatment that turn on these factors are subject to the most rigorous review standard, called *strict scrutiny*. Under this standard, the statute is presumed unconstitutional and will be struck down unless the government establishes a *compelling reason* for treating members of one race, religion, or nationality different from members of another.[114] Because a *compelling reason* is more difficult to establish than a *legitimate reason* (low-level scrutiny) or an *exceedingly persuasive justification* (intermediate scrutiny), distinctions based on race, color, religion, and nationality are generally found to be unconstitutional.

While strict scrutiny has traditionally been used to invalidate laws that impose disadvantages on members of suspect classes, the same analysis applies to laws that treat them more favorably.[115] Affirmative action programs were once thought to represent "benign discrimination" because the government's intention was to raise the economic status of disadvantaged minorities, and not to discriminate. However, benign intentions provide no excuse. Whenever the government deliberately treats members of one race less favorably than members of another, the equal protection clause is

---

[112] Heller v. Doe, 509 U.S. 312, 113 S. Ct. 2637, 125 L. Ed. 2d 257 (1993) (legislative classifications that do not involve race, creed, color, religion, national origin, or gender violate equal protection only if the disparity of treatment is not rationally related to any legitimate government purpose); Kimel v. Florida Board of Regents, 528 U.S. 62, 120 S. Ct. 631, 145 L. Ed. 2d 522 (2000) (age-based distinctions violate the equal protection clause only when there is no rational relationship between the disparity in treatment and any legitimate state interest).

[113] United States v. Virginia, 518 U.S. 515, 116 S. Ct 2264, 135 L. Ed. 2d 735 (1996). *See also* Tuan Anh Nguyen v. Immigration and Naturalization Service, 533 U.S. 53, 121 S. Ct. 2053, 150 L. Ed. 2d 115 (2001).

[114] Johnson v. California, 543 U.S. 499, 125 S. Ct. 1141, 160 L. Ed. 2d 949 (2005); *Shaw v. Hunt*, 517 U.S. 899, 116 S. Ct. 1894, 135 L. Ed. 2d 207 (1996); Adarand Constructors, Inc. v. Pena, *supra* note 108; Richmond v. J.A. Croson Co., 488 U.S. 469, 491, 109 S. Ct. 706, 720, 102 L. Ed. 2d 854 (1989).

[115] *See* cases *supra* note 114.

violated unless the government has a *compelling reason* for the difference in treatment, regardless of which race is disadvantaged.[116]

The Supreme Court has not yet decided the proper standard for reviewing distinctions based on sexual orientation. This issue is central to whether persons who are homosexual can be denied the same rights, such as the right to marry, adopt children, and serve in the military, as persons who are not homosexual enjoy.[117] Most courts apply the lowest review standard. To prevail, the challenger must establish that the challenged distinctions based on sexual orientation bear no rational relationship to *any* legitimate government purpose.[118] This standard makes sexual orientation discrimination claims hard to win.[119] However, there are signs that public attitudes toward gay and lesbian issues are changing, producing a corresponding change in judicial attitudes. Gay and lesbian couples are now permitted to marry in Connecticut, Iowa, Massachusetts, New Hampshire, New York, Vermont, and the District of Columbia,[120] and are permitted to enter into civil unions in several other states.[121] In late 2010, Congress repealed the decades-old ban on gays and lesbians serving openly in the military.[122] These changes have prompted a small but growing number of courts to elevate the review standard for sexual orientation discrimination claims to intermediate scrutiny, which is the standard used for gender-based discrimination

---

[116]   *Id*. Use of race and sex as criteria in police employment decisions is covered in § 10.8 *infra*.

[117]   *See, e.g.*, Hernandez v. Robles, 7 N.Y.3d 338, 855 N.E.2d 1 (N.Y. 2006); Anderson v. King County, 158 Wash.2d 1, 138 P.3d 963 Wash. 2006); Kerrigan v. Commissioner of Public Health, 289 Conn. 135, 957 A.2d 407 (2008); Anderson v. King County, 158 Wash.2d 1, 138 P.3d 963 Wash. 2006); Holmes v. California National Guard, 124 F.3d 1126 (9th Cir. 1997), cert. denied, 525 U.S. 1067, 119 S. Ct. 794, 142 L. Ed. 2d 657 (1999); Richenberg v. Perry, 97 F.3d 256 (8th Cir. 1996); Quinn v. Nassau County Police Dep't, 53 F. Supp. 2d 347 (E.D.N.Y. 1999).

[118]   *See, e.g.*, Hernandez v. Robles, *supra* note 117 (statute denying homosexual couples the right to marry did not violate the equal protection clause); Anderson v. King County, *supra* note 117 (same); Lofton v. Secretary of Dept. of Children and Family Services, 358 F.3d 804 (11th Cir. 2004) (statute denying homosexual couples the right to adopt children did not violate the equal protection clause); Holmes v. California National Guard, *supra* note 117 (Pentagon's "don't ask/don't tell policy" barring gays and lesbians from serving openly in the military did not deny gays and lesbians equal protection); Richenberg v. Perry, *supra* note 117 (same).

[119]   *See* cases *supra* note 118. Lofton v. Secretary of Dept. of Children and Family Services, 358 F.3d 804 (11th Cir. 2004) (prohibiting homosexual couple from adopting children did not violate the equal protection clause).

[120]   Same-sex marriages are permitted in Massachusetts, Connecticut, and Iowa by court decisions, and in Vermont, New Hampshire, the District of Columbia, and New York by statute. *See* Goodridge v. Department of Public Health, 440 Mass., 798 N.E. 2d 941 (2003); Kerrigan v. Commissioner of Public Health, *supra* note 117; Varnum v. Brien, 763 N.W.2d 862 (Iowa 2009); 15 VERT. STAT. ANN. § 1a, *et seq*.; N.H. R.S.A. 457; D.C. Code § 46-401(a) (Supp. 2010).

[121]   *See, e.g.*, Lewis v. Harris, 908 A.2d 196 (N.J. 2006) (state's constitution equal protection clause requires that committed same-sex couples receive the same statutory rights as married couples; state legislature has discretion to decide whether to extend full marriage rights to same-sex couples or create a "separate statutory structure, such as a civil union").

[122]   *See* Carl Hulse, *Senate Ends Military Ban on Gays Serving Openly*, NEW YORK TIMES at 1A (December 19, 2010).

claims.[123] Elevation of the review standard makes a world of difference in the outcome. When the government is required to establish an *exceedingly persuasive justification* for treating persons differently solely because of their sexual orientation, the government more often than not comes up short.[124]

The equal protection clause applies to the enforcement of laws as well as their enactment. Selective enforcement of the law based on race violates the equal protection clause.[125] The perception that police inappropriately consider race in making enforcement decisions, a practice known as racial profiling, has emerged as one of the most critical issues facing law enforcement today. Few things poison race relations more thoroughly than selective enforcement. Racially biased policing fosters deep resentment, fear, and distrust of police, but the poison goes deeper:

> People who see the criminal justice system as fundamentally unfair will be less likely to cooperate with police, to testify as witnesses, to serve on juries, and to convict guilty defendants when they do serve. In addition, people who have lost respect for the law's legitimacy are more likely to break the law themselves . . . . Finally, the perception and reality of a fundamentally unfair criminal justice system contribute to broader racial divisions in society. If we cannot believe that our nation's law enforcement officers will enforce the law in a racially neutral manner, then we will be left with a society where members of the minority community always view the actions of any police officer with great suspicion . . .[126]

Law enforcement agencies need to promulgate written policies condemning racial profiling and establish formal guidelines spelling out when officers may legitimately consider race in discretionary enforcement decisions (*i.e.*, decisions on whom to stop, question, take into custody, arrest, search, use force on, *etc.*) and when they may not. The United States Department of Justice, Civil Rights Division, has issued the following guidelines regarding the use of race by federal law enforcement agents:

> Two standards in combination should guide use by Federal law enforcement authorities of race or ethnicity in law enforcement activities:
>
> • In making routine or spontaneous law enforcement decisions, such as ordinary traffic stops, Federal law enforcement officers may not use race or ethnicity to any degree, except that officers may rely on race and ethnicity in a specific suspect description. This prohibition applies even where the use of race or ethnicity might otherwise be lawful.
> • In conducting activities in connection with a specific investigation, Federal law enforcement officers may consider race and ethnicity only to the extent that there is trustworthy information relevant to the locality or time frame that links persons of a particular race or ethnicity to an identified criminal incident, scheme, or organization. This standard applies even where the use of race or ethnicity might otherwise be lawful."[127]

---

[123] *See* cases *supra* 120–22.

[124] *Id.*

[125] Whren v. United States, 517 U.S. 806, 813, 116 S. Ct. 1769, 135 L. Ed. 2d 89 (1996).

[126] Martinez v. United States, 92 F. Supp. 2d 780 (N.D. Ill. 2000).

§ 1.17 Adjudication of Constitutional Questions

The Constitution is not self-defining. Determining what the Constitution demands in different contexts requires an ongoing process of interpretation. The Supreme Court is the ultimate authority on what the Constitution means. The Supreme Court's decisions interpreting the Constitution become the law of the land, establishing standards that are binding on police officers.

Most of the Supreme Court's criminal justice decisions stem from appeals brought by state prisoners. Non-lawyers are often curious about how a prisoner's case gets to the Supreme Court. This section examines how constitutional issues reach the Supreme Court.

Federalism results in a dual system of federal and state courts. Within each system, there are two types of courts —trial courts and appeals courts. Trial courts determine the facts, apply the law to the facts, and reach verdicts. Appeals courts do not retry facts. Their function is to review the trial judge's rulings on questions of law in order to determine if they were correct. Appeals courts have the power to reverse criminal verdicts only if the verdict resulted from incorrect rulings on questions of constitutional or statutory law, or rules of evidence.

Understanding how cases reach the Supreme Court requires a brief sketch of state judicial systems. Most states have three levels of courts. The trial courts are at the bottom. This is where criminal prosecutions take place. Directly above the trial courts are middle-level appeals courts. Their function is to hear cases that are appealed from trial courts. Appeal to middle-level appeals courts generally exists as a matter of right. The highest state court, often called the supreme court, is at the top of the judicial pyramid. Two levels of appeals courts exist to ensure that everyone has an opportunity to have a higher court review trial court rulings on questions of law and decide if the rulings were correct. Middle-level appeals courts perform this function. Review at the highest level — the supreme court level — is normally discretionary. State supreme courts generally have discretion whether to hear a particular appeal. This allows the state's highest court to control its docket and hear only cases that raise issues of special importance to the legal system.

This is also how it works with the United States Supreme Court. The Supreme Court has discretion whether to hear a particular appeal. Requests to the Supreme Court for discretionary review are instituted by filing a petition for a *writ of certiorari*. If at least four members of the Supreme Court vote to hear the case, the petition will be

127   United States Department of Justice, Civil Rights Division, GUIDANCE REGARDING THE USE OF RACE BY FEDERAL LAW ENFORCEMENT AGENTS (June 2003), available at http://www.justice.gov/crt/about/spl/documents/guidance_on_race.pdf (last visited on 2/09/2011) *See also*, Farm Labor Org. Comm. v. Ohio State Highway Patrol, 308 F.3d 523 (6th Cir. 2002); United States v. Montero-Camargo, 208 F.3d 1122 (9th Cir. 2000); MN ST § 626.8471 (2010).

granted and the appeal will be allowed; if less than four are interested, the petition will be denied and the appeal will be dismissed. Each term (which begins the first Monday of each October and usually continues through June), the Supreme Court receives thousands of petitions seeking discretionary (certiorari) review. The Supreme Court usually hears about 150 appeals per term. The remaining petitions for discretionary review are rejected. Denial of certiorari does not mean that the Supreme Court agrees with the legal principles that were applied by the court below. This is a mistake commonly made in news reports. The only meaning that can be attributed to the Supreme Court's denial of certiorari is that less than four Supreme Court justices were interested in hearing the appeal.

Constitutional issues raised by state prisoners generally reach the Supreme Court through one of two routes: direct review and habeas corpus review.

Direct review. Criminal prosecutions for state crimes are tried in state courts. If the trial results in a conviction, the defendant can petition the United States Supreme Court for direct review after he or she receives a final judgment from the highest state court available.[128] In other words, a defendant seeking direct review must go up the state appellate ladder to the highest court available before petitioning the Supreme Court to have his or her case heard on direct review. State prisoners cannot ask the Supreme Court to review claimed violations of state law; their appeals must involve a substantial federal question.

Habeas corpus review. Constitutional errors are not always discovered in time to seek direct review. Federal law gives state prisoners a post-conviction remedy called habeas corpus.[129] Habeas corpus is a remedy used to secure release from an unlawful confinement. A state prisoner commences this action by filing a petition in federal court, alleging that he or she is being detained in prison in violation of his or her constitutional rights and requesting the issuance of a writ of habeas corpus. A writ of habeas corpus directs the party having custody, usually the warden, to produce the prisoner in court, so that the court can inquire into the matter.[130] The writ of habeas corpus enables state prisoners to have a federal judge review the constitutionality of their state court convictions. Federal habeas corpus involves a collateral attack on a state court judgment. The reason it is called a collateral attack is that the courts of one jurisdiction (federal) are exercising review powers over a case decided by the courts of another jurisdiction (state).

Federal habeas corpus is a common path that state prisoners travel on their road to the Supreme Court. A petition is filed in a federal district court.[131] If the prisoner's claim is denied by the federal district court, the prisoner appeals to the United States

---

[128]   28 U.S.C. § 1257.
[129]   28 U.S.C. § 2241.
[130]   28 U.S.C. § 2254(a).
[131]   United States district courts are the federal court system's trial courts. They have both criminal and civil jurisdiction. There are a total of 94 federal judicial districts — at least one for each state, the District of Columbia, and Puerto Rico. The 94 judicial districts are organized into 12 regional circuits, each of which has a United States Court of Appeals. The United States Courts of Appeals hear appeals from the district courts located within their circuits.

Court of Appeals and, from there, petitions the Supreme Court for discretionary (certiorari) review.

The number of state prisoners filing habeas corpus petitions in federal courts has increased exponentially through the years, growing from 127 in 1941 to 12,000 in 1990.[132] The flood of habeas corpus petitions from state prisoners became so heavy that lower federal courts were having difficulty managing their other dockets. In 1996, Congress restricted the availability of habeas corpus review, eliminating second and successive habeas corpus petitions[133] and review of claims previously litigated in a state court unless the state court decision is contrary to clearly established constitutional standards.[134] These procedural changes have made it more difficult for state prisoners to make their way to the Supreme Court.

§ 1.18   Federal Remedies for Constitutional Abuses

Why are students in training to become law enforcement officers required to study the United States Constitution?

There are three reasons. First, all citizens should have a basic knowledge of the Constitution, because preservation of our constitutional liberties depends on an informed citizenry. Second, police officers are regularly required to make decisions with constitutional implications. The decision to detain a suspect for investigation, make an arrest, conduct a frisk, use force, search for evidence, and interrogate a suspect are some of the many decisions police routinely make that are regulated by the Constitution. Professionalism means taking constitutional rights seriously. In the words of the late Justice Brandeis:

> Our government is the potent, the omnipresent teacher. For good or for ill, it teaches the whole people by its example …. If the government becomes a lawbreaker, it breeds contempt for law …. To declare that in the administration of the criminal law the end justifies the means to declare that the government may commit crimes in order to secure the conviction of a private criminal would bring terrible retribution. Against that pernicious doctrine this court should resolutely set its face.[135]

Finally, constitutional violations carry serious consequences for the person whose rights are violated, for the criminal justice system, and for the officer personally. Constitutional misconduct can lead to:

1. Exclusion of evidence procured in violation of the Constitution.
2. Reversal of criminal convictions.

---

[132]   Withrow v. Williams, 507 U.S. 680, 697, 113 S. Ct. 1745, 123 L. Ed. 2d 407 (1993) (O'Connor, J., concurring).
[133]   28 U.S.C. § 2254 and 2255.
[134]   28 U.S.C. § § 2254 (d).
[135]   Olmstead v. United States, 277 U.S. 438, 468, 48 S. Ct. 564, 72 L. Ed. 944 (1928) (Brandeis, J., dissenting).

3.   Disciplinary action.
4.   Civil liability.
5.   Criminal prosecution.

These sanctions are covered in later chapters. We briefly mention them here to underscore the importance of the material that follows. Thus, it is extremely important that police officers "know the rules" and obey them.

§ 1.19   Summary

The Constitution of the United States is the highest law of the land. It contains seven articles. The first three articles apportion the powers of the national government among three branches (legislative, executive, and judicial) and describe the powers of each. The separation of powers among the three branches is permanently fixed. Encroachment and delegation are forbidden.

The apportionment of power between the national government and the states is accomplished by: (1) delegating a broad range of powers to the federal government (Article I, Section 8); (2) expressly prohibiting the exercise of specified powers by the states (Article I, Section 10); and (3) declaring that all powers not expressly delegated to the federal government, nor forbidden to the states, belong to the states (Tenth Amendment). When Congress enacts legislation within the scope of its delegated powers, federal law nullifies contrary state law. This results from the supremacy clause, which makes the Constitution and laws of the United States the supreme law of the land, superseding contrary state law. Our dual federal/state system of government requires a distinction between matters that are truly national and matters that are purely local. Congress can regulate the former, but not the latter.

The Constitution establishes a process for amendment. There are now 27 Amendments. The first 10, known as the Bill of Rights, were adopted in 1791, two years after the Constitution was ratified. The Bill of Rights addresses many aspects of criminal procedure that are discussed in later chapters. Although the Bill of Rights originally limited only the federal government, the most important safeguards have been incorporated into the Fourteenth Amendment and are now binding on state governments as well.

The Fourteenth Amendment contains the due process and equal protection clauses. The due process clause provides two kinds of protection —one procedural and the other substantive. Procedural due process requires fair procedures before the government may take away a citizen's life, liberty, or property. Substantive due process prohibits: (1) arbitrary restrictions on "fundamental rights" and (2) conscience-shocking behavior by public officials. The equal protection clause prohibits state legislatures from making arbitrary distinctions between classes of citizens, and police officers from engaging in discriminatory enforcement of neutral laws.

The Supreme Court has discretion whether to hear an appeal. Criminal appeals generally reach the Supreme Court through one of two routes —direct review and habeas corpus review. Direct review requires the aggrieved party to take her case to the highest state court available before petitioning the Supreme Court for certiorari (discretionary) review. Habeas corpus review is a postconviction remedy. The prisoner brings an action in federal court, challenging the constitutionality of her state court conviction and resulting confinement.

Violating constitutional rights can lead to five different sanctions: (1) exclusion of evidence procured in violation of the Constitution, (2) reversal of a criminal conviction, (3) disciplinary action, (4) civil liability, and, in extreme cases, (5) criminal prosecution.

Freedom of Speech

2

Congress shall make no law ... abridging the freedom of speech, or of the press; or the right of the people peaceably to assemble, and to petition the Government for a redress of grievances.

First Amendment

Chapter Outline

KEY TERMS AND CONCEPTS

Child pornography   Nonpublic forum
Commercial speech   Panhandling
Expressive conduct   Public forum
Fighting words   Public forum by designation
Hate speech   Symbolic speech
Obscenity   Traditional public forum
                           Vulgar speech

§ 2.1   Historical Background

Many portions of the Bill of Rights have origins that go back to the Magna Charta or descend from time-honored English traditions. This is not so with the First Amendment. Freedom of speech, press, religion, and assembly was pioneered on American soil.[1] The merger of church and state in England provided a fertile ground for religious and political repression. Censorship of the press originated with the efforts of the Church to suppress heretical writings. In 1585, the Court of the Star Chamber issued a decree prohibiting books from being printed unless they were reviewed and licensed by the Archbishop.[2] The function of licensing laws was to weed out unorthodox religious thought or criticism of the crown. Licensing laws ended in 1694, only to be succeeded by seditious libel laws.[3] The crime of seditious libel consisted of criticizing public officials. During the heyday of these laws, a person could be punished for this crime if she read libelous material, heard it read and laughed at it, or repeated it to another.[4]

The framing of a bill of rights was the first order of business facing the Congress that met after the ratification of the Constitution. The foundations for a strong central government had been laid. Now curbs were needed to prevent the repressive English experience from being repeated. In specifying the rights of the American people

---

[1]   BRYANT, THE BILL OF RIGHTS 81 (1965).
[2]   *Id*. at 98–100.
[3]   *Id*. at 94.
[4]   *Id*. at 115.

against their government, it was no coincidence that freedom of speech, press, religion, and assembly were mentioned first. Our colonial forefathers had the vision to realize that without these rights, no rights would be secure. The First Amendment placed these cherished freedoms beyond the federal government's control. With the adoption of the Fourteenth Amendment, which provides, among other things, that no state shall deprive any person of *liberty* without due process of law, the First Amendment became binding on state governments as well.[5]

The United States has experienced more than two centuries of political stability. When viewed against the background of world history, this is remarkable. The First Amendment has played a singularly important role. When citizens can openly criticize their government, changes come about through orderly political processes. When grievances exist, they must be aired, if not through the channels of public debate, then by riots in the streets. The First Amendment functions as a safety valve through which the pressures and frustrations of a heterogeneous society can be ventilated and defused. Professor Emerson has identified another function that free speech serves in a democratic society:

> [F]reedom of expression is an essential process for advancing knowledge and dis-covering truth. An individual who seeks knowledge and truth must hear all sides of the question, consider all alternatives, test his judgment by exposing it to opposition, and make full use of different minds .... The reasons which make open discussion essential for an intelligent individual judgment likewise make it imperative for rational social judgment.[6]

A working knowledge of the First Amendment is a minimum that a nation firmly committed to the value of freedom of expression has a right to expect from those who enforce its laws.

§ 2.2 Overview of Constitutional Protection for Speech and Expressive Conduct

The First Amendment directs that "Congress shall make no law ... abridging the freedom of speech ...." Although this language is addressed to Congress, the First Amendment binds all branches and levels of government, as well as public officials who exercise government authority.[7]

This chapter begins by examining the boundaries of "speech" under the First Amendment. "Speech" for First Amendment purposes goes far beyond written and spo-ken words. It encompasses all known mediums of communication and fields of intel-lectual endeavor, including art, music, theater, dance, entertainment, and much more.

---

[5] Gitlow v. New York, 268 U.S. 652, 45 S. Ct. 625, 69 L. Ed. 1138 (1925).
[6] EMERSON, THE SYSTEM OF FREEDOM OF EXPRESSION 6–7 (1969).
[7] *Id.*

The determination that "speech" is involved is just the beginning. It means that the case will be decided under the First Amendment. However, it does not ordain the outcome. The right to speak is not absolute. A society in which the government is powerless to restrain citizens from speaking at any time or place, on any subject, however loudly they please, would be an insufferable place to live. The First Amendment does not strip the government of power to regulate speech; it prohibits the government from "abridging freedom of speech." Deciding when a restriction "abridges freedom of speech" is what First Amendment jurisprudence is about; this determination calls for complex value judgments.

To the Framers, freedom of speech meant freedom from government control over the content of public discourse. When they wrote "Congress shall make no law . . . abridging the freedom of speech . . ." they were concerned with protecting the free exchange of ideas. They believed that a free marketplace of ideas was essential to creating an informed citizenry capable of self-government.[8] Consequently, in deciding whether freedom of speech has been abridged, an important distinction exists between interventions that are directed at a speaker's *message*, such as arresting a person for expressing unorthodox, provocative, or obnoxious ideas,[9] and those that are directed at a speaker's *conduct*, such as arresting a person for using a loudspeaker in a residential neighborhood after dark.[10]

The First Amendment sharply curtails the government's power to dictate what can be written, spoken, or read. Punishing citizens for what they *say* is, with rare exception, unconstitutional unless their speech falls within a small, narrowly limited category of topics that have been written out of the First Amendment. These topics are discussed in §§ 2.5–2.11.

Punishing people for what they *do* is an entirely different matter. Conduct involved in communicating a message can give rise to regulatory concerns that have nothing to do with the message. Bullhorns, for example, are loud, parades disrupt normal traffic patterns, and door-to-door solicitation intrudes on privacy. The First Amendment gives the government a freer hand to address concerns that stem from a speaker's conduct.

Figure 2.1 contains a flow chart that shows the relationship between the main concepts covered in this chapter.

---

[8] Whitney v. California, 274 U.S. 357, 375–376, 47 S. Ct. 641, 648, 71 L. Ed. 1095 (1927) (Brandeis, J., concurring).

[9] Terminiello v. Chicago, 337 U.S. 1, 69 S. Ct. 894, 93 L. Ed. 1131 (1949).

[10] Kovacs v. Cooper, 336 U.S. 77, 69 S. Ct. 448, 93 L. Ed. 513 (1949) (upholding ordinance prohibiting the operation of vehicles equipped with sound amplifiers or other instruments that emit "loud and raucous noises"); Grayned v. City of Rockford, 408 U.S. 104, 92 S. Ct. 2294, 33 L. Ed. 2d 222 (1972) (upholding ordinance prohibiting noisy demonstrations in front of schools during school hours).

Figure 2.1
Overview of the First Amendment

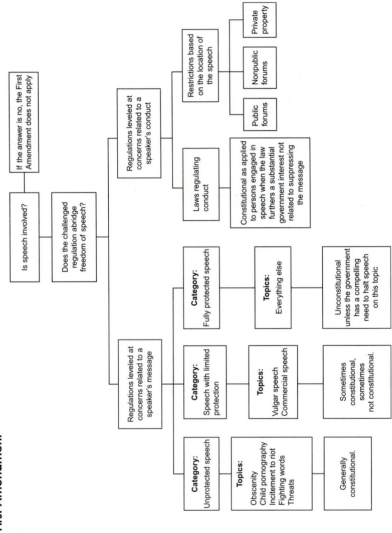

Figure 2.2
First Amendment Concept of Speech

The First Amendment concept of speech includes the right to:

1.   receive information,
2.   maintain ideas and beliefs,
3.   communicate them to others,
4.   engage in ideological silence, and
5.   engage in symbolic speech.

---

§ 2.3   Is Speech Involved?

The First Amendment meaning of "speech" cannot be found in a dictionary. Dictionaries record standard usages. A broader meaning is necessary to fulfill the purpose of the First Amendment. The essence of freedom of speech is the right to share one's beliefs with others. However, because formulating beliefs is necessary to share them, the First Amendment protects the right to receive and take in information as well.[11] There are an infinite variety of techniques for sharing beliefs. A partial list includes: making speeches; participating in parades,[12] marches, pickets, and other public demonstrations[13]; displaying signs and placards; distributing literature, pamphlets, and other written materials; writing letters[14]; soliciting membership in organizations, signatures on petitions, and contributions for causes[15]; broadcasting via radio, television, or cable[16]; communicating and receiving information over the Internet[17]; filing public interest litigation; participating in politically motivated business boycotts[18]; and engaging in artistic forms of expression such as theater, dance, music, and painting.[19] All of these activities constitute "speech" within the meaning of the First Amendment.

---

[11]   *See, e.g.*, Lamont v. Postmaster General, 381 U.S. 301, 85 S. Ct. 1493, 14 L. Ed. 2d 398 (1965) (invalidating federal statute requiring people who wished to receive "communist political propaganda" to notify the post office); Stanley v Georgia, 394 U.S. 557, 89 S. Ct. 1243, 22 L. Ed. 2d 542 (1969) (holding that the government lacks power to make it a crime to possess obscene material in the privacy of one's own home. "[A] State has no business telling a man, sitting alone in his own house, what books he may read or what films he may watch."); Reno v. American Civil Liberties Union, 521 U.S. 844, 117 S. Ct. 2329, 138 L. Ed. 2d 874 (1997) (invalidating provision of the Communications Decency Act of 1996, enacted to protect minors from indecent and patently offensive communications on the Internet, because the law effectively suppressed "a large amount of speech that adults have a constitutional right to receive").

[12]   Hurley v. Irish-American Gay, Lesbian and Bisexual Group of Boston, 515 U.S. 557, 115 S. Ct. 2338, 132 L. Ed. 2d 487 (1995).

[13]   Thornhill v. Alabama, 310 U.S. 88, 60 S. Ct. 736, 84 L. Ed. 1093 (1940); Edwards v. South Carolina, 372 U.S. 229, 83 S. Ct. 680, 9 L. Ed. 2d 697 (1963).

[14]   Procunier v. Martinez, 416 U.S. 396, 94 S. Ct. 1800, 40 L. Ed. 2d 224 (1974).

[15]   **International Soc. for Krishna Consciousness, Inc. v. Lee, 505 U.S. 672, 112 S. Ct. 2701, 120 L. Ed. 2d 541 (1992)**; Thomas v. Collins, 323 U.S. 516, 65 S. Ct. 315, 89 L. Ed. 430 (1945).

[16]   Turner Broadcasting System, Inc. v. FCC, 512 U.S. 622, 114 S. Ct. 2445, 129 L. Ed. 2d 497 (1994).

[17]   Reno v. American Civil Liberties Union, *supra* note 11.

[18]   NAACP v. Claiborne Hardware Co., 458 U.S. 886, 102 S. Ct. 3409, 73 L. Ed. 2d 1215 (1982).

[19]   Ward v. Rock Against Racism, 491 U.S. 781, 109 S. Ct. 2746, 105 L. Ed. 2d 661 (1989); Schad v. Mount Ephraim, 452 U.S. 61, 101 S. Ct. 2176, 68 L. Ed. 2d 671 (1981).

Speech also includes the freedom not to speak or, in other words, to remain silent for ideological reasons. Compulsion to voice public adherence to ideas one finds unacceptable is forbidden by the First Amendment.[20] In *West Virginia State Board of Education v. Barnette*,[21] the Supreme Court struck down a state statute that required schoolchildren, on pain of expulsion, to recite the Pledge of Allegiance while saluting the American flag. The Court wrote:

> If there is any fixed star in our constitutional constellation, it is that no official, high or petty, can prescribe what shall be orthodox in politics, nationalism, religion, or other matters of opinion or force citizens to confess by word or act their faith therein. If there are any circumstances which permit of an exception, they do not now occur to us.[22]

Speech also includes mute conduct like displaying a red flag,[23] wearing a black armband,[24] staging a sit-in demonstration,[25] wearing a Nazi uniform,[26] and burning a cross at a Ku Klux Klan rally.[27] These acts constitute speech because they are intended to communicate a message. Mute conduct intended to communicate a message that is likely to be understood by those who view it is called **symbolic speech**.[28]

§ 2.4 First Amendment Distinction between a Speaker's Message and the Conduct Associated with Communicating It

Some speech dissemination techniques, such as writing a newspaper editorial, have only one ingredient — the message. Others, such as marching, picketing, and handbilling, have two. The second ingredient is public conduct. A large group of people marching down a city street, broadcasting their message over a bullhorn may interrupt traffic, hinder pedestrians, obstruct entrances to buildings, and cause distracting noise. The First Amendment distinguishes between the speaker's conduct and the message. While the message carries almost absolute protection, the speaker's conduct associated with the delivery does not.

In *United States v. O'Brien*,[29] the Supreme Court established the controlling test for when laws prohibiting conduct may be enforced against people engaged in

---

[20] West Virginia State Board of Education v. Barnette, 319 U.S. 624, 63 S. Ct. 1178, 87 L. Ed. 1628 (1943); Wooley v. Maynard, 430 U.S. 705, 97 S. Ct. 1428, 51 L. Ed. 2d 752 (1977).

[21] *Supra* note 20.

[22] *Id*. at 642, 63 S. Ct. at 1187, 87 L. Ed. at 1639.

[23] Stromberg v. California, 283 U.S. 359, 51 S. Ct. 532, 75 L. Ed. 1117 (1931).

[24] Tinker v. Des Moines Independent School Dist., 393 U.S. 503, 89 S. Ct. 733, 21 L. Ed. 2d 731 (1969).

[25] Brown v. Louisiana, 383 U.S. 131, 86 S. Ct. 719, 15 L. Ed. 2d 637 (1966).

[26] Collin v. Smith, 578 F. 2d 1197 (7th Cir.), *cert. denied*, 439 U.S. 916, 99 S. Ct. 291, 58 L. Ed. 2d 264 (1978) (striking down, on First Amendment grounds, several Skokie, Illinois, ordinances prohibiting the National Socialist Party of America from marching through the town).

[27] **Virginia v. Black, 538 U.S. 343, 123 S. Ct. 1536, 155 L. Ed. 2d 535 (2003)**; Brandenburg v. Ohio, 395 U.S. 444, 89 S. Ct. 1827, 23 L. Ed. 2d 430 (1969).

[28] **Texas v. Johnson, 491 U.S. 397, 109 S. Ct. 2533, 105 L. Ed. 2d 342 (1989)**.

[29] 391 U.S. 367, 88 S. Ct. 1673, 20 L. Ed. 2d 672 (1968).

speech. O'Brien burned his draft card during an anti-war demonstration to express his opposition to the war. He was prosecuted under a federal statute that made deliberate destruction of draft cards a crime. He argued that the statute could not be applied to him because he destroyed his draft card as a symbolic substitute for words. The Supreme Court rejected this defense, holding that laws prohibiting conduct may be applied to persons engaged in speech when they: (1) further a substantial government interest that is (2) unrelated to suppressing the message accompanying the conduct. Because the government had a legitimate reason for requiring preservation of draft cards — a reason unrelated to stifling political dissent — O'Brien's conviction was valid.

The holding in *United States v. O'Brien* has broad application in the field of law enforcement. Police are free to apply the general laws of the community (*i.e.*, noise, traffic, trespass, disorderly conduct, breach of the peace, *etc.*) to persons engaged in speech because these laws advance important community interests that are unrelated to suppressing the content of the speech. If the law says it is illegal to use artificial sound amplification equipment, obstruct traffic, block entrances to public buildings, or engage in other disruptive acts, police may arrest people who perform these acts, even when they are engaged in First Amendment activity.

In *Clark v. Community for Creative Non-Violence*,[30] the Supreme Court held that a park regulation prohibiting camping in national parks could be enforced against a group who wanted to hold a sleep-in in the park in front of the White House to dramatize the plight of the nation's homeless. In *Barnes v. Glen Theatre, Inc.*,[31] the Court ruled that laws prohibiting nudity in public places could be applied to erotic dancers in adult entertainment establishments. In both cases, the statute's regulatory focus was on the speaker's conduct, not the message that accompanied it.

The reverse was true in *Schacht v. United States*.[32] In *Schacht*, the Supreme Court struck down a federal statute prohibiting the wearing of military uniforms in dramatic productions under circumstances tending to discredit the armed forces. While this statute ostensibly regulated conduct (wearing military uniforms in dramatic productions), the government's real concern was the message (depicting the armed forces in an unfavorable light). Because the statute's regulatory focus was on the message, the statute was unconstitutional under the *O'Brien* test.

A similar result was reached in *Texas v. Johnson*,[33] which involved a state statute that made it a crime to desecrate an American flag. The defendant was arrested under this statute for burning an American flag during a protest demonstration. The Supreme Court noted that promoting respect for national symbols is the government's only

---

[30] 468 U.S. 288, 104 S. Ct. 3065, 82 L. Ed. 2d 221 (1984).

[31] 501 U.S. 560, 111 S. Ct. 2456, 115 L. Ed. 2d 504 (1991); City of Erie v. Pap's A.M., 529 U.S. 277, 120 S. Ct. 1382, 146 L. Ed. 2d 265 (2000) (same).

[32] 398 U.S. 58, 90 S. Ct. 1555, 26 L. Ed. 2d 44 (1970).

[33] *Supra* **note 28.** This decision so outraged Congress that it enacted federal flag desecration statute. The federal statute was sufficiently different from one struck down in Texas v. Johnson as to give the Supreme Court an opportunity to reconsider. In United States v. Eichman, 496 U.S. 310, 110 S. Ct. 2404, 110 L. Ed. 2d 287 (1990), the Supreme Court reconsidered, but refused to back down.

interest in regulating how Americans treat flags that belong to them. Since this interest is inextricably linked to the message that accompanies the act of flag desecration, the Texas statute was unconstitutional under the *O'Brien* test. The Court cautioned: "We do not consecrate the flag by punishing for its desecration, for in doing so we dilute the freedom that this cherished emblem represents."

The previous discussion in no way exhausts the range of activities that are considered "speech." The determination that "speech" is involved leads to the next question. Does the challenged restriction abridge freedom of speech? As previously noted, this answer often hinges on whether the restriction is directed at the speaker's message or the conduct accompanying it.[34]

Figure 2.3
Expressive Conduct

> General laws that prohibit trespasses, breaches of the peace, disorderly conduct, blocking the public passage, and the like may be applied to people engaged in speech-related conduct because they further important government interests that are unrelated to the message.

§ 2.5   Punishing Speech Because of the Message

The First Amendment sharply limits the government's power to punish people for what they say or for the language they use to say it. Subject to a small number of exceptions that will be discussed shortly, laws that ban speech because of its content rarely survive a constitutional challenge.[35] In *Linmark Associates, Inc. v. Township of Willingboro*,[36] the Supreme Court invalidated an ordinance that prohibited the posting of "For Sale" and "Sold" signs on real estate. The purpose of ordinance was to stem panic selling in newly racially integrated neighborhoods. The Court held that truthful information cannot be suppressed out of fear of how the public will react to it. The choice "between the dangers of suppressing information, and the dangers of its misuse if it is freely available," the Court wrote, "is one the First Amendment has already made

---

[34]   *See, e.g.*, **Brown v. Entertainment Merchants Ass'n, — U.S. —, 131 S. Ct. 2729, 100 L. Ed. 2d – (2011)** (characterizing the government's lack of power to restrict speech based on its content as "the most basic principle in First Amendment jurisprudence").

[35]   *See, e.g.*, **Brown v. Entertainment Merchants Ass'n,** *supra* **note 34** (stating that content-based restrictions on protected speech are invalid unless they further a compelling government interest); United States v. Stevens, _ U.S. _, 130 S. Ct. 1577, 176 L. Ed. 2d 435 (2010) (declining to create an exception to the First Amendment for speech depicting gruesome acts of cruelty to animals).

[36]   431 U.S. 85, 97 S. Ct. 1614, 52 L. Ed. 2d 155 (1977).

for us." [37] In *Brown v. Hartlage*,[38] the Court invalidated a campaign corruption law that prohibited political candidates from promising that, if elected, they would serve at a reduced salary. Mr. Justice Brennan wrote:

> [The First] Amendment embodies our trust in the free exchange of ideas as the means by which the people are to choose between good ideas and bad, and between candidates for political office. The State's fear that voters might make an ill-advised choice does not provide the State with a compelling justification for limiting speech. It is not the function of government to "select which issues are worth discussing or debating,"... in the course of a political campaign.

The belief that truth is most likely to emerge through an unfettered exchange of ideas is central to the First Amendment. Even offensive ideas are protected on the theory that, once expressed, they can be openly debated and that truth will emerge from this process.[39]

A. *Topics That Have Diminished or No Free Speech Protection*

Although free speech generally means freedom to speak on any matter, a small number of speech categories have been excluded from the First Amendment. They include: (1) **obscenity** and **child pornography**;[40] (2) **fighting words**;[41] (3) threats;[42] and (4) incitement to immediate unlawful action.[43] Exclusion has been justified on the grounds that these categories were regarded as unprotected at the time the First Amendment was adopted and hence were not considered part of the freedom of speech that the Amendment was intended to protect.[44] The Supreme Court is unlikely to enlarge this

---

[37] *Id.*

[38] 456 U.S. 45, 102 S. Ct. 1523, 71 L. Ed. 2d 732 (1982). See also Republican Party of Minnesota v. White, 536 U.S. 765, 122 S. Ct. 2528, 153 L. Ed. 2d 694 (2002) (judicial ethics rule prohibiting candidates for judicial election from announcing their views on disputed legal or political issues violated First Amendment because it prohibited speech on basis of content).

[39] Abrams v. United States, 250 U.S. 616, 630, 40 S. Ct. 17, 22, 63 L. Ed. 1173 (1919) (Holmes, J., dissenting); **Virginia v. Black**, *supra* note 27 ("The hallmark of the protection of free speech is to allow free trade in ideas — even ideas that the overwhelming majority of people might find distasteful or discomforting."); **Texas v. Johnson**, *supra* note 28 ("If there is a bedrock principle underlying the First Amendment, it is that the government may not prohibit the expression of an idea simply because society finds the idea itself offensive or disagreeable."); Barry v. Boos, 485 U.S. 312, 108 S. Ct. 1157, 99 L. Ed. 2d 333 (1988) ("[C]itizens must tolerate insulting, and even outrageous speech in order to provide adequate breathing space to the freedoms protected by the First Amendment.").

[40] *See* § 2.6 *infra.*

[41] *See* § 2.7 *infra.*

[42] *See* § 2.8 *infra.*

[43] *See* § 2.9 *infra.*

[44] **Brown v. Entertainment Merchants Association**, *supra* **note 34** (declining to carve out an exception to the First Amendment for speech depicting extreme violence); United States v. Stevens, *supra* note 34 (declining to carve out an exception to the First Amendment for speech depicting gruesome acts of cruelty to animals).

list because it has stated that new categories cannot be recognized unless their exclusion from the First Amendment is historically grounded. In *United States v. Stevens*,[45] for example, the Court declined to exclude videos depicting gruesome acts of cruelty to live animals from the protection of the First Amendment because no historical basis existed for denying protection.

The excluded categories have narrow, well-defined boundaries. Students need to pay close attention to them because police may not arrest people for the contents of their speech unless their speech falls within one of the categories.[46]

§ 2.6   — Obscenity and Child Pornography

A. *The Miller Definition of Obscenity*

In 1957, the Supreme Court ruled that obscenity lacks First Amendment protection, and then struggled for the next 15 years to formulate a constitutional definition. The current test was announced in *Miller v. California*.[47] A work is obscene under the *Miller* test if, taken as a whole, it:

1.   appeals to the prurient interests of the average person;
2.   depicts "hard-core" sexual acts, previously defined by applicable state law, in a patently offensive way; and
3.   lacks any serious literary, artistic, political, scientific, or other value.

Three separate criteria must be satisfied before materials can be branded obscene and excluded from First Amendment protection. First, they must appeal to the *prurient* interest of the average person. Prurient is a pajorative term that suggests unwholesomeness. Materials that arouse a normal, healthy interest in sexual matters are not obscene.[48] They must appeal to an abnormal, voyeuristic, degrading, or shameful interest in sex to satisfy the first requirement. Next, the work must depict hard-core sexual acts, covered in the state's obscenity law, in a patently offensive way. The *Miller* test places the onus on state legislatures to give concrete meaning to the legal definition of obscenity by enumerating specific types of hard-core sexual acts that must be found in a work before it can be branded as obscene. These acts may include: patently offensive verbal or visual depictions of ultimate sexual acts (normal or perverted, real or simulated); masturbation; lewd exhibition of genitals; sadomasochistic sexual behavior; violent sex; bestiality; and sexual perversions. Finally, the work, considered

---

45   United States v. Stevens, *supra* note 35.
46   Roth v. United States, 354 U.S. 476, 77 S. Ct. 1304, 1 L. Ed. 2d 1498 (1957), overruled by Miller v. California, 413 U.S. 15, 93 S. Ct. 2607, 37 L. Ed. 2d 419 (1973).
47   *Supra* note 47.
48   Brockett v. Spokane Arcades, Inc., 472 U.S. 491, 105 S. Ct. 2794, 86 L. Ed. 2d 394 (1985).

as a whole, must lack serious literary, political, scientific, artistic, or other value. Works that have serious value are not obscene even when they describe or depict sexual activity in highly graphic ways.

Figure 2.4
Constitutional Test for Obscenity

> To be considered obscene in the constitutional sense, a literary work must:
>
> 1. appeal to prurient interests of the average person;
> 2. depict hard-core sexual acts previously defined by state law in a patently offensive way; and
> 3. lack serious literary, artistic, political, scientific, or other value.

B. Sale of Obscenity to Minors

The First Amendment permits states to enact separate laws regulating the sale of sexually explicit materials to minors.[49] Enactment of child obscenity laws requires a modification of the first prong of the *Miller* test. The determination whether a work appeals to prurient interests is made from the perspective of a minor rather than the average person. A variable standard enables states to restrict the sale to minors of materials that are inappropriate for them, but that are not obscene under the *Miller* test and, consequently, can be sold to adults.

In *Brown v. Entertainment Merchants Association*,[50] the Supreme Court was asked to expand the definition of obscenity to include graphic violence and to uphold a state statute prohibiting the sale of violent video games to minors based on the notion of variable obscenity—the notion that materials can sometimes be obscene when sold to a minor that would not be so if sold to an adult. The Supreme Court refused, explaining that "the obscenity exception . . . does not cover whatever a legislature finds shocking, but only depictions of 'sexual conduct.'" This statute did not seek to "adjust the boundaries of an existing category of unprotected speech to ensure that a definition designed for adults is not uncritically applied to children." It attempted, instead, "to create a wholly new category of content-based regulation" that applies only to speech directed at children. Legislatures do not have "free-floating power to restrict the ideas to which children may be exposed." It is up to parents, and not the government, to decide whether particular materials are appropriate for their children.

---

[49] Ginsberg v. New York, 390 U.S. 629, 88 S. Ct. 1274, 20 L. Ed. 2d 195 (1968) (upholding use of a variable obscenity standard that restricts the rights of minors to obtain sexually explicit materials that are not obscene as to adults).

[50] *Supra* note 35.

C. Child Pornography

The *Miller* test was formulated as an adult obscenity standard. The psychological damage done to children by exploiting them to produce **child pornography** was not considered. In order to protect children from sexual exploitation, traffic in child pornography can be banned without regard to whether the work is obscene under the *Miller* standard. However, departure from the *Miller* standard is allowed only for works that visually depict real children engaged in sexual activity, not adults posing as children or computer-generated images.[51]

D. Role of Police in Enforcing Obscenity Laws

Because the line between punishable obscenity and free speech is not so sharp that police officers can instantly recognize on which side of the line certain works fall, special rules have been developed for obscenity searches and seizures. The rules are designed to minimize the risk that constitutionally protected materials will be mistakenly seized while enforcing obscenity laws.

First, a search warrant is *always* necessary to seize literary materials.[52] Police must obtain a preliminary determination from a judicial officer that there is probable cause to believe that a particular work is obscene before they may seize it. Undercover purchases are exempt from this requirement because no seizure is involved.[53] Purchases are a convenient way to acquire the evidence that will be needed to support an application for a search warrant.

Second, affidavits used to support an obscenity search warrant must contain a higher than normal degree of specificity. The ideal situation is for the judge to view the materials in person. When this is not feasible, an officer applying for a search warrant must provide detailed factual data regarding the types of hard-core sexual acts, their quantitative and qualitative aspects, and their relationship to the plot, if any. It will not do to supply no more than a conclusory opinion that the *Miller* test has been met. The officer's job is to supply factual data and the judge's job is to evaluate the data in the light of the legal standards. The officer's affidavit must be detailed enough to enable the

---

[51] New York v. Ferber, 458 U.S. 747, 102 S. Ct. 3348, 73 L. Ed. 2d 1113 (1982) (holding that works that visually depict *actual* children engaged in sexual activity may be banned, regardless of whether the works are obscene under the *Miller* test); Ashcroft v. Free Speech Coalition, 535 U.S. 234, 122 S. Ct. 1389, 152 L. Ed. 2d 403 (2002) (holding that trafficking in simulated child pornography — child pornography produced through computer-generated images or adults posing as children — may be prohibited only if the works are obscene under the *Miller* test). *But see* United States v. Williams, 553 U.S. 285, 128 S. Ct. 1830, 170 L.Ed.2d 650 (2008) (holding that governments may prohibit offers to supply or requests to receive child pornography, even though no such material exists, because offers to engage in illegal transactions are not protected by the First Amendment).

[52] Roaden v. Kentucky, 413 U.S. 496, 93 S. Ct. 2796, 37 L. Ed. 2d 757 (1973); Walter v. United States, 447 U.S. 649, 100 S. Ct. 2395, 65 L. Ed. 2d 410 (1983).

[53] Maryland v. Macon, 472 U.S. 463, 105 S. Ct. 2778, 86 L. Ed. 2d 370 (1985).

judge to make an independent determination of probable cause.[54] The sample affidavit in Figure 2.5 illustrates the amount of detail needed.

Figure 2.5
Sample Affidavit for an Obscenity Search Warrant

The affidavit below was upheld as legally sufficient in *New York v. P.J. Video, Inc.*, 475 U.S. 868, 878 106 S. Ct. 1610, 89 L. Ed. 2d 871 (1986).

"I, I.M. VIRTUOUS, being duly sworn, deposes and says:

I am presently a Confidential Criminal Investigator assigned to the Hope County District Attorney's Office and prior to this, was a detective with the State of Confusion Police Department for approximately 25 years.

On October 26, 2011 I rented and viewed the videotape movie "CALIFORNIA VALLEY GIRLS" in a viewing booth at Sex Frolics, an adult entertainment establishment located at 6900 Smut Road. The viewing of "CALIFORNIA VALLEY GIRLS" began at 12:00 Noon and lasted until 1:33 P.M.

The content and character of the above mentioned video movie is as follows: Six white females, approximately 18 to 25 years of age, are unemployed and attempt to make a living by becoming prostitutes. The first scene is a bedroom scene where two females are involved in lovemaking, fondling, and cunnilingus. The second scene depicts a white male and a white female having intercourse in the back of a van. The third scene is a house scene where six girls, all white females, are introduced to the art of lovemaking. One male, approximately 35 years of age, is teaching the girls the art of fellatio with each one of them performing this act on him. The next scene is a bedroom scene in a home where a husband and wife, and the wife's friend, perform various sexual acts which include intercourse, fellatio, anal intercourse, and cunnilingus. The movie ends with some lesbianism where the wife performs cunnilingus on the friend while the latter performs fellatio on the husband and they engage in intercourse and anal intercourse."

Third, the Fourth Amendment requirement that search warrants particularly describe the "things to be seized" is strictly applied when the things to be seized are literary materials. General language authorizing seizure of "all obscene publications" found at a particular location is unconstitutional because it delegates to the executing officer discretion to make on-the-spot determinations of whether particular works are obscene. This determination is one that can only be made by a judge.[55]

Finally, police officers may not seize all copies of items described in their search warrant. Their mission is to obtain evidence for use at trial; one or two copies are enough for this purpose. Police may not halt sales by seizing all

---

[54] Roaden v. Kentucky, *supra* note 52; Heller v. New York, 413 U.S. 483, 93 S. Ct. 2789, 37 L. Ed. 2d 745 (1973), *cert. denied sub. nom.*, Buckley v. New York, 418 U.S. 944, 94 S. Ct. 3231, 41 L. Ed. 2d 1175 (1974).
[55] Marcus v. Search Warrant, 367 U.S. 717, 81 S. Ct. 1708, 6 L. Ed. 2d 1127 (1961); A Quantity of Copies of Books v. Kansas, 378 U.S. 205, 84 S. Ct. 1723, 12 L. Ed. 2d 809 (1964).

copies until after the work has been adjudicated obscene in an adversarial legal proceeding.[56]

§ 2.7 — Fighting Words

In *Chaplinsky v. New Hampshire*,[57] a man was arrested for confronting the city marshal and calling him "a God damned racketeer" and a "damned Fascist" to his face. Prior to *Chaplinsky*, the Court had observed that a "resort to epithets or personal abuse is not in any proper sense communication of information safeguarded by the Constitution . . ."[58] In *Chaplinsky*, the Supreme Court officially excluded "**fighting words**" from the protection of the First Amendment.

Subsequent cases have reaffirmed the holding in *Chaplinsky* and have sought to clarify the scope of this exclusion. The "fighting words" exclusion is not concerned with speech that communicates an idea or makes a statement about the speaker's beliefs.[59] Marching through a Jewish neighborhood wearing Nazi uniforms with swastikas is an example. This conduct is protected by the First Amendment because the marchers are expressing their views.[60] Speech that communicates ideas cannot be punished as fighting words, no matter how insulting, offensive, or provocative the ideas may be.[61] "Fighting words" are used for a different purpose. Their purpose is purely to inflict injury.

There is no judicially established list of words that, when spoken, always constitute "fighting words." Whether language constitutes "fighting words" requires an examination of both the words used and the context in which they are uttered. A person may be arrested for using "fighting words" only if the person's language is:

---

[56]   Marcus v. Search Warrant, *supra* note 55; Heller v. New York, *supra* note 54; Fort Wayne Books, Inc. v. Indiana, 489 U.S. 46, 109 S. Ct. 916, 103 L. Ed. 2d 34 (1989).

[57]   315 U.S. 568, 62 S. Ct. 766, 86 L. Ed. 1031 (1942).

[58]   Cantwell v. Connecticut, 310 U.S. 296, 60 S. Ct. 900, 84 L. Ed. 1221 (1940) (dicta).

[59]   *See, e.g.*, Boos v. Barry, *supra* note 39 (". . . in public debate our own citizens must tolerate insulting, and even outrageous, speech in order to provide adequate 'breathing space' to the freedoms protected by the First Amendment"); Bachellar v. Maryland, 397 U.S. 564, 90 S. Ct. 1312, 25 L. Ed. 2d 570 (1970) (. . . under our Constitution the public expression of ideas may not be prohibited merely because the ideas are themselves offensive to some of their hearers . . .).

[60]   Collin v. Smith, *supra* note 26.

[61]   *See, e.g.*, R.A.V. v. City of St. Paul, 505 U.S. 377, 395, 112 S. Ct. 2538, 120 L. Ed. 2d 305 (1992) (invalidating statute making it an offense to display symbols, such as burning crosses and swastikas, known to arouse anger in others on the basis of race, creed, religion, or gender); Brandenburg v. Ohio, *supra* note 27 (overturning conviction for burning a cross at a Ku Klux Klan rally); Sons of Confederate Veterans, Inc. ex rel. Griffin v. Commissioner of Virginia Dept. of Motor Vehicles, 288 F.3d 610 (4th Cir. 2002) (invalidating statute which prohibited use of Confederate flag on specialty license plates); Church of American Knights of Ku Klux Klan v. Kerik, 232 F. Supp. 2d 205 (S.D.N.Y. 2002) (invalidating statute prohibiting wearing of masks at public gathering).

1.   Abusive, derisive, or insulting.[62]
2.   Spoken in a face-to-face encounter under circumstances likely to provoke the other person into making an immediate violent response.[63]

Whether the second element is present calls for consideration of the factual context, including the time and place of the communication, the characteristics of the parties, and their proximity. Personally abusive remarks made by a feeble old lady or shouted from the window of a passing car, for example, do not constitute "fighting words," because the possibility of provoking an immediate violent response is absent.

The "fighting words" exclusion has a narrow application when the target of verbal abuse is a police officer because police officers are trained not to respond in physical ways.[64] Making profane gestures or calling a police officer an "ass" is not enough to

---

[62]   Common examples include racial slurs ("nigger") and insults about a person's sexual orientation ("faggot'), masculinity ("pussy"), or sexual looseness ("slut"). *See, e.g.,* In re *John,* 201 Ariz. 424, 36 P.3d 772 (2001) (Juvenile's racially hostile outburst — "fuck you, you goddamn nigger" — constituted fighting words that were not constitutionally protected speech. The court observed that "few words convey such an inflammatory message of racial hatred and bigotry as the term 'nigger'"); In re *Spivey,* 345 N.C. 404, 480 S.E.2d 693, 699 (1997) (affirming removal of a district attorney from office for using the derogatory and abusive racial epithet "nigger"; observing that "[n]o fact is more generally known than that a white man who calls a black man a nigger within his hearing will hurt and anger the black man and often provoke him to confront the white man and retaliate"); Gilles v. Davis, 427 F.3d 197 (3rd Cir. 2005) (holding that preacher's remarks addressed to woman who identified herself as both Christian and lesbian, including "Christian lesbo," "lesbian for Jesus," "do you lay down with dogs," and "are you a bestiality lover," constituted fighting words and were not protected by First Amendment.).

[63]   The court in City of Seattle v. Camby, 104 Wash.2d 49, 701 P.2d 499, 501 (1985) broke the definition of fighting words down into three elements: "First, the words must be directed at a particular person or group of persons. There must be an addressee. Second, the words must be personally abusive epithets or insults that "when addressed to the ordinary citizen, are, as a matter of common knowledge, inherently likely to provoke violent reaction. "Third, the words must be evaluated in the context in which they are used to determine if it is likely that the addressee would react violently."

[64]   Heckling an officer, calling the officer names, and yelling insults and obscenities are protected by the First Amendment and will not support an arrest. *See, e.g.,* Lewis v. City of New Orleans, 415 U.S. 130, 94 S. Ct. 970, 39 L. Ed. 2d 214 (1974); Gooding v. Wilson, 405 U.S. 518, 92 S. Ct. 1103, 31 L. Ed. 2d 408 (1972); City of Houston v. Hill, 482 U.S. 451, 107 S. Ct. 2502, 96 L. Ed. 2d 398, *cert. denied,* 483 U.S. 1001, 107 S. Ct. 3222, 97 L. Ed. 2d 729 (1987); **Sandul v. Larion, 119 F.3d 1250 (6th Cir. 1997)**. *See also* Allen T. McGlynn, *The Constitutional Ramifications of Calling a Police Officer an "Asshole,"* 16 S. Ill. U. L.J. 741 (1992). However, the line is crossed when abusive language is accompanied by provocative gestures, such as shaking a finger in an officer's face, raising a fist, or spitting. The words and acts in combination justify an arrest. *See, e.g.,* State v. Bower, 725 N. W. 2d 435 (Iowa 2006) (affirming conviction for entering officer's personal space in an angry, threatening manner and telling him to get off the property or he would be sued). Threats stand on a different footing. Police are justified in arresting citizens who verbally threaten them. *See, e.g.,* Wise v. Com., 49 Va. App. 344, 641 S. E. 2d 134 (Va. App. 2007) (affirming conviction for stating to police officer: "the first thing I'm going to do when I get out is find you. I know where you live, or, I see you all the time in town. You're mine.").

justify an arrest for using "fighting words."[65] While the Supreme Court has stopped short of saying the "fighting words" exclusion can never apply when the object of verbal abuse is a police officer, the indignities must go far beyond what an ordinary person would be expected to endure.[66] In *Lewis v. City of New Orleans*,[67] the Supreme Court overturned the conviction of a woman who hurled a litany of four-letter words at a police officer when he asked her husband for his license. The officer arrested the woman under an ordinance making it a crime to "curse or revile or to use ... opprobrious language toward or with reference to any member of the city police while in the actual performance of his duty." The Supreme Court declared the ordinance unconstitutional because it made cursing at a police officer a crime without regard to whether the words were likely to provoke an immediate violent response. The Court commented that this likelihood is reduced when abusive language is addressed to a police officer because they are trained not to respond in physical ways. The Supreme Court repeated this observation in *City of Houston v. Hill*,[68] this time noting that "freedom of individuals verbally to oppose or challenge police actions without thereby risking arrest is one of the principal characteristics by which we distinguish a free nation from a police state." Consequently, police officers should think twice about arresting citizens who insult them.

§ 2.8   — Threats

Threats are another class of speech that has been excluded from the First Amendment.[69] However, before a person can be punished for making a threat, a true threat must be made. To constitute a true threat, the speaker must intend his statement to be understood as a serious expression of intent to commit an act of unlawful violence against a particular person or group of persons.[70]

Context is everything in determining whether a true threat has been made. In *Watts v. United States*,[71] a young man took the floor at an anti-war rally and said in front of large audience:

---

[65]   *See, e.g.,* **Buffkins v. City of Omaha, 922 F.2d 465 (8th Cir. 1990)**; Sweatt v. Bailey, 876 F. Supp. 1371 (M.D. Ala. 1995); Brockway v. Shepherd, 942 F. Supp. 1012 (M.D. Pa. 1997).

[66]   In the Matter of M.A.H. and J.L.W., 572 N.W.2d 752 (Minn. App. 1997).

[67]   *Supra* note 64.

[68]   *Id.*

[69]   Watts v. United States, 394 U.S. 705, 89 S. Ct. 1399, 22 L. Ed. 2d 664 (1969); **Virginia v. Black**, supra note 27.

[70]   **Virginia v. Black**, *supra* note 27; United States v. Bagdasarian, 625F. 3d 1113 (9th Cir. 2011) (anonymous comments on Internet message board predicting that an African-American presidential candidate would be shot did not constitute an explicit or implicit threat to take action).

[71]   *Supra* note 69.

They always holler at us to get an education. And now I have already received my draft classification as 1-A and I have got to report for my physical this Monday morning. I am not going. If they ever make me carry a rifle, the first man to get in my sights is L.B.J. They are not going to make me kill my black brothers.

The "L.B.J." the young man was referring to was Lyndon Baines Johnson, then President of the United States. Watts was indicted and convicted under a federal statute making it a crime to "knowingly and willfully ... [make] any threat to take the life of or to inflict bodily harm upon the President ..." The Supreme Court set aside the conviction on the grounds that Watts' statement, interpreted in the context in which it was made, constituted nothing more than "a kind of very crude offensive method of stating political opposition to the President" and, consequently, was not a true threat.

The Supreme Court revisited this issue in *Virginia v. Black*.[72] The case involved a statute that made it a crime to burn a cross with intent to intimidate. The Court began by noting that cross-burnings can have different meanings in different contexts. When a cross is burned on a black family's lawn, it communicates a message of impending violence — "Get out or else!" The message constitutes a true threat and is outside the protection of the First Amendment.[73] However, crosses are also burned at Ku Klux Klan rallies as a way of expressing group solidarity and shared commitment to the white supremacist cause. The message, in this context, constitutes core political speech that is protected by the First Amendment.[74] Although states may outlaw cross-burnings done with intent to intimidate, the Virginia statute went too far. It presumed that *all* cross-burning were done with this intent. The context must be examined on a case-by-case basis to determine whether a true threat has been made.[75]

§ 2.9　—Incitement to Immediate Illegal Action

Inflammatory speech at the right time and place can incite action. Establishing the point at which speech advocating violence or other unlawful acts loses First Amendment protection was one of the Supreme Court's major concerns during the first half of the twentieth century. In the 1919 case of *Schenck v. United States*,[76] the Supreme Court adopted a test that would dominate First Amendment jurisprudence for decades to

---

[72]　*Supra* note 27. *See also, generally,* Jennifer E. Rothman, *Freedom of Speech and True Threats*, 25 HARV. J. L. & PUB. POL'Y 283 (2001); John T. Nockleby, Note, *Hate Speech in Context: the Case of Verbal Threats*, 42 BUFF. 653 (1994).

[73]　**Virginia v. Black**, *supra* note 27 (stating that cross-burning done with intent to intimidate is not protected by the First Amendment); United States v. J.H.H., 22 F.3d 821 (8th Cir. 1994) (upholding conviction for cross-burning with intent to intimidate where three boys ignited a cross in the middle of the night in an African-American family's yard).

[74]　**Virginia v. Black**, *supra* note 27.

[75]　*Id.*

[76]　249 U.S. 47, 39 S. Ct. 247, 63 L. Ed. 470 (1919).

come. Schenck, a Socialist Party leader, was convicted under the Espionage Act for mailing circulars to young men who had been called up for the draft, criticizing the war and urging them not to go. At the time of this appeal, the nation had not yet recovered a peacetime mentality. Mr. Justice Oliver Wendell Holmes, writing for the Court, affirmed the conviction, stating:

> We admit that in many places and in ordinary times the defendants, in saying all that was said in the circular, would have been within their constitutional rights. But the character of every act depends upon the circumstances in which it is done .... The question in every case is whether the words used are used in such circumstances and are of such a nature to create a *clear and present danger* that they will bring about the substantive evils that Congress has a right to prevent.[77]

Within a few years, it became apparent to Mr. Justice Holmes that he had set loose a potential Frankenstein monster in the hands of a Court swept up in the post-war tides of a nation beset by hysteria and frenzy. The waves of violence and labor unrest in the 1950s created a panic that all of the nation's woes were being stirred up by an international Communist conspiracy. State legislatures responded in rapid succession by enacting criminal anarchist and syndicalism laws, making it a crime to advocate or teach the doctrine that organized governments should be overthrown by force and violence. A rash of prosecutions directed at left-wing radicals followed.

In a number of cases handed down during the early years following *Schenck*, a majority of the Court affirmed the conviction of harmless political dissidents under the guise of applying the clear and present danger doctrine, with no real effort to determine whether the danger from their speech was either clear or present. The Court stated that advocacy of the doctrine of the violent overthrow of the government was so inherently dangerous to society that the government could stamp the doctrine out in whatever form it took.[78] Justices Holmes and Brandeis opposed this application, taking the position that advocacy of even the most alarming ideas should be protected by the First Amendment, unless the speech posed a clear and present danger of *immediate* unlawful action. In a famous dissenting opinion, they argued:

> Fear of serious injury cannot alone justify suppression of free speech and assembly. Men feared witches and burnt women. It is the function of speech to free men from the bondage of irrational fears. To justify suppression of free speech there must be reasonable ground to fear that serious evil will result if free speech is practiced. There must be reasonable ground to believe that the danger apprehended is imminent. There must be reasonable ground to believe that the evil to be prevented is a serious one ... [E]ven advocacy of violation [of the law], however reprehensible morally,

---

[77] *Id.* at 52, 39 S. Ct. at 249 (emphasis added).
[78] Abrams v. United States, 250 U.S. 616, 40 S. Ct. 17, 63 L. Ed. 1173 (1919); Gitlow v. New York, 268 U.S. 652, 45 S. Ct. 625, 69 L. Ed. 1138 (1925). Some of the same First Amendment issues confronted during the McCarthy era are now resurfacing. *See, e.g.*, Holder v. Humanitarian Law Project, _ U.S. _, 130 S. Ct. 2705, 177 L. Ed. 2d 355 (2010).

is not a justification for denying free speech where ... there is nothing to indicate that the advocacy would be immediately acted on ... Those who won American independence by revolution were not cowards. They did not fear political change. They did not exalt order at the cost of liberty. To courageous, self-reliant men, with confidence in the power of free and fearless reasoning applied through the processes of popular government, no danger flowing from speech could be deemed clear and present, unless the incidence of the evil apprehended is so imminent that it may befall before there is an opportunity for full discussion. If there is time to expose through discussion the falsehoods and fallacies, to avert the evil by the processes of education, the remedy to be applied is more speech, not enforced silence. Only an emergency can justify repression.[79]

A. *Brandenburg Test*

The position taken by Justices Holmes and Brandeis was accepted by the Supreme Court 40 years later in *Brandenburg v. Ohio*[80] and has been the law ever since. Brandenburg, a Ku Klux Klan leader, was convicted under an Ohio statute that made it a crime to advocate "the duty, necessity, or propriety of crime, sabotage, violence, or unlawful methods of terrorism as a means of accomplishing ... political reform ..." His conviction stemmed from a speech he delivered at a Ku Klux Klan rally on a farm outside Cincinnati, Ohio. A local television reporter, who had been invited to witness the rally, filmed the event and later broadcast portions of the footage, in which Brandenburg asserted that "if our President, our Congress, our Supreme Court, continues to suppress the white, Caucasian race, it's possible that there might have to be some revengeance [sic] taken." Brandenburg further stated that "the nigger should be returned to Africa, the Jew returned to Israel." The Supreme Court overturned the conviction, holding that the Constitution does not allow the government to make advocacy of the use of force or other unlawful action a crime unless the advocacy is "both directed toward inciting or producing imminent lawless action, and likely to incite or produce such action."

The *Brandenburg* test limits the authority of the police, as well as the authority of legislatures. Police may not halt ongoing speech and arrest a speaker for inciting unlawful activity unless: (1) the speaker *intends* to incite unlawful action, (2) the unlawful action is *likely to occur*, and (3) the action is *imminent*. In *Hess v. Indiana*,[81] the Supreme Court overturned the disorderly conduct conviction of an anti-war demonstrator for shouting "We'll take the f——ing street later!" as the police were trying to move a crowd of demonstrators off the street and onto the sidewalk so that vehicles could pass. The Court held that the arrest was improper because Hess did not urge *imminent* unlawful action. The action urged ("We'll take the f——ing street later") was to occur at some indefinite future time.

---

[79]   Whitney v. California, 274 U.S. 357, 47 S. Ct. 641, 71 L. Ed. 1095 (1927), *overruled* in Brandenburg v. Ohio, 395 U.S. 444, 89 S. Ct. 1827, 23 L. Ed. 2d 430 (1969).

[80]   *Supra* note 79.

[81]   414 U.S. 105, 94 S. Ct. 326, 38 L. Ed. 2d 303 (1973).

Figure 2.6
Incitement to Immediate Unlawful Action

> Speech advocating violence or other unlawful actions is protected by First Amendment unless it is both:
>
> 1. directed toward inciting *imminent* lawless action and
> 2. is likely to incite such action.

B. Premature Fears

Speech may not be suppressed out of premature fears of what might occur if it is allowed to take place.[82] On April 30, 1992, the day after verdicts of acquittal were announced in a highly publicized trial of several Los Angeles police officers accused of the racially motivated beating of a black motorist, a number of demonstrations occurred in various parts of San Francisco. Most were peaceful, but a few were not. That evening, the mayor of San Francisco declared a local emergency and imposed a 9:00 P.M. curfew. The next day, he and the chief of police decided to ban all demonstrations, peaceful or otherwise, effective May 1, 1992, and to arrest all demonstrators who refused to obey dispersal orders. Later that day, local authorities became aware that a demonstration was planned for the BART (Bay Area Rapid Transit) Plaza area. Police went to the scene, issued dispersal orders, and began arresting people. A federal court ruled that imposing a ban on demonstrating before the demonstrators have done anything illegal is unconstitutional. The court stated:

> The law is clear that First Amendment activity may not be banned simply because prior similar activity led to or involved instances of violence. There are sound reasons for this rule. Demonstrations can be expected when the government acts in highly controversial ways, or other events occur that excite or arouse the passions of the citizenry. The more controversial the occurrence, the more likely people are to demonstrate. Some of these demonstrations may become violent. The courts have held that the proper response to potential and actual violence is for the government to ensure an adequate police presence, and to arrest those who actually engage in such conduct, rather than to suppress legitimate First Amendment conduct as a prophylactic measure.

The court stressed the importance of allowing citizens to express their frustrations with recent events by engaging in spontaneous protest. Banning demonstrations because others have or might abuse the privilege deprives innocent citizens of their First Amendment rights. The court, nevertheless, left open the question whether a city, confronted with widespread violence beyond the capabilities of the police, might in rare instances be justified in imposing a time-limited ban on all demonstrations. The court found it unnecessary to address this question because this point had not been reached in San Francisco at the time the mayor imposed the ban in question.

---

[82] Collins v. Jordan, 110 F.3d 1363 (9th Cir. 1996).

The Ohio Supreme Court expressed a similar view in setting aside an injunction that prohibited two groups with opposing viewpoints from simultaneously picketing outside the home of a Nazi war criminal whose conviction had been overturned by the Israeli Supreme Court.[83] The Coalition for Jewish Concerns was picketing to show their opposition, while the Ku Klux Klan was picketing to show their support. Picketing had been peaceful, but local authorities were concerned. The Ohio Supreme Court overturned the ban on simultaneous picketing, holding that prohibiting speech is not a constitutionally acceptable means of averting a feared disturbance.

C. Hostile Reception

Police intervention is justified when an outbreak appears imminent, but the response depends on whether the speaker[84] or the audience[85] is responsible. When the threat of an outbreak stems from a hostile reaction to an unpopular speaker's views, peacekeeping efforts must be directed at the audience, not the speaker.[86] In *Cox v. Louisiana*,[87] 2,000 African-American university students assembled a few blocks from the courthouse in Baton Rouge to protest segregation. They walked in an orderly fashion, obeying traffic laws, until they reached the courthouse, where they pledged allegiance to the flag, prayed briefly, sang two "freedom songs," and listened to a speech delivered by Cox, their leader. A crowd of 100 to 300 spectators gathered on the sidewalk to watch. There was some angry muttering and jeering, but the protesters did not respond and the police presence at the scene was adequate to maintain order. At the end of his speech, Cox urged the demonstrators to go uptown and "sit in" at various segregated lunch counters. The sheriff, worried about the crowd's reaction, took a bullhorn and ordered the demonstrators to go home. When the order was ignored, the police arrested Cox for

---

[83] City of Seven Hills v. Aryan Nations, 76 Ohio St. 3d 304, 667 N.E.2d 942 (1996). *See also* Grider v. Abramson, 180 F.3d 739 (6th Cir.) (discussing creation of buffer zones and use of metal detectors to address public safety concerns when groups with opposing views seek to demonstrate at the same time and place). Issuance of a permit eases the problems of counter–demonstrations. Once a permit has been issued, police have authority to enforce the permit by excluding hecklers and others who want to drown out the permit holders' message and replace it with their own. *See e.g.,* Torossian v. Hayo, 45 F. Supp. 2d 63 (D.D.C. 1999) (counter-demonstrators do not have a right to express their views by intruding into an area reserved for another event then in progress); Schwitzgebel v. City of Strongsville, 898 F. Supp. 1208 (N.D. Ohio 1995) (forcible removal of AIDS activists from a Bush-Quayle campaign rally did not violate their First Amendment rights because they physically intruded upon another previously permitted event); Kroll v. U.S. Capitol Police, 847 F.2d 893 (D.C. Cir.1988) (issuance of a permit authorizes police to exclude counter-demonstrators who interject themselves into an area reserved for another event).

[84] Feiner v. New York, 340 U.S. 315, 71 S. Ct. 303, 95 L. Ed. 295 (1951).

[85] Cox v. Louisiana, 379 U.S. 536, 85 S. Ct. 453, 13 L. Ed. 2d 471 (1965).

[86] *See, e.g.*, Forsyth County v. Nationalist Movement, 505 U.S. 123, 112 S. Ct. 2395, 120 L. Ed. 2d 101 (1992); Gregory v. City of Chicago, 394 U.S. 111, 89 S. Ct. 946, 22 L. Ed. 2d 134 (1969); Cox v. Louisiana, *supra* note 85.

[87] *Supra* note 85.

causing a breach of the peace. The Supreme Court reversed Cox's conviction, holding that the First Amendment does not allow the police to arrest a speaker because a hostile audience threatens to react with violence.[88] Police, instead, have a constitutional duty to maintain order so that the speech can continue.[89] Accordingly, peacekeeping efforts must be directed at the hecklers.

However, miscalculations occasionally occur about the strength of the peacekeeping force needed to maintain order. Halting speech should never be considered, except as a last resort. Police would be justified in asking demonstrators to suspend their activity in the face of an uncontrollable crowd reaction. If their request is refused, they may take the demonstrators into custody for their own protection, but may not arrest them for the disorderly conduct of spectators who are hostile to them.[90]

§ 2.10   — Hate Speech

Hate speech refers to speech that denigrates, belittles, or expresses contempt for others because of their race, color, religion, sexual orientation, or other characteristic that makes them vulnerable. Freedom to engage in hate speech is one of the most problematic First Amendment issues in modern times.[91] While some argue that society would be better served by excluding hate speech from the protection of the First Amendment, this is not how our Constitution is interpreted.[92] The First Amendment protects the right to preach racism, sexism, anti-Semitism, homophobia, or any other bigoted belief. The Court has upheld the right of Nazi Party members to march through Jewish neighborhoods in full uniform,[93] of private organizers to exclude gays and lesbians from their St. Patrick's Day Parade,[94] and of Ku Klux Klan members to deliver

---

[88]   *See* cases *supra* note 86.

[89]   *See, e.g.*, Glasson v. City of Louisville, 518 F.2d 899, 906 (6th Cir. 1975).

[90]   *See, e.g.*, Gregory v. City of Chicago, *supra* note 86; Wright v. Georgia, 373 U.S. 284, 293, 83 S. Ct. 1240, 1246, 10 L. Ed. 2d 349 (1963) ("the possibility of disorder by others cannot justify exclusion of persons from a place if they otherwise have a constitutional right . . . to be present").

[91]   *See, e.g.*, John P. Cronan, *The Next Challenge for the First Amendment: The Framework for an Internet Incitement Standard*, 51 CATH. U. L. REV. 425 (2002); Richard A. Glenn and Otis H. Stephens, *Campus Hate Speech and Equal Protection: Competing Constitutional Values*, 6 Widener J. PUB. L. 349, 352 (1997).

[92]   *See, e.g.*, R.A.V. v. City of St. Paul, *supra* 61 (declaring municipal hate speech ordinance unconstitutional); Saxe v. State College Area School Dist., 240 F.3d 200 (3d Cir. 2001) (declaring campus hate speech code unconstitutional).

[93]   National Socialist Party of America v. Skokie, 432 U.S. 43, 97 S. Ct. 2205, 53 L. Ed. 2d 96 (1977). *See also* Collin v. Smith, *supra* note 26 (striking down, on First Amendment grounds, several Skokie, Illinois ordinances prohibiting the National Socialist Party of America from marching through the town).

[94]   Hurley v. Irish-American Gay, Lesbian and Bisexual Group of Boston, *supra* note 12.

hate speeches and burn crosses at their rallies[95] while declaring governmental efforts to prohibit hate speech unconstitutional.[96]

Hate speech, nevertheless, is protected only so long as it remains an expressed belief. People have the right to march, carry banners, and deliver speeches about racial superiority and inferiority as long as they like, because they are expressing their views. However, the First Amendment confers absolutely no protection on hate-motivated conduct.[97] When people go beyond expressing bigoted beliefs and act on them, they may be punished.[98] States, for example, can make it a crime to assault another person because of the person's race, religion, or sexual orientation. States are also free to take bigoted motives into account by providing enhanced punishment for defendants who select their victims because of their race, religion, sexual orientation, or other distinguishing characteristics.[99] Offenders whose sentences are increased under statutes providing enhanced punishment for hate crimes are not being punished for their beliefs; they are being punished for their conduct.

Hate speech is not protected when it takes the form of a threat[100] or fighting words[101] because these categories of speech fall outside the First Amendment.

§ 2.11 — Crude and Vulgar Speech

Under traditional First Amendment analysis, speech was either fully protected by the First Amendment or had no protection at all. There was nothing in between. This scheme left no place for crude, profane, or vulgar speech. **Vulgar speech** contributes so little to the free exchange of ideas that full protection seems inappropriate. At the same time, it is not so harmful that complete withdrawal of protection seems appropriate, either. As a result, the Supreme Court had difficulty locating a place within the First Amendment for crude and vulgar speech. The status has unfolded gradually through a series of cases.

---

[95]   Brandenburg v. Ohio, *supra* note 27; **Virginia v. Black**, *supra* note 27.

[96]   R.A.V. v. City of St. Paul, *supra* 62 (declaring ordinance prohibiting the display of symbols likely to arouse anger, alarm or resentment in others based on race, color, creed, religion or gender, unconstitutional because it prohibited otherwise protected speech on the basis of content).

[97]   United States v. McDermott, 971 F. Supp. 939 (E.D. Pa. 1997) (upholding a conviction for burning a cross with the intent to threaten African-Americans who witnessed it); People v. Nitz, 285 Ill. App. 3d 364, 674 N.E.2d 802 (1996) (upholding conviction of hate crime offense, based on defendant's racially motivated harassment of his neighbor).

[98]   *See* authorities *supra* notes 73, 97.

[99]   Wisconsin v. Mitchell, 508 U.S. 476, 113 S. Ct. 2194, 124 L. Ed. 2d 436 (1993) (upholding statute providing enhanced sentence for defendants who intentionally select their victim based on victim's race).

[100] *See* authorities *supra* note 73.

[101] *See* authorities *supra* note 62.

Cohen v. California[102] was the first case in the series. Cohen was arrested for breach of the peace when he appeared in a courtroom wearing a jacket with the message "F—— the Draft!" displayed across the front. The Supreme Court ruled that Cohen's language, while vulgar, was protected by the First Amendment because in a society as diverse as ours, the government has "no right to cleanse public debate to the point where it is grammatically palatable to the most squeamish among us." *Cohen v. California* made it illegal for police to arrest people for using vulgar language in public, although forty years later some officers still fail to appreciate this.[103]

In *Bethel School District v. Fraser*,[104] the Supreme Court upheld the suspension of a high school student for delivering a lewd, racy speech during a high school assembly. The Court explained that it does not follow "simply because the use of an offensive form of expression may not be prohibited to adults . . . , the same latitude must be permitted to children in public school." *Cohen* was again distinguished in *FCC v. Pacifica Foundation*,[105] where the Court upheld the government's authority to prohibit radio stations from airing programs with vulgar language during hours when children were likely to be listening.

Finally, in *Young v. American Mini Theaters, Inc.*,[106] the Supreme Court made a clean break with the traditional notion that speech must be either fully protected or unprotected. Upholding a zoning ordinance that restricted the location of adult movie theaters, the Court wrote:

> . . . [E]ven though we recognize that the First Amendment will not tolerate the total suppression of erotic materials that have some arguably artistic value, it is manifest that society's interest in protecting this type of expression is of . . . different, and lesser, magnitude than the interest in untrammeled political debate . . . Whether political oratory or philosophical discussion moves us to applaud or to despise what is said, every schoolchild can understand why our duty to defend the right to speak remains the same. But few of us would march our sons and daughters off to war to preserve the citizen's right to see "Specified Sexual Activities" exhibited in the theaters of our choice. Even though the First Amendment protects communication in this area from total suppression, we hold that the State may legitimately use the content of these materials as the basis for placing them in a different classification from other motion pictures.

As a result of *Young* and subsequent cases, there are now three categories of speech: (1) fully protected, (2) unprotected, and (3) speech that has limited protection. Vulgar speech falls in the third category. It is protected in some contexts, but not others. However, in the context in which police typically encounter it — on city streets and sidewalks — vulgar speech is protected and does not furnish grounds for arrest.

---

[102]   403 U.S. 15, 91 S. Ct. 1780, 29 L. Ed. 2d 284 (1971).
[103]   Leonard v. Robinson, 477 F.3d 347 (6th. Cir 2007).
[104]   478 U.S. 675, 106 S. Ct. 3159, 92 L. Ed. 2d 549 (1986). *See also* Hazelwood School District v. Kuhlmeier, 484 U.S. 260, 108 S. Ct. 562, 98 L. Ed. 2d 592 (1988).
[105]   438 U.S. 726, 98 S. Ct. 3026, 57 L. Ed. 2d 1073 (1978).
[106]   427 U.S. 50, 96 S. Ct. 2440, 49 L. Ed. 2d 310 (1976).

§ 2.12   — Commercial Speech

Commercial speech refers to speech calculated to stir up interest in a commercial transaction. The Supreme Court has explained that there are "commonsense differences between speech that does 'no more than propose a commercial transaction'" and speech that expresses a viewpoint and invites dialogue, and that these differences justify "a different degree of protection."[107] Accordingly, commercial speech also carries limited protection, being protected in some contexts, but not others. Reduced protection for commercial speech allows the government to do such things as protect consumers from misleading and deceptive advertising;[108] require sellers to warn consumers of health hazards from their product;[109] and prevent overly aggressive advertising.[110] Content controls like these would be unconstitutional if the government tried to impose them on fully protected speech.

§ 2.13   Restraints on Speech Based on Considerations Other Than the Message

We are now ready to consider the government's power to regulate a speaker's conduct. Some speech dissemination techniques involve conduct entwined with speech. Handbilling, parading, picketing, and marching are examples. Freedom of speech would have limited practical value for people of modest means if it did not carry the right to use public spaces to engage in activities like these. For people championing poorly funded causes, streets, sidewalks, and parks are often the only facilities available for making contact with a large audience. These facilities, however, also have important nonspeech uses.

What would a day in the life of the community be like if First Amendment activities like handbilling, marching, parading, and picketing could not be restricted? The following is a grisly sketch. After being kept awake all night by the clamor of sound trucks and the blasts of bullhorns, Jane leaves for work. As she walks down the street, she is accosted by people who want financial contributions, signatures on petitions, and

---

[107]   Virginia State Board of Pharmacy v. Virginia Citizens Consumer Council Inc., 425 U.S. 748, 771 n. 24, 196 S. Ct. 1817, 1830 n. 24, 48 L. Ed. 2d 346 (1976); Central Hudson Gas & Elec. Corp. v. Public Serv. Comm'n of N.Y., 447 U. S. 557, 566, 100 S. Ct. 2343, 65 L. Ed. 2d 341 (1980) (commercial speech may be regulated when the regulation directly advances a substantial governmental regulatory interest and is no more extensive than is necessary to serve that interest).

[108]   Liquormat, Inc. v. Rhode Island, 517 U.S. 484, 116 S. Ct. 1495, 134 L. Ed. 2d 711 (1996); Florida Bar v. Went For It, Inc., 515 U.S. 618, 115 S. Ct. 2371, 132 L. Ed. 2d 541 (1995).

[109]   Virginia State Board of Pharmacy v. Virginia Citizens Consumer Council, Inc., *supra* note 107.

[110]   Florida Bar v. Went For It, Inc., *supra* note 108.

ideological support. Jane finally makes it to her car and, after removing the handbills, begins inching her way to work. Traffic is slow because of the need to stop at intersections to wait for parades and marches to pass. Traffic eventually clears. Jane picks up speed and crashes into an oncoming vehicle that is blocked from view by a cluster of billboards. Noise, congestion, delays, safety hazards, and intrusions on privacy would result if a speaker's conduct was as impervious to regulation as the message.

Fortunately, the First Amendment does not require this.[111] A different approach is used to evaluate restrictions on a speaker's conduct. How does a court decide whether local governments can prohibit individuals from using loudspeakers after dark?[112] Soliciting contributions on public streets?[113] Holding parades during rush hour? Or erecting giant billboards?[114] The answer is through an approach called *forum analysis*.

§ 2.14 Free Speech Access to Government Property: Public Forums and Nonpublic Forums

Members of the public do not have an unrestricted right to use government property for speech simply because the government owns it.[115] Many locations are poorly equipped to accomodate speech activity and serious disruption would result.[116] Recognizing this, the Supreme Court has adopted a forum-based approach to evaluate restrictions on the First Amendment use of government property. Under this approach, the court classifies the location as being either a **public forum** or a **nonpublic forum**, and then tests the restriction using the legal standards established for forums of that type.

Public forums occupy a special status in First Amendment law; speech can be restricted only for important reasons.

---

[111] *See* § 2.4 *supra.*

[112] *See, e.g.,* Kovacs v. Cooper, 336 U.S. 77, 69 S. Ct. 448, 93 L. Ed. 513 (1949) (upholding ordinance prohibiting use of sound trucks emitting "loud and raucous" noise in residential neighborhoods).

[113] *See, e.g.,* **International Soc. for Krishna Consciousness, Inc. v. Lee, 505 U.S. 672, 112 S. Ct. 2701, 120 L. Ed. 2d 541 (1992)** (upholding ban on solicitation of contributions in airport terminals). *See* § 2.15 *infra.*

[114] Metromedia, Inc. v. San Diego, 453 U.S. 490, 101 S. Ct. 2882, 69 L. Ed. 2d 800 (1981) (upholding ban on offsite billboard advertising).

[115] *See, e.g.,* Cornelius v. NAACP Legal Defense & Ed. Fund, Inc., 473 U.S. 788, 105 S. Ct. 3439, 87 L. Ed. 2d 567 (1985) (observing that "[n]othing in the Constitution requires the Government freely to grant access to all who wish to exercise their right to free speech on every type of Government property without regard to the nature of the property or to the disruption that might be caused by the speaker's activities.").

[116] *See, e.g.,* United States v. Kokinda, 497 U.S. 720, 110 S. Ct. 3115, 111 L. Ed. 2d 571 (1990); Greer v. Spock, 424 U.S. 828, 96 S. Ct. 1211, 47 L. Ed. 2d 505 (1976).

A. *Criteria Used to Determine Forum Status*

The status of a public forum can be acquired in one of two ways. The first way is though a long history and tradition of First Amendment use by members of the public. Locations that have traditionally been available for public assembly and free exchange of ideas are called **traditional public forums**. Streets, sidewalks, and parks are the main examples.[117] The second way public forum status can be acquired is through the government's deliberate decision to set a particular facility aside for speech uses by members of the public. Public forums that acquire their status this way are called **public forums by designation**.[118] Municipal auditoriums and public meeting halls are the main examples. Traditional and designated public forums are subject to the same legal standards. All other government locations are classified as **nonpublic forums**.[119] Nonpublic forums represent the property the government uses to conduct its official business, such as post offices, police stations, courthouses, municipal airport terminals, military installations, government office buildings, and the like.

B. *Control Over Speech in Nonpublic Forums*

The government has broad control over speech in nonpublic forums because these facilities have not been set aside for speech uses by members of the public but have, instead, been reserved for the government's own uses. Restrictions on speech are valid so long as they are neutral as to viewpoint and reasonable.[120]

---

[117]   *See, e.g.*, Hague v. CIO, 307 U.S. 496, 5, 59 S. Ct. 954, 83 L. Ed. 1423 (1939) (noting that streets and parks "have immemorially been held in trust for the use of the public, and, time out of mind, have been used for purposes of assembly, communicating thoughts between citizens, and discussing public questions"); United States v. Grace, 461 U.S. 171, 103 S. Ct. 1702, 75 L. Ed. 2d 736 (1983). *See also, generally,* Nathan W. Kellum, *If it Looks like a Duck . . . Traditional Public Forum Status of Open Areas on Public University Campuses,* 33 HASTINGS CONST. L. Q. 1 (2005).

[118]   *See, e.g.*, Southeastern Promotions, Limited v. Conrad, 420 U.S. 546, 95 S. Ct. 1239, 43 L. Ed. 2d 448 (1975) (municipal theater); Widmar v. Vincent, 454 U.S. 263, 102 S. Ct. 269, 70 L. Ed. 2d 440 (1981) (university meeting facilities); City of Madison Joint School District v. Wisconsin Public Employment Relations Comm'n, 429 U.S. 167, 97 S. Ct. 421, 50 L. Ed. 2d 376 (1976) (school board meeting).

[119]   *See, e.g.*, United States v. Kokinda, *supra* note 117 (sidewalks entirely on Postal Service's property in front of post office); Jones v. North Carolina Prisoners' Labor Union, 433 U.S. 119, 97 S. Ct. 2532, 53 L. Ed. 2d 629 (1977) (prison); Lehman v. City of Shaker Heights, 418 U.S. 298, 94 S. Ct. 2714, 41 L. Ed. 2d 770 (1974) (advertising space on vehicles of a city transit system); Greer v. Spock, *supra* note 116 (streets on a military base).

[120]   Perry Educ. Ass'n v. Perry Local Educators' Ass'n., 460 U.S. 37, 103 S. Ct. 948, 74 L. Ed. 2d 794 (1984); **International Soc. for Krishna Consciousness, Inc. v. Lee,** *supra* note 113; Cornelius v. NAACP Legal Defense & Ed. Fund, Inc., *supra* note 115; Arkansas Educ. Television Comm'n v. Forbes, 523 U.S. 666, 118 S. Ct. 1633, 140 L. Ed. 2d 175 (1998).

1. Reasonable

Whether a restriction is reasonable is evaluated in light of the forum's purpose and normal patterns of activity. The government does not have to allow speech uses that are incompatible with the orderly conduct of its business. Handbilling and solicitation of funds, for example, do not have to be permitted inside government office buildings.[121] Reasonable restrictions may also be imposed on the subject matter of the speech and the identity of the speaker. A school district, for example, may grant the union elected as the teachers' exclusive bargaining agent access to the interschool mail system without granting a rival union similar access[122] and a municipal transit authority can refuse to sell advertising space to political candidates while accepting other types of advertising.[123] Subject matter distinctions like these are not allowed in public forums where everyone has an equal right of access.

2. Neutral as to Viewpoint

Viewpoint discrimination is not allowed in either type of forum.[124] The government cannot use its control over access to government facilities to advance some views and suppress others. It cannot, for example, grant access to Republicans, but not Democrats or to pro-life groups, but not pro-choice groups.[125] This would empower

---

[121] For cases classifying the location as a nonpublic forum and upholding the speech restriction as reasonable *see, e.g.,* **International Soc. for Krishna Consciousness, Inc. v. Lee,** *supra* note 113 (ban on soliciting funds inside municipal airport terminal); United States v. Kokinda, *supra* note 116 (ban on leafleting in pedestrian walkway connecting post office building with its parking lot); Members of City Council of Los Angeles v. Taxpayers for Vincent, 466 U.S. 789, 104 S. Ct. 2118, 80 L. Ed. 2d 772 (1984) (ban on attaching signs and posters to municipal lampposts and fire hydrants); Lehman v. City of Shaker Heights, *supra* note 119 (municipal transit authority policy against selling advertising space on buses to persons wanting to use the space for political advertisements); Anderson v. Milwaukee County, 433 F.3d 975 (7th Cir. 2006) (ban on distributing literature inside city buses); Preminger v. Principi, 422 F.3d 815 (9th Cir. 2005) (ban on partisan political activity on campus of the Department of Veterans' Affairs); de la O v. Housing Authority of City of El Paso, Tex., 417 F.3d 495 (5th Cir. 2005) (restrictions on door-to-door solicitation in government-owned low-income housing complexes).

[122] Perry Educ. Ass'n v. Perry Local Educators' Ass'n, *supra* note 120 (First Amendment not violated by granting union elected by public school teachers as their exclusive bargaining representative access to interschool mail system while denying access to rival union).

[123] Lehman v. City of Shaker Heights, *supra* note 119.

[124] *See, e.g.,* Good News Club v. Milford Cen. School, 533 U.S. 98, 121 S. Ct. 2093, 150 L. Ed. 2d 151 (2001) (school's exclusion of religious club from after-hours use of its facilities, while allowing social, civil, recreational, and other uses, constituted impermissible viewpoint discrimination); Lamb's Chapel v. Center Maracas Union Free School District, 508 U.S. 384, 113 S. Ct. 2141, 124 L. Ed. 2d 352 (1993) (after-hours access to public school property may not be withheld based on viewpoint); Rosenberger v. Rector and Visitors of Univ. of Va., 515 U.S. 819, 115 S. Ct. 2510, 132 L. Ed. 2d 700 (1995) (public university's student activities funds may not be disbursed based on viewpoint considerations).

[125] *See* cases note 124 *supra.*

the government to distort public debate by allowing the public to hear only one side of an issue. Few things are more dangerous in a democracy.

C. Control Over Speech in Public Forums

Speech enjoys maximum protection in public forums. The right to freedom of speech would be of little practical importance without the ability to reach a sizeable audience. Public streets, sidewalks, and parks have traditionally served this need. The Supreme Court has stressed the importance of open-air public facilities to groups championing poorly funded causes who lack the resources to hire newspaper space, television time, or billboards. For persons of modest means, public forum facilities offer the only opportunity for making contact with a large audience. However, use of these facilities for speech unavoidably burdens nonspeech uses. A large rally in a park makes the facilities temporarily unavailable for quiet contemplation and recreation, and a march through a busy downtown intersection at rush hour can tie up traffic for miles. Conflicting demands on the use of outdoor public spaces create a need for regulations designed to accommodate the interests of all.

1. Reasonable Time, Place, and Manner Restrictions

The government is allowed to place reasonable restrictions on the time, place, or manner of using public forums for speech.[126] To be sustainable, the restriction must: (1) advance a significant government interest,[127] (2) apply without regard to content,[128] and (3) leave ample alternatives available to reach the desired audience.[129]

---

[126]   Examples of the many laws the Supreme Court has upheld as reasonable time, place, and manner restrictions on speech include a statute prohibiting solicitation of votes within 100 feet of the entrance to polling place on election day, Burson v. Freeman, 504 U.S. 191, 112 S. Ct. 1846, 119 L. Ed. 2d 5 (1992); a municipal noise regulation requiring performers in a park band shell to use the sound system and sound technician provided by city so as not to disturb surrounding residents, Ward v. Rock Against Racism, 491 U.S. 781, 109 S. Ct. 2746, 105 L. Ed. 2d 661 (1989); a statute making it unlawful for persons engaged in demonstrating to interfere with free ingress or egress to public buildings; Cameron v. Johnson, 390 U.S. 611, 88 S. Ct. 1335, 20 L. Ed. 2d 182 (1968); and an ordinance prohibiting persons from making loud noises on grounds adjacent to school buildings while classes are in session, Grayned v. City of Rockford, 408 U.S. 104, 92 S. Ct. 2294, 33 L. Ed. 2d 222 (1972).

[127]   *See, e.g.,* United States v. Grace, *supra* note 117 (ban on carrying flags, banners, or signs on the sidewalk abutting the Supreme Court held unconstitutional because it failed to advance a significant government interest).

[128]   *See, e.g.,* Boos v. Barry, *supra* note 39 (District of Columbia ordinance prohibiting display within 500 feet of a foreign embassy of signs that bring "the foreign government into public disrepute" held unconstitutional because it was content-based).

[129]   *See, e.g.,* Grayned v. City of Rockford, *supra* note 126 (discussing this requirement).

Local governments, for example, can prohibit noisy demonstrations in front of schools while classes are in session. This regulation satisfies all three requirements.[130] It promotes the government's significant interest in undisrupted school sessions, applies without regard to content, and leaves ample alternatives available for reaching the desired audience. Speakers who are prevented from holding a noisy demonstration while classes are in session can wait until classes are over or use a quieter medium, such passing out leaflets. Would-be speakers, therefore, have ample alternatives for communicating their method.

2. Blanket Prohibition on an Entire Medium of Expression

Laws that impose a blanket prohibition on an entire medium of communication, such as residential yard signs,[131] door-to-door canvassing,[132] or handbilling,[133] are not sustainable as a reasonable time, place, or manner restriction. Because they eliminate cheap and convenient means of communicating, they run the risk of preventing persons of modest means from making their voices heard. Laws that forbid use of an entire medium of communication violate First Amendment unless adequate substitutes exist for reaching the desired audience as conveniently and cheaply.[134]

---

[130] *Id.* (Upholding an ordinance prohibiting persons on grounds adjacent to a school building from making loud noises that disturb the peace while the school is in session). An ordinance that prohibits the display of a swastika within 100 feet of a synagogue, in contrast, would not qualify as a valid time, place, and manner restrictions because it is content-based. Content-based distinctions are not allowed in regulating access to public forums. *See, e.g.,* Boos v. Barry, *supra* note 39.

[131] *See, e.g.,* **City of Ladue v. Gilleo, 512 U.S. 43, 114 S. Ct. 2038, 129 L. Ed. 2d 36 (1994)** (invalidating ordinance that prohibited display of residential yard signs because it banned a "unique and important" means of communicating for which "no practical substitute" exists).

[132] *See, e.g.,* Watchtower Bible & Tract Society v. Village of Stratton, 536 U.S. 150, 122 S. Ct. 2080, 153 L. Ed. 2d 205 (2002) (invalidating ordinance making it a misdemeanor to engage in door-to-door canvassing for any cause without first registering with the mayor and receiving a permit); Martin v. Struthers, 319 U.S. 141, 63 S. Ct. 862, 87 L. Ed. 1313 (1943) (striking down ordinance prohibiting door-to-door solicitation and distribution of handbills).

[133] *See, e.g.,* Schneider v. State of New Jersey, 308 U.S. 147, 60 S. Ct. 146, 84 L. Ed. 155 (1939) (invalidating ordinance making it unlawful to circulate or distribute handbills on any sidewalk, street or other public place); Lovell v. City of Griffin, 303 U.S. 444, 58 S. Ct. 666, 82 L. Ed. 949 (1938) (invalidating ordinance that forbade the distribution by hand of literature on city streets without written permission from the city manager); Watchtower Bible & Tract Society of N.Y., Inc. v. Village of Stratton, 536 U.S. 150, 122 S. Ct. 2080, 153 L. Ed. 2d 205 (202).

[134] *See* authorities *supra* notes 131–133; Shuttlesworth v. Birmingham, 394 U.S. 147, 89 S. Ct. 935, 22 L. Ed. 2d 162 (1969) (invaliding prohibition on public marches); Schad v. Mount Ephraim, 452 U.S. 61, 101 S. Ct. 2176, 68 L. Ed. 2d 671 (1981) (invalidating complete ban on live entertainment); McIntyre v. Ohio Elections Comm'n, 514 U.S. 334, 115 S. Ct. 1511, 131 L. Ed. 2d 426 (1995) (striking down law banning distribution of anonymous campaign literature).

Figure 2.7
Government's Power to Limit First Amendment Activity on Government Property

Type of property	Criteria for inclusion	Illustrations	Validity of restrictions on speech
Nonpublic forums	Government's business property	Office buildings, military bases, police stations, jails, municipal airports, etc.	Restrictions are valid if they are: (1) neutral as to viewpoint and (2) reasonable in light of the purpose the particular facility serves.
Public forums Traditional	Long-standing history and tradition of First Amendment use by members of the public	Streets, sidewalks, parks	Reasonable restrictions on the time, place, or manner of using public forums for speech will be upheld when they (1) advance a significant government interest, (2) apply without regard to content, and (3) leave ample alternatives available to reach the desired audience.
By designation	Earmarked by government for First Amendment uses	Municipal auditoriums, meeting halls	

§ 2.15 — Protecting the Community from Nuisances Linked to Speech

Now that we have explored the approach courts use to evaluate restrictions on the First Amendment use of government property, we are ready to discuss the outcomes courts have reached.

A. Anti-Noise Ordinances

Disturbingly loud noises can be an unpleasant by-product of freedom of speech. Local governments can tone noise levels down by enacting reasonable time, place, and manner restrictions. The Supreme Court has upheld the constitutionality of noise control measures regulating use of bullhorns, sound amplification equipment, loud music, and other excessively loud noises.[135]

However, one size does not fit all. What constitutes a reasonable noise control measure in front of schools, churches, or hospitals might be an unconstitutional

---

[135] *See, e.g.*, Madsen v. Women's Health Center, Inc., 512 U.S. 753, 114 S. Ct. 2516, 129 L. Ed. 2d 593 (1994) (upholding a court injunction limiting use of sound amplification equipment in front of abortion clinic); Grayned v. City of Rockford, *supra* note 126 (upholding ordinance prohibiting noisy demonstrations in front of schools during class hours); Ward v. Rock Against Racism, *supra* note 126 (upholding ordinance regulating the sound equipment that could be used in outdoor municipal bandstand); Kovacs v. Cooper, *supra* note 112 (upholding ordinance prohibiting use of sound trucks emitting "loud and raucous" noise in residential neighborhoods); Housing Works, Inc. v. Kerik, 283 F.3d 471 (2d Cir. 2002) (upholding ordinance banning the use of amplified sound on the steps, sidewalks, and plaza area directly in front of New York City Hall); Sharkey's, Inc. v. City of Waukesha, 265 F. Supp. 2d 984 (E.D. Wis. 2003) (upholding noise ordinances prohibiting bars from sponsoring loud entertainment that unreasonably disturbs persons in the neighborhood); Holland v. City of Tacoma, 954 P.2d 290 (Wash. App. 1998) (upholding ordinance prohibiting playing of automobile sound equipment at volumes that could be heard more than 50 feet from car).

infringement on freedom of speech in a downtown business district.[136] The nature of the location and normal patterns of activity determine whether a given noise control measure is reasonable.[137]

B. Ordinances Protecting Residential Privacy

Home is the place where people retreat to escape the stresses of their daily lives. Local governments can protect domestic privacy and tranquility by making it illegal to knock on doors of homes where the owners have posted "No Solicitation" signs.[138] Because posting a sign is adequate to protect the privacy of homeowners who want this protection, the First Amendment does not allow local governments to ban door-to-door canvassing[139] or to require a permit to engage in this activity.[140] Door-to-door canvassing has been an important medium of communication throughout history and cannot be banned altogether.[141]

The Supreme Court, in contrast, has upheld an ordinance banning focused residential picketing (i.e., picketing directed at a particular dwelling).[142] What accounts for the

---

[136] See, e.g., Deegan v. City of Ithaca, 444 F.3d 135 (2d Cir. 1996) (invalidating anti-noise ordinance, interpreted by police to prohibit any noise, including ordinary speech, anywhere in the city, any time of day or night, whether amplified or not, that could be heard 25 feet from its source). See also, generally, Paula P. Bentley, *Line in the Sand: Florida Municipalities Struggle to Determine the Line Between Valid Noise Ordinances and Unconstitutional Restrictions*, 35 STETSON L. REV. 461 (2006); Aaron C. Dunlap, *Come on Feel the Noise: The Problem with Municipal Noise Regulation*, 15 U. MIAMI BUS. L. REV. 47 (2006).

[137] Grayned v. City of Rockford, *supra* note 126.

[138] See, e.g., Village of Schaumberg v. Citizens for Better Government, 444 U.S. 620, 100 S. Ct. 826, 63 L. Ed. 2d 73 (1980) (approving in dictum ordinance giving municipality power to enforce no solicitation signs); Martin v. City of Struthers, *supra* note 132 ("A city can punish those who call at a home in defiance of the previously expressed will of the occupant . . .").

[139] See, e.g., Watchtower Bible & Tract Society v. Village of Stratton, *supra* note 132 (invalidating ordinance making it a misdemeanor to engage in door-to-door canvassing for any cause without first registering with the mayor and receiving a permit); City of Watseka v. Illinois Public Action Council, 796 F.2d 1547 (7th Cir. 1986), *aff'd*, 479 U.S. 1048, 107 S. Ct. 919, 93 L. Ed. 2d 972 (1987) (invalidating ordinance which limited door-to-door soliciting to hours between 9:00 A.M. and 5:00 P.M., Monday through Saturday); Village of Schaumberg v. Citizens for Better Government, *supra* note 138 (invalidating ordinance prohibiting door-to-door solicitation of contributions by charitable organizations not using at least 75% of their receipts for charitable purpose); Martin v. Struthers, *supra* note 132 (invalidating law prohibiting door-to-door distribution of handbills and other literature).

[140] See, e.g., Watchtower Bible & Tract Society of N.Y., Inc. v. Village of Stratton, *supra* note 132 (invalidating village ordinance making it a misdemeanor to go upon private property to promote any cause without first registering with the mayor and receiving a permit); Schneider v. State of New Jersey, *supra* note 133 (invalidating a ban on house-to-house canvassing, solicitation, distribution of circulars, or other matter without a permit from the Chief of Police).

[141] Watchtower Bible & Tract Society of N.Y., Inc. v. Village of Stratton, *supra* note 132.

[142] Frisby v. Schultz, 487 U.S. 474, 108 S. Ct. 2495, 101 L. Ed. 2d 420 (1988) (upholding ordinance banning "picketing before or about the residence or dwelling of any individual" as a valid time, place, and manner restriction on speech in a public forum); Klein v. San Diego County, 463 F.3d 1029 (9th Cir. 2006) (upholding residential picketing ordinance, requiring picketers to remain at least 300 feet from targeted dwelling).

difference? The difference is that homeowners have adequate means to protect them-selves from unwelcome intrusions by canvassers and solicitors; they can post a "No Solicitation" sign. However, they are defenseless against people picketing in front of their home. The fact that they are a "captive audience" allows the government to step in and protect them from unwelcome assaults on their privacy.

C. Anti-Litter Laws and Laws Prohibiting Distribution of Handbills

Anti-litter laws are constitutional, but enforcement efforts must be directed at the people who drop handbills and produce litter, not against those who distribute handbills that are later dropped. The public distribution of handbills cannot be made illegal as a means of controlling litter.[143]

D. Avoiding Traffic Congestion and Interference with Access to Buildings

The government has a substantial interest in avoiding traffic congestion and inter-ference with access to buildings. A large group of people conducting a free speech gath-ering on a public street or sidewalk are likely to obstruct entrances to buildings and interfere with traffic. Laws prohibiting obstruction of the public passage are constitu-tional and may be applied to individuals engaged in speech.[144]

Anti-abortion protesters sometimes deliberately block entrances to abortion clinics to prevent women from obtaining services.[145] A federal law known as the Freedom of Access to Clinic Entrances Act ("FACE")[146] makes this conduct illegal. Many states have enacted laws creating "buffer zones" around abortion clinics to protect women from being harassed. In *Hill v. Colorado*,[147] the Supreme Court upheld, as a valid time, place, and manner restriction on speech, a state statute prohibiting

---

[143] *See, e.g.*, Lovell v. City of Griffin, *supra* note 133 (invalidating ordinance that forbade the distribu-tion by hand of literature on city streets without written permission from the city manager); Schnei-der v. State, *supra* note 133 (invalidating ordinance banning distribution of handbills on any city street, sidewalk, or park; commenting that cities can save street-cleaning costs without banning hand-billing by enforcing anti-litter laws against persons who drop handbills on street); City Council v. Taxpayers for Vincent, 466 U.S. 789, 104 S. Ct. 2118, 80 L. Ed.2d 772 (1984) (stating that "the es-thetic interest in preventing the kind of litter that may result from the distribution of leaflets on the public streets and sidewalks cannot support a prophylactic prohibition against the citizen's exercise of that method of expressing his views").

[144] Cameron v. Johnson, *supra* note 126.

[145] Madsen v. Women's Health Center, Inc., *supra* note 135; Schenck v. Pro-Choice Network New York, 519 U.S. 357, 117 S. Ct. 855, 137 L. Ed. 2d 1 (1997); Cox v. Louisiana, 379 U.S. 536, 85 S. Ct. 453, 13 L. Ed. 2d 471 (1965).

[146] 18 U.S.C. § 248.

[147] 530 U.S. 730, 120 S. Ct. 240, 147 L. Ed. 2d 597 (2000).

anti-abortion protesters from approaching within eight feet of a woman going into an abortion facility, without the woman's consent.

E. *Restrictions on Face-to-Face Solicitation*

Laws prohibiting public begging have been around for years, but problems of homelessness have stepped up enforcement.[148] Because asking for money involves speech, restrictions on begging have frequently been challenged under the First Amendment.[149] Although the Supreme Court has not yet addressed this issue, many lower courts have. The consensus is that public begging or **panhandling**, as it is often called, constitutes expressive activity protected by the First Amendment.[150] As a result, local governments cannot categorically prohibit begging in any place in the city.[151] Citywide bans on begging have uniformly been declared unconstitutional because they deprive beggars of all means to communicate their message.[152] Narrower measures must be employed.

Ordinances that prohibit aggressive begging, unacceptable conduct associated with begging, and begging in nonpublic forums have been upheld as valid." Beggars who harass, touch, block, threaten, or otherwise intimidate persons to extract money from them may be charged with disorderly conduct, assault, or under special statutes dealing with aggressive panhandling.[153] Local governments may also outlaw conduct associated with begging that poses a safety hazard, such as walking up to motorists stopped at a traffic light,[154] and also objectionable nonspeech conduct associated with begging,[155] such as sleeping,[156] sitting, or lying on sidewalks.[157]

Beggars often frequent places like train and subway stations,[158] airport terminals,[159] and lobbies of government office buildings.[160] Local governments can outlaw

---

[148]   For comprehensive treatment of this issue, see Robert C. Ellickson, *Controlling Chronic Misconduct in City Spaces: Of Panhandlers, Skid Rows, and Public-Space Zoning*, 105 YALE L.J. 1165 (1996).

[149]   *See, e.g.,* **International Soc. for Krishna Consciousness v. Lee**, *supra* note 113; **Loper v. New York City Police Department, 999 F.2d 699 (2d Cir. 1993)**.

[150]   *See* cases *supra* note 149.

[151]   *See, e.g.,* **Loper v. New York City Police Department**, *supra* note 149 (striking down ordinance prohibiting begging on any public street); Benefit v. City of Cambridge, 424 Mass. 918, 679 N. E.2d 184 (1997) (same); Ledford v. State, 652 So. 2d 1254 (Fla. Dist. Ct. App. 1995) (same).

[152]   *See* authorities *supra* note 151. *See also* § 2.14 (C).

[153]   *See, e.g.,* Gresham v. Peterson, 225 F. 3d 899 (7th Cir. 2000) (upholding ordinance prohibiting "aggressive panhandling"); Douchette v. City of Santa Monica, 955 F. Supp. 1192 (D. C. Cal. 1997) (same).

[154]   *See, e.g.,* People v. Barton, 12 Misc.3d 322, 816 N.Y.S.2d 853 (2006).

[155]   United States v. O'Brien, *supra* note 29 (First Amendment permits the government to regulate conduct associated with speech when the government's regulatory focus is on the conduct, not the message).

[156]   *See, e.g.,* Clark v. Community for Creative Non-Violence, *supra* note 30.

[157]   *See, e.g.,* Roulette v. City of Seattle, 97 F.3d 300 (9th Cir. 1996) (upholding ordinance prohibiting sitting or lying on sidewalks in commercial areas).

[158]   *See, e.g.,* Young v. New York City Transit Authority, 903 F.2d 146 (2d Cir.), *cert. denied,* 498 U.S. 984, 111 S. Ct. 516, 112 L. Ed. 2d 528 (1990) (upholding ban against begging in municipal subway system).

[159]   **International Soc. for Krishna Consciousness v. Lee**, *supra* note 113.

[160]   *See, e.g.,* United States v. Kokinda, *supra* note 116.

all forms of begging in these locations because they are nonpublic forums. Restrictions on speech in nonpublic forums are constitutional if they are reasonable.[161] This requirement is satisfied because begging in these locations, even when nonaggressive, adds to congestion, slows traffic, and intrudes on people who are in a hurry.

F. Signs and Billboards

Although billboards are a form of speech, they take up space, obstruct views, and pose other problems that call for regulation."[162] As a result, reasonable restrictions may be imposed on the size, location, and physical characteristics of billboards.[163] The posting of signs and advertisement on telephone poles and fire hydrants can also be prohibited.[164]

However, bans on residential yard signs stand on a different footing. Residential yard signs constitute an important means of expression. They enable ordinary citizens to communicate their support for candidates, issues, and causes in ways that no other medium can. A municipality's interest in promoting neighborhood aesthetics is important, but not nearly as important as the right of homeowners to take advantage of this unique, convenient, and economical medium of communication.[165]

G. Permit Regulations

All communities require permits for large-scale marches, parades, and rallies. Advance notice is necessary for orderly scheduling, effective resource allocation, and adequate policing. Requiring a permit is the only practical way to ensure that advance notice is given.[166] The First Amendment, nevertheless, is hostile toward laws

---

[161]   *See* authorities *supra* note 120.

[162]   **City of Ladue v. Gilleo**, *supra* note 131.

[163]   *See, e.g.*, Metromedia, Inc. v. San Diego, 453 U.S. 490, 101 S. Ct. 2882, 69 L. Ed. 2d 800 (1981) (upholding ban on offsite billboard advertising as valid means of furthering city's interest in traffic safety and aesthetics).

[164]   Members of City Council of Los Angeles v. Taxpayers for Vincent, 466 U.S. 789, 104 S. Ct. 2118, 80 L. Ed. 2d 772 (1984).

[165]   **City of Ladue v. Gilleo**, *supra* note 131 (invalidating ordinance banning nearly all residential signs). *See also* Linmark Associates, Inc. v. Township of Willingboro, 431 U.S. 85, 97 S. Ct. 1614, 52 L. Ed. 2d 155 (1977) (invalidating law prohibiting homeowners from posting "For Sale" or "Sold" signs); Arlington County Republican Comm'n v. Arlington County, 983 F.2d 587 (4th Cir. 1993) (invalidating ordinance limiting homeowners to two signs); Whitton v. City of Gladstone, Mo., 54 F.3d 1400 (8th Cir. 1995) (invalidating ordinance imposing time limits on political signs).

[166]   Permits may be required only for gatherings that are large enough to create traffic, public safety, or competing use concerns. *See, e.g.*, Knowles v. City of Waco, Tex., 462 F.3d 430 (5th Cir. 2006); Santa Monica Food Not Bombs v. City of Santa Monica, 450 F.3d 1022 (9th Cir. 2006); American-Arab Anti-Discrimination Committee v. City of Dearborn, 418 F.3d 600 (6th Cir. 2005). Compare Thomas v. Chicago Park District, 534 U.S. 316, 322, 122 S. Ct. 775, 151 L. Ed. 2d 783 (2002) (permits may be required for more-than-50-person events) *with* Douglas v. Brownell, 88 F.3d 1511 (8th Cir. 1996) (expressing doubt whether a permit may be required for groups of 10 persons or less).

that require citizens to obtain advance permission from a public official before exercising their right to free speech.[167] Laws that require advance permission create a danger that permission will be denied to groups whose appearance, lifestyles, or views are unacceptable. Consequently, permit laws are constitutional only if they contain adequate safeguards to prevent censorship. To be constitutional, they must: (1) contain clear, narrow, objective standards for permit officials to follow; (2) not impose unreasonably long advance notice requirements; and (3) not allow overly broad discretion in fixing permit fees.

Overly broad discretion is fatal to permit laws because it creates a risk of censorship. Permit officials cannot be given discretion to consider the applicant's identity, message, or predictions about the amount of public hostility the gathering might arouse.[168] Resource allocation, scheduling, and financial responsibility for damages, in contrast, are legitimate considerations, but even as these matters, the administrators' discretion must be narrowly circumscribed.[169]

Second, permit ordinances may not impose unreasonably long advance notice requirements. Long waiting periods stifle speech that is reactive to late-breaking events and discourage some citizens from applying.[170] An ordinance requiring 30 days advance notice, for example, would have silenced groups who wanted to hold a rally to protest the first Bush Administration's threatened military action in Iraq because the invasion was already in progress by then.

Finally, although a fee may be charged to cover the cost of processing the application, traffic control, and clean-up costs,[171] the administrator may not be given

---

[167]   *See, e.g.*, Forsyth County v. Nationalist Movement, 505 U.S. 123, 112 S. Ct. 2395, 120 L. Ed. 2d 101 (1992); Shuttlesworth v. City of Birmingham, 394 U.S. 147, 89 S. Ct. 935, 22 L. Ed. 2d 162 (1969).

[168]   *See, e.g.*, Shuttlesworth v. City of Birmingham, *supra* note 167 (invalidating ordinance vesting discretion to refuse a permit when required by "public welfare, peace, safety, health, decency, good order, morals or convenience"); Hague v. C.I.O., 307 U.S. 496, 59 S. Ct. 954, 83 L. Ed. 1423 (1939) (invalidating ordinance vesting discretion to refuse a permit when necessary to prevent "riots, disturbances or disorderly assemblage"); Staub v. Baxley, 355 U.S. 313, 78 S. Ct. 277, 2 L. Ed. 2d 302 (1958) (invalidating ordinance vesting discretion to refuse a permit to applicants who are "not of good character" or who are "canvassing for a project not free from fraud").

[169]   *See, e.g.*, Thomas v. City of Park District, *supra* note 166 (upholding ordinance requiring permit to hold a large-scale outdoor gathering where permit could be denied only when the application was incomplete or contained material misrepresentations, the applicant damaged park property on a prior occasion and failed to pay for the damage, a permit was granted to an earlier applicant for the same time and place, or the intended use would endanger health or safety).

[170]   Courts have consistently rejected advance notice requirements that are more than a couple of days. *See, e.g.*, Church of the American Knights of the Ku Klux Klan v. City of Gary, 334 F.3d 676 (7th Cir. 2003) (invalidating a 45-day advance notice requirement); Local 32B-32 J v. Port Auth. of N.Y. & N.J., 3 F. Supp. 2d 413 (S.D.N.Y. 1998) (upholding a 36-hour advance notice requirement); Santa Monica Food Not Bombs v. City of Santa Monica, *supra* note 166 (upholding two-day advance notice requirement).

[171]   Cox v. New Hampshire, 312 U.S. 569, 61 S. Ct. 762, 85 L. Ed. 1049 (1941).

unrestrained discretion to determine the amount.[172] The fee must be established in accordance with a fixed fee schedule or by reference to narrow, objective criteria.[173] The fee may not include the cost of police protection required to keep hostile spectators in line.[174] "Speech cannot be financially burdened, any more than it can be punished or banned, simply because it might offend a hostile mob."[175]

§ 2.16 — Free Speech Access to Private Property

The First Amendment only controls the actions of the government.[176] Private landowners do not have to allow First Amendment activity on their property.

A controversy existed at one time over whether corporate malls and shopping centers were obliged to permit picking, solicitation, and handbilling. Civil libertarians argued that shopping center streets and sidewalks were "functionally" indistinguishable from streets and sidewalks in downtown business districts and, consequently, that shopping center owners should have the same Constitutional responsibilities as the government. The Supreme Court briefly entertained this argument,[177] but later discarded it.[178] Shopping center proprietors are, free to impose any speech restrictions they please.[179] However, police officers should never arrest peaceful First Amendment actors simply

---

[172] *See, e.g.*, Forsyth County v. Nationalist Movement, *supra* note 167 (ordinance requiring administrator to set the permit fee based on the "estimated cost of maintaining order" violated the First Amendment because this language: (1) delegated unfettered discretion to fix the fee, (2) allowed consideration of the content of the message in estimating the cost of maintaining order, and (3) authorized charging applicants for the cost of police protection necessary to keep hostile spectators in line); Sullivan v. City of Augusta, 406 F. Supp. 2d 92 (D. Me. 2003) (invalidating ordinance that provided the cost of the permit "shall be one hundred dollars ($100.00), plus the costs of traffic control . . . as estimated by the Police Department" because it contained no criteria for estimating those costs); Transp. Alternatives, Inc. v. City of New York, 340 F.3d 72 (2d Cir. 2003) (striking down permit ordinance that conferred unfettered discretion both as to whether to charge a fee at all and as to the fee amount).

[173] *See, e.g.*, Center for Auto Safety, Inc. v. Athey, 37 F.3d 139, 145 (4th Cir. 1994), *cert. denied*, 514 U.S. 1036, 115 S. Ct. 1401, 131 L. Ed. 2d 289 (1995); Coalition for the Abolition of Marijuana Prohibition v. City of Atlanta, 219 F.3d 1301 (11th Cir. 2000).

[174] *See, e.g.*, Forsyth County v. Nationalist Movement, *supra* note 167; Church of the American Knights of the Ku Klux Klan v. City of Gary, *supra* note 170.

[175] Forsyth County v. Nationalist Movement, *supra* note 167.

[176] *See, generally,* Weinstein, *Symposium: Free Speech and Community: A Brief Introduction to Free Speech Doctrine*, 29 ARIZ. ST. L.J. 461 (1997).

[177] Amalgamated Food Employees Local v. Logan Valley Plaza, 391 U.S. 308, 88 S. Ct. 1601, 20 L. Ed. 2d 603 (1968).

[178] Lloyd v. Tanner, 107 U.S. 551, 92 S. Ct. 2219, 33 L. Ed. 2d 131 (1976); Central Hardware Co. v. NLRB, 407 U.S. 539, 92 S. Ct. 2238, 33 L. Ed. 2d 122 (1976); Hudgens v. NLRB, 424 U.S. 507, 96 S. Ct. 1029, 47 L. Ed. 2d 196 (1975).

[179] *See* authorities *supra* note 178.

because they are on private property. Their presence becomes a criminal trespass only if they remain after being asked by the owner to leave.

The fact that the First Amendment does not confer a right of speech access to shopping center premises does not mean that state law cannot create such a right. Some states have statutes requiring shopping malls to allow certain speech activities; these statutes constitute a valid exercise of police power.[180]

§ 2.17   —Need for Precision in Regulating Speech

In *Gooding v. Wilson*,[181] a group of anti-war protesters deliberately obstructed the entrance to an army induction center to prevent inductees from entering. When an officer attempted to remove the protesters, the defendant, who was part of the group, angrily remonstrated: "White son of a bitch, I'll kill you." "You son of a bitch, I'll choke you to death." "You son of a bitch, if you ever put your hands on me again, I'll cut you all to pieces." Threats like this are not protected by the First Amendment. The officer arrested the defendant under a statute prohibiting the use of "opprobrious words or abusive language." It may come as a surprise that the Supreme Court overturned the conviction.

What did the officer do wrong? The answer is nothing. The problem was in the statute used to make the arrest. Criminal laws — particularly those designed for application to people engaged in speech — must contain narrow, clear, and precise standards to guide arrest decisions.[182] This requirement serves two equally important purposes.[183] The first is fair notice.[184] Citizens are entitled to know in advance when their behavior will subject them to arrest. The Constitution therefore requires criminal laws to define the prohibited conduct with sufficient clarity that ordinary citizens would understand what they are forbidden to do.[185] Fair notice is particularly important for laws that apply to speech. Cautious citizens faced with laws of uncertain meaning will often choose to forgo exercising their First Amendment rights rather than risk arrest. Vague laws, consequently, cause self-censorship, resulting in the suppression of more speech than the legislature intendes.

Clear standards are also necessary to guide police officers in making arrest decisions.[186] In a "nation of laws and not of men," legislatures may not delegate

---

[180] Pruneyard Shopping Center v. Robins, 447 U.S. 74, 100 S. Ct. 2035, 64 L. Ed. 2d 741 (1980).
[181] 405 U.S. 518, 92 S. Ct. 1103, 31 L. Ed. 2d 408 (1972).
[182] City of Houston v. Hill, *supra* note 64; Kolender v. Lawson, 461 U.S. 352, 357, 103 S. Ct. 1855, 1858, 75 L. Ed. 2d 903 (1983); Grayned v. City of Rockford, *supra* note 126; Gooding v. Wilson, *supra* note 64.
[183] Kolender v. Lawson, *supra* note 182.
[184] *See* authorities *supra* note 182.
[185] *Id.*
[186] *Id.*

standardless discretion to police officers to arrest whomever they please.[187] Laws that lack clear standards lend themselves to arbitrary and discriminatory applications. As a result, courts sometimes allow persons to attack the constitutionality of the statute under which they were arrested, even though their own conduct was not protected by the First Amendment and would have subjected them to arrest under a properly drawn law.[188]

Police, therefore, need to pay special attention to the law they invoke in cases involving speech. Opportunities often exist to choose between several statutes. Police should always prefer statutes that contain precise, narrow, and objective criteria over statutes that confer broad discretion and invite subjective judgments.

There are three kinds of statutes that police should never use in a speech context, even when the speaker's language and conduct are not protected by the First Amendment.

A. Statutes Authorizing Arrests for "Disturbing," "Annoying," or "Offensive" Conduct

In *Coates v. City of Cincinnati*,[189] the Court invalidated an ordinance that made it unlawful for "three or more persons to assemble ... on any sidewalks, and there conduct themselves in a manner annoying to persons passing by." Laws that make arrest decisions turn on an officer's assessment of whether others were offended or annoyed by the arrestee's conduct are unconstitutional for three different reasons.[190] First, they fail to give ordinary citizens adequate notice of the conduct to be avoided because virtually any conduct might annoy at least some people in the vicinity. Second, they vest too much discretion in the police to decide whether the statute has been violated. How is an officer to know whether people passing by were annoyed by the arrestee's conduct? The best an officer can do to gauge the reactions of others is to consider her own reaction. A statute that, read literally, makes it a crime to annoy a police officer comes dangerously close to a police state. Finally, these statutes cover some speech that is protected by the First Amendment. Speech does not cease to have protection because it offends or annoys another person.[191] For these reasons, statutes authorizing arrest

---

[187]   Grayned v. City of Rockford, *supra* note 126 (vague laws are constitutionally objectionable because they "impermissibly delegate basic policy matters to policemen, judges, and juries for resolution on an ad hoc and subjective basis ...").

[188]   Gooding v. Wilson, *supra* note 181; Brockett v. Spokane Arcades, Inc., *supra* note 48; New York v. Ferber, *supra* note 51; Smith v. Goguen, 415 U.S. 566, 582, 94 S. Ct. 1242, 1251, 39 L. Ed. 2d 605 (1974).

[189]   402 U.S. 611, 91 S. Ct. 1686, 29 L. Ed. 2d 214 (1971).

[190]   Cordova v. Reno, 920 F. Supp. 135 (D. Nev. 1997) (invalidating ordinance creating criminal liability for behavior that has the tendency to annoy, insult, or disturb any person passing by).

[191]   Forsyth County, Ga. v. The Nationalist Movement, *supra* note 167; Smith v. Goguen, 415 U.S. 566, 582, 94 S. Ct. 1242, 1251, 39 L. Ed. 2d 605 (1974).

for offensive or annoying conduct should never be used to arrest people engaged in speech, whether or not their speech is protected by the First Amendment.

B. Statutes Authorizing Arrests for Refusal to Obey a Police Officer's Order to Move On

Statutes authorizing police to make an arrest for disobeying an order to "move on" should also be used with extreme caution. Such statutes are constitutional only when they contain objective criteria for when such orders may be issued.[192] Legislatures may not invest police officers with standardless discretion to issue orders to move on and arrest those who disobey.

Shuttlesworth v. City of Birmingham[193] is the leading case on point. Shuttlesworth, a civil rights activist, and several of his companions were standing outside a department store during a protest boycott when a police officer approached them and told them to move on. The others left, but Shuttlesworth stayed behind. When he questioned the officer's authority to order him to leave, he was arrested under an ordinance that made it an offense to "stand ... upon any street or sidewalk of the city after having been requested by any police officer to move on." The Supreme Court reversed Shuttlesworth's conviction on the grounds that legislatures may not give police authority to arrest people who disobey a dispersal order without providing them with objective criteria for when such orders may be issued. The following observations, made in a different case, explain the reason.

> [U]nder our democratic system of government, lawmaking is not entrusted to the moment-to-moment judgment of the policeman on his beat. Laws, that is valid laws, are to be made by representatives chosen to make laws for the future, not by police officers whose duty it is to enforce laws already enacted and to make arrests only for conduct already made criminal ... To let a policeman's command become equivalent to a criminal statute comes dangerously near making our government one of men rather than of laws.[194]

Statutes that treat the failure to obey a police order to move as grounds for arrest are not objectionable when they detail the circumstances under which dispersal orders may be issued. Had the Birmingham ordinance made it an offense to "obstruct the free passage upon any public street and remain after having been requested by an officer to move on," the unconstitutional discretion would have been eliminated.[195] The right to stand on the street no longer depends on an officer's whim because the statute now

---

[192] Shuttlesworth v. City of Birmingham, 382 U.S. 87, 86 S. Ct. 211, 15 L. Ed. 2d 176 (1965); Chicago v. Morales, 527 U.S. 41, 119 S. Ct. 1849, 144 L. Ed. 2d 67 (1999).
[193] *Supra* note 192.
[194] Gregory v. City of Chicago, 394 U.S. 111, 120, 89 S. Ct. 946, 951, 22 L. Ed. 2d 134 (1969).
[195] Boos v. Barry, *supra* note 39 (upholding ordinance prohibiting persons from congregating within 500 feet of the embassy and not dispersing when ordered to do so).

requires the officer to observe overt acts declared unlawful by the legislature before issuing an order, the violation of which becomes grounds for arrest.

The point of this discussion is that law enforcement officers have no inherent power to issue arrest-triggering orders, and legislators may not confer this power on them. But because law enforcement officers have no way of judging the constitutionality of the laws they enforce, the following rule of thumb will reduce the risk of making an unconstitutional arrest:[196] If First Amendment actors are in a place where they have a legal right to be and are conducting themselves in a peaceful and lawful manner, an officer cannot make their conduct a crime by ordering them to disperse and arresting them if they disobey.

C. Statutes Authorizing Arrests for "Loitering"

Loitering statutes that make it a crime to "wander or stroll about in a public place without any apparent purpose" have uniformly been held unconstitutional because they are capable of being applied to large amounts of innocent conduct and contain no guidelines for distinguishing guilty from innocent behavior.[197] Laws that criminalize aimless wandering are too lacking in standards to be enforced in any context, not simply contexts involving speech. This principle is so well established that officers who make an arrest under a loitering statute like this run the risk of being sued.

The problem of standardless discretion is removed if the loitering statute requires proof of an overt act or a specific criminal intent, such as loitering in a public place with intent to commit prostitution. Loitering statutes that require an overt act or a specific criminal intent are constitutional because police no longer have unchecked discretion to arrest whomever they please.[198]

§ 2.18   Summary

The First Amendment prohibits the police from abridging freedom of speech. Speech encompasses a variety of mediums, including parades, pickets, protest demonstrations, and symbolic speech. A critical First Amendment distinction exists between police interventions targeted at a speaker's message and those targeted at his or her conduct.

---

[196]   Although police officers are immune from liability for enforcing laws that are later declared unconstitutional, *see, e.g.*, Pierson v. Ray, 386 U.S. 547, 87 S. Ct. 1213, 18 L. Ed. 2d 288 (1967), society is better served by making arrests that can stick.

[197]   Chicago v. Morales, *supra* note 192; Kolender v. Lawson, *supra* note 182; Papachristou v. City of Jacksonville, 405 U.S. 156, 92 S. Ct. 839, 31 L. Ed. 2d 110 (1972).

[198]   *See, e.g.*, People v. Superior Court (Caswell), 46 Cal. 3d 381, 758 P. 2d 1046 (1988).

A. First Amendment Protection for a Speaker's Message

Police may not arrest people for the content of their speech unless their speech falls outside the First Amendment. The following speech categories have been excluded.

- **Obscenity.** Obscenity refers to materials that appeal to prurient interests, depict hard-core sexual acts in a patently offensive manner, and lack serious literary, artistic, political, scientific, or other value. Police officers are not allowed to make this decision; it must be made by a judge. Materials suspected of being obscene may not be seized unless a judge has issued a search warrant.

- **Child pornography.** Child pornography refers to materials that visually depict real children engaged in sexual acts. In order to protect children from sexual exploitation, states may outlaw production and distribution of child pornography, without regard to whether the materials are obscene under the *Miller* standard.

- **Fighting words.** "Fighting words" are derogatory or abusive remarks spoken to another in a face-to-face encounter under circumstances likely to provoke the other into making an immediate violent response. The fighting words exclusion has a narrow application when the target of verbal abuse is a trained police officer.

- **Threats.** A threat, for purposes of the First Amendment, requires communication of a serious expression of intent to commit an act of unlawful violence

- **Incitement to riot.** Speech advocating violence or other unlawful action ceases to be protected by the First Amendment only if the speech is both directed toward inciting imminent lawless action and is likely to produce such action. A hostile reception does not furnish grounds for arresting individuals engaged in orderly protest.

B. First Amendment Protection for a Speaker's Conduct

Conduct and speech are often intertwined. The First Amendment does not confer the same protection on a speaker's conduct as on the message. General laws prohibiting conduct may be applied to people engaged in speech when they serve a substantial government interest that is not related to suppressing the speaker's message.

The government's authority to restrict speech on government property depends on whether the location is a public forum or a nonpublic forum. Restrictions on speech access to nonpublic forums — such as schools, police stations, military installations, and government buildings — need only be reasonable and neutral as to viewpoint. Speech receives maximum protection in public forums, such as streets, parks, sidewalks, and municipal auditoriums. While reasonable restrictions on the time, place, and manner of using public forums for speech are permitted, restrictions that foreclose an entire medium of expression are unconstitutional. The First Amendment does not guarantee a right of speech access to privately owned property including shopping centers and malls.

Laws that require a permit to hold a parade, march, or demonstration must: (1) contain clear, narrow, objective standards for permit administrators to follow; (2) not impose unreasonably long advance notice requirements; and (3) not allow discretion to establish the permit fee.

Criminal laws that are capable of being applied to speech must contain clear, precise, and objective standards to guide arrest decisions. In policing open-air speech gatherings, an officer must keep several things in mind. First, speakers may not be arrested for inciting a breach of the peace unless they urge imminent lawless action. Urging unlawful action down the road is not enough. Second, police may not arrest an unpopular speaker for a hostile audience reaction. Their duty is to protect the speaker's right to speak.

Authority to Detain and Arrest; Use of Force

3

The right of the people to be secure in their persons . . . against unreasonable . . . seizures, shall not be violated, and no Warrants shall issue, but upon probable cause, supported by Oath or affirmation, and particularly describing the person . . . to be seized.

Fourth Amendment

Chapter Outline

KEY TERMS AND CONCEPTS

Affidavit

Arrest

Arrest warrant

Common law

Exigent circumstances

Felony

Fresh pursuit

Hot pursuit

Investigatory detention

Investigatory stop

Misdemeanor

Pretextual traffic stop

Probable cause

Racial profiling

Reasonable grounds

Reasonable suspicion

Seizure

Show of legal authority

Terry stop

Voluntary encounter

§ 3.1   Introduction

During a routine day, an officer may pull a car over to advise the driver that her tire is dangerously low, ask three men loitering in front of a liquor store what they are doing there, arrest a shoplifter, and use deadly force in self-defense. The Fourth Amendment guarantees citizens the right to go about their business free of *unreasonable* interference by the police. Because the concern is with unreasonable interference, the Fourth Amendment does not treat all police interventions alike. Developing workable principles for when citizens may be detained for questioning, arrested, or forcibly subdued requires a trade-off between society's need for effective law enforcement and the need of its members for freedom from unwarranted interference with their ability to go about their business. This chapter explores the balance that has been struck.

A police officer's authority to detain citizens against their will is regulated by three layers of legal principles — the Fourth Amendment to the United States Constitution, state constitutions, and state arrest laws. The Fourth Amendment guarantees the "right of the people to be secure in their persons . . . against *unreasonable . . . seizures . . .*" Whenever a police officer detains a suspect for investigation, makes an arrest, or uses force to bring a suspect under control, the suspect is seized and the officer's conduct must conform to Fourth Amendment standards of reasonableness. However, the Fourth Amendment is not the only rule police officers must obey. All states have constitutional and statutory provisions covering these matters as well. A police officer's actions must comply with state constitutions and arrest laws, as well as the Fourth Amendment.

The primary focus of this chapter is on the Fourth Amendment. Students will receive in-depth instruction in the arrest laws of their state as part of their police department training programs.

Figure 3.1
Legal Restrictions on Arrest Authority

In order to be lawful, an arrest must comply with:

1. Fourth Amendment standards,
2. State constitutional standards, and
3. State arrest laws.

§ 3.2   Overview of the Fourth Amendment

An arrest results in a deprivation of liberty that carries serious consequences. It can damage important relationships, disrupt the ability to earn a living, and destroy a person's reputation in the community. As a result, common law judges wisely decided at an early date that arrest decisions should not be left to the unfettered discretion of the police. They established safeguards to reduce the likelihood of false arrests. In the case of an arrest for a **misdemeanor**, the **common law** required a prior judicial determination that the arrest was justified, unless the offense was committed in the officer's presence.[1] This is the origin of the modern **arrest warrant**. A warrant was not required to arrest for a **felony** because the threat to the public from having dangerous criminals roaming at large required that police be allowed to make an arrest at once. Protection against arbitrary arrests was provided through the requirement that the officer have **probable cause** to believe that a felony had been committed and that the person to be arrested had committed it.[2] These concepts helped shape the Fourth Amendment and play a central role in contemporary arrest law.[3]

A. Historical Purpose of the Fourth Amendment

General warrants and writs of assistance were the historic evil that led to the Fourth Amendment's adoption. These instruments conferred blanket authority on British customs officials to decide whom to search, where to search, and what to search for.[4] Armed with these dreaded instruments, customs officials could enter anyone's home without grounds for believing they had committed a crime or that contraband would be found there.[5] Hatred of this practice was one of the driving forces behind

---

[1]   10 HALSBURY'S LAWS OF ENGLAND 344–345 (3d ed. 1955); 4 W. BLACKSTONE, COMMENTARIES * 292; 1 J. STEPHEN, A HISTORY OF THE CRIMINAL LAW OF ENGLAND 193 (1883).

[2]   *See* sources *supra* note 1.

[3]   Henry v. United States, 361 U.S. 98, 100, 80 S. Ct. 168, 170, 4 L. Ed. 2d 134 (1959).

[4]   Barbara C. Salken, *The General Warrant of the Twentieth Century? A Fourth Amendment Solution to Unchecked Discretion to Arrest for Traffic Offenses*, 62 TEMP. L. REV. 221 (1989).

[5]   Steagald v. United States, 451 U.S. 204, 101 S. Ct. 1642, 68 L. Ed. 2d 38 (1981).

the American Revolution.[6] The purpose of the Fourth Amendment is announced in the first clause:

> The right of the people to be secure in their persons, houses, papers, and effects, against unreasonable searches and seizures, shall not be violated . . .

B. Overview of Fourth Amendment Detention and Arrest Provisions

The Fourth Amendment recognizes two classes of seizures: **investigatory stops** and **arrests**. Neither is mentioned in the text of the Fourth Amendment. The crucial term is seizure. The Fourth Amendment states that "[t]he right of the people to be secure in their persons . . . against unreasonable . . . seizures shall not be violated."

A seizure occurs when a suspect submits to a police officer's show of legal authority or the officer gains actual physical control over the suspect.[7] When an officer activates lights and siren and stops a vehicle, the motorist has been seized through submission to the officer's **show of legal authority** (*i.e.*, activating the lights and siren). When an officer takes a person from his home to the police station at gunpoint, the person is also seized. Seizures are classified as investigatory stops or arrests according to their duration and intrusiveness. Investigatory stops are limited seizures made for the purpose of conducting a brief investigation.[8] Pulling a vehicle over to check the registration because the vehicle matches the description of a stolen car is an example. Because investigatory stops are shorter and less intrusive than arrests, they are permitted on a lower degree of suspicion.[9] The degree of suspicion needed for an investigatory stop is known as **reasonable suspicion**.[10] When the police restrain a suspect's liberty beyond the degree allowed for an investigatory stop, the seizure automatically becomes an arrest and triggers the full protection of the Fourth Amendment. Arrests can occur either because an officer intends to make an arrest and so states or because a seizure that lasts too long or is too intrusive to qualify as a limited seizure.[11] Taking a suspect to the police station at gunpoint, for example, is so intrusive that it constitutes an arrest, whether or not the officer intends this consequence.

The Fourth Amendment is violated only when the seizure is **unreasonable**. A seizure may be considered unreasonable for any of the following reasons: (1) the officer lacked adequate grounds for the seizure, (2) the officer failed to procure a warrant in a

---

[6] *Id*. at 494 U.S. at 266, 110 S. Ct. at 1056.

[7] **California v. Hodari D., 499 U.S. 621, 111 S. Ct. 1547, 113 L. Ed. 2d 690 (1991)**; United States v. Mendenhall, 446 U.S. 544, 100 S. Ct. 1870, 64 L. Ed. 2d 497 (1980).

[8] **Terry v. Ohio, 392 U.S. 1, 88 S. Ct. 1868, 20 L. Ed. 2d 889 (1968).**

[9] *Id*.

[10] United States v. Cortez, 449 U.S. 411, 101 S. Ct. 690, 66 L. Ed. 2d 621 (1981).

[11] **Kaupp v. Texas, 538 U.S. 626, 123 S. Ct. 1843, 155 L. Ed. 2d 814 (2002)**; Dunaway v. New York, 442 U.S. 200, 209, 99 S. Ct. 2248, 2255, 60 L. Ed. 2d 824 (1979); Brown v. Illinois, 422 U.S. 590, 95 S. Ct. 2254, 45 L. Ed. 2d 416 (1975).

situation in which one was required, or (3) the officer used excessive force to affect the seizure.

The Fourth Amendment requires grounds for a seizure. The officer must be aware of facts that support the degree of suspicion needed for the action that was taken. A higher degree of suspicion is needed for an arrest than for an investigatory stop because it is more intrusive. If the officer lacks adequate grounds to justify the seizure, the seizure will violate the Fourth Amendment.[12]

The Fourth Amendment also regulates the method of affecting a seizure. The police, for example, are required to obtain an arrest warrant before they may enter a private residence to arrest someone inside.[13] Even though the police have probable cause to make the arrest, if they arrest a suspect inside her home without a warrant, the arrest is unconstitutional – not because they lacked grounds, but because they used the wrong method. An arrest warrant was necessary. Finally, the Fourth Amendment regulates the degree of force that may be used to affect a seizure. The force permitted varies with the seriousness of the offense and whether the officer's safety or the safety of others appears to be at risk.[14]

C. Consequences of an Unconstitutional Arrest or Detention for Investigation

Fourth Amendment violations have serious consequences — for the person whose constitutional rights are violated, the criminal justice system, and the officer personally. A false arrest can destroy an innocent person's reputation. It can also hamper the prosecution of a guilty person. Procuring evidence of the crime is one of the main purposes of a criminal investigation. This purpose can be defeated if the suspect's arrest violates the Fourth Amendment. If the arrest is unconstitutional, any search that follows is unauthorized and physical evidence or incriminating statements obtained as a result are inadmissible as evidence.[15] While an unconstitutional arrest does not bar the government from trying a person,[16] if the only evidence that the state has to convict an armed robbery suspect is a gun, stocking, and large roll of bills taken from him during a search incident to an unconstitutional arrest, the offender will go free. Consequently, police officers must be able to recognize when their conduct involves a seizure, whether the seizure constitutes an investigatory stop or an arrest, and whether they have grounds for taking this action. The police also have a personal stake in complying with the Fourth Amendment. Violating a suspect's Fourth Amendment rights can lead to a civil lawsuit and, if the violation is intentional, to criminal prosecution as well.[17]

---

[12]   Beck v. Ohio, 379 U.S. 89, 85 S. Ct. 223, 13 L. Ed. 2d 142 (1964).
[13]   *See* § 3.15 *infra.*
[14]   *See* § 3.16 *infra.*
[15]   The impact of an unconstitutional arrest on the admission of evidence is covered in Chapter 4.
[16]   *See, e.g.,* State v. Crews, 445 U.S. 463, 100 S. Ct. 1244, 63 L. Ed. 2d 537 (1980).
[17]   A police officer's civil liability for violating constitutional rights is covered in Chapter 10.

Figure 3.2
Consequences of an Unconstitutional Seizure

An unconstitutional seizure can:

1.   Ruin an innocent person's reputation.
2.   Destroy admissibility of evidence.
3.   Lead to a civil suit and, in rare cases, criminal prosecution of the officer.

§ 3.3   Crossing the Boundary of the Fourth Amendment

Police encounters with suspects range from contacts in which the suspect's cooperation is voluntary to full-blown arrests. Students must learn to recognize and distinguish among three kinds of interactions — **voluntary encounters**, **investigatory stops**,[18] and **arrests**. Figure 3.3 summarizes the descriptive characteristics and Fourth Amendment relevance of each. Because investigatory stops and arrests are both subcategories of seizures, the concept of a seizure must be understood first.

Voluntary encounters are not regulated by the Fourth Amendment. The police have a "free zone" for investigative work — a zone in which they are at liberty to approach members of the public and ask questions or request other forms of assistance, even though they are acting on nothing more than a hunch. The critical characteristic of the "free zone" is that the suspect's compliance with the officer's request is voluntary

Figure 3.3
Types of Investigatory Encounters and Suspicion Needed to Initiate

	Free Zone	Fourth Amendment Threshold	Encounters Regulated by the Fourth Amendment	
Type of Encounter	Voluntary Encounter	Seizure	Investigatory Stop	Arrest
Descriptive Characteristics	The police ask the suspect to cooperate in the investigation, such as answer questions, consent to a search, take a Breathalyzer test, etc, without restraining the suspect's freedom of movement or indicating, in any manner, that compliance is mandatory.	A seizure occurs when a suspect's freedom of movement is restricted and the suspect is brought under the officer's control, either by a, submission to a show of legal authority, or b, physical restraint, The Fourth Amendment kicks in at this point.	Seizure of limited scope and duration.	Seizure effected with an announced intent to make an arrest or that exceeds the boundaries of an investigatory stop.
Suspicion Needed to Initiate	None		Officer must have a reasonable suspicion that the suspect is involved in criminal activity.	Officer must have probable cause to believe that the suspect has committed or is committing a crime.

---

[18]   "Investigatory stops" are also called "investigatory detentions," "*Terry* stops," and sometimes "stop and frisks."

and consensual. The officer has not done or said anything that would convey the message that compliance is required. The moment this changes and the atmosphere becomes overbearing, threatening, or oppressive, the transition to a seizure is in progress. A seizure occurs when a suspect's freedom of movement is restricted and the suspect is brought under an officer's control, either through submission to the officer's show of legal authority or physical restraint. Seizure is a critical point in Fourth Amendment jurisprudence. Once a seizure occurs, the officer's conduct will be examined for compliance with the Fourth Amendment.

§ 3.4 — "Free Zone" for Investigative Work

Under the Fourth Amendment, as well as under other provisions of the Bill of Rights, people who voluntarily cooperate with the police have no standing to complain that their constitutional rights have been violated. The police do not need probable cause, reasonable suspicion, or any other grounds to initiate a voluntary encounter. Investigative encounters conducted without a seizure are not regulated by the Fourth Amendment. Police officers are free to ask suspects for any form of voluntary assistance — identification,[19] answers to questions,[20] permission to search their luggage,[21] consent to take a Breathalyzer test, *etc.* — provided they do not restrict the suspect's freedom of movement or communicate through words or conduct that compliance with their request is mandatory.[22] It goes without saying that the suspect has a corresponding right to refuse the officer's request. However, the important point is that officers do not need grounds to ask. Evidence is always admissible when a suspect furnishes it voluntarily.

Figure 3.4
Characteristics of a Voluntary Encounter

Voluntary police/suspect encounters are not regulated by the Fourth Amendment. Encounters are considered voluntary only if the police do not:

1. restrict the suspect's freedom of movement, or
2. communicate through words, conduct, or gestures that compliance with their request is mandatory.

No grounds for suspicion are needed to initiate a voluntary encounter. However, the suspect has a corresponding right to refuse to cooperate.

[19] INS v. Delgado, 466 U.S. 210, 104 S. Ct. 1758, 80 L. Ed. 2d 247 (1984).
[20] Florida v. Rodriguez, 469 U.S. 1, 105 S. Ct. 308, 83 L. Ed. 2d 165 (1984).
[21] **United States v. Drayton, 536 U.S. 194, 122 S. Ct. 2105, 153 L. Ed. 2d 242 (2002)**; Florida v. Bostick, 501 U.S. 429, 111 S. Ct. 2382, 115 L. Ed. 2d 389 (1991); Florida v. Royer, 460 U.S. 491, 103 S. Ct. 1319, 1326, 75 L. Ed. 2d 229 (1983).
[22] **United States v. Drayton**, *supra* note 21; Florida v. Bostick, *supra* note 21; Dunaway v. New York, *supra* note 11.

§ 3.5   — "Seizure" Defined

Because seizures trigger the Fourth Amendment, knowing when conduct involves a seizure must become an automatic reflex. Otherwise, violations of the Fourth Amendment will be inevitable. We have invented a petty crook named Sticky-Fingered Sam to illustrate concepts in this book. The assertion that Officer Blake "seized" Sticky-Fingered Sam evokes the image of Officer Blake grabbing Sam. This is one way Officer Blake can seize Sam. However, he can also seize him without laying a hand on him. Suppose Officer Blake, while patrolling a residential neighborhood late at night, sees Sam lugging a stereo down the street. He gets out of his patrol car and, with one hand resting on his revolver, stands in front of Sam and says in an authoritative tone of voice, "Hey bud! Put that stereo down, show me some identification, and tell me where you got that stereo." Sam stops, puts the stereo down, and complies. Sam has been seized.

In order to affect a seizure, the police must gain control over the suspect. Control can be gained through either: (1) physical restraint or (2) the suspect's submission to a show of legal authority.[23] Sticky-Fingered Sam was seized in the second way. Officer Blake made a show of legal authority when, standing with his hand on his gun, he directed Sam to put the stereo down and explain where he got it. Sam complied, not because he wanted to, but because he understood from Officer Blake's words, body language, and tone of voice that he had no choice. Officer Blake brought Sam under his control psychologically. Interactions with a suspect do not have to involve physical contact or a trip to the police station in order to constitute a seizure.[24]

Figure 3.5
Definition of a Seizure

> A suspect is seized when he is deprived of freedom of movement and brought under a police officer's control through either:
>
> 1.   submission to a show of legal authority or
> 2.   physical restraint.

Because submission to a show of legal authority is one way suspects can be seized, police officers must be able to recognize when conduct amounts to a show of legal authority. An objective standard is used to make this determination. Courts are not concerned with whether the officer actually intended to restrict the suspect's freedom of movement or with whether the suspect subjectively believed that the officer had this intent. Some citizens are so intimidated by the police that they never feel free to refuse an officer's request, no matter how politely they are asked. Whether an officer's conduct amounts to a show of legal authority depends on how a reasonable person in the

---

[23]   **California v. Hodari D.**, *supra* note 7; United States v. Mendenhall, *supra* note 7.
[24]   **Terry v. Ohio**, *supra* note 8.

suspect's position would have assessed the situation.[25] If the officer's words and conduct would have conveyed the message to a reasonable person that he/she is not free to ignore the officer's request, terminate the encounter, and go about his/her business, a suspect who complies is seized.

Police interactions with a suspect can start off as voluntary, but then change. It is often necessary for courts to pinpoint the exact moment during an encounter when a suspect was seized. The reason is that evidence procured from a suspect without a seizure is always admissible, whereas evidence procured after a seizure may or may not be. Admissibility will turn on whether the officer had grounds for the seizure.[26] Grounds must exist at the time the seizure was made; a seizure cannot be justified by what an officer learns afterwards. Consequently, courts are regularly called upon to decide whether the police became aware of facts that created grounds for a seizure before or after they made it. This makes it imperative for officers to be able to recognize when they are on the verge of making a seizure and not cross this line until they have constitutional grounds.

A. Submission to a Show of Legal Authority

The consensual aspects of an encounter vanish once a police officer's conduct conveys the message that the suspect is not free to terminate the encounter and leave. Such conduct is called a show of legal authority. A seizure based on submission to a show of legal authority can occur even though the suspect submits without protest. Below are two hypothetical police/suspect encounters. The first is voluntary; the second is a seizure.

> *Encounter 1.* A narcotics detective observes a nervous young man pull out a roll of $100 bills at a Miami airport ticket counter and pay cash for a one-way ticket to New York. Acting on a hunch that he is a drug courier, she approaches him, shows her badge, and says, "Would you mind answering a few questions about the purpose of your travel and the contents of your attaché case?" The young man agrees.[27]

Even though the detective identified herself as a narcotics agent before requesting an interview, this encounter is consensual because she asked permission. A request for permission conveys the message that the suspect is free to decline. Incriminating information procured in response to an approach like this is always admissible.

---

[25] **United States v. Drayton**, *supra* note 21; Florida v. Bostick, *supra* note 21; **California v. Hodari D.**, *supra* note 7; INS v. Delgado, *supra* note 19; United States v. Mendenhall, *supra* note 7.

[26] *See, e.g.*, Brown v. Illinois, *supra* note 11; Wong Sun v. United States, 371 U.S. 471, 83 S. Ct. 407, 9 L. Ed. 2d 441 (1963). The Fourth Amendment exclusionary rule is discussed in Chapter 4.

[27] *See, e.g.*, **United States v. Drayton**, *supra* note 21 (Police did not "seize" bus passengers when, as part of a routine drug and weapons interdiction effort, they boarded a bus at a rest stop and began asking passengers at random for permission to search their luggage); Florida v. Bostick, *supra* note 21 (same).

Encounter 2. The detective, after observing the ticket purchase, approaches the young man, shows her badge, and says in a commanding voice: "Pick up your bags and follow me. I'm taking you to the security office for questioning." The young man complies.[28]

The second interaction constitutes a seizure. The detective did not ask for the young man's cooperation — she ordered him to follow her. Because a reasonable person who is told that he must accompany an officer to another location for questioning does not feel free to refuse, the young man's submission resulted in a seizure.[29]

Application of the "free to leave" test is fact specific. It requires consideration of all the circumstances surrounding an encounter, viewed from the perspective of a reasonable person in the suspect's position.[30] Courts have identified the following factors, among others, as relevant: the time and place of the encounter; the number of uniformed officers present; whether the officers speak in an authoritative tone of voice or use overbearing or threatening language; whether they touch the suspect, surround him, or obstruct his path of exit; whether they draw a weapon; whether they tell him that he is suspected of a crime; and whether the suspect is alone with the police during the encounter or whether others are present.[31] The perception of not being free to leave must arise from the behavior of the police and not from the fact that the encounter takes place on a bus[32] or other location where it would be inconvenient for the suspect to leave.[33] While an encounter can be voluntary without the suspect being told that he is free to leave,[34] informing the suspect dispels any possible confusion about this matter.[35]

Below are three examples of seizures. In all three cases, the actions of the police convey the message that the suspect is not free to ignore their request and go about his or her business.

- An officer activates a siren and pursues the suspect's car. The suspect pulls over.[36]

---

[28]   These facts are taken from Florida v. Royer, *supra* note 21. The court held that a traveler was seized when detectives told him he had to accompany them to the airport security office for questioning. *Id.*

[29]   *Id.*

[30]   Michigan v. Chesternut, 486 U.S. 567, 108 S. Ct. 1975, 100 L. Ed. 2d 565 (1988).

[31]   For a discussion of the factors relevant to free-to-leave analysis, *see, e.g.*, Florida v. Bostick, *supra* note 21, 501 U.S. at 434–435, 111 S. Ct. at 2386–2387; United States v. Watson, 423 U.S. 411, 424, 96 S. Ct. 820, 828, 46 L. Ed. 2d 598 (1976).

[32]   **United States v. Drayton**, *supra* note 21 (bus passenger not seized where officer spoke in non-threatening tone of voice, did not block passenger's path to exit, and said nothing that would lead passenger to believe that he was required to answer officer's question).

[33]   INS v. Delgado, *supra* note 19.

[34]   *See, e.g.*, **United States v. Drayton**, *supra* note 21 (no seizure, despite officer's failure to advise suspect of his right to refuse cooperation, where circumstances surrounding encounter indicated that consent was voluntary).

[35]   *Id.*

[36]   Stopping a moving vehicle by making a show of legal authority is always a seizure. *See* § 3.10 *infra.*

- Police pound on the suspect's door, shouting "Open up! This is the police." The suspect opens the door.[37]
- Five police officers exit squad cars and surround the suspect, while one questions him. The suspect answers.[38]

The following interventions also involve seizures: terminating a suspect's movement by putting up barricades or roadblocks[39]; halting a suspect's flight by drawing a weapon or firing a warning shot[40]; surrounding a suspect on all sides[41]; stopping a suspect through an order to halt or freeze[42]; grabbing,[43] frisking,[44] or putting handcuffs on a suspect[45]; placing the suspect in a locked squad car; retaining possession of a suspect's car keys, driver's license, airline tickets, or other property that prevents the suspect from leaving[46]; and accusing the suspect of involvement in criminal activity.[47] Whenever a suspect pulls over to the shoulder of the road, submits to a search, or complies with any other demand that amounts to a show of legal authority, the suspect has been seized.

---

[37] *See, e.g.,* United States v. Jerez, 108 F.3d 684 (7th Cir. 1997) (seizure occurred when police banged on door, announced their presence, and ordered occupants to open it); United States v. Saari, 272 F.3d 804 (6th Cir. 2001) (seizure occurred when officers positioned themselves in front of the only exit from defendant's apartment with their guns drawn and knocked forcefully, announcing that they were the police and ordering defendant to come outside).

[38] *See, e.g.,* United States v. Alarcon-Gonzalez, 73 F.3d 289 (10th Cir. 1996) (seizure occurred when suspect was surrounded on all sides by uniformed police officers); United States v. Packer, 15 F.3d 654 (7th Cir. 1994) (seizure occurred when two police officers parked their cars on either side of the suspect's vehicle and shined a "take down" light through his window).

[39] *See, e.g.,* Brower v. County of Inyo, 489 U.S. 593, 109 S. Ct. 1378, 103 L. Ed. 2d 628 (1989) (suspect seized when his car crashed into an impassable tractor-trailer barricade deliberately placed across the highway by the police to capture him).

[40] *See, e.g.,* United States v. Mendenhall, *see* note 7 (opinion of Stewart, J.) ("Examples of circumstances that might indicate a seizure, even where the person did not attempt to leave, would be the threatening presence of several officers, the display of a weapon by an officer, some physical touching of the person of the citizen, or the use of language or tone of voice indicating that compliance with the officer's request might be compelled.").

[41] *See* cases *supra* note 38.

[42] United States v. Mendenhall, *supra* note 7.

[43] Sibron v. State, 392 U.S. 40, 88 S. Ct. 1889, 20 L. Ed. 2d 917 (1968) (suspect seized when police officer grabbed him by the collar).

[44] **Terry v. Ohio,** *supra* note 8; Gentry v. Sevier, 597 F. 3d 838 (7th Cir. 2010) (suspect seized where officer told him to hold his hands up and frisked him).

[45] United States v. Wilson, 2 F.2d 226 (7th Cir. 1993).

[46] *See, e.g.,* Florida v. Royer, *supra* note 21 (airline traveler seized when officers took and retained his airline ticket, identification, and baggage claim check, and asked him to accompany them to the security office). *See also* United States v. Chan-Jimenez, 125 F.3d 1324 (10th Cir. 1997); United States v. Sanchez, 89 F.3d 715 (10th Cir. 1996).

[47] *See, e.g.,* United States v. White, 890 F.2d 1413 (8th Cir. 1989) (suspect seized when an officer told him he had been stopped because he exhibited characteristics displayed by drug couriers).

B. Physical Restraint

Most people submit to a police officer's show of legal authority without putting up resistance.[48] When this does not happen, the suspect must be brought under control physically for the seizure to be complete.[49] Pursuing a suspect, shouting "you're under arrest," "stop in the name of the law," "halt," or "freeze" is not a seizure if the suspect continues to flee.[50] Until the suspect is captured, there is no seizure.

This principle was applied in *California v. Hodari D.*,[51] in which a juvenile who was standing on a street corner ran when he saw an approaching unmarked police car. The officers got out of the car and pursued him on foot, yelling at him to stop. The youth discarded a rock of crack cocaine seconds before the officers tackled him. The Supreme Court held that, even though the officers lacked grounds for seizing the youth when they began the chase, the crack cocaine was not subject to suppression because the youth was not seized until he was captured. By then, he had already discarded the cocaine. The discarded cocaine was admissible because it was not the fruit of an unconstitutional seizure. *California v. Hodari D.* stands for the proposition that evidence discarded by a suspect while being pursued by the police is not subject to suppression, even if the police lack grounds for seizing the suspect when they start the chase.

Police, nevertheless, should not knowingly place themselves in a position in which they are forced to rely on *California v. Hodari D.* Chasing a suspect when the officer lacks grounds to capture him has a happy ending only if the suspect discards the contraband during the chase. This happens only by chance. If the suspect still has the contraband in his possession when he is seized, an illegal chase will end in an unconstitutional capture, and the evidence will be suppressed.

§ 3.6   — Fourth Amendment Grounds for a Lawful Seizure

The determination that the suspect was seized leads to the next stage of Fourth Amendment analysis. Did the police have constitutional grounds?

A police officer's constitutional authority to interfere with a suspect's liberty depends on the degree of suspicion concerning the suspect's guilt. Increasingly intrusive interventions are allowed as the degree of suspicion grows. Figure 3.6 shows the relationship between degrees of suspicion and responses permitted by the Constitution.

There are four relevant degrees of suspicion. Figure 3.6 lists them in ascending order. A hunch is the lowest degree of suspicion. Each successively higher degree requires either more or stronger evidence of guilt. When police have nothing more than a

---

[48]   *See, e.g.*, Albright v. Oliver, 510 U.S. 266, 114 S. Ct. 807, 127 L. Ed. 2d 114 (1994) (suspect seized when he voluntarily surrendered to authorities after learning of an outstanding warrant for his arrest).

[49]   *See, e.g.*, Brower v. County of Inyo, *supra* note 39 (suspect seized when his car crashed into a tractor-trailer barricade placed across the highway by police in order to capture him).

[50]   **California v. Hodari D.**, *supra* note 7.

[51]   *Id.*

Figure 3.6
Degrees of Suspicion and Response Permitted by the Constitution

Degree of Suspicion	Response Permitted by the Constitution
Hunch	Interactions with the suspect must be consensual
Reasonable suspicion that the suspect is involved in criminal activity	Suspect may be seized and detained for a brief investigation
Probable cause to believe that the suspect is guilty	Suspect may be arrested
Proof beyond a reasonable doubt	Suspect may be convicted of the crime and punished

raw hunch that the suspect is involved in criminal activity, they may investigate, but their encounter with the suspect must be voluntary—the suspect may not be seized. When police have evidence that justifies a reasonable suspicion of criminal activity, they may conduct an investigatory detention. An **investigatory detention** is a limited seizure made for the purpose of investigating the circumstances that aroused the officer's suspicion. Investigatory detentions must be brief because evidence that forms the basis for a reasonable suspicion does not justify a prolonged detention. Probable cause is the next level of suspicion. Once the police know of enough facts to warrant a reasonable person in believing, not just suspecting, that a particular individual is guilty of a crime, they have probable cause to make an arrest. However, in order to obtain a conviction and deprive a person of her liberty over an extended period, there must be a higher degree of certainty yet. The government must present evidence that establishes guilt beyond a reasonable doubt.

A. Comparison of Reasonable Suspicion and Probable Cause

Both reasonable suspicion and probable cause involve assessments of a suspect's probable guilt. Rational people make assessments based on the strength of the evidence. The evidence on which police officers act comes from a variety of sources. These sources include personal observation, physical evidence found at the crime scene, information supplied by other law enforcement agencies or contained in police records, and reports from citizens and informants.[52] Based on this pool of information, the police draw inferences and make assessments about the suspect's probable guilt. The probability increases as the information pointing to this conclusion mounts. The level of suspicion rises accordingly. Probable cause and reasonable suspicion represent different points on an evidentiary continuum, rather than discrete concepts.

---

[52] United States v. Cortez, 449 U.S. 411, 101 S. Ct. 690, 66 L. Ed. 2d 621 (1981).

B. *Process Used to Evaluate the Existence of Reasonable Suspicion/Probable Cause*

Judges consider the same sources of information for reasonable suspicion and probable cause determinations. The only difference is the amount of evidence needed to satisfy the two standards. The evaluation process is also the same.[53] The process consists of identifying the facts and circumstances known to the officer at the time of the action and then weighing them to decide whether they were sufficient to satisfy the relevant standard.

Figure 3.7
Procedure Used to Evaluate Whether Constitutional Grounds Existed for the Action Taken

In order to determine whether the officer had constitutional grounds (*i.e.*, reasonable suspicion/probable cause) for the action taken, courts:

1. identify all the facts and circumstances known to the officer at the time the action was taken,
2. weigh the facts in combination, and
3. evaluate their implications from the perspective of a trained police officer.

How do judges weigh facts to decide whether they are sufficient to satisfy the relevant standard? First, they view the facts and circumstances known to the officer in combination. In other words, they look at the whole picture. Second, they view them in the way that a trained police officer would view them. Even though each fact, standing by itself, may be innocent, when the facts are viewed in combination through the eyes of an experienced police officer, they may present an entirely different picture. Suppose an officer sees two men standing on a street corner, talking. This behavior is perfectly innocent. Suppose that the time is 1:00 in the morning. This behavior is still innocent. There is nothing particularly unusual about two men conversing at a street corner at 1:00 A.M. Now add one more fact. The site of the rendezvous is a neighborhood in which there have been numerous arrests for drug trafficking. Now there is something worth looking into.

This is where the going gets tough. A hunch does not justify a seizure; interactions with the suspect must remain voluntary. Reasonable suspicion, on the other hand, does; the officer may stop and detain the suspect for a brief investigation. Although different degrees of suspicion carry vastly different legal consequences, there are, unfortunately, no hard-edged boundaries between them. Consequently, deciding when the required level of suspicion exists often presents a difficult judgment call. On the facts just given, the Supreme Court ruled that the officer's observations justified a hunch, but not reasonable suspicion.[54] Why did the Supreme Court find that these facts justified only a hunch?

---

[53] Ornelas v. United States, 517 U.S. 690, 116 S. Ct. 1657, 134 L. Ed. 2d 911 (1996).

[54] Brown v. Texas, 443 U.S. 47, 99 S. Ct. 2637, 61 L. Ed. 2d 357 (1979). *See also* Gentry v. Sevier, 597 F. 3d 838 (7th Cir. 2010) (holding that officers who observed a black male walking through a residential neighborhood at night, pushing a wheelbarrow did not have reasonable suspicion necessary to initiate a *Terry* stop or a pat down).

Reasonable suspicion requires that an officer observe behavior that is out of the ordinary in ways that are suggestive of criminal activity. In this case, the officer cannot point to anything unusual about the actions of these men that justifies suspecting them of anything. The facts that aroused the officer's suspicion were associated with the neighborhood and the time of day. Suspicion that develops solely because of the surrounding circumstances and would apply to any person who happened to be standing there is a hunch, not reasonable suspicion. Had the officer seen one man take out a bundle of money and hand it to the other, the officer's suspicion would now be grounded on facts associated with the conduct of these men that would justify a reasonable suspicion that they had engaged in a drug transaction.

C. *Inferences and Assumptions from Known Facts and Circumstances*

The suspicion that arose when the money changed hands derived from two sources: (1) the things the officer observed and (2) the officer's assumptions and deductions about their meaning. The officer knew four things: (1) the neighborhood was frequented by drug users, (2) drug transactions normally take place in the early morning hours; (3) it was 1:00 A.M., and (4) a large sum of money changed hands between these two men. From these facts, the officer drew an inference that the men might be engaged in a narcotics transaction.

When behavior is observed, inferences are made about its meaning. Three people on a street corner who see a man pushing a screaming and fighting seven year old into a car may see three different things. One may see a beleaguered father harassed by an ill-tempered child, the second an abusive father, and the third a kidnapper. All three witnessed the same sequence of events, but each drew a different inference. Where did their different inferences originate?

Sensory input is meaningless until the observer interprets it. When an event is observed, the information is processed through the lens of the observer's prior experience, and inferences and assumptions are added. These mental additions come from the observer's prior life experiences. The inferences and assumptions that are added bind the pieces of information together and shape their meaning to the observer. Interpretation of sensory input in light of prior experience is a normal part of the human mental process and explains why these three observers saw three different things.

Police officers are trained observers. They are sometimes able to see patterns that are suggestive of criminal activity in ordinary behavior that others without their experience would be unlikely to see. An untrained observer noticing a loose arm panel in the backseat of a car, for example, would be likely to interpret this as a sign of wear and tear. However, a trained narcotics detective who has searched many cars will see another possibility. To the detective, loose panels in the backseats of cars also raise the possibility that drugs may be secreted there.[55]

---

[55]   Ornelas v. United States, *supra* note 53.

The Supreme Court has repeatedly emphasized that law enforcement officers are expected to rely on their prior experience in drawing inferences and using them to assess the probability of criminal activity.[56] In evaluating whether the officer had reasonable suspicion or probable cause, courts look at the facts the way a trained police officer would.[57] However, the ultimate decision of whether the facts known to the officer, along with the inferences that arise from the officer's experience, are sufficient to satisfy the relevant standard rests with the court. The officer's subjective belief that grounds exist has no bearing on this matter.[58]

§ 3.7   Investigatory Stops

Today, seizures are classified as *limited* or *full*. This has not always been the case. Prior to *Terry v. Ohio*,[59] the Fourth Amendment universe was black and white. No degree of suspicion was required for an officer to approach a suspect and attempt to strike up a voluntary investigative encounter, but as soon as the encounter ceased being voluntary, the suspect was seized. There was only one class of seizures and one constitutionally recognized justification. Whenever the police detained a suspect against her will, even momentarily, the seizure constituted an arrest for which probable cause was necessary.[60] The same level of suspicion was needed to stop a vehicle on the highway for a two-minute registration check as to take a suspect under formal arrest to the police station for booking and fingerprinting.

Probable cause is an exacting standard. To have probable cause for an arrest, the officer must possess information that would justify a reasonably cautious person in believing that the person to be arrested committed a crime.[61] This standard hampered effective law enforcement in cases in which an officer's on-the-spot observations prompted a reasonable suspicion of criminal activity, but not probable cause for an arrest.

This predicament is common in law enforcement. A patrol officer on the beat receives a radio dispatch that a liquor store three blocks away has just been robbed. En route to the robbery scene, the officer sees a man running down the street with a bag in his hand, constantly looking back to see whether anyone is following him.

---

[56]   United States v. Arvizu, 534 U. S. 266, 122 S. Ct. 744, 151 L. Ed. 2d 740 (2002); Ornelas v. United States, *supra* note 53; United States v. Sokolow, 490 U.S. 1, 109 S. Ct. 1581, 104 L. Ed. 2d 1 (1989); Florida v. Royer, *supra* note 21; United States v. Cortez, *supra* note 52.
[57]   *See* cases *supra* note 56.
[58]   The constitutionally required levels of suspicion needed for investigatory stops and arrests are discussed in greater depth in §§ 3.8 and 3.13 *infra*.
[59]   **392 U.S. 1, 88 S. Ct. 1868, 20 L. Ed. 2d 889 (1968).**
[60]   Dunaway v. New York, 442 U.S. 200, 99 S. Ct. 2248, 60 L. Ed. 2d 824 (1979).
[61]   Carroll v. United States, 267 U.S. 132, 45 S. Ct. 280, 69 L. Ed. 543 (1925); Beck v. Ohio, 379 U.S. 89, 85 S. Ct. 223, 13 L. Ed. 2d 142 (1964).

The man's dress and running style indicate that he is not jogging for exercise. Although the officer has a sound basis for a reasonable suspicion, he does not have probable cause to make an arrest.

Before *Terry v. Ohio*, officers in this situation faced an impossible choice — let the person run by or make an unconstitutional arrest. The stakes grew higher after *Mapp v. Ohio*,[62] in which the Supreme Court held that evidence procured in violation of the Fourth Amendment is inadmissible. If the police detained this man for investigation and found a gun and a roll of money in his possession, the gun and the money were the product of an unconstitutional arrest, made without probable cause, and could not be used as evidence.

Whether the police should have the power to detain persons for investigation without probable cause for arrest was hotly debated for many decades. In *Terry v. Ohio*,[63] decided in 1968, the Supreme Court spoke. The police would be entrusted with this power, but the scope and duration of the intrusion would be proportionately limited.

A. *Terry v. Ohio*

The facts of *Terry v. Ohio*[64] are similar to thousands of other cases in which the police observe behavior that arouses reasonable suspicion that criminal activity is afoot, but not probable cause for an arrest. While patrolling in downtown Cleveland, a police officer observed three men gazing through a store window, studying what was going on inside. The men walked a short distance, turned back, gazed through the store window again, and then assembled for a conference. They repeated this ritual five or six times. Suspecting them of casing the store in preparation for a robbery, the officer approached them, identified himself, and directed them to recite their names. When Terry who was one of them mumbled something inaudible, the officer grabbed him, spun him around, and held him while patting down his exterior clothing. Feeling a pistol in the left breast pocket, the officer ordered Terry to remove his overcoat, reached in, and retrieved a .38-caliber revolver. Terry was indicted for carrying a concealed weapon. His attorney moved to suppress the revolver on the grounds that the Fourth Amendment does not allow police officers to conduct a weapons frisk unless they have probable cause for an arrest.

The issue in *Terry v. Ohio* centered on the constitutionality of the weapons frisk. However, because the constitutionality of the weapons frisk depended on the constitutionality of stopping Terry for questioning without probable cause to arrest him, the Supreme Court was forced to decide both questions. Concerning the constitutionality of the stop, the Supreme Court ruled that the police may briefly detain individuals for questioning when their conduct arouses a reasonable suspicion that they are involved in criminal activity. The reasonable suspicion standard is less demanding than probable

---

[62] **367 U.S. 643, 81 S. Ct. 1684, 6 L. Ed. 2d 1081 (1961).**
[63] *Supra* note 59.
[64] *Id.*

cause for an arrest. Having granted authority to detain on reasonable suspicion, the Supreme Court went on to rule that:

> When an officer is justified in believing that the individual whose suspicious behavior he is investigating at close range is armed and presently dangerous to the officer or to others, . . . the officer [has] the power to take necessary measures to determine whether the person is in fact carrying a weapon and to neutralize the threat of physical harm.

Terry v. Ohio established two rules that are of central importance to law enforcement. First, police may detain persons for investigation whose conduct arouses reasonable suspicion that they are involved in criminal activity. Second, when a detention is justified, police may conduct a protective weapons search (*i.e.*, frisk) if, in addition, they have a reasonable suspicion that the detainee may be armed and dangerous. *Terry v. Ohio* did not establish the parameters for an investigatory stop, however. This remained for later cases.

B. Purpose of a Terry Investigatory Stop

The purpose of a *Terry* **stop** is to enable the police to investigate the circumstances that prompted the stop in order to confirm or dispel their suspicion within a relatively short period.[65] If the investigation confirms the suspicion, police now have probable cause for an arrest and can proceed to the next stage. However, if additional facts needed to establish probable cause are not forthcoming after a brief investigation, police must let the suspect go. The police may not detain a suspect indefinitely on nothing more than a reasonable suspicion of involvement in criminal activity.[66]

Figure 3.8
Purpose of a Terry Stop

> The purpose of a *Terry* stop is to enable the police to investigate the circumstances that prompted the stop in order to confirm or dispel their suspicion within a relatively short period.

C. Constitutional Requirements for Making a Lawful Terry Investigatory Stop

There are three constitutional requirements for a lawful *Terry* stop. First, police must have reasonable suspicion to initiate the stop. Second, they must conduct the business of the stop as expeditiously as possible so as to not prolong the period of

---

[65]   Florida v. Royer, *supra* note 21; United States v. Brignoni-Ponce, 422 U.S. 873, 880, 95 S. Ct. 2574, 2580, 45 L. Ed. 2d 607 (1975).

[66]   Florida v. Royer, *supra* note 21, 460 U.S. at 709–710, 103 S. Ct. at 2646.

involuntary detention. Third, they must employ the least intrusive means of detention and investigation reasonably available that will achieve their goal. Failure to comply with any of these requirements transforms a detention, valid when made, into a *de facto* arrest for which probable cause is necessary.

Figure 3.9
Requirements for a Constitutional *Terry* Investigatory Stop

There are three requirements for a lawful *Terry* stop. Police must:

1. have reasonable suspicion to initiate the stop;
2. conduct the business of the stop as expeditiously as possible so as to not prolong the period of involuntary detention;
3. employ the least intrusive means of detention and investigation reasonably available that will achieve their goal.

D. *Location of a* Terry *Investigatory Stop*

Although the detention in *Terry* involved a pedestrian standing on a street corner, investigatory stops are not limited to any particular geographic location. They may be made on highways, in airport terminals, on buses,[67] inside buildings, or anywhere a police officer observes facts that arouse her reasonable suspicion that criminal activity is afoot.[68] Homes, however, enjoy special protection under the Fourth Amendment.[69] Police may not make a nonconsensual entry into a private residence to conduct a *Terry* investigation unless there is an urgent need for immediate action.[70]

E. *Suspected Criminal Activity for Which a* Terry *Investigatory Stop May Be Made*

Terry stops are typically made in response to on-the-spot observations that lead an officer to reasonably believe that criminal activity is in progress. The observation of three men casing a store provided the impetus for the stop in *Terry v. Ohio*. However, the suspicion that prompts the stop can also relate to past criminal activity. An officer, for example, may come into contact with a person who matches the description of a suspect wanted by the police for a previous crime and need to detain the person while

---

[67]   *See, e.g.*, United States v. Drayton, *supra* note 21; Florida v. Bostick, *supra* note 21.

[68]   Florida v. Royer, *supra* note 21; **Place v. United States, 462 U.S. 696, 103 S. Ct. 2637, 77 L. Ed. 2d 110 (1983)**; United States v. Mendenhall, *supra* note 7.

[69]   *See, e.g.*, Silverman v. United States, 365 U.S. 505, 81 S. Ct. 679, 5 L. Ed. 2d 734 (1961) ("At the very core [of the Fourth Amendment] stands the right of a man to retreat into his own home and there be free from unreasonable governmental intrusion."). Special Fourth Amendment protection for the sanctity of the home is covered in § 3.15 *infra*.

[70]   *See, e.g.*, Alto v. City of Chicago, 863 F. Supp. 658 (N. D. Ill. 1994) (hot pursuit of suspect fleeing from the scene of a *Terry* stop); Harbin v. City of Alexandria, 712 F. Supp. 67 (E.D. Va. 1989) (same).

looking into this matter.[71] In short, *Terry* stops may be made whenever the police have a reasonable suspicion that the person detained has committed, is committing, or is about to commit a crime.

F. Relevance of the Officer's Intent

Police need not intend to make a *Terry* stop in order to be held responsible for making one. *Terry* stops are seizures. Whenever a person submits to an officer's show of legal authority or is physically restrained, the person is seized. If the seizure is brief and limited in scope, the court will characterize the encounter as a *Terry* stop and move on to the next question. Did the officer have the requisite degree of suspicion?

§ 3.8   — Reasonable Suspicion

A. Definition of Reasonable Suspicion

The Supreme Court has provided the following test for reasonable suspicion:

> The officer must be able to point to specific and articulable facts that, taken together with rational inferences from those facts, provide a particularized and objective basis for suspecting the detainee of criminal activity.[72]

On an evidentiary spectrum (see Figure 3.6), reasonable suspicion lies somewhere between a hunch and probable cause for an arrest. In order to satisfy this standard, the officer must be able to verbalize and explain with particularity why she suspected the detainee of involvement in criminal activity. Further, her reasons must be based on objective facts and circumstances that would justify a reasonable police officer in reaching this conclusion. The Fourth Amendment does not allow suspects to be involuntarily detained on nothing more than a hunch.[73] The difference between a hunch and reasonable suspicion is that reasonable suspicion must be based on objective facts related to the detainee's behavior that suggest involvement in criminal activity — not just a gut reaction.

The facts of *Terry v. Ohio*[74] provide a textbook illustration of the application of the reasonable suspicion standard. The officer in *Terry* watched three men repeatedly go through the ritual of peering into a store window, walking a short distance, conferring, turning back, and peering into the store window again. The implications that arise from this behavior are unmistakable. The grounds for the officer's suspicion in *Terry* can readily be put into words and explained. The Supreme Court held that a police officer

---

[71]   United States v. Hensley, 469 U.S. 221, 105 S. Ct. 675, 83 L. Ed. 2d 604 (1985).

[72]   *See* authorities *supra* note 56.

[73]   *Id.*

[74]   **Supra note 59**.

may detain a person for investigation when "he observes unusual conduct which leads him reasonably to conclude in light of his experience that criminal activity may be afoot."

Figure 3.10
Grounds for Reasonable Suspicion of Involvement in Criminal Activity

> In order to satisfy the reasonable suspicion standard, the officer must possess an objective and particularized basis for suspecting the detainee of committing, having committed, or being about to commit a crime. To satisfy this standard, the officer must be able to:
>
> 1. point to behavior of the detainee that is different from what one might ordinarily expect of an innocent person in the vicinity, and
> 2. explain why the detainee's behavior suggests the possibility of criminal activity.

In *Brown v. Texas*,[75] in contrast, the officers acted on a hunch. Two police officers cruising an area with a high incidence of drug trafficking observed Brown and another man walking away from one another in an alley. They got out of the patrol car, detained Brown, and demanded identification and an explanation for his presence. When he refused to comply, they frisked him. The Supreme Court held that the officers lacked reasonable suspicion for a stop and frisk because Brown's behavior — walking in a high-crime area, protesting an illegal detention, and refusing to provide identification — was as consistent with innocent conduct as with guilty conduct.

In order to have an objective basis for reasonable suspicion, police must be able to point to something specific about the detainee's behavior that caused them to associate it with criminal activity. It must be different from the behavior one would ordinarily expect of an innocent person in the vicinity.[76] In *Reid v. Georgia*,[77] a drug enforcement agent stopped a traveler in the Atlanta airport based on the fact that he (1) arrived from a city that was a principal point of origin for cocaine sold elsewhere in the country; (2) arrived in the early hours of the morning, when law enforcement activity tends to be lax; (3) arrived with no luggage other than a shoulder bag; and (4) occasionally looked back over his shoulder as he walked toward the concourse. The Supreme Court ruled that the behaviors observed did not provide grounds for a reasonable suspicion that the individual was a drug courier because they "describe a very large category of presumably innocent travelers, who would be subject to virtually random seizures were the Court to conclude that as little foundation as there was in this case could justify a seizure."[78]

---

75   *Supra* note 54.
76   *Id.*
77   448 U.S. 438, 100 S. Ct. 2752, 65 L. Ed. 2d 890 (1980).
78   *Id.*

The following behaviors, although insufficient standing alone to provide reasonable suspicion, are capable of adding background, color, and context, and may be considered as part of the totality of facts and circumstances in deciding whether reasonable suspicion is present.[79]

1. The person is spotted in a high-crime area or in close proximity to the scene of a recently committed crime.[80]

2. The person has a criminal record,[81] or is in the company of others who have criminal records.[82]

3. The person attempts to avoid contact with the officer or flees.[83]

4. The person gives suspicious, inconsistent, or false answers to routine questions.[84]

5. The person's race or ethnicity matches the description of the offender or fits the facts of a known offense.[85]

6. The person appears abnormally nervous and fidgety.[86]

---

[79] **Illinois v. Wardlow, 528 U.S. 119, 120 S. Ct. 673, 145 L. Ed. 2d 570 (2000)** (presence in an area with a high incidence of drug trafficking, coupled with sudden flight upon spotting a patrol car, provided reasonable suspicion for *Terry* stop).

[80] *Id.*

[81] *See, e.g.*, United States v. Childs, 256 F.3d 559 (7th Cir. 2001) (although reasonable suspicion cannot be based solely on suspect's prior criminal record, criminal record may be considered in conjunction with other information in forming a reasonable suspicion); United States v. McRae, 81 F.3d 1528 (10th Cir. 1996) (criminal record, nervous behavior, and implausible travel plans deemed sufficient to establish reasonable suspicion).

[82] *See* cases *supra* note 81.

[83] *See, e.g.*, United States v. Arvizu, *supra* note 56 (ignoring sighted police officer); **Illinois v. Wardlow**, *supra* note 79 (flight).

[84] *See, e.g.*, United States v. Gonzales, 328 F.3d 755 (5th Cir. 2003); United States v. Valles, 292 F.3d 678 (10th Cir. 2002); United States v. Zubia-Melendez, 263 F.3d 1155 (10th Cir. 2001); United States v. Acuna-Ramirez, 64 Fed. Appx. 683 (10th Cir. 2003).

[85] Compare People v. Turner, 37 A.D.3d 874, 829 N.Y.S.2d 261 (2007) (Officer had reasonable suspicion for investigatory stop of a pedestrian where the pedestrian's race and clothes were consistent with description of the perpetrator of burglary, he was located close in time and proximity to the crime scene and at an hour of day, *i.e.*, 3:42 A.M., when few people were out on the streets, and was openly using a cell phone that matched the one reportedly stolen from the crime scene) *with* Rodriguez v. State, 948 So. 2d 912 (Fla. App. 2007) (radio bulletin asking police to be on the lookout for robbery suspect, described as a "black male, approximately 5'9" tall, wearing a black hooded shirt or sweater, black baggy pants and black sneakers, and carrying a silver revolver with a brown handle" did not create sufficient reasonable suspicion for investigatory stop of vehicle in which defendant was a passenger that was stopped a half hour later and a quarter of a mile away, where the only information the officer was able to verify before the stop was that the defendant was a black male); United States v. Manzo-Jurado. 457 F.3d 928 (9th Cir. 2006) (stating that the defendant's apparent Hispanic ethnicity, although a relevant factor in the reasonable suspicion inquiry, was insufficient, standing alone, to justify stopping him to investigate whether he was an illegal alien, even near the border).

[86] United States v. Arvizu, *supra* note 56; United States v. Linkous, 285 F.3d 716 (8th Cir. 2002).

B. Rational Deductions and Inferences That Arise from an Officer's Prior Experience

Police officers have special expertise and training that sometimes enables them to spot criminal activity in conduct that would seem innocent to an untrained observer.[87] Recognizing this, courts examine the facts that prompted the stop through the eyes of a trained police officer. *Ornelas v. United States*[88] shows how a veteran narcotics detective's observations, combined with his prior experience in apprehending drug traffickers and a quick check of police records, created a reasonable suspicion justifying an investigatory stop. The officer, an experienced narcotics detective, observed a 1981 two-door Oldsmobile with a California license plate pull into a motel parking lot in downtown Milwaukee at 4:00 A.M. This incident attracted his attention because: (1) California was a "source state" for drugs, (2) older-model General Motors cars were popular with drug couriers, and (3) Milwaukee was an unlikely winter vacation spot for a California visitor. His suspicion aroused, the detective radioed the registration number to his dispatcher, obtained the owner's name, and ran the name through the Narcotics and Dangerous Drugs Information System (NADDIS), a federal database of known and suspected drug traffickers. The NADDIS report identified the vehicle's owner as a heroin dealer from California. These facts, viewed in combination through the eyes of an experienced narcotics detective, provided a particularized and objective basis for suspecting the vehicle's owner of being in Milwaukee on drug business and detaining him for investigation.

Law enforcement agencies have developed an investigative tool called the "drug courier profile," which is used to identify candidates to approach for investigation on suspicion of transporting drugs. The drug courier profile consists of a list of behavioral characteristics commonly seen in persons engaged in drug trafficking. The characteristics, which have been distilled from the collective experience of law enforcement agencies, generally include the following: the suspect is generally between the ages of 20 and 30; travels to or from a major source city; has made numerous trips to or from this destination before; remains in the destination city for only a short time; purchases an airline ticket shortly before the time for departure; uses a false name on the ticket; pays cash for the ticket; carries little or no luggage or, at most, a carry-on bag; travels in the early morning, when law enforcement is likely to be lax; appears nervous; walks hurriedly, constantly scanning the environment in a manner that suggests he is trying to detect and avoid contact with the police; makes a telephone call immediately after deplaning; uses public transportation; and gives a false explanation about the reason for the trip.[89]

---

[87] *See, e.g.,* United States v. Arvizu, *supra* note 56; Ornelas v. United States, *supra* note 53; United States v. Sokolow, *supra* note 56; United States v. Brignoni-Ponce, *supra* note 65.

[88] *Supra* note 53.

[89] 4 WAYNE R. LaFAVE, SEARCH AND SEIZURE: A TREATISE ON THE FOURTH AMENDMENT § 9.4(E) (3d ed. 1996); Kimberly J. Winbush, *Propriety of Stop and Search by Law Enforcement Officers Based Solely on Drug Courier Profile,* 37 A.L.R. 5th 1 (1996).

The Supreme Court has reviewed several cases in which detainees were selected for investigatory stops because their characteristics matched some of the characteristics found in the drug courier profile.[90] In *United States v. Sokolow*,[91] Sokolow was detained for investigation at Honolulu International Airport after a return trip from Miami, based on the officer's knowledge of the following facts: (1) Sokolow paid $2,100 for two round-trip tickets from a roll of $20 bills; (2) he traveled under a name that did not match his name in the telephone directory; (3) he flew from Honolulu to Miami, a source city for illicit drugs; (4) he stayed in Miami for only 48 hours, even though a round-trip flight from Honolulu to Miami takes 20 hours; (5) he appeared nervous during his trip; and (6) he checked none of his luggage. The Supreme Court ruled that, while none of these facts by themselves were indicative of wrongdoing, when viewed in combination through the eyes of an experienced narcotics officer, they provided a reasonable basis for suspecting Sokolow of being a drug courier.

The reader should not jump to the conclusion that exhibiting several characteristics found in the drug courier profile automatically provides grounds for an investigatory stop.[92] Whether it does or does not depends on whether the characteristics the officer has observed sufficiently distinguish the suspect's behavior from that of an ordinary traveler.[93] Some of the characteristics in the drug courier profile, like arriving from a source city late at night with only carry-on luggage and appearing nervous, are too widespread and common to form the basis of a reasonable suspicion of criminal activity.[94] That Sokolow paid cash for his ticket, traveled under an assumed name, and stayed in Miami for a period suspiciously short as compared to the travel time were the characteristics that distinguished Sokolow's behavior from the behavior of an ordinary traveler. Reliance on drug courier profiles does not eliminate the need to observe atypical behavior that suggests involvement in criminal activity.

C. Information Furnished by Members of the Public

Reasonable suspicion does not have to derive solely from an officer's personal observations. Stops may be based on reports received from members of the public that appear reliable or that are corroborated through independent police work.[95] The tipster's credibility and basis for knowledge must be considered in making this call. A tip from a known informant who has given accurate leads in the past can

---

[90] United States v. Sokolow, *supra* note 56; Florida v. Royer, *supra* note 21.

[91] *Supra* note 56.

[92] *See, e.g.*, Reid v. Georgia, *supra* note 77; State v. Young, 569 N.W.2d 84 (Wis. Ct. App. 1997).

[93] *See, e.g.*, United States v. Barrett, 976 F. Supp. 1105 (N.D. Ohio 1997) (fact that bus passenger paid cash for ticket and that his call back number was to an answering machine with a woman's voice did not provide articulable grounds for a reasonable suspicion).

[94] Reid v. Georgia, *supra* note 77.

[95] Adams v. Williams, 407 U.S. 143, 92 S. Ct. 1921, 32 L. Ed. 2d 612 (1972); Alabama v. White, 496 U. S. 325, 110 S. Ct. 2412, 110 L. Ed. 2d 301 (1990); **Florida v. J.L., 529 U.S. 266, 120 S. Ct. 1375, 146 L. Ed. 2d 245 (2000)**.

stand on its own in supplying reasonable suspicion.[96] However, a proven track record is not necessary. The fact that the informant is known to the police and can be tracked down and held accountable if the report is fabricated is enough to impart credibility.[97]

Figure 3.11
Information Furnished by Members of the Public

> Stops may be initiated based on tips provided by members of the public when they carry indicia of reliability or are corroborated through independent police work. The tipster's credibility and basis for knowledge must both be considered in making this call. Tips received from: (1) known informants and (2) concerned citizens, who identify themselves and report matters of which they have personal knowledge, can stand on their own in providing reasonable suspicion. Tips provided by anonymous informants, in contrast, must be corroborated before they can be used.

Police must also consider the tipster's basis for knowledge. If a person calls the police and says, "This is Mary Smith. I live in Apartment 3 at 218 Brook Street. I have heard a rumor that Jack Green, the man who lives directly above me, is a dope peddler," the police must corroborate this information before acting on it because the caller has not demonstrated an adequate basis for knowledge. On the other hand, if the same person calls and reports, "This is Mary Smith. I live in Apartment 3 at 218 Brook Street. Two minutes ago, I saw a heavy-set man wearing a black leather jacket and green pants go upstairs and enter Apartment 13. I just heard gunfire, screaming, and saw this man run down the stairs, get into a 2006 white Chevrolet, and head west on Brook Street," the police may act on this information without corroboration.

A recent Utah case illustrates application of the reasonable suspicion standard to reports from concerned citizens who identify themselves and report criminal activity of which they have personal knowledge.[98] A fast-food restaurant worker noticed a customer drinking a can of beer while waiting for his order at a drive-through window. He immediately telephoned the police and reported what he saw, along with his own telephone number and location, a description of the vehicle's make, model, and license plate number, and the direction it turned when it left the restaurant. This information was dispatched over the police radio and the suspect was stopped a few blocks away. The stop was upheld even though the officer who made it knew nothing about the suspect's behavior beyond what the caller reported. The court stated that when a caller identifies herself, gives a detailed account of a criminal activity he/she has just observed, and provides a description sufficient to enable the police

---

[96]   Adams v. Williams, *supra* note 95 (a tip from a known informant is sufficiently reliable to support a *Terry* stop).

[97]   *Id.*

[98]   City of St. George v. Carter, 945 P. 2d 165 (Utah 1997).

to identify the subject, the report may be presumed reliable and police may use it to make a *Terry* stop.[99]

Anonymous tips are the weakest kind because the tipster's credibility and basis for knowledge are unknown. The tip must be corroborated before police may act upon it.[100] What constitutes sufficient corroboration varies with the facts. When an anonymous tip contains predictive information about a suspect's future activities likely to be known only by someone who has special familiarity with the suspect's private affairs, corroboration of the predictive information is enough for a *Terry* stop. *Alabama v. White*[101] is an example. Police received a tip from an anonymous caller that a woman named White would leave a particular apartment building in a described vehicle at a certain time, that she would be going to a particular motel, and that she would be in possession of cocaine. Officers immediately proceeded to the apartment building, where they saw a woman get into the described vehicle at the designated time, and followed her as she proceeded along the most direct route to the motel. They stopped her just short of the motel, and arrested her after discovering drugs in her car. Although characterizing this as a close case, the Supreme Court concluded that this tip had been corroborated as reliable before the stop was made. The caller's ability to predict White's future behavior was the controlling consideration. The general public would have had no way of knowing that White would leave her apartment building at a certain time, get into a particular car, and drive to a particular motel. The accuracy and detail with which the caller predicted White's future movements demonstrated a special familiarity with her private affairs. Because only a small number of people would be likely to know this information, the police could infer that the caller was someone in whom White had

---

[99]   *See, e.g.*, United States v. Quarles, 330 F.3d 650 (4th Cir. 2003) (information provided by 911 caller, to the effect that defendant was wanted by government on firearms charges, was sufficiently reliable to provide police with reasonable suspicion for a *Terry* stop, where the caller gave enough information to be identified later, arranged for police to meet with him after the phone call, and gave specific information, which included a wealth of detail and indicated personal knowledge of the defendant); State v. Partridge, 29 Kan. App.2d, 33 P. 3d 362 (2001) (motorist's call to law enforcement agency from her cell phone, without more, was sufficient to give rise to reasonable suspicion justifying stop of defendant's automobile where the motorist identified herself and gave firsthand information to the effect that she was following an automobile on a public highway that was being driven in a reckless manner); United States v. Tucker, 305 F.3d 1193 (10th Cir. 2002) (tips received from citizen informants who identify themselves are presumed to be reliable); Frazer v. State, 80 Ark. App. 231, 94 S. W.3d 357 (2002) (telephone tip by a citizen informant who gave his name was sufficient to support an investigatory stop of a vehicle that the informant suspected was being operated by an intoxicated person); State v. Manuel, 796 So. 2d 602 (Fla. App. 2001) ("A tip by a citizen-informant . . . is entitled to a presumption of reliability and does not require further corroboration to provide the requisite reasonable suspicion for a stop.").

[100]   Alabama v. White, *supra* note 95; Florida v. J.L., *supra* note 95 ("Unlike a tip from a known informant whose reputation can be assessed and who can be held responsible if her allegations turn out to be fabricated, 'an anonymous tip alone seldom demonstrates the informant's basis of knowledge or veracity.'").

[101]   *Supra* note 95.

confided and, consequently, that the caller had reliable information about White's criminal activities.

Another way an anonymous tip can be corroborated is through observations made at the scene of the stop. In one case,[102] an officer responding to a radio bulletin relaying an anonymous report that a black male had just fired a pistol at a particular location, immediately went to the location where he observed a black male who matched the tipster's description; the man was in a crouched position, peeking around the corner a short distance from the spot where the shot was allegedly fired. When the officer made eye contact with him, he backed away as if he was trying to hide. The court ruled that this behavior sufficiently corroborated the anonymous tip to justify detaining the man for questioning.

Verification of details relating to a suspect's physical appearance and present location, without more, is not sufficient to corroborate the reliability of an anonymous tip. In *Florida v. J.L.*,[103] an anonymous caller informed the police that a young black male, wearing a plaid shirt and standing at a certain bus stop, was carrying a concealed gun. The caller did not explain how he knew about the gun or provide other information that could be used to could assess his credibility. The police immediately went to the bus stop where they saw three black males, one of whom was wearing a plaid shirt. Although they had no reason apart from the tip for suspecting the man in the plaid shirt of anything, the police frisked him and found a gun. The Supreme Court ruled that the anonymous caller's ability to provide an accurate description of the defendant's readily observable physical appearance and present location was insufficient to establish that the tip was reliable in its assertion that he had a concealed weapon. Anyone who saw him standing at the bus stop could just as well have placed this call. The Court stated that to create reasonable suspicion, an anonymous tip must "be reliable in its assertion of illegality, not just its tendency to identify a determinate person."

D. *Information Transmitted Through Official Law Enforcement Channels*

Suppose Officer Blake receives a radio dispatch advising her to "be on the lookout for the driver of a dilapidated green Mazda van with license plate number G6207, believed to be carrying stolen property." The dispatcher follows the customary practice of not reporting the facts that support the requested action. Two minutes later, Officer

---

[102]   United States v. Sims, 296 F.3d 284 (4th Cir. 2002). *See also* Burkes v. State, 842 N. E. 2d 426 (Ind. App. 2006) (Police officers had reasonable suspicion to justify an investigatory stop and search of defendant; while an anonymous tip that a black male with braided hair, wearing glasses and all-black outfit was at the home of a known drug user, and was in possession of a handgun and marijuana, and selling cocaine, standing alone, was insufficient to support finding of reasonable suspicion; the tip, combined with fact that defendant was in immediate vicinity of woman for whom there was an outstanding warrant and that defendant fled when officers ordered him to "freeze," gave rise to reasonable suspicion that defendant was engaged, or about to engage, in criminal activity.).

[103]   *Supra* note 95.

Blake sees a green van that matches the dispatcher's description and pulls it over. Did Officer Blake have a reasonable suspicion to make the stop?

The answer is no, at least not personally, because he was not informed of the underlying facts that supported the requested action and observed nothing suspicious at the scene. However, this does not mean that the stop was unconstitutional. The Supreme Court has ruled that an officer who makes an investigatory stop or arrest at the direction of another officer need not be informed of the factual basis for the requested action.[104] Requiring police bulletins to communicate the facts supporting a requested action would hamper prompt investigation of criminal activity. Officers who receive official communications must be able to act swiftly and do not have time to conduct a detailed investigation.

However, grounds for the action must exist somewhere. If the officer making the investigatory stop or arrest lacks grounds to support it, the constitutionality of the action will depend on whether the officer or agency requesting the action had such grounds.[105] When a radio dispatch or other communication is supported by adequate grounds, any authorized officer may implement the action without being advised of the factual foundation behind it. This principle was applied in *United States v. Hensley*,[106] in which officers from the Covington Kentucky police department stopped a person based on a teletype communication from a neighboring police department stating that he was wanted in connection with an armed robbery, but disclosing no further details. The Supreme Court, after determining that the department requesting the action had reasonable suspicion to make the stop, upheld the stop as constitutional.

A somewhat related problem arises when information needed to support an action is divided between several officers engaged in a common investigation. Suppose that Officer X, who requests an action, is aware of facts 1 and 2, and that Officer Y, who implements the action, learns of fact 3 when he arrives at the scene. Suppose further that neither officer's separate information will support the action, but that their combined information will. Is the action constitutional?

The Supreme Court has not yet addressed this question. Had Officer X shared facts 1 and 2 with Officer Y, this problem would not arise because Officer Y would now be in possession of all the facts needed to support the action. The problem arises only when the information is not shared. Lower courts are divided on whether the focus should be on the collective knowledge or the separate knowledge of officers acting together, in determining whether grounds exist. In some jurisdictions, X's knowledge will be

---

[104]   United States v. Hensley, 469 U.S. 221, 105 S. Ct. 675, 83 L. Ed. 2d 604 (1985) (holding that a police officer may, in detaining and questioning an individual, rely on a bulletin posted by another police department, as long as the department that posted the bulletin possessed reasonable suspicion to justify the stop). *See also, generally,* 4 WAYNE R LAFAVE, SEARCH AND SEIZURE: A TREATISE ON THE FOURTH AMENDMENT § 9.4(i), at 233–235 (1996).

[105]   Whiteley v. Warden, 401 U.S. 560, 91 S. Ct. 1031, 28 L. Ed. 2d 306 (1971).

[106]   *Supra* note 104.

imputed to Y, even if it is not shared, and the action will be treated as constitutional if X and Y's combined information is sufficient to support the action.[107] In other jurisdictions, uncommunicated information held by other officers working on an investigation will not be imputed to the acting officer.[108] The action will be treated as constitutional only if the officer directing the action (X) or the officer taking it (Y) individually knew of enough facts to support it.

§ 3.9   — Scope and Duration of Investigatory Stops

The constitutional authority of the police to interfere with a suspect's liberty is directly related to their degree of certainty about the suspect's guilt. Police are more restricted in what they can do during *Terry* stops than during arrests, because stops are allowed on a lower degree of suspicion. Limitations on police authority are necessary to maintain the required alignment between the level of suspicion and degree of intrusiveness. When the police overstep the boundaries of a *Terry* stop, the stop automatically escalates into an arrest, resulting in a violation of the detainee's Fourth Amendment rights — unless the police have developed probable cause in the meantime.[109] This is why police must understand and stay within the boundaries allowed for *Terry* stops until they have probable cause for an arrest. This section explores those boundaries. However, before discussing the boundaries, the purpose of the stop needs to be explained.

A. *Purpose of a* Terry *Stop*

The purpose of a *Terry* stop is to enable the police to investigate the underlying suspicion as quickly as possible. If the suspicion is confirmed, the police now have probable cause for an arrest and may move to the next stage. However, if police do not develop grounds for an arrest within a relatively short period, they must release the detainee, even though their investigation remains incomplete. The Fourth Amendment does not allow prolonged detentions on a mere suspicion of criminal activity.

All activities during *Terry* stops must be directed toward one of two goals: (1) securing the officer's safety, when precautions are necessary, and (2) investigating the underlying suspicion as quickly as possible.

---

[107]   *See, e.g.,* United States v. Edwards, 885 F.2d 377 (7th Cir. 1989) (imputing knowledge of one arresting officer to another when officers act together in making arrest); Johnson v. State, 660 So. 2d 648 (Fla. 1995) (imputing knowledge of an outstanding arrest warrant to an arresting officer who was unaware of its existence and otherwise lacked probable cause for the arrest); State v. Soukharith, 253 Neb. 310, 570 N. W. 2d 344 (1997) (reasonable suspicion should be applied to the collective knowledge of officers engaged in a common investigation).

[108]   *See, e.g.,* United States v. Morgan, 997 F.2d 433 (8th Cir. 1993); United States v. Shareef, 100 F.3d 1491 (10th Cir. 1996); United States v. Conner, 948 F. Supp. 821 (N.D. Iowa 1996).

[109]   *See, e.g.,* Florida v. Royer, *supra* note 21.

Figure 3.12
Actions Authorized During a *Terry* Stop

All police actions undertaken during a *Terry* stop must be directed at one of the following two purposes:

1. Securing the officer's safety, when precautions are necessary.
2. Investigating the underlying suspicion as quickly as possible.

B. *Procedures Appropriate During* Terry *Stops*

Requests for identification and questioning are the two most common techniques used during *Terry* stops. Police do not have to administer *Miranda* warnings[110] unless force is necessary.[111] When police draw guns and use handcuffs, the questioning becomes custodial, and warnings are necessary.[112] Police should not otherwise administer them because this might prompt a court to view the encounter as an arrest, resulting in a violation of the Fourth Amendments unless probable cause exists.[113]

Persons detained for investigation are not required to answer questions and police may not treat their refusal as grounds for arrest. Arresting detainees for refusing to answer questions would violate their Fifth Amendment privilege against self-incrimination.[114] However, the same is not true for refusing to disclose their name. Detainees may be arrested for refusing to disclose their name if state law authorizes this.[115] Statues requiring detainees to furnish identification on pain on arrest exist in less than half the states.

Police may also take the following actions when they are relevant to their investigation or safety concerns[116]:

1. Communicate with others to verify the detainee's explanation.
2. Run a check of police records, automobile registration records, and the like.[117]

---

[110] **Miranda v. Arizona, 384 U.S. 436, 86 S. Ct. 1602, 16 L. Ed. 2d 694 (1966)**. The *Miranda* rule is discussed in Chapter 6. Warnings are required only during custodial interrogations (*i.e.*, when a suspect in custody is interrogated.) Because of the comparatively nonthreatening nature and limited scope and nature of the typical *Terry* encounter, detainees are not considered to be in custody unless arrest-like force becomes necessary to execute the stop. See § 6.7 (A) (4) *infra*.

[111] **Berkemer v. McCarty, 468 U.S. 420, 104 S. Ct. 3138, 82 L. Ed. 2d 317 (1984)** (stating that there is no right to *Miranda* warnings during routine traffic stops).

[112] *See, e.g.*, United States v. Perdue, 8 F.3d 1455 (10th Cir. 1993) (holding that *Miranda* warnings were necessary where a detainee was stopped on an isolated, rural road at gunpoint, ordered to lie face-down, and interrogated with guns still drawn). See also § 6.7 (A) (4) *infra*.

[113] *See, e.g.*, United States v. Obasa, 15 F.3d 603 (6th Cir. 1994); State v. Wilkenson, 118 Ohio Misc. 2d 10, 769 N. E. 2d 430 (Ohio Com. Pl. 2001).

[114] **Terry v. Ohio**, *supra* note 59 (White, J. concurring); Kolender v. Lawson, 461 U.S. 352, 103 S. Ct. 1855, 1860, 75 L. Ed. 2d 903 (1983) (Brennan, J. concurring).

[115] Hiibel v. Sixth Judicial Dist. Court, 542 U.S. 177, 124 S. Ct. 2451, 159 L. Ed. 2d 292 (2004).

[116] United States v. Sharpe, 470 U.S. 675, 105 S. Ct. 1568, 84 L. Ed. 2d 605 (1985).

[117] United States v. Hensley, *supra* note 104; United States v. Finke, 85 F.3d 1275 (7th Cir. 1996); United States v. Shareef, *supra* note 108.

3. Transport the detainee back to a nearby fresh crime scene for a show-up identification.[118]
4. Fingerprint the detainee at scene of the stop.[119]
5. Bring a narcotics detection dog to the scene of the stop to perform a sniff test.[120]
6. Request permission to conduct a search, administer a Breathalyzer test, or perform other procedures designed to further the investigation, keeping in mind that these procedures are allowed only if the suspect consents.[121]

Figure 3.13
Investigative Activity Appropriate During *Terry* Stops

After a lawful *Terry* stop, the police may always:

1. Ask for identification, and
2. Question the detainee about the matter that aroused their suspicion.

Police may also pursue the following inquiries when they are relevant to their investigation or safety concerns:

3. Communicate with others to verify the suspect's explanation;
4. Run checks of police records, *etc.*
5. Fingerprint the suspect at the stop location;
6. Bring a drug detection dog to the stop location to perform a sniff test;
7. Transport the detainee back to a nearby fresh crime scene for a show-up identification; and
8. Request consent to search or perform other procedures designed to further the investigation.

C. *Authority to Conduct Protective Weapons Searches*

Authority to frisk detainees for weapons does not arise as an automatic incident of a *Terry* stop. It exists only when the police have reasonable suspicion that the person stopped may be armed and dangerous.[122] Grounds, for example, are present

---

[118] People v. Brown, 277 Ill. App. 3d 989, 661 N. E. 2d 533 (Ill. Ct. App. 1996); People v. Rowe, 236 A. D. 2d 637, 654 N.Y.S.2d 787 (1997).

[119] **Hayes v. Florida, 470 U.S. 811, 817, 105 S. Ct. 1643, 1647, 84 L. Ed. 2d 705 (1985).**

[120] **Illinois v. Caballes, 543 U.S. 405, 125 S. Ct. 834, 160 L. Ed. 2d 842 (2005)** (holding that reasonable suspicion is not required to walk a trained drug-detection dog around the exterior of a vehicle stopped for a traffic violation provided performance of the procedure does not extend the duration of the stop beyond the time reasonably required to process the traffic violation); United States v. Place, 462 U.S. 696, 103 S. Ct. 2637, 77 L. Ed. 2d 110 (1983) (holding that a dog sniff is not a search).

[121] Schneckloth v. Bustamonte, 412 U.S. 218, 93 S. Ct. 2041, 36 L. Ed. 2d 854 (1973).

[122] **Terry v. Ohio,** *supra* note 59. When a suspect is stopped in a car, the police may perform a limited weapons search of the passenger compartment when they have reason to believe that the detainee is dangerous and may have a weapon in the vehicle. *Terry* weapon searches are discussed in greater detail in Chapter 4.

when the crime for which the stop is made is one that makes possession of a weapon likely[123] or the suspect reaches for something that could be a weapon.[124] The traditional "totality of circumstances" approach is used to determine whether grounds exist for a frisk.[125]

Terry searches have only one legitimate object — weapons. Officers may not search for nondangerous contraband during a *Terry* stop.[126] Searching for objects other

---

[123] *See, e.g.*, **Terry v. Ohio**, *supra* note 59, 392 U.S. at 33, 88 S. Ct. 1868 (Harlan, J., concurring) (stating that when an officer suspects a crime of violence, the same information that will support an investigatory stop will, without more, support a frisk); United States v. Bullock, 510 F.3d 342 (D.C. Cir. 2007) ("If an officer possesses reasonable suspicion that the detained suspect committed a violent or serious crime — such as murder, robbery, rape, burglary, assault with a weapon, or various drug offenses — the officer by definition is dealing with an individual reasonably suspected of committing a crime that involves or is associated with carrying or using a weapon."). Numerous courts have held that drug trafficking so often involves the use and possession of weapons that a reasonable suspicion of committing such an offense automatically gives law enforcement officers grounds to perform a frisk. *See, e.g.*, United States v. Jackson, 300 F.3d 740 (7th Cir. 2002) (reasonable suspicion that detainee is engaged in drug-related activity and knowledge that he had been armed in the past supplied grounds for frisk); United States v. Sinclair, 983 F.2d 598 (4th Cir. 1993) (frisk of suspected drug dealer is proper, given the fact that they frequently carry weapons); United States v. Crespo, 868 F. Supp. 79 (M.D. Pa. 1994) ("We join a growing number of courts who have taken judicial notice of the fact that drug dealers are likely to be armed and dangerous.") *See also* 4 WAYNE R LAFAVE, SEARCH AND SEIZURE: A TREATISE ON THE FOURTH AMENDMENT § 9.5 (3d ed. 1996) ("Lower courts have been inclined to view the right to frisk as being "automatic" whenever the suspect has been stopped upon the suspicion that he has committed, was committing, or was about to commit a type of crime for which the offender would likely be armed, whether the weapon would be used to actually commit the crime, to escape if the scheme went awry, or for protection against the victim or others involved. This includes such suspected offenses as robbery, burglary, rape, assault with weapons, homicide, and dealing in large quantities of narcotics.").

[124] *See, e.g.*, United States v. Mitchell, 951 F.2d 1291 (D.C. Cir. 1991) (frisk justified where officer observed defendant "moving both his hands under his coat in a manner suggesting that he was hiding a gun"); United States v. Flippin, 924 F.2d 163 (9th Cir. 1991) (frisk justified where defendant grabbed her makeup bag when officer turned his back); United States v. Lane, 909 F. 2d 895 (6th Cir. 1990) (frisk justified where defendant "twice attempted to reach into his coat pocket").

[125] *See, e.g.*, United States v. Brown, 188 F.3d 860 (7th Cir. 1999) (officer had reasonable suspicion to perform a pat down during a traffic stop based on his knowledge that the vehicle was under FBI surveillance as possibly part of a large-scale drug operation; the smell of marijuana smoke from the car; detainee's unusually nervous demeanor, including his failure to make eye contact; and the fact that the stop occurred in a high-crime area where there was gang and drug activity and had been recent shootings); United States v. Menard, 95 F.3d 9 (8th Cir. 1996) (officer justified in conducting a pat down after arresting the defendant's companion for gun possession where encounter occurred on a relatively deserted highway in the early hours of the morning); Jackson v. Com., *supra* note 99 ("In assessing whether a suspect may be armed and dangerous for purposes of determining whether a pat down search is warranted during an investigatory stop, an officer may consider characteristics of the area surrounding the stop, the time of the stop, the specific conduct of the suspect individual, the character of the offense under suspicion, and the unique perspective of a police officer trained and experienced in the detection of crime.").

[126] **Terry v. Ohio**, *supra* note 59, 392 U.S. at 26, 88 S. Ct. at 1882.

than weapons is permitted only when the police have a search warrant, probable cause for an arrest, or obtain consent. When an officer's search goes beyond what is necessary to determine whether the suspect is armed, the search ceases to be valid under *Terry* and the fruits of the search are inadmissible.[127] If a weapon is found during a lawful pat down, the officer may remove it and hold on to it until the investigation is completed, at which time the officer must return the weapon if the detainee's possession is lawful.[128]

Terry searches have precisely defined boundaries. Officers are limited to patting down the suspect's outer clothing. Reaching inside the detainee's pockets or requiring the detainee to empty them is allowed only if the officer feels an object that might be a weapon and cannot make a conclusive determination through touch alone. After an object is ruled out as being a weapon, an officer may not continue touching it to try to figure out what it is. *Terry* search authority is exhausted once the officer is satisfied that the detainee is unarmed.[129]

While an officer may not search for objects other than weapons, if, while patting down the suspect's outer clothing, the officer feels an object that he immediately recognizes as contraband, the officer may seize it, even though he knows it is not a weapon. This rule is called the "plain feel" doctrine. The "plain feel" doctrine applies only when the identity of the object is immediately apparent to the officer from its shape and the way it feels. An officer may not seize an object that is unmistakably not a weapon, if determining its identity requires further manipulation. The reason for this fine line is that when the incriminating nature of an object is immediately apparent to the officer from its shape and the way it feels, seizing it does not invade the suspect's privacy beyond the degree that is already authorized. When making this determination requires further manipulation, an additional invasion of privacy is necessary and the additional invasion is not allowed.

The Supreme Court applied the "plain feel" doctrine in *Minnesota v. Dickerson*,[130] in which an officer conducting a lawful pat down search felt a lump inside the suspect's pocket that he knew was not a weapon. He continued squeezing and manipulating it until he decided it might be crack cocaine, at which point he removed it. The officer was right. However, the cocaine was inadmissible because it was discovered by the officer while overstepping the bounds of his *Terry* search authority. Once the officer determined that the lump was not a weapon, he lacked the authority to continue touching it.

[127]   Minnesota v. Dickerson, 508 U.S. 366, 113 S. Ct. 2130, 124 L. Ed. 2d 334 (1993).
[128]   **Terry v. Ohio**, *supra* note 59.
[129]   *Id.*
[130]   *Supra* note 127.

D. *Procedures Prohibited During* Terry *Stops*

Terry investigations must be kept as narrowly intrusive as possible. The Supreme Court has expressed this limitation by stating that police must use the least intrusive methods reasonably available to resolve the underlying suspicion within a relatively short period.[131] Taking detainees to the police station for questioning and searching them for evidence are two procedures that are categorically off limits during *Terry* stops.[132] Although they are standard accompaniments of an arrest, the Supreme Court regards them as too intrusive to be allowed on reasonable suspicion.

Unnecessary displays of force are also taboo. Although detainees may be held at gunpoint, handcuffed, and placed in squad cars when police have legitimate concerns for their safety,[133] measures like these are not allowed when their use is unwarranted.[134]

Figure 3.14
Actions Prohibited During *Terry* Stops

The following actions are prohibited during *Terry* stops:

1. Taking detainees to the police station.
2. Searching detainees for anything besides a weapon.
3. Unnecessary displays of force.
4. Unnecessary movement of detainees from the place of the stop to a second location.
5. Delaying completion of stop to investigate unrelated matters without reasonable suspicion.

Investigatory stops must generally be confined to the location where the stop is made. Moving the detainee to a second location is permitted only when a change in

---

[131] Florida v. Royer, *supra* note 21.

[132] *See, e.g.*, Minnesota v. Dickerson, *supra* note 127 (police may not search *Terry* detainees for anything other than weapons); **Kaupp v. Texas, 538 U.S. 626, 123 S. Ct. 1843, 155 L. Ed. 2d 814 (2002)** (suspect was arrested within the meaning of the Fourth Amendment when he was awakened in his bedroom at three in the morning by three police officers, one of whom stated, "we need to go and talk," and taken from his home in handcuffs, without shoes, in his underwear to the police station for questioning); **Hayes v. Florida**, *supra* note 119 (taking a suspect to the police station against his will for questioning is "sufficiently like arres[t] to invoke the traditional rule that arrests may constitutionally be made only on probable cause").

[133] *See, e.g.*, Smoak v. Hall, 460 F.3d 768 (6th Cir. 2006).

[134] Unwarranted use of coercive restraints resulted in an unconstitutional arrest in the following cases: United States v. Lopez-Arias, 344 F.3d 623 (6th Cir. 2003) (drawing weapon, handcuffing, placing the detainee in the backseat of a squad car, and reading *Miranda* rights); United States v. Del Vizo, 918 F.2d 821 (9th Cir. 1990) (drawing weapon, handcuffing, and ordering detainee to lie prone); United States v. Richardson, 949 F.2d 851 (6th Cir. 1991) (locking detainee in the backseat of squad car while interrogating companion).

location is necessary to further the investigation[135] or for safety.[136] The detainee, for example, can be taken to a nearby crime scene for a show-up identification,[137] but not to a second location for fingerprinting or questioning because the latter procedures can be performed at the stop location.[138] A change in location is, therefore, unnecessary. In *Florida v. Royer*,[139] the Supreme Court ruled that a *Terry* stop, lawful when made, was transformed into an unconstitutional arrest when the police required the detainee to accompany them from the airport concourse to the security office for questioning. Moving the detainee to a second location violated the Fourth Amendment because the detainee could have been questioned at the scene of the stop.

E. Permissible Duration of a Terry Stop

Terry stops must be brief. Most last only a few minutes. While the Supreme Court has declined to set a maximum time,[140] it has suggested that 90 minutes is generally too long to hold a suspect on reasonable suspicion,[141] unless the detainee's behavior is responsible for the delay.[142] However, any detention lasts too long if it lasts longer than necessary to effectuate the purpose of the stop.[143] Once a stop is made, police must

---

[135]   *See, e.g.*, United States v. Short, 570 F.2d 1051 (D.C. Cir. 1978) ("Pursuant to a *Terry* stop the officer was free to take the appellant to the nearby scene of the burglary for possible identification, and such an identification would have given the police officer probable cause for arrest."); Buckingham v. State, 482 A.2d 327(Del. 1984) ("In cases where it is known that a crime has been committed, a suspect may be detained in order to be viewed by eyewitnesses, unless such travel would unduly prolong the detention."); Speight v. United States, 671 A.2d 442 (D.C. 1996) ("Pursuant to a lawful *Terry* stop police also may transport an individual to a nearby crime scene for a show-up identification."). See also 4 Wayne LaFave, Search and Seizure § 9.2(g) (3d ed. 1996).

[136]   *See, e.g.*, United States v. Pino, 855 F.2d 357 (6th Cir. 1988) (permissible to take suspect, stopped on freeway off-ramp, to area underneath overpass to get out of rain and for safety); United States v. Richards, 500 F.2d 1025 (9th Cir. 1974) (permissible to take detainee, stopped on airport runway, into terminal, where it was easier to talk and phone could be used); Commonwealth v. Revere, 585 Pa. 262, 888 A.2d 694 (2005) (holding that police may change the site of an investigative detention when such a movement is a reasonable response to security and safety concerns).

[137]   *See* authorities *supra* note 135. *But see* State v. Solano, 187 Ariz. 512, 930 P.2d 1315 (Ariz. Ct. App. 1996) (transporting *Terry* detainee back to the crime scene for questioning converted the stop into an arrest where the officer was aware witnesses had already left).

[138]   **Hayes v. Florida**, *supra* note 119 (fingerprinting); State v. Solano, *supra* note 137 (questioning).

[139]   *Supra* note 21.

[140]   United States v. Sharpe, 470 U.S. 675, 105 S. Ct. 1568, 84 L. Ed. 2d 605 (1985).

[141]   This limitation stems from **United States v. Place, 462 U.S. 696, 103 S. Ct. 2637, 77 L. Ed. 2d 110 (1983).** While the Supreme Court has upheld a 16-hour detention of a suspected "alimentary canal" drug smuggler at the national border, United States v. Montoya De Hernandez, 473 U.S. 531, 105 S. Ct. 3304, 87 L. Ed. 2d 381 (1985), the Court emphasized that detentions at the nation's border of people seeking entry constitute a special situation and that this ruling did not apply to domestic law enforcement.

[142]   United States v. Sharpe, *supra* note 140.

[143]   *Id.*

proceed expeditiously in conducting the investigation. A 30-minute detention is acceptable if this amount of time is necessary to complete the investigation,[144] whereas a 15-minute detention is too long if it is not.[145]

Unnecessary delay in completing the investigation carries a stiff penalty — the stop escalates into a *de facto* arrest. In *United States v. Place*,[146] police officers failed to arrange to have a narcotics detection dog present to perform a "sniff test," even though they knew several hours in advance that the detainee would be arriving at LaGuardia on a particular flight, carrying luggage believed to contain narcotics. The detainee was kept waiting until the narcotics detection dog arrived. The Supreme Court held that the detention violated the Fourth Amendment because the police prolonged it unnecessarily. The clear message is that police must conduct *Terry* investigations as expeditiously as possible. When officers know beforehand that a particular person will be stopped and that special arrangements will be needed to conduct the investigation, the arrangements must be made in advance.

Investigative activity undertaken during *Terry* stops must ordinarily be confined to the suspicious circumstances that justified the stop. Police may not prolong the stop to inquire into unrelated criminal activity for which they lack reasonable suspicion.[147] Once their investigation has been completed, police must either arrest the detainee or let him go. Continued detention after the purpose of the stop has been accomplished violates the Fourth Amendment unless reasonable suspicion of unrelated criminal activity surfaces during the stop or the detainee consents to remain.[148]

Although the Supreme Court has declined to impose a fixed outer time limit on the duration of *Terry* stops, legislatures in several states have. In Arkansas, for example, an officer must complete the business of the stop within 15 minutes. At the end of

---

[144]   *See, e.g.*, Cady v. Sheahan, 467 F.3d 1057 (7th Cir. 2006) (30 minutes was not excessive where officers worked diligently to resolve the situation, most of the delay was attributable to the suspect's evasive action and refusal to provide identification, and the suspect was released as soon as the officers determined that he was not a threat to courthouse security); United States v. Donnelly, 475 F.3d 946 (8th Cir. 2007) (80-minute detention to wait arrival of drug detection dog not unreasonable where dog had to be brought a considerable distance to a remote, rural location, there was no lack of diligence, and no way to have completed the investigation any faster); United States v. Street, 472 F.3d 1298 (11th Cir. 2006) (60 minutes did not exceed bounds of a legitimate *Terry* where the crime under investigation — bank robbery — was a serious one, officer diligently pursued the investigation and each segment of questioning increased the quantum of reasonable suspicion sufficient to allow continuation of the detention).

[145]   *See, e.g.*, United States. v. Boyce, 351 F.3d 1102 (11th Cir. 2003) (finding unnecesary delay in compelting the stop where motorist was detained an additional twelve minutes after warning ticket was issued to await arrival of drug detection dog).

[146]   *Supra* note 141.

[147]   *See, e.g.*, State v. Chapman, 921 P. 2d 446 (Utah 1996) (officers exceeded scope of stop by running a stolen weapons check on a gun found in the possession of suspect who was stopped on suspicion of unrelated criminal activity).

[148]   United States v. Sanchez-Valdeuten, 11 F.3d 985 (10th Cir. 1993).

15 minutes, officers must let the detainee go unless they have probable cause for an arrest.[149] Students should check the statutes of their state to determine if there are time limits on *Terry* stops.

Figure 3.15
Duration of a *Terry* Stop

> A *Terry* stop must be:
>
> 1. brief — 90 minutes probably being the outer limit;
> 2. conducted efficiently so the period of involuntary detention lasts no longer than necessary;
> 3. limited in scope to the suspicious circumstances that prompted the stop, unless: (1) police acquire reasonable suspicion of unrelated criminal activity or (2) the detainee consents to an extension.

§ 3.10 Traffic and Vehicle Stops

Stopping a motorist is always a seizure, whether the officer's purpose is to make an arrest, issue a traffic citation, investigate a nontraffic offense, or simply to check the motorist's license and vehicle registration.[150] The requirements of the Fourth Amendment do not change when a pedestrian climbs into a motor vehicle. Police officers are held to identical Fourth Amendment standards. They must have probable cause to make a traffic arrest or to issue a traffic citation, and reasonable suspicion to stop a motorist for investigation.

Contrary to popular belief, police do not have the authority to stop motorists at random and demand to see their drivers' license and vehicle registration.[151] Police must have grounds to suspect a motorist of wrongdoing before the stop is made.[152] The Fourth Amendment demands individualized suspicion. Suspicion that some motorists are driving under the influence of alcohol or without a license, although undoubtedly correct, does not supply grounds for stopping a particular motorist. Police must have grounds to suspect the motorist who is stopped.

---

[149] Ark. Code Ann. § 16-81-204(b) (15 minutes). See also Guam Code Ann. § 30.30 (15 minutes); Nev. Rev. Stat. § ST 171.123(4) (60 minutes).

[150] United States v. Martinez-Fuerte, 428 U.S. 543, 96 S. Ct. 3074, 49 L. Ed. 2d 1116 (1976); United States v. Brignoni-Ponce, *supra* note 65; Delaware v. Prouse, 440 U.S. 648, 99 S. Ct. 1391, 59 L. Ed. 2d 660 (1979). Not only is the driver seized, the passengers are seized as well. Brendlin v. California, 551 U.S. 249, 127 S. Ct. 2400, 168 L. Ed. 2d 132 (2007) (suppressing evidence seized from a passenger who police recognized as a parole violator during a traffic stop made without adequate grounds).

[151] Brendlin v. California, *supra* note 150; Delaware v. Prouse, *supra* note 150.

[152] *See, e.g.*, United States v. Brignoni-Ponce, *supra* note 65 (random stops by border patrol officer to check for the presence of illegal aliens are unconstitutional).

A. *Special Rules for Checkpoint Stops*

However, an exception is made for stops conducted at a fixed checkpoint.[153] Individualized suspicion of wrongdoing is not required. The Fourth Amendment, instead, imposes the following requirements.

First, the checkpoint program must serve a "special need" — one that goes beyond the ordinary need for effective law enforcement.[154] Protecting our national borders from illegal entry,[155] performing vehicle safety inspections and driver's license checks,[156] keeping alcohol-impaired drivers off the road,[157] and intercepting kidnappers and escaped prisoners believed to be traveling along a particular route[158] are examples of special needs that justify a checkpoint. Checkpoints may not be used to investigate ordinary criminal wrongdoing. They may not be used, for example, where their primary programmic purpose is detecting drugs.[159] While drug trafficking is a serious social problem, it does not pose the type of immediate threat to the public safety that justifies establishing a checkpoint.

Figure 3.16
Fourth Amendment Requirements for Checkpoint Stops

Checkpoint programs must comply with the following requirements in order to satisfy the Fourth Amendment. They must:

1. further a special need beyond the normal need to control crime;
2. be authorized by a supervisory-level police department official;
3. be operated under systematic procedures that limit discretion in selecting which vehicles to stop; and
4. be conducted so as to avoid unnecessary fear, danger, and inconvenience to motorists.

---

[153] *See, e.g.*, Illinois v. Lidster, 124 U.S. 885, 124 S. Ct. 885, 157 L. Ed. 2d 843 (2004); United States v. Martinez-Fuerte, *supra* note 150.

[154] Indianapolis v. Edmond, 531 U.S. 32, 121 S. Ct. 447, 148 L. Ed. 2d 333 (2000).

[155] United States v. Martinez-Fuerte, *supra* note 150.

[156] Delaware v. Prouse, *supra* note 150; Mullinax v. State, 327 Ark. 41, 938 S.W.2d 801 (1997); State v. Williams, 85 Wash. App. 271, 932 P.2d 665 (1997).

[157] Michigan Department of State Police v. Sitz, 496 U.S. 444, 450, 110 S. Ct. 2481, 2485, 110 L. Ed. 2d 412, 420 (1990).

[158] *See, e.g.*, United States v. O'Mara, 963 F.2d 1288 (9th Cir. 1992); United States v. Harper, 617 F.2d 35 (4th Cir. 1980); State v. Gascon, 119 Idaho 932, 812 P. 2d 239 (1991). *See also* Illinois v. Lidster, *supra* note 153 (upholding brief checkpoint stop at which highway police sought information about recent fatal hit-and-run accident on that highway).

[159] Indianapolis v. Edmond, *supra* note 154. In Indianapolis v. Edmond, the City of Indianapolis set up a drug interdiction checkpoint at which they used trained narcotics detection dogs to sniff vehicles passing through. The Supreme Court held that this practice violated the Fourth Amendment, stating that "[w]hen law enforcement authorities pursue . . . general crime control purposes at checkpoints such as here, . . . stops can only be justified by some quantum of individualized suspicion."

Second, the checkpoint must be properly authorized. The decision to conduct a checkpoint and the site selection must be made by supervisory-level officials, not by officers operating in the field.[160]

Third, checkpoints must be operated under standardized procedures that limit discretion in deciding which vehicles to stop.[161]

Finally, operations must be conducted so as to avoid unnecessary fear, danger, and inconvenience to motorists.[162] There must be signs warning motorists that they are approaching a checkpoint. The site must be illuminated and police control visible so that motorists will not be placed in fear that they are being ambushed. Routine inter-actions should rarely last longer than a few minutes. If reasonable suspicion is aroused, the motorist may be referred to a second location for a *Terry* investigation.[163] Other-wise, the motorist must be allowed to go on once routine interactions are over. Vehicles stopped at checkpoints may not be searched unless police have probable cause or the motorist consents.[164]

§ 3.11 — Pretextual Traffic Stops

A pretextual traffic stop is a traffic stop made for an observed traffic violation in which the officer's real motive is to check out a hunch about unrelated criminal activity. Pretextual stops are widely used in drug interdiction. An officer who has a hunch that a motorist is transporting drugs, but lacks grounds for an investigatory stop, will follow the vehicle until the motorist commits a minor traffic violation and then pull the vehicle over for the chance to peer inside the passenger compartment and interact with the motorist.

The Supreme Court gave this practice a thumbs-up in *Whren v. United States*.[165] Two plainclothes police officers patrolling a neighborhood known for drug trafficking noticed a truck with a temporary license plate paused at a stop sign. The driver turned without signaling when he saw their vehicle headed toward him. They followed and

---

[160] *See, e.g.*, People v. Fullwiley, 710 N. E. 2d 491 (Ill. Ct. App. 1999); State v. Downey, 945 S. W. 2d 102 (Tenn. 1997); State v. Park, 810 P. 2d 456 (Utah Ct. App. 1991).

[161] *See, e.g.*, Brown v. Texas, *supra* note 54; People v. Fullwiley, *supra* note 160; State v. Manos, 516 S. E. 2d 548 (Ga. Ct. App. 1999).

[162] *See, e.g.*, United States v. Martinez-Fuerte, *supra* note 150; Mullinax v. State, 327 Ark. 41, 938 S. W. 2d 801 (1997).

[163] State v. Eggleston, 109 Ohio App. 3d 217, 671 N.E.2d 1325 (1996).

[164] United States v. Ortiz, 422 U.S. 891, 95 S. Ct. 2585, 45 L. Ed. 2d 623 (1975).

[165] **517 U.S. 806, 116 S. Ct. 1769, 135 L. Ed. 2d 89 (1996).** The Supreme Court has consistently taken the position that a police officer's motives or state of mind have no bearing on the Fourth Amendment validity of the officer's conduct. Ashcroft v. Al-Kidd, 563 U.S. — 131 S. Ct. 2074, 179 L.Ed.2d 1149 (2011) is the latest case. The Court ruled that, where the requirements of the federal material witness statute are met, use of the statute to detain persons suspected of ties to terrorist organizations does not violate the Fourth Amendment, even though the government lacks grounds to charge the person with a crime.

pulled the driver over. Upon approaching the vehicle, they saw two plastic bags in the passenger compartment containing a substance that looked like crack cocaine. They seized the bags and arrested the occupants. The question before the Court was whether stopping a motorist for an observed traffic violation offends the Fourth Amendment if the officer's real reason is to check out a hunch about unrelated criminal activity. The Supreme Court ruled that a police officer's subjective state of mind or motives have no bearing on the Fourth Amendment validity of his/her conduct. The Fourth Amendment imposes an objective standard. If the officer has objectively valid grounds for making the stop, the stop is valid under the Fourth Amendment, regardless of the officer's reasons for making it. Improper motives do not invalidate an otherwise valid traffic stop.

Whren significantly expanded the investigative authority of the police because virtually any motorist, if followed long enough, is likely to drive a mile or two above the speed limit or commit some other minor traffic infraction. Consequently, police now have the authority to stop motorists when they have reasonable suspicion that the motorist is engaged in criminal activity and also when they do not, if they observe the motorist commit a minor traffic violation.

Pretextual traffic stops have become a mainstay in the war on drugs. Knowing how to perform one is essential for effective police work.

A. Grounds for a Traffic Stop

A valid pretextual traffic stop requires grounds for a stop. Otherwise evidence uncovered during the stop will be suppressed.[166] Most traffic stops are based on an observed traffic or equipment violation. However, reasonable suspicion of a violation will also suffice.[167]

In a pretextual traffic stop, the traffic violation justifies stopping the vehicle and provides an opportunity to take a quick look inside. But the officer must stick to administering the traffic violation unless reasonable suspicion of unrelated criminal activity surfaces during the stop.

B. Safety Precautions During Traffic Stops

A large percentage of police shootings occur during routine traffic stops.[168] Police officers are allowed to take precautions for their safety. After making a lawful traffic stop, they may take the following precautions as a matter of course: (1) order the motorist to step out of the automobile and remain outside for the duration of the stop,[169]

---

[166]   Wong Sun v. United States, 371 U.S. 471, 83 S. Ct. 407, 9 L. Ed. 2d 441 (1963).

[167]   *See, e.g.*, United States v. Banuelos-Romero, 597 F. 3d 763 (5th Cir. 2010).

[168]   In 1999 alone, 6,048 officers were assaulted and eight were killed while enforcing traffic laws. *See* United States v. Holt, 264 F.3d 1215 (110th Cir. 2001) (citing Federal Bureau of Investigation, Uniform Crime Reports: Law Enforcement Officers Killed and Assaulted 82, 28 (1999)).

[169]   Pennsylvania v. Mimms, 434 U.S. 106, 98 S. Ct. 330, 54 L. Ed. 2d 331 (1977) (*per curiam*) (once a motor vehicle has been lawfully detained for a traffic violation, officers may order the driver to get out of the vehicle without violating the Fourth Amendment).

(2) inquire whether there are loaded guns or other weapons in the vehicle,[170] (3) visually look inside and shine a flashlight around the interior,[171] and (4) run a criminal records check.[172] Police have the same authority with respect to passengers.[173] They may order the passengers to step out of the vehicle and detain them for the duration of the stop, even though they lack grounds to suspect them of criminal activity.[174]

Pat downs are not permitted as a matter of course. They require reasonable suspicion that the person frisked is armed and dangerous.[175] The same is true for vehicle protective weapon searches. They may be performed only when an officer has reasonable suspicion that one or more occupants are dangerous and might have a weapon inside the vehicle.[176]

Figure 3.17
Precautions for Safety During Traffic Stops

Officers who make a valid traffic stop may take the following precautions for their safety, as a matter of course: (1) order the motorist and passengers to remain outside of the vehicle, (2) ask them whether they have guns or weapons, (3) visually look inside the vehicle and shine a flashlight around the interior, and (4) run a criminal records check. Frisking the occupants and searching the passenger compartment for weapons require reasonable suspicion that the occupants may be armed and dangerous.

[170] *See, e.g.,* United States v. Holt, 264 F.3d 1215 (10th Cir. 2001) (*en banc*).
[171] *See, e.g., Id.*; United States v. Beatty, 170 F.3d 811 (8th Cir. 1999); United States v. Weatherspoon, 82 F.3d 697 (6th Cir. 1996).
[172] *See, e.g.,* United States v. Purcell, 236 F.3d 1274 (11th Cir. 2001) (upholding computer check for criminal history and inquiry whether motorist has weapons in vehicle as a reasonable precaution for officer's safety).
[173] Brendlin v. California, 551 U.S. 249, 127 S. Ct. 2400, 168 L. Ed. 2d 13 (2007) (holding that passengers in an automobile pulled over for a traffic stop are "seized," just as the driver, from the moment the automobile came to a halt on the roadside and, therefore, are entitled to challenge the constitutionality of the traffic stop); Maryland v. Wilson, 519 U.S. 408, 117 S. Ct. 882, 137 L. Ed. 2d 41 (1997) (An officer making a traffic stop may order the passengers to get out of the vehicle pending completion of the stop.); **Arizona v. Johnson, 555 U.S. 323, 129 S. Ct. 781, 172 L. Ed. 2d 694 (2009)** (holding that passengers, as well as the driver, may be frisked on reasonable suspicion that they may be armed and dangerous).
[174] **Arizona v. Johnson, *supra* note 173** (holding that during a lawful traffic stop police may pat down passengers reasonably suspected of being armed and dangerous, without cause to believe that they are involved in the criminal activity for which the stop was made).
[175] *Id.*
[176] Michigan v. Long, 463 U.S. 1032, 103 S. Ct. 3469, 77 L. Ed. 2d 1201 (1983) (police have the authority to perform a limited protective search of the passenger compartment during a traffic stop when they reasonably believe the occupants are dangerous and could gain immediate control of a weapon when permitted to re-enter).

C. Scope and Duration of Traffic Stops

A lawful roadside stop begins when a vehicle is pulled over for a traffic violation. The temporary seizure of the driver and passengers ordinarily continues for the duration of the stop. Normally, the stop ends when the police have no further need to control the scene, and inform the driver and passengers that they are free to leave.

Routine traffic stops more closely resemble *Terry* stops than arrests. They must be brief, minimally intrusive, and last no longer than necessary to process the traffic violation.[177] Police may request the driver's license, vehicle registration and insurance papers, run a computer check on them, run a criminal records check, check for outstanding warrants, and ask a few general questions about the driver's destination and travel plans.[178] They may also ask passengers for identification and run a background check on them.[179] After this, they must conclude the business of the stop, issue a citation or warning, and allow the vehicle to leave. Further detention is permitted only if reasonable suspicion of unrelated criminal activity arises during the stop or the occupants consent to remain.[180]

The Fourth Amendment is concerned with the duration of the stop, but not with the scope of questioning that occurs during it. Police are allowed to inquire into matters unrelated to the stop, such as whether there are drugs or weapons in the vehicle, if it does not prolong the duration of the stop by more than a few minutes.[181] The time

---

[177] United States v. Holt, *supra* note 170; United States v. Jones, 234 F.3d 234 (5th Cir. 2000).

[178] *See, e.g.*, United States v. Alcaraz-Arellano, 441 F.3d 1252 (10th Cir. 2006); United States v. Holt, *supra* note 170; United States v. Jones, *supra* note 177; United States v. Purcell, *supra* note 172; United States v. Linkous, 285 F.3d 716 (8th Cir. 2002). *See also* United States v. Zabalgo, 346 F.3d 1255 (l0th Cir. 2003) ("The detaining officer may also question the vehicle's occupants regarding their identities, travel plans, and ownership of the vehicle.").

[179] **Arizona v. Johnson, *supra* note 173**; United States v. Rice, 483 F.3d 1079 (10th Cir. 2007).

[180] *See, e.g.*, **Illinois v. Caballes, *supra* note 120** (The Fourth Amendment is violated if a lawful traffic stop is extended beyond the time reasonably required to process the traffic violation in order to inquire into unrelated matters for which police lack reasonable suspicion); United States v. Jones, *supra* note 177 (although the initial stop of the defendants' vehicle was valid, their continued involuntary detention, after completion of computer check on drivers' licenses and vehicle rental papers, for three additional minutes, violated Fourth Amendment); United States v. West, 219 F.3d 1171 (10th Cir. 2000) (A driver must be permitted to proceed after a routine traffic stop if a license and registration check reveal no reason to detain the driver further unless the officer has reasonable suspicion of other crimes or the driver voluntarily consents to further questioning.").

[181] **Arizona v. Johnson, *supra* note 173** (Fourth Amendment not violated by questioning passenger about gang activity during a traffic stop unless it measurably extends the duration); Muehler v. Mena, 544 U.S. 93, 125 S. Ct. 1465, 161 L. Ed. 2d 299 (2005) (questioning detainees about matters unrelated to the reason for the detention does not violate the Fourth Amendment unless it adds to the duration of the detention); **Illinois v. Caballes, *supra* note 120** (walking a drug detection dog around a vehicle during a traffic stop violates the Fourth Amendment only if it results in the motorist being detained beyond the time reasonably necessary to process the traffic violation); United States v. Alcaraz-Arellano, *supra* note 178 (questioning motorists about matters unrelated to the purpose of the stop violates the Fourth Amendment only if it prolongs the duration of the stop). For a general discussion of this topic, *see* Wayne R. LaFave, *The "Routine Traffic Stop" From Start to Finish: Too Much "Routine," Not Enough Fourth Amendment*, 102 MICH. L. REV. 1843 (2004).

spent waiting for the results of the computer check or while writing out a ticket may be used for this purpose because this is "dead time." Another time to inquire into unrelated criminal activity is after the stop is over if the motorist consents to remain.

D. *Fourth Amendment Authority to Search for Evidence During Traffic Stops*

Police have no authority to search for evidence when they issue a traffic citation because neither justification for allowing police to perform a search incident to arrest - the need to disarm suspects before taking them into custody and to gather evidence for use at trial - are present.[182]

A traffic arrest confers authority to search the motorist's person, but seldom the vehicle.[183] The Supreme Court sharply limited police authority to search vehicles in *Arizona v. Gant*.[184] Gant was arrested for driving with a suspended license. After he was handcuffed and locked in a patrol car, police searched his vehicle and discovered cocaine in the pocket of a jacket in the back seat. The Court suppressed the evidence, holding that "[p]olice may search a vehicle incident to a recent occupant's arrest only if the arrestee is within reaching distance of the passenger compartment at the time of the search or it is reasonable to believe the vehicle contains evidence of the offense of arrest."

Neither justification existed in *Gant* or in most cases where a motorist is arrested for a traffic violation. The first justification is based on the need to prevent the arrestee from gaining access to a weapon inside the vehicle. This justification did not exist in *Gant* because he was handcuffed and locked in a patrol car when his vehicle was searched. The Court opined that "[b]ecause officers have many means of ensuring the safe arrest of vehicle occupants, it will be the rare case in which an officer is unable to fully effectuate an arrest so that a real possibility of access to the arrestee's vehicle remains." The second justification — reason to believe the vehicle contains evidence of the offense of arrest — has no application when an arrest is made for a traffic violation because traffic violations are, by their nature, offenses for which no physical evidence exists. The officer's observation of the commission of the offense is the only evidence that exists, and this evidence is not located inside the vehicle.

Arizona v. Gant virtually eliminates the authority of police to search vehicles incident to arrest for a traffic violation. However, this is exactly what the Supreme Court intended. The Court stated that "[a] rule that gives police the power to conduct . . . a

---

[182]   Knowles v. Iowa, 525 U.S. 113, 119 S. Ct. 484, 142 L. Ed. 2d 492 (1998) (Issuance of a traffic citation does not authorize police to search a vehicle for evidence, even if the officer has probable cause to make a custodial arrest, but decides to ticket the motorist instead.).

[183]   **United States v. Robinson, 414 U.S. 218, 94 S. Ct. 467, 38 L. Ed. 2d 427 (1973)** (police may search the motorist's person after making a valid traffic arrest).

[184]   **553 U.S. 232, 129 S. Ct. 1710, 173 L. Ed. 2d 485 (2009)** (police may search the vehicle interior after arresting the motorist for traffic offense only if the motorist is unsecured and within reaching distance at the time of the search).

search whenever an individual is caught committing a traffic offense, when there is no basis for believing evidence of the offense might be found in the vehicle, creates a serious and recurring threat to the privacy of countless individuals."

No search authority is needed to walk a drug-detection dog around a lawfully stopped vehicle because this procedure is not considered a search.[185] However, the dog needs to be close at hand because police may not detain a motorist beyond the time needed to process the traffic violation unless they acquire reasonable suspicion of drug activity during the stop.[186]

Figure 3.18
Search Authority During a Traffic Stop

Police have authority to:

1. search the motorist's person after making a traffic arrest.
2. walk a trained drug-detection dog around the exterior of a lawfully stopped vehicle if it does not prolong the duration of the stop.

Police have no authority to:

1. search the motorist or the vehicle after issuing a traffic citation.
2. search a vehicle incident to a traffic arrest after the motorist has been handcuffed and secured.

---

[185]   **Illinois v. Caballes,** *supra* **note 120** (reasonable suspicion is not required to walk a drug-detection dog around the exterior of a lawfully stopped vehicle if it does not prolong the duration of the stop); United States v. Place, *supra* note 120 (A canine examination by a trained narcotics detection dog is not a search within the meaning of the Fourth Amendment because it discloses only the presence or absence of a contraband item for which there is no legitimate expectation of privacy.). *See* § 4.2 (C) (2), *infra*, for a fuller discussion of this matter.

[186]   **Illinois v. Caballes,** *supra* **note 120**; Carter v. State, 143 Md. App. 670, 795 A. 2d 790 (2002) ("***Whren***-inspired traffic stops ... present only a limited window of opportunity for the police who would exploit them in order to serve some extraneous investigative purpose, such as checking for the possession of contraband drugs. Once a reasonable time for the processing of a traffic charge has expired, even a minimal further delay to accommodate the arrival of a drug-sniffing canine is not permitted. That foreclosure is for the obvious reason that the dog sniff, however valuable it might be for other investigative purposes, does not in any way serve the purpose of the justifying traffic stop. Once the purpose of the traffic stop has been fully and reasonably served, no further detention is permitted — unless, in the course of the traffic stop, some independent articulable or reasonable suspicion has arisen to create some new and self-sufficient investigative purpose.") However, courts do not split hairs. The Fourth Amendment is not violated where the detention is prolonged by no more than a minute or two. *See, e.g.,* United States v. Martin, 411 F.3d 998 (8th Cir. 2005) ("[W]hen a police officer makes a traffic stop and has at his immediate disposal the canine resources to employ this uniquely limited investigation procedure, it does not violate the Fourth Amendment to require that the offending motorist's detention be momentarily extended for a canine sniff of the vehicle's exterior."); Hugueley v. Dresden Police Department, 469 F. Supp. 2d 507 (W.D. Tenn. 2007) (dog sniff lasting two minutes after completion of the traffic stop was *de minimis* and did not violate the Fourth Amendment).

E. De-escalation from Traffic Stop into a Voluntary Investigative Encounter

Just as consensual encounters can escalate into seizures, seizures can de-escalate into consensual encounters. The metamorphosis can occur without the motorist being expressly told that he is free to leave. In *Ohio v. Robinette*,[187] an officer, while handing the motorist's license back, said: "One question before you get gone: are you carrying any illegal contraband in your car? Any weapons of any kind, drugs, anything like that?" When Robinette replied "no," the officer asked for and received permission to search his car. The search turned up narcotics, which Robinette sought to suppress on the grounds that his consent was the product of an illegal detention. The Supreme Court disagreed, holding that formal notice that the motorist is legally free to go is not required for a traffic stop to end and be followed by a consensual investigative encounter. A successful transition requires two things. The officer must: (1) return the motorist's license and registration so the motorist is, in fact, free to go, and (2) then ask the motorist, in a courteous and nonthreatening manner, if he would mind answering a few more questions.[188]

F. Racial Targeting

Recent studies show that African-American and Hispanic motorists are more likely to be targeted for pretextual traffic stops and treated differently during them than members of other demographic groups.[189] This problem is often referred to as

---

[187]   519 U.S. 33, 117 S. Ct. 417, 136 L. Ed. 2d 347 (1996). Post-traffic stop dialogues like the one in *Robinette* are exceptionally common. The officer who conducted the traffic stop in *Robinette* testified in a separate case that, in one year alone, he had asked almost 800 motorists for permission to search their vehicle. *See* State v. Retherford, 93 Ohio App. 3d 586, 639 N.E.2d 498 (1994), *discussed in* LEWIS R. KATZ AND PAUL C. GIANELLI, OHIO ARREST, SEARCH AND SEIZURE § 16.7 (2002 ed.).

[188]   *See, e.g.,* United States v. West, *supra* note 180 (A traffic stop may become a consensual encounter, requiring no reasonable suspicion, if the officer returns the license and registration and asks questions without further constraining the driver by an overbearing show of authority); United States v. Walker, 933 F.2d 812 (10th Cir. 1991) (traffic stop cannot become consensual until motorist's license and papers are returned); United States v. Gregory, 79 F.3d 973 (10th Cir. 1996) (traffic stop had not yet ended where officer leaned on motorist's car when he asked about drugs, because a reasonable person would not feel free to leave while an officer is leaning on his car).

[189]   Blacks and Hispanics, for example, are more likely, after being stopped for a traffic violation, to be asked to step out of their vehicle, questioned about drugs, frisked, searched, or asked for consent to search than members of other demographic groups. *See, e.g.,* State v. Soto, 324 N.J. Super. 66, 734 A.2d 350 (1996) (statistical evidence that blacks were 4.85 times more likely than whites to be stopped for traffic violations established a prima facie case of racially discriminatory enforcement); Interim Report of the State Police Review Team Regarding Allegations of Racial Profiling ("Interim Report"), released in April of 1999, http://www.state.nj.us/lps/intm_419.pdf (concluding that the problem of disparate treatment during traffic stops is real and not imagined). Although racial profiling is generally associated with enforcement of traffic laws, the problem of racially biased policing goes deeper. *See, e.g.,* Anderson v. Corneyo, 284 F. Supp. 2d 1008 (N.D. Ill. 2003) (class action

racial profiling. Racial profiling has received widespread media attention and is the focus of a large number of lawsuits[190] mainly brought under the equal protection clause.[191]

Although racial profiling suits have enjoyed some success in the courts, litigation is not an effective technique for addressing this problem. The perception that police engage in racially biased policing leads to hostility, mistrust, and resentment, and drives a wedge into the relationship between the police and the minority community.[192] Professor David A. Harris writes:

---

challenging disproportionate targeting of African-American women for pat down and strip searches by customs officials following their arrival on international flights); Carrasca v. Pomeroy, 313 F.3d 823 (3d Cir. 2002) (complaint that officer singled out plaintiffs who were Hispanic, rather than other similarly situated non-Hispanics, for enforcement of the swimming hours regulations, stated claim for selective enforcement). A wealth of literature can be found on the Department of Justice (http://www.usdoj.gov), the U.S. Commission on Civil Rights (http://www.usccr.gov), the American Civil Liberties Union (http://www.aclu.org); and the Police Executive Research Forum (http://policeforum.mn-8.net) Web sites. *See, e.g.,* U.S. Dept. J., A Resource Guide on Racial Profiling Data Collection Systems: Promising Practices and Lessons Learned, http://www.ncjrs.org/pdffiles1/bja/184768.pdf; David A. Harris, Driving While Black: Racial Profiling on Our Nation's Highways, http://www.aclu.org/profiling/report/index.html; U.S. Dept. J., Civil Rights, Guidance Regarding the Use of Race by Federal Law Enforcement Agencies (June, 2003), http://www.usdoj.gov/crt/split/documents/guidance_on_race.htm; U.S. Dept. J., Fact Sheet on Racial Profiling (June 17, 2003), http://www.usdoj.gov/opa/pr/2003/June/racial_profiling_fact_sheet.pdf; Lorie Fridell et al., Racially Biased Policing: A Principled Response (Police Executive Research Forum, 2001), available at http://www.cops.usdoj.gov/html/cd_rom/inaction1/pubs/RaciallyBiasedPolicing.pdf; Interim Report of the State Police Review Team Regarding Allegations of Racial Profiling ("Interim Report"), released in April of 1999, http://www.state.nj.us/lps/intm_419.pdf.

[190] *See, e.g.,* Melendres v. Arpaio, 598 F. Supp. 2d 1025 (D. Ariz. 2009) (holding that complaint alleging that deputies from sheriff's office profiled, targeted, and ultimately stopped and detained plaintiffs based on their race stated a claim for violating the Fourth and Fourteenth Amendments); **Maryland State Conference of NAACP Branches v. Maryland State Police, 454 F. Supp. 2d 339 (D. Md. 2006)** (holding that complaint filed by African-American motorists alleging that they were subjected to illegal traffic stops and searches by state troopers engaged in racial profiling stated a claim for violating their Fourteenth Amendment right to equal protection of the laws).

[191] **Wren v. United States**, *supra* note 165 (Racial targeting does not violate the Fourth Amendment if objectively valid grounds exist for the action that is taken. Victims of racial targeting must look to Fourteenth Amendment equal protection clause for protection.).

[192] *See, e.g.,* Minn. St. Ann. § 626.8471 (1) ("The legislature finds that the reality or public perception of racial profiling alienates people from police, hinders community policing efforts, and causes law enforcement to lose credibility and trust among the people law enforcement is sworn to protect and serve."); U.S. Dept. J., A Resource Guide on Racial Profiling Data Collection Systems: Promising Practices and Lessons Learned, supra note 189 at 3 ("When law enforcement practices are perceived to be biased, unfair, or disrespectful, communities of color are less willing to trust and confide in police officers, report crimes, participate in problem-solving activities, be witnesses at trials, or serve on juries.").

Pretextual traffic stops aggravate years of accumulated feelings of injustice, resulting in deepening distrust and cynicism by African-Americans about police and the entire criminal justice system. But the problem goes deeper. If upstanding citizens are treated like criminals by the police, they will not trust those same officers as investigators of crimes or as witnesses in court.[193]

Racial profiling rests on the erroneous assumption that African-Americans and Hispanics are more likely than whites to be involved in drug activity. This assumption becomes a self-fulfilling prophecy, as the following passage shows:

Because police will look for drug crimes among black drivers, they will find it disproportionately among black drivers. More black drivers will be arrested, prosecuted, convicted, and jailed, thereby reinforcing the idea that blacks constitute the majority of drug offenders. This will provide a continuing motive and justification for stopping more black drivers as a rational way of using resources to catch the most criminals. At the same time, because police will focus on black drivers, white drivers will receive less attention, and the drug dealers and possessors among them will be apprehended in proportionately smaller numbers than their presence in the population would predict.[194]

More than 20 states and hundreds of local governments across the nation have enacted legislation condemning racial profiling.[195] The typical statute contains a policy statement declaring racial profiling illegal,[196] provides for the collection and analysis of data on traffic stops to determine the nature and extent of the problem,[197]

[193] David A. Harris, The Stories, the Statistics, and the Law: Why "Driving While Black" Matters, 84 MN. L. REV. 265, 268–269 (1999). The Police Executive Research Forum cautions: "There are grave dangers in neglecting to take the issue of biased policing seriously and respond with effective initiatives . . . . If a substantial part of the population comes to view the justice system as unjust, they are less likely to be cooperative with police, withholding participation in community problem-solving and demonstrating their disaffection in a variety of ways. The loss of moral authority could do permanent injury to the legal system, and deprive all of society of the protection of the law." Lorie Fridell et al., Racially Biased Policing: A Principled Response, supra note 189, at 6.

[194] Harris, supra note 193, 84 MINN. L. REV. at 297.

[195] See, e.g., Arizona (ARIZ. STAT. § 12-12-1401 et seq.); California (WEST'S ANN. CAL. PENAL CODE § 13519.4); Colorado (COLO. REV. STAT. § 24-31-309); Connecticut (CONN. GEN. STAT. § 54-11); Kentucky (K.R.S. § 15A.19); Minnesota (MINN. STAT. ANN. § 626.8471); Missouri (MO. REV. STAT. § 590.650); Nebraska (NEB. REV. STAT. § 20-501 et seq.); Nevada (WEST'S NEV. REV. STAT § 289.820); Rhode Island (R.I. STAT. § 31-21.1-2 et seq.); West Virginia (W. VA. CODE § 30-29-19).

[196] See authorities supra note 195.

[197] See, e.g., Colorado (COLO. REV. STAT. § 42-4-115); Louisiana (LSA-R.S. 32:398.10); Maryland (MD. CODE. ANN., TRANSP. § 25-113); Minnesota (MINN. STAT. ANN. § 626.8471(5)), Nebraska (NEB. REV. STAT. § 20-504); North Carolina (N.C. GEN. STAT. § 114-10); Tennessee (TENN. CODE. ANN. § 38-1-402); Texas (VERNON'S ANN. TEXAS CODE CRIM. PRO. ARTS. 2.131, 2132 (b)); Washington (WASH. REV. CODE. ANN. § 43.43.480(1)).

establishes training programs to teach police how to avoid racial profiling,[198] and puts mechanisms in place to strengthen police accountability.[199]

Police departments need to show their commitment to unbiased policing by providing officers with concrete guidance as to when they may appropriately consider race and ethnicity in law enforcement decision making, and when they may not. The United States Department of Justice, the Police Execution Research Forum, and other highly respected police organizations have all come to the same conclusion — that race and ethnicity may legitimately be considered only when this characteristic is part of the description of a specific suspect.[200] The United States Department of Justice, Civil Rights Division's written guidelines on *The Use of Race by Federal Law Enforcement Agencies* state that "[i]n making routine . . . enforcement decisions, such as ordinary traffic stops, Federal Law enforcement officers may not use race or ethnicity *to any degree*" unless they have specific, trustworthy information to be on the lookout for a specific individual or individuals who are connected to a particular unlawful incident and who are identified in part by race or ethnicity.[201]

§ 3.12   Requirements for a Constitutional Arrest

A. *Arrest Defined*

Prior to *Terry v. Ohio*, defining "arrest" was simple. "Arrest" and "seizure" were one and the same. Whenever the police detained a person against her will, even momentarily, the person was seized, the encounter was an arrest, and probable cause was necessary.[202] *Terry v. Ohio* carved out an exception to the probable cause requirement for brief, limited seizures conducted for investigation.

One consequence of *Terry* is that defining an arrest has ceased to be simple. There are now two kinds of arrests — formal and *de facto*. Formal arrests are intentional. The officer intends to make an arrest, generally announces this intent to the suspect, and the suspect either submits or is brought under the officer's control. Thus, a formal

---

[198] *See*, *e.g.*, California (WEST'S ANN. CAL. PENAL CODE § 13519.4); Missouri (MO. REV. STAT. § 590.050); Minnesota Oklahoma (OKLA. STAT. TIT 22, § 34.5); Texas (TEXAS OCC. CODE ANN. § 1701.253); Washington (WASH. REV. CODE ANN. § 43.43.490).

[199] *See*, *e.g.*, Minnesota (MINN. STAT. ANN. § 626.9517 (providing for installation of automatically activated video cameras on all police vehicles to record traffic stops and monitor compliance with anti-racial profiling policies); Oklahoma (OKLA. STAT. TIT. 22, § 34.4 (2002) (authorizing victims of racial profiling to file a complaint with Human Rights Commission or district attorney for the county in which the stop or arrest occurred).

[200] *See* U.S. Dept. J., Civil Rights, Guidance Regarding the Use of Race by Federal Law Enforcement Agencies (June, 2003), *supra* note 189; Lorie Fridell et al., Racially Biased Policing: A Principled Response, *supra* note 189; New Jersey Attorney General's "Interim Report," *supra* note 189.

[201] *See* U.S. Dept. J., Civil Rights, Guidance Regarding the Use of Race by Federal Law Enforcement Agencies (June, 2003), *supra* note 189.

[202] Dunaway v. New York, 442 U.S. 200, 99 S. Ct. 2248, 60 L. Ed. 2d 824 (1979).

arrest has two ingredients — an announced intent to make an arrest combined with a seizure. Merely saying "you're under arrest," without bringing the suspect under control, is insufficient to constitute an arrest because the suspect has not yet been seized.[203]

De facto arrests, in contrast, are unintentional. They arise by operation of law when police exceed the boundaries allowed for a *Terry* stop. These boundaries were explored in § 3.9. When a stop lasts too long or is too intrusive to be justified on reasonable suspicion, the seizure automatically escalates into an arrest and probable cause becomes necessary.[204]

B. *Probable Cause for an Arrest*

Probable cause depends upon the reasonable conclusion to be drawn from the facts known to the arresting officer at the time of the arrest. It exists when the facts within the officer's knowledge would warrant a reasonably prudent person in believing that an offense has been committed by the person to be arrested.[205]

When the officer is aware of facts that provide probable cause for arrest, the arrest is valid even though the officer states the wrong reason. In *Devenpeck v. Alford*,[206] an officer pulled a motorist over on suspicion of impersonating a police officer but arrested him for violating the state's privacy law after noticing that he was recording their conversation. The officer was mistaken in his belief that this conduct violated the state's privacy law and was sued for making a false arrest after the charges were dismissed. The Supreme Court ruled that the probable cause that supports the arrest does not have to arise out of the grounds stated at the time of arrest. Fourth Amendment analysis is objective. Consequently, an officer's subjective beliefs about the nature of the offense committed are irrelevant. An arrest is valid under the Fourth Amendment whenever the facts within the officer's knowledge justify the action that was taken.[207] The Court remanded the case for retrial on the issue of whether the arresting officer had probable cause to arrest the motorist for impersonating a police officer. If he did, the arrest would be valid, regardless of the stated reason. Persons are lawfully arrested whenever the facts known to the arresting officers provide probable cause to arrest them for *any* offense.

---

[203]   *See* § 3.5(B) *supra.*

[204]   *See* § 3.9 *supra.*

[205]   *See, e.g.,* Gerstein v. Pugh, 420 U.S. 103, 95 S. Ct. 854, 43 L. Ed. 2d 54 (1975); Beck v. Ohio, 379 U. S. 89, 85 S. Ct. 223, 13 L. Ed. 2d 142 (1964). United States v. Cortez, *supra* note 52; Illinois v. Gates, 462 U.S. 213, 103 S. Ct. 2317, 76 L. Ed. 2d 527 (1983); Draper v. United States, 358 U.S. 307, 79 S. Ct. 329, 3 L. Ed. 2d 327 (1959); Brinegar v. United States, 338 U.S. 160, 69 S. Ct. 1302, 93 L. Ed. 1879 (1949).

[206]   543 U.S. 146, 125 S. Ct. 588, 160 L. Ed. 2d 537 (2004).

[207]   The Supreme Court has consistently taken the position that a police officer's subjective reasons and motivations for making an arrest has no bearing on the Fourth Amendment validity. *See, e.g.,* **Whren v. United States,** *supra* **note 165.**

C. Procedures for Determining Whether Probable Cause Exists for an Arrest

An officer who makes an investigatory stop must decide on the spot whether he has enough evidence to justify this action. With arrests, officers have an alternative. They can apply for an arrest warrant and have a magistrate decide this question for them. An officer applies for an arrest warrant by preparing a sworn affidavit detailing the results of the investigation. The magistrate reviews the officer's **affidavit** and determines whether the facts set forth establish probable cause for an arrest. Although the same probable cause standard applies whether the arrest is made with or without a warrant, there are important reasons for having a magistrate decide this question when time permits. Before discussing them, we will briefly outline when the Fourth Amendment requires an arrest warrant.

D. Fourth Amendment Requirement of an Arrest Warrant

The first clause of the Fourth Amendment guarantees citizens the right to be free from unreasonable searches and seizures; the second clause states that "no Warrant shall issue, but upon probable cause." It is unclear whether the Framers meant these clauses to be connected, making arrests unreasonable unless carried out under a warrant. However, the Supreme Court has read them separately. Under settled interpretation, an arrest warrant is necessary only when an arrest is made inside a private dwelling.[208] In all other instances, a warrant is optional, even when there is time to obtain one.[209]

E. Advantages of an Arrest Warrant

There are several reasons police officers should develop the habit of applying for arrest warrants whenever they have time, even when a warrant is not necessary. First, because magistrates are neutral and have more experience in making probable cause determinations, putting this decision in a magistrate's hands reduces the risk of mistakes. Because of this, the Supreme Court has expressed a strong preference for actions taken under a warrant.[210]

Second, a magistrate's determination of probable cause carries a presumption of correctness.[211] As a result of this presumption, a magistrate's determination will be set aside only if the officer who applied for the warrant: (1) deliberately or recklessly included false information in the affidavit[212] or (2) failed to provide enough facts in the

---

[208] Kirk v. Louisiana, 153 U.S. 636, 622 S. Ct. 2458, 153 L. Ed. 2d 599 (2002); **Payton v. New York, 445 U.S. 573, 100 S. Ct. 1371, 63 L. Ed. 2d 639 (1980).** This restriction is discussed in § 3.15 *infra*.
[209] United States v. Watson, 423 U.S. 411, 96 S. Ct. 820, 46 L. Ed. 2d 598 (1976). However, state statutes occasionally impose more stringent warrant requirements. *See infra* §§ 3.17–3.18.]
[210] Illinois v. Gates, *supra* note 205.
[211] *Id.*
[212] Franks v. Delaware, 438 U.S. 154, 98 S. Ct. 2674, 57 L. Ed. 2d 667 (1978).

affidavit to enable the magistrate to make an independent determination of probable cause.[213] Both of these deficiencies are within the officer's control. If the officer's affidavit truthfully recounts the facts, and recounts enough facts to enable a magistrate to make an independent decision, the magistrate's decision that probable cause exists for the arrest is final and cannot be challenged.

The warrant arms the officer with an "insurance policy," which is important for two reasons. First, because the admissibility of evidence seized during an arrest turns on the constitutionality of the arrest itself, admissibility has now been guaranteed. A police officer's determination of probable cause carries no presumption of correctness. If the constitutionality of the arrest is later challenged, the judge will make an independent determination. If probable cause is found to be lacking, evidence seized during the arrest will be suppressed.

Finally, an arrest warrant protects an officer against civil liability.[214] An officer who makes an arrest under a facially valid warrant cannot be sued for making an unconstitutional arrest unless the officer: (1) deliberately or recklessly falsified information in her affidavit[215] or (2) prepared an affidavit that fell so far short of establishing probable cause that the decision to apply for a warrant reflected gross incompetence.[216]

What are the drawbacks of applying for an arrest warrant, assuming there is time to obtain one? There are none. If the magistrate refuses to issue a warrant, this does not mean that the officer's investigative efforts have been for naught. A magistrate's refusal to issue a warrant means that the officer needs to gather more evidence to satisfy the probable cause standard. An officer is fortunate to learn this beforehand, because the

Figure 3.19
Advantages of an Arrest Warrant

Arrests made under the authority of a warrant carry two advantages over arrests without a warrant. A facially valid warrant:

1. ensures admissibility of evidence seized during a search incident to the arrest, and
2. protects the officer against liability in a civil suit.

However, both advantages are lost if the officer:

1. deliberately or recklessly falsifies information in her affidavit in support of the warrant, or
2. fails to include enough information to enable the magistrate to make an independent determination that probable cause exists for the arrest.

---

[213] Illinois v. Gates, *supra* note 205, 462 U.S. at 239, 103 S. Ct. at 2332 ("Sufficient information must be provided to the magistrate to allow that official to determine probable cause; his action cannot be a mere ratification of the bare conclusions of others."); Whiteley v. Warden, 401 U.S. 560, 91 S. Ct. 1031, 28 L. Ed. 2d 306 (1971).
[214] Malley v. Briggs, 475 U.S. 335, 106 S. Ct. 1092, 89 L. Ed. 2d 271 (1986).
[215] Franks v. Delaware, *supra* note 212.
[216] Malley v. Briggs, *supra* note 214.

officer has been spared the consequences of making an unconstitutional arrest. Consequently, police officers have nothing to lose and everything to gain from seeking a judicial determination of probable cause in advance. Uncertainties in the application of the probable cause standard make advance confirmation the most prudent course of action.

F. Prompt Judicial Review of Warrantless Arrests

While a police officer's determination of probable cause will support an arrest, it does not provide legal justification for incarcerating the arrestee for more than a short period. Arrested persons may not be deprived of their liberty for any extended period without a judicial determination that probable cause existed for their arrest. When the arrest is made without a warrant, such that this determination was not made in advance, the arrestee is entitled to a prompt judicial determination of probable cause after the arrest. The purpose of a post-arrest judicial determination is to prevent lengthy unconstitutional confinements. Consequently, this procedure is required only for persons who are: (1) arrested without a warrant and (2) not released on bail.[217] Absent extraordinary circumstances, a post-arrest probable cause determination must be made within 48 hours of a warrantless arrest.[218] The Fourth Amendment does not require an adversarial hearing in which the arrestee is represented by counsel and has a right to put on evidence. Post-arrest judicial review procedures need not be any more elaborate than the procedures that would have been used to decide whether to issue a warrant in advance of the arrest.

§ 3.13   — Probable Cause

To be lawful, an arrest must be based on probable cause. For probable cause to exist, an officer must know of facts that warrant a belief that the person to be arrested committed a crime.[219] Probable cause is identical to reasonable suspicion in all ways but one. It requires a higher probability of guilt, and thus requires more evidence or more reliable evidence. Consequently, earlier discussions of reasonable suspicion are also relevant here.[220]

The Fourth Amendment requires probable cause for four different purposes. Probable cause must exist to: (1) obtain an arrest warrant, (2) make an arrest without a warrant, (3) obtain a search warrant, and (4) conduct some searches without a warrant.

---

[217]   Gerstein v. Pugh, *supra* note 205; County of Riverside v. McLaughlin, 500 U.S. 44, 111 S. Ct. 1661, 114 L. Ed. 2d 49 (1991).

[218]   *See* authorities *supra* note 217.

[219]   Maryland v. Pringle, 540 U.S. 366, 370, 124 S. Ct. 795, 800 157 L. Ed.2d 769 (2003) ("[P]robable cause is a fluid concept — turning on the assessment of probabilities in particular factual contexts — not readily, or even usefully, reduced to a neat set of legal rules."); Beck v. Ohio, *supra* note 205.

[220]   *See* § 3.6 *supra*.

The difference between probable cause for an arrest and probable cause for a search is what the officer must have probable cause to believe. To secure an arrest warrant or make an arrest without a warrant, the officer must have probable cause to believe that the person to be arrested committed an offense. To obtain a search warrant, an officer must have probable cause to believe that the evidence sought will be found at the location to be searched. However, the amount of supporting evidence needed to satisfy all four probable cause standards is the same. Consequently, courts regularly rely on cases from one context as authority in the other. Having pointed this out, it will not be necessary to repeat the same information in Chapter 4.

Probable cause may be based on evidence from a variety of sources other than the officer's personal observations. These sources include physical evidence found at the scene; information supplied by other law enforcement officers or agencies, or in police records; reports received from eyewitnesses, victims, and informants; and rational inferences drawn from the officer's prior experience.[221] Determinations of probable cause are case specific. Each case turns on its own unique combination of facts. No two cases are ever exactly alike. Knowing when evidence is sufficient to establish probable cause for an arrest requires experience and sound professional judgment. There is no better way to acquire this judgment than by routinely applying for arrest warrants and observing when a magistrate will issue one.

Officers occasionally observe the commission of a crime with their own eyes, but this is rare. In most cases, probable cause derives from a combination of mutually reinforcing facts. In evaluating whether the officer's evidence is sufficient to satisfy the probable cause standard, the magistrate will identify all the facts and circumstances known to the officer at time of the action, view them in combination, and evaluate their evidentiary significance in the way a trained police officer would. A single piece of evidence, weak on its own, can be reinforced when other evidence points to the same conclusion.

Investigations are often initiated by information received from members of the public. In determining the weight that should be given to such information in assessing probable cause for an arrest, the officer must consider the information provider's trustworthiness and basis for knowledge. When information comes from the victim or an eyewitness, veracity and basis for knowledge may be assumed.[222] When the information comes from an anonymous informant, veracity and basis for knowledge must be corroborated, either by confirming details that are not easily obtainable or through independent police work.[223]

In *Illinois v. Gates*,[224] police received an anonymous letter accusing Lance Gates and his wife of trafficking in drugs and predicting that, in early May, Gates' wife would

[221] *Id.*
[222] United States v. Armstrong, 16 F.3d 289 (8th Cir. 1993); Buggs v. State, 693 So. 2d 57 (Fla. Dist. Ct. App. 1997); Anderson v. State, 932 S.W.2d 502 (Tex. Crim. App. 1996) (en banc); Belton v. State, 900 S.W.2d 886 (Tex. Ct. App. 1995).
[223] Illinois v. Gates, *supra* note 205.
[224] *Id.*

drive from Chicago to Florida, leave their car there to be loaded with drugs, and Gates would fly to Florida a few days later, pick up their car, and drive it back to Chicago. Gates was arrested on his return from the predicted itinerary. The Supreme Court held that the police were justified in considering the anonymous tip reliable because it contained a large number of details that were not easily obtainable. From the informant's ability to predict the Gates' future travel plans in precise and accurate detail, police could infer that the informant acquired the information directly from Gates or his wife and that the information was therefore reliable.

Suppose that police receive a tip from an anonymous caller who reports that a woman who lives at 1105 Brook Street, named Mary Wanna, is a drug dealer. Officers confirm that Mary Wanna resides at that location and further learn that Mary Wanna has a criminal record for drug trafficking. Have the police corroborated enough details to have probable cause for an arrest?

This situation is readily distinguishable from *Illinois v. Gates*. The details the police have corroborated are easily obtainable. Corroboration of easily obtainable details gives no assurance that an anonymous caller is trustworthy or that the information provided is reliable.[225] The caller could be playing a prank on Mary Wanna, seeking revenge, or reporting a rumor. When an anonymous tip lacks indicia of reliability, it must be corroborated through independent police work.

Probable cause depends entirely on the facts of each case. The hazards of assessing when evidence is sufficient to satisfy this standard can be removed by applying for an arrest warrant.

§ 3.14   — Requirements for a Valid Arrest Warrant

The Fourth Amendment warrant clause reads that "no Warrants shall issue, but upon probable cause, supported by Oath or affirmation, and particularly describing ... the persons ... to be seized." This language establishes three requirements for the issuance of an arrest warrant: (1) a judicial officer, normally a magistrate, must determine that probable cause exists for the arrest; (2) this determination must be supported by information given under oath; and (3) the warrant must contain a particularized description of the person to be seized. As previously noted, an arrest warrant insulates the fruits of an arrest from suppression and the officer from civil suit.[226] However, to perform these functions, it must be issued in conformity with the three requirements listed above.[227] A warrant that fails to satisfy these requirements is subject to challenge.

---

[225] Parish v. State, 939 S.W.2d 201 (Tex. Ct. App. 1997).
[226] *See* § 3.12(E) *supra*.
[227] *Id.*

A. *Determination of Probable Cause by a Magistrate*

The Fourth Amendment divides responsibility for the issuance of a warrant between the magistrate and the officer who applies for the warrant. The magistrate is responsible for deciding whether probable cause exists for an arrest or search. However, because the magistrate lacks independent knowledge of the underlying facts, the Fourth Amendment places responsibility for supplying this information on the applicant. A police officer begins the warrant process by preparing a sworn written statement, called an affidavit, in which the officer sets forth the facts on which her application is made. The magistrate reviews the officer's affidavit and decides whether the facts stated in it are sufficient. In making this decision, the magistrate considers both the content of the information and the reliability of the officer's sources.

Figure 3.20
Fourth Amendment Requirements for a Valid Arrest Warrant

The Fourth Amendment warrant clause imposes three requirements for a constitutional arrest warrant:

1. The magistrate must make an independent determination that probable cause exists for the arrest.
2. The magistrate's determination must be supported by information given under oath.
3. The warrant must contain a particularized description of the person to be arrested.

B. *Supported by Oath or Affirmation*

The Fourth Amendment requires that the magistrate's probable cause determination be based on information given under oath. An oath is required to ensure that the information on which the magistrate acts is trustworthy. Magistrates normally rely exclusively on the information contained in the officer's sworn affidavit; they rarely take oral testimony or call other witnesses. This means that the validity of the warrant will hinge on whether the officer's affidavit contains enough information to enable the magistrate to make an independent determination of probable cause.[228] On a scale of 1 to 10 of the skills needed to be a police investigator, knowing how to prepare a constitutionally sufficient affidavit rates a "10."

To support the issuance of a warrant, the officer's affidavit must contain a detailed account of the facts uncovered by the investigation, the source of these facts, and any other information that the magistrate will need to evaluate the reliability of the officer's sources. If the officer has observed a particular matter with her own eyes, the officer should say so. If the officer heard about it from a third party, she should

---

[228]   Aguilar v. Texas, 378 U.S. 108, 111, 84 S. Ct. 1509, 1512, 12 L. Ed. 2d 723 (1964).

identify the third party and then explain the third party's basis for knowledge and the officer's reasons for believing that the third party's information is reliable. This is particularly important when the existence of probable cause depends on information supplied by a police informant.[229] Courts consider police informants disreputable and their information suspect.[230] Consequently, special attention must be given to providing information that will enable the magistrate to evaluate an informant's credibility and basis of knowledge. Below are two sample affidavits. The first is constitutionally deficient.

Figure 3.21
Sample Affidavit I

I, Officer Susan Blake, based on information received from reliable persons, do solemnly swear that sometime between 8:00 and 10:00 P.M. on October 27, 2011, Sam Wanna (alias Sticky-Fingered Sam) did unlawfully break into and enter a home owned by Vicki Royce, located at 406 Meadow Lane in Euphoria County, and did then and there steal property worth in excess of $12,000.

/s/ Susan Blake
      Affiant

Subscribed and sworn to before me this 29th day of October, 2011.

      /s/ Betty Hitchcock
      Clerk, Associate Division
      Circuit Court of Euphoria County

This affidavit is constitutionally deficient because it sets forth Officer Blake's conclusion that Sticky-Fingered Sam committed a burglary, but discloses none of the underlying facts that lead Officer Blake to reach this conclusion.[231] It is impossible for a magistrate to make an independent determination of probable cause from an affidavit like this. All the magistrate can do is act as a rubber stamp. Issuance of a warrant on an affidavit that is devoid of facts violates the Fourth Amendment. A competent magistrate will not issue a warrant and, if a magistrate issues one, it will not insulate evidence from suppression[232] or the officer from civil liability.[233] When a warrant is issued on an insufficient affidavit, the problem cannot be cured through testimony that the officer knew more facts than were included in the affidavit.[234] It is therefore important that officers learn how to prepare a constitutionally sufficient affidavit.

The affidavit below shows the details that Officer Blake should have put in her application for a warrant.

---

[229]   Illinois v. Gates, *supra* note 205; Spinelli v. United States, 393 U.S. 410, 89 S. Ct. 584, 21 L. Ed. 2d 637 (1969); Aguilar v. Texas, 378 U.S. 108, 84 S. Ct. 1509, 12 L. Ed. 2d 723 (1964).
[230]   People v. Kurland, 28 Cal. 3d 376, 168 Cal. Rptr. 667, 618 P.2d 213 (1980).
[231]   Whiteley v. Warden, 401 U.S. 560, 91 S. Ct. 1031, 28 L. Ed. 2d 306 (1971).
[232]   United States v. Leon, 468 U.S. 897, 914, 104 S. Ct. 3405, 3416, 82 L. Ed. 2d 677 (1984).
[233]   Malley v. Briggs, *supra* note 214.
[234]   Whiteley v. Warden, *supra* note 231.

Figure 3.22
Sample Affidavit II

Comes now Susan Blake, being first duly sworn and upon oath, does state:

I am a Euphoria County Police Detective. The date of this Affidavit In Support of an Application for an Arrest Warrant is October 29, 2011. I have been employed as a Euphoria Police Officer for the past seven years. During this period, I have participated in more than 150 arrests for burglary, larceny, and armed robbery.

Sometime between 8:00 P.M. and 10:00 P.M. on October 27, 2011, a burglary occurred at the home of Vicki Royce at 406 Meadow Lane. The burglary was discovered at 10:15 P.M. when Vicki Royce returned home. The property stolen during the burglary included a large Indian Head coin collection stored in a maroon and gold case, jewelry, and sterling silver place settings. I was given a detailed description of the stolen property when I interviewed Vicki Royce at her residence after the burglary was discovered.

While I was there, Alan Polk, a neighbor who lives at 408 Meadow Lane, saw my squad car and came over. He stated that he was out walking his dog about 9:20 P.M. that evening and that he saw a man leave Vicki Royce's house, get into a maroon or rust-colored "K-car type" station wagon, and drive off. He described the man as white, bald, approximately 5'9", of medium build, and in his early fifties.

On the morning of October 28, 2011, Officer Dave Fox of the Euphoria County Police Department received a telephone call from a woman who stated that she wished to remain anonymous. This individual informed Officer Fox that a man named Sam M. Wanna, who lives in a rented house at 721 Preston Street, invited her into his home the previous evening shortly before midnight, and offered to sell her some Indian Head coins, jewelry, and silverware.

I ran criminal records check and learned that Sam M. Wanna (alias Sticky-Fingered Sam) has three convictions for burglary (1990, 1997, 2004) and one for check forgery (2007). The criminal records show that Sam Wanna is 48 years old, 5'10", and weighs 170 pounds.

I went to 721 Preston Street and saw a maroon Chrysler station wagon parked in front, bearing an in-state license plate, number 256-JRV. I ran a vehicle registration check and verified that this vehicle is registered to Sam M. Wanna.

As a result of this information, it is my belief that Sam M. Wanna burglarized Vicki Royce's home on October 27, 2011.

/s/ Susan Blake
          Affiant

Subscribed and sworn to before me this 29th day of October, 2011.

/s/ Betty Hitchcock
Clerk, Associate Division
Circuit Court of Euphoria County

This affidavit is sufficient to enable a magistrate to make an independent determination of whether probable cause exists for an arrest. If the magistrate issues a warrant, the existence of probable cause will be conclusively established unless Officer Blake recklessly or deliberately falsified the facts on which the magistrate's determination was based.[235]

Note the certification above Betty Hitchcock's signature, at the bottom of Officer Blake's affidavit. The certification recites that the information in Officer Blake's affidavit was subscribed and sworn (*i.e.*, given under oath), as required by the Fourth Amendment. Officers should make certain that their affidavit contains a signed certification like this, or the warrant will not comply with the Fourth Amendment and the arrest will be unconstitutional.

C. The Person to Be Seized Must Be Particularly Described

Arrest warrants must also "particularly describ[e] the . . . persons . . . to be seized." The usual method of describing the person to be arrested is by their name. Minor discrepancies in spelling do not invalidate a warrant. However, when the arrested person's name is the only identifying information on the face of the warrant, the name provided must be at least similar to the person's real name.[236] A warrant for the arrest of "Sam Cook" does not confer authority to arrest "Sam Wanna" if he has never been known by this name, even though Sam Wanna was the person the officer had in mind, but was confused about his real name.[237] When police have probable cause for arrest but are uncertain of the individual's real name, they will need to describe him by a combination of other characteristics that are sufficient to identify him. The characteristics may variously include the person's occupation, age, date of birth, physical appearance, place of residence, aliases, nicknames, the vehicle the person drives, distinguishing features like scars or limps, etc.[238]

Figure 3.23
Particularized Description of the Person to Be Arrested

> In order to satisfy the Fourth Amendment requirement of a particularized description of the person to be arrested, the warrant must either designate them by:
>
> 1. their actual name, or
> 2. if their name is unknown, by some other combination of characteristics that leaves little room for doubt as to the person intended.

Police may not select an arbitrary name like "John Doe" and use it as the sole means of identification.[239] A warrant for the arrest of "John Doe" does not contain

---

[235] **United States v. King, 227 F.3d 732 (6th Cir. 2000).** This case contains an unusually clear discussion of what an affidavit must contain in order to satisfy the probable cause requirement.

[236] West v. Cabell, 153 U.S. 78, 85, 14 S. Ct. 752, 753, 38 L. Ed. 643 (1894).

[237] *Id.*

[238] People v. Montoya, 255 Cal. App. 2d 137, 63 Cal. Rptr. 73 (1967).

[239] Powe v. City of Chicago, 664 F.2d 639 (7th Cir. 1981).

a particularized description of anyone.[240] The combination of characteristics on the face of the warrant must leave little doubt about the identity of the party intended.[241] A warrant for the arrest of "John Doe, alias Sticky-Fingered Sam, who lives at 721 Preston Street and drives a maroon Chrysler station wagon" contains a particularized description of the person to be arrested.[242]

A different problem arises when the warrant's description is correct, but the police arrest the wrong person. Suppose a warrant is issued for the arrest of "Sam Wanna (alias Sticky-Fingered Sam)," but police mistakenly arrest his cousin George who looks almost exactly like him. In this example, the warrant is issued in conformity with the Fourth Amendment. The problem arose in the execution. The police arrested the wrong person. Victims of mistaken identity have no recourse if the mistake was reasonable, because a warrant issued in conformity with the Fourth Amendment furnishes probable cause to arrest any person whom the police reasonably believe is the person named in the warrant.[243] Since police had probable cause, George's Fourth Amendment rights were not violated.

D. Form and Content of the Warrant

Arrest warrants are short, one-page documents. Below is a sample warrant for Sticky-Fingered Sam's arrest.

Figure 3.24
Sample Arrest Warrant

The State of Confusion
To any Sheriff, Constable, Marshal, or Police Officer of the State of Confusion:
It appearing that there are reasonable grounds for believing that Sam M. Wanna (alias Sticky-Fingered Sam) committed the offense of burglary in the County of Euphoria on October 27, 2011, you are therefore commanded, forthwith, to arrest Sam M. Wanna, and bring him before some magistrate of Euphoria, to be dealt with according to law.

Given under my hand the 29th day of October, 2011
Betty Bright,
Justice of the Peace for Euphoria County

---

[240] United States v. Doe, 703 F.2d 745 (3d Cir. 1983).
[241] People v. Simmons, 210 Ill. App. 3d 692, 569 N.E.2d 591 (1991).
[242] United States v. Espinosa, 827 F.2d 604, *cert. denied*, 485 U.S. 968, 108 S. Ct. 1243, 99 L. Ed. 2d 441 (1987) (description of arrestee by physical appearance, place of residence, and vehicle he drives is sufficient to satisfy the Fourth Amendment); United States v. Ferrone, 438 F.2d 381, 389 (3d Cir. 1971) (description of arrestee as "John Doe, a white male with black wavy hair and stocky build observed using the telephone in Apartment 4-C, 1806 Patricia Lane, East McKeesport, Pennsylvania" is sufficient to satisfy the Fourth Amendment).
[243] Baker v. McCollan, 443 U.S. 137, 99 S. Ct. 2689, 61 L. Ed. 2d 433 (1979); Hill v. California, 401 U.S. 797, 91 S. Ct. 1106, 28 L. Ed. 2d 484 (1971).

The form and content of arrest warrants are prescribed by statute. State statutes typically impose the following seven requirements and sometimes additional ones.[244] The arrest warrant must:

1. be issued in the name of the state or a municipality.
2. contain the date and the county or municipality where it was issued.
3. designate the officer or class of officers who are directed to execute it. The usual practice, as shown in the sample arrest warrant, is to designate all peace officers in the state so that any of them can execute it.
4. name or otherwise identify the person to be arrested.
5. command that this person be arrested and brought before the nearest accessible court for an initial appearance.
6. describe the offense charged in general terms sufficient to apprise the arrested person of the nature of the charges.
7. be signed by the judge of the court who issued it.

Examine the sample arrest warrant above and identify the place in it where each of these requirements is satisfied.

E. Proper Execution

A warrant must also be properly executed in order for an arrest to be valid. The requirements for proper execution include the following:

1. The party executing the warrant must be the specific officer or member of the class of officers to whom the warrant is directed.
2. The warrant must be executed within the territorial jurisdiction of the magistrate who issued it.[245]
3. The officer must either serve the warrant or advise the arrestee that a warrant has been issued. The common law required arresting officers to have the warrant in their possession at the time of the arrest so that they could show it on demand. While a person who has been arrested unquestionably has a right to see the warrant, the modern trend is toward allowing greater flexibility in the timing. The Federal Rules of Criminal Procedure[246] and many state codes[247] provide that the arresting officer need not have the warrant in his or her possession at the time of the arrest, but must, upon request, show the warrant to the defendant as soon thereafter as practical.

Special requirements exist when the arrest requires a nonconsensual entry into a private dwelling. The requirements for making an arrest inside a private dwelling are covered in the next section.

---

[244]   *See, e.g.,* IOWA CODE ANN. § 804.2 (West 1994); MONT. CODE ANN. § 46-6-214 (1991); OKLA. STAT. ANN.§ 2203 (West 1996).
[245]   *See § 3.18 infra.*
[246]   FED. R. CRIM. P. 4(d)(3).
[247]   *See, e.g.,* ARIZ. REV. STAT. ANN. § 13-3887 (1989).

§ 3.15   — Arrests Inside a Private Residence

While probable cause is enough to authorize an arrest in a public place, it is not enough to authorize entry into a private dwelling to arrest someone inside. Fear of warrantless intrusions by British customs officials searching for goods imported in violation of British law was the catalyst that led to the Fourth Amendment's adoption.[248] This concern is reflected in the language of the Fourth Amendment, which declares that: "the right of the people to be secure in their . . . houses . . . shall not be violated." The Supreme Court has established a firm and inflexible rule concerning arrests inside private dwellings. Absent consent or exigent circumstances, police may not enter a private dwelling to arrest someone inside unless a magistrate issues a warrant.[249]

Figure 3.25
Requirements for Making an Arrest Inside a Private Dwelling

	Type of Warrant	Procedure for Execution	Excuse for Noncompliance
Arrestee's residence	Arrest warrant	Knock-and-announce presence	• Consent to enter given by person with authority
Third party's residence	Arrest warrant and residence search warrant	Knock-and-announce presence	• Hot pursuit of a suspect wanted for a felony • Danger to officer's safety • Danger to a third party • Risk of the suspect's escape • Risk of destruction of evidence

A. Type of Warrant Required

The Fourth Amendment makes provisions for two kinds of warrant — arrest and search. The type of warrant needed to make an arrest inside a private residence depends on who resides there. When the person to be arrested resides on the premises, police are only required to have an arrest warrant. When the residence belongs to someone else, police must also have a search warrant, because they may have to search the person's home in order to find the suspect.[250] Thus, when police officers come to B's house to arrest A, who does not reside there, they must come armed with two warrants — a search warrant authorizing them to search B's residence and an arrest warrant authorizing them to arrest A.[251] If A and B both reside on the premises, an arrest warrant will suffice. In a society in which people frequently move in with friends or family for

---

[248]   United States v. United States District Court, 407 U.S. 297, 92 S. Ct. 2125, 32 L. Ed. 2d 752 (1972).
[249]   Kirk v. Louisiana, *supra* note 208; **Payton v. New York, *supra* note 208.**
[250]   Steagald v. United States, 451 U.S. 204, 101 S. Ct. 1642, 68 L. Ed. 2d 38 (1981).
[251]   *Id.*

extended periods, deciding whether a suspect "resides" at a particular location or is simply visiting can be problematic. When in doubt about this matter, officers should come equipped with both warrants.

B. *Locations Covered by the Warrant Requirement*

The police are required to obtain a warrant only when the arrest is made inside a private dwelling. They do not have to procure a warrant to make an arrest in a public place or inside a commercial establishment. Dwellings, for purposes of the Fourth Amendment, include hotel and motel rooms and temporary residences, as well as permanent residences.[252]

Fourth Amendment protection against warrantless arrests starts on the other side of the front door. Police do not need a warrant to arrest people who are standing in their yard, on their front porch, or even in an open doorway, because people who stand in a place where they are visible to the public have a reduced expectation of privacy.[253]

Moreover, because the purpose of requiring a warrant is to protect the sanctity of the home, the Fourth Amendment is not violated by the use of noncoercive ploys to induce suspects to leave their home so that police can arrest them without a warrant outside.[254] People who voluntarily leave the confines of their home cannot complain if they are arrested without a warrant.

C. *"Knock and Announce" Requirement*[255]

The Fourth Amendment requires police to knock and announce their identity and purpose before forcing their way into a person's home to make an arrest.[256] This requirement can be traced to the early common law and has withstood the test of time because it makes good sense. Compliance protects privacy by giving the occupants an opportunity to collect themselves, avoids unnecessary destruction of property, and protects police from being shot in the mistaken belief that they are burglars.

---

[252]   Hoffa v. United States, 385 U.S. 293, 87 S. Ct. 408, 17 L. Ed. 2d 374 (1966); Stoner v. California, 376 U.S. 483, 84 S. Ct. 889, 11 L. Ed. 2d 856 (1964).

[253]   United States v. Santana, 427 U.S. 38, 96 S. Ct. 2406, 49 L. Ed. 2d 300 (1976) (open doorway); Dyer v. State, 680 So. 2d 612 (Fla. Dist. Ct. App. 1996) (yard).

[254]   Alvarez v. Montgomery County, Maryland, 963 F. Supp. 495 (D. Md. 1997); United States v. Vasiliavitchious, 919 F. Supp. 1113 (N.D. Ill. 1996).

[255]   The procedures described in this section apply to execution of both arrest and search warrants.

[256]   United States v. Banks, 540 U.S. 31, 124 S. Ct. 521, 157 L. Ed. 2d 343 (2003); United States v. Ramirez, 523 U.S. 65, 118 S. Ct. 992, 140 L. Ed. 2d 191 (1998); Richards v. Wisconsin, 520 U.S. 385, 117 S. Ct. 1416, 137 L. Ed. 2d 615 (1997); Wilson v. Arkansas, 514 U.S. 927, 115 S. Ct. 1914, 131 L. Ed. 2d 976 (1995). A civil action for damages is the only remedy available for violations of the knock-and-announce requirement. When police have a valid warrant, the exclusionary rule does not apply. In Hudson v. Michigan, 547 U.S. 586, 126 S. Ct. 2159, 165 L. Ed. 2d 56 (2006), the Court explained that illegality in the manner of the entry is not sufficiently related to the subsequent discovery of evidence to justify invoking the suppression remedy when a search is conducted under a valid search warrant.

Accordingly, police must normally do two things before they can force their way into a person's home to make an arrest: (1) secure the appropriate warrant or warrants and (2) knock and announce their presence.

D. Exceptions that Excuse Compliance with the Warrant and/or Knock and Announce Requirements

There are three exceptions that excuse both the need for a warrant or for knocking: (1) consent, (2) **hot pursuit**, and (3) exigent circumstances. However, police must still have probable cause to believe that the person to be arrested committed an offense and a reasonable belief that the person will be found inside.[257]

Consent. Police officers do not need an arrest warrant to walk up to a person's front door, ring the bell, and ask for permission to enter. Permission given by someone with authority eliminates the need for a warrant. To have authority, the person must live on the premises.[258] Any person of sufficient age who resides on the premises can give valid consent. Hotel clerks,[259] landlords,[260] nonresident caretakers,[261] and occasional babysitters[262] lack authority to give police permission to enter because they do not reside on the premises.

Consent is effective only if it is given voluntarily. Consent given in response to an ordinary knock on the door and a nonauthoritarian request for permission to enter is considered voluntary[263]; consent procured by pounding on the door and shouting "open in the name of the law" is not.[264] Police do not have to advise the person answering the door that she has the right to withhold consent in order for consent to be voluntary.[265] Nor do police have to reveal their true identity.[266] People who invite a police officer into their home expose themselves to a warrantless arrest, even though they are mistaken as

---

[257] **Payton v. New York**, *supra* note 208.
[258] United States v. Matlock, 415 U.S. 164, 94 S. Ct. 988, 39 L. Ed. 2d 242 (1974); Illinois v. Rodriguez, 497 U.S. 177, 110 S. Ct. 2793, 111 L. Ed. 2d 148 (1990); Humphrey v. State, 327 Ark. 753, 940 S. W.2d 860 (1997).
[259] Stoner v. California, 376 U.S. 483, 84 S. Ct. 889, 11 L. Ed. 2d 856 (1964).
[260] United States v. Elliott, 50 F.3d 180 (2d Cir. 1995).
[261] Peterson v. People, 939 P.2d 824 (Colo. 1997) (*en banc*).
[262] People v. Walter, 890 P.2d 240 (Colo. Ct. App. 1994).
[263] United States v. Vaneaton, 49 F.3d 1423 (9th Cir. 1995), *cert. denied*, 516 U.S. 1176, 116 S. Ct. 1271, 134 L. Ed. 2d 218 (1996).
[264] United States v. Conner, 127 F.3d 663 (8th Cir. 1997).
[265] **United States v. Drayton**, *supra* note 21; Ohio v. Robinette, *supra* note 187; Schneckloth v. Busta-monte, *supra* note 121.
[266] Lewis v. United States, 385 U.S. 206, 87 S. Ct. 424, 17 L. Ed. 2d 312 (1966) (consent valid even though officer gained entry by pretending to be a drug buyer); United States v. Bramble, 103 F.3d 1475 (9th Cir. 1996) (consent valid even though officer gained entry by pretending to respond to advertisement); State v. Johnston, 84 Wis. 2d 794, 518 N.W.2d 759 (1994) (consent valid even though officer gained entry by posing as an invited party guest); People v. Catania, 140 Mich. App. 755, 366 N.W.2d 38 (1985) (consent valid even though officer gained entry by posing as a motorist experiencing car trouble who needed to make a phone call).

to their visitor's identity. However, consent is not voluntary when entrance is gained under a false assertion that police have a warrant because the occupant is misled into believing that she has no authority to resist the entry.[267]

Exigent circumstances. Police officers are not required to obtain a warrant or to knock and announce their presence before making a nonconsensual entry when they are confronted with exigent circumstances.[268] For exigent circumstances to exist, the officer must have reason to believe that complying with one or both of these require-ments will: (1) endanger the lives or safety of the officer, the suspect, or a third party; (2) enable the suspect to escape; or (3) lead to the destruction of evidence.[269]

The exigent circumstances exception applies only to arrests for serious offenses. It does not apply to arrests for traffic violations and misdemeanors.[270]

Hot pursuit. Police are also allowed to enter a private residence, without a warrant and without knocking, when they are in continuous hot pursuit of a suspected felon, encountered in a public place, who flees and takes refuge inside.[271] Suspects are not allowed to thwart an otherwise proper arrest that has been set in motion in a public place by retreating into their home. Police may follow them inside and arrest them. This rule was announced in United States v. Santana.[272] Police went to a known stash house to arrest a suspect who had earlier sold drugs to an undercover officer. They were within 15 feet of the house when they recognized the suspect standing in the entranceway of her home. As soon as she saw them, she ran into the house. The police followed in hot pursuit and arrested her in the vestibule. The Supreme Court ruled that when the police undertake to make a lawful arrest without a warrant in a public place and the suspect flees into his or her home, the police may follow and make the arrest inside. The Court treated the suspect's entranceway as a public place, for purposes of this rule, because

---

[267] Bumper v. North Carolina, 391 U.S. 543, 88 S. Ct. 1788, 20 L. Ed. 2d 787 (1968) (Fourth Amend-ment violated when consent to enter was obtained only after officer falsely asserted that he had a warrant); Truelove v. Hung, 67 F. Supp. 2d 569 (D.S.C. 1999) (Fourth Amendment violated when police gained entry into home under a forged custody order issued by nonexistent court).

[268] **Brigham City v. Stuart, 547 U.S. 398, 126 S. Ct. 1943, 164 L. Ed. 2d 650 (2006)**; United States v. Santana, *supra* note 253; Griffin v. City of Clanton, 932 F. Supp. 1359 (M.D. Ala. 1996) (third party's home).

[269] **Brigham City v. Stuart**, *supra* note 268 (Officers, responding to a complaint about a loud party, who heard fighting and yelling inside and observed a youth through the window striking an adult with enough force to cause the adult to spit blood, were justified in entering a home without a warrant, under exigent circumstances exception to warrant requirement); Richards v. Wisconsin, 520 U.S. 385, 117 S. Ct. 1416, 137 L. Ed. 2d 615 (1997) (Officers conducting felony drug investigation are justified in making no-knock entry where they have reasonable suspicion that knocking and an-nouncing their presence will lead to destruction of evidence).

[270] United States v. Banks, *supra* note 256; Welsh v. Wisconsin, 466 U.S. 740, 104 S. Ct. 2091, 80 L. Ed. 2d 732 (1984).

[271] United States v. Santana, *supra* note 253 (suspect may not defeat a felony arrest set in motion in a public place by fleeing into her house).

[272] *Id.*

she was as visible to the public while standing there as she would have been if she had been standing on a public street.

The hot pursuit exception, like the exigent circumstances exception, only applies to serious crimes. Police may not pursue suspects into their home to arrest them for a minor offense, such as drunk driving.[273] When a petty offender manages to flee and takes sanctuary inside his or her home, officers must stop at the threshold, turn around, and get an arrest warrant.

Figure 3.26
Fourth Amendment Restrictions on Force

The force used in making an arrest or other seizure must be objectively reasonable in light of the facts and circumstances confronting the officer, including the seriousness of the crime, whether the suspect poses an immediate threat to the safety of the officer or others, actively resists arrest, or attempts to flee.

Deadly force — force likely to cause death or serious bodily harm — is allowed only when the officer has probable cause to believe that such force is necessary for self-defense or to protect others from serious bodily harm. A warning ("Stop or I'll shoot") must be given before using deadly force, whenever feasible.

§ 3.16 Use of Force in Making an Arrest or Other Seizure

Our Constitution accepts that force is sometimes necessary to maintain law and order, but regulates unconstitutional applications in three separate provision — the Fourth, Eighth, and Fourteenth Amendments. Each covers a different phase of the criminal process and imposes a different standard for when force is excessive. The Fourth Amendment prohibits excessive force in making investigatory stops, arrests, and other seizures.[274] The Eighth Amendment prohibits use of unconstitutional force on prisoners serving sentence,[275] and the Fourteenth Amendment regulates the period in between arrest and conviction.[276] Thus, our Constitution protects persons in the custody of the law from unconstitutional applications of force continuously from their initial seizure until they have completed their sentence.

---

[273] Welsh v. Wisconsin, *supra* note 270 (hot pursuit exception to warrant requirement does not apply to DUI arrest).

[274] Graham v. Connor, 490 U.S. 386, 109 S. Ct. 1865, 104 L. Ed. 2d 443 (1989).

[275] Hope v. Pelzer, 536 U.S. 730, 122 S. Ct. 2508, 153 L. Ed. 2d 666 (2002) (holding that handcuffing a prisoner to a hitching post in the hot sun for an extended period violated the Eighth Amendment ban on cruel and unusual punishment).

[276] Graham v. Connor, *supra* note 274.

A. *Fourth Amendment Requirement of Objective Reasonableness*

The Fourth Amendment prohibits excessive force in making arrests or other seizures.[277] The standard used to determine when force is excessive is objective reasonableness. *The question is whether a reasonable police officer, confronted with the same facts, would have believed that this level of force was necessary.*[278]

There are three legitimate reasons for using force: (1) for self-defense or protection of others from physical harm, (2) to overcome resistance, or (3) to prevent escape.[279] All others are illegitimate. Police, for example, are not justified in using their nightsticks on people who "mouth off" at them.[280] Further, although force may be justified to overcome resistance, once a suspect has been subdued, the force must cease.[281] Striking, hitting, kicking, and tasering suspects after they have been brought under control violates the Fourth Amendment[282] and, in extreme cases, can result in federal criminal prosecution.[283]

The severity of the crime, whether the suspect posed an immediate threat to the safety of the officer or others, actively resisted arrest, or attempted to flee, is the primary consideration in evaluating whether the level of force used was reasonable.[284] The Supreme Court has cautioned that appropriate allowance must be made "for the fact that police officers are often forced to make split-second judgments — in circumstances that are tense, uncertain, and rapidly evolving — about the amount of force that is necessary in a particular situation."[285] In judging reasonableness, courts are required to focus on the particular moment when the force was used. The issue is not whether the officer made prior errors of judgment that contributed to the need for force or whether alternative strategies existed; the question is whether the officer made a reasonable split-second judgment at this precise moment in time.[286]

B. *Special Limitations on the Use of Deadly Force*

The Fourth Amendment imposes additional limitations on the use of deadly force — force likely to cause death or seriously bodily injury. Society's interest in effective law enforcement does not always justify taking a human life in order to

---

[277]   *Id.*; Tennessee v. Garner, 471 U.S. 1, 105 S. Ct. 1694, 85 L. Ed. 2d 1 (1985).

[278]   *See* cases *supra* note 277.

[279]   *Id.*

[280]   Stewart v. Bailey, 876 F. Supp. 1571 (N.D. Ala. 1996).

[281]   Ellis v. Wynalda, 999 F.2d 243 (7th Cir. 1993).

[282]   Frazell v. Flanigan, 102 F.3d 877 (7th Cir. 1996); Rambo v. Daley, 68 F.3d 203 (7th Cir. 1995).

[283]   18 U.S.C. § 242 is a federal statute that imposes criminal liability on persons who willfully violate federal constitutional rights while acting under the color of the law.

[284]   Graham v. Connor, *supra* note 274.

[285]   *Id.*, 490 U.S. at 396, 109 S. Ct. at 1872.

[286]   *See, e.g.*, Carter v. Buscher, 973 F.2d 1328 (7th Cir. 1992); Schultz v. Long, 44 F.3d 643 (8th Cir. 1995); Forrett v. Richardson, 112 F.3d 416 (9th Cir. 1997); Stephens v. City of Butler, 509 F. Supp. 2d 1098 (S.D. Ala. 2007).

prevent a suspect from escaping. In some circumstances, the Fourth Amendment requires that police officers allow a suspect to escape rather than kill him or her.[287]

This has not always been the rule. The common law allowed police to use all necessary force, including deadly force, to effect an arrest for any felony. In *Tennessee v. Garner*,[288] the Supreme Court decided that the value of human life must also be considered in determining whether deadly force is reasonable. The decision arose out of the tragic death of a 15-year-old youth who had burglarized a house. The officer interrupted the burglary and chased the youth until cornering him against a six-foot chain-link fence. The officer observed the youth with a flashlight, determined that he was unarmed, and ordered him to stop. The youth disobeyed and began climbing the fence. The officer shot the youth in the back of the head to prevent him from escaping, as he was authorized to do under state law because the burglary was a felony. A purse with $10 was found beside the youth's body.

The Supreme Court, horrified by the boy's senseless death, wrote:

> The use of deadly force to prevent the escape of all felony suspects, whatever the circumstances, is constitutionally unreasonable. It is not better that all felony suspects die than that they escape. Where the suspect poses no immediate threat to the officer and no threat to others, the harm resulting from failing to apprehend him does not justify the use of deadly force to do so.... A police officer may not seize an unarmed, non-dangerous suspect by shooting him dead.[289]

The Court stated that for the use of deadly force to be constitutionally reasonable, the officer must have "probable cause to believe that the suspect poses a threat of serious physical harm, either to the officer or to others." The Court went on to identify two situations where this standard is met: (1) when the suspect threatens the officer or someone else with a weapon and (2) when it is necessary to prevent escape of a suspect who has committed a crime involving the infliction or threatened infliction of serious physical harm, and his escape will be dangerous to society. In the second situation, the officer is required to issue a warning ("stop or I'll shoot") before resorting to deadly force, if it is feasible to do so.[290] The youth in *Tennessee v. Garner* was unarmed and not dangerous. The Court ruled that police may not shoot to kill an unarmed, nondangerous suspect who is trying to escape on foot.

In *Scott v. Harris*,[291] the Supreme Court was asked to apply *Tennessee v. Garner* in the context of a high-speed chase. The chase began when police tried to pull a motorist

---

[287] **Tennessee v. Garner,** *supra* note 277.

[288] *Id.*

[289] *Id.*

[290] *Id.*

[291] **550 U.S. 372, 127 S. Ct. 1769, 167 L. Ed. 2d 290 (2007)** (Officer's use of his vehicle to ram fleeing motorist's vehicle, causing the motorist to lose control and crash, was objectively reasonable because the motorist's high-speed, reckless flight imminently endangered the lives of innocent bystanders). *See also* Brosseau v. Haugen, 543 U.S. 194, 125 S. Ct. 596, 160 L. Ed. 2d 583 (2004) (holding that shooting was not necessarily unreasonable where disturbed felon attempted to flee in a vehicle, endangering the safety of officers on foot and others in the immediate area).

over for a speeding violation. The motorist sped away and led the police on a high-speed chase, traveling 85 miles per hour down a two-lane road in the dead of the night, running red lights and crossing double yellow traffic lines. After ten minutes, police decided to terminate the dangerous pursuit by ramming the motorist's car from behind. The motorist lost control of the vehicle, crashed, and was rendered a quadriplegic. He sued, claiming that the police were not justified in using potentially deadly force because he had not threatened anyone with a weapon and had no known record of crimes involving serious bodily harm.

The Court held that the illustrations mentioned in *Tennessee v. Garner* were not intended as an exhaustive list of instances in which deadly force may be employed. That case involved "an application of the Fourth Amendment's 'reasonableness test' to the use of a particular type of force in a particular situation.'" The question in this case was not whether the factors mentioned in *Tennessee v. Garner* were present, but whether the officer's actions were reasonable under the circumstances.

A police video of the chase persuaded the Court that the plaintiff's flight endangered innocent bystanders, as well as the officers involved in the chase. In weighing the lesser probability of injuring or killing numerous innocent bystanders against the greater probability of injuring or killing the suspect, police were entitled to consider not only the number of lives at risk, but also their relative culpability. The suspect had "intentionally placed himself and the public in danger by unlawfully engaging in the reckless, high-speed flight that ultimately produced the choice between [these] two evils . . . ."

The Court rejected the motorist's further argument that "the innocent public [could] have been protected, and the tragic accident entirely avoided, if police had simply ceased their pursuit." The Court pointed out that there was no certainty that the motorist would have slowed down if the police abandoned their pursuit; he might have construed this as simply the beginning of a new strategy for his capture. More important, laying down a rule "requiring the police to allow fleeing suspects to get away whenever they drive so recklessly that they put other lives in danger" would create a "perverse incentive" for suspects, trying to elude the police, to drive faster and even more recklessly. The Court concluded that the officer had acted reasonably in using deadly force to neutralize an actual and immediate threat to the lives of innocent bystanders.

Whether use of deadly force is reasonable requires an objective assessment of the danger a suspect poses *at that moment*. Even though the suspect has committed a crime involving the use or threatened use of serious physical harm, deadly force is not justified if the suspect does not pose an imminent threat of harm to others at the time when he is shot.[292] Deadly force was not justified in a case where FBI snipers, conducting surveillance of a cabin occupied by a person believed to be responsible for killing an officer the previous day, shot him in the back, without warning, as he

---

[292]   Harris v. Roderick, 126 F.3d 1189 (9th Cir. 1997).

ran toward the cabin for safety.[293] Although the suspect had exchanged fire with the police the previous day, at the time he was shot, he posed no danger to anyone. The court stated:

> Law enforcement officials may not kill suspects who do not pose an immediate threat to their safety or to the safety of others simply because they are armed . . . . A desire to prevent an armed suspect from entering the place he is residing because it may be difficult to persuade him to reemerge is insufficient cause to kill him. Other means exist for bringing the offender to justice, even if additional time and effort are required.

§ 3.17   State Arrest Laws

The Fourth Amendment establishes the constitutional minimum for a lawful arrest. States remain free, as a matter of local law, to impose more stringent requirements.[294] Violations of state requirements generally have the same consequences as violations of the Fourth Amendment. This means that detaining suspects for investigation longer than state law allows, or failing to obtain a warrant when state law requires one, will probably result in suppression of evidence, even if the arrest satisfies the Fourth Amendment. Compliance with state arrest laws is more important today than in former times. The Supreme Court's gradual retrenchment from the liberal Fourth Amendment jurisprudence of the Warren and Burger Court eras has created a situation in which state law often affords greater protection than the Fourth Amendment. This shift has led defense attorneys to scrutinize for state law violations more carefully than they once did. Because arrest laws vary from state to state, only a cursory examination is possible. Each student is responsible for determining whether the laws of her state impose special restrictions on a police officer's arrest authority.

A. *Distinctions between Authority to Arrest for Felonies and Misdemeanors*

All states have statutes defining the conditions under which arrests are authorized.[295] They diverge from federal law primarily in their treatment of misdemeanors. In a majority of states, a warrant is necessary to arrest for a misdemeanor unless the

---

[293]   *Id.*

[294]   Oregon v. Hass, 420 U.S. 714, 95 S. Ct. 1215, 43 L. Ed. 2d 570 (1975). An arrest is valid under the Fourth Amendment whenever police have probable cause to make the arrest, even though the arrest violates state law. *See, e.g.*, Virginia v. Moore, 553 U.S. 164, 128 S. Ct. 1598, 170 L. Ed. 2d 559 (2008) (police did not violate the Fourth Amendment by arresting motorist whom they had probable cause to believe was driving with suspended license, even though the misdemeanor offense of driving with a suspended license was one for which they were required to issue a summons under state law).

[295]   *See, e.g.*, KY. REV. STAT. § 431.005(1).

misdemeanor is committed in the officer's presence.[296] This distinction is not required by the Fourth Amendment[297]; it is a relic that survives from the common law.[298]

The statute below codifies the common law.

(1) A peace officer may make an arrest:

    (a) In obedience to a warrant; or

    (b) Without a warrant when a felony is committed in his presence; or

    (c) Without a warrant when he has probable cause to believe that the person being arrested has committed a felony; or

    (d) Without a warrant when a misdemeanor . . . has been committed in his presence . . .[299]

This statute is modeled on the common law. Under subsection (1)(a), peace officers may arrest for any offense when they have an arrest warrant. When they do not, their arrest authority depends on whether the offense is a felony or a misdemeanor. If the offense is a misdemeanor, subsection (d) controls; they may arrest without a warrant only if the misdemeanor is committed in their presence. If the offense is a felony, subsection (c) controls; they may arrest without a warrant based on probable cause alone. Subsection (b) is redundant because, when a felony is committed in the officer's presence, the officer almost invariably has probable cause to believe the person committed a felony and thus already has authority to arrest under subsection (c).

A growing number of states are now moving toward a unified standard that grants arrest authority to the full extent allowed under the Fourth Amendment.[300] In Illinois, for example, "[a]ny law enforcement officer may make an arrest without a warrant if the officer has probable cause to believe that the person has committed or is committing any crime, . . . even if the crime was not committed in the presence of the officer."[301] A unified standard based on the Fourth Amendment is simpler and offers fewer opportunities for mistakes. Officers do not have to make an on-the-spot determination whether the crime is a felony or misdemeanor, or whether the offense took place in his/her presence.

---

[296] *See. generally*, William A. Schroeder, *Warrantless Misdemeanor Arrests and the Fourth Amendment*, 58 Mo. L. Rev. 771 (1993).

[297] Although the Supreme Court has never squarely faced this issue, there are numerous lower federal court cases holding that the Fourth Amendment does not require that a misdemeanor be committed in the arresting officer's presence. Arrests are valid under the federal Constitution based on probable cause alone. *See, e.g.*, Woods v. City of Chicago, 234 F.3d 979 (7th Cir. 2000) (Warrantless arrest for misdemeanor assault did not violate Fourth Amendment, even though alleged assault did not did not occur in arresting officers' presence); Street v. Surdyka, 492 F.2d 368 (4th Cir.1974) (warrantless arrests by police officers for misdemeanors committed outside of their presence . . . do not violate the Fourth Amendment so long as the arrest is supported by probable cause).

[298] 10 Halsbury's Laws of England 344–345 (3d ed. 1955); 4 W. Blackstone Commentaries* 292; 1 J. STEPHEN A HISTORY OF THE CRIMINAL LAW OF ENGLAND 193 (1883).

[299] KY. REV. STAT. § 431.005(1).

[300] *See, e.g.*, COLO. REV. STAT. § 16-3-102.

[301] ILL. COMP. STAT. § 5.112A-26(2).

A few states take an intermediate position, authorizing warrantless arrests for misdemeanors not committed in the officer's presence when the officer is confronted with exigent circumstances.[302] In Nebraska, for example, police have the authority to make a warrantless arrest for a misdemeanor when the offender is likely to flee, destroy or conceal evidence, cause injury to self or others, or cause damage to property unless apprehended immediately.[303] Another variation is to authorize warrantless arrests for designated misdemeanors or classes of misdemeanors.[304]

B. Determining Whether an Offense is a Misdemeanor or a Felony

Whether an offense is a felony or misdemeanor turns on the punishment. Offenses punishable by death or imprisonment (usually of one year or more) are classified as felonies, while those punishable by fines or jail sentences are treated as misdemeanors. In jurisdictions where arrest laws make a distinction between felony and misdemeanor arrests, officers are required to make an on-the-spot determination of the nature of the offense involved. Remembering the punishments for every offense is next to impossible. When in doubt, the officer should get a warrant because this ensures that the arrest will be valid for either.

C. Meaning of "In the Officer's Presence"

For a misdemeanor to be committed "in the officer's presence," the officer must be aware that it is taking place while it is still in progress. This does not mean that the officer has to observe it from beginning to end. However, the misdemeanor is not committed in the officer's presence if it is completed before she arrives. The officer does not actually have to see it for the misdemeanor to occur in her presence. It is enough that the officer is aware that it is taking place through any of her natural senses — sight, touch, hearing, smell, or taste. The first three illustrations below satisfy this requirement. We will let you decide for yourself whether the fourth one does.

1. Officer Blake answers a 911 domestic disturbance call. While waiting for the door to be opened, she hears a man shouting "I'll kill you, you bitch!" the sound of struggling, and a woman screaming "Please, don't hit me again!"[305]
2. While conducting a traffic stop, Officer Blake smells alcohol on the driver's breath and marijuana smoke in the passenger compartment.
3. A government informant agrees to wear a radio transmitter concealed under his clothing while making a drug purchase. Officer Blake electronically monitors the transaction from a squad car several blocks away.[306]

---

[302] *See, e.g.*, NEB. REV. STAT. § 29-404.02(2); WYO. STAT. ANN. § 7-2-103(4).
[303] NEB. REV. STAT. § 29-404.02(2).
[304] MD. ANN. CODE art. 27, § 594B (d)(e).
[305] State v. Bryant, 678 S. W. 2d 480 (1984).
[306] *See, e.g.*, Carranza v. State, 266 Ga. 263, 467 S.E.2d 315 (1996).

4. Officer Blake, walking a beat, rounds a corner where she spots Sticky-Fingered Sam, standing beside a puddle of liquid, zipping up his trousers. Was Sam's offense of public urination committed in Officer Blake's presence?[307]

When arrest authority derives from the commission of a misdemeanor in the officer's presence, the arrest must be made on the spot or in hot pursuit. If the arrest is not made until later, a warrant is necessary. As an illustration, suppose that Officer Blake sees Sticky-Fingered Sam steal a bike and ride away. Several hours later, she spots Sam on foot. If she works in a jurisdiction that requires a warrant to arrest for misdemeanors unless committed in an officer's presence and bike theft is a misdemeanor, she would lack the authority to arrest Sam unless she has procured an arrest warrant in the meantime.

§ 3.18   — Territorial Limits on a Police Officer's Arrest Authority

State and local police officers have territorial limits on their arrest authority — both intrastate (within the state) and interstate (between states).

A. Intrastate Territorial Limits

In the absence of a statute, a police officer lacks the authority to take official action outside the boundaries of the government unit in which he holds appointment.[308] However, many states today have statutes authorizing statewide service of arrest warrants.[309] A warrant issued by a magistrate in one part of the state can also have an indirect effect in other parts of the state. Suppose, for example, that Sticky-Fingered Sam is stopped for a traffic violation in County A and the officer learns from a computer check that County B has an outstanding warrant for Sam's arrest on a felony charge. Knowledge that County B has issued a warrant for Sam's arrest provides probable cause to believe that Sam committed a felony, and thus furnishes grounds for making a warrantless arrest in County A.[310]

Fresh pursuit is an important exception to the rule that police lack the authority to make an arrest outside their territorial jurisdiction. Fresh pursuit refers to the immediate, uninterrupted pursuit of a person who is trying to avoid apprehension. Under the common law and the statutes of most states, police are allowed to enter other parts of the state in order to make an arrest when they are in fresh pursuit. The common law limited this privilege to felony arrests. For misdemeanors and traffic violations,

[307] United States v. Williams, 754 F.2d 1001 (D.C. Cir. 1985).
[308] State v. Masat, 239 Neb. 849, 479 N. W. 2d 131 (1992).
[309] *See, e.g.,* N.J. STAT. ANN. § 39:5-28.
[310] People v. Gouker, 665 P.2d 113 (Colo. 1983) (*en banc*).

the chase had to end at the district or county line.[311] Although a few states retain this limitation, a growing number of states now authorize statewide fresh pursuit for all offenses.[312] The Delaware statute below is typical:

> Any peace officer of a duly organized county, municipality, town, interstate bridge or university peace unit . . . may carry out fresh pursuit of any person anywhere within this State, regardless of the original territorial jurisdiction of such officer, in order to arrest such person pursued, when there are reasonable grounds to suspect that a felony, misdemeanor, or violation of the Motor Vehicle Code has been committed in this State by such person.[313]

If Sticky-Fingered Sam lives in Delaware, Officer Blake may pursue him across district or county lines and chase him throughout the state to arrest him for any offense. While investigatory stops are rarely mentioned in fresh pursuit statutes, fresh pursuit statutes are generally interpreted to cover them as well.[314]

B. *Interstate Territorial Limits*

Each state is a sovereign political entity. Authority conferred by state law ends at the state line. Police officers do not carry their authority with them when they enter a second state. This limitation stems from the nature of our federal union. Under our federal system, no state can confer authority effective in another state. Before a police officer can take official action in another state, the state in which the action is taken must grant this authority.

Interstate cooperation within the law enforcement community is on the increase. Most states provide for issuance of "fugitive arrest warrants," directing the arrest of persons found inside the state who are wanted elsewhere so they can be returned for trial.[315] Most states also have interstate fresh pursuit statutes, authorizing out-of-state police officers to enter the state in fresh pursuit to make an arrest for a felony.[316] The Delaware statute below, which authorizes interstate fresh pursuit for any offense, is broader than most.

> Any member of a duly organized state, county, or municipal peace unit of another state of the United States who enters this State in fresh pursuit, and continues within this State in such fresh pursuit, of a person in order to arrest the person on the ground that the person is believed to have committed a felony, a misdemeanor or a violation of the motor vehicle code in such other state, shall have the same authority to arrest and hold such person in custody, as has any member of any duly organized state, county or municipal peace unit of this State, to arrest . . .[317]

---

[311]   *See, e.g.,* State v. Stahl, 838 P.2d 1193 (Wyo. 1992).
[312]   *See, e.g.,* DEL. CODE ANN. TIT. 11, § 1935.
[313]   *Id.*
[314]   People v. Pollard, 216 Ill. App. 3d 591, 575 N.E.2d 970 (1991).
[315]   *See, e.g.,* CAL. PENAL CODE § 1551; NEB. REV. STAT. at § 29-409.
[316]   *See, e.g.,* TEX. CODE CRIM. P. ANN. art. 14.051.
[317]   DEL. CODE ANN. TIT. 11, § 1932(a).

Application of the fresh pursuit doctrine has become increasingly common as means of rapid transportation have improved. To understand the exact territorial limits of their arrest authority, officers must be familiar with the fresh pursuit statutes of all neighboring states, as well as their own.

An officer who makes an extraterritorial arrest not authorized by the laws of the jurisdiction in which the arrest is made has the same authority as a private citizen.[318] State laws vary on the circumstances in which citizens may make an arrest, but whatever authority a citizen has can generally be claimed by an out-of-state police officer.[319]

§ 3.19   Summary and Practical Suggestions

The Fourth Amendment prohibits unreasonable seizures of persons. A seizure occurs when a person submits to a police officer's show of legal authority or the officer gains actual physical control over him or her. Police officers do not need any grounds to approach members of the public and ask for their voluntary cooperation in resolving the officer's suspicion of them. To determine whether the suspect's cooperation was voluntary or resulted from a seizure, the court inquires into whether a reasonable person in the suspect's position would have believed that he was free to disregard the officer's request and leave. If a reasonable person would not have felt free to leave, a suspect who cooperates is seized.

Seizures are broken down into two categories — investigatory stops and arrests. Under *Terry v. Ohio*, an officer is permitted to detain a person for investigation when the officer is aware of specific, articulable facts that, in light of the officer's prior experience, would warrant a reasonable police officer in suspecting that the person detained is committing, has committed, or is about to commit a crime. Once the stop is made, the officer may conduct a weapons frisk if, in addition to the grounds for the stop, the officer has a reasonable suspicion that the detainee may be armed and dangerous. An officer may not search a detainee for objects other than weapons, but may seize nondangerous contraband when it is in plain view or is detected through plain "feel" or touch without overstepping the boundaries of a *Terry* pat down search. The officer must proceed with the investigation expeditiously in order to avoid unnecessarily prolonging the period of involuntary detention. *Miranda* warnings are not necessary unless the encounter becomes a custodial arrest.

There is no bright line separating *Terry* stops from custodial arrests. Factors that courts consider in determining when a stop, made on a reasonable suspicion, has escalated into an arrest, for which probable cause is necessary, include the duration of the detention, the diligence with which the officers pursue the investigation, and the scope and intrusiveness of the detention. If the detention lasts too long or is too intrusive to be allowed on reasonable suspicion, the encounter becomes a *de facto* arrest.

---

[318]   Stevenson v. State, 287 Md. 504, 413 A.2d 1340 (1980).

[319]   *Id.*

During *Terry* stops, police officers are not allowed to conduct evidentiary searches, take detainees to a police station, or perform any acts that are more intrusive than necessary to conduct the investigation or for safety and security. As a general rule, the stop may not last longer than 90 minutes.

To justify an arrest, police officers must have probable cause to believe the person has committed or is committing a crime. Probable cause for an arrest may be based on a variety of sources other than the officer's own observations. These sources include physical evidence found at the scene; information supplied by other law enforcement officers or agencies, or in police records; reports received from victims, eyewitnesses, and informants; and rational inferences drawn from the officer's prior experience. The facts and circumstances known to the officer are considered in combination and evaluated from the perspective of a trained police officer. Probable cause exists when the facts and circumstances known to the officer at the moment of arrest are sufficient to warrant a belief that the person to be arrested committed a crime.

The same standard is also used to evaluate whether probable cause exists for the issuance of an arrest warrant. Absent exigent circumstances or hot pursuit, police officers must obtain an arrest warrant before making a nonconsensual entry into a private dwelling to arrest someone inside. When the dwelling belongs to someone else, the Fourth Amendment also requires a search warrant. A majority of states, by statute, also require police officers to obtain an arrest warrant in order to arrest for a misdemeanor, unless the misdemeanor is committed in the officer's presence.

The preferable method of making an arrest is under the authority of a warrant, even when one is not required. A properly issued arrest warrant ensures the admissibility of evidence seized during the arrest and immunizes the arresting officer from liability for making an unconstitutional arrest. However, these advantages will be lost if the officer deliberately or recklessly misstates facts in the affidavit, or if the affidavit fails to contain enough information about the underlying facts to enable the magistrate to make an independent determination of probable cause. Persons arrested without a warrant are entitled to a post-arrest judicial review of grounds for their arrest no later than 48 hours after the arrest unless they have already been released on bail.

Traffic stops involve seizures and require probable cause or reasonable suspicion unless they are made at a fixed checkpoint. Evidence of drugs uncovered during a pretextual traffic stop is admissible if police have grounds for the underlying stop and do not exceed the limits on scope and duration, which are similar to *Terry* stops.

The Fourth Amendment prohibits excessive force in making a seizure. Force is excessive if it is more than a reasonable police officer on the scene would have considered necessary. The severity of the crime, whether the suspect posed an immediate threat to the safety of the officer or others, actively resisted arrest, or attempted to flee, is the primary considerations bearing on the degree of force that may be used. Additional restrictions exist on the use of deadly force — force likely to cause death or serious bodily harm. Deadly force may not be used unless the suspect poses an imminent danger of serious physical harm to an officer or others; a warning must be given, whenever feasible, before resorting to deadly force.

Search and Seizure

4

The right of the people to be secure in their persons, houses, papers, and effects, against unreasonable searches and seizures, shall not be violated, and no Warrants shall issue, but upon probable cause, supported by Oath or affirmation, and particularly describing the place to be searched, and the persons or things to be seized.

Fourth Amendment

Chapter Outline

KEY TERMS AND CONCEPTS

Anticipatory search warrant
Apparent authority
Arrest
Arrest warrant
Container
Contraband
Curtilage
Facially valid warrant
Frisk
Fruits (of a crime)
Fruits (of an illegal search
   or seizure)
Full search
Impoundment
Instrumentalities
Intensity (of a search)
Inventory search
Investigatory detention

Limited weapons search
Mere evidence
Open fields
Open view
Pat down
Plain view doctrine
Probable cause (to arrest)
Probable cause (to search)
Probable cause (to seize)
Protective sweep
Reasonable expectation of privacy
Scope (of a search)
Search
Search warrant
Seizable evidence of crime
Seizure (of persons)
Seizure (of things)
Testimony

§ 4.1   Overview of the Law of Search and Seizure

The Fourth Amendment regulates three activities in addition to those covered in Chapter 3: (1) searching persons for evidence, (2) searching places and things for evidence, and (3) seizing evidence. These three activities are grouped together into a single category called "search and seizure" law. The work that police officers do often requires them to coordinate the rules covered in Chapter 3 with those covered in Chapter 4. Gathering evidence is usually necessary to develop probable cause for an arrest. Further evidence gathering generally occurs during an arrest and often afterward to develop the case for trial. The same Fourth Amendment language that regulates investigatory detentions and arrests also regulates searches and seizures. It should, therefore, come as no surprise that the requirements in both contexts are similar.

We will begin this chapter by examining a recent police investigation known as the Curious Case of the Artless Art Thief. What makes this case unique is that Inspector

Clueso's compliance with the Fourth Amendment was, for once in his career, impeccable.

The Curious Case of the Artless Art Thief

Prologue

Several summers ago, a collection of famous works of art, on loan from the Louvre museum in Paris, was on tour in the United States and exhibited in various local museums. While these works were on display at the Whosville Art Institute, a brazen burglary took place. The burglar broke in under cover of night and stole two paintings — Leonardo da Vinci's *Mona Lisa* and Marcell du Chump's *Nude Descending a Fireman's Pole*. There were no witnesses and the only physical evidence recovered by the Whosville Police Department (WPD) at the crime scene was a single left-handed white glove bearing the monogram SS.

The Investigation

The WPD's finest, Inspector Clueso, surmised that the glove belonged to none other than Sticky-Fingered Sam, Whosville's most infamous criminal. Glove in hand, Clueso headed straight to the local magistrate, Judge Stickler, and requested a warrant to search Sam's home. After reviewing the evidence, Stickler denied the warrant, exclaiming with exasperation:

"You dunce, you should know by now that a glove bearing the initials SS is not enough evidence to establish probable cause to believe that the stolen works of art will be found in Sam's house. You had no business asking for a search warrant on such meager evidence. It shows a complete disregard for the rights of the citizens who elected me."

Undaunted, Clueso set up surveillance outside Sam's home. He waited on the street outside Sam's house each morning, followed Sam to his office, waited outside, and then followed Sam home again. In the evenings, when Sam took his garbage out to the curb, Clueso rummaged through the cans, looking for incriminating materials. He also put in a requisition for a pair of Super-Spy X-Ray Binoculars, explaining that he needed the equipment to look through Sam's walls. His request was denied with advice that he "could get in big trouble for using a device like that without a search warrant."

After one week, Clueso had observed nothing unusual, but his garbage rummaging had turned up several art magazines and a receipt for one pair of gloves. Once again Clueso applied for a search warrant and once again was told against that his evidence was not sufficient to satisfy the Fourth Amendment.

Feeling like a failure, Clueso sank into a depression and was unable to work for several weeks. However, on the first night that he returned to work, Clueso hit what he thought would be a pay dirt — a right-handed white glove, discarded in Sam's garbage, bearing the initials SS. This time Stickler agreed that there was probable cause, but not the kind for which Sam had hoped. The matching glove, considered in combination with Sam's criminal record, established probable cause to believe that Sam committed the theft, allowing for issuance of an arrest warrant, but not a search warrant. A search warrant, Stickler explained, required probable cause to believe that the stolen paintings would be found in Sam's home. Because the burglary had happened almost a month before and Clueso had not kept Sam's house under observation for much of this period, it was just as probable that Sam had already disposed of the paintings. As a result, no search warrant would be issued.

A big break in the case came several months later. Fortunately for Clueso, Sam loved art more than his privacy and installed a large display window facing the street to let in the northern light. As Clueso drove by Sam's house one day, he saw a painting of a woman resembling the *Mona Lisa*, clearly visible through the window.

Believing that he now had enough evidence to support a search warrant, but afraid to let the painting out of his sight, he rang Sam's doorbell and introduced himself as Joe, a world-renowned art critic. He told Sam that he couldn't help but notice the dazzling painting he saw through the window, and asked whether he could come in to admire it up closer. Flattered, Sam agreed, and took Clueso into his living room.

Once inside, Clueso could see that the painting looked very much like the *Mona Lisa*, but could not be sure. The famous smile on the painting was all wrong and the paint appeared to be wet. Either this was a common reproduction of the famous painting or Sam had been altering it to suit his own sense of aesthetics. To solve this mystery, Clueso took the painting from the wall and sniffed around the smile. Sure enough, the paint was wet. Confident that the painting was authentic, Clueso placed Sam under arrest. He then scanned the room and looked inside a closet near where Sam was standing, but the du Chump painting was nowhere to be seen. However, he spotted a set of finger paints, which he seized.

When advised of these developments, Judge Stickler hastily issued a warrant to search Sam's home for "Du Chump's *Nude Descending a Fireman's Pole*, tools used in connection with the theft, and any other items evidencing Sam's responsibility." Armed with the search warrant, Clueso returned to Sam's home and, this time, looked in every room and closet. He found the *Nude Descending a Fireman's Pole* unharmed behind the bureau in Sam's bedroom. As he moved the bureau, he dislodged a plastic sandwich bag containing what appeared to be several ounces of marijuana that was wedged behind it and seized that as well. Sam's motion to suppress the evidence taken from his home was denied and he was convicted of two counts of grand theft, one count of willful destruction of property, and one count of possession of a controlled substance. Sam's conviction was upheld on appeal.

Epilogue

Clueso was promoted to head of the WPD, Sam finished out his sentence, and the investigation has been hailed as a resounding success.

§ Analysis of the Investigation

Inspector (now Chief) Clueso's investigation fully complied with the Fourth Amendment. "Privacy" and "property" are the centerpieces of Fourth Amendment search and seizure law. A **search** occurs when police intrude on a **suspect's reasonable expectation of privacy**. A **seizure** occurs when they interfere with a suspect's possessory rights in property. As with **seizures of persons**, searches and seizures of property are graded according to invasiveness. Some evidence-gathering is not regulated by the Fourth Amendment because there is no interference with the suspect's privacy or property rights. Other evidence-gathering involves an intrusion, but the intrusion is sufficiently brief and limited as to call for less stringent regulation. Finally, some intrusions are sufficiently serious as to constitute full-blown searches or seizures. Clueso's investigation contains examples of each, as well as a host of other concepts that will be covered in this chapter.

> A search occurs when police intrude on a suspect's reasonable expectation of privacy. A seizure occurs when they interfere with a suspect's possessory rights in property.

A. Nonsearch Activity

Investigative activity that does not interfere with interests protected by the Fourth Amendment constitutes a "free zone" for police work. In detention and arrest law, this zone is defined in terms of the suspect's freedom to go about his or her business.

In search and seizure law, it is defined in terms of the suspect's privacy and property rights. Police operate in the free zone as long as their investigative activity does not infringe on any of these three interests.

Investigative activity that infringes on a suspect's reasonable expectation of privacy results in a search. A search can occur either because police make a trespassory entry into a constitutionally protected location or because they use high-tech surveillance devices that invade privacy.[1] Inspector Clueso was careful not to perform a search until he developed Fourth Amendment grounds. The initial stages of his investigation were conducted on the public streets. He was standing on the street when he saw what appeared to be the stolen *Mona Lisa* through Sam's front window where it was visible to anyone who looked. Suspects have no reasonable expectation of privacy in matters they knowingly expose to the public. Consequently, police surveillance of activities exposed to public view is not a search. This also explains why rummaging through Sam's garbage container was not a search. Once Sam placed the garbage container on the curb for collection, he no longer had any reasonable expectation of privacy in the contents. Just as the public could see the *Mona Lisa* through Sam's undraped window, so vagabonds, children, and snooping neighbors could have picked through his garbage. Consequently, Clueso was free to rummage through it as well.[2]

Clueso also refrained from seizing evidence before he developed grounds. A **seizure** occurs when police interfere with a suspect's property rights.[3] Removing items from Sam's garbage container was not a seizure because Sam deliberately abandoned his property rights in the objects he discarded as trash.

B. Consent Searches and Seizures

Sam's house is a location that is protected by the Fourth Amendment. A physical entry into a constitutionally protected location constitutes a **search**[4] and normally requires a **search warrant**.[5] However, consent voluntarily given by someone who resides on the premises eliminates the need for a warrant. Clueso's misrepresentation of his police identity did not destroy the voluntariness of Sam's consent.[6] Accordingly, his entry into Sam's home did not violate the Fourth Amendment.

C. Brief, Limited Searches and Seizures

When Inspector Clueso removed the *Mona Lisa*-like painting from Sam's wall, he interfered with Sam's property rights because he had only been given permission to look at the painting. Removing it from the wall was, therefore, a seizure. Probable cause

[1]   **Katz v. United States**, 389 U.S. 347, 88 S. Ct. 507, 19 L. Ed. 2d 576 (1967).
[2]   **California v. Greenwood**, 486 U.S. 35, 108 S. Ct. 1625, 100 L. Ed. 2d 30 (1988).
[3]   Maryland v. Macon, 472 U.S. 463, 105 S. Ct. 2778, 86 L. Ed. 2d 370 (1985).
[4]   **Katz v. United States**, *supra* note 1.
[5]   Carroll v. United States, 267 U.S. 132, 45 S. Ct. 280, 69 L. Ed. 543 (1925).
[6]   Lewis v United States, 385 U.S. 206, 17 L. Ed. 2d 312, 87 S. Ct. 424 (1966).

to believe that property is connected to a crime is necessary before police may seize it for use as evidence.[7] Because Inspector Clueso had not yet developed this degree of certainty, he would have violated Sam's Fourth Amendment rights had he put the painting under his arm and left with it. However, Clueso removed the painting for a lesser purpose — to examine it to determine whether it was stolen. Police are allowed to perform brief, limited seizures for investigation when they have a reasonable suspicion that property is connected to criminal activity.[8] This authority is based on the principles announced in *Terry v. Ohio*[9] and is governed by the same standard. Clueso's reasonable suspicion that the painting was the stolen *Mona Lisa* justified his removing it from Sam's wall for a closer examination. Once satisfied that it was the real thing, Inspector Clueso now had probable cause to seize it as evidence.

D. Full Searches and Seizures

A search for criminal evidence is called a **full search** (short for full-blown). Unlike arrests, in which a warrant is usually optional, full-blown searches always require a search warrant unless an established exception to the warrant requirement applies. However, a number of exceptions exist and consent is one of them. Sam's consent was, nevertheless, limited. He invited Clueso into his living room to look at his painting. When Clueso developed probable cause to believe that the painting on the wall was the stolen *Mona Lisa* and placed Sam under arrest, however, a second exception to the search warrant requirement became applicable. Clueso was entitled to perform a search incident to the arrest.

Searches incident to arrest, and indeed all searches, have defined boundaries. An arrest only justifies a search of the arrestee's person and the area under his or her immediate control, which is defined as the area within arm's reach. Consequently, it was necessary for Clueso to get a search warrant before he could search the rest of Sam's home. Judge Stickler, who had previously refused to grant a search warrant because Clueso's evidence failed to establish probable cause to believe that the stolen works of art were still in Sam's home, was now willing to do so. Discovery of the stolen *Mona Lisa* created probable cause to believe that the du Chump painting was probably still there, too.

The search warrant only authorized the seizure of the du Chump painting and articles related to the theft. Police, nevertheless, are not required to ignore criminal evidence and **contraband** discovered in **plain view** during an authorized search, even when they are not listed in the warrant.[10] The plain view exception to the warrant requirement supplied the basis for Clueso's seizure of the marijuana.[11]

---

[7]   Warden v. Hayden, 387 U.S. 294, 87 S. Ct. 1642, 18 L. Ed. 2d 782 (1967).

[8]   United States v. Place, 462 U.S. 696, 103 S. Ct. 2637, 77 L. Ed. 2d 110 (1983).

[9]   **392 U.S. 1, 88 S. Ct. 1868, 20 L. Ed. 2d 889 (1968).**

[10] Coolidge v. New Hampshire, 403 U.S. 443, 467, 91 S. Ct. 2022, 2038, 29 L. Ed. 2d 564 (1971).

[11] The plain view doctrine is discussed in § 4.4.

Now that the Curious Case of the Artless Art Thief has been solved, we are ready to explore the law of search and seizure.

§ 4.2 — Definition of a Search

Every Fourth Amendment analysis begins with the basic question: "Did the conduct of the police constitute a "search" or a "seizure?" If the answer is "no," no further Fourth Amendment inquiry is necessary. As you learned in Chapter 3, there is a free zone in which police are able to investigate without having to worry about the Fourth Amendment. In fact, the Fourth Amendment covers only two activities — searches and seizures. As long as the police avoid doing either, their activity is not regulated by the Fourth Amendment.

The Fourth Amendment restricts the search authority of the police to protect privacy. The colonists' experience with general warrants and writs of assistance, which gave British customs officials authority to enter any home and search at will for smuggled goods or anything else that might be incriminating, without grounds for believing that anything incriminating would be found, made the colonists acutely aware of this need.[12] Concern for privacy is also the controlling consideration in determining whether there has been a search. The Supreme Court defines a search as police activity that intrudes upon a citizen's reasonable expectation of privacy. However, this has not always been the case.

A. *Fourth Amendment Interpretation from* Olmstead *to* Katz

The Supreme Court originally interpreted the term "search" to require a physical intrusion into a constitutionally protected location. Persons, houses, papers, and effects are the four subjects mentioned in the Constitution. This interpretation was adequate to protect the privacy of citizens for the first 200 years of American history. However, as technology became more sophisticated, the government acquired the ability to monitor private activities without a physical trespass. Technology created new ways to communicate, eliminating the need to conduct private business face-to-face behind closed doors. Invention of the telephone made it possible to communicate at a distance. While parties to telephone conversations intend their communications to be private, the conversation can easily be intercepted without physically entering either party's home. The telephone was just the beginning of the new technology. Developments in police surveillance technologies created new ways for the government to snoop. The traditional concept of a search as involving a physical intrusion into a constitutionally protected location was no longer capable of protecting citizens' full range of privacy expectations.

---

[12]   James Otis, *Against the Writs of Assistance* (1761) in 1 ORATORS OF AMERICA 23–28 (G. Carlton Lee ed., 1900).

The Supreme Court's first encounter with the impact of the new technologies on Fourth Amendment analysis occurred in *Olmstead v. United States*.[13] Olmstead, a bootlegger, was convicted of violating the National Prohibition Act based on evidence obtained by tapping his telephone line from a junction box located on a public street. The Supreme Court stood by the traditional interpretation, holding that Olmstead's Fourth Amendment rights were not violated because the police listened to his conversation without trespassing on any property that belonged to him.

Olmstead remained the Supreme Court's official position until the 1967 case of *Katz v. United States*,[14] which marked the beginning of modern Fourth Amendment jurisprudence. Katz, a bookie, was convicted of transmitting wagering information based on evidence overheard by FBI agents who attached a recording device to the exterior of a public telephone booth Katz regularly used to conduct his business. The conduct of the police did not violate the Fourth Amendment under traditional analysis because the recording device did not penetrate the wall of the booth. As a result, there was no physical intrusion into a constitutionally protected location. The Supreme Court, nevertheless, ruled that a person who occupies a telephone booth, shuts the door, and pays the toll has a reasonable expectation that his telephone conversation is private and that this expectation is entitled to Fourth Amendment protection. The Court declared:

> . . . the Fourth Amendment protects people, not places. What a person knowingly exposes to the public, even in his own home or office, is not a subject of Fourth Amendment protection. But what he seeks to preserve as private, even in an area accessible to the public, may be constitutionally protected.

Katz redefined the term *search*. A search occurs whenever the police intrude on a suspect's reasonable expectation of privacy. This definition does not withdraw the protection that previously existed against physical intrusions into constitutionally protected locations.[15] The Supreme Court's goal in *Katz* was to make the Fourth Amendment responsive to changes in surveillance technology that made it possible for the police to invade privacy without committing a physical trespass.

B. Search Defined

We are now ready to formulate a working definition of the term search. A search occurs whenever police invade a suspect's reasonable expectation of privacy. An invasion can occur because the police either: (1) physically intrude into a constitutionally protected location (*i.e.*, a location in which the suspect has a reasonable expectation of privacy)[16] or (2) use advanced surveillance technologies to spy on activities that citizens reasonably expect are private.[17]

---

[13] **277 U.S. 438, 48 S. Ct. 564, 72 L. Ed. 944 (1928).**
[14] **Katz v. United States**, *supra* note 1.
[15] **United States v. Jones, _S. Ct._ , 2012 WL 171117 (U.S. 2012)** (holding that the *Katz* reasonable expectation-of-privacy test was intended to augment, not to supplant the original test which required a physical intrusion into a constitutionally protected location).
[16] Silverman v. United States, 365 U.S. 505, 81 S. Ct. 679, 5 L. Ed. 2d 734 (1961).
[17] **Katz v. United States**, *supra* note 1.

> A search occurs whenever police invade a suspect's reasonable expectation of privacy, either by physically intruding into a constitutionally protected location or by using advanced surveillance technologies to spy on activities that citizens reasonably expect are private.

1. Physical Intrusion into a Constitutionally Protected Location

The most common way a search occurs is by physically intruding into a constitutionally protected location. The Fourth Amendment mentions four subjects — persons, houses, papers, and effects — as having constitutional protection. These subjects have been interpreted expansively as denoting broad general categories.

Persons. The term *persons*, for search purposes, encompasses those parts of a suspect's body and clothing that are not exposed to the public, such as private parts of the anatomy, biological materials, and pockets and undergarments. Examining private parts of a suspect's body[18] or clothing[19] for evidence of a crime constitutes a search and requires Fourth Amendment search authority. Searches of clothing and personal belongings are covered in §§ 4.6 to 4.8. Highly intrusive body searches, such as strip searches and body cavity searches, and the taking of blood and urine samples, are subject to special rules that are covered in Chapter 7.

Houses. Houses includes homes and their surrounding buffer zone known as the **curtilage**, apartments, hotel rooms, private offices and warehouses, telephone booths, and even fixtures like file cabinets and lockers. In fact, this term has been defined to include any premises, structure, or fixture in which a reasonable expectation of privacy exists.[20] Shopping malls and retail establishments, in contrast, are constitutionally protected locations only during hours when they are closed to the public. Searches of protected premises are covered in §§ 4.13 to 4.16.

Papers and personal effects. *Papers* encompasses letters, journals, records, films, and other private documents. *Personal effects* encompasses handbags, briefcases, packages, luggage and other closed **containers**, and vehicles, among other things. Searches involving papers and effects are discussed at various points in this chapter.

Police may not physically enter a suspect's home,[21] reach into his pocket,[22] look inside his luggage,[23] or intrude into any other location in which the suspect has a reasonable expectation of **privacy,** without a recognized source of Fourth Amendment search authority.

---

18   **Schmerber v. California**, 384 U.S. 757, 86 S. Ct. 1826, 16 L. Ed. 2d 908 (1966).
19   Minnesota v. Dickerson, 508 U.S. 366, 113 S. Ct. 2130, 124 L. Ed. 2d 334 (1993).
20   Maryland v. Macon, *supra* note 3.
21   **Payton v. New York**, 445 U.S. 573, 100 S. Ct. 1371, 63 L. Ed. 2d 639 (1980).
22   Minnesota v. Dickerson, *supra* note 19.
23   **United States v. Place**, *supra* note 8.

2. Technological Invasions of Privacy

Today a search can also occur through a technological invasion of privacy. *Olmstead* and *Katz* both involved intrusions into the privacy of telephone conversations. In *Katz*, the Supreme Court held that a person who enters a public telephone booth and closes the door, shutting out the world, has a reasonable expectation that the conversation will be private and that this expectation is protected by the Fourth Amendment. Telecommunication surveillance is now regulated by a federal statute. Six months after *Katz*, Congress enacted the Omnibus Crime Control and Safe Streets Act of 1968,[24] which brought law enforcement use of wiretapping and other interception devices under judicial control by requiring prior court authorization.

Despite the promise held out in *Katz* that citizens would enjoy broad protection against the government's surreptitious monitoring of their comings and goings, this has not turned out to be the case. Technological advances since *Katz* have furnished the police with sophisticated devices that enable them to obtain much of the same information that once required a physical trespass, and the Supreme Court has given police considerable latitude to use the tools of modern science to fight crime.[25] Practically speaking, there are only two limitations on surreptitious surveillance of matters other than communications. First, surveillance devices must be employed from a location where the officer has a right to be. Second, police may not use special surveillance equipment that is not generally available to the public to spy on activities inside a residence.[26] Had Inspector Clueso used Super-Spy X-Ray Specs to monitor activities inside Sam's home, such use would have constituted a search and a search warrant would have been necessary.

Constitutional and statutory limitations on wiretapping and other technological invasions of privacy are covered in greater depth in Chapter 5.

Figure 4.1
Nonsearch Investigative Activity

> The Fourth Amendment does not treat the following activities as searches:
>
> 1. Searches and seizures performed by private parties without government complicity;
> 2. Searches and seizures of abandoned property;
> 3. Investigation of matters exposed to public view; and
> 4. Canine inspections to detect for the presence of narcotics

---

[24] 18 U.S.C. §§ 2510–2520.

[25] *See, e.g.*, United States v. Knotts, 460 U.S. 276, 103 S. Ct. 1081, 75 L. Ed. 2d 55 (1983) (approving use of electronic tracking devices to monitor location and movement of suspect's vehicle); California v. Ciraolo, 476 U.S. 27, 106 S. Ct. 1809, 90 L. Ed. 2d 210 (1986) (permitting aerial surveillance and photographing of suspect's backyard).

[26] **Kyllo v. United States, 533 U.S. 27, 121 S. Ct. 2038, 150 L. Ed. 2d 94 (2001)** (use of thermal-imaging device to detect whether the amount of heat emanating from suspect's home was consistent with the presence of high-intensity lamps used in marijuana growth constitutes search).

C. Nonsearches

A search, as we have seen, is defined as police activity that invades a suspect's reasonable expectation of privacy. This definition has two components: (1) police activity and (2) an invasion of a suspect's reasonable expectation of privacy. If either of these components is missing, there is no search and the Fourth Amendment does not apply.

1. Private-Party Searches

Our Constitution operates as a limitation only on the actions of the government. Searches conducted by private parties without police complicity are not regulated by the Fourth Amendment. As a result, police may use evidence received from private parties, without concern for how they obtained it.[27] Furthermore, police activity that would otherwise be considered a search is not a search if it merely duplicates activity that a private party has already performed. Suppose an airline traveler inadvertently leaves her travel bag on an airplane and an airline employee opens it to determine the owner's identity. Upon discovering a vial of cocaine, the employee closes the bag and hands it over to the police. Although opening a travel bag and inspecting the contents would normally be considered a search, it is not a search after a private party has done this because the owner's reasonable expectation of privacy has already been compromised.[28] However, police activity becomes a search when it exceeds the previous exploratory activity and invades privacy interests that have not yet been invaded. If an apartment maintenance worker discovers a vial of cocaine while fixing a leaking faucet and turns it over to the police, police may not re-enter and search the apartment in its entirety. Unlike the travel bag, which was fully examined before being turned over to the police, a person's apartment contains countless other possessions that have not yet been viewed. The occupant's reasonable expectation of privacy in the unviewed objects is still intact.[29] Consequently, a police inspection, following a private-party search, is not considered a search only if it goes no farther.

2. Police Investigations Conducted Without Invading Privacy

The Fourth Amendment does not regulate police investigations conducted without encroaching on a suspect's reasonable expectations of privacy. Because suspects lack a reasonable expectation of privacy in matters exposed to the public and abandoned property, police surveillance of these matters falls outside the Fourth Amendment.

Matters in open view. Police are free to make the same observations that members of the public could make. Anything visible to members of the public from a vantage

---

[27] United States v. Jacobsen, 466 U.S. 109, 104 S. Ct. 1652, 80 L. Ed. 2d 85 (1984). However, if the police affirmatively encourage a private search and the private individual acts to assist the police rather than for independent reasons, the search must satisfy the Fourth Amendment. *See, e.g.*, United States v. Jarrett, 338 F.3d 339 (4th Cir. 2003); Dawson v. State, 106 S. W. 3d 388 (Tex. Ct. App. 2003).

[28] United States v. Jacobsen, *supra* note 27.

[29] *See, e.g.*, Walter v. United States, 447 U.S. 649, 100 S. Ct. 2395, 65 L. Ed. 2d 410 (1980); United States v. Runyan, 275 F.3d 449 (5th Cir. 2001); United States v. Allen, 106 F.3d 695 (6th Cir. 1997).

point where the officer is lawfully present is said to be in "**open view**."[30] Police sur-veillance of matters in "open view" is not regarded as a search because people do not have a reasonable expectation of privacy in matters they expose to the public. If there is an undraped window, a knothole in a fence, or a garbage can on the sidewalk, police are free to peek inside.

The fact that it takes special effort to reach a vantage point from which a view is possible does not prevent the matter observed from being in "open view." Even though an officer has to climb 20 flights of stairs to reach the outdoor fire escape of a public building to get to the rooftop garden that overlooks the defendant's backyard, the back-yard is still considered to be in open view. What matters is that the officer is standing in a place accessible to members of the public when the officer observes things that any-one else standing there could have observed.[31] Police are allowed to use flashlights, binoculars, telescopes, and other artificial aids in general public use to enhance their ability to make the observation.[32] In *California v. Ciraolo*,[33] police officers, acting on an anonymous tip, flew a helicopter over the defendant's backyard, which was shielded from ground-level view by a 10-foot-high fence, and observed marijuana plants grow-ing below. The Supreme Court held that this was not a search because the observation occurred in navigable airspace and anyone else flying in this airspace who glanced down could have observed the very same things.

The same principle applies to evidence detected through the senses of smell or hear-ing. Police officers are allowed to use any of their natural senses when they are lawfully present at the place where their senses are used.[34] Listening with the naked ear to goings-on inside a motel room from an adjoining room or a common hallway,[35] and sniffing the exterior of a car parked on a public street for the odor of drugs are not searches.[36]

---

[30] *See, generally,* 1 WAYNE R. LAFAVE, SEARCH & SEIZURE § 2.2 (3d ed. 1996).

[31] *Id.*

[32] **United States v. Dunn, 480 U.S. 294, 107 S. Ct. 1134, 94 L. Ed. 2d 326 (1987)** (holding that use of flashlight to illuminate inside of a barn did not violate Fourth Amendment); Texas v. Brown, 460 U.S. 730, 103 S. Ct. 1535, 75 L. Ed. 2d 502 (1983) (holding that shining a flashlight to illuminate the interior of a car did not violate the Fourth Amendment); United States v. Dellas, 355 F. Supp. 2d 1095 (N.D. Cal. 2005) (holding that a government agent's use of night vision goggles from a lawful viewing point to observe an outbuilding used for the purpose of growing marijuana did not constitute a search within the meaning of the Fourth Amendment).

[33] *Supra* note 25.

[34] *See, e.g.*, LAFAVE, *supra* note 30 ("As a general proposition, it is fair to say that when a law enforce-ment officer is able to detect something by utilization of one or more of his senses while lawfully present at the vantage point where those senses are used, that detection does not constitute a "search" within the meaning of the Fourth Amendment.").

[35] United States v. Jackson, 588 F.2d 1046 (5th Cir. 1979); United States v. Agapito, 477 F. Supp. 706 (S.D.N.Y. 1979).

[36] United States v. Marlar, 828 F. Supp. 415 (N. D. Miss. 1993) (canine sniff conducted outside motel room door did not constitute a search); Jennings v. Joshua Independent School District, 877 F.2d 313 (5th Cir. 1989) (use of trained dogs to sniff cars parked in a public parking lot does not constitute Fourth Amendment search), *cert. denied*, 496 U.S. 935, 110 S. Ct. 3212, 110 L. Ed. 2d 660 (1990).

The Supreme Court has extended this principle to the use of trained drug detection dogs. In *United States v. Place*,[37] the Supreme Court ruled that the use of a trained drug detection dog to sniff luggage is not a search because it does not require opening the luggage or exposing the contents. Trained narcotics detection dogs function as little more than an extension of the officer's own senses.

Drug detection dogs are now being used to perform inspections at airports, bus terminals, train stations, and other places.[38] No suspicion is needed to walk a trained narcotics detection dog down a public street, through a parking lot, airport terminal, train station, hotel corridor, or any other location accessible to members of the public.[39] Drug-detection dogs may also be used during routine traffic stops if their use does not extend the duration of the stop beyond the time required to process the traffic violation.[40]

Police, nevertheless, do not have the right to touch and feel everything they are free to look at or smell. Exploratory touching involves a greater intrusion on privacy. In *Bond v. United States*,[41] a border patrol agent boarded a bus to check the immigration status of the passengers. As he walked forward to exit the bus after completing the check, he squeezed the soft luggage passengers had placed in the overhead storage bins to feel for the presence of contraband objects. He felt a brick-like object in the defendant's luggage that turned out to be a brick of methamphetamine. The Supreme Court ruled that the border patrol agent's tactile examination of the defendant's luggage to determine the contents involved a search. Although bus passengers who store luggage in overhead storage bins expect that other passengers may move or shove their luggage to make room for their own, they do not expect that others will touch their bags in the exploratory manner the border patrol agent did here. As a result, the border patrol agent's exploratory touching could not be sustained under the open view doctrine and involved a search.

---

[37]   *Supra* note 8.

[38]   Kenneth R. Vallentin, *Dogs Are a Prosecutor's Best Friend: Canine Search and Seizure Law*, PROS-ECUTOR 31 (October 1997).

[39]   *See, e.g.*, **Illinois v. Caballes, 543 U.S. 405, 125 S. Ct. 834, 160 L. Ed. 2d 842 (2005)** (vehicle stopped for traffic violation); United States v. Place, *supra* note 8 (luggage); United States v. Jacobsen, *supra* note 27 (postal package); Commonwealth v. Welch, 420 Mass. 646, 651 N.E.2d 392 (1995) (lockers in fire department's common room); United States v. Friend, 50 F.3d 548 (8th Cir. 1995) (car parked on private property beyond the curtilage); United States v. Roby, 122 F.3d 1120 (8th Cir. 1997) (common corridor of a motel); United States v. Marlar, *supra* note 36 (outside motel room door); United States v. Lingenfelter, 997 F.2d 632 (9th Cir. 1993) (exterior of commercial warehouse); State v. Carter, 697 N.W.2d 199 (Minn. 2005) (outside self-storage unit); United States v. Colyer, 878 F.2d 469 (D.C. Cir. 1989) (Amtrak sleeper car); Scott v. State, 927 P.2d 1066 (Okla. Crim. App. 1996) (luggage checked with bus company); United States v. Reyes, 349 F.3d 219 (5th Cir. 2003) (non-contact canine sniff of person).

[40]   **Illinois v. Caballes**, *supra* note 39.

[41]   **529 U.S. 334, 120 S. Ct. 1462, 146 L. Ed. 2d 365 (2000).**

Abandoned property. A person who abandons property voluntarily relinquishes any reasonable expectation of privacy in that property. This explains why rummaging through the contents of garbage cans that have been placed on the curb for collection is not a search.[42]

Figure 4.2
Essentials for a Lawful Search

For a search to be lawful, the officer must:

1. act under a recognized source of search authority, and
2. confine the search activity to authorized search boundaries.

Grounds for search authority and search boundaries vary with the purpose of the search.

§ 4.3 — Sources of Search Authority

Whenever police perform an act that the Fourth Amendment treats as a search, they must have search authority. What is necessary to have search authority varies with the purpose of the search. The three main purposes for searching are to gather evidence, to disarm suspects for self-protection, and to make an inventory of property that the police have impounded. The first kind of search is called a **full search**, the second a **limited weapons search** or **frisk**, and the third an **inventory search.**

Rummaging through a person's belongings for anything incriminating without probable cause to believe that anything will be found is a general search, the evil against which the Fourth Amendment is directed.[43] To guard against general searches, the Fourth Amendment requires that police: (1) have search authority and (2) confine their search to the authorized search boundaries.[44] Each ground for search authority has companion rules delineating the boundaries of the search. Descriptions of search boundaries have two features: the **scope**, which defines the locations that may be searched, and the **intensity**, which defines the thoroughness with which they may be searched. However, there is one overriding limitation that governs all searches: *The scope and intensity of a search may never be greater than necessary to locate the objects for which an officer has search authority.*

---

[42] **California v. Greenwood**, *supra* note 2.
[43] **Payton v. New York**, *supra* note 21.
[44] **Chimel v. California**, 395 U.S. 752, 89 S. Ct. 2034, 23 L. Ed. 2d 685 (1969); Arizona v. Hicks, 480 U.S. 321, 107 S. Ct. 1149, 94 L. Ed. 2d 347 (1987).

Figure 4.3
Categories of Searches

Category	Purpose of Search	Grounds for Conducting
Full Search	Gather evidence	Search warrant or recognized exception to warrant requirement
Limited Weapons Search	Disarm person to protect officer's safety	Reasonable suspicion that a person lawfully detained is armed and dangerous
Inventory Search	Catalogue property that police have taken into custody	Authority to impound and adherence to police department regulations governing conduct of inventory searches

A. Full Searches

Searches conducted to gather criminal evidence are called full searches. When the purpose of the search is to gather evidence, the Fourth Amendment always requires either a search warrant or a recognized exception to the warrant requirement.[45] The exceptions are generally based on circumstances that create an urgent need for a search at a time when it is impractical to obtain a warrant.

Figure 4.4
Probable Cause for a Search Warrant

In order to secure a search warrant, an officer must possess facts sufficient to warrant a person of reasonable caution in believing three things:

1. That a crime has been (or is being) committed;
2. That specific objects associated with the crime exist; and
3. That they will be found in the place to be searched.

1. Searches Under the Authority of a Warrant

The Supreme Court has expressed a strong preference for searches and seizures to be conducted under the authority of a warrant, because a warrant places the decision of whether there is probable cause for the search in the hands of a neutral and detached judge.[46] Fourth Amendment search and seizure analysis starts with the presumption

---

[45]   **Flippo v. West Virginia**, 528 U.S. 11, 120 S. Ct. 7, 145 L. Ed. 2d 16 (1999).
[46]   **Payton v. New York**, *supra* note 21.

that a search warrant is necessary and then carves out an abundance of exceptions that cut deep inroads into the general rule. Nevertheless, it is good policy to obtain a warrant, even when an exception applies, because search warrants carry at least two advantages. First, a facially valid search warrant shields the officer from civil and criminal liability.[47] Second, it also insulates the fruits of the search from suppression.[48]

The Fourth Amendment provides that "no Warrants shall issue, but upon probable cause, supported by Oath or affirmation." Probable cause for a search warrant is similar to probable cause for an arrest warrant. It requires the same level of certainty, which is more than a hunch or even a reasonable suspicion, but less than proof beyond a reasonable doubt.[49] The facts upon which probable cause for a search are based may be gathered from the same sources and must have the same degree of reliability as those supporting probable cause to arrest.[50] The major difference is what the officer must have probable cause to believe. Probable cause for a search warrant requires facts sufficient to justify a person of reasonable caution in believing three things: (1) that criminal activity has taken place, (2) that specific objects associated with that crime exist, and (3) that they will be found at the place to be searched. Courts do not insist on direct evidence that the objects of the search are located at the place to be searched; it is enough that they are probably there.[51] Courts, for example, will assume that the gun used to commit a crime and the clothing worn during its commission are probably at the suspect's home, absent evidence to the contrary.[52]

A second difference is the freshness of the information needed to support an application for a search warrant.[53] Unlike facts that support probable cause to believe that a suspect has committed a crime, facts supporting probable cause to believe that items of evidence will be found at a given location can grow stale. If the information is too old, it may have little value in showing that the evidence is still present at the place for which the warrant is sought. This is why Judge Stickler, although willing to issue an arrest warrant once the second glove was found, refused to issue a search warrant. By the time Clueso developed probable cause to believe that Sam had stolen the paintings, several weeks had passed and Sam could have sold or removed them in the meantime. Consequently, even though Clueso now had enough evidence for an arrest, the passage of time prevented him from making the showing needed for a search warrant.

---

[47] Malley v. Briggs, 475 U.S. 335, 106 S. Ct. 1092, 89 L. Ed. 2d 271 (1986).

[48] *Id.*

[49] Illinois v. Gates, 462 U.S. 213, 103 S. Ct. 2317, 76 L. Ed. 2d 257 (1983).

[50] *Id.*

[51] United States v. Hernandez, 80 F.3d 1253 (9th Cir. 1996).

[52] State v. Smith, 868 S. W. 2d 561 (Tenn. 1993).

[53] *See, e.g.*, People v. Rodriguez, 758 N.Y.S.2d 172, 303 A.D.2d 783 (2003) (finding that information used to obtain a search warrant was stale where it was based on single purchase of cocaine that occurred 28 days prior to search).

Finally, the Fourth Amendment requires that search warrants contain a particularized description of the place to be searched and the things to be seized. The warrant's description of the place to be searched limits the search to locations for which police have demonstrated probable cause to believe that the objects of the search will be found, while the description of the things to be seized prevents the police from rummaging more extensively than necessary to discover them. The two requirements combine to guard against general searches.

a. Scope of a Search Under a Warrant

The warrant's description of the place to be searched defines the permissible **scope of the search**. Although warrants are usually issued for searches of homes and businesses, they can also be issued for searches of vehicles, containers, and even people. Search authority under a warrant extends only to the locations described in it. If a warrant is issued to search Sam's kitchen, police may not search the bedroom, garage, or the cabana behind his pool. However, descriptions like this are exceedingly rare. It is more common to describe the premises to be searched by address. When the premises are described by address, search authority extends to the residence, the yard, and all structures and vehicles inside the curtilage.[54]

b. Intensity of a Search Under a Warrant

The warrant's description of the premises to be searched grants authority to enter. Once inside, the **intensity** of the search — whether the officer may look inside closets, open drawers or containers, read mail, etc. — is controlled by the warrant's description of the objects to be seized. Police may only look in places that are potential repositories of the objects for which they have search authority.[55] If the police secure a warrant to search Sam's home for a stolen pink baby elephant named Cha Cha, they may look in the basement and walk through all the rooms, but they may not open envelopes or look inside drawers, behind furniture, or under beds, because it would be impossible for a stolen elephant to be hidden there. Looking in places where Cha Cha could not possibly be violates the Fourth Amendment. On the other hand, when a search warrant is issued for small, easily concealed objects such as money or drugs, which can be hidden almost anywhere, police may meticulously go over every square inch of the premises with a fine-tooth comb.

---

[54] *See, e.g.,* United States v. Earls, 42 F.3d 1321 (10th Cir. 1994) (search warrant for "premises" at a certain street address included outbuildings within the curtilage such as detached garage and shed); United States v. Asselin, 775 F.2d 445 (1st Cir. 1985) (search warrant for premises at a certain address carried authority to search car next to carport); United States v. Napoli, 530 F. 2d 1198 (5th Cir. 1976) (search warrant for premises at a certain address carried authority to search camper in driveway).

[55] *See, e.g.,* **United States v. Weinbender, 109 F.3d 1327 (8th Cir. 1997)**; People v. Llanos, 288 Ill. App.3d 592, 681 N. E. 2d 598 (1997).

Figure 4.5
Warrant Requirement for Evidentiary Searches

A search warrant is necessary to conduct a full search, except when:

1. police obtain consent from someone who has authority to give it.
2. the search is conducted as an incident to a lawful custodial arrest.
3. police have probable cause to believe that a motor vehicle contains property they may lawfully seize.
4. police are confronted with exigent circumstances that require immediate warrantless action.

2. Full Searches Conducted Under an Exception to the Warrant Requirement

The Supreme Court has expressed a strong preference that searches be conducted under the authority of a warrant because the decision of whether probable cause exists is made by a neutral and detached magistrate in a calm atmosphere rather than a hurried decision by an officer on the scene.[56] However, search warrants are necessary only for full-blown searches. Even then, four exceptions exist. Full searches are permitted without a warrant: (1) with consent, (2) as an incident to a lawful arrest, (3) when police have probable cause to believe a motor vehicle contains evidence that is subject to seizure, and (4) when exigent circumstances are present. Each of these exceptions is briefly described below and in greater detail later in this chapter. Pay close attention to what is necessary to have search authority under each of the exceptions and the scope and intensity of search activity that is permitted.

a. Consent to Search

A warrant is not required to search premises if the suspect or a fellow occupant, such as a spouse or roommate, consents to the search.[57] The rationale behind third-party consent is that when multiple parties share joint access and mutual use of the premises, each

---

[56] "[S]earches conducted outside the judicial process, without prior approval by judge or magistrate, are *per se* unreasonable under the Fourth Amendment-subject only to a few specifically established and well-delineated exceptions." **Arizona v. Gant, 556 U.S. 332, 129 S. Ct. 1710, 173 L. Ed. 2d 485 (2009);** United States v. Ventresca, 380 U.S. 102, 85 S. Ct. 741, 13 L. Ed. 2d 684 (1965); United States v. Jeffers, 342 U.S. 48, 72 S. Ct. 93, 96 L. Ed. 59 (1951).

[57] *See, e.g.*, United States v. Matlock, 415 U.S. 164, 94 S. Ct. 988, 39 L. Ed. 2d 242 (1974) ("voluntary consent of any joint occupant of a residence to search the premises jointly occupied is valid against the co-occupant, permitting evidence discovered in the search to be used against him at a criminal trial"); United States v. Hylton, 349 F.3d 781 (4th Cir. 2003) (consent given by defendant's girlfriend to search apartment and bedroom that she shared with defendant valid); United States v. Kimoana, 383 F.3d 1215 (10th Cir. 2004) (individual who had stayed overnight in motel room with other parties, who left his possessions there, and who had room key, had authority to consent to search of room). Although oral consent is legally sufficient, it is customary to have the person sign a "Permission to Search" form, something like the following: "I, Charles T Brown, do hereby voluntarily authorize L. Jones, of the Whosville Police Department, with such assistance as he/she deems proper, to search _____ (description). I am giving this written permission freely and voluntarily, without any threats or promises having been made to me, and after having been informed that I have the right to refuse to permit this search."

assumes the risk that one of their numbers may permit the premises to be searched. Third-party consent can rest on apparent, as well as actual, authority. **Apparent authority** exists when the facts available to the officer at the time of the search would lead a reasonable person to believe that the consent-giver has joint access and control over the premises to be searched, even though the person does not. In *Illinois v. Rodriguez*,[58] the Supreme Court upheld a search conducted with the consent of the suspect's former girlfriend, even though she no longer occupied the premises, where she referred to the apartment as "ours" and unlocked the door with her own key, creating the impression that she lived there. Landlords, hotel clerks, and others who, to the officer's knowledge, are not occupants lack apparent authority to admit the police.[59]

A third-party's consent extends to the areas shared in common. Whether it also extends to the suspect's private bedroom and closed containers that house personal be longings, such as purses, suitcases, briefcases, and footlockers, turns on whether police know that the room or container belongs to the suspect and that the consent-giver has no right of access. When this information is lacking, the search can generally be sustained based on apparent authority.[60] However, when police are aware that the room or container belongs to the suspect and that the consent-giver has no right of access, the consent is ineffective.[61] Police, for example, cannot rely on a male occupant's consent

---

[58] 497 U.S. 177, 110 S. Ct. 2793, 111 L. Ed. 2d 148 (1990) (upholding search where suspect's former girlfriend who no longer occupied premises produced a key to suspect's apartment, referred to the apartment as "ours," and granted police permission to enter).

[59] *See, e.g.*, Chapman v. United States, 365 U.S. 610, 81 S. Ct. 776, 5 L. Ed. 2d 828 (1961) (landlord cannot validly consent to search of tenant's residence); Stoner v. California, 376 U.S. 483, 84 S. Ct. 889, 11 L. Ed. 2d 856 (1964) (hotel clerk cannot validly consent to search of guest's room); United States v. Jeffers, 342 U.S. 48, 72 S. Ct. 93, 96 L. Ed. 59 (1951) (hotel staff who have access to room for purposes of cleaning lack authority to admit police); People v. Superior Court, 143 Cal. App. 4th 1183, 49 Cal. Rptr. 3d 831 (2006) (university may not validly consent to a search of a university student's dormitory room).

[60] *See, e.g.*, United States. v. Melgar, 227 F.3d 1038 (7th Cir. 2000) (consent to search defendant's purse was valid based on apparent authority where police had no reason to know that the purse in question did not belong to woman authorizing the search); Glenn v. Commonwealth, 49 Va. App. 413, 642 S.E.2d 282 (2007) (Consent given by defendant's grandfather to search of his home included permission to open a backpack found on the floor in one of the rooms sometimes used by defendant where the backpack had no identifying information on it that revealed who owned it, used it, or had access to it, and nothing about the backpack itself put the officers on notice that defendant claimed an exclusive privacy interest in it.); People v. Goforth, 564 N.W.2d 526 (Mich. App. 1997) (Police had authority to search son's bedroom on his mother's consent when they reasonably believe that mother has common authority over the room with the right to enter.).

[61] *See, e.g.*, United States v. Davis, 332 F.3d 1163 (9th Cir. 2003) (Officers who conducted search of defendant's gym bag did not have reasonable belief that apartment tenant had actual authority to grant consent to search of bag, which was located underneath bed in bedroom that they were told was occupied by the tenant's roommate and the defendant.); United States v. Jimenez, 419 F.3d 34 (1st Cir. 2005) (Consent to search, given by lessee of residence, did not extend to defendant's bedroom where the lessee characterized the bedroom as defendant's space and said she was not supposed to enter the room, and she did not have a key to the room); Krise v. State, 746 N.E.2d 957 (Ind. 2001) (male housemate's consent to search of female suspect's purse invalid, even though the purse was found in a bathroom they shared, because police knew that purse did not belong to the consent giver). *See also* WAYNE R. LAFAVE, SEARCH & SEIZURE § 8.3 (f) (3d ed. 1996).

to search his female roommate's purse, even if the purse is located in an area of the house under the control of both, because they are aware that the purse does not belong to the consent-giver and that he has no right of access.

A fellow occupant's consent to search is ineffective, even as to the areas shared in common, if the suspect is present and objects to the search.[62] When a dispute exists about whether to admit the police, police must remain outside and obtain a search warrant.

The scope of a search based on consent is confined to the terms of the authorization. When a general statement of consent is given without express limitations, search authority extends to anything a reasonable police officer could interpret the terms of the authorization as encompassing.[63] The express object of the search is the most important consideration. A suspect's consent to search his apartment for drugs, for example, would permit the police to open closets and drawers, search clothing, and look in any other place in which drugs might be found.

Consent to search must be voluntary to be effective. However, police are not required to advise people of their right to refuse when asking for permission to search.[64]

b. Search Incident to a Lawful Arrest

A lawful custodial arrest carries automatic authority to search the arrested individual's person.[65] This source of warrantless search authority is justified by the need to disarm suspects before taking them into custody and to prevent them from destroying evidence. The scope of the search extends to the suspect's person, clothing, and wallet or handbag,[66] but not to luggage, packages, or other containers in close proximity unless a realistic possibility exists that the suspect could gain access to a weapon or evidence from inside them at the time of the search.[67]

---

[62]   Georgia v. Randolph, 547 U.S.103, 126 S. Ct.1515, 74 L. Ed. 2d 4176 (2005).

[63]   **Florida v. Jimeno, 500 U.S. 248, 111 S. Ct. 1801, 114 L. Ed. 2d 297 (1991)** (permission to search automobile for narcotics, unless qualified, carries authority to open any closed containers that might contain the object of the search); State v. Roberts, 110 Ohio St. 3d 71, 850 N.E.2d 1168 (2006) (defendant's general consent to search the premises of her home extended to the garage and the vehicle inside).

[64]   **United States v. Drayton, 536 U.S. 194, 122 S. Ct. 2105, 153 L. Ed. 2d 242 (2002)**; Schneckloth v. Bustamonte, 412 U.S. 218, 93 S. Ct. 2041, 36 L. Ed. 2d 854 (1973); Ohio v. Robinette, 519 U.S. 33, 117 S. Ct. 417, 136 L. Ed. 2d 347 (1996).

[65]   **United States v. Robinson, 414 U.S. 218, 94 S. Ct. 467, 38 L. Ed. 2d 427 (1973).**

[66]   *See, e.g.,* **United States v. Robinson,** *supra* **note 65** (upholding search of a crumpled pack of cigarettes found in the pocket of person arrested for a traffic violation).

[67]   **Arizona v. Gant,** *supra* **note 56** (holding that the search incident to arrest exception does "not authorize a vehicle search incident to a recent occupant's arrest after the arrestee has been secured and cannot access the interior of the vehicle"); United States v. Taylor, 656 F. Supp. 2d 998 (E.D. Mo. 2009) (applying same rule to an arrest made inside a residence).

c. Vehicle Search Based on Probable Cause to Believe that the Vehicle Contains Criminal Evidence or Contraband

Police may conduct a warrantless search of a vehicle whenever they have probable cause to believe that the vehicle contains contraband or evidence of criminal activity.[68] This exception to the warrant requirement exists because of the ease with which motor vehicles can be moved. Within the time it takes to return with a search warrant, the vehicle may be gone. Accordingly, a search warrant is not necessary when officers have probable cause to believe that the vehicle contains evidence that they may lawfully seize. The scope of the search extends to the entire vehicle and everything inside, although police, of course, may only look in places where the object of their search could be located. For example, they may not look inside the motorist's handbag when searching for a stolen television.

d. Exigent Circumstances and Hot Pursuit

Police are allowed to enter private premises without a search warrant when they are confronted with exigent circumstances that create an urgent need for immediate action.[69] The three main circumstances that fall within this exception are hot pursuit of a fleeing suspect, threats to safety, and threatened destruction of evidence.[70]

Exigent circumstances searches are limited, both in scope and intensity, to action immediately necessary to address the exigency that justified the entry.[71] For example, if the exigency concerns destruction of evidence, police may enter for the sake of securing the premises to prevent people inside from destroying or removing the evidence while applying for a search warrant, but must postpone the search until a warrant is obtained.

---

[68]   Maryland v. Dyson, 527 U.S. 465, 119 S. Ct. 2013, 144 L. Ed. 2d 442 (1999); California v. Acevedo, 500 U.S. 566, 111 S. Ct. 1982, 114 L. Ed. 2d 619 (1991); United States v. Ross, 456 U.S. 798, 102 S. Ct. 2157, 72 L. Ed. 2d 472 (1982).

[69]   **Brigham City v. Stuart, 547 U.S. 398, 126 S. Ct. 1943, 164 L. Ed. 2d 650 (2006)** ("[W]arrants are generally required to search a person's home or his person unless the exigencies of the situation make the needs of law enforcement so compelling that the warrantless search is objectively reasonable under the Fourth Amendment.").

[70]   United States v. Santa, 236 F.3d 662 (11th Cir. 2000) (exigent circumstances include danger of flight or escape; danger of harm to police officers or the general public; risk of loss, destruction, removal, or concealment of evidence; and "hot pursuit" of a fleeing suspect); Ingram v. City of Columbus, 185 F.3d 579 (6th Cir. 1999) (same). Exigent circumstances searches are covered in § 4.16.

[71]   Segura v. United States, 468 U.S. 796, 104 S. Ct. 3380, 82 L. Ed. 2d 599 (1984) (when police have probable cause to believe that a drug operation is being conducted inside an apartment, they may enter to secure the premises and prevent removal or destruction of evidence while applying for warrant); Illinois v. McArthur, 531 U.S. 326, 121 S. Ct. 946, 148 L. Ed. 2d 838 (2001) (where police have probable cause to believe that drugs are located inside a dwelling and good reason to fear that residents will destroy the evidence before they return with a warrant, they may seal off the premises and prevent residents from entering, pending issuance of a search warrant).

B. *Limited Weapons Searches: Frisks and Protective Sweeps*

The traditional Fourth Amendment requirements of probable cause and a search warrant apply only to full searches. Searches conducted for reasons besides discovery of evidence, such as to disarm a suspect or to prepare an inventory of property that has been impounded, are governed by different Fourth Amendment standards.

Police may perform a limited weapons search or frisk when they have reason to believe that a person they have lawfully detained may be armed and dangerous.[72] The purpose of a frisk is to disarm the suspect so that police can conduct the investigation without fear for their safety. Weapons frisks are limited searches. They are limited both in the objects for which police may search and in their scope and intensity. Police may search only for weapons and are limited to patting down the suspect's outer clothing. If the detention involves a vehicle, they are limited to performing a cursory visual inspection of areas and receptacles inside the passenger compartment that are capable of housing a weapon.[73]

Protective sweeps are another type of limited search. When police make an arrest inside a residence, they are allowed to perform a cursory visual inspection of closets and other spaces immediately adjoining the place of arrest in which cohorts who pose a danger to the officers might be hiding.[74]

C. *Inventory Searches*

An impoundment occurs when police take custody of property for reasons other than use as evidence. Vehicles and personal belongings taken from arrestees before placing them in a detention facility are the articles most often impounded.[75] The Fourth Amendment allows lawfully impounded property to be searched without a warrant.[76] The reason traditional Fourth Amendment requirements do not apply is that the search is not investigatory. The purpose of the search is to protect the owner's property while it is in police custody and to protect the police department against false claims of lost or stolen property. The Fourth Amendment is satisfied if police have legal authority for

---

[72] **Terry v. Ohio**, *supra* note 9. *Terry* stops are covered in §§ 3.7–3.9.
[73] *Terry* pat down searches are discussed in greater detail in § 4.7.
[74] Protective sweeps are covered in greater detail in § 4.15.
[75] South Dakota v. Opperman, 428 U.S. 364, 96 S. Ct. 3092, 49 L. Ed. 2d 1000 (1976) (inventory search of abandoned automobile impounded by police); Illinois v. Lafayette, 462 U.S. 640, 103 S. Ct. 2605, 77 L. Ed. 2d 65 (1983) (inventory search of contents of arrestee's shoulder bag before placing arrestee in detention facility); Florida v. Wells, 495 U.S. 1, 110 S. Ct. 1632, 109 L. Ed. 2d 1 (1990).
[76] *See* cases *supra* note 75.

the impoundment and conduct the search according to standardized inventory procedures.[77]

§ 4.4   — Fourth Amendment Requirements for Seizing Property

So far this chapter has discussed only searches. The Fourth Amendment also protects "[t]he right of the people to be secure in their . . . houses, papers, and effects, against unreasonable . . . seizures." Although seizures normally occur in tandem with searches, this is not always the case. There can be searches without seizures and seizures without searches, and the Fourth Amendment imposes separate requirements for each.[78]

There are at least four different reasons police seize property: (1) to use it as evidence at a trial, (2) to detain it while conducting a brief investigation into its ownership or contents, (3) to prevent it from being moved while applying for a search warrant to open it, and (4) to impound it for safekeeping. As with searches, Fourth Amendment requirements vary with the purpose of the seizure. Each purpose has its own set of rules. However, we are getting ahead of ourselves. We will start by defining the term seizure, as applied to things:

> A seizure, in the Fourth Amendment sense, occurs when police commit a meaningful interference with a person's possessory interest in property.

A. Seizure Defined

Under property law, the possessor of property has the exclusive right to use it and the absolute right to exclude others from using it. Even the slightest touching constitutes a trespass if done without permission. However, Fourth Amendment protection does not go this far. A seizure in the Fourth Amendment sense requires a meaningful interference with a person's possessory interest in property.[79] This definition has two key phrases — "meaningful interference" and "possessory interest in property." Both must be understood in order to grasp the concept of a seizure. The following example will help explain.

---

[77]   Inventory searches are discussed in greater detail in §§ 4.8 and 4.12. There are other reasons for searching besides the ones covered in this chapter. Searches conducted at international borders by customs officials, for example, require no level of suspicion. *See, e.g.*, United States v. Flores-Montano, 124 U.S. 1582, 124 S. Ct. 1582, 158 L. Ed. 2d 311 (2004) (approving removal and disassembly of gas tank, without reasonable suspicion, as part of a border search). The same is true of parolee searches in jurisdictions where consent to being searched at any time is made a statutory condition of parole. *See* Samson v. California, 126 U.S. 2193, 126 S. Ct. 2193, 165 L. Ed. 2d 250 (2006).

[78]   Searches and seizures compromise different interests in property. A search compromises the suspect's interest in privacy while a seizure deprives the suspect of the right to possession. These are separate invasions and one can occur without the other.

[79]   Maryland v. Macon, *supra* note 3.

Duffel Trouble for Officer Caesar

Ralph Riefer (the second stupidest drug dealer in Whosville history) recently placed an anonymous telephone call to the Whosville Police Department to report a theft. Riefer told police that Mary Wanna (the stupidest drug dealer in Whosville) had just stolen a duffel bag full of his "personal stash" and was planning to smuggle it across the border into Mexico. Officer Caesar, who took the call, believed it was a practical joke and asked the caller to identify himself. When Riefer refused, Caesar told him that he could do nothing without more information, "What do you want me to do, arrest every woman in Whosville carrying a duffel bag?"

"No, you idiot," Riefer replied, "just look at the name tag on the duffel. If it says 'Ralph Riefer,' that's the one." Riefer then hung up quickly, hoping that the call would not be traced, but he was too late.

Caesar sent a car down to Riefer's house to determine whether the call was a joke, but decided in the meantime to check Whosville Air's next flight to Mexico, just in case Riefer was telling the truth. Sure enough, when he arrived at the airport, Caesar observed three women in line at the check-in counter, each traveling with a duffel bag.

The first woman had already checked her bag with the ticket agent, so Caesar stepped behind the counter, checked the tag, and determined that the bag did not belong to Riefer. The second woman had her duffel strapped to her back with a name tag dangling from it. Caesar snuck up, flipped it over, and read it without her noticing. Again, not Riefer's bag.

The third woman, who had been watching Caesar the whole time, clutched her bag tightly to her chest as he approached. Caesar politely asked her if he could examine the name tag on her luggage, but she refused. Caesar did not bother her further. Instead, he headed straight to the airport security office to telephone his superior for instructions. The superior instructed Caesar to keep the woman under observation and to see if she checked in under the name "Mary Wanna." In the meantime, the third woman became nervous, tossed her duffel in a nearby garbage can, and headed out of the airport. When Caesar returned, he found the duffel, opened it, and located Riefer's stash. The duffel bag and the stash were admitted into evidence against Mary and Ralph and both were convicted of drug offenses.

Caesar touched all three bags, but none of his acts amounted to a meaningful interference with possession each for a different reason.

1. Touching or Moving an Object Outside the Owner's Presence

Caesar did not interfere with the first owner's possessory rights because the bag was not in her possession when he touched it. She had already relinquished possession to the airline and had no intention of reclaiming her bag until she reached her destination. Touching or moving luggage outside the owner's presence is not a seizure if the acts of the police do not damage the luggage, delay its arrival, or interfere with the owner's travel plans.[80]

2. Touching or Moving Property in the Owner's Presence without Depriving the Owner of Possession

Caesar touched the second duffel bag while the owner was carrying it. However, his touching did not amount to a *meaningful* interference with the second owner's possessory rights because he did not deprive the owner of possession and control of her bag.[81] The Supreme Court has decided two cases in which the police handled property in the owner's presence. In one case, the police detained a traveler's luggage for 90 minutes. The Court found that this was a seizure because the owner was denied access to his luggage and was prevented from taking it with him.[82] Depriving a traveler of his right to take his luggage with him, even for a short period, constitutes a meaningful interference with possession. In the second case, the police turned stereo equipment around to examine the serial numbers to determine whether it was stolen, also in the owner's presence. The Court held that this handling was not a seizure.[83] Putting these cases together, the following principle emerges: To constitute a meaningful interference with possession, the police must deprive the suspect of possession, if only

---

[80] *See, e.g.*, United States v. Gant, 112 F.3d 239 (6th Cir. 1997) (removal of unattended luggage from overhead compartment of bus to subject it to examination by drug-sniffing dog constituted neither search nor seizure); United States v. Johnson, 990 F.2d 1129 (9th Cir. 1993) (removing traveler's luggage from airline luggage cart and subjecting it to canine inspection to detect for odor of narcotics is not a seizure when procedure is completed prior to time the luggage is scheduled to be placed on airplane). *See also* WAYNE R. LaFAVE, SEARCH & SEIZURE § 9.7(e) (3d ed. 1996) (no seizure occurs when an airline or bus passenger's luggage is moved slightly to facilitate a canine inspection, at a time when the luggage is outside the passenger's immediate presence, if the investigation does not delay the journey of the passenger or the luggage). However, handling luggage outside a suspect's presence may constitute a Fourth Amendment search if police touch or feel it in an exploratory manner that is different from the kind of touching that the suspect could reasonably anticipate. *See, e.g.*, **Bond v. United States**, *supra* note 41 (holding that tactile examination of soft luggage constitutes a search).

[81] *See, e.g.*, **Arizona v. Hicks**, *supra* note 44 (1987) (turning stereo equipment around to examine serial number to determine whether it was stolen was not a seizure); **United States v. McIver, 186 F.3d 1119 (9th Cir. 1999)** (placement of small electronic tracking device on undercarriage of suspect's vehicle did not constitute a seizure because it did not damage the vehicle or deprive the owner of dominion or control over it).

[82] **United States v. Place**, *supra* note 8 (removing luggage from passenger's custody and detaining it for investigation constitutes a seizure).

[83] **Arizona v. Hicks**, *supra* note 44.

temporarily, such as by taking the property away, detaining it, or preventing the suspect from retrieving it from a third party.

3. Abandoned Property

Caesar did not seize the third duffel bag when he fished it out of the garbage can because Mary abandoned her property rights when she threw it there. Tossing something into a garbage can constitutes an unequivocal act of abandonment. A person who abandons property has no right to complain of a seizure.[84]

Denying ownership is another common way property can be abandoned. Had Caesar approached Mary as she stood a few feet away from the bag, asked Mary if the bag was hers, and had she denied ownership, this, too, would have constituted abandonment.[85]

Figure 4.6
Fourth Amendment Requirements for Seizing Property

Purpose of the Seizure	Fourth Amendment Requirements
Use the object as evidence	Probable cause to associate the object with a crime and either a search warrant describing it or a plain view discovery.
Detain the object for investigation	Reasonable suspicion that the object is or contains criminal evidence or contraband.
Prevent the object from being moved while applying for a search warrant	Probable cause to obtain a search warrant coupled with the risk that the object will be moved unless the police seize it now.
Impound the property	Legal authority to impound.

B. Seizure of Property for Use as Evidence

The requirements for seizing property vary with the purpose. Figure 4.6 shows the four main purposes for seizing property and summarizes the requirements for each. In order to seize property for use as evidence, the officer must have probable cause to believe that the property is connected to a crime.[86] Otherwise, officers conducting a lawful search would seize everything that looked even slightly suspicious.[87] The officer must, in addition, either have a search warrant authorizing the seizure or discover the item

---

[84]   United States. v. Basinski, 226 F.3d 829 (7th Cir. 2000)

[85]   United States v. Leshuk, 65 F.3d 1105 (4th Cir. 1995).

[86]   **Arizona v. Hicks**, *supra* note 44; United States v. Wick, 52 F. Supp. 2d 1310 (D.N.M. 1999).

[87]   United States v. Wick, *supra* note 86 (storage locker rental agreement could not be seized because officer lacked probable cause to believe that it was an incriminating document).

in plain view.[88] More will be said about the second requirement shortly. We must first consider the kinds of objects police are permitted to seize as evidence.

> There are four categories of objects police may seize for use as evidence: fruits of a crime, instrumentalities of its commission, other evidence of its commission, and contraband.

1. Objects that May Be Seized as Evidence: The Requirement of Probable of Cause

There are four categories of items that police may seize as evidence: (1) fruits of a crime, such as stolen money or goods; (2) the instrumentalities used to commit it, such as a weapon; (3) contraband, which includes anything that it is a crime to possess, such as an unregistered gun or narcotics; and (4) "mere evidence," a catch-all phrase that includes any other evidence that links a suspect to a crime or furnishes evidence of its commission, such as a mask worn by a bank robber, a shoe with a tread pattern that matches footprints found at the crime scene, or a receipt for the purchase of the murder weapon.[89]

A police officer must be able to make a reasoned determination that the object viewed falls into one of these four categories before the officer may seize it without a search warrant and, to some extent, even when the officer has a warrant.[90] Police officers' experience and training generally enable them to recognize fruits, instrumentalities, and contraband without much difficulty.[91] Cash in unusual quantities or packaged in particular ways sends up a "red flag" that it is probably the fruits of a crime.[92] Police officers do not have to know what the crime was or who committed it in order to have probable cause to treat bundles of $100 bills crammed into a briefcase as seizable evidence. Experience also helps police officers to recognize instrumentalities of a crime and contraband. In *Texas v. Brown*,[93] for example, the Supreme Court held that a police officer had probable cause to seize a balloon knotted a half-inch from the tip, even though he could not see what was inside, because the officer knew from prior experience that balloons knotted this way are often used to transport drugs. Based on similar

---

[88]   *See* § 4.4(B)(3) *infra.*

[89]   Warden v. Hayden, *supra* note 7; Zurcher v. Stanford Daily, 436 U.S. 547, 98 S. Ct. 1970, 56 L. Ed. 2d 525 (1978). Rule 41(b) of the Federal Rules of Criminal Procedure provides that "[a] warrant may be issued under this rule to search for and seize any (1) property that constitutes evidence of the commission of a criminal offense; or (2) contraband, the fruits of crime, or things otherwise criminally possessed; or (3) property designed or intended for use or which is or has been used as the means of committing a criminal offense . . ."

[90]   *See, e.g.,* **Arizona v. Hicks**, *supra* note 44; Warden v. Hayden, *supra* note 7.

[91]   *See, e.g.,* United States v. Padilla, 819 F.2d 952 (10th Cir. 1987).

[92]   United States v. Bono, 946 F. Supp. 972 (M. D. Fla. 1996).

[93]   460 U.S. 730, 103 S. Ct. 1535, 75 L.Ed.2d 502 (1983).

reasoning, a Maryland court held that police officers investigating a recent burglary had probable cause to seize a crowbar in the possession of the man they arrested, even though they were not yet unaware of the means used to gain entry, because a crowbar is a burglar's "stock in trade."[94]

2. Seizure Under a Search Warrant

As in the case of searches, the Supreme Court has expressed a strong preference for seizures under the authority of a warrant because a warrant protects against mistaken seizures.[95] An officer is not forced to decide on the spot whether an object that comes into view constitutes the fruits, instrumentalities, or other evidence of a crime or contraband. The judge has already decided this. The listing of an object in a search warrant carries a judicial finding that there is probable cause to believe that the object is properly subject to seizure. All the officer has to do is find it. The particularized description that search warrants must contain reduces the danger of mistaken seizures.[96]

Figure 4.7
Authority to Seize Evidence in Plain View

Police may seize evidence, without a warrant, if they discover it and develop probable cause to believe that it is connected to criminal activity without exceeding their lawful search authority. Evidence is considered to be in plain view only if:

1. the initial intrusion that brings the officer in contact with the evidence is lawful;
2. it is immediately apparent to the officer that the object observed is criminal evidence or contraband; and
3. the officer is able to gain physical access to seize it without violating the Fourth Amendment.

3. Plain View Exception to the Warrant Requirement

The only time police are allowed to seize an object for use as evidence without a search warrant describing it is when the plain view exception to the warrant requirement applies. This exception permits police to perform a warrantless seizure when: (1) the initial intrusion that brings them in contact with the evidence is lawful, (2) it is immediately apparent that the object viewed is associated with criminal activity, and (3) they have a lawful right of access to it.[97] The Supreme Court has explained that once an officer is lawfully in a position to view an object, the owner's privacy interest in

---

[94] Williams v. State, 342 Md. 724, 679 A.2d 1106 (1996).
[95] *See, e.g.*, Coolidge v. New Hampshire, *supra* note 10.
[96] The requirements for a valid search warrant are covered in § 4.5.
[97] **Arizona v. Hicks**, *supra* note 44; Coolidge v. New Hampshire, *supra* note 10; **United States v. Weinbender**, *supra* note 55.

that object is lost and it would be a needless inconvenience and sometimes even dangerous to require the officer to obtain a search warrant, to say nothing of the risk that the object might be removed or destroyed in the meantime.

The plain view exception originally applied only to objects discovered by accident. The thinking was that if the officer knew of the object's existence in advance, he/she should obtain a warrant. This limitation was abandoned in *Horton v. California*.[98] Consequently, even though plain view discoveries normally occur by chance, chance discovery is no longer necessary.

a. The Initial Intrusion That Brings the Officer in Contact with the Evidence Must Be Lawful

Police must have a legitimate reason for being present at the precise location where the discovery is made for the plain view exception to apply.[99] This requirement is often phrased as being whether the initial intrusion that brought the officer in contact with the evidence was lawful.

There can be any number of legitimate explanations for the officer's presence at the scene of the discovery. The incriminating object, for example, may have been found while the police were on the premises executing a valid warrant to search for other evidence, while they were conducting an appropriately limited search under an exception to the warrant requirement, while they were inventorying the contents of an impounded vehicle, while they were rendering emergency aid to a motorist who is having a seizure, while they were walking up to a driveway to ring the doorbell to ask the occupant a few questions, ad nauseam. The possibilities are unlimited.

It is often necessary for the court to decide whether police were exceeding their search authority at the time of discovery because, if they were, the initial intrusion that brought them in plain view of the evidence is not lawful, and the seizure cannot be justified by the plain view doctrine. For example, if police discover a bag of marijuana in a medicine cabinet while executing a search warrant to search for a stolen television, the evidence will be suppressed because they had no business looking inside a medicine cabinet for a stolen television.

The plain view rule is not limited to items that can be seen. It also applies to objects recognized through the sense of touch. For example, if an officer, while conducting a lawful *Terry* pat-down search to determine whether a suspect is armed, feels an object

---

[98] 496 U.S. 128, 110 S. Ct. 2301, 110 L. Ed. 2d 112 (1990). However, a number of states retain the inadvertent discovery requirement on the theory that if police had probable cause to believe they would encounter the object, they should have gotten a search warrant. *See, e.g.*, Commonwealth. v. King, 67 Mass. App. Ct. 823, 858 N.E.2d 308 (2006).

[99] Minnesota v. Dickerson, *supra* note 19 ("[i]f police are lawfully in a position from which they view an object, if its incriminating character is immediately apparent, and if the officers have a lawful right of access to the object, they may seize it without a warrant. If, however, the police lack probable cause to believe that an object in plain view is contraband without conducting some further search of the object — i.e., if its incriminating character is not immediately apparent — the plain view doctrine cannot justify its seizure.").

that he or she instantly recognizes as contraband from its shape and the way it feels, the officer may seize it.[100]

b. The Object's Criminal Nature Must Be Immediately Apparent

The second prong of the plain view exception requires that the incriminating nature of the object be "immediately apparent." This raises two questions. How much certainty must the officer possess about an object's incriminating nature in order to seize it? And second, what additional exploratory activity is an officer allowed to perform in making this determination? As to the first question, the plain view doctrine does not require absolute certainty that the object viewed constitutes criminal evidence or contraband. The "immediately apparent" requirement is satisfied if the officer has probable cause to associate the object with criminal activity.[101]

The answer to the second question is more complicated. Examining a suspicious object to determine its criminal identity constitutes a search. The plain view doctrine does not give police an iota of search authority beyond what they already have. Some grounds for search authority, such as searches incident to a lawful arrest, allow police to examine objects that come into view before deciding whether to seize them; others do not carry this authority. To satisfy the "immediately apparent" requirement, police must develop probable cause to believe that the object viewed is associated with criminal activity, with no additional exploratory activity beyond what is authorized.[102] Moving a suspicious object as little as an inch to take a closer look is not allowed if this activity is unrelated to the justification that brought the officer in contact with it.

Arizona v. Hicks[103] is an illustrative case. Police entered the defendant's apartment in search of a shooter who had fired a bullet through the floor that struck a person in the apartment below. While on the premises, one of them noticed high-end stereo equipment that seemed out of place in the surroundings and, suspecting that it might be stolen, moved the turntable to read the serial number. A call to headquarters confirmed the officer's suspicion. Application of the plain view exception was denied because the officer had to move the stereo to develop probable cause to seize it. If an officer has to pick up, move, feel, or otherwise examine an object to determine its criminal identity and this activity is unrelated to justification that brought police in contact with it, the plain view exception does not apply.

The same principle applies to writings. Unless police are operating under an exception to the warrant requirement that allows them to read writings, they may not examine writings that come into view during a search beyond glancing at what is plainly visible. *United States v. Silva*[104] illustrates this principle. Police obtained a warrant authorizing

---

[100]   Minnesota v. Dickerson, *supra* note 19; State v. Wilson, 112 N.C. App. 777, 437 S.E.2d 387 (1993).

[101]   Minnesota v. Dickerson, *supra* note 19; Arizona v. Hicks, *supra* note 44; Coolidge v. New Hampshire, *supra* note 10; State v. Wilson, *supra* note 100; Texas v. Brown, *supra* note 93.

[102]   **Arizona v. Hicks**, *supra* note 44; Minnesota v. Dickerson, *supra* note 19.

[103]   *Supra* note 44.

[104]   714 F. Supp. 693 (S.D.N.Y. 1999) (plain view exception did not justify examination of contents of a notebook where there was nothing on its cover to suggest that it contained evidence of a crime).

them to search the home of a bank robbery suspect for a gun, a holster, ammunition, certain items of clothing, business suits, ties, ski masks, and a pair of wide-rimmed sunglasses. In the course of the search, one of the officers came across a brown satchel, opened it, and found a spiral notebook. As he thumbed through the notebook, a five-page letter fell out, which he read as well. He discovered an incriminating passage on the third page. The court rejected application of the plain view exception because the officer had no justification for inspecting the contents of the notebook. The notebook was not listed in the warrant and was incapable of containing any of the objects that were.

For the plain view exception to apply, the incriminating nature of a writing must be ascertainable without opening, inspecting, or disturbing it in any way beyond reading what is plainly visible.[105]

c. The Officer Must Have a Lawful Right of Access to the Object

The last requirement for a plain view seizure is that the officer must have a lawful right of access to the object. Simply because the police lawfully observe an object that they have probable cause to seize does not give them authority to seize it if it would require a warrantless entry into a constitutionally protected location to gain physical access.[106] This happened when Clueso saw what he thought was the stolen *Mona Lisa* through Sam's living room window. Even though his off-premises view was lawful and created probable cause for a seizure, it was necessary for Sam to obtain a search warrant or consent to enter.

Objects recognized as criminal evidence or contraband may be seized without a search warrant only if the officer is able to gain physical access to them without violating the Fourth Amendment. If a physical intrusion into a constitutionally protected location is necessary to gain access, the officer must obtain a search warrant or consent to enter.

---

[105] *See, e.g.,* United States v. Silva, *supra* note 104; State v. Oswald, 232 Wis. 2d 103, 606 N.W.2d 238 (Wis. App. 1999) (police may seize writings that are plainly incriminatory on their face, even if a cursory examination of the exposed parts is necessary to make this determination); State v. Keup, 265 Neb. 96, 655 N.W.2d 25 (2003) (warrantless seizure of notebook was justified under the plain view exception where the notebook was opened to a page that contained incriminating content at the time of discovery).

[106] *See, e.g.,* Illinois v. Andreas, 463 U.S. 765, 103 S. Ct. 3319, 77 L. Ed. 2d 1003 (1983) (for plain view doctrine to operate, not only must the officer be lawfully located in a place from which the object can be plainly seen, but he or she must also have a lawful right of access to the object itself); State v. Fisher, 154 P.3d 455 (Kan. 2007) (holding that officer's off-property open view of a trash bag that was located within the curtilage of defendant's home did not justify seizure of the trash bag under plain view doctrine). *See also* Howard E. Wallin, *Plain View Revisited,* 22 Pace L. Rev. 307, 325 (2002) ([When] police officers stand outside a constitutionally protected location observing items within that protected area . . . they may employ the information they have garnered through their observation, for example, in seeking a warrant, [but] the view in and of itself does not justify an intrusion into the protected area. Simply because they have seen an item that they have a legitimate right to observe does not justify a warrantless intrusion into an otherwise constitutionally protected area.").

C. Brief, Limited Seizures

When police have suspicions about an object, but lack a search warrant or authority to seize it under the plain view doctrine, they may be able to detain it for a brief investigation or prevent it from being moved while applying for a search warrant.[107] The Fourth Amendment imposes less rigorous requirements for brief, limited seizures.

Brief, limited seizures are generally used to detain closed containers, such as briefcases, suitcases, and mailed parcels. **Containers** are personal effects in which suspects have both privacy and property rights. Opening a closed container to look inside constitutes a search and requires either a search warrant or an exception to the warrant requirement that authorizes the opening of a closed container. When search authority is lacking, police may be able to temporarily seize it for investigation or while applying for a search warrant.

1. Seizure Pending Issuance of a Search Warrant

Because a search warrant requires probable cause, police must have probable cause to believe that a container houses criminal evidence or contraband coupled with reason to fear that it might be moved in order to seize it while applying for a search warrant to open it.[108] Seizures pending application for a search warrant rest on exigent circumstances. Suppose that police learn that Sam has left a package with $10,000,000 worth of stolen diamonds with UPS for delivery to his "French connection," and that the plane containing the package is about to take off for Paris. Even though police have no warrant, exigent circumstances justify seizing the package from UPS. This preserves the status quo, pending application for a search warrant. Once the container has been secured, police must obtain a search warrant before they may look inside.[109]

2. Brief, Limited Seizures for Investigation

Police cannot obtain a search warrant if they only have reasonable suspicion to believe that a container houses seizable evidence. However, reasonable suspicion is enough to seize the container for a brief investigation.[110] Investigatory detentions of property are based on the principles established in *Terry v. Ohio*[111] and are subject

---

[107] **United States v. Place**, *supra* note 8; United States v. Jacobsen, *supra* note 27.
[108] United States v. Van Leeuwen, 397 U.S. 294, 90 S. Ct. 1029, 25 L. Ed. 2d 282 (1970) (upholding detention of a suspicious package in the hands of a postal inspector for 29 hours while developing probable cause and obtaining a search warrant); Illinois v. McArthur, *supra* note 71 (where police have probable cause to believe that drugs are located inside a dwelling and a good reason to fear that residents will destroy the evidence before they return with a warrant, they may seal off the premises and prevent residents from entering, pending issuance of a search warrant.).
[109] United States v. Jacobsen, *supra* note 27 ("Even when government agents may lawfully seize a sealed package to prevent loss or destruction of suspected contraband, the Fourth Amendment requires that they obtain a warrant before examining contents of such a package.").
[110] United States v. Place, *supra* note 8.
[111] *Supra* note 9.

to the same rules.[112] For example, if police spot a woman in an airport who matches a drug courier profile, they may temporarily detain her for investigation and also her luggage.[113] However, because reasonable suspicion does not confer authority to open a closed container, investigatory detentions of containers are of little use to the police unless they can confirm their suspicion without looking inside.

The chief application of this exception occurs in narcotics work. As you learned earlier, canine examinations are not searches.[114] Consequently, when police have reasonable suspicion that there are drugs in a traveler's luggage, they may seize the luggage and detain it to subject it to a canine examination. Because no search is involved, the only requirement necessary to perform this procedure is grounds for an investigatory detention. If the dog detects drugs, the officer will then have probable cause for a lengthier seizure, pending application for a search warrant to open the luggage.

No degree of suspicion is necessary to subject a container to a canine examination if police can gain access to the container without seizing it. Unoccupied parked vehicles,[115] checked luggage,[116] and packages in the control of the postal service[117] are examples of containers that may be exposed to a sniff, without suspicion, because the owner's possessory rights are not disturbed.

D. Seizures of Vehicles and Personal Belongings for Impoundment

Traditional Fourth Amendment requirements do not apply when property is seized for a noninvestigative reason, such as to **impound** it (*i.e.*, take custody for safekeeping).[118] Vehicles and the clothing worn at the time of arrest are the two articles most

---

[112] **United States v. Place**, *supra* note 8 (removing luggage from a passenger's custody and detaining it for investigation constitutes seizure; suppression required because 90-minute detention went beyond police authority to detain luggage reasonably suspected to contain narcotics for brief investigation). Although reasonable suspicion permits law enforcement officials to temporarily detain a package pending further investigation, often involving a canine test, it does not give them the option to take the package to the police station. State v. Ressler, 701 N.W.2d 915 (N.D. 2005) (holding that police violated the Fourth Amendment in transporting a package left with shipping company for next-day-air service to a nearby police station for canine testing). They must detain it at the location where the reasonable suspicion originated, pending arrival of a drug-detection dog. Removing it to the police station constitutes a full-fledged seizure that requires either probable cause supported by an exception to the warrant requirement or a warrant to be valid.

[113] *Id.*

[114] *See* § 4.2(C)(2).

[115] *See, e.g.*, United States v. Dyson, 639 F.3d 230 (6th Cir. 2011).

[116] *See* cases *supra* notes 36–40, 80, and 115.

[117] *See, e.g.*, United States v. Vasquez, 213 F.3d 425 (8th Cir. 2000) (package on delivery truck); United States v. Terriques, 319 F.3d 1051 (8th Cir. 2003) (package in possession of postal authorities). United States v. Quiroz, 57 F. Supp. 2d 805 (D. Minn. 1999) (mail).

[118] Florida v. White, 526 U.S. 559, 119 S. Ct. 1555, 143 L. Ed. 2d 748 (1999) (vehicle forfeitable as contraband); Florida v. Wells, *supra* note 75 (driver arrested and taken to jail); South Dakota v. Opperman, *supra* note 75 (abandoned automobile); Colorado v. Bertine, 479 U.S. 367, 107 S. Ct. 738, 93 L. Ed. 2d 739 (1987) (driver arrested and taken to jail); United States v. Coccia, 446

often impounded. Statutes generally give police authority to impound vehicles when they are abandoned, illegally parked, not drivable, or when no one is available to take charge of them after a driver's arrest.[119] The clothing worn at the time of arrest is generally taken from arrested persons and impounded when they are booked into a detention facility.[120]

Once property is impounded, a search will be conducted to produce an inventory. The Fourth Amendment regulates inventory searches, but not by the same standards that are used for evidentiary searches, because the purpose of the search is to protect the owner's property while in police custody and to deter false claims of loss or theft.[121] The Fourth Amendment requirements for inventory searches are designed to ensure that they are used for this purpose and not as a subterfuge to search for evidence. For the search to be valid, (1) there must be a law or police department regulation authorizing the impoundment and (2) the search must be conducted according to established police department operating procedures.[122]

§ 4.5 — The Fourth Amendment Search Warrant

Much has been made of the fact that a search warrant is generally necessary to search for or seize evidence. Little, however, has been said of the search warrant itself. Before proceeding further, we will pause to examine what a search warrant looks like, how one is obtained, and what is necessary for proper execution. Because Fourth Amendment requirements for an arrest warrant (§§ 3.14–3.15) also apply, for the most part, to search warrants, the following explanation focuses on the differences.

A. Applying for a Search Warrant

The mechanics of applying for search and arrest warrants are similar. For both, the officer must submit an affidavit under oath to a magistrate setting forth facts showing probable cause.[123] The facts must be true to the best of the officer's knowledge[124]

F.3d 233 (1st Cir. 2006) (owner taken by ambulance to the hospital); United States v. Gordon, 23 F. Supp. 2d 79 (D. Me. 1998) (car parked four feet away from curb).
[119] See cases supra note 118.
[120] Illinois v. Lafayette, supra note 75 (1983) (inventory search of contents of arrestee's shoulder bag before placing arrestee in a detention facility).
[121] Id.
[122] Colorado v. Bertine, supra note 118 (in the absence of showing that police, who followed standardized caretaking procedures, acted in bad faith for the sole purpose of investigation in conducting inventory search of a defendant's van, evidence discovered during search was admissible. Reasonable police regulations relating to inventory procedures administered in good faith satisfy Fourth Amendment).
[123] Illinois v. Gates, supra note 49.
[124] Malley v. Briggs, supra note 47.

and must be sufficiently detailed to enable the magistrate to make an independent determination of probable cause.[125] The main difference is what the facts in the affidavit must show. For a search warrant, the facts must establish probable cause to believe that: (1) a crime has been committed,[126] (2) the items the officer seeks constitute evidence of that offense, and (3) the items are located at the place to be searched.[127]

To satisfy the second requirement, the officer must describe the items to be seized and explain their connection to the crime. When authority is sought to search for the **fruits** or **instrumentalities of a crime** or **contraband**, the connection is generally self-evident and simply describing the object in the application is generally enough.[128] For example, if the application establishes probable cause to believe that Mary Wanna is dealing in drugs from her home, it will be easy for the judge to see why a balance scale could be an instrumentality of that crime.[129] However, if police wish to search for and seize **mere evidence**, such as "one black overcoat" (allegedly worn by the perpetrator of the crime), they should be sure to include in the application the facts that lead them to believe that the item furnishes evidence of the crime — such as, the fact that an eyewitness saw the perpetrator fleeing the scene of the crime while wearing such a coat.

To satisfy the last requirement, the affidavit must set forth facts that establish probable cause to believe that the items described in the warrant are located at the place to be searched.[130] In the typical case, police seek permission to search for evidence that is now there. However, courts also have authority to issue anticipatory search warrants authorizing police to search for evidence that is not currently there, but is expected to be there at the time of execution.[131] The most common use for anticipatory warrants is in drug investigations. Police arrange for a controlled delivery of drugs and then apply for a warrant authorizing them to search the premises after the delivery has occurred. Anticipatory warrants are not that different from ordinary search warrants

---

[125]   Illinois v. Gates, *supra* note 49.

[126]   Zurcher v. Stanford Daily, *supra* note 89 (it is not necessary that the owner or possessor of the premises to be searched be suspected of involvement in the crime for a search warrant to be issued).

[127]   *See* Figure 4.4 *supra*.

[128]   See Warden v. Hayden, *supra* note 7.

[129]   United States v. Jones, 543 F.2d 627 (8th Cir.), cert. denied, 429 U.S. 1051, 97 S. Ct. 763, 50 L. Ed. 2d 767 (1976).

[130]   Sgro v. United States, 287 U.S. 206, 53 S. Ct. 138, 77 L. Ed. 2d 260 (1932) (holding that probable cause requirement was not satisfied where warrant was issued based on information relating to an alleged violation of the National Prohibition Act that occurred more than 20 days before).

[131]   United States v. Grubbs, 547 U.S. 90, 126 S. Ct. 1494, 164 L. Ed. 2d 195 (2006) (upholding anticipatory search warrant issued on the basis of probable cause to believe that a videotape containing child pornography purchased from a Web site operated by an undercover postal inspector would be at the suspect's residence when the warrant was executed). The Court stated that to satisfy the probable cause requirement for an anticipatory search warrant, the supporting affidavit must establish probable cause to believe that contraband or evidence of a crime will be found in a particular place when the triggering event occurs, and also that there is probable cause to believe the triggering condition will occur. A few states lack statutory authority to support issuance of anticipatory search warrants. *See*, *e.g.*, Dodson v. State, 150 P.3d 1054 (Okla. Crim. App. 2006).

because all warrants require probable cause to believe that the objects listed in the warrant will be at the placed to be searched when the warrant is executed.

Facts establishing probable cause to search can grow stale with the passage of time because, even though the police had probable cause to believe that the objects were there a month ago, they may not be there now. The staleness of the facts in Clueso's affidavit was one of the reasons Judge Stickler initially refused to issue a search warrant. If a significant amount of time passes between the facts relied on to establish probable cause and the application for a search warrant, police must include facts showing why they believe the objects described are still at that location. For example, had Clueso kept Sam's house under observation for the entire month, and had Stickler been informed of that fact, the passage of time would not have precluded issuance of the search warrant.

B. Contents and Form of the Search Warrant

The Fourth Amendment requires that search warrants "particularly describe" the place to be searched and the things to be seized. The purpose of this requirement is to ensure that police do not seize the wrong property and that they search only in locations where there is probable cause to believe that the objects of their search will be found.

1. Particular Description of the Place to be Searched

Oftentimes a search warrant will be executed by a person other than the one who knows the facts of the case and who swore to them in the application. Accordingly, the search warrant must describe the place to be searched with sufficient particularity to allow an executing officer who is unfamiliar with the facts to locate and identify it with reasonable certainty.[132] If a warrant is issued to search premises, a street address will suffice unless the building is subdivided into units — in which case the unit number must also be included.[133] If a warrant is issued to search a vehicle, reference to the vehicle's make and license number or make and owner is sufficient, but other facts, such as color, model, model year, or vehicle identification number (VIN), should be included, if this information is known.

2. Particular Description of the Things to be Seized

The Fourth Amendment requires a particularized description of the items to be seized for two reasons — to avoid seizing the wrong property and to prevent indiscriminate rummaging. The more precisely an object is described, the more limited the search of the premises is likely to be. Accordingly, the warrant must describe the

---

[132]   Steele v. United States, 267 U.S. 498, 45 S. Ct. 414, 69 L. Ed. 757 (1925); **United States v. King, 227 F.3d 732 (6th Cir. 2000).**

[133]   Maryland v. Garrison, 480 U.S. 79, 107 S. Ct. 1013, 94 L. Ed. 2d 72 (1987).

objects of the search with sufficient particularity to avoid misidentification and to prevent the police from invading privacy to any greater extent than necessary.[134]

Whether a particular warrant description is adequate to accomplish these purposes varies with the nature of the object, the ease of describing it, the amount of detail known to the police, and the risk of misidentification.[135] For example, a warrant authorizing a search for "drug paraphernalia" in a tobacco shop should contain a fairly specific description of what items are considered "paraphernalia." Otherwise, the executing officers could end up seizing tobacco pipes even though there is no probable cause to believe that they are associated with the use of illegal drugs.

Even when the risk of seizing innocent items is low, as, for example, when a warrant authorizes the seizure of drug paraphernalia from a video store, the warrant's description must be as specific as the circumstances of the case permit.[136] Failure to do so violates the Fourth Amendment because it leads to overly broad searches and unnecessary invasions of privacy.[137] For example, a warrant issued to search a robbery suspect's home for "weapons used in the robbery" would violate the particularity requirement if the police knew that the weapon used was a machine gun because "weapons" is a category that includes everything from missiles with multiple warheads to tiny razor blades. Failure to describe the weapon sought as a machine gun will result in unnecessary intrusions on privacy because it allows police to look inside places a "weapon" would fit, but a machine gun would not.

3. The "Facially Valid" Warrant

A warrant that appears to contain a particularized description of the place to be searched and the items to be seized is said to be **"facially valid."**[138] Even though the description turns out to be less precise than it appears to be and the warrant is held invalid, evidence seized under it will not be suppressed as long as the executing officer reasonably failed to appreciate the warrant's deficiency.[139] *Maryland v. Garrison*[140] is

---

[134] Coolidge v. New Hampshire, *supra* note 10; Marron v. United States, 275 U.S. 192, 48 S. Ct. 74, 72 L. Ed. 231 (1927); State v. Lefort, 248 Kan. 332, 806 P.2d 986 (1991); People v. Bennett, 171 Misc. 2d 264, 653 N. Y. S. 2d 835 (1996).

[135] *See, e.g.,* United States v. Ford, 184 F.3d 566 (6th Cir. 1984) ("Degree of specificity required in a search warrant depends on what information is reasonably available to the police in the case; thus, a general description may suffice when the police could supply no better information, but fail when a narrower description was available."). *See also* Marcus v. Search Warrant, 367 U.S. 717, 81 S. Ct. 1708, 6 L. Ed. 2d 1127 (1961) (a higher degree of particularity is required when the items to be seized carry the protection of the First Amendment).

[136] United States v. Ford, *supra* note 135 (failure to limit broad descriptive terms renders search warrant invalid when further descriptive information is available to the police); Sate v. Schrager, 472 So. 2d 896 (Fla. Dist. Ct. App. 1985).

[137] United States v. Guidry, 199 F.3d 1150 (10th Cir. 1999); United States v. Robertson, 21 F.3d 1030 (10th cir. 1994).

[138] United States v. Wood, 6 F. Supp.2d 1213 (D. Kan. 1998).

[139] United States v. Leon, 468 U.S. 897, 104 S. Ct. 3405, 82 L. Ed. 2d 677 (1984).

[140] 480 U.S. 79, 107 S. Ct. 1013, 94 L. Ed. 2d 72 (1987).

an example. Police obtained and executed a search warrant for premises known as "2036 Park Avenue, third floor apartment" and learned later that the third floor was divided into two apartments and that they had searched the wrong unit. The Supreme Court, nevertheless, upheld the admissibility of the evidence, despite the warrant's invalidity, because the executing officers were excusably ignorant that there were two separate units on the third floor.

Whether the executing officer should have recognized the warrant's defects depends on a number of considerations, including the degree to which the officer participated in the investigation and preparation of the affidavit. For example, a description of the items to be seized as "women's jewelry" could seem perfectly adequate to an officer who is unfamiliar with the case, but overly broad to an officer who is intimately familiar and knows that only a small portion of the jewelry likely to be found on the premises will be relevant. Likewise, an officer who prepared the affidavit might review the list of items in the warrant and understand that extraneous items have been included. Thus, the reasonableness of the officer's reliance on a defective warrant must be determined on a case-by-case basis.[141]

However, reliance on a warrant that fails to give any description of the place to be searched or the items to be seized is never reasonable.[142] The search warrant in Figure 4.8 is facially invalid because it completely fails to list any of the items for which it is issued.

Figure 4.8
Sample Search Warrant/Without Item Listing

> To any Sheriff, Constable, Marshal, or Police Officer of the State of Confusion:
>
> You are hereby authorized and directed to search the following premises located: 2443 Morris Avenue, Apartment/Room # 7, IN THE COUNTY OF WHADYASAY, STATE OF CONFUSION.
>
>   This search warrant must be executed between 6:00 a.m. and 9:00 p.m.
>   This search warrant must be executed not more than 10 days after the date of issuance.
>   The search warrant and any property seized must be returned and delivered without any unnecessary delay.
>
>   Given under my hand this 13th Day of May 2011
>   /s/ Betty Bright
>   Justice of the Peace, Whadyasay County

---

[141] *See, e.g.*, People v. Bradford, 15 Cal. 4th 1229, 939 P.2d 259 (1997).

[142] Groh v. Ramirez, 540 U.S. 551, 124 S. Ct. 1284, 157 L. Ed. 2d 1068 (2004) ("Fourth Amendment, by its terms requires particularity in the warrant. A search warrant that utterly fails to describe the persons or things to be seized is invalid on its face, notwithstanding that requisite particularized description was provided in search warrant application.").

C. *Requirements for Executing the Warrant*

The procedure for executing search warrants is similar to the procedure for executing arrest warrants. In both cases, only the persons to whom the search warrant is addressed may execute it,[143] the warrant must be presented upon execution, and officers must knock and announce their presence before making a forcible entry unless compliance will jeopardize their safety or risk destruction of evidence. However, there are two important differences.

First, search warrants must be executed within a reasonably short time after their issuance.[144] This is in contrast to arrest warrants, which can remain valid for a long time — even years. Once facts make it reasonable to believe that a given person is guilty of a crime, the reasonableness of that belief will not change over time. The same is not true of search warrants, which require probable cause to believe that the objects described in the warrant are located at the place to be searched. Even though there was probable cause to believe that the objects were there when the warrant is issued, this probability weakens with the passage of time. Delay in executing a search warrant violates the Fourth Amendment if the probable cause that supported its issuance no longer exists when it is executed.

Second, after completing the search, the executing officer must prepare an inventory of the property seized, give the owner a copy, and return the warrant, together with a copy of the inventory, to the judge who issued it.[145] Although failure to make a timely return will rarely invalidate an otherwise lawful search, it can cause other problems because the prosecutor is required to authenticate objects offered into evidence (*i.e.*, establish that they are what they purport to be and have not been tampered with). A timely return is important because the longer the police wait, the more difficult it will be for the prosecutor to establish authenticity.

---

[143] Hanlon v. Berger, 526 U.S. 808, 119 S. Ct 1706, 143 L. Ed. 2d 978 (1999) (police may not take reporters, photographers, or other third parties whose presence is not necessary with them during execution of search warrant because this leads to unnecessary invasion of privacy); Wilson v. Layne, 526 U.S. 603, 119 S. Ct. 1692, 143 L. Ed. 2d 818 (1999) (same).

[144] Statutes and court rules often require that search warrants be executed or returned within a specified period after their issuance. Federal search warrants, for example, must command the officer to execute the warrant within a specified time no longer than 10 days. *See* FED. R. CRIM. P. 41. However, execution within the time specified in the warrant does not necessarily ensure compliance with the Fourth Amendment. Delay in execution will violate the Fourth Amendment if the probable cause that supported the issuance of the warrant no longer exists at the time of execution. *See, e.g.*, United States v. Grant, 108 F. Supp. 2d 1172 (D. Kan. 2000) (finding violation of the Fourth Amendment where search warrant, issued on an affidavit showing a single sale of rock cocaine at the address to be searched, was executed six and one-half months later); State v. Nelson, 817 So. 2d 158 (La. App. 2002) (validity of the warrant depends upon whether the probable cause recited in the affidavit continues until the time of execution of the warrant.). *See also* 2 WAYNE R. LAFAVE, SEARCH AND SEIZURE § 3.7(a) at p. 342 (1996) ("Absent additional facts tending to show otherwise, a one-shot type of crime, such as a single instance of possession or sale of some form of contraband, will support a finding of probable cause only for a few days at best.").

[145] *See* Berger v. New York, 388 U.S. 41, 87 S. Ct. 1873, 18 L. Ed. 2d 1040 (1967).

We have just completed a condensed tour of the main principles governing search and seizure law. Police are called upon to apply these principles in three primary settings: searches involving people, searches involving vehicles, and searches involving premises. Examining the rules a second time in the settings in which police are called upon to apply them will solidify their understanding. The rules need to be instantly accessible because most searches are conducted without a warrant, forcing police to make on-the-spot decisions about the scope of their authority. Their decisions need to be correct, because the admissibility of evidence can be destroyed if they overstep their lawful search authority.[146]

§ 4.6   Searches Involving People and Personal Effects

Although search warrants may be issued to search a specific individual,[147] most such searches are conducted without a warrant. *Terry* pat-down searches and searches incident to custodial arrests are the two most common grounds for searching individuals.

We begin with the following example.

Operation Grab 'n' Sniff

The Whosville PD recently implemented Operation "Grab 'n' Sniff" at the Whosville international airport. The operation involves placing trained dogs in the baggage handling area to detect illegal drugs. As soon as the bags from an arriving flight are unloaded, Whosville officers separate out bags that appear suspicious and present them for a canine examination.[148] Usually, the dogs detect nothing and the bags are returned to the airline for standard handling. When a dog detects something, police officers seize the bag and proceed to the magistrate for a warrant to search the bag and a second warrant to arrest the owner.

Last week, Officer Caesar of the Whosville PD separated out a Gucci gym bag that looked suspicious and exposed it to a canine examination. Sure enough, the dog detected something. The name tag on the bag showed that it was owned by Bugsy Boss. Recognizing the name as the head of Whosville's biggest crime syndicate, Caesar decided that instead of following the standard procedure, he would place the bag back on the carousel and arrest Boss when he claimed it. That way, Caesar reasoned, Boss

---

[146]   The requirements for the plain view doctrine are discussed in § 4.4(B).

[147]   *See, e.g.*, Ybarra v. Illinois, 444 U.S. 85, 88, 100 S. Ct. 338, 340, 62 L. Ed. 2d 238, 243 (1979).

[148]   It is not a search or a seizure to expose luggage and other packages to a canine inspection while they are outside the owner's immediate custody and control. *See* cases *supra* notes 36, 39, and 80.

would not be able to extricate himself with high priced attorneys. Caesar returned the Gucci bag to the airline and staked out the baggage claim area, but Boss was nowhere to be seen.

A young man named Tom Thug, also familiar to Caesar because of a prior armed robbery conviction, retrieved the Gucci bag. Caesar watched him go outside, hand the bag to Boss, and return to the baggage claim area. Suspecting Tom of being an accomplice, Caesar radioed for a second officer to arrest Boss while he kept Tom under surveillance.

Officer Fromkin responded to the call. After placing Boss under arrest, he grabbed the Gucci bag from him, performed a pat down, and then hastily searched the contents for drugs and weapons. All he found was two rocks of crack cocaine. He then handcuffed Boss' arms behind his back, and went through his pockets and wallet where he found a note titled "Things to do today." The note read: "1. Buy milk, 2. Bribe Mayor Kruger re: road contract, 3. Blackmail jurors in RICO trial." There were check marks beside "2" and "3." Because the note dealt with matters unrelated to Boss' arrest, Fromkin put it back in Boss' wallet and returned it to him.

Meanwhile, Caesar watched Tom remove two more bags from the carousel. As he carried them from the airport, Caesar approached Tom and asked if he would answer a few questions.

"I'm too busy," Tom replied, and kept walking. Caesar said, "Not so fast buddy! WPD – let me see some identification." As Tom reached for his wallet, Caesar noticed a strange bulge underneath his coat and proceeded to pat him down for weapons. The bulge was bumpy but pliable and clearly not a weapon. As Caesar poked, squeezed, lifted, and pushed on the bulge, he heard a "clinking" sound like glasses tapping each other. As a result, Caesar was able to conclude that the bulge was a baggie containing several glass vials of the kind used to package illegal drugs. At that point, Caesar reached into Tom's pocket and removed a bag full of glass vials containing crack, just as he had expected, and placed Tom under arrest.

The Boss, Torn, the bag containing vials of crack cocaine, and the three pieces of luggage were transported to the Whosville police station. Upon arrival, Caesar searched the remaining two bags and made a huge bust — he found several kilograms of crack cocaine. At the arraignment the next day, the judge denied bail for Boss (due to his prior record), but ruled that Tom had been illegally arrested and released him.

After the arraignment, Caesar placed Boss in lockup, exchanged his street clothes for an orange jumpsuit, and searched his wallet again. Coming across the "things to do" note, he read it and set it aside for use as evidence. He then searched the Gucci bag and he discovered a bound ledger book that Officer Fromkin had missed. He thumbed through it to determine whether it contained anything incriminating. Sure enough, it contained vast records of drug transactions, bribery, and corrupt dealings. After completing the inventory, Caesar took the ledger and the "things to do" note to the evidence room, and the rest of Boss' belongings to the property room for safekeeping. At the trial, the judge suppressed everything except the two rocks of crack cocaine recovered from Boss' Gucci bag at the scene of his arrest and the "things to do" note. As you read the materials that follow, try to figure out why the rest of the evidence was inadmissible.

§ 4.7 — The *Terry* Search Revisited

A number of searches were performed in Operation Grab 'n' Sniff — some legal, some not. We will begin our analysis with Officer Caesar's *Terry* search of Tom. Although the search began properly, it quickly went awry. As a result, all the evidence against Tom had to be suppressed.

A. *Required Grounds*

Police perform weapons frisks during investigatory encounters when they have reasonable concerns for their safety. Although this practice is longstanding, the Supreme Court did not have occasion to rule on its constitutionality until 1968 in the landmark case of *Terry v. Ohio*,[149] covered in Chapter 3. The Court laid down two requirements for protective weapons searches. First, the officer must have adequate grounds to initiate the encounter. The usual reason is to check out circumstances that arouse their reasonable suspicion.[150] That is why Officer Caesar initiated his encounter with Tom. The canine alert in response to Boss' luggage, Caesar's observation that Tom appeared to be working with Boss, and his knowledge that both had previously been involved in criminal activity provided ample justification for initiating the stop.

However, a lawful stop does not automatically justify a weapons frisk.[151] A frisk is permitted only if the officer has reasonable suspicion that the detainee is armed and could be dangerous.[152] The crime under investigation, knowledge of the detainee's

---

[149] *Supra* note 9.

[150] *Id.*

[151] *Id.*; State v. Garland, 270 N.J. Super. 31, 636 A.2d 541 (1994).

[152] **Terry v. Ohio**, *supra* note 9; **Florida v. J.L., 529 U.S. 266, 120 S. Ct. 1375, 146 L. Ed. 2d 254 (2000).**

criminal past, weapon-like bulges in the detainee's clothing, hostile behavior, furtive gestures, and the late hour or secluded location of the stop are some of the many factors that might justify a frisk. Caesar's observation of the bulge in Tom's jacket,[153] combined with his knowledge of Tom's prior armed robbery conviction,[154] provided adequate justification for a frisk.

B. Permissible Scope

The scope of a *Terry* weapons search extends to the detainee's person[155] and any unlocked containers within grabbing distance that might contain a weapon.[156] Officer Caesar's *Terry* search authority did not extend to the luggage Tom was carrying at the time of his arrest because the bags were probably locked, rendering weapons inside inaccessible. Moreover, the probability of their containing weapon was low because they had previously cleared airport security.

C. Permissible Intensity

Officer Caesar's search went bad, not because he lacked grounds for frisking Tom, but because he exceeded the intensity permitted for this kind of search. A *Terry* weapons search is limited to activity necessary to determine whether the suspect is armed. When the search is directed at the suspect's person, the intensity is limited to patting down the suspect's outer clothing.[157] When authority exists to search a container, the intensity is limited to a cursory visual inspection of the contents — just enough to determine whether there is a weapon inside.[158]

Once Officer Caesar determined that the bulge under Tom's coat was not a weapon, he reached the limits of his *Terry* search authority. When he continued to poke, squeeze, and push the bulge, he was no longer searching for weapons, but was trying to determine other things about the object. Because these acts were not necessary to rule the object out as being a weapon, Caesar's continued tactile examination exceeded the boundaries of his *Terry* search authority, requiring suppression of the glass vials of cocaine removed from Tom's pocket.[159]

---

[153] Pennsylvania v. Mimms, 434 U.S. 106, 98 S. Ct. 330, 54 L. Ed. 2d 331 (1977).

[154] *See* Adams v. Williams, 406 U.S. 143, 92 S. Ct. 1921, 32 L. Ed. 2d 612 (1972).

[155] **Terry v. Ohio**, *supra* note 9.

[156] United States v. Flippin, 924 F.2d 163 (9th Cir. 1991) (officer justified in looking inside makeup bag when suspect grabbed it after he turned away); State v. Ortiz, 67 Haw. 181, 683 P.2d 822 (1984) (officer justified in looking inside knapsack when detainee made quick grab for it after stating that it was empty).

[157] **Terry v. Ohio**, *supra* note 9.

[158] Michigan v. Long, 463 U.S. 1032, 103 S. Ct. 3469, 77 L. Ed. 2d 1201 (1983).

[159] Minnesota v. Dickerson, *supra* note 19; **State v. Wilson, 112 N.C. App. 777, 437 S.E.2d 387 (1993)**.

Figure 4.9
Requirements for a "Plain Feel" Seizure during a *Terry* Stop

1.	Police feel an object in the course of a weapons pat down.
2.	They immediately recognize the object as "feeling" something like a specific kind of contraband.
3.	Other circumstances surrounding the encounter reinforce the belief that the object is what it feels like.

D. *Seizure of Evidence in "Plain Feel" During a* Terry *Pat-Down Search*

Although police officers may not initiate a pat-down search solely because they suspect that a detainee has contraband, they may seize it if they discover it during a lawful pat-down search. The plain view doctrine has an analog known as the "plain feel" doctrine, which applies to *Terry* searches. If an officer feels an object during a lawful pat down and its contours and mass make it immediately apparent that the object is contraband, the officer may to seize it without a warrant.[160] "Immediately apparent" means that the officer must develop probable cause to believe that the object felt is contraband without exceeding the boundaries of the officer's *Terry* search authority. Once the officer rules the object out as being a weapon, *Terry* search authority ends. Continued manipulation to determine an object's identity, as Officer Caesar did, violates the Fourth Amendment.

Police are seldom able to develop probable cause to believe that an unseen object is contraband solely from the light touch that is permissible during a pat-down search. What feels like a rock of crack cocaine could be just a rock,[161] a "one-hitter" pipe could be a pen, and a film canister might actually contain only film.[162] However, police officers are allowed to take other information into account.[163] For example, if an officer feels what he or she believes could be a rock of crack cocaine in a suspect's shirt pocket during a pat-down search, this alone does not provide probable cause to seize it.[164] However, if the officer also observes a glass tube and a box of Brillo pads on the front seat of the suspect's car, which he or she knows from prior experience are often used to smoke crack, the officer would then have grounds to seize it.[165]

---

[160]   *See* cases *supra* note 159.

[161]   State v. Bridges, 963 S. W. 2d 487 (Tenn. 1997); Campbell v. State, 864 S. W. 2d 223 (Tex. Ct. App. 1993).

[162]   *Id.*

[163]   Illinois v. Gates, *supra* note 49; Taylor v. People, 454 Mich. 580, 564 N.W.2d 24 (1997). *See also* United States v. Chien, 266 F.3d 1 (1st Cir. 2001) ("[E]ven though an officer may not seize an object during a *Terry* frisk unless he or she has probable cause to believe that it is contraband, nothing prevents an officer from inquiring into the nature of an object that he feels is suspicious.").

[164]   Minnesota v. Dickerson, *supra* note 19.

[165]   **State v. Wilson**, *supra* note 159; People v. Mitchell, 65 Ill. 2d 211, 650 N. E. 2d 1014 (1995).

§ 4.8　— Search Following a Custodial Arrest

Bugsy Boss and Tom Thug were both arrested and searched. The Boss search derived from a lawful arrest and was conducted in a proper manner, producing evidence that could be used at his trial. Tom's arrest, in contrast, derived from a *Terry* search violation. The unconstitutionality of the arrest tainted the search that followed. Tom was released because there was no evidence that could be used against him.

A. *Justifications for Performing the Search*

In studying the search incident to arrest exception to the warrant requirement, you need to stay focused on the justifications for the search. The search serves two purposes: (1) to protect the officer's safety by removing weapons that could be used to assault the officer or effect an escape and (2) to prevent persons under arrest from destroying or concealing evidence. The justifications that support the search also define the boundaries. Search authority only extends to the arrestee's person[166] and objects within the area under his immediate control (defined as the area from within which he/she might reach to gain access to a weapon or destructible evidence).[167]

The "immediate control" test was announced in *Chimel v. California*.[168] The defendant was arrested in his home for the burglary of a coin shop. After his arrest, police conducted a warrantless search of his entire home, which lasted almost an hour. They recovered some of the stolen coins in a drawer in the bedroom.

The Supreme Court ruled that this search vastly exceeded their search authority. The Court explained:

> When an arrest is made, it is reasonable for the arresting officer to search the person arrested in order to remove any weapons that the latter might seek to use in order to resist arrest or effect his escape . . . . In addition, it is entirely reasonable for the arresting officer to search for and seize any evidence on the arrestee's person in order to prevent its concealment or destruction. And the area into which an arrestee might reach in order to grab a weapon or evidentiary items must, of course, be governed by a like rule. A gun on a table or in a drawer in front of one who is arrested can be as dangerous to the arresting officer as one concealed in the clothing of the person arrested.

However, "[t]here is no comparable justification . . . for searching any room other than that in which an arrest occurs — or, for that matter, for searching through all the desk drawers or other closed or concealed areas in that room itself. Such searches, in the

---

[166] **United States v. Robinson,** *supra* **note 65** (upholding seizure of heroin capsules discovered while examining contents of cigarette pack in pocket of motorist arrested for driving with a revoked license); United States v. Armstrong, 16 F.3d 289 (8th Cir. 1994) (wallet); United States v. Phillips 607 F.2d 808 (8th Cir. 1979) (wallet); Corrasco v. State, 712 S.W. 2d 120 (TEX. CRIM. APP. 1986) (handbag). *See also* WAYNE R. LAFAVE, 3 SEARCH & SEIZURE § 5.3 (3d. ed. 1996).

[167] Chimel v. California, *supra* note 44.

[168] *Id.*

absence of well-recognized exceptions, may be made only under the authority of a search warrant."

The search incident to arrest exception to the warrant requirement has two sub rules, one which deals with searches of an arrested individual's person and the other with searches of objects within arm's reach.

Figure 4.10
Authority to Search the Arrestee's Person Incident to Arrest

A lawful custodial arrest carries automatic authority to search the arrested individual's person, clothing, and articles closely associated with his person that are on or carried by him. The officer's authority does not depend upon the nature of the offense of arrest or the probability that the search will turn up weapons or evidence. The search may be performed either at the scene of arrest, the police station, or at both places, and may be as methodical as the police wish to make it.

B. Search of the Arrested Individual's Person

1. Authority to Perform

The majority of searches performed by the police are made after an arrest. A lawful custodial arrest carries automatic authority to search the arrested individual's person, clothing, and articles closely associated with his person that are on or carried by him. Authority to perform the search does not depend on the nature of the offense or the probability that the search will turn up weapons or evidence.

This rule was established in *United States v. Robinson*.[169] Robinson was arrested for driving with a revoked operator's permit. After his arrest, the officer performed a field search that included inspecting the contents of a crumpled cigarette pack in Robinson's pocket where 14 heroin capsules were found. Robinson moved to suppress this evidence on the grounds that the nature of the offense for which he was arrested — driving on a suspended license — made the search unreasonable because the officer lacked probable cause to believe that the search would turn up weapons or evidence of the crime he was arrested for. The Supreme Court rejected this argument, explaining that the danger to an officer from the extended exposure, which follows taking a suspect into custody and transporting him to the police station, makes it reasonable to perform a full search of the arrested individual's person in *all* cases, and not just those where the officer has probable cause to believe the person arrested possesses a weapon or destructible evidence. An actual custodial arrest is necessary to perform the search. Police are not allowed to search for evidence when they issue a citation in lieu of making an arrest.[170]

---

[169] **United States v. Robinson**, *supra* note 65.
[170] Knowles v. Iowa, 525 U.S. 113, 119 S. Ct. 484, 142 L. Ed. 2d 492 (1998).

The validity of the search depends on the legality of the arrest. If the arrest is made without probable cause or the probable cause derives from tainted evidence, the search that follows is not authorized, and the evidence will be suppressed.[171] That is why the crack cocaine in Tom's luggage was suppressed. Tom's arrest was illegal because it derived from a *Terry* search violation.

2. Scope and Intensity of the Search

The search of the arrested individual's person includes his clothing and articles closely associated with his person that are on or carried by him, such as his wallet, handbag or cellphone, but does not include backpacks, packages, luggage, or other objects that are not closely associated with his person.[172] Their searchability depends on second rule.

The search of the arrested individual's person can be quite thorough. Police can examine everything in his pockets, go through his wallet, read his receipts and private papers, retrieve information from his cell phone or pager, and even inspect the contents of his cigarette pack, in search of evidence of *any* offense, not just the crime for which the arrest was made.[173]

However, a lawful custodial arrest does not confer automatic authority to perform highly intrusive searches, such as strip and bodily cavity, or searches that extend below the surface of the body, such as taking blood samples. Additional grounds are necessary for searches like these. Bodily intrusive searches are covered in Chapter 7.

3. Timing of the Search

The search of the arrested individual's person may be performed at the scene of arrest, at the police station, or at both places.[174] The Supreme Court has not been troubled even by substantial delays in performing the search. In *United States*

---

[171] Wong Sun v. United States, 371 U.S. 471, 83 S. Ct. 407, 9 L. Ed. 2d 441 (1963).

[172] *See, e.g.,* **United States v. Robinson**, *supra* **note 65** (upholding search of crumpled cigarette package in arrested person's pocket as incident to arrest); United States v. Molinaro, 877 F.2d 1341 (7th Cir.1989) (upholding search of wallet as incident to arrest); United States v. Rodriguez, 995 F.2d 776 (7th Cir.1993) (upholding the search and photocopying of address book found in arrestee's pocket as incident to arrest); United States. v. Curtis, 635 F.3d 704 (5th Cir. 2011) (upholding search of cell phone found in arrestee's pocket as incident to arrest); United States v. Murphy, 552 F. 3d 405 (4th Cir. 2009) (same); United States v. Finley, 477 F.3d 250 (5th Cir. 2007) (same); People v. Diaz, 51 Cal.4th 84, 244 P.3d 501 (Cal. 2011) (same). *But see* State v. Robinson, 131 Ohio App.3d 356, 722 N.E.2d 573 (1998) (holding that search of arrested person's handbag is not incident to arrest unless it was on her person at the time of arrest). For a more complete discussion of cell phone searches incident to arrest, *see, generally,* Allen M. Gershowitz, *The iPhone Meets the Fourth Amendment*, 56 UCLA L. Rev. 27 (2008); Justin M. Wolcott, *Are Smartphones Like Footlockers or Crumpled Up Cigarette Packages? Applying the Search Incident to Arrest Doctrine to Smartphones in South Carolina Courts*, 61 S.C. L. Rev. 843 (2010).

[173] *See* authorities note 172 *supra*.

[174] United States v. Edwards, 415 U.S. 800, 94 S. Ct. 1234, 39 L. Ed. 2d 771 (1974).

v. Edwards,[175] for example, police searched the defendant's clothing at the police station hours after his arrest for attempting to break and enter a post office. The arrest was made at 11:00 P.M. and the defendant was taken to jail. An investigation of the burglary scene after the defendant's arrest revealed that the attempted entry had been made through a wooden window, which had been pried up, leaving paint chips on the window sill. The next morning, the defendant's shirt, trousers and other articles of clothing were taken from him and tested for paint chips. A positive match was found. The Supreme Court upheld the delayed search, stating:

> ... [O]nce the accused is lawfully arrested and is in custody, the effects in his possession at the place of detention that were subject to search at the time and place of his arrest may lawfully be searched and seized without a warrant even though a substantial period of time has elapsed between the arrest and subsequent administrative processing, on the one hand, and the taking of the property for use as evidence, on the other. This is true where the clothing or effects are immediately seized upon arrival at the jail, held under the defendant's name in the "property room" of the jail, and at a later time searched and taken for use at the subsequent criminal trial. The result is the same where the property is not physically taken from the defendant until sometime after his incarceration.

The Supreme Court has never explained why delayed searches are permitted for articles that are closely associated with the arrestee's person (*i.e.*, clothing, wallet, handbag, pocket notebooks, cell phones, and pagers) but not of other things.[176] Perhaps it is because a thorough examination of the suspect's clothing and personal effects at the scene of the arrest would be embarrassing, inconvenient, and impracticable, or because an inventory search will take place, in any event, when the suspect is booked into a detention facility. Whatever the reason, the line has been drawn at articles closely associated with the arrested individual's person that are on or carried by him.[177] Searches of articles not associated with the person, such as backpacks, briefcases, suitcases, and packages are governed by a different rule.[178] This rule is discussed in the next section.

> Articles not closely associated with the arrested individual's person that were on or carried by him at the time of arrest may be searched without a warrant only if the arrestee is unsecured and within reaching distance at the *time of the search*.

---

[175] *Id.*

[176] *See* authorities note 172 *supra*.

[177] *See, e.g.*, United States v. Edwards, *supra* note 174 (upholding warrantless search of clothing taken from the arrestee after he was placed in jail); United States v. Phillips, 607 F.2d 808 (8th Cir. 1979) (upholding warrantless search of arrestee's wallet at police station); State v. Wade, 215 Wis. 2d 684, 573 N.W.2d 228 (1997) (upholding warrantless search of arrestee's handbag at police station); Curd v. City Court of Judsonia, Arkansas, 141 F.3d 839 (8th Cir. 1998) (same).

[178] *See, e.g.*, United States v. Chadwick, 433 U.S. 1, 97 S. Ct. 2476, 53 L. Ed. 2d 538 (1977) (station house search of 200 pound footlocker, suspected of containing marijuana, more than an hour after suspect's arrest not justified as incident to his arrest).

C. Search of Articles Not Closely Associated with the Arrested Individual's Person

The broad authority police have to search the arrested individual's person does not extend to articles not closely with his person that were under his control at the time of arrest such as his backpack, briefcase, suitcase, or vehicle. Articles like these may be searched without a warrant only if the arrestee is unsecured and within reaching distance of them at the time of the search. Once the arrestee has been secured and can no longer grab a weapon or evidence from inside them, the search can no longer be justified as an incident to his arrest, and police must obtain a search warrant.[179]

Although this restriction makes perfect sense, it was not the law until recently. Authority to search containers that were under the arrested person's immediate control at the time of arrest was viewed as the spoils of a lawful arrest.[180] So long as the search occurred reasonably close in time to the arrest and was an integral part of the arrest process, the search was valid even through the arrestee was securely in police custody and no longer had access to them.[181]

In *Arizona v. Gant*,[182] the Supreme Court eliminated this windfall. Gant was arrested for driving with a suspended license. After he was handcuffed and locked in a patrol car, police searched his vehicle and found cocaine in the pocket of a jacket in the backseat. The Supreme Court ruled that the right to search a motorist's vehicle after his arrest is not a police entitlement. It is a precaution police are allowed to take when the search is necessary to protect their safety or prevent destruction of evidence. If no realistic possibility exists that the arrestee could retrieve a weapon or evidence from his vehicle when it is searched, the search is unjustified and violates the Fourth Amendment.

1. Application of *Arizona v. Gant* Outside the Vehicle Context

Arizona v. Gant left many questions unanswered, the most important being whether the ruling applies outside the vehicle context. In his dissenting opinion in *Arizona v. Gant*, Justice Alito observed that "there is no logical reason why the same rule should not apply to all arrestees."[183] Justice Alito's prediction has proven correct. *Gant*[1] has

---

[179] **Arizona v. Gant, 556 U.S. 332, 129 S. Ct. 1710, 173 L. Ed. 2d 485 (2009)** (holding that the search incident to arrest exception does "not authorize a vehicle search incident to a recent occupant's arrest after the arrestee has been secured and cannot access the interior of the vehicle").

[180] *See, e.g.,* United States v. Tehada, 524 F.3d 809 (7th Cir. 2008) (upholding search of cabinet as incidental to arrest where the arrestee was lying face down in another room with his hands cuffed behind his back, surrounded by police officers, at the time); United States v. Hudson, 100 F.3d 1409 (9th Cir. 1996) (upholding search of rifle case as incidental to arrest where it was performed after arrestee was handcuffed and removed from the scene).

[181] *See* cases *supra* note 180.

[182] *Supra* **note 179**.

[183] *Gant*, 129 S. Ct. at 1731 (Alito, J., dissenting).

been generally understood as applying to all searches incident to arrest, and not just those involving a vehicle.[184]

As a result, police are not allowed to search backpacks, briefcases, suitcases and other containers that were under the arrestee's immediate control unless the arrestee is unsecured and within reaching distance of them when they are searched.[185]

D. *Analysis of the Searches Performed in Operation Grab 'N' Sniff*

Police searched Bugsy Boss's wallet twice, once at the scene of the arrest and a second time at the police stations. Both searches were valid because the Fourth Amendment allows police to search an arrested individual's person and clothing, either at the scene of the arrest, the police station, or at both places. A wallet in the arrested individual's pocket is regarded as part of his clothing. Consequently, the "things to do" note seized from Boss's wallet during the second search can be used as evidence. The Gucci bag Boss was carrying at the time of his arrest is governed by a different rule. Objects under the arrested individual's immediate control that are not associated with his person or part of his clothing may be searched without a warrant, incident to arrest, only if the arrestee is unsecured and within reaching distance of them when they are searched. Once the arrestee has been incapacitated and is no able to retrieve a weapon or destroy evidence inside them, the search can no longer be justified as incident to arrest and a search warrant is necessary. Based on this analysis, the search of Boss's Gucci bag at the scene of the arrest was valid because he was unsecured and within reaching distance of it at the time of the search, but the second search at the police station was not. However, station house searches that fail to qualify as a valid search incident to the arrest can sometimes be justified under a different exception to the warrant requirement—the **inventory search** exception.[186]

---

[184]   *See, e.g.,* United States v. Shakir, 616 F.3d 315 (3rd Cir. 2010) (applying *Arizona v. Gant* to search of handcuffed arrestee's gym bag on floor beside him in the hotel lobby); United States v. Taylor, 656 F. Supp.2d 998 (E.D. Mo. 2009) (applying *Arizona v. Gant* to search of residential premises incident to arrest; search of area within suspect's reach at the time of arrest not justified after he was removed from his residence, handcuffed, and placed in a police car.); People v. Leal, 178 Cal. App. 4th 1051, 100 Cal. Rptr. 3d 856 (2009) (same). *See, generally,* Angad Singh, Comment, *Stepping out of the Vehicle: the Potential of* Arizona v. Gant *to End Automatic Searches Incident to Arrest Beyond the Vehicular Context,* 59 AM. U. L. Rev. 1749 (2010) (concluding that *Arizona v. Gant* abrogates automatic searches incident to arrest outside the vehicle context; searches are not permitted after the arrestee has been secured and is no longer in a position to grab a weapon or destroy evidence).

[185]   *See* authorities *supra* note 184.

[186]   *See, e.g.* State v. Rodriguez, 122 Hawai'i 229, 225 P. 3d 671 (Hawaii App. 2010) (Evidence recovered from otherwise illegal search incident to arrest is admissible under the inevitable discovery exception to the exclusionary rule if the evidence would have been inevitably discovered during an inventory search conducted at the police cell block); Thompson v. State, 192 Md. App. 653, 995 A. 2d 1030 (2010) (holding that the seizure of a handgun in the trunk of an arrestee's vehicle was lawful, notwithstanding *Arizona v. Gant,* because it would inevitably have been discovered during a valid inventory search).

E. *Inventory Searches Incident to Booking an Arrestee into Jail*

When a person is arrested at a place other than his home, belongings in his possession at the time of arrest will be bundled up and taken to the police station unless there is someone present who can take charge of them.[187] During routine booking procedures incident to incarceration, the suspect's clothing and other belongings will be impounded and an inventory search will be performed. The purpose of an inventory search is not to discover evidence. The purpose is to secure valuables, protect the police department against false claims of loss or theft, and prevent weapons and contraband from being introduced into the jail community.[188] The search should not be performed until it is determined that the suspect will not be released on bail.[189] If the inventory search is conducted properly, evidence that comes to light during the search will be admissible under the plain view rule.[190] Evidence missed during a search incident to an arrest is sometimes discovered later during an inventory search.

Inventory searches must be conducted in accordance with standard police department operating procedures concerning the time, place, and manner for conducting such searches.[191] The purpose of this requirement is to ensure that police do not use inventory searches as a subterfuge to search for evidence. For example, if the department's standard operating procedures do not provide for opening closed containers and inventorying their contents separately, but instead require them to be securely taped and sealed and placed into a locker, opening and searching them will violate the Fourth Amendment and evidence uncovered will be inadmissible.[192]

The permissible intensity of an inventory search also differs from a search incident to arrest because police are performing an administrative and caretaking function, not looking for evidence. Accordingly, police may not examine the articles they are inventorying to any greater extent than necessary to describe them on an inventory.[193] A superficial examination is generally enough. Caesar's reading of Boss' ledger book, for example, exceeded the permissible intensity of an inventory search because reading the contents was not necessary to describe it on an inventory. Because the reading occurred too late to qualify as a search incident to arrest and was too intensive for an inventory search, the ledger book could not be used as evidence.

---

[187] United States v. Perea, 986 F.2d 633 (2d Cir. 1993).

[188] Inventory searches are discussed in § 4.3 *supra* and 4.12 *infra*.

[189] United States v. Mills, 472 F.2d 1231 (D.C. Cir. 1972).

[190] Illinois v. Lafayette, *supra* note 75; South Dakota v. Opperman, note 75 (inventory searches satisfy the Fourth Amendment when they are part of routine police practice and are not conducted as a pretext for evidentiary search).

[191] *See* cases *supra* note 190.

[192] Colorado v. Bertine, *supra* note 118; Florida v. Wells, *supra* note 75.

[193] United States v. Khoury, 901 F.2d 948 (11th Cir. 1990) (reading contents of notebook during inventory search not permitted because it does not further purposes of inventory search).

F. Searches Preceding an Arrest

Police sometimes do things out of sequence. They search the suspect before placing him under arrest. This is not a problem if police have probable cause for making an arrest before the search is begun. When grounds for arrest are present, the fact that the search precedes the arrest does not violate the Fourth Amendment. However, the fruits of a search cannot supply grounds for an arrest that follows. If the police do not have grounds for arrest before they start the search, the search and subsequent arrest are both illegal.[194]

§ 4.9   Vehicle Searches

Although it is a wise practice to obtain a search warrant when feasible, for obvious reasons, this is often not feasible in the case of motor vehicle searches. As a result, most motor vehicle searches are conducted without a warrant. There are four theories, in addition to consent, for searching motor vehicles without a warrant: (1) vehicular limited weapons searches, (2) searches incident to the arrest of a motorist or passenger, (3) searches based on probable cause to believe that the vehicle contains criminal evidence or contraband (referred to as the "motor vehicle exception"), and (4) inventory searches. Officers need a strong grasp of these theories, because there is rarely time to ponder when the need to search arises.

These four theories can work in tandem, with one theory triggering another. An officer develops grounds for conducting a vehicular limited weapons search during a *Terry* or traffic stop and, while conducting the search, comes across drugs or contraband. The officer places the motorist under arrest, conducts a more intensive search (allowed as an incident to arrest), and finds additional drugs or contraband. This discovery gives the officer probable cause to believe that there may be more evidence in areas yet unsearched and enlarges the scope of the officer's search authority by triggering the third exception. The officer performs a highly intensive search based on probable cause to believe that the vehicle contains criminal evidence. When this search is completed, because the motorist has been arrested and there is no one to take charge of the vehicle, it is towed to the police impound lot where it is searched a fourth time, this time under the inventory search exception.

In studying the four theories for searching motor vehicles without a warrant, pay close attention to the grounds for search authority and areas that can be searched, because they differ markedly from theory to theory. Consider the following example.

---

[194] *Compare* United States v. Bell, 692 F. Supp. 2d 606 (W. D. Va. 2010) (fact that search precedes arrest is irrelevant if probable cause for search already exits) *with* Smith v. Ohio, 494 U.S. 541, 110 S. Ct. 1288, 108 L. Ed. 2d 464 (1990) (warrantless search of suspect's bag could not be justified as incident to his arrest on drug charges where the arrest was not made until after drug paraphernalia was found in his bag).

A Mid-Summer's Nightmare

Back before the rock group The Thankless Incarnates broke up, Mary Wanna and Ralph Riefer decided to spend a whole summer following the band. Although Ralph's parents told him to "get a haircut and earn some money for once," Ralph convinced them he could make a killing going from concert to concert selling knickknacks and trinkets to the other Incarnate Heads. Ralph's parents finally gave up and agreed to lend him the family's blue Volkswagen Bug. Due to a series of mishaps that Ralph would later describe to his lawyer as "an unforeseeable bummer," Ralph and Mary got arrested and spent the last part of the summer behind bars.

As Ralph and Mary wound their way through Whosville, they were stopped by Officer Bobby Weird, who was acting on a tip from the WPD's most reliable informant that a "major drug dealer named Ray V. Gravy would be passing through town in a blue VW Bug, carrying a large stash of marijuana in the trunk." The informant also told Weird that Gravy was "usually heavily armed, uses numerous aliases, and often travels with girlfriends." Weird felt confident that Ralph was the suspect he'd been waiting for since he'd been watching the highway all week and this was the first blue Bug he had seen.

Weird pulled Ralph over with his siren and lights, and approached the vehicle with his hand on his holster. Rich from the sales of counterfeit Incarnate sweatshirts and trinkets, Ralph offered Weird a roll of twenties, saying: "Look, we're in a hurry to get to a concert. I don't know what I did, but I'm sure this is enough to pay the fine."

Weird pushed the money aside, ordered Ralph and Mary to step outside, and patted them down for weapons. Finding none, he proceeded to search the VW. He saw a couple of fliers on the floor, advertising "Ralph's Thankless Knock-Off-Knickknacks: We cut out the band's share and pass the savings on to you." He put them in his pocket and continued to search. He found two large bags of marijuana and a bundle of $20 bills in the glove compartment, and a vial of cocaine in a cigarette pack inside Mary's handbag, that she had left on the seat when she exited. As things turned out, Ralph had expanded the business model during the trip to include drug trafficking. Weird then placed Ralph and Mary under arrest, handcuffed them, and put them in the squad car. He also took the keys from Ralph and opened the trunk, where he found some scales and other materials used in connection with drug distribution but, to his consternation, no drugs or counterfeit goods.

Officer Weird had Ralph's Bug towed to the impound lot where the contents of the vehicle were inventoried. Miscellaneous trash and spare change were the only things found. Later that same day, the real Ray V. Gravy passed through Whosville in a beaten-up, blue VW Bug and he, too, was arrested.

Weird was puzzled by the scantiness of his find and knew that the couple would get off light unless he found more evidence. Two days later, it came to Weird like a flash; he had been looking in the wrong places. Luckily, Ralph's father had not yet traveled to Whosville to pick up the vehicle, so Weird jumped on the chance and used some tools to take out the steering wheel hub, door panels, dashboard, and back seat. Sure enough, Weird found 30 pounds of marijuana, a case of counterfeit glow-in-the-dark Thankless Incarnate action figures, and nearly $37,000 in cash (mostly $20 bills).

Ralph was charged with possession of marijuana with intent to distribute, possession of counterfeit goods, and attempted bribery of a police officer; Mary was charged with possession of a vial of cocaine. The judge denied all of their motions to suppress and both of them are now serving sentences in the Whosville jail.

Figure 4.11
Vehicle Limited Weapons Search

- The sole object of the search is weapons
- The officer must have reasonable suspicion that weapons are located inside a lawfully stopped vehicle
- The scope of the search is confined to the passenger compartment
- The intensity is limited to a cursory visual inspection of areas (and containers) inside the passenger compartment in which a weapon would fit.

§ 4.10 — Search of Vehicles Pursuant to a Detention or Arrest

Terry vehicular limited weapons searches and vehicle searches incident to arrest share one feature in common. Both searches are confined to the passenger compartment. However, this is where the similarity ends. Significant differences exist in the grounds for the search, the lawful objects, and intensity of search activity permitted.

A. Terry Searches of Vehicles

1. Grounds for Search Authority

A limited weapons search, as the name suggests, is strictly limited to searching for weapons that could be used to harm the officer. Officers who make a valid *Terry* or traffic stop may order the driver and passengers to step out of the vehicle and remain outside for the duration of the stop. This precaution may be taken as a matter of course, with no additional grounds beyond grounds for the stop.[195] Frisks and vehicular weapon searches, in contrast, require reasonable suspicion that weapons are present.[196] A vehicle weapons search may be performed even though the driver and passengers have been ordered to step out of the vehicle because they will have access to weapons inside once they are permitted to re-enter.[197]

2. Scope and Intensity

The scope of a vehicular weapons search is limited to the passenger compartment.[198] The trunk is off-limits because a locked trunk is not a place from which the occupants can gain immediate access to a weapon. The intensity of the search is limited to a cursory visual inspection of areas within the passenger compartment in which a weapon could fit.[199] These areas include the floors, dashboard, seats, area under the seats, glove compartment, console, storage compartments, rear window ledge, and all containers inside the passenger compartment in which a weapon could fit. A cursory visual inspection of these areas is all that is permitted.[200] If criminal evidence or contraband is discovered by the police while searching within these confines, they may seize it under the plain view exception.[201]

Officer Weird cannot be faulted for his decision to stop Ralph's car, frisk Ralph and Mary, and perform a vehicle weapons search. He had received a tip from a reliable informant that a heavily armed drug dealer, possibly accompanied by a female companion, would be passing through Whosville and he had every reason to believe that Ralph was the suspect he had been waiting for.[202] Ralph's car matched the informant's description in every detail: he was traveling with a woman companion, as Gravy normally did, and because traffic rarely passes through Whosville, Officer Weird was reasonable in concluding that Ralph was the suspect he had been waiting for, and that he and Mary were armed and dangerous.[203]

---

[195]   Pennsylvania v. Mimms, *supra* note 153 (driver); Maryland v. Wilson, 519 U.S. 408, 117 S. Ct. 882, 137 L. Ed. 2d 41 (1998) (passenger).

[196]   Michigan v. Long, *supra* note 158.

[197]   *Id.*

[198]   *Id.*

[199]   *Id.*

[200]   *Id.*

[201]   The plain view doctrine is discussed in § 4.4(B)(3) *supra*.

[202]   United States v. Taylor, 162 F.3d 12 (1st Cir. 1998) (detailed tip from a reliable informant that occupants of an automobile were in possession of crack cocaine and weapons exhibited sufficient indicia of reliability to justify investigatory stop of automobile).

[203]   United States v. Perrin, 45 F.3d 869, 873 (4th Cir. 1995) (noting that "it is certainly reasonable for an officer to believe that a person engaged in selling crack cocaine may be carrying a weapon for protection").

However, Officer Weird twice exceeded the boundaries of a *Terry* vehicle weapons search. The first time was when he examined the contents of the crumpled cigarette pack in Mary's handbag. Because he knew that the cigarette pack did not contain a weapon, he had no authority to examine the contents.[204] The second time was when he searched the trunk. Trunks are beyond the scope of a vehicle weapons search because weapons hidden in a locked trunk are not immediately accessible.[205]

Even though Officer Weird exceeded the bounds for a vehicular weapons search, he did not violate the Fourth Amendment because he had probable cause to arrest Ralph for being a drug dealer before the search began. A tip from a reliable informant establishes probable cause to arrest a person whom the officer reasonably believes is the suspect, even though the officer is mistaken.[206] Accordingly, the search Weird performed needs to be analyzed under the search incident to arrest exception to the warrant requirement. We turn now to an examination of this exception.

Figure 4.12
Vehicle Searches Incident to an Occupant's Arrest

- Police may perform a vehicle search incident to arrest only if: (1) the arrestee is unsecured and within reaching distance of the passenger compartment at the time of the search or (2) police have reason to believe that the vehicle might contain evidence of the crime for which the arrest is made.
- The scope of the search extends to the entire passenger compartment and all containers located inside, without regard for ownership.
- The intensity may be as thorough as necessary to find offense-related evidence.
- The timing of the search depends on the justification. If the justification is protecting the officer's safety, the search must be performed while the suspect is unsecured and within reaching distance of the passenger compartment. If the justification is reason to believe that the vehicle contains evidence of the crime for which the arrest was made, the search may be postponed until after the arrest scene has been secured.

---

[204] Minnesota v. Dickerson, *supra* note 19; Commonwealth v. Silva, 318 N.E.2d 895 (Mass. 1974) (police exceeded their *Terry* vehicular weapon search authority when they unzipped a small pouch, found under the front seat, because it was inconceivable that a pouch that size could contain a weapon).

[205] *See*, *e.g.*, United States v. Perea, *supra* note 187 (search of duffel a bag in a trunk could not be justified as search incident to arrest).

[206] *See*, *e.g.*, Hill v. California, 401 U.S. 797, 91 S. Ct. 1106, 28 L. Ed. 2d 484 (1971) (upholding the search of an individual named Miller where the police had probable cause to arrest Hill and reasonably, but mistakenly believe that Miller was Hill); Jordan v. Fournier, 324 F. Supp.2d 242 (D. Me 2004) (when the police have probable cause to arrest one party, and reasonably mistake a second party for the first party, the arrest of the second party is a valid arrest and evidence seized during subsequent search is admissible).

B. Vehicle Searches Incident to the Custodial Arrest of an Occupant

Until recently, police could automatically search the passenger compartment whenever they arrested a vehicle occupant[207] or recent occupant[208] for *any* offense, including a traffic violation. This overly broad search authority led to the wisespread practice of using arrests for traffic violations as a cover to search for drugs.[209] Countless motorists had their privacy invaded for nothing more serious than a speeding or seatbelt violation. In *Arizona v. Gant*,[210] discussed in § 4.8, the Supreme Court rewrote the law of vehicle searches incident to arrest.

Gant was arrested for driving with a suspended license. After he was handcuffed and locked in a squad car, police searched his vehicle and found drugs. The Supreme Court recognized two justifications for searching a vehicle incident to the arrest of an occupant — a safety justification and an evidence-gathering justification. The police are permitted to search the passenger compartment if: (1) the arrestee is unsecured and within reaching distance at the time of the search (safety justification) or (2) it is reasonable to believe that evidence relevant to the crime of arrest might be found inside the vehicle (evidence-gathering justification). Neither justification was present in *Gant*. Police had no concerns for their safety because Gant was handcuffed and locked in the back seat of a squad car when his vehicle was searched. Nor did they have the slightest hope of finding evidence of the crime for which Gant was arrested. Gant was arrested for driving on a suspended license, a crime for which no tangible evidence existed. Since the officers had absolutely no reason to search Gant's vehicle, the search was unreasonable and violated the Fourth Amendment.

The first justification for searching a vehicle incident to arrest derives from *Chimel v. California*,[211] which allows police to search objects under the arrested person's immediate control as an incident to his arrest. *Gant* clarified the immediate control test by requiring that control be measured as of the time of the search, and not the time of arrest. Once the arrestee has been secured the first justification for searching is over.

---

[207]   New York v. Belton, 453 U.S. 454, 101 S. Ct. 2860, 69 L. Ed. 2d 768 (1981) (holding that "when a policeman has made a lawful custodial arrest of the occupant of an automobile, he may, as a contemporaneous incident of that arrest, search the passenger compartment of that automobile.").

[208]   Thornton v. United States, 541 U.S. 615, 124 S. Ct. 2127, 158 L. Ed. 2d 905 (2004) (holding that police may search the passenger compartment when they arrest a person who just exited the vehicle, but is still in close proximity, when police initiate contact).

[209]   *See, e.g.*, Carson Emmons, Comment, Arizona v. Gant: *An Argument for Tossing out* Belton *and All Its Bastard Kin*, 36 ARIZ. ST. L. J. 1067 (2004).

[210]   **Supra note 179**.

[211]   *Supra* note 44 (discussed in §4.8).

The second justification is new. The Supreme Court took with one hand, but gave with the other. Police may search a vehicle incident to arrest, even after the safety concerns have been eliminated, if it is *reasonable to believe* that evidence relevant to the crime of arrest *might be found* in the vehicle."[212] "Reasonable to believe" and "might be found" establish a lenient standard, one considerably lower than probable cause.[213] The offense for which the arrest is made is the most important consideration, and according to many courts, the only factor police need to consider in determining whether evidence of the offense of arrest might be found inside the vehicle.[214] When the offense is, by its nature, one for which physical evidence might exist, such as a DUI or drug offense, then evidence of that offense *might* be in the vehicle and police are entitled to perform an evidence-gathering search.[215] On the other hand, if the defendant is arrested for a nonevidentiary offense like speeding, driving with a suspended license, or resisting arrest, no evidence of that offense can be expected to be found in the vehicle and an evidence-gathering search is not allowed.

The Court stressed that the second justification for searching is based on "circumstances unique to the vehicle context,"[216] but did not explain why. It is probably because vehicles are mobile, creating a risk that a family member or nonarrested

---

[212] **Arizona v. Gant**, *supra* note 179, 129 S. Ct. at 1719, 1723.

[213] *See, e.g.*, United States v. Reagan, 713 F. Supp. 2d 724 (E.D. Tenn. 2010) (equating "reasonable belief" to "reasonable suspicion"); People v. McCarthy, 229 P. 3d 1041 (Colo. 2010 (same).

[214] *See, e.g.*, Brown v. State, 24 So. 3d 671 (Fla. Dist. Ct. App. 2009) ("We conclude ... that the reasonable belief that evidence might be found prong of *Gant* can be satisfied solely from the inference that might be drawn from the offense of arrest itself ... .). *See also,* WAYNE R. LaFAVE, SEARCH & SEIZURE § 7.1., at 111-12 (4th ed. Supp. 2009) (stating that a reasonable belief should be found to exist whenever the crime of arrest is one for which evidence is possible and might conceivably be found in the arrestee's vehicle).

[215] Grant v. State, 43 So.3d 864 (Fla. App. 2010) ("When the offense of arrest of an occupant of a vehicle is, by its nature, a crime that might yield physical evidence, then as an incident to that arrest, police may search the passenger compartment of the vehicle, including containers, to gather evidence, irrespective of whether the arrestee has access to the vehicle at the time of the search."); State v. Cantrell, 233 P.3d 178, 183 (Idaho App.2010) (Police are justified in searching the vehicle interior after the motorist has been secured, when the arrest is made for DUI because open or empty alcohol containers or other evidence of alcohol use might be found inside); People v. Chamberlain, 229 P. 3d 1054 (Colo. 2010) (same); United States v. Davis, 569 F. 3d 813 (8th Cir. 2009) (Police are justified in searching the vehicle interior when an arrest is for a drug offense); McCloud v. Commonwealth, 286 S.W.3d 785 (Ky. 2009) (same); United States v. Grote, 629 F. Supp. 2d 1201 (E.D. Wash. 2009) (same); United States v. Vinton, 594 F. 3d 15 (C.A.D.C. 2010) (Arrest for unlawful weapon possession provides reason to believe there might be more weapons inside the vehicle, justifying a search of the passenger compartment); Brown v. State, *supra* note 214 (Outstanding warrant for theft established reason to believe that evidence of the offense of arrest might be found inside the vehicle.).

[216] **Arizona v. Gant**, *supra* note 179, 129 S. Ct. at 1719.

occupant might move the vehicle before the officer returns with a search warrant. Consequently, the officer needs authority to search the vehicle without a warrant. Otherwise, evidence of the crime for which the arrest was made might not be available at the trial. This problem is not encountered when an arrest is made inside a residence or other fixed location and, consequently, police are not allowed to search for evidence after the arrest scene has been secured unless they obtain a search warrant.[217]

1. Scope and Intensity of the Search

When a vehicle search is authorized incident to arrest, the scope of the search extends to the entire passenger compartment (*i.e.*, the seats, floor, glove compartments, consoles, etc.) and everything inside that could house a weapon or evidence of the crime for which the arrest was made (*i.e.*, luggage, boxes, bags, briefcases, jackets, handbags, etc.).[218] Search authority does not extend to the engine compartment or the trunk[219] unless the rear component is accessible without exiting the vehicle.[220] No authority exists to rip up upholstery or remove structural parts.[221]

2. Timing of the Search

The timing of the search depends on the justification. If the justification is preventing the arrestee from gaining access to a weapon, the search must be performed while the arrestee is unsecured and within reaching distance of the vehicle.[222] The *Gant* Court observed in a footnote that "[b]ecause officers have many means of ensuring the safe

---

[217] *See, e.g.*, United States v. Taylor, 656 F. Supp. 2d 998 (E. D. Mo. 2009) (Exception to the Fourth Amendment warrant requirement allowing search of a vehicle for evidence relevant to the crime of arrest did not apply so as to justify search of the defendant's residence after he was removed, placed in handcuffs, and put in a police vehicle.).

[218] New York v. Belton, *supra* note 207 (jacket on backseat of car); United States v. Bell, 692 F. Supp. 2d 606 (W. D. Va. 2010) (When police have reason to believe that a vehicle contains evidence of the offense of arrest, they may search the entire passenger compartment and every purse, briefcase, or other container inside that is capable of housing the object of their search, regardless of ownership.).

[219] *See, e.g.*, United States v. Perea, *supra* note 187 (trunk); United States v. Lugo, 978 F.2d 631 (10th Cir. 1992) (trunk); United States v. Marchena-Borjas, 209 F.3d 698, 700 (8th Cir.2000) (engine compartment).

[220] *See, e.g.*, United States v. Pino, 855 F.2d 357 (6th Cir. 1988) (search authority incident to arrest extends to rear component of station wagon); United States v. Russell, 670 F.2d 323 (D.C. Cir.) (same, hatchback).

[221] *See, e.g.*, United States v. Barnes, 374 F.3d 601 (6th Cir. 2004) (search authority incident to arrest does not extend to areas inside the passenger compartment that can be reached only through elaborate dismantling of the vehicle); State v. Cuellar, 211 N.J. Super. 299, 511 A.2d 745 (1986) (removal of rear seat and door panel exceeded scope of search incident to arrest).

[222] **Arizona v. Gant, *supra* note 179**. *Arizona v. Gant* is also discussed in § 4.8 (C).

arrest of vehicle occupants, it will be the rare case in which an officer is unable to fully effectuate an arrest so that a real possibility of access to the arrestee's vehicle remains." This suggests that officers who rely on the first justification should be prepared to explain why they were unable to fully effectuate the arrest, making it necessary to search the vehicle to ensure their safety.

If the search is justified by the need to gather offense-related evidence, police may secure the arrest scene first. However, the search must be performed close in time to the arrest, and generally before the arrestee or the vehicle has been removed from the scene.[223]

3. Further Analysis of A Mid-Summer's Nightmare

Officer Weird had both justifications for searching the vehicle incident to Ralph and Mary's arrest. They were unsecured, standing near the vehicle, and outnumbered him two to one, creating a risk that they might try to overpower him and lunge for a weapon inside. Weird also had reason to believe that there were drugs in the vehicle, because he had received a tip from a reliable informant that a drug dealer would be passing through and he had probable cause to believe that Ralph was that person. The fact that Weird performed the search before placing Ralph under arrest is not objectionable. When police have probable cause for arrest, the timing of the search vis-à-vis the arrest is inconsequential.[224]

Weird's incident-to-arrest search authority extended to the entire passenger compartment and all containers inside capable of housing drugs. Mary's handbag was such a container. The fact that it belonged to a passenger whom Weird did not yet have probable cause to arrest was no obstacle. In *Wyoming v. Houghton*,[225] a patrol officer stopped a car for speeding. During the stop, the officer noticed a syringe in the driver's pocket. When asked about the syringe, the driver candidly admitted that he used it to take drugs, giving the officer probable cause to search the vehicle. During the search, the officer spotted a handbag on the backseat. He searched it even though he knew that it belonged to a passenger, and arrested her when he found drugs found inside. The Supreme Court upheld the search even though the officer lacked probable cause to suspect the passenger of criminal activity before searching her handbag. The Court stated that, when police have probable cause to search a vehicle, requiring them to determine the ownership of belongings found inside before searching them would encourage

---

[223] *See, e.g.,* New York v. Belton, *supra* note 207 (stating that [a] warrantless search incident to arrest is not valid if it is remote in time or place from the arrest"); United States v. Dennison, 410 F.3d 1203 (10th Cir. 2005) (stating that search of the passenger compartment conducted after suspect is removed from the scene is not justified as incident to arrest); United States v. Vasey, 834 F. 2d 782 (9th Cir. 1987) (search of passenger compartment conducted between 30 and 45 minutes after defendant was arrested, handcuffed, and placed in rear of police vehicle not sufficiently contemporaneous to qualify as a search incident to arrest).

[224] *See* § 4.3 *supra.*

[225] **526 U.S. 295, 119 S. Ct. 1297, 143 L. Ed. 2d 408 (1999).**

drivers to stash their contraband in passengers' belongings or induce passengers to claim ownership to thwart the search. This would impair the ability of the police to do their job. Accordingly, when police have probable cause to search a vehicle, they may search all containers, packages, and belongings found inside that are capable of housing the object of their search, without concern for ownership.

Although *Houghton* involved a vehicle search conducted under the motor vehicle exception, courts have extended the ruling to searches of a passenger's belongings incident to the motorist's arrest.[226] As one court explained:

> When police stop a car with multiple passengers and arrest one of them, the need for the police to discover either hidden weapons that could be turned upon them or evidence that could be destroyed is no less acute than when the police stop a vehicle and arrest its sole occupant. Indeed, because of the number of people involved, the need may be even greater. Given that third-party ownership of an item within a car's passenger compartment would not necessarily prevent an arrestee from gaining access to it, third-party ownership of an item should not bar police from searching that item in the same manner as if it were owned by the arrestee.[227]

However, Officer Weird cannot rely on the search incident to arrest exception to justify his search of Ralph's trunk or the search he conducted two days later.[228] Authority to search vehicle trunks or to search a vehicle at a time and place remote from the scene of an arrest can derive only from the exceptions covered in the next two sections.

Figure 4.13
Vehicle Searches Based on Probable Cause ("Automobile Exception")

- The officer must have probable cause to believe that the vehicle contains criminal evidence or contraband
- The scope of the search extends to the entire vehicle, from motor compartment to trunk and all the contents
- The intensity is limited to search activity necessary to find the objects the officer has probable cause to believe are hidden in the vehicle

---

[226] *See, e.g.*, People v. Morales, 799 N.E.2d 986 (Ill. Ct. App. 2003) (search authority incident to driver's arrest extended to the passenger's jacket found on the backseat); State v. Ray, 260 Neb. 868, 620 N.W.2d 83 (2000) (search authority incident to driver's arrest extended to passenger's knapsack); State v. Tognotti, 663 N.W.2d 642 (N.D. 2003) (arresting officer could search the contents of a non-arrested occupant's purse); Purnell v. State, 171 Md. App. 582, 911 A.2d 867 (2006) (stating that passengers' personal belongings may be searched incident to the driver's arrest because passengers also have a reduced expectation of privacy with regard to property they transport in automobiles).

[227] People v. Morales, *supra* note 226. Search authority recognized in Wyoming v. Houghton does not extend to a nonarrested passenger's person or the clothing on his back. *See, e.g.*, State v. Tognotti, *supra* note 226.

[228] *See* authorities cited in notes 219 and 223 *supra*.

§ 4.11 — Search of Vehicles Based on Probable Cause ("Automobile Exception")

A. Grounds for Search Authority

The third exception, known as the "automobile exception," permits the police to search motor vehicles without a warrant whenever they have probable cause to believe that the vehicle contains evidence that they may lawfully seize (*i.e.*, criminal evidence or contraband).[229] This exception is based on the ready mobility of motor vehicles, which creates a risk that they might be gone by the time the police return with a search warrant,[230] and also on the reduced expectation of privacy of people seated inside a vehicle because the passenger compartment is exposed to anyone who wants to look.[231]

This is the broadest of the four exceptions relating to motor vehicles. Police do not need a search warrant to search a vehicle that is stopped on the highway, parked on a curb, or encountered elsewhere[232] if they have probable cause to believe that the vehicle contains criminal evidence or contraband, even if they have time to obtain a warrant.[233] A handful of states use an older, more restrictive version of the automobile exception that requires exigent circumstances in addition to probable cause.[234] Police in these jurisdictions are not allowed to search unoccupied parked vehicles because there is no emergency. One officer can be left at the scene to watch the vehicle while another goes to get a search warrant.

---

[229] Pennsylvania v. Labron, 518 U.S. 938, 116 S. Ct. 2485, 135 L. Ed. 2d 1031 (1996); California v. Acevedo, *supra* note 68.

[230] Carroll v. United States, 267 U.S. 132, 151, 45 S. Ct. 280, 284, 69 L. Ed. 543 (1925) ("A necessary difference [exists] between a search of a store, dwelling house or other structure in respect of which a proper official warrant readily may be obtained, and a search of a ship, motor boat, wagon or automobile, for contraband goods, where it is not practicable to secure a warrant because the vehicle can be quickly moved out of the locality or jurisdiction in which the warrant must be sought.").

[231] Cardwell v. Lewis, 417 U.S. 583, 94 S. Ct. 2464, 41 L. Ed. 2d 325 (1974) (noting that vehicles often contain personal effects, which are in plain view); Cady v. Dombrowski, 413 U.S. 433, 93 S. Ct. 2523, 37 L. Ed. 2d 706 (1973) (explaining that use of automobiles is highly regulated, bringing law enforcement in contact with persons in their vehicles where contraband may be in plain view).

[232] Cardwell v. Lewis, *supra* note 231; State v. Colvin, 123 N.J. 428, 433, 437, 587 A.2d 1278 (1991). However, the automobile exception does not apply to vehicles parked on residential property. *See, e.g.*, State v. LeJeune, 576 S. E. 2d 888 (Ga. 2003) (holding that automobile exception does not apply where the suspect's car is legally parked in his residential parking space).

[233] Maryland v. Dyson, 527 U.S. 465, 467, 119 S. Ct. 2013, 144 L. Ed. 2d 442 (1999); Pennsylvania v. Labron, *supra* note 229.

[234] *See, e.g.*, State v. Cooke, 751 A.2d 92 (N. J. 2000); State v. Coleman, 2 P.3d 399 (Or. Ct. App. 2000); Fletcher v. State, 990 P.2d 192 (Nev. 1999).

B. Scope and Intensity

Search authority under the motor vehicle exception extends from bumper to bumper.[235] Police may search the vehicle as thoroughly as if they had a search warrant,[236] even to the point of removing structural parts.[237] Their search authority also extends to containers within the vehicle.[238] They may open any container that is capable of housing the objects of their search, regardless of ownership.[239] However, their search authority does not automatically carry over to the occupants. The occupants may be searched only if police have probable cause to believe that the objects of the search are secreted on their persons or in their clothing.[240]

As is true for all searches, searches conducted under the automobile exception may not be broader than necessary to locate the objects for which the police have search authority. For example, if the police have probable cause to believe that drugs are hidden somewhere in the vehicle, they may search the entire vehicle from engine compartment to trunk and everything inside. On the other hand, if the only thing they have is probable cause to believe that there is a briefcase containing drugs in the trunk, they are limited to opening the trunk and looking inside the briefcase.[241]

C. Timing of the Search

Searches conducted under the automobile exception do not have to be performed on the spot.[242] Requiring police to stop everything and conduct an immediate search at the roadside whenever they have probable cause to believe that a vehicle contains

---

[235]   United States v. Ross, *supra* note 68 ("If probable cause justifies the search of a lawfully stopped vehicle, it justifies the search of every part of the vehicle and its contents that may conceal the object of the search.").

[236]   *Id.*

[237]   *See, e.g.*, Carroll v. United States, *supra* note 228 (upholstery); Ornelas v. United States, 517 U.S. 690, 116 S. Ct. 1657, 134 L. Ed. 2d 911 (1996) (side door panel); Cardwell v. Lewis, *supra* note 229 (paint sample); United States v. Zucco, 860 F. Supp. 363 (E. D. Tex. 1994) (wall paneling in recreational vehicle).

[238]   United States v. Ross, *supra* note 68.

[239]   **Wyoming v. Houghton**, *supra* note 230 (upholding search of a passenger's purse based on fact that police had probable cause to believe that the driver was a drug user and had controlled substances somewhere in his car, even though the police had no reason to suspect the passenger of anything).

[240]   Ybarra v. Illinois, 444 U.S. 85, 91, 100 S. Ct. 338, 62 L. Ed. 2d 238 (1979) (warrant authorizing search of tavern and bartender did not carry authority to search customers present on the premises at the time of the search); United States v. Di Re, 332 U.S. 581, 68 S. Ct. 222, 92 L. Ed. 210 (1948) (probable cause to search a car did not justify a body search of a passenger).

[241]   California v. Acevedo, *supra* note 68; United States v. Ross, *supra* note 68.

[242]   *See, e.g.,* United States v. Johns, 469 U.S. 478, 105 S. Ct. 881, 83 L. Ed. 2d 890 (1985) (upholding warrantless search of packages three days after their seizure from the vehicle); Florida v. Meyers, 466 U.S. 380, 104 S. Ct. 1852, 80 L. Ed. 2d 381 (1984) (per curiam) (upholding warrantless search of automobile at police impound lot conducted approximately eight hours after initial search); Chambers v. Maroney, 399 U.S. 42, 90 S. Ct. 1975, 26 L. Ed. 2d 419 (1970) (explaining that whenever the police could have searched the vehicle without a warrant earlier at the scene, had they so chosen, they may search it at the police station later).

evidence subject to seizure would hamper thorough and efficient criminal investiga-tions.[243] Consequently, the search may be delayed until the vehicle reaches the police impoundment lot.[244]

D. *Further Analysis of A Mid-Summer's Nightmare*

Officer Weird's search of the passenger compartment at the scene of the stop gave him reason to believe that there was more criminal evidence and contraband as yet undiscovered. It was obvious from the fliers that Ralph was a traveling peddler who sold counterfeit wares. The two bags of marijuana and large wad of $20 bills found in the passenger compartment suggested that Ralph was also peddling drugs. These discoveries supplied probable cause to believe that there were counterfeit trinkets and drugs in other parts of the vehicle, triggering the automobile exception and broad-ening Officer Weird's search authority.[245] Weird was no longer restricted to searching the passenger compartment. He could now search the car from bumper to bumper, including the trunk.

Officer Weird's superficial roadside search did not exhaust his search authority under the automobile exception because he remained convinced, despite this search, that there were undiscovered drugs and counterfeit trinkets elsewhere in the vehicle.[246] Search authority under the automobile exception does not have to be exercised at the scene of the stop.[247] When police have probable cause to believe that a vehicle contains criminal evidence or contraband, they may seize it and search it later at a more conve-nient location.[248]

---

[243] Michigan v. Thomas, 458 U.S. 259, 102 S. Ct. 3079, 73 L. Ed. 2d 750 (1982) (per curiam) (the jus-tification to conduct a warrantless search under the automobile exception does not disappear merely because the vehicle is immobilized and impounded); United States v. Henderson, 241 F.3d 638 (9th Cir. 2000) (authority to search defendant's rental car, under automobile exception to warrant requirement, did not evanesce because officers decided to impound the vehicle and search it later). *But see* United States v. Brookins, 228 F. Supp. 2d 732 (E.D. Va. 2002) (although police officers had probable cause to search vehicle at the time of suspect's arrest, probable cause no longer existed where suspect was allowed to leave scene and vehicle was found parked at his residence 15 minutes later, because the suspect could have disposed of the contraband in the meantime).

[244] *See* authorities *supra* notes 242, 243.

[245] Myles v. State, 946 S.W.2d 630 (Tex. Ct. App. 1997) (discovery of marijuana in interior of vehicle stopped for traffic violation provided probable cause for more thorough search of entire vehicle, in-cluding inside of spare tire); United States v. Bullock, 94 F.3d 896 (4th Cir. 1996) (discovery of wad of money, two cellular telephones, and a beeper, combined with the motorist's nervous behavior, at-tempts to conceal console, and incredible explanation of his trip, provided probable cause to believe vehicle contained contraband and justified search under the automobile exception).

[246] *See* authorities *supra* note 243.

[247] *Id.*

[248] Michigan v. Thomas, *supra* note 243.

The fact that two days elapsed between the seizure of Ralph's car and the second search is not a problem because searches under the automobile exception do not have to occur simultaneously with the seizure.[249] Courts have upheld searches under the automobile exception even in the face of substantial delays.[250] In one case, police searched a hidden compartment behind the radio in the dashboard for drugs more than a month after the vehicle was impounded.[251] The court upheld the search notwithstanding the delay.

The scope and intensity of searches under the automobile exception are also different from searches conducted as an incident to an arrest. When the police have probable cause to search a motor vehicle, they may search any location where the objects of their search could be hidden, even if it requires disassembling parts of the vehicle.[252] Officer Weird was, accordingly, justified in looking inside the steering wheel column and behind the dashboard, and removing the door panels and backseat because they are locations where drug dealers sometimes hide drugs and that could also serve as hiding places for counterfeit trinkets.

Figure 4.14
Vehicle Inventory Search

- The purpose of the search is to secure the owner's valuables and protect the police department against liability for loss and theft
- Police must have legal authority to impound the vehicle
- Police must follow standard procedures for inventorying the contents of impounded vehicles
- The scope of the search is governed by these procedures
- The intensity is limited to activity necessary to catalog and safeguard the items

---

[249] *See, e.g.,* United States v. Gastiaburo, 16 F.3d 582 (4th Cir. 1994) (warrantless search of hidden compartment behind the radio in the dashboard conducted 38 days after vehicle was impounded upheld as valid search under automobile exception); Bayless v. City of Frankfort, 981 F. Supp. 1161 (S. D. Ind. 1997) (warrantless search of vehicle more than four months after impoundment upheld as valid search under automobile exception).

[250] *See* cases *supra* note 249.

[251] United States v. Gastiaburo, *supra* note 249.

[252] *See, e.g.,* United States v. McSween, 53 F.3d 684 (5th Cir. 1995) (suspect's four prior arrests on narcotics charges and smell of odor of burned marijuana provided probable cause to search entire vehicle, including under the hood, where officer found marijuana in hole in fire wall); United States v. Zucco, 71 F.3d 188 (5th Cir. 1995) (proper to remove door panel after canine alert created probable cause to search vehicle for drugs); United States v. Gastiaburo, *supra* note 249 (upholding search of hidden compartment behind radio in console of car); United States v. Anderson, 114 F.3d 1059 (10th Cir. 1997) (upholding search of gas tank). *See also* authorities *supra* note 237.

§ 4.12 — Inventory Searches of Impounded Vehicles

A. Grounds for Search Authority

The first requirement for a lawful inventory search is a valid impoundment. Statutory authority exists to impound vehicles for a variety of reasons, including illegal parking, unpaid traffic tickets, abandonment, mechanical failures, and disablement due to accidents.[253]

In addition the decision to impound must be reasonable.[254] Police, for example, may not impound a vehicle after a driver's arrest if there are other licensed drivers present who are able of take charge of it.[255] Evidence that comes to light after a wrongful impoundment will be suppressed.[256]

Once a vehicle has been impounded, an inventory search will follow. Inventory searches are exempt from conventional Fourth Amendment requirements because police are performing a caretaking function.[257] To be sustainable as an inventory search, the search must be conducted in accordance with "standardized criteria" specifying where, when, and how inventory searches are to be conducted (i.e., whether the search is to be conducted at the scene before the vehicle is released to a third-party towing company or when it reaches the impoundment lot, what parts of the vehicle may be searched, whether police may open closed containers, etc.).[258] Standardized procedures are necessary to ensure that inventory searches are used for their intended purposes and not as a ruse to search for evidence.[259] It is up to each individual police department to formulate inventory search procedures. Once policies and procedures have been put into place, they must be routinely followed in order for the search to be upheld under the inventory search exception.

---

[253] United States v. Foreman, 993 F. Supp. 186 (S. D. N. Y. 1998).
[254] People v. Williams, 145 Cal. App. 4th 756, 52 Cal. Rptr. 3d 162 (2006); Miranda v. City of Cornelius, 429 F.3d 858 (9th Cir. 2005).
[255] Miranda v. City of Cornelius, *supra* note 254; United States v. Duquay, 93 F.3d 346 (7th Cir. 1996); State v. Lark, 748 A.2d 1103 (N.J. 2000); Butler v. Com, 525 S.E.2d 58 (Va. Ct. App. 2000); Philips v. State, 167 Ga. App. 260, 305 S.E.2d 918 (1983).
[256] United States v. Cooley, 119 F. Supp. 2d 824 (N.D. Ind. 2000).
[257] South Dakota v. Opperman, *supra* note 75; Colorado v. Bertine, *supra* note 118.
[258] *See, e.g.,* California v. Bertine, *supra* note 118 (police may not open locked containers in impounded vehicles unless inventory procedures mandate opening of all such containers).
[259] South Dakota v. Opperman, *supra* note 75 (emphasizing standardized procedures as means of curbing abuses); United States v. Thompson, 29 F.3d 62, 65 (2d Cir. 1994) (fruits of inventory searches will be suppressed when the searching officers act in bad faith solely for the purpose of investigation); United States v. Prescott, 599 F.2d 103 (5th Cir. 1979) (inventories used as pretext for investigatory search are unlawful).

B. *Scope and Intensity of Inventory Searches*

All search activity performed during an inventory search must be geared toward one or more of the following purposes: (1) safeguarding valuables inside the vehicle, (2) protecting law enforcement agencies against unjustified claims of loss or damage, or (3) locating potentially hazardous articles like weapons and flammables.[260] Police, for example, are not allowed to open and read journals, diaries, and planners, search cellular phones for telephone numbers, or listen to tapes during an inventory search because these activities advance none of the purposes for which an inventory search may be conducted.[261] Nor are they allowed to dismantle parts of the vehicle, such as removing steering wheel hubs and door panels, because the police department is not responsible for safeguarding valuables stored in places like these.[262] A noted authority on the law of search and seizure writes:[263]

> The inventory must be reasonably related to its purpose, which is the protection of the car owner from loss, and the police or other custodian from liability or unjust claim. It extends to the open areas of the vehicles, including areas under seats, and other places where property is ordinarily kept, e.g., glove compartments and trunks. It does not permit a search of hidden places, certainly not the removal of car parts in an effort to locate contraband or other property. The owner having no legitimate claim for protection of property so hidden, the police could have no legitimate interest in seeking it out.

C. *Inventory Search Exception and the Inevitable Discovery Rule*

Standard operating procedures for conducting inventory searches are important for a second reason. Their existence can salvage evidence from suppression under a doctrine known as the inevitable discovery rule. As will be explained in § 4.17, evidence that comes to light through unlawful means may nonetheless be used at trial if it would inevitably have been revealed in some other lawful way.[264] Consequently, even though

---

[260]   WAYNE R. LaFAVE, SEARCH & SEIZURE § 7.4 (3d ed. 1996).

[261]   United States v. Flores, 122 F. Supp. 2d 491 (S.D.N.Y. 2000) (suppressing evidence gained by reading planner and searching cellular telephone for numbers); United States v. Chan, 830 F. Supp. 531 (N.D. Cal. 1993) (suppressing evidence gained by warrantless activation of a pager); State v. Jewel, 338 So. 2d 633 (La. 1976) (suppressing evidence gained from inspecting contents of Excedrin bottle); Crowley v. State, 25 Md. App. 417, 334 A.2d 557 (1975) (suppressing LSD capsules found in can of mechanics' cleansing soap).

[262]   United States v. Best, 135 F.3d 1223 (8th Cir. 1998) (suppressing drugs discovered while shining flashlight to look inside door panel to find out what was obstructing front window from rolling down); United States v. Lugo, 978 F.2d 631 (10th Cir. 1992) (searching behind door panels does not qualify as standard inventorying procedure or serve the purpose of protecting the car and its contents); People v. Rutovic, 193 Colo. 397, 566 P.2d 705 (1977) (looking inside zipped seat covers impermissible during inventory search); Fields v. State, 382 So. 2d 1098 (Miss. 1980) (vacuuming car cannot be justified as inventory search).

[263]   LaFAVE, *supra* note 260.

[264]   Nix v. Williams, 467 U.S. 431, 104 S. Ct. 2501, 81 L. Ed. 2d 377 (1984).

a vehicle search violates the Fourth Amendment, the evidence can be used if it would, in any case, have been discovered during a routine inventory search.[265]

D. Final Analysis of A Mid-Summer's Nightmare

The search Officer Weird performed at the police impoundment lot was not sustainable as an inventory search because he dismantled parts of the vehicle. The search was, nevertheless, valid under the automobile exception because he had probable cause to believe that drugs and other incriminating evidence were hidden somewhere in the vehicle. Police officers do not need to have a particular exception in mind when they conduct a warrantless search. The search is valid if it can be sustained under any exception to the warrant requirement.

§ 4.13   Search of Protected Premises

When police officers cross the threshold of a home in search of evidence, the values protected by the Fourth Amendment are most at risk. Accordingly, it is at this point that the Fourth Amendment affords maximum protection. A search warrant is required so that the decision to invade a resident's privacy will be made only after proper consideration and the boundaries for the search will be established in advance. Unlike searches of people and vehicles, in which warrants are more the exception than the rule, there are only two circumstances that justify a warrantless search of protected premises — consent and exigent circumstances.

Consider this last example as you examine the rules for premises searches.

A Final "Tail"

Something evil has been taking place in Officer Goodfellow's neighborhood. One by one, his neighbors' pets have vanished. In the once peaceful suburb where cats and dogs roamed freely, people are now frightened and lock their animals up with them at night. Still, the disappearances continue.

---

[265] *See, e.g.*, United States v. Kimes, 246 F.3d 800 (6th Cir. 2001) (applying inevitable discovery rule); United States v. Blaze, 143 F.3d 585 (10th Cir. 1998) (evidence unlawfully seized from a briefcase inside a trunk is admissible under theory of inevitable discovery because it would have been inevitably discovered in a subsequent inventory search); United States v. Haro-Salcedo, 107 F.3d 769 (10th Cir. 1997) (cocaine seized from trunk during overly broad search incident to arrest admissible under inevitable discovery doctrine; when police officers lawfully impounded vehicle after defendant's arrest, police department procedures mandated inventory search to secure personal items found in defendant's seized vehicle, and proper inventory search would have uncovered cocaine in trunk of vehicle).

The first disappearance occurred at about the same time that a strange old woman, Mrs. Metzger, moved into the neighborhood. Metzger purchased the largest lot in the neighborhood, known as "the Farm." The lot consists of three acres surrounded by a hog wire fence. Located inside are a main house, a separate three-car garage, and a dilapidated barn situated at the far rear in an area overgrown with weeds and brush.

The neighbors first put two and two together when they learned that Mrs. Metzger had started her own sausage company and was running it out of the barn and garage. Metzger Sausages were rumored to have a "curiously gamey flavor," unlike any other brand on the market. Time and time again a pet would disappear early in the evening, and the sausage trucks would pull up to the barn the next morning.

Neighbors called various government offices to report the atrocities, but little attention was paid to them. They ultimately persuaded an inspector from the county's Board of Food Safety to conduct a surprise search. The inspector went to Mrs. Metzger's home, demanded to see the sausage production facilities in the barn and garage, pronounced the facilities "safe," left, and reported that he did not see anything unusual. So the neighbors turned to Officer Goodfellow and begged him to stop the carnage.

Goodfellow agreed. That night, he hopped over the fence, flashlight in hand, and began examining the barn. Immediately outside the barn door he found two animal collars, one with the name "Fido" on it, the other "Boogums." He entered the barn through an unlocked door, inspected the machinery and found what looked like cat hair near one of the grinders. He took the hair with him.

Goodfellow proceeded to the garage. Using his flashlight, he observed a large meat grinder and a car parked in a far corner of the building. Unfortunately, the doors were locked and he could not enter. Leaving, Goodfellow noticed some garbage cans outside the garage. Out of curiosity, he opened one, and found something that sent a chill down his spine — a shoe box filled with animal collars. Too scared to look further without backup, Goodfellow grabbed the box and headed straight to the local magistrate, seeking a warrant to search the entire estate and an arrest warrant for Mrs. Metzger. The magistrate refused both, saying: "Just because you found some animal collars doesn't mean that there is probable cause to believe that Mrs. Metzger committed a crime or that evidence of a crime will be found on her property. I'm sorry, but you need to do some more police work."

The next evening, Goodfellow made the rounds of the

neighborhood, knocking on doors and asking if anyone could identify the Fido and Boogums' collars. Goodfellow finally felt that he had probable cause when Jason P. Thomas, a neighbor for many years whom Goodfellow knew to be trustworthy, told him that "Fido" and "Boogums" were two of the pets that had disappeared from the neighborhood within the last week. But before Goodfellow could get back to the magistrate, a frightened young girl came running up to him, screaming "Please save Snowball! She didn't come back tonight." Eerily, at that same moment, they heard the low hum of machinery coming from Mrs. Metzger's place and the lights in the garage came on.

Believing that Snowball had only a few minutes left, Goodfellow ran into the garage to save her. He burst through the door screaming "Stop! You're under arrest." As soon as Mrs. Metzger saw him, she dropped a white fluffy cat to the floor and ran into the main house. Goodfellow chased her inside, and began a systematic search, looking in rooms, closets, and under beds in an effort to find her, bending down to pick up pet collars as he made his way. When he opened the door to the basement, approximately 50 animals, cats and dogs, came running out. Mrs. Metzger came out behind them and asked that she be allowed to speak to a lawyer.

As it turns out, all of the neighborhood's pets were unharmed. Mrs. Metzger, a zoophile, simply wanted them all to herself. She received a suspended sentence and is currently undergoing counseling.

In the sections that follow, we will explore whether Mrs. Metzger's Fourth Amendment rights were violated by the warrantless incursions onto her property. Because her property was used as a business as well as a residence, we will analyze the Fourth Amendment protection for each.

§ 4.14   — Premises Protected by the Fourth Amendment

While a literal reading of the Fourth Amendment would suggest that "houses" are the only premises protected by the Fourth Amendment because they are the only ones mentioned, the term "house" has never been interpreted this narrowly.[266] Protection extends to any location, including business premises, for which there exists a reasonable expectation of privacy.[267]

---

[266]   *See, e.g.,* **Katz v. United States,** *supra* note 1 (public telephone booth); Wayne R. LaFave, Search & Seizure § 2.1[d] (3d ed. 1996).

[267]   **Katz v. United States,** *supra* note 1.

A. *Fourth Amendment Protection for Business Premises*

Fourth Amendment protection for business premises depends on whether they are open to the public, such as retail establishments, or closed to the public, such as private offices and warehouses.[268] Police do not need a search warrant to enter business premises that are open to the public,[269] but they may only enter during business hours and go into areas that members of the public are invited to enter.[270] Officers acting on a tip on that the defendant is running an illegal bingo hall, for example, are free to enter while a bingo game is in progress, but not to sneak into the back offices or break into the bingo hall during hours when the establishment is closed.[271]

> The Fourth Amendment protects any location for which there exists a reasonable expectation of privacy.

B. *Fourth Amendment Protection of Residences*

The Fourth Amendment affords maximum protection to homes.[272] Police may not enter a home without a warrant, exigent circumstances, or consent.[273] A home, for Fourth Amendment purposes, includes any structure occupied as a dwelling. It does not have to be a permanent residence. Hotel rooms, motel rooms, and bedrooms occupied by an overnight guest are entitled to the same protection as a permanent residence.[274]

C. *Outdoor Spaces: Areas Within the Curtilage and "Open Fields"*

Outdoor spaces surrounding a home are broken down into two categories — areas within the **curtilage** and **open fields**. The curtilage refers to the area immediately surrounding the home, which is regularly used for domestic and family purposes, such as the garage and yard. The curtilage carries the same Fourth Amendment protection as

---

[268] Maryland v. Macon, *supra* note 3 (it is not a search for an officer to enter an adult bookstore and examine merchandise displayed for sale).

[269] *Id.*

[270] *Id.*

[271] State v. Foreman, 662 N. E. 2d 929 (Ind. 1996).

[272] **Payton v. United States,** *supra* note 21 ("The Fourth Amendment protects the individual's privacy in a number of settings, but in none is the zone of privacy more clearly defined than when bounded by the unambiguous physical dimensions of an individual's home — a zone that finds its route in clear and specific constitutional terms. . . . [T]he Fourth Amendment has drawn a firm line at the entrance to the home."); Lewis v. United States, *supra* note 6.

[273] Donovan v. Dewey, 452 U.S. 594, 101 S. Ct. 2534, 69 L. Ed. 2d 262 (1981).

[274] Minnesota v. Olson, 495 U.S. 91, 110 S. Ct. 1684, 109 L. Ed. 2d 85 (1990) (overnight guests); Stoner v. California, 376 U.S. 483, 84 S. Ct. 889, 11 L. Ed. 2d 856 (1964) (hotel room); United States v. Sandoval, 200 F.3d 659 (9th Cir. 2000) (tent).

the home.[275] Consequently, police need a search warrant to enter the curtilage in search of evidence, although they have the same right as visitors, deliverymen, and other members of the public to enter, using the regular access route, when they come on legitimate business.[276]

The rest of the land is classified as an open field and carries no Fourth Amendment protection. The phrase "open field" is misleading because the area need not be open or a field in any literal sense; it can be a thickly wooded area, a condominium parking lot, or even a lake.[277] Police do not need any Fourth Amendment justification to enter an open field, even though their presence constitutes a trespass under property law.[278]

There is no fixed formula for drawing the line between the curtilage and an "open field." The Supreme Court has identified four factors that are relevant to this inquiry: (1) the proximity to the home, (2) whether the area is included within an enclosure surrounding the home, (3) whether it is used for family purposes, and (4) the steps taken by the residents to shield the area from view by passersby.[279] No single factor is determinative, but they each inform a court's decision as to whether the outlying area is "so intimately tied to the home itself that it should be placed under the home's 'umbrella' of Fourth Amendment protection."[280] While there is no fixed distance at which the curtilage ends, the Supreme Court has indicated that it would be rare for the curtilage to extend more than 150 feet beyond the home.[281]

The curtilage concept does not apply to business establishments, but the grounds surrounding a business may receive analogous protection when special precautions are taken by the occupants to protect their privacy by putting up a tall fence with a locked gate.[282]

---

[275] **United States v. Dunn**, *supra* note 32.

[276] State v. Christensen, 131 Idaho 143, 953 P.2d 583 (1998) (noting that police with legitimate business, like other citizens, are entitled to enter areas of the curtilage impliedly open to public use, such as sidewalks, driveways, and pathways to an entry); Hardister v. State, 849 N.E.2d 563 (Ind. 2006) (no search occurs when police enter areas of curtilage impliedly open to use by the public to conduct legitimate business; legitimate business includes a knock and talk where police use normal routes of ingress and egress from a residence to make appropriate inquiries of the occupants). *See also* WAYNE R. LAFAVE, SEARCH & SEIZURE: A TREATISE ON THE FOURTH AMENDMENT § 2.3(C) (4th ed. 2004) (summarizing cases).

[277] *See, e.g.*, State V. Matthews, 805 S.W.2d 776 (Tenn. Crim. App. 1990) (apartment complex parking lot). *See also* 1 WAYNE R. LAFAVE, SEARCH & SEIZURE § 2.4 (3d ed. 1996).

[278] **United States v. Dunn**, *supra* note 32.

[279] *Id.*

[280] *Id.*

[281] *Id.*

[282] Dow Chemical Co. v. United States, 476 U.S. 227, 106 S. Ct. 1819, 90 L. Ed. 2d 226 (1986) (noting that a lesser expectation of privacy exists in lands surrounding commercial buildings); United States v. Elkins, 300 F.3d 638, 654 (6th Cir. 2002) (areas adjoining commercial buildings that are accessible to members of the public do not receive curtilage-like protection); United States v. F.M.C. Corp., 428 F. Supp. 615 (D.C.N.Y. 1977) (curtilage-like protection recognized for a commercial facility surrounded by an 8-foot-high fence, topped with barbed wire, and a locked gate).

D. *Analysis of A Final Tail*

Officer Goodfellow violated the Fourth Amendment when he entered Mrs. Metzger's curtilage in search of evidence. The more difficult question is determining the curtilage's boundaries. Mrs. Metzger's garage was within the curtilage both because of its proximity to her home and because garages are commonly used for domestic purposes, even though hers was being used partly for business. Consequently, Goodfellow performed a search when he walked up to her garage, shined a flashlight to look inside, and retrieved a shoe box full of pet collars from a garbage can just outside. The fact that the shoe box had been placed in a garbage can did not destroy Fourth Amendment protection because until a garbage can is placed outside the curtilage for collection, the contents are not yet abandoned.[283] The garbage can is just another container that is being used for a domestic purpose.

The pet collars found near the barn stand on a different footing because the barn was situated in an "open field." The reason the land around the barn was an open field was its substantial distance from Mrs. Metzger's house, its dilapidated condition, which suggested that the barn was not being put to domestic use, and the fact that it was actually being used for business.[284] Had the barn been closer to the home and used for domestic purposes, the characterization would have been more difficult.

E. *Outbuildings*

Even though the barn was situated in an "open field," and Goodfellow was free to walk around outside, his warrantless entry constituted a search because the barn itself was entitled to the same Fourth Amendment protection as any other closed building used for business.[285] Police may not enter a closed building used for business without exigent circumstances, consent, or a warrant.[286]

This does not mean that barns and outbuildings situated in an open field enjoy the same privacy protection as structures located inside the curtilage. If a barn is situated in an open field, police are free to walk up, peer through the windows, and use a flashlight to illuminate the interior.[287] Police are not allowed to do this for buildings that lay within the curtilage because they have no right to enter the curtilage to search for evidence without a search warrant.

---

[283] **California v. Greenwood**, *supra* note 2 (no Fourth Amendment protection exists for the contents of garbage can once it is placed outside the curtilage for collection); State v. Hauser, 115 N.C. App. 431, 445 S.E.2d 73 (N.C. App. 1995) (search of garbage container located inside the curtilage violated Fourth Amendment).

[284] **United States v. Dunn**, *supra* note 32 (holding that a barn located 60 yards from the dwelling that was used to manufacture drugs lay outside curtilage).

[285] Fite v. State, 873 P.2d 293 (Okla. Crim. App. 1993).

[286] *Id.*

[287] **United States v. Dunn**, *supra* note 32.

Figure 4.15
Premises Searches Conducted Under the Authority of a Warrant

- The scope of the search extends to the residence, curtilage, and all structures and vehicles inside the curtilage.
- Police may search everything found on the premises that is a plausible repository for the objects described in the warrant, regardless of ownership.
- The occupants may be detained while the search is in progress
- The occupants may be frisked only if police have *Terry* grounds for a frisk
- The occupants may be searched for objects listed in the warrant only if: (1) the search warrant expressly confers this authority, (2) the search is incidental to a lawful arrest, or (3) police have probable cause to believe that objects of the kind listed in the warrant are secreted on their person.

§ 4.15 — Entry and Search of Premises Under a Warrant

Most premises searches are conducted under the authority of either a search warrant or an arrest warrant. The search authority conferred by each warrant is different.

A. *Searches Conducted Under the Authority of a Search Warrant*

None of the problems encountered in A Final Tail would have arisen if Officer Goodfellow had been able to get a search warrant. A search warrant that describes the premises by address confers authority to search the residence, the curtilage, and all structures and vehicles within the curtilage.[288]

The permissible intensity is controlled by the warrant's description of the articles to be seized. Officers may search any place, receptacle, or effects that are plausible repositories for articles of the kind described in their warrant. When the articles sought are small, police may look under beds, in drawers and closets, and even in the pockets of the clothing hanging inside.[289]

Whether a premises search warrant confers authority to search containers found on the premises that belong to visitors, although formerly unclear,[290] has now been settled. In *Wyoming v. Houghton*,[291] a case that arose under the automobile exception, police

---

[288]   *See, e.g.,* United States v. Pennington, 287 F.3d 739 (8th Cir. 2002); United States v. Gottschalk, 915 F.2d 1459 (10th Cir. 1990); United States v. Asselin, 775 F.2d 445 (1st Cir. 1985); United States v. Napoli, 530 F.2d 1198 (5th Cir. 1976).

[289]   United States v. Lucas, 932 F.2d 1210 (8th Cir. 1991).

[290]   *See, e.g.,* Zachary H. Johnson, *Personal Container Searches Incident to Execution of Search Warrants: Special Protection for Guests?* 75 TEMP. L. REV. 313 (2002); Diane L. Schmauder, *Propriety of Search of Nonoccupant Visitor's Belongings Pursuant to Warrant Issued for Another's Premises,* 51 A.L.R. 5th 375 (1997).

[291]   **Wyoming v. Houghton,** *supra* note 225 (holding that search authority under the automobile exception extended to search of passenger's handbag located in the back seat). *See also* State v. Reid,

searched a passenger's handbag even though the probable cause that supported the search was directed at the driver. The Supreme Court held that when police have probable cause to search a vehicle, they may search any container that is a plausible repository for the objects of their search, regardless of ownership. A close reading of the opinion leaves little room for doubt that the Court would have reached the same conclusion had the case involved a premises search conducted under a search warrant.

1. Authority to Detain the Occupants During the Execution of a Search Warrant

A search warrant carries automatic authority to detain persons who regularly occupy the premises for the duration of the search.[292] Detention is justified because a search warrant embodies a judicial finding of probable cause to believe that someone on the premises has committed a crime and that evidence of the crime will be found there. This finding casts suspicion on all who regularly occupy the premises, making it constitutionally reasonable to detain them while the search is in progress.

Police do not have automatic authority to detain nonoccupants, such as visitors and others who are coincidentally present.[293] Detention of nonoccupants requires

---

190 Or. App. 49, 77 P.3d 1134 (2003) (holding that the visitor's jacket fell within scope of a premises search warrant where it was capable of containing objects described in search warrant, and was not on him or in his immediate physical possession when it was searched.); State v. Andrews, 201 Wis. 2d 383, 549 N.W.2d 210 (1996) (holding that police may search all personal belongings found on the premises, except those worn by or in the actual physical possession of a visitor).

[292] Michigan v. Summers, 452 U.S. 692, 101 S. Ct. 2587, 69 L. Ed. 2d 640 (1981) (announcing rule). In Michigan v. Summers, the officers were about to execute a search warrant upon the suspect's house as he was descending the front steps to leave. They made him turn around and go back, and detained him while they conducted the search. The Supreme Court held that the detention was reasonable, stating that "[i]f the evidence that a citizen's residence is harboring contraband is sufficient to persuade a judicial officer that an invasion of the citizen's property is justified, it is constitutionally reasonable to require that the citizen remain while the officers execute a valid warrant to search his house." For cases applying Michigan v. Summers, see United States v. Cochran, 939 F.2d 337 (6th Cir. 1991) (no constitutional violation occurred when police, who were preparing to execute a premises search warrant, detained an occupant who had already left the premises and was getting into his car, and made him return); United States v. Bohannon, 225 F.3d 615 (6th Cir. 2000) (officers could reasonably infer that the man who drove down the long driveway while they were executing the warrant to search for drugs was either a drug distributor or customer because his quick exit from car and rapid approach to the residence indicated apparent familiarity; police were, therefore, justified in detaining him).

[293] Hummel-Jones v. Strope, 25 F.3d 647 (8th Cir. 1994) ("*Summers* did not announce a per se rule authorizing . . . detention of anyone found on any premises being searched subject to a warrant, regardless of the circumstances, but simply permits the temporary detention of those residents of a house rendered suspect by a contraband warrant for that house."); Commonwealth v. Gray, 896 A.2d 601 (Pa. Super. 2006) (police could not detain customers during a drug raid of a store open to public, absent reasonable suspicion that they were connected to criminal activity under investigation); Lippert v. State, 664 S.W.2d 712 (Tex. Crim. App. 1984) (stating that a valid premises search warrant, standing alone, carries no authority to detain persons found on the premises who are not directly associated with the premises or named or specifically described in the warrant).

reasonable suspicion that they are connected to the crime,[294] but even nonoccupants may be detained long enough to establish their identity and the reason for their presence.[295]

2. Authority to Frisk Persons Present During the Execution of a Search Warrant

Authority to detain persons present on the premises covered by a search warrant does include the authority to frisk them. A frisk requires reasonable suspicion.[296] In *Ybarra v. Illinois*,[297] police prior to executing a warrant to search a tavern and the bartender for drugs frisked all of the patrons. A pat down of Ybarra yielded six packets of heroin. The Supreme Court held the pat down was not justified because the presence in a tavern covered by a narcotics search warrant does not furnish reasonable suspicion for a frisk.

Presence in a crack house is an entirely different matter. Guns and weapons are widely known to be used in narcotics trafficking and, unlike the patrons of a public tavern, there are no innocent explanations for a person's presence there. The potential dangers associated with execution of drug search warrants have persuaded a growing number of courts to uphold frisks of all persons encountered on the premises, based on this fact alone.[298] In the words of an Ohio court:[299]

> It is common knowledge that, in this day and age and in this area, drugs and weapons are frequently found in close proximity . . .; therefore, although the search warrant did not specifically authorize a search for weapons, the trial court could have concluded that it was reasonable for the police, out of concern for their own safety, to perform a *Terry* frisk for weapons upon anyone present in a suspected crack house.

---

[294]   Brown v. State, 397 Md. 89, 916 A.2d 245 (2007) (upholding detention of an individual who knocked on the door of known "open-air drug house" at 1:00 A.M. while police were executing a search warrant); Burchett v. Kiefer, 310 F.3d 937 (6th Cir. 2002) (upholding detention of an individual who approached the premises, paused at the property line, and then fled when he saw the police); State v. Reynolds, 155 P.3d 712 (Idaho App. 2007) (holding that facts known to police did not support independent reasonable suspicion that a person leaving premises when police arrived to conduct a premises search for drugs was connected to the criminal activity).

[295]   State v. Reynolds, *supra* note 294 (stating that individuals found on the premises at the inception of the search whose identity and connection to the premises are unknown may be detained for the time necessary to determine those facts).

[296]   Ybarra v. Illinois, 444 U.S. 85, 100 S. Ct. 338, 62 L. Ed. 2d 238 (1979). *See also* Denver Justice and Peace Committee, Inc. v. City of Golden, 405 F.3d 923 (10th Cir. 2005) (rejecting argument that police have categorical authority to frisk any person who seeks to enter an area where a search warrant is being executed).

[297]   Ybarra v. Illinois, *supra* note 296.

[298]   Dashiell v. State, 374 Md. 85, 821 A.2d 372 (Md. 2003) (holding that police were justified in frisking everyone present in a private residence during execution of a search warrant for drugs where an affidavit included information that there were firearms on the premises); State v. Taylor, 82 Ohio App. 3d 434, 612 N.E.2d 728 (1992) (holding that execution of a search warrant in a suspected crack house alone justifies a *Terry* search for weapons).

[299]   State v. Taylor, *supra* note 298.

The bottom line is that police do not have automatic authority to frisk all persons present during the execution of a search warrant unless the place to be searched happens to be a crack house. Otherwise individualized reasonable suspicion of weapon possession is necessary.

3. Authority to Search the Occupants for the Objects Described in the Warrant

A premises search warrant covers things, not people. People encountered on the premises are not like containers that police are free to search at will. The search of persons is permitted only: (1) when the search warrant expressly confers this authority, (2) the search is conducted as an incident to a lawful arrest, or (3) there is probable cause to believe that the person searched has objects described in the warrant on him.

Authorization under the search warrant. A search warrant can authorize the search of persons, as well as locations.[300] If police have advance knowledge that individuals likely to be in possession of objects of the kind listed in the warrant will be present on the premises during the search, they should name them in their application and seek authority to search them. While courts may, under limited circumstances, issue a warrant to search "all persons present" at a particular location, such warrants are valid only when there is probable cause to believe that all persons present at that location at the time of the search are likely to be involved in the crime and have evidence of it on their persons.[301] This situation generally exists only when the location is a crack house.[302]

Searches incident to an arrest. Persons encountered on the premises may also be searched when police have probable cause to arrest them.[303] A search may qualify as "incident" to an arrest, even though it precedes the arrest, if police have probable cause before the search is undertaken.[304] However, police should keep in mind that presence on the premises covered by a search warrant does not automatically supply grounds for an arrest.

---

[300]   The search warrant in Ybarra v. Illinois, *supra* note 296, authorized police to search the bartender as well as the tavern.

[301]   *See, e.g.,* Owens ex rel. Owens v. Lott, 372 F.3d 267 (4th Cir. 2004) (Deputy sheriff's affidavit did not supply sufficient information to establish probable cause that every person who happened to be on premises to be searched was involved in sale of illegal drugs, and thus, the "all persons" warrant, authorizing search of the residence and all persons located therein for drugs, was not supported by probable cause particularized with respect to occupants of residence searched.); 2 WAYNE R. LAFAVE, SEARCH & SEIZURE § 4.5(e) (3d ed. 1996).

[302]   *See, e.g.,* State v. Allard, 674 A.2d 921 (Me. 1996).

[303]   United States v. Holder, 990 F.2d 1327 (D.C. Cir. 1993) (defendant's presence in an apartment standing a few feet away from a table full of cocaine gave police probable cause to arrest him because he was clearly either the owner or a customer).

[304]   *See* § 4.8 (F).

Probable cause to believe that objects of the kind listed in the warrant are on the person searched. The last ground arises when police have probable cause to believe that the person searched has objects described in the warrant on his/her person. A noted authority on the law of search and seizure[305] writes that the

> requisite probable cause is most likely to be deemed present if the person searched lives at the place searched, was implicated by the search warrant affidavit in the crimes under investigation, had engaged in suspicious or incriminating conduct, or was found in the immediate proximity of contraband in open view.[306]

A person standing next to a table full of drugs, for example, can be searched. We turn now to search authority that arises pursuant to an arrest warrant.

B. Search of Premises Pursuant to an Arrest Warrant

Under the *Payton* rule discussed in Chapter 3, a person cannot be arrested inside their own home without an arrest warrant.[307] If the home belongs to someone else, a search warrant is also required.[308] Both warrants confer authority to perform a cursory visual inspection of places inside the home where the person to be arrested could hide.[309] Once the suspect is found and placed under arrest, two new grounds for search authority arise. Police are entitled to perform a protective sweep and a search incident to the arrest.

1. Protective Sweeps

A protective sweep consists of a cursory visual inspection of closets and other spaces immediately adjoining the place of arrest in which accomplices and others who pose a danger to the officers could be hiding.[310] Authority to conduct a protective

---

[305] 3 WAYNE R. LaFAVE, LAW OF SEARCH & SEIZURE § 6.6(a) (3d ed. 1996).

[306] *See, e.g.,* United States v. Khounsavanh, 113 F.3d 279 (1st Cir. 1997) (police had probable cause to search occupants after informant made controlled purchase of drugs from them and they attempted to flee when police entered the apartment to execute search warrant); State v. Farrell, 242 Neb. 877, 497 N.W.2d 17 (1993) ("it was reasonable for the officers to believe that defendant was concealing evidence on his person," as he whispered to his wife "I've got it" and then asked to use the bathroom); Patton v. State, 148 Ga. App. 793, 252 S.E.2d 678 (1979) (police had probable cause to search person seated beside the table with marijuana when he surreptitiously put hand in pocket); United States v. Savides, 664 F. Supp. 1544 (N.D. Ill. 1987) (presence in the home with large quantities of narcotics and weapons in plain view creates probable cause for a search, even if the person is only a visitor); People v. Gutierrez, 109 Ill. 2d 59, 92, 485 N.E.2d 845 (1985) (police had probable cause to search defendant for illegal drugs, even though he was not listed in warrant, where drugs were found on premises, defendant had bulges in pants pockets, had attempted forcibly to bar police from entering, and was nervous and unable to sit still).

[307] *See* § 3.15 *supra.*

[308] *Id.*

[309] Maryland v. Buie, 494 U.S. 325, 110 S. Ct. 1093, 108 L. Ed. 2d 276 (1990).

[310] *Id.*

sweep arises as an automatic incident of arrests made inside a dwelling and does not require reasonable suspicion that potential attackers are, in fact, present.[311] However, such suspicion is necessary to conduct a broader sweep.[312] Protective sweeps may last no longer than necessary to dispel any suspicion of danger, and in any event no longer than it takes to complete the arrest and depart from the premises.

2. Search Incident to Arrest Made Inside a Dwelling

When an arrest is made inside a dwelling, the scope of the search is confined to the area under the arrested person's immediate control, defined as "the area from within which he might gain possession of a weapon or destructible evidence."[313] Police may not automatically search this area. A search is permitted only if the arrestee is unsecured and within reaching distance of this area at the time of the search.[314] If a more complete premises search is needed, police may take reasonable precautions to secure the premises, but must then apply for a search warrant.[315]

§ 4.16   — Entry and Search of Premises Without a Warrant

There are only two justifications for searching protected premises without a search warrant: exigent circumstances and consent.[316]

Figure 4.16
Exigent Circumstances Exception

The exigent circumstances exception authorizes the police to make a warrantless entry when: 1. they have reason to believe that life or property is in imminent danger or that a serious crime is in progress; 2. they have reason to believe that evidence will be destroyed or removed unless they act immediately; or 3. they are in hot pursuit of a felon who flees and takes refuge inside.

---

[311] *Id.*

[312] *Id.*; In re *Sealed Case*, 153 F.3d 759 (D.C. Cir. 1997) (protective sweep could extend to the small bedroom located between the bedroom where the arrest was made and the top of the stairs because it was a space from which an attack could be launched).

[313] **Chimel v. California**, *supra* note 44.

[314] *See* authorities *supra* notes 184, 217.

[315] *See* authorities *supra* note 71.

[316] **Payton v. New York**, *supra* note 21; Steagald v. United States, 451 U.S. 204, 101 S. Ct. 1642, 68 L. Ed. 2d 38 (1981).

A. *Grounds for Warrantless Entry Under the Exigent Circumstances Exception*

Films and television programs regularly portray police officers bursting through the door in the nick of time to save a victim, but never show them waiting nervously outside the magistrate's door for a search warrant. That is because the Fourth Amendment excuses the police from obtaining a warrant when they are confronted with an emergency that requires immediate action. There are an endless number of emergencies that can justify an immediate warrantless entry. Fires,[317] shootings,[318] domestic violence reports,[319] screams,[320] hot pursuit of dangerous criminals,[321] the belief that a burglary is in progress,[322] concerns for the safety of children[323] or colleagues inside,[324] and fears that evidence is about to be destroyed[325] are just a few.

Exigent means urgent. The exigent circumstances exception to the warrant requirement deals with urgent circumstances in which there is no time to obtain a warrant.[326] There are three broad categories of cases that come within this exception.

---

[317]   State v. Loh, 275 Mont. 460, 914 P.2d 592 (1996) (exigent circumstances of apparent fire and the possibility that individuals were still inside justified warrantless entry).

[318]   People v. Dixon, 721 N. Y. S. 2d 402 (N. Y. A.D. 2001) (entry justified where made in response to radio transmission that a man had just killed his wife and was alone with their baby in the apartment).

[319]   Fletcher v. Town of Clinton, 196 F.3d 41 (1st Cir. 1999) (officer who, responding to a domestic disturbance report, was informed by neighbors that shouting had ended right before his arrival, was justified in concluding that someone inside might have been injured and in need of medical care or protection; police may enter dwelling without warrant to render emergency aid and assistance to persons whom they reasonably believe to be in distress).

[320]   **Brigham City v. Stuart**, *supra* note 69 (Officers, responding to complaint about a loud party, justified in entering without a warrant when they heard yelling inside and observed a youth striking an adult through the window); United States v. Barone, 330 F.2d 543 (2d Cir. 1964) (screams coming from inside apartment); United States v. Gillenwaters, 890 F.2d 679 (4th Cir. 1989) (call from stab victim requesting help).

[321]   Warden v. Hayden, *supra* note 7.

[322]   In re *Sealed Case*, *supra* note 312.

[323]   State v. Peterson, 543 S. E. 2d 692 (Ga. 2001) (entry for the purposes of making sure children left without adult supervision were safe).

[324]   People v. Lee, 723 N. Y. S. 2d 833 (N. Y. City Crim. Ct. 2001) (police justified in entering prostitute's apartment without search warrant when an undercover officer working with the vice squad unit failed to emerge after prearranged 20-minute period inside and his team members became concerned that his life might be in danger).

[325]   Illinois v. McArthur, *supra* note 71 (same); United States v. Rivera, 248 F.3d 677 (7th Cir. 2001) (warrantless search of defendant's residence was justified by exigent circumstances, where at moment of entry, agents had reason to believe that evidence might be destroyed or removed before a warrant could be secured; agents observed defendant transport packages containing marijuana to his residence, other individuals continuously entered defendant's residence and left with small packages that agents presumed to be narcotics).

[326]   *See, e.g.*, In re *Sealed Case*, *supra* note 312 ("[t]he test for exigent circumstances is whether police had an 'urgent need' or 'an immediate major crisis in the performance of duty afford[ing] neither time nor opportunity to apply to a magistrate.'").

Failure to obtain a warrant before entering a residence is excused when police reasonably believe that: (1) lives or property are in imminent danger or that a serious crime is in progress,[327] (2) evidence will be destroyed or moved if they postpone taking action until a search warrant can be obtained,[328] or (3) they are in hot pursuit of a felon who flees and takes refuge inside.[329]

B. *Exigent Circumstances and the Plain View Exception*

Discovery of incriminating evidence while on the premises generally provides the context in which questions about the exigent circumstances exception arise. Two police officers, patrolling a residential neighborhood in the early hours of the morning, see a man run up a path leading to a dark residence, strike the main door with his shoulder, force it open, and enter without turning on the lights. Believing that a burglary is in progress and that lives and property are in danger, the police stop the car, follow the man into the house, and guess what? It turns out that the man was entering his own house, but the police, while on the premises investigating, see a large quantity of marijuana in plain view.

This scenario requires the court to determine whether the entry was justified by exigent circumstances,[330] because if the initial intrusion that brings the police in contact with evidence is lawful, they immediately recognize its incriminating nature, and

---

[327] *See, e.g.*, **Arizona v. Hicks**, *supra* note 44 (exigent circumstances justified entry to search for person who fired a shot through the floor, injuring a man in the apartment below); *Brigham City v. Stuart*, *supra* note 69 (police may enter a home without a warrant when they have an objectively reasonable basis for believing that an occupant is seriously injured or imminently threatened with serious injury); Michigan v. Fisher, —U.S. —, 130 S. Ct. 546, 175 L. Ed. 2d 410 (2009) (officers are justified in making warrantless entry into a residence when they have an objectively reasonable belief that a person inside is in need of immediate assistance); Michigan v. Tyler, 436 U.S. 499, 509, 98 S. Ct. 1942, 56 L. Ed. 2d 486 (1978) (burning building presents exigency of sufficient proportions to render warrantless entry reasonable); Mincey v. Arizona, 437 U.S. 385, 392, 98 S. Ct. 2408, 57 L. Ed. 2d 290 (1978) (recognizing the need to protect or preserve life or avoid serious injury justifies warrantless entry); Minnesota v. Olson, 495 U.S. 91, 100, 110 S. Ct. 1684, 109 L. Ed. 2d 85 (1990) (recognizing that warrantless entry may be justified by the risk of danger to the police or to other persons inside or outside the dwelling); In re *Sealed Case*, *supra* note 312 (warrantless entry justified where officers, while patrolling a residential neighborhood, observed what they reasonably thought was a burglary in progress).

[328] Because of the ease with which narcotics can be destroyed, cases invoking this exception frequently involve narcotics busts. *See, e.g.*, Illinois v. McArthur, *supra* note 71.

[329] Warden v. Hayden, *supra* note 7 (warrantless search for suspect and weapons was justified where delay posed grave danger); Welsh v. Wisconsin, 466 U.S. 740, 748, 104 S. Ct. 2091, 80 L. Ed. 2d 732 (1984) (exigent circumstances do not justify warrantless entry to search for nondangerous suspect).

[330] The facts recited in the previous paragraph are from In re *Sealed Case*, *supra* note 312. The court held that warrantless action was justified.

they are able to gain physical access without violating the Fourth Amendment, they may seize it under the plain view exception.[331]

C. *Search Activity Permitted Under the Exigent Circumstances Exception*

When an entry is made under the exigent circumstances exception, search authority is limited to actions immediately necessary to address the exigency that justified the entry.[332] As to what the police may do once inside, one authority writes:

> [T]his must be assessed upon a case-by-case basis, taking into account the type of emergency which appeared to be present.... The officer's post-entry conduct must be carefully limited to achieving the objective which justified the entry.[333]

For example, if the entry is made to render emergency assistance, the officer is limited to determining whether someone is in need of aid and providing it.[334] When the entry is to prevent destruction of evidence, the police may perform a cursory visual inspection of rooms, closets, and other locations in which persons who might destroy the evidence could hide.[335] If the evidence sought is discovered in plain view while performing a cursory visual inspection, the police may seize it under the plain view doctrine. If no evidence is discovered, the police may secure the premises, but must then apply for a search warrant.[336]

Police may not deviate to investigate unrelated matters; they must stick to addressing the exigency that justified their entry. In *Arizona v. Hicks*,[337] a bullet was fired through the floor of the defendant's apartment, striking and injuring a man in the apartment below. The police entered the defendant's apartment and, while searching for the shooter and the weapon, noticed some very expensive stereo equipment that seemed out of place. Acting on a hunch that the equipment was stolen, they turned the stereo around and read the serial numbers to a radio operator who confirmed that it was stolen. The Supreme Court held that, while the initial entry was justified by exigent circumstances, turning the stereo around to read the serial numbers resulted in an additional search unrelated to the exigency that justified the entry and violated the Fourth Amendment.

---

[331]   The plain view exception to the warrant requirement is discussed in § 3.4.

[332]   Mincey v. Arizona, *supra* note 327 (search activity while on the premises is "'strictly circumscribed by the exigencies which justify its initiation.'").

[333]   3 WAYNE R. LAFAVE, SEARCH & SEIZURE § 6.6(a) (3d ed. 1996).

[334]   *Id.*

[335]   Mincey v. Arizona, *supra* note 327; Illinois v. McArthur, *supra* note 71; Arizona v. Hicks, *supra* note 44.

[336]   *See* authorities *supra* note 335.

[337]   *Supra* note 44.

D. *Entry to Prevent Emminent Destruction of Evidence*

Police may enter a person's home without a warrant to prevent destruction of evidence if they have: (1) probable cause to secure a search warrant and (2) an objectively reasonable belief that there are persons inside who will destroy the evidence if they do not act right now.[338] When both conditions are present, police may enter for the limited purpose of securing the premises while they apply for a search warrant, but must postpone the search until after a warrant is obtained.[339] Entry even for this limited purpose is not permitted if the risk of destruction can be adequately controlled by conducting a perimeter stakeout (*i.e.,* sealing off the premises and preventing anyone from entering).[340]

E. *Police-Created Exigent Circumstances*

In *Kentucky v. King,*[341] the Supreme Court was asked to decide whether police can rely on the exigent circumstances exception to justify entering a home without a warrant when the exigent circumstances are police-created. In *King,* police followed a drug dealer into an apartment building after watching him engage in a controlled sale of crack cocaine with a police informant. They lost sight of him, but heard a door slam and mistakenly assumed that he had entered the apartment on the left because they smelled a strong odor of marijuana wafting around door. They pounded on the door and shouted "Police!" No one answered, but they heard movement inside that they interpreted as an attempt to destroy drug-related evidence. The officers kicked in the door and found the Hollis King and two companions smoking marijuana, along with a cache of drugs. The trial court denied King's motion to suppress, finding that the police were justified in entering his apartment without a warrant to prevent destruction of evidence. King argued on appeal that the exigent circumstances exception did not apply because the officers created the exigency by pounding on his door and shouting "Police!" The attempted destruction of evidence would never have occurred had this not happened. Since the exigent circumstances were police-created, the police were barred from relying on the exigent circumstances exception to justify entering his home without a warrant.

---

[338]   *See, e.g.,* Illinois v. McArthur, *supra* note 71 (after defendant's wife informed police that defendant had illegal drugs inside their home, police justified in preventing defendant from entering his residence without an officer until a search warrant was obtained).

[339]   *See* authorities *supra* note 335.

[340]   Illinois v. McArthur, *supra* note 71 (when police have probable cause to believe there are illegal drugs inside a residence and reason to fear evidence will be destroyed, they may seal off a residence and refuse to allow occupants to enter, unless accompanied by a police officer, until a warrant can be obtained); Mincey v. Arizona, *supra* note 327 (exigent circumstances do not justify search where police guard at door could prevent loss of evidence).

[341]   _ U.S. _, 31 S. Ct. 1849, 179 L. Ed. 2d 865 (2011).

The Supreme Court disagreed, holding that the pertinent question was not whether the actions of the police caused the attempted destruction of evidence, but whether their prior actions were lawful under the Fourth Amendment. Police may enter a home without a warrant to prevent destruction of evidence so long as they do not cause the attempted destruction of evidence "by engaging or threatening to engage in conduct that violates the Fourth Amendment."

Applying the test to the facts, the Court concluded that the prior actions of the police were lawful. In knocking on the defendant's door and requesting an opportunity to speak with him, they did nothing more than a private citizen might do. The defendant was not obliged to open his door. He could have stood on his constitutional right and told the police that he would not let them in unless they returned with a search warrant. However, he did not do this. He, instead, attempted to dispose of drug-related evidence. "Occupants who choose not to stand on their constitutional rights, but instead elect to destroy evidence have only themselves to blame for the warrantless exigent-circumstances search that may ensue."

F. Analysis of A Final Tail

A Final Tail contains two examples of the exigent circumstances exception. The first occurred when Officer Goodfellow burst into Mrs. Metzger's garage and the second when he pursued her into her home. Officer Goodfellow was justified in bursting into Mrs. Metzger's garage without a warrant because he had probable cause to believe that Snowball was inside and, at the moment of entry, he had reason to believe that Snowball was about to be destroyed. He had just confirmed that the pet collars found the previous day belonged to cats that had mysteriously disappeared; moments later, he learned that Snowball had disappeared, too; Goodfellow had previously seen the grinding machines inside Mrs. Metzger's barn and garage; and now he heard them start up and begin humming. In his mind, there was only one explanation that could account for this bizarre sequence of events. Snowball was about to be ground up and would be no more by the time he returned with a search warrant. Snowball was more than just a pet[342]; he was evidence of criminal activity. Consequently, Goodfellow was justified in rushing in to prevent what he believed was the imminent destruction of evidence.

Mrs. Metzger's retreat into her home to avoid arrest provided the second occasion for applying the exigent circumstances exception. This time the exception concerned hot pursuit. Officer Goodfellow encountered Mrs. Metzger outside her home, where he

---

[342]   Suss v. American Society for the Prevention of Cruelty to Animals, 823 F. Supp. 181 (S.D.N.Y. 1993) (recognizing that exigent circumstances exception may, in limited situations, allow warrantless action to protect animals against cruelty).

attempted to arrest her. She could not defeat his attempt by fleeing inside. Officer Goodfellow was entitled to pursue her.[343]

Officer Goodfellow did a commendable job of complying with the Fourth Amendment. Unfortunately, no medals are given for capturing little old ladies who love animals.

G. Consent

Consent affords the second and only other justification for entering protected premises without a search warrant. Actual consent is necessary to enter a home or its curtilage. A fiction known as implied consent is used to justify warrantless inspections of business premises to determine compliance with government regulations.

1. Actual Consent

Police are always free to walk up to a suspect's door, ring the bell, and ask for permission to enter. A warrantless entry is justified when police receive knowing, voluntary, and intelligent consent[344] from someone who has authority.[345]

The person answering the door does not have to be informed of the right to refuse in order for the consent to be valid.[346] Concealment of police identity does not destroy consent.[347] However, there are limits on allowable police duplicity. Police may not secure admission by misrepresenting that they have a warrant[348] or by threatening to obtain one when they lack grounds.[349] To be effective, the consent must be given by someone who has actual or apparent authority.[350]

The boundaries of the search are determined by the authorization that has been given.[351] Police may only look in places and for things that a reasonable officer would believe are within the scope of the consent.[352] The consenter also controls the duration of the search. The consenter can limit the duration at the outset[353] or ask police to leave at any time.[354] However, after the police discover incriminating evidence, it is generally too late, because at this point other warrant exceptions generally arise.

---

[343] See §3.15 (D).

[344] Schneckloth v. Bustamonte, *supra* note 64; United States v. Conner, 127 F.3d 663 (8th Cir. 1997) (unconstitutional search occurs when officers gain physical access to a motel room after an occupant opens the door in response to a demand issued under color of authority).

[345] Illinois v. Rodriguez, *supra* note 58. See also §§ 3.15(D), 4.3(A)(2)(a) *supra*.

[346] Schneckloth v. Bustamonte, *supra* note 64.

[347] Lewis v. United States, *supra* note 6.

[348] Bumper v. North Carolina, 391 U.S. 543, 88 S. Ct. 1788, 20 L. Ed. 2d 797 (1968).

[349] State v. Apodaca, 839 P.2d 352 (Wash. 1992); Orhorhaghe v. INS, 38 F.3d 488 (9th Cir. 1994) (agent represented to alien that he had authority to enter without a warrant).

[350] Illinois v. Rodriguez, *supra* note 58. See also § 4.3(A)(2)(a) *supra*.

[351] United States v. Dichiarinte, 445 F.2d 126 (7th Cir. 1971) (police exceeded consent to search for narcotics when they read defendant's personal papers).

[352] *Id.*

[353] State v. Douglass, 123 Wis. 2d 13, 365 N. W. 2d 580 (1985).

[354] See, e.g., State v. Mer, 441 N. W. 2d 762 (Iowa 1989); Mason v. Pullman, 557 F.2d 426 (5th Cir. 1977); United States v. Million-Rodriguez, 759 F. 2d 1558 (11th Cir. 1985).

2. Implied Consent — Statutory Authority and Administrative Searches

The Fourth Amendment permits warrantless inspections of business premises to determine compliance with government regulations.[355] This exception to the warrant requirement rests on the fiction of implied consent. The warrantless inspection performed by the official from the Board of Food Safety can be justified on this basis. The theory proceeds as follows. When Mrs. Metzger began producing sausages, she knew that food service is a heavily regulated industry and that the regulations often include periodic, unannounced inspections. Consequently, when she went into business, she impliedly consented to this practice and is in no position to complain that her Fourth Amendment rights were violated when an official from the Board of Food Safety arrived and demanded to inspect her sausage production facilities.

§ 4.17 The Exclusionary Rule

The principal remedy for unconstitutional police action is to exclude the illegally obtained evidence from admission in a criminal prosecution. The remedy serves two purposes: to undo the damage that the defendant has suffered by preventing illegally seized evidence from being used against her,[356] and to discourage police from future violations by depriving them of the fruits of their transgressions.[357]

> The exclusion of evidence is a criminal defendant's remedy for police violations of his or her constitutional rights.

A. History of the Exclusionary Rule

The exclusionary rule has been attacked ever since its recognition, but no one has ever summarized the frustration that many feel about the rule better than Justice (then Judge) Cardozo did in his opinion in *People v. Defore*,[358] when he lamented: "The criminal is to go free because the constable has blundered."

---

[355]   Donovan v. Dewey, 452 U.S. 594, 101 S. Ct. 2534, 69 L. Ed. 2d 262 (1981) (upholding warrantless inspections by federal mine inspectors of underground mines to ensure compliance with health and safety standards); United States v. Biswell, 406 U.S. 311, 92 S. Ct. 1593, 32 L. Ed. 2d 87 (1972) (upholding warrantless inspection of premises of licensed gun dealers to determine compliance with the Gun Control Act).

[356]   Mapp v. Ohio, 367 U.S. 643, 81 S. Ct. 1684, 6 L. Ed. 2d 1081 (1961).

[357]   Wong Sun v. United States, 371 U.S. 471, 83 S. Ct. 407, 9 L. Ed. 2d 441 (1963).

[358]   242 N. Y. 13, 150 N. E. 585 (1926).

In recent years, the Supreme Court has attempted to balance the costs to the criminal justice system inherent in allowing the guilty to "go free" against the benefits of discouraging police violations of the Constitution. In the process, it has reshaped the rule and created many exceptions to it. As you read through the following materials, ask whether it is still the case today that the criminal who would otherwise have been convicted "goes free" simply because "the constable has blundered."

1. Recognition and Framing of the Rule

The Supreme Court first announced the exclusionary rule in *Weeks v. United States*.[359] In that case, a federal marshal working with state police entered Weeks' house without a warrant and seized his private papers — some of which showed that he was guilty of running an illegal lottery. Prior to trial, Weeks moved unsuccessfully to have the prosecution return the papers to him to prevent the prosecution from using them. The Supreme Court overturned the conviction, but not because Weeks had a constitutional right to suppress evidence seized in violation of the Fourth Amendment. Reversal was required because the defendant had a constitutional right to the return of his property, which was violated when the prosecution refused to give it back.[360]

It was not until the Court's later decisions that it came to regard suppression itself as the proper remedy for an illegal search and seizure.[361] However, the rule lost its characterization as a constitutional right and became simply a judicially created remedy for an illegal search and seizure that judges could apply or refuse to apply, depending on whether it furthered the deterrent goals of the exclusionary rule.[362] This remains the prevailing view today.[363]

2. Application of the Rule to the States

The exclusionary rule originally applied only to evidence seized by federal authorities.[364] It was not until almost 50 years after *Weeks* that the Supreme Court finally made the exclusionary rule binding on the states in the now famous case of *Mapp v. Ohio*.[365] The facts of the case were particularly egregious and highlighted the need for suppression as a remedy to curb police abuses.

Mapp involved a prosecution for the possession of obscene materials. Police officers initially sought entry after learning that an unnamed person, wanted for questioning in connection with a recent bombing, might be hiding in Mapp's home, and that she also

---

[359]   232 U.S. 383, 34 S. Ct. 341, 58 L. Ed. 652 (1914).

[360]   *Id.*

[361]   Silverthorn Lumber Co. v. United States, 251 U.S. 385, 40 S. Ct. 182, 64 L. Ed. 319 (1920).

[362]   United States v. Leon, *supra* note 139; Davis v. United States, — U.S.—, 131 S. Ct. 2419, 177 L. Ed. 2d 894 (2010).

[363]   Arizona v. Evans, 514 U.S. 1, 115 S. Ct. 1185, 131 L. Ed. 2d 34 (1995); **Herring v. United States, 355 U.S. 135, 129 S. Ct. 695, 172 L. Ed. 2d 496 (2009)**.

[364]   Wolf v. Colorado, 338 U.S. 25, 69 S. Ct. 1359, 93 L. Ed. 1782 (1949).

[365]   ***Supra*** note 356.

had a large amount of revolutionary literature. Mapp refused to admit them without a warrant, so the officers left and returned three hours later with a fake warrant. When Mapp demanded to see it, a scuffle ensued, in which Mapp was forcibly subdued and placed under arrest. Police officers proceeded to scour the home. The obscene materials for which Mapp was eventually charged were found in a locked trunk in her basement.

Faced with these facts, the Supreme Court ruled that a mandatory exclusionary rule was necessary:

> The ignoble shortcut to conviction left open to the State tends to destroy the entire system of constitutional restraints on which the liberties of the people rest. Having once recognized that the right to privacy embodied in the Fourth Amendment is enforceable against the States, and that the right to be secure against rude invasions of privacy by state officers is, therefore, constitutional in origin, we can no longer permit that right to remain an empty promise. Because it is enforceable in the same manner and to like effect as other basic rights secured by the Due Process Clause, we can no longer permit it to be revocable at the whim of any police officer who, in the name of law enforcement itself, chooses to suspend its enjoyment.[366]

Since *Mapp v. Ohio*, suppression of illegally obtained evidence has been required in both federal and state courts.

B. Scope of the Rule

The defendant's right to suppression includes not only evidence uncovered during an illegal search or seizure but also any other evidence that police discover as a result of it.[367] This is known as the "fruit of the poisonous tree doctrine," or the *Wong Sun* doctrine — after the case in which it was recognized. The recognition of the fruit of the poisonous tree doctrine means that illegal police activity can have far-ranging effects on a prosecution. Once police obtain evidence by violating the Fourth Amendment, the prosecution will not only lose the benefit of that evidence; it will bear the burden of showing that all other evidence that it seeks to introduce was acquired from a source untainted by the illegal evidence-gathering activity.[368]

C. Standing to Assert the Rule

The exclusionary rule is a remedy for criminal defendants whose Fourth Amendment rights have been violated. Because it is a remedy (rather than a general prohibition on the use of illegally obtained evidence), only a defendant whose rights were violated when police obtained the evidence can demand suppression.[369] If the illegally obtained

---

[366] *Id.*

[367] Wong Sun v. United States, *supra* note 357.

[368] Murray v. United States, 487 U.S. 533, 108 S. Ct. 2529, 101 L. Ed. 2d 472 (1988).

[369] Rakas v. Illinois, 439 U.S. 128, 99 S. Ct. 421, 58 L. Ed. 2d 387 (1978); Minnesota v. Carter, 525 U.S. 83, 119 S. Ct. 469, 142 L. Ed. 2d 373 (1998) (capacity to claim protection of Fourth Amendment depends on whether the person who claims it has a reasonable expectation of privacy in the place invaded; a person present in another's apartment for a few hours to package cocaine lacks a reasonable expectation of privacy in the premises).

evidence is offered against a person whose rights were not violated, the person has no standing to complain.

Suppose, for example, that police break into Mary Wanna's home without a warrant or probable cause, looking for evidence of drug trafficking. While inside, they find five kilograms of cocaine and a photograph of her brother Sam cultivating a marijuana garden in his basement. Based on the photograph, police obtain a warrant for Sam's home. They seize the plants and a photograph depicting Mary assisting Sam in his basement operation. Mary is charged on both cocaine and marijuana counts. She will "walk" on both counts because all the evidence against her derives either directly (the cocaine) or indirectly (the photographs linking her to Sam's marijuana operations) from the illegal search of her home. Sam, on the other hand, is going to jail because the police did not violate his Fourth Amendment rights. He cannot complain that police acquired probable cause for his search warrant and some of the evidence used against him by violating his sister Mary's rights.

D. Exceptions to the Rule

Because the Supreme Court has come to regard the exclusionary rule as a judge-made remedy, rather than a constitutional right, it has recognized a number of exceptions based on whether the rule will have an appreciable deterrent effect in a given situation and whether this benefit outweighs the cost of suppressing reliable evidence and letting a guilty person go free.

Figure 4.17
Exceptions to the Exclusionary Rule

Suppression is not required if:
1. the same evidence inevitably would have been discovered through lawful means;
2. the officer acted in objective good faith;
3. the illegality related only to the manner of entering to execute a valid search warrant;
4. the evidence is offered for the limited purpose of impeaching (i.e., discrediting) the defendant's own testimony; or
5. the evidence is offered in a proceeding other than the defendant's criminal trial.

1. Inevitable Discovery/Independent Source Exception

Because the exclusionary rule is designed to undo the effects of a Fourth Amendment violation and to discourage future violations, the Supreme Court has determined that suppression is not required in cases in which the police obtain no advantage from their unlawful conduct. Accordingly, illegally obtained evidence will be admitted if the prosecution can show that the same evidence inevitably would have found its way into the hands of the police through lawful means in the absence of the illegal discovery. The reasoning behind this exception is that the government should not be better off as a result of unlawful activity, but neither should it be worse off.[370]

The inevitable discovery exception often works in conjunction with the inventory search exception to wash out earlier errors committed by the police. For example, if the police perform an overly broad motor vehicle search after arresting a motorist, but the same evidence inevitably would have been discovered during a routine inventory search, the evidence is admissible because the police did not reap any advantage from their wrongdoing.[371]

2. Good Faith Exception

The exclusionary rule cannot deter all violations of the Fourth Amendment because accidental violations occur no matter how hard police try to avoid them. Because the exclusionary rule only applies when suppression will have a deterrent effect, the rule does not apply when the officer who violated the Fourth Amendment acted in objective good faith. To be acting in objective good faith, the officer must reasonably believe that she is complying with the Fourth Amendment.

The most important application of the good faith exception involves reasonable reliance on a **facially valid warrant** that is later determined to be defective.[372] The Court recognized this application in *United States v. Leon*.[373] In *Leon*, police officers investigating suspected drug activity prepared an affidavit stating facts that they believed established probable cause to search Leon's home for drugs. The magistrate reviewed the affidavit, found probable cause, and issued a search warrant. At a later suppression hearing, the trial court ruled that the magistrate's finding of probable cause was erroneous and suppressed the evidence. On appeal, the Supreme Court accepted that probable cause was lacking, but held that the exclusionary rule did not apply because the officers conducting the search reasonably believed that the search warrant

---

[370]   *See, e.g.*, Nix v. Williams, *supra* 264; State v. Rodriguez, 122 Hawai'i 229, 225 P. 3d 671 (Hawaii App. 2010) (Evidence recovered from otherwise illegal search incident to arrest is admissible under the inevitable discovery exception to exclusionary rule if the evidence would have been inevitably discovered during an inventory search conducted at the police cell block); Thompson v. State, 192 Md. App. 653, 995 A. 2d 1030 (2010) (Seizure of handgun in the trunk of arrestee's vehicle was lawful, notwithstanding *Arizona v. Gant*, because it would inevitably have been discovered during a valid inventory search.).

[371]   United States v. George, 971 F.2d 1113 (4th Cir. 1992) (government must prove that it would have found same evidence under the police department's standard inventory procedures).

[372]   United States v. Leon, 468 U.S. 897, 104 S. Ct. 3405, 82 L. Ed. 2d 677 (1984); Massachusetts v. Sheppard, 468 U.S. 981, 104 S. Ct. 3424, 82 L. Ed. 2d 737 (1984).

[373]   *Supra* note 372.

was valid.[374] Where an officer reasonably believes that she is acting under a valid warrant, the exclusionary rule does not apply because there is misconduct that can be deterred.

The early cases applying the good faith exception followed a common pattern. The unconstitutionality of the search was caused by the mistake of a third party on whose judgment the officer reasonably relied. In *Leon*, the mistake was made by the magistrate who issued the search warrant. The officer relied on the magistrate's determination of probable cause and, as a result, reasonably believed that his conduct was lawful. Since the officer was blameless, the exclusionary rule did not apply because there was no wrongful conduct that could be deterred. This pattern was also present in *Illinois v. Krull*,[375] the second case in which the Supreme Court applied the good faith exception. In *Krull*, the mistake was made by the legislature. The legislature enacted an unconstitutional procedural statute. The officer reasonably relied on the statute in performing a search. The Court ruled that the exclusionary rule does not apply when police conduct a search in reliance on a procedural statute that is subsequently held unconstitutional.

In *Arizona v. Evans*,[376] the mistake was made by a court clerk. Police ran a warrant check during a routine traffic stop and received a computer report that there was an outstanding warrant for the driver's arrest. They made an arrest and conducted a search in reliance on this report. The report turned out to be inaccurate. The warrant had been quashed 17 days earlier, but the court clerk had failed to notify the police department. The Court ruled that the good faith exception applies when an officer makes an arrest based on a reasonable, but mistaken, belief that there is an outstanding warrant authorizing the arrest. The Court stressed the fact that the mistake was made by a person outside law enforcement, stating that the exclusionary rule was designed to deter "police misconduct, not mistakes by court employees."

In *Herring v. United States*,[377] the Supreme Court broke new grounds. The facts were superficially similar to *Arizona v. Evans* — an arrest was made in reliance on an

---

[374] The officer must reasonably believe that the search warrant is valid for the good faith exception to apply. The *Leon* Court listed four situations where such a belief is lacking and where suppression remains an appropriate remedy, even though the officer obtains a search warrant: (1) where police include information in their affidavit they know or should know is false; (2) where the magistrate rubber-stamps the warrant application without reviewing it; (3) where the affidavit used to obtain the warrant is so lacking in indicia of probable cause as to render any belief as to its existence unreasonable; and (4) where the warrant fails to contain a particularized description of the place to be searched or things to be seized and is, thus, deficient on its face.

[375] 475 U.S. 868, 107 S. Ct. 1160, 94 L. Ed. 2d 364 (1978) (holding that evidence obtained through a search conducted in reliance on statutory authority later found unconstitutional is not subject to suppression). *See also* Davis v. United States, *supra* note 362 (holding that evidence obtained though a search conducted in reasonable reliance on binding judicial precedent is not subject to suppression).

[376] *Supra* note 363 (holding that evidence seized in violation of the Fourth Amendment as result of clerical errors of court employees, causing incorrect computer records, falls within good faith exception to exclusionary rule).

[377] ***Supra* note 363.**

wrong or incorrect

(erroneous) computer report that there was an outstanding warrant — but there was one key difference. The error was made by a police employee. The police department had been notified of the warrant's recall, but the recall information was not entered into the police database due to the carelessness of a police employee. By the time the error was discovered, the defendant had already been searched, and methamphetamine and a pistol had been found in his possession. The Court held that the good faith exception applied, even though the unconstitutional arrest was caused by a police error, because the error resulted in "isolated negligence attenuated from the arrest." The Court noted that suppression is "not an automatic consequence of a Fourth Amendment violation." "To trigger the exclusionary rule, police conduct must be sufficiently deliberate that exclusion can meaningfully deter it, and sufficiently culpable that such deterrence is worth the price paid by the justice system." The Court observed that the deterrence value of suppression varies "with the culpability of the law enforcement conduct" at issue. Suppression is justified when the Fourth Amendment violation results from "deliberate, reckless, or grossly negligent conduct, or in some circumstances, recurring or systemic negligence," but not when it results from "isolated negligence attenuated from the arrest," as occurred here. Applying the exclusionary rule would not deter isolated acts of bad record keeping and any minimal deterrence that might result from applying the exclusionary rule was outweighed by the heavy cost of excluding reliable evidence.

Herring is a game changer on several scores. First, it requires trial courts to conduct a cost benefit analysis to determine whether the exclusionary rule should be applied. To justify suppression, the deterrence benefits must be real and must outweigh the heavy costs to the legal system of suppressing highly probative and trustworthy evidence. Second, the fact that the Fourth Amendment violation results from police error does not automatically require suppression. Whether suppression is required depends on the degree of culpability.[378] Suppression is required when the Fourth Amendment violation results from "deliberate, reckless, or grossly negligent conduct," but not when it results from nonrecurring acts of negligence because the marginal deterrence achieved by excluding evidence based on negligent mistakes is not sufficient to overcome the social costs of exclusion.

The big question left unanswered is whose negligent mistakes does the good faith exception excuse? Only negligent mistakes that are "attenuated from the arrest" (the type that occurred in *Herring*) or also negligent mistakes of the officer who made the arrest, such as mistakes in determining the existence of probable cause and reasonable suspicion? If the ruling applies only to the former, *Herring*'s impact on existing law will be relatively minor. If it applies to the latter, the decision will have far-reaching consequences. Exclusionary sanctions will be reserved for extreme cases where the conduct of the police is grossly negligent or worse. Such cases are rare since most

---

[378] For scholarly comments on Herring v. United States, *see, e.g.,* Albert W. Alschuler, *Herring v. United States; A Minnow or a Shark?*, OHIO ST. J. CRIM L. 463 (2009); WAYNE R. LAFAVE, *The Smell of Herring: A Critique of the Supreme Court's Latest Assault on the Exclusionary Rule*, 99 J. CRIM. L. & CRIMINOLOGY 757 2009).

officers genuinely try to comply with the Fourth Amendment and when they overstep the Fourth Amendment, it is because they have made an honest mistake.

3. Illegality in the Manner of Entering to Execute a Valid Search Warrant

Suppression is not required where the illegality relates to the manner of entry to execute a valid warrant. In *Hudson v. Michigan*,[379] police waited only three to five seconds after knocking before entering through the defendant's unlocked front door to execute a search warrant. They discovered large quantities of drugs and a loaded firearm, which the defendant sought to suppress on the grounds that the premature entry violated his Fourth Amendment rights. His motion was denied, he was convicted, and he appealed. The Supreme Court began by stating that the exclusionary rule should be applied only when the deterrence benefits from applying the rule exceed the social costs. The deterrence benefits from applying the exclusionary rule to knock and announce violations[380] were, in the court's view, negligible since the failure of knock does not lead to discovery of incriminating evidence that could not have been obtained lawfully. "Whether that preliminary misstep had occurred or not, the police would have executed the warrant, and would have discovered the gun and drugs inside the house."

On the cost side, the Supreme Court found that the social costs of applying the exclusionary rule to knock and announce violations were considerable. In addition to the loss of evidence and the accompanying risk of setting guilty criminals free, application of the exclusionary rule would open a floodgate to endless allegations that police did not wait long enough, and would discourage police from making a timely entry after knocking and announcing their presence for fear that a later court might agree. Putting all this together, the Court concluded that the exclusionary rule should not be applied to knock and announce violations because social costs of applying the rule were considerably greater than the deterrence benefits.

4. Impeachment

The exclusionary rule prevents the prosecution from offering illegally obtained evidence to prove its case. However, if the defendant takes the witness stand and commits perjury, the prosecution may offer the evidence for the limited purpose of impeaching (*i.e.*, discrediting) the defendant's own testimony.[381] Impeachment consists of offering evidence that contradicts the defendant's testimony for the sake of showing that the defendant is lying. The exception for impeachment is narrow because it applies only if the defendant takes the stand and gives contradictory testimony at the trial and, as is explained in later chapters, the defendant is not required to testify.

---

[379] 547 U.S. 586, 126 S. Ct. 2159, 165 L. Ed. 2d 57 (2006).

[380] The knock-and-announce rule was covered in § 3.15.

[381] Walder v. United States, 347 U.S. 62, 74 S. Ct. 354, 98 L. Ed. 503 (1954) (permitting the prosecutor to introduce into evidence heroin obtained through an illegal search to undermine the credibility of the defendant's claim that he had never possessed narcotics).

5. Use Outside Criminal Trials

The only kind of proceeding in which the exclusionary rule applies is a criminal trial.[382] The Supreme Court has repeatedly declined to extend the rule to other proceedings. Thus, for example, illegally obtained evidence can be offered in grand jury proceedings,[383] parole hearings,[384] civil trials,[385] and administrative hearings for deportation.[386] The Court has limited the exclusionary rule to the criminal trial because it believes that suppression in other contexts has no deterrent effect. Its reasoning is that when police intentionally violate the Fourth Amendment, they do so in order to obtain evidence for a conviction, not to convince a grand jury that a criminal should be prosecuted, or an immigration official that an alien should be deported. Because the Court believes that the Fourth Amendment's deterrent policy would not be served under these circumstances, it refuses to apply the rule.

§ 4.18   Summary and Practical Suggestions

The Fourth Amendment prohibits unreasonable searches and seizures. A search occurs whenever police invade a suspect's reasonable expectation of privacy, either by physically intruding into a constitutionally protected location (*i.e.*, persons, houses, papers, and effects) or by committing a technological invasion of privacy. A seizure occurs when police commit a meaningful interference with a suspect's possessory interest in property. Minor interferences with possession do not trigger Fourth Amendment protection.

The Fourth Amendment generally requires a search warrant before police may search for or seize property for use as evidence. A search warrant protects against general searches by interposing between a citizen and the police the disinterested determination of a neutral, detached magistrate that there is probable cause for the search and by specifying where the police may search or what they may search for. The warrant's description of the place to be searched limits the scope of the search to locations where the police have demonstrated probable cause to believe that the objects of the search are likely to be found. The description of the things to be seized limits the intensity of the search activity to that necessary to uncover the items listed in the warrant. Police are allowed to search for evidence without a warrant in four situations: consent, searches incident to a lawful arrest, exigent circumstances, and vehicle searches. The Fourth Amendment also allows warrantless limited weapons searches and inventory searches.

---

[382] Pennsylvania Board of Probation and Parole v. Scott, 524 U.S. 357, 118 S. Ct. 2014, 141 L. Ed. 2d 344 (1998).

[383] United States v. Calandra, 414 U.S. 338, 94 S. Ct. 613, 38 L. Ed. 2d 561 (1974).

[384] Pennsylvania Board of Probation and Parole v. Scott, *supra* note 382.

[385] United States v. Janis, 428 U.S. 433, 96 S. Ct. 3021, 49 L. Ed. 2d 1046 (1976).

[386] INS v. Lopez-Mendoza, 468 U.S. 1032, 104 S. Ct. 3479, 82 L. Ed. 2d 778 (1984).

Property may be seized for various reasons, the most common being to use it as evidence. When the purpose of the seizure is to obtain criminal evidence, the Fourth Amendment requires probable cause to believe that the property is connected to a crime and either a search warrant describing it or discovery in plain view. There are four general categories of articles that may be seized: fruits of crime, instrumentalities of crime, contraband, and "mere evidence." The "plain view" doctrine allows police to seize evidence without a warrant when they discover it in plain view without violating the Fourth Amendment and immediately develop probable cause to believe that it constitutes the fruits, instruments, or evidence of a crime or contraband. Brief, limited seizures are permitted on a lesser showing. When the police have probable cause to believe that a container houses criminal evidence or contraband, they may seize it without a warrant, but must obtain a warrant before opening and searching it. Police may act on reasonable suspicion in seizing containers for the purpose of subjecting them to a canine examination for illegal drugs, but the period of detention must be brief. Finally, police may impound property without a warrant under various circumstances unrelated to the discovery of evidence.

When evidence is obtained in violation of these requirements, the exclusionary rule applies. Under this rule, a person whose Fourth Amendment rights have been violated can move to have all resulting evidence excluded from his or her criminal trial. There are a number of exceptions to this rule, the most important of which allows admission of evidence obtained in violation of the Fourth Amendment as long as the officer made a reasonable, good faith error.

Laws Governing Police Surveillance

5

The Congress makes the following findings: There has been extensive wiretapping carried on without legal sanctions, and without the consent of any of the parties to the conversation. Electronic, mechanical, and other intercepting devices are being used to overhear oral conversations made in private, without the consent of any of the parties to such communications. . . . To safeguard the privacy of innocent persons, the interception of wire or oral communications . . . should be allowed only when authorized by a court [and] with assurances that the interception is justified and that the information obtained thereby will not be misused.

Congressional Findings, Omnibus Crime Control and Safe Streets
Act of 1968

Chapter Outline

KEY TERMS AND CONCEPTS

Curtilage

Device

Eavesdropping

Electronic communication

Foreign intelligence information

Interception

Open field

Open view

Oral communication

Reasonable expectation of privacy

Search

Search warrant

Wire communication

Wiretap order

§ 5.1   Introduction to the Laws Governing Police Surveillance

In modern times, it is not unusual for police to use a host of surveillance techniques in a single investigation, such as wiretapping, interception of e-mail messages, video surveillance, and electronic tracking. This chapter discusses the constitutional and statutory rules that apply to police surveillance. It builds on the search and seizure principles developed in Chapter 4.

Police surveillance tools have grown increasingly sophisticated, enabling police to monitor a suspect's movements, communications, and activities in ways that would have been unthinkable years ago.[1] Wiretapping was just the beginning. Capabilities now exist for capturing conversations from several blocks away. A noted authority on the law of search and seizure writes:

> Tiny microphones can be secreted behind a picture or built into a coat button. Highly directive microphones known as "parabolic microphones" are capable of eavesdropping on a conversation taking place in an office on the opposite side of a busy street or on a park bench or outdoor restaurant terrace hundreds of feet away. Laser beams can pick sound waves off closed windows. A small, continuously operating

---

[1]   For a description of the vast range of police surveillance technologies now available, *see, e.g.*, Michael Froomkin, *The Death of Privacy*, 52 STAN. L. R. 1461 (2000); Christopher Slobogin, *Symposium, Public Privacy: Camera Surveillance of Public Places and the Right to Anonymity*, 72 MISS. L.J. 213 (2002); Christopher Slobogin, *Technologically Assisted Physical Surveillance: The American Bar Association's Tentative Draft Standards*, 10 HARV. J. L. & TECH. 383, 406 (1997); Andrew W.J. Tarr, *Recent Development, Picture It: Red Light Cameras Abide by the Law of the Land*, 80 N.C. L. REV. 1879 (2002); Christopher S. Milligan, Note, *Facial Recognition Technology, Video Surveillance, and Privacy*, 9 S. CAL. INTERDISC. L.J. 295, 301 (1999).

transmitter can be placed beneath the fender of an automobile and its signal picked up by a receiver in another car or in a fixed plant. A special gun developed for American military authorities can shoot a small dart containing a wireless radio microphone into a tree, window pane, awning or any other object near the subject of investigation.[2]

During the 2001 Super Bowl game, the Tampa Police Department used cutting-edge video surveillance and facial recognition technology that scanned the faces of 100,000 spectators as they passed through the stadium turnstiles and compared the digitized images with a database of known or suspected terrorists.[3] Cutting-edge technology like this is not yet widely used in law enforcement, but may represent the wave of the future. This chapter covers more commonly used surveillance techniques, such as wiretapping; "bugging"; access to e-mail, voice mail, and text messages; pen registers and track-and-trace devices; video surveillance; electronic tracking; and detection devices such as heat sensors, metal detectors, and drug-sniffing dogs. This chapter begins with older forms of surveillance because the Fourth Amendment rules applicable to technologically assisted surveillance build on these principles.

The threshold question in police surveillance law is whether the activity in question constitutes a search. If the answer is yes, a search warrant, interception order, or other form of judicial approval will be necessary. If the answer is no, then police may conduct their investigations, without concern for the Fourth Amendment, though occasionally there are statutory requirements.

§ 5.2   Fourth Amendment Foundation of Police Surveillance Law: The *Katz* Standard

A. *Historical Development*

To our colonial forefathers, a search and seizure meant an actual physical intrusion into their homes and a ransacking of their private papers and effects. In the Fourth Amendment, they protected "the right of the people to be secure in their persons, houses, papers, and effects, against unreasonable searches and seizures." However, they did not have telephones and had no way to anticipate future technological developments. As a result, they listed only persons, houses, papers, and effects as entitled

---

[2]   WAYNE LAFAVE, SEARCH & SEIZURE § 2.2 (3d ed. 1996).

[3]   Rudy Ng, *Catching up to Our Biometric Future: Fourth Amendment Privacy Rights and Biometric Identification Technology*, 28 HASTING COM. & ENT. L.J. 425 (2006); Cathryn L. Claussen, *The Constitutionality of Mass Searches of Sports Spectators*, J. LEGAL ASPECTS OF SPORTS 153 (2006); Marc Jonathan Blitz, *Video Surveillance and the Constitution of Public Space; Fitting the Fourth Amendment to a World That Tracks Image and Identity*, 82 TEX. L. REV. 1349 (2004); Martin Kasindorf, *"Big Brother" Cameras on Watch for Criminals*, USA TODAY, Aug. 2 2001, at A3; Mary Huhn, *Just a Face in the Crowd? Superbowl Kicked Off the Use of Face Recognition Software, but Is This an Invasion of Privacy?*, N.Y. POST, June 26, 2001, at 51.

to Fourth Amendment protection. Modern invention and technology have produced far more refined and sophisticated techniques for garnering information relating to criminal activity and have revolutionized law enforcement. No longer is it necessary for the police to stand under windows or physically enter homes to learn a great deal about what is going on inside.

The question of Fourth Amendment protection against technological intrusions on privacy first reached the Supreme Court in the 1928 case of *Olmstead v. United States.*[4] The issue was whether wiretapping constituted a "search" for purposes of the Fourth Amendment. Olmstead was convicted of conspiring to violate the National Prohibition Act based on evidence obtained by tapping his telephone line from a junction box located on the public street. The tap was conducted without probable cause or a search warrant. The Court, nevertheless, rejected Olmstead's claim that his Fourth Amendment rights were violated. A "search," the Court declared, requires a physical intrusion into a constitutionally protected location and a "seizure," the taking of tangible things. Olmstead's Fourth Amendment rights were not violated by the interception of his telephone conversations because government agents never set foot on his property or took anything tangible; his telephone conversations were "acquired" through their sense of hearing only. *Olmstead* restricted the protection of the Fourth Amendment to activities our founding fathers considered a search.

Justice Brandeis dissented, arguing that technological advances had made it necessary to reconceptualize the notion of a search.

> ... [I]n the application of a Constitution, our contemplation cannot be only of what has been, but of what may be. The progress of science in furnishing the government with means of espionage is not likely to stop with wire tapping. Ways may some day be developed by which the government, without removing papers from secret drawers, can reproduce them in court, and by which it will be enabled to expose to a jury the most intimate occurrences of the home. Advances in the psychic and related sciences may bring means of exploring unexpressed beliefs, thoughts and emotions. ... Can it be that the Constitution affords no protection against such invasions of individual security?

B. *The Katz Standard*

Forty years later in *Katz v. United States,*[5] the Supreme Court recognized that it had taken the wrong turn and embarked upon a new course. Katz, a bookie, was convicted of illegal wagering based on evidence obtained by attaching a small listening and recording device to the exterior of a public telephone booth that he regularly used for wagering calls. Because the listening device did not penetrate the walls of the phone booth, the interception would not have been considered a search under *Olmstead.* The Supreme Court overruled *Olmstead,* declaring:

---

[4]   277 U.S. 438, 48 S. Ct. 564, 72 L. Ed. 944 (1928).
[5]   **Katz v. United States**, 389 U.S. 347, 88 S. Ct. 507, 19 L. Ed. 2d 576 (1967).

... the Fourth Amendment protects people, not places. What a person knowingly exposes to the public, even in his own home or office, is not a subject of Fourth Amendment protection. But what he seeks to preserve as private, even in an area accessible to the public, may be constitutionally protected.[6]

Whether the secret recording of Katz's telephone conversation constituted a search depended on whether he had a "reasonable expectation" that his conversation was private. The Court had no trouble concluding that a person who enters a telephone booth and closes the door has a right to expect privacy. The presence of the concealed tape recorder violated the privacy on which Katz justifiably relied in placing calls, and resulted in a search.

The Court then turned its attention to whether the search was conducted according to Fourth Amendment standards. Even though the police had probable cause to believe that Katz was using the phone booth to conduct illegal gambling operations, probable cause was not enough to justify covertly monitoring his phone calls. A search warrant was necessary.

Shortly afterward, Congress enacted Title III of the Omnibus Crime Control and Safe Streets Act of 1968,[7] known as the Wiretap Act, which requires law enforcement officials to obtain a wiretap order (*i.e.*, a specialized search warrant) to engage in wiretapping and electronic surveillance. The Wiretap Act was subsequently amended to provide protection for electronic communications. The Wiretap Act is covered in §§ 5.8–5.15 of this chapter.

Figure 5.1
Application of the Fourth Amendment to Non-assisted Surveillance

> - Matters in open view are not protected by the Fourth Amendment. Police are free to investigate, using their natural senses in any location where they are lawfully present.
> - The home carries heightened Fourth Amendment protection. Warrantless surveillance may not be conducted from a vantage point inside the curtilage, but an open field carries no Fourth Amendment protection.
> - Information voluntarily disclosed to a third party carries no Fourth Amendment protection.

§ 5.3   Application of the *Katz* Standard to Non-assisted Surveillance

Physical surveillance the old-fashioned way — with footwork rather than fancy high-tech devices — has not gone out of style. Older techniques are still used, and used frequently, to acquire probable cause for the issuance of a search warrant. *Katz*

---

[6]   *Id.*
[7]   18 U.S.C. § 2510 *et seq.*

established the constitutional standard and guiding principle that governs police surveillance law. What a person knowingly exposes to the public is not protected by the Fourth Amendment, and is a legitimate subject for police surveillance. However, what a person seeks to conceal from the public and reasonably expects is private is protected and requires a search to uncover.[8]

The rules that govern technologically assisted surveillance evolved from principles developed in earlier cases involving non-assisted surveillance. Three are of central importance and constantly re-emerge, in slightly changed forms, across the entire field of police surveillance law. First, no Fourth Amendment protection exists in matters exposed to public view. Second, no Fourth Amendment protection exists in matters that have been voluntarily disclosed to a third party. And third, the home carries heightened Fourth Amendment protection. Police need a search warrant to enter a suspect's home or curtilage, whether the intrusion is physical or technological. These three principles are discussed immediately below.

A.　Police Surveillance of Matters in Open View

Anything that can be detected through any of an officer's natural senses from a location where the officer is lawfully present is said to be in "**open view**."[9] Police surveillance of matters in "open view" is not a **search** because suspects have no **reasonable expectation of privacy** in illegal activities conducted in a place where they can be seen, heard, or otherwise detected by members of the public. Listening with the naked ear to goings-on inside a motel room from an adjoining room or common hallway,[10] sniffing the exterior of a car parked on a public street for the odor of drugs,[11] and peering through an undraped window do not implicate the Fourth Amendment.[12] The fact that the officer has to crane his neck, bend over, or squat in order to make an observation does not render the open view doctrine inapplicable, as long as what the officers saw or heard could have been observed by any member of the public who happened to be standing there. In one case, narcotics detectives had to lie prone on the floor of the

---

[8]　**Katz v. United States**, *supra* note 5.

[9]　The principle that observation of matters in open view is not a search was discussed in § 4.2 (C)(2) *supra*. *See also*, 1 WAYNE R. LAFAVE, SEARCH & SEIZURE § 2.2 (3d ed. 1996) ("As a general proposition, it is fair to say that when a law enforcement officer is able to detect something by utilization of one or more of his senses while lawfully present at the vantage point where those senses are used, that detection does not constitute a "search" within the meaning of the Fourth Amendment.").

[10]　United States v. Jackson, 588 F.2d 1046 (5th Cir. 1979) (no reasonable expectation of privacy existed in conversation audible in adjoining hotel room).

[11]　United States v. Marlar, 828 F. Supp. 415 (N.D. Miss. 1993) (canine sniff conducted outside motel room door did not constitute a search); Jennings v. Joshua Independent School District, 877 F.2d 313 (5th Cir. 1989) (use of trained dogs to sniff cars parked on public parking lots does not constitute Fourth Amendment search), *cert. denied*, 496 U.S. 935, 110 S. Ct. 3212, 110 L. Ed. 2d 660 (1990).

[12]　People v. Oynes, 920 P.2d 880 (Colo. App. 1996) (holding that law enforcement officer's viewing of interior of defendant's residence through binoculars, while standing in open field, was not search); State v. Kennedy, 193 Wis. 2d 578, 535 N.W.2d 43 (1995) (same).

adjoining hotel room and press their ears against a three-quarter inch crack at the bottom of the connecting door to hear the suspect's conversations in the next room.[13] The court was not troubled by this fact because the officers were able to overhear the conversation, using nothing more than their normal powers of hearing, in a place where they were lawfully present. The court stated that people who hold an incriminating conversation in a motel room, aware that the walls are thin and neighbors are just a few feet away, have only themselves to blame if a police officer in the next room is listening.

There are, nevertheless, limits to how far police may go in positioning themselves to make the observation, and still claim that the matter was in open view. These limits were exceeded in a case where an officer had to climb three-quarters of the way up a high fence, brace himself on a fellow officer's shoulders, and use a 60-power telescope to obtain a view of marijuana plants growing in the defendant's backyard.[14] The court declined to apply the open view exception, explaining that the notion that it is not a search for police to observe anything that can be observed from a vantage point where the officer is lawfully present is limited to situations where their ability to make the observation is facilitated by the suspect's failure to take adequate steps to protect his privacy. When police have to take extraordinary steps to position themselves in a place where members of the public would not be expected to go, the matters observed are not in open view, and their observation constitutes a search.

B. Heightened Fourth Amendment Protection for the Home

In *Payton v. United States*,[15] the Supreme Court observed:

> The Fourth Amendment protects the individual's privacy in a number of settings, but in none is the zone of privacy more clearly defined than when bounded by the unambiguous physical dimensions of an individual's home — a zone that finds its route in clear and specific constitutional terms. . . . [T]he Fourth Amendment has drawn a firm line at the entrance to the home.

Police are not allowed to conduct warrantless surveillance of a suspect's home from a vantage point inside the curtilage. Fourth Amendment protection afforded the home does not necessarily extend to the property line; only the "**curtilage**" — *i.e.*, "the land immediately surrounding and associated with the home" — is protected by the Fourth Amendment.[16] The area that lies beyond the curtilage is called an

---

[13] United States v. Jackson, *supra* note 10.

[14] State v. Kender, 60 Haw. 301, 588 P.2d 447 (1978) (marijuana was not in open view where defendant had surrounded the plants to shield them against discovery and police officers had to stand on each other's shoulders to make observation). *See also* Pate v. Municipal Court, 11 Cal. App. 3d 721, 89 Cal. Rptr. 893 (5th Dist. 1970) (search resulted when officer climbed a trellis to look into a second floor motel room through a 1-inch gap in the curtain).

[15] 445 U.S. 573, 100 S. Ct. 1371, 63 L. Ed. 2d 639 (1980).

[16] Review § 4.14 *supra*.

"**open field**." Open fields are treated like public places. Police do not need any Fourth Amendment justification to enter an open field, even though their presence constitutes a trespass under property law. In *United States v. Dunn*,[17] the Supreme Court held that no search occurred when police entered a field enclosed by stock fences and looked inside the open doors of a barn, which was located outside the curtilage. The Court stated that "there is no constitutional difference between police observations conducted while in a public place and while standing in an open field." Consequently, when police conduct their surveillance while standing in an open field, the suspect has no Fourth Amendment grounds for complaint, even when the matter surveilled is the interior of the suspect's home.[18]

C. Information Voluntarily Conveyed to a Third Party

1. Conversations Between the Suspect and a Police Informant

The Fourth Amendment does not protect a wrongdoer whose trusted confidant turns out to be a police informant. In *Hoffa v. United States*,[19] Teamster President James Hoffa, was under investigation for jury tampering. Federal authorities worked out a deal with Edward Partin, a local teamster official, to cooperate with the government. Partin attended numerous meetings with Hoffa and other union officials in Hoffa's hotel suite and reported what he heard to the authorities. Hoffa was convicted of jury tampering, largely on the strength of Partin's testimony. Hoffa appealed, claiming that the government's use of a secret informant to listen to his conversations inside his own hotel suite violated the Fourth Amendment. The Supreme Court sided with the government. Although Hoffa's hotel suite was a location protected by the Fourth Amendment, his conversations with Partin were not. Partin was not a trespassing eavesdropper. He "was in the suite by invitation, and every conversation which he heard was either directed to him or knowingly carried on in his presence." The Fourth Amendment does not protect "a wrongdoer's misplaced belief that a person to whom he voluntarily confides his wrongdoing will not reveal it." Hoffa knowingly took this risk. Defendants lack a constitutionally protected privacy interest in information they knowingly disclose to a third party. This principle is known as the *Hoffa* doctrine.

---

[17] **488 U.S. 445, 109 S. Ct. 693, 102 L. Ed. 2d 835 (1989)**. *See also* **Oliver v. United States, 466 U.S. 170, 104 S. Ct. 1735, 80 L. Ed. 2d 214 (1984)** (holding that no search occurred when police entered private property with No Trespassing signs to observe marijuana plants in an "open field" that were not visible from outside the property).

[18] People v. Oynes, *supra* note 12 (holding that the law enforcement officer did not perform a search when he viewed the interior of the defendant's home through binoculars, while standing in an open field); State v. Kennedy, *supra* note 12 (same).

[19] 385 U.S. 293, 302, 87 S. Ct. 408, 413, 17 L. Ed. 2d 374 (1966) (holding that individuals take the risk that person to whom they are speaking will report what was said to the authorities).

2. Information Contained in Records and Files in the Hands of a Third Party

In our information era, information is power and today a greater wealth of information is available to the police than ever before. Bank records; credit card records; employment records; financial records; telephone, cell phone, and Internet service provider records; insurance records; car rental records; electricity bills — you name it — all this information can be relevant to a criminal investigation, and none of it is protected by the Fourth Amendment.[20] The *Hoffa* doctrine has been extended beyond false confidants. A defendant forfeits Fourth Amendment protection in *any* information that is knowingly revealed to a third party, even though it is revealed for a limited purpose and on the assumption that the third party will keep the information confidential. In *United States v. Miller*,[21] the Supreme Court ruled that a depositor has no Fourth Amendment protection in his bank records because the information is known to the bank. "The depositor takes the risk, in revealing his affairs to another, that the information will be conveyed by that person to the Government." The Court repeated this message in *Maryland v. Smith*,[22] holding that the attachment of a pen register to a phone line to record the telephone numbers dialed from the suspect's phone did not violate the Fourth Amendment because this information was available to the telephone company. The Court stated that because people "know that they must convey numerical information to the phone company," they cannot "harbor any general expectation that the numbers they dial will remain secret."

It does not follow from the fact that records in the hands of a third party carry no Fourth Amendment protection that the third party must turn them over voluntarily. The police will need to subpoena the records if the third party refuses. However, the requirements for a subpoena are much less onerous than for a search warrant. Police do not have to establish probable cause to believe that records contain evidence of criminal activity. This makes records in the hands of a third party accessible before police have developed probable cause for a search warrant.

---

[20] United States v. Miller, 425 U.S. 435, 96 S. Ct. 1619, 48 L. Ed. 2d. 71 (1976) (bank records); Smith v. Maryland, 442 U.S. 735, 99 S. Ct. 2577, 61 L. Ed. 2d 220 (1979) (numbers dialed from subscriber's telephone); United States v. Payner, 447 U.S. 727, 100 S. Ct. 2439, 65 L. Ed. 2d 468 (1980) (financial records in hands of bank); Couch v. United States, 409 U.S. 322, 93 S. Ct. 611, 34 L. Ed. 2d 548 (1973) (tax records turned over to accountant); United States v. Hamilton, 434 F. Supp. 2d 974 (D. Or. 2006) (employment records and utilities company subscriber and power consumption information). *See also, generally,* Daniel J. Sokolove, *Digital Dossiers and the Dissipation of Fourth Amendment Privacy,* 75 S. CAL. L. REV. 1083 (2002).

[21] *Supra* note 20.

[22] *Supra* note 20.

Figure 5.2
Application of the Fourth Amendment to Technologically Assisted Surveillance

Surveillance Activity	Fourth Amendment/ Statutory Requirements
Use of surveillance devices, such as flashlights, telescopes, tracking devices, video surveillance cameras, helicopters, etc., to observe activities in open view	None
Employment of sense-enhancing devices, not in general public use, to acquire information about activities inside a home not visible from outside	Search warrant
Interception of wire, electronic, or oral communications with a device	Generally requires a wiretap order
Surreptitious audio or video surveillance of contacts between the suspect and a cooperating informant	None

§ 5.4   Application of the *Katz* Standard to Technologically Assisted Surveillance: An Overview

Technology has markedly improved the surveillance capabilities of police. Electronic beepers and GPS devices make it possible to track people, vehicles, and objects without maintaining visual contact. Hidden video cameras sometimes catch criminals in the act. Metal detectors can reveal whether a person is carrying a weapon. Thermal sensors can detect movement and activity via heat patterns and determine whether a person is growing marijuana. These are just a few of the many police surveillance technologies in current use.[23]

---

[23]   For a survey of current literature on police surveillance technology and the Fourth Amendment, see Marc Jonathan Blitz, *Video Surveillance and the Constitution of Public Space; Fitting the Fourth Amendment to a World That Tracks Image and Identity*, 82 TEX L. REV. 1349 (2004); Quentin Burrows, *Scowl Because You're on Candid Camera: Privacy and Video Surveillance*, 31 VAL. U. L. REV. 1079 (1997); Orin S. Kerr, *Internet Surveillance Law After the USA Patriot Act: The Big Brother That Isn't*, 97 NW. U. L. REV. 607, 630 (2003); Christopher S. Milligan, Note, *Facial Recognition Technology, Video Surveillance, and Privacy*, 9 S. CAL. INTERDISC. L.J. 295, 301 (1999); Ric Simmons, *Technologically Enhanced Surveillance by Law Enforcement Officials*, 60 N.Y.U. ANN. SURV. AM. L. 711, 717 (2005); Christopher Slobogin, Symposium, *Public Privacy: Camera Surveillance of Public Places and the Right to Anonymity*, 72 MISS. L.J. 213 (2002); Christopher Slobogin, *Technologically Assisted Physical Surveillance: The American Bar Association's Tentative Draft Standards*, 10 HARV. J. L. & TECH. 383, 406 (1997); Daniel J. Sokolove, 75 S. CAL. L. REV. 1083 (2002); Andrew W. J. Tarr, Recent Development, *Picture It: Red Light Cameras Abide by the Law of the Land*, 80 N.C. L. REV. 1879 (2002); Mark G. Young, *What Big Eyes and Ears You Have!: A New Regime for Covert Governmental Surveillance*, 70 FORDHAM L. REV. 1017 (2001).

Fourth Amendment restrictions on technologically enhanced surveillance generally depend on the nature of the information obtained, not the device used to obtain it. The Fourth Amendment does not restrict the use of sense-enhancing devices to observe more efficiently, cost-effectively, or at a greater distance, matters that are in open view,[24] but it does restrict their use to encroach on privacy.[25]

A. Technologically Assisted Surveillance of Matters in Open View

Courts have never been troubled by the use of everyday mechanical devices like flashlights, binoculars, and telescopes to increase an officer's powers of observation from a lawful viewing point.[26] In *Dow Chemical Co. v. United States,*[27] the Court extended this principle to aerial photography, holding that use of a precision camera to photograph an industrial complex was not a search because the pictures were taken from navigable airspace and any member of the public flying in that space could have seen and filmed everything below. In *California v. Ciraolo,*[28] the Court used this reasoning to uphold aerial surveillance of a suspect's back yard. Police flew a helicopter over the suspect's back yard, which was shielded from street level view by a fence, to check out an anonymous tip that he was growing marijuana. The Court held that this was not a search because the observation was made within publicly navigated airspace and any member of the public flying in this airspace who glanced down could have seen everything the police observed. As long as police have a right to be in a position to make the observation and the observation is one that any member of the public could have made, there is no search even though police use sense-enhancing equipment to augment their normal powers of observation.

---

[24] *See, e.g.,* United States v. Knotts, 460 U.S. 276, 103 S. Ct. 1081, 75 L. Ed. 2d 55 (1983) (approving use of electronic tracking devices to monitor location and movement of suspect's vehicle); California v. Ciraolo, 476 U.S. 27, 106 S. Ct. 1809, 90 L. Ed. 2d 210 (1986) (permitting aerial surveillance of suspect's back yard).

[25] *See, e.g.,* **Katz v. United States,** *supra* note 5 (holding that telephone conversations are protected from covert interception by government); United States v. Karo, 468 U.S. 705, 104 S. Ct. 3296, 82 L. Ed. 2d 530 (1984) (holding that warrantless beeper monitoring of objects inside a home violates the Fourth Amendment); **Kyllo v. United States, 533 U.S. 27, 121 S. Ct. 2038, 150 L. Ed. 2d 94 (2001)** (holding that warrantless use of thermal imaging device to detect whether the amount of heat emanating from suspect's home is consistent with the presence of high-intensity lamps used to grow marijuana indoors violates the Fourth Amendment).

[26] **United States v. Dunn,** 480 U.S. 294, 107 S. Ct. 1134, 94 L. Ed. 2d 326 (1987) (flashlight); Texas v. Brown, 460 U.S. 730, 103 S. Ct. 1535, 75 L. Ed. 2d 502 (1983) (flashlight); Dow Chemical Co. v. United States, 476 U.S. 227, 106 S. Ct. 1819, 90 L. Ed. 2d 226 (1986) (aerial photography); United States v. Dellas, 355 F. Supp. 2d 1095 (N.D. Cal. 2005) (night vision goggles); People v. Oynes, *supra* note 12 (binoculars); State v. Kennedy, *supra* note 12 (same).

[27] *Supra* note 26.

[28] Supra note 24. *See also* Florida v. Riley, 488 U.S. 445, 109 S. Ct. 693, 102 L. Ed. 2d 835 (1989) (aerial observations by police officer in a helicopter 400 feet above the defendant's greenhouse did not violate Fourth Amendment).

This principle also makes it lawful for police to use tracking devices to monitor a suspect's public movements. In *Knotts v. United States*,[29] the Court held that police do not need a search warrant to use an electronic beeper to track the public movements of a suspect's vehicle because a car traveling down a street is exposed to public view. The beeper revealed nothing that the police could not have discovered through close physical surveillance. It simply enabled them to follow the suspect's vehicle at a greater distance while remaining in contact. Use of surveillance technologies that enable police to monitor activities in open view more cost effectively or from a greater distance do not violate the Fourth Amendment.

B. Technologically Assisted Surveillance of Matters Carried on in Private

Technologically assisted surveillance becomes a search and requires a search warrant when police use surveillance devices not in general public use to spy on activities carried on in private that they could not otherwise observe. Wiretapping and technologically enhanced surveillance of activities occurring inside a home are the two main areas of surveillance law where this principle applies.

Wiretapping is qualitatively different from other searches because it is ongoing and unavoidably intrudes into private aspects of the suspect's life well beyond the information sought. The Fourth Amendment requires heightened procedural safeguards to engage in wiretapping. These safeguards are supplied by the Federal Wiretap Act, which is covered in §§ 5.8–5.15 of this chapter.[30]

Use of sense-enhancing devices to monitor activities occurring inside a home that are not visible from the outside is the second situation where a search warrant is required.[31] The home is a privacy zone that police are not allowed to enter without a search warrant, whether the entry is physical or virtual. The Supreme Court has twice applied this limitation to technological intrusions into the privacy of the home.[32] In *United States v. Karo*,[33] the Supreme Court held that the warrantless monitoring of a beeper after the beeperized object is taken into a private residence violates the Fourth Amendment. In *Kyllo v. United States*,[34] the Court reached the same conclusion in a case where police scanned the suspect's home with a thermal detector to determine

---

[29]　*Supra* note 24.

[30]　Covert video surveillance inside homes and other private locations is as intrusive on privacy as wiretapping. As a result, most courts borrow from the procedural requirements of the Wiretap Act in framing video surveillance search warrants. *See* § 5.6 (B) *infra*.

[31]　United States v. Karo, *supra* note 25 (holding that warrantless beeper surveillance inside a home violates the Fourth Amendment); **Kyllo v. United States, *supra* note 25** (holding that warrantless use of thermal imaging device to detect whether amount of heat emanating from suspect's home was consistent with presence of high-intensity lamps used to grow marijuana violated the Fourth Amendment).

[32]　*See* authorities *supra* note 31.

[33]　*Supra* note 25.

[34]　*Supra* note 25.

whether the amount of heat emanating from his roof was consistent with presence of high-intensity lamps used to grow marijuana indoors. These cases, taken together, stand for the proposition that use of surveillance devices to gather information about activities inside a home that are not visible from the outside constitutes a search and requires a search warrant.

C. Technologically Assisted Surveillance with the Consent of a Cooperating Informant

In *Hoffa v. United States*,[35] discussed in Section 5.3.C. the Supreme Court held that the Fourth Amendment does not protect a wrongdoer's misplaced belief that the person in whom he confides will not reveal what was said to the authorities. In *United States v. White*,[36] the Court extended this principle to the electronic monitoring of conversations with the consent of a wired informant. The defendant was convicted of narcotics violations based on incriminating statements overheard by government agents through the use of a tiny transmitter concealed on the informant's person. The Court reasoned that, since the informant could have testified to the conversation from memory, it made no difference, for constitutional purposes, that instead, he carried a hidden transmitter that relayed the conversation to the agents so that they can listen directly.

The *Hoffa* doctrine applies across the entire field of police surveillance law. Electronic eavesdropping and wiretapping, made possible through the cooperation of a party to the conversation, not only removes the conversation from the protection of the Fourth Amendment, but also removes it from the operation of the Wiretap Act.[37] The same is true for video surveillance. Police do not need a search warrant to conduct secret video surveillance of contacts between a suspect and a cooperating informant. Because the informant could have reported everything said and done in his presence from memory, secret video surveillance does not violate the Fourth Amendment.[38]

---

[35]   *Supra* note 19.

[36]   401 U.S. 745, 91 S. Ct. 1122, 28 L. Ed. 2d 453 (1971) (suspects take the risk that the other party to the conversation might record or transmit it so that police can listen to it).

[37]   *See* § 5.13 (1) *infra*; United States v. Longoria, 177 F.3d 1179 (10th Cir. 1999) (holding that the defendant had no reasonable expectation that a person in whose presence he conducts a conversation will not reveal the conversation to the authorities and, thus, assumed the risk that other person might record it).

[38]   **United States v. Lee, 359 F.3d 194 (3d Cir. 2004)** (warrantless audio and video monitoring of conversations between the defendant and a cooperating informant does not violate the defendant's Fourth Amendment rights); United States v. Brathwaite, 458 F.3d 376 (5th Cir. 2006) (videotaping of defendant's living quarters by a consenting informant using a video camera hidden in her purse did not violate the defendant's Fourth Amendment rights); United States v. Corona-Chavez, 328 F.3d 974 (8th Cir. 2003) (warrantless videotaping of meeting in a hotel room between a suspect and consenting informant did not violate suspect's Fourth Amendment rights).

Figure 5.3
Application of the Fourth Amendment to Electronic Tracking

> - Use of electronic beepers to monitor a suspect's public movements is a "free zone" activity.
> - Use of electronic beepers to monitor the movement of objects inside a home or other location protected by the Fourth Amendment requires a search warrant.

§ 5.5　— Electronic Tracking

Visual surveillance of a suspect's movements from one place to another has never raised constitutional concerns because the route the suspect travels and where he goes are exposed to public view. Electronic beeper and GPS technology have made this task easier and more precise.

A. *Beeper Tracking of Public Movements*

An electronic beeper is a small radio transmitter, usually battery operated, that can be attached to the undercarriage of a suspect's vehicle or other object of surveillance. The beeper emits periodic signals that can be picked up by a radio receiver in the officer's vehicle, enabling the officer to track the beeper by determining its position relative to his or her own. The strength of the signal increases as the distance between the beeper and the receiver narrows.[39] Beepers are used to assist visual surveillance. They enable the police to follow at a greater distance, reducing the risk of detection, without losing contact.

In *Knotts v. United States*,[40] police placed a beeper inside a container of chloroform they suspected would be used to manufacture illegal drugs. After a police informant sold the chloroform to the suspect and they watched him load the container into his car, they tracked the vehicle over a 100-mile journey to a secluded cabin in Wisconsin, using a combination of visual surveillance and beeper monitoring. At one point during the tracking, police lost visual contact and had to rely on the beeper signal to re-establish it. After the suspect reached the cabin, police obtained a search warrant, raided the cabin, and found the container and an illegal drug laboratory.

Though candidly acknowledging that the beeper "enabled the law enforcement officials . . . to ascertain the ultimate resting place of the [chemicals] when they would

---

[39] *See, e.g.*, Michael Froomkin, *The Death of Privacy*, 52 STAN L. REV. 1461 (2000); Richard S. Julie, *High-Tech Surveillance Tools and the Fourth Amendment: Reasonable Expectation of Privacy in the Technological Age*, 37 AM. CRIM. L. REV. 127 (2000).

[40] 460 U.S. 276, 103 S. Ct. 1081, 75 L. Ed. 2d 55 (1983) (holding that warrantless use of an electronic beeper to monitor the public movements of a suspect's vehicle does not violate the Fourth Amendment).

not have been able to do so had they relied solely on their naked eyes," the Supreme Court, nevertheless, dismissed the defendant's argument that the Fourth Amendment was violated:

> A person traveling . . . on public thoroughfares has no reasonable expectation of privacy in his movements from one place to another. When [the suspect] traveled over the public streets[,] he voluntarily conveyed to anyone who wanted to look the fact that he was traveling over particular roads in a particular direction, the fact of whatever stops he made, and the fact of his final destination when he exited from public roads onto private property.

The installation of the beeper may sometimes raise Fourth Amendment concerns apart from the information obtained. In *United States v. Jones*,[41] police attached a tracking device to the undercarriage of the suspect's vehicle while it was parked in a public parking lot and used it to monitor his movements over an extended period of time. The government argued that this method of installation did not violate the Fourth Amendment because suspects have no reasonable expectation of privacy in the exterior of their vehicle. The Court held ruled against the government on the grounds that attaching a tracking device to a suspect's car is like trespassing on his property. The Fourth Amendment is violated when the government trespasses on a suspect's property to obtain evidence. The Court distinguished *Knotts* on the grounds that the beeper was placed in the cannister, with the consent of the owner, before Knotts purchased it; police, accordingly, did not trespass on any property that belonged to him. A person's property is legally sacred. The warrantless attachment of a tracking device to the exterior of suspect's vehicle constitutes a physical intrusion on his property and violates the Fourth Amendment.

> The attachment of a tracking device to the suspect's property requires either a search warrant or an exception to the warrant requirement.

B. GPS Tracking

Global position system (GPS) tracking systems are an advanced technology with more powerful and precise capabilities. The system uses satellite signals that indicate the device's precise location and direction of travel and stores the information in a computer. When the device is later retrieved and the information downloaded, police will have before them the car's complete travel history since the installation of the device. GPS tracking systems completely eliminate the need to conduct visual surveillance; the subject's movements can be monitored in real time by an officer sitting in front of a screen. The technology has been described as follows:

---

[41] _ S. Ct._, 2012 WL 171117 (U.S. 2012) (The warrantless installation of a GPS device on the exterior of the suspect's vehicle while it was parked in a public parking lot amounted to a physical intrusion on his property and violated the Fourth Amendment.)

Global Positioning System (GPS) devices used by law enforcement agencies are small, but usually larger than beepers. They contain not only a GPS satellite communications function that pinpoints the device's location. They also contain computerized recording devices, or logs. Law enforcement agents attach a GPS device to the underside of a vehicle, in a place where it will not be noticed. From then on the device automatically keeps a detailed time and place itinerary of everywhere the vehicle travels and when and how long it remains at various locations. Later, law enforcement agents remove the device and download the detailed itinerary of where and when the vehicle has traveled. Unlike beepers, GPS devices do not require continuous monitoring by a law enforcement agent.[42]

The Supreme Court has not yet decided whether the use of GPS device to monitor a suspect's public comings and goings over an extended period of time constitutes a search under the Fourth Amendment. Clandestine GPS surveillance has the potential to be far more intrusive of privacy than beeper tracking, which is normally used in conjunction with physical surveillance to enable police to follow the beeperized object without losing track of it.

Suppose police know in their heart-of-hearts that Sticky-Fingered Sam is responsible for almost all of the local burglaries, but they have never been able to pin even one on him because he's too smart for them. They devise a plan to catch him. They attach a GPS memory storage unit to the undercarriage of his car while it is parked on a public street and leave it on for a month. They then remove the device, download the information, and line up Sam's travel itinerary with the local burglaries occurring the previous months. Sure enough, Sam was there for all of them. Is GPS tracking something police should be allowed to do without a search warrant?[43] Does GPS tracking simply provide the same information that police could have obtained through close visual surveillance or does it yield a great deal more?

In one sense, it does nothing more because if the police wanted to increase their manpower a hundredfold and put the additional officers to work tracking people like Sam, then GPS memory storage tracking units accomplish the same result they could have accomplished through visual surveillance, just more cheaply and efficiently. On the other hand, we all know that the police department is not going to do this. Realistically, the GPS memory storage system has provided the police with information about Sam's comings and goings that they could not have obtained through visual surveillance alone, and has done so at considerable cost to Sam's privacy. Police now know every place Sam has visited over the last month and how long he stayed. Some of the places he visited could be a source of embarrassment, without revealing criminal activities.

Since both sides represent legitimate ways to view the situation, courts are divided on whether use of GPS memory tracking systems to conduct long term surveillance of

---

[42]   Dorothy J. Glancy, *Privacy on the Open Road*, 30 Ohio N. U. L. Rev. 295, 316–317 (2004).

[43]   *See, e.g.*, People v. Lacey, 3 Misc. 3d 1103, 787 N.Y.S.2d 689 (2004) (holding that a search warrant is required for long term GPS surveillance to determine whether a burglary suspect's car would be present at the scene of subsequent burglaries).

a suspect's public movements constitutes a search and requires a search warrant.[44] In *United States v. Jones*,[45] the Supreme Court sidestepped the chance to clarify this issue, choosing to focus on the method of installation instead. The Court held that attaching a GPS device to the undercarriage of a suspect's vehicle is equivalent to trespassing on his property and violates the Fourth Amendment in the absence of a warrant or an exception to the warrant requirement.

C. *Electronic Tracking of Objects Inside Homes and Other Protected Locations*

The Fourth Amendment requires a search warrant whenever either type of tracking device is used to obtain information about activities inside a private residence that are not visible from the outside. In *Karo v. United States*,[46] Drug Enforcement Administration (DEA) agents installed a beeper in a drum of chemicals, which they suspected would be used to extract cocaine. The drum was sold by a government informant to the defendant. The agents used the beeper to track the drum's movement through a succession of homes and commercial storage facilities over a course of several months, until the drum finally came to rest in a house in Taos. They kept the house under surveillance, periodically spot-monitoring the beeper to verify that the drum was still there, until they observed the windows wide open on a cold day. Suspecting that the chemicals were being used, they obtained a search warrant and found a drug laboratory.

The Court ruled that the continued monitoring of the beeper after the drum was withdrawn from public view and taken inside a private residence violated the Fourth Amendment because it revealed information about activities inside the residence that

---

[44] *Compare* United States v. Garcia, 474 F.3d 994 (7th Cir. 2007) (holding that a search warrant is not required to use a GPS memory tracking unit to monitor a suspect's public movements); States v. Marquez, 605 F.3d 604, 610 (8th Cir.2010) (same); United States v. Pineda-Moreno, 591 F.3d 1212 (9th Cir.2010) (same) *with* State v. Jackson, 150 Wash. 2d 251, 76 P.3d 217 (2003) (holding that under the state constitution, a GPS device cannot be used without a search warrant because GPS tracking devices constitute "a particularly intrusive method of surveillance, making it possible to acquire an enormous amount of personal information about the citizen under circumstances where the individual is unaware that every single vehicle trip taken and duration of every stop may be recorded by the government."); People v. Lacey, *supra* note 43 (holding that a search warrant is necessary to use a GPS memory tracking unit for an extended period to determine whether a burglary suspect's car would be present at the scene of subsequent burglaries). See also John S. Ganz, Comment, It's Already Public: Why Federal Officers Should Not Need Warrants to Use GPS Vehicle Tracking Devices, 95 J. Crim L. & Criminology 1325 (2005); Renee McDonald Hutchins, Tied Up in Knotts? GPS Technology and the Fourth Amendment, 419 UCLA L.Rev. 409 (2007).

[45] *Supra* note 41.

[46] *Supra* note 25.

were not visible from the outside. The monitoring of the beeper told the authorities that the drum they were tracking had been taken into this residence and that it was still there. This information could not have been obtained through visual surveillance alone. Once a beeperized object is withdrawn from public view and taken inside a residence, continued monitoring constitutes a search and requires a search warrant.

D. *Use of the Suspect's Cell Phone as a Tracking Device*

Even though cellular phones are not designed as tracking devices, a person's present location is capable of being tracked, often with a high degree of accuracy through his cell phone, using a method known as triangulation. Triangulation involves estimating the caller's location based on the relative positions of the different cellular receiving towers that carry the signals from his phone.[47] A majority of courts require a Fourth Amendment search warrant to compel cellular service providers to make real-time cell tower location information available so that law enforcement officials can use the suspect's cell phone to locate him. [48] Older cases relied on the lack of federal statutory authorization for such orders as the reason for requiring a search warrant, while more recent cases cite the fact that cell phones are frequently used inside homes. This fact brings cell phone location tracking squarely within the rule that a search

---

[47] A description as to how law enforcement can use triangulation to track the exact location of a cell phone is found in the following cases and articles: *In re* U.S. for an Order Directing a Provider of Electronic Communication Service to Disclose Records to the Government, 534 F. Supp. 2d 585 (W. D. Pa. 2008); *In re* App of the U.S. for an Order for Prospective Cell Site Location Information on a Certain Cellular Telephone, 460 F. Supp. 2d 448, 451 n. 3 (S.D.N.Y. 2006); Recent Developments, *Who Knows Where You've Been? Privacy Concerns Regarding the Use of Cellular Phones as Personal Locators*, 18 Harv. J.L. & Tech. 307 (2004); Derek P. Richmond, Comment, *Can You Find Me Now? — Tracking the Limits on Government Access to Cellular GPS Location Data*, 16 Comm Law Conspectus 283 (2007); Kevin McClaughlin, Comment, *The Fourth Amendment and Cell Phone Location Tracking: Where Are We?*, 29 Hastings Comm. & Ent. L.J. 421 (2007).

[48] *In re* Application of U.S. for an order relating to Target Phone 2, 733 F. Supp. 2d 939 (N.D. Ill. 2009) (holding that a search warrant is necessary to compel disclosure of real-time cell tower location information because there are no federal statutes authorizing entry of such an order on a lesser showing); *In re* U.S. for an Order Directing a Provider of Electronic Communication Service to Disclose Records to the Government, 534 F. Supp. 2d 585 (W. D. Pa. 2008) (holding that when the government seeks access to cellular phone-derived location information, the Fourth Amendment requires a search issued based on probable cause because location information that produces a record of a person's travels over an extended period of time can reveal highly personal information about an individual, such as "an extra-marital liaison or other information regarding sexual orientation/activity; physical or mental health treatment/conditions (including, *e.g.*, drug or alcohol treatment and/or recovery programs/associations); political and religious affiliations; financial difficulties; domestic difficulties and other family matters (such as marital or family counseling, or the physical or mental health of one's children); and many other matters of a potentially sensitive and extremely personal nature. It is likely to reveal precisely the kind of information that an individual wants and reasonably expects to be private.").

warrant is required to monitor a tracking device after the object to which it is attached is removed from public view and taken inside a dwelling.

If police do not need real-time cell tower location information and are content with past records of the suspect's cell phone use and locations, this information is readily obtainable without a search warrant under the Stored Wire and Electronic Communication and Transactional Records Act.[49] In the highly publicized 2004 trial of Scott Peterson for murdering his wife Laci and their unborn child, the state introduced cell phone records to contradict Peterson's testimony that he left the house at 9:30 A.M. on the morning of the murder.[50] Cell phone records, which placed him at home until 10:08 A.M., were instrumental in convicting him.[51]

Figure 5.4
Constitutional and Statutory Requirements for Video Surveillance

Surveillance Activity	Fourth Amendment/ Statutory Requirements
Video surveillance of activities exposed to public view	None
Video surveillance of interactions between the target and a cooperating informant	None
Video surveillance of interiors of homes and other protected locations	Search warrant
Video surveillance that produces a soundtrack	Video aspects must comply with the Fourth Amendment and audio aspects with the Wiretap Act

---

[49]　A majority of courts interpret Section 2703 (d) of the Stored Wire and Electronic Communications and Transactional Records Act to authorize compelled disclosure of past cell phone location and use records upon a showing of relevance to an ongoing investigation, a standard far lower than probable cause for a search warrant. *See, e.g., In re* Application of the United States for an Order Directing a Provider of Electronic Communication Service to Disclose Records to the Government, 620 F.3d 304 (3rd Cir. 2010); *In re* Applications of the United States of America for Orders Pursuant to Title 18, United States Code, Section 2703(d), 509 F. Supp. 2d 76 (D. Mass. 2007) (holding that disclosure of past cell phone location and use records does not implicate the Fourth Amendment). The Stored Wire and Electronic Communications Act is discussed in greater detail in § 5.15 of this chapter.

[50]　Recent Developments, *Who Knows Where You've Been? Privacy Concerns Regarding the Use of Cellular Phones as Personal Locators, supra* note 47 (discussing criminal cases in which law enforcement's access to cell phone location information may have been critical).

[51]　*See, e.g.,* State v. Marinello, 49 So. 3d 488 (La.App. 3 Cir. 2010) (holding that a search warrant is not required to obtain cellular telephone records needed to reconstruct murder suspect's past whereabouts); Mitchell v. State, 25 So. 3d 632 (Fl. D.C.A. 2009) (same).

§ 5.6   — Video Surveillance

A. *Video Surveillance of Activities in Open View*

Police do not need a search warrant to use video cameras to monitor activities in open view.[52] The video surveillance cameras perform the same function as a stakeout, allowing the police to observe more efficiently what they have always been free to observe using only their own senses.[53] Surveillance cameras may be used without a warrant in any location where an officer could lawfully make the observation in person.

In *United States v. McIver*,[54] United States Forest Service law enforcement officers observed transplanted marijuana plants growing in a remote area of the Kootenai National Forest. They installed motion-activated video cameras focused on the plants. Over the course of the next few weeks, the video surveillance cameras photographed two men working on the marijuana plants and later harvesting them. The men were subsequently identified through other means, arrested, and convicted. The court held that

---

[52] United States v. McIver, 186F. 3d 1119 (9th Cir. 1999) *supra* note 41 (warrant not required to install motion-activated video cameras near marijuana plants growing in national forest); United States v. Jackson, 213 F.3d 1269 (10th Cir. 2000) (warrant not required to install video surveillance camera on telephone pole outside defendant's residence); Hudspeth v. State, 349 Ark. 315, 78 S. W.3d 99 (2002) (suspect lacked reasonable expectation of privacy in methamphetamine laboratory operations captured on video surveillance cameras where activities occurred in an open field); State v. Costin, 168 Vt. 175, 720 A.2d 866 (1998) (suspect had no reasonable expectation of privacy in marijuana plants growing in a wooded section of his property that lay beyond the curtilage and police were free to conduct warrantless video surveillance); People v. Wemette, 285 A.D.2d 729, 728 N.Y.S.2d 805 (2001) (suspect lacked reasonable expectation of privacy in activities occurring on his open front porch that were captured on video surveillance cameras); Cowles v. State, 23 P.3d 1168 (Alaska 2001) (warrantless video surveillance of box office did not violate box officer manager's Fourth Amendment rights where her activities were observable by members of public through the ticket window and by co-employees circulating through the office); State v. Augafa, 92 Hawaii 454, 992 P.2d 723 (Haw. Ct. App. 1999) (no reasonable expectation of privacy existed in drug transaction captured on video surveillance camera installed on public sidewalk); State v. McLellan, 144 N.H. 602, 744 A.2d 611 (1999) (school custodian's Fourth Amendment rights not violated by warrantless video surveillance of classroom because classroom was accessible to other staff members and students); State v. Holden, 964 P.2d 318 (Utah Ct. App. 1998) (warrantless use of a video camera placed in a neighbor's home to record the comings and goings of persons in the front yard of the defendant's home did not violate the Fourth Amendment); Vega-Rodriguez v. Puerto Rico Telephone Co., 110 F.3d 174 (1st Cir. 1997) (holding that employees of a quasi-public telephone company had no legitimate expectation to be free from videotaping in open workplace areas).

[53] State v. Costin, *supra* note 52.

[54] *Supra* note 41 (warrantless video surveillance of marijuana garden in National Forest did not violate the Fourth Amendment).

the warrantless placement of unmanned surveillance cameras on national forest land did not violate their reasonable expectation of privacy because the video cameras photographed only what any member of the public who visited that area could have observed. The court stated "we reject the notion that the visual observation of the site became unconstitutional merely because law enforcement chose to use a more cost-effective 'mechanical eye' to continue the surveillance." The use of a motion-activated camera constituted "a prudent and efficient use of modern technology."

B. *Video Surveillance Inside Homes and Other Private Places*

A search warrant is necessary to use hidden surveillance cameras inside private homes,[55] offices,[56] and other locations in which a reasonable expectation of privacy exists.[57] A search warrant, for example, is required to conduct video surveillance of a suspect's enclosed backyard that it is complete shielded from the ground-level view,[58] police department locker rooms,[59] and enclosed bathroom stalls in public rest rooms.[60]

When a search warrant is necessary, an ordinary search warrant does not suffice because nothing is more Orwellian than secretly watching a person's activities inside his home or office. Courts have looked to the requirements of the Wiretap Act for guidance in framing video surveillance warrants on the theory that the Wiretap Act codifies Fourth Amendment procedural requirements for hyper-intrusive searches.[61] Issuance of a video surveillance search warrant requires heightened procedural safeguards similar to those imposed by the Wiretap Act.[62]

---

[55] United States v. Torres, 751 F.2d 875 (7th Cir. 1984), *cert. denied*, 470 U.S. 1087, 105 S. Ct. 1853, 85 L. Ed. 2d 150 (1985) (terrorist organization safe house).

[56] United States v. Taketa, 923 F.2d 665 (9th Cir. 1991) (employee's private office); United States v. Biasucci, 786 F.2d 504 (2d Cir.1986) (interior of business office); United States v. Williams, 124 F.3d 411 (3d Cir. 1997) (office believed to be the headquarters of gambling operation).

[57] Truhillo v. City of Ontario, 428 F. Supp. 2d (C.D. Cal. 2006) (police locker room); United States v. Mesa-Rincon, 911 F.2d 1433 (10th Cir. 1990) (warehouse).

[58] United States v. Cuevez-Sanches, 821 F.2d 248 (5th Cir. 1987).

[59] Trujillo v. City of Ontario, *supra* note 57.

[60] People v. Dezek, 107 Mich. App. 78, 308 N.W.2d 652 (1981) (enclosed bathroom stalls in public rest room); Cowles v. State, 23 P.3d 1168 (Alaska 2001) (same).

[61] United States v. Torres, *supra* note 55; United States v. Williams, *supra* note 56; United States v. Falls, 34 F.3d 674 (8th Cir. 1994); United States v. Mesa-Rincon, *supra* note 57.

[62] *See* authorities *supra* note 61.

C. Video Surveillance of Interactions Between the Target and a Cooperating Informant

A video surveillance warrant is not required to conduct covert video surveillance of interactions between the suspect and a cooperating informant.[63] This result derives from an application of our old friend, the *Hoffa* misplaced confidence doctrine.[64] In *United States v. Lee*,[65] Lee, the President of the International Boxing Foundation, was under investigation for accepting bribes in exchange for giving boxers favorable ratings. The government prevailed on Beavers, one of Lee's associates, to become a government informant and allow his meeting with Lee to be audio- and videotaped. The FBI, without obtaining a video surveillance warrant, rented two adjoining hotel suites, one for Lee and the other for monitoring. The audio and video equipment were installed in the suite that was rented for Lee. The government agents stationed in the adjoining room were instructed to switch the monitor and recorder on only when Beavers was present in the suite, and to keep them switched off at all other times. Lee was captured on tape accepting cash from Beavers obtained as bribes from boxing promoters.

Lee argued that a video surveillance search warrant was required because the video surveillance was conducted in his hotel suite, which is treated like a home under the Fourth Amendment. Justice (then Judge) Alito ruled against him on the grounds that a suspect who invites an informant into his room has no reasonable expectation of privacy with respect to anything he permits the informant to see or hear. Because the video surveillance cameras captured nothing that Beavers could not have testified to from memory, a video surveillance warrant was not necessary.

In *United States v. Nerber*,[66] the video camera continued to roll after the informant departed from the hotel room, and captured the defendants brandishing weapons and snorting cocaine. The court suppressed this evidence on the grounds that the *Hoffa* doctrine does not justify continued video surveillance after the informant departs. Once the informant departed, the defendants did not knowingly expose their actions to anyone. They believed they were alone in the hotel room and had a reasonable expectation of

---

[63]   *See, e.g.*, **United States v. Lee, 359 F.3d 194 (3d Cir. 2004)** (covert video surveillance, conducted in a hotel room rented for the suspect, did not violate the Fourth Amendment where it was carried on in the presence of a consenting informant who heard and saw everything that was captured on the tape); United States v. Shyrock, 342 F.3d 948 (9th Cir. 2003) (covert video surveillance of drug transaction conducted in consenting informant's hotel room did not violate Fourth Amendment); United States v. Brathwaite, *supra* note 38 (no violation of Fourth Amendment occurred where the suspect invited an informant into his home, and informant used a hidden video surveillance camera to record the meeting and transmit the information to government agents).

[64]   The *Hoffa* doctrine is discussed in §§ 5.3 (C), 5.4 (C).

[65]   **Supra note 63**.

[66]   222 F.3d 597 (9th Cir. 2002). *See also, generally,* Marc Jonathan Blitz, *Video Surveillance and the Constitution of Public Space: Fitting the Fourth Amendment to a World That Tracks Image and Identity*, 82 TEX L. REV. 1349 (2004).

privacy. When warrantless video surveillance rests on an informant's consent, the surveillance must cease once the participating informant leaves.

D. Use of Video Surveillance Equipment That Produces a Soundtrack

For maximum effectiveness of video surveillance, a soundtrack is often necessary. If the government uses video equipment that produces a soundtrack, the video portion must satisfy the Fourth Amendment, while the audio portion must satisfy the Wiretap Act.[67] The Wiretap Act[68] does not cover silent video surveillance,[69] but a wiretap order is necessary to use video equipment that produces a soundtrack[70] unless: (1) the suspect lacks a reasonable expectation of freedom from interception[71] or (2) a participant consents.[72] The reasons for this will be clearer after you study the Wiretap Act.

E. Mass Video Surveillance as a Tool of Social Control

Video cameras are taking on an increasingly important role in modern law enforcement. In England, "[c]ameras now encircle the center of London in a 'ring of steel,' photographing the license plate and driver of every vehicle that enters."[73] Baltimore, Chicago, Washington D.C.,[74] and a growing number of other American cities have installed networks of video cameras and use them on a smaller scale, often for traffic control at intersections and surveillance in high-crime areas. While a number of

---

[67] United States v. Torres, *supra* note 55 (holding that the audio component of a video recorder falls within the scope of the Wiretap Act); United States v. Shyrock, 342 F.3d 948 (9th Cir. 2003) (same); State v. O'Brien, 774 A.2d 89 (R.I. 2001) (same). *See also* James G. Carr, The Law of Electronic Surveillance § 3.8 at 3-144 (2d ed.1996) ("If * * * law enforcement officers use equipment which records sounds as well as sights, so that spoken communications can be overheard or recorded, [the Wiretap Act] will be applicable with reference to the audio portion of the videotape. The conversations are oral communications under § 2510(2), which are intercepted by the audio component of the video camera, and are regulated accordingly.").

[68] 18 U.S.C. § 2510 *et seq.* The Wiretap Act is covered in §§ 5.8–5.15 of this chapter.

[69] United States v. Falls, *supra* note 61; United States v. Biasucci, *supra* note 56; United States v. Torres, *supra* note 55; State v. Diaz, 308 N.J. Super. 504, 706 A.2d 264 (1998) (Wiretap Act did not apply to silent video portion of videotape, which included a sound component).

[70] The Wiretap Act applies when a device of any kind is used to acquire access to the contents of a protected communication. *See* 18 U.S.C. § 2510(5) (defining "interception device").

[71] The Wiretap Act only protects oral communications when they are "uttered by a person exhibiting an expectation that such communication is not subject to interception under circumstances justifying such expectation." 18 U.S.C. § 2510(2).

[72] A wiretap order is not required under the Wiretap Act when a party to conversation consents to the interception. 18 U.S.C. § 2511(2)(C).

[73] Marc Jonathan Blitz, *supra* note 66 at 1351.

[74] *Id.* at 1352.

scholars,[75] judges,[76] and civil libertarians have expressed alarm at mass surveillance aimed indiscriminately that captures lawful activities of ordinary citizens, the government is not alone in this practice. Members of the public are under regular video surveillance when they enter banks, retail establishments, schools, apartment buildings, parking lots, office building lobbies, at ATMs, and in dozens of other places where security is an issue. Mass video surveillance has become so common that people have come to expect that they are being watched a great deal of the time. Moreover, when people venture out in public places, they knowingly expose themselves to public view. Consequently, for these and other reasons, it would be surprising if courts were to hold that mass video surveillance of public places conducted in the hopes of capturing criminals in the act violates the Fourth Amendment.[77]

Figure 5.5
Detection Devices

Detection Device	Fourth Amendment Requirements
Detection devices capable of revealing only the presence of contraband	None
Magnetometers (metal detectors) and X-ray scanning machines	Compliance with the administrative search exception to warrant requirement or individualized suspicion
Thermal sensors aimed at a home	Search warrant

§ 5.7   — Detection Devices

Detection devices disclose things that are incapable of being detected by the ordinary senses. This section explores Fourth Amendment restrictions on four widely used police detection devices — drug and bomb-sniffing dogs, magnetometers, X-rays, and thermal detectors.

---

[75]   *Id.*; Christopher S. Milligan, *Facial Recognition Technology, Video Surveillance, and Privacy*, 9 S. CAL. INTERDISCIP L.J. 295 (1999); Christopher Slobogin, *Public Privacy: Camera Surveillance of Public Places and the Right to Anonymity*, 72 MISS. L.J. 213 (2002); Andrew W.J. Tarr, *Recent Development, Picture It: Red Light Cameras Abide by the Law of the Land*, 80 N.C. L. REV. 1879 (2002).

[76]   State v. Costin, *supra* note 52.

[77]   Robert C. Power, *Changing Expectations of Privacy and the Fourth Amendment*, 16 WIDENER L.J. 43 (2006).

Detection devices that detect only the presence of contraband — objects that it is always a crime to possess — are not regulated by the Fourth Amendment.[78] The Supreme Court has determined that suspects have no legitimate expectation of privacy in contraband and, therefore, have no Fourth Amendment right to object to devices that detect only its presence.[79] However, few devices are this content-discriminating. An X-ray, for example, may reveal the presence of a gun in a suitcase, but it can also reveal the outlines of numerous innocent objects. The same is true of magnetometers used to screen for weapons in airports and elsewhere. Magnetometers reveal the presence of any object that has a sufficient metallic content, not just weapons. Use of detection devices that are capable of disclosing hidden innocent activity results in a search under the Fourth Amendment.[80]

You are probably wondering whether any technological devices exist that are so discriminating that they are able to detect guilty objects without exposing innocent ones. Under the present state of technology, there are only two devices — bomb and drug-sniffing dogs and chemical tests — that can perform this task.

A. Canine Examinations

The Supreme Court regards canine sniffs as "*sui generis*" because they disclose only the presence of narcotics, a contraband item, without providing information about lawful activity.[81] *United States v. Place*,[82] the first case that presented this issue, involved a canine examination of luggage at an airport. The Court could have ruled that use of a drug-detection dog was not a search because the odor emanating from the suspect's luggage had been knowingly exposed to the public and the dog was simply a sensory enhancement device, similar to a flashlight or binoculars. This would have gotten the job done. However, the Court did not say this. Instead, it came up with what was, at that time, the rather startling proposition that suspects have no legitimate expectation of privacy in contraband and, consequently, have no right to object to the use of devices that expose only its presence.

In the same term, the Supreme Court decided *United States v. Jacobsen*,[83] where it extended the rationale to chemical testing that reveals only the presence of a particular drug. A package was damaged during shipment by a common carrier. To determine the amount of damage, the carrier opened the package and observed four white bags of

---

[78]   United States v. Place, 466 U.S. 109, 104 S. Ct. 1652, 80 L. Ed. 2d 85 (1984); United States v. Jacobsen, 466 U.S. 109, 104 S. Ct. 1652, 80 L. Ed. 2d 85 (1984).

[79]   *See* cases *supra* note 78.

[80]   Bourgeois v. Peters, 387 F.3d 1303 (11th Cir. 2004) (holding that magnetometer screening constitutes a search); United States v. Epperson, 454 F.2d 769 (4th Cir. 1972), *cert. denied*, 406 U.S. 947, 92 S. Ct. 2050, 32 L. Ed. 2d 334 (same); United States v. Young, 350 F.3d 1302 (11th Cir. 2003) (holding that use of an X-ray device that reveals, in picture form, the shape of objects inside a package constitutes a search within the meaning of the Fourth Amendment).

[81]   *See* authorities *supra* note 78.

[82]   *Supra* note 78.

[83]   *Supra* note 78.

powder inside. The carrier immediately contacted federal agents, who ran chemical tests on the substance, confirming that the powder was cocaine. The defendants were arrested. The Supreme Court ruled that because the chemical test only reacted to narcotics, there was no search. *United States v. Place* was recently reaffirmed in a case involving a traffic stop. In *Illinois v. Caballes*,[84] the defendant was stopped for speeding on an interstate highway. While one officer was writing a ticket, another officer arrived and walked a narcotics detection dog around the defendant's car. The dog alerted on the trunk of the car, and based on that alert, officers searched the trunk, found marijuana, and arrested the defendant. The court upheld the constitutionality, stating that "[a] dog sniff conducted during a concededly lawful traffic stop that reveals no information other than the location of a substance that no individual has any right to possess does not violate the Fourth Amendment."

Dog sniffs and chemical tests are the only two situations where the *United States v. Place* rationale has been applied. The reason is that, under the current state of technology, no other devices exist that react only to the presence of contraband. Someday, perhaps, there may be. Life would certainly be much easier if police were blessed with infallible detection devices that exposed criminals, without disturbing the privacy of innocent citizens.[85] When this happens, the Fourth Amendment will quietly pass into oblivion.

As a final note in passing, the fact that no Fourth Amendment justification is needed to perform a canine examination does not mean that police can go around snatching objects from suspects and exposing them to canine sniffs. They must have either a lawful right of access to the object or Fourth Amendment grounds to seize it.[86] Dog sniffs may be performed, without reasonable suspicion, in any location that the officer is lawfully present[87] on any object an officer has a lawful right of access to.[88] Otherwise, police need Fourth Amendment grounds to seize the object in order to expose it to a canine sniff.

---

[84] **543 U.S. 405, 125 S. Ct. 834, 160 L. Ed. 2d 842 (2005).**

[85] *See, generally,* Ric Simmons, *From* Katz *to* Kyllo: *A Blueprint for Adapting the Fourth Amendment to Twenty-First Century Technologies*, 53 HASTINGS L.J. 1303 (2002).

[86] Review § 4.4.

[87] **Illinois v. Caballes,** *supra* note 84 (vehicle stopped for traffic violation); United States v. Place, *supra* note 78 (luggage in airport); Commonwealth v. Welch, 420 Mass. 646, 651 N.E.2d 392 (1995) (lockers in fire department's common room); United States v. Friend, 50 F.3d 548 (8th Cir. 1995) (car parked on private property outside curtilage); United States v. Roby, 122 F.3d 1120 (8th Cir. 1997) (common corridor of a motel); Fitzgerald v. State, 384 Md. 484, 864 A.2d 1006 (Md. 2004) (common hallway of apartment building); United States v. Marlar, 828 F. Supp. 415 (N.D. Miss. 1993) (outside motel room door); United States v. Lingenfelter, 997 F.2d 632 (9th Cir. 1993) (exterior of commercial warehouse); State v. Carter, 697 N.W.2d 199 (Minn. 2005) (outside self-storage unit); United States v. Colyer, 878 F.2d 469 (D.C. Cir. 1989) (Amtrak sleeper car); Scott v. State, 927 P.2d 1066 (Okla. Crim. App. 1996) (luggage checked with bus company); United States v. Reyes, 349 F.3d 219 (5th Cir. 2003) (non-contact canine sniff of person). However, police may not conduct a sniff inside the curtilage of a suspect's home, because they have no right to enter in search of evidence without a search warrant. State v. Rabb, 920 So. 2d 1175 (Fla. App. 2006).

[88] United States v. Place, *supra* note 78; *see also* § 4.4 of this book.

B. X-Ray and Magnetometer Searches

Everyone who boards an airplane today has to walk through a magnetometer (metal detector) and put their carry-on luggage on a conveyor belt to pass through an X-ray scanning machine. Similar screening procedures have become regular features at entrances to courthouses, jails, military installations, and other government locations where security is a concern.[89] Use of screening devices that reveal the presence of hidden objects the owner has a right to possess results in a search,[90] but the search is valid under the administrative search exception when the devices are used in government locations that have heightened security needs.[91] Searches conducted as part of a general regulatory scheme in furtherance of an administrative purpose (here preventing hijackings, and bombings), rather than as part of a criminal investigation to secure evidence of a crime, are permissible under the Fourth Amendment without individualized suspicion when the government's need to conduct the search exceeds the invasion of privacy which the search entails.[92] The need for the search — to prevent hijacking and bombings — outweighs the limited intrusion of having to pass through an airport security checkpoint before boarding. The fact that passengers may avoid the search by electing not to fly further limits the intrusiveness. Finally, the screening procedures are no surprise. No one in the post-9/11 era expects that they will be able to board an airplane without passing through a magnetometer and having their carry-on luggage X-rayed.[93]

Because magnetometer and X-ray searches are valid at airports, courthouses, and other places with high security needs does not mean they can be used, without individualized suspicion, everywhere. In *Bourgeois v. Peters*,[94] the court held that a city policy requiring all persons wishing to participate in a large protest demonstration to undergo magnetometer screening violated the Fourth Amendment. The court stated: "While the

---

[89] LaTasha v. People, 60 Cal. App. 4th 1524, 79 Cal. Rptr. 2d 886 (Cal. 1998) (holding that random metal detector weapon searches of high school students do not violate the Fourth Amendment); Minich v. County of Jefferson, 919 A.2d 356 (Pa. Commw. 2007) (upholding ordinance requiring everyone entering the courthouse to pass through a magnetometer).

[90] *See* authorities *supra* note 80.

[91] **United States v. Hartwell, 436 F.3d 174 (3d Cir. 2006)** (holding that airport screening procedures are valid under the administrative search exception to the warrant requirement); United States v. Marquez, 410 F.3d 612 (9th Cir. 2005) (same). A few courts, however, have upheld them under the consent exception to the warrant requirement. *See, e.g.,* Torbet v. United Airlines, Inc., 298 F.3d 1087 (9th Cir. 2002) (upholding that airline screening procedures on the theory that airline passengers impliedly consent to the search by placing their bag on the X-ray conveyor belt).

[92] United States v. Hartwell, *supra* note 91; United States v. Marquez, *supra* note 91.

[93] United States v. Allman, 336 F.3d 555, 557 (7th Cir. 2003) (observing that "we have trouble seeing how, in this age of routine, soon to be universal, X-raying of containers shipped by air, the defendant could have had a reasonable expectation that his package would not be X-rayed at any point during transit.").

[94] *Supra* note 80.

threat of terrorism is omnipresent, we cannot use it as the basis for restricting the scope of the Fourth Amendment's protections in any large gathering of people. In the absence of some reason to believe that international terrorists would target or infiltrate this protest, there is no basis for using September 11 as an excuse for searching the protestors."[95] Other courts agree that there must be a substantial and real risk of terrorism to justify a mass invasion of privacy.[96]

C. *Thermal Image Devices (Heat Sensors)*

Indoor marijuana gardens require heat lamps that produce substantial amounts of heat. Thermal imagers (heat sensors) create a picture based on heat emissions. When directed at a building suspected of being used to grow marijuana, the device can confirm those suspicions by detecting an abnormal heating pattern suggestive of a marijuana growing operation.[97] However, heat sensors are not as smart as drug-sniffing dogs. They reveal information about innocent activities inside a home, such as when the occupants take their daily bath, as well as guilty secrets.

In *Kyllo v. United States*,[98] police aimed a thermal imaging device at the suspect's home from a public street to determine whether the amount of heat emanating from his home was consistent with the presence of high-intensity lamps used to grow marijuana. The Supreme Court held that the Fourth Amendment is implicated whenever the police use sense-enhancing technologies, not in general public use, to explore details inside a home that would previously have been unknowable without a physical intrusion. The thermal imaging device told the police that some areas of the roof were warmer than others and that the dwelling as a whole was warmer than other dwellings in the neighborhood as a result of activities going on inside. The government argued that a search warrant should not be required because a thermal imager only measures heat output and is incapable of revealing intimate details. The Court took issue with this argument, replying that "[i]n the home ... all details are intimate details, because the entire area is held safe from prying government eyes." The information the police obtained through use of the thermal-imaging device was not exposed to public view and was

---

[95]   *Id.*

[96]   Johnston v. Tampa Sports Authority, 442 F. Supp.2d 1257 (M.D. Fla. 2006) (holding that public stadium authority violated Fourth Amendment by conditioning admission to professional football games on consent to be subjected to a pat-down search, for purpose of preventing terrorist activities). *See also* Cathryn L. Claussen, *The Constitutionality of Mass Searches of Sports Spectators*, J. LEGAL ASPECTS OF SPORTS 153 (2006).

[97]   *See, e.g.*, Jonathan Todd Laba, *If You Can't Stand the Heat, Get Out of the Drug Business: Thermal Imagers, Emerging Technologies, and the Fourth Amendment*, 84 CAL L. REV. 1437 (1996) (describing technology and function of thermal imaging devices and their current uses in law enforcement).

[98]   **533 U.S. 27, 121 S. Ct. 2038, 150 L. Ed. 2d 94 (2001)** (use of thermal-imaging device to detect whether amount of heat emanating from suspect's home was consistent with presence of high-intensity lamps used in marijuana growth constitutes search).

not otherwise obtainable without an entry. Technological devices not in general public use may not be used to explore activities inside a home, not visible from outside, without a search warrant.

The question of whether a search warrant is necessary to conduct a thermal scan of business or commercial premises remains unsettled.[99]

§ 5.8 The Wiretap Act

Wiretapping and electronic surveillance are vital to the investigation of certain crimes. Since 1968, this area of the law has been regulated by a federal statute known as the Wiretap Act.[100] It was enacted in response to the Supreme Court's holding in *Katz v. United States*[101] that telephone conversations cannot be intercepted without a search warrant. The Wiretap Act originally covered only wiretapping and electronic eavesdropping, but rapid changes in telecommunications technology soon made the Wiretap Act hopelessly out of date. In 1986, Congress amended the Wiretap Act to bring the newer forms of communication under its protection,[102] explaining:

> Today we have large-scale electronic mail operations, computer-to-computer data transmissions, cellular and cordless telephones, paging devices, and video teleconferencing. A phone call can be carried by wire, by microwave or fiber optics. It can be transmitted in the form of digitized voice, data or video. Since the divestiture of AT&T and deregulation, many different companies, not just common carriers, offer a wide variety of telephone and other communications services. It does not make sense that a phone call transmitted via common carrier is protected by the current federal wiretap statute, while the same phone call transmitted via a private telephone network such as those used by many major U.S. corporations today, would not be covered by the statute.[103]

If one had to summarize what law enforcement officials need to know about the Wiretap Act in a single paragraph, it would be this: the Act prohibits the government from intercepting a protected communication with a device unless a judge issues a

---

[99] Compare State v. Schumaker, 136 Idaho 509, 37 P.3d 6 (2001) (holding that warrantless thermal imaging of a barn was unlawful search, and thus the resulting evidence of heat patterns could not be used to support issuance of search warrant or employed against the defendant at a trial) with United States v. Johnson, 42 Fed. Appx. 959 (9th Cir. 2002) (warrantless thermal imaging of suspect's barn during an over flight of the property did not violate the Fourth Amendment).

[100] 18 U.S.C. § 2510 *et seq.*

[101] *Supra* note 5.

[102] Electronic Communications Privacy Act of 1986, Pub. L. 99-508, 100 Stat. 1848 (1986) (codified at 18 U.S.C. §§2510-22, 2701- 09, 3121-27). Because of various changes instituted by the 1986 Act and by subsequent amendments, older decisions rendered under earlier versions of the Wiretap Act should always be checked against the language of the current provisions. In some instances, amendments have overridden interpretations placed on former statutory language.

[103] S. Rpt. No. 99-541, at 3 (1986).

wiretap order or one of the parties consents.[104] Violations carry serious consequences. The Act imposes criminal penalties on violators,[105] creates a damage remedy for those whose rights are violated,[106] and requires exclusion of illegally intercepted wire or oral communications in both federal and state prosecutions.[107]

The Wiretap Act is not the only statute that protects the privacy of communications. Communications surveillance in national security cases is regulated by a separate statute known as the Foreign Intelligence Surveillance Act,[108] which is covered in § 5.17 of this chapter. In addition, all but five states (Alabama, Kentucky, Michigan, Montana, and Vermont) have state electronic surveillance laws that are patterned on Title III.[109] State wiretap laws can be more protective of privacy (and some are), but not less protective.[110]

Figure 5.6
Overview of the Wiretap Act

- A wiretap order is necessary to intercept a protected communication unless one of the parties consents.
- An interception occurs when a device is used to acquire access to the contents of a protected communication in the course of its transmission.
- The Wiretap Act protects three kinds of communications:

  1. Wire (*i.e.*, communications containing the human voice that travel through wires at some point in their transmission);
  2. Oral (*i.e.*, communications carried by sound waves). Oral communications are protected only when they are "uttered by a person exhibiting an expectation that such communication is not subject to interception under circumstances justifying such expectation;" and
  3. Electronic (*i.e.*, signs, signals, writings, images, and other data transmitted over a wide range of mediums).

---

[104]   18 U.S.C. § 2511. The Wiretap actually does far more than this. It outlaws the use of interception devices by private citizens. 18 U.S.C. § 2511(1). In addition, it regulates the manufacture, possession, and sale of interception devices and provides for confiscation of illegal devices. 18 U.S.C. §§ 2512, 2513. However, these aspects of the Wiretap Act are beyond the scope of this chapter.

[105]   18 U.S.C. § 2511(4), (5).

[106]   18 U.S.C. § 2520.

[107]   18 U.S.C. §§ 2515, 2518(9).

[108]   50 U.S.C. § 1801 *et seq.*

[109]   State v. Mullins, 221 W. Va. 70, 79, 650 S. E. 2d 169, 178 (W. Va. 2007). *See also* JAMES G. CARR, THE LAW OF ELECTRONIC SURVEILLANCE § 2.4(a) (2002); Stacy L. Mills, *He Wouldn't Listen to Me Before, But Now . . . : Interspousal Wiretapping and an Analysis of State Wiretapping Statutes*, 37 BRANDEIS L.J. 415, 429 (1998) (discussing differences among state wiretapping statutes generally); Susan L. Kopecky, *Dealing with Intercepted Communications: Title III of the Omnibus Crime Control and Safe Streets Act in Civil Litigation*, 12 REV. LITIG. 441 (1993); Carol N. Bast, *What's Bugging You? Inconsistencies and Irrationalities of the Law of Eavesdropping*, 47 DEPAUL L. REV. 837 (1998).

[110]   *See, e.g.*, Commonwealth v. Barboza, 54 Mass. App. Ct. 99, 763 N.E.2d 547, 553 (2002) ("Although a state wiretap statute may adopt standards more stringent than the requirements of federal law, thus excluding from state courts evidence that would be admissible in federal courts, a state may not adopt standards that are less restrictive and would thereby allow evidence in state court that would be inadmissible in federal court.").

§ 5.9 — Scope of the Wiretap Act

A wiretap order is needed to intercept a protected communication unless one of the parties consents. The definition of an **"interception"** is central to the coverage. An interception occurs when: (1) a device is used (2) to acquire access to the contents (3) of a protected communication during the course of its transmission.[111] Study this definition carefully because every word is meaningful. We are going to discuss the requirements in reverse order.

A. *Protected Communications*

The Wiretap Act covers three kinds of communications: wire, electronic, and oral. **Wire communications** are communications containing the human voice that travel through wires at some point in their transmission.[112] The term "wire communication" accurately described land-line telephone systems, the only kind that existed in 1968. However, coverage has since been expanded to include cordless and cellular telephone systems. Interoffice telephone and private intercom systems are not covered because they do not affect interstate or foreign commerce.

Oral communications also contain the human voice. However, they do not travel through wires but are, instead, carried by sound waves. They commonly take the form of a face-to-face conversation. Interception is generally accomplished through hidden, unattended tape recorders and "bugging" devices.

Oral communications are protected by the Wiretap Act only when they are "uttered by a person exhibiting an expectation that such communication is not subject to interception under circumstances justifying such expectation."[113] This is the Wiretap Act's version of the *Katz* "reasonable expectation of privacy" test.[114]

---

[111]   *See* 18 U.S.C. § 2510(4) defines an interception as "the aural or other acquisition of the contents of any wire, electronic, or oral communication through the use of any electronic, mechanical, or other device."

[112]   18 U.S.C. § 2510 (1) defines a wire communication as "any aural transfer made in whole or in part through the use of facilities for the transmission of communications by the aid of wire, cable, or other like connection between the point of origin and the point of reception (including the use of such connection in a switching station) furnished or operated by any person engaged in providing or operating such facilities for the transmission of interstate or foreign communications or communications affecting interstate or foreign commerce."

[113]   18 U.S.C. § 2510(2) defines an oral communication as a "communication uttered by a person exhibiting an expectation that such communication is not subject to interception under circumstances justifying such expectation."

[114]   **Katz v. United States**, *supra* note 5.

If police secretly bug Sticky-Fingered Sam's home and overhear his end of a telephone conversation, they have intercepted an oral communication, not a wire one, because access to Sam's voice was not acquired as it passed through wires.[115] The voice they heard was carried by sound waves. On the other hand, if police secretly record Sam's end of a telephone conversation while standing next to him as he talks on his cell phone in a grocery store, poor Sam is out of luck because oral communications are protected only when the person speaking reasonably expects privacy. With a stranger standing next to him who could hear his every word, Sam had no such expectation.[116] The Wiretap Act tracks the Fourth Amendment, requiring a wiretap order only when the conduct of the police constitutes a search under the Fourth Amendment.

Electronic communications include transmissions of matters other than the human voice, such as written words, signs, signals, symbols, images, or other data transmitted over a wide range of media, including wire, radio, electromagnetic, and photo optical.[117] Examples of electronic communications include e-mail messages, telegrams, faxes, computer data transmissions, and display pager messages, but not tone-only paging devices, which are expressly excluded from coverage.

B. *Acquire Access to the Contents*

To constitute an **interception**, the device used must provided access to the *contents* of a communication. Devices that provide access to other information, such as the telephone numbers dialed to or from a particular phone, are beyond the scope of the Wiretap Act.[118] Access to the contents, moreover, must be acquired *while the message*

---

[115]   United States v. Carroll, 332 F. Supp. 1288 (D.D.C. 1971) ("The overhearing and recording of one end of a telephone conversation without the actual interception of a communication passing through the wires, was not intended to be included within the definition of the term 'wire communication' but under the statute is simply another form of oral communication."); People v. Siripongs, 45 Cal. 3d 548, 745 P.2d 1301 (1988), *cert. denied*, 488 U.S. 1019, 109 S. Ct. 820, 102 L. Ed. 2d 810 (1989) (same).

[116]   People v. Siripongs, *supra* note 115 (defendant whose telephone conversation was overheard by a police officer standing within three feet of defendant "could not have justifiably expected his conversation was not being intercepted, because he could clearly see that at least one police officer could hear every word he said.").

[117]   18 U.S.C. § 2510(12). Although a wiretap order is required to intercept electronic communications, they receive less protection under the Wiretap Act than wire and oral communications in three respects. First, any U.S. attorneys may seek judicial authorization to intercept electronic communications. § 2516(3). Second, authorization may be sought in the investigation of any federal felony. § 2516(3). Finally, and most important of all, the statutory suppression remedy does not apply to illegally obtained electronic communications. § 2515.

[118]   United States v. New York Tel. Co., 434 U.S. 159, 98 S. Ct. 364, 54 L. Ed. 2d 376 (1977).

is being transmitted.[119] It is not an interception, for example, to replay a tape-recording of a past telephone conversation.[120]

The requirement of a capture in transit virtually eliminates protection for e-mail. E-mail is protected under the Wiretap Act only for the few seconds between the time the sender hits the "send" button and it reaches its destination.[121] After this, the e-mail message becomes a stored communication. Access to stored communications is regulated by a separate federal statute — the Stored Wire and Electronic Communications and Transactional Records Act.[122] Stored communications receive far less protection, making it easier for law enforcement officials to gain access to them.[123] Access to stored communications is covered later in this chapter.[124]

C. *Use of a Device*

The type of device used is the least important of the three requirements. The device does not have to be unusual, technologically sophisticated, or specially designed for spying activity. It can be a parabolic microphone that picks up conversations miles away; an electronic "bug"; wiretapping apparatus; a concealed, unattended tape-recorder; or some other device.[125] The nature of the device does not matter. What matters is how it is used.[126] If it is used to obtain access to the contents of a protected communication while it is being transmitted, the device constitutes an interception device. A garden-variety extension phone, for example, constitutes an interception device

---

[119] *See, e.g.,* Steve Jackson Games, Inc. v. U.S. Secret Service, 36 F.3d 457 (5th Cir. 1994) (seizure of e-mail from electronic storage is not an interception under the Wiretap Act, even if the e-mail has not yet have been retrieved by the recipient and read); United States v. Steiger, 318 F.3d 1039 (11th Cir. 2003) (acquisition of e-mail by hacking information stored on computer hard drive does not involve an interception); Konop v. Hawaiian Airlines, Inc., 302 F.3d 868 (9th Cir. 2002) (to constitute an interception under the Wiretap Act, acquisition of e-mail must occur while they are being transmitted, not while they are in storage).

[120] United States v. Turk, 526 F.2d 654 (5th Cir. 1976).

[121] *See* authorities *supra* note 119. Wiretap Act protection for e-mail is discussed in great detail in § 5.14 of this chapter.

[122] Stored Wire & Electronic Communications & Transactional Records Access, 18 U.S.C.A. § 2701 *et seq.*

[123] *See, e.g.,* United States v. Jones, 451 F. Supp. 2d 71 (D.D.C. 2006) (access to stored text messages is governed by the Stored Wire & Electronic Communications Act, not the Wiretap Act); United States v. Moriarty, 962 F. Supp. 217, 220 (D. Mass.1997) (same, stored voice mail messages).

[124] § 5.15 *infra.*

[125] *See, e.g.,* Malpas v. State, 16 Md. App. 69, 695 A.2d 588 (1997) (parabolic microphone); United States v. Lucht, 18 F.3d 541 (8th Cir. 1993) (electronic bug); State v. Denman, 100 F.3d 399 (5th Cir. 1996) (wiretap apparatus); **United States v. McIntyre, 582 F.2d 1221 (9th Cir. 1978)** (microphone and transmitter concealed in a brief case that was left in the assistant chief of police's office to monitor his conversations).

[126] 18 U.S.C. § 2510(5) defines an interception device as "any device or apparatus which can be used to intercept a wire, oral, or electronic communication. . . ." other than a hearing aid or similar device used to correct subnormal hearing.

when it is used to listen to a telephone conversation without the knowledge or consent of either party.[127]

Figure 5.7
Procedural Requirements for a Wiretap Order

The procedural requirements for a wiretap order exceed Fourth Amendment requirements for an ordinary search warrant. The Wiretap Act:

- Limits the crimes for which wiretap orders may be issued.
- Requires approval by a high-ranking official within the Justice Department before the application may be submitted to the court.
- Requires proof that traditional investigative techniques have been tried and failed, appear unlikely to succeed, or are too dangerous to try.
- Requires establishment of probable cause to believe that: (1) a person is committing a crime for which an interception order may be issued; (2) the targeted facilities are being used in connection with that crime; and (3) an interception will produce communications relevant to that crime.
- Limits the duration of wiretap orders to a maximum of 30 days or attainment of the authorized objective, whichever occurs first. A fresh application is required for an extension.
- Requires that wiretap orders be executed so as to minimize intrusions into communications not related to the investigation.
- Limits disclosure and use of communications intercepted under a wiretap order to: (1) furtherance of the investigation, (2) national defense and security, and (3) giving testimony in court.

§ 5.10   — Procedural Requirements for Intercepting Protected Communications

The procedural requirements for a wiretap order exceed the Fourth Amendment requirements for an ordinary search warrant. In addition to incorporating the Fourth Amendment probable cause and specificity requirements, the Act restricts the crimes for which wiretap orders may be issued, limits their duration, permits them to be issued only as a last resort, requires that efforts be made to minimize the interception of communications beyond the scope of the order, and provides for continuing judicial oversight of the entire process. The following passage summarizes why these heightened procedural safeguards are necessary:

---

[127]   *See, e.g., In re* State Police Litigation, 888 F. Supp. 1235 (D. Conn. 1995) (holding that use of a telephone extension without the consent of either party constitutes an interception); United States v. Murdock, 63 F.3d 1391 (6th Cir. 1995) (holding that a recorder connected to an extension phone that was automatically activated when the extension phone handset was lifted constituted an interception); Commonwealth v. Brachbill, 520 Pa. 533, 555 A.2d 82 (Pa. 1989) (holding that surreptitious listening over an extension phone violated state version of the Wiretap Act).

> Title III was Congress's carefully thought out . . . effort to implement the requirements of the Fourth Amendment with regard to the necessarily unconventional type of warrant that is used to authorize electronic eavesdropping. In a conventional search the police go through a home or an office looking for contraband or evidence of a crime, and they either find what they are looking for or not, and then they leave. By rummaging through a person's possessions in search of what they came for they invade the person's privacy, and much of what they examine may be at once personal and irrelevant to the objective of the search, but the search is usually brief. Electronic interception, being by nature a continuing rather than one-shot invasion, is even less discriminating than a physical search, because it picks up private conversations (most of which will usually have nothing to do with any illegal activity) over a long period of time. Whether because it is more indiscriminate, or because people regard their conversations as more private than their possessions, or for both reasons, electronic interception is thought to pose a greater potential threat to personal privacy than physical searches, and Congress therefore pitched the requirements for a valid intercept warrant higher than those for a conventional Rule 41 warrant . . .[128]

Because of the heightened procedural safeguards, wiretap orders have aptly been described as "super-warrants."[129]

A. *Crimes for Which Interception Orders Can Be Obtained*

Interceptions are more intrusive than traditional investigative techniques and, consequently, may only be used when important law enforcement interests are at stake. Federal officials may seek interception orders only for serious crimes such as espionage, sabotage, terrorism, treason, murder, kidnapping, robbery, extortion, counterfeiting, dealing in drugs, and crimes dangerous to life, limb, or property.[130]

B. *"Necessity Requirement"*

A wiretap order may not be issued unless traditional investigative techniques have been tried and failed, appear unlikely to succeed, or are too dangerous to try.[131] This is referred to as the "necessity requirement." The purpose of the necessity requirement is to ensure that wiretapping and electronic surveillance are not used in situations where less intrusive methods of investigation techniques would suffice to expose the crime.[132] The traditional investigative techniques judges consider in deciding whether the necessity requirement has been satisfied include: (1) physical surveillance, (2) examination of public records, (3) questioning and interrogation of witnesses, (4) use of search

---

[128]　United States v. Torres, *supra* note 55.

[129]　Orin S. Kerr, *Internet Surveillance Law After the USA Patriot Act: The Big Brother That Isn't*, 97 NW. U. L. REV. 607, 630 (2003).

[130]　18 U.S.C. § 2516(1). State wiretap statutes may authorize issuance of interception orders for the following crimes: murder, kidnapping, gambling, robbery, bribery, extortion, or dealing in narcotic drugs, marijuana or other dangerous drugs, or other crime dangerous to life, limb, or property, and punishable by imprisonment for more than one year. 18 U.S.C. § 2516(2).

[131]　18 U.S.C. § 2518(3) (C).

[132]　United States v. Kahn, 415 U.S. 143, 94 S. Ct. 977, 39 L. Ed. 2d 225 (1974) (10th Cir. 2002).

warrants, (5) infiltration of conspiratorial groups by undercover agents or informants, and (6) use of pen registers and trap-and-trace devices.[133] The Wiretap Act does not require proof that no stones have been left unturned. What courts insist on is that the government demonstrates that it has made a good faith effort to utilize a range of conventional law enforcement techniques before seeking a wiretap order.[134]

C. Authorization to Apply for an Interception Order

The decision to apply for a wiretap order is not left to criminal investigators. Congress wanted authority and responsibility for this decision to be in the hands of politically accountable government officials. In federal investigations, applications for wiretap orders must be reviewed and approved by the United States Attorney General or another designated ranking official within the Justice Department before they may be submitted to a judge.[135] In state investigations, responsibility for making the application rests with the principal prosecuting officer of the state or political subdivision.[136]

> Prosecutors, not the police, are primarily responsible for applying for and overseeing implementation of wiretap orders.

D. Probable Cause and Particularity Requirement

Wiretap orders are a specialized kind of search warrant. They authorize law enforcement officials to search for and seize communications. Being a search warrant, they must comply with the Fourth Amendment directive that "no Warrants shall issue, but upon probable cause, . . . particularly describing the place to be searched, and the persons or things to be seized." The court may issue a wiretap order only if it finds probable cause to believe that: (1) a person is committing a crime for which an interception order may be issued, (2) the targeted facilities are being used in connection with that crime, and (3) an interception will produce communications relevant to that crime.[137] The contents of a wiretap order are similar to those of a traditional search warrant. The order must identify the person, if known, whose communications will be intercepted and contain a particularized description of the types of communications

---

[133]   United States v. Ramirez-Encarnacion, 291 F.3d 1219 (10th Cir. 2002).

[134]   United States v. Jones, *supra* note 123.

[135]   18 U.S.C. § 2516(1). The authorization requirement for interception of electronic communications is not as strict. Any attorney for the government may apply for court authorization to intercept electronic communications in connection with the investigation of "any federal felony." 18 U.S.C. § 2516(3).

[136]   18 U.S.C. § 2516(2).

[137]   18 U.S.C. § 2518(3).

that may be intercepted and the facilities from which, or place where, interception is authorized.[138]

E. Duration of Interception Orders

Wiretap orders are required to specify a period during which they remain in effect. Unlike conventional searches, which rarely take longer than a few hours, ongoing interception operations sometimes continue for days or even months.[139] As a way of preserving judicial oversight, the Wiretap Act limits the duration for which wiretap orders may be approved to 30 days, subject to any number of additional extensions.[140] Each extension requires a fresh application with the same showing required for the initial application.[141] This enables the judge to monitor the progress and evaluate the need for continued interception. Wiretap orders terminate upon attainment of the authorized objective or expiration of the period specified in them, whichever occurs first.[142]

F. Access and Assistance in Placing the Interception Device

Most interceptions are accomplished either through wiretapping or "bugging." Bugging is performed by installing a small microphone or recorder in the room to be bugged. For the operation to be effective, the equipment must be installed without the suspect's knowledge. This generally requires a covert entry. An order granting authority to conduct interception surveillance at a described location confers implied authority to secretly enter for the sake of installing and servicing the necessary equipment.[143] A separate warrant is unnecessary. A judge who issues a wiretap order may, in addition, direct landlords, custodians, and others to furnish information, facilities, or technical assistance necessary to accomplish the interception without discovery.[144]

When the target of a wiretap order is itinerant, or purposely changes locations or uses different telephone booths to thwart detection, the judge can authorize a "roving wiretap" — a wiretap order that authorizes surveillance of any phone that the subject may use, instead of a specific facility or location.[145] Roving wiretap warrants were developed partly in response to the increased use of cellular telephones. Suspects frequently change cellular phones to elude interception. The Communication Assistance for Law Enforcement Act requires cellular providers to engineer systems capable of accommodating roving wiretaps.[146]

---

[138]   18 U.S.C. § 2518(4).
[139]   Congressional findings, Omnibus Crime Control and Safe Streets Act of 1968, § 801.
[140]   18 U.S.C. § 2518(5).
[141]   Id.
[142]   Id.
[143]   Dalia v. United States, 441 U.S. 238, 99 S. Ct. 1682, 60 L. Ed. 2d 177 (1979).
[144]   18 U.S.C. § 2518(4).
[145]   18 U.S.C. § 2518(11); United States v. Hermanek, 289 F.3d 1076 (9th Cir. 2002).
[146]   47 U.S.C. § 1002(d).

G. Duty to Minimize Interceptions of Conversations Beyond the Scope of the Order

Interception orders are required to specify the kinds of communications that maybe intercepted. During the surveillance, it is inevitable that police will find themselves listening to communications beyond the scope of their order. Some of the conversations will be truly innocent: a crime boss still calls his mother on Sunday, and drug dealers have been known to send out for pizza. Indeed many, if not most, communications intercepted during ongoing operations have nothing to do with the crimes under investigation. The Federal Bureau of Investigation reported that in listening to more than 1.3 million conversations using wiretaps and bugs, only 15 percent contained incriminating information.[147] To complicate matters, criminals engaged in organized crime often converse in code. This can make differentiating truly innocent conversations from seemingly innocent ones challenging.

The Fourth Amendment prohibits general searches. Even criminal suspects have a right to keep their private lives private. Herein lays the dilemma. With searches involving tangible objects, the requirement that police limit their search to areas and containers capable of housing the object of the search keeps the intrusiveness of the search within bounds. However, with interception orders, there is no way to tell whether a given communication contains information relating to the crimes under investigation other than to intercept the communication and listen.

While recognizing that interception of innocent communications is unavoidable, the Wiretap Act nevertheless requires investigators to conduct their operations so as to minimize intrusions into communications beyond the scope of the order.[148]

Normally, the prosecutor in charge of the investigation will issue protocols for officers to follow regarding proper minimization. The usual practice is to monitor every communication for a couple of minutes to determine whether the conversation concerns crimes specified in the interception order.[149] Once satisfied that the call is irrelevant or after listening for a couple of minutes without anything materializing, the officer must stop listening.[150] If the officer overhears a conversation about an unrelated crime during the first few minutes, the officer may continue listening, but should notify the prosecutor immediately afterward so that the prosecutor can bring this matter to the attention of the judge who issued the order and seek the judge's approval.[151] Only if the judge finds that the government was following the minimization procedures when it

---

[147] David Burnham, *The F.B.I.*, THE NATION, Aug. 11, 1997, at 11.
[148] Every authorization and extension must contain a provision requiring that the execution to "be conducted in such a way as to minimize the interception of communications not otherwise subject to interception." 18 U.S.C. § 2518(5).
[149] *See, e.g.*, United States v. Abascal, 564 F.2d 821 (9th Cir. 1977); United States v. Chavez, 533 F.2d 491 (8th Cir. 1976); United States v. Scott, 516 F.2d 751 (D.C. Cir. 1975); United States v. Borrayo-Gutierrez, 119 F. Supp. 2d 1168 (D. Colo. 2000).
[150] *See* cases *supra* note 149.
[151] 18 U.S.C. § 2517(5).

stumbled across evidence of an unrelated crime will the government be permitted to use this evidence in a judicial proceeding.[152]

H. *Limitations on Disclosure and Use of Intercepted Communications*

The Wiretap Act imposes a lid on the use and disclosure of communications intercepted under a wiretap order. The information may be used and disclosed for only one of three purposes. The first is to further a criminal investigation. Criminal investigators may use information intercepted under a judicial interception order to perform their official duties and may disclose the information to other criminal investigators when the information is appropriate to the latter's duties.[153] Officers who are informed of the communication are bound by the same restrictions. The second purpose concerns national security. When the contents of an intercepted communication relate to foreign intelligence or counterintelligence, the communication may be disclosed to other federal law enforcement, intelligence, immigration, national defense, and national security officers to assist them in performing their duties.[154] The final purpose is to further a criminal prosecution. Officers may disclose information while giving testimony in court and the recordings of the conversation may be introduced as evidence.[155] No other use or disclosure is permitted. Thus, while it would be appropriate for an officer to share information about a large drug buy with a DEA agent, sharing it with a local news reporter violates the Wiretap Act.

I. *The Emergency Exception*

Emergency situations occasionally arise in which police must act promptly or risk losing critical evidence. Anticipating this, Congress included a provision that allows police, under limited circumstances, to commence intercepting before a judge issues an interception order and to apply for an order afterward. This provision is patterned on the "exigent circumstances" exception to the Fourth Amendment warrant requirement, which permits the police to take action without a search warrant when they are confronted with an emergency that requires prompt action. For the emergency surveillance provision to apply, the following four conditions are necessary.[156]

First, the police must be confronted with an emergency that involves: (1) immediate danger of death or serious physical injury to a person, (2) conspiratorial activity

---

152 *Id. See also* State v. Gerena, 653 F. Supp. 974 (D. Conn. 1987).
153 18 U.S.C. § 2517(1)(2).
154 18 U.S.C. § 2517(6). This provision was added as part of the USA Patriot Act to promote closer working relationships between criminal investigators, immigration authorities, and the intelligence community. Lack of information-sharing hampered efforts to gather and utilize information that might have prevented the 9/11/01 terrorist attacks.
155 18 U.S.C. § 2517(3).
156 18 U.S.C. § 2518(7).

threatening national security, or (3) conspiratorial activity characteristic of organized crime.

Second, grounds must exist for believing that an interception order would have been granted had the authorities had time to apply for one.

Third, authorization to initiate emergency surveillance must be obtained from a high-ranking official within the Justice Department in federal investigations and from the principal prosecuting attorney of the state or political subdivision in state investigations.

Finally, application must be made to a judge for an order approving the interception within 48 hours after emergency interception surveillance has begun. If the order is denied, the interception must terminate immediately.

The emergency surveillance provision has not been widely used. The Justice Department has invoked it sparingly, in life-threatening situations only.[157]

Figure 5.8
Communication Surveillance That Is Not Regulated by the Wiretap Act

A wiretap order is not required to conduct communications surveillance when: 1. The conversation is overheard naturally (*i.e.*, without the aid of a device). 2. The target of the surveillance lacks a reasonable expectation that the communication is not being intercepted, or 3. A party to the conversation performs or consents to the interception.

§ 5.11   Communication Surveillance Not Regulated by the Wiretap Act

A wiretap order is not required to listen to conversations when: (1) the conversation is overheard naturally (*i.e.*, without the aid of a device), (2) the target of the surveillance lacks a reasonable expectation that the communication will not be intercepted, or (3) a party to the conversation intercepts it or consents to the interception. These situations are explored in the sections that follow.

§ 5.12   — Listening with the Unaided Ear

The coverage of the Wiretap Act is limited to interception of communications with a device. When government agents listen with their naked ear, the only requirements are those imposed by the Fourth Amendment. If the agent is lawfully present where the

---

[157]   Clifford S. Fishman, *Interception of Communications in Exigent Circumstances: The Fourth Amendment, Federal Legislation, and the United States Department of Justice*, 22 GA. L. REV. 1, 47 (1987).

listening takes place, no search results because people who speak loudly enough to be overheard by others who are or might be present lack a reasonable expectation of privacy.[158]

A listening device is used when government agents are not in a position to hear a conversation naturally.[159] This occurred in *Katz v. United States*.[160] Federal agents attached a concealed, unattended tape recorder to the top of a telephone booth so that they could monitor Katz's phone calls. The Supreme Court held that this constituted a search and violated the Fourth Amendment. The same result would be reached today under Wiretap Act because the federal agents used a device to obtain access to the contents of a protected communication without a wiretap order.

A wiretap order is not required when a conversation captured on tape is actually overheard because the tape recorder is not the means of "acquiring" the conversation.[161] The conversation is "acquired" through normal powers of hearing; the tape recorder is merely a means of preserving it. Officers engaged in communications surveillance should, use an ordinary cassette-type recorder with a standard microphone because a device more sensitive might pick up parts of the conversation that were not heard independently, resulting in a violation of the Wiretap Act.

§ 5.13   — Interception of an Oral Communication Where the Target Lacks a Reasonable Expectation of Freedom from Interception

The Wiretap Act protects **oral communications** only when they are "uttered by a person exhibiting an expectation that such communication is not subject to interception under circumstances justifying such expectation."[162] This is the Wiretap Act's version of the *Katz* reasonable expectation of privacy test. Whether a person has a reasonable expectation that an oral communication will not be intercepted depends on a number of

---

[158]   United States v. Jackson, *supra* note 10 (no reasonable expectation of privacy existed in conversation audible to police officers in an adjoining hotel room); 1 WAYNE LAFAVE, SEARCH & SEIZURE § 2.2 (3d ed. 1996) ("As a general proposition, it is fair to say that when a law enforcement officer is able to detect something by utilization of one or more of his senses while lawfully present at the vantage point where those senses are used, that detection does not constitute a 'search' within the meaning of the Fourth Amendment.").

[159]   1 WAYNE LAFAVE, SEARCH & SEIZURE § 2.2 (e) at 437 (3d ed.1996).

[160]   *Supra* note 5.

[161]   *See, e.g.*, People v. Siripongs, 45 Cal. 3d 548, 745 P.2d 1301 (1988), cert. denied, 488 U.S. 1019, 109 S. Ct. 820, 102 L. Ed. 2d 810 (1989) (holding that the Wiretap Act was not violated where officer standing beside prisoner as he talked on the phone secretly recorded the words he spoke into the receiver); Matter of John Doe, Trader Number One, 722 F. Supp. 419 (N.D. Ill. 1989) (holding that the Wiretap Act was not violated where an undercover FBI agent standing next to the suspect on the floor of a stock exchange recorded his conversations).

[162]   *Id.*

factors, the most important of which are the nature of the location, the presence and proximity of others, and how loudly the person speaks.[163]

The clearest example of a reasonable expectation that an oral communication will not be intercepted exists when the conversation takes place in the person's own home or office.[164] However, this is not the only setting in which oral communications are protected. In the foundation case of *Katz v. United States*,[165] the Supreme Court determined that Katz had a reasonable expectation that his conversation would not be intercepted, even though he was in a public telephone booth when he spoke. The Court stated that when a person enters a public telephone booth and closes the door, he has a right to expect that the words he utters into the receiver will remain private.

Two situations exist where Wiretap Act protection for oral communications is routinely denied: (1) when the conversation is carried on while third parties are within normal hearing range, and (2) where it takes place in a highly controlled police environment where surreptitious monitoring is so common that it is almost expected.

Kee v. City of Rowlett[166] is an example of the first situation. Police planted an electronic surveillance microphone in a funeral urn next to the graves of two murdered children. The device picked up a conversation between their father and grandmother during an outdoor gravesite memorial service. The court ruled that the father and

---

[163] *See, e.g.*, Kee v. City of Rowlett, 247 F.3d 206, 212 (5th Cir. 2001) (conversation between father and grandmother occurring during outdoor grave site service for murdered children not protected against interception accomplished by placing electronic surveillance microphone in funeral urn); Hornberger v. American Broadcasting Companies, Inc., 351 N.J. Super. 577, 799 A.2d 566 (2002) ("Courts have identified several factors relevant to evaluating the existence of a reasonable expectation of privacy in oral communications made in publicly accessible places. These factors include: (1) the volume of the communication or conversation; (2) the proximity or potential of other individuals to overhear the conversation; (3) the potential for communications to be reported; (4) the affirmative actions taken by the speakers to shield their privacy; (5) the need for technological enhancements to hear the communications; and (6) the place or location of the oral communications as it relates to the subjective expectations of the individuals who are communicating."); United States v. Carroll, 337 F. Supp. 1260 (D.D.C. 1971) (conversation in hotel room not protected against interception where it could be heard in adjoining room, by the unassisted ear, and was recorded by using a cassette-type recorder with a standard microphone no more sensitive than the human ear); United States v. Burns, 624 F.2d 95 (10th Cir. 1980) ("Legitimate privacy expectations cannot be separated from a conversation's context. Bedroom whispers in the middle of a large house on a large, private tract of land carry quite different expectations of privacy, reasonably speaking, than does a boisterous conversation occurring in a crowded supermarket or subway.").

[164] United States. v. Duncan, 598 F.2d 839 (4th Cir.), *cert. denied*, 444 U.S. 871, 100 S. Ct. 148, 62 L. Ed. 2d 96 (1979) (holding that the bank's "bugging" of an office assigned to IRS auditors while they were in the bank conducting an audit violated the Wiretap Act); **United States v. McIntyre, 582 F.2d 1221 (9th Cir. 1978** (holding that assistant chief of police had a reasonable expectation of privacy in conversations carried on in his office, even though the door to his office was open and there were other persons present because none were within normal hearing range).

[165] **Katz v. United States,** *supra* note 5.

[166] *Supra* note 163.

grandmother failed to establish that they had a reasonable expectation that their conversation would not be intercepted. The cemetery was publicly accessible and the memorial service was well attended. The plaintiffs did not establish that their "conversations were conducted in a manner inaudible to others and provide[d] no information about who was present," or whether "third parties were in close proximity." "[M]ost damaging" of all, "they failed to present evidence demonstrating any affirmative steps taken to preserve their privacy."

United States v. Turner[167] illustrates the second situation. A couple carried on an incriminating conversation in the back seat of a patrol car while their own car was being searched, oblivious to the fact that their conversation was being recorded. The court held that their conversation was not protected. The fact that patrol cars "bristle with electronics, including microphones to a dispatcher, possible video recording with audio pickup, and other electronic and recording devices" should have made realities of the situation "starkly apparent" to them. The same analysis applies to oral conversations carried on in police station interrogation rooms, jails, and prisons.[168] As one court bluntly put it, anyone "who expects privacy under the circumstances of prison visiting is, if not actually foolish, exceptionally naive."[169] Because privacy is not expected in highly controlled police environments, a wiretap order is not required to use an interception device to eavesdrop on prisoner conversations.[170]

§ 5.14   — Interception Conducted with the Consent of a Party

Under the *Hoffa* doctrine, the Fourth Amendment is not violated when a communication is intercepted with the cooperation of someone who is a party to it.[171] The Wiretap Act incorporates this exception. Title 18 U.S.C. § 2511(2) (C) states that "[i]t shall not be unlawful . . . for a person acting under color of law to intercept a wire, oral, or electronic communication, where such person is a party to the communication or one of the parties to the communication has given prior consent to such interception."

---

[167] **United States v. Turner,** 209 F.3d 1198 (10th Cir. 2000).

[168] *See, e.g.,* United States v. Clark, 22 F.3d 799 (8th Cir. 1994) (no reasonable expectation of freedom from interception exists in the backseat of a police car); United States v. McKinnon, 985 F.2d 525 (11th Cir.), *cert. denied,* 510 U.S. 843, 114 S. Ct. 130, 126 L. Ed. 2d 94 (1993) (same); People v. Riel, 22 Cal. 4th 1153, 998 P.2d 969, 96 Cal. Rptr. 1 (2000) (same, jail visitors' room); *Ex parte* Graves, 853 S.W.2d 701 (Tex. Ct. App. 1993) (same, inmate's cellblock conversation with fellow inmate); State v. Owen, 643 N.W.2d 735 (S.D. 2003) (same, call from telephone in police station interrogation room).

[169] United States v. Harrelson, 754 F.2d 1153, 1169 (5th Cir. 1985).

[170] *See* authorities *supra* note 168.

[171] *See* § 5.4 (C) *supra.*

Consent can be implied as well as expressed. The most common situation where consent is implied is where a person is given notice that calls made from a particular phone will be monitored, but makes the call anyway.[172] Suppose Sam is in jail, awaiting trial on burglary charges. He uses the jail phone to make arrangements for his escape. His call is intercepted and his escape plans are thwarted. The Wiretap Act will not protect Sam because inmates are given repeated notice — during their orientation, in correctional facility handbooks, and through signs posted near the telephone — that calls are monitored. If Sam uses the telephone with notice that calls made from the jail are monitored, his consent to the monitoring will be implied.[173] The intercepted phone call can also be used as evidence against Sam's partner in crime, even though he did not consent to the interception, because the consent of one party is enough to eliminate protection under the federal Wiretap Act for both.[174]

Figure 5.9
Requirements for Obtaining E-mail, Voice Mail, and Text Messages

Different statutory schemes apply to e-mail, depending on when it is intercepted.

- The Wiretap Act governs the interception of e-mail during the transmission stage while the message is traversing the Internet.
- The Stored Wire and Electronic Communications and Transactional Records Act governs access to e-mail after the message has reached its intended destination and is held in electronic storage.
- The Stored Wire and Electronic Communications and Transactional Records Act also governs access to voice mail, text messages, and transactional records.

§ 5.15   — E-mail, Voice Mail, and Text Messages

The Internet is widely used as a method of communication by criminals as well as ordinary citizens, making access to e-mail and stored electronic communications increasingly important in modern law enforcement. E-mail messages are protected by

---

[172] *See, e.g.,* **United States v. Willoughby, 860 F.2d 15 (2d Cir. 1988)** (holding that when inmates are given notice that their telephone conversations may be monitored and/or recorded for security and they use the phone anyway, they impliedly consent to the interception and their telephone conversation is not protected by the Wiretap Act); PBA Local No. 38 v. Woodbridge Police Dept., 832 F. Supp. 808 (D.N.J. 1993) (holding that police officers impliedly consented to the interception when they placed personal calls from police headquarter, using "beeped" telephone).

[173] United States v. Faulkner, 439 F.3d 1221 (10th Cir. 2006); **United States v. Willoughby**, *supra* note 172; Griggs-Ryan v. Smith, 904 F.2d 112 (1st Cir. 1990).

[174] **United States v. Willoughby**, *supra* note 172. Although consent of one party is sufficient under the federal Wiretap Act, we recommend checking state law before taking action. Statutes in a number of states make it illegal to use a device to listen to or record a conversation unless all of the parties consent. *See, e.g.*, Ill. Rev. Stat., Ch. 38, par. 14-2(a) (1991).

the Wiretap Act only during the brief interval they are transversing the Internet.[175] The protection ends once the message reaches its intended destination, which generally takes only a few seconds. The reason Wiretap Act protection for e-mail is so short-lived is the definition of an "interception." An interception requires that access to the contents of a communication be acquired during its transmission.[176] Once an e-mail message reaches its intended destination, it becomes a stored communication. Access to stored communications (such as e-mail after arrival, voice mail, and text messages) is regulated by a separate federal statute — the Stored Wire and Electronic Communications and Transactional Records Act.[177] Stored communications receive a lower level of protection than communications covered by the Wiretap. This makes it easier for law enforcement to obtain access to them.

The Stored Communications Act begins by prohibiting electronic communication service providers from voluntarily divulging their customers' stored communications to any person.[178] It then sets forth procedures that law enforcement officials must follow to compel disclosure.[179] These procedures are much less cumbersome than the elaborate scheme imposed by the Wiretap Act. During the first 180 days of storage, access requires a search warrant issued on a showing of probable cause. Protection dwindles with the passage of the time.[180] After 180 days, if notice is given to the subscriber, disclosure can be compelled through a subpoena or court order issued on a showing that the contents are relevant to an ongoing criminal investigation.[181] Notice to the subscriber may be delayed for up to 90 days if giving notice might have serious adverse consequences, such as jeopardizing the investigation, endangering lives, or promoting flight.[182] The court may, upon application, further extend the time for giving notice. As a result, access to e-mails that have been in storage for 180 days may, in many cases, be obtained without notice to the subscriber on the scanty showing that the

---

[175] 18 U.S.C. §§ 2511, 2518; United States v. Councilman, 418 F.3d 67 (1st Cir. 2005).

[176] *See, e.g.*, United States v. Steiger, 318 F.3d 1039 (11th Cir. 2003); Konop v. Hawaiian Airlines, Inc., 302 F.3d 868 (9th Cir. 2002); Steve Jackson Games, Inc. v. United States Secret Serv., 36 F.3d 457 (5th Cir. 1994); *see also* CLIFFORD S. FISHMAN & ANNE T. MCKENNA, WIRETAPPING AND EAVESDROPPING § 2:5 (West, 2d ed. 1995) ("An interception [of an electronic communication] occurs ... only if the contents are acquired as the communication takes place, not if they are acquired while the communications are in storage."); Orin S. Kerr, *Internet Surveillance Law After the USA Patriot Act: The Big Brother That Isn't,* 97 Nw. U. L. Rev. 607, 613-14 (2003).

[177] 18 U.S.C. §§ 2701 *et seq. See, e.g.*, United States v. Jones, 451 F. Supp. 2d 71 (D.D.C. 2006) (holding that the Wiretap Act does not apply to the government's acquisition of text messages held in storage at an electronic communication service provider). *See generally*, Patricia L. Bellia & Susan Freiwald, *Fourth Amendment Protection for Stored E-Mail,* 2008 U. CHI. LEGAL F. 121 (2008); Alexander Scolnik, Note, *Protections for Electronic Communications: The Stored Communications Act and the Fourth Amendment*, 78 FORDHAM L. REV. 349 (2009).

[178] 18 U.S.C. § 2702.

[179] **18 U.S.C. § 2703**. This statute is reproduced in Part II.

[180] 18 U.S.C. § 2703 (a).

[181] 18 U.S.C. § 2703 (b) (d).

[182] 18 U.S.C. § 2705.

information is likely to be relevant to a criminal investigation. This is a far cry from the elaborate procedural requirements imposed by the Wiretap Act.

The same mechanisms can be used to compel disclosure of subscriber-identifying information and records of the subscriber's use of the service.[183] The information that must be turned over includes the subscriber's name and address, local and long-distance telephone connection records, or records of session times and durations, the length of service (including start date), types of service utilized, the subscribers' login and user names, passwords, and IP addresses, and the source of payment for such services, including credit card or bank account numbers.[184]

Electronic communications remain admissible even when they are illegally obtained,[185] because the Wiretap Act's statutory suppression remedy, for reasons unclear, covers illegally obtained wire and oral communications, but not electronic ones.[186]

§ 5.16   — Pen Registers and Trap-and-Trace Devices

Pen registers and trap-and-traces are recording devices attached to a telephone line, usually at a central telephone office, that identify the source and destination of all calls made to (pen registers) or from (trap-and-trace devices) a particular telephone, much like a secret Caller ID. They are normally used to obtain information needed to satisfy the probable cause requirement for a wiretap order. Their use, nevertheless, is not regulated by the Wiretap Act because they do not yield access to the contents of the call and, thus, there is no interception.

In *Smith v. Maryland*,[187] the Supreme Court ruled that subscribers lack a reasonable expectation of privacy in dialing information.

> Telephone users … typically know that they must convey numerical information to the phone company; that the phone company has facilities for recording this information; and that the phone company does in fact record this information for a variety of legitimate business purposes.… [I]is too much to believe that telephone subscribers, under these circumstances, generally harbor any general expectation that the numbers they dial will remain secret.

Smith v. Maryland stripped dialing information of Fourth Amendment protection.

Eight years later, Congress enacted the Electronic Communications Privacy Act (ECPA),[188] which made it illegal to install pen/traps without a court order. However,

---

[183]   18 U.S.C. § 2703 (C).
[184]   *Id.*
[185]   *See, e.g.*, United States v. Jones, 364 F. Supp. 2d 1303 (D. Utah 2005) (finding no provision in the Act to allow for suppression of electronic communications intercepted in violation of the Act); *United States v. Meriwether*, 917 F.2d 955 (6th Cir.1990) (same); United States v. Steiger, *supra* note 176 (same)
[186]   18 U.S.C. § 2514.
[187]   442 U.S. 735, 745, 99 S. Ct. 2577, 61 L. Ed. 2d 220 (1979).
[188]   18 U.S.C. § 3121 *et seq.*

because there is no Fourth Amendment protection for dialing information, the threshold for obtaining a pen/trap order is quite low. Law enforcement officials are not required to set forth facts establishing probable cause to believe that the surveillance will uncover identified evidence, as they must for a conventional search warrant or a wiretap order. The only thing necessary to obtain a pen/trap order is an application that names the applicant and the law enforcement agency conducting the investigation and certifies under oath that the information likely to be obtained is relevant to an on-going criminal investigation.[189] Upon that certification, the judge is required to enter an order authorizing collection of dialing information; the judge has no authority to independently assess the factual predicate underlying the certification.[190]

Orders authorizing the installation and use of pen/traps may be issued for up to 60 days and are subject to renewal. Comparable orders are available for the collection of source and addressee information for e-mail.[191]

Figure 5.10
Foreign Intelligence Surveillance Act

> The Foreign Intelligence Surveillance Act establishes a special statutory procedure governing electronic surveillance conducted inside the United States for the purpose of gathering foreign intelligence. Surveillance orders require probable cause to believe that the target of the surveillance is a foreign power, agent of a foreign power, or a member of an international terrorist organization.
>
> A surveillance order is not required to conduct electronic surveillance of communications between persons inside the United States and persons overseas when the target of the surveillance is the person overseas.

§ 5.17   Foreign Intelligence Surveillance Act

There is a second federal statute that deals with wiretapping and electronic surveillance — the Foreign Intelligence Surveillance Act, better known as FISA.[192] This statute regulates electronic surveillance *conducted inside the United States* to gather intelligence about foreign powers, agents of foreign powers, and international

---

[189]   18 U.S.C. § 3122.

[190]   J. CARR & P. BELLIA, THE LAW OF ELECTRONIC SURVEILLANCE § 1:26, at 1-25 (West 2004).

[191]   18 U.S.C. § 3131, 3123.

[192]   50 U.S.C. § 1801 *et seq.* The Foreign Intelligence Surveillance Act, as originally enacted, covered only electronic surveillance warrants, but it was amended in 1994 to cover physical searches and video surveillance. *See* 50 U.S.C. §§ 1821–1829. The provisions regarding physical search warrants are similar to those for electronic surveillance orders and are beyond the scope of this chapter. For a general discussion of the Foreign Intelligence Surveillance Act, *see, generally,* Alison A. Bradley, Comment, *Extremism in the Defense of Liberty? The Foreign Intelligence Surveillance Act and the Significance of the USA Patriot Act,* 77 TUL. L. REV. 465 (2002); William Michael, *A Window on Terrorism: The Foreign Intelligence Surveillance Act,* 58 NOV. BENCH & B. MINN. 23 (2001).

terrorist organizations. This is the statute that intelligence agencies use when they investigate suspected al-Qaeda cells inside the United States, spying activity by foreign embassies, and other domestic threats to our national security. Electronic surveillance abroad is not regulated.

A. *Overview of the Foreign Intelligence Surveillance Act*

FISA establishes a special statutory procedure governing electronic surveillance conducted for the purpose of gathering "foreign intelligence." "Foreign intelligence" refers to information about terrorism, spying, espionage, sabotage, political assassinations, and similar threats to our national security.[193] The Act establishes a special secret court — the Foreign Intelligence Surveillance Court (FISC) — to oversee this process. The FISC is composed of 11 federal district court judges, selected by the Chief Justice of the U.S. Supreme Court, to hear applications for orders authorizing electronic surveillance and physical searches in national security cases.[194] The court's proceedings are secret, records of the proceedings are sealed after the application is heard, and the subject never learns of the surveillance unless criminal charges are later brought.[195]

B. *Authorized Targets of FISA Surveillance Orders*

A FISA surveillance order requires probable cause to believe the target surveillance is a foreign power, agent of a foreign power, or member of an international terrorist organization.[196] FISA orders cannot be obtained to investigate persons or groups inside the United States who lack foreign ties. Authorization for electronic surveillance must, instead, be sought under the stricter requirements of the Wiretap Act.

---

[193] Foreign intelligence is defined in the statute as information that relates to actual or potential attacks, clandestine spying activity, sabotage, international terrorism, and information relevant to national defense, security, or the conduct of foreign affairs. 50 U.S.C. § 1801(e).

[194] 50 U.S.C. § 1803.

[195] The FISA court operates in extreme secrecy and the opportunities for review of its decisions are limited. *See, e.g.*, United States v. Rahman, 861 F. Supp. 247 (S.D.N.Y. 1994) (upholding admission of wiretap evidence obtained under a FISA surveillance order in the prosecution of Omar Ahmad Ali Abdel Rahman over the defendant's objection that the government had misused its FISA surveillance authority. The court stated that once the reviewing court finds that an authorized executive branch official has certified that the purpose of the investigation was to gather intelligence information, and "his certification is supported by probable cause to believe that the target is an agent of a foreign power as defined in the statute, and that the location is one being or to be used by the target, and it appears from the application as a whole that the certification is not clearly erroneous, the task of that court is at an end.... A reviewing court is not to 'second-guess' the certification.").

[196] 50 U.S.C. § 1805(a)(2). "Foreign power" is defined broadly to include, *inter alia*, "a group engaged in international terrorism or activities in preparation therefore" and "a foreign-based political organization, not substantially composed of United States persons." §§ 1801(a)(4), (5). The definition of an "agent of a foreign power" includes any person who "knowingly engages in clandestine intelligence gathering activities for or on behalf of a foreign power[,]" or any person who "knowingly engages in sabotage or international terrorism, or activities that are in preparation therefore, for or on behalf of a foreign power."

C. *Procedures for Obtaining FISA Surveillance Authority*

All applications for FISA surveillance orders must be personally approved by the Attorney General.[197] The application must state facts establishing probable cause to believe that the target of the surveillance is a foreign power, agent of a foreign power, or an international terrorist organization, describe the manner in which the order will be implemented, and contain the certification of a senior national security official, typically the Director of the FBI, that the information sought is foreign intelligence information and that the information cannot "be obtained by normal investigative techniques."[198] The FISC judge is required to approve the application if, based on the facts established in the application, there is probable cause to believe that the target of the surveillance is a foreign power, agent of a foreign power, or an international terrorist organization, and all necessary certifications are attached.[199] Judicial scrutiny of FISA applications is minimal. Of the thousands of applications for FISA orders made since 1978, only a few have ever been denied.[200]

D. *The Terrorist Surveillance Program*

In 2002, President Bush signed an order creating the Terrorist Surveillance Program, which authorized the National Security Agency (NSA) to engage in the warrantless surveillance of international phone calls and e-mail messages between persons in the United States and persons abroad, when one of the parties was suspected of being an al-Qaeda member.[201] The program was conducted without a warrant, wholly outside the framework of FISA. A heated national debate was sparked when the *New York Times* broke the story of the NSA spying program. The President staunchly defended the program, claiming that he had inherent constitutional power, by virtue of his position as Commander-in-Chief, to conduct national security surveillance of enemy activity inside the United States without seeking judicial approval.[202] He further claimed that compliance with FISA procedural requirements would impede the government's ability to detect and prevent imminent terrorist attacks.

As a direct result of the debate, Congress amended FISA to allow warrantless surveillance of international communications between persons in the United States and persons overseas, so long as the target of the surveillance is the person overseas.[203] The Department of Justice and the Director of National Intelligence are required to

---

[197]   50 U.S.C. §§ 1801 (a)(4), (b)(2)(C).

[198]   50 U.S.C. §§ 1804 (a)(7), 1805(a)(2).

[199]   50 U.S.C. §§ 1804 (a)(4), (7), 1801(h).

[200]   *See, e.g.*, Stephanie Cooper Blum, *What Really Is at Stake with the FISA Amendments Act of 2008 and Ideas for Future Surveillance Reform*, 18 B. U. PUB. INT. L.J. 269 (2009).

[201]   James Risen & Eric Lichtblau, *Bush Lets U.S. Spy on Callers Without Courts*, N.Y. TIMES, Dec. 16, 2005, at A1.

[202]   *The President's News Conference* (Dec. 19, 2005), 41 Weekly Comp. Pres. Doc. 1885, 1885 (Dec. 26, 2005).

[203]   FISA Amendments Act of 2008, Pub. L. No. 110–261, §403, 122 Stat. 2463, 2473 (2008).

certify to the FISC, in advance of surveillance activity, that a significant purpose of the surveillance is to acquire foreign intelligence information and that the targeting and minimization procedures in place meet the statutory standards.[204] Oversight of the program is provided through frequent audits by inspectors general, and periodic reporting to congressional committees charged with oversight responsibilities.[205]

The warrantless surveillance program does not supersede traditional FISA; the program can be used only when the target of the surveillance resides outside the United States. When the target is a person inside the United States, a FISA surveillance order is necessary.

§ 5.18　Summary and Practical Suggestions

This chapter covered both technologically assisted and non-assisted surveillance. A search warrant is necessary only when the surveillance intrudes on a suspect's reasonable expectation of privacy.

A warrant is not required to perform surveillance of matters in open view. Officers are free to use any of their natural senses in any location where they are lawfully present. They are also allowed to use technological enhancements, such as flashlights, binoculars, telescopes, tracking devices, and aerial and video surveillance to augment their observation of matters in open view.

The Fourth Amendment does not protect "a wrongdoer's misplaced belief that a person to whom he voluntarily confides his wrongdoing will not reveal it." This is known as the *Hoffa* doctrine. The *Hoffa* doctrine justifies clandestine use of recording and transmitting devices, wiretapping, and audio and video surveillance, when this activity is carried by or on in the presence of a cooperating an informant.

The home carries heightened protection. Physical and technologically assisted surveillance must be conducted from a vantage point outside the curtilage unless police have a search warrant. A search warrant is also needed to use sense-enhancing technologies, not in general public use, to monitor activities inside a home that are not visible from the outside.

The Wiretap Act makes it illegal for police to intercept wire, electronic, or oral communications with a device unless a judge issues a wiretap order, there is an emergency, or a party to the intercepted communication consents. Wiretap orders are specialized search warrants that authorize seizure of communications. Because of the extremely intrusive nature of wiretapping and electronic surveillance, their issuance is clothed with restrictions that go well beyond the Fourth Amendment requirements

---

[204]　FISA Amendments Act of 2008 (FAA), Pub. L. No. 110–261, § 702(g)(2).

[205]　The 2008 Amendment is discussed in Paul M. Schwartz, *Warrantless Wiretapping, FISA Reform, and the Lessons of Public Liberty: A Comment on Holmes's Jorde Lecture*, 97 CAL. L. REV. 407 (2009); Stephanie Cooper Blum, *supra* note 214; William C. Bank, *Responses to the Ten Questions*, 35 WM. MITCHELL L. REV. 5007 (2009).

for an ordinary search warrant. The decision to apply for an interception order must be approved by a designated high-ranking prosecutorial official. Orders are available only for the investigation of serious crimes. They may be sought only after normal investigative procedures have been tried and failed or appear unlikely to succeed. In executing the order, efforts must be made to minimize interception of unrelated conversations. The order terminates on the attainment of the authorized objective or 30 days from issuance, whichever comes first, but the court may grant extensions. Restrictions exist on the use and disclosure of information obtained under an interception order. The information may only be used for law enforcement purposes and may be disclosed only to another law enforcement officer when appropriate to the other's duties or when giving testimony in court.

A wiretap order is necessary to intercept a protected communication with a device. An interception occurs when a devise is used to acquire, access to the contents of a protected communication during the transmission stage — before the message reaches its intended destination and held in some kind of storage. Stored communications, such as stored e-mail, voice mail, and text messages, fall outside the Wiretap Act. They are covered by a separate federal statute — the Stored Communications Act — and receive a lower level of protection. The Wiretap Act also does not regulate the use of silent video cameras, tracking devices, or other devices that record information other than communications. However, the Fourth Amendment applies and requires a search warrant when the surveillance is conducted inside private homes, offices, and other locations protected by the Fourth Amendment.

A wiretap order is not required when: (1) a conversation is overheard naturally (*i.e.*, without the aid of a device), (2) the target of the surveillance lacks a reasonable expectation that the conversation will not be intercepted, or (3) the interception is conducted with the consent of a party. Consent can be implied as well as expressed. Implied consent arises when a person uses a telephone with notice that calls made on that phone are monitored.

FISA establishes a special statutory procedure governing electronic surveillance conducted inside the United States to gather foreign intelligence. Surveillance orders require probable cause to believe that the target of the surveillance is a foreign power, agent of a foreign power, or a member of an international terrorist. An order is not required to conduct electronic surveillance of international communications between persons inside the United States and persons overseas when the target of the surveillance is the person overseas.

Interrogations and Confessions

6

No person shall be . . . compelled in any criminal case to be a witness against himself . . .

Fifth Amendment

Chapter Outline

KEY TERMS AND CONCEPTS

Arraignment

Arrest

Corpus delicti

Custodial interrogation

Custody

Derivative evidence

Formal charges

Grand jury

Indictment

Information

Interrogation

Investigative questioning

Investigatory stop

Seizure

§ 6.1   Introduction

The law of **interrogations** and confessions is not set out in any single article or amendment to the Constitution. The restrictions come from five constitutional provisions, combined with federal and state statutes requiring prompt **arraignment** of suspects in **custody**. The five constitutional provisions that bear on the admissibility of confessions are the Fourth Amendment exclusionary rule, the Fifth Amendment privilege against self-incrimination, the Sixth Amendment right to counsel, and the Fifth and Fourteenth Amendment due process clauses.

Constitutional restrictions on the admission of confessions are designed to ensure that confessions are voluntary and trustworthy. Coerced statements are considered unreliable. However, even if this were not so, restrictions on admission serve to discourage police officers from engaging in practices that our society does not tolerate.

A.   *Five Requirements for Admissibility*

Admission of a confession may be challenged on at least five different grounds. The first stems from the Fifth and Fourteenth Amendment due process clauses. It is a violation of due process to admit an involuntary confession into evidence.[1] Coerced confessions are considered unreliable because even an innocent person may confess when the pressures become unbearable.

The second requirement stems from the Fourth Amendment exclusionary rule, which was covered in Chapter 4. The Fourth Amendment exclusionary rule applies to confessions as well as to physical evidence. Police are aware that people tend to confess when the "cat is out of the bag." To reduce the temptation to force the cat out of the

---

[1]   *See* § 6.2 *infra.*

Figure 6.1
Legal Hurdles That Confessions Must Pass in Order to be Admissible as Evidence

> Confessions that fail to satisfy any of the following requirements are inadmissible as evidence of guilt.
>
> 1.   The due process free and voluntary rule,
> 2.   The Fourth Amendment exclusionary rule,
> 3.   The Fifth Amendment privilege against self-incrimination, and
> 4.   The Sixth Amendment right to counsel.
>
> Confessions may also be suppressed for violating federal and state delay-in-arraignment statutes.

bag illegally, the Fourth Amendment requires suppression of confessions that are causally related to an illegal *Terry* stop, **arrest**, or **seizure** of property, even if the confession was voluntary and its reliability is not in question.[2]

The third requirement, known as the *McNabb-Mallory* delay-in-arraignment rule,[3] is based on federal and state statutes that require suspects to be taken before a magistrate for arraignment "without undue delay" after the arrest. The period between arrest and arraignment is inherently coercive because the suspect is generally held incommunicado, without counsel or access to the outside world. Concerns for the voluntariness of confessions given during this period prompted the Supreme Court to adopt the *McNabb-Mallory* rule, which requires suppression of confessions given during the interval between a suspect's arrest and arraignment if police officers are guilty of unnecessary delay in taking the arrestee before a magistrate.

The fourth requirement, known as the *Miranda* rule,[4] is grounded in the Fifth Amendment privilege against self-incrimination.[5] This requirement applies to confessions elicited during police **custodial interrogations**. Confessions given by suspects while in police custody will be suppressed unless the prosecution proves that the suspect was warned of his or her *Miranda* rights and voluntarily waived them before making the statement.

The fifth requirement stems from the Sixth Amendment right to counsel.[6] The Sixth Amendment right to counsel attaches upon initiation of prosecution. During all subsequent investigative contacts pertaining to the charges, police must obtain a valid waiver of the right to counsel or see to it that counsel is present, whether the defendant is in custody or at large.

Confessions provide powerful evidence of guilt and are often necessary for a conviction. However, they are easily contaminated. Violation of the rules discussed in this chapter will result in suppression. Consequently, police officers must be thoroughly

---

[2]   *See* § 6.3 *infra.*
[3]   *See* § 6.5 *infra.*
[4]   **Miranda v. Arizona, 384 U.S. 436, 86 S. Ct. 1602, 16 L. Ed. 2d 694 (1966).**
[5]   *See* §§ 6.6–6.8 *infra.*
[6]   *See* § 6.9 *infra.*

versed in the law of interrogations and confessions. Although restrictions on police interrogations are designed to protect the accused, compliance serves the interests of society by producing confessions that can be used as evidence.

B. *Legally Relevant Phases in the Development of a Criminal Case*

Police questioning may take place at different stages in the development of a criminal case, with the tone varying from inquisitive to accusatory. The legal requirements that police officers must observe are not the same across the entire spectrum of questioning situations. Although confessions must pass five legal hurdles in order to be admissible, all five do not materialize the instant a police officer asks a question. The requirements in effect during police questioning vary with the stage when questions are asked and the tone of the questioning. In developing an overview of the law of interrogations and confessions, it is useful to break down the development of criminal cases into three phases and focus on the legal requirements that police officers must observe during each stage. This will lead to a clearer understanding of what police officers are required to do, and when they are required to do it, in order to preserve the admissibility of confessions. The time line at the top of Figure 6.2 identifies three legally relevant phases in the development of a criminal case.

Figure 6.2

Time Line in the Development of a Criminal Case Showing the Periods During Which Each of the Five Hurdles Operates

Time line	Phase I: Noncustodial Investigative Questioning of Suspects Who Are Not in Custody		Phase II: Interrogation of Suspects Who Are in Custody	Phase III: Interrogation of Defendants After Formal Charges Have Been Filed
	Consensual encounter	Investigatory detentions and traffic stops		
Due process free and voluntary rule				
Fourth Amendment exclusionary rule				
McNabb-Mallory rule				
Miranda rule				
Sixth Amendment right to counsel				

The first phase (noncustodial **investigative questioning**) spans the period between the unfolding of a hunch and the time when a suspect is placed under formal arrest or taken into custody. The tone of questioning is inquisitive during the first phase, but becomes accusatory once the case enters the second phase. The second phase (**custodial interrogation**) begins when the suspect is placed under formal arrest or is taken into custody and continues until formal charges have been made. Once formal charges are filed, the case enters the third phase, which continues until the trial. The five legal requirements discussed in this chapter are shown along the left-hand margin of Figure 6.2. The shaded areas show the periods during which each of them is in effect.

The typical criminal case begins when an officer develops a hunch that a person has committed, is committing, or is about to commit a crime, and decides to investigate further. The officer approaches the suspect, introduces him or herself, and asks whether the suspect would be willing to answer some questions. As long as a reasonable person in the suspect's position would feel free to decline the interview, terminate the encounter, and go about his or her business, the investigative encounter is consensual, and none of the five requirements applies. In Chapter 3, we used the phrase "free zone" to describe police activity that is not regulated by the Constitution.[7] The "free zone" concept applies here as well. Incriminating statements elicited during consensual investigative encounters will always be admissible.

However, investigative encounters are not always consensual. This is true of investigatory detentions and traffic stops. Although the suspect has not yet been arrested or taken into custody, investigatory detentions and traffic stops are not consensual because the suspect has been seized. Statements made during these encounters are capable of being contaminated because two of the five legal requirements — the due process free and voluntary rule and the Fourth Amendment exclusionary rule — are in effect.

The second phase, the *custodial interrogation phase*, begins when police officers place a suspect under formal arrest or take a suspect into custody. Once the investigation enters this phase, the tone of the questioning changes. The questioning is no longer inquisitive; it becomes accusatory. The mere fact of being in police custody puts pressure, both internal and external, on a suspect. As a result, restrictions on police questioning tighten and, as Figure 6.2 shows, four of the five requirements are now in effect.

At some point after the arrest, formal charges will be filed. When this happens, the suspect officially becomes an accused and the Sixth Amendment right to counsel attaches. The case now enters the third phase — the *prosecutorial* stage — and protection for the defendant's right to counsel broadens.

---

[7]   For the characteristics of a voluntary investigative encounter, *see* Chapter 3, §§ 3.3–3.5.

§ 6.2   The Free and Voluntary Rule

At early common law, confessions were admissible as evidence of guilt even when they were tortured from suspects. As time passed, judges came to appreciate that coerced confessions are not reliable. Everyone has a breaking point. When exposed to extreme pressure, even an innocent person may confess. This insight led to the adoption, both in England and the United States, of the rule that confessions must be voluntary in order to be admissible as evidence of guilt. This requirement is incorporated into the Fifth and Fourteenth Amendment due process clauses. Suppression of coerced confessions serves three main purposes. It (1) protects against convictions based on unreliable evidence, (2) preserves a suspect's freedom of choice, and (3) deters police from engaging in interrogation practices our society does not tolerate.

Figure 6.3
Due Process Free and Voluntary Requirement

> Confessions are not voluntary and will be suppressed when: (1) coercive pressures exerted by the government (2) induce the making of a statement the suspect would not otherwise have made.

A. *The Two-Part Test of "Voluntariness"*

A confession is involuntary under the due process clause if it results from coercive pressures exerted by the government that overcome the suspect's free will and induce the making of a statement the suspect would not otherwise have made.[8] The due process test of voluntariness has two components — the first is concerned with the source of the pressure and the second with its impact on the suspect.

The confession must derive from improper government activity to be involuntary in the constitutional sense. Internal pressures and external ones exerted without government complicity do not render a confession involuntary in the constitutional sense. Suppose that Sticky-Fingered Sam suffers a head injury in an auto accident that temporarily incapacitates the "lying" center of his brain. For a few (poorly timed) moments, Sam is unable to speak anything but the truth. When the police reach the accident scene, Sam confesses to all of his past crimes. Although Sam's confession was not a product of his free will, his confession satisfies the due process test of voluntariness because the police did nothing improper to induce the confession.

The Supreme Court used this reasoning in a case in which a chronic schizophrenic suffering from auditory hallucinations walked into a police station and confessed to murdering a young girl.[9] The Supreme Court refused to suppress the confession,

---

[8]   Nix v. Williams, 467 U.S. 431, 104 S. Ct. 2501, 81 L. Ed. 2d 377 (1984); *Colorado v. Connelly*, 479 U.S. 157, 107 S. Ct. 515, 93 L. Ed. 2d 473 (1986).

[9]   Colorado v. Connelly, *supra* note 8.

despite psychiatric testimony that the deranged man believed that God's voice had ordered him to confess, because the confession was obtained without improper activity by the police. Improper police activity is necessary for a confession to be involuntary in a due process sense.

B. *Factors Considered in Determining Voluntariness*

Physical force and violence are so obviously coercive that confessions extracted through their use are involuntary as a matter of law.[10] When the pressures to confess are less extreme, voluntariness is determined by examining the circumstances surrounding the making of the confession, with emphasis on three factors: (1) the pressures exerted by the police, (2) the suspect's degree of susceptibility, and (3) the conditions under which the interrogation took place.[11]

Figure 6.4
Factors Relevant to Voluntariness

Physical brutality and threats of violence render a confession involuntary as a matter of law. When the pressures are less extreme, voluntariness is determined by examining the totality of circumstances surrounding the confession, with emphasis on three factors:

1. the pressures exerted by the police;
2. the suspect's degree of susceptibility; and
3. the conditions under which the interrogation took place.

Pressures exerted by the police. Courts first examine the methods used by the police to elicit the confession. Force and brutality render confessions involuntary as a matter of law. While "beating" confessions out of suspects is rare in modern times, it is unfortunately not rare enough. The following is an unnerving account of testimony given by a defendant in an Illinois case concerning the circumstances surrounding his confession.[12]

---

[10]   Beecher v. Alabama, 389 U.S. 35, 88 S. Ct. 189, 19 L. Ed. 2d 35 (1967) (statement obtained after police held a gun to suspect's head and threatened to kill him if he did not tell the truth); Brown v. Mississippi, 297 U.S. 278, 56 S. Ct. 461, 80 L. Ed. 682 (1936) (statement obtained after police whipped suspect).

[11]   **Arizona v. Fulminante, 499 U.S. 279, 111 S. Ct. 1246, 113 L. Ed. 2d 302 (1991)**; Schneckloth v. Bustamonte, 412 U.S. 218, 93 S. Ct. 2041, 36 L. Ed. 2d 854 (1973).

[12]   People v. Banks, 549 N.E.2d 766 (Ill. 1989). Cases like People v. Banks are not unique. On January 11, 2003, two days before leaving office, Illinois governor George Ryan pardoned four inmates on death row who were convicted based on confessions tortured from them using tactics similar to those used in the *Banks* case. *See* James Webb, *Illinois Governor Pardons Four Inmates Condemned to Death*, COURIER JOURNAL A7 (Jan. 11, 2003). On the following day, Governor Ryan commuted all 167 remaining Illinois death sentences to prison terms, stating: "The facts that I have seen in reviewing each and every one of these cases raised questions not only about the innocence of people on death row, but about the fairness of the death penalty as a whole." Jodi Wilgoren, *Illinois Governor Cleans Out Death Row*, COURIER JOURNAL A1 (Jan. 12, 2003).

The defendant testified that, following his arrest, he was taken to an interrogation room where he was interrogated for six hours with his wrists handcuffed behind his back. When he persisted in denying knowledge of the crime, one of the detectives put a chrome .45 caliber automatic gun in his mouth and told him that he would blow off his head because he knew that the defendant was lying. The defendant further testified that the detective struck him in the stomach with a flashlight three or four times and, when he fell out of the chair, stomped on him and hit him with the flashlight. When he continued denying knowledge of the crime, the detective put a plastic bag over his head while another officer kicked him. Thereafter, three officers took him to another room and again placed a plastic bag over his head, this time for about two minutes. At this point, the defendant confessed.

The officers denied these incidents, but their testimony was not convincing. A physician who examined the defendant found lacerations on both wrists, multiple scrapes and scratches on his chest and abdomen, bruises on both legs and upper thighs, swollen muscles, and a lump under the skin in his lower rib cage. Confessions procured through tactics like these are involuntary as a matter of law.

Threats and false promises also raise constitutional concerns.[13] Police may not threaten to arrest innocent family members or take the suspect's children away to induce a confession.[14] Nor may they promise immunity from prosecution, a lighter sentence, or another form of leniency.[15] However, it is not improper to tell suspects that the prosecutor will be informed of their cooperation,[16] or to refer to the jail time or

---

[13]   *See, e.g.*, Payne v. Arkansas, 356 U.S. 560, 78 S. Ct. 844, 2 L. Ed. 2d 975 (1958) (invalidating confession obtained after police threatened to turn the suspect over to an angry lynch mob); Rogers v. Richmond, 365 U.S. 534, 81 S. Ct. 735, 5 L. Ed. 2d 760 (1961) (invalidating confession made in response to bogus threat to arrest suspect's ailing wife); Lynum v. Illinois, 372 U.S. 528, 83 S. Ct. 917, 9 L. Ed. 2d 922 (1963) (invalidating confession made in response to bogus threat to take away suspect's children); Spano v. New York, 360 U.S. 315, 79 S. Ct. 1202, 3 L. Ed. 2d 1265 (1959) (invalidating confession where officer lied to childhood friend that he would lose his job and this would create a family hardship if suspect did not cooperate); Hopkins v. Cockrell, 325 F.3d 579 (5th Cir. 2003) (holding confession involuntary where the police detective conducting an interview with the defendant assured the defendant that "their conversation was confidential, telling [the defendant], 'This is for me and you. This is for me. Okay. This ain't for nobody else.'" The court stated that "[a]n officer cannot read the defendant his *Miranda* warnings and then turn around and tell him that despite those warnings, what the defendant tells the officer will be confidential and still use the resultant confession against the defendant"; Spence v. State, 281 Ga. 697, 642 S.E.2d 856 (2007) (same).

[14]   Rogers v. Richmond, *supra* note 13.

[15]   *See, e.g.*, United States v. LeBrun, 306 F.3d 545 (8th Cir. 2002); State v. Sturgill, 469 S.E.2d 557 (N.C. Ct. App. 1996); State v. Rush, 174 Md. App. 259, 921 A.2d 334 (2007) (holding that confessions are involuntary as a matter of law when they are induced by false promises that the suspect will be given special consideration from a prosecuting authority or some other form of assistance in exchange for his confession). However, vague assurances that cooperation is in the suspect's best interest are not considered improper. *See, e.g.*, United States v. Ruggles, 70 F.2d 262 (2d Cir. 1995); United States v. Nash, 910 F.2d 749 (11th Cir. 1990); Collins v. State, 509 N.E.2d 827 (Ind. 1987).

[16]   United States v. Westbrook, 125 F.3d 996 (7th Cir. 1997).

maximum penalty they face.[17] Police officers are allowed to make truthful representations about the suspect's legal predicament.

Interrogation strategies designed to convince the suspect that the case against him is stronger than it really is, on the other hand, seldom render a confession involuntary because they are unlikely to cause an innocent person to confess.[18]

If the court determines that the police used improper interrogation tactics, it will next consider whether the suspect's will was overborne. The suspect's degree of susceptibility is the central focus of this inquiry.

Suspect's degree of susceptibility. People vary in the degree and types of pressure they can withstand. The suspect's background, education, intellect, prior experience with the criminal justice system, physical and mental condition, ability to cope with stress, and other traits will be examined to decide whether the suspect's free will was overcome by the pressures that were placed on him or her.[19]

Conditions under which the interrogation took place. Because a suspect's capacity to resist pressures can be worn down by the length, intensity, and frequency of the interrogation sessions; food and sleep deprivation; the intimidating presence of large numbers of police officers; and other circumstances, these factors will be examined as well.[20]

---

[17] United States v. Braxton, 112 F.3d 777 (4th Cir. 1997) (telling a suspect "if you don't come clean, you can get five years" is not improperly coercive).

[18] For cases holding that police trickery does not render a confession involuntary, *see* Frazier v. Cupp, 394 U.S. 731, 89 S. Ct. 1420, 22 L. Ed. 2d 684 (1969) (misrepresentation that a suspect's associate had confessed to the crime and implicated him); United States v. Rodgers, 186 F. Supp. 2d 971 (E.D. Wis. 2002) (misrepresentation that defendant's fingerprints had been found on the firearm); Sovalik v. State, 612 P.2d 1003 (Alaska 1980) (misrepresentation that defendant's fingerprints were found at the crime scene); Ledbetter v. Edwards, 35 F.3d 1062 (6th Cir. 1994) (misrepresentation that the victim and two witnesses had identified suspect); State v. Pitts, 936 So. 2d 1111 (Fla. App. 2006) (appeal to suspect for assistance in finding the victim's body so that the family can arrange a decent burial); State v. Woods, 280 Ga. 758, 632 S.E.2d 654 (2006) (same); People v. Dishaw, 30 A.D.3d 689, 816 N.Y.S.2d 235 (2006) (telling defendant that her actions were caught on video surveillance, and placing fake videotape on table in front of defendant); 2 Wayne R. LaFave, Jerold H. Israel, & Nancy J. King, Criminal Procedure (2d Ed. 1999) § 6.2(C), p. 456 ("as a general matter it may be said that the courts have not deemed [police trickery and deception] sufficient by itself to make a confession involuntary"). However, trickery and deception may not be used to tease out a confession after the suspect has invoked his/her *Miranda* rights. See § 6.7(B)(2) *infra*.

[19] *See, e.g.,* **Arizona v. Fulminante**, *supra* note 11 (below-average intelligence, fourth-grade education, poor coping skills).

[20] Mincey v. Arizona, 437 U.S. 385, 98 S. Ct. 2408, 57 L. Ed. 2d 290 (1978) (statement obtained from suspect under sedation in intensive care unit); Greenwald v. Wisconsin, 390 U.S. 519, 88 S. Ct. 1152, 20 L. Ed. 2d 77 (1968) (statement obtained from suspect interrogated nonstop for more than 18 hours without food or sleep); Reck v. Pate, 367 U.S. 433, 81 S. Ct. 1541, 6 L. Ed. 2d 948 (1961) (statement obtained after depriving suspect of adequate food, sleep, and contact with family); Malinski v. New York, 324 U.S. 401, 65 S. Ct. 781, 89 L. Ed. 1029 (1945) (statement obtained after forcing suspect to remain naked).

C. Procedures for Determining the Voluntariness of a Confession

The question of whether a confession is voluntary is one that the judge must decide before admitting the confession. The judge may not admit the confession and leave it up to the jury to decide whether the confession was voluntary, with instructions to disregard the confession if they find it involuntary.[21] It is unrealistic to expect lay jurors to disregard a confession once they have heard it. Consequently, when the voluntariness of a confession is challenged, the judge must hold a hearing outside the presence of the jury and take testimony about the circumstances surrounding the making of the confession.[22]

The burden of proof at the voluntariness hearing is on the government. To secure admission, the government must prove that the defendant confessed of his own free will. In *Lego v. Twomey*,[23] the defendant argued, without success, that the government should be required to prove this fact "beyond a reasonable doubt." The Court disagreed, holding that, while the government must establish guilt beyond a reasonable doubt, the Constitution does not require this degree of certainty to secure the admission of a confession. The Court adopted a "preponderance of the evidence" standard; the government must establish that it is more probable than not that the defendant confessed of his or her own free will. If the evidence at the suppression hearing is equally weighted, the confession will be suppressed because the government has not shouldered its burden of proof.

Summarizing, involuntary confessions — confessions that are a product of police misconduct that overbears a suspect's free will — are inadmissible. Voluntariness is determined by examining the methods police used to elicit the confession, the suspect's degree of susceptibility, and the conditions under which the interrogation took place. The government bears the burden of proving by a preponderance of the evidence (*i.e.*, that it is more probable than not) that the defendant confessed of his or her own free will.

§ 6.3 The Fourth Amendment Exclusionary Rule

The second ground for challenging a confession stems from the Fourth Amendment exclusionary rule. The Fourth Amendment exclusionary rule applies to confessions as well as to physical evidence. If the police conduct an illegal search, find drugs, and the suspect confesses when confronted with the evidence, the confession will be suppressed even if it was otherwise voluntary. The same holds true for confessions caused by unconstitutional arrests and stops. Moreover, when a confession is

---

[21] Jackson v. Denno, 378 U.S. 368, 84 S. Ct. 1774, 12 L. Ed. 2d 908 (1964).
[22] This position is codified in 18 U.S.C.A. § 3501(a).
[23] 404 U.S. 477, 489, 92 S. Ct. 619, 626, 30 L. Ed. 2d 618 (1972).

contaminated by violation of the Fourth Amendment, the taint normally destroys the admissibility of **derivative evidence** discovered as a result of the confession.

This branch of the Fourth Amendment exclusionary rule is known as the "fruit of the poisonous tree" doctrine. The fruit of the poisonous tree doctrine derives from the case of *Wong Sun v. United States*.[24] The facts of *Wong Sun* are convoluted, but every fact matters. Narcotics agents barged into Blackie Toy's apartment and arrested him, without probable cause or a warrant. Toy confessed at the scene and implicated another man named Johnny Yee. The agents immediately went to Yee's home and arrested him. They found heroin in Yee's possession, which he said he got from Toy and Wong Sun. The agents next arrested Wong Sun. Wong Sun was released on his own recognizance and several days later voluntarily returned to the police station and confessed. The Supreme Court dealt with each confession separately. Concerning Blackie Toy, the Supreme Court ruled that Toy's confession given at the scene of his arrest and the heroin found in Johnny Yee's possession, which was discovered as a result of his confession, were the fruits of Toy's unconstitutional arrest and could not be used as evidence against him.

Figure 6.5
Fourth Amendment Exclusionary Rule

> The Fourth Amendment exclusionary rule requires suppression of confessions that are: (1) causally connected (2) to a violation of the suspect's Fourth Amendment rights (*i.e.*, illegal *Terry* stop, arrest, or search). Further, when a confession is tainted beyond use, derivative evidence that would not have been discovered without the confession will also be suppressed.

The Court, nevertheless, declined to hold that the violation of a defendant's Fourth Amendment rights renders the defendant permanently incapable of making an admissible confession. Admissibility turns on whether the illegal conduct of police caused the defendant to confess or whether his confession was the result of an independent act of free will. Courts consider the following three factors in deciding this: (1) the length of time between the violation and the confession, (2) the presence of intervening circumstances, and (3) purpose and flagrancy of the violation.[25]

Length of time. The length of time between the Fourth Amendment violation and the confession is the first consideration. When the confession occurs at the scene of the violation, there is no break in the causal chain and suppression is required.[26] Blackie

---

[24]   371 U.S. 471, 83 S. Ct. 407, 9 L. Ed. 2d 441 (1963).

[25]   **Kaupp v. Texas**, 538 U.S. 626, 123 S. Ct. 1843, 155 L. Ed. 2d 814 (2003); New York v. Harris, 495 U.S. 14, 110 S. Ct. 1640, 109 L. Ed. 2d 13 (1990); Taylor v. Alabama, 457 U.S. 687, 102 S. Ct. 2664, 73 L. Ed. 2d 314 (1982); Dunaway v. New York, 442 U.S. 200, 99 S. Ct. 2248, 60 L. Ed. 2d 824 (1979); Brown v. Illinois, 422 U.S. 590, 95 S. Ct. 2254, 45 L. Ed. 2d 416 (1975).

[26]   Wong Sun v. United States, *supra* note 24, 371 U.S. at 484–488, 83 S. Ct. at 416.

Toy's confession, which occurred when the police barged into his home, was suppressed for this reason. When the confession occurs hours or days later, the remaining two factors will be examined.[27]

Presence of intervening circumstances. The passage of time alone is not enough to break the causal chain. There must be intervening circumstances that show that the suspect's decision to confess was an independent act of free will, and not a panicked reaction to an illegal arrest or search. Speaking with family members, consulting with an attorney, and voluntarily returning to the police station after being released are the three circumstances most often relied on to establish this.[28] The presence of intervening circumstances was the reason for the Supreme Court's decision to admit Wong Sun's confession. The fact that he voluntarily returned to the police station to confess several days after he was released convinced the Court that his decision to confess was an independent act of free will. Providing *Miranda* warnings, in contrast, is not enough to break the causal chain.[29] The Supreme Court has entertained several cases in which illegally arrested suspects confessed at the police station after receiving *Miranda* warnings.[30] In only one case[31] was the confession admitted, and it was admitted for an entirely different reason.

Purpose and flagrancy of the violation. The purpose and flagrancy of the violation is the last consideration. This factor is tied to the policy behind the exclusionary rule, which is to deter unconstitutional conduct by taking away the incentive.[32] Suppression, accordingly, is not required when police do not profit from their wrong. The Court relied on this factor in a case[33] where the suspect confessed at the police station after being arrested inside his home, without a warrant, in violation of the *Payton* rule.[34] The Court ruled that the confession was admissible because the *Payton* rule violation did not enable police to obtain a confession they could not have obtained lawfully. Since police had probable cause for arrest, they could have waited until the suspect left his home and arrested him lawfully outside.

However, this is not the case when an arrest is made without probable cause. When a suspect confesses after being arrested without probable cause, the violation enables the police to obtain a confession they could not have obtained by lawful means, and permitting them to keep it will encourage future violations. As a result, suppression

---

[27]   *See* cases *supra* note 25.

[28]   Wong Sun v. United States, *supra* note 24; United States v. Patino, 862 F.2d 128 (7th Cir. 1988).

[29]   *See* authorities, *supra* note 25; State v. Ford, 30 S.W.3d 378 (Tenn. Crim. App. 2000).

[30]   *See* authorities *supra* note 25.

[31]   New York v. Harris, *supra* note 25.

[32]   *See, e.g.*, United States v. Leon, 468 U.S. 897, 906, 104 S. Ct. 3405, 3411, 82 L. Ed. 2d 677 (1984).

[33]   New York v. Harris, *supra* note 25 ("[W]here the police have probable cause to arrest a suspect, the exclusionary rule does not bar the State's use of a statement made by the defendant outside of his home, even though the statement is taken after an arrest made in the home in violation of *Payton*.").

[34]   The rule of **Payton v. New York**, 445 U.S. 573, 100 S. Ct. 1371, 63 L. Ed. 2d 639 (1980) requires an arrest warrant to make an arrest inside a home. This rule was discussed in § 3.15.

is required unless there are intervening circumstances, such as in *Wong Sun*, which break the causal chain.[35]

The three factors used to determine causation — length of time between the violation and the confession, the presence of intervening circumstances, and the purpose and flagrancy of the police misconduct — admittedly do not yield a high degree of predictability. However, the lack of predictability will not prevent police from properly discharging their duties, because causation analysis takes place after the Fourth Amendment violation has occurred. Police officers do not need to know in advance how long the effects of their Fourth Amendment violation will linger in order to properly discharge the responsibilities of their job.

§ 6.4   Overview of the Rules Governing Custodial Interrogation

At this point, two grounds for suppression have been discussed. First, confessions are inadmissible unless they are a product of the suspect's own free will. Second, they are inadmissible if a police violation of the suspect's Fourth Amendment rights caused the suspect to confess. Notice in Figure 6.2 that both grounds carry over and continue to provide the basis for challenging confessions made during the second and third phases of a criminal case. Notice further that confessions made during the second phase are vulnerable to challenge on two additional grounds: the *McNabb-Mallory* rule and the *Miranda* rule.

These requirements were developed to counterbalance the pressures that arise from the fact of being in police custody. Once a suspect is arrested or taken into custody, the tone of the questioning changes. The questions are no longer inquisitive; they are now accusatory. Moreover, once in custody, suspects find themselves in strange surroundings, often behind closed doors, and experience interrogation methods that may be new to them, but with which their interrogators have considerable expertise and experience. Most important, the suspect is alone, without an advocate or even an impartial witness.

As a result, the atmosphere is inherently coercive, even when police interrogation methods are not. Consequently, there are fewer guarantees that confessions elicited during police custodial interrogations will be a product of the suspect's free will and voluntary choice. To counteract this danger, the Supreme Court has imposed two additional safeguards that become effective once the suspect is arrested or taken into custody — the *McNabb-Mallory* rule and the *Miranda* requirement.

The *McNabb-Mallory* rule seeks to alleviate the pressured atmosphere of a police custodial interrogation by requiring the police to present the arrested person to a magistrate promptly after the arrest. Presentment to a magistrate reassures the suspect that

---

[35]   **Kaupp v. Texas**, *supra* note 25; Taylor v. Alabama, *supra* note 25; Dunaway v. New York, *supra* note 25; Brown v. Illinois, *supra* note 25.

the outside world is aware that she is in police custody and that the police are accountable to the courts. This procedure also reinforces protection for an arrested person's constitutional rights. The magistrate will inform the suspect of her constitutional rights and confirm that she understands them and knows that she is free to exercise them. The *McNabb-Mallory* rule enforces compliance with this requirement by suppressing confessions obtained during a period of unnecessary delay in presenting the arrested person to a magistrate.

This is also the point at which that the *Miranda* rule goes into effect. The *Miranda* rule requires the police to issue a detailed set of warnings — "you have the right to remain silent, anything you say can and will be used against you, you have a right to an attorney, and one will be appointed for you if you cannot afford one" — before initiating a custodial interrogation and to cease the interrogation if the suspect at any time thereafter expresses a desire to exercise her rights. Failure to give the required warnings or to cease interrogation if the suspect invokes her rights will result in the suppression of any resulting confession.

§ 6.5   The *McNabb-Mallory* Delay in Arraignment Rule

Rule 5(a) of the Federal Rules of Criminal Procedure and the procedural rules of most, if not all, states, require officers to take persons under arrest "forthwith" or "without unnecessary delay" before the nearest available magistrate or other committing officer for an arraignment. The purpose of this requirement is to ensure that prisoners are given timely notice of their rights and are not subjected to lengthy secret interrogations. This requirement was routinely ignored in the period before the *McNabb-Mallory* rule because statutes requiring a prompt arraignment imposed no penalties for their violation.

A. *Statement and Discussion of the McNabb-Mallory Rule*

The Supreme Court took steps to correct this problem in *McNabb v. United States*[36] by announcing that confessions obtained in violation of Rule 5(a) of the Federal Rules of Criminal Procedure (the federal prompt arraignment statute) would henceforth be inadmissible in federal criminal prosecutions, even if they were voluntary.

The Court reaffirmed this position in *Mallory v. United States*.[37] Mallory, a rape suspect, was arrested between 2:00 and 2:30 P.M. the day after the rape and taken to police headquarters, where he was questioned for about 30 minutes before agreeing to submit to a polygraph test. The polygraph operator was not located until later that evening. Mallory was detained at police headquarters for four hours while the police waited for the polygraph operator to arrive, even though several magistrates were

---

[36]   318 U.S. 332, 63 S. Ct. 608, 87 L. Ed. 819 (1943), *reh'g denied*, 319 U.S. 784, 63 S. Ct. 1322, 87 L. Ed. 1727 (1943).

[37]   354 U.S. 449, 77 S. Ct. 1356, 1 L. Ed. 2d 1479 (1957).

available in the immediate vicinity. The polygraph questioning began at around 8:00 P.M. Approximately 90 minutes into the interview, Mallory stated that he "might" have done it. At this point, the police made their first attempt to reach a United States Commissioner, but when they were unsuccessful, asked Mallory to repeat his confession, which he agreed to do. Between 11:30 P.M. and 12:30 A.M., Mallory dictated his confession to a typist. Mallory was not brought before a United States Commissioner until the next morning. Notwithstanding the delay in taking him before a magistrate, his confession was admitted into evidence, he was found guilty, and sentenced to death. The Supreme Court reversed his conviction, stating:

> We cannot sanction this extended delay, resulting in a confession, without subordinating the general rule of prompt arraignment to the discretion of arresting officers. In every case where the police resort to interrogation of an arrested person and secure a confession, they may well claim, and quite sincerely, that they were merely trying to check the information given by him . . . . It is not the function of the police to arrest, as it were, at large and to use an interrogation process at police headquarters in order to determine whom they should charge . . . .

B. Determining Whether a Delay in Arraignment Is "Unnecessary"

The *McNabb-Mallory* rule does not impose a fixed time period within which arrested persons must be taken before a magistrate. The question turns on whether the confession was obtained during a period of "*unnecessary* delay." Each case is evaluated on its own facts. Delays due to causes beyond the government's control, such as lack of an available magistrate,[38] the distance that needs to be traveled,[39] transportation problems,[40] mechanical breakdowns, and hazardous weather conditions are disregarded in applying the *McNabb-Mallory* rule because they are unavoidable. The same holds true for delays needed to complete booking,[41] sober prisoners up,[42] or obtain needed medical treatment.[43]

The purpose of the *McNabb-Mallory* rule is to prevent prolonged questioning of suspects before bringing them into the open. When an arrest is made during normal business hours, a judicial officer is readily available, and police have no excuse for not taking the suspect before a magistrate other than a desire to question him, the delay is unnecessary and statements taken during the delay are generally inadmissible.[44]

---

[38]   United States v. Gorel, 622 F.2d 100 (5th Cir. 1979).
[39]   United States v. McCormick, 468 F.2d 68 (10th Cir. 1972).
[40]   United States v. Odom, 526 F.2d 339 (5th Cir. 1976).
[41]   United States v. Rubio, 709 F.2d 146 (2d Cir. 1983); United States v. Johnson, 467 F.2d 630 (2d Cir. 1972).
[42]   United States v. Christopher, 956 F.2d 536 (6th Cir. 1991), *cert. denied*, 505 U.S. 1207, 112 S. Ct. 2999, 120 L. Ed. 2d 875 (1992); United States v. Bear Killer, 534 F.2d 1253 (8th Cir. 1976).
[43]   United States v. Isom, 588 F.2d 858 (2d Cir. 1978).
[44]   McNabb v. United States, *supra* note 36; Mallory v. United States, *supra* note 37.

Figure 6.6
McNabb-Mallory Rule

> The *McNabb-Mallory* or "delay in arraignment" rule requires suppression of confessions obtained during a period of unnecessary delay in presenting the suspect to a magistrate for arraignment.

C. Current Status of the McNabb-Mallory Rule in Federal Courts

In 1968, Congress passed § 3501 of the Omnibus Crime Control and Safe Streets Act.[45] The avowed purpose was to abrogate the *Miranda* rule. While Congress was unsuccessful,[46] the statute had the unintentional effect of calling the continued existence of the *McNabb-Mallory* rule into question. Subsection (a) provided that confessions "shall be admissible in evidence if voluntarily given." Subsection (b) listed several factors to be considered in deciding whether a confession was voluntary. Unnecessary delay in presentment was one of them. Subsection (c) provided that confessions should "not be inadmissible solely because of delay in bringing" an arrested person before a magistrate judge "if such confession was made or given by such person within six hours immediately following his arrest."

The intended effect of § 3501 on the *McNabb-Mallory* rule was unclear. There were two plausible readings. The first was that subsection (a) abolished the *McNabb-Mallory* rule by making voluntariness the sole test for the admissibility of confessions in federal court. Subsection (b) permitted courts to consider unnecessary delay in presentment as a factor bearing on voluntariness, but not as independent grounds for suppressing confessions found to be voluntary. Subsection (c) barred courts from suppressing confessions given within the first six hours after the suspect's arrest as involuntary solely because of delay in bringing the arrested person to a magistrate.[47] The second interpretation was that subsection (c) is the only part of § 3501 that applies to the *McNabb-Mallory*. This subsection modified the rule by excluding the first six hours after an arrest from its operation, but otherwise left the rule intact.

The Supreme Court held that the second interpretation was accepted in *Corley v. United States*.[48] The Supreme Court held that subsection (c) insulates confessions given during the first six hours after an arrest on federal charges from suppression based on unnecessary delay in arraignment. However, once the six-hour safe harbor period expires, the rule springs back into full force and effect. Confessions given

---

[45]   **18 U.S.C. § 3501.** This statute is reproduced in Part II.

[46]   Dickerson v. United States, 530 U.S. 28, 120 S. Ct. 2326, 147 L. Ed. 2d 405 (2000) (holding that the *Miranda* decision is based on the Constitution and cannot be abrogated by statute).

[47]   United States v. Christopher, *supra* note 42 (interpreting § 3501 as abrogating the *McNabb-Mallory* rule); Glover v. United States, 104 F.3d 1570 (10th Cir. 1997) (same).

[48]   556 U.S. 303, 129 S. Ct. 1558, 173 L. Ed. 2d. 443 (2009).

outside the six-hour period will be suppressed if they were obtained during a period of unnecessary delay in presenting the suspect to a magistrate, even if they are voluntarily.

> The *McNabb-Mallory* rule, as modified by § 3501, requires suppression of confessions given more than six hours after an arrest during a period of unnecessary delay in presenting the defendant for arraignment, but immunizes confessions given during the first six hours from being challenged on these grounds.

D. *Status of the McNabb-Mallory Rule in State Courts*

The *McNabb-Mallory* rule was promulgated by the Supreme Court under its supervisory authority to establish rules of evidence for the federal courts and was never binding on state courts.[49] Some states have voluntarily adopted the *McNabb-Mallory* rule as a means of enforcing their speedy arraignment statutes, but most treat unnecessary delay in presentment for arraignment as a factor bearing on the voluntariness of the confession, rather than as independent grounds for suppression.[50]

§ 6.6 Protection for the Fifth Amendment Privilege Against Self-Incrimination During Police Interrogations: The *Miranda* Rule

In 1966, the Supreme Court handed down the most famous of all criminal justice decisions — *Miranda v. Arizona*.[51] The decision was based on the Fifth Amendment privilege against self-incrimination, which the Court extended to police custodial interrogations. After surveying police interrogation manuals recommending strategies designed to capitalize on the isolated surroundings of a custodial interrogation to break down and overcome resistance to pressures to confess, the Court concluded that station house interrogations were inherently coercive and that special procedures were needed

---

[49]   United States v. Alvarez-Sanchez, 511 U.S. 350, 114 S. Ct. 1599, 128 L. Ed. 2d 319 (1994).

[50]   *See Romualdo P. Eclavea*, Annotation, *Admissibility of Confession or Other Statement Made by Defendant as Affected by Delay in Arraignment — Modern State Cases*, 28 A.L.R. 4th 1121 (1984). While older cases tended to treat unnecessary delay in arraignment as automatic grounds for suppression, *see, e.g.*, Duncan v. State, 291 Ark. 521, 726 S. W. 2d 653 (1987), more recent cases generally treat it as a factor in evaluating the overall voluntariness of the confession and admit the confession if it was given voluntarily, *see, e.g.*, Commonwealth v. Perez, 577 Pa. 360, 845 A. 2d 779 (Pa. 2004); Williams v. State, 75 Md. 404, 825 A.2d 1078 (2003); Rhiney v. State, 935 P.2d 828 (ALASKA CT. APP. 1997); Landrum v. State, 328 Ark. 361, 944 S.W.2d 101 (1997); People v. Cipriano, 431 Mich. 315, 429 N.W.2d 781 (1987).

[51]   384 U.S. 436, 86 S. Ct. 1602, 16 L. Ed. 2d 694 (1966).

to ensure that suspects in police custody were aware of their constitutional rights and that the police respected their decision to exercise them. The Court laid out the procedures that the police henceforth would be required to follow in order to obtain an admissible confession during a police custodial interrogation.

The *Miranda* decision was so controversial in the beginning that Congress immediately tried to overturn it by enacting a statute, 18 U.S.C. § 3501, requiring federal judges to admit confessions found to be voluntary, even though they were given without the benefit of warnings. Courts ignored the statute on the assumption that it was unconstitutional, an assumption that was later borne out in *Dickerson v. United States*.[52] Although many predicted that *Miranda* would make it impossible for the police to obtain confessions, this has not turned out to be the case. Law enforcement officials have managed to live comfortably with the *Miranda* rule now for more than 40 years.

Figure 6.7
Statement of the *Miranda* Rule

> The *Miranda* rule is activated whenever police interrogate a suspect who is then in custody. To procure an admissible confession, police must:
>
> 1. warn the suspect of his or her Fifth Amendment rights;
> 2. secure a knowing, intelligent, and voluntary waiver; and
> 3. cease interrogation if the suspect, at any time during the interrogation, manifests a desire to remain silent or to consult with an attorney.

A. Overview of the Miranda Rule

There are two aspects of the *Miranda* rule that police officers must commit to memory — when it applies and what it requires. *Miranda* procedural safeguards must be observed when the police **interrogate** a suspect who is then in police **custody**. Prior to initiating a **custodial interrogation**, the officer must warn the suspect: (1) that he has the right to remain silent, (2) that anything he says can be used against him in a court of law, (3) that he has the right to the presence of an attorney, and (4) that one will be appointed if he cannot afford one.[53] The officer must then make sure that the suspect understands his rights and afford him an opportunity to exercise them before initiating questioning.[54] Unless the prosecution can demonstrate that the required warnings were given and that the suspect made a knowing and voluntary waiver of his *Miranda* rights, statements made during the custodial interrogation will be suppressed.[55]

---

[52] *Supra* note 46.

[53] *Supra* note 51 at 467–474, 479, 86 S. Ct. at 1624–1628, 1630.

[54] *Id.*, at 475, 86 S. Ct. at 1628.

[55] Suppression of evidence is a criminal defendant's only remedy for *Miranda* violations. The defendant cannot bring a civil action for damages. Chavez v. Martinez, 538 U.S. 760, 123 S. Ct. 1994, 155 L. Ed. 2d 984 (2003) (plurality opinion); Olaniyi v. District of Columbia, 416 F. Supp. 2d 43 (D. D.C. 2006) (holding that failure to provide *Miranda* warnings, standing alone, cannot be the basis for a civil suit).

§ 6.7 — Custodial Interrogation Defined

Two factors combine to determine when warnings are necessary. These factors are *custody* and *interrogation*. *Miranda* safeguards are necessary only when police interrogate a suspect who is then in custody. They are not required in any other legal setting.[56] For example, warnings do not have to be given to grand jury witnesses, even when they are the focus of the investigation.[57] Custodial interrogations are unique. Being questioned in police custody, with no one else around, brings into play feelings of fear, isolation, and vulnerability that place suspects at a psychological disadvantage, making it difficult for them to resist the pressure to confess. *Miranda* warnings were developed to neutralize the inherently coercive atmosphere of a police custodial interrogation.

Figure 6.8
Definition of Custodial Interrogation

Miranda safeguards must be observed whenever police interrogate a suspect who is then in custody.

1. Custody requires a formal arrest or a restraint of the suspect's freedom of action to the degree associated with a formal arrest.
2. An interrogation occurs when the police ask investigative questions or engage in other words or actions that they should know are reasonably likely to elicit an incriminating response from the suspect.

A. Custody Defined

A custodial interrogation has two components: *custody* and *interrogation*. When both are present warnings are necessary, whether the offense is a felony or a misdemeanor.[58]

1. Objective Nature of the Inquiry

Custody requires either a formal arrest or a restraint of a suspect's freedom of action to the "degree associated with a formal arrest."[59] The inquiry is objective. The focus is on how a *reasonable person* in the suspect's position would have experienced the encounter.[60] A suspect is in custody if a reasonable person would have experienced

---

[56] Minnesota v. Murphy, 465 U.S. 420, 104 S. Ct. 1136, 79 L. Ed. 2d 409 (1984) ("The mere fact that an investigation has focused on a suspect does not trigger the need for *Miranda* warnings in noncustodial settings...").

[57] United States v. Washington, 431 U.S. 181, 97 S. Ct. 1814, 52 L. Ed. 2d 238 (1977); United States v. Mandujano, 425 U.S. 564, 96 S. Ct. 1768, 48 L. Ed. 2d 212 (1976); United States v. Wong, 431 U.S. 174, 97 S. Ct. 1823, 52 L. Ed. 2d 231 (1977).

[58] **Berkemer v. McCarty, 468 U.S. 420, 104 S. Ct. 3138, 82 L. Ed. 2d 317 (1984).**

[59] Thompson v. Keohane, 511 U.S. 318, 116 S. Ct. 457, 133 L. Ed. 2d 383 (1995); Stansbury v. California, 511 U.S. 318, 114 S. Ct. 1526, 128 L. Ed. 2d 293 (1994).

[60] Stansbury v. California, *supra* note 59.

the encounter as an arrest.[61] The traits of the particular suspect, such as his age, intelligence, education, and previous experience with the criminal justice system, are not considered in determining whether he is in custody.[62] The objectivity of the test is designed to give clear guidance to police by sparing them the need to guess how each suspects' individual characteristics might color his/her actual understanding. However, an exception is made for juvenile suspects. When police know or should know that they are dealing with a juvenile, they cannot ignore the suspect's age.[63] Since juveniles as a class are more vulnerable to outside pressures than adults, police must take a juvenile suspect's age into consideration in determining the need for warnings.

The time, place, and manner of the interrogation are the most important considerations in deciding whether a suspect is in custody. Although most custodial interrogations occur at a police station, the questioning does not have to occur at the police station to be custodial, and the reverse is also true.[64] In *Oregon v. Mathiason*,[65] a suspect voluntarily went to the police station on his own after receiving a communication that the police wanted to talk to him. When he arrived, he was told that he was not under arrest and could leave at any time. He gave a confession after a brief interview, got up, and was allowed to leave. The Supreme Court held that the suspect was not in custody because his presence at the police station was voluntary at all times.

2. Custody Indicators

While there is no infallible checklist for when a suspect is in custody, a number of factors can give a police/suspect encounter the coercive atmosphere of an arrest. These factors include[66]: (1) prolonged questioning; (2) isolated surroundings; (3) the

---

[61]   Students should not confuse the *Miranda* test for when a suspect is in "custody" with the Fourth Amendment test for when a suspect is "seized." "Seizure" and "custody" are not congruent concepts. The "free to leave" test is used to determine when a suspect is seized. A suspect is seized when a reasonable person under the circumstances of the encounter would believe that he or she is no longer free to leave. At this point, the suspect acquires Fourth Amendment protection. *See* § 6.3 *supra. Miranda* protection requires more. The suspect's liberty must be been restrained to a degree associated with a formal arrest. A suspect can be seized without being in custody. This explains why warnings are not required during traffic and *Terry* stops. *See* § 6.7 (A)(3) *infra*. These encounters involve seizures but not custody.

[62]   Yarborough v. Alvarado, 541 U.S. 652, 124 S. Ct. 2140, 158 L. Ed. 2d 311 (2004) (whether a suspect is in custody for warning purposes calls for an objective inquiry into how a reasonable person would have experienced the encounter; the suspect's individual characteristics, such as age and lack of prior experience with the criminal justice system are not relevant); Stansbury v. California, *supra* note 59.

[63]   J.D.B. v. North Carolina , _ U.S._, 131 S. Ct. 2394, _ L. Ed.2d _ (2011).

[64]   Oregon v. Mathiason, 429 U.S. 492, 97 S. Ct. 711, 50 L. Ed. 2d 714 (1977).

[65]   *Supra* note 64.

[66]   The Supreme Court found that the suspect was in custody in New York v. Quarles, 467 U.S. 649, 104 S. Ct. 2626, 81 L. Ed. 2d 550 (1984) (suspect surrounded by four police officers and handcuffed); Orozco v. Texas, 394 U.S. 324, 89 S. Ct. 1095, 22 L. Ed. 2d 311 (1969) (suspect awakened in middle of the night by four police officers who entered his bedroom); Mathis v. United States, 391 U.S. 1, 88 S. Ct. 1503, 20 L. Ed. 2d 381 (1968) (suspect questioned while incarcerated in jail for unrelated offense). The Court reached the opposite conclusion in **Berkemer v. McCarty, supra note 58** (motorist detained for routine traffic stop).

threatening presence of several police officers; (4) weapon displays; (5) physical touching; (6) a hostile demeanor; (7) an intimidating tone of voice or language; (8) restrictions on movements, handcuffs, or other forms of restraint; and (9) confronting the suspect with evidence of guilt.[67] This is not an exhaustive list of factors and all of them need not be present; they are mentioned simply as factors to look out for. Deciding whether a suspect is in custody can be a tricky call.[68] Officers should consider whether they would feel intimidated, vulnerable, and under pressure to answer if the tables were turned. If the answer is "yes," *Miranda* warnings should be given. If the answer is "perhaps," they should also be given because it is better to give them when they are not required than to neglect them when they are.

3. Suspect's Awareness That He Is Speaking with a Police Officer

Miranda warnings are not required when the suspect is unaware that the interrogator is a police officer.[69] In *Illinois v. Perkins*,[70] the Supreme Court ruled that an inmate was not in custody for *Miranda* purposes when he was questioned by a police undercover agent who had been planted in his cell because the pressures that make warnings necessary during police custodial interrogations are not present when a suspect speaks freely to a person who he believes is a fellow inmate. Requiring warnings when the suspect is unaware that his interrogator is a police officer would impede undercover operations without advancing the concerns behind the *Miranda* rule and, consequently, they are not required in this setting.[71]

---

[67] For cases containing a good general discussion of factors bearing on "custody," *see, e.g.,* United States v. Kim, 292 F.3d 969 (9th Cir. 2002) (suspect was in custody for *Miranda* purposes where police, while executing a search warrant, locked the door to her shop with her inside, deliberately isolating her from her husband, before conducting lengthy interrogation session); United States v. Johnson, 64 F.3d 1120, 1126 (8th Cir. 1995), *cert. denied,* 516 U.S. 1139, 116 S. Ct. 971, 133 L. Ed. 2d 891 (1996) (defendant was in custody for *Miranda* purposes where he was ordered out of his vehicle at gunpoint, handcuffed, placed in the back of a patrol car, and questioned by detectives); United States v. Smith, 3 F.3d 1088 (7th Cir. 1993), *cert. denied,* 510 U.S. 1061, 114 S. Ct. 733, 126 L. Ed. 2d 696 (1994) (defendant was in custody for *Miranda* purposes where police stopped the cab in which the defendant was riding and frisked, handcuffed, and surrounded him while he was questioned); State v. Rucker, 821 A.2d 439 (Md. 2003) (defendant was not "in custody" for *Miranda* purposes when he made incriminating statement during investigatory stop in public parking lot, detention was brief, no weapons were drawn, and defendant was not handcuffed or physically restrained until after he admitted having cocaine).

[68] Oregon v. Elstad, 470 U.S. 298, 105 S. Ct. 1285, 84 L. Ed. 2d 222 (1985).

[69] Illinois v. Perkins, 496 U.S. 292, 110 S. Ct. 2394, 110 L. Ed. 2d 243 (1990) ("*Miranda* forbids coercion, not mere strategic deception by taking advantage of a suspect's misplaced trust in one he supposes to be a fellow prisoner.")

[70] *Id.*

[71] In Illinois v. Perkins, the suspect had not been formally charged with the offense under investigation. The rules change once formal charges are lodged. Undercover questioning is no longer allowed. *See* § 6.9(C) *infra.*

4. Traffic Stops, *Terry* Stops, and the *Miranda* Rule

Have you ever been stopped for a traffic violation? If so, did the officer administer warnings? My bet is that this did not happen. Roadside questioning during a traffic stop does not involve custody which means that there is no right to *Miranda* warnings.[72] How many of the factors listed on pages 331-332 are present during the typical traffic stop? The answer is none of them. Traffic stops occur on a public street, generally with other people around, there is no prolonged questioning, the period of detention is brief, and the police do not draw weapons or use handcuffs. In fact, motorists are generally treated fairly courteously during traffic stops. Because traffic stops normally lack the coercive atmosphere of an arrest, there is no right to *Miranda* warnings.[73]

This is true for most *Terry* stops. Brief *Terry* encounters in which the officer requests identification and asks a moderate number of questions do not equate to custody.[74] However, the situation can change. Police are permitted during *Terry* stops to draw weapons, use handcuffs, order detainees to lie prone on the ground, and place them in squad cars when they have reasonable concerns for their safety.[75] Intrusive precautions like these, nevertheless, render the detainee in custody, and make warnings necessary.[76] As one court bluntly put it, "Police officers must make a choice — if they are going to take highly intrusive steps to protect themselves from danger, they must similarly provide protection to their suspects by advising them of their constitutional rights."[77]

---

[72] **Berkemer v. McCarty,** *supra* **note 58** (holding that roadside questioning of a motorist detained for a routine traffic stop does not constitute a "custodial interrogation"). Traffic stops are discussed in Chapter 3, §§ 3.10–3.11.

[73] *Terry* stops are discussed in §§ 3.7–3.9.

[74] **Berkemer v. McCarty,** *supra* **note 58**.

[75] *See, e.g.,* United States. v. Perdue, 8 F.3d 1544 (10th Cir. 1993); United States v. Clemons, 201 F. Supp. 2d 142 (D.D.C. 2002).

[76] *See, e.g.,* United States v. Foster, 70 Fed. Appx. 415 (9th Cir. 2003) (Defendant was in custody during *Terry* stop, requiring suppression of his statements made in absence of *Miranda* warning where he was (1) stopped by a combined unit of four armed federal and local officers on a remote rural highway, (2) had three police and Border Patrol vehicles positioned in single file behind him, (3) was accused by the officers of engaging in the trafficking of illegal narcotics, (4) was informed that the officers had discovered a large quantity of illegal drugs nearby and that they believed he was in the area to pick it up, (5) had his driver's license and car registration seized, and (6) was pressured by the officers to be "honest" and to confess that the marijuana belonged to him); United States v. Perdue, 8 F.3d 1455 (10th Cir. 1993) (officers who draw weapons and force detainees to the ground while conducting *Terry* stop create a custodial situation in which *Miranda* warnings are required); United States v. Clemons, 201 F. Supp. 2d 142 (D.D.C. 2002) (*Terry* detainee was in custody for *Miranda* purposes when he was removed from vehicle, handcuffed, and forced to lie on the ground); State v. Morgan, 254 Wis. 2d 602, 648 N.W.2d 23 (2002) (*Terry* detainee was in custody for *Miranda* purposes where police drew weapons, four officers were present, suspect was frisked and handcuffed, and the questioning occurred while suspect was detained in squad car).

[77] United States v. Perdue, *supra* note 75.

B. *Interrogation Defined*

Interrogation is the second component. *Miranda* procedural safeguards come into play only when a person in custody is subjected to an interrogation. Suspects sometimes blurt out incriminating statements before the police have time to Mirandize them. While being taken into custody, they may say things like "How did you find me so quickly?" "Did Joe blow the whistle on me?" or "Why are you arresting both of us when I did it?"[78] Spontaneous, unsolicited statements are not affected by the *Miranda* rule because they are not the product of an interrogation.[79]

The test for what constitutes an interrogation was established in *Rhode Island v. Innis*.[80] The term interrogation includes both express questioning and any other words or actions that police should know are reasonably likely to elicit an incriminating response from the suspect.[81]

1. Express Questioning

Interrogations usually take the form of express questions, but express questions do not invariably involve an interrogation. "Would you like to make a phone call?" is an example. To constitute an interrogation, the officer must have reason to expect that the question is likely to elicit an incriminating response from the suspect.[82] Small talk about matters unrelated to the investigation and questions asked for administrative purposes are not treated as interrogations. For example, if Officer Quizzard, while driving Mary Wanna to the police station during a heavy snowstorm, attempts to make small talk by saying, "What do you think about this weather?" and she replies "Terrible! You caught me with two kilos because I haven't made a sale for the last two days," her unwarned statement is admissible because it is not the product of an interrogation.[83] The same is true for routine booking questions covering matters such as name, address, height, weight, eye

---

[78]   United States v. Crowder, 62 F.3d 782 (6th Cir. 1995); United States v. Montano, 613 F.2d 147 (6th Cir. 1980); United States v. Gonzalez, 954 F. Supp. 48 (D. Conn. 1997).

[79]   *See, e.g.*, **Miranda v. Arizona,** *supra* **note 51**, 384 U.S. at 478, 86 S. Ct. at 1630; United States v. Hawkins, 102 F.3d 973 (8th Cir. 1996); United States v. Hayes, 120 F.3d 739 (8th Cir. 1997); United States v. Sherwood, 98 F.3d 402 (9th Cir. 1996). However, police must administer warnings before asking follow-up questions if the answers are likely to be incriminating. *See, e.g.*, State v. Walton, 41 S.W.3d 75 (Tenn. 2001).

[80]   **446 U.S. 291, 100 S. Ct. 1682, 64 L. Ed. 2d 297 (1980)** ("[T]he term "interrogation" under *Miranda* refers not only to express questioning but also to any words or actions on the part of the police (other than those normally attendant to arrest and custody) that the police should know are reasonably likely to elicit an incriminating response from the suspect.").

[81]   Pennsylvania v. Muniz, 496 U.S. 582, 601, 110 S. Ct. 2638, 2650, 110 L. Ed. 2d 528 (1990); **Rhode Island v. Innis,** *supra* **note 80**.

[82]   Pennsylvania v. Muniz, *supra* note 81; United States v. Pacheco-Lopez, 531 F. 3d 420 (6th Cir.2008) (routine biographical information elicited during the booking process does not constitute interrogation); State v. Griffin, 814 A.2d 1003 (Me. 2003) ("Even in a custodial situation, an officer may, without giving *Miranda* warnings, ask questions designed to identify the suspect, check her identification and resolve any health or safety concerns regarding the suspect or others.").

[83]   *See, e.g.*, State v. Tucker, 81 Ohio St. 3d 431, 692 N.E.2d 171 (1998).

color, date of birth, age, and the like.[84] Routine booking questions may be asked without administering *Miranda* warnings because they are not asked for an investigative purpose.[85] However, questions like how much alcohol a person arrested for drunk driving has consumed are not booking questions.[86] Police may not ask investigative questions, even during the booking process, without administering *Miranda* warnings.

2. Functional Equivalent of Express Questioning

The definition of interrogation also includes words or actions that are the "functional equivalent" of an express question. "Functional equivalent" includes ruses designed to trick suspects into confessing. The test for whether something is the "functional equivalent" of an express question is whether the police knew or should have known that their actions were reasonably likely to elicit an incriminating response from the suspect.[87] Any knowledge that police have about a suspect's unique susceptibility to a particular form of persuasion is taken into consideration in deciding this.

In *Rhode Island v. Innis*,[88] two police officers, while transporting an armed robbery suspect to the police station, held a conversation between themselves concerning the missing shotgun. One of the officers mentioned to the other that there was a school for handicapped children near the vicinity of the robbery and said "God forbid one of the children should find the gun and hurt herself." The suspect, who was listening in the back seat, interrupted the conversation and told the officers to turn the squad car around and go back to the robbery scene so he could show them where the gun was located.

Were these officers engaged in the functional equivalent of express questioning? This depends on whether the officers should have anticipated that their actions were reasonably likely to elicit an incriminating response from the suspect. Had the officers known that the suspect was unusually susceptible to the theme of their conversation and staged this conversation to provoke an incriminating response, their actions would have constituted an interrogation. However, the Supreme Court did not read the facts this way. The Court viewed the conversation as "offhand remarks" between two police officers for which no response from the suspect was expected. Viewed this way, the police were not responsible for the suspect's unforeseen response.

However, the Supreme Court reached the opposite conclusion in a case in which the use of a similar strategy was deliberate. Police, knowing of the murder suspect's deep religious convictions, told him that the victim's missing body deserved a "Christian" burial. This statement prompted the suspect to tell the officers where the body was

---

[84] *See, e.g.*, **Pennsylvania v. Muniz**, *supra note 81*; Vasquez v. Filion, 210 F. Supp. 2d 194 (E.D.N.Y. 2002); Colon v. State, 568 S.E.2d 811 (Ga. Ct. App. 2002).

[85] **Pennsylvania v. Muniz**, *supra* note 81.

[86] State v. Chrisicos, 813 A.2d 513 (N.H. 2002) (booking officer's question of how much alcohol defendant arrested for drunk driving had consumed was not a routine booking question, but was instead designed to elicit incriminating statement).

[87] **Rhode Island v. Innis**, *supra* **note 80**.

[88] *Id.*

located.[89] The Supreme Court held that the statement was the product of a police interrogation.

Telling suspects that they have been implicated by someone else, identified by eye-witnesses, or that their alibi was not confirmed are examples of actions that are the functional equivalents of an express question because they are ploys deliberately used to trick suspects into incriminating themselves.[90] In one case, police falsely told a murder suspect that his father had lived long enough to identify him as the killer.[91] The son then admitted to the acts, explaining that he had performed them in a blacked-out state. "[I]t wasn't me, it was like another Marty Tankleff that killed them." Even though the son's unwarned confession was the product of an interrogation, it was admitted because the son had gone to the police station voluntarily and, consequently, was not in custody when he made the statement. When a suspect is interrogated without being in custody, warnings are not necessary.

3. Public Safety Exception

Police officers may dispense with *Miranda* safeguards before interrogating a suspect in custody when they are confronted with an emergency that requires immediate action to protect the public safety or their own safety.[92] This is known as the "public safety" exception. The Supreme Court articulated the public safety exception in a case in which two police officers on patrol encountered a woman who stated that she had just been raped by a man with a gun, and that he had gone into a nearby grocery store. The police entered the store and saw a man fitting the suspect's description approaching the checkout counter.

---

[89]   Brewer v. Williams, 430 U.S. 387, 97 S. Ct. 1232, 51 L. Ed. 2d 424 (1977) (decided under the Sixth Amendment right to counsel).

[90]   *See, e.g.,* Drury v. State, 368 Md. 331, 793 A.2d 567 (2002) (officers engaged in functional equivalent of an interrogation when they confronted suspect with physical evidence of the crime and told him that they were going to send the evidence to be examined for fingerprints); United States v. Orso, 266 F.3d 1030 (9th Cir. 2001) (suspect subjected to the functional equivalent of an interrogation when officer engaged in detailed discussion of the evidence and witnesses against the suspect and penalties for the crime of which she was suspected, going so far as to make up some of the evidence); United States v. Collins, 43 Fed. Appx. 99 (9th Cir. 2002) (defendant's statement "I've heard enough, you got me," in response to playing of incriminating audiotape was inadmissible because defendant was subjected to functional equivalent of an interrogation); United States v. Guerra, 237 F. Supp. 2d 795 (E.D. Mich. 2003) (*Miranda* violated where police told defendant that his accomplice had confessed and invited him to discuss the case after defendant had invoked his right to remain silent); State v. Brown, 592 So. 2d 308 (Fla. Dist. Ct. App. 1991) (confessions obtained in violation of *Miranda*, where, after defendant clearly invoked his rights, officer informed defendant that victim named him as suspect, that three witnesses placed him at scene of crime, that his girlfriend implicated him in burglary, and that he had been seen in possession of items stolen in burglary, causing defendant to state later that he wanted to tell "the truth" or "his side of the story.") *But see* White v. State, 374 Md. 232, 821 A.2d 459 (2003) (conduct of police in providing defendant with statement of charges, after he had invoked his *Miranda* rights, was not the functional equivalent of an interrogation where notification of the charges was a routine part of the booking process.).

[91]   Tankleff v. Senkowski, 993 F. Supp. 151 (E.D.N.Y. 1997).

[92]   New York v. Quarles, *supra* note 66.

When the suspect saw the police, he dropped his items and fled into the aisles. After the suspect was apprehended and frisked, the police discovered an empty shoulder holster, and before warning the suspect of his *Miranda* rights, asked him where the gun was. The suspect pointed to some empty cartons and said "The gun is over there." The officers retrieved a loaded .38-caliber revolver from one of the cartons.

The suspect was later prosecuted for possession of a weapon and moved to suppress his unwarned statement and the weapon discovered as a result of it. The Supreme Court ruled that *Miranda* warnings may be delayed temporarily when police officers are confronted with an immediate need for answers to questions in a situation posing a threat to the public safety or to the officer's own safety. The exception applies only when the officer's perception of danger is "objectively reasonable."[93] Police, moreover, are restricted to asking questions necessary to address the immediate danger.[94] They may ask an unwarned suspect "Where is the gun?" but not "Who owns it?" "Where did you buy it?" or "Do you have a license for it?" Investigative questions such as these must be postponed until after *Miranda* warnings have been administered.

4. Non-police Interrogators

Private detectives and security officers are not bound by the *Miranda* rule[95] because the Fifth Amendment, like other portions of the Bill of Rights,[96] regulates only the actions of the government.[97] Although the interrogator has to be a government agent, he/she does not have to be a police officer. Government officials employed in other capacities are required to administer warnings when they conduct custodial

---

[93] *Id.* at 659 n. 8, 104 S. Ct. at 2633 n. 8; **Benson v. State, 698 So. 2d 333 (Fla. Dist. Ct. App. 1997)** (warnings unnecessary when police need to ask questions to address what they reasonably believe is a life-threatening emergency); United States v. Reyes, 249 F. Supp. 2d 277 (S.D.N.Y. 2003) (asking suspect about to be searched about the possible presence of objects that could pose a danger to the officer comes within the public safety exception only when officer has some genuine, particularized reason for believing that dangerous, undetected objects might exist); United States v. DeJear, 552 F.3d 1196, 1201 (10th Cir.2009) (holding that officer's questioning of defendant as to what he was stuffing under a seat without first giving proper *Miranda* warnings was excused under the public safety exception; an officer may ask a suspect, "[d]o you have any guns or sharp objects on you," without first giving the *Miranda* warnings even after a suspect has been handcuffed, only if the officer has reason to believe (1) that the defendant might have a weapon, and (2) that an accomplice or someone else might gain access to it and inflict harm). *But see* United States v. Brathwaite, 458 F.3d 376 (5th Cir. 2006) (The "public safety" exception to the *Miranda* rule did not apply to the defendant's unwarned statement concerning the presence of guns in his house where, at time of questioning, agents had performed two sweeps of the house, and the only two occupants were both in handcuffs.).

[94] United States v. Simpson, 974 F.2d 845 (7th Cir. 1992).

[95] *See, e.g.,* United States v. Garlock, 19 F.3d 441 (8th Cir. 1994); United States v. Antonelli, 434 F.2d 335 (2d Cir. 1970); United States v. Birnstihl, 441 F.2d 368 (9th Cir. 1971); *United States v. Bolden,* 461 F.2d 998 (8th Cir. 1972) (per curiam); United States v. Casteel, 476 F.2d 152 (10th Cir. 1973); Woods v. City of Tucson, 128 Ariz. 477, 626 P.2d 1109 (1981); State v. Brooks, 862 P.2d 57 (N.M. Ct. App. 1992).

[96] *See, e.g.,* Burdeau v. McDowell, 256 U.S. 465, 475, 41 S. Ct. 574, 576, 65 L. Ed. 1048 (1921) (Fourth Amendment provides no protection against private searches).

[97] *See* cases *supra* note 95.

interviews seeking information designed for use in a criminal prosecution.[98] Prison psychiatrists, for example, are required to administer *Miranda* warnings before eliciting information from prison inmates when the information is intended for use at the trial, but not when they are seeking information for use in diagnosis and treatment.[99]

Summarizing, the *Miranda* rule applies only during custodial interrogations. A custodial interrogation has two ingredients: custody and interrogation. Custody requires a formal arrest or a restraint of the suspect's liberty to the degree usually associated with a formal arrest. The latter is determined from the vantage point of a reasonable person in the suspect's shoes. An interrogation includes not only express questions, but any words or actions on the part of the police that they should know are reasonably likely to elicit an incriminating response from the suspect. Volunteered statements are not subject to *Miranda* warnings because they are not elicited through interrogation. To constitute an interrogation, the questioning must be reasonably likely to elicit an incriminating response; routine booking questions are not considered interrogations and, consequently, do not have to be preceded by warnings. Undercover questioning is also not covered by the *Miranda* rule because the suspect must be aware that the other person is a police officer. Otherwise, the encounter lacks the coercive atmosphere of a police custodial interrogation. Police officers may temporarily postpone giving *Miranda* warnings before interrogating a suspect when they are confronted with an emergency that requires immediate action to protect their own safety or the safety of the public.

§ 6.8   — Procedural Requirements for Custodial Interrogations: *Miranda* Warnings and Waivers

The *Miranda* warnings are the best known aspect of this Supreme Court opinion, but they are only part of the steps necessary to obtain an admissible statement. *Miranda* established a complete set of rules that remain in effect throughout the interrogation.[100] These rules are summarized in the next paragraph.

---

[98]   *See, e.g.,* Mathis v. United States, *supra* note 66 (*Miranda* violated by IRS civil investigator's failure to warn inmate before questioning him about matters that could lead to a criminal prosecution); Estelle v. Smith, 451 U.S. 454, 101 S. Ct. 1866, 68 L. Ed. 2d 359 (1981) (unwarned statement made to psychiatrist during court-ordered psychiatric evaluation is inadmissible); State v. Bankes, 57 P.3d 284 (Wash. Ct. App. 2002) (same). *See also* 2 WAYNE R. LaFAVE ET AL., CRIMINAL PROCEDURE § 6.10(C), at 622–624 (2d ed. 1999) (custodial questioning by any government employee comes within *Miranda* whenever prosecution of the defendant being questioned is among the purposes, definite or contingent, for which the information is elicited; this is generally the case whenever the government questioner's duties include investigation or reporting of crimes).

[99]   Estelle v. Smith, *supra* note 98 (interrogation conducted by a court-appointed competency psychiatrist at the county jail implicates *Miranda* rights).

[100]   Four Justices on the Supreme Court have taken the position that *Miranda* does not impose any duties on the police. It functions purely as a limitation on the admissibility of evidence. Police must give warnings if they want to use the confession as evidence, but not if they want to use it to develop leads or for some other purposes. *See* Chavez v. Martinez, *supra* note 55. *See, generally,* Steven D. Clymer, *Are the Police Free to Disregard* Miranda? 112 YALE L.J. 447 (2002).

After administering a complete set of warnings, police must ascertain whether the suspect understands his rights and afford him an opportunity to exercise them. They may start the interrogation if the suspect does not invoke his rights, but the suspect remains free to change his mind at any time. If, at any time before or during the interrogation, the suspect makes a clear and unambiguous request for an attorney, questioning must stop immediately and may resume only if (1) counsel is made available, (2) the suspect reopens the dialog, or (3) there is a break in custody, lasting at least 14 days, between the first and second interrogations. If the suspect makes a clear and unambiguous assertion of the right to remain silent, questioning must also cease and may resume only if the suspect reopens the dialog or there is a 14-day break in custody. However, police may resume questioning about an unrelated crime after waiting a reasonable period of time.

Violation of *Miranda* rules at any point will prevent police from using statements obtained thereafter to establish the suspect's guilt. Consequently, police officers must be able to recognize when they may start questioning and when they must stop.

A. The Requirement to Warn the Suspect

1. Required Content of *Miranda* Warnings

Anyone who regularly watches television or attends movies can probably recite from memory the *Miranda* warnings scripted by Chief Justice Warren:

> [You have] the right to remain silent, anything [you say] can and will be used against [you] in court. [You have] the right to consult with a lawyer and to have the lawyer with [you] during [questioning]. [If you are unable to afford] a lawyer, one will be appointed to represent [you].[101]

Four "warnings" or explanations are necessary. The suspect must be warned that:

1. She has the right to remain silent;
2. Anything she says can and will be used against her in a court of law;
3. She has the right to have an attorney present during interrogation; and
4. If she cannot afford an attorney, one will be appointed for her.[102]

Although police departments equip officers with *Miranda* script copies to carry with them and read at appropriate times, in the haste and confusion surrounding an arrest, they sometimes use their own wording. When this happens, a court must decide whether the officer's wording was legally sufficient. While departures from the Supreme Court's carefully scripted language are not fatal if the warnings given

---

[101]   **Miranda v. Arizona**, *supra* note 51.
[102]   *Id.*

are adequate to inform the suspect of all four rights,[103] deviations should be avoided because they engender needless controversy.

2. Frequency of Warnings

Miranda warnings are required on three occasions. First, warnings are always necessary before interrogating a suspect for the first time. The prevailing practice is to administer the first set of warnings immediately after the arrest. The reason is that police officers sometimes inadvertently elicit incriminating statements without being aware that they are engaged in an interrogation. The notion of an interrogation is not limited to formal interrogation sessions. An officer is engaged in an interrogation, for *Miranda* purposes, any time the officer asks a question, even a casual one, that the officer should know is reasonably likely to elicit an incriminating response. Saying to Sticky-Fingered Sam, "You look familiar. Weren't you the guy I stopped on Primrose Avenue about two months ago for questioning in connection with a burglary?" constitutes an interrogation. Consequently, to avoid slip-ups, police should issue the first set of *Miranda* warnings immediately after the arrest. Second, *Miranda* warnings can lose their efficacy and grow stale with the passage of time. To avoid controversies about whether earlier warnings had grown stale, police should issue a fresh set of *Miranda* warnings each time they initiate a new interrogation. Finally, warnings should be given before resuming interrogation of a suspect who initiates dialog with the police after invoking *Miranda* rights.[104]

B. *Waiver of* **Miranda** *Rights*

To secure admission of a confession made during a custodial interrogation, the prosecution must establish that the accused made a voluntary and knowing waiver of *Miranda* rights.[105] It is customary to ask suspects to sign a written waiver like the one in Figure 6.9. A waiver such as this will simplify the prosecution's task.

However, a waiver of *Miranda* rights does not have to be written or even verbalized to be effective. It can be implied from a suspect's conduct. The law presumes that a person who with full knowledge of his rights, acts in a manner inconsistent with their

[103] *See, e.g.,* Florida v. Powell, 560 U.S.__, 130 S. Ct. 1195, 176 L. Ed. 2d 1089 (2010) (Advising the suspect that he had "the right to talk to a lawyer before answering" was adequate to advise him of the right to have counsel present during the interrogation, where police also told him that he could exercise any of "these rights at any time he wanted during this interview"); Duckworth v. Eagan, 492 U.S. 195, 109 S. Ct. 2875, 106 L. Ed. 2d 166 (1989); California v. Prysock, 453 U.S. 355, 101 S. Ct. 2806, 69 L. Ed. 2d 696 (1981) (per curiam).

[104] The rules concerning resumption of interrogation when the suspect seeks further communication with police after invoking *Miranda* rights are discussed below.

[105] Withrow v. Williams, 507 U.S. 680, 113 S. Ct. 1745, 127 L. Ed. 2d 407 (1993); North Carolina v. Butler, 441 U.S. 369, 99 S. Ct. 1755, 60 L. Ed. 2d 286 (1979); Tague v. Louisiana, 444 U.S. 469, 100 S. Ct. 652, 62 L. Ed. 2d 622 (1980).

Figure 6.9
Advice of Rights and Waiver

> Prior to any questioning, I was advised that I have the right to remain silent, that whatever I say can or will be used against me in a court of law, that I have a right to speak with a lawyer and have a lawyer present during questioning, and that, if I cannot afford a lawyer, one will be appointed for me. I was further advised that, even if I sign this waiver, I have the right to stop the interview and refuse to answer further questions or ask to speak with an attorney at any time I so desire. I fully understand my rights. I am willing to answer questions and make a statement. I do not wish to consult with a lawyer or to have a lawyer present.

exercise intends to waive them. Establishing an implied waiver of *Miranda* rights requires proof that (1) police administered adequate warnings, (2) the suspect understood his rights, and that (3) he voluntarily answered questions without invoking them.[106] The second requirement is important. Proof that police administered warnings and that the suspect subsequently answered questions is not enough to establish a waiver. The prosecution must make the additional showing that the accused understood his rights. Although implied waivers are legally as effective as signed written ones, they are not as easy to prove. Consequently, police should obtain a written waiver if the suspect is willing to give one.

> Where the prosecution shows that adequate warnings were given and understood by the suspect, the suspect's subsequent uncoerced statement establishes an implied waiver of *Miranda* rights.

What happens if the police administer warnings and ask the suspect to sign a waiver, and the suspect refuses? Does this count as an invocation of *Miranda* rights, requiring police to cut off questioning? This issue arose in *Berghuis v. Thompkins.*[107] Thompkins was arrested on murder charges and taken to the police station for questioning. Before starting the interrogation, Officer Helgert presented him with a copy of *Miranda* warnings and asked him to read one out loud to determine whether he could read and understand English. Helgert then read the others to him and asked him to sign the form to acknowledge that he had been notified of his rights and understood them. Thompkins declined, but Helgert began the interrogation anyway.

---

[106] **Berghuis v. Thompkins,** 560 U.S. __, 130 S. Ct. 2250, 176 L.Ed.2d 1098 (2010); Moran v. Burbine, 475 U.S. 412, 421, 106 S. Ct. 1135, 89 L.Ed.2d 410 (1986); Tague v. Louisiana, *supra* note 105.

[107] *Supra* note 106.

Thompkins remained largely silent and unresponsive throughout the interrogation, but at no point did he say that he wanted an attorney or that he did not want to talk with the police. Near the end of the three hour session, Officer Helgert asked Thompkins whether he prayed to God to forgive him for the shooting. This question jarred Thompkins. Tears welled up in his eyes, and he answered "yes." His one-word confession was admitted into evidence over his objection and he was found guilty of first-degree murder.

Thompkins made two arguments on appeal. He first argued that he effectively invoked the right to remain silent by refusing to sign a form acknowledging that he had been warned, and remaining unresponsive for a lengthy period. Since police could infer from his actions that he was unwilling to discuss the case, they were required to end the interrogation long before he incriminated himself. The Supreme Court rejected this argument in reliance on a prior case holding that an accused who wishes to invoke the right to counsel must make a clear and unambiguous request for an attorney.[108] The Court held that this requirement applies equally to the right to remain silent and requires a suspect who wishes to invoke this right to say so in clear language. Silence is not an effective means of invoking the right to remain silent because the conduct is ambiguous. A suspect's silence could mean that he is unwilling to answer the questions asked, but might be willing to answer others, or that he is unwilling to discuss the matter at all. The same was true about Thompkins' refusal to sign the form. Since the meaning of Thompkins' behavior was unclear, police were not required to stop the interrogation. They could continue interrogating Thompkins until he either answered their questions or clearly stated he was unwilling to speak to them.

Thompkins' second argument was that police were required to obtain a waiver of *Miranda* rights *before* commencing interrogation. This argument correctly stated the law as it stood before *Berghuis v. Thompkins*, but not afterwards. *Berghuis v. Thompkins* is a game changer.[109] The Court held that police may start the interrogation after administering *Miranda* warnings and determining that the suspect understands his rights, and may continue interrogating until the suspect either answers their questions or clearly invokes his rights. If the suspect answers without invoking his rights, an implied waiver will be established then. Thompkins' response to the question whether he prayed to God to forgive him for the shooting was effective to waive his *Miranda* right to remain silent, even though it occurred almost three hours into the interview and Thompkins had remained silent and unresponsive until then.

---

[108] **Davis v. United States,** 512 U.S. 452, 114 S. Ct. 2351, 129 L. Ed. 2d 362 (1994).

[109] *See, e.g.,* **Davis v. United States,** *supra* note 108 ("If the suspect effectively waives his right to counsel after receiving the *Miranda* warnings, law enforcement officers are free to question him."); **Missouri v. Seibert,** 542 U.S. 600, 124 S. Ct. 2601, 159 L. Ed. 2d 642 (2004) (**Plurality Opinion**) (noting that "failure to give the prescribed warnings and obtain a waiver of rights *before custodial questioning* generally requires exclusion of any statements obtained).

Berghuis v. Thompkins waters down the *Miranda* rule by making it easier for suspects to waive their *Miranda* rights and harder for them to invoke them. Police are not required to obtain a waiver of the suspect's rights before commencing interrogation. A waiver will be inferred from the suspect's conduct if the suspect, at any time during the interview, answers a question with awareness and understanding of his rights and without asserting them. A clear and unambiguous assertion of his rights is required cut off questioning.

> Police are not required to obtain an express waiver for *Miranda* rights before commencing interrogation. The *Miranda* rule and its requirements are met if a suspect receives adequate *Miranda* warnings, understands them, and has an opportunity to invoke the rights before giving any answers or admissions.

C. *Police Duties When a Suspect Invokes* Miranda *Rights*

The interrogation must stop if at any time prior to or during the interrogation, the suspect invokes the right to remain silent or to speak with an attorney. Suspects who desire to invoke either right must make the wishes clear.[110] Ambiguous or equivocal statements such as "maybe I should talk to a lawyer" or "I probably shouldn't be talking to you, should I?" do not constitute a sufficiently clear and unequivocal assertion of rights to counsel[111] (first statement) or to remain silent[112] (second statement) to obligate police to cease interrogating.[113] While it would be just as easy to require the police to ask for clarification when a suspect makes a statement that creates uncertainty about his intentions, this is not the law. Police may disregard an unclear request and are not required to ask clarifying questions.[114]

---

[110] **Berghuis v. Thompkins,** *supra* note 106; **Davis v. United States,** *supra* note 108. The following statements have been ruled insufficient to invoke the right to counsel: Clark v. Murphy, 317 F.3d 1038 (9th Cir. 2003) ("I think I would like to talk to a lawyer" and "Should I be telling you, or should I talk to an attorney?"); United States v. Mendoza-Cecelia, 963 F.2d 1467 (11th Cir. 1992) ("I don't know if I need a lawyer, maybe I should have one, but I don't know if it would do me any good at this point."); Poyner v. Murray, 964 F.2d 1404 (4th Cir. 1992) ("Didn't you tell me I had the right to an attorney?"); Lord v. Duckworth, 29 F.3d 1216 (7th Cir. 1994) ("I can't afford a lawyer, but is there any way I can get one?"); State v. Harris, 741 N.W.2d 1 (Iowa 2007) ("If I need a lawyer, tell me now.") The following statements, in contrast, have been found sufficient: Alvarez v. Gomez, 185 F.3d 995 (9th Cir. 1999) ("Can I get an attorney right now, man?"); Com. v. Barros, 779 N. E.2d 693 (Mass. App. Ct. 2002) ("I don't think I want to talk to you anymore without a lawyer").

[111] **Davis v. United States,** *supra* note 108.

[112] **Berghuis v. Thompkins,** *supra* note 106.

[113] *Id.*; **Davis v. United States,** *supra* **note 108**

[114] See cases *supra* note 113.

D. Resumption of Questioning After Miranda Rights Have Been Invoked

Once the suspect makes a clear invocation of *Miranda* rights, the questioning must cease immediately.[115] If the police persist and the suspect gives in, statements subsequently obtained are inadmissible.[116] The purpose is to prevent police from badgering suspects into waiving their previously invoked *Miranda* rights.

1. Resuming Questioning After a Suspect Has Invoked the Right to Counsel

After a suspect invokes the right to counsel, questioning may resume only if (1) counsel is made available, (2) the suspect reopens the dialog, or (3) the suspect experiences a break in custody between the first and second interrogations, lasting at least 14 days.[117] The first two protection-terminating events stem from *Edwards v. Arizona*.[118] Edwards was questioned by the police until he said that he wanted an attorney. Questioning then ceased, but police came to the jail the following day and, after stating that they wanted to talk to Edwards and again informing him of his *Miranda* rights. This time Edwards waived his rights and confessed. The Supreme Court ruled that after a suspect expresses a desire to deal with the police only through counsel, no waiver of this right will be recognized during a police-initiated contact. Accordingly, police officers may not interrogate a suspect who has invoked the right to counsel unless counsel is made available or the suspect, without police prodding, reopens the dialog.

To reopen the dialog, the suspect must initiate further communications with the police in a manner that shows a willingness and desire to engage in a generalized discussion of the case. Breaking the silence with a statement like "What time is it?" or "May I have a drink of water?" does not indicate a desire to resume discussion of the crime and, consequently, does not authorize resumption of questioning. The clearest example of reopening the dialog would be the case in which a suspect, who previously invoked the right to counsel, sends a message to police that he has changed his mind and now wants to tell his side of the story. However, this degree of clarity rarely exists and courts do not insist on it. Asking a question like "What is going to happen to me now?" after invoking the right to counsel, allows the police to explore whether the suspect wants to resume a generalized discussion of the

---

[115] Edwards v. Arizona, 451 U.S. 477, 101 S. Ct. 1880, 68 L. Ed. 2d 378 (1981) ("[A]n accused, . . . having expressed his desire to deal with the police only through counsel, is not subject to further interrogation by the authorities until counsel has been made available to him, unless the accused himself initiates further communication, exchanges, or conversations with the police.").

[116] *Id.*

[117] *Id.*

[118] *Id.*

crime.[119] However, in order to avoid misunderstandings, police officers must issue a fresh set of *Miranda* warnings. Only if the suspect willingly participates after manifesting a desire to resume the discussion and receiving fresh a fresh set of *Miranda* warnings will the suspect be considered to have reopened the dialog.

The third protection-terminating event derives from *Maryland v. Shatzer*.[120] A police detective tried to question Shatzer about allegations that he had sexually abused his son while he was in prison serving a sentence for an unrelated child-sexual-abuse offense. The interview ended when Shatzer invoked his right to counsel. Shatzer was released back into the general prison population. Two and a half years later, a second detective contacted Shatzer, who was still in prison, about the same allegations. This time Shatzer waived his *Miranda* rights and made an inculpatory statement. The Supreme Court ruled that a suspect who invokes the right to counsel does not gain permanent immunity from interrogation. Protection ends if there is a significant break in custody, lasting at least 14 days, between the first and second interrogations. A break in custody of this duration "provides plenty of time for the suspect to get reacclimated to his normal life, to consult with friends and counsel, and to shake off any residual coercive effects of prior custody." A suspect who agrees to discuss the case with police, after being free of police custody for at least 14 days, does so because he has thought the matter through and now believes that it is in his best interest, and not because he feels badgered into submission. The bar on police-initiated questioning ends because the reason for it — preventing police from badgering suspects into relinquishing their previously invoked *Miranda* rights — is absent.

The Court next considered whether Shatzer's return to the general prison population constituted a sufficient break in custody for *Miranda* purpose to allow resumption of questioning and found that it did. Shatzer was returned to the surroundings he had grown accustomed to, his life regained the sense of normalcy it previously had, and he had plenty of opportunity to deliberate. Accordingly, his question proof status ended14 days after he invoked the right to counsel during the first interrogation and police were free to attempt a new interrogation.

Returning a pretrial detainee to his jail cell, in contrast, does not constitute a break in *Miranda* custody. The two-week period commences to run for pretrial detainees only if they are released on bail. Fourteen days after their release, police may contact them, read them their *Miranda* rights, and seek to ascertain whether they are willing to speak in the absence of counsel.

---

[119] Oregon v. Bradshaw, 462 U.S. 1039, 103 S. Ct. 2830, 77 L. Ed. 2d 405 (1983) (plurality opinion); Clayton v. Gibson, 199 F.3d 1162 (10th Cir. 1999) ("I have something I want to get off my chest" sufficient to reopen dialog); Vann v. Small, 187 F.3d 650 (9th 1999) ("What is going to happen to me? What do you think I should do?" authorizes police to explore whether suspect wants to reopen dialog); United States v. Michaud, 268 F.3d 728 (9th Cir. 2001) (contact reinitiated where defendant's cellmate told police, in the defendant's presence, that he wanted to speak to someone "about a murder" and defendant did not object).

[120] **559 U.S. _ 130 S. Ct. 1213, 175 L. Ed. 2d 1045 (2010).**

2. Resuming Questioning After a Suspect Has Invoked the Right to Remain Silent

After a suspect invokes the right to remain silent, questioning must also cease. Police may not re-question the suspect about the same offense unless (1) the suspect re-opens the dialog or (2) there is a 14-day break in custody. However, police are allowed to question him about an unrelated offense after waiting a reasonable period of time.[121] This option does not exist when a suspect invokes the right to counsel. Once a suspect expresses a desire to deal with police only through counsel, the police may not question the suspect about *any* offense, even one that is unrelated, unless counsel is present, the suspect initiates the dialog, or there is a 14-day break in custody.[122]

To summarize, *Miranda* warnings must be given each time a suspect is subjected to a custodial interrogation. The suspect must waive his *Miranda* rights for his confession to be admissible, but the waiver does not have to be expressed. A waiver will be inferred from the suspect's conduct if the suspect responds to the questions, having been advised of his rights and with full awareness that he is not required to answer. Police may begin questioning after administering *Miranda* warning and ascertaining that they are understood, and may continue the interrogation unless or until the suspect expresses a clear request for an attorney or a clear wish to remain silent. If the suspect, either before or during the questioning, makes a clear request for an attorney, questioning must stop immediately and may not resume unless (1) counsel is present, (2) the suspect reopens the dialog, or (3) there is a break in custody, lasting at least 14 days between the first and second interrogations. If a suspect makes a clear assertion of the right to remain silent, questioning must also stop and may not resume as to the same offense unless (1) the suspect reopens the dialog or (2) there is a 14-day break in custody. However, the police may initiate questioning about an unrelated offense, after waiting a reasonable period of period.

§ 6.9   The Sixth Amendment Right to Counsel During Interrogations Conducted After the Commencement of Adversary Judicial Proceedings

The Sixth Amendment provides that "[i]n all criminal prosecutions, the accused shall enjoy the right . . . to have the assistance of counsel for his defense." Upon the lodging of formal charges, the suspect officially becomes an "accused" and the case enters the third phase. The system has now become fully adversarial and restrictions on police interrogations tighten. Figure 6.10 summarizes the restrictions that go into effect when the case enters the third phase.

---

[121]   Michigan v. Mosley, 423 U.S. 96, 96 S. Ct. 321, 46 L. Ed. 2d 313 (1975).

[122]   **Maryland v. Shatzer,** *supra* note 120; Edwards v. Arizona, *supra* note 115; Arizona v. Robertson, 486 U.S. 675, 108 S. Ct. 2093, 100 L. Ed. 2d 704 (1988).

Figure 6.10
Sixth Amendment Restrictions on Police Questioning

- The Sixth Amendment right to counsel attaches when adversary judicial proceedings are initiated.
- From this point forward, the government is prohibited from deliberately eliciting incriminating information from the defendant outside the presence of counsel unless the defendant gives a valid waiver of the right to counsel.
- Sixth Amendment restrictions on interrogation are offense specific. The restrictions apply only when the questions relate to a charged offense; they do not apply when the questions relate to other uncharged criminal activity.
- The Sixth Amendment right to counsel can be waived by a defendant in the same way that the *Miranda* right to counsel can be waived.

A. *Attachment of the Sixth Amendment Right to Counsel*

The Sixth Amendment right to counsel attaches when adversary judicial proceedings are commenced.[123] This generally occurs at the earliest of any of the following four events: (1) an **arraignment** (*i.e.*, the defendant's initial appearance before a judicial officer where he is informed of the charges, a probable cause determination is made, and bail is set); (2) a **grand jury indictment**; (3) an **information** (*i.e.*, a formal complaint filed by a prosecutor); or (4) a preliminary hearing (*i.e.*, a hearing at which the judge finds that there is enough evidence to bind the accused for trial).[124] Criminal prosecutions are not commenced by the issuance of an arrest warrant[125] or the making of an arrest.[126] Although police have authority to conduct investigations and make arrests, only judges, prosecutors, and grand juries have the ability to initiate a criminal prosecution.

The most common ways criminal prosecutions are initiated are at arraignments and preliminary hearings held after an arrest. However, other sequences are possible. The prosecutor can convene a grand jury and seek an indictment without waiting for the

---

[123] *See, e.g.*, Moran v. Burbine, 475 U.S. 412, 106 S. Ct. 1135, 89 L. Ed. 2d 410 (1986) (The Sixth Amendment, "[b]y its very terms . . . becomes applicable only when the government's role shifts from investigation to accusation. For it is only then that the assistance of one versed in the 'intricacies . . . of law' is needed to assure that the prosecution's case encounters 'the crucible of meaningful adversarial testing.'"); Kirby v. Illinois, 406 U.S. 682, 92 S. Ct. 1877, 32 L. Ed. 2d 411 (1972) (The right to counsel attaches only when "the government has committed itself to prosecute, [for it is] only then that the adverse positions of government and defendant have solidified."); **Rothgery v. Gillespie County, *Tex.*, 554 U.S. 191, 128 S. Ct. 2578, 177 L. Ed. 2d 366 (2008)** (a criminal defendant's initial appearance before a magistrate is one of several events that trigger attachment of Sixth Amendment right to counsel).

[124] *See* cases note 123 *supra*.

[125] *See, e.g.*, United States v. D'Anjou, 16 F.3d 604, 608 (4th Cir.), *cert. denied*, 512 U.S. 1242, 114 S. Ct. 2754, 129 L. Ed. 2d 871 (1994).

[126] *See, e.g.*, United States v. Langley, 848 F.2d 152 (11th Cir. 1988).

police. If an indictment is returned, the judge will issue a warrant for the accused's arrest. When a prosecution is initiated in this manner, the Sixth Amendment right to counsel will already have attached and there will be no *Miranda* phase.

B. *Deliberate Elicitation Standard*

Once adversary judicial proceedings are initiated, the case enters the Sixth Amendment phase and protection for the right to counsel expands. No longer is this right available only during *custodial interrogations*.[127] "*Deliberate elicitation*" is the triggering event that activates the Sixth Amendment right to counsel.[128] Defendants under formal charges have a right to have counsel present whenever the government deliberately elicits incriminating information from them pertaining to the charges, whether they are in custody, the interview constitutes an interrogation, or they are even aware that they are speaking with a police officer.[129]

The *deliberate elicitation* standard requires neither custody nor interrogation. In *Fellers v. United States*,[130] the Supreme Court found that this standard was met where police paid a post-indictment visit to the defendant's home and told him that they had come to discuss his involvement in drug distribution, that he had been indicted for conspiracy to distribute drugs, and that they had at warrant for his arrest. They went on to mention the names of four persons listed in the indictment. The defendant responded that he knew all four and had used methamphetamine with them. The officers then transported him to the county jail where they, for the first time, advised him of his *Miranda* rights." The Supreme Court held that the defendant's Sixth Amendment rights were violated when police engaged him in a discussion of the criminal charges that were pending against in the absence of counsel or a valid waiver of the right to counsel. The Court asserted "there is no question that the officers in this case 'deliberately elicited' information from the petitioner. Indeed, the officers, upon arriving at petitioner's house, informed him that their purpose in coming was to discuss his involvement in the distribution of methamphetamine and his association with certain charged co-conspirators."

---

[127] Review § 6.7 *supra*.

[128] *See, e.g.*, Fellers v. United States, 540 U.S. 519, 124 S. Ct. 1019, 157 L. Ed. 2d 1016 (2004); **Kuhlmann v. Wilson, 477 U.S. 436, 106 S. Ct. 2616, 91 L. Ed. 2d 364 (1986)** ("[O]nce a defendant's Sixth Amendment right to counsel has attached, he is denied that right when federal agents 'deliberately elicit' incriminating statements from him in the absence of his lawyer.").

[129] *See, e.g.*, Fellers v. United States, *supra* note 128 (holding that officers violated the Sixth Amendment by deliberately eliciting information from a defendant during a post-indictment visit to his home absent counsel or waiver of counsel, regardless of whether the officer's conduct constituted an "interrogation"); United States v. Henry, 447 U.S. 264, 100 S. Ct. 2183, 65 L. Ed. 2d 115 (1980) (defendant's Sixth Amendment right to counsel was violated when a paid informant, planted in his cellblock, "deliberately elicited" incriminating statements from him, even though the defendant was unaware he was speaking with a police informant).

[130] *Supra* note 128.

The lesson to be learned from *Fellers* is that police must administer *Miranda* warnings and obtain a valid waiver of the Sixth Amendment right to counsel before questioning defendants about criminal charges pending against them, even when the interview is voluntary and the defendant is not in custody.

C. Secret Interrogations Using Police Undercover Agents, Paid Informants, and Jailhouse Snitches

The deliberate elicitation standard originated in cases involving secret interrogations. In *Massiah v. United States*,[131] Massiah was arrested and indicted on a federal narcotics charge. He retained a lawyer and was released on bail. Federal agents prevailed on his co-defendant to allow them to install a hidden radio transmitter in his car. The co-defendant engaged Massiah in an incriminating conversation while the federal agents secretly listened. The Supreme Court reversed Massiah's conviction on the grounds that the government violated his Sixth Amendment right to counsel when, acting in collusion with his co-defendant, they deliberately elicited incriminating information from him, in the absence of his counsel, after he was indicted.

The practice condemned in *Messiah* would have been lawful during the *Miranda* phase for two reasons. First, Massiah was not in custody when he was secretly interrogated; he was at large. Second, warnings are not required during the *Miranda* phase when the suspect is unaware that his questioner is a police officer.[132] Both rules change during the Sixth Amendment phase. Secret interrogations using undercover agents, paid informants, and jailhouse snitches are not allowed.

However, the Sixth Amendment is not violated if the stealth interrogator does nothing to stimulate the conversation and merely serves as an attentive listener. In *Kuhlmann v. Wilson*,[133] police planted an inmate-informant in the defendant's jail cell, with instructions to "keep his ears open" and report what he heard, but not to ask questions. The informant did as instructed and, over time, the defendant made incriminating statements that were introduced against him at his trial. The Court held that

> a defendant does not make out a violation [of the Sixth Amendment] by showing that an informant, either through prior arrangement or voluntarily, reported his incriminating statements to the police. Rather, the defendant must demonstrate that the police and their informant took some action, beyond merely listening, that was designed deliberately to elicit incriminating remarks.[134]

---

[131]   377 U.S. 201, 84 S. Ct. 1199, 12 L. Ed. 2d 246 (1964) (Sixth Amendment right to counsel was violated when informant working for police elicited incriminating statements subsequent to indictment).

[132]   *See* Illinois v. Perkins, *supra* note 69 (holding that a prisoner's *Miranda* rights were not violated when he was questioned, without warnings, by a government undercover agent posing as a fellow inmate). Illinois v. Perkins is discussed in § 6.7(A)(3).

[133]   **Supra note 128.**

[134]   *Id.*

D. *Procedural Requirements for Conducting Post-Attachment Interrogations*

The procedural requirements for conducting pre- and post-attachment interrogations are now the same.[135] Before seeking to engage a criminal defendant in a discussion of the charges pending against him, police must administer *Miranda* warnings, obtain a valid waiver, and conduct the interview the same as she would a *Miranda*-phase interrogation. Former rules that prevented police from obtaining a valid waiver from a defendant who had previously retained or requested appointment of counsel have now been swept away.[136] Nothing bars police from approaching any defendant, whether represented or not, and seeking to determine whether he is willing to waive his Sixth Amendment right to counsel and discuss the charges outside his attorney's presence.

E. *Offense-Specific Nature of the Sixth Amendment Right to Counsel*

The Sixth Amendment right to counsel is *offense-specific*. That means that it applies only when police question a defendant under formal charges about that offense.[137] The defendant may be questioned about separate uncharged criminal activity, subject only to the *Miranda* rule.

In *Texas v. Cobb*,[138] the Supreme Court was asked to carve out an exception for crimes that are factually related. The police received a report that a home was burglarized and that a woman and child who occupied the home were missing. Acting on an anonymous tip that Cobb, who lived across the street, was involved in the burglary, the police questioned him about the events. Cobb gave a written confession to the burglary, but denied knowledge of the disappearances. He was subsequently indicted for the burglary and an attorney was appointed to represent him. While he was out on bail, Cobb admitted to his father that he had killed the missing woman and child, and his father contacted the police. Cobb was arrested and taken to the police station where he was given *Miranda* warnings and confessed to the murders. He later sought suppression, claiming that the police violated his Sixth Amendment right to counsel. His theory was that, when the Sixth Amendment right to counsel attaches, it attaches not only for the charged offense (*i.e.*, the burglary), but also for other uncharged offenses that are "closely related factually" (*i.e.*, the murders). The Supreme Court found this argument unpersuasive, and reaffirmed that when a person under formal charges for one offense is questioned about a separate uncharged offense, the Sixth Amendment right to counsel has no application. Because Cobb had not yet been charged with the murders when

---

[135]   **Montejo v. Louisiana, 556 U.S. 778, 129 S. Ct. 2079, 173 L. Ed. 2d 955 (2009),** *overruling* Michigan v. Jackson, 475 U.S. 625, 106 S. Ct. 1404, 89 L. Ed. 2d 631 (1986).

[136]   *Id.*

[137]   McNeil v. Wisconsin, 501 U.S. 171, 111 S. Ct. 2204, 115 L. Ed. 2d 158 (1991); Texas v. Cobb, 532 U.S. 162, 121 S. Ct. 1335, 149 L. Ed. 2d 321 (2001) (same).

[138]   *Supra* note 137.

he confessed to them, his only right was the right to *Miranda* warnings, and he received them. His confession was, therefore, admissible as evidence.

Figure 6.11, summarizes the key points covered in this section.

Figure 6.11
Comparison of the Right to Counsel Under the *Miranda* Rule and the Sixth Amendment

> - The *Miranda* right to counsel applies before formal charges are lodged, the Sixth Amendment right to counsel afterward.
> - The *Miranda* right to counsel is available only during custodial interrogations. The Sixth Amendment right to counsel is available whenever the police deliberately elicit information from a defendant about pending criminal charges, whether the interview constitutes an interrogation or the defendant is in custody or at large.
> - The *Miranda* right to counsel is not violated by secret interrogations conducted through undercover agents, informants, and jailhouse snitches; the Sixth Amendment right to counsel is.
> - The Sixth Amendment right to counsel is offense specific; it applies only when a defendant is questioned about a crime he has already been charged with. The *Miranda* rule is not offense specific; it applies whenever a suspect in custody is interrogated about any uncharged criminal activity.
> - Both rights to counsel may be waived and the procedures for obtaining a valid waiver and conducting the interview are the same for both.

§ 6.10   Use of Inadmissible Confession for Impeachment

Confessions must be freely and voluntarily given, not caused by a violation of the accused's Fourth Amendment rights, and not obtained in violation of the *Miranda* rule or the Sixth Amendment right to counsel in order to be admissible as evidence of guilt. However, confessions that fail these requirements are not entirely useless. They can be used for a limited purpose — **impeachment**.[139]

Impeachment involves an attack on a witness's credibility. One way to attack a witness's credibility is to show that the witness previously made statements that are inconsistent with his trial testimony. If the accused takes the witness stand and tells the jurors a story different from the one he previously told the police, the prosecution may, during cross-examination, use an inadmissible confession as impeachment evidence. In *Walder v. United States*,[140] the Supreme Court explained that "it is one

---

[139]   Harris v. New York, 401 U.S. 222, 91 S. Ct. 643, 28 L. Ed. 2d 1 (1971) (voluntary statements obtained in violation of *Miranda* rule are admissible to impeach a defendant's inconsistent trial testimony); Michigan v. Harvey, 494 U.S. 344, 110 S. Ct. 1176, 108 L. Ed. 2d 293 (1990) (voluntary statements obtained in violation of the Sixth Amendment right to counsel may be used for impeachment purposes); Kansas v. Ventris, 556 U.S. 586, 129 S. Ct. 1841, 173 L. Ed. 2d 801 (2009) (statements elicited by police informant after attachment of Sixth Amendment right to counsel can be used to impeach the defendant's inconsistent trial testimony).

[140]   347 U.S. 62, 74 S. Ct. 354, 98 L. Ed. 503 (1954).

thing to say that the Government cannot make an affirmative use of evidence unlawfully obtained. It is quite another to say that the defendant can turn the illegal method by which evidence in the Government's possession was obtained to his own advantage, and provide himself with a shield against contradiction of his untruths."[141] However, even this use is prohibited if the confession was in voluntary.[142] Involuntary confessions are considered too unreliable to be used for any purpose, including impeachment.

Figure 6.12
Impeachment Use of Inadmissible Confessions

An inadmissible confession may be used for impeachment only if:

1.   the defendant takes the stand and testifies in her own behalf.
2.   she tells the jurors a story different from the one she told the police, and
3.   the confession was freely and voluntarily given.

When a confession is admitted for impeachment purposes, the jurors may consider it for the sake of evaluating the trustworthiness of the defendant's trial testimony, but not as evidence of guilt.

When a confession has been contaminated so that it can be used only for impeachment, its value to the government is greatly reduced. A confession is one of the most powerful pieces of evidence that can be put before a jury. When a confession is introduced as substantive evidence of guilt, the impact on the defense is devastating. However, only an admissible confession (*i.e.*, one obtained in conformity with the requirements discussed in this chapter) may be introduced as evidence of guilt. The prosecution's potential gains from a contaminated confession are meager by comparison. First, it is the defense, not the prosecution, which controls whether an inadmissible confession can be introduced as impeachment evidence. The defense can thwart impeachment use by having the accused not testify, a right the accused enjoys under the Fifth Amendment. This generally happens in cases in which an accused has previously given an inadmissible confession because the accused now has little to gain and much to lose by testifying. Second, even if the accused takes the witness stand and tells the jurors a different story from the one he or she told the police, when a confession is used on cross-examination as impeachment evidence, the jurors may consider it for only one purpose — to evaluate whether the accused's trial testimony is trustworthy. The jurors will be instructed that they may not consider the confession as evidence of guilt.

---

[141]   *Id.* 347 U.S. at 65, 74 S. Ct. at 356.
[142]   Harris v. New York, *supra* note 139; Michigan v. Harvey, *supra* note 139.

§ 6.11   Restrictions on the Use of Derivative Evidence

Statements given in response to an interrogation are often instrumental in uncovering other evidence. The suspect, for example, may tell the police the location of physical evidence, such as the murder weapon or drugs, or identify potential prosecution witnesses. The initial statement may also prompt the suspect to give a subsequent statement in which further damaging disclosures are made. Evidence that derives from a confession is called "**derivative evidence**." Derivative evidence is generally treated the same as the confession. When a confession is obtained in compliance with all applicable legal requirements, the evidence is admissible. On the other hand, when a confession is tainted by illegal police practices, the taint generally carries over and destroys the admissibility of derivative evidence.[143]

The rule requiring suppression of derivative evidence is known as the "fruit of the poisonous tree" doctrine. The fruit of the poisonous tree doctrine was developed to destroy the incentive for police to violate the Constitution by taking away all gains.[144] Suppose Sticky-Fingered Sam is arrested on burglary charges and taken to the police station, where he is deprived of food and sleep for two days until he finally confesses. Sam admits to the crime, tells the police where he hid the stolen property, and names Joe as his accomplice. Several hours after he has eaten and slept, Sam, believing his situation is hopeless, gives a second confession, this time in writing. The police locate the stolen property where Sam said it was, prevail on Joe to testify, and offer the stolen property, Joe's testimony, and Sam's second confession into evidence. None of this evidence can be used because it constitutes of the fruits of an involuntary confession.[145] Allowing police to benefit from the coercive interrogation practices they used on Sam will give them an incentive to continue using them. Consequently, when police use coercion to obtain a confession, courts will invoke the poisonous tree doctrine and suppress the fruits of the confession along with the confession.[146] The same generally also holds true for the fruits of statements obtained in violation of the Fourth Amendment search and seizure clause[147] and the Sixth Amendment right to counsel.[148]

---

[143]   Nardone v. United States, 308 U.S. 338, 60 S. Ct. 2663, 84 L. Ed. 307 (1939); Wong Sun v. United States, *supra* note 24. *See also, generally,* Yale Kamisar, *On the "Fruits" of Miranda Violations, Coerced Confessions, and Compelled Testimony,* 93 Mich. L. Rev. 929 (1995).

[144]   *See* authorities *supra* note 143.

[145]   *See, e.g.,* Clewis v. Texas, 386 U.S. 707, 87 S. Ct. 1338, 18 L. Ed. 2d 423 (1967).

[146]   *Id.*

[147]   *See, e.g.,* Wong Sun v. United States, *supra* note 24 (physical evidence derived from confession procured in violation of suspect's Fourth Amendment rights inadmissible); Brown v. Illinois, *supra* note 25 (subsequent confession suppressed where police violation of suspect's Fourth Amendment rights caused suspect's initial confession).

[148]   *See, e.g.,* Brewer v. Williams, *supra* note 89; Nix v. Williams, *supra* note 8; United States v. Wade, 388 U.S. 218, 87 S. Ct. 1926, 18 L. Ed. 2d 1149 (1967) (same); United States v. Johnson, 196 F. Supp. 2d 795 (N.D. Iowa 2002).

The fruit of the poisonous tree doctrine, nevertheless, does not apply to *Miranda* warning violations. Although a failure to warn contaminates the unwarned statement, the fruits are admissible if the statement was voluntarily given.[149] This probably comes as a surprise. However, the fruits doctrine only applies to evidence obtained in violation of the Constitution. Although, the *Miranda* rule is based on the Fifth Amendment privilege against compulsory self-incrimination, a failure to warn, standing alone, does not violate a suspect's Fifth Amendment rights. The Fifth Amendment is violated only when a statement is compelled.[150] Consequently, the fruits of voluntary, unwarned statements can be used as evidence.

Figure 6.13
Restrictions on Admission of Derivative Evidence

1. The fruits of statements obtained in violation of the due process free and voluntary requirement, the Fourth Amendment search and seizure clause, and the Sixth Amendment right to counsel are inadmissible.
2. The fruits of statements obtained in violation of the *Miranda* rule are admissible, despite the violation, unless the statement was involuntary or the police violation was deliberate.

This does not mean that police can deliberately violate the *Miranda* rule and walk away with usable derivative evidence.[151] In *Oregon v. Elstad*,[152] the Supreme Court held that a simple failure to warn, not accompanied by coercion or other improper

---

[149] *See, e.g.*, United States v. Patane, 542 U.S. 630, 124 S. Ct. 2620 159 L. Ed. 2d 667 (2004) (failure to warn does not require suppression of the physical fruits of a statement if the statement is voluntary); Michigan v. Tucker, 417 U.S. 433, 94 S. Ct. 2357, 41 L. Ed. 2d 182 (1990) (failure to warn does not require suppression of the testimony of witness whose identity is discovered as a result of an unwarned, voluntary statement); Oregon v. Elstad, *supra* note 68 (a noncoercive, unintentional failure to warn does not require suppression of a subsequent voluntary confession given after warnings are administered). *But see* **Missouri v. Seibert, 542 U.S. 600, 124 S. Ct. 2601, 159 L. Ed. 2d 643 (2004)** (deliberately interrogating a suspect about the same matters twice, the first time without *Miranda* warnings and the second time after warnings are administered as part of a calculated strategy to undermine the exercise of *Miranda* rights requires suppression of both confessions).

[150] *See, e.g.*, Michigan v. Tucker, 417 U.S. 433, 444, 94 S. Ct. 2357, 2364, 41 L. Ed. 2d 182 (1974) ("[P]rophylactic *Miranda* warnings . . . are 'not themselves rights protected by the Constitution but [are] instead measures to ensure that the right against compulsory self-incrimination [is] protected'"); Oregon v. Elstad, *supra* note 68 (same).

[151] **Missouri v. Seibert**, *supra* note 149; United States v. Faulkingham, 295 F.3d 85 (1st Cir. 2002) (expressing view that suppression is required when police deliberately fail to give *Miranda* warnings in the hopes of obtaining admissible derivative or impeachment evidence or leads). *See also, generally*, Charles D. Weisselberg, *Deterring Police from Deliberately Violating* Miranda*: In The Stationhouse after Dickerson*, 99 Mich. L. Rev. 1121 (2001).

[152] *Supra* note 68 (holding that a suspect who responds to unwarned, noncoercive questioning is not disabled from subsequently waiving his rights and giving an admissible statement after warnings are properly administered).

conduct, does not destroy the admissibility of a subsequent statement that is given after warnings are administered. Specialists in police training took this to mean that the only thing at risk in withholding *Miranda* warnings was loss of the original unwarned statement, but that subsequent repetitions and derivative evidence could still be used. Based on this understanding, they developed an interrogation strategy known as "two-step" or "question-first" strategy. The strategy consisted of purposefully withholding *Miranda* warnings until a full confession was obtained, providing warnings, getting the suspect to confess again, and then offering the second confession into evidence. The effectiveness of this strategy was put to the test in *Missouri v. Seibert*.[153] In that case, police deliberately withheld *Miranda* warnings and interrogated the suspect until she confessed. They then took a 15-minute break, administered warnings, obtained a written waiver, turned the tape recorder on, and went over the details of the confession. The second confession was reduced to writing, signed, and offered into evidence. The Supreme Court held that the two-step interrogation strategy rested on a misunderstanding of its holding in *Oregon v. Elstad*. The failure to administer warnings the first time around in that case resulted from a good faith mistake, not a calculated strategy designed to undermine the effectiveness of the warnings by withholding them until after the suspect made a full confession, as the police did here. Police cannot magically transform inadmissible confessions into admissible ones by deliberately withholding warnings until after a confession is obtained, administering them, and then asking the suspect to repeat the confession. When officers deliberately use a two-step interrogative strategy to obtain a confession, derivative evidence will be suppressed along with the confession.[154]

§ 6.12   Restrictions on the Use of Confessions Given by Accomplices

This section begins with another story about Sticky-Fingered Sam. Sam pulled off a big "after hours" bank robbery by working a deal with Tillie Teller to share half the loot in exchange for keys to the bank vault. Unfortunately for Sam, his driver's license fell out while stuffing money into his pockets and the police quickly caught up with him. Sam was taken to the police station, where he was subjected to coercive interrogation methods. He confessed and named Tillie as his accomplice. Tillie is now facing trial. May she object to the prosecutor's introduction of Sam's confession as evidence against her?

---

[153] *Supra* note 153.
[154] *See, e.g.,* United States. v. Gilkeson, 431 F. Supp. 2d 270 (N.D.N.Y. 2006) (holding that fruit of poisonous tree doctrine bars admission of evidence that derives from a deliberate violation of the *Miranda* rule); State v. Knapp, 285 Wis. 2d 86, 700 N.W.2d 899 (2005) (reaching same result under state constitutional provision).

This question raises a problem that prosecutors encounter when they try to introduce one accomplice's confession as evidence against another. There are two constitutional objections Tillie might raise — one valid and the other invalid. The most obvious objection — that the police violated Sam's constitutional rights to obtain the confession — is not valid. The problem is lack of standing. Only a person whose constitutional rights have been violated has standing to challenge the admissibility of evidence on the grounds that it was unconstitutionally obtained.[155] That the confession was coerced is an objection that only Sam can raise.

However, Tillie has a valid objection to the prosecutor's introduction of Sam's confession against her. The Sixth Amendment confrontation clause guarantees that "[i]n all criminal prosecutions, the accused shall enjoy the right . . . to be confronted with the witnesses against him."[156] The purpose of this guarantee is to enable an accused to cross-examine prosecution witnesses and expose weaknesses and inaccuracies in their testimony.

An accused's Sixth Amendment right to confront prosecution witnesses bars the government from using an out-of-court statement given by an accomplice, implicating the accused, as evidence against the latter unless the government can prevail on the accomplice who gave the statement to testify at the trial where he can be cross-examined.[157] This means that Sam's confession cannot be introduced as evidence against Tillie unless Sam is willing to testify. Unfortunately for the prosecution, Sam can invoke the Fifth Amendment and refuse to testify because his testimony is self-incriminatory. Consequently, a prosecutor who wants to use one accomplice's confession as evidence against another is generally forced to grant immunity or work out a plea deal in exchange for this testimony.

§ 6.13   The Requirement of Corroboration of Valid Confessions

In order to secure a conviction, the prosecution must prove that a crime was committed and that the defendant was the person who committed it. Under early English common law, the defendant's confession could be used to establish both elements. This practice increased the danger that an innocent person might be convicted — even of a crime that never happened. To combat this danger, most American jurisdictions adopted the rule that in order to secure a conviction based on a confession, the prosecution must produce some evidence independent of the confession that the crime was

---

[155] Alderman v. United States, 394 U.S. 165, 89 S. Ct. 961, 22 L. Ed. 2d 176 (1969).

[156] The Sixth Amendment confrontation clause applies to the states through the Fourteenth Amendment. Pointer v. Texas, 380 U.S. 400, 85 S. Ct. 1065, 13 L. Ed. 2d 923 (1965).

[157] Lilly v. Virginia, 527 U.S. 116, 119 S. Ct. 1887, 144 L. Ed. 2d 117 (1999) (admission of nontestifying accomplice's confession violated defendant's confrontation clause rights).

committed by someone or, in other words, that there was in fact a crime.[158] The independent proof requirement is known as the **corpus delicti** rule.

The phrase *corpus delicti* means the "body of the crime" (*i.e.*, the fact that the crime charged was committed by someone). In the case of an unlawful homicide, for example, the prosecution would have to prove that a person is dead, and that his or her death was caused by a crime, before a confession given by the accused may be introduced as evidence. Courts differ on the amount of proof necessary to satisfy the foundation required by the *corpus delicti* rule. However, the modern tendency is to minimize this requirement by establishing a low threshold of proof.[159] The *corpus delicti* requirement is generally stated as demanding "some evidence" or "slight evidence," independent of the defendant's confession, that the confessed crime was committed.[160]

The *corpus delicti* requirement made sense when no safeguards existed against the admission of confessions secured by coercion. The danger that innocent people might be coerced into confessing to crimes that were never committed was real. However, with *Miranda* safeguards and the due process free and voluntary requirement, the legal situation has changed. With these changes, the original purpose of the *corpus delicti* requirement no longer exists,[161] and some have expressed misgivings about whether this requirement should be retained.[162] Requiring the prosecution to present independent evidence that the confessed crime was in fact committed before introducing a confession rarely accomplishes anything other than allowing the guilty to go free.[163]

§ 6.14   Summary and Practical Suggestions

A confession must pass at least four, and in some jurisdictions five, legal hurdles before it will be received as evidence of guilt. Voluntary confessions that fail some of these requirements may be used as impeachment evidence (*i.e.*, to attack the credibility of the accused's trial testimony if he takes the witness stand and tells the jurors a different story from the one he told the police). However, this use is relatively unimportant. Consequently, students need a solid grounding in the requirements for a valid confession and the phases in the development of a criminal case when each applies.

---

[158]   For a general discussion of the corroboration requirement, see Thomas A. Mullen, *Rule Without Reason: Requiring Independent Proof of the Corpus Delicti as a Condition of Admitting an Extrajudicial Confession*, 27 U.S.F. L. REV. 385 (1993) (recommending elimination of *corpus delicti* rule).

[159]   *Id.* at 390–391.

[160]   State v. Van Hook, 39 Ohio St. 3d 256, 261–262, 530 N.E.2d 883, 888–889 (1988); Thomas A. Mullen, *supra* note 159, at 390–391.

[161]   Willoughby v. State, 552 N.E.2d 462, 466 (Ind. 1990).

[162]   Thomas A. Mullen, *supra* note 162.

[163]   *See, e.g.*, State v. Thompson, 560 N.W.2d 535 (N.D. 1997) (confession insufficient to sustain conviction for sexual contact with young child when there was no independent evidence establishing the *corpus delicti*).

Due process free and voluntary requirement. When a confession is offered as evidence, the government bears the burden of proving by a preponderance of the evidence that the confession was given voluntarily. A confession is considered involuntary under the due process clause when: (1) an agent of the government applies improper pressures that (2) overcome the suspect's free will. Voluntariness is determined by examining the totality of circumstances under which the confession was given, with emphasis on: (1) the interrogation methods used by the police, (2) the suspect's degree of susceptibility, and (3) the conditions under which the interrogation took place.

Fourth Amendment exclusionary rule. Confessions that are causally related to a police violation of the suspect's Fourth Amendment rights (*i.e.*, unconstitutional investigatory stop, arrest, or search) are inadmissible, even if voluntary. Courts consider the following three factors in deciding whether a causal relationship exists: the length of time between the violation and the confession, the presence of intervening circumstances, and the purpose and flagrancy of the violation.

***McNabb-Mallory* rule**. The *McNabb-Mallory* rule was developed to enforce compliance with Rule 5(a) of the Federal Rules of Criminal Procedure, which requires federal officers to act without unnecessary delay in presenting persons arrested on federal charges to a magistrate for arraignment. It does this by requiring suppression confessions obtained during a period of unnecessary delay in complying with this requirement. Section 3501 of Omnibus Crime Control and Safe Streets Act of 1968 limited the *McNabb-Mallory* rule by preventing confessions obtained during the first six hours after an arrest on federal charges from being suppressed on this ground. The *McNabb-Mallory* rule was based on the Supreme Court's supervisory powers to establish rules of evidence for federal courts and is not binding on state courts, although some have voluntarily adopted it.

Fifth Amendment/*Miranda* rule. The *Miranda* rule, which is grounded in the Fifth Amendment privilege against self-incrimination, was developed to counteract the coercive atmosphere of a police custodial interrogation. *Miranda* warnings must be administered whenever the police: (1) interrogate a suspect, (2) who is then in custody, (3) about an offense with which he has not yet been charged. (If the suspect has already been charged with the offense, police must observe the Sixth Amendment right to counsel procedures, which are summarized below.) A suspect is considered "in custody" whenever the objective circumstances surrounding the encounter are such that a reasonable person would assess the situation as equivalent to an arrest. The suspect must be aware that the questioner is a police officer for *Miranda* custody to exist. An interrogation occurs when police ask questions or engage in other words or actions that they should know are reasonably likely to elicit an incriminating response from the suspect. Unless confronted with an emergency requiring immediate action to protect the public safety or their own safety, police must warn the suspect before initiating questioning. If the suspect, either before or during the questioning, clearly expresses a desire to speak with an attorney or to remain silent, questioning must stop immediately and may resume only under narrowly defined circumstances. Failure to comply with *Miranda* requirements results in suppression of the confession, but not derivative evidence unless police are guilty of coercion.

Sixth Amendment right to counsel. The Sixth Amendment right to counsel attaches upon the initiation of adversary criminal proceedings by way of a preliminary hearing, indictment, information, or arraignment. Once the Sixth Amendment right to counsel attaches, police may not deliberately elicit incriminating statements from the accused at a time when counsel is not present, unless the accused gives a valid waiver. This restriction applies whether the accused is in custody or at large. However, it only applies when the questioning relates to the pending charges; it does not apply when police question an accused about other uncharged criminal activity. The Sixth Amendment right to counsel can be waived. The procedures for obtaining a valid waiver and for conducting the interrogation are the same as under the *Miranda* rule.

Compulsory Self-Incrimination

7

No person . . . shall be compelled in any criminal case to be a witness against himself . . .

Fifth Amendment, 1791

Chapter Outline

KEY TERMS AND CONCEPTS

Absolute immunity	Reasonable suspicion
Appearance evidence	Search
Arrest	Seizure
Bodily evidence	Self-incrimination
Contempt	Strip search
Custodial interrogation	Subpoena (*ad testificatum*)
Investigatory detention	Subpoena (*duces tecum*)
Manual body cavity search	Testimony/testimonial evidence
Physical evidence	Use, including derivative use, immunity
Privilege	Witness
Probable cause to arrest	

§ 7.1   Introduction

The power to compel testimony is central to the existence of a legal system. Without it, there could be no trials. Our Constitution, nevertheless, limits the government's ability to use this power against the accused. The terrifying practices of the Court of the Star Chamber, in which suspects were interrogated in secret for hours until they finally confessed, were still fresh in memory when our nation was founded. The Framers of the Constitution made the choice to establish an accusatorial system — a system in which the government carries the burden of proving the charges through its own independent investigation, rather than by twisting confessions from the mouth of the accused. The cornerstone of this protection is found in the self-incrimination clause of the Fifth Amendment which provides that no "person . . . shall be compelled in any criminal case to be a witness against himself."

However, it is incorrect to think that criminal defendants may never be compelled to assist the government in building a criminal case against them. Our Constitution distinguishes between compelled testimony and compelled production of other forms of evidence.

Suspects have a monopoly on many forms of evidence that are needed to establish their guilt. Suppose Veronica Victim is found dead in her apartment, shot in the head with her own gun. Forensic analysis reveals that there are two sets of fingerprints on the gun and that it was fired twice, but the bullet in Veronica Victim's head is the only one found in her apartment. Investigators take samples from a trail of blood leading away

Figure 7.1
Constitutional Restrictions on Compulsory Self-Incrimination

Constitutional provision	Type of incriminating evidence	Scope of restriction
Fifth Amendment	Testimony	The government is prohibited from compelling suspects to disclose knowledge of their criminal activity.
Fourth Amendment	Physical evidence	The government may compel suspects to permit use of their body to produce evidence when it has grounds for the initial seizure and for any further invasion of privacy or bodily integrity that the compelled production of the evidence entails.

from her apartment. A lab report establishes that the blood belongs to someone else. Based on this, police surmise that Victim shot her assailant, who then grabbed her gun and killed her. A woman living in the apartment next door, Nosie Neighbor, reports seeing a heavy-set, well-dressed man in his early thirties, about six feet tall, leave Victim's apartment at about the time of death. Victim's ex-husband, Stephan Bullette, matches this description and is known to have made previous threats on Victim's life.

Unless Bullette can be compelled to cooperate, the police will probably not be able to solve this crime. The police would like to compel Bullette to assist them in the following ways: (1) answer questions about his relationship with Victim and his activities at the time of the crime; (2) appear before Neighbor in a lineup; (3) provide fingerprints for comparison; (4) provide a blood sample for forensic analysis; (5) submit to an examination of his body to determine whether he was shot and, if he was; and (6) undergo surgery to have the bullet removed for ballistics testing. The first form of compulsory assistance involves **testimony** and is regulated by the Fifth Amendment.

The remaining five involve **physical evidence**[1] and are regulated by the Fourth Amendment.

A. *Fifth Amendment Protection Against Testimonial Self-Incrimination*

The Fifth Amendment is the only provision that explicitly addresses compulsory **self-incrimination**, but its coverage is limited to testimony. The Fifth Amendment declares that "[n]o person ... shall be compelled in any criminal case to be a **witness** against himself." Witnesses provide testimony. Although the Fifth Amendment speaks of compulsion in a criminal case, this language has never been interpreted literally.

---

[1] Physical evidence includes all forms of evidence that do not involve testimony.

A person is considered to be a "witness against himself in a criminal case" when he is compelled to disclose information that could *later* be used against him in a criminal case, no matter where or when the compulsion occurs.[2]

The Fifth Amendment has a narrow sphere of operation — compelled testimony — but provides absolute protection within this sphere. The government may not compel Bullette to disclose knowledge of his own criminal activities, whether inside or outside a courtroom. However, the Fifth Amendment does not protect Bullette against being forced to assist the government in other ways. This has been the settled interpretation of the Fifth Amendment going back to 1910, when the Supreme Court declared:

> ... [T]he prohibition of compelling a man in a criminal court to be a witness against himself is a prohibition of the use of physical or moral compulsion to extort communications from him, not an exclusion of his body as evidence when it may be material.[3]

B. *Fourth Amendment Protection Against Bodily Self-Incrimination*

Constitutional protection for Bullette's body derives from the Fourth Amendment, which protects that "[t]he right of the people to be secure in their persons ... against unreasonable searches and seizures." Bullette's right to security in his person reaches three interests he has in his body. The first is his interest *freedom of movement*. In order to use Bullette's body as a source of evidence, the police must gain physical control over him. Consequently, evidence obtained from using Bullette's body without his consent will be suppressed unless the police have constitutional grounds for seizing and detaining him long enough to obtain the evidence.

Bullette also has an interest in his *bodily privacy*. This interest does not reach parts that are exposed to the public,[4] such as his voice, handwriting, physical appearance, and fingerprints,[5] but it does reach the parts that are not. Examining Bullette's nude body for evidence of a bullet wound will intrude on his privacy. Finally, Bullette has an interest in his bodily integrity. Drawing blood and performing surgery to retrieve the bullet will intrude on this interest.[6] When the police perform procedures that invade a suspect's privacy or *bodily integrity*, they must satisfy two sets of Fourth Amendment requirements. They must have grounds for the initial seizure and also for any further invasion of privacy or bodily integrity that compulsory production of the evidence entails.

---

[2] Garner v. United States, 424 U.S. 648, 96 S. Ct. 1178, 47 L. Ed. 2d 370 (1976) (on income tax returns); Lefkowitz v. Turley, 414 U.S. 70, 94 S. Ct. 316, 38 L. Ed. 2d 274 (1973) (in any legal proceeding, civil or criminal, formal or informal); **Miranda v. Arizona, 384 U.S. 436, 86 S. Ct. 1602, 16 L. Ed. 2d 694 (1966)** (during custodial interrogations).

[3] Holt v. United States, 218 U.S. 245, 31 S. Ct. 2, 53 L. Ed. 1021 (1910).

[4] **Katz v. United States, 389 U.S. 347, 88 S. Ct. 507, 19 L. Ed. 2d 576 (1967).**

[5] United States v. Dionisio, 410 U.S. 1, 93 S. Ct. 764, 35 L. Ed. 2d 67 (1973).

[6] **Schmerber v. California, 384 U.S. 757, 86 S. Ct. 1826, 16 L. Ed. 2d 908 (1966).**

§ 7.2 Fifth Amendment Protection Against Testimonial Self-Incrimination

The Fifth Amendment privilege against self-incrimination was adopted as a direct response to the horrors that took place in the Court of the Star Chamber in seventeenth-century England. The accused could be placed under oath and forced to reveal knowledge of his own criminal activities on pain of being thrown into prison for perjury if he lied and for contempt of court if he remained silent.[7] The text of the Fifth Amendment self-incrimination clause, which applies to the states through the Fourteenth Amendment,[8] reads: "[n]o person . . . shall be compelled in any criminal case to be a witness against himself." While this language seems to be limited to compulsion during criminal trials, the Fifth Amendment has never been interpreted this narrowly. A person is compelled to be a witness against herself in a criminal case whenever she is compelled to disclose information to the government that might later be used against her in a criminal case. Fifth Amendment protection is available in all legal proceedings, judicial or administrative, formal or informal, criminal or civil.[9] Moreover, protection is not limited to legal proceedings. The Fifth Amendment also applies outside the courtroom. In Chapter 6, you saw an important out-of-court application of the Fifth Amendment — its application during police **custodial interrogations**.[10]

The Fifth Amendment affords two levels of protection: (1) the right to remain silent and (2) the privilege not to answer self-incriminating questions. The right to remain silent involves a complete exemption from the citizen's normal duty to testify. This protection is available in only two settings — during police custodial interrogations and at a defendant's criminal trial. Suspects in police custody have an absolute right to remain silent. They do not have to answer any police questions, even questions that lack incriminating potential.[11] If the suspect invokes the right to remain silent, questioning must cease. Defendants also enjoy the right to remain silent (*i.e.*, not to testify) at their criminal trial.[12] If they decide not to testify, the prosecution may not call them as a witness.

In no other proceedings do citizens enjoy this level of protection. They are required to appear as a witness, but are privileged not to reveal incriminating information.[13] The

---

[7]   Murphy v. Waterfront Comm'n of New York Harbor, 378 U.S. 52, 84 S. Ct. 1594, 12 L. Ed. 2d 678 (1964); Doe v. United States, 487 U.S. 201, 108 S. Ct. 2341, 101 L. Ed. 2d 184 (1988); **Pennsylvania v. Muniz, 496 U.S. 582, 110 S. Ct. 2638, 110 L. Ed. 2d 528 (1990).**

[8]   Malloy v. Hogan, 378 U.S. 1, 84 S. Ct. 1489, 12 L. Ed. 2d 653 (1963).

[9]   Lefkowitz v. Turley, *supra* note 2; Maness v. Meyers, 419 U.S. 449, 95 S. Ct. 584, 42 L. Ed. 2d 574 (1975).

[10]   *See* §§ 6.8–6.11.

[11]   **Miranda v. Arizona**, *supra* note 2. The *Miranda* rule is covered in §§ 6.8–6.11.

[12]   Murphy v. Waterfront Comm., *supra* note 7; Malloy v. Hogan, *supra* note 8.

[13]   Hoffman v. United States, 341 U.S. 479, 71 S. Ct. 814, 95 L. Ed. 1118 (1951).

Figure 7.2
Levels of Fifth Amendment Protection

1. Suspects have the right to remain silent during custodial interrogations.
2. Criminal defendants have a right to remain silent at their criminal trial.
3. In all other legal contexts, citizens have a right not to answer specific questions that might incriminate them, but are not exempt from testifying.

difference between these two levels of protection is illustrated by the following example. Suppose Bullette receives a subpoena to appear before a grand jury, which is investigating whether he should be indicted for murdering Victim. Bullette has no choice about whether to testify.[14] If subpoenaed, he must appear and make himself available for questioning. However, if asked a question that calls for a self-incriminating response, he may invoke the Fifth Amendment and refuse to answer.[15] To be regarded as incriminating, the answer need not exhibit guilt outright. A witness is privileged not to answer questions if the answer could provide a link in a chain of facts evidencing his guilt.[16] "Did you ever threaten Victoria Victim's life?" "Did you see her the night she died?" or "Did you know she owned a gun?" are examples of questions that call for answers that "tend to incriminate." If Bullette is asked questions like these, he may invoke the Fifth Amendment and refuse to answer. Furthermore, Bullette does not have to explain what it is about the answer that would be incriminating. If witnesses had to do this, they would be compelled to surrender the very protection that the privilege guarantees. The judge is required to sustain a claim of privilege unless it is perfectly clear, considering the implications of the question and the setting in which it is asked, that the answer could not possibly be incriminating.[17]

With this introduction, we are now going to take a closer look at the Fifth Amendment.

§ 7.3   — Prerequisites for Application of the Fifth Amendment

The most efficient way to analyze the Fifth Amendment is to break the language down into components. The text prohibits the government from: (1) compelling a person (2) to be a witness (3) against himself in a criminal case. Three requirements are necessary to invoke the protection: (1) compulsion, (2) testimony, and (3) self-incrimination.

---

[14] United States v. Dionisio, *supra* note 5.
[15] *Id.*
[16] Hoffman v. United States, *supra* note 13.
[17] *Id.*

A. *Testimony*

The Fifth Amendment only applies to testimony.[18] Testimony in a Fifth Amendment sense includes any words or actions that disclose things a person knows.[19] Compulsion to speak does not invariably involve testimony. Suspects in lineups, for example, are sometimes required to repeat words spoken by the perpetrator to determine whether their voice characteristics are recognizable. Voice characteristics may be the only way a victim can identify a person whose voice was heard but whose face was never seen. Compulsion to repeat words spoken by a perpetrator does not involve testimony because the suspect is not being compelled to disclose anything he knows. The compulsion, instead, relates to voice characteristics.[20] Compulsion to exhibit physical characteristics involves physical evidence and is protected, if at all, by the Fourth Amendment.[21]

Figure 7.3
Prerequisites for Application of the Fifth Amendment

> Testimony, compulsion, and self-incrimination are necessary for the Fifth Amendment to apply.
>
> 1. Testimony includes words or actions that disclose things a person knows.
> 2. Compulsion occurs when the disclosure is obtained by threatening serious consequence if the information is withheld.
> 3. Information is self-incriminating when it exposes the maker to a risk of criminal prosecution.

B. *Compulsion*

Compulsion occurs when information is extracted by threatening serious consequence if the information is withheld. The normal manner in which our legal system compels testimony is by issuing a subpoena. A **subpoena (*ad testificatum*)** is a court order to appear and testify, on penalty of being held in **contempt** of court and fined or imprisoned. However, any threatened harm will suffice as long as it is serious. Suppose that a police officer suspected of taking a bribe is summoned to appear before a police disciplinary board and told that he will be fired unless he makes a full disclosure. He

---

[18]   **Schmerber v. California**, *supra* note 6.

[19]   *See, e.g.*, Doe v. United States, *supra* note 7 ("[I]n order to be testimonial, an accused's communication must, explicitly or implicitly, relate a factual assertion or disclose information. Only then is a person compelled to be a 'witness' against himself."); Pennsylvania v. Muniz, *supra* note 7 (same).

[20]   United States v. Dionisio, *supra* note 5.

[21]   *See* § 7.7 *infra*.

capitulates and admits to his wrongdoing. The officer's statement may not be used against him in a criminal prosecution because it was compelled.[22]

Compulsion also has a temporal dimension. The relevant time for evaluating whether a person has been compelled to incriminate herself in violation of the Fifth Amendment is when the statement was made originally. The Fifth Amendment prohibits the government from compelling individuals to *make* incriminating statements, not from using incriminating statements they previously made voluntarily. The contents of voluntarily prepared incriminating records, journals, and documents, accordingly, are not protected by the Fifth Amendment. Consequently, when the government is aware of their existence and location, it may seize them under a search warrant and use them as evidence.[23]

When the government does not know their existence or location, a **subpoena** (***duces tecum***) will have to be used to obtain them. A subpoena (*duces tecum*) is an order, issued by a court or legislative body, which commands the person named in it to appear and produce designated documents. Even though voluntarily prepared documents lack Fifth Amendment protection, a person served with a subpoena to turn them over can invoke the Fifth Amendment in situations where the act of production has self-incriminating testimonial aspects apart from the content. Suppose that government issues a subpoena *duces tecum* ordering Bullette to appear before the grand jury and bring with him receipts and cancelled checks for all weapon purchases made during the past 24 months. Compliance with this subpoena tacitly admits that such documents exist, are in Bullette's possession, and are the ones sought by the subpoena. Since these admissions are self-incriminating, Bullette can invoke the Fifth Amendment and refuse to comply.[24]

---

[22] *See, e.g.*, Garrity v. New Jersey, 385 U.S. 493, 87 S. Ct. 616, 17 L. Ed. 2d 562 (1967) (testimony compelled where police officer was given a choice between incriminating himself or losing his job); Uniformed Sanitation Men Ass'n, Inc. v. Commissioner of Sanitation of City of New York, 392 U.S. 280, 88 S. Ct. 1917, 20 L. Ed. 2d 1089 (1968) (same); Spevack v. Klein, 385 U.S. 511, 87 S. Ct. 625, 17 L. Ed. 2d 574 (1967) (testimony compelled where attorney was given a choice between incriminating himself or disbarment).

[23] **United States v. Hubbell, 530 U.S. 27, 20 S. Ct. 2037, 147 L. Ed. 2d 24 (2000)**; Fisher v. United States, 425 U.S. 391, 96 S. Ct. 1569, 48 L. Ed. 2d 39 (1976); *Packwood v. Senate Select Committee On Ethics*, 510 U.S. 1319, 114 S. Ct. 1036, 127 L. Ed. 2d 530 (1994); Couch v. United States, 409 U.S. 322, 93 S. Ct. 611, 34 L. Ed. 2d 548 (1973); United States v. Moody, 977 F.2d 1425 (11th Cir. 1992) (personal writings); State v. Barrett, 401 N.W.2d 184 (Iowa 1987) (journal); State v. Andrei, 574 A.2d 295 (Me. 1990) (diary).

[24] *See, e.g.*, **United States v. Hubbell**, *supra* note 23 (recognizing that the act of producing self-incriminatory documents in response to a subpoena has communicative aspects of its own, apart from the contents of the documents produced); Fisher v. United States, *supra* note 23 (same); People v. Havrish, 8 N.Y.3d 39, 866 N.E.2d 1009 (2007) (holding that Fifth Amendment protects the accused from being compelled to surrender evidence, even evidence that is not otherwise cloaked with Fifth Amendment protection, if the act of production has testimonial or communicative aspects. *See also, generally*, Lance Cole, *The Fifth Amendment And Compelled Production of Personal Documents after United States v. Hubbell — New Protection For Private Papers?* 29 Am. J. Crim. L. 123 (2002): Thomas Kiefer Wedeles, Note, *Fishing for Clarity in a Post-Hubbell World: The Need for a Bright-line Rule in the Self-incrimination Clause's Act of Production Doctrine*, 56 Vand. L. Rev. 613 (2003).

Hubbell case

C. Self-Incrimination

Fifth Amendment protection can only be claimed for disclosures that are incriminating. To be incriminating, they must do more than reveal criminal activity. They must create a risk of the person's being convicted of the crimes revealed.[25] The government is permitted to compel disclosure of information that lacks this potential. People under arrest, for example, may be compelled to furnish biographical information (*i.e.*, name, address, Social Security number, etc.) needed for booking because this information is not incriminating.[26]

Even when disclosures relate to criminal activity, they may be compelled if they do not expose the person to a risk of conviction.[27] This risk is removed if the person has already been tried for the crime because the double jeopardy clause will bar re-prosecution.[28] Suppose that Sticky-Fingered Sam commits a burglary and stores the stolen property at his sister Mary Wanna's house. Mary Wanna is guilty of aiding and abetting. However, she can be forced to testify against Sam if she has already been tried, even though her testimony will require disclosure of her own criminal activity, because her testimony is no longer incriminating. The double jeopardy clause has removed the risk of reconviction and Fifth Amendment protection along with it.

The most common way in which claims of privilege are overridden is through grants of immunity.[29] Grants of immunity are used when the government needs the testimony of a "small fish" to convict a "big fish." Two forms of immunity are available — absolute and use. **Absolute immunity** (also called transactional immunity) bars the government from prosecuting the witness for crimes revealed through compelled testimony.[30] Because the government is barred from prosecuting, the testimony is no longer incriminating and may be compelled.

The government, nevertheless, is not required to grant absolute immunity in order to compel testimony. The Fifth Amendment is satisfied if the government grants the witness immunity from the government's use of the testimony and its fruits in any prosecution it later brings.[31] This level is called **use immunity**, or **use, including derivative use**, **immunity**. The reason use immunity is adequate to satisfy the Constitution is that it grants legal protection equivalent to the "fruit of the poisonous tree" remedy given for evidence procured in violation of constitutional rights. By providing this remedy in advance, the government removes the witness' objection to testifying, while retaining the

---

[25]   Kastigar v. United States, 406 U.S. 441, 92 S. Ct. 1653, 32 L. Ed. 2d 212 (1972).

[26]   *See, e.g.*, **Pennsylvania v. Muniz**, *supra* note 7.

[27]   Kastigar v. United States, *supra* note 25.

[28]   *In re Keijam*, 226 Conn. 497, 628 A.2d 562 (1993). *See also In re Grand Jury Subpoena to Doe*, 41 F. Supp. 2d 616 (W.D. Va. 1999) (a witness may not invoke the privilege against self-incrimination when prosecution is barred by such legal barriers as the statute of limitations, the doctrine of double jeopardy, or grants of immunity); *Ex parte Moore*, 804 So. 2d 245 (Ala. Civ. App. 2001) (same).

[29]   Kastigar v. United States, *supra* note 25.

[30]   *Id.*

[31]   *Id.*

right to prosecute. If the government later decides to prosecute after granting immunity, it will be required to prove that all evidence it seeks to introduce was derived independently of the compelled testimony.[32]

When the same criminal act is punishable under both state and federal law, grants of immunity given by either jurisdiction will bind the other to the extent of use immunity.[33] While the other jurisdiction remains free to prosecute, it must establish that the evidence it plans to introduce was obtained through its own independent investigation and not, directly or indirectly, from the previously immunized testimony.[34]

Grants of immunity must be recommended by the prosecutor and approved by the judge. Police lack authority to promise suspects that they will receive immunity if they cooperate. Confessions induced through false promises of immunity are considered involuntary and cannot be used as evidence.[35]

§ 7.4 — Rules for Invoking and Waiving Fifth Amendment Protection

A. Invoking the Fifth Amendment

Criminal defendants have the right to remain silent at their trial. They invoke this right by not taking the witness stand. A defendant's decision not to testify is final; the prosecutor is not permitted to call the defendant as a witness. The decision not to testify is a difficult choice for defendants because jurors tend to speculate about why they failed to take the stand and deny the charges. The Fifth Amendment prohibits the prosecutor from capitalizing on this tendency. In a leading case, the prosecutor, during closing arguments, told the jurors that the defendant was the only person who could provide information relating to the victim's murder, and yet he had "not seen fit to take the stand and deny or explain."[36] The Supreme Court reversed the conviction, holding that the prosecutor's comment impermissibly infringed on the defendant's Fifth Amendment right to remain silent. Adverse comments on a defendant's failure to testify penalize the exercise of a constitutional right and make assertion costly. When a defendant chooses to remain silent, the prosecution is prohibited from drawing attention to this choice by arguing to the jurors that it furnishes evidence of guilt. The judge must also, on request, instruct the jurors that they may not infer guilt from a defendant's silence.[37]

Other witnesses are required to testify, but are privileged not to answer questions that call for an incriminating response. The privilege against self-incrimination is not

---

[32]   *Id.*

[33]   Murphy v. Waterfront Comm., *supra* note 7.

[34]   Kastigar v. United States, *supra* note 25.

[35]   See § 6.4 *supra.*

[36]   Griffin v. California, 380 U.S. 609, 85 S. Ct. 1229, 14 L. Ed. 2d 106 (1965).

[37]   Carter v. Kentucky, 405 U.S. 288, 101 S. Ct. 1112, 67 L. Ed. 2d 241 (1981).

self-executing. A witness who desires its protection must expressly invoke it. This puts the judge on notice that the witness considers the answer incriminating. If the witness voluntarily answers the question without invoking the privilege, the answer will not be considered "compelled."[38]

Witnesses invoke the privilege by stating in response to a specific question: "I refuse to answer on the grounds that it might incriminate me." When a witness invokes the privilege, the judge must determine whether a truthful answer would, in fact, have this tendency. Because the judge has no way of knowing what the witness' answer would be, the judge must rule on the witness's claim of privilege based on the incriminating potential of the question. When the incriminating potential is unclear, the judge faces a dilemma. The Supreme Court has indicated that claims of privilege should be honored unless there is no rational basis for believing that a truthful answer to the question could be incriminating.[39] If the judge erroneously instructs the witness to answer, the witness's testimony has been compelled and cannot be used against him or her in subsequent criminal proceedings.

B. *Waiver of the Privilege*

A waiver occurs when a person who has a Fifth Amendment privilege voluntarily testifies without invoking it. Under *Miranda*, a valid waiver requires a fourfold warning. Although the Supreme Court has declined to impose a similar requirement in other contexts,[40] judges generally take extreme precautions to ensure that the decision of a criminal defendant to waive the protection of the Fifth Amendment is made intelligently and with full knowledge of the consequences.

C. *Scope of the Waiver*

Criminal defendants who take the witness stand waive the privilege, but only concerning the matters about which they have testified.[41] They cannot waive the privilege for the sake of putting forth their version of the facts and then invoke it to block cross-examination. A contrary rule would give them an unfair advantage. However, they

---

[38] *See, e.g.*, United States v. Monia, 317 U.S. 424, 63 S. Ct. 409, 87 L. Ed. 376 (1943); Johnson v. United States, 318 U.S. 189, 63 S. Ct. 549, 87 L. Ed. 704 (1943). *See also* Minnesota v. Murphy, 465 U.S. 420, 104 S. Ct. 1136, 79 L. Ed. 2d 409 (1984) (defendant's failure to assert the privilege against self-incrimination during a meeting with a probation officer left him in no position to complain that his statement admitting commission of rape and murder was compelled); Garner v. United States, 424 U.S. 648, 96 S. Ct. 1178, 47 L. Ed. 2d 370 (1976) (failure to claim privilege against self-incrimination before disclosing incriminating information on a federal tax return forfeited the right to object to use of information in a criminal prosecution on the grounds that it was compelled).

[39] Maness v. Meyers, *supra* note 9.

[40] *See, e.g.*, Minnesota v. Murphy, *supra* note 38 (probation officers are not required to administer warnings before asking questions that call for incriminating response); United States v. Washington, 431 U.S. 181, 97 S. Ct. 1814, 52 L. Ed. 2d 238 (1977) (judges are not required to issue warnings to witnesses called to testify before grand juries investigating them).

[41] Mitchell v. United States, 526 U.S. 314, 119 S. Ct. 1307, 143 L. Ed. 2d 424 (1999); Brown v. United States, 356 U.S. 148, 78 S. Ct. 622, 2 L. Ed. 2d 589 (1958).

retain the right to invoke the privilege if they are cross-examined about matters beyond the scope of their testimony.[42] If Bullette takes the witness stand and limits his testimony to the fact that he was at a bar, drinking with friends, when Victim was killed, he may be cross-examined about his alibi, but not about whether he hated Victim, knew she owned a gun, or threatened her life, because he did not testify about these matters. This strikes a fair balance between the interests of the defendant and the government. A defendant is permitted to limit the subjects he is willing to discuss, but not to distort the truth.

§ 7.5 — Protection Against Adverse Consequences from Exercising the Privilege Against Self-Incrimination

When people invoke the Fifth Amendment, the natural tendency is to think that they have something to hide. The Fifth Amendment prohibits the government from capitalizing on this tendency in criminal trials[43] and sentencing proceedings.[44] Neither the prosecutor nor the judge is allowed to call attention to the fact that the defendant failed to take the witness stand and deny the charges at his trial or to suggest that it furnishes evidence of guilt.[45] Allowing jurors to draw a negative inference from a defendant's failure to testify would discourage exercise of the Fifth Amendment privilege out of fear that silence would be equally incriminating. For similar reasons, jurors are not allowed to be told that the defendant invoked the Fifth Amendment during a police interrogation.[46]

The rule prohibiting adverse inferences from being drawn from a defendant's reliance on the Fifth Amendment only applies during criminal trials and sentencing proceedings; it does not apply in civil cases, parole revocation hearings, police disciplinary actions, or other proceedings.[47] Although witnesses have a right to invoke the Fifth Amendment in these proceedings, the Fifth Amendment does not guarantee that their decision to do so will be cost-free. Chapter 10 considers the consequences of invoking the privilege in police disciplinary proceedings.

---

[42] *See* authorities *supra* note 41.

[43] Griffin v. California, *supra* note 36 (prosecutor may not comment on defendant's failure to testify); Carter v. Kentucky, *supra* note 37 (upon defendant's request, court must charge jury that no adverse inference may be drawn from defendant's failure to testify).

[44] Mitchell v. United States, *supra* note 41.

[45] Griffin v. California, *supra* note 36.

[46] Doyle v. Ohio, 426 U.S. 610, 96 S. Ct. 2240, 42 L. Ed. 2d 91 (1976).

[47] *See, e.g.,* Baxter v. Palmigiano, 425 U.S. 308, 96 S. Ct. 1551, 47 L. Ed. 2d 810 (1976) (Noting that "the prevailing rule [is] that the Fifth Amendment does not forbid adverse inferences against parties to civil actions when they refuse to testify in response to probative evidence against them"; holding that adverse inferences may be drawn from prisoner's silence in prison disciplinary proceedings); United States v. Stein, 233 F.3d 6 (1st Cir. 2000) (bar discipline proceeding); United States v. Serafino, 82 F.3d 515 (1st Cir. 1996) (civil tort action).

§ 7.6 — Self-Reporting Laws and the Fifth Amendment

Each year, millions of Americans are compelled, on penalty of criminal prosecution, to fill out a report to the federal government, detailing their year's economic activity. The report is a 1040 income tax return. What protection does the Fifth Amendment confer on citizens like Sticky-Fingered Sam, whose income derives exclusively from crime?

Whether the Fifth Amendment privileges citizens not to file government reports that could draw attention to their criminal activity depends on the government's purpose in requiring the report. Citizens are not excused from complying with reporting statutes like the Internal Revenue Code, which serve a valid regulatory purpose. Sam must file a federal income tax return and pay his taxes just like the rest of us.[48] He may, however, refuse to answer specific questions on the form that could incriminate him, such as the nature of his occupation or the source of his income.[49] Income tax laws, sales tax laws, occupational tax laws, and hit-and-run motorist statutes are examples of some of the many statutes with reporting requirements that serve a legitimate regulatory purpose.[50] The Fifth Amendment provides no defense for failing to comply with them.

People engaged in criminal activity, on the other hand, do not have to comply with statutes that are enacted purely for the sake of entrapping them. Suppose that Congress enacts a statute that imposes a special tax on income from the sale of stolen property. Taxpayers subject to this "tax" are required, on penalty of criminal prosecution, to file a tax return, disclosing their name, Social Security number, and source of income. The purpose of this so-called tax law is not to raise revenue. Its purpose is to force people who traffic in stolen property to identify themselves to the government. Citizens may ignore reporting statutes that (1) apply to a highly select group engaged in criminal activity and (2) require them to report information that could, and probably will, lead to their prosecution.[51] Laws with these characteristics are not legitimate regulatory measures. The Fifth Amendment provides a complete defense against prosecution for violating them.

---

[48] Garner v. United States, 424 U.S. 648, 96 S. Ct. 1178, 47 L. Ed. 2d 370 (1975); United States v. Sullivan, 274 U.S. 259, 47 S. Ct. 607, 71 L. Ed. 1037 (1927).
[49] Garner v. United States, *supra* note 48.
[50] California v. Byers, 402 U.S. 424, 91 S. Ct. 1535, 29 L. Ed. 2d 748 (1983) (hit-and-run motorist statute); United States v. Sullivan, *supra* note 48 (federal income tax).
[51] Marchetti v. United States, 390 U.S. 39, 88 S. Ct. 697, 19 L. Ed. 2d 889 (1968) (invalidating statute requiring gamblers to register with the Internal Revenue Service); Grosso v. United States, 390 U.S. 62, 88 S. Ct. 709, 19 L. Ed. 2d 906 (1968) (invalidating statute imposing an excise tax on gambling); Haynes v. United States, 390 U.S. 85, 88 S. Ct. 722, 19 L. Ed. 2d 923 (1968) (invalidating statute requiring registration of firearms, used to prosecute persons engaged in criminal activity); Leary v. United States, 395 U.S. 6, 89 S. Ct. 1532, 23 L. Ed. 2d 57 (1969) (invalidating statute requiring persons trafficking in marijuana to register and pay an occupational tax).

§ 7.7 Fourth Amendment Protection Against Bodily Self-Incrimination

Information stored in a suspect's memory is not the only thing that can incriminate him. His appearance, fingerprints, footprints, breath, blood, hair, saliva, and other biological characteristics can be equally incriminating. However, the Fifth Amendment does not protect suspects from compulsory self-incrimination through evidence that derives from their body because this evidence is physical, not testimonial.

The constitutional distinction between compelled testimony and compulsory production of **physical evidence** was dramatically illustrated during the O.J. Simpson murder trial when Simpson was forced to try on a glove found at the murder scene in front of the jury. Had the glove fit, the effect could have been almost as devastating as a confession. The Fifth Amendment gave Simpson no protection against being forced to try on the glove because he was being compelled to exhibit physical characteristics (*i.e.*, the size of his hand), not to reveal his thoughts. Simpson, on the other hand, did not take the witness stand and the prosecution did not call him because the Fifth Amendment protected him from being forced to testify.

The Framers relegated protection for the suspect's body to the Fourth Amendment, which guarantees " (t)he right of the people to be secure in their persons . . ., against unreasonable searches and seizures . . ." The right to security in one's person encompasses the three interests people have in their bodies — (1) freedom of movement, (2) bodily privacy, and (3) bodily integrity. Concentrating on these three interests is the key to understanding Fourth Amendment protection against compulsory production of physical evidence. Freedom of movement is always implicated when the police perform procedures that require use of the suspect's body. This means that the police always need grounds for a seizure. Whether they need grounds beyond this depends on whether the procedures subsequently performed invade the suspect's privacy or bodily integrity. When police perform procedures that invade privacy or bodily integrity, they must have separate grounds for the second invasion. Grounds for arrest alone are not enough to justify highly intrusive bodily searches.

Clarity is promoted by grouping physical evidence obtained from a suspect's body into two categories: (1) **appearance evidence** and (2) **bodily evidence**.

A. Appearance Evidence

Appearance evidence refers to evidence that derives from body characteristics that are routinely displayed to the public.[52] Compulsory submission to photographing, lineups, fingerprinting, handwriting and voice samples, and field sobriety

---

[52] **United States v. Dionisio**, *supra* note 5 (voice exemplar); United States v. Mara, 410 U.S. 19, 93 S. Ct. 774, 35 L. Ed. 2d 99 (1973) (handwriting exemplar); United States v. Wade, 388 U.S. 218, 87 S. Ct. 1926, 18 L. Ed. 2d 1149 (1967) (compulsion to repeat the perpetrator's words during a lineup); **Pennsylvania v. Muniz**, *supra* note 7 (field sobriety test).

tests[53] are examples of such procedures.[54] Because a person's physical appearance, voice, handwriting, fingerprints, and body coordination are external characteristics that are exposed to public view, neither privacy nor bodily integrity is invaded when the police compel suspects to use these characteristics to produce evidence. Only one interest is implicated — the suspect's interest in freedom of movement. Police must gain physical control over the suspect to perform these procedures.

> Because only one interest is implicated, the rule for when police may compel suspects to participate in producing appearance evidence is easy to remember: Police are permitted to compel participation whenever they have constitutional grounds to seize the suspect and detain him long enough to perform the procedure.

B. Bodily Evidence

Bodily evidence refers to physical evidence obtained by searching areas of a suspect's body not normally exposed to the public, penetrating the body surface or removing biological materials[55] or foreign substances.[56] In the hypothetical posed at the beginning of this chapter, searching Bullette's naked body for evidence of a gunshot wound,[57] taking a blood sample for analysis,[58] and surgically removing the bullet[59] are examples of bodily evidence. These procedures implicate two interests. The police must restrain Bullette's freedom of movement (the first invasion) long enough to perform a highly intrusive procedure (the second invasion). When procedures performed on a suspect's body intrude upon the suspect's privacy or bodily integrity, having grounds for the initial seizure is not enough. There must be separate grounds for the second invasion.

§ 7.8   — Requirements for Appearance Evidence

The most common procedures involving appearance evidence are: (1) station house lineups; (2) showup identifications at the crime scene; (3) photographing, measuring, fingerprinting, and taking handwriting and voice exemplars; and (4) field sobriety tests. These procedures invade the suspect's interest in freedom of movement and, consequently, require grounds for a seizure, but that is all. Because a person's

---

[53]   Field sobriety tests are based on the relationship between intoxication and loss of coordination. Tests for sobriety include such things as having the suspect walk heel-to-toe, stand on one foot, or touch the tip of the nose with his or her finger.

[54]   *See* authorities note 52.

[55]   **Schmerber v. California**, *supra* note 6; Skinner v. Railway Labor Executives' Ass'n, 489 U.S. 602, 109 S. Ct. 1402, 103 L. Ed. 2d 639 (1989).

[56]   Cupp v. Murphy, 412 U.S. 291, 93 S. Ct. 2000, 36 L. Ed. 2d 900 (1973).

[57]   Bell v. Wolfish, 441 U.S. 520, 99 S. Ct. 1861, 60 L. Ed. 2d 447 (1979).

[58]   **Schmerber v. California**, *supra* note 6.

[59]   Winston v. Lee, 470 U.S. 753, 105 S. Ct. 1611, 84 L. Ed. 2d 662 (1985).

physical appearance, fingerprints, footprints, handwriting, voice, body coordination, and gait are exposed to public view, there is no privacy interest in them. As a result, a lawful arrest is the only constitutional requirement needed to compel participation.[60] Even *Miranda* warnings are unnecessary because there is no interrogation.[61]

Figure 7.4
Appearance Evidence

Appearance evidence refers to evidence that can be taken from a suspect's body without: (1) searching areas not normally exposed to the public, (2) penetrating the surface, or (3) removing biological or foreign materials. The main examples include:

1. Station house lineups.
2. Showup identifications at the crime scene.
3. Photographs, fingerprints, footprints, body measurements, and voice and handwriting exemplars.
4. Field sobriety tests.

These procedures are considered routine incidents of a lawful arrest and require no justification beyond grounds for arrest.

A. *Compulsory Production of Appearance Evidence During* Terry *Stops*

Since *Terry* stops are required to be brief and minimally intrusive, procedures that are time-consuming or too much like an arrest are beyond their scope. *Terry* detainees, for example, may not be taken to the police station, without their consent, for lineups, questioning, or other procedures.[62] Virtually the only time a detainee may be moved from the place of the stop is when the movement is to a nearby crime scene for a showup identification.[63]

---

[60] *See* cases *supra* note 53.

[61] Williams v. State, 257 Ga. App. 54, 570 S.E.2d 362 (Ga. Ct. App. 2002) (*Miranda* warnings not required before taking blood sample for DNA testing); State v. Harmon, 952 P.2d 402 (Idaho Ct. App. 1998) (same, blood-alcohol test); Com. v. Cameron, 44 Mass. App. Ct. 912, 689 N.E.2d 1365 (1998) (same, field sobriety test); State v. Lee, 184 Ariz. 230, 908 P.2d 44 (1995) (same, Breathalyzer test); State v. Acosta, 951 S.W.2d 291 (Tex. Ct. App. 1997) (same, asking suspect to count backward as test for intoxication).

[62] *See, e.g.*, Hayes v. Florida, 470 U.S. 811, 105 S. Ct. 1643, 84 L. Ed. 2d 705 (1985); Dunaway v. New York, 442 U.S. 200, 99 S. Ct. 2248, 60 L. Ed. 2d 824 (1979); 4 W. LaFave, Treatise on Search & Seizure § 9.2 (f) (g) (3d ed. 1996).

[63] *See, e.g.*, People v. Ross, 317 Ill. App. 3d 26, 739 N.E.2d 50 (2000) (officers conducting a field investigation into a fresh crime are permitted to transport suspect a short distance to a nearby crime scene for a showup identification where witnesses are available who can confirm or deny that police have apprehended the right person); Commonwealth v. Barros, 425 Mass. 572, 682 N.E.2d 849 (1997) (same); State v. Lund, 853 P.2d 1379 (Wash. Ct. App. 1993) (same).

Nonintrusive procedures like fingerprinting and photographing may be performed at the scene of the stop when this can be done expeditiously.[64]

B. Special Statutory Procedures for Obtaining Nontestimonial Identification Evidence

In some jurisdictions, an alternative statutory procedure exists for obtaining appearance evidence.[65] The judge is given authority, upon the request of a prosecutor, to enter an order (commonly called a "nontestimonial identification order") directing a suspect to appear at a particular place and time to undergo a covered procedure. The covered procedures generally include lineups; photographing; fingerprinting; foot printing; measurements; handwriting and voice exemplars; and hair, blood, urine, semen, and saliva samples.[66] The court-ordered alternative is particularly attractive because judges have the authority to issue nontestimonial identification orders on a reduced showing that resembles **reasonable suspicion**.[67] This makes nontestimonial identification orders a useful investigative tool. Once reasonable suspicion exists, the prosecutor can seek a court order compelling the suspect to appear for a lineup or other covered procedure to gather the additional evidence needed to establish probable cause for an arrest.

Court orders to appear are enforced through contempt sanctions. The failure to appear in response to a court order is punishable as contempt of court.

C. Consequences of Violating the Fourth Amendment

An illegal arrest taints appearance evidence just like it taints other things. If the police arrest Sticky-Fingered Sam without probable cause and obtain a positive match between his fingerprints and the ones found at the crime scene, and then put him in a lineup where he is identified by the victim, the fingerprint match and lineup

---

64   See, e.g., Hayes v. Florida, *supra* note 62; People v. Green, 298 Ill. App. 3d 1054, 233 Ill. Dec. 389, 700 N.E.2d 1097 (1998) (photographing suspect at stop location permissible during lawful *Terry* stop); State v. Eastman, 691 A.2d 179 (Me. 1997) (administering field sobriety test permissible during *Terry* stop).

65   See, e.g., Alaska R. Ct. 16(c)(1)-(2); ARIZ. REV. STAT. ANN. § 13-3905; COLO. R. CRIM. P. 41.1; IDAHO CODE ANN. § 19-625; IOWA CODE § 810.1 et seq.; NEB. REV. STAT. §§ 29-3301 et seq.; N.C. GEN. STAT. § 15A-271 et seq.; UTAH CODE ANN. §§ 77-8-1 et seq.; VERMONT R. CRIM. P. 41. See also 4 W. LAFAVE, TREATISE ON SEARCH & SEIZURE § 9.7(b), at 327 (3d ed.1996).

66   See, e.g., N.C. GEN. STAT. § 15A-271 (1999); VERMONT R. CRIM. P. 41.1.

67   See, e.g., In re Nontestimonial Identification Order Directed to R.H., 171 Vt. 227, 762 A.2d 1239 (2000) (upholding nontestimonial identification order, issued on reasonable suspicion, requiring suspect to submit to collection of saliva for DNA comparison); Bousman v. Iowa Dist. Court, 630 N.W. 2d 789 (Iowa 2001) (nontestimonial identification orders do not violate Fourth Amendment because their issuance is based on reasonable suspicion, rather than probable cause).

identification will be suppressed as the tainted fruits of the poisonous tree.[68] However, the taint does not affect subsequent prosecutions for unrelated crimes. If police illegally arrest Sam, take his mug shot, and put it in the mug shot book, and months or years later the victim of a different offense identifies him from his mug shot, suppression is not required because the use of a mug shot to obtain an identification in the investigation of an unrelated offense months or years later is sufficiently attenuated from the illegal arrest as to be free of the taint.[69]

§ 7.9 — Requirements for Bodily Evidence

A lawful custodial arrest confers automatic authority to search a suspect's outer clothing for evidence of crime, contraband, and weapons, even though police lack probable cause to believe that anything incriminating will be found.[70] However, it does not confer authority to: (1) inspect the suspect's private parts; (2) search below the surface of the body; or (3) remove bodily fluids, tissues, or residues. Physical evidence obtained by invading a suspect's privacy or bodily integrity is called bodily evidence. Examples include:

- Removal of incriminating residue from the body's surface
- Taking X-rays
- Performing strip searches and body cavity searches
- Taking body tissue and fluids for forensic analysis
- Reaching inside a suspect's mouth or pumping a suspect's stomach to recover evidence
- Operating on a suspect under general anesthesia to retrieve a foreign object needed as evidence

---

[68] *See, e.g.,* **Hayes v. Florida**, *supra* note 62 (suppressing fingerprints obtained during illegal detention); Davis v. Mississippi, 394 U.S. 721, 89 S. Ct. 1394, 22 L. Ed. 2d 676 (1969) (same); United States v. Crews, 445 U.S. 463, 100 S. Ct. 1244, 63 L. Ed. 2d 537 (1980) (suppressing pretrial identification through use of photograph taken during illegal detention); United States. v. Guevara-Martinez, 262 F.3d 751 (8th Cir. 2001) (suppressing fingerprints obtained during unlawful stop); United States v. Fisher, 702 F.2d 372 (2d Cir. 1982) (suppressing eyewitness identification made after illegal arrest); *In re* T.L.L., 729 A.2d 334 (D.C. 1999) (suppressing eyewitness identification that was product of illegal detention); State v. Rolle, 265 N.J. Super. 482, 627 A.2d 1157 (1993) (suppressing lineup identification that derived from illegal arrest); United States v. Perez, 732 F. Supp. 347, 352 (E.D.N.Y. 1990) (suppressing photograph obtained after illegal detention).

[69] *See, e.g.,* United States v. Beckwith, (D. Utah 1998) (suppression of photograph taken during routine booking procedures following an illegal arrest is not required in a subsequent prosecution on an unrelated charge); People v. McInnis, 6 Cal. 3d 821, 100 Cal. Rptr. 618, 494 P.2d 690 (1972) (same); United States v. Olivares-Rangel, 458 F.3d 1104 (10th Cir. 2006) (fingerprint evidence obtained as part of a routine book procedure may be used in a subsequent prosecution on an unrelated charge). *See also* WAYNE R. LAFAVE, 3 SEARCH & SEIZURE § 11.4 (g) (3d ed. 1996).

[70] United States v. Robinson, 414 U.S. 218, 94 S. Ct. 467, 38 L. Ed. 2d 427 (1973); United States v. Edwards, 415 U.S. 800, 94 S. Ct. 1234, 39 L. Ed. 2d 771 (1974). *See also, generally,* Wayne R. LAFAVE, 3 SEARCH & SEIZURE § 5.3 (3d ed. 1996).

Although all of these procedures involve searches, they are not routine searches included within the search incident to arrest exception to the warrant clause. A separate justification is necessary.[71] The precise justification required varies with the seriousness of the intrusion. Highly intrusive bodily searches are allowed only when: (1) the government's need for the evidence exceeds the intrusion into the suspect's privacy or bodily integrity necessary to retrieve it, (2) there is a clear indication that the desired evidence will be found, (3) a search warrant is obtained (or is excused due to exigent circumstances), and (4) the procedure used to retrieve the evidence is reasonable and is performed in a reasonable manner.

Figure 7.5
Bodily Evidence

> Bodily evidence refers to evidence taken from a suspect's body by: (1) searching parts not normally exposed to the public, (2) penetrating the body's surface, or (3) taking biological or foreign materials. Examples include:
>
> - Removing incriminating residues from the body's surface
> - Taking X-rays
> - Conducting strip searches and body cavity searches
> - Taking body tissue and fluids for forensic analysis
> - Reaching into a suspect's mouth or pumping his or her stomach to recover evidence

A. The Framework for Evaluating Compelled Production of Bodily Evidence: Schmerber v. California

The modern framework for evaluating when highly intrusive bodily searches may be performed to retrieve evidence was established in *Schmerber v. California*.[72] Schmerber was convicted of driving while intoxicated based on the chemical analysis of a blood sample taken from his body without his consent. The blood was drawn by a physician, at the direction of the police, while Schmerber was in the hospital, where he had been taken from the scene of the accident following his arrest for drunk driving. Schmerber objected to this evidence on the grounds that drawing blood without his consent violated his Fifth Amendment privilege against self-incrimination and Fourth Amendment right to be free from unreasonable searches and seizures. The Supreme Court made short shrift of his first claim. Because the evidence was physical, not testimonial, the Fifth Amendment privilege did not apply. Schmerber's Fourth Amendment claim raised a more serious question.

---

[71] *See, e.g.,* Illinois v. Lafayette, 462 U.S. 640, 103 S. Ct. 2605, 77 L. Ed. 2d 65 (1983); Fuller v. M.G. Jewelry, 950 F.2d 1437 (9th Cir. 1991); Mary Beth G. v. City of Chicago, 723 F.2d 1263 (7th Cir. 1983).

[72] **384 U.S. 757, 86 S. Ct. 1826, 16 L. Ed. 2d 908 (1966).**

After establishing that drawing blood from a suspect's body without consent constitutes a search, the Court established a framework for evaluating when searches below the body surface satisfy Fourth Amendment standards of reasonableness. Four factors must be considered: (1) the reasonableness of compelling the suspect to submit to the procedure, (2) the probability that the desired evidence will be found, (3) whether a search warrant is obtained, and (4) whether the procedure is reasonable and is performed in a reasonable manner.

The first factor — the reasonableness of compelling the suspect to submit to the procedure — is determined by balancing the government's need for the evidence against the invasiveness of the procedure required to obtain it. The government's need must be greater than the invasiveness for forced submission to be Constitutionally reasonable. Second, bodily invasive searches are not allowed on a mere chance that evidence will be found; there must be a "clear indication" that the desired evidence is present. Third, police must obtain a search warrant unless the evidence will be dissipate or destroyed as a result of the delay needed to obtain a warrant. Finally, the procedure performed to retrieve the evidence must be reasonable and must be performed in a reasonable manner.

Applying these factors, the Supreme Court concluded that drawing blood from Schmerber for chemical analysis was reasonable under the circumstances, even though it was done without a search warrant. The smell of alcohol on Schmerber's breath, as well as his bloodshot eyes, provided a clear indication that he was intoxicated. Consequently, there was a high probability that a blood-alcohol test would be successful in recovering evidence. Second, drawing blood is a routine medical procedure that carries no threat to health and almost no pain. Consequently, the government's need for the evidence, outweighed the seriousness of intrusion required to obtain the evidence. Third, although a search warrant is normally required before forcing a suspect to undergo a medical procedure, none was required here because the percentage of alcohol in the blood begins to diminish shortly after drinking stops. Delaying the search to obtain a warrant would have resulted in the destruction of this evidence. Finally, because the blood extraction was performed in a hospital setting by a trained professional, the procedure was reasonable and was performed in a reasonable manner. The Court stressed that drawing blood is a routine medical procedure that carries no risk and almost no pain and cautioned that this decision should not be understood as applying to highly invasive and dangerous procedures.[73]

B. Surgical Intrusions to Recover Evidence

Nine years later, the Supreme Court was asked to decide whether a suspect could be compelled to undergo surgery. In *Winston v. Lee*,[74] a prosecutor sought a court order to compel a suspect who was shot during a robbery to undergo surgery to remove a

[73] *Id.* at 772, 86 S. Ct. at 1836.
[74] 470 U.S. 753, 105 S. Ct. 1611, 84 L. Ed. 2d 662 (1985).

bullet lodged in his collarbone so the prosecutor could use it as evidence. Using the approach outlined in *Schmerber*, the Court ruled against the government. The surgical procedure for which the authorization was sought was far more painful, dangerous, and invasive than the blood extraction authorized in *Schmerber*, while the evidence was less necessary because the prosecutor already had ample evidence to secure a conviction.[75] This being the case, forced surgery was constitutionally unreasonable. The general tone of the opinion, nevertheless, makes it doubtful that the government's need for evidence could ever be great enough to force a suspect to undergo surgery under general anesthesia, putting his or her life at risk.

§ 7.10   — Necessity of a Search Warrant to Explore for Bodily Evidence

Schmerber and *Winston* both involved searches that intruded below the body's surface. In *Schmerber*, the intrusion resulted from insertion of a needle to draw blood, while in *Winston* the intrusion resulted from performing surgery. In discussing the need for a search warrant before performing searches that penetrate the surface of the body, the *Schmerber* Court wrote:

> Search warrants are ordinarily required for searches of dwellings, and absent an emergency, no less could be required where intrusions into the human body are concerned . . . The importance of informed, detached and deliberate determinations of the issue whether or not to invade another's body in search of evidence is indisputable and great.

Although the quoted language stresses the fact that the contemplated procedure — drawing blood — intruded into the body, courts have not treated this as a limiting factor. A search warrant is normally required before a suspect can be compelled to undergo procedures involving: (1) penetration of the body's surface; (2) taking saliva,[76] urine,[77] semen, pubic hair,[78] or other bodily tissues or fluids; (3) manual inspection of rectal or genital cavities[79]; (4) severe pain or discomfort; (5) risks to health; or (6) intense

---

[75]   *Id.* at 765B766, 105 S. Ct. at 1619B1620.

[76]   United States v. Nicolosi, 885 F. Supp. 2d 50 (E.D.N.Y. 1995); State v. Ostroski, 201 Conn. 534, 518 A.2d 915 (1986); State v. Garcia-Salgado, 170 Wash.2d 176, 240 P.3d 153 (Wash., 2010).

[77]   National Treasury Employees Union v. Von Raab, 489 U.S. 656, 109 S. Ct. 1384, 103 L. Ed. 2d 685 (1989) (requiring a person to provide a urine sample involves a search); United States v. Edmo, 140 F.3d 1289 (9th Cir. 1998) (search warrant required unless evidence will be destroyed by delay).

[78]   *See, e.g.,* United States v. Nobel, 433 F. Supp. 2d 129, 133 n. 3 (D. Md. 2006) ("Courts have erred on the side of applying the *Schmerber* balancing test to requests for saliva samples even though, technically, procedures to collect such samples entail no intrusion beneath the skin."); *In re* Grand Jury Proceeding, 455 F. Supp. 2d (D.N.M. 2006) (search warrant is required to obtain a saliva sample); United States v. Nicolosi, 855 F. Supp. 2d 50 (E.D.N.Y. 1995) (same).

[79]   Rodrigues v. Furtado, 950 F.2d 805 (1st Cir. 1991); Fuller v. M.G. Jewelry, *supra* note 71; State v. Fontenot, 383 So. 2d 365 (La. 1980); People v. More, 738 N.Y.S.2d 667, 764 N.E.2d 967 (N.Y. 2002).

humiliation.[80] On the other hand, courts have not insisted on a search warrant before performing benign procedures like "the placing of the arrestee's hands under an ultra-violet lamp; examining the arrestee's arms to determine the age of burn marks; swabbing the arrestee's hands with a chemical substance; taking scrapings from under the arrestee's fingernails; [or] taking a small hair sample from the arrestee's head."[81]

Figure 7.6
Bodily Evidence Procedures for Which a Search Warrant Is Necessary

Unless confronted with an emergency in which the delay could cause evidence to be destroyed, the officer should obtain a search warrant before performing or arranging for the performance of procedures that involve:

- taking bodily tissues or fluids,
- penetration of the surface of the body,
- manual probing of rectal or genital cavities,
- significant pain or physical discomfort,
- risks to health, or
- intense humiliation.

When a search warrant is required, searching without a warrant violates the Fourth Amendment unless the exigent circumstances exception applies. This exception allows the police to conduct a warrantless search to preserve evidence when they have grounds for a search coupled with probable cause to believe that the evidence will be destroyed if they delay action to obtain a warrant.[82] Courts have applied the exigent circumstances exception to the three situations involving bodily intrusive searches: (1) taking blood, breath, or urine samples to perform tests for alcohol intoxication; (2) swabbing residues left on the skin; and (3) reaching into a suspect's mouth to prevent evidence from being swallowed. Police do not need to obtain a search warrant in these three situations, but the other *Schmerber* requirements still apply.

A. *Testing for Alcohol Intoxication*

Because the percentage of alcohol in the blood begins to decrease rapidly once drinking stops, police officers need to take immediate action to preserve this evidence once they make an alcohol-related arrest. The exigent circumstances exception formed the basis for the Supreme Court's holding in *Schmerber*, allowing blood to be drawn without a search warrant for alcohol testing. Breathalyzer tests and chemical analysis

---

[80]   State v. Williams, 15 Kan. App. 2d 656, 815 P.2d 569 (1991).

[81]   3 WAYNE R. LAFAVE, SEARCH & SEIZURE § 5.3 (3d ed. 1996).

[82]   Michigan v. Tyler, 436 U.S. 499, 98 S. Ct. 1942, 56 L. Ed. 2d 486 (1978); Ker v. California, 374 U.S. 23, 83 S. Ct. 1623, 10 L. Ed. 2d 726 (1963).

of urine are alternative procedures for measuring the presence of alcohol in the body and, consequently, may also be performed without a search warrant.

Students should not conclude that a warrant is never necessary to have blood drawn for chemical analysis. The properties for which the blood will be tested determine whether a warrant is necessary. When the properties are stable and do not change over time, such as DNA or blood type, there are no exigent circumstances and a warrant must be obtained before blood may be drawn.[83]

B. Swabbing Incriminating Residue on the Skin

Many crimes leave incriminating residue on the perpetrator's skin. Firing a gun leaves microscopic chemical residue; physical contact with the victim may leave biological tissue and fiber residue. Residue evidence must be taken as soon as police officers are aware of its existence because residue can be washed off, wiped off, and disappears naturally in the normal course of living. Techniques for obtaining residue evidence are even less intrusive than for drawing blood. Residue can be removed by rubbing a cotton swab over the suspect's skin where the residue is located and sending the specimen to a laboratory for analysis. In *Cupp v. Murphy*,[84] the police, while questioning the murder victim's husband, noticed debris under his fingernails that looked like dried blood and asked for permission to take a scraping. When the suspect refused, put his hands in his pockets, and started abrading his fingernails against coins and keys, the officers grabbed him and took the scraping without his consent. A lab analysis of the scraping revealed traces of his wife's blood. The Supreme Court held that the police were justified in taking the scraping without a warrant because they had probable cause to believe that Cupp had murdered his wife and was in the process of destroying evidence and were, therefore, confronted with exigent circumstances.

C. Reaching Inside a Suspect's Mouth to Prevent Evidence from Being Swallowed

Suspects, particularly in narcotics cases, sometimes try to swallow evidence to prevent discovery. With the suspect chomping on evidence, there is no time to get a warrant. Because a suspect's mouth is not considered a "sacred orifice,"[85] police may use reasonable force it pry it open.[86] When this fails, officers sometimes try to prevent swallowing through a maneuver called a "chokehold," which consists of grabbing the suspect by the throat and applying pressure. While this maneuver is effective to

---

[83] McBride v. State, 840 S.W.2d 111 (Tex. Ct. App. 1992).
[84] 412 U.S. 291, 93 S. Ct. 2000, 36 L. Ed. 2d 900 (1973).
[85] People v. Johnson, 231 Cal. App. 3d 1, 15, 282 Cal. Rptr. 114, 122 (1991).
[86] *See, e.g.,* State v. Strong, 493 N.W.2d 834 (Iowa 1992).

prevent swallowing, it also cuts off breathing and, as a result, some courts consider it too dangerous to be used.[87]

When a suspect succeeds in swallowing evidence, stomach pumping is sometimes tried as a last resort. In *Rochin v. California*,[88] the Supreme Court found this practice unconstitutional. However, *Rochin* was decided before *Schmerber* and it is unlikely that it would be decided the same way today. Stomach pumping is not life-threatening and causes no lasting trauma or pain. As a result, most courts consider stomach pumping and use of laxatives to be a constitutionally acceptable means of recovering evidence when performed in a hospital setting by a trained physician.[89]

§ 7.11 — Strip Searches and Manual Body Cavity Searches

Strip and body cavity searches are used for two main law enforcement purposes: (1) to obtain evidence for use at the trial, and (2) to prevent contraband and weapons from being introduced into detention facilities. This section explores the Fourth Amendment requirements for each kind of search.

A. Definitions

The term "**strip search**" does not have a single precise meaning. Varying definitions can be found in case law, statutes, police department regulations, and jail policy manuals. However for Fourth Amendment purposes, the term refers to "any [forced] exposure or observation of a portion of a person's body where the person has a 'reasonable expectation of privacy.'"[90] "Deeply imbedded in our culture . . . is the belief that people have a reasonable expectation not to be unclothed involuntarily, to be observed unclothed or to have their private parts observed . . . by others."[91] Strip searches, in a Fourth Amendment sense, refers to everything from forced removal of outer clothing to visual inspections of a person's genitals and anus at close range,

---

[87] *See, e.g.*, Merriweather v. State, 228 Ga. App. 246, 491 S.E.2d 467 (1997) (allowed); People v. Fulkman, 235 Cal. App. 3d 555, 286 Cal. Rptr. 728 (1992) (allowed); **State v. Tapp, 353 So. 2d 265 (La. 1977) (not allowed).**

[88] 342 U.S. 165, 72 S. Ct. 205, 96 L. Ed. 183 (1952).

[89] *See, e.g.*, State v. Payano-Roman, 290 Wis. 2d 380, 714 N.W.2d 548 (2006); **State v. Tapp, 353 So. 2d 265 (La. 1977)**; Hendrix v. State, 843 So. 2d 1003 (Fla. Dist. Ct. App. 2003); Lewis v. State, 56 S.W.3d 617 (Tex. Ct. App. 2001); Beck v. State, 216 Ga. App. 532, 455 S.E.2d 110 (1995); State v. Strong, 493 N.W.2d 834 (Iowa 1992); Oviedo v. State, 767 S.W.2d 214 (Tex. Ct. App. 1989). *But see* Williams v. Payne, 73 F. Supp. 2d 785 (E.D. Mich. 1999) (forcible stomach pumping to retrieve evidence violates Fourth Amendment).

[90] Doe v. Calumet City, 754 F. Supp. 1211, 1216 n.9 (N.D. Ill. 1990).

[91] *Id.*

but without touching.[92] Touching converts the search into a **manual body cavity search** and requires a stronger justification.

Although strip searches normally involve a complete disrobing, this is not necessary. The Supreme Court recently applied this term in a case where a middle school student was required to remove her outer clothing and pull her bra and underpants away from her body in the presence of two school officials.[93] Although the school officials testified that they were unable to see her privates, the Supreme Court declined to include "who was looking and how much was seen" in the definition of a strip search. The fact that the student was forced to remove her outer clothing in the presence of school officials was enough to warrant treating the incident as a strip search. The Court found that the student's Fourth Amendment rights were violated because school officials lacked reasonable suspicion that she had drugs hidden in her underwear. The Court noted that strip searches are categorically distinct from searches of outer clothing and ruled that a search that exposes private parts of the body requires reasonable suspicion that it will pay off.

B. Post-Arrest Investigative Strip Searches

Although the strip search in *Unified School District # 1 v. Redding* occurred in a school setting, lower courts have applied the same standard to investigatory strip searches performed by police. Reasonable suspicion the person arrested has evidence of the crime of arrest hidden underneath his/her clothing is necessary to perform an investigatory strip search incident to arrest.[94]

---

[92] *See, e.g.*, Masters v. Crouch, 872 F. 2d 1248 (6th Cir. 1989) (requiring suspect to unbutton her blouse and expose her chest for inspection analyzed as a strip search.); Jones v. City of Brunswick, 704 F. Supp. 2d 721 (N.D. Ohio 2010) (requiring suspect to remove outer layer of clothing and expose her underwear treated as strip search); Foster v. City of Oakland, 675 F. Supp. 2d 992 (N.D. Cal. 2009) (pulling suspect's pants out and shining a flashlight down the front constituted a strip search); Mason v. Village of Babylon, 124 F. Supp. 2d 807 (E.D.N.Y. 2001) (requiring suspect to raise her shirt exposing her bra and then to pull her bra out so as to dislodge anything that might be hidden underneath, and lower her pants to her thighs analyzed as a strip search). Strip and body cavity searches are defined by statute in some states. *See, e.g.*, Wa. Stat. § 10.79.070 *et seq.* defining "strip search" as having "a person remove or arrange some or all of his or her clothing so as to permit an inspection of the genitals, buttocks, anus, or undergarments of the person or breasts of a female person" and "body cavity search" as "touching or probing the stomach or rectum of a person or the vagina of a female person."

[93] Unified Sch. Dist. # 1 v. Redding, _U.S._, 129 S. Ct. 2633, 174 L. Ed. 2d 354 (2009).

[94] *See, e.g.*, Swain v. Spinney, 117 F. 3d 1 (1st Cir. 1997) (stating that a strip search requires at the very least reasonable suspicion that an arrestee is concealing drugs, weapons, or contraband); Evans v. Stephens, 407 F. 3d 1272 (11th Cir. 2005) (same); People v. Mothersell, 14 N.Y.3d 358, 926 N. E. 2d 1219 (2010) ("[E]ven where there is probable cause for an arrest, and a suspect has been arrested . . . , there must, in addition to the predicate for the arrest, be grounds to justify the very significant intrusion of a strip or visual body cavity search . . . , *i.e.*, specific facts to support a reasonable suspicion that a particular person has secreted contraband beneath his or her clothes or in a body cavity.").

A strip search performed for an investigative purpose incident to an arrest must be founded on reasonable suspicion that the arrestee is concealing evidence underneath his clothing, and the search must be conducted in a reasonable manner.

1. Reasonable Suspicion

Investigatory strip searches are most often performed in connection with drug trafficking arrests because drug dealers often hide their inventory in their buttocks to avoid detection. However, this fact alone does not automatically justify a strip search.[95] The Fourth Amendment requires *individualized* suspicion. The suspicion must relate to the person searched, and not just the class of offenders to which the person belongs. However, it does not take much additional evidence to establish reasonable suspicion for a strip search when an arrest is made for drug trafficking.[96]

2. Method of Conducting

Strip searches must be performed in a reasonable and professional manner. This normally means that they must be performed by an officer of the same sex in an enclosed area away from the view of all persons except those conducting the search.[97] Roadside strip searches are strongly disfavored. In a recent case, the court held that a female suspect's Fourth Amendment rights were violated when police lowered her

---

[95] *See, e.g.*, United States v. Barnes, 506 F. 3d 58 (1st Cir. 2007) (Knowledge that the suspect was a drug dealer and that some drug dealers conceal drugs between their buttocks did not provide reasonable suspicion for a strip search); People v. Colon, 80 A.D.3d 440, 913 N. Y. S. 2d 658 (N.Y.A.D. 1 Dept. 2011) ("The police officers' generalized knowledge that drug sellers often keep drugs in their buttocks, and the fact that no drugs were found in a search of defendant's clothing" is not enough to justify a strip search.).

[96] *See, e.g.*, People v. Hunter, 73 A.D. 3d 1279, 902 N. Y. S. 2d 678 (N.Y.A.D. 3 Dept. 2010) (individualized reasonable suspicion found where confidential informant told police that suspect had a habit of carrying narcotics in his rectum and the suspect kept fidgeting with his hands down the back of his pants); State v. Harris, 66 Wash. App. 636, 833 P.2d 402 (1992) (individualized reasonable suspicion found where the arrestee clenched his buttocks tightly during the pat down and asked to use the bathroom immediately upon arrival at the precinct).

[97] *See, e.g.*, Foster v. City of Oakland, *supra* note 92 (Strip search of drug suspect during which arresting officer, while standing in middle of street, pulled front of suspect's pants out and shined flashlight down front of pants violated suspect's Fourth Amendment rights); Evans v. Stephens, 407 F. 3d 1272 (11th Cir. 2005) (Fourth Amendment violated where strip search was performed in a broom closet, detainees were forced to disrobe in the presence of each other, and a police baton was used to lift their testicles and perform a rectal examination.); McIllwain v. Weaver, 686 F. Supp. 2d 894 (E.D. Ark. 2010) (Absent special circumstances, strip search performed by a member of the opposite sex violates Fourth Amendment.); Young v. County of Cook, 616 F. Supp. 2d 834 (N.D. Ill. 2009) (The Fourth Amendment does not allow group searches in a single room without privacy screens); Lopez v. Youngblood, 609 F. Supp. 2d 1125 (E.D. Cal. 2009) (Blanket policy of conducting group strip and visual body cavity searches of pretrial detainees violated Fourth Amendment.).

pants and examined her buttocks on the side of the road in broad daylight. The court stated that "[i]n order for a roadside strip search to pass constitutional muster, there must be . . . exigent circumstances that show some significant government or public interest would be endangered were the police to wait until they could conduct the search in a more discreet location — usually at a private location within a police facility.[98]

C. Detention Facility Strip Searches

The most common occasion for a strip search occurs when an arrestee is booked into a detention facility. The purpose for the search is to prevent drugs, weapons, and contraband from being introduced into the facility. Newly arriving detainees are typically required to remove all their clothing. An intake officer then looks inside their ears, mouth, and nostrils, runs his fingers through their hair, has them lift their penises and testicles to provide a clear view of their groin area, and then has them bend over and spread their rectum to provide a clear view of this area. Female detainees are normally required to lift their breasts and bend forward while spreading the cheeks of the buttocks to facilitate visual inspection of their vaginal and anal cavities.[99]

As this book went to press, the Supreme Court agreed to decide whether a jail policy requiring all newly arriving detainees to undergo a strip search at the time of intake, regardless of the crime charged and without individualized reasonable suspicion, violates the Fourth Amendment.[100] Lower federal courts are split on this question. A majority hold that jail intake strip searches may not be routinely performed on everyone booked into a detention facility, regardless of the nature of the crime or other individualized factors. Reasonable suspicion to believe drugs, weapons, or contraband will be found is necessary before jail officials can force newly arriving detainees to undergo the indignity of a strip search.[101] *Florence v. Board of Chosen Freeholders*

---

[98]   *See, e.g.*, State v. Battle, 688 S. E. 2d 805 (N. C. App. 2010).

[99]   *See, e.g.*, Rhode Island Department of Corrections Policy & Procedure 9.14-1 Part III.B.2. (dated January 27, 1997), *quoted in* Roberts v. State of Rhode Island, 239 F. 3d 107, 108 (1st Cir. 2001). *See also* Murcia v. County of Orange, 226 F. Supp. 2d 489 (S.D.N.Y. 2002).

[100]   Florence v. Board of Chosen Freeholders of County of Burlington, 621 F.3d 296 (3 rd Cir. 2011), *cert granted*, 131 S. Ct. 1816, 179 L. Ed. 2d 772 (2011). Powell v. Barrett, 541 F. 3d 1298 (11th Cir. 2008) (*en banc*) (strip searching all jail detainees entering general population for first time was constitutional, regardless of whether detainees had been arrested for minor offenses or misdemeanors, overruling prior cases).

[101]   *See, e.g.*, Swain v. Spinney, 117 F. 3d 1 (1st Cir. 1997) (jail intake strip search requires particularized reasonable suspicion that arrestee has contraband hidden beneath his clothing); Wilson Wilson v. Jones, 251 F. 3d 1340 (11th Cir. 2001) (reasonable suspicion required as a predicate to strip searching newly admitted detainees); Brown v. City of Boston, 154 F. Supp. 2d 131 (D. Mass. 2001) (concern for jail security does not justify blanket policy of strip searching all arrestees admitted to jail, regardless of crimes with which they are charged or other individual factors); Murcia v. County of Orange, 226 F. Supp. 2d 489 (S.D.N.Y. 2002) (blanket policy of strip-searching all newly arrested detainees before placement in correctional facility without individualized reasonable suspicion that the person searched has drugs, weapons, or contraband secreted on his or her person violates the Fourth Amendment).

of County of Burlington,[102] the case the Supreme Court recently agreed to hear, reached the opposite conclusion. When the Supreme Court agrees to hear a case that goes against the strong weight of authority, it is generally because the Supreme Court has decided that the time has come to change the law. This author would not be surprised if that is what is at play in the Supreme Court's decision to hear this case.

D. *Manual Body Cavity Searches*

It is hard to image anything more humiliating than having a stranger poke around inside one's rectal or genital cavity searching for evidence believed to have been stashed there. Because manual rectal and genital cavity searches are more intrusive than strip searches, a stronger justification is necessary. Most courts require a search warrant.[103]

Manual body cavity searches are regarded as medical procedures and must be performed under sanitary conditions by a trained medical professional, not by a police officer.[104] This reduces the intrusiveness because rectal and vaginal cavity examinations performed by medical professionals are regarded as normal and are accepted in everyday life while similar examinations performed by a police officer are not.

§ 7.12   Summary and Practical Suggestions

Constitutional restrictions on the government's power to compel suspects to provide assistance in building a case against them depend on whether the government is seeking physical evidence or testimony.

Compulsion to provide incriminating testimony is regulated by the Fifth Amendment, which bars the government from compelling defendants to take the witness stand at their criminal trial and from introducing previously compelled self-incriminating

---

102   *Supra* note 100.

103   *See, e.g.*, United States v. Oyekan, 786 F. 2d 832 (8th Cir. 1986) (stating that "a body cavity search must be conducted consistently with the *Schmerber* factors"); Giles v. Ackerman, 746 F. 2d 614 (9th Cir. 1984) (stating that *Schmerber* "implies that intrusions into the arrestee's body, including body cavity searches . . . are not authorized by arrest alone"); Arizona v. Barnes, 215 Ariz. 279, 281, 159 P.3d 589 (2007) ("an officer must secure a warrant to remove items partially protruding from an arrestee's rectum"); People v. Moore, 738 N.Y.S.2d 667, 764 N. E. 2d 967 (N.Y. 2002) (manual body cavity searches must be conducted consistent with *Schmerber* requirements); People v. Hall, 10 N.Y.3d 303, 856 N.Y.S.2d 540, 546, 886 N. E. 2d 162 (2008), *cert. denied*, 129 S. Ct. 159, 172 L. Ed. 2d 241 (2008) ("If an object is visually detected or other information provides probable cause that an object is hidden inside the arrestee's body, *Schmerber* dictates that a warrant be obtained before conducting a body cavity search unless an emergency situation exists.").

104   *See, e.g.*, United States ex rel. Guy v. McCauley, 385 F. Supp. 193 (E.D. Wis.1974) (female arrestee's constitutional rights were violated where plastic bag containing heroin was extracted from her vagina during a manual body cavity search conducted by police women rather than a trained medical professional).

statements as evidence against them. Protection of the Fifth Amendment privilege against self-incrimination may be invoked in all legal proceedings, whether judicial or administrative, criminal or civil, or formal or informal, and also during police custodial interrogations. The Fifth Amendment provides two forms of protection: (1) the right to remain silent and (2) the privilege not to answer incriminating questions. The right to remain silent involves a complete exemption from a citizen's normal duty to give testimony. This protection is available in only two contexts — during police custodial interrogations and at the defendant's criminal trial. In all other contexts, citizens are privileged to not answer incriminating questions, but are not privileged to refuse to testify.

Three factors are necessary to invoke the protection of the Fifth Amendment: (1) testimony, (2) compulsion, and (3) self-incrimination. Testimony encompasses any behavior that explicitly or implicitly makes a statement or discloses information. Compulsion occurs when the government threatens a serious consequence unless information is divulged. Self-incrimination requires that the statement subject the maker to a risk of criminal prosecution. This risk can be removed by granting immunity. Witnesses who have been granted immunity from the government's use of their testimony may not invoke the Fifth Amendment because the testimony is no longer self-incriminating.

The Fifth Amendment provides no protection against compulsory self-incrimination through evidence that derives from a suspect's body because this evidence is physical, not testimonial. The source of protection for a suspect's body is the Fourth Amendment, which confers protection on a suspect's (1) freedom of movement, (2) bodily privacy, and (3) bodily integrity.

Evidence that derives from body characteristics that are exposed to the public is called appearance evidence. Station house lineups; showups at the crime scene; photographing; measurements; fingerprinting, handwriting and voice samples; and field sobriety tests are the main examples of police procedures that yield appearance evidence. Because these procedures do not invade a suspect's privacy or bodily integrity, they may be performed whenever police have constitutional grounds to seize a suspect and detain him long enough to perform the procedure.

Evidence obtained by searching a suspect's private parts, penetrating inside the body or removing biological or other substances from the body is called bodily evidence. Searches for bodily evidence are generally allowed only when: (1) the government's need for the evidence outweighs the bodily intrusion required to obtain it, (2) there is a clear indication that the desired evidence will be found, (3) the police obtain a search warrant (or are confronted with exigent circumstances that excuse the need for obtaining one), and (4) the procedure used to retrieve the evidence is medically reasonable and is performed in a medically reasonable manner. Unless confronted with exigent circumstances, police should obtain a search warrant before compelling suspects to undergo any procedure that involves penetrating the body surface; taking blood, saliva, urine, public hair, semen or other tissue samples; or that involves severe discomfort or risk to health.

Strip and manual body cavity searches exceed the scope of a routine search incident to arrest. Particularized reasonable suspicion that the person arrested is concealing evidence underneath his clothing is necessary to justify a post-arrest investigatory strip search. Compliance with the requirements laid down in *Schmerber* is necessary to arrange for a manual body cavity search. Whether jail intake strip searches require individualized reasonable suspicion is a question that is now before the Supreme Court.

Schmerber = drunk driver caused car crash and police took his blood. USSC ruled it lawful bc of the circumstances

invoke – symptoms
cite or appeal
cite. refer to.
something solicit

Right to Counsel

8

*In all criminal prosecutions, the accused shall enjoy the right . . . to have
the Assistance of Counsel for his defense.*

Sixth Amendment, 1791

Chapter Outline

KEY TERMS AND CONCEPTS	
Accused	Interrogation
Appointed counsel	Lineup
Arraignment	Photographic identification
Confrontation	Prosecution
Critical stage	Retained counsel
Indictment	Showup
Information	Suspect

§ 8.1   Overview of the Sixth Amendment Right to Counsel

The Sixth Amendment right to counsel represents a departure from the English common law. Accused felons did not acquire the right to counsel in England until 1836.[1] Counsel was less important during the early years because criminal cases were prosecuted by the victim, not the state.[2] Consequently, the **accused** and accuser stood on relatively equal footing, reducing the need for professional assistance.

In the United States, in contrast, criminal cases have always been prosecuted by the government, using highly trained professionals.[3] The advent of our system made it imperative for defendants to hire lawyers to do battle for them. This was the background against which the Framers adopted the Sixth Amendment which guarantees that "[i]n all criminal prosecutions, the accused shall enjoy the right . . . to have the Assistance of Counsel for his defense."[4]

The Sixth Amendment right to counsel performs two functions important to the fair administration of justice. First and foremost, counsel is necessary to avoid unjust convictions. The average layperson lacks the legal skills needed to put forth an effective

---

[1]   Powell v. Alabama, 287 U.S. 45, 68, 53 S. Ct. 55, 64, 77 L. Ed. 2d 158 (1932) (stating that the common law, as it existed in England at the time the U.S. Constitution was adopted, generally denied counsel to felony defendants); Adam D. Young, *An Analysis of the Sixth Amendment Right to Counsel as It Applies to Suspended Sentences and Probation: Do* Argersinger *and* Scott *Blow a Flat Note on Gideon's Trumpet?* 107 Dick. L. R. 699 (2003) (stating that, while the English common law recognized the right to counsel for individuals charged with treason, misdemeanor offenses, and in civil litigation, there was no right to counsel for individuals accused of felonies until 1836).

[2]   Powell v. Alabama, *supra* note 1.

[3]   *Id.*; United States v. Ash, 413 U.S. 300, 93 S. Ct. 2568, 37 L. Ed. 2d 919 (1973).

[4]   U.S. Const. Amend. VI (1971).

defense. This places uncounseled defendants at risk of being convicted, even though innocent. The Supreme Court has repeatedly stressed the importance of legal assistance in avoiding unjust convictions:

> The right to be heard would be, in many cases, of little avail if it did not comprehend the right to be heard by counsel. Even the intelligent and educated layman has small and sometimes no skill in the science of law. If charged with crime, he is incapable, generally, of determining for himself whether the indictment is good or bad. He is unfamiliar with the rules of evidence. Left without the aid of counsel he may be put on trial without a proper charge, and convicted upon incompetent evidence, or evidence irrelevant to the issue or otherwise inadmissible. He lacks both the skill and knowledge adequately to prepare his defense, even though he have a perfect one. He requires the guiding hand of counsel at every step in the proceedings against him. Without it, though he be not guilty, he faces the danger of conviction because he does not know how to establish his innocence.[5]

The right to counsel is so important to the fair administration of justice that in modern times counsel must be made available, free of charge, to defendants who cannot afford to hire one on their own and ineffective assistance of counsel renders a conviction vulnerable to challenge.

The right to counsel also performs a second function. Representation is necessary for the effective assertion of a criminal defendant's other constitutional rights. Protections like the right to remain silent during custodial interrogations and to have the fruits of an illegal search suppressed are basic to our adversarial system but would have little practical application without counsel, because few defendants are sufficiently versed in constitutional law to claim these rights on their own. Moreover, because important rights may be lost during stages of the criminal process other than the trial, the right to counsel is no longer just a "trial right." It is also available in a variety of pre- and post-trial contexts.[6]

§ 8.2   — The Indigent Person's Right to Appointed Counsel

At common law and throughout most of the Sixth Amendment's history, assistance of counsel was available only to defendants who could afford an attorney. The Sixth Amendment right to counsel was interpreted to mean only that this right could not be denied to defendants who had the means to hire an attorney. The government was under no duty to provide counsel for defendants who lacked means. This interpretation seems unjust by modern standards. If, as the founders believed, assistance of counsel was necessary to ensure a fair trial, then it followed that defendants who lacked means were being unfairly convicted, imprisoned, and even executed.[7]

---

[5]   Powell v. Alabama, *supra* note 1 (emphasis added).
[6]   *See* § 8.3 *infra*.
[7]   Powell v. Alabama, *supra* note 1.

Powell v. Alabama[8] was the first case to recognize the right of an indigent criminal defendant to court-appointed counsel. In *Powell*, nine indigent and illiterate African-American youths were charged with raping two white girls. They were tried in a racially tense environment in which the state militia had to be called in to protect them from an angry mob waiting outside the courthouse. The youths were tried without the aid of counsel. Eight of the nine were convicted and sentenced to death.

The Supreme Court set aside their convictions, holding that they were denied the right to **appointed counsel**. The source of this right was not the Sixth Amendment right to counsel. *Powell* involved a state court conviction and, at the time it was decided, the safeguards contained in the Bill of Rights were not binding on the states. The Supreme Court located the right of state criminal defendants to court-appointed counsel in the due process clause of the Fourteenth Amendment which guarantees a fair trial. The Court reasoned that placing illiterate youths on trial for their life without affording them the help of a lawyer rendered the trial fundamentally unfair, violating the Fourteenth Amendment prohibition against depriving citizens of "life . . . without due process of law." *Powell v. Alabama* was an exceedingly narrow ruling, as the following passage reveals:

> We are of opinion that, under the circumstances . . . counsel was so vital and imperative that the failure of the trial court to make an effective appointment of counsel was . . . a denial of due process within the meaning of the Fourteenth Amendment. Whether this would be so in other criminal prosecutions, or under other circumstances, we need not determine. All that it is necessary now to decide . . . is that in a capital case, where the defendant is unable to employ counsel, and is incapable adequately of making his own defense because of ignorance, feeble-mindedness, illiteracy, or the like, it is the duty of the court, whether requested or not, to assign counsel for him as a necessary requisite of due process of law.[9]

Powell gave state criminal defendants facing serious charges the right to court-appointed counsel if they were illiterate or otherwise at a disadvantage in defending themselves. Predicated on the due process right to a fair trial, Powell required proof of special circumstances that caused the failure to provide court-appointed counsel to result in an unfair trial. Six years later, the Supreme Court conferred a broader right to counsel on indigent criminal defendants facing federal criminal charges, a right that derived from the Sixth Amendment, and did not depend on proof that they were illiterate or otherwise handicapped in defending themselves.[10] The right to court-appointed counsel was made available to any defendant facing serious federal charges who lacked the means to hire a lawyer.[11]

The law stood at this point for the next 25 years. Federal courts had to provide counsel for any criminal defendant facing serious charges who lacked the means to hire

---

[8] *Id*

[9] *Id.*

[10] Johnson v. Zerbst, 304 U.S. 458, 58 S. Ct. 1019, 82 L. Ed. 1462 (1938).

[11] *Id.*

an attorney, while state courts had to provide counsel only for defendants who, because of "special circumstances," were incapable of receiving a fair trial without representation by counsel.

The Supreme Court erased this distinction in the landmark case of *Gideon v. Wainwright*.[12] Gideon was charged by the state of Florida with a felony that carried a five-year sentence. He demanded that the trial court appoint an attorney for him, his only reason being that he could not afford one. The court denied Gideon's demand, explaining that because he was not illiterate or otherwise hindered from representing himself, he was not entitled to appointment of counsel. Gideon was convicted and eventually brought a *habeas corpus* petition challenging the constitutionality of his imprisonment on the basis that he was denied the Sixth Amendment right to court-appointed counsel. The Supreme Court agreed, ruling that court-appointed counsel must henceforth be furnished to state criminal defendants facing felony charges who lack the means to hire a lawyer on their own.[13]

The Sixth Amendment today entitles indigent criminal defendants charged with a felony to representation at the state's expense. In the case of misdemeanor prosecutions, the right to counsel turns on the sentence actually imposed, not on the potential sentence faced.[14] Indigent defendants charged with a misdemeanor cannot be incarcerated, even for a short time, unless counsel is appointed to represent them. However, no right to counsel exists when a fine alone is imposed.[15] This limitation is based on practical considerations. The cost of providing court-appointed counsel in cases where a fine alone is imposed would be too burdensome on state governments. If Sam is apprehended for tricycle theft, a misdemeanor punishable by incarceration of up to 60 days, $1,000 fine, or both, the judge will have to decide before his trial starts whether, if Sam is convicted, the offense would merit jail time. If so, counsel must be appointed to represent him. If the judge fails to appoint counsel, a fine alone may be imposed even though facts brought to light at the trial establish that Sam has a tricycle fetish and that this is the sixth one he has purloined this month.[16]

Once the right to appointment of trial counsel became firmly established, a period of rapid expansion followed. Indigent criminal defendants today have the right to have counsel appointed to represent them during all critical pretrial stages,[17] post-trial

12 **372 U.S. 335, 83 S. Ct. 792, 9 L. Ed. 2d 799 (1963).**
13 *Id.*
14 Argersinger v. Hamlin, 407 U.S. 321, 92 S. Ct. 2006, 32 L. Ed. 2d 530 (1972) (holding that, in the absence of a waiver, indigent criminal defendants may not be sentenced to incarceration for any offense, no matter how petty, unless represented by counsel).
15 Argersinger v. Hamlin, *supra* note 14; Alabama v. Shelton, 535 U.S. 654, 122 S. Ct. 1764, 152 L. Ed.2d 888 (2002) (holding that a suspended sentence may not be imposed on an unrepresented indigent defendant because the sentences may lead to an actual deprivation of liberty in the future).
16 Scott v. Illinois, 440 U.S. 367, 99 S. Ct. 1158, 59 L. Ed. 2d 383 (1979) (holding that there is no right to counsel when a fine alone is imposed).
17 United States v. Wade, 388 U.S. 218, 87 S. Ct. 1926, 18 L. Ed. 2d 1149 (1967).

sentencing proceedings,[18] and the first appeal of a conviction or sentence.[19] The right to counsel during these stages is covered in the next section.

§ 8.3 — The Right to Assistance of Counsel in Pre- and Post-Trial Proceedings: Critical Stages of the Prosecution and Criminal Appeals

When the Sixth Amendment was adopted, the trial was the only adversarial confrontation between the government and the accused.[20] There were no pretrial judicial proceedings, and no police force to engage the defendant in interrogations or other investigative procedures.[21] As a result, the Sixth Amendment right to counsel was originally viewed as a trial right.[22]

Criminal procedures have changed and trials have become more elaborate. Today, there are numerous pre- and post-trial proceedings in which decisions must be made and important rights may be lost if the defendant is forced to proceed without counsel. These changes made expansion of the Sixth Amendment right to counsel necessary.

A. Right to Counsel During Critical Stages

"**Critical stage**" is the phrase the Supreme Court has coined to describe those pre- and post-trial proceedings in which the accused has a Sixth Amendment right to have counsel present.[23] To be regarded as a "critical stage," the event must have the following characteristics.

First, it must take place after a criminal prosecution has been initiated.[24] This is the point at which the suspect officially becomes an "accused" and the Sixth Amendment right to counsel attaches.[25] Criminal prosecutions are generally initiated in one of the following four ways: (1) a preliminary hearing during which the defendant is taken before the magistrate, informed of the charges, and bail is set; (2) the filing of an **information** by the prosecutor; (3) the return of an **indictment** by a grand jury; and (4) an **arraignment** during which the defendant is read the charges and asked to enter a plea.[26]

---

[18] Mempa v. Rhay, 389 U.S. 128, 88 S. Ct. 254, 19 L. Ed. 2d 336 (1967).
[19] Douglass v. California, 372 U.S. 363, 83 S. Ct. 814, 9 L. Ed. 2d 811 (1963).
[20] United States v. Wade, *supra* note 17.
[21] *Id.*
[22] *Id.*
[23] Kirby v. Illinois, 406 U.S. 682, 92 S. Ct. 1877, 32 L. Ed. 2d 411 (1972).
[24] *Id.*
[25] The point at which a criminal prosecution is commenced, for Sixth Amendment purposes, is covered in greater depth in § 6.9(A).
[26] **Rothgery v. Gillespie County, Texas, 554 U.S. 191, 128 S. Ct. 2578, 171 L. Ed. 2d 366 (2008)** (holding that a defendant's initial appearance before a judge or magistrate where the defendant is informed of the charges and restrictions are imposed on his liberty is one event that signals the initiation of a criminal prosecution).

*Second, the event must involve an adversarial **confrontation** between the government and the accused or, in other words, an encounter in which the accused and a representative of the government are both present.*[27] No right to counsel exists, for example, during government interviews of prosecution witnesses and crime lab tests because the accused has no right to be present.[28]

Finally, the encounter must be of such a nature that important rights may be lost, defenses waived, or the fairness of the trial placed in jeopardy if the defendant is forced to proceed without the guiding hand of counsel.[29]

B. Pretrial Events Recognized as Critical Stages

The following pretrial judicial proceedings have been recognized as critical stages: (1) preliminary hearings at which evidence is presented and a decision on bail is made, (2) bail hearings, and (3) arraignments.[30] All three involve confrontations between the government and the accused, occurring after the initiation of prosecution, in which defenses may be waived,[31] admissible statements made,[32] or the defendant may even plead guilty. As a result, the assistance of counsel is necessary. The Supreme Court also considers interrogations,[33] lineups,[34] and showups[35] occurring after the initiation of prosecution to be critical stages.

C. Right to Counsel in Post-Trial Proceedings

The Sixth Amendment right to counsel continues to apply after the trial to post-conviction sentencing proceedings[36] and the first appeal of a conviction or sentence.[37] There is no Sixth Amendment right to appointed counsel in subsequent appeals or

---

27 United States v. Ash, *supra* note 3.
28 *Id.*
29 *Id.*
30 *See, e.g.,* Iowa v. Tovar, 541 U.S. 77, 124 S. Ct. 1379, 158 L. Ed. 2d 209 (2004) (arraignment); Coleman v. Alabama, 399 U.S. 1, 90 S. Ct. 1999, 26 L. Ed. 2d 387 (1970) (preliminary hearing in which evidence is presented and decision on bail is made); McMann v. Richardson, 397 U.S. 759, 90 S. Ct. 1441, 25 L. Ed. 2d 682 (1965) (plea hearing). The defendant also enjoys the right to counsel during court-ordered psychiatric exams to determine competency to stand trial. Estelle v. Smith, 451 U.S. 454, 101 S. Ct. 1866, 68 L. Ed. 2d 359 (1981).
31 *See* Hamilton v. Alabama, 368 U.S. 52, 82 S. Ct. 157, 7 L. Ed. 2d 114 (1961) (insanity defense).
32 *See* White v. Maryland, 373 U.S. 59, 83 S. Ct. 1050, 10 L. Ed. 2d 193 (1963).
33 Maine v. Moulton, 474 U.S. 159, 106 S. Ct. 477, 88 L. Ed. 2d 481 (1985).
34 United States v. Wade, *supra* note 17.
35 Moore v. Illinois, 434 U.S. 220, 98 S. Ct. 458, 54 L. Ed. 2d 424 (1973).
36 Mempa v. Rhay, *supra* note 18.
37 Douglass v. California, *supra* note 19 (holding that indigent criminal defendants are entitled to appointed counsel on their first appeal); Halbert v. Michigan, 545 U.S. 605, 125 S. Ct. 2582, 162 L. Ed. 2d 552 (2005) (holding that this right exists even when the defendant's conviction results from a guilty plea).

habeas corpus proceedings,[38] but defendants who can afford an attorney have a due process right to be represented.

§ 8.4   —The Defendant's Right to Self-Representation

In addition to the right to the assistance of counsel and the appointment of counsel in an appropriate case, the Sixth Amendment guarantees yet a third right: the right to waive assistance of counsel and conduct one's own defense.[39] In striking contrast to the *Gideon* case, the Supreme Court, in *Faretta v. California*,[40] set aside a conviction not because the defendant was denied appointed counsel, but because he was convicted after the trial court forced him to accept a public defender:

> There can be no blinking the fact that the right of an accused to conduct his own defense seems to cut against the grain of this Court's holdings that the Constitution requires that no accused can be convicted and imprisoned unless he has been accorded the right to counsel. For it surely is true that the basic thesis of those decisions is that the help of a lawyer is essential to assure the defendant a fair trial.... [But] it is not inconceivable that ... the defendant might present his case more effectively by conducting his own defense.... The defendant, not the lawyer or the State, will bear the personal consequences of a conviction. It is the defendant, therefore, who must be free personally to decide ...[41]

Before accepting a waiver of the right to counsel, the judge must make sure that the defendant is mentally competent to make this decision and that the decision has been knowingly, intelligently, and voluntarily made.

Competence to waive the right to counsel. The Constitution does not permit trial of individuals who are mentally incompetent. Mental competence to stand trial requires the capacity to understand the nature of the proceedings and to cooperate with an attorney.[42] However, a stronger showing of competence is required to waive the right to counsel and engage in self-representation. Defendants who suffer from severe mental illness to the point where they are not competent to conduct trial proceedings on their own may be denied this right, even though they are competent to be tried.[43]

---

[38]   *See* cases *supra* note 37.

[39]   Faretta v. California, 422 U.S. 806, 95 S. Ct. 2525, 45 L. Ed. 2d 562 (1975). However, the Sixth Amendment right to self-representation is a trial right. Criminal defendants do not have the constitutional right to conduct their own appeals, although courts sometimes exercise their discretion in permitting them to do so. Martinez v. Court of Appeals of California, Fourth Appellate Dist., 528 U.S. 152, 120 S. Ct. 684, 145 L. Ed. 2d 597 (2000).

[40]   *Supra* note 39.

[41]   *Id.*

[42]   Dusky v. United States, 362 U.S. 402, 80 S. Ct. 788, 4 L. Ed. 2d 824 (1960) (*per curiam*); Drope v. Missouri, 420 U.S. 162, 95 S. Ct. 896, 43 L. Ed. 2d 103 (1975).

[43]   Indiana v. Edwards, 554 U.S. 164, 128 S. Ct. 2379, 171 L. Ed. 2d 345 (2008).

Requirements for a valid waiver. For a valid waiver, the defendant must be advised of his Sixth Amendment rights and warned of the dangers and disadvantages of self-representation.[44] There is no preset script or formula that must be read. While a defendant need not have the knowledge and skills of a lawyer to make this choice, it must be made with full awareness of the consequences. Consideration is given to the defendant's education, prior experience with the criminal justice system, and the complexity of the charges in deciding whether the judge's warning was sufficient to enable the defendant to make an intelligent choice.

When a mentally competent criminal defendant makes an informed choice to represent himself, the decision must be honored.[45] Although the trial judge has discretion to appoint standby counsel to provide legal assistance, a *pro se* defendant is entitled to act as his own attorney and to present his defense in his own way.[46]

§ 8.5 — Ineffective Assistance of Counsel

The Sixth Amendment right to counsel requires more than the mere presence of counsel in the courtroom. A defendant is entitled to reasonably effective representation. This requirement was first imposed in cases involving appointed counsel. After *Gideon v. Wainwright*,[47] the Court began hearing challenges to the effectiveness of the representation that indigent criminal defendants were receiving. Because a person represented by an attorney who does nothing is no better off than one who has no representation at all, the Court made it clear that a state's Sixth Amendment duty is not discharged unless appointed counsel provides reasonably effective assistance and that ineffective assistance renders a conviction vulnerable to challenge.[48]

Defendants who can afford an attorney are entitled to counsel of their choice.[49] This generally suffices to ensure effective assistance, but in *Cuyler v. Sullivan*[50] it did not. The defendant's own attorney made him the "fall guy" for his co-defendants.

---

[44] Faretta v. California, *supra* note 39; Iowa v. Tovar, *supra* note 30 ("warnings of the pitfalls of proceeding to trial uncounseled must be 'rigorous [ly]' conveyed").

[45] Faretta v. California, *supra* note 39 (Sixth Amendment violated when judge forced unwanted representation on mentally competent defendant).

[46] McKaskle v. Wiggins, 465 U.S. 168, 104 S. Ct. 944, 79 L. Ed. 2d 122 (1984) (Unsolicited appointment of standby counsel did not violate a defendant's right to conduct his own defense where the defendant was allowed to control the organization and content, make motions, argue points of law, question witnesses, and address the judge and jurors at appropriate points in the trial.).

[47] Gideon v. Wainwright, *supra* note 14.

[48] McMann v. Richardson, *supra* note 30.

[49] United States v. Gonzalez-Lopez, 548 U.S. 140, 126 S. Ct. 2557, 165 L. Ed. 2d 409 (2006) (holding that reversal of conviction is required where a criminal defendant is deprived of his Sixth Amendment right to be represented by counsel of his choice due to the trial court's erroneous refusal to grant his out-of-state attorney's application for admission *pro hoc vice*).

[50] 446 U.S. 335, 100 S. Ct. 1708, 64 L. Ed. 2d 33 (1980).

"Friends" of his co-defendants hired the same attorney to represent all three of them. The defendant's case came to trial first and his attorney put on no evidence. As a result, the defendant was convicted while both of his co-defendants were acquitted. He subsequently brought a *habeas corpus* petition based on ineffective assistance of counsel. The Supreme Court granted the petition, rejecting the state's argument that because the defendant was represented by retained counsel, he had only himself to blame. The Court wrote:

> The vital guarantee of the Sixth Amendment would stand for little if the often uninformed decision to retain a particular lawyer could reduce or forfeit the defendant's entitlement to constitutional protection. Since the State's conduct of a criminal trial itself implicates the State in the defendant's conviction, we see no basis for drawing a distinction between retained and appointed counsel that would deny equal justice to defendants who have to choose their own lawyers.

Claims of ineffective representation can be raised on appeal and also through *habeas corpus review.*[51] Although numerous claims are lodged each year, few are found meritorious because the defendant must prove not only that (1) counsel's performance was deficient (*i.e.*, fell below reasonable professional standards), but also that (2) the outcome would probably have been different had the representation been adequate.[52]

The first requirement is difficult to establish because courts start with a strong presumption that there are a wide range of professionally competent ways to defend a criminal case, and that counsel's performance fell within that range.[53] To overcome this presumption, the defendant must convince the court that the acts or omissions complained of resulted from neglect or incompetence rather than a reasonable defense strategy gone awry.

The second requirement calls for proof of prejudice. The defendant must establish the existence of a reasonable probability that he would have been acquitted or received

---

[51] *See, e.g.*, United States v. Booker, 981 F.2d 289 (7th Cir. 1992).

[52] *See* Strickland v. Washington, 466 U.S. 668, 689, 104 S. Ct. 2052, 2052, 80 L. Ed. 2d 674 (1984) ("Judicial scrutiny of counsel's performance must be highly deferential. It is all too tempting for a defendant to second-guess counsel's assistance after conviction or adverse sentence, and it is all too easy for a court, examining counsel's defense after it has proved unsuccessful, to conclude that a particular act or omission of counsel's was unreasonable.... [A] court must indulge a strong presumption that counsel's conduct falls within the wide range of reasonable professional assistance; that is, the defendant must overcome the presumption that, under the circumstances, the challenged action "might be considered sound trial strategy."); Yarborough v. Gentry, 540 U.S. 1, 124 S. Ct. 1, 157 L. Ed. 2d 1 (2003) (noting that given the deferential review standard, it would be a rare case in which ineffective assistance of counsel would be found based upon a deficient closing argument); Wright v. Van Patten, 552 U.S. 120, 128 S. Ct. 743, 169 L. Ed. 2d 583 (2008) (reaffirming Strickland v. Washington standard).

[53] Strickland v. Washington, *supra* note 52; Bell v. Cone, 535 U.S. 685, 122 S. Ct. 1843, 152 L. Ed. 2d 914 (2002); Yarborough v. Gentry, *supra* note 52; Premo v. Moore, __U.S. __, 131 S. Ct. 733, 178 L. Ed. 2d 649 (2011).

a lighter sentence but for counsel's unprofessional errors.[54] When the evidence against the defendant is overwhelming this is impossible, even though counsel's errors may have caused the prosecution's case to appear stronger than it really was.

Because of the heavy burden defendants face, claims of ineffective representation succeed only in the clearest cases, such as where counsel represents co-defendants with conflicting interests, making effective representation of both impossible,[55] fails to seek suppression of clearly illegal and prejudicial evidence,[56] or fails to present clearly exculpatory evidence during the penalty phase of a capital case.[57]

§ 8.6   Sixth Amendment Restrictions on the Conduct of the Police

The Sixth Amendment right to counsel places two restrictions on the police. Both spring into existence immediately upon initiation of prosecution. First, police must secure a valid waiver of the right to counsel or see to it that counsel is present before conducting critical stage interrogations, lineups, showups, or other investigatory encounters that require the presence of the accused. Second, police must abstain from improper interference with the attorney–client relationship.

---

[54] Strickland v. Washington, *supra* note 52; **Smith v. Spisak, __ U.S.__, 130 S. Ct. 676, 175 L. Ed. 2d 595 (2010)** (finding no reasonable probability that a better closing argument would have made a difference in the outcome); Berghuis v. Thompkins, __ U.S. __, 130 S. Ct. 2250, 176 L. Ed. 2d 1098 (2010) (finding no reasonable probability that effective representation would have changed the outcome in light of the overwhelming evidence of guilt presented at the defendant's trial); *But see* Porter v. McCollum, __ U.S. __, 130 S. Ct. 447, 175 L. Ed. 2d 398 (2009) (defense counsel's failure to uncover and present *any* mitigating evidence regarding defendant's abusive childhood, heroic military service, the trauma he suffered because of it, his long-term substance abuse, and his impaired mental health, during penalty phase of capital murder prosecution constituted ineffective assistance of counsel); Sears v. Upton, __ U.S. __, 130 S. Ct. 3259, 177 L. Ed. 2d 1025 (2010) (holding that defense counsel's expenditure of less than half a day to uncover mitigation evidence and resulting failure to discover substantial evidence of child abuse constituted ineffective assistance of counsel in penalty phase of capital murder trial).

[55] *See, e.g.*, Cuyler v. Sullivan, *supra* note 50.

[56] *See, e.g.*, Tomlin v. Myers, 30 F.3d 1235 (9th Cir. 1994).

[57] *See, e.g.*, Wiggins v. Smith, 539 U.S. 510, 123 S. Ct. 2527, 156 L. Ed. 2d 471 (2003) (failure to investigate and present mitigating evidence of defendant's dysfunctional background during death penalty sentencing proceedings violated defendant's Sixth Amendment right to counsel); Rompilla v. Beard, 545 U.S. 374, 125 S. Ct. 2456, 162 L. Ed. 2d 360 (2005) (Failure to examine file of prior convictions, readily available at the courthouse, that counsel knew prosecution would use during sentencing phase of capital murder trial violated defendant's Sixth Amendment right to effective assistance of counsel); Porter v. McCullom, *supra* note 54; Sears v. Upton, *supra* note 54.

A. *Investigatory Interactions with Defendants After Prosecution Has Been Commenced*

The Sixth Amendment requirements for interrogations, lineups, and showups conducted after initiation of prosecution are straightforward. Police must administer *Miranda*-type warnings and secure a knowing, intelligent, and voluntary waiver of the right to counsel.[58] If the defendant invokes the right to counsel, police must postpone the proceedings until counsel is present. The same procedural requirements apply during critical stage interrogations as during *Miranda* custodial interrogations.[59]

1. Police Responsibility to Provide Counsel

If the defendant, having been warned of her Sixth Amendment right to counsel, expresses a wish to have counsel present during a critical stage event, the police must respect this wish. Police department procedures specify what officers must do to secure appointed counsel for defendants who lack the means to hire a lawyer on their own. Indigent criminal defendants are not entitled to counsel of their choice.[60] Representation is usually provided by a public defender. If the defendant has the means to retain a lawyer, police must wait for the defendant's counsel of choice to arrive before starting the procedure.[61] However, the police do not have to wait forever. If the lawyer the defendant retains fails to arrive after a reasonable waiting period or if urgent circumstances require immediate action, police may secure appointed counsel to provide temporary representation and go on with the procedure.[62]

2. Participation by Counsel

The degree to which the police must allow defense counsel to play an active role varies with the procedure. With lineups and showups, counsel is present to observe the manner in which the procedure is conducted so that she will be in a position to object to testimony at the trial if it was improperly conducted.[63] Police do not have to comply with counsel's objections, but if a slight modification will satisfy the objection and avert a later challenge at trial, they would be foolish not to comply.[64]

---

[58] Review § 8.3 for what constitutes a *"critical stage."*

[59] **Montejo v. Louisiana, __ U.S. __, 129 S. Ct. 2079, 173 L. Ed. 2d 955 (2009)**, overruling Michigan v. Jackson, 475 U.S. 625, 106 S. Ct. 1404, 89 L. Ed. 2d 631 (1986); Patterson v. Illinois, 487 U.S. 285, 108 S. Ct. 2389, 101 L. Ed. 2d 261 (1988).

[60] United States v. Wheat, 406 U.S. 153, 108 S. Ct. 153, 100 L. Ed. 2d 140 (1988).

[61] *Id.*

[62] United States v. Wade, *supra* note 17; *see also* United States v. Clark, 346 F. Supp. 428 (E.D. Pa. 1972).

[63] United States v. Wade, *supra* note 17; Goodwin v. Superior Court, 90 Cal. App. 4th 215, 108 Cal. Rptr. 2d 553 (2001) ("[T]he right to counsel at a lineup is a limited one. Thus, the attorney 'may not insist law enforcement officials hear his objection to procedures employed, nor may he compel them to adjust their lineup to his views of what is appropriate. At most, defense counsel is merely present at the lineup to silently observe and to later recall his observations for purposes of cross-examination or to act in the capacity of a witness. . . .'").

[64] Stovall v. Denno, 388 U.S. 263, 87 S. Ct. 1951, 18 L. Ed. 2d 1199 (1967).

Suspects are also entitled to have counsel present during critical stage interrogations. The purpose for counsel's presence is to ensure that his client understands his rights, participates voluntarily, and does not say things that will make defense of his case impossible. The suspect must be allowed to consult with his lawyer in private. The lawyer is entitled to call the shots on the degree of participation. The lawyer can limit the subjects that can be covered, object to particular questions and instruct the client not to answer them, and end the interrogation at any time.[65]

B. *Improper Interference with the Attorney–Client Relationship*

Confidentiality is of utmost importance in the attorney–client relationship and is essential for effective assistance of counsel. Police must refrain from improper intrusions into the attorney–client relationship, such as surreptitiously monitoring or recording private conversations,[66] intercepting telephone calls,[67] or inducing disloyalty.[68] Conduct like this will lead to suppression of evidence[69] and, in extreme cases, dismissal of the criminal charges.[70]

Having discussed the right to counsel in this chapter and its application to interrogations in Chapter 6, we will now consider its application to pretrial identification procedures. However, the Sixth Amendment is not the only constitutional provision that

---

[65]   *See, e.g.*, People v. Settles, 46 N.Y.2d 154 (1978).

[66]   *See, e.g.*, **State v. Quattlebaum, 338 S.C. 441, 527 S.E.2d 105** (2001) (government's clandestine videotaping of defendant's conversation with his attorney violated defendant's Sixth Amendment right to counsel, requiring reversal of his conviction), Wilson v. Superior Court of Los Angeles County, 70 Cal. App. 3d 751, 139 Cal. Rptr. 61 (2d Dist. 1997) suppressing evidence obtained through surreptitious recording of a conversation between a defendant and his attorney while they were conferring in a private conference room at the police station); Shillinger v. Haworth, 70 F.3d 1132 (10th Cir. 1995) (reversing conviction where deputy sheriff eavesdropped on inmate's conversation with attorney and divulged contents to prosecutor).

[67]   *See, e.g.*, Tucker v. Randall, 948 F.2d 388 (7th Cir. 1991) (surreptitious recording of inmate's telephone conversations with attorney violated Sixth Amendment); State v. Pecard, 196 Ariz. 371, 998 P.2d 453 (2000) (same).

[68]   *See, e.g.*, United States v. DiDomenico, 78 F.3d 294 (7th Cir. 1996) (offering inducement to counsel to betray client).

[69]   *See, e.g.*, Wilson v. Superior Court of Los Angeles County, *supra* note 66.

[70]   **State v. Quattlebaum**, *supra* note 66 (reversing conviction and disqualifying solicitor's office from prosecuting defendant at his new trial where deputy solicitor participated in clandestine videotaping of defendant's conversation with his attorney); United States v. Marshank, 777 F. Supp. 1507 (N.D. Cal. 1991) (dismissing indictment where federal agents used defendant's attorney as a government informant); United States v. Orman, 417 F. Supp. 1126 (D. Colo. 1976) (dismissing indictment where police interfered with the right to counsel by eavesdropping on a conversation between defendant and counsel); State v. Cory, 62 Wash. 2d 371, 382 P.2d 1019 (1963) (same). *But see* Weatherford v. Bursey, 429 U.S. 545, 97 S. Ct. 837, 51 L. Ed. 2d 2130 (1977).

applies. The rest of this chapter discusses the various constitutional provisions that regulate pretrial identification.

§ 8.7 Pretrial Identification Procedures

Pretrial identification procedures are used for two main purposes: to verify that the police have apprehended the right person and to generate evidence for use at trial. Police use three separate procedures: (1) **photographic identifications** (the witness is shown a photograph of the suspect, either alone or as part of a photo spread); (2) **show-ups** (the witness views a lone suspect); and (3) **lineups** (the witness views the suspect, along with others who possess similar physical characteristics, to determine whether an identification can be made). Each procedure fulfills a different law enforcement need. Figure 8.1 shows the main use for each. Photographic identifications are mainly used to narrow the focus of an investigation when the witness and the police are uncertain of the offender's identity. Showups are used when swift action is required to confirm that the police have apprehended the "right person." Lineups are used to confirm that the police have apprehended the "right person" when swift action is not required. All three procedures, when conducted in conformity with the Constitution, generate evidence that can be admitted at trial. A positive eyewitness identification made shortly after the crime furnishes convincing evidence of guilt.

Despite the faith jurors place in eyewitness testimony, extensive published research reveals that eyewitnesses often make mistakes and that their mistakes have sent many an innocent person to prison. A noted researcher writes that "mistaken eyewitness identification is the single largest source of wrongful convictions."[71] Recognizing this, the Supreme Court has crafted several constitutional doctrines designed to minimize the risk of police-induced mistaken identifications. Depending on the circumstances, admission of pretrial identification testimony may be challenged under four separate constitutional provisions — the Fifth and Fourteenth Amendment due process clauses, the Sixth Amendment right to counsel, and the Fourth Amendment search and seizure clause. The Fourth Amendment search and seizure clause and the Fifth and Fourteenth Amendment due process clauses apply to *all* pretrial identification procedures, while the Sixth Amendment right to counsel applies only to lineups and showups, and is further limited to those conducted after a prosecution has been initiated. Figure 8.2 summarizes the requirements laid down by each provision.

---

[71] *See, e.g.,* Gary L. Wells & Eric P. Seelau, *Eyewitness Identification: Psychological Research and Legal Policy on Lineups,* 1 PSYCHOL., PUB. POL'Y, & L. 765, 765 (1995). *See also* United States Department of Justice Office of Research Programs, Eyewitness Evidence: A Guide for Law Enforcement (Oct. 1999); Donald P. Judges, *Two Cheers for the Department of Justice's Eyewitness Evidence: A Guide for Law Enforcement,* 53 A.R.L.R. 231 (2000); Elizabeth F. Loftus, Eyewitness Testimony (1996 ed.); GARY L. WELLS & ELIZABETH F. LOFTUS, EYEWITNESS TESTIMONY: PSYCHOLOGICAL PERSPECTIVE (Cambridge University Press 1987); Mark Hansen, *Second Look at the Line-Up,* 87 A.B.A.J. 20 (Dec. 2001) (stating that faulty eyewitness identification is the leading cause of wrongful convictions).

Figure 8.1
Main Use of Each Identification Procedure

Identification Procedure	Main Use in Law Enforcement
Photographic Identification	Used to narrow the focus of an investigation in cases in which the witness and the police are uncertain of the offender's identity.
Showup identification	Used when swift action is necessary to confirm that the police have apprehended the right person.
Lineup Identification	Used when swift action is not necessary to confirm that the police have apprehended the right person.

Figure 8.2
Constitutional Requirements for Pretrial Identification

Procedure	Fourth Amendment Requirements	Due Process Requirements	Sixth Amendment Requirements
Photographic identification	Photograph must be acquired without violating suspect's Fourth Amendment rights.	Police must: (1) select an identification procedure that is appropriate under the circumstances and (2) avoid unnecessary suggestiveness in conducting the procedure.	The Sixth Amendment is inapplicable.
Showup	Police must have constitutional grounds to seize the suspect. This procedure is permitted after both investigatory detentions and arrests.	Same as above.	The Sixth Amendment applies only to showups conducted after initiation of prosecution. Before conducting a critical stage showup, police must either obtain a waiver of the right to counsel, (2) secure appointed counsel, or (3) wait for retained counsel to arrive.
Lineup	Police must have constitutional grounds to make an arrest. This procedure is not allowed after an investigatory detention. A valid arrest is necessary.	Same as above.	Same as above.

§ 8.8 — Fourth Amendment Limitations on Admission of Pretrial Identification Testimony

The Fourth Amendment exclusionary rule applies to witness identification testimony as well as physical evidence. Testimony concerning a positive out of court identification will be suppressed if it constitutes the fruits of an illegal arrest or detention.[72] If police arrest Sticky Fingered Sam without probable cause and place him in a lineup where the victim identifies him, the testimony cannot be used because it derives from an illegal arrest.[72] Photo identifications are rarely vulnerable to challenge on this ground. The only way the Fourth Amendment could be violated is if the police make a bogus arrest to acquire the suspect's photograph. Evidence of a positive identification made from a photograph acquired in this manner would be suppressed.[73]

Fourth Amendment issues are more likely with lineups and showups because police must seize the suspect to perform the procedures. A lawful arrest carries automatic authority to compel participation in all witness identification procedures.[74] Compelled participation infringes on only one interest protected by the Fourth Amendment — the suspect's interest in freedom of movement.[75] Because probable cause for an arrest justifies infringement, authority to compel participation in lineups and showups arises as an automatic incident of a lawful arrest.[76]

Police authority is more limited during *Terry* stops. Showups are permitted,[77] but lineups are not because they occur at the police station, a location off-limits to police during *Terry* stops.[78]

A positive lineup or showup identification that derives from an illegal seizure is inadmissible as evidence.[79] A witness who makes an inadmissible out-of-court

---

[72] *See, e.g.,* Gary L. Wells & Eric P. Seelau, *Eyewitness Identification: Psychological Research and Legal Policy on Lineups*, 1 PSYCHOL. PUB. POL'Y, & L. 765, 765 (1995). *See also* United States Department of Justice Office of Research Programs, Eyewitness Evidence: A Guide for Law Enforcement (Oct. 1999); Donald P. Judges, *Two Cheers for the Department of Justice's Eyewitness Evidence: A Guide for Law Enforcement*, 53 A.R.L.R. 231 (2000); Elizabeth F. Loftus, Eyewitness Testimony (1996 ed.); GARY L. WELLS & ELIZABETH F. LOFTUS, EYEWITNESS TESTIMONY: PSYCHOLOGICAL PERSPECTIVE (Cambridge University Press 1987); Mark Hansen, *Second Look at the Line−Up*, 87 A. B.A.J. 20 (Dec. 2001) (stating that faulty eyewitness identification is the leading cause of wrongful convictions).

[73] *See* United States v. Crews, 445 U.S. 463, 100 S. Ct. 1244, 63 L. Ed. 2d 537 (1980).

[74] *See, e.g.,* Kirby v. Illinois, *supra* note 24 (admitting evidence obtained in showup conducted after lawful arrest); United States v. Fisher, 702 F.2d 372 (2d Cir. 1982) (suppressing evidence of showup conducted pursuant to an illegal arrest); Goodwin v. Superior Court, *supra* note 63 (a suspect who police have probable cause to arrest has no Fourth or Fifth Amendment right to refrain from participating in a lineup).

[75] §§ 7.7–7.8 *supra.*

[76] *See* cases *supra* note 74.

[77] Dempsey v. Town of Brighton, 749 F. Supp. 1215 (W.D.N.Y. 1990), *aff'd*, Curenton v. Town of Brighton, 940 F.2d 648 (2d Cir. 1991), *cert. denied*, Dempsey v. Town of Brighton, 502 U.S. 925, 112 S. Ct. 338, 116 L. Ed. 2d 278 (1991).

[78] Hayes v. Florida, 470 U.S. 811, 105 S. Ct. 1643, 84 L. Ed. 2d 705 (1985). This limitation is discussed in § 3.9(D).

[79] United States v. Crews, *supra* note 73.

identification will also be barred from identifying the defendant in the courtroom un-less the judge finds that the witness's ability to make the courtroom identification stemmed from independent recollections acquired at the time of the crime, and not from having observed him in police custody after the illegal seizure.[80] A violation of Fourth Amendment, consequently, can deprive government of the ability to establish that the defendant was the person who perpetrated the crime.

§ 8.9   — Due Process Requirements for Pretrial Identification Procedures

The most important basis for challenging pretrial witness identification testimony stems from the due process clause, which prohibits convictions based on unreliable evidence.[81] Experimental memory research has demonstrated that the memory of eye-witnesses is capable of being transformed through exposure to suggestive influences after an event is witnessed.[82] Faulty eyewitness identification has sent many an inno-cent person to prison. To reduce the risk of wrongful convictions, the due process clause prohibits admission of pretrial identification testimony obtained under circ-umstances that are so unnecessarily suggestive as to create a substantial risk of misidentification.[83]

Challenges based on due process grounds are resolved under a two-step analysis.[84] Courts first consider whether the police used an unnecessarily suggestive identifica-tion procedure. If so, the Court next determines whether the unnecessary suggestive-ness created a substantial risk of misidentification. Because people who have sharp and clear memories of an event are less susceptible to suggestion, courts consider the following five factors in assessing this risk: (1) whether the witness had an adequate opportunity to view the suspect at the time of the crime, (2) the witness' degree of attention, (3) the accuracy of the witness' prior description of the suspect, (4) the level of certainty exhibited at the time of the identification, and (5) the length of time between the crime and the identification.[85] The greater the witness' observation time and degree of attention, the more accurate the witness' prior description, the higher the witness' level of certainty, and the shorter the interval between the crime and the iden-tification, the more likely it is that a court will admit evidence of a positive eyewitness identification despite flaws in conducting the identification procedure.[86] Police, nev-ertheless, should strive to make their procedures as accurate and reliable as possible.

---

[80]   *Id.*

[81]   Neil v. Biggers, 409 U.S. 188, 93 S. Ct. 375, 34 L. Ed. 2d 401 (1972); Manson v. Brathwaite, 432 U.S. 98, 97 S. Ct. 2243, 53 L. Ed. 2d 140 (1970); Simmons v. United States, 390 U.S. 377, 88 S. Ct. 967, 19 L. Ed. 2d 1247 (1968); Stovall v. Denno, *supra* note 64; **United States v. Downs, 230 F.3d 272 (7th Cir. 2000)**.

[82]   WELLS & LOFTUS, EYEWITNESS TESTIMONY: PSYCHOLOGICAL PERSPECTIVES (Cambridge 1984).

[83]   *See* cases *supra* note 81.

[84]   *Id.*

[85]   *Id.*

[86]   *See, e.g.,* **United States v. Downs**, *supra* note 81 (although the lineup in which the defendant was the only person without a moustache was unduly suggestive, the bank teller's identification was sufficiently

A. *Choosing the Proper Procedure for Identification*

Unnecessary suggestiveness can be introduced in one of two ways — either by selecting an inappropriate witness identification procedure (*i.e.*, one that is unnecessarily suggestive under the circumstances) or conducting an appropriate procedure in an unnecessarily suggestive way.

Challenges based on choice of procedures generally involve showups. Showups are the most inherently suggestive of the three identification procedures because only one person is presented for identification, that person is in police custody, and the clear implication is that the police think "he's the one." As a general rule, showups should be used only when police have a strong need for a quick confirmation that they have apprehended the right person.[87] The ideal case is one in which the showup takes place close in time to the crime and the public safety would be threatened if the perpetrator were to remain at large.

Suppose that Veronica Victim reports that she has just been robbed at gunpoint by a 4′ tall white man with long green hair and an artificial leg, wearing a T-shirt that reads "Kiss the Chef." Police dispatch a car to her residence. En route, they spot a man matching the description hobbling at his best speed away from her neighborhood and

---

reliable to be admitted where the teller had ample opportunity to observe the suspect at the time of the robbery, the lineup was held five days later, and she expressed certainty when she saw him that he was the one); State v. Gross, 776 N.E.2d 1061 (Ohio 2002) (circumstances of showup identification of capital murder defendant by two witnesses, in which witnesses, sitting in separate police cars, identified defendant as he stood with his hands behind his back between two officers, although suggestive, were not so suggestive as to create very substantial likelihood of irreparable misidentification, where both witnesses had time to view defendant during commission of crimes, focused their attention on him, described him prior to showup identification, were confident in their respective identifications, and made the identification mere hours after witnessing the crime); State v. Meyers, 153 Ohio App. 3d 547, 795 N.E.2d 77 (2003) (identification procedure was sufficiently reliable to allow admission of alleged rape victim's identification of defendant as her assailant, even though alleged victim was presented with a second photograph array that included defendant after she failed to identify defendant as her assailant in first photograph array; alleged victim got a good look at assailant, had a high degree of attention while observing assailant, provided the detective with complete description of assailant shortly after incident, and rated her level of certainty as a seven out of ten upon identifying defendant from second photograph array, and length of time between attack and identification of defendant was six weeks). *But see* Wise v. Commonwealth, 6 Va. App. 178, 367 S.E.2d 197 (1988) (showing Virginia bank employees single bank surveillance photo depicting defendant as robber of Maryland bank five months after the Virginia robbery tainted employees' subsequent identifications of defendant from photographic array where employees were unable, prior to seeing the single photograph, to describe robber's facial features or to identify him in earlier photographic identification array).

87　*See, e.g.*, Fite v. State, 60 S.W. 3d 314 (Tex. Ct. App. 2001) (showup proper where police picked up suspect who fit the victim's description of a man who, moments before, had forced his way into her home, threatened her life, and spent 20 minutes rummaging through her belongings); State v. Mansfield, 343 S.C. 66, 538 S.E.2d 257 (2000) (showup proper where eyewitness observed the defendant trying break into a neighbor's home and had an opportunity to get a good look at him, and showup occurred within minutes after he fled the scene). *But see Ex parte Appleton*, 828 So. 2d 894 (Ala. 2001) (showup improper where witness was unable to see robber's face at the time of the crime because it was covered with a mask and there was no urgency); *In re* Duane F., 764 N.Y.S.2d 434 (2003) (Precinct house showup at which witness identified juvenile was unduly suggestive where showup did not take place near the crime scene nor did it result from the culmination of an unbroken chain of fast-paced events).

apprehend him. This is a proper case for a showup. First, swift action is necessary because of the violent nature of the crime and Veronica's report that the perpetrator was armed. A photographic identification would delay confirmation while a dangerous criminal remains at large. Moreover, the risk that a showup will induce a misidentification is negligible because the showup occurred close in time to the crime, the victim furnished a detailed description of a perpetrator who had unique identifying characteristics, the suspect was apprehended near the scene of the crime, and his unique appearance matched the victim's description of him. A quick viewing in the immediate aftermath of a crime is justified by the need to determine whether the person detained is the right person while the perpetrator's image is still fresh in the victim's memory. Rapid identification enables the police to focus their investigation, enhances the reliability of the identification, and minimizes the risk that innocent persons will be unjustly detained.

Suppose instead that Mrs. Lucy Marbles calls to report that she just discovered that her prized 24-carat gold lawn flamingo is missing. "I kept it in my front yard for years," she says, "and no one ever took it. What's the world coming to?!" After racking her brain for a few days, she calls again, this time to report that she knows who has taken it. She believes it was taken by a man who briefly came to her door a week ago and offered to pave her driveway "for cheap." Her description of the man, a 5′4″ white male with a mustache, matches many of the usual suspects known to local police, including Sticky-Fingered Sam. Under these circumstances, it would be inappropriate to use a showup identification. First, there is no urgency. The crime is not a violent one, the public safety is not at risk, and the police have no special need to know whether Sam is the perpetrator right now. They know where Sam lives and can pick him up any time they want. Because there is no rush, a photographic identification will serve the needs of law enforcement equally well. Moreover, there is a substantial risk that a showup will induce a mistaken identification. Mrs. Marbles viewed the perpetrator briefly a week before and had no reason to focus attention on his appearance because she was unaware of the theft at that time. Memories of the facial characteristics of strangers observed momentarily during a chance encounter tend to fade rapidly. The fact that the police think Sam is the perpetrator may prompt Mrs. Marbles to mistakenly "remember" him. These considerations make the use of a showup identification a poor choice on these facts.

B. Avoiding Suggestive Measures During Identification Procedures

Unnecessary suggestiveness can also be introduced by the way in which a procedure is conducted. Police must avoid saying or doing things that might influence the witness' decision. While it is rare for police to point out a suspect and say "We've caught our man. He's the one," their conduct can say this as loudly as their language. *Foster v. California*[88] is an illustrative case. Police first placed the suspect in a police station lineup along with two other men, both of whom were half a foot shorter. The suspect was the only one wearing a leather jacket, a characteristic that played prominently in the witness' description of the robber. When the lineup did not lead to a positive identification, police arranged a one-on-one confrontation between the witness and the defendant. The

[88] 394 U.S. 440, 89 S. Ct. 1127, 22 L. Ed. 2d 402 (1969).

witness continued to be uncertain. A week later, the police arranged a second lineup, in which there were five participants. The suspect was the only person in the second lineup who had also participated in the first lineup. This time the witness made a positive identification. The Supreme Court threw the identification testimony out, stating:

> The suggestive elements in this identification procedure made it all but inevitable that David would identify petitioner whether or not he was in fact "the man." In effect, the police repeatedly said to the witness, "This is the man." This procedure so undermined the reliability of the eyewitness identification as to violate due process.

1. Conducting Photographic Identification Procedures

The United States Department of Justice recently promulgated a series of guidelines for handling eyewitness evidence. Many of the Justice Department's recommendations have been incorporated into the discussions that follow.[89]

When conducting a photographic identification, police should prepare a photo spread that includes at least five photographs in addition to the suspect's. The suspect's photograph should be reasonably contemporary. The photographs of the fillers — i.e., non-suspects — should match the witness' description of the criminal rather than the person the police suspect. However, the fillers should not so closely resemble the suspect that even people familiar with the suspect might have difficulty distinguishing the two. The photo spread should include only one photograph of the suspect. Repeatedly showing the suspect's picture increases the risk of misidentification by reinforcing that suspect's image in the witness' mind. It also contains an implied suggestion that the police think that person whose picture is being repeatedly shown is the perpetrator.[90]

Before starting the procedure, the investigator should caution the witness that the person who committed the crime may or may not be in the photo spread, thus eliminating pressure on the witness to select someone. If there are multiple eyewitnesses, officers should conduct separate identifications to prevent them from influencing each other.[91] It goes without saying that police should abstain from saying anything during the procedure that might influence the witness' decision.

---

[89] In 1999, the United States Department of Justice published a research report titled *United States Department of Justice Office of Research Programs, Eyewitness Evidence: A Guide for Law Enforcement* (Oct. 1999). This document can be obtained free of charge from the Office of Justice Programs at http://www.ojp.usdoj.gov. The Justice Department's Eyewitness Evidence Guide offers valuable recommendations for interviewing eyewitnesses and conducting witness identifications. For favorable commentary, see Donald P. Judges, *Two Cheers for the Department of Justice's Eyewitness Evidence: A Guide for Law Enforcement*, 53 Ark. L. Rev. 231 (2000). The Eyewitness Evidence Guide's recommendations for conducting photographic identifications are found at pp. 39–40 of the Guide.

[90] *Id.*

[91] *See, e.g.*, United States v. Bagley, 772 F.2d 482 (9th Cir. 1985) (photographic display was unnecessarily suggestive where one witness looked over another's shoulder as she was viewing the pictures and saw her select Bagley's mug shot. The court stated: "A joint confrontation is a disapproved identification procedure. Clearly, the better procedure is to keep witnesses apart when they view photographic spreads."). *But see* United States v. Bowman, 215 F.3d 951 (9th Cir. 2000) (allowing witnesses to attend a lineup as a group and to write down their observations on a written form did not create substantial likelihood of misidentification where they were instructed not to talk to one another, not to let anyone see their choices, and not to make comments or gestures as they viewed lineups, and where a law enforcement officer remained in the room to ensure that these instructions were followed).

Showing a single photograph is occasionally justified.[92] A Maryland court, for example, upheld admission of identification testimony based on the showing of a single photograph where the victim had been in the suspect's presence for more than four hours and had escaped shortly before the photograph was shown.[93] Police had a second reason for showing only the suspect's photograph. There was an outstanding warrant for the suspect's arrest on unrelated charges and the police wanted to know whether the victim could identify him and provide information on his whereabouts. Consequently, police had a legitimate reason for showing a single photograph.

2. Lineups

Lineups have been described as "the most useful and least questionable witness identification procedure."[94] They are more reliable than photographic identifications and less suggestive than one-man showups and, consequently, should be employed whenever feasible.

However, the reliability of a lineup depends on how it is conducted.[95] Police must avoid making the suspect conspicuous. A suspect can be made conspicuous either by selecting stand-ins whose age, race, physique, etc., bear no resemblance to the victim's description of the perpetrator[96] or by presenting the suspect in a way that draws attention, such as by having only the suspect wear the distinctive clothing worn by the perpetrator.[97] However, presenting the suspect in ways that draw attention may

---

[92]   United States v. Lumpkin, 192 F.3d 280 (2d Cir. 1999) (suppressing pretrial identification made from single photograph, but finding that officers had independently reliable bases upon which to make in-court identification); Hyppolite v. State, 774 N.E.2d 584 (Ind. Ct. App. 2002) (while exhibiting a single photograph to a crime witness for identification is normally an unnecessarily suggestive procedure, an exception is sometimes made when the crime witness is an investigating police officer).

[93]   Smith v. State, 6 Md. App. 59, 250 A.2d 285 (1969), *cert. denied*, 397 U.S. 1057, 90 S. Ct. 1402, 25 L. Ed. 2d 674 (1970).

[94]   Wayne LaFave, Jerold H. Israel, & Nancy King, Criminal Procedure § 7.3(c) (2d ed. 1999).

[95]   The Justice Department's recommendations for conducting to lineups are similar to its recommendations for photographic identifications. *See* United States Department of Justice Office of Research Programs, *supra* note 89 at 40–42.

[96]   Frazier v. New York, 187 F. Supp. 2d 102 (S.D.N.Y. 2002) (lineup unnecessarily suggestive where hairstyle was the only consistent, distinctive feature in victim's descriptions of perpetrator, defendant was only participant in the lineup whose dreadlocks hairstyle matched the description, and police could have disguised this feature by making participants wear hats); Solomon v. Smith, 645 F.2d 1179, 1183 (2d Cir. 1981) (lineup unnecessarily suggestive where victim described the assailant as 5′7″ tall and weighing 145 and all participants but the defendant were either much taller or heavier); United States v. Downs, *supra* note 81 (lineup unnecessarily suggestive where bank robbery suspect was only participant who had no facial hair).

[97]   Raheem v. Kelly, 257 F.3d 122 (2d Cir. 2001) (lineup unnecessarily suggestive where defendant was the only participant who appeared in black leather coat, a characteristic that featured prominently in witness' description of suspect. The court stated that a "lineup is unduly suggestive as to a given defendant if he meets the description of the perpetrator previously given by the witness and the other lineup participants plainly do not."); Bell v. State, 847 So. 2d 880 (Miss. Ct. App. 2002) (photographic identification was impermissibly suggestive, where defendant's photograph was the only one in which a person was depicted with long hair, in an orange jumpsuit, and with shackles or handcuffs).

occasionally be unavoidable. Suppose that a bank is robbed by a bearded man, and the next day several eyewitnesses identify Sticky-Fingered Sam from a photo array of known bearded bank robbers. Police arrest Sam and place him in a lineup with other bearded men to see whether the witnesses will identify him. Unfortunately, Sam shaved his beard before his arrest and he is the only person in the lineup with an artificial beard. Forcing Sam to wear an artificial beard is permissible, even though it is likely to draw attention to him, because Sam created the situation that made it necessary to alter his appearance.

Police do not have to go to extraordinary lengths to find stand-ins who look like the suspect.[98] They are only required to make a reasonable effort. Police, for example, would have no excuse for assembling a lineup in which the suspect is the only African-American when this feature is part of the witness' description of the perpetrator. However, if the suspect has a unique identifying characteristic, such as a star-shaped birthmark or tattoo on his cheek, police do not have to find stand-ins with a similar characteristic. They nevertheless should try to conceal this characteristic by requiring all lineup participants to wear a bandage covering this part of their face.

C. Consequences of an Unduly Suggestive Identification

Testimony about an out-of-court identification will be suppressed if the pretrial identification procedure is so unnecessarily suggestive that it creates a substantial likelihood of a mistaken identification.[99] A witness who has been exposed to such a procedure will, in addition, be barred from making an identification in the courtroom during the trial unless the judge concludes that the witness' testimony stems from independent recollection acquired at the time of the crime and not from having observed the accused at the suggestive pretrial identification procedure.[100] The amount of time the witness was in the presence of the defendant, the distance between them, the lighting conditions, the witness' degree of attention to the defendant, the accuracy of any prior description of the perpetrator by the witness; the witness' level of certainty at the pretrial identification, and the length of time between the crime and the tainted identification are among the factors the judge will consider in deciding this.[101] However, even if the judge permits the witness to make an identification in the courtroom during the trial, defense counsel can argue to the jury why it should distrust this

---

[98] *See, e.g.*, United States v. Traeger, 289 F.3d 461 (7th Cir. 2002) (lineup not unnecessarily suggestive, even though bank robbery suspect's mammoth 6′ 5″ height, 350-pound weight made him stand out from other participants because finding five or six other men who approximated suspect's size is very difficult); Roldan v. Artuz, 78 F. Supp. 2d 260 (S.D.N.Y. 2000); Taylor v. Kuhlmann, 36 F. Supp. 2d 534 (E.D.N.Y. 1999); United States v. Shakur, 560 F. Supp. 353 (S.D.N.Y. 1983).

[99] Neil v. Biggers, *supra* note 81; Stovall v. Denno, *supra* note 64.

[100] United States v. Lumpkin, *supra* note 92 (finding that investigating officers had independently reliable basis upon which to make in-court identifications where officers had unobstructed view of the suspect selling crack cocaine during daylight on two occasions, and immediately recognized him on the second occasion); Hyppolite v. State, *supra* note 92.

[101] *See* cases *supra* notes 99, 100.

testimony. Thus, no matter what the judge decides, an unnecessarily suggestive pretrial identification can weaken the prosecution's case.

§ 8.10 — Right to Counsel During Pretrial Identification Procedures

The Sixth Amendment guarantees the right to counsel during all "critical stages." Lineups and showups conducted after the initiation of prosecution are regarded as critical stage events because improper suggestiveness in the manner in which the procedure is conducted might never come to light unless counsel is present as an observer.[102] The possibilities for suggestive influences during lineups and showups are numerous and subtle and effective representation requires that counsel be allowed to observe the procedure so that she can mount an effective challenge to unreliable witness identification testimony at the trial.[103]

The same is not true for photographic identification sessions.[104] A photo display can be reconstructed for counsel's benefit after the fact and any suggestiveness that did occur can usually be flushed out at the trial through cross-examination. Because photo spreads can be reconstructed, counsel's presence during the actual event is not critical. For this reason, the Sixth Amendment guarantees the right to counsel during critical stage lineups and showups (i.e., those conducted after initiation of prosecution), but not during photographic identification sessions.[105]

A. Determining Whether Prosecution Has Commenced

To be a critical stage lineup or showup, it must take place after prosecution has been initiated.[106] The Supreme Court has identified the following actions as initiating prosecution: (1) a preliminary hearing. (2) the **arraignment** of the defendant pursuant to an arrest warrant or on charges filed in the form of a criminal complaint, (3) the filing of an **information** by the prosecutor, and (4) the return of a grand jury **indictment**.[107] Although the prosecution certainly is commenced by the time any of the above events

102   United States v. Wade, *supra* note 17; Moore v. Illinois, 434 U.S. 220, 98 S. Ct. 458, 54 L. Ed. 2d 424 (1977) (defendants have no constitutional right to the presence of counsel during identification procedures conducted before prosecution is initiated).
103   United States v. Wade, *supra* note 17.
104   United States v. Ash, *supra* note 3.
105   United States v. Wade, *supra* note 17; United States v. Ash, *supra* note 3.
106   United States v. Wade, *supra* note 17.
107   **Rothgery v. Gillespie County, Tex.,** *supra* **note 26** (criminal defendant's initial appearance before magistrate judge, where he learns the charge against him and his liberty is subject to restriction, is one of several events that mark initiation of adversary proceedings, triggering attachment of Sixth Amendment right to counsel); Kirby v. Illinois, *supra* note 24 (pre-indictment showup not critical stage); *In re* Groban, 352 U.S. 330, 77 S. Ct. 510, 1 L. Ed. 2d 376 (1957).

takes place, some states hold that the government commits itself to prosecute at earlier stages[108] — even at the time the suspect is booked.[109] Accordingly, officers should familiarize themselves with the rules in their jurisdiction.

B. Consequences of Failing to Provide Counsel

If police officers conduct a showup or lineup after prosecution is initiated without obtaining a waiver or providing counsel, the results can be devastating to the prosecution. First, evidence of the pretrial identification will be excluded from trial, regardless of whether there was undue suggestiveness.[110] Second, any witness who participates in the illegal pretrial identification is presumptively incompetent to identify the accused at trial. In accordance with the "fruit of the poisonous tree" doctrine,[111] the prosecution must show by clear and convincing evidence that the in-court identification has a sufficient basis in the witness' observation of the accused other than at the pretrial identification.[112] If the prosecution cannot meet this burden, and there are no other witnesses to identify the accused or other evidence proving his or her identity as the perpetrator, the result will be a complete acquittal.

§ 8.11   Summary and Practical Suggestions

The Sixth Amendment guarantees those accused of crime the assistance of counsel for their defense. The right to assistance of counsel includes the right to retain counsel of one's own choosing, to have counsel appointed, to reasonably competent representation, and to engage in self-representation.

The right to counsel applies prior to trial during several critical stages, including the preliminary hearing, bail hearing, arraignment, and certain investigative procedures, such as critical stage interrogations, lineups, and showups. The Sixth Amendment right to counsel attaches at the earliest of several events: a preliminary hearing, arraignment of the defendant pursuant to an arrest warrant or on charges filed in the form of a criminal complaint, the filing of information by the prosecutor, or the

---

[108] *See* United States v. Zelker, 468 F.2d 159, 163 (2d Cir. 1972), *cert. denied*, 411 U.S. 939, 93 S. Ct. 1892, 36 L. Ed. 2d 401 (1973) (right attached upon issuance of arrest warrant under New York penal law); Cannistraci v. Smith, 470 F. Supp. 586, 592 n.16 (S.D.N.Y. 1979) (right attached after arrest and booking); United States v. Cuyler, 439 F. Supp. 1173, 1180–1181 (E.D. Pa. 1977), *aff'd*, 582 F.2d 1278 (3d Cir. 1978) (right attached upon issuance of arrest warrant under Pennsylvania law); People v. Hinton, 23 Ill. App. 3d 369, 372, 319 N.E.2d 313, 316 (1974) (right attached upon filing of complaint and issuance of arrest warrant); Commonwealth v. Richman, 458 Pa. 167, 170, 320 A.2d 351, 353 (1974) (right attached upon filing of complaint and issuance of arrest warrant).
[109] See Cannistraci v. Smith, *supra* note 108.
[110] United States v. Wade, *supra* note 17; *see also* cases *supra* note 108.
[111] Wong Sun v. United States, 371 U.S. 471, 83 S. Ct. 407, 9 L. Ed. 2d 444 (1963).
[112] *See* United States v. Wade, *supra* note 17.

return of a grand jury indictment. State courts, however, sometimes recognize earlier points.

Pretrial identification procedures can be challenged under three separate constitutional provisions — the Fourth Amendment, the due process clause, and the Sixth Amendment right to counsel. The Fourth Amendment requires grounds for a seizure. When police have probable cause for arrest, they may conduct either a lineup or a showup. When they only have reasonable suspicion for a detention, showups alone are allowed. The due process clause regulates the manner in which photographic identifications, lineups, and showings are conducted. They must be conducted in a manner that avoids unnecessary suggestiveness conducive to a misidentification. The Sixth Amendment right to counsel applies to lineups and showups that take place after the prosecution has been initiated. Police must observe warning and waiver requirements and abstain from interfering with the attorney–client relationship.

Trial and Punishment

9

[No] person [shall] be subject for the same offense to be twice put in jeopardy of life or limb . . .

Fifth Amendment, 1791

In all criminal prosecutions, the accused shall enjoy the right to a speedy and public trial, by an impartial jury . . . and to be informed of the nature and cause of the accusation [and] to be confronted with the witnesses against him . . .

Sixth Amendment, 1791

Excessive bail shall not be required, nor excessive fines imposed, nor cruel and unusual punishments inflicted.

Eighth Amendment, 1791

421

Chapter Outline

KEY TERMS AND CONCEPTS

Aggravating circumstances
Contraband
Elements (of a crime)
Grand jury
Instrumentalities (of a crime)
Jury pools
Jury venire
Mitigating circumstances
Petit jury

Peremptory challenge
"Same elements" test
"Same transaction" test
Sequester (a jury)
Sovereign
Statutes of limitation
Tribunal
Voir dire

§ 9.1   Overview of Constitutional Safeguards During the Trial and Punishment Phases of a Criminal Case

An inscription on the walls of the Department of Justice reads: "The United States wins its points when justice is done its citizens in the courts." This sentiment is echoed throughout the Constitution, but is especially apparent in the constitutional provisions covered in this chapter: the double jeopardy clause of the Fifth Amendment, which prohibits the government from placing an accused person twice in jeopardy of conviction or punishment for the same offense; the Fifth and Fourteenth Amendment due process clauses; the Sixth Amendment guarantee of a fair trial; and the Eighth Amendment prohibition against cruel and inhuman punishment. Citizens have not always enjoyed these rights. There was a time in the Western world when people accused of a crime could be condemned without a trial and subjected to barbaric, torturous punishments. The first major triumph in the evolution of the Anglo-American criminal justice system occurred at Runnymede, England, in 1215, when King John was forced to capitulate to the demands of insurgent barons and signed the historic document known as the Magna Charta. The Magna Charta guaranteed that no free man would be condemned to death or sent to prison "except by the legal judgment of his peers or by the law of the land."[1]

This phrase is the precursor of the due process clause enshrined in the Fifth and Fourteenth Amendments to the United States Constitution. However, the Framers were not content to rely on the general assurance of due process to perpetuate the numerous

---

[1]   MAGNA CHARTA, ch. 39, reprinted in R. PERRY & J. COOPER, SOURCES OF OUR LIBERTIES 17 (1959).

procedural safeguards that, over the centuries, had come to be associated with a fair trial. In the Bill of Rights, they laid out what would be required. This chapter examines the safeguards that the Framers incorporated to ensure that criminal justice is fairly administered.

§ 9.2   The Fifth Amendment Double Jeopardy Prohibition

The double jeopardy clause of the Fifth Amendment mandates that no person shall "be subject for the same offense to be twice put in jeopardy of life or limb . . ." This clause prohibits the government from twice prosecuting or punishing a criminal defendant for the same offense.[2] Although double jeopardy is not mentioned in the Magna Charta, the seeds were already sown[3] and this protection was fully entrenched in the English legal system by the colonial period.[4]

A. Reasons for Prohibiting Double Jeopardy

The prohibition of double jeopardy reflects society's judgment that a person who has stood trial for an offense should be able to put this ordeal behind him and go on to other things. A criminal trial is a heavy strain, both personal and financial. An acquittal would not end the defendant's ordeal if he or she could be retried.[5] Even a conviction would not have this effect because the government could retry the defendant in the hopes of obtaining a more severe punishment. The double jeopardy safeguard prevents the government from using its vast resources to imprison innocent people by repeatedly trying them until they are too worn out, psychologically and financially, to put forth an adequate defense.[6]

B. Scope of the Prohibition Against Double Jeopardy

The double jeopardy clause imposes two closely related restraints. First, it prevents the government from retrying a criminal defendant for the same offense following an acquittal or conviction.[7] Second, it prevents the government from imposing multiple punishments for the same offense.[8] If a defendant is convicted, the sentence imposed fixes the punishment and may not thereafter be augmented or changed. Moreover, the power to prosecute may be lost if the government has previously "punished" the

---

[2]   Benton v. Maryland, 395 U.S. 784, 89 S. Ct. 2056, 23 L. Ed. 2d 707 (1969).

[3]   Bartkus v. Illinois, 359 U.S. 121, 79 S. Ct. 676, 3 L. Ed. 2d 684 (1959) (Black, J., dissenting).

[4]   J.A. Sigler, Double Jeopardy 22 (1969).

[5]   Green v. United States, 355 U.S. 184, 78 S. Ct. 221, 2 L. Ed. 2d 199 (1957).

[6]   Id.

[7]   Fong Foo v. United States, 369 U.S. 141, 82 S. Ct. 671, 7 L. Ed. 2d 629 (1962).

[8]   United States v. DiFrancesco, 449 U.S. 117, 101 S. Ct. 426, 66 L. Ed. 2d 328 (1980); North Carolina v. Pearce, 395 U.S. 711, 89 S. Ct. 2072, 23 L. Ed. 2d 656 (1969).

defendant for the same offense in some other way, such as by seizing his property as a penalty.[9]

Although the double jeopardy clause seems straightforward, it is actually complex. There are two sources of difficulty. The first is the meaning of "same offense." Suppose a masked man enters a federally insured bank, takes a gun from his pocket, points it at the teller, demands that she fill a bag with cash, and speeds away in his car. During this period, our masked bandit has committed at least four separate crimes in addition to the bank robbery. The other crimes were carrying a concealed weapon, making a terroristic threat, reckless endangerment of the lives of other persons present in the bank, and speeding. The double jeopardy clause bars a second prosecution only when it is brought for the "same offense." The number of offenses determines how many times a defendant can be tried. How many "offenses" did our masked bandit commit — one or five?[10]

A second problem is with the meaning of "punishment." When do government-imposed sanctions amount to "punishment?" Suppose Mary Wanna and Thrifty Penny are convicted of operating a multi-million dollar drug ring and each is sentenced to five years in the penitentiary. Thrifty Penny is in a hurry to "pay her debt to society" so that she can get out and spend the millions she amassed from her drug business. Mary is indifferent because she has already blown her share. Suppose further that, while in prison, the government confiscates all of Penny's drug money. Since Penny suffered a second burden that Mary did not, does this mean that she has been punished twice for the same offense?[11] Both questions call upon courts to make difficult choices.

§ 9.3 — Prohibition of Multiple Prosecutions for the Same Offense

Three conditions are necessary for a defendant to have double jeopardy protection against a second prosecution. First, an earlier prosecution must progress to the point of jeopardy attachment. Second, a subsequent prosecution must involve the same offense. Finally, both prosecutions must be brought by the same government entity. Because the federal government and the states are separate sovereign entities, each is separately empowered to prosecute for violations of its laws.[12]

---

[9] *See, e.g.*, Department of Revenue of Montana v. Kurth Ranch, 511 U.S. 767, 114 S. Ct. 1937, 128 L. Ed. 2d 767 (1994); United States v. Bajakajian, 524 U.S. 321, 118 S. Ct. 2028, 141 L. Ed. 2d 314 (1998); United States v. Halper, 490 U.S. 435, 109 S. Ct. 1892, 104 L. Ed. 2d 487 (1989).

[10] United States v. Dixon, 509 U.S. 688, 704, 113 S. Ct. 2849, 2860, 125 L. Ed. 2d 556 (1993); Ashe v. Swenson, 397 U.S. 436, 90 S. Ct. 1189, 25 L. Ed. 2d 469 (1970).

[11] *See* United States v. Ursery, 518 U.S. 267, 116 S. Ct. 2135, 135 L. Ed. 2d 549 (1996).

[12] United States v. Lanza, 260 U.S. 377, 43 S. Ct. 141, 67 L. Ed. 314 (1922); Bartkus v. Illinois, 359 U.S. 121, 79 S. Ct. 676, 3 L. Ed. 2d 684 (1959).

Figure 9.1

Conditions Necessary for Double Jeopardy Protection Against Reprosecution

---

Three conditions are necessary to acquire double jeopardy protection against reprosecution:

1.   An earlier prosecution must progress to the point of jeopardy attachment;
2.   The subsequent prosecution must involve the same offense; and
3.   Both prosecutions must be brought by the same government entity.

A. Did Jeopardy "Attach" in the Prior Proceedings?

Because the Fifth Amendment prohibits the government from placing a criminal defendant twice in jeopardy for the same offense, a defendant is not protected from reprosecution unless he or she has already once before been placed in jeopardy of a conviction for this offense. If an earlier prosecution is scuttled before this point is reached, the government is free to start over.

The jeopardy attachment point is the point at which it is too late for the government to turn back and retain the right to prosecute. There are a number of points in a criminal case that could have been selected. The earliest is when formal charges are filed. However, selecting this point is undesirable because it would force the government to try everyone it charges, whether or not it then has enough evidence, or be barred from trying them later. This position would benefit no one and is the reason for the Supreme Court's rejection. None of the steps preliminary to placing a defendant on trial constitute jeopardy. A defendant who is released after being arrested or who otherwise succeeds in having charges against him dismissed without a trial acquires no constitutional protection against being forced to face them again later.[13]

The latest point for the attachment of jeopardy is when a jury (or judge) returns a verdict on the charges. Selection of this point would mean that the government could reprosecute a defendant as many times as necessary to have the charges resolved on the merits. The English common law selected this point.[14] However, the U.S. Supreme Court has opted for an earlier attachment point. When a defendant is tried before a jury, jeopardy attaches as soon as the jury has been empaneled and sworn.[15] In nonjury trials, jeopardy attaches when the first witness is sworn and the judge has begun hearing testimony.[16] The American attachment rule reflects the judgment that, once a trial has

---

[13]   Serfass v. United States, 420 U.S. 377, 95 S. Ct. 1055, 43 L. Ed. 2d 265 (1975); Collins v. Loisel, 262 U.S. 426, 43 S. Ct. 618, 67 L. Ed. 1062 (1922); Bassing v. Cady, 208 U.S. 386, 28 S. Ct. 392, 52 L. Ed. 540 (1908).

[14]   Note, *Double Jeopardy: The Reprosecution Problem*, 77 HARV. L. REV. 1272, 1273 (1964).

[15]   Illinois v. Somerville, 410 U.S. 458, 93 S. Ct. 1066, 35 L. Ed. 2d 425 (1973); Downum v. United States, 372 U.S. 734, 83 S. Ct. 1033, 10 L. Ed. 2d 100 (1963); Crist v. Bretz, 437 U.S. 28, 98 S. Ct. 2156, 57 L. Ed. 2d 24 (1978).

[16]   Serfass v. United States, *supra* note 13.

started, the defendant has a valued right to have the charges resolved by the first tribunal chosen so that his ordeal can be brought to a close. This means that, once the trial begins, it will normally be the government's one and only shot at establishing the defendant's guilt. However, the Supreme Court has recognized three situations in which the defendant's interest in having his ordeal end with one trial will be subordinated to society's interest in pressing forward until a verdict is reached. When any of the following exceptions apply, the defendant can be retried for the same offense despite the fact that the first trial progressed beyond the jeopardy attachment point.

1. Retrial After an Early Termination Requested by the Defendant

The first exception arises when the defendant requests a mistrial. A defendant who requests an early termination cannot object to being retried because this request operates as a deliberate election to forego the valued right to have the charges resolved by the first tribunal.[17] However, it will not be treated as an election if the need for making the request is caused by the prosecutor's deliberate commission of a prejudicial error to force the defendant into aborting a trial that is going poorly for the government.[18] A defense request made under these circumstances operates as a bar to retrial.

2. Retrial After an Early Termination Based on "Manifest Necessity"

Forcing a defendant to undergo a second trial that he has not solicited frustrates the defendant's interest in having his ordeal ended with one trial. On the other hand, freeing a defendant whenever his first trial progresses beyond the jeopardy attachment point but ends without a verdict, regardless of the underlying reason, makes too light of society's stake in criminal prosecutions. In *United States v. Perez*,[19] the Supreme Court struck a compromise. Under the *Perez* doctrine, retrial is permissible despite the absence of a defense request for a mistrial whenever, taking all the circumstances into account, there is a "manifest necessity" for ending the first trial prematurely.

Jury "deadlock" is the most common situation calling for application of the *Perez* principle.[20] In most jurisdictions, jury verdicts must be unanimous. This is true for both acquittals and convictions. When the jury is unable to reach a verdict, there is no choice but to end the trial. Because a hung jury does not constitute an acquittal, the defendant may be retried. The *Perez* doctrine also allows retrial when

---

[17] United States v. Dinitz, 424 U.S. 600, 96 S. Ct. 1075, 47 L. Ed. 2d 267 (1976); United States v. Scott, 437 U.S. 82, 98 S. Ct. 2187, 57 L. Ed. 2d 65 (1978).

[18] Oregon v. Kennedy, 456 U.S. 667, 102 S. Ct. 2083, 72 L. Ed. 2d 416 (1982).

[19] 22 U.S. (9 Wheat.) 579, 6 L. Ed. 165 (1824).

[20] Logan v. United States, 144 U.S. 263, 12 S. Ct. 617, 36 L. Ed. 429 (1892); Richardson v. United States, 468 U.S. 317, 104 S. Ct. 3081, 82 L. Ed. 2d 242 (1984).

supervening events like wars make it impossible to complete the first trial[21] and when the judge,[22] a juror,[23] or the accused[24] becomes too ill to continue. The Supreme Court has refused to establish rigid criteria for what constitutes a "manifest necessity" for bringing a criminal trial to a premature close, choosing instead to resolve each case on its facts.

3. Retrial After the Successful Appeal of a Conviction

A defendant who is acquitted of the charges at his trial gains absolute constitutional immunity against reprosecution for the same offense.[25] It makes no difference that the acquittal resulted from trial errors prejudicial to the prosecution or that the prosecutor later discovers evidence that conclusively demonstrates the defendant's guilt.[26] An acquittal is final and ends the defendant's ordeal, regardless of the underlying reasons.

A conviction has the same constitutional finality — that is, if the defendant is willing to acquiesce in the outcome. However, if the defendant appeals and secures a reversal,[27] the defendant can be retried unless the conviction is reversed because the prosecutor failed to prove the defendant's guilt beyond a reasonable doubt. A reversal on this ground means that the defendant should have been acquitted and is the legal equivalent of an acquittal.[28] However, if the conviction is reversed for any other reason, such as that the judge erred in admitting a coerced confession or illegally seized evidence, the defendant can be retried. The Supreme Court has pointed out that appeals courts would scarcely be as solicitous of a defendant's constitutional rights if the reversal of a conviction meant that the defendant could not be retried.[29] Retrying a defendant after a successful appeal does not violate double jeopardy because this is the very relief that a defendant requests when he brings a criminal appeal.

---

[21] Wade v. Hunter, 336 U.S. 684, 69 S. Ct. 834, 93 L. Ed. 974 (1949).

[22] Freeman v. United States, 237 F. 815 (2d Cir. 1916).

[23] United States v. Potash, 118 F.2d 54 (2d Cir.), *cert. denied*, 313 U.S. 584, 61 S. Ct. 1103, 85 L. Ed. 1540 (1941).

[24] United States v. Stein, 140 F. Supp. 761 (S.D.N.Y. 1956).

[25] Smith v. Massachusetts, 543 U.S. 462, 125 S. Ct. 1129, 160 L. Ed. 2d 914 (2005); Fong Foo v. United States, *supra* note 7; Green v. United States, *supra* note 5; Kemper v. United States, 195 U.S. 100, 24 S. Ct. 797, 49 L. Ed. 114 (1904); United States v. Ball, 163 U.S. 662, 16 S. Ct. 1192, 41 L. Ed. 300 (1896).

[26] *See* authorities *supra* note 25.

[27] United States v. Tateo, 377 U.S. 463, 84 S. Ct. 1587, 12 L. Ed. 2d 448 (1964); Sattazahn v. Pennsylvania, 537 U.S. 101, 123 S. Ct. 732, 154 L. Ed. 2d 588 (2003) (A defendant who is convicted of murder and sentenced to life imprisonment is not protected by the double jeopardy clause against imposition of a death sentence if he succeeds in having his conviction set aside on appeal and is convicted again on retrial).

[28] Burks v. United States, 437 U.S. 1, 98 S. Ct. 2141, 57 L. Ed. 2d 1 (1978).

[29] United States v. Tateo, *supra* note 27.

B. Does the Subsequent Prosecution Involve the "Same Offense"?

When the new charges differ from the charges the defendant was previously tried for, the court must decide whether they represent the "same offense" or a different one. Only if they represent the "same offense" will the second prosecution be foreclosed.

Deciding when new charges brought under a different section of the penal code represent the "same offense" is the most difficult question in double jeopardy law. When the Constitution was adopted, the number of crimes was relatively small and each crime covered a broad spectrum of conduct. Consequently, there were few opportunities for a prosecutor, displeased with the outcome of the first trial, to indict the defendant under a different section of the penal code and start all over again. This is no longer true. Modern criminal codes are replete with instances of overlapping and duplicating statutes dealing with slightly different aspects of the same underlying conduct.

Faced with the problem of determining when charges brought under different sections of the penal code represent the "same offense," courts have taken one of two approaches.[30] The first, and most widely used approach, is called the *Blockburger*[31] or "**same elements**" test. As you probably already know, legislatures define crimes by the acts that must be performed, the required mental state, and the consequences. These are the **elements** of the crime. The "same elements" test determines whether charges brought under different sections of the penal code represent the same offense by comparing the elements the prosecutor must prove in order to obtain a conviction under each statute. Crimes defined under different sections of the penal code are considered different offenses as long as each statute requires proof of at least one distinct element.[32] If the crime charged at the second trial requires proof of at least one new element, the second prosecution may go forward, even though it is based on the same underlying criminal conduct and the variations in the required elements of proof are slight.[33] The hypothetical bank robber mentioned earlier in the chapter committed five distinct, same-element-test offenses — bank robbery, carrying a concealed weapon, making a terroristic threat, reckless endangerment, and speeding — and, consequently, may be tried five separate times. The "same elements" test provides

---

[30] For a discussion of these approaches, see Kirchheimer, *The Act, the Offense, and Double Jeopardy*, 58 YALE L.J. 513 (1949); Thomas, *The Prohibition of Successive Prosecutions for the Same Offense in Search of a Definition*, 71 IOWA L. REV. 323 (1986); Note, *Twice in Jeopardy*, 75 YALE L. REV. 262 (1965).

[31] Blockburger v. United States, 284 U.S. 299, 304, 52 S. Ct. 180, 182, 76 L. Ed. 306 (1932).

[32] United States v. Dixon, *supra* note 10; Carter v. United States, 530 U.S. 225, 120 S. Ct. 2159, 147 L. Ed. 2d 203 (2000) (finding that offense of taking and carrying away, with intent to steal anything of value exceeding $1,000 belonging to a bank was an offense distinct from taking from the person or presence of another, by force, violence, or intimidation, anything of value belonging to a bank, because the former offense contained three elements not included in the latter offense, namely, specific intent to steal, asportation, and valuation exceeding $1,000. The fact that the two statutory offenses were similar and arose out of the same underlying conduct does not make them the same offense).

[33] *See* cases *supra* note 32.

scant protection against successive prosecutions for the same underlying conduct.[34] It nevertheless satisfies the Fifth Amendment and is the test used by federal courts and a majority of state courts.[35]

The second approach, known as the "**same transaction**" test, focuses on the underlying conduct to determine the number of times a defendant can be tried. Under this approach, all criminal charges that derive from the same underlying conduct must be joined for prosecution in a single trial.[36] The prosecutor cannot hold some of the charges in reserve to start over again if disappointed with the outcome of the first trial, because the prosecutor is barred from bringing multiple prosecutions for the same criminal conduct.

C. Is the Same Governmental Entity Prosecuting?

The double jeopardy prohibition applies only when both prosecutions are brought by the same government entity. It does not prevent separate prosecutions by different sovereign entities when the offense is a crime against the laws of each. Bank robbery is a classic example. Robbing a federally insured bank (a category that today includes virtually all banks) is a federal crime; robbing a bank located within the jurisdiction of the state is a state crime. Thus, our bank robber can be prosecuted for the same bank robbery by the federal government and the state in which the bank is located without violating the double jeopardy clause.[37] The same is true for crimes that cross state lines; all states whose laws are violated are permitted to prosecute.[38]

§ 9.4   — Prohibition of Multiple Punishments for the Same Offense

There is a second aspect to double jeopardy — the prohibition against multiple punishments for the same offense. This aspect has come before the Court repeatedly as states have undertaken increasingly aggressive measures to deal with criminals who are not deterred by traditional forms of punishment. These measures have taken a variety of forms, including laws authorizing confiscation of money and property

---

[34] Two doctrines, the included offense doctrine and collateral estoppel, block retrial in limited situations. *See* Brown v. Ohio, 432 U.S. 161, 97 S. Ct. 2221, 53 L. Ed. 2d 187 (1977) (recognizing included offense doctrine); Ashe v. Swenson, 397 U.S. 436, 90 S. Ct. 1189, 25 L. Ed. 2d 469 (1970) (applying collateral estoppel). Discussion of these doctrines is beyond the scope of this book.
[35] United States v. Dixon, *supra* note 10.
[36] For cases following this approach, *see* Neal v. State, 55 Cal. 2d 11, 357 P.2d 839 (1960), *cert. denied*, 365 U.S. 823, 81 S. Ct. 708, 5 L. Ed. 2d 700 (1961); State v. Corning, 289 Minn. 354, 184 N.W.2d 603 (1971); State v. Brown, 262 Or. 442, 497 P.2d 1191 (1972).
[37] United States v. Lanza, *supra* note 12; Bartkus v. Illinois, *supra* note 12.
[38] Heath v. Alabama, 474 U.S. 82, 106 S. Ct. 433, 88 L. Ed. 2d 387 (1985).

gained from criminal activity[39]; "Megan's" laws, requiring convicted sexual offenders to register with the local police when they move into a community[40]; sexual predator laws requiring involuntary civil commitment of habitual sexual offenders upon completion of their criminal sentences[41]; and laws imposing enhanced sentences on habitual offenders.[42] Because they impose additional penalties following a conviction, such laws raise the question of what constitutes "punishment" for double jeopardy purposes.

Whether burdens like these constitute a punishment is not determined from the offender's point of view.[43] From the offender's point of view, any burden that accrues because of the commission of a crime feels like a punishment. However, the Eighth Amendment distinguishes between civil and criminal penalties. The ban on multiple punishments for the same offense is violated only when multiple *criminal* penalties are exacted. It is not violated when one penalty is criminal and the other is civil. Whether a penalty is civil or criminal depends on the government's purpose for imposing it. If the purpose is nonpunitive and the legislature characterizes the remedy as civil, courts will normally treat it this way.[44]

Megan's laws and laws requiring involuntary commitment of habitual sexual offenders upon completion of their criminal sentences are regarded as civil, not criminal, because their purpose is to protect the community against future crimes, not to punish sex offenders for their past ones.[45] The same is true for forfeiture laws authorizing confiscation of proceeds from criminal activity, instrumentalities used to commit the crime, and contraband.[46] Confiscation of "guilty property" furthers the nonpunitive goals of preventing wrongdoers from using the property to commit future crimes and also from profiting from their wrongs.[47]

---

[39] United States v. Ursery, *supra* note 11.

[40] McAllister, *The Constitutionality of Kansas Laws Targeting Sex Offenders*, 36 W.B.N. L.J. 419, 436 (1997) ("sexual offender registration laws which exist in every state generally have not been successfully challenged on constitutional grounds").

[41] Selig v. Yount, 531 U.S. 250, 121 S. Ct. 727, 148 L. Ed. 2d 734 (2001) (state court's determination that the sexual predator statute was civil rather than criminal precluded inmate's double jeopardy challenge because there is no constitutional protection against successive civil and criminal remedies; involuntary civil commitment following completion of criminal sentence was justified by state's interest in protecting the public from dangerous individuals with untreatable mental conditions); Kansas v. Hendricks, 521 U.S. 346, 117 S. Ct. 2072, 138 L. Ed. 2d 501 (1997) (involuntary civil commitment of habitual sexual offenders following completion of their prison sentence does not violate double jeopardy clause).

[42] Monge v. California, 524 U.S. 721, 118 S. Ct. 2246, 141 L. Ed. 2d 615 (1998) (laws imposing enhanced sentences on repeat offenders do not violate double jeopardy protection against multiple punishments for the same offense because the sentence enhancement is not imposed as additional punishment for the previous offense, but as a stiffened penalty for the present offense, which is regarded as more serious by virtue of its repetition).

[43] Department of Revenue of Mont. v. Kurth Ranch, 511 U.S. 767, 114 S. Ct. 1937, 128 L. Ed. 2d 767 (1994).

[44] Seling v. Young, *supra* note 41.

[45] *See* authorities *supra* notes 41 and 42.

[46] United States v. Ursery, *supra* note 11.

[47] *Id.*

Most jurisdictions also have statutes imposing enhanced sentences, often as much as double, on repeat offenders. These laws have also been upheld, over double jeopardy challenge, on the grounds that they do not punish the offender a second time for past crimes; the enhanced punishment is imposed for the present crime, which is considered a more aggravated offense due to its repetition.[48]

§ 9.5   Sixth Amendment and Due Process Requirements for Fair Trials

We will now take up consideration of the constitutional requirements for a fair trial. Most are found in the Sixth Amendment. You are already familiar with one of the most important provisions for ensuring a fair trial — the Sixth Amendment right to assistance of counsel. As explained in Chapter 8, the right to counsel is essential to protect innocent people from being convicted because they lack the legal skill and knowledge needed to defend themselves. This chapter investigates other provisions that are also essential to a fair trial, including the guarantee of a speedy and public trial; the requirement that the tribunal be fair and impartial; the right to trial by jury; and the right to confront and cross-examine adverse witnesses.

§ 9.6   —Speedy Trial

The Sixth Amendment guarantees defendants, in both state and federal prosecutions, the right to a speedy trial.[49] Delays in the administration of justice jeopardize several interests. First, for those unable to obtain release on bail, delays result in a loss of freedom, a consequence that is particularly tragic for defendants who are later acquitted.[50] Even for defendants who are able to afford bail, time spent waiting for trial is emotionally and financially taxing. Outstanding criminal charges can damage a person's reputation, curtail employment opportunities, disrupt important relationships, and cause intense anxiety.[51] Most important of all, when the wheels of justice turn too slowly, the integrity of the proceedings may be compromised. Time has a dulling effect on memory. Key defense witnesses, in addition, may die or disappear.[52] The

---

[48]   *See* Monge v. California, *supra* note 42; *see also* United States v. Watts, 519 U.S. 148, 117 S. Ct. 633, 136 L. Ed. 2d 554 (1997); Witte v. United States, 515 U.S. 389, 115 S. Ct. 2199, 132 L. Ed. 2d 351 (1995).
[49]   Klopfer v. North Carolina, 386 U.S. 213, 87 S. Ct. 988, 18 L. Ed. 2d 1 (1967).
[50]   Barker v. Wingo, 407 U.S. 514, 92 S. Ct. 2182, 33 L. Ed. 2d 101 (1972).
[51]   *Id.*; Smith v. Hooey, 393 U.S. 374, 89 S. Ct. 575, 21 L. Ed. 2d 607 (1972); Klopfer v. North Carolina, *supra* note 49.
[52]   *See* authorities *supra* note 51.

problem is particularly serious for defendants who are incarcerated during this period. The Supreme Court has noted:[53]

why U.S.S.C. thinks speedy trial is important

> ...[T]he possibilities that long delay will impair the ability of an accused to defend himself" are markedly increased when the accused is incarcerated.... Confined in a prison, ... his ability to confer with potential defense witnesses, or even to keep track of their whereabouts, is obviously impaired. And, while "evidence and witnesses disappear, memories fade, and events lose their perspective," a man isolated in prison is powerless to exert his own investigative efforts to mitigate these erosive effects of the passage of time.[54]

Although the speedy trial guarantee is intended to protect the accused, society also suffers when justice is delayed. The testimony of prosecution witnesses is subject to the same time hazards; they, too, can die, disappear, or forget, depriving the government of crucial evidence.[55] In *Barker v. Wingo*,[56] the Supreme Court elaborated on the consequences of tardy justice:

> ... [T]here is a societal interest in providing a speedy trial which exists separate from, and at times in opposition to, the interests of the accused. The inability of courts to provide a prompt trial has contributed to a large backlog of cases in urban courts which, among other things, enables defendants to negotiate more effectively for pleas of guilty to lesser offenses and otherwise manipulate the system. In addition, persons released on bond for lengthy periods awaiting trial have an opportunity to commit other crimes.... Moreover, the longer an accused is free awaiting trial, the more tempting becomes his opportunity to jump bail and escape. Finally, delay between arrest and punishment may have a detrimental effect on rehabilitation.

When all the costs of delay are taken into account, it becomes apparent that the maxim that "justice delayed is justice denied" rings true for everyone.

A. Attachment of the Right to a Speedy Trial

Criminal trials represent the culmination of a process that begins with the commission of a crime and proceeds through discovery of the crime, investigation, the defendant's arrest, indictment, arraignment, and beyond. It is necessary to select a point to mark the start of the period in which the government must bring the accused to trial or lose the right to prosecute — i.e., the point at which the right to a speedy trial attaches. In *United States v. Marion*,[57] the Supreme Court ruled that the Sixth Amendment guarantee of a speedy trial starts to run only after the prosecutorial phase commences. By conferring the right to a speedy trial on an "accused," the drafters manifested an intent

---

[53] Smith v. Hooey, *supra* note 51.
[54] *Id*. at 379–380, 89 S. Ct. at 578.
[55] Dickey v. Florida, 398 U.S. 30, 42, 90 S. Ct. 1564, 1571, 26 L. Ed. 2d 26 (1970) (Brennan, J., concurring); see also Ponzi v. Fessenden, 258 U.S. 254, 264, 42 S. Ct. 309, 312, 66 L. Ed. 2d 607 (1922).
[56] *Supra* note 50.
[57] 404 U.S. 307, 92 S. Ct. 455, 30 L. Ed. 2d 468 (1971); *see also* United States v. MacDonald, 456 U.S. 1, 102 S. Ct. 1497, 71 L. Ed. 2d 696 (1982).

to exclude pre-accusatory delays from consideration in determining whether the right to a speedy trial has been denied. As with the right to counsel, the suspect stands "accused" only after the government decides to prosecute by obtaining an indictment or filing formal charges. Delays before a suspect has been charged with a crime are not taken into account in determining whether a speedy trial has been denied.

Postponing the time of attachment serves the interests of both the public and the accused. The prosecution benefits because it will not lose the right to prosecute if it is slow to learn of the crime or to develop the case. Likewise, the would-be defendant benefits because the prosecution will conduct a more thorough examination before lodging formal charges, making it less likely that innocent persons will be accused. Moreover, criminal defendants already have other legal protection against delays in charging them. First, for most crimes there are **statutes of limitation** that require that criminal charges be made within a fixed number of years after the crime has been committed. If the delay exceeds the period of limitation, prosecution will be barred. Second, the due process clause provides a further basis for relief in cases in which the prosecution deliberately delays filing charges in order to obtain a tactical advantage over the defendant or does so with knowledge of an appreciable risk that the delay will cripple the defendant's ability to put forth an adequate defense.[58]

Even though the right to a speedy trial has attached, the prosecution[59] or defense[60] can stop the clock by having the charges dismissed. If the prosecution subsequently reinstates the charges, the period in between will be excluded from Sixth Amendment computation. Only the period during which a defendant bears the status of an accused is taken into account in determining whether a speedy trial has been denied.

B. Determining Whether the Right Has Been Denied

There is no set period in which a trial must take place after prosecution has begun. Rather, in determining whether the right to a speedy trial has been denied, the Supreme Court balances four factors[61]: (1) the length of the delay, (2) the reasons for the delay, (3) whether the defendant asserted his or her right to a speedy trial or sat idly by, and (4) whether the delay prejudiced the defendant's case.

There is only one remedy for deprivation of the right to a speedy trial — permanent dismissal of the charges. The government cannot compensate the accused for unconstitutional delay by proceeding with the trial and subtracting the period of unconstitutional delay from the sentence imposed.[62] Freeing defendants without trial even though they may be guilty is a serious action. Consequently, the finding that delay has denied the defendant a speedy trial is reserved only for the most egregious cases.

---

[58] United States v. Lovasco, 431 U.S. 783, 97 S. Ct. 2044, 52 L. Ed. 2d 752 (1977) (dicta).
[59] United States v. MacDonald, *supra* note 57.
[60] United States v. Loud Hawk, 474 U.S. 302, 106 S. Ct. 648, 88 L. Ed. 2d 640 (1986).
[61] Barker v. Wingo, *supra* note 50.
[62] Strunk v. United States, 412 U.S. 434, 93 S. Ct. 2260, 37 L. Ed. 2d 56 (1973).

1. Length of Delay

The first factor, duration of the delay, operates as a red flag signaling the need to inquire into the other three factors. An inquiry is necessary only when the delay is long enough to be presumptively prejudicial.[63] What constitutes a presumptively prejudicial delay varies with the nature of the case. A presumptively prejudicial delay in the case of an ordinary street crime, for example, would be less than for a tax evasion case, both because less time is needed to prepare for trial and because eyewitness testimony, the kind used to prove street crimes, grows stale more rapidly than documentary evidence, the kind typically presented in a tax evasion case.[64] Although the Constitution does not set an absolute time limit, some jurisdictions have adopted statutes requiring automatic dismissal of charges against non-violent offenders who are incarcerated while awaiting trial unless the trial is brought within a relatively short, fixed period.[65]

2. Reasons for Delay

The second factor in speedy trial analysis focuses on allocating responsibility for the delay. The Sixth Amendment does not protect an accused against delays he has requested or for which he is responsible.[66] An accused cannot complain of delays resulting from the government's inability to locate him while a fugitive from justice,[67] of trial postponements caused by his own illness[68] or due to defense motions seasonably acted upon,[69] or for periods during which he was mentally incompetent to stand trial.[70] The only delays relevant for Sixth Amendment purposes are those attributable to the government.

However, some reasons for prosecutorial delay are dealt with more harshly than others. When the delay results from reasons beyond the government's control, such as the inability to locate a crucial prosecution witness, an appropriate delay may be excused. Deliberate delays interjected in order to impair the defense, in contrast, are weighed heavily against the government.[71] Even negligent delays can, at times, work

[63] Barker v. Wingo, *supra* note 50.

[64] *Id.*

[65] *See* United States v. West, 504 F.2d 253 (D.C. Cir. 1974).

[66] *See, e.g.,* Dickey v. Florida, *supra* note 55 (Brennan, J., concurring); United States v. Loud Hawk, *supra* note 60; United States v. Lustman, 258 F.2d 475 (2d Cir.), *cert. denied,* 358 U.S. 880, 79 S. Ct. 118, 3 L. Ed. 2d 109 (1958); United States v. Ferguson, 498 F.2d 1001 (D.C. Cir.), *cert. denied,* 419 U.S. 900, 95 S. Ct. 183, 42 L. Ed. 2d 145 (1974). A defendant is also chargeable, for speedy trial purposes, with delays caused by his attorney, whether defense counsel is privately retained or has been assigned by the government. Vermont v. Brillon, ___ U.S. ___, 129 S. Ct. 1283, 173 L. Ed. 2d 231 (2009).

[67] United States v. Simmons, 338 F.2d 804 (2d Cir. 1964), *cert. denied,* 380 U.S. 983, 85 S. Ct. 1352, 14 L. Ed. 2d 276 (1965).

[68] Joy v. United States, 416 F.2d 962 (9th Cir. 1969).

[69] United States v. Jones, 524 F.2d 834 (D.C. Cir. 1975).

[70] United States v. Cartano, 420 F.2d 362 (1st Cir.), *cert. denied,* 397 U.S. 1054, 90 S. Ct. 1398, 25 L. Ed. 2d 671 (1970); Nickens v. United States, 323 F.2d 808 (D.C. Cir. 1963), *cert. denied,* 379 U.S. 905, 85 S. Ct. 198, 13 L. Ed. 2d 178 (1964); United States v. Lustman, *supra* note 66.

[71] Barker v. Wingo, *supra* note 50. *See also* United States v. Loud Hawk, *supra* note 60.

a speedy trial violation. For example, in *Doggett v. United States*,[72] the authorities did nothing to search for the defendant for six years due to an erroneous assumption that he was out of the country. Had they made an effort to locate him, they could have discovered his whereabouts in minutes, because he was living and working openly under his own name. Characterizing this delay as extraordinary, the Supreme Court ruled that Doggett had been denied his right to a speedy trial.

3. Defendant's Assertion of Rights

Prior to *Barker v. Wingo*, a majority of federal courts adhered to the so-called "demand-waiver" rule. This rule required the court to disregard any delays occurring before the accused demanded that his case be docketed for trial.[73] The defendant's silence in the face of delay was regarded as an automatic waiver. The *Barker* Court acknowledged that the defendant's timely assertion of his rights was "one of the factors to be considered," and that the "failure to assert the right" would "make it difficult for a defendant to prove that he was denied a speedy trial," but declined to treat this factor as automatic grounds for rejecting a claim. A defendant, for example, cannot be faulted with delay in making a demand when he is unaware that charges against him are outstanding.[74] Even when the defendant is aware of the charges, the impact of not demanding a speedy trial varies with the facts. The failure, for example, would be weighed more heavily against a defendant who, on the advice of his attorney, makes a strategic decision to acquiesce in the delay, hoping that the government will abandon the prosecution, than against one who is uncounseled and whose failure to make a timely demand for trial is caused by ignorance.

4. Prejudice to Defendant

Whether the defendant was damaged by the delay is the last and most important factor. This factor is evaluated in light of the interests that the constitutional guarantee of a speedy trial protects. Accordingly, delays are more serious for defendants who are subjected to oppressive pretrial confinements than for those who are free on bail.[75] However, even for defendants who are free on bail, delay can be harmful because job opportunities may be foreclosed, important relationships may be strained, and anxieties over the future can be immobilizing. However, the most serious damage is that which occurs to a defendant's ability to defend. Defendants who are able to demonstrate that crucial defense witnesses have died, disappeared, or forgotten important facts during an extended delay for which the government is responsible have a strong basis for claiming they were denied their constitutional right to a speedy trial.

---

[72]   505 U.S. 647, 112 S. Ct. 2628, 120 L. Ed. 2d 520 (1992).

[73]   Barker v. Wingo, *supra* note 50.

[74]   Doggett v. United States, *supra* note 72.

[75]   Petition of Provoo, 17 F.R.D. 183 (D. Md.), *aff'd sub nom.*, United States v. Provoo, 350 U.S. 857, 76 S. Ct. 101, 100 L. Ed. 761 (1955); United States ex rel. Von Cseh v. Fay, 313 F.2d 620 (2d Cir. 1963).

§ 9.7   — Public Trial

The Sixth Amendment also guarantees the right to a public trial. The oppressive practices of the English Court of Star Chamber sparked fear and distrust of secret trials.[76] The guarantee of a public trial was included to safeguard against arbitrary abuses of judicial power behind closed door. Public trials are also important because they afford citizens an opportunity to observe trials and to evaluate whether judges and juries are fulfilling their constitutional responsibility to administer justice.[77] Conducting criminal trials in open courtroom enhances "both the basic fairness of the criminal trial and the appearance of fairness so essential to public confidence in the system."[78]

The right to a public trial extends to ancillary pretrial proceedings, such as the jury selection phase[79] and hearings on motions to suppress illegally seized evidence,[80] as well as the trial itself. However, it does not apply to **grand jury** proceedings, which have always been conducted in secret.[81] Secrecy is important in grand jury proceedings to protect the reputation of innocent people should the evidence be found insufficient to return an indictment.[82]

Although the Supreme Court has vigorously protected a criminal defendant's right to a public trial, this right is not absolute. Occasions may arise when a judge considers it necessary to exclude members of the public from the courtroom. Before taking this action, the judge must make findings that this action is necessary to advance an overriding interest and that there are no reasonable alternatives to protect this interest.[83]

---

[76]   *In re* Oliver, 333 U.S. 257, 68 S. Ct. 499, 92 L. Ed. 682, 690–692 (1948).

[77]   *See* Gannett Co. v. DePasquale, 443 U.S. 368, 99 S. Ct. 2898, 61 L. Ed. 2d 608 (1979); Globe Newspaper Co. v. Superior Court, 457 U.S. 596, 102 S. Ct. 2613, 73 L. Ed. 2d 248 (1982); United States v. Kobli, 172 F.2d 919 (3d Cir. 1949); State v. Schmit, 273 Minn. 78, 139 N.W.2d 800 (1966); People v. Jelke, 308 N.Y. 56, 123 N.E.2d 769 (1954).

[78]   Press-Enterprise Co. v. Superior Court, 464 U.S. 501, 508, 104 S. Ct. 819, 823, 78 L. Ed. 2d 629 (1984).

[79]   Presley v. Georgia, __ U.S. __, 130 S. Ct. 721, 175 L. Ed. 2d 675 (2010); Press-Enterprise Co. v. Superior Court, *supra* note 78.

[80]   Waller v. Georgia, 467 U.S. 39, 104 S. Ct. 2210, 81 L. Ed. 2d 31 (1984).

[81]   *See* Fed R. Crim. P. 6; *see also* Douglas Oil Co. v. Petrol Stops, etc., 441 U.S. 211, 222, 99 S. Ct. 1167, 1674, 60 L. Ed. 2d 156 (1979).

[82]   United States v. Procter & Gamble Co., 356 U.S. 677, 78 S.C. 983, 986, 2 L. Ed. 2d 1077 (1958).

[83]   Waller v. Georgia, *supra* note 80, provided the standard for courts to apply before excluding the public from any phase of a criminal trial to which the right applies. "[T]he party seeking to close the hearing must advance an overriding interest that is likely to be prejudiced, the closure must be no broader than necessary to protect that interest, the trial must consider reasonable alternatives to closing the proceeding, and it must make findings adequate to support closure." *See also* Press-Enterprise Co. v. Superior Court, *supra* note 78 (holding that the right to a public trial extends beyond the trial phase to the jury selection process); Presley v. Georgia, *supra* note 79 (holding that defendant's Sixth Amendment right to a public trial was violated when the trial court excluded the public from the *voir dire* of prospective jurors without considering whether the existence of alternatives to closure).

Closure, for example, is allowed when a child witness is called to testify about matters too embarrassing or frightening to discuss in public.[84] Even here, the judge must make case-specific findings that, because of the sensitive nature of the testimony and the child's age, closure is necessary to protect the child's physical and psychological well-being.

The right to a public trial extends beyond the accused. Members of the public and the media have a corresponding right to attend criminal trials, but their right derives from the First Amendment, not the Sixth. The First Amendment guarantees members of the public and the media the right to attend criminal trials so that they can observe and evaluate the workings of the judicial system. Even when a defendant asks the judge to clear the courtroom, and this sometimes happens, judges must consider the interest of the public and press in ruling on the motion. Exclusion of members of the public and press from the courtroom, at the defendant's request, is proper only when this action is necessary to protect the defendant's right to a fair trial.[85]

§ 9.8 — Confrontation of Adverse Witnesses

The Sixth Amendment also guarantees an accused the right to confront witnesses who testify against her in open court. A courtroom confrontation enhances the reliability of testimony in several ways.[86] First, testimony in court is given under oath and on penalty of perjury. Second, jurors have an opportunity to observe the witness's demeanor and decide whether the witness is telling the truth. Finally, and most important of all, testimony given in open court is subject to cross-examination. Cross-examination has been described as the "greatest legal engine ever invented for discovery of truth."[87] The witness may have had an inadequate opportunity to observe the matters about which she testifies, her memory may be faulty and language imprecise, or she may not be telling the truth. Cross-examination gives the accused an opportunity to challenge a witness's veracity and expose weaknesses in her testimony. Cross-examination is so central to the right of confrontation that the Supreme Court has often spoken of the Sixth Amendment as guaranteeing the "right to confront and cross-examine" adverse witnesses as if both terms appeared in the Constitution.[88] Because the confrontation clause provides a fundamental mechanism for ensuring the reliability of the evidence offered against an accused, it is regarded as an integral part of due process and is binding on the states.[89]

---

[84] Globe Newspaper Co. v. Superior Court, *supra* note 77 (decided under First Amendment).

[85] Richmond Newspapers, Inc. v. Virginia, 448 U.S. 555, 100 S. Ct. 2814, 65 L. Ed. 2d 973 (1980); Globe Newspaper Co. v. Superior Court, *supra* note 77.

[86] Chambers v. Mississippi, 410 U.S. 284, 93 S. Ct. 1038, 35 L. Ed. 2d 297 (1973); Maryland v. Craig, 497 U.S. 836, 845–846, 110 S. Ct. 3157, 3165, 111 L. Ed. 2d 666 (1990).

[87] California v. Green, 399 U.S. 149, 90 S. Ct. 1930, 26 L. Ed. 2d 489 (1970).

[88] Chambers v. Mississippi, *supra* note 86.

[89] Pointer v. Texas, 380 U.S. 400, 85 S. Ct. 1065, 13 L. Ed. 2d 923 (1965).

Historically, the right to confront adverse witnesses meant the right to confront them face-to-face. While a defendant could forfeit this right by not showing up for trial[90] or by being so disruptive that it was necessary to remove him from the courtroom, this right could not otherwise be denied.[91] However, the Supreme Court has since carved out an exception for child sex abuse trials.[92] Putative child sexual abuse victims may be permitted to testify via one-way, closed-circuit television if the judge determines that facing the accused in the courtroom would cause severe trauma and impair the child's ability to testify.

§ 9.9　　—Fair and Impartial Tribunal

Few rights are more important than the right to be tried before an impartial tribunal. The Sixth Amendment guarantees the right to an impartial jury, but impartiality is also an ingredient of due process of law and applies in bench trials as well. There are many potential sources of bias. The trier of fact (the judge or jury) may harbor racial or religious prejudice against the defendant; they may stand to gain, in some way, from his conviction; they may have past ties that cause them to believe the defendant is capable of diabolical deeds; or they may harbor animosity toward the defendant because of things they have heard or read about the case. Each of these influences can be corrupting.

Figure 9.2
Elements of an Impartial Tribunal

The judge sitting as a trier of fact or the members of the jury panel must:

1. not have a stake in the outcome of the case;
2. not bear any personal animosity toward the specific defendant;
3. be able to set aside any general prejudice toward a class to which the defendant belongs;
4. be able to set aside any preconceived notions about the proper outcome of the case and be able to render a verdict based solely on the evidence presented at trial.

An obviously biasing influence exists when the judge or a juror has a financial stake in the outcome. In *Tumey v. Ohio*,[93] the Supreme Court set aside a conviction because the judge who tried the case was paid from the fines and costs levied against

---

[90]　Taylor v. United States, 414 U.S. 17, 94 S. Ct. 194, 38 L. Ed. 2d 174 (1973).

[91]　Illinois v. Allen, 397 U.S. 337, 90 S. Ct. 1057, 25 L. Ed. 2d 353 (1970).

[92]　Maryland v. Craig, *supra* note 86.

[93]　273 U.S. 510, 47 S. Ct. 437, 71 L. Ed. 749 (1927); *see also* Ward v. Village of Monroeville, 409 U.S. 57, 93 S. Ct. 80, 34 L. Ed. 2d 267 (1972).

persons found guilty, rather than out of the general funds, which is the normal way judges are compensated. This method of compensation created an incentive to resolve doubtful cases in favor of fee-generating guilty verdicts.

In *Mayberry v. Pennsylvania*,[94] the judge who tried the case harbored animosity toward the defendant for reasons that were richly deserved. The defendant, who insisted on representing himself, showed contemptuous disdain for the judge's authority. When he disagreed with a ruling, he would deride the judge, calling him names like "hatchet man for the state," "dirty sonofabitch," and "tyrannical old dog." His conduct eventually became so insufferable that he had to be gagged in order for the trial to proceed. After the jury returned a verdict, the judge held the defendant in contempt of court and sentenced him to between 11 and 22 years in prison. The Supreme Court set the contempt conviction aside. Characterizing the defendant's trial demeanor as "a shock to those raised in the Western tradition," the Court ruled that a judge who has been the target of repeated vitriolic attacks must turn the trial of contempt charges over to another judge who does not bear the "sting of . . . slanderous remarks."[95] A defendant has a right to be tried before an impartial tribunal even when the defendant is responsible for the animosity of which he or she complains.

Special precautions are sometimes necessary during jury trials that would not be required during a trial before a judge. The defendant, for example, may not be forced to appear before the jury in prison clothing because jurors might construe this as evidence of guilt.[96] This does not mean that a defendant is entitled to have the courtroom purified of everything from which jurors might infer guilt. Some practices, like the presence of armed guards in the courtroom, are necessary for security. When a practice is necessary for security, the defendant cannot complain that it may create an unfavorable impression on the minds of the jurors.[97]

Finally, and most importantly, a fair trial means one in which the defendant's guilt is determined based on testimony developed in open court, and not on preconceived notions and prejudices.[98] Of course, a panel of jurors that is totally free of prejudice is a goal that is seldom realized. All human beings are prejudiced, at least on some level, about some issues. To ferret out the worst prejudices, defense counsel is permitted to conduct a *voir dire* examination of prospective jurors during the jury selection process to determine whether they have "disqualifying attitudes" about the case. If so, the potential juror will be "struck" from the panel. What constitutes a disqualifying attitude depends on the issues involved in the case. A prospective juror's admission that he favors the death penalty and would automatically vote to impose it if the defendant is

---

[94] 400 U.S. 455, 91 S. Ct. 499, 27 L. Ed. 2d 532 (1971).
[95] *Id.*
[96] Estelle v. Williams, 425 U.S. 501, 96 S. Ct. 1691, 48 L. Ed. 2d 126 (1976). *See also* Deck v. Missouri, 545 U.S. 622, 125 S. Ct. 2007, 161 L. Ed. 2d 953 (2005) (holding that criminal defendants may not be made to appear before the jury in physical restraints or shackles unless the judge makes case-specific findings that their use is warranted by security concerns).
[97] Holbrook v. Flynn, 475 U.S. 560, 106 S. Ct. 1340, 89 L. Ed. 2d 525 (1986).
[98] Parker v. Gladden, 385 U.S. 363, 87 S. Ct. 468, 17 L. Ed. 2d 420 (1966).

found guilty would be a disqualifying attitude in a death penalty case because it would prevent the juror from considering mitigating factors in imposing the sentence.[99] The same attitude, however, would not disqualify the juror from sitting in a non-capital trial, even though this attitude may indicate a slant in favor of conviction.

§ 9.10 — Pretrial Publicity

A fair and impartial tribunal is one that reaches its decision solely from the evidence presented at the trial, rather than from information learned elsewhere. The rules of evidence, which are designed to filter reliable facts from unsubstantiated rumors, would mean little if the jurors came to the trial already knowing the "correct outcome" based on things they read in the newspaper.

There is usually no problem assembling a jury panel that will make its decision based solely on the evidence presented at trial because members of the jury usually have no independent knowledge of the case. To help ensure that no one with independent knowledge finds his way onto the jury, trial counsel will be allowed to examine prospective jurors to learn whether they know the defendant or the victim, or have some other connection to the case that might provide a source of independent knowledge. If a potential juror indicates having preconceived notions about the case that could affect his decision, the judge will excuse the juror so that another, without a connection to the case, can be selected.

However, in this day of mass media, some cases are of such intense public interest that it may be impossible to find a juror who has not heard of the case before being selected to sit on the jury. Mr. Justice Frankfurter summarized this problem when he questioned:

> How can fallible men and women reach a disinterested verdict based exclusively on what they heard in court when, before they entered the jury box, their minds were saturated by press and radio for months preceding by matters designed to establish the guilt of the accused?[100]

The trial of Dr. Sam Sheppard during the 1950s is the case that galvanized support for reform. Sheppard was a prominent osteopathic physician whose pregnant wife was found bludgeoned to death in their suburban Cleveland home. He claimed that his wife had been attacked by an intruder who overpowered him. The case featured high society, sex, murder, and mystery and enthralled the public. The media lost all sense of perspective. Even before Dr. Sheppard had been charged with murder, the front pages of

---

[99] Morgan v. Illinois, 504 U.S. 719, 112 S. Ct. 2222, 119 L. Ed. 2d 492 (1992).

[100] Irvin v. Dowd, 366 U.S. 717, 729–730, 81 S. Ct. 1639, 1646, 6 L. Ed. 2d 751, 760 (1961) (Frankfurter, J., concurring). *See also, generally*, Robert Hardaway & Douglas B. Tumminello, *Pretrial Publicity in Criminal Cases of National Notoriety: Constructing a Remedy for the Remediless Wrong*, 46 AM. U. L. REV. 39 (1996).

newspapers were proclaiming his guilt and demanding "justice." During the weeks and months before the trial, headlines were saturated with stories of Sheppard's lack of co-operation, his refusal to take a lie detector test, his secret love affairs, interviews with "bombshell witnesses," and other prejudicial disclosures. The courtroom was packed with reporters throughout the trial. The reporters often commented on the evidence right in front of the jury. The state appeals court described the trial as "a 'Roman holiday' for the news media" while the Supreme Court called it a "carnival atmosphere."[101] Sheppard spent 10 years in prison before the U.S. Supreme Court declared that he had received an unfair trial and ordered that he be released. Although he was acquitted at the new trial, he and his family were ruined.

A. Constitutional Standards for Choosing an Impartial Jury When There Has Been Significant Pretrial Publicity

In a nation in which most citizens either read the newspaper or own radios or televisions, the facts associated with names like O.J. Simpson and Scott Peterson are likely to come to the attention of virtually every person qualified for jury service. If media exposure to some of the facts of the case was enough to disqualify prospective jurors, selecting a constitutionally acceptable jury would be impossible except in routine cases. The due process standard for impartiality does not require that the prospective juror be unfamiliar with the case, or even that the juror hold no "preconceived notion as to the guilt or innocence of the accused."[102] Rather, the test is whether the "juror can lay aside his impression or opinion and render a verdict based on evidence presented in court."[103]

During their *voir dire* examination, prospective jurors will be asked if they are familiar with the case and, if so, whether they believe that they can decide the defendant's guilt based solely on the evidence. A juror's affirmation that she can make an unbiased determination does not conclusively establish this fact. The defendant can still attempt to show that the panel was biased. For example, in *Irvin v. Dowd*,[104] the entire community was flooded with prejudicial media reports during the six months prior to the trial. Ninety percent of those questioned expressed uncertainty about whether they could render an impartial verdict based on the evidence developed at the trial and 8 of the 12 jurors who were eventually selected to sit in the case admitted to having preconceived notions about the defendant's guilt. However, because they stated that they could put their beliefs aside and act impartially, the trial court allowed them to sit in the case. The Supreme Court was skeptical about their ability to do this and reversed the

[101] Sheppard v. Maxwell, 384 U.S. 333, 86 S. Ct. 1507, 16 L. Ed. 2d 600, 608 (1966).
[102] Irvin v. Dowd, *supra* note 100. *See also* Murphy v. Florida, 421 U.S. 794, 95 S. Ct. 2031, 44 L. Ed. 2d 589 (1975).
[103] Rideau v. Louisiana, 373 U.S. 723, 83 S. Ct. 1417, 10 L. Ed. 2d 663 (1963); Patton v. Yount, 467 U.S. 1052, 104 S. Ct. 2885, 81 L. Ed. 2d 847 (1984). Irvin v. Dowd, *supra* note 100; Skilling v. United States, __ U.S. __, 130 S. Ct. 2896, 177 L. Ed. 2d 619 (2010).
[104] *Supra* note 100.

conviction, stating, "[w]here so many, so many times, admitted prejudice, such a statement of impartiality [by the jurors actually selected] can be given little weight."[105]

Courts consider the following factors in deciding whether prejudicial news coverage compromised the impartiality of the jury.

1. Prejudicial Nature of the Publicity

Factual news reports containing straightforward, unemotional accounts of unfolding events are less likely to be prejudicial than editorialized indictments. However, even factual accounts can compromise the integrity of the proceedings when they lead to disclosure of incriminating evidence that is later ruled inadmissible.[106] Reports about inadmissible confessions are particularly damaging because people usually remember them. In *Rideau v. Louisiana*,[107] the accused confessed to the details of a brutal rape-murder during a televised interview from jail. The Supreme Court set his conviction aside on the grounds that it was impossible for the accused to receive a fair trial after the entire community had seen him confess on television.

2. Extent of Publicity

The extent of the publicity is also important.[108] Adverse publicity must be pervasive before an accused can complain of being denied a fair trial.

3. Proximity to Time of Trial

The length of time between the damaging disclosures and the trial is a third consideration.[109] Memories tend to fade with time. Consequently, the chances of finding an impartial jury improve as the interval between the damaging disclosures and the trial grows.[110] Jury exposure to contaminating news stories during the trial is the most dangerous, but is also the easiest to prevent.[111] The judge can order the jurors not to read, watch, or listen to any reports, or may even **sequester** them in order to prevent all contact with the outside world while the trial is in progress.

4. Attitudes Revealed on *Voir Dire* Examination

Prospective jurors are subject to ***voir dire*** examination. The attitudes they reveal on *voir dire* are likely to mirror the sentiments of the community. In *Murphy v. Florida*,[112] the Supreme Court observed:

---

[105] *Id.*

[106] Rideau v. Louisiana, *supra* note 103.

[107] *Id.*

[108] See Sheppard v. Maxwell, *supra* note 101.

[109] Patton v. Yount, *supra* note 103.

[110] *Id.*

[111] United States v. Concepcion Cueto, 515 F.2d 160 (1st Cir. 1975); United States v. Bowe, 360 F.2d 1 (2d Cir. 1966), cert. denied, 385 U.S. 961, 87 S. Ct. 401, 17 L. Ed. 2d 306 (1967).

[112] 421 U.S. 794, 95 S. Ct. 2031, 44 L. Ed. 2d 589 (1975).

The length to which the trial judge must go in order to select jurors who appear to be impartial is ... [a] factor relevant in evaluating those jurors' assurances of impartiality. In a community where most veniremen will admit to a disqualifying prejudice, the reliability of the others' protestations may be drawn into question; for it is then more probable that they are part of a community deeply hostile to the accused, and more likely that they may unwittingly have been influenced by it.[113]

B. Methods of Counteracting Media Contamination After It Has Taken Place

Once a community has been exposed to media contamination, there are several precautions a trial judge can take in an attempt to preserve the accused's right to a fair and impartial trial. First, special efforts can be made in the jury selection process to identify and eliminate prospective jurors who hold fixed opinions about the defendant's guilt by asking probing questions on *voir dire*. However, as *Irvin v. Dowd* shows, once a community has been thoroughly saturated, probing *voir dire* examinations may not be enough to prevent the damage from seeping into the jury box. A second alternative is to postpone the trial until the case has lost its notoriety. Although delay has antiseptic value, this method of securing a fair trial has serious drawbacks: repairing damage to one constitutional right is achieved at the cost of injury to another. By the time the case has lost its notoriety, it may no longer be possible to afford the accused a speedy criminal trial. In the trade-off, the accused has been forced to give up his right to a speedy trial in order to obtain an impartial jury, both of which are his constitutional due.

Changing the venue of the trial to a different community may afford an alternative to delay.[114] However, this solution will work only if the publicity has been localized. No community is so remote that a name such as O.J. Simpson is unknown. For cases in which contaminating disclosures have been plastered across the front pages of newspapers all over the country, finding a constitutionally acceptable jury may be next to impossible.

None of the methods for trying to undo damage after it has occurred are entirely satisfactory. Their efficacy is incapable of being measured, and their use is often accompanied by added costs, delays, or the sacrifice of other constitutional rights.

C. Proactive Measures Designed to Avert Media Contamination of Criminal Trials

During the 1970s, criminal trial judges began experimenting with new measures designed to protect an accused's right to a fair trial. The older methods focused on reducing damage after it happened. The newer approaches were bolder — they

---

[113]   *Id*. at 803–804, 95 S. Ct. at 2037. But see Patton v. Yount, *supra* note 103.

[114]   Groppi v. Wisconsin, 400 U.S. 505, 91 S. Ct. 490, 27 L. Ed. 2d 571 (1971). *See also* Sheppard v. Maxwell, *supra* note 101.

attempted to keep inflammatory information out of print. The media's response was to claim the protection of the First Amendment.

1. Restraining Publication: Media Gag Orders

Media "gag orders" were one of the first approaches to be tried. Trial judges in high-profile cases would enter orders directing media representatives to refrain from reporting specified details that posed a threat to the fairness of the proceedings. This approach was reviewed in *Nebraska Press Association v. Stuart*.[115] A few days after the accused was arrested in a small, rural community for murdering six members of the same family, the trial judge issued an order prohibiting representatives of the media from publishing information about the existence and contents of confessions, inculpatory statements, or other "strongly implicative" details. The Supreme Court unanimously ruled that the First Amendment prevents trial judges from restraining publication of news reports about what transpires in open court. Criminal trials are public events and what goes on in the court room is public property. The Justices, nevertheless, split on whether the First Amendment prevents trial judges from restraining publication of damaging information learned from other sources, such as from attorneys or the police. Three took the position that media gag orders are always unconstitutional while the remainder stopped just short of this. However, the gist of this case is that of all the various methods for controlling prejudicial pretrial publicity, ordering media representatives to refrain from publishing lawfully gathered information is the least acceptable.

2. Preventing Media Access to Newsworthy Information: Closure Orders

After *Nebraska Press Association*, criminal trial judges switched to "closure orders." Trial judges would close the proceedings to media representatives and members of the public when testimony and arguments were being presented that the judge did not want reported. The use of closure orders set the stage for a second round of constitutional litigation. The issue was no longer whether criminal trial judges could restrain publication of lawfully gathered information, but whether they could prevent the media from learning the facts in the first place.

Gannett Co. v. DePasquale[116] was the first closure case to reach the U.S. Supreme Court. The trial judge, at the request of both the prosecutor and the accused, closed the court during arguments on a pretrial motion to suppress evidence alleged to have been illegally seized. The Supreme Court upheld the closure order, noting that the purpose of a pretrial suppression hearing is to eliminate inadmissible evidence so that jurors will

---

[115] 427 U.S. 539, 96 S. Ct. 2791, 49 L. Ed. 2d 683 (1976).
[116] 443 U.S. 368, 99 S. Ct. 2898, 61 L. Ed. 2d 608 (1979).

not be made aware of its existence at the trial. This purpose could be defeated if the outcome of a pretrial suppression hearing were carried in the news. The rule that emerges from *Gannett Co. v. DePasquale* and subsequent cases[117] is that trial judges may close specified portions of criminal proceedings if, but only if: (1) there is a substantial probability that publicity from open proceedings will compromise the accused's right to a fair trial and (2) alternatives short of closure would be inadequate to protect this right. An order clearing the courtroom for the entire duration of the trial, for example, would violate the First Amendment because publicity about what happens at the trial discloses nothing the jurors have not already heard.[118] The real threat is that jurors (actual or potential) will read about damaging information that was not introduced at the trial or comments on evidence that was introduced. This danger can be managed, at least in part, by excluding media from pretrial suppression hearings, admonishing the jurors not to read news articles or to listen to radio or television reports about the case and, if necessary, by sequestering them during the trial.

3. Controlling the Release of Information to the Media

Although media gag orders violate the First Amendment, there is nothing wrong with ordering prosecutors, defense attorneys, prospective witnesses, and police officers to refrain from discussing specific aspects of a case with the media.[119] The American Bar Association (ABA) has promulgated a set of guidelines governing pretrial release of information by lawyers, prosecutors, judges, and law enforcement officers.[120] Disclosure of the following matters carries a "substantial likelihood of prejudicing criminal proceedings" and, therefore, should be avoided:

1. a suspect's prior criminal record;
2. a suspect's character or reputation;
3. opinions about the suspect's guilt, the merits of the case, or the strength of the government's evidence;
4. the existence or contents of confessions or inculpatory statements, or a suspect's refusal to make a statement;
5. the outcome of examinations or laboratory tests or the suspect's refusal to cooperate;
6. the identity, expected testimony, criminal records, or credibility of prospective witnesses;
7. the possibility of a plea bargain, guilty plea, or other disposition; and
8. any other information that the officer knows or has reason to know would be inadmissible as evidence in a trial.

---

[117] Press-Enterprise Co. (II) v. Superior Court, 478 U.S. 1, 106 S. Ct. 2735, 92 L. Ed. 2d 1 (1986).

[118] 448 U.S. 555, 100 S. Ct. 2814, 65 L. Ed. 2d 973 (1980).

[119] Sheppard v. Maxwell, *supra* note 101.

[120] **ABA STANDARDS FOR CRIMINAL JUSTICE, FAIR TRIAL AND FREE PRESS §§ 8-1.1, 8-2.1 (1992).** The ABA Standards are reproduced in Part II.

The following matters, on the other hand, are considered appropriate subjects for public comment:

1.   the accused's name, age, residence, occupation, and family status;
2.   the identity of the victim (if release of this information is not otherwise prohibited by law);
3.   information necessary to aid in a suspect's apprehension or to warn the public of dangers;
4.   requests for assistance from the public in obtaining evidence;
5.   general information about the investigation, including its length and scope, and the identity of the investigating officers;
6.   the facts and circumstances surrounding the arrest, including its time and place, and the identity of the arresting officer;
7.   the general nature of the charges against the defendant, with an accompanying explanation that the charges are merely accusations and that the defendant is presumed innocent until proven guilty;
8.   the scheduling or results of any judicial proceeding; and
9.   any information contained in a public record.

The ABA guidelines also address the propriety of granting media representatives access to persons in police custody. While police are not required to take special precautions to shield persons in custody from news cameras, they should not pose them for picture-taking sessions or make them available for press conferences unless they consent after being informed of their right to refuse.

The ABA standards are binding on lawyers, who can be disciplined for violating them.[121] The standards can become effective against police officers through a different route, by encouraging police professional organizations and departments to adopt them in codes of professional responsibility and departmental regulations. Law enforcement agencies would do well to study the ABA standards. Because the First Amendment limits the power of judges to halt publication of damaging information once it finds its way into the hands of the media, prosecutors, attorneys, and law enforcement agencies must be careful about releasing information. There is no First Amendment duty to grant media representatives access to crime information that is not available to the general public.[122] If law enforcement agencies restrict press releases along the lines contained in the ABA standards, this will go a long way toward protecting the right of the accused to a fair trial.

---

[121]   Gentile v. State Bar of Nevada, 501 U.S. 1030, 111 S. Ct. 2720, 115 L. Ed. 2d 888 (1991).
[122]   The Florida Star v. BJF, 491 U.S. 524, 109 S. Ct. 2603, 105 L. Ed. 2d 445 (1989); Houchins v. KQED, Inc., 438 U.S. 1, 98 S. Ct. 2588, 57 L. Ed. 2d 553 (1979).

§ 9.11 — Trial by Jury

Trial by jury is an ancient and venerable institution. In 1215, the Magna Charta proclaimed that no free man could be condemned to death or sent to prison except by the legal judgment of his peers.[123] While the Magna Charta laid the foundation for the jury, there is little evidence of the existence of a jury concept even remotely resembling the modern jury until the fourteenth century.[124] For a while, the jury method of determining guilt existed in competition with several older, barbaric methods, such as "trial by ordeal" and "trial by battle."[125] Gradually, the older methods fell into disuse and the jury method emerged as the sole procedure. By the time the United States was settled, the institution of trial before a panel of 12 laymen, known as a **petit jury**, had a tradition dating back several centuries.

Figure 9.3
Constitutional Right to Trial by Jury

Constitutional Entitlement	Required Number of jurors	Selection Process	Need for Unanimity
Only for offenses carrying a penalty of six months or more in jail.	Twelve in federal courts; no fewer than six in state courts.	Jury venires must be drawn from a source that is fairly representative of the community. Peremptory strikes may not be used to exclude potential jurors solely because of their race or gender.	Required in federal trials, but not in state trials unless the jury is comprised of only six persons.

William Blackstone, writing in 1768, hailed the jury principle as the "glory of English law" and "the most transcendent privilege which any subject can enjoy or wish for."[126] While Blackstone's praise seems lavish by modern standards, his words reflect eighteenth-century sentiments. Those who drafted our Constitution held the jury principle in such high esteem that they took double precautions to ensure its preservation. In Article III, section 2 of the original Constitution, they declared that "[t]he Trial of all

[123] MAGNA CHARTA, ch. 39, reprinted in R. PERRY AND J. COOPER, SOURCES OF OUR LIBERTIES 17 (1959).
[124] 1 F. POLLOCK & R. MAITLAND, THE HISTORY OF ENGLISH LAW BEFORE THE TIME OF EDWARD I, 173 n. 3 (2d ed. 1909); 2 J. STORY, COMMENTARIES ON THE CONSTITUTION OF UNITED STATES, 540–541 (4th ed. 1873); Frankfurter and Corcoran, *Petty Federal Offenses and the Constitutional Guaranty of Trial by Jury*, 39 HARV. L. REV. 917, 923 (1926).
[125] Wells, *The Origin of the Petty Jury*, 27 L.Q. REV. 347, 357 (1911); *see also* CORNISH, THE JURY 10–12 (1968).
[126] 3 W. BLACKSTONE COMMENTARIES 379.

Crimes, except in Cases of Impeachment, shall be by Jury ...." When the Bill of Rights was added two years later, they repeated in the Sixth Amendment that "[i]n all criminal prosecutions, the accused shall enjoy the right to ... trial, by an impartial jury ...."

The jury system offers at least three advantages over other methods of determining guilt. First, it gives citizens an opportunity to participate and, through shared participation, to evaluate the workings of the criminal justice system. Second, it imparts humanizing qualities and the community's sense of justice into the guilt-determining process. Finally, it enhances public confidence in criminal verdicts. In *Duncan v. Louisiana*,[127] the Supreme Court observed:

> A right to jury trial is granted to criminal defendants in order to prevent oppression by the Government. Those who wrote our constitutions knew from history and experience that it was necessary to protect against unfounded criminal charges brought to eliminate enemies and against judges too responsive to the voice of higher authority. The framers of the constitution strove to create an independent judiciary but insisted upon further protection against arbitrary action. Providing an accused with the right to be tried by a jury of his peers gave him an inestimable safeguard against the corrupt or overzealous prosecutor and against the complacent, biased, or eccentric judge. If the defendant preferred the common-sense judgment of a jury to the more tutored but perhaps less sympathetic reaction of the single judge, he was to have it ....[128]

The Sixth Amendment right to trial by jury is deemed a fundamental right that constitutes an integral part of due process of law. Accordingly, states are required to provide jury trials in all cases in which this right is available in federal court.[129]

A. Proceedings in Which a Jury Trial Is Available

The English common law recognized limited instances in which defendants did not enjoy the right to trial by jury. Defendants, for example, were not entitled to a jury trial in criminal prosecutions brought for "petty offenses."[130] Although the Sixth Amendment uses sweeping language, proclaiming that the accused shall enjoy the right to trial by jury in "all criminal prosecutions," the Supreme Court has consistently interpreted this language as perpetuating the historic distinction between petty and serious offenses.[131] The only dispute has been about where to draw the line.

---

[127]   391 U.S. 145, 88 S. Ct. 1444, 20 L. Ed. 2d 491 (1968).

[128]   *Id.* at 155–156, 88 S. Ct. at 1451 (footnote omitted).

[129]   *Id.*

[130]   *Frankfurter & Corcoran, Petty Federal Offenses and the Constitutional Guaranty of Trial by Jury*, 39 HARV. L. REV. 917, 934 (1926).

[131]   Baldwin v. New York, 399 U.S. 66, 90 S. Ct. 1886, 26 L. Ed. 2d 437 (1970); Frank v. United States, 395 U.S. 147, 89 S. Ct. 1503, 23 L. Ed. 2d 162 (1969); Cheff v. Schnackenberg, 384 U.S. 373, 86 S. Ct. 1523, 16 L. Ed. 2d 629 (1966) (plurality opinion); District of Columbia v. Clawans, 300 U.S. 617, 57 S. Ct. 660, 81 L. Ed. 843 (1937); Callan v. Wilson, 127 U.S. 540, 8 S. Ct. 1301, 32 L. Ed. 223 (1888).

The Supreme Court early on rejected the felony-misdemeanor distinction because some misdemeanors carry substantial penalties, as well as significant stigma.[132] This matter was finally settled in *Baldwin v. New York*,[133] where the Supreme Court ruled that the punishment authorized by the legislature is the best indicator of the seriousness of an offense. The Court drew the line at six months in prison. Where the maximum punishment authorized by the legislature does not exceed six months in prison, the advantages of speedy, inexpensive nonjury trials outweigh the hardship to the defendant of being tried by a judge. The offense is, therefore, petty and there is no constitutional right to a jury trial.[134] The Supreme Court has expanded the right to be tried by jury to criminal contempt charges, even though no such right was recognized under the common law.[135] Six months is the maximum sentence a judge may impose for criminal contempt without empaneling a jury.[136]

There are several other proceedings in which there is no right to trial by jury. They include: (1) proceedings before a military tribunal,[137] (2) juvenile court proceedings,[138] and (3) sentencing proceedings.[139] However, defendants facing capital punishment are entitled to have a jury determine the existence or nonexistence of aggravating circumstances before the death penalty may be imposed.[140]

Legislatures may not authorize juries to impose the death penalty, while making life imprisonment the maximum sentence that can be imposed by a judge.[141] The

---

[132]   Callan v. Wilson, *supra* note 131.

[133]   *Supra* note 131.

[134]   Baldwin v. New York, *supra* note 131; Blanton v. City of North Las Vegas, 489 U.S. 538, 109 S. Ct. 1289, 103 L. Ed. 2d 550 (1989) (driving under the influence (DUI) for first-time offenders was a petty offense where the maximum punishment was six months' imprisonment, even though conviction also carried a mandatory fine of between $200 and $1,000, automatic loss of driver's license for 90 days, and compulsory attendance in alcohol abuse education course); Lewis v. United States, 518 U.S. 322, 116 S. Ct. 2163, 135 L. Ed. 2d 590 (1996) (offense carrying maximum authorized prison term of six months was a petty offense for which defendant was not entitled to jury trial, even though he was charged with multiple counts in single proceeding so that aggregate maximum prison term exceeded six months).

[135]   Bloom v. Illinois, 391 U.S. 194, 88 S. Ct. 1477, 20 L. Ed. 2d 522 (1968).

[136]   Taylor v. Hayes, 418 U.S. 488, 94 S. Ct. 2697, 41 L. Ed. 2d 897 (1974) (contempt of court is a petty offense that may be tried without jury when the sentence actually imposed does not exceed six months); Frank v. United States, *supra* note 131.

[137]   *Ex parte Milligan*, 71 U.S. (4 Wall.) 2, 122, 18 L. Ed. 281, 296 (1886). *See also* Dennis, *Jury Trial and the Federal Constitution*, 6 Colum L. Rev. 423 (1906).

[138]   McKeiver v. Pennsylvania, 403 U.S. 528, 91 S. Ct. 1976, 29 L. Ed. 2d 647 (1971).

[139]   Libretti v. United States, 516 U.S. 29, 116 S. Ct. 356, 133 L. Ed. 2d 271 (1995). *But see* United States v. Booker, 543 U.S. 220, 125 S. Ct. 738. 160 L. Ed. 2d 621 (2005) (holding that defendants are entitled to have any factor that will enhance a prison sentence other than a prior conviction tried by a jury); Blakely v. Washington, 542 U.S. 296, 124 S. Ct. 2531, 159 L. Ed. 2d 403 (2004) (same).

[140]   Ring v. Arizona, 1536 U.S. 584, 22 S. Ct. 2428, 153 L. Ed. 2d 556 (2002).

[141]   United States v. Jackson, 390 U.S. 570, 88 S. Ct. 1209, 20 L. Ed. 2d 138 (1968). *But see* Corbitt v. New Jersey, 439 U.S. 212, 99 S. Ct. 492, 58 L. Ed. 2d 466 (1980).

natural tendency of such a provision would be to discourage defendants from asserting their constitutional right to be tried by a jury.

B. *Required Number of Jurors*

The common law trial jury (**petit jury**) consisted of a body of 12 individuals selected at random from the community, whose function was to hear evidence presented in open court and to render a unanimous verdict.[142] This pattern continues to exist today in the federal courts and in most states.

However, at least five states — Florida, Louisiana, South Carolina, Texas, and Utah — provide for less than 12-member juries in the trial of felony cases and at least eight states provide for them in the trial of misdemeanor cases.[143] Once the U.S. Supreme Court decided in *Duncan v. Louisiana*[144] that the Sixth Amendment right to trial by jury was binding on the states, it was forced to determine whether the Constitution requires 12-person juries in state criminal prosecutions, the same as in federal courts. This question came before the Court in *Williams v. Florida*,[145] in which a felony conviction was returned by a six-person jury. The Court determined that the number "12" was not an immutable corollary of the Sixth Amendment right to a jury trial. Justice White, who wrote the majority opinion, stated that the relevant inquiry was not whether a particular feature was buttressed by centuries of tradition, but whether it was critical to the jury's constitutional role. Having cast the inquiry in this form, Justice White concluded:

> [T]he essential feature of a jury obviously lies in the interposition between the accused and his accuser of the commonsense judgment of a group of laymen, and in the community participation and shared responsibility that results [sic] from that group's determination of guilt or innocence. The performance of this role is not a function of the particular number of the body that makes up the jury. To be sure, the number should probably be large enough to promote group deliberation, free from outside attempts at intimidation, and to provide a fair possibility for obtaining a representative cross-section of the community. But we find little reason to think that these goals are in any meaningful sense less likely to be achieved when the jury numbers six, than when it numbers 12.... And, certainly the reliability of the jury as a factfinder hardly seems likely to be a function of its size.[146]

A six-person jury is the smallest constitutionally acceptable size. In *Ballew v. Georgia*,[147] the Supreme Court ruled that a state criminal defendant was deprived of his Sixth and Fourteenth Amendment rights when he was tried before a five-person jury for a nonpetty offense. A five-person panel, the Court stated, is too small to achieve the

---

[142]   1 W. Holdsworth, A. History of English Law 325 (1927).

[143]   Williams v. Florida, 399 U.S. 78, 99 n. 45, 90 S. Ct. 1893, 1905, n. 45, 26 L. Ed. 2d 446, 459, n. 45 (1970).

[144]   391 U.S. 145, 88 S. Ct. 1444, 20 L. Ed. 2d 491 (1968).

[145]   *Supra* note 143.

[146]   *Id.*

[147]   435 U.S. 223, 98 S. Ct. 1029, 55 L. Ed. 2d 234 (1978).

broad-based representation and diverse points of view that the constitutional right to a jury trial is designed to ensure.

C. *Requirement of Unanimity*

Under the common law, jury verdicts had to be unanimous. If the jurors could not agree, a mistrial would be declared leaving the accused subject to retrial. This requirement was firmly entrenched in Anglo-American jurisprudence when the Constitution was drafted and continues to be the prevailing practice today. However, a few states have abandoned it.[148] In Louisiana and Oregon, for example, verdicts can be returned in non-capital felony cases by a vote of 10 out of 12 jurors,[149] but unanimity continues to be required in capital cases.[150] Several other jurisdictions have eliminated the requirement of unanimity for misdemeanor trials.

The Oregon statute allowing 10 out of 12 jurors to return a verdict was upheld in *Apodaca v. Oregon*.[151] The Court ruled that the Sixth Amendment requires unanimous verdicts in federal criminal proceedings, but not in state trials. In *Burch v. Louisiana*,[152] the Supreme Court was asked to decide whether states could combine less-than-unanimous verdicts with a substantial reduction in the jury's size. The statute under review allowed a verdict to be returned in nonpetty misdemeanor trials by a vote of five out of six jurors. This time Supreme Court balked, holding that when a state cuts the jury's size in half, the Sixth Amendment requires that the verdict must be unanimous.

D. *Demographic Composition of the Jury*

The right to a jury trial means the right to be tried before a jury that is drawn from a representative cross-section of the community. There are two theories for challenging an unrepresentative jury.

1. Jury Pools and Venires

The first theory derives from the Sixth Amendment guarantee of an impartial jury. The Supreme Court has interpreted an impartial jury to mean one that is drawn from a fair cross-section of the community.[153] Juries representing a fair cross-section of the community are more likely to reflect the values of the community, act impartially, and engender confidence in the judicial system.[154] This does not mean that trial juries must contain proportional representation of the various demographic groups in the community. Defendants are not entitled to a jury of any particular composition. The fair cross-section requirement guarantees criminal defendants the *opportunity* for a

---

[148]   Comment, *Should Jury Verdicts Be Unanimous in Criminal Cases?* 47 OR. L. REV. 417 (1968).

[149]   LA. CODE CRIM. PROC. ANN. art. 782; OR. REV. STAT. ANN. § 136.450.

[150]   *Id.*

[151]   406 U.S. 404, 92 S. Ct. 1628, 32 L. Ed. 2d 184 (1972).

[152]   441 U.S. 130, 99 S. Ct. 1623, 60 L. Ed. 2d 96 (1979).

[153]   Taylor v. Louisiana, 419 U.S. 522, 95 S. Ct. 692, 42 L. Ed. 2d 690 (1975).

[154]   Peters v. Kiff, 407 U.S. 493, 92 S. Ct. 2163, 33 L. Ed. 2d 83 (1972).

representative jury by prohibiting systematic exclusion of distinctive groups within the community from the **jury pools** and **venires** that provide the source from which juries are selected to sit in a particular trial are drawn.[155] To establish a fair cross-section claim, the defendant must prove that members of a distinctive group were not fairly represented in the jury venire from which his trial jury was drawn, and that systematic exclusion in the jury-selection process was responsible for the underrepresentation.[156]

2. Prosecution's Use of Peremptory Challenges

The second theory for challenging the demographic characteristics of the trial jury is the Fourteenth Amendment equal protection clause.[157] This theory focuses on the prosecution's exercise of **peremptory challenges**.[158] Both sides in a criminal case are allowed to strike a certain number of potential jurors without cause (*i.e.*, without having to show that the potential juror is biased). These are called peremptory challenges. Although the prosecutor does not have to give any particular reason for exercising a peremptory challenge, they may not be used to exclude potential jurors solely because of their race or gender.[159]

E. *Waiver of the Right to Jury Trial*

Under the common law of England, trial by jury was required for all serious offenses. The defendant could not waive a jury and be tried by a judge.[160] Although "consent" was technically required, the defendant could be tortured into

---

[155]   Taylor v. Louisiana, *supra* note 153. The criteria for being considered a "distinctive group" is articulated in United States v. Raszkiewicz, 169 F.3d 459 (7th Cir. 1999). There must be: (1) qualities that define a group; (2) a similarity of attitudes, beliefs, or experiences; and (3) a community of interest among the members. African-Americans (Peters v. Kiff, *supra* note 154), Mexican-Americans (Castaneda v. Partida, 430 U. S. 482, 97 S. Ct. 1272, 51 L. Ed. 2d 498 (1977)), women (Taylor v. Louisiana, *supra* note 153), and Jews (United States v. Gelb, 881 F.2d 1155 (2d Cir. 1989) have been found to constitute distinctive groups, but blue-collar workers (Anaya v. Hansen, 781 F.2d 1 (1st Cir. 1986)), college students (United States v. Fletcher, 965 F.2d 781 (9th Cir. 1992)), and persons under or over a particular age (Brewer v. Nix, 963 F.2d 1111 (8th Cir. 1992) have not.

[156]   Berghuis v. Smith, __ U.S. __, 130 S. Ct. 1382, 176 L. Ed. 2d 249 (2010)

[157]   Criminal defendants may object to the prosecutor's misuse of peremptory challenges to exclude prospective jurors solely because of their race (Batson v. Kentucky, 476 U.S. 79, 106 S. Ct. 1712, 90 L. Ed. 2d 69 (1986)), gender (J.E.B. v. Alabama, 511 U.S. 127, 114 S. Ct. 1419, 128 L. Ed. 2d 89 (1994)), or ethnicity (Hernandez v. New York, 500 U.S. 352, 111 S. Ct. 1859, 114 L. Ed. 2d 395 (1991)), even though they do not share the demographic traits as the excluded groups. *See, e.g.,* Powers v. Ohio, 499 U.S. 400, 111 S. Ct. 1364, 113 L. Ed. 2d 411 (1991) (holding that defendants do not have to have the same demographic characteristics as the improperly struck jurors to raise an equal protection challenge).

[158]   *See* cases *supra* note 157.

[159]   Miller-El v. Dretke, 545 U.S. 231, 125 S. Ct. 2317, 162 L. Ed. 2d 196 (2005); Snyder v. Louisiana, 552 U.S. 472, 128 S. Ct 1203, 170 L. Ed. 2d 175 (2008).

[160]   Singer v. United States, 380 U.S. 24, 85 S. Ct. 783, 13 L. Ed. 2d 630, 633–634 (1965) (defendant's only constitutional right concerning method of trial is to an impartial trial by jury).

submission.[161] Even after torture ceased, the accused had no choice as to the mode of trial. Jury trials were the only type available.

In modern times, all jurisdictions offer bench trials as an alternative to jury trials. Still, the ability to waive a jury trial is often restricted. The right to waive a jury trial and be tried by a judge is often conditioned upon the approval of the court, the prosecutor, or both. Conditioning the right to waive a jury trial upon approval of the prosecutor or court does not violate the Sixth Amendment because the only constitutional right a defendant has concerning the mode of trial is the right to be tried by a jury.[162]

§ 9.12   —Preservation and Disclosure of Evidence Favorable to the Defense

The prosecutor occupies a unique position in our adversarial system of criminal justice. Several decades ago, the Supreme Court observed:

> The United States Attorney is the representative not of an ordinary party to a controversy, but of a sovereignty whose obligation to govern impartially is as compelling as its obligation to govern at all; and whose interest, therefore, in a criminal prosecution is not that it shall win a case, but that justice shall be done. As such, he is, in a peculiar and very definite sense the servant of the law, the twofold aim of which is that guilt shall not escape or innocence suffer. He may prosecute with earnestness and vigor — indeed, he should do so. But, while he may strike hard blows, he is not at liberty to strike foul ones. It is as much his duty to refrain from improper methods calculated to produce a wrongful conviction as it is to use every legitimate means to bring about a just one.[163]

This observation marked the beginning of a line of cases that eventually developed into two constitutional duties imposed on the prosecution and, indirectly, the police. The first duty is to disclose to the accused any evidence within the government's possession or knowledge that is favorable to the accused and material to guilt or punishment. The second duty is to preserve evidence that might be expected to play a significant role in the defense. Both obligations are grounded on the fundamental fairness implicit in due process, rather than on specific language found in the Constitution.

A. The Requirements for Disclosure of Exculpatory Information

The prosecution's constitutional duty to disclose exculpatory evidence to the accused evolved from cases in which the prosecutor had either knowingly used false testimony[164] or allowed false testimony to go uncorrected.[165] When this happened, the Supreme Court

[161] *Id.*
[162] Note, *Constitutional Law: Criminal Procedure: Waiver of Jury Trial: Singer v. United States*, 308 U.S. 24 (1965), 51 Cornell L. Rev. 339, 342–343 (1966).
[163] Berger v. United States, 295 U.S. 78, 88, 55 S. Ct. 629, 633, 79 L. Ed. 1314, 1321 (1935).
[164] Mooney v. Holohan, 294 U.S. 103, 55 S. Ct. 340, 79 L. Ed. 791 (1935).
[165] Alcorta v. Texas, 355 U.S. 28, 78 S. Ct. 103, 2 L. Ed. 2d 9 (1957).

Figure 9.4
Comparison of Police Obligations to Preserve and Disclose Exculpatory Evidence

Duty to Preserve	Duty to Disclose
Police have a duty to preserve physical evidence that: 1. has an exculpatory value that is apparent to them and 2. is of a type that the defense cannot obtain by other means.	Police have a duty to make sure that the prosecutor is aware of all evidence known to the police or anyone under their control that may help to: 1. show that the defendant is innocent; 2. counter the prosecution's version of the events; or 3. challenge the credibility of key prosecution witnesses.

Brady v.s. maryland

had little trouble concluding that use of perjured testimony denied the defendant due process. However, in *Brady v. Maryland*,[166] the Supreme Court took a broad leap and transformed what had begun as a narrow doctrine concerned with the use of perjured testimony into a broad obligation to disclose all evidence within the government's possession or control, favorable to the accused, that is material to guilt or punishment.

In *Brady*, the prosecutor failed to disclose that one of Brady's accomplices had confessed to the killing for which Brady was charged, even though his attorney made a formal request for any such statements. Brady was sentenced to death, but the Supreme Court reversed, announcing what has become known as the *Brady* rule:

> [T]he suppression by the prosecution of evidence favorable to an accused upon request violates due process where the evidence is material either to guilt or to punishment, irrespective of the good faith or bad faith of the prosecution. The principle . . . is not punishment of society for misdeeds of a prosecutor but avoidance of an unfair trial to the accused. . . . A prosecution that withholds evidence on demand of an accused which, if made available, would tend to exculpate him or reduce the penalty helps shape . . . a proceeding that does not comport with standards of justice, even though, as in the present case, his action is not "the result of guile . . ."[167]

The duty established in *Brady* does not depend upon proof that the prosecutor acted in bad faith. The rule is premised on recognition that whenever the government withholds evidence that could change the outcome of a case, the integrity of the verdict is compromised. Failure to comply with *Brady* created a near crisis in the Timothy McVeigh prosecution. McVeigh was convicted of bombing the Oklahoma City federal building and killing 168 people. Shortly before his scheduled execution, the FBI discovered 3,135 pages of documents that McVeigh's lawyers had never seen. The execution was postponed so that a judge could review the material to determine whether it

---

[166] 373 U.S. 83, 83 S. Ct. 1194, 10 L. Ed. 2d 215 (1963).
[167] *Id.* at 87–88, 83 S. Ct. 1196–1197.

contained anything that might have changed the outcome. Nothing was found and the execution was rescheduled.[168] Had the evidence against McVeigh been less clear, the FBI's blunder could have cost the government a conviction that took millions of dollars and years to obtain, and left the families of the victims without closure.

1. Types of Evidence That Must Be Disclosed

The constitutional duty to disclose extends to evidence that is favorable to the accused and material either to guilt or to punishment. It is impossible to formulate a comprehensive list of evidence that must always be disclosed because this list varies with the nature of the crime, the background (including criminal histories) of government witnesses, the prosecution's theory of the case, and other factors. Favorable evidence includes evidence that may help establish the defendant's innocence, counter the prosecution's version of the events, or impeach the credibility of key prosecution witnesses.[169] Certainly, a defendant is entitled to know whether someone else has confessed to the crime, whether a key prosecution witness has a criminal record or received

---

[168]   Neil A. Lewis & David Johnston, *Cleanup That Made a Mess: Putting Together Story on McVeigh Files, Government, So Far, Finds No Culprit*, SEATTLE TIMES at A3 (May 13, 2001); Editorial, *The Final Verdict. McVeigh's Fate Weighed Reasonably. Is the Story Finished?* AKRON BEACON JOURNAL, at A14, June 10, 2001. McVeigh was executed June 11, 2001, almost one month after his first execution was scheduled. McVeigh's execution was the first federal execution in 38 years.

[169]   Stickler v. Green, 527 U.S. 263, 119 S. Ct. 1936, 144 L. Ed. 2d 286 (1999) ("[T]he duty to disclose . . . is applicable even though there has been no request by the accused and . . . encompasses impeachment evidence as well as exculpatory evidence. Such evidence is material 'if there is a reasonable probability that, had the evidence been disclosed to the defense, the result of the proceeding would have been different.' Moreover, the rule encompasses evidence 'known only to police investigators and not to the prosecutor.' In order to comply with *Brady*, therefore, 'the individual prosecutor has a duty to learn of any favorable evidence known to the others acting on the government's behalf in this case, including the police.'"); Youngblood v. West Virginia, 547 U.S. 867, 126 S. Ct. 2188, 165 L. Ed. 2d 269 (2006) (reversing conviction where police failed to advise prosecutor of existence of a note written by putative rape victim indicating that the sex had been consensual; this evidence was material because it contradicted the prosecuting witness's testimony and was consistent with the theory of the defense). *See also, generally.* R. Michael Cassidy, *Toward a More Independent Grand Jury: Recasting and Enforcing the Prosecutor's Duty to Disclose Exculpatory Evidence*, 13 GEO. J. LEGAL ETHICS 361, fn 33 (2000) ("Stated simply, the prosecution must disclose to the defense prior to trial any 'information known to or available to them which may develop doubt about the government's narrative.' The *Brady* line of cases has established a broad definition of constitutionally exculpatory evidence, including evidence that would impeach a government witness (such as prior inconsistent statements or inconsistent identification), evidence that would show bias on the part of a government witness (such as promises, rewards, or inducements), evidence that would cast doubt on any essential element of the crime charged, or evidence that would suggest that someone other than the defendant committed the crime. Exculpatory evidence includes not only documents or testimony admissible in evidence, but also inadmissible materials that, if defense counsel had access to them, might lead to admissible evidence.").

a promise of leniency,[170] or whether there are documented errors on police crime laboratory reports[171] or negative results that indicate that the accused may not be guilty.[172]
In *Barbee v. Warden*,[173] the prosecutor introduced the defendant's revolver into evidence without informing the defense that the police had run ballistics and fingerprint
tests on the revolver and had learned that it was not the weapon used in the crime. The
prosecutor failed to inform the defense because the prosecutor was unaware of the test
results. The Fourth Circuit reversed the defendant's conviction, holding that the prosecutor was responsible for disclosing this information to the defense because it was in
the hands of the police.

2. Scope of the Disclosure Obligation

The Supreme Court has consistently broadened the scope of the prosecutor's disclosure obligations. Today, it is settled law that the prosecutor is responsible for disclosing all evidence known to anyone assisting the prosecutor, including the police,[174]
when the evidence is both favorable to the defense and material to guilt or punishment,
regardless of whether the defense has specifically requested disclosure.[175]

Normally, the prosecutor will contact police to learn whether any exculpatory
information is known to the department. However, when the police know of information favorable to the defense, they should advise the prosecutor of its existence without
waiting to be asked. Sometimes a harried prosecutor may neglect to ask for the police
file. Police can botch a prosecution by not taking the initiative to ensure that the
prosecutor is aware of *Brady* material.

In *Kyles v. Whitley*,[176] the prosecution at a murder trial argued that the killer drove
to the lot where the murder occurred, killed the victim, and drove off in the victim's car,
leaving his own behind. The prosecutor showed the jury a blurry photo of the cars in the
parking lot, which the prosecutor claimed substantiated this fact. However, he failed to
disclose that the police had recorded the license plate numbers of all the cars in the

---

[170] Giglio v. United States, 405 U.S. 150, 92 S. Ct. 763, 31 L. Ed. 2d 104 (1972) (due process violated by
       failure to disclose promise of leniency given to key prosecution witness in exchange for testimony);
       United States v. Bagley, 473 U.S. 667, 105 S. Ct. 3375, 87 L. Ed. 2d 481 (1975); **People v. Wright,
       86 N.Y.2d 591, 658 N.E.2d 1009, 635 N.Y.S.2d 136 (1995)**.
[171] United States v. Sebring, 44 M.J. 805 (1996).
[172] **Kyles v. Whitley, 514 U.S. 419, 115 S. Ct. 1555, 131 L. Ed. 2d 490 (1995)**.
[173] 331 F.2d 842 (4th Cir. 1964).
[174] *Id.*; *see also* Giglio v. United States, *supra* note 170.
[175] **Kyles v. Whitley**, *supra* note 172. Reversal is required only when a reasonable possibility exists that
       the outcome of the trial might have been different had the evidence been disclosed. *See, e.g.*, Smith v.
       Cain, ___ S.Ct. ___, 2012 WL 43512 (U.S., 2012) (Reversing conviction on *Brady* grounds where pros-
       ecutor failed to disclose to defense that prosecution witness whose testimony at the trial was only
       evidence linking the defendant to the crime, had told the police on the night of murder that he "could
       not ID anyone because [he] couldn't see faces" and "would not know them if [he] saw them.").
[176] *Supra* note 172 ("The prosecution has the duty to learn of any evidence known to others acting on the
       government's behalf, including police, and to disclose this information to the defense. Failure to dis-
       close is not excused because the prosecutor was unaware of the information.").

parking lot when they took the photo, and that the defendant's car was not among them. The reason the prosecutor failed to disclose this information was that the police did not tell him. The government's argument that prosecutors are not accountable for information known to the police, but not to them, fell on deaf ears. The Court held that prosecutors have a duty to find out whether the police have uncovered *Brady* material. Knowledge of information in the hands of the police will be imputed to the prosecutor for the sake of determining whether the government has discharged its *Brady* responsibilities. A contrary rule, the Court stated, would "substitute the police for the prosecutor, and even for the courts themselves, as the final arbiters of the government's obligation to ensure fair trials."[177]

B. *Police Responsibility to Preserve Evidence*

Police are also under a second, closely related duty — the duty to *preserve evidence*. This duty was first recognized in *California v. Trombetta*.[178] The prosecutor was unable to produce a breath sample taken from the defendant at the time of his DUI arrest because police destroyed it after receiving a positive result on an Intoxilyzer test. The Supreme Court held that destruction of evidence by the police constitutes a denial of due process only if the evidence (1) has an exculpatory value that is apparent to police at the time it is destroyed and (2) is of such a nature that it cannot be replaced by other reasonable available means. Neither requirement was met here. The breath sample had no apparent exculpatory value because it had tested positive for intoxication. Since Intoxilyzer tests are highly accurate, the possibility that a second test would produce a negative result was slim. The defendant, moreover, could challenge the test result without the sample by hiring an expert to testify about the margin of error on Intoxilyzer tests.

---

[177]   *Id*. at 514 U.S. at 438, 115 S. Ct. at 1568, 131 L. Ed. 2d at 509. However, federal prosecutors are not accountable under *Brady* for information possessed by state officials and vice versa. *See, e.g.*, United States v. Beers, 189 F.3d 1297 (10th Cir. 1999) (holding that a state's knowledge and possession of potential impeachment evidence cannot be imputed to a federal prosecutor for purposes of establishing a *Brady* violation). The same is true for information possessed by private third parties. *See, e.g.*, United States v. Levitt, 198 F.3d 259 (10th Cir. 1999) (prosecutor not guilty of *Brady* violation in failing to disclose personal medical records of key government witness where the records were not in the government's possession and the prosecutor had no knowledge of them). Even for information in the government's possession, the prosecutor is not accountable if the person who knows of the information is employed in a different office that does not regularly work with the prosecutor's office. Imputing knowledge of all information within the government's possession, regardless of who knows it, would impose an impossible burden on prosecutors. *See, e.g.*, United States v. Avellino, 136 F.3d 249 (2d Cir.1998).

[178]   467 U.S. 479, 104 S. Ct. 2528, 81 L. Ed. 2d 413 (1984).

The *Trombetta* decision was clarified four years later in *Arizona v. Youngblood*.[179] Police failed to refrigerate a semen sample taken from a child sexual molestation victim. Tests run on the semen sample were inconclusive because it had been left unrefrigerated too long. The defendant argued that he had been mistakenly identified, that had the semen sample been preseved he could have established this, and that the police mishandling of the semen sample denied him due process. The Court began by noting that "[w]henever potentially exculpatory evidence is permanently lost, courts face the treacherous task of divining the import of materials whose contents are unknown and, very often, disputed." This was not a case where the evidence had an exculpatory value that was unmistakable to the police at the time it was destroyed. It was a case where the most that could be said about the evidence was that it *might have been useful to the defense*. To keep the obligation of police to preserve evidence within constitutional bounds, the defendant must prove that police destroyed the evidence in bad faith to make out a violation of due process. Here, the semen sample was destroyed before the investigation had focused on a particular suspect and at a time when the police had no way of knowing whether it would inculpate or exculpate the person they eventually charged. Consequently, the most that could be said was that the police were negligent in their handling of the semen sample. Defendants have no constitution remedy for the negligent failure of police to preserve evidence that might have been useful to them

As things turned out, Youngblood was in fact innocent. He released from prison 15 years later when DNA testing, not available at the time of his trial, established that he did not commit the crime for which he had been convicted.[180] The careless handling of the semen sample by the police caused a miscarriage of justice, even though it did not deprive Youngblood of due process.

---

[179]   **488 U.S. 51, 109 S. Ct. 333, 102 L. Ed. 2d 281 (1988)** ("Unless a criminal defendant can show bad faith on the part of the police, failure to preserve potentially useful evidence does not constitute a denial of due process of law"). The holding in *Arizona v. Youngblood* was reaffirmed in *Illinois v. Fisher*, 540 U.S. 544, 124 S. Ct. 1200, 157 L. Ed.2d 1060 (2004) (holding that a showing of bad faith is necessary where the most that can be said about destroyed evidence is that it might have been useful to the defense).

[180]   *DNA Evidence Frees Tucson Man Convicted in Sex Case 15 Years Ago*, COURIER JOURNAL1 at A10 (Aug. 11, 2000).

§ 9.13   Eighth Amendment Requirements for Punishment

The Eighth Amendment, which applies to the states through the Fourteenth Amendment, prohibits excessive fines and "cruel and unusual punishments." Humane punishment has not always been practiced. There was a time in England when a person convicted of a crime could be burned at the stake, boiled in oil, or have his or her hands or ears cut off. Blackstone, in his Commentaries on the Law of England, published in 1769, reported that for the crime of treason an Englishman might be dragged to the gallows, hanged, cut down, disemboweled while still living and, finally, put to death by decapitation and quartering.[181] Public hangings, floggings, and cropping of ears were still being practiced when our Constitution was adopted.[182] Thomas Jefferson, one of the most enlightened thinkers of his day, advocated castrating men found guilty of rape, polygamy, or sodomy, and mutilating the faces of women found guilty of similar crimes.[183] These recommendations, although barbaric by modern standards, were not particularly radical back then. In deciding whether a punishment is cruel and unusual, should a court consider opinions prevalent when the Constitution was adopted or enlightened modern opinion?

To ask this question is to answer it. The Court has repeatedly emphasized the Eighth Amendment's "expansive and vital character"[184] and its capacity for evolutionary growth.[185] The constitutional definition of "cruelty" embodies "contemporary standards of decency,"[186] and changes as "public opinion becomes enlightened."[187] Should the time come when enlightened public opinion has advanced to a point where the death penalty is no longer acceptable to a majority of Americans, these attitudes will work their way into the Eighth Amendment, and the death penalty will be prohibited. Nevertheless, as of this writing, that time has not yet arrived.

§ 9.14   — Constitutionally Acceptable Punishments

The Eighth Amendment generally limits the kinds of punishments that may be imposed to fines, prison terms, and executions carried out in a humane fashion. Other kinds of punishment are certainly unusual in modern times and, when they involve unnecessary physical pain, humiliation, or degradation, are also cruel. Perpetual

---

[181]   Robinson v. California, 370 U.S. 660, 82 S. Ct. 1417, 8 L. Ed. 2d 758 (1962).

[182]   4 W. BLACKSTONE COMMENTARIES 92.

[183]   Mr. Justice Brennan traced the history of the Eighth Amendment in his concurring opinion in Furman v. Georgia, 408 U.S. 238, 257, 92 S. Ct. 2726, 2736, 33 L. Ed. 2d 346, 360 (1972).

[184]   VAN DEN HAAG, PUNISHING CRIMINALS 193–194 (1975).

[185]   Weems v. United States, 217 U.S. 349, 377, 30 S. Ct. 544, 553, 54 L. Ed. 793, 802 (1910); Trop v. Dulles, 356 U.S. 86, 78 S. Ct. 590, 2 L. Ed. 2d 630 (1958).

[186]   Hudson v. McMillian, 503 U.S. 1, 112 S. Ct. 995, 117 L. Ed. 2d 156 (1992).

[187]   Weems v. United States, *supra* note 185.

surveillance[188] and forfeiture of citizenship,[189] for example, have been held constitutionally unacceptable punishments. So has conditioning a sex offender's early release on his willingness to undergo castration.[190]

Even ordinary punishments (*i.e.*, fines, incarceration, and death) violate the Eighth Amendment when they are disproportionately severe to the crimes for which they are imposed."[191] The Supreme Court has observed that "[i]t is a precept of justice that punishments for crime should be graduated and proportioned to [the] offense [charged].[192] This precept is rooted in the language of the Eighth Amendment, which declares that "excessive fines [shall not be] imposed."

The proportionality limitation has been applied most often to the death penalty. Death may be imposed only when the underlying offense involves the taking of a human life.[193] It is regarded as too severe for crimes that do not involve the taking of a human life, such as rape.

The Supreme Court has been reluctant to apply the proportionality principle to the length of a prison sentence, explaining:[194]

> ... [T]he "seriousness" of an offense or pattern of offenses in modern society is not a line, but a plane. Once the death penalty and other punishments different in kind from fine or imprisonment have been put to one side, there remains little in the way of objective standards for judging whether or not a life sentence imposed ... for ... felony convictions not involving "violence" violates the cruel-and-unusual punishment prohibition of the Eighth Amendment.... . Whatever views may be entertained regarding severity of punishment, whether one believes in its efficacy or its futility, ... these are peculiarly questions of legislative policy.[195]

The Supreme Court recently made a limited exception for juvenile offenders. Noting that juveniles offenders are less culpable and have a greater chance of rehabilitation than adults, the Court ruled that life without parole is constitutionally excessive punishment for juvenile offenders convicted of nonhomicidal crimes. Such offenders must

---

[188]   *Id.*

[189]   Trop v. Dulles, *supra* note 185.

[190]   State v. Brown, 284 S.C. 407, 326 S.E.2d 410 (1985) (physical castration); People v. Gauntlett, 134 Mich. App. 737, 352 N.W.2d 310 (1984) (mandatory use of sex drive suppressant).

[191]   Weems v. United States, *supra* note 185, 217 U.S. at 367, 30 S. Ct. at 549.

[192]   *Id.*

[193]   Coker v. Georgia, 433 U.S. 584, 97 S. Ct. 2861, 53 L. Ed. 2d 982 (1977).

[194]   Ewing v. California, 538 U.S. 11, 123 S. Ct. 1179, 155 L. Ed. 2d 108 (2003) (noting that "federal courts should be reluctant to review legislatively mandated terms of imprisonment" and that "outside the context of capital punishment, successful challenges to the proportionality of particular sentences have been exceedingly rare"); Harmelin v. Michigan, 501 U.S. 957, 111 S. Ct. 268, 115 L. Ed. 2d 836 (1991); Solem v. Helm, 463 U.S. 277, 103 S. Ct. 3001, 77 L. Ed. 2d 637 (1983); Lockyer v. Andrade, 538 U.S. 63, 123 S. Ct. 1166, 155 L. Ed. 2d 144 (2003) (upholding a sentence of life imprisonment with no possibility of parole for 50 years for the crime of shoplifting under California's "three strike law").

[195]   Rommel v. Estelle, 445 U.S. 263, 283 n. 27, 100 S. Ct. 1133, 1143–1144 n. 27, 63 L. Ed. 2d 381 (1980) (holding that mandatory life sentence imposed under Texas recidivist statute following defendant's third felony conviction for obtaining $120.75 by false pretenses did not violate Eighth Amendment).

be afforded an opportunity to earn their release by demonstrating that they have matured and changed.[196]

§ 9.15   — The Death Penalty

The death penalty has been the center of a stormy debate that has gone on for decades. There are conflicting views about the morality of putting a fellow human being to death, conflicting evidence about the effectiveness of this punishment in deterring violent crimes, and the omnipresent specter of discovering, after the fact, that an innocent person has been executed.[197] However, the most serious and statistically best supported indictment of the death penalty is socioeconomic. It has been documented, time and again, that the death penalty is imposed disproportionately on racial minorities and the poor.

None of these issues is likely to be resolved soon. For now, the Supreme Court has chosen to err on the side of allowing the death penalty, but has limited the crimes for which the death penalty may be imposed, and has developed special procedures designed to ensure, to the greatest extent possible, that the decision to impose this penalty will be based on appropriate considerations and not motivated by passion or prejudice.

Figure 9.5
Requirements for Death Penalty Sentencing Laws

To be constitutional, death penalty sentencing laws must incorporate all six of the following safeguards:

1. The death penalty may be imposed only for crimes that involve the taking of a human life;
2. The sentencer must have the discretion to decide whether the death penalty is appropriate;
3. Sentencing discretion must be channeled by establishing statutory aggravating factors that must be present to warrant imposition of the death penalty;
4. Defendants must be afforded an unrestricted opportunity to offer evidence that might convince the tribunal to show compassion and withhold the death penalty;
5. The trial must be conducted in two phases, with the sentencing phase kept separate from the guilt phase; and
6. The death penalty may not be imposed on offenders who are under the age of 18, mentally retarded, or criminally insane.

---

[196]   Graham v. Florida, __ U.S. __ , 130 S. Ct. 2011,176 L. Ed. 2d 825 (2010) (Eighth Amendment prohibits the imposition of a life without parole sentence on a juvenile offender for crimes other than homicide).

[197]   Recent DNA exonerations of large numbers of death row prisoners have raised fresh concerns, causing a decline in public support for the death penalty. *See, e.g.*, Carol S. Steiker, *Things Fall Apart, but the Center Holds: The Supreme Court and the Death Penalty*, 77 N.Y.U. L. Rev. 1475 (2002) ("Public opinion polling data has shown dramatic drops in public support for capital punishment, documenting a rapid descent from a high of 80% in favor in 1994 to a low of 65% in favor in 2001, the lowest level of support in nineteen years.").

A. Crimes for Which the Death Penalty May Be Imposed

The death penalty may be imposed only for crimes that result, or that are intended to result, in the taking of a human life.[198] The Supreme Court has repeatedly invalidated state statutes that authorize the death penalty for crimes such as rape or kidnapping where the victim is not killed.[199] Unless a human life is taken, the Eighth Amendment prohibits imposition of the death penalty.

B. Procedures Required for Death-Eligible Crimes

Even when a human life is taken, the defendant may not be sentenced to death in an impersonal, mechanical fashion. The tribunal must have the discretion to decide whether the circumstances surrounding this particular homicide were heinous enough to warrant the death penalty and also whether the accused's age, background, character, or other traits make it appropriate to show mercy and spare him. This has not always been the law.

The Supreme Court's death penalty reforms began when it handed down the landmark case of *Furman v. Georgia*.[200] Furman invalidated capital punishment laws around the nation. The Court was disenchanted with the capital punishment sentencing procedures in use at that time. These procedures conferred unguided discretion on sentencing bodies to decide whether to impose the death penalty. The result was random and unequal justice, with the death penalty being imposed almost exclusively on minorities and the poor. The *Furman* Court ruled that unguided discretion to impose the death penalty was constitutionally unacceptable.

Furman resulted in a moratorium on the executions of death row prisoners. Chaos ensued as legislatures around the nation met for the purpose of remodeling their capital punishment laws. Because broad and unguided sentencing discretion had led to the death penalty's downfall, it was clear that this feature had to be removed from capital punishment sentencing procedures if the death penalty was to be salvaged. Legislatures took two different approaches. Some retained sentencing discretion but provided standards to guide the sentencing body in its decision to impose the death penalty, while others eliminated sentencing discretion entirely, making death the mandatory punishment for specified crimes. No one knew what the Supreme Court's reaction to the new approaches would be.

In 1976, the Supreme Court issued a number of opinions regarding the states' post-*Furman* capital punishment sentencing procedures.[201] It carefully selected the cases for review so that it could discuss all the various "do's and don'ts" of capital punishment sentencing. The following summarizes the law of capital punishment sentencing as it has evolved since 1976.

---

[198]   **Coker v. Georgia**, *supra* note 193 (kidnapping and rape of adult woman); Kennedy v. Louisiana, 554 U.S. 407, 128 S. Ct. 2641, 171 L. Ed. 2d 525 (2008) (rape of child whose life was not taken).

[199]   *See* cases *supra* note 198.

[200]   408 U.S. 238, 92 S. Ct. 2726, 33 L. Ed. 2d 346 (1972).

[201]   Gregg v. Georgia, 428 U.S. 153, 96 S. Ct. 2909, 49 L. Ed. 2d 859 (1976); Proffitt v. Florida, 428 U.S. 242, 96 S. Ct. 2960, 49 L. Ed. 2d 913 (1976); Jurek v. Texas, 428 U.S. 262, 96 S. Ct. 2950, 49 L. Ed. 2d 929 (1976); Woodson v. North Carolina, 428 U.S. 280, 96 S. Ct. 2978, 49 L. Ed. 2d 944 (1976); Roberts v. Louisiana, 428 U.S. 325, 96 S. Ct. 3001, 49 L. Ed. 2d 974 (1976).

1. The Tribunal Must Have Discretion to Determine Whether the Death Penalty Is Appropriate

When a person's life is at stake, the Eighth Amendment demands individualized sentencing discretion.[202] Mandatory death penalty laws are unconstitutional because they treat "all persons convicted of a designated offense, not as uniquely individual human beings, but as members of a faceless, undifferentiated mass to be subjected to the blind infliction of the [death] penalty."[203] This treatment is incompatible with the Eighth Amendment's mandate of respect for human dignity. Thus, legislatures may not make death a mandatory punishment for any crime, even for the deliberate slaying of a police officer.[204]

2. Sentencing Discretion Must Be Channeled by Establishing Statutory Aggravating Factors that Must Be Present to Warrant Imposition of the Death Penalty

Although sentencing discretion is essential, the Supreme Court recognized in *Furman v. Georgia* that unguided sentencing discretion leads to arbitrary and unequal applications of the death penalty. To minimize this risk, death penalty sentencing laws must incorporate concrete, clear, and objective guidelines that focus the sentencer's attention on factors accompanying the taking of a human life that make the death penalty appropriate, and distinguish them from other cases involving the taking of a human life for which death is not an appropriate penalty.[205] These factors are called **aggravating circumstances** or aggravating factors.[206] The function of statutory aggravating factors is to "narrow the class of persons eligible for the death penalty and . . . reasonably justify the imposition of a more severe sentence on certain offenders found guilty of the same crime."[207] Unless the sentencer finds the existence of one or more aggravating factors, the death penalty may not be imposed.

Aggravating factors must be specific enough to guide the tribunal's discretion. Aggravating factors typically mentioned in death penalty sentencing statutes include the fact that the killing was accompanied by rape, performed for hire, or the victim was a police officer. In *Godfrey v. Georgia*,[208] the Supreme Court ruled that a statute authorizing imposition of the death penalty upon a finding that the murder "was outrageously or wantonly vile, horrible or inhuman in that it involved . . . depravity of

---

[202]   Woodson v. North Carolina, *supra* note 201.

[203]   *Id.*, *supra* note 201, 428 U.S. at 304, 96 S. Ct. at 2991, 49 L. Ed. 2d at 961.

[204]   Roberts v. Louisiana, 431 U.S. 633, 97 S. Ct. 1993, 52 L. Ed. 2d 637 (1977); *see also* Sumner v. Shuman, 483 U.S. 66, 107 S. Ct. 2716, 97 L. Ed. 2d 56 (1987).

[205]   Gregg v. Georgia, *supra* note 201.

[206]   Lockett v. Ohio, 438 U.S. 586, 89 S. Ct. 2954, 57 L. Ed. 2d 973 (1978); Eddings v. Oklahoma, 455 U.S. 104, 102 S. Ct. 869, 71 L. Ed. 2d 1 (1982); Richmond v. Lewis, 506 U.S. 40, 113 S. Ct. 528, 121 L. Ed. 2d 411 (1992); Tuilaepa v. California, 512 U.S. 967, 114 S. Ct. 2630, 129 L. Ed. 2d 750 (1994).

[207]   Zant v. Stephens, 462 U.S. 862, 103 S. Ct. 2733, 77 L. Ed. 2d 235 (1983).

[208]   446 U.S. 420, 100 S. Ct. 1759, 64 L. Ed. 2d 398 (1980).

mind, or an aggravated battery to the victim" did not furnish an adequate standard for differentiating between murderers who deserved to die and those who should be spared, because these factors normally accompany every intentional homicide. The statute failed to furnish the type of concrete differentiating standards the Constitution demands before a person convicted of homicide can be put to death.

3. Defendants Facing the Death Penalty Must Be Afforded an Unrestricted Opportunity to Offer Evidence That Might Convince the Tribunal to Show Mercy

The fact that the tribunal finds an aggravating circumstance does not mean that it must impose the death penalty; it means that the tribunal has the authority to do so. However, mercy still remains an option. To this end, sentencing procedures must afford the accused an opportunity to establish the existence of factors that make him deserving of mercy. These factors are sometimes called mitigating factors or circumstances. **Mitigating circumstances** include such things as the defendant's age, good character, lack of a criminal record, subaverage intellectual functioning, abusive childhood, or any other factor that might influence the tribunal to show mercy and spare him.[209]

In *Lockett v. Ohio*,[210] the Supreme Court struck down a death penalty statute that required the sentencing body, upon finding that the murder was accompanied by an aggravating circumstance, to impose the death penalty unless it found that the victim had provoked the offense, the crime resulted from duress, or the accused was suffering from mental illness. The Court ruled that this statute unduly limited the sentencer's discretion to show compassion. For a death sentence to be valid under the Eighth Amendment, the sentencer must be permitted to hear and consider all possible mitigating evidence that the accused elects to offer in the hopes of escaping the death penalty.

4. The Tribunal's Consideration of Guilt and Sentencing Must Be Kept Separate

In *Gregg v. Georgia*,[211] the Supreme Court approved Georgia's approach to capital sentencing, and that approach has become the prototype for the laws of other jurisdictions. Not only did the Georgia approach list aggravating and mitigating circumstances, it employed a bifurcated proceeding. The trial was divided into two phases — a guilt phase and a separate sentencing phase. During the first phase, the issue before the tribunal is whether the accused committed the crime. If the guilt phase results in a conviction, the trial enters a second phase, during which the tribunal hears testimony bearing on the appropriateness of the death penalty. Separating the sentencing phase from the guilt phase is constitutionally necessary because much evidence relevant to

---

[209] Lockett v. Ohio, 438 U.S. 586, 89 S. Ct. 2954, 57 L. Ed. 2d 973 (1978); Buchanan v. Angelone, 522 U.S. 269, 118 S. Ct. 757, 139 L. Ed. 2d 702 (1998); Penry v. Johnson, 532 U.S. 782, 121 S. Ct. 1910, 150 L. Ed. 2d 9 (2001).
[210] *Supra* note 209.
[211] *Supra* note 201.

fixing the appropriate punishment, such as the accused's character and prior criminal record, is irrelevant to his guilt of the crimes for which he is on trial, and would be highly prejudicial if introduced at the guilt phase of the trial.

5. Offenders Who Are Ineligible for the Death Penalty

The death penalty may be imposed only on offenders "whose extreme culpability make them 'most deserving of execution.'"[212] Juveniles under the age of 18 at the time of the crime,[213] mentally retarded offenders,[214] and the criminally insane[215] are not eligible for the death penalty.

C. Lingering Problems of Unfairness in the Application of the Death Penalty

The Supreme Court's sentencing reforms were an attempt to eliminate arbitrary sentencing discretion by focusing the sentencer's attention on factors that would give them a rational basis for making distinctions between offenders, separating those who deserved the death penalty from those who deserved to be spared. These reforms have not achieved all that was hoped for them. It remains true today that racial minorities and the poor are much more likely than others to receive the death penalty. The Supreme Court has acknowledged and lamented this fact. Still, it holds that the death penalty is constitutional.

---

[212] Roper v. Simmons, 543 U.S. 551, 125 S. Ct. 1183, 161 L. Ed. 2d 1 (2005) (*overruling* Stanford v. Kentucky, 492 U.S. 361, 109 S. Ct. 2969, 106 L. Ed. 2d 306 (1989) which had set the age of death penalty eligibility at 16).

[213] *Id.*

[214] Atkins v. Virginia, 536 U.S. 304, 122 S. Ct. 2242, 153 L. Ed. 2d 335 (2002), *overruling* Penry v. Lynaugh, 492 U.S. 302, 109 S. Ct. 2934, 106 L. Ed. 2d 256 (1989). The *Atkins* Court left to the states the task of developing criteria for deciding which offenders will be spared the death penalty because of mental retardation, although it approvingly cited the widely accepted clinical definition. This definition requires (1) significantly subaverage intellectual functioning and (2) significant limitations in adaptive skills, such as communication, self-care, and self-direction, manifested before the age of 18. This definition has been incorporated into a number of state statutes prohibiting the execution of the mentally retarded. *See, e.g.,* Ariz. Rev. Stat. § 13-703.02(J)(2) (2001); Ark. Code Ann. § 5-4-618 (Michie 1993); Colo. Rev. Stat. § 18-1.3-1101(2) (2002); Conn. Gen. Stat. § 1-1 g (2001); Fla. Stat. Ann. § 921.137(1) (West 2002); Ga. Code Ann. § 17-7-131(a)(3) (1997); Ind. Code § 35-36-9-2 (1998); Kan. Stat. Ann. § 21-4623(e) (1995); Mo. Rev. Stat. § 565.030(6) (2001); N.Y. Crim. Proc. Law § 400.27(12)(e) (McKinney 2002); S.D. Codified Laws § 23A-27A-26.2 (Michie 2002). "Significantly subaverage intellectual functioning" is generally defined as having an IQ of 70 or below. *See, e.g.,* Ky. Rev. Stat. Ann. § 532.130(2) (Michie 1999); Neb. Rev. Stat. § 28-105.01(3) (2000); N.M. Stat. Ann. § 31-20A-2.1(A) (Michie 2000); N.C. Gen. Stat. § 15A-2005(a)(1)(a) (2001); Tenn. Code Ann. § 39-13-203(a) (1997); Wash. Rev. Code § 10.95.030(2)(a)(2002).

[215] Panetti v. Quarterman, 551 U.S. 930, 127 S. Ct. 2842, 168 L. Ed. 2d 662 (2007) (holding that the Eighth Amendment prohibits execution of prisoners whose mental illness deprives them of the mental capacity to understand that they are being executed as a punishment for a crime); Ford v. Wainwright, 477 U.S. 399, 106 S. Ct. 2595, 91 L. Ed. 2d 335 (1986).

In *McCleskey v. Kemp*,[216] McCleskey, an African-American man sentenced to death by a Georgia jury for killing a white police officer during a robbery, used statistical evidence to drive home how little the Supreme Court's reforms had genuinely accomplished. McCleskey's statistics showed that African-American defendants charged with killing white victims were four times more likely than anyone else to receive the death penalty. McCleskey contended that these statistics demonstrated that racial considerations continued to play a role in Georgia's capital punishment sentencing and that, as a consequence, the Georgia system still violated the Eighth Amendment. This was a serious challenge — a challenge that, as the Court recognized, went to the legitimacy of permitting juries in a multiracial society to decide who will receive the death penalty. A sharply divided Supreme Court (5-4) voted to affirm McCleskey's sentence in an opinion that admitted with sadness that the current system is still imperfect, but apologized that it was the best the Supreme Court could do. Mr. Justice Powell, who wrote the majority opinion, proclaimed that there can be "no perfect procedure for deciding in which cases governmental authority should be used to impose death."[217]

§ 9.16 — Eighth Amendment Protection Inside Prison Walls

Eighth Amendment protection does not end when a sentence is imposed. Prisoners have a right to be free from cruel and inhumane treatment during their confinement.[218] However, courts take the realities of prison life into account in applying the Eighth Amendment. Harsh conditions and rough disciplinary treatment reach Eighth Amendment proportions only when they lack penological justification and involve wanton and unnecessary infliction of pain.[219] Despite this low standard, correctional officers and officials are sued more often than any other criminal justice professionals. This does not mean they are less competent. Prisoners, who have years on their hands with little

---

[216] 481 U.S. 279, 107 S. Ct. 1756, 95 L. Ed. 2d 262 (1987).

[217] *Id*. at 313, 107 S. Ct. at 1778.

[218] Brown v. Plata, __ U.S. __, 131 S. Ct. 1910, 179 L. Ed. 2d 969 (2011) (finding that massive overcrowding and chronic failure to provide basic medical and mental health treatment resulted in prison conditions so overwhelming as to constitute cruel and unusual punishment; affirming lower court judgment ordering release of prisoners as the only remedy able to correct violation of the Eighth Amendment); Hope v. Pelzer, 536 U.S. 730, 122 S. Ct. 2508, 153 L. Ed. 2d 666 (2002) (inmate's complaint alleging that he was handcuffed to hitching post for seven hours without regular water or bathroom breaks as punishment for disruptive behavior that had long since ended stated claim under the Eighth Amendment). *But see* Overton v. Mazzetta, 539 U.S. 126, 123 S. Ct. 2162, 156 L. Ed. 2d 162 (2003) (two-year ban on visitations for inmates serving sentences for substance abuse offenses did not violate Eighth Amendment ban on cruel and unusual punishment because it did not deprive them of basic necessities or entail gratuitous infliction of wanton and unnecessary pain).

[219] *See, e.g.*, Hope v. Pelzer, *supra* note 218; Farmer v. Brennan, 511 U.S. 825, S. Ct. 1970, 128 L. Ed. 2d 811 (1994); Estelle v. Gamble, 429 U.S. 97, 104 S. Ct. 285, 50 L. Ed. 2d 251 (1976).

else to do, file thousands of lawsuits each year claiming that their Eighth Amendment rights have been violated.[220]

A. *Sadistic Use of Force Against Inmates*

The Eighth Amendment, which controls use of force by prison guards, imposes a standard that is less demanding than the Fourth Amendment, which governs the use of force in making an arrest.[221] The Eighth Amendment is violated only when excessive force is used with a sadistic intent to inflict injury.

Hudson v. McMillian[222] and *Whitley v. Albers*[223] illustrate application of the Eighth Amendment inside prisons. In *Hudson*, prison guards gratuitously punched an inmate in the mouth, eyes, chest, and stomach on the way to the penitentiary's administrative lockdown. The Supreme Court held that the prisoner's Eight Amendment rights were violated, even though he was not seriously injured, because the punches

Figure 9.6
Eighth Amendment Standards for Treatment of Prisoners

Conduct Regulated by the Eighth Amendment	Mental State Necessary to Incur Liability
1. Application of physical force 2. Failure to attend to a prisoner's basic human needs	Sadistic intent to injure the prisoner Deliberate indifference in the face of awareness that a prisoner's basic human needs are not being met

---

[220]   In 1995, inmates filed nearly 40,000 federal civil lawsuits — 19 percent of the entire federal civil docket. Margo Schlanger, *Inmate Litigation*, 116 Harv. L. R. 1555, 1558 (2003). Inmate lawsuits were placing such a heavy strain on the federal courts that Congress found it necessary to put curbs in place. The Prison Litigation Reform Act of 1996 prevents inmates from filing lawsuits in *forma pauperis* (*i.e.*, without paying filing fees) and imposes other restrictions. See 28 U.S.C. § 1915.

[221]   Fourth Amendment restrictions on the use of force are covered in § 3.16.

[222]   503 U.S. 1, 112 S. Ct. 995, 117 L. Ed. 2d 156 (1992) (holding that correctional officers' malicious use of excessive force against an inmate may constitute cruel and unusual punishment, even though the inmate does not sustain serious injury). *See also* Wilkins v. Gaddy, __ U.S. __, 130 S. Ct. 1175, 175 L. Ed. 2d 995 (2010) (The core judicial inquiry is not whether a prisoner sustained a certain quantum of injury, but rather "whether force was applied in a good-faith effort to maintain or restore discipline, or maliciously and sadistically to cause harm."); Hope v. Pelzer, *supra* note 218 (Inmate's Eighth Amendment rights were violated when he was handcuffed to a hitching post and exposed to the heat of the sun, thirst, taunting, and deprivation of bathroom breaks for a 7-hour period as punishment for disruptive behavior. Because the prisoner had already been subdued, this treatment amounted to gratuitous infliction of "wanton and unnecessary" pain); Despain v. Uphoff, 264 F.3d 965 (10th Cir. 2001) (allegation that prison guard discharged pepper spray in inmate's face as a sadistic prank stated Eighth Amendment claim).

[223]   Whitley v. Albers, 475 U.S. 312, 106 S. Ct. 1078, 89 L. Ed. 2d 251 (1986).

were administered sadistically and served no penological purpose. In *Whitley v. Albers*, correction officers shot an inmate while attempting to quell a cellblock disturbance. The Supreme Court ruled that the inmate's Eighth Amendment rights were not violated, even though he was not one of the rioters, because the prison guards used the force in good faith belief that it was necessary to restore order.

B. *Deliberate Indifference to an Inmate's Basic Human Needs*

Correctional officials also have a constitutional duty to provide for an inmate's "basic human needs." This duty arises because the government has stripped the prisoner of ability to provide for his/her own needs.[224] The Eighth Amendment, therefore, imposes a corresponding duty on the government.

A prisoner's "basic human needs" are sparse. Prisoners have a constitutional entitlement to minimally decent conditions of habitation,[225] safety from attack, care for serious medical needs,[226] and little more. They are not entitled to education, entertainment, or any of the other amenities of life that people who are not incarcerated enjoy.[227] The harshness of prison life has penological value. It reinforces the deterrent goal of criminal punishment.

---

[224] DeShaney v. Winnebago County Dep't of Soc. Servs., 489 U.S. 189, 109 S. Ct. 998, 103 L. Ed. 2d 249 (1989) (explaining that " when the State takes a person into its custody and holds him there against his will, the Constitution imposes upon it a corresponding duty to assume some responsibility for his safety and general well-being"); Brown v. Plata, *supra* note 118 (same).

[225] Hutto v. Finney, 437 U.S. 678, 98 S. Ct. 2565, 57 L. Ed. 2d 522 (1978) (lengthy punitive confinement of a prisoner in filthy, overcrowded eight-by-ten-foot cells where violence was rampant and where the prisoner was served a diet limited to a paste called "gruel" violated the Eighth Amendment); Helling v. McKinney, 509 U.S. 25, 113 S. Ct. 2475, 125 L. Ed. 2d 22 (1993) (housing nonsmoker in cell with inmate who smoked five packs of cigarettes per day violated the Eighth Amendment); Gates v. Collier, 501 F.2d 1291 (5th Cir. 1974) (threat to personal safety by exposed electrical wiring, deficient firefighting measures, and housing inmates with others who had serious contagious diseases violated Eighth Amendment); Phelps v. Kapnolas, 308 F.3d 180 (2d Cir. 2002) (complaint stating that inmate was placed on nutritionally inadequate diet for 14 days as punishment for throwing a bowl of cereal stated claim under the Eighth Amendment).

[226] Estelle v. Gamble, 429 U.S. 97, 97 S. Ct. 285, 50 L. Ed. 2d 251 (1976) (Eighth Amendment violated by deliberate indifference to a prisoner's known, serious medical needs); Wilson v. Seiter, 501 U.S. 305, 111 S. Ct. 2321, 115 L. Ed. 2d 271 (1991).

[227] Rhodes v. Chapman, 452 U.S. 337, 349, 101 S. Ct. 2392, 2400, 69 L. Ed. 2d 59 (1981) (the Constitution "does not mandate comfortable prisons"); Beard v. Banks, 548 U.S. 521, 126 S. Ct. 2572, 165 L. Ed. 2d 697 (2006) (holding that prison policy restricting access to television, radio, newspapers, magazines, etc. by violent inmates placed in the prison's most restrictive long-term segregation unit, was justified by need to provide incentives for improved prison behavior, and consequently, did not violate their constitutional rights).

Failure to provide for an inmate's basic human needs constitutes cruel and unusual punishment only when it is accompanied by a culpable mental state described as "deliberate indifference." This mental state requires proof that prison officials actually knew of and disregarded an excessive risk to an inmate's health or safety.[228]

C. Methods of Execution

Methods of putting condemned prisoners to death have changed over time. Hanging was the primary method during the nineteenth century and electrocution throughout most of the twentieth. Lethal injections were introduced toward the end of the century and are now used in every jurisdiction that imposes the death penalty.

Most jurisdictions use a combination of three drugs. The initial drug — sodium thiopental — anesthetizes the prisoner and induces unconsciousness, the second — pancuronium bromide — causes paralysis and stops breathing, and the third — potassium chloride — causes a cardiac arrest. The three-drug protocol, if properly administered, leads to a peaceful and painless death. However, significant pain can result if an insufficient dose of the sedating drug is administered during the initial phase. The risk of pain is exacerbated by the fact that physicians are ethically prohibited from participating in prison executions.

In *Baze v. Rees*,[229] a death row prisoner challenged Kentucky's three-drug lethal injection protocol under the Eighth Amendment. The Supreme Court ruled against him, stating that no method of execution is totally painless and the Eighth Amendment does not require this. The test is whether the method of execution poses a "*substantial* risk of severe pain." Kentucky's three-drug protocol was constitutional because it incorporated adequate safeguards to minimize the risk of maladministration.

§ 9.17 Summary and Practical Suggestions

This chapter examined a variety of constitutional safeguards designed to ensure fair trials and humane punishments. These safeguards include the Fifth Amendment prohibition of double jeopardy, Sixth Amendment right to a speedy and public trial before an impartial jury, the Sixth Amendment right to confront adverse witnesses, and the Eighth Amendment ban on cruel and unusual punishments.

---

[228] *See, e.g.*, Farmer v. Brennan, 511 U.S. 825, 114 S. Ct. 1970, 128 L. Ed. 2d 811 (1994) (prison official may be held liable for "deliberate indifference" to a prisoner's Eighth Amendment right to protection against violence while in custody if the official "knows that [the] inmat[e] face[s] a substantial risk of serious harm and disregards that risk by failing to take reasonable measures to abate it"); Erickson v. Pardus, 551 U.S. 89, 127 S. Ct. 2197, 167 L. Ed. 2d 1081 (2007) (prison officials are liable under the Eighth Amendment for "deliberate indifference" to a prisoner's serious medical needs).

[229] 553 U.S. 35, 128 S. Ct. 1520, 170 L. Ed. 2d 420 (2008) (widely used three-drug lethal injection method of capital punishment does not pose an unacceptable risk of significant pain and, consequently, does not involve cruel and unusual punishment).

A. Double Jeopardy

The double jeopardy clause prevents the government from trying or punishing an accused person more than once for the same offense. Three conditions must combine in order to have protection against reprosecution: (1) an earlier prosecution must have progressed at least to the point of jeopardy attachment, (2) the subsequent prosecution must have involved the "same offense," and (3) both prosecutions must have been brought by the same government entity.

In jury trials, jeopardy attaches, so as to bar reprosecution for the same offense, when the jury is empaneled, and in bench trials when the first witness has been sworn and the judge begins taking testimony. Nevertheless, there are three instances in which an accused can be retried for the same offense even though the first trial has proceeded beyond the jeopardy attachment point. Retrial is permissible when: (1) the defense requests the declaration of a mistrial; (2) factors beyond either side's control — such as a deadlocked jury — prevent a verdict from being reached; and (3) the defendant is convicted, appeals, and the conviction is reversed.

When new charges are brought against a defendant who has previously been tried for the same underlying conduct, the court must decide whether the new charges represent the same or different offense. There are two tests used to determine whether prosecutions brought under different sections of the penal code involve the "same offense." The *Blockburger* ("same elements") test, which is used in federal courts and most state courts, allows reprosecution if both crimes have at least one distinct element. The less common test, known as the "same transaction" test, bars multiple prosecutions for crimes that were committed as part of the same underlying criminal transaction.

B. Speedy Trial

The Sixth Amendment guarantees the right to a speedy trial. This right attaches when formal charges are filed. Courts consider the following four factors in evaluating whether the right to a speedy trial has been denied: (1) the length of the delay, (2) the reasons for the delay, (3) whether the defendant made a timely assertion of his or her rights, and (4) whether he or she was prejudiced by the delay.

C. Jury Trial

The Sixth Amendment guarantees the right to a jury trial. This right is available only for serious offenses (*i.e.*, offenses punishable by at least six months in prison). Although the prevailing pattern is to use a 12-person jury and to require a unanimous verdict, neither feature is required in state criminal prosecutions.

D. Fair and Impartial Trial

The Sixth Amendment and the due process clause work together to ensure that the accused receives a fair trial. There are numerous factors that go into the making of a fair trial. They include the right to have a trial that is open to the public, to confront and cross-examine adverse witness, to be tried by an impartial tribunal, and to receive disclosure of all exculpatory evidence in the possession of the police or the prosecutor that is favorable to the defendant and material to guilt or punishment.

E. Cruel and Unusual Punishment

The Eighth Amendment generally limits the types of punishments that may be imposed to fines, prison terms, and executions carried out in a humane fashion. Death is the most severe penalty that any society can impose. There are six different Eighth Amendment restrictions surrounding the imposition of the death penalty: (1) death is a constitutionally acceptable punishment only for crimes that involve the death or intended death of another human being; (2) the sentence may not be imposed as an automatic consequence of commission of the crime — sentencing discretion is necessary; (3) sentencing discretion must be channeled by establishing statutory aggravating factors that must accompany commission of the crime to warrant imposition of the death penalty; (4) defendants must be afforded an unrestricted opportunity to convince the tribunal that they deserve mercy; (5) guilt and sentencing phases of a capital punishment case must be conducted separately; and (6) the death penalty may not be imposed on juveniles under 18, the mentally retarded, or the criminally insane.

The Eighth Amendment imposes two restrictions on prison officials. They must: (1) refrain from unnecessary and sadistic applications of force and (2) provide for an inmate's "basic human needs." "Basic human needs" fall into three categories: (1) minimally decent conditions of habitation, (2) safety from attack, and (3) care for serious medical needs. Correctional officials are liable for failing to provide for an inmate's basic needs only when they are actually aware that these needs are not being met and act with deliberate indifference.

Constitutional Rights and Liabilities in the Workplace   10

Twentieth Century America has a right to demand for itself, and the obligation to secure for its citizens, law enforcement personnel whose conduct is above and beyond reproach. The police officer is expected to conduct himself lawfully and properly to bring honor and respect to the law which he is sworn and bound to uphold. He who fails to so comport brings upon the law grave shadows of public distrust. We demand from our law enforcement officers, and properly so, adherence to demanding standards which are higher than those applied in many other professions. It is a standard which demands more than forbearance from overt and indictable illegal conduct. It demands that in both an officer's private and official lives he do nothing to bring dishonor upon his noble calling and in no way contribute to a weakening of the public confidence and trust.

Cerceo v. Darby, 281 A.2d 251, 255 (Pa. 1971)

Chapter Outline

KEY TERMS AND CONCEPTS

Disparate impact discrimination
Disparate treatment discrimination
Hostile work environment
sexual harassment
Qualified immunity

Quid pro quo sexual harassment
Under color of state law
Use, including derivate use,
immunity

§ 10.1   Introduction

Courts have long struggled to determine the appropriate level of constitutional protection in government workplaces. In 1892, Supreme Court Justice Oliver Wendell Holmes, then on the Massachusetts Supreme Court, wrote that a police officer "may have a constitutional right to talk politics, but he has no constitutional right to be a policeman."[1] What Justice Holmes meant is that public employment is a privilege, not a right, and that the government can grant this privilege on whatever terms it pleases, including terms that require public employees to give up their First Amendment rights. While this is no longer true today, the constitutional rights studied in earlier chapters often have a narrower application in the workplace. Government employees retain constitutional rights only to the extent that their exercise is compatible with the government's need for operational efficiency. Even so, government employees have more constitutional protection than their private sector counterparts, who have no constitutional protection whatsoever.

This chapter examines the workplace constitutional rights of police officers, their protection against employment discrimination, and their accountability under federal law for violating the constitutional rights of others.

§ 10.2   First Amendment Protection for Work-Related Speech

First Amendment protection means protection against adverse employment action for speech that annoys superiors. Very little of a police officer's work-related speech carries this protection. Protection exists only when: (1) the officer speaks in his

---

[1]   McAuliffe v. Mayor of New Bedford, 155 Mass. 216, 29 N.E. 517 (1892).

capacity as a private citizen, (2) about a matter of public concern, and (3) the value of the speech outweighs its adverse effect on the police department.[2]

Figure 10.1
First Amendment Protection for Work-Related Speech

Police officers are entitled to First Amendment protection for work-related speech only when they:

1.   Speak in their capacity as a private citizen (rather than as an employee);
2.   About a matter of public (as opposed to private) concern; and
3.   The value of the speech outweighs its adverse effect on the police department.

A. *Did the Officer Speak as an Employee or as a Citizen?*

The first prong of the free speech test focuses on the capacity in which the officer spoke. The Supreme Court has drawn a sharp distinction between the speech of public employees in their capacity as an employee and their speech as a private citizen. When they speak as an employee "pursuant to their official duties," they have no constitutional protection.

The official duties exclusion stems from *Garcetti v. Ceballos*.[3] Ceballos, a supervising deputy district attorney, was asked by defense counsel to review an affidavit prepared by police to obtain a critical search warrant, which defense counsel claimed contained serious misrepresentations. Ceballos verified the claim and wrote a memo to his supervisors recommending dismissal of the case. His supervisors disregarded his recommendation and permitted the case to go forward. Shortly thereafter, Ceballos experienced a series of job setbacks. He sued, claiming that the adverse employment actions were retaliatory and violated his First Amendment rights.

---

[2]   The first prong of this test comes from **Garcetti v. Ceballos**, 547 U.S. 410, 126 S. Ct. 1951, 164 L. Ed. 2d 689 (2006), the second from **Connick v. Myers**, 461 U.S. 138, 103 S. Ct. 1684, 75 L. Ed. 2d 708 (1983), and the third from Pickering v. Board of Education, 391 U.S. 563, 88 S. Ct. 1731, 20 L. Ed. 2d 811 (1968).

[3]   *Supra* **note 2.** For scholarly comments on the *Garcetti* case, see Helen v. Norton, Constraining Public Employee Speech: Government's Control of its Workers' Speech to Protect its Own Expression, 59 DUKE L. J. 1 (2009); Lawrence Rosenthal, *The Emerging First Amendment Law of Managerial Prerogative*, 77 FORDHAM L. REV. 33 (2008); Ramona L. Paetzold, *When Are Public Employees Not Really Public Employees? In the Aftermath of* Garcetti v. Ceballos, 7 FIRST AMEND. L. REV. 92 (2008); Elizabeth Dale, *Employee Speech & Management Rights: A Counterintuitive Reading* of Garcetti v. Ceballos, 29 BERKELEY J. EMP. & LAB. L. 175 (2008); Steven Stafstrom Jr., Note, *Government Employee, Are You a Citizen?:* Garcetti v. Ceballos *and the Citizenship Prong to the* Pickering/Connick *Protected Speech Test*, 52 ST. LOUIS U. L.J. 589 (2009); Elizabeth M. Ellis, Note, Garcetti v. Ceballos: *Public Employees Left to Decide "Your Conscience or Your Job,"* 41 IND. L. REV. 187 (2008).

The Supreme Court denied his claim, holding that when government employees *make statements pursuant to their official duties,* they speak as employees, not as citizens, and the Constitution does not insulate their communications from managerial discipline. The Court emphasized the government's need for control over communications its employees make on its behalf. "Official communications," the Court wrote, "have official consequences, creating a need for substantive consistency and clarity. Supervisors must ensure that their employees' official communications are accurate, demonstrate sound judgment, and promote the employer's mission." The Court further explained that the speech the government pays employees a salary to make on its behalf belongs to the government, not the employees, and that they have no First Amendment interest in it. "Restricting speech that owes its existence to a public employee's professional responsibilities does not infringe any liberties the employee might have enjoyed as a private citizen. It simply reflects the exercise of employer control over what the employer itself has commissioned or created."

Turning to Ceballos' claim, the Court stated that neither the fact that Ceballos' speech occurred at work nor that the subject matter concerned his employment was dispositive. The controlling factor was that his expressions were made pursuant to his duties as a calendar deputy. He "wrote his disposition memo because that is part of what he, as a calendar deputy, was employed to do." "When he went to work and performed the tasks he was paid to perform, Ceballos acted as a government employee. The fact that his duties sometimes required him to speak or write does not mean his supervisors were prohibited from evaluating his performance."

Because Garcetti conceded that his memorandum was written pursuant to his official duties, the Court declined to establish "a comprehensive framework for defining the scope of an employee's duties in cases where there is room for serious debate." It noted, however, that the proper inquiry is a practical one that focuses on the duties an employee actually is expected to perform, rather than formal job descriptions. "The listing of a given task in an employee's written job description is neither necessary nor sufficient to demonstrate that conducting the task is within the scope of the employee's professional duties for First Amendment purposes."

Left with incomplete guidance, lower courts generally decide whether an employee's speech arose "pursuant an official duty" on a case-by-case basis, looking at the totality of the circumstances. They have considered a range of factors, such as the employee's written job description, daily work responsibilities, agency regulations, statutory duties, whether the speech was made internally or externally, occurred during working hours, and other considerations.[4] No consensus has emerged on how

---

[4]   For a sampling of cases treating a police officer's work-related speech as pursuant to his official duties, *see, e.g.,* Callahan v. Fermon, 526 F.3d 1040 (7th Cir. 2008) (report to supervisors of fellow officer's misconduct); Foraker v. Chaffinch, 501 F.3d 231 (3d Cir. 2007) (state trooper's complaint, made up the chain of command, about hazardous health and safety conditions in the workplace); **Vose v. Kliment, 506 F.3d 565 (7th Cir. 2009)** (police sergeant's complaint that detectives in a

closely related to the speaker's job responsibilities the speech must be to constitute speech "pursuant to an official duty." Some courts limit the official duties exclusion to speech that is *required* by the speaker's job.[5] Most courts, however, apply the exclusion broadly to any statement that is *job related* and made while on duty, even though it is not part of the employee's normal job responsibilities.[6] In *Nixon v. City of Houston*,[7] for example, the court held that a patrol officer who criticized his department's high-speed chase policy in a statement made to the media at the scene of a high-speed chase accident, was acting pursuant to his official duties, even though he was not a media spokesman and was not authorized to make the statement in question. Upholding his dismissal, the court wrote:

> The fact that Nixon's statement was unauthorized . . . and that speaking to the press was not part of his regular job duties is not dispositive. Nixon's statement was made while he was performing his job, and the fact that Nixon performed his job incorrectly, in an unauthorized manner, or in contravention of the wishes of his superiors does not convert his statement at the accident scene into protected citizen speech.

Garcetti permits retaliation against public employees who report improprieties and misdeeds pursuant to their official duties, even when their reports are accurate. In *Sigworth v. City of Aurora, Illinois*,[8] a police detective who reported to his supervisors that he believed that members of his drug investigation task force had broken the law by tipping off suspects regarding arrest warrants, was removed from the task force and passed up for a promotion. The court denied his First Amendment claim on the grounds

---

different unit were violating department procedures for obtaining search warrants); Sigsworth v. City of Aurora, Ill., 487 F.3d 506 (7th Cir. 2007) (police detective's report to supervisors that members of drug investigation task force had broken the law by tipping off suspects); **Spiegla v. Hull, 481 F.3d 961 (7th Cir. 2007)** (prison guard's report made to assistant superintendent of suspected security lapse by immediate supervisor); Bradley v. James, 479 F.3d 536 (8th Cir. 2007) (investigative report containing findings that superior officer was intoxicated on the job); Mills v. City of Evansville, Indiana, 452 F.3d 646 (7th Cir. 2006) (criticism of chief's plan to reduce the number of crime prevention officers under officer's command); Haynes v. City of Circleville, Ohio, 474 F.3d 357 (6th Cir. 2007) (internal complaint about cuts in dog training budget); *Freitag v. Ayers*, 468 F.3d 528 (9th Cir. 2006) (correctional officer's internal complaint of sexual harassment by inmates); Nixon v. City of Houston, 511 F.3d 494 (5th Cir. 2007) (on-duty, uniformed police officer's unauthorized statements to the media at accident scene); Williams v. Riley, 481 F. Supp. 2d 582 (N.D. Miss. 2007) (internal report of prisoner abuse committed by fellow officer).

5   *See, e.g.*, Sassone v. Quartararo, 598 F. Supp. 2d 459 (S.D.N.Y 2009); Paola v. Spada, 498 F. Supp. 2d 502 (D. Conn. 2007); Densmore v. City of Maywood, 2008 W L 5077582 (9th Cir. 2008); Ventura v. Town of Manchester, 2008 WL 4080099 (D. Conn. Sept. 2, 2008).

6   *See, e.g.*, Nixon v. Houston, 511 F.3d 494 (5th Cir. 2007); **Vose v. Kliment,** *supra* note 4; Mills v. City of Evansville, Indiana, *supra* note 4; Abdul-Rahman v. Walker, 567 F.3d 1278 (11th Cir. 2009).

7   *Supra* note 6.

8   *Supra* note 4.

that reporting wrongdoing to his supervisor fell within the scope of his official duties. Cases like *Sigworth v. City of Aurora, Illinois* are far from rare.[9]

Garcetti makes it safer for government employees who fear retaliation to voice their concerns to an outside agency, instead of expressing them internally, because they have greater First Amendment protection. In *Freitag v. Ayers*,[10] for example, a female corrections officer in a maximum-security prison filed numerous incident reports complaining that two prisoners repeatedly masturbated in her presence. When nothing was done to address her grievance, she complained up the prison hierarchy to the director of the California Department of Corrections, and still nothing happened. She eventually wrote a letter to a state senator chronicling her sexual harassment by prisoners and her department's failure to take any corrective action. The senator forwarded her letter to the Inspector General's Office, which investigated and wrote a report supporting her allegations. She was terminated in retaliation. The Court of Appeals ruled that the incident reports and complaints made inside the Department of Corrections lacked First Amendment protection because they were made pursuant to the correction officer's official duties, but that her complaint to an outside agency was protected.

> It certainly was not part of her official tasks to complain to the senator or the [Inspector General] about the state's failure to perform its duties properly, and specifically its failure to take corrective action to eliminate sexual harassment in its workplace. Rather, it was Freitag's responsibility as a citizen to expose such official malfeasance to broader scrutiny. Accordingly, in these instances, for purposes of the First Amendment she spoke as a citizen.

As *Freitag v. Ayers* illustrates, the choice of forums is generally decisive on the capacity of the speech. When concerns are expressed internally, the speech is normally treated as made pursuant to official duties because this is what government employees are expected to do when they encounter problems in the workplace. When the same concerns are expressed to an outside agency or the media, in contrast, the employee

---

[9]   *See, e.g.,* **Vose v. Kliment,** *supra* **note 4** (police sergeant's complaint that detectives in another unit were violating department procedures for obtaining search warrants was made pursuant to official duties); Morales v. Jones, 494 F.3d 590 (7th Cir. 2007) (police officer's allegation of misconduct by superior made to District Attorney was pursuant to official duties); **Spiegla v. Hull,** *supra* note 4 (prison guard's report to assistant superintendent of suspected security lapse by immediate supervisor unprotected); Haynes v. City of Circleville, Ohio, *supra* note 4 (police canine handler's internal memorandum to chief protesting cuts to dog training budget unprotected); Freitag v. Ayers, *supra* note 4 (correctional officer's internal complaint of sexual harassment by inmates unprotected); Williams v. Riley, *supra* note 4 (police officer's internal report detailing beating of prisoner by fellow officer unprotected); Harrison v. Oakland County, 612 F. Supp. 2d 848 (E.D. Mich. 2009) (report to supervisor about co-worker's sexually inappropriate conduct unprotected); Callahan v. Fermon, 526 F.3d 1040 (7th Cir. 2008) (report made to supervisors of a fellow officer's misconduct unprotected).

[10]   *Supra* note 6. *See also* Eberz v. Oregon Dept. of State Police, 2008 WL 69 (D. Or. 2008) (finding that a police officer's duties required him to report misconduct to his supervisor, but a report of the alleged misconduct to the Attorney General was protected speech); Morales v. Jones, *supra* note 9 (police officer's allegation of misconduct by superior to District Attorney was unprotected because it was made as part of his duties, but subsequent deposition testimony in a related civil suit was protected speech).

is considered to be speaking as a citizen unless external reporting is part of the employee's job responsibilities. Consequently, the safest course for government employees who fear retaliation is to bypass internal reporting procedures and go directly to the public — contact an elected public official, call a press conference, write a letter to the editor, or complain to an independent government agency.[11] The *Garcetti* case makes it impossible for conscientious government employees to speak out in the interests of the public without compromising their loyalty and professionalism placing their jobs at risk.

B. Did the Speech Address a Matter of "Public Concern?"

When police officers speak outside their official duties, they speak as a private citizen.[12] However, this does not mean they are home free. They still have to prevail on two more tests.

The second test focuses on the content of the speech. The speech must address a matter of "public concern" to have First Amendment protection.[13] "Public concern" has been defined broadly as speech on any matter of "political, social, or other concern to the community,"[14] "of legitimate news interest,"[15] or "about which information is needed or appropriate to enable the members of society to make informed decisions about the operation of their government."[16]

The public concern requirement was established in *Connick v. Myers*.[17] The case involved an assistant district attorney who was fired for circulating a questionnaire

---

[11]   *See, e.g.*, Pickering v. Davis, *supra* note 2 (letter to newspaper protected); Marcos v. City of Atlanta, 364 F.3d 567 (5th Cir. 2004) (media statement about attempted cover-up of police shooting incident protected); *In re* Disciplinary Action Against Gonzalez, 405 N.J. Super. 336, 964 A.2d 811 (N.J. Super., A.D. 2009) (televised interview protected); Alaska v. E.E.O.C., 564 F.3d 1062 (9th Cir. 2009) (media allegations of sexual harassment of co-worker protected); Freitag v. Ayers, *supra* note 4 (external complaints to inspector general and legislator protected); Reilly v. City of Atlantic City, 532 F.3d 216 (3d Cir. 2008) (courtroom testimony for prosecution in trial of fellow officer — protected); Morales v. Jones, *supra* note 9 (deposition testimony given in a civil suit protected); Schlarp v. Dern, 610 F. Supp. 2d (W.D. Pa. 2009) (testimony before State Ethics Commission protected); Turner v. Perry, 278 S.W.2d (Tex. Ct. App. 2009) (report of suspected misconduct by fellow officers to the district attorney's office protected); Davis v. McKinney, 518 F.3d 304 (5th Cir. 2008) (surveying post-*Garcetti* case law and concluding that complaints made up the chain of command are generally viewed as pursuant to official duties, but when public employees take their complaints to persons outside the work place, those "external communications are ordinarily not made as an employee, but as a citizen").

[12]   *See* authorities *supra* note 11.

[13]   **Connick v. Myers,** *supra* **note 2**. *See also, generally,* Stephen Allred, *From* Connick *to Confusion: the Struggle to Define Speech on Matters of Public Concern,* 64 IND. L. J. 43 (1988).

[14]   *Id.*

[15]   City of San Diego v. Roe, 543 U.S. 77, 125 S. Ct. 521, 160 L. Ed. 2d 410 (2004) (defining "public concern" as "matters concerning government policies that are of interest to the public at large," "a subject of legitimate news interest; that is, a subject of general interest and of value and concern to the public at the time of publication").

[16]   *See, e.g.*, Desrochers v. City of San Bernardino, 572 F.3d 703 (9th Cir. 2009) (defining a matter of public concern as pertaining to "issues about which information is needed or appropriate to enable the members of society to make informed decisions about the operation of their government").

[17]   ***Supra* note 2**.

soliciting the views of her co-workers on the office transfer policy, their level of confidence in supervisors, their morale, and whether a grievance committee should be formed. The Court stated that whether a public employee's work-related speech addresses a matter of public or private concern requires consideration of the *content*, *form*, and the *context* of the speech. After examining these factors, the Court concluded that the district attorney's speech did not address a matter of public concern. The *content* focused on internal office affairs of scant interest to the public; the *form* was an internal questionnaire, not intended for public consumption, and the *context* was an ongoing dispute with her supervisors over her scheduled transfer. The point of her speech was not that her supervisors were failing to discharge their responsibilities to the public. She was angry about the way they had treated her and was seeking ammunition to contest her transfer. The Court observed that government agencies could not function properly if every employment grievance was treated as a constitutional matter. Government employees have no First Amendment protection when they speak about their private concerns in the workplace.

Figure 10.2
"Public Concern" Requirement

Whether speech involves a matter of public or private concern is determined from the:

1. *Content.* Speech alleging official misconduct, waste of public funds, systematic discrimination, and hazards to public health or safety are always a matter of public concern. Speech that deals with personnel grievances and internal office affairs is almost never a matter of private concern.
2. *Form*, including whether the speech was addressed to a public or private audience.
3. *Context*, such as whether the communication was made against the background of an employment dispute or had a broader public purpose.

Content is the most important consideration in applying the public concern test. Some topics like allegations of official misconduct,[18] waste of public funds,[19]

---

[18] *See, e.g.*, Markos v. City of Atlanta, Tex., *supra* note 11 (attempted cover up of excessive force incident); Oladeine v. City of Birmingham, 230 F.3d 1275 (11th Cir. 2000) (alleged tampering with public records to cover up criminal conduct of mayor's daughter); Dill v. City of Edmond, Okla., 155 F.3d 1193 (10th Cir. 1998) (alleged withholding of exculpatory evidence in a murder case); Putnam v. Town of Saugus, Mass., 365 F. Supp. 2d 151 (D. Mass. 2005) (testimony before state ethics committee that the police chief ordered officers not to arrest an apparently intoxicated town selectman for drunken driving); Bergeron v. Cabral, 535 F. Supp. 2d 204 (D. Mass. 2008) (stating that official malfeasance, abuse of office, and neglect of duties are matters of inherent public concern); Branton v. City of Dallas, 272 F.3d 730 (5th Cir. 2001) (observing that "[t]here is perhaps no subset of "matters of public concern" more important than bringing official misconduct to light").

[19] For a sampling of cases finding the employee's speech addressed a matter of public concern, *see, e.g.*, Chappel v. Montgomery County Fire Protection District No. 1, 131 F.3d 564 (6th Cir. 1997) (allegations of corruption and misappropriation of public funds are inherently matters of public concern); Wulf v. City of Wichita, 883 F.2d 842 (10th Cir. 1989) (allegation that chief misappropriated and misused public funds, dealt with matter of public concern); Johnson v. Multnomah County, 48 F.3d 420,

discrimination by public agencies,[20] and hazards to the public health and safety[21] are *inherently* matters of *public concern* because they raise issues critical to the public's evaluation of the performance of their government. Other topics, such as private personnel grievances, individual employment disputes, and workaday internal office matters *never* reach this level because they involve matters that concern only the employees involved and others who work inside the agency.[22]

Most work-related topics fall between these extremes. When a topic is neither inherently a matter of public concern or inherently not a matter of public concern, the form and context of the speech take on added importance. The fact that the communication was made internally, arose in the context of an employment dispute,

---

425 (9th Cir.1995); Roth v. Veteran's Admin., 856 F.2d 1401 (9th Cir. 1988) ("The misuse of public funds, wastefulness, and inefficiency in managing and operating government entities are matters of inherent public concern.").

[20] *See*, *e.g.*, Robinson v. York, 566 F.3d 817 (9th Cir. 2009) (testimony in a class action lawsuit that county had engaged in systematic discrimination related to a matter of public concern); Mandell v. County of Suffolk, 316 F.3d 368 (2d Cir. 2003) (deputy police inspector's testimony before public safety committee criticizing police department's systemic racism and anti-Semitism was on a matter of public concern").

[21] For cases finding that the employee's speech addressed a matter of public concern, *see*, *e.g.*, Abad v. City of Marathon, *Fl.*, 472 F. Supp. 2d 1374 (S.D. Fla. 2007) (media comment that quality of services provided by firefighters and paramedics was at risk due to an insufficient number of emergency workers and below average wages); Pattee v. Georgia Ports Authority, 477 F. Supp. 2d 1253 (S.D. Ga. 2006) (complaint made to Georgia's Homeland Security Task Force about security flaws at the Port of Savannah where the officer worked); Wallace v. Suffolk County Police Dept., 396 F. Supp. 2d 251 (E.D.N.Y. 2005) (criticism of police department's emergency services unit for inadequate training protocols and equipment); Lauretano v. Spada, 339 F. Supp. 2d 391 (D. Conn. 2004) (criticism of police department's systematic failure to develop proper procedures for investigating and prosecuting child sexual assault cases); Bates v. Mackay, 321 F. Supp. 2d 173 (D. Mass. 2004) (letter to newspaper discussing safety issues related to inadequate security at night clubs); Campbell v. Towse, 99 F.3d 820 (7th Cir. 1996) (expressing view that community-oriented police program carried a risk of compromising the department's ability to assure the safety of all segments of the public); Biggs v. Village of Dupo, 892 F.2d 1298 (7th Cir. 1990) (comment on inadequate police funding); Moore v. City of Kilgore, Tex., 877 F.2d 364 (5th Cir. 1989) (media comment about staff shortages).

[22] For cases holding that the employee's speech did not address a matter of public concern, *see*, *e.g.*, **Connick v. Meyers,** *supra* **note 2**; Borough of Duryea, Pennsylvania v. Guarnieri, _ U.S. _,131 S. Ct. 2488, 180 L. Ed. 2d 408 (2011) (employee grievance regarding changes in his duties); Alexander v. Eeds, 392 F.3d 138 (5th Cir. 2004) (criticism of promotional process); Tiltti v. Weise, 155 F.3d 596 (2d Cir. 1998) (speech expressing dissatisfaction with work assignments, working conditions, personnel actions, and other employee grievances); Potter v. Arkansas Game & Fish Comm'n, 839 F. Supp. 638 (E.D. Ark. 1993) (employee speech pertaining to distrust of his supervisors); Gros v. The Port Washington Police Dist., 944 F. Supp. 1072 (E.D.N.Y. 1996) (officer's speech involving his own promotion); Murray v. Gardner, 741 F.2d 434 (D.C. Cir. 1984) (speech criticizing of method used to determine layoffs).

or was motivated by self-interest may prompt the court to conclude that the speech does not involve a matter of public concern.[23]

C. Balancing the Value of the Officer's Speech Against Its Adverse Effect on the Police Department

The final step requires the court to balance the value of the officer's speech against its adverse effect on the police department.[24] On the officer's side, the court will consider not only the officer's interest in speaking, but also the public's interest in hearing what the officer had to say.[25] On the department's side, the court will consider whether the speech damaged close working relationships for which personal loyalty and confidence are necessary, undermined the authority of superiors, caused morale problems, impaired the officer's ability to perform his duties, or otherwise interfered with the normal operation of the police department.[26]

Officers disciplined for speech face an uphill battle and few make it to the top. Courts regard police departments as paramilitary organizations and give them wider latitude in their decisions regarding discipline than other government agencies.[27] If the officer's speech has an adverse effect on the police department, the balance will be struck in the department's favor unless the speech addresses a matter of highest

---

[23]   *See, e.g.*, Borough of Duryea, Pennsylvania v. Guarnieri, *supra* note 22 ("The forum in which a petition is lodged will be relevant to the determination of whether the petition relates to a matter of public concern. A petition filed with an employer using an internal grievance procedure in many cases will not seek to communicate to the public or to advance a political or social point of view beyond the employment context."); Marcos v. City of Atlanta, *supra* note 11 (observing that "[i]n a close case, when the subject matter of a statement is only marginally related to issues of public concern, the fact that it was made because of a grudge or other private interest or to co-workers rather than to the press may lead the court to conclude that the statement does not substantially involve a matter of public concern").

[24]   Pickering v. Board of Education, *supra* note 2.

[25]   In Pickering v. Board of Education, *supra* note 2, the Court has noted that government employees are "members of a community most likely to have informed and definite opinions" about problems in the agency where they work and that "[t]he interest at stake is as much the public's interest in receiving informed opinion as it is the employee's own right to disseminate it."

[26]   *See, e.g.*, Rankin v. McPherson, 483 U.S. 378, 107 S. Ct. 2891, 97 L. Ed. 2d 811 (1968) (relevant considerations on the employer's side include whether the speech "impairs discipline by superiors or harmony among co-workers, has a detrimental impact on close working relationships for which personal loyalty and confidence are necessary, or impedes the performance of the speaker's duties or interferes with the regular operation of the enterprise").

[27]   *See, e.g.*, Nixon v. Houston, *supra* note 6 (observing that because police departments function as paramilitary organizations, they are entitled to more latitude in their decisions regarding discipline than an ordinary government employer); Stanley v. City of Dalton, Georgia, 219 F.3d 1280 (11th Cir. 2000) (stating that police departments have a stronger interest in maintaining close working relationships, mutual respect, discipline, and trust than other government agencies); Busby v. City of Orlando, 931 F.2d 764 (11th Cir. 1991) (quasi-military organizations such as law enforcement agencies have a unique need for maintaining loyalty, discipline, and good working relationships).

public concern.[28] Communications that exposes malfeasance, breaches of the public trust, and hazards to public health and safety are the most likely to be protected, but not if the communication is made in carrying out official duties.[29]

Figure 10.3
First Amendment Protection for Work-Related Speech on a Matter of Public Concern

> If the officer prevails on the first two inquiries, protection will be determined by balancing:
>
> 1.   the value of the officer's speech against
> 2.   its adverse effect on the police department.

D. Off-Duty Speech Away from the Workplace on Subjects Unrelated to the Speaker's Employment

The police department's legitimate interests as an employer do not end when the officer leaves the workplace. Officers can be disciplined for off-duty speech if their speech impairs the police department's efficiency or brings their profession into

---

[28]   For cases striking the balance in the police department's favor, *see, e.g.*, Magri v. Giarrusso, 379 F. Supp. 353 (E.D. La. 1974) (upholding dismissal of police sergeant who, as head of the police union, made a public statement during a battle about pay raises in which he called the police superintendent a "coward" and a "liar" and demanded his resignation); Kokkinis v. Ivkovich, 185 F.3d 840 (7th Cir. 1999) (affirming dismissal for stating during a televised interview that everyone was afraid of the police chief's vindictiveness, and that if anyone dared to question one of the chief's decisions, that person's life would be "made miserable."); Greer v. Amesqua, 212 F.3d 358 (7th Cir. 2000) (affirming dismissal for accusing fire chief in a news release of favoring homosexuals and imposing overly lenient discipline on female firefighters); Tyler v. City of Mountain Home, Ark., 72 F.3d 568 (8th Cir. 1995) (upholding disciplinary measures for violating chain of command in writing letter to another law enforcement agency); Ely v. Honnaker, 451 F. Supp. 16 (W.D. Va. 1977), *aff'd*, 588 F.2d 1348 (4th Cir. 1978) (upholding dismissal for discussing an ongoing investigation into a suspected prostitute ring with a television reporter).

[29]   *See, e.g.*, **Connick v. Myers**, *supra* **note 2** (noting that speech merits strong First Amendment protection when employee seeks to bring to light actual or potential wrongdoing or breach of the public trust); Hufford v. McEnaney, 249 F.3d 1142 (9th Cir. 2001) ("The public's interest in learning about illegal conduct by public officials and other matters at the core of First Amendment protection outweighs a state employer's interest in avoiding a mere potential disturbance to the workplace."); Solomon v. Royal Oak Twp., 842 F.2d 862 (6th Cir. 1988) (overturning termination for breaching department confidentiality rules by informing newspaper reporter about corruption within the police department, stating that "the public interest in the disclosure of corruption outweighs the state's interest in confidentiality").

disrepute.[30] In *City of San Diego, California v. Roe*,[31] the Supreme Court upheld the dismissal of a police officer who was fired after his supervisor discovered he was selling sexually explicit videos on the Internet that depicted him stripping off a police uniform and masturbating. The Court stated:

> ... Although Roe's activities took place outside the workplace and purported to be about subjects not related to his employment, the SDPD demonstrated legitimate and substantial interests of its own that were compromised by his speech. Far from confining his activities to speech unrelated to his employment, Roe took deliberate steps to link his videos and other wares to his police work, all in a way injurious to his employer. The use of the uniform, the law enforcement reference in the Web site, the listing of the speaker as in the field of law enforcement, and the debased parody of an officer performing indecent acts while in the course of official duties brought the mission of the employer and the professionalism of its officers into serious disrepute.

Police officers can also be disciplined for off-duty speech that is racially derogatory or bigoted. In *Locurto v. Giuliani*,[32] the court upheld the dismissal of three officers who blackened their faces, put on Afro wigs, and poked fun at African-Americans during a Labor Day Parade. The court stated that the department's interest in maintaining a relationship of trust with the communities it serves outweighed the interest of the officers in publicly expressing their views on race. The same sentiments were expressed in another case[33] involving a police officer who was fired for disseminating anti-black

---

[30]   *See, e.g.*, City of San Diego v. John Roe, 543 U.S. 77, 80, 125 S. Ct. 521, 160 L. Ed. 2d 410 (2004) (upholding officer's termination for eBay sale of home videos depicting the officer stripping off a generic police uniform and masturbating); Thaeter v. Palm Beach County Sheriff's Office, 449 F.3d 1342 (11th Cir. 2006) (affirming dismissal for participating in pornographic videos offered for paid viewing on the Internet); Dibble v. City of Chandler, 515 F.3d 918 (9th Cir. 2008) (upholding dismissal for maintaining a sexually explicit Web site featuring officer and wife); **Locurto v. Giuliani, 447 F.3d 159 (2d Cir. 2006)** (upholding dismissal for mocking African-Americans during a Labor Day Parade). However, police departments cannot restrict off-duty expressive activities that have no real potential to adversely affect the department. *See, e.g.*, United States v. Treasury Employees, 513 U.S. 454, 115 S. Ct. 1003, 130 L. Ed.2d 964 (1995) (striking down a ban on accepting fees for article writing and speech making); Ramirez v. U.S. Customs and Border Protection, 477 F. Supp. 2d 150 (D. D.C. 2007) (striking down order directing border patrol officer to resign from serving on nonpartisan small town city council); Edwards v. City of Goldsboro, 178 F.3d 231 (4th Cir. 1991) (overturning discipline for teaching public course on concealed handgun safety); Flanagan v. Munger, 890 F.2d 1557 (10th Cir. 1989) (overturning discipline for owning an interest in a video store that rented videos, a small portion of which were sexually explicit).

[31]   *Supra* note 30.

[32]   ***Supra* note 30.**

[33]   Pappas v. Giuliani, 290 F.3d 143 (2d Cir. 2002). *See also* Pereira v. Commissioner of Social Services, 432 Mass. 251, 733 N. E. 2d 112 (Mass. 2000) (upholding termination for telling a racist joke in a speech at a retirement dinner); Tindle v. Caudell, 56 F.3d 966 (8th Cir. 1995) (upholding discipline for appearing at a Halloween party in blackface, wearing bib overalls and a curly wig, and carrying a watermelon); Karins v. Atlantic City, 152 N.J. 532, 706 A.2d 706 (1998) (upholding discipline for off-duty firefighter's directing of racial epithet at on-duty police officer during traffic stop); City of Indianapolis v. Heath, 686 N.E.2d 940 (Ind. Ct. App. 1997) (upholding discipline for making off-duty anti-Semitic remark at a public meeting).

and anti-Semitic materials. Affirming the dismissal, the Court stated that "[t]he effectiveness of a city's police department depends importantly on the respect and trust of the community and on the perception in the community that it enforces the law fairly, even-handedly, and without bias. If the police department treats a segment of the population of any race, religion, gender, national origin, or sexual preference, etc., with contempt, so that the particular minority comes to regard the police as oppressor rather than protector, respect for law enforcement is eroded and the ability of the police to do its work in that community is impaired."

E. Political Activity and Patronage Practices

Many states have laws (called Hatch Acts) that prohibit government employees from taking an active role in political campaigns. The Supreme Court has upheld their constitutionality on the grounds that restrictions on partisan political activity foster impartial execution of the laws and ensure that the government workforce is not used to maintain powerful and corrupt political machines.[34]

Government employees, conversely, enjoy First Amendment protection against discharge because of party affiliation unless they occupy a policymaking position. The age-old practice of cleaning house and restaffing government agencies with patronage appointments was declared unconstitutional in *Elrod v. Burns*[35] on the grounds that it interferes with a government employee's freedom of political beliefs and association. Political affiliation may not be used as a factor in hiring, transfer, or promotion decisions unless the job is a "policymaking position" in which the employee acts as an advisor or spokesperson for an elected official or is privy to confidential information, making party loyalty and shared ideological beliefs an appropriate requirement for the job.[36]

§ 10.3 Fourth Amendment Protection Against Workplace Searches

When the police department acts as a criminal investigator gathering evidence for use in a trial, the Fourth Amendment requires probable cause and usually a search warrant.[37] However, neither requirement applies when the police department, acting as an

---

[34] United Public Workers of America v. Mitchell, 330 U.S. 75, 67 S. Ct. 556, 91 L. Ed. 754 (1947); United States Civil Service Commission v. National Assn. of Letter Carriers, 413 U.S. 548, 93 S. Ct. 2880, 37 L. Ed. 2d 796 (1973); Broadrick v. Oklahoma, 413 U.S. 601, 93 S. Ct. 2908, 37 L. Ed.2d 830 (1973).

[35] 427 U.S. 347, 96 S. Ct. 2673, 49 L. Ed. 2d 547 (1976). *See also* Branti v. Finkel, 445 U.S. 507, 100 S. Ct. 1287, 63 L. Ed. 2d 574 (1980) (holding that an assistant public defender could not be terminated for his political allegiance).

[36] Rutan v. Republican Party of Illinois, 497 U.S. 62, 110 S. Ct. 2729, 111 L. Ed. 2d 52 (1990).

[37] *See* Chapter 4.

employer, conducts a workplace search. The Supreme Court has explained that government employees generally have a diminished expectation of privacy in the workplace, and that requiring probable cause and a search warrant would be unduly burdensome.[38]

A. *Constitutionality of Searching Desks, Lockers, File Cabinets, Computers, and Squad Cars for a Work-Related Purpose*

The Fourth Amendment framework for analyzing government workplace searches was established in *O'Connor v. Ortega*.[39] Application of the Fourth Amendment requires the Court to answer two questions: (1) Did the officer have a reasonable expectation of privacy in the subject of the search? (2) If so, was the police department's work-related intrusion into the officer's privacy justified? Unless the answer to the first question is "yes" and the second "no," the officer has no Fourth Amendment protection.

1. Did the Employee Have a Reasonable Expectation of Privacy in the Location Searched?

Police officers generally fare poorly on the first question, making consideration of the second one unnecessary. No constitutionally protected privacy interest generally exists in a police officer's workstation, desk, locker, file cabinets, squad car, or other departmental property issued for use on the job unless the property has been given over to the officer's exclusive use and no one else has a right of access.[40] If the officer's

---

[38]   O'Connor v. Ortega, 480 U.S. 709, 107 S. Ct. 1492, 94 L. Ed. 2d 714 (1987) (plurality opinion) ("requiring an employer to obtain a warrant whenever the employer wished to enter an employee's office, desk, or file cabinets for a work-related purpose would seriously disrupt the routine conduct of business and would be unduly burdensome"). *See also*, **City of Ontario, California v. Quon, _ U.S. _, 130 S. Ct. 2619, 177 L. Ed. 2d 216 (2010);** Skinner v. Railway Labor Executives' Ass'n, 489 U.S. 602, 109 S. Ct. 1402, 103 L. Ed. 2d 639 (1989); 4 LaFave, Search & Seizure § 10.3(d), at 487–88 (3d ed. 1996) (warrant requirement does not apply when department is engaged in internal investigation of work-related misconduct); Brian R. Lemons, *Public Privacy and Warrantless Workplace Searches of Public Employees*, 7 U. Pa. J. Lab. & Empl. L. (2004).

[39]   *Supra* note 38. *See also* **City of Ontario, California v. Quon, *supra* note 38;** Rakas v. Illinois, 439 U.S. 128, 99 S. Ct. 421, 58 L. Ed. 2d 387 (1978); Gossmeyer v. McDonald, 128 F.3d 481 (7th Cir. 1997); State v. Nelson, 189 W. Va. 778, 434 S. E. 2d 697 (1993).

[40]   Compare Thornton v. University Civil Service Merit Board, 507 N. E. 2d 1262 (Ill. App. Ct. 1987) (police officer had no expectation of privacy in an office shared with others that was not his private office); Sacramento County Deputy Sheriff's Ass'n v. County of Sacramento, 51 Cal. App. 4th 1468, 59 Cal. Rptr. 2d 834 (1997) (jail employee had no reasonable expectation of privacy in office that was not assigned to his exclusive use and that had no lock on the door); *with* O'Connor v. Ortega, *supra* note 38 (reasonable expectation of privacy existed in contents of locked file cabinet in locked office provided for employee's exclusive use); United States v. Taketa, 923 F.2d 665 (9th Cir. 1991) (reasonable expectation of privacy existed in airport DEA agent's office where the office was provided for his exclusive use, was not open to the public, was not subject to regular inspection visits by DEA personnel, and no regulation provided for a right of inspection); United States v. Slanina, 283 F.3d 670 (5th Cir. 2002) (fire marshal had reasonable expectation of privacy in pornographic files stored on his work computer located in his office where: (1) his office was private, (2) the door was kept

workstation is located in an unenclosed space accessible to co-workers or members of the public, no Fourth Amendment protection exists in documents on top of the desk, or even documents inside, if others have keys and regularly enter the desk to retrieve correspondence, files, and reports.[41] The same holds true for an officer's locker; no Fourth Amendment protection exists if the officer's supervisor has a master key or a copy of the combination and routinely enters to remove work-related materials.[42]

Police department regulations can also affect whether an officer's expectation of privacy is reasonable. Police department regulations, for example, commonly reserve the right to inspect lockers and squad cars at any time and for any reason. The retention of an unlimited right of inspection eliminates the existence of a reasonable expectation of privacy.[43] A police officer, for example, does not have a reasonable expectation of privacy in objects placed in the trunk of her patrol car if police department regulations reserve an unlimited right of inspection.[44]

---

locked, (3) access to his computer was protected by a password, and (4) the city had no policy forbidding employees from storing personal information on city computers or warning them that their computer usage would be monitored); Leventhal v. Knapek, 266 F.3d 64 (2nd Cir. 2001) (finding reasonable expectation of privacy in contents of department head's computer where it was (1) located in his private office, (2) he had exclusive use of it, and (3) the agency's computer use policy did not prohibit storage of personal materials on it). *See also*, *generally*, L. Camille Hebert, *Searches of Employer Property in Which Employees Have Interest*, 1 EMPL. PRIVACY LAW § 8:6 (2002).

[41]   O'Connor v. Ortega, *supra* note 38 ("Public employees' expectations of privacy in their offices, desks and file cabinets, like similar expectations of employees in the private sector, may be reduced by virtue of actual office practices and procedures . . ."); United States v. Simons, 206 F.3d 392 (4th Cir. 2000) (holding that in light of employer policy to inspect and monitor Internet activity, the government employee had no reasonable expectation of privacy in files transferred from Internet); Sacramento County Deputy Sheriff's Ass'n v. County of Sacramento, *supra* note 40 (jail employee did not have a reasonable expectation of privacy in an office that was not assigned to his exclusive use and that had no lock on the door).

[42]   Shaffer v. Field, 339 F. Supp. 997 (C. D. Cal. 1972); Moore v. Constantine, 191 A. D. 2d 769, 594 N. Y. S. 2d 395 (1993).

[43]   American Postal Workers Union v. United States Postal Serv., 871 F.2d 556 (6th Cir. 1989) (concluding that employees lacked a reasonable expectation of privacy in lockers because regulations allowed for inspections); Los Angeles Police Protection League v. Gates, 579 F. Supp. 36 (C. D. Cal. 1984) (same); People v. Rosa, 928 P.2d 1365 (Colo. Ct. App. 1996) (same); *but see* United States v. Speights, 557 F.2d 362 (3d Cir. 1977) (reasonable expectation of privacy existed in lockers where officers supplied their own locks and department regulations did not provide for inspections or searches).

[44]   State v. Stoddard, 909 S. W. 2d 454 (Tex. Crim. App. 1994). *See also* People v. Neal, 109 Ill. 2d 216, 486 N.E.2d 898 (1985) (police officer lacked a reasonable expectation of privacy in his patrol car and police-department issued raincoat pouch because both were subject to departmental inspection, with and without notice); Martin v. State, 686 A. 2d 1130 (Md. Ct. App. 1996) (Defendant lacked reasonable expectation of privacy in police vehicle he was authorized to use where department placed restrictions on vehicle's use; vehicle was subject to inspections by supervisor at any time; vehicle could be operated by common key and used by other officers if necessary; and defendant testified that he, in his supervisory capacity, believed he had the right to enter and inspect vehicles similarly entrusted to other officers.).

The same principles apply to workplace searches of computers, e-mail, and text messages. No constitutionally protected privacy interest is recognized in computer files, e-mail, and text-messages sent, received, or downloaded on electronic equipment furnished for use on the job if the police department has an electronic equipment use policy that prohibits personal use, provides for routine monitoring, and reserves a right of access.[45]

However, officers retain a constitutionally protected privacy interest in personal belongings brought into the workplace, such as handbags, lunch pails, closed luggage, and their own vehicle.[46]

2. Was the Police Department's Work-Related Intrusion Justified?

If the officer establishes a reasonable expectation of privacy in the location or object searched, the court will have to decide whether the search was justified. To be justified, the police department must either have: (1) a noninvestigatory work-related reason for the search, or (2) reasonable suspicion that the search will turn up evidence of work related misconduct.[47]

---

[45] *See, e.g.*, United States v. Thorn, 375 F.3d 679 (8th Cir. 2004) (finding no reasonable expectation of privacy in contents of computer where employer's computer use policy prohibited personal use, reserved a right to access to audit use, and specifically provided that employees had no personal right of privacy); Biby v. Board of Regents, of University of Nebraska at Lincoln, 419 F.3d 845 (8th Cir. 2005) (plaintiff lacked a constitutionally protected privacy interest in his work computer, in light of the university policy informing employees not to expect privacy when the university has a legitimate reason to search); United States v. Ziegler, 456 F. 3d 1138 (9th Cir. 2006) (the regular monitoring of the employees' use of workplace computers, issuance of a company policy announcing that such monitoring would take place, and dissemination to employees of a prohibition on using the computer for private matters defeated any privacy expectations employees might have had in their workplace computers); United States v. Simons, *supra* note 41) (finding no legitimate expectation of privacy in Internet use where employer's publicized computer use policy reserved the right to monitor all file transfers, Web sites visited, and e-mail messages). *But see* United States v. Slanina, 283 F.3d 670 (5th Cir. 2002) (finding reasonable expectation of privacy in pornographic files stored on fire marshal's work computer located in his office where: (1) his office was private, (2) the door was kept locked, (3) access to his computer was protected by a password, and (4) city had no policy forbidding employees from storing personal information on city computers or warning them that their computer usage would be monitored); Leventhal v. Knapek, 266 F.3d 64 (2nd Cir. 2001) (finding reasonable expectation of privacy in contents of department head's office computer where it was (1) located in his private office, (2) he had exclusive use of it, and (3) the agency's computer use policy did not prohibit storage of personal materials on it).

[46] *See, e.g.,* O'Connor v. Ortega, *supra* note 38 (Although "the workplace includes those areas and items that are related to work and are generally within the employer's control . . . , not everything that passes through the confines of the business address can be considered part of the workplace context.").

[47] **City of Ontario, Cal. v. Quon, *supra* note 38** (No justification is need when the intrusion on employee's privacy is for a noninvestigatory, work-related reason); O'Connor v. Ortega, *supra* note 38 (A government employer may initiate an investigatory search whenever it has "reasonable grounds for suspecting that the search will turn up evidence that the employee is guilty of work-related misconduct . . . ."); Narducci v. Moore, 572 F. 3d 313 (7th Cir. 2009) (a work-related intrusion on a public employer's privacy is justified when there are reasonable grounds for suspecting that the search will turn up evidence that the employee is guilty of work-related misconduct).

Noninvestigatory workplace searches. The most common reasons for workplace searches are noninvestigatory. The Fourth Amendment allows government employers to intrude on an employee's workplace privacy, with no degree of suspicion, when they have a legitimate, noninvestigatory work-related reason. Entering an employee's locked office in the employee's absence to retrieve a needed report, repair equipment, or empty the wastebasket are examples.[48] The business of the government cannot come to a halt every time an employee with a privacy interest is temporarily away from the job. Noninvestigatory, work-related intrusions on privacy are permitted whenever the employer has a legitimate work reason.

The Supreme Court applied this principle in a case where the police department audited a SWAT Team officer's text messages sent and received on his official pager for a noninvestigative work-related reason.[49] Officer Quon was one of the two highest users of text-messaging services on the police force and regularly exceeded his monthly 25,000 character (*i.e.*, letters, numbers, symbols, etc.) allotment. The police chief requested copies of Quon's text messages covering a two-month period to determine whether the monthly character allotment under the City's contract with its service provider was high enough to cover Quon's work-related use or whether the overage was due to personal use. The audit revealed that most of Quon's on-duty text messages had nothing to do with his job and that many were salacious. The matter was referred to internal affairs and Quon was disciplined.

Quon sued, claiming that the informal arrangement he had with the officer in charge of administering the pager program — that his text messages would not be audited for billing purposes so long as he paid the overage charges — created a reasonable expectation of privacy, undermining the effectiveness of the department's written policy prohibiting employees from making personal use of work-related electronic equipment, and notifying them that they should not expect privacy.

The Supreme Court declined to determine whether Quon's informal billing arrangement created a reasonable expectation of privacy, explaining that it made no difference to the outcome because the audit was performed for the legitimate noninvestigatory purpose of "ensuring that officers were not being forced to pay out of their own pockets for work-related expenses, or on the other hand that the City was not paying for extensive personal communications." The police department needed to know what percent of Quon's text messages was business versus personal to determine whether its contract with the text-messaging service provider was adequate to cover the department's needs. Auditing Quon's usage was a convenient way to acquire this information. The scope of the audit was consistent with this purpose. The police department did not audit all of Quon's text messages; it audited only the ones that were sent and received during working hours, and only during a two-month sample period. Since the police department had a legitimate noninvestigative, work-related reason for performing the audit, and the scope of the audit was not excessive in relation to

---

[48]   *See* authorities *supra* note 47.
[49]   **City of Ontario, Cal. v. Quon**, *supra* note 38.

the need, Quon's Fourth Amendment rights were not violated. The Supreme Court added, as an aside, that employees who need to use their cell phones for personal matters while on the job should purchase and pay for their own if they want privacy.

Figure 10.4
Justification Needed for a Work-Related Search

[handwritten: Non investigatory search = no search warrant/NO RS]

> The justification needed for a search that intrudes on an officer's workplace privacy varies with the police department's reason for searching.
>
> ■ Noninvestigatory workplace searches require no justification beyond a legitimate work-related need.
> ■ Investigatory workplace searches require reasonable suspicion that the search will turn up evidence of work-related misconduct.
> ■ Criminal investigations into work-related misconduct require probable cause and a search warrant.

[handwritten: evidence = search warrant]
[handwritten: Investigatory search = search warrant / R.S.]

Investigatory workplace searches. When a government employer performs a workplace search to discover evidence for use in a disciplinary proceeding, the Fourth Amendment requires a justification. However, the required justification is not probable cause and a search warrant, the standard used in criminal investigations. Work-related investigatory intrusions on privacy are governed by the standard of *reasonable suspicion*.[50] The police department must have reasonable suspicion that the search will turn up evidence that an employee is guilty of work-related misconduct. The *reasonable suspicion* needed for a workplace investigatory search is the same reasonable suspicion that you learned about in Chapters 3 and 4. An anonymous tip that an officer has child pornography in his briefcase, for example, would not justify an investigatory workplace search because an anonymous tip is not reliable enough to establish reasonable suspicion.[51]

Criminal investigations of work-related misconduct. When the police department's role changes from employer to criminal investigator, the requirements of the Fourth Amendment also change. Police officers do not lose their constitutional protection merely because they are employed by the police department. The traditional standard of probable cause and a search warrant applies when the police department

---

[50] *See, e.g.*, O'Connor v. Ortega, *supra* note 38 ("Ordinarily, a search of an employee's office by a supervisor will be 'justified at its inception' when there are reasonable grounds for suspecting that the search will turn up evidence that the employee is guilty of work-related misconduct."); True v. Nebraska, 612 F. 3d 676 (8th Cir. 2010) (holding that search of vehicles belonging to correctional employees parked outside the institution's confines in a location where inmates had no access to them requires reasonable suspicion that the vehicle to be searched contains contraband).

[51] *See, e.g.*, Whiley v. Dep't. of Justice, 328 F. 3d 1346 (Fed. Cir. 2003) (government employee's dismissal for refusing to consent to his employers request to search his car, based on anonymous letter alleging that he kept a loaded 9 mm weapon in it, violated the Fourth Amendment; anonymous letter lacked sufficient indicia of reliability to establish reasonable suspicion).

conducts a criminal investigation.[52] In *Cerrone v. Cahill*,[53] an officer suspected of criminal wrongdoing was transported in a squad car to a second location where he was read his *Miranda* rights, informed that he was the target of a criminal investigation, and questioned for six hours. The court held that the traditional probable cause standard applied, even though the suspected wrongdoing was work-related, because the police were seeking evidence to build a criminal case against him.

The original purpose of the search dictates the standard used to evaluate the constitutionality. If the search is conducted pursuant to an internal investigation, the reasonable suspicion standard applies even though the search turns up evidence that is later offered against the officer in a criminal prosecution.[54]

B. Mandatory Drug Testing

Drug abuse affects all levels of society. No one knows for certain how prevalent this problem is in the ranks of police departments, but considering the high stress levels associated with police work, there is no reason to assume that it is less prevalent here than elsewhere. Many police departments have mandatory drug testing programs. Compulsory production of a urine sample for drug testing involves a search.[55] Consequently, mandatory drug testing must satisfy the Fourth Amendment. Police officers may be forced to undergo drug testing only when (1) the department has reasonable suspicion that they are abusing drugs or (2) the testing is done pursuant to a systematic drug-screening program.

1. Drug Testing Based on Reasonable Suspicion

When the police department selectively singles out a particular officer to undergo drug testing, the Fourth Amendment demands reasonable suspicion of drug use.[56] Reasonable suspicion may derive from a combination of mutually reinforcing facts, such a deficient job performance, unexplained excessive absenteeism, apparent

---

[52] United States v. Taketa, *supra* note 40 ("[W]here the search is conducted by the government employer to further a criminal investigation, the traditional requirements of probable cause and warrant are applicable."); Trujillo v. City of Ontario, 428 F. Supp. 2d 1094 (C.D. Cal. 2006) (same).

[53] 84 F. Supp. 2d 330 (N.D.N.Y. 2000).

[54] *See, e.g.*, United States v. Thorn, *supra* note 45; United States v. Simons, *supra* note 41.

[55] **Schmerber v. California, 384 U.S. 757, 87 S. Ct. 1826, 16 L. Ed. 2d 908 (1966)**; Skinner v. Railway Labor Executives' Ass'n, 489 U.S. 602, 109 S. Ct. 1402, 103 L. Ed. 2d 639 (1989); National Treasury Employees Union v. Von Raab, 489 U.S. 656, 109 S. Ct. 1384, 103 L. Ed. 2d 685 (1989).

[56] Copeland v. Philadelphia Police Department, 840 F.2d 1139 (3d Cir. 1988), *cert. denied*, 490 U.S. 1004, 109 S. Ct. 1639, 104 L. Ed. 2d 153 (1989); Ford v. Dowd, 931 F.2d 1286 (8th Cir. 1991); Jackson v. Gates, 975 F.2d 648 (9th Cir. 1992); Nocera v. New York City Fire Commissioner, 921 F. Supp. 192 (S. D. N. Y. 1996). The suspected drug abuse does not have to involve conduct while on duty. See Palm Bay v. Bauman, 475 So. 2d 1322 (Fla. Dist. Ct. App. 1985) (testing for off-duty drug use justified by physical, mental, and psychological effects of drug use and on the need to have police officers abide by the laws they enforce). The same is true for alcohol testing. Officers may be compelled to undergo alcohol testing based on reasonable suspicion of off-duty alcohol intoxication. *See, e.g.*, Grow v. City of Milwaukee, 84 F. Supp. 2d 990 (E.D. Wis. 2000) (off-duty police officer, encountered under circumstances in which intoxication could present a danger to public safety, may be compelled to undergo alcohol testing based on reasonable suspicion of intoxication).

substance-related impairments, aberrant behavior, and/or financial difficulties.[57] It was found in a case where an officer was arrested for trespassing in a location frequented by drug dealers, failed to report his arrest as department regulations required, and had excessive absenteeism.[58] On the other hand, it did not exist where the department's sole basis for suspecting drug use was the officer's friendship with another officer suspected of drug use.[59]

2. Drug Testing Pursuant to Systematic Screening Programs

Drug impairment can be present before an officer exhibits outward signs, making discovery through close supervision unreliable. Because police officers carry weapons and drive high-speed vehicles, and momentary lapses of attention can cause fatal accidents, police departments have a special need to discover drug abuse before accidents happen. The Fourth Amendment recognizes an exception to the requirement of individualized suspicion when the search serves a special need beyond the general need for crime control.[60] The Supreme Court has held that this exception justifies the establishment of suspicionless drug-screening programs for government employees in safety-sensitive positions, a category that includes police officers.[61] As a result, police officers may be compelled to undergo drug testing, without individualized suspicion, when the testing is conducted as part of a systematic drug-screening program.[62]

To be justifiable under the special needs exception, the process of selection must be nondiscretionary.[63] Testing, for example, may be required at the time of employment; at scheduled periodic intervals; when applying for a promotion[64]; as part of regularly scheduled routine medical exams[65]; after accidents[66] or other triggering events[67]; or based on computerized random selection.[68]

---

[57]   Fraternal Order of Police Lodge No. 5 v. Tucker, 868 F.2d 74 (3d Cir. 1989); Copeland v. Philadelphia Police Department, *supra* note 56.

[58]   Nocera v. New York City Fire Commissioner, *supra* note 56. *See also* Felder v. Kelly, 210 A. D. 2d 78, 619 N. Y. S. 2d (1994).

[59]   Jackson v. Gates, *supra* note 56.

[60]   National Treasury Employees Union v. Von Raab, *supra* note 55.

[61]   *Id.*

[62]   *Id.*

[63]   *Id.*; National Federation of Federal Employees v. Cheney, 884 F. 2d 603 (D.C. Cir. 1989), *cert. denied*, 493 U.S. 1056, 110 S. Ct. 864, 107 L. Ed. 2d 948 (1990); McCloskey v. Honolulu Police Dep't, 71 Haw. 568, 799 P.2d 953 (1990); New Jersey Transit PBA Local 304 v. New Jersey Transit Corp., 151 N. J. 531, 701 A.2d 1243 (1997).

[64]   National Treasury Employees Union v. Von Raab, *supra* note 55 (upholding Customs Service regulation requiring employees seeking transfer or promotions to certain Customs Service positions to submit to urinalysis).

[65]   Wrightsell v. Chicago, 678 F. Supp. 727 (N. D. Ill. 1988).

[66]   Skinner v. Railway Labor Executives' Ass'n, *supra* note 55 (permitting suspicionless drug testing of railroad employees conducted pursuant to government regulations requiring testing of employees involved in major train accidents).

[67]   Delaraba v. Nassau County Police Department, 83 N. Y. 2d 367, 632 N.E.2d 1251, 610 N. Y. S. 2d 928 (1994).

[68]   *Id.*

§ 10.4   Fifth Amendment Protection Against Self-Incrimination

When a police officer is suspected of misconduct, the police department internal affairs division will normally conduct an investigation into whether discipline is warranted. When the investigation involves matters that could lead to a criminal prosecution, there is a clash between the department's need for answers and the officer's Fifth Amendment privilege against self-incrimination. This section explores two related questions. First, can an officer be compelled, under a threat of job termination, to disclose information pertaining to criminal activity? And second, if an officer can be compelled to answer, can the officer's statement be used against her in a criminal prosecution?

The answer to both questions requires a brief review of the self-incrimination clause of the Fifth Amendment. The Fifth Amendment provides that "[n]o person . . . shall be compelled in any criminal case to be a witness against himself." The Fifth Amendment privilege against self-incrimination can be asserted during administrative proceedings, as well as judicial ones.[69] Consequently, police officers undergoing an internal affairs investigation are protected by the Fifth Amendment.

The police department as an employer, nevertheless, has a right to demand that officers account for their official conduct. Departmental regulations frequently make refusal to answer questions relating to an officer's performance of his duties grounds for dismissal.[70] You may be wondering how, if the Fifth Amendment privilege against self-incrimination applies, an officer can be fired for refusing to answer questions that relate to criminal activity.

The answer lies in immunity, a concept that was covered in Chapter 7.[71] Officers can be compelled to answer questions pertaining to criminal activity provided they are granted immunity from the use of compelled statements (and evidence derived from them) in a criminal prosecution. In fact, immunity attaches by operation of law when

---

[69]   Lefkowitz v. Turley, 414 U.S. 70, 77, 94 S. Ct. 316, 322, 38 L. Ed. 2d 274 (1973) ("The [Fifth] Amendment not only protects the individual against being involuntarily called as a witness against himself in a criminal prosecution but also privileges him not to answer official questions put to him in any other proceeding, civil or criminal, formal or informal, where the answers might incriminate him in future criminal proceedings.").

[70]   *See, e.g.*, New York Police Department Patrol Guide, Procedure 206-13 (Jan. 1, 2000) (warning officers that "if [they] refuse to testify or to answer questions relating to the performance of [their] official duties, [they] will be subject to departmental charges, which could result in [their] dismissal from the Police Department"); 1 Los Angeles Police Dep't Manual § 210.47 (2000) ("When police officers acquire knowledge of facts which will tend to incriminate any person, it is their duty to disclose such facts to their superiors and to testify freely concerning such facts when called upon to do so, even at the risk of self-incrimination. It is a violation of duty for police officers to refuse to disclose pertinent facts within their knowledge, and such neglect of duty can result in disciplinary action up to and including termination.") *quoted in* Steven D. Clymer, *Compelled Statements from Police Officers and Garrity Immunity*, 76 N.Y.U. L. Rev. 1309 at fn. 15 (2001).

[71]   Testimony compelled under a grant of immunity was covered in § 7.3(C).

a police officer makes incriminating statements under threat of job termination. This immunity is called *Garrity* immunity because it derives from *Garrity v. New Jersey.*[72]

In *Garrity*, a police officer undergoing an internal investigation for "fixing" traffic tickets was told that he could invoke the Fifth Amendment, but that if he did so, he would be discharged. The officer disclosed incriminating information for which he was later prosecuted. The Supreme Court ruled that when an officer makes a statement under threat of dismissal for refusing to answer, the statement is compelled and cannot be used against the officer in a criminal prosecution. In a subsequent case,[73] the Court explained that the Fifth Amendment does not bar compulsion to extract self-incriminating statements. Rather, it bars the courtroom use of compelled statements in the criminal prosecution of the maker. However, no violation occurs if the statement is never used. Accordingly, the department may threaten an officer with dismissal to obtain information needed for an internal investigation,[74] but is limited to making disciplinary use, because compelled statements may not be used in a criminal prosecution of the maker.[75]

Officers undergoing internal affairs investigations may be tempted to deny the charges and lie, but this, too, will lead to forfeiture of their job if the department has other evidence.[76]

---

[72] 385 U.S. 493, 87 S. Ct. 616, 17 L. Ed. 2d 562 (1967) (Fifth Amendment prohibits use in subsequent criminal proceedings of statements obtained under threat of removal from office). For a discussion of "*Garrity* immunity," *see*, *generally*, Steven D. Clymer, *supra* note 70; J. Michael McGuinness, *Representing Law Enforcement Officers in Personnel Disputes and Employment Litigation*, 77 Am. Jur. Trials 1, § 10 (2000); Kate E. Bloch, *Police Officers Accused of Crime: Prosecutorial and Fifth Amendment Risks Posed by Police-Elicited "Use Immunized" Statements*, 1992 U. Ill. L. Rev. 625 (1992). For cases applying "*Garrity* immunity," *see* United States v. Koon, 34 F.3d 1416 (9th Cir. 1994); United States. v. Vangates, 287 F.3d 1315 (11th Cir. 2002).

[73] Chavez v. Martinez, 538 U.S. 760, 123 S. Ct. 1994, 155 L. Ed. 2d 984 (2003) ("[G]overnments may penalize public employees . . . with loss of their jobs . . . to induce them to respond to relevant inquiries, so long as the answers elicited (and their fruits) are immunized from use in any criminal case against the speaker.").

[74] **Lingler v. Fechko, 312 F.3d 237 (6th Cir. 2002)** (Fifth Amendment is not violated by compelling officers to furnish potentially incriminating information as part of an internal affairs investigation where the statement was not used against them in a criminal prosecution); Wiley v. Mayor & City Council of Baltimore, 58 F.3d 773 (4th Cir. 1995) (officers' Fifth Amendment rights were not violated when they were required as a condition of continued employment to take a polygraph examination during an internal investigation into a shooting incident, but were not asked to waive their Fifth Amendment privilege against self-incrimination and were never charged with any offense); Aguilera v. Baca, 394 F. Supp. 2d 1203 (C.D. Cal. 2005) (coercive questioning of police officers suspected of assaulting a civilian did not violate their Fifth Amendment privilege against self-incrimination where they were not prosecuted for the assault); Erwin v. Price, 778 F.2d 668 (11th Cir. 1986) (affirming dismissal of police officer who refused to answer specific questions about an alleged gun-pointing incident).

[75] *See, e.g.*, Driebel v. Milwaukee, 298 F.3d 622 fn. 8 (7th Cir. 2002); Riggins v. Walter, 279 F.3d 422 (7th Cir. 1995) (per curiam); Confederation of Police v. Conlisk, 489 F 2d 891 (7th Cir. 1973).

[76] LaChance v. Erickson, 522 U.S. 262, 118 S. Ct. 753, 130 L. Ed. 2d 695 (1998). *See also* United States v. Veal, 153 F.3d 1233 (11th Cir. 1998) (the Fifth Amendment does not protect an officer who makes false statements under oath during an internal investigation from a later criminal prosecution for perjury).

§ 10.5 Fourteenth Amendment Protection for a Police Officer's Personal Liberty

Police department regulations often impose significant restrictions on a police officer's liberty, both on and off the job. In fact, the profession is more highly regulated than any career outside the military. One court commented on this while discussing a 72-page manual of police department rules and regulations.[77] We have culled a few of the regulations mentioned in the opinion to provide a sampling of the range of subjects that police department regulations address:

- **Standard of Conduct.** Members and employees shall conduct their private and professional lives in such a manner as to avoid bringing the department into disrepute.

- **Debts — Incurring and Payment.** Members and employees shall pay all just debts and legal liabilities incurred by them.

- **Persons and Places of Bad Reputation.** Members and employees shall not frequent places of bad reputation, nor associate with persons of bad reputation, except as may be required in the course of police duty.

- **Liquor.** Employees of the department shall refrain from drinking intoxicating beverages for a period of at least four (4) hours before going on duty.

- **Smoking While On Duty.** Members shall not smoke on duty while in direct contact with the public nor when in uniform in public view, except that smoking is permitted in public view at mealtimes and while patrolling in police automobiles, at which times it shall be as inconspicuous as possible.

- **Grooming.** Hair shall be evenly trimmed at all times while on duty. The hair shall at no point extend downward over the shirt collar in normal posture. Sideburns shall not extend below the bottom of the ear. The maximum width at the bottom of the sideburns shall not exceed 1¾ inches. A clean-shaven appearance is required, except that mustaches are permitted. Mustaches shall be neatly trimmed and shall not extend more than ¼inch beyond the corners of the mouth nor more than ¼inch below the corners of the mouth. Remainder of the face shall be clean shaven.

- **Use of Derogatory Terms.** Members and employees shall neither speak disparagingly of any race or minority group, nor refer to them in insolent or insulting terms of speech, whether prisoners or otherwise.

The justification for heightened regulation is found in the unique service that police officers perform a service that sets them apart from ordinary citizens and from civil servants in other branches of government. Courts often use the phrase "paramilitary organization" to explain why restrictions on a police officer's conduct are condoned

[77] *Policemen's Benevolent Association of New Jersey*, Local 318 v. Township of Washington, 850 F.2d 133 (3d Cir. 1988).

that would not be condoned if imposed on employees in other branches of government service. The explanation goes as follows:

> Police officers are members of quasi-military organizations called upon for duty at all times, armed at almost all times, and exercising the most awesome and dangerous power that a democratic state possesses with respect to its residents — the power to use lawful force to arrest and detain them. The need in a democratic society for public confidence, respect and approbation of the public officials on whom the state confers that awesome power is significantly greater than the state's need to instill confidence in the integrity of [other employees].[78]

When a police officer is unable to find a constitutional basis for challenging a police department regulation under any specific Bill of Rights guarantee, the officer is likely to claim that the regulation violates substantive due process.[79] This theory is grounded in the Fourteenth Amendment, which prohibits the government from arbitrarily depriving individuals of their liberty. In challenging a regulation on this ground, the officer is claiming that the regulation is arbitrary. This theory rarely succeeds because the officer must convince the court that the regulation has no rational relationship to any legitimate interest of the police department as an employer.[80] Perception of the police department as a paramilitary organization makes this task difficult indeed.

Police department regulations most frequently challenged are discussed below.

A. *Regulation of Height, Weight, Grooming, and Personal Appearance*

No one seriously questions the authority of police departments to require police officers to wear uniforms and to be neat and clean in appearance. However, police department regulations often go beyond this and regulate height, weight, hairstyle, and other aspects of an officer's personal appearance.

In *Kelley v. Johnson*,[81] a Patrolmen's Benevolent Association lodged an unsuccessful attack on a police department grooming standard that prescribed style and length of hair and prohibited beards and goatees. The Supreme Court pointed to the fact that the overwhelming majority of police departments require officers to wear uniforms and regulate their appearance as evidence that those in charge of directing the operations of police department regard similarity in appearance as desirable. Whether the reason was to make police officers readily recognizable to the public or for the *esprit de corps* that similarity in appearance fosters did not matter — either justification was sufficient to defeat the plaintiff's claim that the regulation had no rational relationship to the department's interest as an employer.

Challenges to police department regulations establishing *maximum* weight restrictions have met the same fate.[82] Police departments have a legitimate interest in an

---

[78]   *Id.*
[79]   Substantive due process was covered in § 1.15(B).
[80]   Kelley v. Johnson, 425 U.S. 238, 96 S. Ct. 1440, 47 L. Ed. 2d 708 (1976).
[81]   *Id.*
[82]   *See, e.g.*, Dade County v. Wolf, 274 So. 2d 584 (Fla. 1973), *cert. denied*, 414 U.S. 1116, 94 S. Ct. 849, 38 L. Ed. 2d 743 (1973); Gray v. City of Florissant, 588 S. W. 2d 722 (Mo. 1979).

officer's weight because obesity is likely to make it difficult for an officer to execute some of the more strenuous tasks that the job requires. Constitutional challenges to regulations establishing maximum weights have, therefore, failed.

Challenges to police department regulations establishing *minimum* height and weight, in contrast, often succeed — but not on constitutional grounds. Title VII of the Civil Rights Act of 1964 prohibits employers from discriminating against job applicants based on their race, color, religion, gender, or national origin.[83] Minimum height and weight requirements disproportionately disqualify women and members of certain minority groups from securing jobs as police officers. Requirements that have this effect are illegal under Title VII unless they measure traits that are necessary for the successful performance of the job.[84] Police departments have had difficulty sustaining minimum height and weight requirements.[85]

B. Citizenship Requirements

A majority of states require police officers to be United States citizens. In *Foley v. Connelie*,[86] a resident alien, turned down for a position as a New York state trooper, challenged this requirement as a denial of equal protection of the laws. The Supreme Court disagreed. Pointing out that police officers are vested with broad discretion that operates "in the most sensitive areas of daily life," the Court held that it is legitimate for states to confine police employment to those whom it "may reasonably presume to be more familiar with and sympathetic to American traditions."

C. Residency Requirements

Many jurisdictions also have residency rules, requiring police officers to live in the political subdivision in which they are employed. The job relatedness of residency requirements was upheld in *McCarthy v. Philadelphia Civil Service Commission*[87] on the grounds that residing in the district improves an officer's job effectiveness by increasing an officer's knowledge of local geography, problems of the local community, and stake in its progress, and decreases problems of tardiness.

D. Restrictions on Outside Employment

Police officers are generally prohibited from holding outside employment. Courts have shown little sympathy to suits challenging moonlighting restrictions, explaining that because police officers are required to make split-second decisions that tax their mental and physical capabilities to the limits, it is reasonable for police

---

[83]	Title VII protection against employment discrimination is discussed in § 10.7 *infra*.
[84]	Evans, Height, Weight and Physical Agility Requirements: Title VII and Public Safety Employment, 8 J. Pol. Sci. & Admin. 414 (1980).
[85]	**Dothard v. Rawlinson, 433 U.S. 321, 97 S. Ct. 2720, 53 L. Ed. 2d 786 (1977).**
[86]	435 U.S. 291, 98 S. Ct. 1067, 55 L. Ed. 2d 287 (1978).
[87]	424 U.S. 645, 96 S. Ct. 1154, 47 L. Ed. 2d 366 (1976).

departments to insist that officers forego other employment that might lead to fatigue on the job.[88]

E. Regulation of Smoking

As society has become more health conscious, regulations banning smoking in the workplace are becoming increasingly common. In *Grusendorf v. City of Oklahoma City*,[89] a firefighter trainee unsuccessfully challenged a fire department regulation that prohibited firefighters from smoking cigarettes either on or off duty for one year after being hired. The officer argued that this regulation impermissibly infringed on his Fourteenth Amendment liberty outside the workplace. The court disagreed. Noting that public safety employers have a legitimate interest in the health and fitness of employees, the court rejected the officer's claim that a total ban on smoking was arbitrary.

F. Off-Duty Sexual Activity

Police department regulations typically require police officers to conduct their private lives so as avoid bringing the department into disrepute.[90] When a police officer is disciplined for having an extramarital affair, the court must decide whether it is legitimate for a police department to delve into this aspect of an officer's life. It is unquestionably legitimate when the officer's private life adversely affects the police department.[91] Dismissal, for example, was upheld in a case in which a police chief's adulterous affair became front-page news when he was sued for nonsupport of an illegitimate child.[92] Dismissals have also been upheld when the officer's affair is with another officer or with the spouse of another officer.[93] When officers keep their sexual activity out of the workplace and off the front page, case law is divided on whether they can be disciplined for having an illicit affair. Older cases treated police

---

[88]   Reichelderfer v. Ihrie, 59 F.2d 873 (D.C. Cir. 1932), *cert. denied*, 287 U.S. 631, 53 S. Ct. 82, 77 L. Ed. 2d 547 (1932); Hayes v. Civil Service Comm'n, 348 Ill. App. 346, 108 N.E.2d 505 (1952); Hopwood v. Paducah, 424 S. W. 2d 134 (Ky. 1968); Isola v. Belmar, 112 A. 2d 738 (N. J. 1955); Flood v. Kennedy, 12 N. Y. 2d 345, 239 N. Y. S. 2d 665, 190 N. E. 2d 13 (1963). *But see* Firemen v. City of Crowley, 280 So. 2d 897 (La. 1973).

[89]   816 F.2d 539 (10th Cir. 1987).

[90]   *See, e.g.*, City of San Diego, Cal. v. Roe, *supra* note 30 (affirming dismissal of police for auctioning on eBay videotapes of himself him stripping off his police uniform and masturbating).

[91]   *See, e.g.*, Fugate v. Phoenix Civil Service Board, 791 F.2d 736 (9th Cir. 1986) (affirming discharge for patronizing prostitutes).

[92]   Borough of Riegelsville v. Miller, 162 Pa. Commw. 654, 939 A. 2d 1258 (1994).

[93]   Mercure v. Van Buren Township, 81 F. Supp. 2d 814 (E.D. Mich. 2000) (affirming dismissal for having affair with estranged wife of superior officer); City of Sherman v. Henry, 928 S. W. 2d 464 (Tex. 1996) (same); Shawgo v. Spradlin, 701 F.2d 470 (5th Cir. 1983) (upholding a police department's anti-cohabitation policy forbidding members of the department, especially those different in rank, to share an apartment or to cohabit).

officers as role models, placed them on a moral pedestal and punished them when they fell off.[94] Modern cases, however, generally require proof that a police officer's off-duty sexual conduct adversely affected the police department.[95]

§ 10.6 Procedural Due Process in Police Disciplinary Actions

The Fourteenth Amendment may entitle an officer facing termination, suspension, or demotion to a hearing to contest whether grounds exist for the department's action.[96] This right is rooted in the Fourteenth Amendment, which provides that no state shall deprive any person of *life, liberty,* or *property* without due process. Accordingly, this right is available only to officers who have either a property right in their job or a liberty interest in pursuing their chosen profession.[97]

To have a property right in a job, the officer's job must be one that cannot be taken away without just cause.[98] "Just cause" is a legal concept that refers to serious

---

[94] Fabio v. Civil Service Commission of the City of Philadelphia, 30 Pa. Commw. 203, 373 A.2d 751 (1977), *aff'd*, 489 Pa. 309, 414 A.2d 82 (1980) (rejecting claim that police officer's constitutional rights were violated as a result of his dismissal for adultery; observing that police officers are held to a higher standard of conduct than other citizens).

[95] Briggs v. North Muskegon Police Dep't, 563 F. Supp. 585 (W. D. Mich. 1983), *aff'd mem.*, 746 F.2d 1475 (6th Cir. 1984), *cert. denied*, 473 U.S. 909, 105 S. Ct. 3535, 87 L. Ed. 2d 659 (1985) (married police officer's constitutional rights were violated when he was fired for living with a married woman who was not his wife); Thorne v. City of El Segundo, 726 F.2d 459 (9th Cir. 1983), *cert. denied*, 469 U.S. 979, 105 S. Ct. 380, 83 L. Ed. 2d 315 (1984) (female applicant's constitutional rights were violated when she was denied employment as a police officer because of prior affair with a married police officer on the force); Reuter v. Skipper, 832 F. Supp. 1420 (D. Or. 1993) (female corrections officer could not be terminated for having relationship with ex-felon).

[96] Board of Regents v. Roth, 408 U.S. 564, 92 S. Ct. 2701, 33 L. Ed. 2d 548 (1972); Cleveland Bd. of Education v. Loudermill, 470 U.S. 532, 105 S. Ct.1487, 84 L. Ed. 2d 494 (1985). Police officers may also have other sources of hearing rights. State statutes, local ordinances, department regulations, and collective bargaining agreement, for example, may entitle police officers to a hearing. These sources of hearing rights are beyond the scope of this chapter.

[97] A life, liberty, or property interest is necessary to claim procedural protection under the Fourteenth Amendment. *See, e.g.,* Wilkinson v. Austin, 545 U.S. 209, 125 S. Ct. 2384, 162 L. Ed. 2d 175 (2005) ("The Fourteenth Amendment's due process clause protects persons against deprivations of life, liberty, or property, and those who seek to invoke its procedural protection must establish that one of those interests are at stake."); Board of Regents v. Roth, *supra* note 96 ("To have a property interest in a benefit, a person . . . must . . . have a legitimate claim of entitlement . . ."); Cleveland Bd. of Education v. Loudermill, *supra* note 96 (classified civil service employee had property interest in continued employment because a state statute provided that such employees could not be dismissed except for certain specified reasons); Ciambriello v. County of Nassau, 292 F.3d 307 (2d Cir. 2002) (A police officer has a property interest in continued employment if the officer is guaranteed continued employment absent just cause for discharge).

[98] *See* authorities *supra* notes 96 and 97.

misconduct, not occasional lateness or isolated acts of rudeness.[99] Whether a property right exists depends on sources outside the Fourth Amendment, such as personnel regulations, employee handbooks, ordinances, and collective bargaining agreements.[100] Probationary officers do not have a property right in their job.[101] They can be fired for any reason or no reason at all.

The Fourteenth Amendment entitles employees who have a property right in their job to a hearing to contest the department's decision to terminate them.[102] A hearing provides a valuable safeguard against mistaken decisions. The hearing must, at a minimum, include: (1) notice of the charges, (2) a hearing before an impartial decision maker, (3) an opportunity to challenge the department's evidence, and (4) an opportunity to present testimony.[103]

The Fourteenth Amendment also protects "liberty." Even though probationary officers lack a property right in their job, they have a "liberty interest" in pursuing their chosen profession.[104] This interest is infringed if they are terminated based on stigmatizing charges, disclosed to the public, which could foreclose their ability to obtain other employment in the law enforcement field.[105] Should this happen, they, too, are entitled to a hearing, but not a hearing to try to get their job back. Their hearing serves a lesser purpose — it provides an opportunity to clear their name.[106]

The right to a name-clearing hearing is available only if the charges on which a probationary officer is dismissed are both stigmatizing and disclosed to the public.

---

[99]   J. Michael McGuinness, *Representing Law Enforcement Officers in Personnel Disputes and Employment Litigation*, 77 AM. JUR. TRIALS 1, at § 15 (2000).

[100] Bishop v. Wood, 426 U.S. 341, 344, 96 S. Ct. 2074, 2077, 48 L. Ed. 2d 684 (1976); Golem v. Village of Put-In Bay, 222 F. Supp. 2d 924 (N.D. Ohio 2002).

[101] Blanding v. Pennsylvania State Police,12 F.3d 1303 (3d Cir. 1993) (probationary officer did not have property right in continued employment); Davis v. City of Chicago, 841 F.2d 186 (7th Cir. 1988) (same); Pipkin v. Pennsylvania State Police, 693 A.2d 190 (Pa. 1997) (same).

[102] *See* authorities *supra* note 96.

[103] *Id*.; Schweiker v. McClure, 456 U.S. 188, 102 S. Ct. 1665, 72 L. Ed. 2d 1 (1982); Brown v. Los Angeles, 102 Cal. App. 4th 155, 125 Cal. Rptr. 2d 474 (2002) ("At a minimum, an individual entitled to procedural due process should be accorded: written notice of the grounds for the disciplinary measures; disclosure of the evidence supporting the disciplinary grounds; the right to present witnesses and to confront adverse witnesses; the right to be represented by counsel; a fair and impartial decision maker; and a written statement from the fact finder listing the evidence relied upon and the reasons for the determination made.").

[104] Paul v. Davis, 424 U.S. 693, 96 S. Ct. 1155, 47 L. Ed. 2d 405 (1976); Graham v. Johnson, 249 F. Supp. 2d 563 (E. D. Pa. 2003) (probationary police officer entitled to name-clearing hearing in order to refute charges of statutory sexual assault and corrupting the morals of a minor that led to termination of his employment).

[105] Paul v. Davis, *supra* note 104; *Palmer v. City of Monticello*, 31 F.3d 1499, 1503 (10th Cir. 1994) (to establish claim of deprivation of liberty interest, plaintiff must prove "termination based on a publicized charge of sufficient opprobrium that would make plaintiff an unlikely candidate" for employment).

[106] *See* cases *supra* note 104.

To be stigmatizing, the charges must impugn the officer's honesty or integrity, not simply her professional competence.[107] Placing a stigmatizing letter in a probationary officer's personnel file is not enough to satisfy the public disclosure requirement.[108] The information must actually be released to a prospective employer or other person outside the department.[109]

The right to a name-clearing hearing is a limited remedy. The officer is entitled to a hearing in which to refute the charges, but not to challenge the personnel action taken on the basis of them. Because probationary officers are dismissible without cause, the only right they have when wrongfully dismissed is the right to clear their name.

§ 10.7 Employment Discrimination Based on Race, Color, Religion, Gender, or National Origin

Title VII of the Equal Employment Opportunities Act of 1964[110] prohibits employment discrimination based on race, color, religion, gender, or national origin.[111] Law enforcement agencies, long criticized for under utilization of women and minorities, have frequently been called upon to defend their employment practices. There are three types of discrimination claims: (1) disparate treatment, (2) disparate impact, and (3) harassment.

---

[107]   Gibson v. Caruthersville School Dist. No. 8, 36 F.3d 768 (8th Cir. 2003) ("The requisite stigma has been found when the allegations involve 'dishonesty, immorality, criminality, racism, or the like.'"). The following charges have been held to be stigmatizing: Palmer v. City of Monticello, 31 F.3d 1499 (10th Cir. 1994) (falsifying a speeding ticket); Hade v. City of Fremont, 246 F. Supp. 2d 837 (N.D. Ohio 2003) (sexual improprieties); Rosenstein v. Dallas, 876 F.2d 392 (5th Cir. 1989) (making harassing and obscene telephone calls to fellow officer); Cronin v. Town v. Amesbury, 895 F. Supp. 375 (D. Mass. 1995) (lying). The following charges did not satisfy this requirement: Shands v. City of Kennett, 993 F.2d 1337 (8th Cir. 1992) (statement to television news reporter that officer was discharged for "acts of insubordination"); Robinson v. City of Montgomery City, 809 F.2d 1355 (8th Cir. 1987) (press release issued by city stating that chief of police was dismissed because of city's dissatisfaction with his performance).

[108]   Clark v. Maurer, 824 F.2d 565, 566 (7th Cir. 1987).

[109]   Palmer v. City of Monticello, 31 F.3d 1499 (10th Cir 1994) (requirement satisfied when charges for which officer was dismissed were discussed during a city council meeting attended by members of the public).

[110]   Civil Rights Act of 1964, § 701 et seq., as amended, 42 U.S.C.A. § 2000e et seq. There are a vast array of federal, state, and local regulations that affect the employment relationship of police officers. Only a small handful of them are covered in this chapter. For an overview of the broad range of regulations, see, generally, JAMES BAIRD & RONALD J. KRAMER, MUNICIPAL PERSONNEL PRACTICES, MUNICIPAL LAW & PRACTICE IN ILLINOIS 10–1 (September, 2000); J. Michael McGuinness, Representing Law Enforcement Officers in Personnel Disputes and Employment Litigation, 77 AM. JUR. TRIALS 1 (2000).

[111]   Because sexual orientation is not the same thing as gender, Title VII does not cover employment discrimination based on sexual orientation. See, e.g., De Santis v. Pacific Tel. & Tel. Co., 608 F.2d 327 (9th Cir. 1979); Holloway v. Arthur Andersen & Co., 566 F.2d 659 (9th Cir. 1977).

A. Disparate Treatment Discrimination

Disparate treatment discrimination occurs when an employer intentionally treats some people less favorably than others because of their race, color, religion, sex, or national origin.[112] Although a discriminatory intent must be established to recover on this theory, such intent will be inferred when the plaintiff proves that he or she: (1) belongs to a protected class, (2) was qualified and/or performed satisfactorily, (3) was subjected to adverse employment action, and (4) that similarly situated individuals not in his or her protected class received more favorable treatment.[113] At this point, the burden shifts to the employer to articulate a legitimate, nondiscriminatory reason for the treatment. If the employer shoulders this burden, the presumption of discrimination dissolves, and the employee must then prove that the employer's nondiscriminatory explanation is pretextual and not the real reason.

Title VII's prohibition of workplace discrimination cuts in both directions. White employees who suffer adverse employment action because of their race can also sue under Title VII. *Ricci v. DeStefano* was such a case.[114] The City of New Haven discarded the results of firefighter promotional exams to fill vacant lieutenant and captain positions because of a statistical disparity in the pass rates of minority and nonminority candidates. The racial distribution of the test results was such that the city could not have considered black candidates for any of the 15 vacant positions.

A group of white firefighters and one Hispanic who would have been promoted based on their exam scores sued the city for disparate treatment discrimination, alleging that they were unfairly denied promotions because of their race. The Supreme Court ruled that Title VII does not allow employers to discard exam results because of a racial disparity in the pass rates unless they have a strong basis in evidence to believe that the disparity resulted from flaws in the test design so that the test fails to reliably measure the knowledge, skills, and abilities required for the job. The promotional exams used by the City of New Haven were developed by an outside consulting firm after a detailed job analysis and painstaking efforts to ensure that the questions were job-related. There was nothing wrong with the exams. Consequently, the decision to discard the results, to the detriment of the white firefighters and the Hispanic who would have received promotions, constituted disparate treatment discrimination in violation of Title VII.[115]

---

[112] International Bhd. of Teamsters v. United States, 431 U.S. 324, 335 n. 15, 97 S. Ct. 1843, 1854 n. 15, 52 L. Ed. 2d 396 (1977).

[113] McDonnell Douglas Corp. v. Green, 411 U.S. 792, 93 S. Ct. 1817, 36 L. Ed. 2d 668 (1973).

[114] **Ricci v. DeStefano, _____ U.S. _____, 129 S. Ct. 2658, 174 L. Ed. 2d 490 (2009)**.

[115] *Id*.

B. *Disparate Impact Discrimination*

Most police departments have long since ceased intentionally discriminating. However, compliance with Title VII requires more than pure motives. In *Griggs v. Duke Power Company*,[116] the Supreme Court recognized a second theory, called **disparate impact discrimination**, which measurably increases the burdens of Title VII compliance. In *Griggs*, a private company used a professionally administered aptitude test to screen job applicants. Although the test was fair in form and was not employed with a discriminatory intent, it had the effect of disproportionately eliminating African-American applicants without being an accurate indicator of the knowledge, traits, or skills necessary for the job in question. Denouncing the use of this test as discriminatory, the Court declared:

> . . . [G]ood intent or absence of discriminatory intent does not redeem employment procedures or testing mechanisms that operate as "built-in headwinds" for minority groups and are unrelated to measuring job capability.

The form of discrimination recognized in *Griggs* is called *disparate impact* discrimination. Disparate impact discrimination occurs when an employer uses selection criteria that disproportionately eliminate members of a protected class without being valid predictors of the knowledge, skills, or traits necessary for the job in question. To establish a disparate impact discrimination claim, the plaintiff must demonstrate that the challenged selection requirement disproportionately eliminates members of a protected class (*i.e.*, that they have significantly lower pass rates or are less likely to be hired or promoted than others to whom this requirement is applied). Once the plaintiff establishes this, there is a rebuttable presumption of discrimination and the burden shifts to the employer to justify its use of this selection requirement. Title VII does not prevent employers from attempting to ensure that persons hired or promoted are qualified for the job or from adopting appropriate screening devices to this end. What it does require is that when selection criteria disproportionally eliminate members of a protected class, the criteria be shown to be valid predictors of the knowledge, skills, or traits necessary for the successful performance of the job.

Statistically significant disparities in the representation of women and minorities in the ranks of police departments have made police departments ready targets for disparate impact discrimination suits. Most police departments, for example, have minimum height, weight, strength, and agility qualifications. These qualifications unquestionably have a disparate impact on women and certain ethnic minorities and, consequently, are illegal under Title VII unless they can be shown, by professionally

---

[116] 401 U.S. 424, 91 S. Ct. 849, 28 L. Ed. 2d 158 (1971). The theory recognized in *Griggs* was subsequently codified in the Civil Rights Act of 1991, Pub. L. No. 102–166, § 3, 105 Stat. 1071, 1071 (1992).

accepted methods, to be job related.[117] In *Dothard v. Rawlinson*,[118] the Supreme Court threw out a five feet, two inches, 120-pound minimum height and weight requirement for the position of correctional officer because the corrections department was unable to establish this. While it may seem intuitively obvious that being at least five feet two inches and weighing at least 120 pounds or being able to do 25 sit-ups or run an obstacle course in 25 seconds is necessary to have the physical strength and agility needed to be a police officer, courts do not take judicial notice of matters simply because they seem intuitively obvious to those who established the requirement. When hiring and promotional requirements are challenged, the department must be able to prove, through professionally accepted methods, that the challenged selection criteria are predictive of or significantly correlated with important elements of the job. Designing employment exams is complex and requires consultation with experts.

In *Ricci v. DeStefano*,[119] the City of New Haven, Connecticut, hired an outside consulting firm, at a cost of $100,000, to develop examinations to identify firefighters best qualified for promotion to the ranks of lieutenant and captain positions. The consulting firm took painstaking efforts to ensure that the questions were job related. When the exam results showed a statistical disparity in pass rates for minority and nonminority candidates, a rancorous public debate ensured. Both sides threatened lawsuits — the minority candidates for *disparate impact* discrimination if the city certified the exam results, and the nonminority candidates for *disparate treatment* discrimination if it did not. Caught in the middle, the city decided to throw the exam results out. The firefighters who would have been promoted based on their exam scores — 17 white and one Hispanic — sued the city, alleging that the city had discriminated against them because of their race in violation of Title VII. The city defended by asserting that it had discarded the test results to avoid being sued for disparate impact discrimination. The Supreme Court ruled that this defense is available only if the employer has a *strong basis in evidence* for believing that it *would be liable for disparate impact discrimination* if it did not take race-conscious action. A statistical racial disparity in pass rates, without more, does not establish liability. The city would be liable for disparate impact discrimination only if the statistical disparity resulted from flaws in the exam's design

---

[117]   Lanning v. Southeastern Pennsylvania Transportation Authority (SEPTA), 181 F.3d 487 (3d Cir. 1999) (aerobic fitness test requiring applicant to run 1.5 miles within 12 minutes, which disproportionately eliminated women applicants, held discriminatory when test was not shown, by professionally acceptable methods, to be significantly correlated with important elements of the job for which candidates are being evaluated); United States v. Commonwealth of Virginia, 620 F.2d 1018 (4th Cir. 1980) (requirement that state troopers be at least five feet nine inches tall and weigh at least 156 pounds, which effectively eliminated 98 percent of all women, violated Title VII when there was no showing of need for such requirement); United States v. City of Erie, Pa, 411 F. Supp. 2d 524 (W.D. Pa. 2005) (physical agility test that disproportionately eliminated female applicants for entry-level police officer positions violated Title VII where municipality was unable to demonstrate that the screening test used traits necessary for successful proper performance of job).

[118]   **433 U.S. 321, 97 S. Ct. 2720, 53 L. Ed. 2d 786 (1977)**.

[119]   *Supra* note 114.

so that the exam failed to operate as a valid predictor of the knowledge, skills, and abilities required for the position. The City of New Haven had no basis, much less a strong basis in evidence, for believing this. The exams had been painstakingly prepared by an outside consulting firm after conducting detailed job analyses and taking numerous precautions to ensure that the questions used on the exam were job related.

The lesson to be learned from *Ricci* is that municipalities cannot disregard employment exam results simply because they disproportionately eliminate minority candidates. If there is nothing wrong with the exam design, the department must allow the cards to fall where they fall.

C. *Workplace Harassment*

Title VII also condemns workplace harassment based on race, color, religion, gender, or national origin.[120] Most people have an idea (not always correct) about when conduct constitutes sexual harassment. There are two distinct forms of sexual harassment recognized under Title VII: *quid pro quo* and *hostile work environment*.

1. *Quid Pro Quo* Sexual Harassment

Quid pro quo is a Latin phrase that means "this for that." **Quid pro quo sexual harassment** occurs when a superior threatens to take a negative action or to withhold a positive action unless a subordinate acquiesces in his or her sexual demands. The message communicated is "put out or else." The threatened action can involve hiring, firing, promotions, work assignments, pay, vacations, travel, or any other tangible employment benefit.

2. Hostile Work Environment Sexual Harassment

Hostile work environment sexual harassment occurs when unwelcome sexual behavior becomes so pervasive or severe that it alters the conditions of a person's employment and creates a hostile, intimidating, abusive, or offensive work environment. Factors that courts consider in deciding whether unwelcome sexual conduct has reached this level include: whether the conduct is verbal, physical, or both; whether it is physically threatening or humiliating; how often the acts are repeated; whether

---

[120]   Meritor Savings Bank v. Vinson, 477 U.S. 57, 106 S. Ct. 2399, 91 L. Ed. 2d 49 (1986); Shipbuilding & Dry Dock Co. v. EEOC, 462 U.S. 669, 103 S. Ct. 2622, 77 L. Ed. 2d 89 (1983); Oncale v. Sundowner Offshore Services, 523 U.S. 75, 118 S. Ct. 998, 140 L. Ed. 2d 201 (1998). EEOC guidelines define sexual harassment, for purposes of Title VII, as follows:

Unwelcome sexual advances, requests for sexual favors, and other verbal or physical conduct of a sexual nature constitutes sexual harassment when: (1) submission to such conduct is made either explicitly or implicitly a term or condition of an individual's employment, (2) submission to or rejection of such conduct by an individual is used as a basis for decisions affecting such individual, or (3) such conduct has the purpose or effect of unreasonably interfering with an individual's work performance or creating an intimidating, hostile, or offensive working environment. 29 C.F.R. § 1604.11(a) (1983).

Quid pro quo sexual harassment is covered in subsections (1) and (2), while subsection (3) covers hostile work environment sexual harassment.

it is perpetrated by a co-worker or supervisor; whether other people joined in the harassment; and whether the harassment unreasonably interfered with the employee's work performance.[121] Conduct does not have to be overtly sexual in order to constitute sexual harassment. Demeaning gender-related comments, sexual jokes, and obscene graffiti are also considered forms of sexual harassment.

3. Police Department Liability for Sexual Harassment by Supervisors and Co-Workers

Title VII imposes liability on employees who commit sexual harassment and, in some cases, also on their employers. When the sexual harasser is a supervisor and the victim suffers tangible employment harm, such as being discharged, demoted, or transferred to a less desirable position, the employer is liable along with the harasser.[122] When no tangible employment harm results, the employer is permitted to defend by establishing that it had a strong and effective anti-harassment policy and complaint mechanism, and that the victim unreasonably failed to take advantage of it.[123] The existence of this defense makes it crucial for police departments to formulate strong policies prohibiting sexual harassment, publicize them, put a complaint mechanism in place, and follow through with prompt and thorough investigations and swift remedial action if the complaint is determined to be well-founded. When the sexual harasser is a co-worker, the employer is liable only if the harasser's supervisor is aware of the harassment and does nothing to stop it.[124]

4. Racial, Ethnic, and Religious Harassment

Protection against workplace harassment under Title VII is not limited to sexual harassment. The Supreme Court has declared that all employees have a "right to work in an environment free from discriminatory intimidation, ridicule, and insult" based on their race, color, religion, national origin, or sex.[125] The requirements for racial, ethnic, or religious harassment are the same as for sexual harassment.[126] The harassment must be sufficiently severe or pervasive as to alter the conditions of the officer's employment and create a hostile, intimidating, or abusive working environment.[127] In *Ways v. City of Lincoln*,[128] an African-American police officer successfully sued his department for

---

[121]   Harris v. Forklift Sys., Inc., 510 U.S. 17, 114 S. Ct. 367, 126 L. Ed. 2d 295 (1993).

[122]   Faragher v. City of Boca Raton, 524 U.S. 775, 118 S. Ct. 2275, 141 L. Ed. 2d 662 (1998); Burlington Industries, Inc. v. Ellerth, 524 U.S. 742, 118 S. Ct. 2257, 141 L. Ed. 2d 633 (1998); Pennsylvania State Police v. Suders, 542 U.S.129, 124 S. Ct. 2342, 159 L. Ed. 2d. 204 (2004).

[123]   *See* cases *supra* note 122.

[124]   McKenzie v. Illinois Dept. of Transp., 92 F.3d 473, 480 (7th Cir. 1996); Yamaguchi v. United States Dept. of Air Force, 109 F.3d 1475, 1483 (9th Cir. 1997).

[125]   Meritor Savings Bank v. Vinson, *supra* note 120.

[126]   *See, e.g.*, Ways v. City of Lincoln, 871 F.2d 750 (8th Cir. 1989); Ross v. Douglas County, Nebraska, 234 F.3d 391 (8th Cir. 2000); Schwapp v. Town of Avon, 118 F.3d 106 (2d Cir. 1997).

[127]   Harris v. Forklift Sys., Inc., *supra* note 121.

[128]   *Supra* note 126.

hostile work environment harassment. The officer proved that he had been subjected to a steady barrage of racial slurs, derogatory comments, and offensive jokes, and that he complained, but nothing was done. The court ruled that when police officials are aware of racial harassment and fail to investigate or take appropriate remedial action, the department is liable under Title VII.

§ 10.8 Equal Protection in the Police Workplace

The equal protection clause requires government employers to make hiring and promotion decisions based on job qualifications, rather than race or gender, except under narrow conditions. Employment policies that give preferences to women and minorities are called *affirmative action plans*.[129] The Supreme Court has long struggled to reconcile affirmative action with the Fourteenth Amendment guarantee of equal protection.[130] Early cases viewed affirmative action as benign discrimination because the reason for the preferential treatment was to elevate the status of women and minorities, not to discriminate against white male employees who were passed over for jobs or promotions.[131] However, the Supreme Court has more recently come to appreciate that no discrimination seems benign to a person whose career is put on hold for someone else's benefit.[132]

Under established case law, police departments may undertake affirmative action only if: (1) they have a compelling need either to remedy workforce imbalances caused by their own prior discriminatory employment practices or to increase diversity to operate more efficiently[133] and (2) the plan is narrowly tailored to minimize the disadvantage to persons who are not beneficiaries.[134] Unless both requirements are met, police departments can be sued for "reverse discrimination" by persons who suffer career setbacks because of the plan.

---

[129] The equal protection clause was discussed in § 1.16.

[130] *See, generally,* Lara Hudgins, *Rethinking Affirmative Action in the 1990s: Tailoring the Cure to Remedy the Disease,* 47 BAYLOR. L. REV. 815 (1995); John Cocchi Day, Comment, *Retelling the Story of Affirmative Action: Reflections on a Decade of Federal Jurisprudence in the Public Workplace,* 89 CAL. L. REV. 59 (2001).

[131] University of California Regents v. Bakke, 438 U.S. 265, 98 S. Ct. 2733, 57 L. Ed. 2d 750 (1978) (holding that a public university may consider the race or ethnicity of an applicant for admission as one factor to be weighed against all others in the admissions process).

[132] Adarand Constructors, Inc. v. Pena, 515 U.S. 200, 115 S. Ct. 2097, 132 L. Ed. 2d 158 (1995); City of Richmond v. J.A. Croson Co., 488 U.S. 469, 109 S. Ct. 706, 102 L. Ed. 2d 854 (1989) (plurality opinion); United States v. Paradise, 480 U.S. 149, 107 S. Ct. 1053, 94 L. Ed. 2d 203 (1987); Wygant v. Jackson Board of Education, 476 U.S. 267, 106 S. Ct. 1842, 90 L. Ed. 2d 260 (1986). *See also* Reynolds v. City of Chicago, 296 F.3d 524 (7th Cir. 2002) ("Racial discrimination even of the 'affirmative action' sort, when practiced by a public agency and thus subject to the equal protection clause, requires proof, and not merely argument, that the agency had a compelling need to discriminate and that it went no further in discrimination than necessary to meet that need.").

[133] *See* cases *supra* note 132.

[134] *Id.*

A. Compelling Need to Remedy Past Discrimination or Achieve Diversity

There are only two situations that can justify affirmative action. The first is the need to correct workforce imbalances caused by the police department's own prior discriminatory employment practices.[135] If the police department has a documented history of discrimination, it can undertake affirmative action to eliminate the workforce imbalances that it is responsible for causing.[136] Eradicating the present effects of past discrimination takes time. The effects can linger years after intentional discrimination has ceased.[137] In a recent federal case, the court approved out-of-rank promotions of several African-American police officers to correct the effects of discrimination in the hiring of minorities that had occurred decades before.[138] Discrimination at the entry level had limited the opportunities for minorities to move up through the ranks and racial disparities in the higher ranks of the police department were still present almost 30 years later.

The second justification for taking affirmative action is the police department's operational need for a racially diverse police force.[139] At a time when charges of

---

[135]   *Id. See also* Reynolds v. City of Chicago, *supra* note 132 (affirmative action promotions of minority and female officers over higher scoring Caucasian officers did not violate equal protection clause where past discrimination had depressed hiring of minority and female officers, leading to a deficit of minority and female officers in senior positions); Majeske v. City of Chicago, 218 F.3d 816, 823 (7th Cir. 2000), *cert. denied*, 531 U.S. 1079, 121 S. Ct. 779, 148 L. Ed. 2d 676 (2001) (holding that statistical evidence of disparity within a police department coupled with anecdotal evidence of past discrimination sufficiently establishes a compelling state interest that justifies an affirmative action plan).

[136]   *See* authorities *supra* notes 132, 135.

[137]   Reynolds v. City of Chicago, *supra* note 132 (holding that the police department's discrimination in hiring of blacks, leading to a deficit of blacks in senior positions, justified affirmative action promotions decades later); Cotter v. City of Boston, 323 F.3 160 (1st Cir. 2003) (same).

[138]   Cotter v. City of Boston, *supra* note 137.

[139]   *See, e.g., Petit v. City of Chicago*, 352 F.3d 1111 (7th Cir. 2004) (police department's operational need for diversity in its workforce constituted compelling interest for engaging in affirmative action promotions of African-American and Hispanic officers); Reynolds v. City of Chicago, *supra* note 132 (holding that affirmative-action promotion of Hispanic officer to rank of lieutenant over higher scoring Caucasian officers was justified by operational need of police department for diversity among higher level administrators); Patrolmen's Benevolent Ass'n of N.Y., Inc. v. City of N.Y., 310 F.3d 43, 52 (2d Cir. 2002) ("[A] law enforcement body's need to carry out its mission effectively, with a workforce that appears unbiased, is able to communicate with the public and is respected by the community it serves, may constitute a compelling state interest."); Wittmer v. Peters, 87 F.3d 916 (7th Cir. 1996) (finding operational need for promotion of black lieutenant in prison boot camp with 70% black inmates); Barhold v. Rodriguez, 863 F.2d 233, 238 (2d Cir. 1988) (holding that "a law enforcement body's need to carry out its mission effectively, with a workforce that appears unbiased, is able to communicate with the public and is respected by the community it serves" constitutes a compelling state interest for purpose of equal protection analysis); Talbert v. City of Richmond, 648 F.2d 925 (4th Cir. 1981) (decision to promote black police officer from rank of captain to major over higher scoring white police officer did not violate equal protection where city took into account the operational need for diversity in the police department's upper ranks); Detroit Police Officers'

racially biased policing have emerged as one of the most challenging issues facing police departments in large, racially divided metropolitan cities, the visible presence of racial and ethnic minorities in all ranks of the police department is critical to effective police work. As one court has explained:[140]

> The argument that police need more minority officers is not simply that blacks communicate better with blacks or that a police department should cater to the public's desires. Rather, it is that effective crime prevention and solution depend heavily on the public support and cooperation which result only from public respect and confidence in the police. In short, the focus is not on the superior performance of minority officers, but on the public's perception of law enforcement officials and institutions.

A police department's operational need for diversity has been widely accepted by lower courts as a justification for making race-conscious employment decisions,[141] but the Supreme Court has not yet considered this issue.[142]

B. Plan to Address the Need Must Be Narrowly Tailored

The police department's plan of action must be narrowly tailored so that it does not unnecessarily burden nonminorities.[143] To satisfy this requirement: (1) The police department must explore race-neutral alternatives and conclude that they are inadequate to accomplish its goal before undertaking affirmative action.[144] (2) The plan's treatment of race or gender must be flexible. Race and gender may be considered as a "plus" factor in making individualized assessments of competing candidates. This is commonly referred to as a *preference*. However, the government is not allowed to set aside a fixed number or proportion of opportunities exclusively for women and minorities. That is a *quota*. Quotas are unconstitutional because they prevent Caucasians and males from competing for the opportunities that have been set aside.[145] (3) The department's need for diversity cannot be met by taking jobs away from people who already have them or by hiring or promoting unqualified candidates.[146]

Ass'n v. Young, 608 F.2d 671 (6th Cir. 1979) (recognizing operational needs of police department as a compelling interest for purposes of equal protection analysis); Wygant v. Jackson Board of Education, *supra* note 128, 476 U.S., at 314, 106 S. Ct., at 1868 (Stevens, J., dissenting) ("[A]n integrated police force could develop a better relationship with the community and do a more effective job of maintaining law and order than a force composed only of white officers,").

[140] Detroit Police Officers' Ass'n v. Young, *supra* note 139 at 695–696.

[141] *See* authorities *supra* note 139.

[142] The Supreme Court confronted a related issue in Grutter v. Bolinger, 539 U.S. 306, 123 S. Ct. 2325, 156 L. Ed. 2d 304 (2003). The case involved whether law schools could consider the need for diversity in their admission policies, and the Supreme Court held that they could.

[143] Grutter v. Bolinger, *supra* note 138; United States v. Paradise, *supra* note 132; Hiller v. County of Suffolk, 977 F. Supp. 202 (E. D. N. Y. 1997).

[144] *Id.*; City of Richmond v. J.A. Croson Co., *supra* note 132;

[145] United States v. Paradise supra note 122; Wygant v. Jackson Board of Education, *supra* note 132.

[146] *See* cases *supra* note 144.

(4) Fourth, the plan must be temporary and must end when its remedial goals have been achieved.[147]

Finally, the plan must also be capable of being reviewed by a court. The Chief of Police and Board of Police Commissioners of a major metropolitan police department were recently successfully used for reverse discrimination where they gave preferential treatment to women and minority candidates in making promotions based on a vague goal of increasing diversity, but with no written policy or standards.[148] Decisions were made on an informal, *ad hoc* basis. The court stated that "[t]he record therefore discloses no policy, no set parameters and no means of assessing how race should be weighed with other promotional criteria .... Our cases approving of a race-conscious promotion policy for a public employer as a narrowly tailored response to a compelling governmental interest have never approved such a loose and indeed effectively standardless approach."

§ 10.9   Constitutional Accountability Under Federal Law

The final section of this chapter deals with civil liability. Title 42 U.S.C. § 1983[149] is a widely used federal statute that hopefully you will never have an occasion to learn about firsthand. It imposes civil liability on police officers who act **under color of state law** in depriving someone of a constitutional right.[150] We live in a litigious society. Section 1983 civil actions against police officers are on the rise[151] and staggering

---

[147]   Detroit Police Officers Ass'n v. Young, 989 F.2d 225 (6th Cir. 1993) (holding that affirmative action plan was no longer valid when goal of 50 percent black sergeants had been virtually attained).
[148]   Alexander v. City of Milwaukee, 474 F.3d 437 (7th Cir. 2007).
[149]   Section 1983 reads as follows:

Every person who, under color of any statute, ordinance, regulation, custom, or usage, of any State or Territory or the District of Columbia, subjects, or causes to be subjected, any citizen of the United States or other person within the jurisdiction thereof to the deprivation of any rights, privileges, or immunities secured by the Constitution and laws, shall be liable to the party injured in an action at law, suit in equity, or other proper proceeding for redress, except that in any action brought against a judicial officer for an act or omission taken in such officer's judicial capacity, injunctive relief shall not be granted unless a declaratory decree was violated or declaratory relief was unavailable. For the purposes of this section, any Act of Congress applicable exclusively to the District of Columbia shall be considered to be a statute of the District of Columbia.

Section 1983 has a criminal counterpart. Eighteen U.S.C. § 242, makes it a federal crime for police officers to willfully deprive persons of their constitutional rights while acting under the color of their legal authority.
[150]   *Id.*
[151]   *See, e.g.*, Andrew Fulkerson, *If the Constable Blunders, Does the County Pay? Liability under 42 U.S.C. § 1983*, 28 U. ARK. LITTLE ROCK L. REV. 519 (2006) ("Civil litigation against law enforcement and other government officials has grown so large, in the words of one commentator, that 'suing public officials has become the second most popular indoor sport in the country.'"); Marc L. Miller & Ronald F. Wright, *Secret Police and the Mysterious Case of the Missing Tort Cases*, 52 BUFF. L. REV. 757 (2004) (stating that statistics on the actual numbers of § 1983 suits filed against police officers and the amount of the judgment or settlement are hard to come by).

seven-figure recoveries are far from rare.[152] The threat of civil suit, at some point in a police officer's professional career, looms as a real possibility in contemporary times.

Figure 10.5
Elements of a 42 U.S.C. § 1983 Claim

> Police officers are civilly liable under § 1983 when they:
>
> 1. act under color of state law;
> 2. in depriving an individual of a constitutional right.

A. *Elements of a § 1983 Claim*

Section 1983 imposes civil liability on persons who (1) act under "color of state law" in (2) depriving an individual of a constitutional right.[153] "Color" means an appearance or pretense. When the government issues police officers a uniform and badge, it creates an appearance of authority for their actions. This appearance continues even when they abuse their authority. "Under color of state law" refers to the "misuse of power, possessed by virtue of state law and made possible only because the wrongdoer is clothed with the authority of state law."[154]

A police officer's constitutional misdeeds are considered to have been committed under color of his legal authority in two situations: (1) when the wrong occurs while undertaking official action[155] and (2) when the wrong is committed for personal

---

[152] *See, e.g.*, Michael Brick, *City to Pay $2 Million to Parents of Man Fatally Shot by an Officer*, N.Y. TIMES, May 24, 2007, at B1, col. 4; Stephen Esposito, *We Finally Got Justice for Him": City to Pay $5 Mil. For Fatal Shooting of Paraplegic Man*, CHI. SUN-TIMES, Feb. 13, 2007, at 16; Maurice Possley & Gary Washburn, *Deal on Wrongful Conviction, City Panel Approves $2 Million Settlement*, CHI. TRIB., Oct. 31, 2006, at B3; Matt O'Connor, *Jury Believes Ex-Chicago Cop Framed by FBI, $6 Million-plus Damages Awarded*, CHI. TRIB., Jan. 1, 2005, at A1; Steve Warmbir, *U.S. Jury Fines City $1 Million ; Lax Official Discipline Cited in Brutality Case of an Off-duty Cop*, CHI. SUN-TIMES, May 3, 2003, at 2; Curtis Lawrence, *$1.5 Million in Shooting by Cop; Jury Says Testimony by Officer Who Killed Man Was Not Credible*, CHI. SUN-TIMES, Aug. 8, 2003, at 9; Janet Rausa Fuller, *$2 Mil. Awarded in Alleged Cop Beating; Jury Finds Police Liable but Rejects Gay Man's Hate-crime Contention*, CHI. SUN-TIMES, Nov. 2, 2002, at 2; Matt O'Connor, *Jury Awards Paralyzed Man $28 Million, Most Ever in Chicago Cop Case*, CHI. TRIB., Oct. 26, 1999, at A1.

[153] *Supra* note 149.

[154] Monroe v. Pape, 365 U.S. 167, 81 S. Ct. 473, 5 L. Ed. 2d 492 (1961), *overruled in part*, Monell v. Department of Social Services, 436 U.S. 658, 98 S. Ct. 2018, 56 L. Ed. 2d 611 (1978).

[155] Monroe v. Pape, *supra* note 154; Stengel v. Belcher, 522 F.2d 438 (6th Cir. 1975) (off-duty police officer having a drink in a bar, acted under color of state law when he shot and killed two men and paralyzed another while intervening in barroom brawl, although he was out of uniform, where police department regulations required officers to carry pistol and mace at all times and to take action to maintain the peace 24 hours a day).

reasons under a false pretense of exercising legal authority.[156] *Johnson v. Cannon*[157] illustrates the second situation. A deputy sheriff stopped a woman for a traffic violation and threatened her with arrest unless she had sex with him. He then took her to her home and sexually assaulted her. The court found that he acted under color of state law because he used his legal authority to coerce his victim into having sex. Although his actions had nothing to do with the performance of his job, the wrongdoing would not have been possible but for the legal authority vested in him by the state. This is enough to satisfy the requirement of action under color of state law.

Section 1983 does not provide a remedy for wrongs committed for personal reasons if the officer neither undertakes nor purports to undertake official action, even if the officer is in uniform and on duty at the time.[158]

Federal officers cannot be sued under § 1983 because they act under color of federal law. However, this does not give them a free pass to engage in unconstitutional conduct. They can be sued directly under the Constitution. Their constitutional liability is the same as state and local police officers sued under § 1983.[159]

Defendants in a § 1983 action are liable only for their own acts and omissions, not for what someone else did.[160] The city, police department, and supervisory personnel, for example, cannot be sued for a rank-and-file police officer's violation of the Constitution unless they did or failed to do something that caused the violation to occur,

---

[156]   **Rogers v. City of Little Rock, 152 F.3d 790 (8th Cir. 1998)** (officer acted under color of state law in intimidating motorist stopped for a traffic violation into having sex with him); Crews v. United States, 160 F.2d 746 (5th Cir. 1947) (officer acted under color of state law when he took a man into custody under the pretext of arresting him, drove him to a bridge, and forced him to leap to his death because physical control over the victim was obtained through misuse of his legal authority); Romero v. City of Clanton, 220 F. Supp. 2d 1313 (M.D. Ala. 2002) (officer acted under color of state law when he used his position as a police officer to detain plaintiff, and then made sexual advances).

[157]   947 F. Supp. 1567 (M.D. Fla. 1996).

[158]   Martinez v. Colon, 54 F.3d 980 (1st Cir.), *cert. denied*, 516 U.S. 987, 116 S. Ct. 515, 133 L. Ed. 2d 423 (1995) (officer not acting under color of state law when he accidentally shot fellow officer while harassing him about his sexual orientation, even though shooting occurred in the police station while both were on duty); Delcambre v. Delcambre, 635 F.2d 407 (5th Cir. 1981) (police chief not acting under color of state law, even though he was on duty and at the police station, when he assaulted his sister-in-law during personal argument over family matter); Bonsignore v. City of New York, 683 F.2d 635 (2d Cir. 1982) (off-duty police officer not acting under color of state law when he used his service revolver to shoot his wife and commit suicide); Johnson v. Hackett, 284 F. Supp. 933 (D. C. Pa. 1968) (on-duty officer not acting under color of law when he called a group of African-Americans racially derogatory names and offered to fight, without undertaking any law enforcement action); Lyons v. Adams, 257 F. Supp. 2d 1125 (N.D. Ill. 2003) (off-duty, out-of-uniform police officer was not acting under "color of state law" when he beat up a bar patron during an altercation in the bar's parking lot prompted by the officer's calling the man a faggot, where the officer neither took nor purported to take any official action).

[159]   Bivens v. Six Unknown Named Agents of Fed. Bureau of Narcotics, 403 U.S. 388, 91 S. Ct. 1999, 29 L. Ed. 2d 619 (1971).

[160]   Monell v. Department of Social Services, 436 U.S. 658, 98 S. Ct. 2018, 56 L. Ed. 2d 11 (1978) (A municipality cannot be held liable under § 1983 because the wrongdoer is its employee; it is liable only if its official policies or customs caused the wrong).

such as by not adequately training or supervising the offending officer.[161] However, police officers who passively stand by and watch their comrades commit unlawful acts of violence are liable along with them, not for what their comrades did, but for what they failed to do. The Constitution imposes a duty on *them* to protect persons in custody against violence, including violence committed by their fellow officers.[162]

While claims involving excessive force are the most common, police have been sued for violating every conceivable constitutional right arising under the First through Fourteenth Amendments. Each time the Supreme Court announces a new constitutional ruling, it enlarges the decisional base on which § 1983 claims can be brought.

Figure 10.6
Qualified Immunity

Police are immune from liability for violating a constitutional right if:

1. The right was not clearly established at the time of the challenged action or
2. A reasonable public official, faced with these facts, could have believed that the action taken complied with the existing constitutional standard.

B. *Qualified Immunity Defense*

This section ends on a more positive note. If police officers stay abreast of constitutional decisions and perform their duty in an objectively reasonable fashion, they will win any § 1983 action brought against them. This is because of a widely used defense known as **qualified immunity**. This defense was developed under the common law out of concern that fear of personal liability would paralyze police officers and cause them to hesitate in situations requiring them to act swiftly and with conviction. The purpose of the qualified immunity defense is to provide a margin for reasonable errors of judgment.

The defense of qualified immunity has been incorporated into § 1983 actions.[163] It insulates police officers from liability "insofar as their conduct does not violate clearly

---

[161] Board of County Comm'rs of Bryan County v. Brown, 520 U.S. 397, 117 S. Ct. 1382, 137 L. Ed. 2d 626 (1997) (negligent hiring); Harris v. City of Canton, 489 U.S. 378, 109 S. Ct. 1197, 103 L. Ed. 3d 412 (1989) (failure to train); Beck v. City of Pittsburgh, 89 F.3d 966, 971 (3d Cir. 1996), *cert. denied*, 519 U.S. 1151, 117 S. Ct. 1086, 137 L. Ed. 2d 219 (1997) (failure to investigate prior charges of excessive force made against violence-prone officer); Davis v. City of Ellensburg, 869 F.2d 1230, 1235 (9th Cir. 1989) (negligent supervision); Benavides v. County of Wilson, 955 F.2d 968, 972 (5th Cir.), *cert. denied*, 506 U.S. 824, 113 S. Ct. 79, 121 L. Ed. 2d 43 (1992) (negligent hiring); **Vann v. City of New York, 72 F.3d 1040 (2d Cir. 1995)** (failure to supervise and monitor officer who had a known, long history of violent behavior).

[162] **Yang v. Hardin, 37 F.3d 282 (7th Cir. 1994)**.

[163] Harlow v. Fitzgerald, 457 U.S. 800, 102 S. Ct. 2727, 73 L. Ed. 2d 396 (1982); Anderson v. Creighton, 483 U.S. 635, 107 S. Ct. 3034, 97 L. Ed. 2d 523 (1987).

established . . . constitutional rights of which a reasonable person should have known."[164] The quoted language gives an officer two shots to avoid liability. There is no liability if the constitutional right the officer is charged with violating had not yet been clearly established at the time of the challenged action. Second, there is no liability, even though the constitutional right was clearly established, if a reasonable police officer faced with the same facts could have believed that the action taken complied with that standard. As a result of the qualified immunity defense, police officers can be successfully sued only for clear violations of clearly established constitutional standards.

In evaluating a claim of qualified immunity, the Court first determines whether the constitutional right the officer is charged with violating was clearly established. The test for when a constitutional right has been established with sufficient clarity that a police officer can be held liable for violating it is whether, based on the current state of the law, a reasonable police officer should have known that the right existed, that it applied to this situation, and that his or her conduct violated it.[165] Normally, the only way imprecise constitutional language can provide concrete guidance in a particular case is if there is an authoritative precedent applying the constitutional language to a case with materially similar facts and declaring the conduct unlawful. An "authoritative precedent" generally requires (1) a closely analogous case decided by the Supreme Court, (2) on-point case law decided by a federal court in the officer's own circuit, or (3) a strong consensus of case law authority from other jurisdictions.[166] If the constitutional right the officer is charged with violating was not established with at least this degree of clarity, then there is no liability. If it was, the court must next determine whether the officer's conduct was objectively reasonable in light of that standard. The second prong of the qualified immunity standard is born of recognition that officers are often called upon to make split-second judgments in tense and rapidly evolving situations during which they have no time to contemplate.[167] Even though they violate the Constitution, they will not be liable if a reasonable police officer, faced with the same facts, could have made the same mistake.[168]

---

[164]   *See* cases *supra* note 163.

[165]   Anderson v. Creighton, *supra* note 163.

[166]   Wilson v. Layne, 526 U.S. 603, 119 S. Ct. 1692, 143 L. Ed. 2d 818 (1999).

[167]   Graham v. Connor, 490 U.S. 386, 396–97, 109 S. Ct. 1865, 104 L. Ed. 2d 443 (1989) (noting that qualified immunity takes into account "the fact that police officers are often forced to make split-second judgments — in circumstances that are tense, uncertain, and rapidly evolving — about the amount of force that is necessary in a particular situation"); Wagner v. Bay City, Tex., 227 F.3d 316 (5th Cir. 2000) (observing that "courts must be careful not to engage in second-guessing police officers in situations in which they have to make split-second, on-the-scene decisions while confronted with violent individuals").

[168]   Saucier v. Katz, 533 U.S. 194, 121 S. Ct. 2151, 150 L. Ed. 2d 272 (2001) (police officer not liable for using excessive force as long as a reasonable officer could have made the same mistake under the particular circumstances); Brousseau v. Haugen, 543 U.S. 194, 125 S. Ct. 596, 160 L. Ed. 2d 583 (2004) (qualified immunity available where officer's conduct in shooting suspect in the back as he tried to flee in his vehicle fell within the "hazy border between excessive and acceptable force").

The greatest test of whether you have mastered the material in this book will occur later in your professional life. In a recent Sixth Circuit decision,[169] the court denied qualified immunity on the grounds that no reasonable police officer could have believed that uttering "God damn" in public furnished probable cause for arrest. We feel confident that no one who has completed this course would have made that mistake.

§ 10.10   Summary

The constitutional provisions studied in earlier chapters often have a narrower application in the government workplace. The First Amendment, for example, protects a police officer's work-related speech only if: (1) the officer speaks as a citizen, (2) about a matter of public concern, and (3) the value of the officer's speech outweighs its adverse effect on the police department.

The Fourth Amendment protects police officers against workplace searches only if: (1) they have a reasonable expectation of privacy in the location searched and (2) the department's decision to search was not justified. Whether police officers have a reasonable expectation of privacy in their work space and equipment depends primarily on whether they have exclusive use and control or the use is shared; whether supervisors, co-workers, or other third parties have access to or a right to enter; and whether employment regulations reserve a right of inspection. Even though an officer has a reasonable expectation of privacy, the department is justified in performing a workplace search whenever it has (1) a legitimate noninvestigatory work-related reason or (2) reasonable suspicion that the search will turn up evidence of work-related misconduct. Mandatory drug testing is considered a search, but is permitted if: (1) the department has a reasonable suspicion that an officer is abusing drugs or (2) the testing is conducted as part of a systematic drug-screening program.

The Fifth Amendment privilege against self-incrimination does not protect officers undergoing a police internal affairs investigation from being compelled, on threat of job termination, to account for their official conduct. However, incriminating statements obtained in this manner are treated as immunized testimony and may not be used against the officer in a criminal prosecution.

The job of police officer is more highly regulated than any career outside the military. Regulations that infringe on an officer's liberty are sometimes challenged as violating substantive due process. Substantive due process challenges rarely succeed because courts look upon police departments as paramilitary organizations and are reluctant to overturn their judgments about what is necessary for the successful operation of a police department. Challenges to regulations affecting a police officer's personal appearance and hairstyle, place of residence, off-duty employment, smoking habits, and even private sexual behavior have generally been unsuccessful.

---

[169]   Leonard v. Robinson, 477 F.3d 347 (6th Cir. 2007).

The Fourteenth Amendment due process clause entitles police officers faced with dismissal, demotion, or suspension who have a property right in their job (*i.e.*, who cannot be dismissed without just cause for removal) to a hearing to refute the charges and get their job back. Probationary police officers have a due process right to a "name clearing" hearing if they are dismissed based on stigmatizing charges disclosed to the public that could foreclose their ability to get another job in the field of law enforcement.

The Equal Employment Opportunity Act, popularly known as Title VII, protects police officers against discrimination based on race, color, religion, gender, or national origin in hiring, promotion, discharge, and other employment decisions. Three different kinds of discrimination claims are recognized: (1) disparate treatment, (2) disparate impact, and (3) harassment. Disparate treatment discrimination occurs when an employer intentionally treats some people less favorably than others because of their race, color, religion, sex, or national origin. Disparate impact discrimination occurs when an employer uses selection criteria that disproportionately eliminate members of a protected class without being valid predictors of traits, skills, or knowledge necessary for successful performance of the jobs for which the selection criteria are being used. Sexual harassment occurs when: (1) a supervisor threatens to take negative action or to withhold positive action unless a subordinate accedes to demands for sexual favors, or (2) when the sexual harassment is so pervasive or severe as to create a hostile work environment. Police departments can be sued for sexual harassment committed by a supervisor and also by a co-worker if a supervisor is aware of the harassment and does nothing to stop it. Title VII also provides a cause of action for harassment based on race, religion, ethnicity, and national origin.

Efforts to increase representation by women and minorities on the police force have induced many police departments to adopt affirmative action plans. When race-conscious employment decisions are necessary, either to remedy the effects of the department's own prior discriminatory employment practices or to achieve diversity, and the plan is narrowly tailored to address a specific and well-documented need, officers disadvantaged by the operation of the plan cannot complain. However, when either requirement is lacking, unequal treatment based on race or gender violates the equal protection clause.

Police officers can be sued under 42 U.S.C. § 1983 when they: (1) act under "color of state law" in (2) depriving an individual of a constitutional right. The first requirement is satisfied when they undertake official action and also when they commit wrongs for personal gain under a false pretense of exercising their official authority. Their accountability under § 1983 is coextensive with the entire Constitution. However, officers who stay abreast of constitutional decisions and perform their duties in an objectively reasonable fashion have a defense against liability. Qualified immunity protects them "insofar as their conduct does not violate clearly established . . . constitutional rights of which a reasonable person should have known."

PART II:

Judicial Decisions and Statutes Relating To Part I

The judicial decisions in this part of the book have been selected to enhance understanding of the materials in Part I. It is not enough to learn the decision or rule of law of a case. To fully appreciate the significance of a rule and to be capable of applying the rule intelligently, the reasoning of the court in reaching the decision must also be considered. Although a court decides only the case that is before it, the decision rendered would be of little use if it did not serve as a guideline for future cases in which similar factual patterns arise. Therefore, the facts are important, and careful attention must be paid to them in reading the cases. The cases that follow have been selected either because of their importance as precedents or because of their "typicality." They interpret constitutional provisions and demonstrate the judicial processes followed when the United States Supreme Court or lower federal courts reach a decision involving a constitutional question. Due to space limitations, considerable editing has been necessary.

Cases Relating to Chapter 1

History, Structure, and Content of the United States Constitution

UNITED STATES
v.
LOPEZ

514 U.S. 549, 115 S. Ct. 1624, 131 L. Ed. 2d 626 (1995)

[Citations and footnotes omitted.]

[Lopez, a 12th-grade student, was convicted of violating the Gun-Free School Zones Act, which made it a federal offense for any individual knowingly to possess a firearm in a school zone. The issue before the Supreme Court was whether Congress had the power to enact the Gun-Free School Zones Act under the Commerce Clause.]

Chief Justice REHNQUIST delivered the opinion of the Court.

* * *

. . . The Constitution creates a Federal Government of enumerated powers. As James Madison wrote, "[t]he powers delegated by the proposed Constitution to the federal government are few and defined. Those which are to remain in the State governments are numerous and indefinite." This constitutionally mandated division of authority "was adopted by the Framers to ensure protection of our fundamental liberties. Just as the separation and independence of the coordinate branches of the Federal Government serve to prevent the accumulation of excessive power in any one branch, a healthy balance of power between the States and the Federal Government will reduce the risk of tyranny and abuse from either front."

The Constitution delegates to Congress the power "[t]o regulate Commerce with foreign Nations, and among the several States, and with the Indian Tribes." . . .

* * *

. . . [W]e have identified three broad categories of activity that Congress may regulate under its commerce power. First, Congress may regulate the use of the channels of interstate commerce. " '[T]he authority of Congress to keep the channels of interstate commerce free from immoral and injurious uses has been frequently sustained, and is no longer open to question.' " Second, Congress is empowered to regulate and protect the instrumentalities of interstate commerce, or persons or things in interstate commerce, even though the threat may come only from intrastate activities. "[F]or example, the destruction of an aircraft or . . . thefts from interstate shipments. Finally, Congress' commerce authority includes the power to regulate those activities having a substantial relation to interstate commerce, i.e., those activities that substantially affect interstate commerce.

* * *

We now turn to consider the power of Congress, in the light of this framework, to enact [The Gun-Free School Zones Act] 922(q). The first two categories of authority may be quickly disposed of: 922(q) is not a regulation of the use of the channels of interstate commerce, nor is it an attempt to prohibit the interstate transportation of a commodity through the channels of commerce; nor can 922(q) be justified as a regulation by which Congress has sought to protect an instrumentality of interstate commerce or a thing in interstate commerce. Thus, if 922(q) is to be sustained, it must be under the third category as a regulation of an activity that substantially affects interstate commerce.

First, we have upheld a wide variety of congressional Acts regulating intrastate economic activity where we have concluded that the activity substantially affected interstate commerce. Examples include the regulation of intrastate coal mining; intrastate extortionate credit transactions, restaurants utilizing substantial interstate supplies, inns and hotels catering to interstate guests, and production and consumption of home-grown wheat. These examples are by no means exhaustive, but the pattern is clear. Where economic activity substantially affects interstate commerce, legislation regulating that activity will be sustained.

* * *

Section 922(q) is a criminal statute that by its terms has nothing to do with "commerce" or any sort of economic enterprise, however broadly one might define those terms. Section 922(q) is not an essential part of a larger regulation of economic activity, in which the regulatory scheme could be undercut unless the intrastate activity were regulated. It cannot, therefore, be sustained under our cases upholding regulations of activities that arise out of or are connected with a commercial transaction, which, viewed in the aggregate, substantially affects interstate commerce.

* * *

. . . The possession of a gun in a local school zone is in no sense an economic activity that might, through repetition elsewhere, substantially affect any sort of interstate commerce. Respondent was a local student at a local school; there is no indication that he had recently moved in interstate commerce, and there is no requirement that his possession of the firearm have any concrete tie to interstate commerce.

To uphold the Government's contentions here, we would have to pile inference upon inference in a manner that would bid fair to convert congressional authority under the Commerce Clause to a general police power of the sort retained by the States. Admittedly, some of our prior cases have

taken long steps down that road, giving great deference to congressional action. The broad language in these opinions has suggested the possibility of additional expansion, but we decline here to proceed any further. To do so would require us to conclude that the Constitution's enumeration of powers does not presuppose something not enumerated, and that there never will be a distinction between what is truly national and what is truly local. This we are unwilling to do.

For the foregoing reasons the judgment of the Court of Appeals is

Affirmed.

JUSTICE KENNEDY, with whom JUSTICE O'CONNOR joins, concurring.

* * *

Of the various structural elements in the Constitution, separation of powers, checks and balances, judicial review, and federalism, only concerning the last does there seem to be much uncertainty respecting the existence, and the content, of standards that allow the judiciary to play a significant role in maintaining the design contemplated by the Framers. Although the resolution of specific cases has proved difficult, we have derived from the Constitution workable standards to assist in preserving separation of powers and checks and balances. These standards are by now well accepted. Judicial review is also established beyond question, and though we may differ when applying its principles, its legitimacy is undoubted. Our role in preserving the federal balance seems more tenuous.

There is irony in this, because of the four structural elements in the Constitution just mentioned, federalism was the unique contribution of the Framers to political science and political theory. Though on the surface the idea may seem counterintuitive, it was the insight of the Framers that freedom was enhanced by the creation of two governments, not one. "In the compound republic of America, the power surrendered by the people is first divided between two distinct governments, and then the portion allotted to each subdivided among distinct and separate departments. Hence a double security arises to the rights of the people. The different governments will control each other, at the same time that each will be controlled by itself." . . .

The theory that two governments accord more liberty than one requires for its realization two distinct and discernable lines of political accountability: one between the citizens and the Federal Government; the second between the citizens and the States. . . . Were the Federal Government to take over the regulation of entire areas of traditional state concern, areas having nothing to do with the regulation of commercial activities, the boundaries between the spheres of federal and state authority would blur and political responsibility would become illusory . . .

* * *

The statute before us upsets the federal balance to [the] degree that renders it an unconstitutional assertion of the commerce power, and our intervention is required. As the Chief Justice explains, unlike the earlier cases to come before the Court here neither the actors nor their conduct have a commercial character, and neither the purposes nor the design of the statute have an evident commercial nexus. The statute makes the simple possession of a gun within 1,000 feet of the grounds of the school a criminal offense. In a sense any conduct in this interdependent world of ours has an ultimate commercial origin or consequence, but we have not yet said the commerce power may reach so far. If Congress attempts that extension, then at the least we must inquire whether the exercise of national power seeks to intrude upon an area of traditional state concern.

An interference of these dimensions occurs here, for it is well established that education is a traditional concern of the States. The proximity to schools, including of course schools owned and operated by the States or their subdivisions, is the very premise for making the conduct criminal. In these circumstances, we have a particular duty to insure that the federal-state balance is not destroyed . . .

While it is doubtful that any State, or indeed any reasonable person, would argue that it is wise policy to allow students to carry guns on school premises, considerable disagreement exists about how best to accomplish that goal. In this circumstance, the theory and utility of our federalism are revealed, for the States may perform their role as laboratories for experimentation to devise various solutions where the best solution is far from clear.

If a State or municipality determines that harsh criminal sanctions are necessary and wise

to deter students from carrying guns on school premises, the reserved powers of the States are sufficient to enact those measures. Indeed, over 40 States already have criminal laws outlawing the possession of firearms on or near school grounds.

* * *

The statute now before us forecloses the States from experimenting and exercising their own judgment in an area to which States lay claim by right of history and expertise, and it does so by regulating an activity beyond the realm of commerce in the ordinary and usual sense of that term. . . .

* * *

. . . While the intrusion on state sovereignty may not be as severe in this instance as in some of our recent Tenth Amendment cases, the intrusion is nonetheless significant. Absent a stronger connection or identification with commercial concerns that are central to the Commerce Clause, that interference contradicts the federal balance the Framers designed and that this Court is obliged to enforce.

For these reasons, I join in the opinion and judgment of the Court.

UNITED STATES v. COMSTOCK

560 U.S. —, 130 S. Ct. 1949, 176 L. Ed. 2d 878 (2010)

[Citations and footnotes omitted.]

[Congress enacted a federal statute authorizing civil commitment, after completion of their prison sentences, of federal prisoners who had previously engaged in sexually violent conduct or child molestation or who, as a result of mental illness, would have serious difficulty in refraining from such conduct. The question before the Court was whether Congress had constitutional power to enact this statute. The Court concluded that the power existed under the Necessary and Proper Clause.]

Justice BREYER delivered the opinion of the Court.

* * *

... [T]he Necessary and Proper Clause grants Congress broad authority to enact federal legislation. Nearly 200 years ago, this Court stated that the Federal [G]overnment is acknowledged by all to be one of enumerated powers, which means that [e]very law enacted by Congress must be based on one or more of_ those powers. But, at the same time, a government, entrusted with such powers must also be entrusted with ample means for their execution. Accordingly, the Necessary and Proper Clause makes clear that the Constitution's grants of specific federal legislative authority are accompanied by broad power to enact laws that are convenient, or useful or conducive to the authority's beneficial exercise. Chief Justice Marshall emphasized that the word necessary does not mean absolutely necessary. In language that has come to define the scope of the Necessary and Proper Clause, he wrote:

> "Let the end be legitimate, let it be within the scope of the constitution, and all means which are appropriate, which are plainly adapted to that end, which are not prohibited, but consist with the letter and spirit of the constitution, are constitutional."

We have since made clear that, in determining whether the Necessary and Proper Clause grants Congress the legislative authority to enact a particular federal statute, we look to see whether the statute constitutes a means that is rationally related to the implementation of a constitutionally enumerated power.

* * *

Thus, the Constitution, which nowhere speaks explicitly about the creation of federal crimes beyond those related to counterfeiting, treason, or Piracies and Felonies committed on the high Seas or against the Law of Nations, nonetheless grants Congress broad authority to create such crimes. And Congress routinely exercises its authority to enact criminal laws in furtherance of, for example, its enumerated powers to regulate interstate and foreign commerce, to enforce civil rights, to spend funds for the general welfare, to establish federal courts, to establish post offices, to regulate bankruptcy, to regulate naturalization, and so forth.

Similarly, Congress, in order to help ensure the enforcement of federal criminal laws enacted in furtherance of its enumerated powers, can cause a prison to be erected at any place within the jurisdiction of the United States, and direct that all persons sentenced to imprisonment under the laws of the United States shall be confined there. Moreover, Congress, having established a prison system, can enact laws that seek to ensure that system's safe and responsible administration by, for example, requiring prisoners to receive medical care and educational training, and can also ensure the safety of the prisoners, prison workers and visitors, and those in surrounding communities by, for example, creating further criminal laws governing entry, exit, and smuggling, and by employing prison guards to ensure discipline and security.

Neither Congress' power to criminalize conduct, nor its power to imprison individuals who engage in that conduct, nor its power to enact laws governing prisons and prisoners, is explicitly mentioned in the Constitution. But Congress nonetheless possesses broad authority to do each of those things in the course of carrying into Execution the enumerated powers vested by the Constitution in the Government of the United States –authority granted by the Necessary and Proper Clause.

* * *

... [E]ven the dissent acknowledges that Congress has the implied power to criminalize any conduct that might interfere with the exercise of an enumerated power, and also the additional power to imprison people who violate those (inferentially authorized) laws, and the additional power to provide for the safe and reasonable management of those prisons, and the additional power to regulate the prisoners' behavior even after their release.... [E]ach of those powers ... is ultimately derived from an enumerated power.... And the same enumerated power that justifies the creation of a federal criminal statute, and that justifies the additional implied federal powers that the dissent considers legitimate, justifies civil commitment under § 4248 as well....

* * *

The judgment of the Court of Appeals for the Fourth Circuit with respect to Congress' power to enact this statute is reversed, and the case is remanded for further proceedings consistent with this opinion.

It is so ordered.

PRINTZ
v.
UNITED STATES

521 U.S. 98, 117 S. Ct. 2365, 138 L. Ed. 2d 914 (1997)

[Citations and footnotes omitted.]

[In 1993, Congress enacted the Brady Handgun Violence Prevention Act, which required the Attorney General of the United States to establish a national system for instantly checking prospective handgun purchasers' backgrounds. As an interim measure, the law directed the "chief law enforcement officer" (CLEO) of each local jurisdiction to conduct background checks of would-be gun purchasers until such time as the national system became operative. A group of sheriffs for counties in Montana and Arizona sought to enjoin enforcement of this provision on the grounds that it was a violation of principles of federalism and state sovereignty for Congress to make state law enforcement officers administer federal programs.]

Justice SCALIA delivered the opinion of the Court.

* * *

... [T]he Brady Act purports to direct state law enforcement officers to participate, albeit only temporarily, in the administration of a federally enacted regulatory scheme. Regulated firearms dealers are required to forward Brady Forms not to a federal officer or employee, but to the CLEOs, whose obligation to accept those forms is implicit in the duty imposed upon them to make "reasonable efforts" within five days to determine whether the sales reflected in the forms are lawful....

The petitioners here object to being pressed into federal service, and contend that congressional action compelling state officers to execute federal laws is unconstitutional. Because there is no constitutional text speaking to this precise question, the answer to the CLEOs' challenge must be sought in historical understanding and practice, in the structure of the Constitution, and in the jurisprudence of this Court....

* * *

It is incontestable that the Constitution established a system of "dual sovereignty." Although the States surrendered many of their powers to the new Federal Government, they retained "a residuary and inviolable sovereignty." This is reflected throughout the Constitution's text, including (to mention only a few examples) the prohibition on any involuntary reduction or combination of a State's territory, Art. IV, § 3; the Judicial Power Clause, Art. III, § 2, and the Privileges and Immunities Clause, Art. IV, § 2, which speak of the "Citizens" of the States; the amendment provision, Article V, which requires the votes of three-fourths of the States to amend the Constitution; and the Guarantee Clause, Art. IV, § 4, which "presupposes the continued existence of the states and ... those means and instrumentalities which are the creation of their sovereign and reserved rights." Residual state sovereignty was also implicit, of course, in the Constitution's conferral upon Congress of not all governmental powers, but only discrete, enumerated ones, Art. I, § 8, which implication was rendered express by the Tenth Amendment's assertion that "[t]he powers not delegated to the United States by the Constitution, nor prohibited by it to the States, are reserved to the States respectively, or to the people."

The Framers' experience under the Articles of Confederation had persuaded them that using the States as the instruments of federal governance was both ineffectual and provocative of federal-state conflict. ... [T]he Framers rejected the concept of a central government that would act upon and through the States, and instead designed a system in which the state and federal governments would exercise concurrent authority over the people — who were, in Hamilton's words, "the only proper objects of government." We have set forth the historical record in more detail elsewhere, and need not repeat it here. It suffices to repeat the conclusion: "The Framers explicitly chose a Constitution that confers upon Congress the power to regulate individuals, not States." The great innovation of this design was that "our citizens would have two political capacities, one state and one federal, each protected from incursion by the other"— "a legal system unprecedented in form and design, establishing two orders of government, each with its own direct relationship, its own privity, its own set of mutual rights and obligations to the people who sustain it and are governed by it." The Constitution thus contemplates that a State's government will represent and remain accountable to its own citizens.... As Madison expressed it: "[T]he local or municipal authorities form distinct and independent portions of the supremacy, no more subject, within their respective spheres, to the general authority than the general authority is subject to them, within its own sphere."

This separation of the two spheres is one of the Constitution's structural protections of liberty. "Just as the separation and independence of the coordinate branches of the Federal Government serve to prevent the accumulation of excessive power in any one branch, a healthy balance of power between the States and the Federal Government will reduce the risk of tyranny and abuse from either front." To quote Madison once again: "In the compound republic of America, the power surrendered by the people is first divided between two distinct governments, and then the portion allotted to each subdivided among distinct and separate departments. Hence a double security arises to the rights of the people. The different governments will control each other, at the same time that each will be controlled by itself." The power of the Federal Government would be augmented immeasurably if it were able to impress into its service — and at no cost to itself — the police officers of the 50 States.

We have thus far discussed the effect that federal control of state officers would have upon the first element of the "double security" alluded to by Madison: the division of power between State and Federal Governments. It would also have an effect upon the second element: the separation and equilibration of powers between the three branches of the Federal Government itself. The Constitution does not leave to speculation who is to administer the laws enacted by Congress; the President, it says, "shall take Care that the Laws be faithfully executed," Art. II, § 3, personally and through officers whom he appoints.... The Brady Act effectively transfers this responsibility to thousands of CLEOs in the 50 States, who are left to implement the program without meaningful Presidential control (if indeed meaningful Presidential control is possible without the power to appoint and remove). The insistence of the Framers upon unity in the Federal Executive — to insure both vigor and accountability — is well known. That unity would be shattered, and the power of the President would be subject to reduction, if Congress could act as effectively without the President as with him, by simply requiring state officers to execute its laws.

The dissent of course resorts to ... the Necessary and Proper Clause. It reasons that the power to regulate the sale of handguns under the Commerce Clause, coupled with the power to "make all Laws which shall be necessary and proper for carrying into Execution the foregoing Powers," Art. I, § 8, conclusively establishes the Brady Act's constitutional validity, because the Tenth Amendment imposes no limitations on the exercise of delegated powers but merely prohibits the exercise of powers "not delegated to the United States." What destroys the dissent's Necessary and Proper Clause argument, however, is not the Tenth Amendment but the Necessary and Proper Clause itself. When a "La[w] ... for carrying into Execution" the Commerce Clause violates the principle of state sovereignty reflected in the various constitutional provisions we mentioned earlier, it is not a "La[w] ... proper for carrying into Execution the Commerce Clause," and is thus, in the words of The Federalist, "merely [an] ac[t] of usurpation" which "deserve[s] to be treated as such." . . . "[E]ven where Congress has the authority under the Constitution to pass laws requiring or prohibiting certain acts, it lacks the power directly to compel the States to require or prohibit those acts. . . .

* * *

We held in New York that Congress cannot compel the States to enact or enforce a federal regulatory program. Today we hold that Congress cannot circumvent that prohibition by conscripting the State's officers directly. The Federal Government may neither issue directives requiring the States to address particular problems, nor command the States' officers, or those of their political subdivisions, to administer or enforce a federal regulatory program. It matters not whether policymaking is involved, and no case-by-case weighing of the burdens or benefits is necessary; such commands are fundamentally incompatible with our constitutional system of dual sovereignty. Accordingly, the judgment of the Court of Appeals for the Ninth Circuit is reversed.

It is so ordered.

[Concurring and dissenting opinions omitted.]

DISTRICT OF COLUMBIA
v.
HELLER

554 U.S. 570, 128 S. Ct. 2783, 171 L. Ed. 2d 637 (2008)

[Citations and footnotes omitted.]

Justice SCALIA delivered the opinion of the Court.

We consider whether a District of Columbia prohibition on the possession of usable handguns in the home violates the Second Amendment to the Constitution.

The District of Columbia generally prohibits the possession of handguns. It is a crime to carry an unregistered firearm, and the registration of handguns is prohibited. . . . District of Columbia law also requires residents to keep their lawfully owned firearms, such as registered long guns, "unloaded and dissembled or bound by a trigger lock or similar device" unless they are located in a place of business or are being used for lawful recreational activities.

Respondent Dick Heller is a D.C. special police officer authorized to carry a handgun while on duty at the Federal Judicial Center. He applied for a registration certificate for a handgun that he wished to keep at home, but the District refused. He thereafter filed a lawsuit in the Federal District Court for the District of Columbia seeking, on Second Amendment grounds, to enjoin the city from enforcing the bar on the registration of handguns, the licensing requirement insofar as it prohibits the carrying of a firearm in the home without a license, and the trigger-lock requirement insofar as it prohibits the use of "functional firearms within the home." . . . We turn first to the meaning of the Second Amendment.

The Second Amendment provides: "A well regulated Militia, being necessary to the security of a free State, the right of the people to keep and bear Arms, shall not be infringed." . . . The two sides in this case have set out very different interpretations of the Amendment. Petitioners and today's dissenting Justices believe that it protects only the right to possess and carry a firearm in connection with militia service. Respondent argues that it protects an individual right to possess a firearm unconnected with service in a militia, and to use that arm for traditionally lawful purposes, such as self-defense within the home.

The Second Amendment is naturally divided into two parts: its prefatory clause and its operative clause. The former does not limit the latter grammatically, but rather announces a purpose. The Amendment could be rephrased, "Because a well regulated Militia is necessary to the security of a free State, the right of the people to keep and bear Arms shall not be infringed." Although this structure of the Second Amendment is unique in our Constitution, other legal documents of the founding era, particularly individual-rights provisions of state constitutions, commonly included a prefatory statement of purpose.

* * *

. . . The prefatory clause does not suggest that preserving the militia was the only reason Americans valued the ancient right; most undoubtedly thought it even more important for self-defense and hunting. But the threat that the new Federal Government would destroy the citizens' militia by taking away their arms was the reason that right-unlike some other English rights-was codified in a written Constitution. . . . Besides ignoring the historical reality that the Second Amendment was not intended to lay down a "novel principl[e]" but rather codified a right "inherited from our English ancestors," petitioners' interpretation does not even achieve the narrower purpose that prompted codification of the right. If, as they believe, the Second Amendment right is no more than the right to keep and use weapons as a member of an organized militia, that is, the *organized* militia is the sole institutional beneficiary of the Second Amendment's guarantee — it does not assure the existence of a "citizens' militia" as a safeguard against tyranny. For Congress retains plenary authority to organize the militia, which must include the authority to say who will belong to the organized force. . . . Thus, if petitioners are correct, the Second Amendment protects citizens' right to use a gun in an organization from which Congress has plenary authority to exclude them. It guarantees a select militia of the sort the Stuart kings found useful, but not the people's militia that was the concern of the founding generation.

* * *

Like most rights, the right secured by the Second Amendment is not unlimited. From Blackstone through the 19th-century cases, commentators and courts routinely explained that the right was not a right to keep and carry any weapon whatsoever in any manner whatsoever and for whatever purpose. For example, the majority of the 19th-century courts to consider the question held that prohibitions on carrying concealed weapons were lawful under the Second Amendment or state analogues. Although we do not undertake an exhaustive historical analysis today of the full scope of the Second Amendment, nothing in our opinion should be taken to cast doubt on longstanding prohibitions on the possession of firearms by felons and the mentally ill, or laws forbidding the carrying of firearms in sensitive places such as schools and government buildings, or laws imposing conditions and qualifications on the commercial sale of arms.

We also recognize another important limitation on the right to keep and carry arms. *Miller* said, as we have explained, that the sorts of weapons protected were those "in common use at the time." We think that limitation is fairly supported by the historical tradition of prohibiting the carrying of "dangerous and unusual weapons."

It may be objected that if weapons that are most useful in military service — M-16 rifles and the like — may be banned, then the Second Amendment right is completely detached from the prefatory clause. But as we have said, the conception of the militia at the time of the Second Amendment's ratification was the body of all citizens capable of military service, who would bring the sorts of lawful weapons that they possessed at home to militia duty. It may well be true today that a militia, to be as effective as militias in the 18th century, would require sophisticated arms that are highly unusual in society at large. Indeed, it may be true that no amount of small arms could be useful against modern-day bombers and tanks. But the fact that modern developments have limited the degree of fit between the prefatory clause and the protected right cannot change our interpretation of the right.

We turn finally to the law at issue here. As we have said, the law totally bans handgun possession in the home. It also requires that any lawful firearm in the home be disassembled or bound by a trigger lock at all times, rendering it inoperable.

As the quotations earlier in this opinion demonstrate, the inherent right of self-defense has been central to the Second Amendment right. The handgun ban amounts to a prohibition of an entire class of "arms" that is overwhelmingly chosen by American society for that lawful purpose. The prohibition extends, moreover, to the home, where the need for defense of self, family, and property is most acute. Under any of the standards of scrutiny that we have applied to enumerated constitutional rights, banning from the home the most preferred firearm in the nation to "keep" and use for protection of one's home and family" would fail constitutional muster.

* * *

It is no answer to say, as petitioners do, that it is permissible to ban the possession of handguns so long as the possession of other firearms (*i.e.,* long guns) is allowed. It is enough to note, as we have observed, that the American people have considered the handgun to be the quintessential self-defense weapon. There are many reasons that a citizen may prefer a handgun for home defense: It is easier to store in a location that is readily accessible in an emergency; it cannot easily be redirected or wrestled away by an attacker; it is easier to use for those without the upper-body strength to lift and aim a long gun; it can be pointed at a burglar with one hand while the other hand dials the police. Whatever the reason, handguns are the most popular weapon chosen by Americans for self-defense in the home, and a complete prohibition of their use is invalid.

We must also address the District's requirement (as applied to respondent's handgun) that firearms in the home be rendered and kept inoperable at all times. This makes it impossible for citizens to use them for the core lawful purpose of self-defense and is hence unconstitutional. The District argues that we should interpret this element of the statute to contain an exception for self-defense. But we think that is precluded by the unequivocal text, and by the presence of certain other enumerated exceptions. . . .

* * *

In sum, we hold that the District's ban on handgun possession in the home violates the Second Amendment, as does its prohibition against rendering any lawful firearm in the home operable for the purpose of immediate self-defense.

Assuming that Heller is not disqualified from the exercise of Second Amendment rights, the District must permit him to register his handgun and must issue him a license to carry it in the home.

* * *

We are aware of the problem of handgun violence in this country, and we take seriously the concerns raised by the many *amici* who believe that prohibition of handgun ownership is a solution. The Constitution leaves the District of Columbia a variety of tools for combating that problem, including some measures regulating handguns. But the enshrinement of constitutional rights necessarily takes certain policy choices off the table. These include the absolute prohibition of handguns held and used for self-defense in the home. Undoubtedly some think that the Second Amendment is outmoded in a society where our standing army is the pride of our Nation, where well-trained police forces provide personal security, and where gun violence is a serious problem. That is perhaps debatable, but what is not debatable is that it is not the role of this Court to pronounce the Second Amendment extinct.

We affirm the judgment of the Court of Appeals.

It is so ordered.

LAWRENCE
v.
TEXAS

539 U.S. 558, 123 S. Ct. 2472, 156 L. Ed. 2d 508 (2003)

[Citations and footnotes omitted.]

[Houston police officers, responding to a hoax call about a weapons disturbance in John Lawrence's apartment, entered and saw Lawrence and Tyrone Garner, another adult male, engaging in homosexual conduct. They arrested both men and charged them with "deviate sexual intercourse," defined under Texas law as having "oral or anal sex, with a member of the same sex." Lawrence and Garner were both found guilty and appealed.]

JUSTICE KENNEDY delivered the opinion of the Court.

* * *

We granted certiorari to consider three questions:

1. Whether Petitioners' criminal convictions under the Texas 'Homosexual Conduct' law — which criminalizes sexual intimacy by same-sex couples, but not identical behavior by different-sex couples — violate the Fourteenth Amendment guarantee of equal protection of laws?
2. Whether Petitioners' criminal convictions for adult consensual sexual intimacy in the home violate their vital interests in liberty and privacy protected by the Due Process Clause of the Fourteenth Amendment?
3. Whether Bowers v. Hardwick should be overruled?

* * *

The facts in *Bowers* had some similarities to the instant case. A police officer, whose right to enter seems not to have been in question, observed Hardwick, in his own bedroom, engaging in intimate sexual conduct with another adult male. The conduct was in violation of a Georgia statute making it a criminal offense to engage in sodomy. One difference between the two cases is that the Georgia statute prohibited the conduct whether or not the participants were of the same sex, while the Texas statute, as we have seen, applies only to participants of the same sex. Hardwick was not prosecuted, but he brought an action in federal court to declare the state statute invalid. He alleged he was a practicing homosexual and that the criminal prohibition violated rights guaranteed to him by the Constitution. The Court, in an opinion by Justice White, sustained the Georgia law. . . .

The Court began its substantive discussion in *Bowers* as follows: "The issue presented is whether the Federal Constitution confers a fundamental right upon homosexuals to engage in sodomy and hence invalidates the laws of the many States that still make such conduct illegal and have done so for a very long time." That statement, we now conclude, discloses the Court's own failure to appreciate the extent of the liberty at stake. To say that the issue in *Bowers* was simply the right to engage in certain sexual conduct demeans the claim the individual put forward, just as it would demean a married couple were it to be said marriage is simply about the right to have sexual intercourse. The laws involved in *Bowers* and here are, to be sure, statutes that purport to do no more than prohibit a particular sexual act. Their penalties and purposes, though, have more far-reaching consequences, touching upon the most private human conduct, sexual behavior, and in the most private of places, the home. The statutes do seek to control a personal relationship that, whether or not entitled to formal recognition in the law, is within the liberty of persons to choose without being punished as criminals.

This, as a general rule, should counsel against attempts by the State, or a court, to define the meaning of the relationship or to set its boundaries absent injury to a person or abuse of an institution the law protects. It suffices for us to acknowledge that adults may choose to enter upon this relationship in the confines of their homes and their own private lives and still retain their dignity as free persons. When sexuality finds overt expression in intimate conduct with another person, the conduct can be but one element in a personal bond that is more enduring. The liberty protected by the Constitution allows homosexual persons the right to make this choice.

* * *

It must be acknowledged, of course, that the Court in *Bowers* was making the broader point that for centuries there have been powerful voices to condemn homosexual conduct as immoral. The condemnation has been shaped by religious beliefs, conceptions of right and acceptable behavior, and respect for the traditional family. For many persons these are not trivial concerns but profound and deep convictions accepted as ethical and moral principles to which they aspire and which thus determine the course of their lives. These considerations do not answer the question before us, however. The issue is whether the majority may use the power of the State to enforce these views on the whole society through operation of the criminal law. "Our obligation is to define the liberty of all, not to mandate our own moral code."

. . . "[O]ur laws and traditions in the past half-century are of most relevance here. These references show an emerging awareness that liberty gives substantial protection to adult persons in deciding how to conduct their private lives in matters pertaining to sex. . . . This emerging recognition should have been apparent when Bowers was decided. In 1955 the American Law Institute promulgated the Model Penal Code and made clear that it did not recommend or provide for "criminal penalties for consensual sexual relations conducted in private." It justified its decision on three grounds: (1) The prohibitions undermined respect for the law by penalizing conduct many people engaged in; (2) the statutes regulated private conduct not harmful to others; and (3) the laws were arbitrarily enforced and thus invited the danger of blackmail. In 1961 Illinois changed its laws to conform to the Model Penal Code. Other States soon followed.

* * *

. . . [T]he deficiencies in *Bowers* became even more apparent in the years following its announcement. The 25 States with laws prohibiting the relevant conduct referenced in the *Bowers* decision are reduced now to 13, of which 4 enforce their laws only against homosexual conduct. In those States where sodomy is still proscribed, whether for same-sex or heterosexual conduct, there is a pattern of nonenforcement with respect to consenting adults acting in private. The State of Texas admitted in 1994 that as of that date it had not prosecuted anyone under those circumstances.

Two principal cases decided after *Bowers* cast its holding into even more doubt. In *Planned Parenthood of Southeastern Pa. v. Casey,* the Court reaffirmed the substantive force of the liberty protected by the Due Process Clause. The *Casey* decision again confirmed that our laws and tradition afford constitutional protection to personal decisions relating to marriage, procreation, contraception, family relationships, child rearing, and education. In explaining the respect the Constitution demands for the autonomy of the person in making these choices, we stated as follows:

These matters, involving the most intimate and personal choices a person may make in a lifetime, choices central to personal dignity and autonomy, are central to the liberty protected by the Fourteenth Amendment. At the heart of liberty is the right to define one's own concept of existence, of meaning, of the universe, and of the mystery of human life. Beliefs about these matters could not define the attributes of personhood were they formed under compulsion of the State.

Persons in a homosexual relationship may seek autonomy for these purposes, just as heterosexual persons do. The decision in Bowers would deny them this right.

The second post-*Bowers* case of principal relevance is *Romer v. Evans*. There the Court struck down class-based legislation directed at homosexuals as a violation of the Equal Protection Clause. *Romer* invalidated an amendment to Colorado's constitution which named as a solitary class persons who were homosexuals, lesbians, or bisexual either by "orientation, conduct, practices or relationships," and deprived them of protection under state antidiscrimination laws. We concluded that the provision was "born of animosity toward the class of persons affected" and further that it had no rational relation to a legitimate governmental purpose.

As an alternative argument in this case, counsel for the petitioners and some amici contend that *Romer* provides the basis for declaring the Texas statute invalid under the Equal Protection Clause. That is a tenable argument, but we conclude the instant case requires us to address whether Bowers itself has continuing validity. Were we to hold the statute invalid under the Equal Protection Clause some might question whether a prohibition would be valid if drawn differently, say, to prohibit the conduct both between same-sex and different-sex participants.

Equality of treatment and the due process right to demand respect for conduct protected by the substantive guarantee of liberty are linked in important respects, and a decision on the latter point advances both interests. If protected conduct is made criminal and the law which does so remains unexamined for its substantive validity, its stigma might remain even if it were not enforceable as drawn for equal protection reasons. When homosexual conduct is made criminal by the law of the State, that declaration in and of itself is an invitation to subject homosexual persons to discrimination both in the public and in the private spheres. The central holding of Bowers has been brought in question by this case, and it should be addressed. Its continuance as precedent demeans the lives of homosexual persons.

The stigma this criminal statute imposes, moreover, is not trivial. The offense, to be sure, is but a class C misdemeanor, a minor offense in the Texas legal system. Still, it remains a criminal offense with all that imports for the dignity of the persons charged. The petitioners will bear on their record the history of their criminal convictions. Just this Term we rejected various challenges to state laws requiring the registration of sex offenders. We are advised that if Texas convicted an adult for private, consensual homosexual conduct under the statute here in question the convicted person would come within the registration laws of a least four States were he or she to be subject to their jurisdiction. This underscores the consequential nature of the punishment and the state-sponsored condemnation attendant to the criminal prohibition. Furthermore, the Texas criminal conviction carries with it the other collateral consequences always following a conviction, such as notations on job application forms, to mention but one example.

The foundations of *Bowers* have sustained serious erosion from our recent decisions in *Casey* and *Romer*. When our precedent has been thus weakened, criticism from other sources is of greater significance. In the United States criticism of *Bowers* has been substantial and continuing, disapproving of its reasoning in all respects, not just as to its historical assumptions. The courts of five different States have declined to follow it in interpreting provisions in their own state constitutions parallel to the Due Process Clause of the Fourteenth Amendment.

To the extent *Bowers* relied on values we share with a wider civilization, it should be noted that the reasoning and holding in *Bowers* have been rejected elsewhere. The European Court of Human Rights has followed not *Bowers* but its own decision in *Dudgeon v. United Kingdom*. Other nations, too, have taken action consistent with an affirmation of the protected right of homosexual adults to engage in intimate, consensual conduct. The right the petitioners seek in this case has been accepted as an integral part of human freedom in many other countries. There has been no showing that in this country the governmental interest in circumscribing personal choice is somehow more legitimate or urgent.

* * *

Bowers was not correct when it was decided, and it is not correct today. It ought not to remain binding precedent. *Bowers v. Hardwick* should be and now is overruled.

The present case does not involve minors. It does not involve persons who might be injured or coerced or who are situated in relationships where consent might not easily be refused. It does not involve public conduct or prostitution. It does not involve whether the government must give formal recognition to any relationship that homosexual persons seek to enter. The case does involve two adults who, with full and mutual consent from each other, engaged in sexual practices common to a homosexual lifestyle. The petitioners are entitled to respect for their private lives. The State cannot demean their existence or control their destiny by making their private sexual conduct a crime. Their right to liberty under the Due Process Clause gives them the full right to engage in their conduct without intervention of the government. "It is a promise of the Constitution that there is a realm of personal liberty which the government may not enter." The Texas statute furthers no legitimate state interest which can justify its intrusion into the personal and private life of the individual.

Had those who drew and ratified the Due Process Clauses of the Fifth Amendment or the Fourteenth Amendment known the components of liberty in its manifold possibilities, they might have been more specific. They did not presume to have this insight. They knew times can blind us to certain truths and later generations can see that laws once thought necessary and proper in fact serve only to oppress. As the Constitution endures, persons in every generation can invoke its principles in their own search for greater freedom.

The judgment of the Court of Appeals for the Texas Fourteenth District is reversed, and the case is remanded for further proceedings not inconsistent with this opinion.

It is so ordered.

MARYLAND STATE CONFERENCE OF NAACP BRANCHES
v.
MARYLAND STATE POLICE

454 F. Supp. 2d 339 (D. Md. 2006)

[Citations and footnotes omitted.]

This action asserts claims of the plaintiffs that they were subjected to illegal traffic stops and/or searches by Maryland state troopers. At its heart,

the action asserts that the stops and searches were the result of racial profiling and were otherwise legally infirm in violation of the Fourth and Fourteenth Amendments to the U.S. Constitution. . . .

* * *

Johnston Williams, a black Liberian citizen and resident alien of the United States, was stopped by Trooper Billy White. Mr. Williams had four passengers in his vehicle, three Liberian and one Guinean, all black.

Mr. Williams claims that he was traveling at the speed limit with the flow of traffic in the middle lane of I-95 when Trooper White pulled in behind him and followed him for several miles. The trooper eventually engaged his emergency lights, and Mr. Williams pulled over. According to Mr. Williams, Trooper White advised him that he had been stopped for speeding and immediately asked him if he was Jamaican. Mr. Williams claims that when he asked why that information was necessary Trooper White replied in a raised voice that he had a right to know, screamed at him and his passengers that he had the right to ask them whatever he pleased and told them that "you Jamaicans" were known to be involved in drug smuggling and gang-related activities. Trooper White purportedly continued to refer to Mr. Williams and his passengers as drug-running Jamaicans and when Mr. Williams attempted to protest that he was Liberian Trooper White cut him off and told him and his passengers that all foreigners of African descent were trouble makers and problem makers.

Mr. Williams avers that Trooper White then opened his car door and pulled him from his car, shoved him against the car and kicked his legs apart, and placed one of his hands on his sidearm. He claims that as Trooper White patted him down he told the other passengers that if they tried to get out of the car during the search he would shoot them and make it look like self-defense. Mr. Williams alleges that Trooper White then divided the group and searched through the car, the engine compartment and the trunk-the search yielding no contraband. The search purportedly was done without the consent of Mr. Williams.

Mr. Williams claims that Trooper White, after checking his license, registration and immigration documents, returned to Mr. Williams' vehicle and gave him two tickets-one for speeding and one for refusing to sign a ticket. Mr. Williams avers that when he and one of his passengers protested that Mr. Williams had not refused to sign anything, Trooper White told the passenger to shut up and told Mr. Williams to take the two tickets or risk being arrested.

Trooper White avers that Mr. Williams was stopped because his vehicle was detected by laser unit traveling at 80 mph in a 65 mph zone. He denies following the vehicle for several miles. He avers that there was no search and that the occupants never left the vehicle. He denies making any racial or ethnic references.

The Court finds that the conduct alleged by Mr. Williams, and the reasonable inferences that can be drawn therefrom, would be violations of his constitutional rights to equal protection and freedom from unreasonable search and seizure and that a reasonable police officer in Trooper White's position would have been aware that his conduct violated Plaintiff Williams' constitutional rights. Therefore Trooper White is not entitled to qualified immunity.

In regard to the substantive constitutional claims asserted, Mr. Williams contends that there was no valid reason for the stop and asserts that Trooper White engaged in ethnic slurs, an unjustified non-consensual search of his person and his vehicle, and deadly threats to his passengers. The facts alleged by Mr. Williams, if fully credited, would give rise to a reasonable inference that Trooper White's conduct was race/national origin based and that the purported search of Mr. Williams and his vehicle were in violation of Mr. Williams' constitutional rights pursuant to the 4th and 14th Amendments. Moreover, if Mr. Williams' version of events is fully credited, the diametrically variant statement of facts presented by Trooper White would impeach Trooper White's credibility generally. By separate Order, summary judgment will be denied as to the constitutional claims of Plaintiff Williams.

Cases Relating to Chapter 2

Freedom of Speech

TEXAS
v.
JOHNSON

491 U.S. 397, 109 S. Ct. 2533,
105 L. Ed. 2d 342 (1989)

[Citations and footnotes omitted.]

[Johnson participated in a political protest demonstration in Dallas during the 1984 Republican National Convention. The demonstration ended in front of City Hall, where Johnson unfurled an American flag, doused it with kerosene, and set it on fire while the demonstrators chanted, "America, the red, white, and blue, we spit on you." No one was physically injured or threatened with injury, although several witnesses testified that they had been seriously offended by Johnson's behavior. Johnson was charged with and convicted of desecrating an American flag in violation of Tex. Penal Code Ann. § 42.09 (a)(3). The question before the Supreme Court was whether criminalizing flag burning violates the First Amendment.]

JUSTICE BRENNAN delivered the opinion of the Court.

* * *

The First Amendment literally forbids the abridgment only of "speech," but we have long recognized that its protection does not end at the spoken or written word. While we have rejected "the view that an apparently limitless variety of conduct can be labeled 'speech' whenever the person engaging in the conduct intends thereby to express an idea," we have acknowledged that conduct may be "sufficiently imbued with elements of communication to fall within the scope of the First and Fourteenth Amendments." In deciding whether particular conduct possesses sufficient communicative elements to bring the First Amendment into play, we have asked whether "[a]n intent to convey a particularized message was present, and [whether] the likelihood was great that the message would be understood by those who viewed it." Hence, we have recognized the expressive nature of students' wearing of black armbands to protest American military involvement in Vietnam; of a sit-in by blacks in a "whites only" area to protest segregation; of the wearing of American military uniforms in a dramatic presentation criticizing American military involvement in Vietnam; and of picketing about a wide variety of causes.

* * *

The State of Texas conceded for purposes of its oral argument in this case that Johnson's conduct was expressive conduct. . . . Johnson burned an American flag as part—indeed, as the culmination—of a political demonstration that coincided with the convening of the Republican Party and its renomination of Ronald Reagan for President. The expressive, overtly political nature of this conduct was both intentional and overwhelmingly apparent. At his trial, Johnson explained his reasons for burning the flag as follows: "The American Flag was burned as Ronald Reagan was being renominated as President. And a more powerful statement of symbolic speech, whether you agree with or not, couldn't have been made at that time. It's quite a just position [juxtaposition]. We had new patriotism and no patriotism." In these circumstances, Johnson's burning of the flag was conduct "sufficiently imbued with elements of communication to fall within the scope of the First and Fourteenth Amendments."

The Government generally has a freer hand in restricting expressive conduct than it has in restricting the written or spoken word. It may not, however, proscribe particular conduct because it has expressive elements. "[W]hat might be termed the more generalized guarantee of freedom of expression makes the communicative nature of conduct an inadequate basis for singling out that conduct for proscription. A law directed at the communicative nature of conduct must, like a law directed at speech itself, be justified by the substantial showing of need that the First Amendment requires." It is, in short, not simply the verbal or nonverbal nature of the expression, but the governmental interest at stake, that helps to determine whether a restriction on that expression is valid.

Thus, although we have recognized that where " 'speech' and 'nonspeech' elements are combined in the same course of conduct, a sufficiently important governmental interest in regulating the nonspeech element can justify incidental limitations on First Amendment freedoms," we have limited the applicability of O'Brien's relatively lenient standard to those cases in which "the governmental interest is unrelated to the suppression of free expression." . . .

In order to decide whether O'Brien's test applies here, therefore, we must decide whether Texas has asserted an interest in support of Johnson's conviction that is unrelated to the suppression of expression. . . . The State offers two separate interests to justify this conviction: preventing breaches of the peace, and preserving the flag as a symbol of nationhood and national unity. We hold that the first interest is not implicated on this record and that the second is related to the suppression of expression.

Texas claims that its interest in preventing breaches of the peace justifies Johnson's conviction for flag desecration. However, no disturbance of the peace actually occurred or threatened to occur because of Johnson's burning of the flag. . . . The only evidence offered by the State at trial to show the reaction to Johnson's actions was the testimony of several persons who had been seriously offended by the flag-burning. The State's position, therefore, amounts to a claim that an audience that takes serious offense at particular expression is necessarily likely to disturb the peace and that the expression may be prohibited on this basis. Our precedents do not countenance such a presumption. On the contrary, they recognize that a principal "function of free speech under our system of government is to invite dispute. It may indeed best serve its high purpose when it induces a condition of unrest, creates dissatisfaction with conditions as they are, or even stirs people to anger." . . .

Thus, we have not permitted the Government to assume that every expression of a provocative idea will incite a riot, but have instead required careful consideration of the actual circumstances surrounding such expression, asking whether the expression "is directed to inciting or producing imminent lawless action and is likely to incite or produce such action." To accept Texas' arguments that it need only demonstrate "the potential for a breach of the peace," and that every flag-burning necessarily possesses that potential, would be to eviscerate our holding in Brandenburg. This we decline to do.

Nor does Johnson's expressive conduct fall within that small class of "fighting words" that are "likely to provoke the average person to retaliation, and thereby cause a breach of the peace." No reasonable onlooker would have regarded Johnson's generalized expression of dissatisfaction with the policies of the Federal Government as a direct personal insult or an invitation to exchange fisticuffs.

We thus conclude that the State's interest in maintaining order is not implicated on these facts. The State need not worry that our holding will disable it from preserving the peace. We do not suggest that the First Amendment forbids a State to prevent "imminent lawless action." And, in fact, Texas already has a statute specifically prohibiting breaches of the peace, Tex. Penal Code Ann. § 42.01 (1989), which tends to confirm that Texas need not punish this flag desecration in order to keep the peace.

The State also asserts an interest in preserving the flag as a symbol of nationhood and national unity. In Spence, we acknowledged that the

Government's interest in preserving the flag's special symbolic value "is directly related to expression in the context of activity" such as affixing a peace symbol to a flag. We are equally persuaded that this interest is related to expression in the case of Johnson's burning of the flag. The State, apparently, is concerned that such conduct will lead people to believe either that the flag does not stand for nationhood and national unity, but instead reflects other, less positive concepts, or that the concepts reflected in the flag do not in fact exist, that is, we do not enjoy unity as a Nation. These concerns blossom only when a person's treatment of the flag communicates some message, and thus are related "to the suppression of free expression" within the meaning of *O'Brien*. We are thus outside of *O'Brien's* test altogether.

It remains to consider whether the State's interest in preserving the flag as a symbol of nationhood and national unity justifies Johnson's conviction.

As in *Spence* "[w]e are confronted with a case of prosecution for the expression of an idea through activity," and "[a]ccordingly, we must examine with particular care the interests advanced by [petitioner] to support its prosecution." Johnson was not, we add, prosecuted for the expression of just any idea; he was prosecuted for his expression of dissatisfaction with the policies of this country, expression situated at the core of our First Amendment values.

* * *

If there is a bedrock principle underlying the First Amendment, it is that the Government may not prohibit the expression of an idea simply because society finds the idea itself offensive or disagreeable.

We have not recognized an exception to this principle even where our flag has been involved. In Street v. New York, we held that a State may not criminally punish a person for uttering words critical of the flag. Rejecting the argument that the conviction could be sustained on the ground that Street had "failed to show the respect for our national symbol which may properly be demanded of every citizen," we concluded that "the constitutionally guaranteed 'freedom to be intellectually . . . diverse or even contrary,' and the 'right to differ as to things that touch the heart of the existing order,' encompass the freedom to express publicly one's opinions about our flag, including those opinions which are defiant or contemptuous." Nor may the Government, we have held, compel conduct that would evince respect for the flag. "To sustain the compulsory flag salute we are required to say that a Bill of Rights which guards the individual's right to speak his own mind, left it open to public authorities to compel him to utter what is not in his mind."

* * *

In short, nothing in our precedents suggests that a State may foster its own view of the flag by prohibiting expressive conduct relating to it. To bring its argument outside our precedents, Texas attempts to convince us that even if its interest in preserving the flag's symbolic role does not allow it to prohibit words or some expressive conduct critical of the flag, it does permit it to forbid the outright destruction of the flag. The State's argument cannot depend here on the distinction between written or spoken words and nonverbal conduct. That distinction, we have shown, is of no moment where the nonverbal conduct is expressive, as it is here, and where the regulation of that conduct is related to expression, as it is here. In addition, both *Barnette* and *Spence* involved expressive conduct, not only verbal communication, and both found that conduct protected.

* * *

We are fortified in today's conclusion by our conviction that forbidding criminal punishment for conduct such as Johnson's will not endanger the special role played by our flag or the feelings it inspires. . . .

We are tempted to say, in fact, that the flag's deservedly cherished place in our community will be strengthened, not weakened, by our holding today. Our decision is a reaffirmation of the principles of freedom and inclusiveness that the flag best reflects, and of the conviction that our toleration of criticism such as Johnson's is a sign and source of our strength. Indeed, one of the proudest images of our flag, the one immortalized in our own national anthem, is of the bombardment it survived at Fort McHenry. It is the Nation's resilience, not its rigidity, that Texas sees reflected in the flag—and it is that resilience that we reassert today.

The way to preserve the flag's special rule is not to punish those who feel differently about these matters. . . . We do not consecrate the flag by punishing its desecration, for in doing so we dilute the freedom that this cherished emblem represents.

Johnson was convicted for engaging in expressive conduct. The State's interest in preventing breaches of the peace does not support his conviction because Johnson's conduct did not threaten to disturb the peace. Nor does the State's interest in preserving the flag as a symbol of nationhood and national unity justify his criminal conviction for engaging in political expression. The judgment of the Texas Court of Criminal Appeals is therefore

Affirmed.

SANDUL
v.
LARION

119 F.3d 1250 (6th Cir. 1997)

[Citations and footnotes omitted.]

[As the truck in which he was riding passed a group of abortion protesters at a high rate of speed, John Sandul leaned out, extended his middle finger to the group, and shouted "f——k you." The truck was then separated from the protesters by a line of traffic, a grassy median strip, and a sidewalk. Officer Larion, who witnessed this incident, pursued the truck and arrested Sandul for disorderly conduct. Sandul was acquitted and sued Officer Larion under 42 U.S.C. § 1983, for violating his First Amendment rights. The trial court dismissed Sandul's complaint and he appealed.]

NATHANIEL R. JONES, Circuit Judge.

* * *

It is well-established that "absent a more particularized and compelling reason for its actions, [a] State may not, consistently with

the First and Fourteenth Amendments, make the simple public display . . . of [a] four-letter expletive a criminal offense." In *Cohen [v. California]*, the words of individual expression were also "f——k you." The *Cohen* Court explained why such language is entitled to First Amendment protection although it appears to have little redeeming value:

> [W]hile the particular four-letter word being litigated here is perhaps more distasteful than most others of its genre, it is nevertheless often true that one man's vulgarity is another's lyric. Indeed, we think it is largely because governmental officials cannot make principled distinctions in this area that the Constitution leaves matters of taste and style so largely to the individual.

Thus, the use of the "f-word" in and of itself is not criminal conduct.

First Amendment protection is very expansive. The only type of language that is denied First Amendment protection is "fighting words." *Chaplinsky [v. New Hampshire]* defined "fighting words" as:

> those which by their very utterance inflict injury or tend to incite an immediate breach of the peace. . . . [S]uch utterances are no essential part of any exposition of ideas, and are of such slight social value . . . that any benefit that may be derived from them is clearly outweighed by the social interest in order and morality.

The fighting words exception is very limited because it is inconsistent with the general principle of free speech recognized in our First Amendment jurisprudence. Fighting words are words that are likely to cause an average person to react thus causing a breach of the peace. They are words which an onlooker would consider a "direct personal insult or an invitation to exchange fisticuffs."

Sandul's words and actions do not rise to the level of fighting words. The actions were not likely to inflict injury or to incite an immediate breach of the peace. Sandul's vehicle was traveling at a high rate of speed on the opposite side of the street, a considerable distance away from the protesters to whom the language was directed. Sandul was in a moving vehicle; the entire incident was over in a matter of seconds. There is no evidence in the record that any abortion protester was offended, nor did anyone acknowledge Sandul's behavior with the exception of Officer Larion. There was no face-to-face contact between Sandul and the protestors. Thus, it is inconceivable that Sandul's fleeting actions and words would provoke the type of lawless action alluded to in *Chaplinsky*. Sandul's action was not fighting words and therefore was speech protected by the First Amendment.

* * *

We conclude that Larion is not entitled to qualified immunity because his actions violated Sandul's clearly established First Amendment rights of which a reasonable officer should have known. Accordingly, the judgment of the district court is REVERSED, and the case is REMANDED for further proceedings consistent with this opinion.

BUFFKINS
v.
CITY OF OMAHA

922 F.2d 465 (8th Cir. 1990)

[Citations and footnotes omitted.]

[On March 17, 1987, Omaha police received a tip that a black person arriving on a flight from Denver some time before 5:00 P.M. would be importing cocaine into the Omaha area. Officers Grigsby and Friend went to the airport to check out this tip. They noticed that Lu Ann Buffkins, the only black passenger to deplane on the 3:40 P.M. from Denver, was carrying a teddy bear with seams that appeared to have been resewn. They approached her, identified themselves as officers conducting a narcotics investigation, and asked her to bring her luggage and come with them to the security office to answer questions. She went, complaining that their conduct was racist and unconstitutional all along the way. The investigation in the security office turned up nothing and when the officers told Ms. Buffkins that she was free to go and to "have a nice day," she replied "I will have a nice day, asshole." The officers immediately arrested her for disorderly conduct.

Buffkins was acquitted and sued Grigsby and Friend under 42 U.S.C. § 1983 for violating her First Amendment rights by arresting her without cause to believe that her language constituted "fighting words." The jury returned a verdict in favor of the officers and Buffkins appealed.]

LAY, Chief Judge

* * *

The Supreme Court held in *Chaplinsky v. New Hampshire* that "fighting words" are not protected speech under the First and Fourteenth Amendments. The *Chaplinsky* Court defines "fighting words" as words "which by their very utterance inflict injury or tend to incite an immediate breach of the peace." "Fighting words" are words that are "likely to cause an average addressee to fight." . . .

We conclude that the district court should have found as a matter of law that the officers did not have probable cause to arrest Buffkins for using "fighting words." There is no evidence that Buffkins' speech was an incitement to immediate lawless action. Neither arresting officer contended that Buffkins became violent or threatened violence. Moreover, both officers admitted that nobody outside the interview room heard Buffkins' comment. In addition, Buffkins' use of the word "asshole" could not reasonably have prompted a violent response from the arresting officers. In *Houston v. Hill,* the Supreme Court recognized that the "fighting words" doctrine may be limited in the case of communications addressed to properly trained police officers because police officers are expected to exercise greater restraint in their response than the average citizen. The *Houston* Court stated:

> The First Amendment protects a significant amount of verbal criticism and challenge directed at police officers. . . . The freedom of individuals verbally to oppose or challenge police action without thereby risking arrest is one of the principal characteristics by which we distinguish a free nation from a police state.

* * *

. . . We . . . hold that Buffkins' speech directed at the officers did not constitute "fighting words." . . .

VIRGINIA
v.
BLACK

538 U.S. 343, 123 S. Ct. 1536, 155 L. Ed. 2d 535 (2003)

[Citations and footnotes omitted]

[Barry Black led a Ku Klux Klan rally, attended by 25 to 30 people, in an open field on private property. During the rally, the members took turns delivering hate speeches. At the conclusion of the rally, a 25- to 30-foot cross was set on fire. A sheriff who observed the rally from the side of the road arrested Black and charged him with violating a Virginia statute (§ 18.2-423) that made it unlawful to burn a cross with the intent to intimidate any person or group of persons. The statute further declared that the act of cross-burning was prima facie evidence of the existence of such intent. Black was convicted and appealed, arguing that the prima facie evidence provision rendered the statute unconstitutional.]

Justice O'CONNOR announced the judgment of the Court.

* * *

To this day, regardless of whether the message is a political one or whether the message is also meant to intimidate, the burning of a cross is a "symbol of hate." And while cross burning sometimes carries no intimidating message, at other times the intimidating message is the only message conveyed. For example, when a cross burning is directed at a particular person not affiliated with the Klan, the burning cross often serves as a message of intimidation, designed to inspire in the victim a fear of bodily harm. Moreover, the history of violence associated with the Klan shows that the possibility of injury or death is not just hypothetical. The person who burns a cross directed at a particular person often is making a serious threat, meant to coerce the victim to comply with the Klan's wishes unless the victim is willing to risk the wrath of the Klan . . . In sum, while a burning cross does not inevitably convey a message of intimidation, often the cross burner intends that the recipients of the message fear for their lives. And when a cross burning is used to intimidate, few if any messages are more powerful.

The First Amendment, applicable to the States through the Fourteenth Amendment, provides that "Congress shall make no law . . . abridging the freedom of speech." The hallmark of the protection of free speech is to allow "free trade in ideas"—even ideas that the overwhelming majority of people might find distasteful or discomforting. Thus, the First Amendment "ordinarily" denies a State "the power to prohibit dissemination of social, economic and political doctrine which a vast majority of its citizens believes to be false and fraught with evil consequence." The First Amendment affords protection to symbolic or expressive conduct as well as to actual speech.

The protections afforded by the First Amendment, however, are not absolute, and we have long recognized that the government may regulate certain categories of expression consistent with the Constitution. The First Amendment permits "restrictions upon the content of speech in a few limited areas, which are 'of such slight social value as a step to truth that any benefit that may be derived from them is clearly outweighed by the social interest in order and morality.' "

Thus, for example, a State may punish those words "which by their very utterance inflict injury or tend to incite an immediate breach of the peace." We have consequently held that fighting words—"those personally abusive epithets which, when addressed to the ordinary citizen, are, as a matter of common knowledge, inherently likely to provoke violent reaction"—are generally proscribable under the First Amendment. Furthermore, "the constitutional guarantees of free speech and free press do not permit a State to forbid or proscribe advocacy of the use of force or of law violation except where such advocacy is directed to inciting or producing imminent lawless action and is likely to incite or produce such action." The First Amendment also permits a State to ban a "true threat."

"True threats" encompass those statements where the speaker means to communicate a serious expression of an intent to commit an act of unlawful violence to a particular individual or group of individuals. The speaker need not actually intend to carry out the threat. Rather, a prohibition on true threats "protect[s] individuals from the fear of violence" and "from the disruption that fear engenders," in addition to protecting people "from the possibility that the threatened violence will occur." Intimidation in the constitutionally proscribable sense of the word is a type of true threat, where a speaker directs a threat to a person or group of persons with the intent of placing the victim in fear of bodily harm or death. Respondents do not contest that some cross burnings fit within this meaning of intimidating speech, and rightly so.... [T]he history of cross burning in this country shows that cross burning is often intimidating, intended to create a pervasive fear in victims that they are a target of violence.

* * *

As the history of cross burning indicates, a burning cross is not always intended to intimidate. Rather, sometimes the cross burning is a statement of ideology, a symbol of group solidarity. It is a ritual used at Klan gatherings, and it is used to represent the Klan itself. Thus, "[b]urning a cross at a political rally would almost certainly be protected expression." Indeed, occasionally a person who burns a cross does not intend to express either a statement of ideology or intimidation. Cross burnings have appeared in movies such as Mississippi Burning, and in plays such as the stage adaptation of Sir Walter Scott's The Lady of the Lake.

The prima facie provision makes no effort to distinguish among these different types of cross burnings. It does not distinguish between a cross burning done with the purpose of creating anger or resentment and a cross burning done with the purpose of threatening or intimidating a victim. It does not distinguish between a cross burning at a public rally or a cross burning on a neighbor's lawn. It does not treat the cross burning directed at an individual differently from the cross burning directed at a group of like-minded believers. It allows a jury to treat a cross burning on the property of another with the owner's acquiescence in the same manner as a cross burning on the property of another without the owner's permission. . . .

. . . The prima facie evidence provision in this case ignores all of the contextual factors that are necessary to decide whether a particular cross burning is intended to intimidate. The First Amendment does not permit such a shortcut.

For these reasons, the prima facie evidence provision . . . is unconstitutional on its face.

* * *

It is so ordered.

HESS
v.
INDIANA

414 U.S. 105, 94 S. Ct. 326, 8 L. Ed. 2d 303 (1973)

[Citations and footnotes omitted.]

[The events leading to Hess' conviction began with an antiwar demonstration on the campus of Indiana University. In the course of the demonstration, approximately 100 to 150 of the demonstrators moved onto a public street and blocked the passage of vehicles. When the demonstrators did not respond to verbal directions from the sheriff to clear the street, the sheriff and his deputies began walking up the street, and the demonstrators in their path moved to the curbs on either side, joining a large number of spectators who had gathered. Hess was standing off the street as the sheriff passed him. The sheriff heard Hess utter the words "We'll take the fucking street later," or "We'll take the fucking street again." and immediately arrested him on disorderly conduct charges. Two witnesses who were in the immediate vicinity testified, apparently without contradiction, that they heard Hess' words and witnessed his arrest. They indicated that Hess did not appear to be exhorting the crowd to go back into the street, that he was facing the crowd and not the street when he uttered the statement, that his statement did not appear to be addressed to any particular person or group, and that his tone, although loud, was no louder than that of the other people in the area.]

PER CURIAM.

* * *

Indiana's disorderly conduct statute was applied in this case to punish only spoken words. It hardly needs repeating that "the constitutional guarantees of freedom of speech forbid the States to punish the use of words or language not within 'narrowly limited classes of speech.' " The words here did not fall within any of these "limited classes." In the first place, it is clear that the Indiana court specifically abjured any suggestion that Hess' words could be punished as obscene under *Roth v. United States* and its progeny. Indeed, after *Cohen v. California,* such a contention with regard to the language at issue would not be tenable. By the same token, any suggestion that Hess' speech amounted to "fighting words," could not withstand scrutiny. Even if under other circumstances this language could be regarded as a personal insult, the evidence is undisputed that Hess' statement was not directed to any person or group in particular. Although the sheriff testified that he was offended by the language, he also stated that he did not interpret the expression as being directed personally at him, and the evidence is clear that appellant had his back to the sheriff at the time. Thus, under our decisions, the State could not punish this speech as "fighting words."

. . . The Indiana Supreme Court placed primary reliance on the trial court's finding that Hess' statement "was intended to incite further lawless action on the part of the crowd in the vicinity of appellant and was likely to produce such action." At best, however, the statement could be taken as counsel for present moderation; at worst, it amounted to nothing more than advocacy of illegal action at some indefinite future time. This is not sufficient to permit the State to punish Hess' speech. Under our decisions, "the constitutional guarantees of free speech and free press do not permit a State to forbid or proscribe advocacy of the use of force or of law violation except where such advocacy is directed to inciting or producing imminent lawless action and is likely to incite or produce such action." Since the uncontroverted evidence showed that Hess' statement was not directed to any person or group of persons, it cannot be said that he was advocating, in the normal sense, any action. And since there was no evidence, or rational inference from the import of the language, that his words were intended to produce, and likely to produce, imminent disorder, those words could not be punished by the State on the ground that they had "a 'tendency to lead to violence.' "

Accordingly, the motion to proceed in forma pauperis is granted and the judgment of the Supreme Court of Indiana is reversed.

[Dissenting opinion omitted.]

BROWN
v.
ENTERTAINMENT MERCHANTS ASSOCIATION

– U.S. –, 131 S. Ct. 2729, 180 L. Ed. 2d (2011) 708

[Footnotes and citations omitted.]

JUSTICE SCALIA delivered the opinion of the Court.

We consider whether a California law imposing restrictions on violent video games comports with the First Amendment.

California Assembly Bill 1179 (2005) prohibits the sale or rental of "violent video games" to minors, and requires their packaging to be labeled "18." The Act covers games "in which the range of options available to a player includes killing, maiming, dismembering, or sexually assaulting an image of a human being, if those acts are depicted" in a manner that "[a] reasonable person, considering the game as a whole, would find appeals to a deviant or morbid interest of minors," that is "patently offensive to prevailing standards in the community as to what is suitable for minors," and that "causes the game, as a whole, to lack serious literary, artistic, political, or scientific value for minors." Violation of the Act is punishable by a civil fine of up to $1,000.

Respondents, representing the video-game and software industries, brought a preenforcement challenge to the Act in the United States District Court for the Northern District of California. That court concluded that the Act violated the First Amendment and permanently enjoined its enforcement. The Court of Appeals affirmed, and we granted certiorari.

California correctly acknowledges that video games qualify for First Amendment protection.

The Free Speech Clause exists principally to protect discourse on public matters, but we have long recognized that it is difficult to distinguish politics from entertainment, and dangerous to try. "Everyone is familiar with instances of propaganda through fiction. What is one man's amusement, teaches another's doctrine." Like the protected books, plays, and movies that preceded them, video games communicate ideas and even social messages through many familiar literary devices (such as characters, dialogue, plot, and music) and through features distinctive to the medium (such as the player's interaction with the virtual world). That suffices to confer First Amendment protection. Under our Constitution, "esthetic and moral judgments about art and literature are for the individual to make, not for the Government to decree, even with the mandate or approval of a majority." And whatever the challenges of applying the Constitution to ever-advancing technology, "the basic principles of freedom of speech and the press, like the First Amendment's command, do not vary" when a new and different medium for communication appears.

The most basic of those principles is this: "[A]s a general matter, government has no power to restrict expression because of its message, its ideas, its subject matter, or its content." There are of course exceptions. "'From 1791 to the present, the First Amendment has permitted restrictions upon the content of speech in a few limited areas, and has never include[d] a freedom to disregard these traditional limitations.'" These limited areas such as obscenity, incitement, and fighting words represent "well-defined and narrowly limited classes of speech, the prevention and punishment of which have never been thought to raise any Constitutional problem."

Last Term, in *Stevens*, we held that new categories of unprotected speech may not be added to the list by a legislature that concludes certain speech is too harmful to be tolerated. *Stevens* concerned a federal statute purporting to criminalize the creation, sale, or possession of certain depictions of animal cruelty. The statute covered depictions in which a living animal is intentionally maimed, mutilated, tortured, wounded, or killed. . . . We held that statute to be an impermissible content-based restriction on speech. There was no American tradition of forbidding the *depiction of* animal cruelty though States have long had laws against *committing* it.

The Government argued in *Stevens* that lack of a historical warrant did not matter; that it could create new categories of unprotected speech by applying a "simple balancing test" that weighs the value of a particular category of speech against its social costs and then punishes that category of speech if it fails the test. We emphatically rejected that startling and dangerous proposition. "Maybe there are some categories of speech that have been historically unprotected, but have not yet been specifically identified or discussed as such in our case law." But without persuasive evidence that a novel restriction on content is part of a long (if heretofore unrecognized) tradition of proscription, a legislature may not revise the "judgment [of] the American people," embodied in the First Amendment, "that the benefits of its restrictions on the Government outweigh the costs."

That holding controls this case. . . . Our cases have been clear that the obscenity exception to the First Amendment does not cover whatever a legislature finds shocking, but only depictions of "sexual conduct."

* * *

Because speech about violence is not obscene, it is of no consequence that California's statute mimics the New York statute regulating obscenity-for-minors that we upheld in *Ginsberg* v. *New York*. That case approved a prohibition on the sale to minors of *sexual* material that would be obscene from the perspective of a child. We held that the legislature could "adjus[t] the definition of obscenity 'to social realities by permitting the appeal of this type of material to be assessed in terms of the sexual interests . . . ' of . . . minors." And because "obscenity is not protected expression," the New York statute could be sustained so long as the legislature's judgment that the proscribed materials were harmful to children "was not irrational."

The California Act is something else entirely. It does not adjust the boundaries of an existing category of unprotected speech to ensure that a definition designed for adults is not uncritically applied to children. . . . Instead, it wishes to create a wholly new category of content-based regulation that is permissible only for speech directed at children.

That is unprecedented and mistaken. "[M]inors are entitled to a significant measure of First Amendment protection, and only in relatively narrow and well-defined circumstances may government bar public dissemination of protected materials to them." No doubt a State possesses legitimate power to protect children from harm, but that does not include a free-floating power to restrict the ideas to which children may be exposed. "Speech that is neither obscene as to youths nor subject to some other legitimate proscription cannot be suppressed solely to protect the young from ideas or images that a legislative body thinks unsuitable for them."

* * *

California claims that video games present special problems because they are "interactive," in that the player participates in the violent action on screen and determines its outcome. The latter feature is nothing new: Since at least the publication of The Adventures of You: Sugarcane Island in 1969, young readers of choose-your-own-adventure stories have been able to make decisions that determine the plot by following instructions about which page to turn to. As for the argument that video games enable participation in the violent action, that seems to us more a matter of degree than of kind. As Judge Posner has observed, all literature is interactive. "[T]he better it is, the more interactive. Literature when it is successful draws the reader into the story, makes him identify with the characters, invites him to judge them and quarrel with them, to experience their joys and sufferings as the reader's own."

* * *

Because the Act imposes a restriction on the content of protected speech, it is invalid unless California can demonstrate that it passes strict scrutiny that is, unless it is justified by a compelling government interest and is narrowly drawn to serve that interest. The State must specifically identify an "actual problem" in need of solving and the curtailment of free speech must be actually necessary to the solution. That is a demanding standard. "It is rare that a regulation restricting speech because of its content will ever be permissible."

* * *

The State's evidence is not compelling. California relies primarily on the research of Dr. Craig Anderson and a few other research psychologists whose studies purport to show a connection between exposure to violent video games and harmful effects on children. These studies have been rejected by every court to consider them and with good reason: They do not prove that violent video games *cause* minors to *act* aggressively (which would at least be a beginning). Instead, "[n]early all of the research is based on correlation, not evidence of causation, and most of the studies suffer from significant, admitted flaws in methodology." They show at best some correlation between exposure to violent entertainment and minuscule real-world effects, such as children's feeling more aggressive or making louder noises in the few minutes after playing a violent game than after playing a nonviolent game.

* * *

California's effort to regulate violent video games is the latest episode in a long series of failed attempts to censor violent entertainment for minors. While we have pointed out above that some of the evidence brought forward to support the harmfulness of video games is unpersuasive, we do not mean to demean or disparage the concerns that underlie the attempt to regulate them concerns that may and doubtless do prompt a good deal of parental oversight. We have no business passing judgment on the view of the California Legislature that violent video games (or, for that matter, any other forms of speech) corrupt the young or harm their moral development. Our task is only to say whether or not such works constitute a "well-defined and narrowly limited clas[s] of speech, the prevention and punishment of which have never been thought to raise any Constitutional problem" (the answer plainly is no) and if not, whether the regulation of such works is justified by that high degree of necessity we have described as a compelling state interest (it is not). Even where the protection of children is the object, the constitutional limits on governmental action apply.

* * *

We affirm the judgment below.

It is so ordered.

INTERNATIONAL SOCIETY FOR KRISHNA CONSCIOUSNESS
v.
LEE

505 U.S. 672, 112 S. Ct. 2701, 120 L. Ed. 2d 541 (1992)

[Citations and footnotes omitted.]

[International Society for Krishna Consciousness, Inc. (ISKCON) is a not-for-profit religious corporation whose members perform a ritual known as sankirtan. The ritual consists of going into public places, disseminating religious literature, and soliciting funds to support the religion. The primary purpose of this ritual is raising funds for the movement. The Port Authority, which owns and operates three major airports in the greater New York City area (John F. Kennedy International Airport, La Guardia Airport, and Newark International Airport) adopted a regulation forbidding solicitation of money or distribution of literature inside the terminals. ISKCON brought suit to have this regulation declared unconstitutional under the First Amendment.]

CHIEF JUSTICE REHNQUIST delivered the opinion of the Court.

In this case we consider whether an airport terminal operated by a public authority is a public forum and whether a regulation prohibiting solicitation in the interior of an airport terminal violates the First Amendment.

* * *

It is uncontested that the solicitation at issue in this case is a form of speech protected under the First Amendment. But it is also well settled that the government need not permit all forms of speech on property that it owns and controls. Where the government is acting as a proprietor, managing its internal operations, rather than acting as lawmaker, its action will not be subjected to the heightened review to which its actions as a lawmaker may be subject. Thus, we have upheld a ban on political advertisements in city-operated transit vehicles, even though the city permitted other types of advertising on those vehicles. Similarly, we have permitted a school district to limit access to an internal mail system used to communicate with teachers employed by the district.

These cases reflect, either implicitly or explicitly, a "forum-based" approach for assessing restrictions that the government seeks to place on the use of its property. Under this approach, regulation of speech on government property that has traditionally been available for public expression is subject to the highest scrutiny. Such regulations survive only if they are narrowly drawn to achieve a compelling state interest. The second category of public property is the designated public forum, property that the state has opened for expressive activity by part or all of the public. Regulation of such property is subject to the same limitations as that governing a traditional public forum. Finally, there is all remaining public property. Limitations on expressive activity conducted on this last category of property must survive only a much more limited review. The challenged regulation need only be reasonable and not an effort to suppress the speaker's activity due to disagreement with the speaker's view.

The parties do not disagree that this is the proper framework. Rather, they disagree whether the airport terminals are public fora or nonpublic fora. They also disagree whether the regulation survives the "reasonableness" review governing nonpublic fora, should that prove the appropriate category. Like the Court of Appeals, we conclude that the terminals are nonpublic fora and that the regulation reasonably limits solicitation.

The suggestion that the government has a high burden in justifying speech restrictions relating to traditional public fora made its first appearance in Hague v. Committee for Industrial Organization. Justice Roberts, concluding that individuals have a right to use "streets and parks for communication of views," reasoned that such a right flowed from the fact that "streets and parks . . . have immemorially been held in trust for the use of the public and, time out of mind, have been used for purposes of assembly, communicating thoughts between citizens, and discussing public questions." . . .

Our recent cases provide additional guidance on the characteristics of a public forum. In Cornelius, we noted that a traditional public forum is property that has "as a principal purpose . . . the free exchange of ideas." Moreover, consistent with the notion that the government—like other property owners—"has power to preserve the property under its control for the use to which it is lawfully dedicated," the government does not create a public forum by inaction. Nor is a public forum created "whenever members of the public are permitted freely to visit a place owned or operated by the Government." The decision to create a public forum must instead be made "by intentionally opening a nontraditional forum for public discourse." . . .

These precedents foreclose the conclusion that airport terminals are public fora. Reflecting the general growth of the air travel industry, airport terminals have only recently achieved their contemporary size and character. But given the lateness with which the modern air terminal has made its appearance, it hardly qualifies for the description of having "immemorially . . . time out of mind" been held in the public trust and used for purposes of expressive activity. . . . Thus, the tradition of airport activity does not demonstrate that airports have historically been made available for speech activity. Nor can we say that these particular terminals, or airport terminals generally, have been intentionally opened by their operators to such activity; the frequent and continuing litigation evidencing the operators' objections belies any such claim. . . .

* * *

[A]irports are commercial establishments funded by users fees and designed to make a regulated profit and where nearly all who visit do so for some travel related purpose. As commercial enterprises, airports must provide services attractive to the marketplace. In light of this, it cannot fairly be said that an airport terminal has as a principal purpose "promoting the free exchange of ideas." To the contrary, the record demonstrates that Port Authority management considers the purpose of the terminals to be the facilitation of passenger air travel, not the promotion of expression. Even if we look beyond the intent of the Port Authority to the manner in which the terminals have been operated, the terminals have never been dedicated (except under the threat of court order) to expression in the form sought to be exercised here: i.e., the solicitation of contributions and the distribution of literature.

The terminals here are far from atypical. Airport builders and managers focus their efforts on providing terminals that will contribute to efficient air travel. . . . Thus, we think that neither by tradition nor purpose can the terminals be described as satisfying the standards we have previously set out for identifying a public forum.

The restrictions here challenged, therefore, need only satisfy a requirement of reasonableness. We reiterate what we stated in *Kokinda,* the restriction "need only be reasonable; it need not be the most reasonable or the only reasonable limitation." We have no doubt that under this standard the prohibition on solicitation passes muster.

We have on many prior occasions noted the disruptive effect that solicitation may have on business. "Solicitation requires action by those who would respond: The individual solicited must decide whether or not to contribute (which itself might involve reading the solicitor's literature or hearing his pitch), and then, having decided to do so, reach for a wallet, search it for money, write a check, or produce a credit card. Passengers who wish to avoid the solicitor may have to alter their path, slowing both themselves and those around them. The result is that the normal flow of traffic is impeded. This is especially so in an airport, where air travelers, who are often weighted down by cumbersome baggage . . . may be hurrying to catch a plane or to arrange ground transportation. Delays may be particularly costly in this setting, as a flight missed by only a few minutes can result in hours' worth of subsequent inconvenience.

* * *

The inconveniences to passengers and the burdens on Port Authority officials flowing from solicitation activity may seem small, but viewed against the fact that pedestrian congestion is one of the greatest problems facing the three terminals, the Port Authority could reasonably worry that even such incremental effects would prove quite disruptive. Moreover, "the justification for the Rule should not be measured by the disorder that would result from granting an exemption solely to ISKCON." For if petitioner is given access, so too must other groups. "Obviously, there would be a much larger threat to the State's interest in crowd control if all other religious, nonreligious, and noncommercial organizations could likewise move freely. As a result, we conclude that the solicitation ban is reasonable. For the foregoing reasons, the judgment of the Court of Appeals sustaining the ban on solicitation in Port Authority terminals is

Affirmed.

CITY OF LADUE
v.
GILLEO

512 U.S. 43, 114 S. Ct. 2038,
129 L.Ed.2d 36 (1994)

[Citations and footnotes omitted.]

[The City of Ladue, a suburb of St. Louis, Missouri, had an ordinance that banned nearly all residential signs. Margaret P. Gilleo, a resident of the City of Ladue, put up a 24- by 36-inch sign in front of her house protesting the first Gulf War. When the authorities removed her sign, she sued, claiming that the ordinance violated her First Amendment right of free speech.]

Justice STEVENS delivered the opinion of the Court.

* * *

In *Linmark* we held that the city's interest in maintaining a stable, racially integrated neighborhood was not sufficient to support a prohibition of residential "For Sale" signs. We recognized that even such a narrow sign prohibition would have a deleterious effect on residents' ability to convey important information because alternatives were "far from satisfactory." Ladue's sign ordinance is supported principally by the City's interest in minimizing the visual clutter associated with signs, an interest that is concededly valid but certainly no more compelling than the interests at stake in *Linmark*. Moreover, whereas the ordinance in *Linmark* applied only to a form of commercial speech, Ladue's ordinance covers even such absolutely pivotal speech as a sign protesting an imminent governmental decision to go to war.

* * *

Here, in contrast, Ladue has almost completely foreclosed a venerable means of communication that is both unique and important. It has totally foreclosed that medium to political, religious, or personal messages. Signs that react to a local happening or express a view on a controversial issue both reflect and animate change in the life of a community. Often placed on lawns or in windows, residential signs play an important part in political campaigns, during which they are displayed to signal the resident's support for particular candidates, parties, or causes. They may not afford the same opportunities for conveying complex ideas as do other media, but residential signs have long been an important and distinct medium of expression.

Our prior decisions have voiced particular concern with laws that foreclose an entire medium of expression. Thus, we have held invalid ordinances that completely banned the distribution of pamphlets within the municipality, handbills on the public streets, the door-to-door distribution of literature, and live entertainment. Although prohibitions foreclosing entire media may be completely free of content or viewpoint discrimination, the danger they pose to the freedom of speech is readily apparent-by eliminating a common means of speaking, such measures can suppress too much speech.

Ladue contends, however, that its ordinance is a mere regulation of the "time, place, or manner" of speech because residents remain free to convey their desired messages by other means, such as hand-held signs, "letters, handbills, flyers, telephone calls, newspaper advertisements, bumper stickers, speeches, and neighborhood or community meetings." However, even regulations that do not foreclose an entire medium of expression, but merely shift the time, place, or manner of its use, must "leave open ample alternative channels for communication. In this case, we are not persuaded that adequate substitutes exist for the important medium of speech that Ladue has closed off.

Displaying a sign from one's own residence often carries a message quite distinct from placing the same sign someplace else, or conveying the same text or picture by other means. Precisely because of their location, such signs provide information about the identity of the "speaker." As an early and eminent student of rhetoric observed, the identity of the speaker is an important component of many attempts to persuade. A sign advocating "Peace in the Gulf" in the front lawn of a retired general or decorated war veteran may provoke a different reaction than the same sign in a

10-year-old child's bedroom window or the same message on a bumper sticker of a passing automobile. An espousal of socialism may carry different implications when displayed on the grounds of a stately mansion than when pasted on a factory wall or an ambulatory sandwich board.

Residential signs are an unusually cheap and convenient form of communication. Especially for persons of modest means or limited mobility, a yard or window sign may have no practical substitute. Even for the affluent, the added costs in money or time of taking out a newspaper advertisement, handing out leaflets on the street, or standing in front of one's house with a handheld sign may make the difference between participating and not participating in some public debate. Furthermore, a person who puts up a sign at her residence often intends to reach neighbors, an audience that could not be reached nearly as well by other means.16

A special respect for individual liberty in the home has long been part of our culture and our law; that principle has special resonance when the government seeks to constrain a person's ability to speak there. Most Americans would be understandably dismayed, given that tradition, to learn that it was illegal to display from their window an 8- by 11-inch sign expressing their political views. Whereas the government's need to mediate among various competing uses, including expressive ones, for public streets and facilities is constant and unavoidable, its need to regulate temperate speech from the home is surely much less pressing.

Our decision that Ladue's ban on almost all residential signs violates the First Amendment by no means leaves the City powerless to address the ills that may be associated with residential signs. It bears mentioning that individual residents themselves have strong incentives to keep their own property values up and to prevent "visual clutter" in their own yards and neighborhoods-incentives markedly different from those of persons who erect signs on others' land, in others' neighborhoods, or on public property. Residents' self-interest diminishes the danger of the "unlimited" proliferation of residential signs that concerns the City of Ladue. We are confident that more temperate measures could in large part satisfy Ladue's stated regulatory needs without harm to the First Amendment rights

of its citizens. As currently framed, however, the ordinance abridges those rights.

Affirmed.

LOPER
v.
NEW YORK CITY POLICE DEPARTMENT

999 F.2d 699 (2d Cir. 1993)

[Citations and footnotes omitted.]

[The plaintiffs, a class of needy persons who beg on the public streets or in the public parks of New York City, brought an action seeking a declaratory judgment that N.Y. Penal Law § 240.35(1) violated the First Amendment and an injunction prohibiting the City Police from enforcing it. The statute provided: "A person is guilty of loitering when he . . . remains or wanders about in a public place for the purpose of begging." The trial court found for the plaintiffs and City Police appealed.]

MINER, Circuit Judge:

* * *

The City Police regard the challenged statute as an essential tool to address the evils associated with begging on the streets of New York City. They assert that beggars tend to congregate in certain areas and become more aggressive as they do so. Residents are intimidated and local businesses suffer accordingly. Panhandlers are said to station themselves in front of banks, bus stops, automated teller machines and parking lots and frequently engage in conduct described as "intimidating" and "coercive." Panhandlers have been known to block the sidewalk, follow people down the street and threaten those who do not give them money. It is said that they often make false and fraudulent representations to induce passers-by to part with their money. The City Police have begun to focus more attention on order maintenance activities in a program known as "community policing." They contend that it is vital to the program to have the statute available for the officers on the "beat" to deal with those who threaten and harass the citizenry through begging.

Although it is conceded that very few arrests are made and very few summonses are issued for begging alone, officers do make frequent use of the statute as authority to order beggars to "move on." The City Police advance the theory that panhandlers, unless stopped, tend to increase their aggressiveness and ultimately commit more serious crimes. According to this theory, what starts out as peaceful begging inevitably leads to the ruination of a neighborhood. It appears from the contentions of the City Police that only the challenged statute stands between safe streets and rampant crime in the city.

It is ludicrous, of course, to say that a statute that prohibits only loitering for the purpose of begging provides the only authority that is available to prevent and punish all the socially undesirable conduct incident to begging described by the City Police. There are, in fact, a number of New York statutes that proscribe conduct of the type that may accompany individual solicitations for money in the city streets. For example, the crime of harassment in the first degree is committed by one who follows another person in or about a public place or places or repeatedly commits acts that place the other person in reasonable fear of physical injury. If a panhandler, with intent to cause public inconvenience, annoyance or alarm, uses obscene or abusive language or obstructs pedestrian or vehicular traffic, he or she is guilty of disorderly conduct. A beggar who accosts a person in a public place with intent to defraud that person of money is guilty of fraudulent accosting. The crime of menacing in the third degree is committed by a panhandler who, by physical menace, intentionally places or attempts to place another person in fear of physical injury.

The distinction between the statutes referred to in the preceding paragraph and the challenged statute is that the former prohibit conduct and the latter prohibits speech as well as conduct of a communicative nature. Whether the challenged statute is consonant with the First Amendment is the subject of our inquiry. We do not write upon a clean slate as regards this inquiry, since the Supreme Court as well as this Court has addressed restrictions on the solicitation of money in public places.

* * *

. . . Despite government ownership, it is the nature of the forum that we must examine in order to determine the extent to which expressive activity may be regulated. It long has been settled that all forms of speech need not be permitted on property owned and controlled by a governmental entity.

* * *

The forum-based approach for First Amendment analysis subjects to the highest scrutiny the regulation of speech on government property traditionally available for public expression. Such property includes streets and parks, which are said to "have immemorially been held in trust for the use of the public and, time out of mind, have been used for purposes of assembly, communicating thoughts between citizens, and discussing public questions."

In these quintessential public forums, the government may not prohibit all communicative activity. For the State to enforce a content-based exclusion it must show that its regulation is necessary to serve a compelling state interest and that it is narrowly drawn to achieve that end. . . . The State may also enforce regulations of the time, place, and manner of expression which are content-neutral, are narrowly tailored to serve a significant government interest, and leave open ample alternative channels of communication.

* * *

. . . The regulation of expressive activity on public property neither traditionally available nor designated for that purpose is subject only to a limited review—the regulation must be reasonable and not designed to prohibit the activity merely because of disagreement with the views expressed. . . .

* * *

It cannot be gainsaid that begging implicates expressive conduct or communicative activity. . . .

* * *

. . . While we indicated in *Young* that begging does not always involve the transmission of a particularized social or political message, . . . begging frequently is accompanied by speech indicating the need for food, shelter, clothing, medical care or transportation. Even without particularized speech, however, the presence of an unkempt and disheveled person holding out his or her hand or a cup to receive a donation itself conveys a message of need for support and assistance. We see little difference between those who solicit for organized charities and those who solicit for themselves in regard to the message conveyed. The former are communicating the needs of others while the latter are communicating their personal needs. Both solicit the charity of others. The distinction is not a significant one for First Amendment purposes.

Having established that begging constitutes communicative activity of some sort and that, as far as this case is concerned, it is conducted in a traditional public forum, we next examine whether the statute at issue: (1) is necessary to serve a compelling state interest and is narrowly tailored to achieve that end; or (2) can be characterized as a regulation of the time, place and manner of expression that is content neutral, is narrowly tailored to serve significant government interests and leaves open alternate channels of communication.

First, it does not seem to us that any compelling state interest is served by excluding those who beg in a peaceful manner from communicating with their fellow citizens. Even if the state were considered to have a compelling interest in preventing the evils sometimes associated with begging, a statute that totally prohibits begging in all public places cannot be considered "narrowly tailored" to achieve that end. Because of the total prohibition, it is questionable whether the statute even can be said to "regulate" the time, place and manner of expression but even if it does, it is not content neutral because it prohibits all speech related to begging; it certainly is not narrowly tailored to serve any significant governmental interest, as previously noted, because of the total prohibition it commands; it does not leave open alternative channels of communication by which beggars can convey their messages of indigency.

* * *

. . . The New York statute does not square with the requirements of the First Amendment. The plaintiffs have demonstrated that they are entitled to the relief they seek.

The judgment appealed from is affirmed.

Cases Relating to Chapter 3

Authority to Detain and Arrest; Use of Force

UNITED STATES
v.
DRAYTON

536 U.S. 194, 122 S. Ct. 2105,
153 L. Ed. 2d 242 (2002)

[Citations and footnotes omitted.]

Christopher Drayton and Clifton Brown, Jr. were traveling on a Greyhound bus. When the bus made a scheduled stop in Tallahassee, Florida, Officers Hoover, Lang, and Blackburn of the Tallahassee Police Department boarded the bus as part of a routine drug and weapons interdiction effort. Once on board, Officer Hoover knelt beside the driver's seat, facing the rear of the bus where he could observe the passengers and ensure the safety of the two other officers without blocking the aisle or otherwise obstructing the bus exit. Officers Lang and Blackburn went to the rear of the bus. Blackburn remained there, facing forward while Lang worked his way toward the front of the bus, speaking with individual passengers about their travel plans.

Drayton and Brown were seated next to each other on the bus. Lang approached from the rear, leaned over Drayton's shoulder, held up his badge long enough for them to identify him as a police officer and then, with his face 12-to-18 inches away from Drayton's, said: "I'm Investigator Lang with the Tallahassee Police Department. We're conducting bus interdiction [sic], attempting to deter drugs and illegal weapons being transported on the bus. Do you have any bags on the bus?"

When both men pointed to a green bag in the overhead luggage rack, Lang asked, "Do you mind if I check it?" Brown responded, "Go ahead." Lang handed the bag to Officer Blackburn to check. The bag contained no contraband.

Noticing that both men were wearing heavy jackets and baggy clothing despite the warm weather which, in Lang's experience, drug traffickers often do to conceal weapons or narcotics, Lang asked Brown if he had any weapons or drugs in his possession, stating: "Do you mind if I check your person?" Brown answered, "Sure," and cooperated by leaning up in his seat, pulling a cell phone out of his pocket, and opening up his jacket. Lang reached across Drayton and patted down Brown's jacket and pockets, including his waist area, sides, and upper thighs. In both thigh areas, Lang detected hard objects similar to drug packages detected on other occasions. Lang arrested and handcuffed Brown and Officer Hoover escorted him from the bus.

Lang then asked Drayton, "Mind if I check you?" Drayton responded by lifting his hands. Lang conducted a pat-down and detected hard objects similar to those found on Brown. He placed Drayton under arrest. A further search revealed that Brown possessed three bundles containing 483 grams of cocaine. Drayton possessed two bundles containing 295 grams of cocaine.

Justice KENNEDY delivered the opinion of the Court.

* * *

Law enforcement officers do not violate the Fourth Amendment's prohibition of unreasonable seizures merely by approaching individuals on the street or in other public places and putting questions to them if they are willing to listen. Even when law enforcement officers have no basis for suspecting a particular individual, they may pose questions, ask for identification, and request consent to search luggage—provided they do not induce cooperation by coercive means. If a reasonable person would feel free to terminate the encounter, then he or she has not been seized.

* * *

[W]e conclude that the police did not seize respondents when they boarded the bus and began questioning passengers. The officers gave the passengers no reason to believe that they were required to answer the officers' questions. When Officer Lang approached respondents, he did not brandish a weapon or make any intimidating movements. He left the aisle free so that respondents could exit. He spoke to passengers one by one and in a polite, quiet voice. Nothing he said would suggest to a reasonable person that he or she was barred from leaving the bus or otherwise terminating the encounter.

There were ample grounds for the District Court to conclude that "everything that took place between Officer Lang and [respondents] suggests that it was cooperative" and that there "was nothing coercive [or] confrontational" about the encounter. There was no application of force, no intimidating movement, no overwhelming show of force, no brandishing of weapons, no blocking of exits, no threat, no command, not even an authoritative tone of voice. It is beyond question that had this encounter occurred on the street, it would be constitutional. The fact that an encounter takes place on a bus does not on its own transform standard police questioning of citizens into an illegal seizure. Indeed, because many fellow passengers are present to witness officers' conduct, a reasonable person may feel even more secure in his or her decision not to cooperate with police on a bus than in other circumstances.

Respondents make much of the fact that Officer Lang displayed his badge. In Florida v. Rodriguez, however, the Court rejected the claim that the defendant was seized when an officer approached him in an airport, showed him his badge, and asked him to answer some questions. . . . Officers are often required to wear uniforms and in many circumstances this is cause for assurance, not discomfort. Much the same can be said for wearing sidearms. That most law enforcement officers are armed is a fact well known to the public. The presence of a holstered firearm thus is unlikely to contribute to the coerciveness of the encounter absent active brandishing of the weapon.

Officer Hoover's position at the front of the bus also does not tip the scale in respondents' favor. Hoover did nothing to intimidate passengers, and he said nothing to suggest that people could not exit and indeed he left the aisle clear. In Delgado, the Court determined there was no seizure even though several uniformed INS officers were stationed near the exits of the factory. The Court noted: "The presence of agents by the exits posed no reasonable threat of detention to these workers, . . . the mere possibility that they would be questioned if they sought to leave the buildings should not have resulted in any reasonable apprehension by any of them that they would be seized or detained in any meaningful way."

* * *

Drayton contends that even if Brown's cooperation with the officers was consensual, Drayton was seized because no reasonable person would feel free to terminate the encounter with the officers after Brown had been arrested. The Court of Appeals did not address this claim; and in any event the argument fails. The arrest of one person does not mean that everyone around him has been seized by police. If anything, Brown's arrest should have put Drayton on notice of the consequences of continuing the encounter by answering the officers' questions. Even after arresting Brown, Lang addressed Drayton in a polite manner and provided him with no indication that he was required to answer Lang's questions.

We turn now from the question whether respondents were seized to whether they were subjected to an unreasonable search, i.e., whether their consent to the suspicionless search was involuntary. In circumstances such as these, where the question of voluntariness pervades both the search and seizure inquiries, the respective analyses turn on very similar facts. And, as the facts above suggest, respondents' consent to the search of their luggage and their persons was voluntary. Nothing Officer Lang said indicated a command to consent to the search. Rather, when respondents informed Lang that they had a bag on the bus, he asked for their permission to check it. And when Lang requested to search Brown and Drayton's persons, he asked first if they objected, thus indicating to a reasonable person that he or she was free to refuse. Even after arresting Brown, Lang provided Drayton with no indication that he was required to consent to a search. To the contrary, Lang asked for Drayton's permission to search him ("Mind if I check you?"), and Drayton agreed.

The Court has rejected in specific terms the suggestion that police officers must always inform citizens of their right to refuse when seeking permission to conduct a warrantless consent search. Nor do this Court's decisions suggest that ... a presumption of invalidity attaches if a citizen consented without explicit notification that he or she was free to refuse to cooperate. Instead, the Court has repeated that the totality of the circumstances must control, without giving extra weight to the absence of this type of warning. Although Officer Lang did not inform respondents of their right to refuse the search, he did request permission to search, and the totality of the circumstances indicates that their consent was voluntary, so the searches were reasonable.

In a society based on law, the concept of agreement and consent should be given a weight and dignity of its own. Police officers act in full accord with the law when they ask citizens for consent. It reinforces the rule of law for the citizen to advise the police of his or her wishes and for the police to act in reliance on that understanding. When this exchange takes place, it dispels inferences of coercion.

We need not ask the alternative question whether, after the arrest of Brown, there were grounds for a *Terry* stop and frisk of Drayton, though this may have been the case. It was evident that Drayton and Brown were traveling together—Officer Lang observed the pair reboarding the bus together; they were each dressed in heavy, baggy clothes that were ill-suited for the day's warm temperatures; they were seated together on the bus; and they each claimed responsibility for the single piece of green carry-on luggage. Once Lang had identified Brown as carrying what he believed to be narcotics, he may have had reasonable suspicion to conduct a Terry stop and frisk on Drayton as well. That question, however, has not been presented to us. The fact the officers may have had reasonable suspicion does not prevent them from relying on a citizen's consent to the search. It would be a paradox, and one most puzzling to law enforcement officials and courts alike, were we to say, after holding that Brown's consent was voluntary, that Drayton's consent was ineffectual simply because the police at that point had more compelling grounds to detain him. After taking Brown into custody, the officers were entitled to continue to proceed on the basis of consent and to ask for Drayton's cooperation.

The judgment of the Court of Appeals is reversed, and the case is remanded for further proceedings consistent with this opinion.

It is so ordered.

[Dissenting opinion omitted.]

CALIFORNIA
v.
HODARI D.

499 U.S. 621, 111 S. Ct. 1547, 113 L. Ed. 2d 290 (1991)

[Citations and footnotes omitted.]

[Hodari, a juvenile, took off running as two police officers, rounding a corner, came into view. The officers gave chase. Hodari tossed away a small rock as he ran. A moment later, he was tackled. The rock Hodari discarded turned out to be crack cocaine. The California state court ruled that the rock should have been suppressed because Hodari was seized when the officers began chasing him. Because the officers lacked probable cause to believe that Hodari had committed a crime when the chase began, the seizure was illegal and that the rock should have been suppressed. The government appealed.]

JUSTICE SCALIA delivered the opinion of the Court.

* * *

As this case comes to us, the only issue presented is whether, at the time he dropped the drugs, Hodari had been "seized" within the meaning of the Fourth Amendment. If so, respondent argues, the drugs were the fruit of that seizure and the evidence concerning them was properly excluded. If not, the drugs were abandoned by Hodari and lawfully recovered by the police, and the evidence should have been admitted....

We have long understood that the Fourth Amendment's protection against "unreasonable ... seizures" includes seizure of the person. From the time of the founding to the present, the word "seizure" has meant a "taking possession." For most purposes at common law, the word connoted not merely grasping, or applying physical force to, the animate or inanimate object in question, but actually bringing it within physical control. . . .

* * *

. . . Hodari was untouched by Officer Pertoso at the time he discarded the cocaine. His defense relies instead upon the proposition that a seizure occurs "when the officer, by means of physical force or show of authority, has in some way restrained the liberty of a citizen." Hodari contends (and we accept as true for purposes of this decision) that Pertoso's pursuit qualified as a "show of authority" calling upon Hodari to halt. The narrow question before us is whether, with respect to a show of authority as with respect to application of physical force, a seizure occurs even though the subject does not yield. We hold that it does not.

The language of the Fourth Amendment, of course, cannot sustain respondent's contention. The word "seizure" readily bears the meaning of a laying on of hands or application of physical force to restrain movement, even when it is ultimately unsuccessful. ("She seized the purse-snatcher, but he broke out of her grasp.") It does not remotely apply, however, to the prospect of a policeman yelling "Stop, in the name of the law!" at a fleeing form that continues to flee. That is no seizure. Nor can the result respondent wishes to achieve be produced—indirectly, as it were—by suggesting that Pertoso's uncomplied-with show of authority was a common-law arrest, and then appealing to the principle that all common-law arrests are seizures. An arrest requires either physical force (as described above) or, where that is absent, submission to the assertion of authority.

Mere words will not constitute an arrest, while, on the other hand, no actual, physical touching is essential. The apparent inconsistency in the two parts of this statement is explained by the fact that an assertion of authority and purpose to arrest, followed by submission of the arrestee, constitutes an arrest. There can be no arrest without either touching or submission.

We do not think it desirable, even as a policy matter, to stretch the Fourth Amendment beyond its words and beyond the meaning of arrest, as respondent urges. Street pursuits always place the public at some risk, and compliance with police orders to stop should therefore be encouraged. Only a few of those orders, we must presume, will be without adequate basis, and since the addressee has no ready means of identifying the deficient ones, it almost invariably is the responsible course to comply. Unlawful orders will not be deterred, moreover, by sanctioning through the exclusionary rule those of them that are not obeyed. Since policemen do not command "Stop!" expecting to be ignored, or give chase hoping to be outrun, it fully suffices to apply the deterrent to their genuine, successful seizures.

* * *

In sum, assuming that Pertoso's pursuit in the present case constituted a "show of authority" enjoining Hodari to halt, since Hodari did not comply with that injunction, he was not seized until he was tackled. The cocaine abandoned while he was running was, in this case, not the fruit of a seizure, and his motion to exclude evidence of it was properly denied. We reverse the decision of the California Court of Appeal, and remand for further proceedings not inconsistent with this opinion.

It is so ordered.

TERRY
v.
OHIO

392 U.S. 1, 88 S. Ct. 1868, 20 L. Ed. 2d 889 (1968)

[Citations and footnotes omitted.]

[Officer McFadden was patrolling in downtown Cleveland when his attention was attracted to two men standing on the corner. He observed one man leave the other, walk past some stores, pause for a moment to look in a store window, walk a short distance beyond, turn around and walk back, pausing to look in the same store window again before returning to his companion. He and his companion conferred briefly and then his companion went through the same series of motions. The two men alternated in repeating this ritual approximately five or six times each. A third man subsequently joined them. These observations caused Officer McFadden to suspect that the three men were casing the store, preparing for a robbery, and that they might have guns. He approached the three men, identified himself as a police officer, and asked for their names. When the men "mumbled something" in response to his inquiry, Officer McFadden grabbed one of them (Terry), spun him around, and patted down the outside of his clothing. Feeling a pistol in Terry's left breast pocket, Officer McFadden ordered all three men to enter Zucker's store. As they went in, he removed Terry's overcoat, retrieved a .38-caliber revolver from the pocket, and ordered all three men to face the wall with their hands raised. He proceeded to pat down the outer clothing of Chilton and Katz, the other two men. He discovered a revolver in the outer pocket of Chilton's overcoat, but no weapons were found on Katz. He testified that he only patted the men down to see whether they had weapons, and that he did not put his hands beneath the outer garments of either Terry or Chilton until he felt their guns. The trial court denied the defendants' motion to suppress the guns on the ground that Officer McFadden, on the basis of his experience, "had reasonable cause to believe that the defendants were conducting themselves suspiciously, and some interrogation should be made of their action."]

Mr. Chief Justice WARREN delivered the opinion of the Court.

This case presents serious questions concerning the role of the Fourth Amendment in the confrontation on the street between the citizen and the policeman investigating suspicious circumstances.

* * *

...Unquestionably petitioner was entitled to the protection of the Fourth Amendment as he walked down the street in Cleveland. The question is whether in all the circumstances of this on-the-street encounter, his right to personal security was violated by an unreasonable search and seizure.

We would be less than candid if we did not acknowledge that this question thrusts to the fore difficult and troublesome issues regarding a sensitive area of police activity—issues which have never before been squarely presented to this Court. Reflective of the tensions involved are the practical and constitutional arguments pressed with great vigor on both sides of the public debate over the power of the police to 'stop and frisk'—as it is sometimes euphemistically termed—suspicious persons.

On the one hand, it is frequently argued that in dealing with the rapidly unfolding and often dangerous situations on city streets the police are in need of an escalating set of flexible responses, graduated in relation to the amount of information they possess. For this purpose it is urged that distinctions should be made between a "stop" and an "arrest" (or a "seizure" of a person), and between a "frisk" and a "search." Thus, it is argued, the police should be allowed to "stop" a person and detain him briefly for questioning upon suspicion that he may be connected with criminal activity. Upon suspicion that the person may be armed, the police should have the power to "frisk" him for weapons. If the "stop" and the "frisk" give rise to probable cause to believe that the suspect has committed a crime, then the police should be empowered to make a formal "arrest," and a full incident "search" of the person. This scheme is justified in part upon the notion that a 'stop' and a 'frisk' amount to a mere "minor inconvenience and petty indignity," which can properly be imposed upon the citizen in the interest of effective law enforcement on the basis of a police officer's suspicion.

On the other side the argument is made that the authority of the police must be strictly circumscribed by the law of arrest and search as it has developed to date in the traditional jurisprudence of the Fourth Amendment. It is contended with some force that there is not—and cannot be—a variety of police activity which does not depend solely upon the voluntary cooperation of the citizen and yet which stops short of an arrest based upon probable cause to make such an arrest. The heart of the Fourth Amendment, the argument runs, is a severe requirement of specific justification for any intrusion upon protected personal security, coupled with a highly developed system of judicial controls to enforce upon the agents of the State the commands of the Constitution. Acquiescence by the courts in the compulsion inherent in the field interrogation practices at issue here, it is urged, would constitute an abdication of judicial control over, and indeed an encouragement of, substantial interference with liberty and personal security by police officers whose judgment is necessarily colored by their primary involvement in "the often competitive enterprise of ferreting out crime." This, it is argued, can only serve to exacerbate police-community tensions in the crowded centers of our Nation's cities.

In this context we approach the issues in this case mindful of the limitations of the judicial function in controlling the myriad daily situations in which policemen and citizens confront each other on the street. . . .

. . . Street encounters between citizens and police officers are incredibly rich in diversity. They range from wholly friendly exchanges of pleasantries or mutually useful information to hostile confrontations of armed men involving arrests, or injuries, or loss of life. Moreover, hostile confrontations are not all of a piece. Some of them begin in a friendly enough manner, only to take a different turn upon the injection of some unexpected element into the conversation. Encounters are initiated by the police for a wide variety of purposes, some of which arc wholly unrelated to a desire to prosecute for crime. Doubtless some police "field interrogation" conduct violates the Fourth Amendment.

* * *

Our first task is to establish at what point in this encounter the Fourth Amendment becomes relevant. That is, we must decide whether and when Officer McFadden "seized" Terry and whether and when he conducted a "search." There is some suggestion in the use of such terms as "stop" and "frisk" that such police conduct is outside the purview of the Fourth Amendment because neither action rises to the level of a "search" or "seizure" within the meaning of the Constitution. We emphatically reject this notion. It is quite plain that the Fourth Amendment governs "seizures" of the person which do not eventuate in a trip to the station house and prosecution for crime—"arrests" in traditional terminology. It must be recognized that whenever a police officer accosts an individual and restrains his freedom to walk away, he has "seized" that person. And it is nothing less than sheer torture of the English language to suggest that a careful exploration of the outer surfaces of a person's clothing all over his or her body in an attempt to find weapons is not a "search." Moreover, it is simply fantastic to urge that such a procedure performed in public by a policeman while the citizen stands helpless, perhaps facing a wall with his hands raised, is a "petty indignity." It is a serious intrusion

upon the sanctity of the person, which may inflict great indignity and arouse strong resentment, and it is not to be undertaken lightly.

* * *

We therefore reject the notions that the Fourth Amendment does not come into play at all as a limitation upon police conduct if the officers stop short of something called a "technical arrest" or a "full-blown search."

In this case there can be no question, then, that Officer McFadden "seized" petitioner and subjected him to a "search" when he took hold of him and patted down the outer surfaces of his clothing. We must decide whether at that point it was reasonable for Officer McFadden to have interfered with petitioner's personal security as he did. And in determining whether the seizure and search were "unreasonable" our inquiry is a dual one—whether the officer's action was justified at its inception, and whether it was reasonably related in scope to the circumstances which justified the interference in the first place.

If this case involved police conduct subject to the Warrant Clause of the Fourth Amendment, we would have to ascertain whether "probable cause" existed to justify the search and seizure which took place. However, that is not the case. . . . Instead, the conduct involved in this case must be tested by the Fourth Amendment's general proscription against unreasonable searches and seizures.

. . . In order to assess the reasonableness of Officer McFadden's conduct as a general proposition, it is necessary "first to focus upon the governmental interest which allegedly justifies official intrusion upon the constitutionally protected interests of the private citizen," for there is "no ready test for determining reasonableness other than by balancing the need to search (or seize) against the invasion which the search (or seize) entails." And in justifying the particular intrusion the police officer must be able to point to specific and articulable facts which, taken together with rational inferences from those facts, reasonably warrant that intrusion. . . . Anything less would invite intrusions upon constitutionally guaranteed rights based on nothing more substantial than inarticulate hunches, a result this Court has consistently refused to sanction. And simple "good faith on the part of the arresting officer is not enough." . . . If subjective good faith alone were the test, the protections of the Fourth Amendment would evaporate, and the people would be 'secure in their persons, houses, papers and effects,' only in the discretion of the police."

... One general interest is of course that of effective crime prevention and detection; it is this interest which underlies the recognition that a police officer may in appropriate circumstances and in an appropriate manner approach a person for purposes of investigating possibly criminal behavior even though there is no probable cause to make an arrest. It was this legitimate investigative function Officer McFadden was discharging when he decided to approach petitioner and his companions. He had observed Terry, Chilton, and Katz go through a series of acts, each of them perhaps innocent in itself, but which taken together warranted further investigation. There is nothing unusual in two men standing together on a street corner, perhaps waiting for someone. Nor is there anything suspicious about people in such circumstances strolling up and down the street, singly or in pairs. Store windows, moreover, are made to be looked in. But the story is quite different where, as here, two men hover about a street corner for an extended period of time, at the end of which it becomes apparent that they are not waiting for anyone or anything; where these men pace alternately along an identical route, pausing to stare in the same store window roughly 24 times; where each completion of this route is followed immediately by a conference between the two men on the corner; where they are joined in one of these conferences by a third man who leaves swiftly; and where the two men finally follow the third and rejoin him a couple of blocks away. It would have been poor police work indeed for an officer of 30 years' experience in the detection of thievery from stores in this same neighborhood to have failed to investigate this behavior further.

The crux of this case, however, is not the propriety of Officer McFadden's taking steps to investigate petitioner's suspicious behavior, but rather, whether there was justification for McFadden's invasion of Terry's personal security by searching him for weapons in the course of that investigation. We are now concerned with more than the governmental interest in investigating crime; in addition, there is the more immediate interest of the police officer in taking steps to assure himself that the person with whom he is dealing is not armed with a weapon that could unexpectedly and

fatally be used against him. Certainly it would be unreasonable to require that police officers take unnecessary risks in the performance of their duties. American criminals have a long tradition of armed violence, and every year in this country many law enforcement officers are killed in the line of duty, and thousands more are wounded. Virtually all of these deaths and a substantial portion of the injuries are inflicted with guns and knives.

In view of these facts, we cannot blind ourselves to the need for law enforcement officers to protect themselves and other prospective victims of violence in situations where they may lack probable cause for an arrest. When an officer is justified in believing that the individual whose suspicious behavior he is investigating at close range is armed and presently dangerous to the officer or to others, it would appear to be clearly unreasonable to deny the officer the power to take necessary measures to determine whether the person is in fact carrying a weapon and to neutralize the threat of physical harm.

We must still consider, however, the nature and quality of the intrusion on individual rights which must be accepted if police officers are to be conceded the right to search for weapons in situations where probable cause to arrest for crime is lacking. Even a limited search of the outer clothing for weapons constitutes a severe, though brief, intrusion upon cherished personal security, and it must surely be an annoying, frightening, and perhaps humiliating experience. Petitioner contends that such an intrusion is permissible only incident to a lawful arrest, either for a crime involving the possession of weapons or for a crime the commission of which led the officer to investigate in the first place. However, this argument must be closely examined.

Petitioner does not argue that a police officer should refrain from making any investigation of suspicious circumstances until such time as he has probable cause to make an arrest; nor does he deny that police officers in properly discharging their investigative function may find themselves confronting persons who might well be armed and dangerous. Moreover, he does not say that an officer is always unjustified in searching a suspect to discover weapons. Rather, he says it is unreasonable for the policeman to take that step until such time as the situation evolves to a point where there is probable cause to make an arrest. When that point has been reached, petitioner would concede the officer's right to conduct a search of the suspect for weapons, fruits or instrumentalities of the crime, or "mere" evidence, incident to the arrest.

There are two weaknesses in this line of reasoning however. First, it fails to take account of traditional limitations upon the scope of searches, and thus recognizes no distinction in purpose, character, and extent between a search incident to an arrest and a limited search for weapons. The former, although justified in part by the acknowledged necessity to protect the arresting officer from assault with a concealed weapon is also justified on other grounds, and can therefore involve a relatively extensive exploration of the person. A search for weapons in the absence of probable cause arrest, however, must, like any other search, be strictly circumscribed by the exigencies which justify its initiation. Thus it must be limited to that which is necessary for the discovery of weapons which might be used to harm the officer or others nearby, and may realistically be characterized as something less than a "full" search, even though it remains a serious intrusion.

A second, and related, objection to petitioner's argument is that it assumes that the law of arrest has already worked out the balance between the particular interests involved here—the neutralization of danger to the policeman in the investigative circumstance and the sanctity of the individual. But this is not so. . . .

Our evaluation of the proper balance that has to be struck in this type of case leads us to conclude that there must be a narrowly drawn authority to permit a reasonable search for weapons for the protection of the police officer, where he has reason to believe that he is dealing with an armed and dangerous individual, regardless of whether he has probable cause to arrest the individual for a crime. The officer need not be absolutely certain that the individual is armed; the issue is whether a reasonably prudent man in the circumstances would be warranted in the belief that his safety or that of others was in danger. And in determining whether the officer acted reasonably in such circumstances, due weight must be given, not to his inchoate and unparticularized suspicion or "hunch," but to the specific reasonable inferences which he is entitled to draw from the facts in light of his experience.

* * *

The scope of the search in this case presents no serious problem in light of these standards. Officer McFadden patted down the outer clothing of petitioner and his two companions. He did not place his hands in their pockets or under the outer surface of their garments until he had felt weapons, and then he merely reached for and removed the guns. He never did invade Katz' person beyond the outer surfaces of his clothes, since he discovered nothing in his patdown which might have been a weapon. Officer McFadden confined his search strictly to what was minimally necessary to learn whether the men were armed and to disarm them once he discovered the weapons. He did not conduct a general exploratory search for whatever evidence of criminal activity he might find.

We conclude that the revolver seized from Terry was properly admitted in evidence against him. At the time he seized petitioner and searched him for weapons, Officer McFadden had reasonable grounds to believe that petitioner was armed and dangerous, and it was necessary for the protection of himself and others to take swift measures to discover the true facts and neutralize the threat of harm if it materialized. The policeman carefully restricted his search to what was appropriate to the discovery of the particular items which he sought. Each case of this sort will, of course, have to be decided on its own facts. We merely hold today that where a police officer observes unusual conduct which leads him reasonably to conclude in light of his experience that criminal activity may be afoot and that the persons with whom he is dealing may be armed and presently dangerous, where in the course of investigating this behavior he identifies himself as a policeman and makes reasonable inquiries, and where nothing in the initial stages of the encounter serves to dispel his reasonable fear for his own or others' safety, he is entitled for the protection of himself and others in the area to conduct a carefully limited search of the outer clothing of such persons in an attempt to discover weapons which might be used to assault him. Such a search is a reasonable search under the Fourth Amendment, and any weapons seized may properly be introduced in evidence against the person from whom they were taken.

Affirmed.

[Concurring and dissenting opinions have been omitted.]

ILLINOIS
v.
WARDLOW

528 U.S. 119, 120 S. Ct. 673, 145 L. Ed. 2d 570 (2000)

[Citations and footnotes omitted.]

CHIEF JUSTICE REHNQUIST delivered the opinion of the Court.

* * *

On September 9, 1995, Officers Nolan and Harvey were working as uniformed officers in the special operations section of the Chicago Police Department. The officers were driving the last car of a four-car caravan converging on an area known for heavy narcotics trafficking in order to investigate drug transactions. The officers were traveling together because they expected to find a crowd of people in the area, including lookouts and customers.

As the caravan passed 4035 West Van Buren, Officer Nolan observed respondent Wardlow standing next to the building holding an opaque bag. Respondent looked in the direction of the officers and fled. Nolan and Harvey turned their car southbound, watched him as he ran through the gangway and an alley, and eventually cornered him on the street. Nolan then exited his car and stopped respondent. He immediately conducted a protective pat-down search for weapons because in his experience it was common for there to be weapons in the near vicinity of narcotics transactions. During the frisk, Officer Nolan squeezed the bag respondent was carrying and felt a heavy, hard object similar to the shape of a gun. The officer then opened the bag and discovered a .38-caliber handgun with five live rounds of ammunition. The officers arrested Wardlow.

* * *

... An individual's presence in an area of expected criminal activity, standing alone, is not enough to support a reasonable, particularized suspicion that the person is committing a crime. But officers are not required to ignore the relevant characteristics of a location in determining whether the circumstances are sufficiently suspicious to warrant further investigation. Accordingly, we have previously noted the fact that the stop occurred in a "high crime area" among the relevant contextual considerations in a Terry analysis.

In this case, moreover, it was not merely respondent's presence in an area of heavy narcotics trafficking that aroused the officers' suspicion but his unprovoked flight upon noticing the police. Our cases have also recognized that nervous, evasive behavior is a pertinent factor in determining reasonable suspicion. Headlong flight—wherever it occurs—is the consummate act of evasion: it is not necessarily indicative of wrongdoing, but it is certainly suggestive of such. In reviewing the propriety of an officer's conduct, courts do not have available empirical studies dealing with inferences drawn from suspicious behavior, and we cannot reasonably demand scientific certainty from judges or law enforcement officers where none exists. Thus, the determination of reasonable suspicion must be based on commonsense judgments and inferences about human behavior. We conclude Officer Nolan was justified in suspecting that Wardlow was involved in criminal activity, and, therefore, in investigating further.

Such a holding is entirely consistent with our decision in *Florida v. Royer*, where we held that when an officer, without reasonable suspicion or probable cause, approaches an individual, the individual has a right to ignore the police and go about his business. And any "refusal to cooperate, without more, does not furnish the minimal level of objective justification needed for a detention or seizure." But unprovoked flight is simply not a mere refusal to cooperate. Flight, by its very nature, is not "going about one's business"; in fact, it is just the opposite. Allowing officers confronted with such flight to stop the fugitive and investigate further is quite consistent with the individual's right to go about his business or to stay put and remain silent in the face of police questioning.

Respondent and amici also argue that there are innocent reasons for flight from police and that, therefore, flight is not necessarily indicative of ongoing criminal activity. This fact is undoubtedly true, but does not establish a violation of the Fourth Amendment. Even in *Terry,* the conduct justifying the stop was ambiguous and susceptible of an innocent explanation. The officer observed two individuals pacing back and forth in front of a store, peering into the window and periodically conferring. All of this conduct was by itself lawful, but it also suggested that the individuals were casing the store for a planned robbery. *Terry* recognized that the officers could detain the individuals to resolve the ambiguity.

In allowing such detentions, *Terry* accepts the risk that officers may stop innocent people. Indeed, the Fourth Amendment accepts that risk in connection with more drastic police action; persons arrested and detained on probable cause to believe they have committed a crime may turn out to be innocent. The *Terry* stop is a far more minimal intrusion, simply allowing the officer to briefly investigate further. If the officer does not learn facts rising to the level of probable cause, the individual must be allowed to go on his way. But in this case the officers found respondent in possession of a handgun, and arrested him for violation of an Illinois firearms statute. No question of the propriety of the arrest itself is before us.

The judgment of the Supreme Court of Illinois is reversed, and the cause is remanded for further proceedings not inconsistent with this opinion.

It is so ordered.

FLORIDA
v.
J.L.

529 U.S. 266, 120 S. Ct. 1375, 146 L. Ed. 2d 254 (2000)

[Citations and footnotes omitted.]

Justice GINSBURG delivered the opinion of the Court.

The question presented in this case is whether an anonymous tip that a person is carrying a gun is, without more, sufficient to justify a police officer's stop and frisk of that person. We hold that it is not.

On October 13, 1995, an anonymous caller reported to the Miami-Dade Police that a young black male standing at a particular bus stop and wearing a plaid shirt was carrying a gun. So far as the record reveals, there is no audio recording of the tip, and nothing is known about the informant. Sometime after the police received the tip—the record does not say how long—two officers were instructed to respond. They arrived at the bus stop about six minutes later and saw three black males "just hanging out [there]." One of the three, respondent J.L., was wearing a plaid shirt. Apart from the tip, the officers had no reason to suspect any of the three of illegal conduct. The officers did not see a firearm, and J.L. made no threatening or otherwise unusual movements. One of the officers approached J.L., told him to put his hands up on the bus stop, frisked him, and seized a gun from J.L.'s pocket. The second officer frisked the other two individuals, against whom no allegations had been made, and found nothing.

J.L., who was at the time of the frisk "10 days shy of his 16th birth[day]," was charged under state law with carrying a concealed firearm without a license and possessing a firearm while under the age of 18. He moved to suppress the gun as the fruit of an unlawful search, and the trial court granted his motion. . . .

* * *

In the instant case, the officers' suspicion that J.L. was carrying a weapon arose not from any observations of their own but solely from a call made from an unknown location by an unknown caller. Unlike a tip from a known informant whose reputation can be assessed and who can be held responsible if her allegations turn out to be fabricated, "an anonymous tip alone seldom demonstrates the informant's basis of knowledge or veracity." As we have recognized, however, there are situations in which an anonymous tip, suitably corroborated, exhibits "sufficient indicia of reliability to provide reasonable suspicion to make the investigatory stop." The question we here confront is whether the tip pointing to J.L. had those indicia of reliability.

In *[Alabama v.] White*, the police received an anonymous tip asserting that a woman was carrying cocaine and predicting that she would leave an apartment building at a specified time, get into a car matching a particular description, and drive to a named motel. Standing alone, the tip would not have justified a *Terry* stop. Only after police observation showed that the informant had accurately predicted the woman's movements, we explained, did it become reasonable to think the tipster had inside knowledge about the suspect and therefore to credit his assertion about the cocaine. Although the Court held that the suspicion in *White* became reasonable after police surveillance, we regarded the case as borderline. Knowledge about a person's future movements indicates some familiarity with that person's affairs, but having such knowledge does not necessarily imply that the informant knows, in particular, whether that person is carrying hidden contraband. We accordingly classified *White* as a "close case."

The tip in the instant case lacked the moderate indicia of reliability present in *White* and essential to the Court's decision in that case. The anonymous call concerning J.L. provided no predictive information and therefore left the police without means to test the informant's knowledge or credibility. That the allegation about the gun turned out to be correct does not suggest that the officers, prior to the frisks, had a reasonable basis for suspecting J.L. of engaging in unlawful conduct: The reasonableness of official suspicion must be measured by what the officers knew before they conducted their search. All the police had to go on in this case was the bare report of an unknown, unaccountable informant who neither explained how he knew about the gun nor supplied any basis for believing he had inside information about J.L. If *White* was a close case on the reliability of anonymous tips, this one surely falls on the other side of the line.

Florida contends that the tip was reliable because its description of the suspect's visible attributes proved accurate: There really was a young black male wearing a plaid shirt at the bus stop. The United States as amicus curiae makes a similar argument, proposing that a stop and frisk should be permitted "when (1) an anonymous tip provides a description of a particular person at a particular location illegally carrying a concealed firearm, (2) police promptly verify the pertinent details of the tip except the existence of the firearm, and (3) there are no factors that cast doubt on the reliability of the tip. . . ." These contentions misapprehend the reliability needed for a tip to justify a Terry stop.

An accurate description of a subject's readily observable location and appearance is of course reliable in this limited sense: It will help the police correctly identify the person whom the tipster means to accuse. Such a tip, however, does not show that the tipster has knowledge of concealed criminal activity. The reasonable suspicion here at issue requires that a tip be reliable in its assertion of illegality, not just in its tendency to identify a determinate person. Cf. 4 W. LaFave, Search and Seizure § 9.4(h), p. 213 (3d ed. 1996) (distinguishing reliability as to identification, which is often important in other criminal law contexts, from reliability as to the likelihood of criminal activity, which is central in anonymous-tip cases).

A second major argument advanced by Florida and the United States as amicus is, in essence, that the standard *Terry* analysis should be modified to license a "firearm exception." Under such an exception, a tip alleging an illegal gun would justify a stop and frisk even if the accusation would fail standard pre-search reliability testing. We decline to adopt this position.

Firearms are dangerous, and extraordinary dangers sometimes justify unusual precautions. Our decisions recognize the serious threat that armed criminals pose to public safety; *Terry's* rule, which permits protective police searches on the basis of reasonable suspicion rather than demanding that officers meet the higher standard of probable cause, responds to this very concern. But an automatic firearm exception to our established reliability analysis would rove too far. Such an exception would enable any person seeking to harass another to set in motion an intrusive, embarrassing police search of the targeted person simply by placing an anonymous call falsely reporting the target's unlawful carriage of a gun. Nor could one securely confine such an exception to allegations involving firearms. Several Courts of Appeals have held it per se foreseeable for people carrying significant amounts of illegal drugs to be carrying guns as well. If police officers may properly conduct Terry frisks on the basis of bare-boned tips about guns, it would be reasonable to maintain under the above-cited decisions that the police should similarly have discretion to frisk based on bare-boned tips about narcotics. As we clarified when we made indicia of reliability critical in *Adams* and *White*, the Fourth Amendment is not so easily satisfied.

The facts of this case do not require us to speculate about the circumstances under which the danger alleged in an anonymous tip might be so great as to justify a search even without a showing of reliability. We do not say, for example, that a report of a person carrying a bomb need bear the indicia of reliability we demand for a report of a person carrying a firearm before the police can constitutionally conduct a frisk. Nor do we hold that public safety officials in quarters where the reasonable expectation of Fourth Amendment privacy is diminished, such as airports and schools, cannot conduct protective searches on the basis of information insufficient to justify searches elsewhere.

Finally, the requirement that an anonymous tip bear standard indicia of reliability in order to justify a stop in no way diminishes a police officer's prerogative, in accord with *Terry,* to conduct a protective search of a person who has already been legitimately stopped. We speak in today's decision only of cases in which the officer's authority to make the initial stop is at issue. In that context, we hold that an anonymous tip lacking indicia of reliability of the kind contemplated in *Adams* and *White* does not justify a stop and frisk whenever and however it alleges the illegal possession of a firearm.

The judgment of the Florida Supreme Court is affirmed.

It is so ordered.

UNITED STATES
v.
PLACE

462 U.S. 696, 103 S. Ct. 2637, 77 L. Ed. 2d 110 (1983)

[Citations and footnotes omitted.]

[After receiving a tip that Place, a man fitting a drug courier profile, was en route on a plane from Miami to New York, two DEA agents waited at the arrival gate at LaGuardia Airport in New York. Place's behavior aroused the suspicion of the agents. After he had claimed his two bags and called a limousine, the agents decided to approach him. When Place refused to consent to a search of his luggage, one of the agents told him that they were going to take the luggage to a federal judge to try to obtain a search warrant and that Place was free to accompany them. Place declined, but obtained from one of the agents telephone numbers at which the agents could be reached. The agents then took the bags to Kennedy Airport, where they subjected the bags to a "sniff test" by a trained narcotics detection dog. The dog reacted positively to the smaller of the two bags but ambiguously to the larger bag. Approximately 90 minutes had elapsed since the seizure of respondent's luggage. Because it was late on a Friday afternoon, the agents retained the luggage until Monday morning, when they secured a search warrant from a magistrate for the smaller bag. Upon opening that bag, the agents discovered 1,125 grams of cocaine.]

JUSTICE O'CONNOR delivered the opinion of the Court.

This case presents the issue whether the Fourth Amendment prohibits law enforcement authorities from temporarily detaining personal luggage for exposure to a trained narcotics detection dog on the basis of reasonable suspicion that the luggage contains narcotics. Given the enforcement problems associated with the detection of narcotics trafficking and the minimal intrusion that a properly limited detention would entail, we conclude that the Fourth Amendment does not prohibit such a detention. On the facts of this case, however, we hold that the police conduct exceeded the bounds of a permissible investigative detention of the luggage.

* * *

At the outset, we must reject the Government's suggestion that the point at which probable cause for seizure of luggage from the person's presence becomes necessary is more distant than in the case of a *Terry* stop of the person himself. The premise of the Government's argument is that seizures of property are generally less intrusive than seizures of the person. While true in some circumstances, that premise is faulty on the facts we address in this case. The precise type of detention we confront here is seizure of personal luggage from the immediate possession of the suspect for the purpose of arranging exposure to a narcotics detection dog. Particularly in the case of detention of luggage within the traveler's immediate possession, the police conduct intrudes on both the suspect's possessory interest in his luggage as well as his liberty interest in proceeding with his itinerary. The person whose luggage is detained is technically still free to continue his travels or carry out other personal activities pending release of the luggage. Moreover, he is not subjected to the coercive atmosphere of a custodial confinement or to the public indignity of being personally detained. Nevertheless, such a seizure can effectively restrain the person since he is subjected to the possible disruption of his travel plans in order to remain with his luggage or to arrange for its return. Therefore, when the police seize luggage from the suspect's custody, we think the limitations applicable to investigative detentions of the person should define the permissible scope of an investigative detention of the person's luggage on less than probable cause. Under this standard, it is clear that the police conduct here exceeded the permissible limits of a Terry-type investigative stop.

The length of the detention of respondent's luggage alone precludes the conclusion that the seizure was reasonable in the absence of probable cause. Although we have recognized the reasonableness of seizures longer than the momentary ones involved in *Terry, Adams,* and *Brignoni-Ponce,* the brevity of the invasion of the individual's Fourth Amendment interests is an important factor in determining whether the seizure is so minimally intrusive as to be justifiable on reasonable suspicion. Moreover, in assessing the effect of the length of the detention, we take into account whether the police diligently pursue their investigation. We note that here the New York agents knew the time of Place's scheduled arrival at La Guardia, had ample time to arrange for their additional investigation at that location, and thereby could have minimized the intrusion on respondent's Fourth Amendment interests. Thus, although we decline to adopt any outside time limitation for a permissible Terry stop, we have never approved a seizure of the person for the prolonged 90-minute period involved here and cannot do so on the facts presented by this case.

Although the 90-minute detention of respondent's luggage is sufficient to render the seizure unreasonable, the violation was exacerbated by the failure of the agents to accurately inform respondent of the place to which they were transporting his luggage, of the length of time he might be dispossessed, and of what arrangements would be made for return of the luggage if the investigation dispelled the suspicion. In short, we hold that the detention of respondent's luggage in this case went beyond the narrow authority possessed by police to detain briefly luggage reasonably suspected to contain narcotics.

* * *

...Consequently, the evidence obtained from the subsequent search of his luggage was inadmissible, and Place's conviction must be reversed. The judgment of the Court of Appeals, accordingly, is affirmed.

It is so ordered.

HAYES
v.
FLORIDA

470 U.S. 811, 105 S. Ct. 1643, 84 L. Ed. 2d 705 (1985)

[Citations and footnotes omitted.]

[Police suspected the defendant of having committed a string of crimes and wanted a fingerprint sample to compare with those found at the crime scenes. They decided to visit the defendant's home to obtain his fingerprints or, if he was uncooperative, to arrest him. When he expressed reluctance to voluntarily accompany them to the station for fingerprinting, one of the investigators explained that they would therefore arrest him. The defendant stated that he would rather go voluntarily then be arrested. He was taken to the station house, where he was fingerprinted. When police determined that his prints matched those left at the scene of the crime, petitioner was placed under formal arrest.]

JUSTICE WHITE delivered the opinion of the Court.

The issue before us in this case is whether the Fourth Amendment to the Constitution of the United States, applicable to the States by virtue of the Fourteenth Amendment, was properly applied by the District Court of Appeal of Florida, Second District, to allow police to transport a suspect to the station house for fingerprinting, without his consent and without probable cause or prior judicial authorization.

* * *

... There is no doubt that at some point in the investigative process, police procedures can qualitatively and quantitatively be so intrusive with respect to a suspect's freedom of movement and privacy interests as to trigger the full protection of the Fourth and Fourteenth Amendments. And our view continues to be that the line is crossed when the police, without probable cause or a warrant, forcibly remove a person from his home or other place in which he is entitled to be and transport him to the police station, where he is detained, although briefly, for investigative purposes. We adhere to the view that such seizures, at least where not under judicial supervision, are sufficiently like arrests to invoke the traditional rule that arrests may constitutionally be made only on probable cause.

None of the foregoing implies that a brief detention in the field for the purpose of fingerprinting, where there is only reasonable suspicion not amounting to probable cause, is necessarily impermissible under the Fourth Amendment. In addressing the reach of a *Terry* stop in *Adams v. Williams,* we observed that "[a] brief stop of a suspicious individual, in order to determine his identity or to maintain the status quo momentarily while obtaining more information, may be most reasonable in light of the facts known to the officer at the time." Also, just this Term, we concluded that if there are articulable facts supporting a reasonable suspicion that a person has committed a criminal offense, that person may be stopped in order to identify him, to question him briefly, or to detain him briefly while attempting to obtain additional information. There is thus support in our cases for the view that the Fourth Amendment would permit seizures for the purpose of fingerprinting, if there is reasonable suspicion that the suspect has committed a criminal act, if there is a reasonable basis for believing that fingerprinting will establish or negate the suspect's connection with that crime, and if the procedure is carried out with dispatch. Of course, neither reasonable suspicion nor probable cause would suffice to permit the officers to make a warrantless entry into

a person's house for the purpose of obtaining fingerprint identification.

* * *

[Concurring opinion omitted.]

WHREN
v.
UNITED STATES

517 U.S. 806, 116 S. Ct. 1769, 135 L. Ed. 2d 89 (1996)

[Citations and footnotes omitted.]

[Officers were patrolling a "high drug area" of the city in an unmarked car. Their suspicions were aroused when they passed a dark Pathfinder truck with temporary license plates and youthful occupants waiting at a stop sign, the driver looking down into the lap of the passenger at his right. The truck remained stopped at the intersection for what seemed an unusually long time—more than 20 seconds. When the police car executed a U-turn in order to head back toward the truck, the Pathfinder turned suddenly to its right, without signaling, and sped off at an "unreasonable" speed. The policemen followed, and in a short while overtook the Pathfinder when it stopped behind other traffic at a red light. They pulled up alongside, and Officer Ephraim Soto stepped out and approached the driver's door, identifying himself as a police officer and directing the driver, petitioner Brown, to put the vehicle in park. When Soto drew up to the driver's window, he immediately observed two large plastic bags of what appeared to be crack cocaine in petitioner Whren's hands. Both were arrested, and quantities of several types of illegal drugs were retrieved from the vehicle. Petitioners challenged the legality of the stop and the resulting seizure of the drugs. They argued that the stop had not been justified by probable cause to believe, or even reasonable suspicion, that petitioners were engaged in illegal drug-dealing activity; and that Officer Soto's asserted ground for approaching the vehicle— to give the driver a warning concerning traffic violations—was pretextual. The District Court denied the suppression motion. Petitioners were convicted of the counts at issue here. The Court of Appeals affirmed the convictions, holding with respect to the suppression issue that, "regardless of whether a police officer subjectively believes that the occupants of an automobile may be engaging in some other illegal behavior, a traffic stop is permissible as long as a reasonable officer in the same circumstances could have stopped the car for the suspected traffic violation."]

Scalia, J., delivered the opinion for a unanimous Court.

* * *

... In this case we decide whether the temporary detention of a motorist who the police have probable cause to believe has committed a civil traffic violation is inconsistent with the Fourth Amendment's prohibition against unreasonable seizures unless a reasonable officer would have been motivated to stop the car by a desire to enforce the traffic laws.

* * *

The Fourth Amendment guarantees "[t]he right of the people to be secure in their persons, houses, papers, and effects, against unreasonable searches and seizures." Temporary detention of individuals during the stop of an automobile by the police, even if only for a brief period and for a limited purpose, constitutes a "seizure" of "persons" within the meaning of this provision. An automobile stop is thus subject to the constitutional imperative that it not be "unreasonable" under the circumstances. As a general matter, the decision to stop an automobile is reasonable where the police have probable cause to believe that a traffic violation has occurred.

Petitioners accept that Officer Soto had probable cause to believe that various provisions of the District of Columbia traffic code had been violated. They argue, however, that "in the unique context of civil traffic regulations" probable cause is not enough. Since, they contend, the use of automobiles is so heavily and minutely regulated that total compliance with traffic and safety rules is nearly impossible, a police officer will almost invariably be able to catch any given motorist in a technical violation. This creates the temptation to use traffic stops as a means of investigating other law violations, as to which no probable cause or even articulable suspicion exists. Petitioners, who are both black, further contend that police officers might decide which motorists to stop based on decidedly impermissible factors, such as the

race of the car's occupants. To avoid this danger, they say, the Fourth Amendment test for traffic stops should be, not the normal one (applied by the Court of Appeals) of whether probable cause existed to justify the stop; but rather, whether a police officer, acting reasonably, would have made the stop for the reason given.

* * *

Petitioners urge as an extraordinary factor in this case that the "multitude of applicable traffic and equipment regulations" is so large and so difficult to obey perfectly that virtually everyone is guilty of violation, permitting the police to single out almost whomever they wish for a stop. But we are aware of no principle that would allow us to decide at what point a code of law becomes so expansive and so commonly violated that infraction itself can no longer be the ordinary measure of the lawfulness of enforcement. And even if we could identify such exorbitant codes, we do not know by what standard (or what right) we would decide, as petitioners would have us do, which particular provisions are sufficiently important to merit enforcement.

For the run-of-the-mine [sic] case, which this surely is, we think there is no realistic alternative to the traditional common-law rule that probable cause justifies a search and seizure.

Here the District Court found that the officers had probable cause to believe that petitioners had violated the traffic code. That rendered the stop reasonable under the Fourth Amendment, the evidence thereby discovered admissible, and the upholding of the convictions by the Court of Appeals for the District of Columbia Circuit correct.

Judgment affirmed.

ARIZONA
v.
JOHNSON

555 U.S. 323, 129 S. Ct. 781, 172 L. Ed. 2d 694 (2009)

Justice GINSBURG delivered the opinion of the Court.

[While patrolling near a Tucson neighborhood associated with the Crips, a violent street gang, three officers serving on Arizona's gang task force pulled an automobile over after a license-plate check indicated that the vehicle's registration had been suspended for an insurance violation. At the time of the stop, the officers had no reason to suspect the car's occupants of criminal activity. Officer Trevizo attended to Johnson, the back-seat passenger, while another officer attended to the driver. She noticed that, as the she approached, Johnson looked back and kept his eyes on her. She also noticed that he had a police scanner in his pocket and was wearing blue clothing and a bandana, which she believed indicated his membership in the Crips. After learning that Johnson was from an area that she knew was home to a Crips gang and had been in prison, she asked him to step out of the vehicle. Suspecting from his appearance and responses that he was armed, she patted him down, felt a gun near his waist, and placed him under arrest. Johnson was charged with being a felon in possession of a firearm. The trial court denied his motion to suppress the evidence, concluding that the stop was lawful and that Trevizo had cause to suspect Johnson was armed and dangerous. Johnson was convicted and appealed.]

Justice GINSBURG delivered the opinion of the Court.

This case concerns the authority of police officers to "stop and frisk" a passenger in a motor vehicle temporarily seized upon police detection of a traffic infraction. In a pathmarking decision, *Terry v. Ohio*, the Court considered whether an investigatory stop (temporary detention) and frisk (patdown for weapons) may be conducted without violating the Fourth Amendment's ban on unreasonable searches and seizures. The Court upheld "stop and frisk" as constitutionally permissible if two conditions are met. First, the investigatory stop must be lawful. . . . Second, to proceed from a stop to a frisk, the police officer must reasonably suspect that the person stopped is armed and dangerous.

For the duration of a traffic stop, we recently confirmed, a police officer effectively seizes "everyone in the vehicle," the driver and all passengers. Accordingly, we hold that, in a traffic-stop setting, the first *Terry* condition—a lawful investigatory stop—is met whenever it is lawful for police to detain an automobile and its occupants pending inquiry into a vehicular violation. The

police need not have, in addition, cause to believe any occupant of the vehicle is involved in criminal activity. To justify a patdown of the driver or a passenger during a traffic stop, however, just as in the case of a pedestrian reasonably suspected of criminal activity, the police must harbor reasonable suspicion that the person subjected to the frisk is armed and dangerous.

* * *

A lawful roadside stop begins when a vehicle is pulled over for investigation of a traffic violation. The temporary seizure of driver and passengers ordinarily continues, and remains reasonable, for the duration of the stop. Normally, the stop ends when the police have no further need to control the scene, and inform the driver and passengers they are free to leave. An officer's inquiries into matters unrelated to the justification for the traffic stop, this Court has made plain, do not convert the encounter into something other than a lawful seizure, so long as those inquiries do not measurably extend the duration of the stop.

* * *

For the reasons stated, the judgment of the Arizona Court of Appeals is reversed, and the case is remanded for further proceedings not inconsistent with this opinion.

It is so ordered.

ARIZONA
v.
GANT

556 U.S. 332, 129 S. Ct. 1710, 173 L. Ed. 2d 485 (2009)

[Rodney Gant was arrested for driving on a suspended license. After he was handcuffed and locked in a patrol car, police officers searched his car and found cocaine in the pocket of a jacket on the back seat. The trial court denied his motion to suppress the evidence, and he was convicted of a drug offenses The Arizona Supreme Court reversed, holding that the search-incident-to-arrest exception, as defined in *Chimel v. California*, and as applied to vehicle searches in *New York v. Belton*, did not justify the search conducted in this case because Gant could not have accessed his car to retrieve weapons or evidence at the time of the search. It distinguished *New York v. Belton*, holding that police may search the passenger compartment of a vehicle and any containers therein as a contemporaneous incident of a recent occupant's lawful arrest—on the basis that *Belton* concerned the scope of a search incident to arrest but did not answer the question whether officers may conduct such a search once the scene has been secured.]

Justice STEVENS delivered the opinion of the Court.

* * *

Consistent with our precedent, our analysis begins, as it should in every case addressing the reasonableness of a warrantless search, with the basic rule that "searches conducted outside the judicial process, without prior approval by judge or magistrate, are *per se* unreasonable under the Fourth Amendment—subject only to a few specifically established and well-delineated. Among the exceptions to the warrant requirement is a search incident to a lawful arrest. The exception derives from interests in officer safety and evidence preservation that are typically implicated in arrest situations.

In *Chimel*, we held that a search incident to arrest may only include "the arrestee's person and the area 'within his immediate control'—construing that phrase to mean the area from within which he might gain possession of a weapon or destructible evidence." That limitation, which continues to define the boundaries of the exception, ensures that the scope of a search incident to arrest is commensurate with its purposes of protecting arresting officers and safeguarding any evidence of the offense of arrest that an arrestee might conceal or destroy. If there is no possibility that an arrestee could reach into the area that law enforcement officers seek to search, both justifications for the search-incident-to-arrest exception are absent and the rule does not apply.

In *Belton*, we considered *Chimel*'s application to the automobile context. A lone police officer in that case stopped a speeding car in which Belton was one of four occupants. While asking for the driver's license and registration, the officer smelled burnt marijuana and observed an envelope on the car floor marked "Supergold"—a name he associated with marijuana. Thus having probable cause to believe the occupants had committed a drug offense, the officer ordered them out of the vehicle, placed them under arrest, and patted them down. Without handcuffing the arrestees, the officer " 'split them up into four separate areas of the Thruway . . . so they would not be in physical touching area of each other' " and searched the vehicle, including the pocket of a jacket on the backseat, in which he found cocaine.

* * *

. . . [W]e held that when an officer lawfully arrests "the occupant of an automobile, he may, as a contemporaneous incident of that arrest, search the passenger compartment of the automobile" and any containers therein. That holding was based in large part on our assumption "that articles inside the relatively narrow compass of the passenger compartment of an automobile are in fact generally, even if not inevitably, within "the area into which an arrestee might reach.' "

The Arizona Supreme Court read our decision in *Belton* as merely delineating "the proper scope of a search of the interior of an automobile" incident to an arrest. That is, *when* the passenger compartment is within an arrestee's reaching distance, *Belton* supplies the generalization that the entire compartment and any containers therein may be reached. On that view of *Belton,* the state court concluded that the search of Gant's car was unreasonable because Gant clearly could not have accessed his car at the time of the search. It also found that no other exception to the warrant requirement applied in this case.

* * *

Despite the textual and evidentiary support for the Arizona Supreme Court's reading of *Belton,* our opinion has been widely understood to allow a vehicle search incident to the arrest of a recent occupant even if there is no possibility the arrestee could gain access to the vehicle at the time of the search. This reading may be attributable to Justice Brennan's dissent in *Belton,* in which he characterized the Court's holding as resting on the "fiction . . . that the interior of a car is *always* within the immediate control of an arrestee who has recently been in the car." Under the majority's approach, he argued, "the result would presumably be the same even if [the officer] had handcuffed Belton and his companions in the patrol car" before conducting the search.

Since we decided *Belton,* Courts of Appeals have given different answers to the question whether a vehicle must be within an arrestee's reach to justify a vehicle search incident to arrest, but Justice Brennan's reading of the Court's opinion has predominated. As Justice O'Connor observed, lower court decisions seem now to treat the ability to search a vehicle incident to the arrest of a recent occupant as a police entitlement rather than as an exception justified by the twin rationales of *Chimel.* Justice SCALIA has similarly noted that, although it is improbable that an arrestee could gain access to weapons stored in his vehicle after he has been handcuffed and secured in the backseat of a patrol car, cases allowing a search in "this precise factual scenario . . . are legion. Indeed, some courts have upheld searches under Belton "even when . . . the handcuffed arrestee has already left the scene."

Under this broad reading of *Belton,* a vehicle search would be authorized incident to every arrest of a recent occupant notwithstanding that in most cases the vehicle's passenger compartment will not be within the arrestee's reach at the time of the search. To read *Belton* as authorizing a vehicle search incident to every recent occupant's arrest would thus untether the rule from the justifications underlying the *Chimel* exception–a result clearly incompatible with our statement in *Belton* that it "in no way alters the fundamental principles established in the *Chimel* case regarding the basic scope of searches incident to lawful custodial arrests." Accordingly, we reject this reading of *Belton* and hold that the *Chimel* rationale authorizes police to search a vehicle incident to a recent occupant's arrest only when the arrestee is unsecured and within reaching distance of the passenger compartment at the time of the search.

Although it does not follow from *Chimel,* we also conclude that circumstances unique to the vehicle context justify a search incident to a lawful arrest when it is "reasonable to believe evidence relevant to the crime of arrest might be found in the vehicle." In many cases, as when a recent occupant is arrested for a traffic violation, there will be no reasonable basis to believe the vehicle contains relevant evidence. But in others, including *Belton* and *Thornton,* the offense of arrest will supply a basis for searching the passenger compartment of an arrestee's vehicle and any containers therein.

Neither the possibility of access nor the likelihood of discovering offense-related evidence authorized the search in this case. Unlike in *Belton,* which involved a single officer confronted with four unsecured arrestees, the five officers in this case outnumbered the three arrestees, all of whom had been handcuffed and secured in separate patrol cars before the officers searched Gant's car. Under those circumstances, Gant clearly was not within reaching distance of his car at the time of the search. An evidentiary basis for the search was also lacking in this case. Whereas *Belton* and *Thornton* were arrested for drug offenses, Gant was arrested for driving with a suspended license—an offense for which police could not expect to find evidence in the passenger compartment of Gant's car. Because police could not reasonably have believed either that Gant could have accessed his car at the time of the search or that evidence of the offense for which he was arrested might have been found therein, the search in this case was unreasonable.

The State does not seriously disagree with the Arizona Supreme Court's conclusion that Gant could not have accessed his vehicle at the time of the search, but it nevertheless asks us to uphold the search of his vehicle under the broad reading of *Belton* discussed above. The State argues that *Belton* searches are reasonable regardless of the possibility of access in a given case because that expansive rule correctly balances law enforcement interests, including the interest in a bright-line rule, with an arrestee's limited privacy interest in his vehicle.

For several reasons, we reject the State's argument. First, the State seriously undervalues the privacy interests at stake. Although we have recognized that a motorist's privacy interest in his vehicle is less substantial than in his home, the former interest is nevertheless important and deserving of constitutional protection. It is particularly significant that *Belton* searches authorize police officers to search not just the passenger compartment but every purse, briefcase, or other container within that space. A rule that gives police the power to conduct such a search whenever an individual is caught committing a traffic offense, when there is no basis for believing evidence of the offense might be found in the vehicle, creates a serious and recurring threat to the privacy of countless individuals. Indeed, the character of that threat implicates the central concern underlying the Fourth Amendment—the concern about giving police officers unbridled discretion to rummage at will among a person's private effects.

At the same time as it undervalues these privacy concerns, the State exaggerates the clarity that its reading of *Belton* provides. Courts that have read *Belton* expansively are at odds regarding how close in time to the arrest and how proximate to the arrestee's vehicle an officer's first contact with the arrestee must be to bring the encounter within *Belton*'s purview and whether a search is reasonable when it commences or continues after the arrestee has been removed from the scene. The rule has thus generated a great deal of uncertainty, particularly for a rule touted as providing a "bright line."

Contrary to the State's suggestion, a broad reading of *Belton* is also unnecessary to protect law enforcement safety and evidentiary interests. Under our view, *Belton* and *Thornton* permit an officer to conduct a vehicle search when an arrestee is within reaching distance of the vehicle or it is reasonable to believe the vehicle contains evidence of the offense of arrest. Other established exceptions to the warrant requirement authorize a vehicle search under additional circumstances when safety or evidentiary concerns demand. For instance, *Michigan v. Long*, permits an officer to search a vehicle's passenger compartment when he has reasonable suspicion that an individual, whether or not the arrestee, is "dangerous" and might access the vehicle to "gain immediate control of weapons." If there is probable cause to believe a vehicle contains evidence of criminal activity, *United States v. Ross* authorizes a search of any area of the vehicle in which the evidence might be found. . . . Finally, there may be still other circumstances in which safety or evidentiary interests would justify a search.

These exceptions together ensure that officers may search a vehicle when genuine safety or evidentiary concerns encountered during the arrest of a vehicle's recent occupant justify a search. Construing *Belton* broadly to allow vehicle searches incident to any arrest would serve no purpose except to provide a police entitlement, and it is anathema to the Fourth Amendment to permit a warrantless search on that basis. For these reasons,

we are unpersuaded by the State's arguments that a broad reading of *Belton* would meaningfully further law enforcement interests and justify a substantial intrusion on individuals' privacy.

Our dissenting colleagues argue that the doctrine of *stare decisis* requires adherence to a broad reading of *Belton* even though the justifications for searching a vehicle incident to arrest are in most cases absent. The doctrine of *stare decisis* is of course "essential to the respect accorded to the judgments of the Court and to the stability of the law," but it does not compel us to follow a past decision when its rationale no longer withstands "careful analysis."

We have never relied on *stare decisis* to justify the continuance of an unconstitutional police practice. And we would be particularly loath to uphold an unconstitutional result in a case that is so easily distinguished from the decisions that arguably compel it. The safety and evidentiary interests that supported the search in *Belton* simply are not present in this case. Indeed, it is hard to imagine two cases that are factually more distinct, as *Belton* involved one officer confronted by four unsecured arrestees suspected of committing a drug offense and this case involves several officers confronted with a securely detained arrestee apprehended for driving with a suspended license. This case is also distinguishable from *Thornton,* in which the petitioner was arrested for a drug offense. It is thus unsurprising that Members of this Court who concurred in the judgments in *Belton* and *Thornton* also concur in the decision in this case.

We do not agree with the contention in JUSTICE ALITO's dissent (hereinafter dissent) that consideration of police reliance interests requires a different result. Although it appears that the State's reading of *Belton* has been widely taught in police academies and that law enforcement officers have relied on the rule in conducting vehicle searches during the past 28 years, many of these searches were not justified by the reasons underlying the *Chimel* exception. Countless individuals guilty of nothing more serious than a traffic violation have had their constitutional right to the security of their private effects violated as a result. The fact that the law enforcement community may view the State's version of the *Belton* rule as an entitlement does not establish the sort of reliance interest that could outweigh the countervailing interest that all individuals share in having their constitutional rights fully protected. If it is clear that a practice is unlawful, individuals' interest in its discontinuance clearly outweighs any law enforcement "entitlement" to its persistence. . . .

* * *

The experience of the 28 years since we decided *Belton* has shown that the generalization underpinning the broad reading of that decision is unfounded. We now know that articles inside the passenger compartment are rarely "within 'the area into which an arrestee might reach,' " and blind adherence to *Belton*'s faulty assumption would authorize myriad unconstitutional searches. The doctrine of *stare decisis* does not require us to approve routine constitutional violations.

Police may search a vehicle incident to a recent occupant's arrest only if the arrestee is within reaching distance of the passenger compartment at the time of the search or it is reasonable to believe the vehicle contains evidence of the offense of arrest. When these justifications are absent, a search of an arrestee's vehicle will be unreasonable unless police obtain a warrant or show that another exception to the warrant requirement applies. The Arizona Supreme Court correctly held that this case involved an unreasonable search. Accordingly, the judgment of the State Supreme Court is affirmed.

It is so ordered.

ILLINOIS
v.
CABALLES

543 U.S. 405, 125 S. Ct. 834, 160 L. Ed. 2d 842 (2005)

[Citations and footnotes omitted.]

JUSTICE STEVENS delivered the opinion of the Court.

Illinois State Trooper Daniel Gillette stopped respondent for speeding on an interstate highway. When Gillette radioed the police dispatcher to report the stop, a second trooper, Craig Graham, a member of the Illinois State Police Drug Interdiction Team, overheard the transmission and immediately headed for the scene with his narcotics-detection dog. When they arrived, respondent's car was on the shoulder of the road and respondent was in Gillette's vehicle. While Gillette was in the process of writing a warning ticket, Graham walked his dog around respondent's car. The dog alerted at the trunk. Based on that alert, the officers searched the trunk, found marijuana, and arrested respondent. The entire incident lasted less than 10 minutes.

Respondent was convicted of a narcotics offense and sentenced to 12 years' imprisonment and a $256,136 fine. . . .

The question on which we granted certiorari is narrow: 'Whether the Fourth Amendment requires reasonable, articulable suspicion to justify using a drug-detection dog to sniff a vehicle during a legitimate traffic stop.' Thus, we proceed on the assumption that the officer conducting the dog sniff had no information about respondent except that he had been stopped for speeding. . . .

Here, the initial seizure of respondent when he was stopped on the highway was based on probable cause, and was concededly lawful. It is nevertheless clear that a seizure that is lawful at its inception can violate the Fourth Amendment if its manner of execution unreasonably infringes interests protected by the Constitution. A seizure that is justified solely by the interest in issuing a warning ticket to the driver can become unlawful if it is prolonged beyond the time reasonably required to complete that mission. In an earlier case involving a dog sniff that occurred during an unreasonably prolonged traffic stop, the Illinois Supreme Court held that use of the dog and the subsequent discovery of contraband were the product of an unconstitutional seizure. We may assume that a similar result would be warranted in this case if the dog sniff had been conducted while respondent was being unlawfully detained.

In the state-court proceedings, however, the judges carefully reviewed the details of Officer Gillette's conversations with respondent and the precise timing of his radio transmissions to the dispatcher to determine whether he had improperly extended the duration of the stop to enable the dog sniff to occur. We have not recounted those details because we accept the state court's conclusion that the duration of the stop in this case was entirely justified by the traffic offense and the ordinary inquiries incident to such a stop.

Despite this conclusion, the Illinois Supreme Court held that the initially lawful traffic stop became an unlawful seizure solely as a result of the canine sniff that occurred outside respondent's stopped car. That is, the court characterized the dog sniff as the cause rather than the consequence of a constitutional violation. In its view, the use of the dog converted the citizen-police encounter from a lawful traffic stop into a drug investigation, and because the shift in purpose was not supported by any reasonable suspicion that respondent possessed narcotics, it was unlawful. In our view, conducting a dog sniff would not change the character of a traffic stop that is lawful at its inception and otherwise executed in a reasonable manner, unless the dog sniff itself infringed respondent's constitutionally protected interest in privacy. Our cases hold that it did not.

Official conduct that does not 'compromise any legitimate interest in privacy' is not a search subject to the Fourth Amendment. We have held that any interest in possessing contraband cannot be deemed 'legitimate,' and thus, governmental conduct that only reveals the possession of contraband 'compromises no legitimate privacy interest.' This is because the expectation 'that certain facts will not come to the attention of the authorities' is not the same as an interest in 'privacy that society is prepared to consider reasonable.' In United States v. Place, we treated a canine sniff by a well-trained narcotics-detection dog as 'sui generis' because it 'discloses only the presence or absence of narcotics, a contraband item . . .

Accordingly, the use of a well-trained narcotics-detection dog—one that 'does not expose noncontraband items that otherwise would remain hidden from public view,'—during a lawful traffic stop, generally does not implicate legitimate privacy interests. In this case, the dog sniff was performed on the exterior of respondent's car while he was lawfully seized for a traffic violation. Any intrusion on respondent's privacy expectations does not rise to the level of a constitutionally cognizable infringement.

This conclusion is entirely consistent with our recent decision that the use of a thermal-imaging device to detect the growth of marijuana in a home constituted an unlawful search. Critical to that decision was the fact that the device was capable of detecting lawful activity—in that case, intimate details in a home, such as 'at what hour each night the lady of the house takes her daily sauna and bath.' The legitimate expectation that information about perfectly lawful activity will remain private is categorically distinguishable from respondent's hopes or expectations concerning the nondetection of contraband in the trunk of his car. A dog sniff conducted during a concededly lawful traffic stop that reveals no information other than the location of a substance that no individual has any right to possess does not violate the Fourth Amendment.

The judgment of the Illinois Supreme Court is vacated, and the case is remanded for further proceedings not inconsistent with this opinion.

It is so ordered.

UNITED STATES
v.
KING

227 F.3d 732 (6th Cir. 2000)

[Kenneth King was charged with possession with intent to distribute cocaine within 1,000 feet of a schoolyard. The cocaine was found during the search of a basement in a two-family dwelling in which he resided. The search was conducted under the authority of a warrant. King filed a motion to suppress the cocaine on the grounds that affidavit submitted in support of the warrant was insufficient to establish probable cause to believe that illegal drugs would be found on the premises. The district court conducted a hearing and thereafter denied the motion to suppress. King was convicted and appealed. This case has been included because of its unusually clear discussion of the factors courts consider in evaluating whether probable cause for the issuance of a warrant has been established.]

CLAY, Circuit Judge.

* * *

The Fourth Amendment guarantees that "no Warrants shall issue, but upon probable cause, supported by Oath or affirmation." The warrant requirement serves to interpose between the police and an individual's personal privacy an orderly procedure involving "a neutral and detached magistrate[,]," who is responsible for making an "informed and deliberate determination" on the issue of probable cause. The warrant process thus avoids allowing the determination of probable cause to rest with the "zealous" actions of the police who are "engaged in the often competitive enterprise of ferreting out crime."

Probable cause is defined as "reasonable grounds for belief, supported by less than prima facie proof but more than mere suspicion," that "there is a fair probability that contraband or evidence of a crime will be found in a particular place." This determination does not lend itself to the application of "[r]igid legal rules," and no one decision may serve to provide a definitive basis upon which to rely inasmuch as "informant's tips, like all other clues and evidence . . . may vary greatly in the value and reliability." Rather, the probable cause standard is a " 'practical non-technical conception . . . [wherein] we deal with probabilities . . . [which are] the factual and practical considerations of everyday life on which reasonable and prudent men, not legal technicians, act.' " Stated otherwise, "probable cause is a fluid concept—turning on the assessment of probabilities in particular factual contexts—not readily, or even usefully, reduced to a neat set of legal rules. Informants' tips doubtless come in many shapes and sizes from many different types of persons. . . . Rigid legal rules are ill-suited to an area of such diversity. One simple rule will not cover every situation." As such, the issuing magistrate must apply a "totality of the circumstances" test to probable cause issues. This test requires the magistrate to "make a practical, common-sense decision whether, given all the circumstances set forth in the affidavit before him, including the 'veracity' and 'basis of knowledge' of persons supplying the hearsay information," probable cause exists.

The Supreme Court identified factors which, although not to be analyzed as "separate and independent requirements to be rigidly exacted in every case," should be weighed by a reviewing court in assessing the value that should be afforded to an informant's tip when determining whether a substantial basis for probable cause exists. These factors, which consist of the "veracity" or "reliability" as well as "basis of knowledge" of the tip, are relative where the strength of one factor may compensate for the deficiency of another. However, "the information presented must be sufficient to allow the official to independently determine probable cause; 'his action cannot be a mere ratification of the bare conclusions of others.' " "In order to ensure that such an abdication of the magistrate's duty does not occur, courts must continue to conscientiously review the sufficiency of affidavits on which warrants are issued." With these standards and cautionary instructions from the Supreme Court in mind, we turn to the affidavit presented to the magistrate in this case to determine whether, under a totality of the circumstances, the affidavit was sufficient to establish probable cause for the warrant to issue.

The affidavit submitted to the court by Detective John Gannon of the Cleveland Police Department in support of the search warrant in question provided as follows:

Before me, a Judge of the Court of Common Pleas, Cuyahoga County, Ohio, personally appeared the undersigned Det. John Gannon, # 2452, who being first duly sworn, deposes and says that he is member of the Police Department of the City of Cleveland, in Cuyahoga County, Ohio, and that his training and experience include: twenty-six years experience with the Cleveland Police, with a current assignment to the Caribbean Gang Task Force; training in the recognition, production, and distribution of controlled substances; over one thousand arrests for drug-related offenses.

Affiant has good cause to believe that on the premises known as 1437 East 116th Street, Cleveland, Cuyahoga County, Ohio, and being more fully described as the downstairs unit in a two family, two and one half story, white wood sided dwelling with green trim, the numbers "1439," the address for the upstairs unit, clearly visible on the south side of the entrance door to the upstairs unit, the structure being located on the east side of East 116th Street, facing west, and in the vehicle described as 1980's model gray Chevrolet Cavalier, Ohio Temporary License Number K591513, there is now being kept, concealed, and possessed the following evidence of criminal offense: Cocaine, and other narcotic drugs, and/or controlled substances; instruments and paraphernalia used in taking or preparing drugs for sale, use, or shipment; records of illegal transactions including computers and computer files, articles of personal property, and papers tending to establish the identity of the persons in control of the premises; other contraband, including, but not limited to, money, communications equipment, motor vehicles, and weapons being illegally possessed therein; and/or any and all evidence pertaining to the violations of the laws of the State of Ohio, to wit:

1. Within the past twenty-four hours, affiant was contacted by another a confidential reliable informant concerning the delivery of a large quantity of crack cocaine to the above-described premises.

2. This information from confidential reliable informant (CRI) indicated that Kenneth King was trafficking in cocaine, and had crack cocaine at the above-described premises having been delivered to King by Antonio Cook within the past day.

3. CRI is made reliable in that CRI has given information to the law enforcement official which has led to the arrest and/or conviction of more than seventy individuals for violations of state and/or federal drug laws, as well as the confiscation of more than $100,000.00 and 5 kilograms of controlled substances.

4. CRI stated that King kept drugs at the above-described premises, giving a description of the premises, and King utilized the above-described vehicle for the purpose of making deliveries of smaller amounts of crack cocaine. Investigation revealed that the above-described address is listed in the records of the Ohio Bureau of Motor Vehicles as an address for vehicles registered to Kenneth King.

5. Affiant is also aware that Antonio Cook is a person known to members of the Task Force as a supplier of cocaine on the east side of Cleveland. Affiant also determined that King has a prior felony conviction for GSI and Aggravated Assault and has done prison time.

6. In the experience of affiant, narcotic drugs are frequently carried or concealed on people who are at locations where drugs are used, kept, or sold, and the size of useable quantities of drugs are small, making them easy to conceal on one's person.

7. Further, in the experience of affiant, persons who traffic in illegal drugs frequently keep records of illegal transactions, at times using computers for such records, and evidence of communications used in the furtherance of drug trafficking activity, including, but not limited to, pagers, cellular telephones, answering machines, and answering machine tapes.

8. Further, in the experience of the affiant, persons who traffic in illegal drugs frequently keep weapons, such as firearms, on or about their person or within their possession, for use against law enforcement officials, as well as other citizens.

9. Permitting a motor vehicle to be used in the commission of a felony drug abuse offense is a violation of R.C. 2925.13.

10. Affiant avers that it is urgently necessary that the above-mentioned premises be searched in the night season forthwith to prevent the above named property from being concealed or removed so as not to be found, and for the safety of the executing officers.

Defendant argues that the affidavit was insufficient to establish probable cause insofar as it fails to provide any basis as to the reliability or veracity of the confidential informant, and fails to indicate that Detective Gannon conducted an independent investigation to corroborate the informant's allegations. Defendant contends that Detective Gannon's verification of Defendant's address, via the Ohio Department of Motor Vehicles, as being that alleged by the informant as a place where drugs were being trafficked, was inadequate to corroborate the informant's claims. Defendant further contends that because the affidavit does not aver that the confidential informant observed drugs or paraphernalia on the premises of Defendant's home, corroboration by Detective Gannon was particularly necessary. We disagree with Defendant's claims, and believe that the affidavit in support of the search warrant was sufficient to establish probable cause that illegal drugs could be found on the premises inasmuch as the affidavit described the area to be searched with particularity, was based upon information provided by a known reliable informant, and was verified by Detective Gannon to the extent possible.

The affidavit described Defendant's residence with particularity as being "the downstairs unit in a two family, two and one half story, white wood sided dwelling with green trim, the numbers '1439,' the address for the upstairs unit, clearly visible on the south side of the entrance door to the upstairs unit, the structure being located on the east side of East 116th Street, facing west." The affidavit further described Defendant's vehicle used in the distribution of cocaine with particularity as a "1980's model gray Chevrolet Cavalier, Ohio Temporary License Number K591513." The affidavit also indicated that in addition to describing the premises and the vehicle in such detail, the confidential reliable informant ("CRI") described the nature of alleged criminal activity in detail. For example, the CRI described the criminal activity as trafficking cocaine, and further stated that a large amount of cocaine had been delivered to the premises described in the affidavit twenty-four hours beforehand for the purposes of distribution. The CRI also stated that the large amount of cocaine had been delivered to the premises by Antonio Cook within the past day. The reliability of the informant was established in the affidavit by Detective Gannon's averments that the CRI had provided credible information in the past which had led to the arrest and/or conviction of "more than seventy individuals for violations of state and/or federal drug laws, as well as the confiscation of more than $100,000.00 and 5 kilograms of controlled substances." Moreover, the informant's tip was corroborated by Detective Gannon's own investigation. For example, the affidavit indicates that Detective Gannon verified with the Ohio Department of Motor Vehicles that the vehicle described by the informant was registered to Defendant and that the address provided by the informant was Defendant's address. Detective Gannon also verified that Defendant had a prior history of criminal offenses for which he had spent time in prison. Finally, Detective Gannon, as an experienced member of the task force established to ferret out drug-related crimes, averred that he was aware that Antonio Cook is a person known to members of the task force as a supplier of cocaine, which further supported the CRI's allegations.

When considering the above information under a totality of the circumstances, we conclude that the affidavit provided a "substantial basis" for the magistrate to believe that "there [was] a fair probability that contraband or evidence of a crime [would] be found in a particular place;" namely, Defendant's residence. Although the affidavit does not indicate that the CRI observed the delivery of a "large quantity of crack cocaine" to Defendant's residence firsthand, the affidavit does indicate that the CRI had provided accurate information in the past and that Antonio Cook, the individual alleged to have delivered the cocaine, was known to be a drug distributor. As a result, the lack of the firsthand observation is not fatal to the affidavit.

The affidavit in question is distinguishable from those cases where the affidavit was found to be insufficient to establish probable cause. For example, unlike in Weaver, where this Court held that the affidavit in support of the search warrant was insufficient to establish probable cause insofar as it presented no underlying factual circumstances to support the informant's knowledge, failed to indicate that the informant had provided information in the past, and failed to establish any independent police corroboration, the affidavit in the present case provides such detail. Similarly, in Leake, the affidavit was insufficient to establish probable cause in that the anonymous caller failed to provide the names of the individuals residing at the home where the marijuana was allegedly being grown, and failed to provide a date upon which the marijuana was allegedly seen; and the police failed to sufficiently corroborate the information. However, none of these insufficiencies [is] present here, even though the CRI did not observe the cocaine being delivered to Defendant's residence firsthand.

We therefore hold that the district court did not err in denying Defendant's motion to suppress the evidence, where the affidavit submitted in support of the warrant was rich in detail, was based upon a tip from a known and reliable informant, and was corroborated by independent police investigation.

* * *

PAYTON
v.
NEW YORK

445 U.S. 573, 100 S. Ct. 137, 163 L. Ed. 2d 639 (1979)

[Citations and footnotes omitted.]

Mr. Justice STEVENS delivered the opinion of the Court.

These appeals challenge the constitutionality of New York statutes that authorize police officers to enter a private residence without a warrant and with force, if necessary, to make a routine felony arrest.

* * *

On January 14, 1970, after two days of intensive investigation, New York detectives had assembled evidence sufficient to establish probable cause to believe that Theodore Payton had murdered the manager of a gas station two days earlier. At about 7:30 a. m. on January 15, six officers went to Payton's apartment in the Bronx, intending to arrest him. They had not obtained a warrant. Although light and music emanated from the apartment, there was no response to their knock on the metal door. They summoned emergency assistance and, about 30 minutes later, used crowbars to break open the door and enter the apartment. No one was there. In plain view, however, was a .30-caliber shell casing that was seized and later admitted into evidence at Payton's murder trial.

In due course Payton surrendered to the police, was indicted for murder, and moved to suppress the evidence taken from his apartment. The trial judge held that the warrantless and forcible entry was authorized by the New York Code of Criminal Procedure, and that the evidence in plain view was properly seized. . . . The Appellate Division, First Department, summarily affirmed.

* * *

It is . . . perfectly clear that the evil the Amendment was designed to prevent was broader than the abuse of a general warrant. Unreasonable searches or seizures conducted without any warrant at all are condemned by the plain language of the first clause of the Amendment. Almost a century ago the Court stated in resounding terms that the principles reflected in the Amendment "reached farther than the concrete form" of the specific cases that gave it birth, and "apply to all invasions on the part of the government and its employŽs of the sanctity of a man's home and the privacies of life." Without pausing to consider whether that broad language may require some qualification, it is sufficient to note that the warrantless arrest of a person is a species of seizure required by the Amendment to be reasonable . . .

The simple language of the Amendment applies equally to seizures of persons and to seizures of property. Our analysis in this case may therefore properly commence with rules that have been well established in Fourth Amendment litigation involving tangible items. As the Court reiterated just a few years ago, the "physical entry of the home is the chief evil against which the wording of the Fourth Amendment is directed." And we have long adhered to the view that the warrant procedure minimizes the danger of needless intrusions of that sort.

* * *

. . . The Fourth Amendment protects the individual's privacy in a variety of settings. In none is the zone of privacy more clearly defined than when bounded by the unambiguous physical dimensions of an individual's home-a zone that finds its roots in clear and specific constitutional terms: "The right of the people to be secure in their . . . houses . . . shall not be violated." That language unequivocally establishes the proposition that "[a]t the very core [of the Fourth Amendment] stands the right of a man to retreat into his own home and there be free from unreasonable governmental intrusion." In terms that apply equally to seizures of property and to seizures of persons, the Fourth Amendment has drawn a firm line at the entrance to the house. Absent exigent circumstances, that threshold may not reasonably be crossed without a warrant.

* * *

The parties have argued at some length about the practical consequences of a warrant requirement as a precondition to a felony arrest in the home. In the absence of any evidence that effective law enforcement has suffered in those States that already have such a requirement, we are inclined to view such arguments with skepticism. More fundamentally, however, such arguments of policy must give way to a constitutional command that we consider to be unequivocal.

Finally, we note the State's suggestion that only a search warrant based on probable cause to believe the suspect is at home at a given time can adequately protect the privacy interests at stake, and since such a warrant requirement is manifestly impractical, there need be no warrant of any kind. We find this ingenious argument unpersuasive. It is true that an arrest warrant requirement may afford less protection than a search warrant requirement, but it will suffice to interpose the magistrate's determination of probable cause between the zealous officer and the citizen. If there is sufficient evidence of a citizen's participation in a felony to persuade a judicial officer that his arrest is justified, it is constitutionally reasonable to require him to open his doors to the officers of the law. Thus, for Fourth Amendment purposes, an arrest warrant founded on probable cause implicitly carries with it the limited authority to enter a dwelling in which the suspect lives when there is reason to believe the suspect is within.

Because no arrest warrant was obtained in either of these cases, the judgments must be reversed and the cases remanded to the New York Court of Appeals for further proceedings not inconsistent with this opinion.

It is so ordered.

[Concurring and dissenting opinions have been omitted.]

TENNESSEE
v.
GARNER

471 U.S. 1, 105 S. Ct. 1694,
85 L. Ed. 2d 1 (1985)

[Citations and footnotes omitted.]

[At about 10:45 p.m. on October 3, 1974, Memphis Police Officers Elton Hymon and Leslie Wright were dispatched to answer a "prowler inside call." Behind the house, Hymon saw someone run across the backyard. The fleeing suspect, who was appellee-respondent's decedent, Edward Garner, stopped at a 6-feet-high chain-link fence at the edge of the yard. With the aid of a flashlight, Hymon was able to see Garner's face and hands. He saw no sign of a weapon, and, although not certain, was "reasonably sure" and "figured" that Garner was unarmed. He thought Garner was 17 or 18 years old and about 5'5" or 5'7" tall. While Garner was crouched at the base of the fence, Hymon called out "police, halt" and took a few steps toward him. Garner then began to climb over the fence. Convinced that if Garner made it over the fence he would elude capture, Hymon shot him. The bullet hit Garner in the back of the head. Garner was taken by ambulance to a hospital, where he died on the operating table. Ten dollars and a purse taken from the house were found on his body. Both a Tennessee statute and

departmental policy authorized Hymon to shoot under these circumstances. Garner's father brought a suit for damages against Hymon and the county claiming that the shooting violated his son's Fourth Amendment right to be free from unreasonable force.]

JUSTICE WHITE delivered the opinion of the Court.

This case requires us to determine the constitutionality of the use of deadly force to prevent the escape of an apparently unarmed suspected felon. We conclude that such force may not be used unless it is necessary to prevent the escape and the officer has probable cause to believe that the suspect poses a significant threat of death or serious physical injury to the officer or others.

* * *

Whenever an officer restrains the freedom of a person to walk away, he has seized that person. While it is not always clear just when minimal police interference becomes a seizure, there can be no question that apprehension by the use of deadly force is a seizure subject to the reasonableness requirement of the Fourth Amendment.

A police officer may arrest a person if he has probable cause to believe that person committed a crime. Petitioners and appellant argue that if this requirement is satisfied, the Fourth Amendment has nothing to say about how that seizure is made. This submission ignores the many cases in which this Court, by balancing the extent of the intrusion against the need for it, has examined the reasonableness of the manner in which a search or seizure is conducted. To determine the constitutionality of a seizure, "[w]e must balance the nature and quality of the intrusion on the individual's Fourth Amendment interests against the importance of the governmental interests alleged to justify the intrusion." We have described "the balancing of competing interests" as "the key principle of the Fourth Amendment." Because one of the factors is the extent of the intrusion, it is plain that reasonableness depends on not only when a seizure is made, but also how it is carried out.

* * *

... [N]otwithstanding probable cause to seize a suspect, an officer may not always do so by killing him. The intrusiveness of a seizure by means of deadly force is unmatched. The suspect's fundamental interest in his own life need not be elaborated upon. The use of deadly force also frustrates the interest of the individual, and of society, in judicial determination of guilt and punishment. Against these interests are ranged governmental interests in effective law enforcement. It is argued that overall violence will be reduced by encouraging the peaceful submission of suspects who know that they may be shot if they flee. Effectiveness in making arrests requires the resort to deadly force, or at least the meaningful threat thereof. "Being able to arrest such individuals is a condition precedent to the state's entire system of law enforcement."

Without in any way disparaging the importance of these goals, we are not convinced that the use of deadly force is a sufficiently productive means of accomplishing them to justify the killing of nonviolent suspects. The use of deadly force is a self-defeating way of apprehending a suspect and so setting the criminal justice mechanism in motion. If successful, it guarantees that that mechanism will not be set in motion. And while the meaningful threat of deadly force might be thought to lead to the arrest of more live suspects by discouraging escape attempts, the presently available evidence does not support this thesis. The fact is that a majority of police departments in this country have forbidden the use of deadly force against nonviolent suspects. If those charged with the enforcement of the criminal law have abjured the use of deadly force in arresting nondangerous felons, there is a substantial basis for doubting that the use of such force is an essential attribute of the arrest power in all felony cases. Petitioners and appellant have not persuaded us that shooting nondangerous fleeing suspects is so vital as to outweigh the suspect's interest in his own life.

The use of deadly force to prevent the escape of all felony suspects, whatever the circumstances, is constitutionally unreasonable. It is not better that all felony suspects die than that they escape. Where the suspect poses no immediate threat to the officer and no threat to others, the harm resulting from failing to apprehend him does not justify the use of deadly force to do so. It is no doubt unfortunate when a suspect who is in sight escapes, but the fact that the police arrive a little late or are a little slower afoot does not always justify killing the suspect. A police officer may not seize an unarmed, nondangerous suspect by shooting him dead. The Tennessee statute is unconstitutional insofar as it authorizes the use of deadly force against such fleeing suspects.

It is not, however, unconstitutional on its face. Where the officer has probable cause to believe that the suspect poses a threat of serious physical harm, either to the officer or to others, it is not constitutionally unreasonable to prevent escape by using deadly force. Thus, if the suspect threatens the officer with a weapon or there is probable cause to believe that he has committed a crime involving the infliction or threatened infliction of serious physical harm, deadly force may be used if necessary to prevent escape, and if, where feasible, some warning has been given. . . .

* * *

Nor do we agree with petitioners and appellant that the rule we have adopted requires the police to make impossible, split-second evaluations of unknowable facts. We do not deny the practical difficulties of attempting to assess the suspect's dangerousness. However, similarly difficult judgments must be made by the police in equally uncertain circumstances. Nor is there any indication that in States that allow the use of deadly force only against dangerous suspects, supra, the standard has been difficult to apply or has led to a rash of litigation involving inappropriate second-guessing of police officers' split-second decisions. Moreover, the highly technical felony/misdemeanor distinction is equally, if not more, difficult to apply in the field. An officer is in no position to know, for example, the precise value of property stolen, or whether the crime was a first or second offense. Finally, as noted above, this claim must be viewed with suspicion in light of the similar self-imposed limitations of so many police departments.

* * *

. . . Officer Hymon could not reasonably have believed that Garner—young, slight, and unarmed—posed any threat. Indeed, Hymon never attempted to justify his actions on any basis other than the need to prevent an escape. The District Court stated in passing that "[t]he facts of this case did not indicate to Officer Hymon that Garner was 'non-dangerous.'" This conclusion is not explained, and seems to be based solely on the fact that Garner had broken into a house at night. However, the fact that Garner was a suspected burglar could not, without regard to the other circumstances, automatically justify the use of deadly force. Hymon did not have probable cause to believe that Garner, whom he correctly believed to be unarmed, posed any physical danger to himself or others.

The dissent argues that the shooting was justified by the fact that Officer Hymon had probable cause to believe that Garner had committed a nighttime burglary. While we agree that burglary is a serious crime, we cannot agree that it is so dangerous as automatically to justify the use of deadly force. The FBI classifies burglary as a "property" rather than a "violent" crime. Although the armed burglar would present a different situation, the fact that an unarmed suspect has broken into a dwelling at night does not automatically mean he is physically dangerous. This case demonstrates as much. In fact, the available statistics demonstrate that burglaries only rarely involve physical violence. During the 10-year period from 1973–1982, only 3.8% of all burglaries involved violent crime.

* * *

The judgment of the Court of Appeals is affirmed, and the case is remanded for further proceedings consistent with this opinion.

So ordered.

[The dissenting opinion has been omitted.]

SCOTT

v.

HARRIS

550 U.S. 372, 176 S. Ct. 1769, 167 L. Ed. 2d 686 (2007)

[Citations and footnotes omitted.]

Justice SCALIA delivered the opinion of the Court.

We consider whether a law enforcement official can, consistent with the Fourth Amendment, attempt to stop a fleeing motorist from continuing his public-endangering flight by ramming the motorist's car from behind. Put another way: Can an officer take actions that place a fleeing motorist at risk of serious injury or death in order to stop the motorist's flight from endangering the lives of innocent bystanders?

In March 2001, a Georgia county deputy clocked respondent's vehicle traveling at 73 miles per hour on a road with a 55-mile-per-hour speed

limit. The deputy activated his blue flashing lights indicating that respondent should pull over. Instead, respondent sped away, initiating a chase down what is in most portions a two-lane road, at speeds exceeding 85 miles per hour. The deputy radioed his dispatch to report that he was pursuing a fleeing vehicle, and broadcast its license plate number. Petitioner, Deputy Timothy Scott, heard the radio communication and joined the pursuit along with other officers. In the midst of the chase, respondent pulled into the parking lot of a shopping center and was nearly boxed in by the various police vehicles. Respondent evaded the trap by making a sharp turn, colliding with Scott's police car, exiting the parking lot, and speeding off once again down a two-lane highway.

Following respondent's shopping center maneuvering, which resulted in slight damage to Scott's police car, Scott took over as the lead pursuit vehicle. Six minutes and nearly 10 miles after the chase had begun, Scott decided to attempt to terminate the episode by employing a "Precision Intervention Technique ('PIT') maneuver, which causes the fleeing vehicle to spin to a stop. Having radioed his supervisor for permission, Scott was told to " '[g]o ahead and take him out.' " Instead, Scott applied his push bumper to the rear of respondent's vehicle. As a result, respondent lost control of his vehicle, which left the roadway, ran down an embankment, overturned, and crashed. Respondent was badly injured and was rendered a quadriplegic.

Respondent filed suit against Deputy Scott and others under Rev. Stat. § 1979, 42 U.S.C. § 1983, alleging, inter alia, a violation of his federal constitutional rights, viz. use of excessive force resulting in an unreasonable seizure under the Fourth Amendment.

* * *

The first step in assessing the constitutionality of Scott's actions is to determine the relevant facts. As this case was decided on summary judgment, there have not yet been factual findings by a judge or jury, and respondent's version of events (unsurprisingly) differs substantially from Scott's version....

... "[T]aking the facts from the [respondent's viewpoint, he] remained in control of his vehicle, slowed for turns and intersections, and typically used his indicators for turns. He did not run any motorists off the road. Nor was he a threat to pedestrians in the shopping center parking lot, which was free from pedestrian and vehicular traffic as the center was closed. Significantly, by the time the parties were back on the highway and Scott rammed [respondent], the motorway had been cleared of motorists and pedestrians allegedly because of police blockades of the nearby intersections."

The videotape tells quite a different story. There we see respondent's vehicle racing down narrow, two-lane roads in the dead of night at speeds that are shockingly fast. We see it swerve around more than a dozen other cars, cross the double-yellow line, and force cars traveling in both directions to their respective shoulders to avoid being hit. We see it run multiple red lights and travel for considerable periods of time in the occasional center left-turn-only lane, chased by numerous police cars forced to engage in the same hazardous maneuvers just to keep up. Far from being the cautious and controlled driver the lower court depicts, what we see on the video more closely resembles a Hollywood-style car chase of the most frightening sort, placing police officers and innocent bystanders alike at great risk of serious injury.

...When opposing parties tell two different stories, one of which is blatantly contradicted by the record, so that no reasonable jury could believe it, a court should not adopt that version of the facts for purposes of ruling on a motion for summary judgment.

That was the case here with regard to the factual issue whether respondent was driving in such fashion as to endanger human life. Respondent's version of events is so utterly discredited by the record that no reasonable jury could have believed him. The Court of Appeals should not have relied on such visible fiction; it should have viewed the facts in the light depicted by the videotape.

... [W]e think it is quite clear that Deputy Scott did not violate the Fourth Amendment. Scott does not contest that his decision to terminate the car chase by ramming his bumper into respondent's vehicle constituted a "seizure." "[A] Fourth Amendment seizure [occurs] ... when there is a governmental termination of freedom of movement through means intentionally applied." It is also conceded, by both sides, that a claim of "excessive force in the course of making [a] ... 'seizure' of [the] person ... [is] properly analyzed under the Fourth Amendment's 'objective reasonableness' standard." The question we need to answer is whether Scott's actions were objectively reasonable.

Respondent urges us to analyze this case as we analyzed Garner. We must first decide, he says, whether the actions Scott took constituted "deadly force." (He defines "deadly force" as "any use of force which creates a substantial likelihood of causing death or serious bodily injury") so, respondent claims that Garner prescribes certain preconditions that must be met before Scott's actions can survive Fourth Amendment scrutiny: (1) The suspect must have posed an immediate threat of serious physical harm to the officer or others; (2) deadly force must have been necessary to prevent escape; and (3) where feasible, the officer must have given the suspect some warning. Since these Garner preconditions for using deadly force were not met in this case, Scott's actions were per se unreasonable.

Respondent's argument falters at its first step; Garner did not establish a magical on/off switch that triggers rigid preconditions whenever an officer's actions constitute "deadly force." Garner was simply an application of the Fourth Amendment's "reasonableness" test to the use of a particular type of force in a particular situation. Garner held that it was unreasonable to kill a "young, slight, and unarmed" burglary suspect, by shooting him "in the back of the head" while he was running away on foot, and when the officer "could not reasonably have believed that [the suspect] ... posed any threat," and "never attempted to justify his actions on any basis other than the need to prevent an escape." Whatever Garner said about the factors that might have justified shooting the suspect in that case, such "preconditions" have scant applicability to this case, which has vastly different facts. "Garner had nothing to do with one car striking another or even with car chases in general.... A police car's bumping a fleeing car is, in fact, not much like a policeman's shooting a gun so as to hit a person." Nor is the threat posed by the flight on foot of an unarmed suspect even remotely comparable to the extreme danger to human life posed by respondent in this case. Although respondent's attempt to craft an easy-to-apply legal test in the Fourth Amendment context is admirable, in the end we must still slosh our way through the fact-bound morass of "reasonableness." Whether or not Scott's actions constituted application of "deadly force," all that matters is whether Scott's actions were reasonable.

In determining the reasonableness of the manner in which a seizure is effected, "[w]e must balance the nature and quality of the intrusion on the individual's Fourth Amendment interests against the importance of the governmental interests alleged to justify the intrusion." Scott defends his actions by pointing to the paramount governmental interest in ensuring public safety, and respondent nowhere suggests this was not the purpose motivating Scott's behavior. Thus, in judging whether Scott's actions were reasonable, we must consider the risk of bodily harm that Scott's actions posed to respondent in light of the threat to the public that Scott was trying to eliminate. Although there is no obvious way to quantify the risks on either side, it is clear from the videotape that respondent posed an actual and imminent threat to the lives of any pedestrians who might have been present, to other civilian motorists, and to the officers involved in the chase. It is equally clear that Scott's actions posed a high likelihood of serious injury or death to respondent-though not the near certainty of death posed by, say, shooting a fleeing felon in the back of the head or pulling alongside a fleeing motorist's car and shooting the motorist. So how does a court go about weighing the perhaps lesser probability of injuring or killing numerous bystanders against the perhaps larger probability of injuring or killing a single person? We think it appropriate in this process to take into account not only the number of lives at risk, but also their relative culpability. It was respondent, after all, who intentionally placed himself and the public in danger by unlawfully engaging in the reckless, high-speed flight that ultimately produced the choice between two evils that Scott confronted. Multiple police cars, with blue lights flashing and sirens blaring, had been chasing respondent for nearly 10 miles, but he ignored their warning to stop. By contrast, those who might have been harmed had Scott not taken the action he did were entirely innocent. We have little difficulty in concluding it was reasonable for Scott to take the action that he did.

But wait, says respondent: Couldn't the innocent public equally have been protected, and the tragic accident entirely avoided, if the police had simply ceased their pursuit? We think the police need not have taken that chance and hoped for the best. Whereas Scott's action—ramming respondent off the road—was certain to eliminate the risk that respondent posed to the public, ceasing pursuit was not. First of all, there would have been no way to convey convincingly to respondent that the chase was off, and that he was free to go. Had respondent looked in his rear-view mirror and seen the police cars deactivate their flashing lights and turn around, he would have had no idea whether they were truly letting him get away, or simply devising a new strategy for capture. Perhaps the police knew a shortcut he didn't know, and would reappear down the road to intercept him; or perhaps they were setting up a roadblock in his path. Given such uncertainty, respondent might have been just as likely to respond by continuing to drive recklessly as by slowing down and wiping his brow.

Second, we are loath to lay down a rule requiring the police to allow fleeing suspects to get away whenever they drive so recklessly that they put other people's lives in danger. It is obvious the perverse incentives such a rule would create: Every fleeing motorist would know that escape is within his grasp, if only he accelerates to 90 miles per hour, crosses the double-yellow line a few times, and runs a few red lights. The Constitution assuredly does not impose this invitation to impunity-earned-by-recklessness. Instead, we lay down a more sensible rule: A police officer's attempt to terminate a dangerous high-speed car chase that threatens the lives of innocent bystanders does not violate the Fourth Amendment, even when it places the fleeing motorist at risk of serious injury or death.

* * *

The car chase that respondent initiated in this case posed a substantial and immediate risk of serious physical injury to others; no reasonable jury could conclude otherwise. Scott's attempt to terminate the chase by forcing respondent off the road was reasonable, and Scott is entitled to summary judgment. The Court of Appeals' decision to the contrary is reversed.

It is so ordered.

Cases Relating to Chapter 4

Search and Seizure

CALIFORNIA
v.
GREENWOOD

486 U.S. 35, 108 S. Ct. 1625, 100 L. Ed. 2d 30 (1988)

[Citations and footnotes omitted.]

[In early 1984, Investigator Jenny Stracner of the Laguna Beach Police Department received information indicating that respondent Greenwood might be engaged in narcotics trafficking. She asked the neighborhood's regular trash collector to pick up the plastic garbage bags that Greenwood had left on the curb in front of his house and to turn the bags over to her without mixing their contents with garbage from other houses. The trash collector cleaned his truck bin of other refuse, collected the garbage bags from the street in front of Greenwood's house, and turned the bags over to Stracner. She searched through the rubbish, found items indicative of narcotics use, and used this information to obtain a search warrant to search Greenwood's home. Narcotics and evidence of narcotics trafficking were found during the search. Greenwood was arrested and prosecuted for trafficking in narcotics.]

JUSTICE WHITE delivered the opinion of the Court.

* * *

The issue here is whether the Fourth Amendment prohibits the warrantless search and seizure of garbage left for collection outside the curtilage of a home. We conclude, in accordance with the vast majority of lower courts that have addressed the issue, that it does not.

* * *

The warrantless search and seizure of the garbage bags left at the curb outside the Greenwood house would violate the Fourth Amendment only if respondents manifested a subjective expectation of privacy in their garbage that society accepts as objectively reasonable. Respondents do not disagree with this standard.

They assert, however, that they had, and exhibited, an expectation of privacy with respect to the trash that was searched by the police: The trash, which was placed on the street for collection at a fixed time, was contained in opaque plastic bags, which the garbage collector was expected to pick up, mingle with the trash of others, and deposit at the garbage dump. The trash was only temporarily on the street, and there was little likelihood that it would be inspected by anyone.

It may well be that respondents did not expect that the contents of their garbage bags would become known to the police or other members of the public. An expectation of privacy does not give rise to Fourth Amendment protection, however, unless society is prepared to accept that expectation as objectively reasonable.

Here, we conclude that respondents exposed their garbage to the public sufficiently to defeat their claim to Fourth Amendment protection. It is common knowledge that plastic garbage bags left on or at the side of a public street are readily accessible to animals, children, scavengers, snoops, and other members of the public. Moreover, respondents placed their refuse at the curb for the express purpose of conveying it to a third party, the trash collector, who might himself have sorted through respondents' trash or permitted others, such as the police, to do so. Accordingly, having deposited their garbage "in an area particularly suited for public inspection and, in a manner of speaking, public consumption, for the express purpose of having strangers take it," respondents could have had no reasonable expectation of privacy in the inculpatory items that they discarded.

Furthermore, as we have held, the police cannot reasonably be expected to avert their eyes from evidence of criminal activity that could have been observed by any member of the public. Hence, "[w]hat a person knowingly exposes to the public, even in his own home or office, is not a subject of Fourth Amendment protection." . . .

Similarly, we held in *California v. Ciraolo*, that the police were not required by the Fourth Amendment to obtain a warrant before conducting surveillance of the respondent's fenced backyard from a private plane flying at an altitude of 1,000 feet. We concluded that the respondent's expectation that his yard was protected from such surveillance was unreasonable because "[a]ny member of the public flying in this airspace who glanced down could have seen everything that these officers observed."

Our conclusion that society would not accept as reasonable respondents' claim to an expectation of privacy in trash left for collection in an area accessible to the public is reinforced by the unanimous rejection of similar claims by the Federal Courts of Appeals. . . .

* * *

We reject respondent Greenwood's alternative argument for affirmance: that his expectation of privacy in his garbage should be deemed reasonable as a matter of federal constitutional law because the warrantless search and seizure of his garbage was impermissible as a matter of California law. . . .

Individual States may surely construe their own constitutions as imposing more stringent constraints on police conduct than does the Federal Constitution. We have never intimated, however, that whether or not a search is reasonable within the meaning of the Fourth Amendment depends on the law of the particular State in which the search occurs. . . . Respondent's argument is no less than a suggestion that concepts of privacy under the laws of each State are to determine the reach of the Fourth Amendment. We do not accept this submission.

* * *

The judgment of the California Court of Appeal is therefore reversed, and this case is remanded for further proceedings not inconsistent with this opinion.

It is so ordered.

[Dissenting opinion omitted.]

BOND
v.
UNITED STATES

529 U.S. 334, 120 S. Ct. 1462, 146 L. Ed. 2d 365 (2000)

[Footnotes and citations omitted.]

CHIEF JUSTICE REHNQUIST delivered the opinion of the Court.

This case presents the question whether a law enforcement officer's physical manipulation of a bus passenger's carry-on luggage violated the Fourth Amendment's proscription against unreasonable searches. We hold that it did.

Petitioner Steven Dewayne Bond was a passenger on a Greyhound bus that left California bound for Little Rock, Arkansas. The bus stopped, as it was required to do, at the permanent Border Patrol checkpoint in Sierra Blanca, Texas. Border Patrol Agent Cesar Cantu boarded the bus to check the immigration status of its passengers. After reaching the back of the bus, having satisfied himself that the passengers were lawfully in the United States, Agent Cantu began walking toward the front. Along the way, he squeezed the soft luggage which passengers had placed in the overhead storage space above the seats.

Petitioner was seated four or five rows from the back of the bus. As Agent Cantu inspected the luggage in the compartment above petitioner's seat, he squeezed a green canvas bag and noticed that it contained a "brick-like" object. Petitioner admitted that the bag was his and agreed to allow

Agent Cantu to open it. Upon opening the bag, Agent Cantu discovered a "brick" of methamphetamine. The brick had been wrapped in duct tape until it was oval-shaped and then rolled in a pair of pants.

Petitioner was indicted for conspiracy to possess, and possession with intent to distribute, methamphetamine in violation of 84 Stat. 1260, 21 U.S.C. § 841(a)(1). He moved to suppress the drugs, arguing that Agent Cantu conducted an illegal search of his bag. Petitioner's motion was denied, and the District Court found him guilty on both counts and sentenced him to 57 months in prison. On appeal, he conceded that other passengers had access to his bag, but contended that Agent Cantu manipulated the bag in a way that other passengers would not. The Court of Appeals rejected this argument, stating that the fact that Agent Cantu's manipulation of petitioner's bag was calculated to detect contraband is irrelevant for Fourth Amendment purposes. Thus, the Court of Appeals affirmed the denial of the motion to suppress, holding that Agent Cantu's manipulation of the bag was not a search within the meaning of the Fourth Amendment. We granted certiorari and now reverse.

The Fourth Amendment provides that "[t]he right of the people to be secure in their persons, houses, papers, and effects, against unreasonable searches and seizures, shall not be violated ... " A traveler's personal luggage is clearly an "effect" protected by the Amendment. Indeed, it is undisputed here that petitioner possessed a privacy interest in his bag.

But the Government asserts that by exposing his bag to the public, petitioner lost a reasonable expectation that his bag would not be physically manipulated. The Government relies on our decisions in *California v. Ciraolo* and *Florida v. Riley* for the proposition that matters open to public observation are not protected by the Fourth Amendment. In *Ciraolo*, we held that police observation of a backyard from a plane flying at an altitude of 1,000 feet did not violate a reasonable expectation of privacy. Similarly, in *Riley*, we relied on *Ciraolo* to hold that police observation of a greenhouse in a home's curtilage from a helicopter passing at an altitude of 400 feet did not violate the Fourth Amendment. We reasoned that the property was "not necessarily protected from inspection that involves no physical invasion," and determined that because any member of the public could have lawfully observed the defendants' property by flying overhead, the defendants' expectation of privacy was "not reasonable and not one 'that society is prepared to honor.' "

But *Ciraolo* and *Riley* are different from this case because they involved only visual, as opposed to tactile, observation. Physically invasive inspection is simply more intrusive than purely visual inspection. For example, in *Terry v. Ohio*, we stated that a "careful [tactile] exploration of the outer surfaces of a person's clothing all over his or her body" is a "serious intrusion upon the sanctity of the person, which may inflict great indignity and arouse strong resentment, and is not to be undertaken lightly." Although Agent Cantu did not "frisk" petitioner's person, he did conduct a probing tactile examination of petitioner's carry-on luggage. Obviously, petitioner's bag was not part of his person. But travelers are particularly concerned about their carry-on luggage; they generally use it to transport personal items that, for whatever reason, they prefer to keep close at hand.

Here, petitioner concedes that, by placing his bag in the overhead compartment, he could expect that it would be exposed to certain kinds of touching and handling. But petitioner argues that Agent Cantu's physical manipulation of his luggage "far exceeded the casual contact [petitioner] could have expected from other passengers." The Government counters that it did not.

Our Fourth Amendment analysis embraces two questions. First, we ask whether the individual, by his conduct, has exhibited an actual expectation of privacy; that is, whether he has shown that "he [sought] to preserve [something] as private." Here, petitioner sought to preserve privacy by using an opaque bag and placing that bag directly above his seat. Second, we inquire whether the individual's expectation of privacy is "one that society is prepared to recognize as reasonable." When a bus passenger places a bag in an overhead bin, he expects that other passengers or bus employees may move it for one reason or another. Thus, a bus passenger clearly expects that his bag may be handled. He does not expect that other passengers or bus employees will, as a matter of course, feel the bag in an exploratory manner. But this is exactly what the agent did here. We therefore hold that the agent's physical manipulation of petitioner's bag violated the Fourth Amendment.

The judgment of the Court of Appeals is affirmed.

MAPP
v.
OHIO

367 U.S. 643, 81 S. Ct. 1684, 6 L. Ed. 2d 1081 (1961)

[Citations and footnotes omitted.]

[After receiving a tip that a man wanted for questioning in connection with a recent bombing was hiding out in Ms. Mapp's house, three Ohio State police officers went there, knocked on the door, and demanded entrance. Ms. Mapp refused to let them in without a search warrant. Three hours later, the officers returned, waiving a piece of paper which they claimed was a search warrant, but which they refused to let Ms. Mapp examine. When she tried to grab the paper, the officers twisted her hand, handcuffed her and forced their way into her house. They then proceeded to search the entire house, even looking through photo albums and private papers. Ms. Mapp was placed under arrest on obscenity charges after the police discovered lewd books in a trunk in the basement. No search warrant probably existed because none was produced at the trial. The trial court admitted the lewd books into evidence, ruling that even if the officers' search of Ms. Mapp's home had violated the Fourth Amendment, this evidence was admissible because the exclusionary rule was not binding on the states. Ms. Mapp was convicted of possessing obscene materials.]

MR. JUSTICE CLARK delivered the opinion of the Court.

* * *

... [I]n the year 1914 in the *Weeks* case, this Court "for the first time" held that "in a federal prosecution the Fourth Amendment barred the use of evidence secured through an illegal search and seizure." This Court has ever since required of federal law officers a strict adherence to that command which this Court has held to be a clear, specific, and constitutionally required—even if judicially implied—deterrent safeguard without insistence upon which the Fourth Amendment would have been reduced to a "form of words." It means, quite simply, that "conviction by means of unlawful seizures and enforced confessions ... should find no sanction in the judgment of the courts ... ," and that such evidence "should not be used at all."

* * *

In 1949, 35 years after *Weeks* was announced, this Court, in *Wolf v. Colorado*, again for the first time, discussed the effect of the Fourth Amendment upon the States through the operation of the Due Process Clause of the Fourteenth Amendment. It said: "We have no hesitation in saying that were a State affirmatively to sanction such police incursion into privacy it would run counter to the guaranty of the Fourth Amendment." Nevertheless, after declaring that the "security of one's privacy against arbitrary intrusion by the police" is "implicit in 'the concept of ordered liberty' and as such enforceable against the States through the Due Process Clause," and announcing that it "stoutly adhere[d]" to the *Weeks* decision, the Court decided that the *Weeks* exclusionary rule would not then be imposed upon the States as "an essential ingredient of the right." ...

... While in 1949, prior to the *Wolf* case, almost two-thirds of the States were opposed to the use of the exclusionary rule, now, despite the *Wolf* case, more than half of those since passing upon it, by their own legislative or judicial decision, have wholly or partially adopted or adhered to the *Weeks* rule. Significantly, among those now following the rule is California, which, according to its highest court, was "compelled to reach that conclusion because other remedies have completely failed to secure compliance with the constitutional provisions ... ." The experience of California that such other remedies have been worthless and futile is buttressed by the experience of other States. The obvious futility of relegating the Fourth Amendment to the protection of other remedies has, moreover, been recognized by this Court since *Wolf*.

* * *

The ignoble shortcut to conviction left open to the State tends to destroy the entire system of constitutional restraints on which the liberties of the people rest. Having once recognized that the right to privacy embodied in the Fourth Amendment is enforceable against the States, and that the right to be secure against rude invasions of privacy by state officers is, therefore, constitutional in origin, we can no longer permit that right to remain an empty promise. Because it is enforceable in the same manner and to like effect as other basic rights secured by the Due Process Clause, we can no longer permit it to be revocable at the whim of any police officer who, in the name of law enforcement itself, chooses to suspend its enjoyment. Our decision, founded on reason and truth, gives to the individual no more than that which the Constitution guarantees him, to the police officer no less than that to which honest law enforcement is entitled, and, to the courts, that judicial integrity so necessary in the true administration of justice.

The judgment of the Supreme Court of Ohio is reversed and the cause remanded for further proceedings not inconsistent with this opinion.

Reversed and remanded.

FLIPPO
v.
WEST VIRGINIA

528 U.S. 11, 120 S. Ct. 7, 145 L. Ed. 2d 16 (1999)

[Citations omitted.]

[One night in 1996, petitioner and his wife were vacationing at a cabin in a state park. After petitioner called 911 to report that they had been attacked, the police arrived to find petitioner waiting outside the cabin, with injuries to his head and legs. After questioning him, an officer entered the building and found the body of petitioner's wife, with fatal head wounds. The officers closed off the area, took petitioner to the hospital, and searched the exterior and environs of the cabin for footprints or signs of forced entry. When a

police photographer arrived at about 5:30 A.M., the officers reentered the building and proceeded to "process the crime scene." For more than 16 hours they took photographs, collected evidence, and searched the contents of the cabin. They found, among other things, a briefcase on a table, which they opened, in which they found and seized various photographs and negatives. The photographs included several taken of a man who appears to be taking off his jeans. He was later identified as Joel Boggess, a friend of petitioner and a member of the congregation of which petitioner was the minister. At petitioner's trial for murder, the prosecution sought to introduce the photographs as evidence of petitioner's relationship with Mr. Boggess in an attempt to establish that the victim's displeasure with this relationship was one of the reasons petitioner killed her. Petitioner sought to suppress the photographs on the grounds that the police did not obtain a warrant and that no exception to the warrant requirement justified the search and seizure.

The trial court denied the motion on the grounds that investigating officers, having secured, for investigative purposes, the homicide crime scene, were within the law in conducting a thorough investigation and examination of anything and everything found within the crime scene area.]

PER CURIAM.

A warrantless search by the police is invalid unless it falls within one of the narrow and well-delineated exceptions to the warrant requirement, none of which the trial court invoked here. It simply found that after the homicide crime scene was secured for investigation, a search of "anything and everything found within the crime scene area" was "within the law."

This position squarely conflicts with *Mincey v. Arizona*, where we rejected the contention that there is a "murder scene exception" to the Warrant Clause of the Fourth Amendment. We noted that police may make warrantless entries onto premises if they reasonably believe a person is in need of immediate aid and may make prompt warrantless searches of a homicide scene for possible other victims or a killer on the premises, but we rejected any general "murder scene exception" as "inconsistent with the Fourth and Fourteenth Amendments— ... the warrantless search of *Mincey*'s apartment was not constitutionally permissible simply because a homicide had recently occurred there." *Mincey* controls here.

* * *

The motion for leave to proceed in forma pauperis and the petition for a writ of certiorari are granted, the judgment of the West Virginia Supreme Court of Appeals is reversed, and the case is remanded for further proceedings not inconsistent with this opinion.

It is so ordered.

UNITED STATES
v.
ROBINSON

414 U.S. 218, 94 S. Ct. 467, 38 L. Ed. 2d 427 (1973)

[Citations and footnotes omitted.]

[The defendant was arrested and taken into custody for driving without a license. Upon arresting him, the officer searched his person, his pockets and the contents and found, inside a crumpled cigarette pack, 14 gelatin capsules of white powder which he thought to be, and which later analysis proved to be, heroin. The lower court suppressed the evidence on the grounds that the search was unconstitutional because the officer lacked grounds to believe that the search would turn up weapons or evidence of the crime for which the defendant was arrested.]

MR. JUSTICE REHNQUIST delivered the opinion of the Court.

* * *

It is well settled that a search incident to a lawful arrest is a traditional exception to the warrant requirement of the Fourth Amendment. This general exception has historically been formulated into two distinct propositions. The first is that a search may be made of the person of the arrestee by virtue of the lawful arrest. The second is that a search may be made of the area within the control of the arrestee.

* * *

Terry v. Ohio did not involve an arrest for probable cause, and it made quite clear that the "protective frisk" for weapons which it approved might be conducted without probable cause. This Court's opinion explicitly recognized that there is a "distinction in purpose, character, and extent between a search incident to an arrest and a limited search for weapons."

"The former, although justified in part by the acknowledged necessity to protect the arresting officer from assault with a concealed weapon, is also justified on other grounds, and can therefore involve a relatively extensive exploration of the person. . . .

". . . An arrest is a wholly different kind of intrusion upon individual freedom from a limited search for weapons, and the interests each is designed to serve are likewise quite different. . . .

* * *

The Court of Appeals in effect determined that the only reason supporting the authority for a full search incident to lawful arrest was the possibility of discovery of evidence or fruits. Concluding that there could be no evidence or fruits in the case of an offense such as that with which respondent was charged, it held that any protective search would have to be limited by the conditions laid down in *Terry* for a search upon less than probable cause to arrest. . . .

* * *

. . . . The standards traditionally governing a search incident to lawful arrest are not, therefore, commuted to the stricter Terry standards by the absence of probable fruits or further evidence of the particular crime for which the arrest is made.

* * *

Nor are we inclined, on the basis of what seems to us to be a rather speculative judgment, to qualify the breadth of the general authority to search incident to a lawful custodial arrest on an assumption that persons arrested for the offense of driving while their licenses have been revoked are less likely to possess dangerous weapons than are those arrested for other crimes. It is scarcely open to doubt that the danger to an officer is far greater in the case of the extended exposure which follows the taking of a suspect into custody and transporting him to the police station than in the case of the relatively fleeting contact resulting from the typical *Terry*-type stop. This is an adequate basis for treating all custodial arrests alike for purposes of search justification.

* * *

... A police officer's determination as to how and where to search the person of a suspect whom he has arrested is necessarily a quick ad hoc judgment which the Fourth Amendment does not require to be broken down in each instance into an analysis of each step in the search. The authority to search the person incident to a lawful custodial arrest, while based upon the need to disarm and to discover evidence, does not depend on what a court may later decide was the probability in a particular arrest situation that weapons or evidence would in fact be found upon the person of the suspect. A custodial arrest of a suspect based on probable cause is a reasonable intrusion under the Fourth Amendment; that intrusion being lawful, a search incident to the arrest requires no additional justification. It is the fact of the lawful arrest which establishes the authority to search, and we hold that in the case of a lawful custodial arrest a full search of the person is not only an exception to the warrant requirement of the Fourth Amendment, but is also a "reasonable" search under that Amendment.

* * *

The search of respondent's person conducted by Officer Jenks in this case and the seizure from him of the heroin, were permissible under established Fourth Amendment law. While thorough, the search partook of none of the extreme or patently abusive characteristics which were held to violate the Due Process Clause of the Fourteenth Amendment in *Rochin v. California*. Since it is the fact of custodial arrest which gives rise to the authority to search, it is of no moment that Jenks did not indicate any subjective fear of the respondent or that he did not himself suspect that respondent was armed. Having in the course of a lawful search come upon the crumpled package of cigarettes, he was entitled to inspect it; and when his inspection revealed the heroin capsules, he was entitled to seize them as "fruits, instrumentalities, or contraband" probative of criminal conduct. The judgment of the Court of Appeals holding otherwise is

Reversed.

[Concurring and dissenting opinions omitted.]

CHIMEL
v.
CALIFORNIA

395 U.S. 752, 89 S. Ct. 2034, 23 L. Ed. 2d 265 (1969)

[Citations and footnotes omitted]

Mr. Justice STEWART delivered the opinion of the Court.

This case raises basic questions concerning the permissible scope under the Fourth Amendment of a search incident to a lawful arrest.

The relevant facts are essentially undisputed. Late in the afternoon of September 13, 1965, three police officers arrived at the Santa Ana, California, home of the petitioner with a warrant authorizing his arrest for the burglary of a coin shop. The officers knocked on the door, identified themselves to the petitioner's wife, and asked if they might come inside. She ushered them into the house, where they waited 10 or 15 minutes until the petitioner returned home from work. When the petitioner entered the house, one of the officers handed him the arrest warrant and asked for permission to "look around." The petitioner objected, but was advised that on the basis of the lawful arrest," the officers would nonetheless conduct a search. No search warrant had been issued.

Accompanied by the petitioner's wife, the officers then looked through the entire three-bedroom house, including the attic, the garage, and a small workshop. In some rooms the search was relatively cursory. In the master bedroom and sewing room, however, the officers directed the petitioner's wife to open drawers and "to physically move contents of the drawers from side to side so that (they) might view any items that would have come from (the) burglary." After completing the search, they seized numerous items—primarily coins, but also several medals, tokens, and a few other objects. The entire search took between 45 minutes and an hour.

At the petitioner's subsequent state trial on two charges of burglary, the items taken from his house were admitted into evidence against him, over his objection that they had been unconstitutionally seized. He was convicted, and the judgments of conviction were affirmed by both the California

Court of Appeal and the California Supreme Court.

* * *

United States v. Rabinowitz [is] the decision upon which California primarily relies in the case now before us. In *Rabinowitz*, federal authorities had been informed that the defendant was dealing in stamps bearing forged overprints. On the basis of that information they secured a warrant for his arrest, which they executed at his one-room business office. At the time of the arrest, the officers "searched the desk, safe, and file cabinets in the office for about an hour and a half," and seized stamps with forged overprints. The stamps were admitted into evidence at the defendant's trial, and this Court affirmed his conviction, rejecting the contention that the warrantless search had been unlawful. The Court held that the search in its entirety fell within the principle giving law enforcement authorities "(t)he right 'to search the place where the arrest is made in order to find and seize things connected with the crime * * *.' " *Harris* was regarded as "ample authority" for that conclusion. The opinion rejected the rule . . .that "in seizing goods and articles, law enforcement agents must secure and use search warrants wherever reasonably practicable." The test, said the Court, "is not whether it is reasonable to procure a search warrant, but whether the search was reasonable."

Rabinowitz has come to stand for the proposition, *inter alia*, that a warrantless search "incident to a lawful arrest" may generally extend to the area that is considered to be in the "possession" or under the "control" of the person arrested. And it was on the basis of that proposition that the California courts upheld the search of the petitioner's entire house in this case. That doctrine, however, at least in the broad sense in which it was applied by the California courts in this case, can withstand neither historical nor rational analysis.

* * *

When an arrest is made, it is reasonable for the arresting officer to search the person arrested in order to remove any weapons that the latter might seek to use in order to resist arrest or effect his escape. Otherwise, the officer's safety might well be endangered, and the arrest itself frustrated. In addition, it is entirely reasonable for the arresting officer to search for and seize any evidence on the arrestee's person in order to prevent its

concealment or destruction. And the area into which an arrestee might reach in order to grab a weapon or evidentiary items must, of course, be governed by a like rule. A gun on a table or in a drawer in front of one who is arrested can be as dangerous to the arresting officer as one concealed in the clothing of the person arrested. There is ample justification, therefore, for a search of the arrestee's person and the area "within his immediate control"—construing that phrase to mean the area from within which he might gain possession of a weapon or destructible evidence.

There is no comparable justification, however, for routinely searching any room other than that in which an arrest occurs—or, for that matter, for searching through all the desk drawers or other closed or concealed areas in that room itself. Such searches, in the absence of well-recognized exceptions, may be made only under the authority of a search warrant. The "adherence to judicial processes' mandated by the Fourth Amendment requires no less.

This is the principle that underlay our decision in *Preston v. United States*. In that case three men had been arrested in a parked car, which had later been towed to a garage and searched by police. We held that search to have been unlawful under the Fourth Amendment, despite the contention that it had been incidental to a valid arrest. Our reasoning was straightforward:

"The rule allowing contemporaneous searches is justified, for example, by the need to seize weapons and other things which might be used to assault an officer or effect an escape, as well as by the need to prevent the destruction of evidence of the crime—things which might easily happen where the weapon or evidence is on the accused's person or under his immediate control. But these justifications are absent where a search is remote in time or place from the arrest.'

* * *

Application of sound Fourth Amendment principles to the facts of this case produces a clear result. The search here went far beyond the petitioner's person and the area from within which he might have obtained either a weapon or something that could have been used as evidence against him. There was no constitutional justification, in the absence of a search warrant, for extending the search beyond that area. The scope of the search was, therefore, "unreasonable" under the Fourth and Fourteenth Amendments and the petitioner's conviction cannot stand.

Reversed.

ARIZONA
v.
GANT

556 U.S. 332, 129 S. Ct. 1710,
173 L. Ed. 2d 485 (2009)

[This case is reproduced on p. 566]

WYOMING
v.
HOUGHTON

526 U.S. 559, 119 S. Ct. 1297,
143 L. Ed. 2d 748 (1999)

[Citations and footnotes omitted.]

In the early morning hours of July 23, 1995, a Wyoming Highway Patrol officer stopped an automobile for speeding and driving with a faulty brake light. There were three passengers in the front seat of the car: David Young (the driver), his girlfriend, and respondent. While questioning Young, the officer noticed a hypodermic syringe in Young's shirt pocket. He left the occupants under the supervision of two backup officers as he went to get gloves from his patrol car. Upon his return, he instructed Young to step out of the car and place the syringe on the hood. The officer then asked Young why he had a syringe; with refreshing candor, Young replied that he used it to take drugs.

At this point, the backup officers ordered the two female passengers out of the car and asked them for identification. Respondent falsely identified herself as "Sandra James" and stated that she did not have any identification. Meanwhile, in light of Young's admission, the officer searched the passenger compartment of the car for contraband. On the back seat, he found a purse, which respondent claimed as hers. He removed from the purse a wallet containing respondent's driver's license, identifying her properly as Sandra K. Houghton. When the officer asked her why she had lied about her name, she replied: "In case things went bad."

Continuing his search of the purse, the officer found a brown pouch and a black wallet-type container. Respondent denied that the former was hers, and claimed ignorance of how it came to be there; it was found to contain drug paraphernalia and a syringe with 60 ccs of methamphetamine. Respondent admitted ownership of the black container, which was also found to contain drug paraphernalia, and a syringe (which respondent acknowledged was hers) with 10 ccs of methamphetamine—an amount insufficient to support the felony conviction at issue in this case. The officer also found fresh needle-track marks on respondent's arms. He placed her under arrest.

The State of Wyoming charged respondent with felony possession of methamphetamine in a liquid amount greater than three-tenths of a gram. After a hearing, the trial court denied her motion to suppress all evidence obtained from the purse as the fruit of a violation of the Fourth and Fourteenth Amendments. The court held that the officer had probable cause to search the car for contraband, and, by extension, any containers therein that could hold such contraband. A jury convicted respondent as charged.

The Wyoming Supreme Court, by divided vote, reversed the conviction . . .

* * *

Justice SCALIA delivered the opinion of the Court.

This case presents the question whether police officers violate the Fourth Amendment when they search a passenger's personal belongings inside an automobile that they have probable cause to believe contains contraband.

* * *

It is uncontested in the present case that the police officers had probable cause to believe there were illegal drugs in the car. *Carroll v. United States* similarly involved the warrantless search of a car that law enforcement officials had probable cause to believe contained contraband—in that case, bootleg liquor. . . . [T]he Court held that "contraband goods concealed and illegally transported in an automobile or other vehicle may be searched for without a warrant" where probable cause exists.

... In *Ross*, we upheld as reasonable the warrantless search of a paper bag and leather pouch found in the trunk of the defendant's car by officers who had probable cause to believe that the trunk contained drugs. . . .

* * *

To be sure, there was no passenger in *Ross*, and it was not claimed that the package in the trunk belonged to anyone other than the driver. Even so, if the rule of law that *Ross* announced were limited to contents belonging to the driver, or contents other than those belonging to passengers, one would have expected that substantial limitation to be expressed. . . .

... [T]he analytical principle underlying the rule announced in *Ross* is fully consistent . . . with the balance of our Fourth Amendment jurisprudence. *Ross* concluded from the historical evidence that the permissible scope of a warrantless car search "is defined by the object of the search and the places in which there is probable cause to believe that it may be found." The same principle is reflected in an earlier case involving the constitutionality of a search warrant directed at premises belonging to one who is not suspected of any crime: "The critical element in a reasonable search is not that the owner of the property is suspected of crime but that there is reasonable cause to believe that the specific 'things' to be searched for and seized are located on the property to which entry is sought.". . .

In sum, neither *Ross* itself nor the historical evidence it relied upon admits of a distinction among packages or containers based on ownership. When there is probable cause to search for contraband in a car, it is reasonable for police officers—like customs officials in the Founding era—to examine packages and containers without a showing of individualized probable cause for each one. A passenger's personal belongings, just like the driver's belongings or containers attached to the car like a glove compartment, are "in" the car, and the officer has probable cause to search for contraband in the car.

Even if the historical evidence, as described by *Ross*, were thought to be equivocal, we would find that the balancing of the relative interests weighs decidedly in favor of allowing searches of a passenger's belongings. Passengers, no less than drivers, possess a reduced expectation of privacy with regard to the property that they transport in cars, which "travel public thoroughfares." "seldom serv[e] as . . . the repository of personal effects," are subjected to police stop and examination to enforce "pervasive" governmental controls "[a]s an everyday occurrence" and, finally, are exposed to traffic accidents that may render all their contents open to public scrutiny.

* * *

Whereas the passenger's privacy expectations are, as we have described, considerably diminished, the governmental interests at stake are substantial. Effective law enforcement would be appreciably impaired without the ability to search a passenger's personal belongings when there is reason to believe contraband or evidence of criminal wrongdoing is hidden in the car. As in all car-search cases, the "ready mobility" of an automobile creates a risk that the evidence or contraband will be permanently lost while a warrant is obtained. In addition, a car passenger . . . will often be engaged in a common enterprise with the driver, and have the same interest in concealing the fruits or the evidence of their wrongdoing. A criminal might be able to hide contraband in a passenger's belongings as readily as in other containers in the car—perhaps even surreptitiously, without the passenger's knowledge or permission. (This last possibility provided the basis for respondent's defense at trial; she testified that most of the seized contraband must have been placed in her purse by her traveling companions at one or another of various times, including the time she was "half asleep" in the car.)

... To require that the investigating officer have positive reason to believe that the passenger and driver were engaged in a common enterprise, or positive reason to believe that the driver had time and occasion to conceal the item in the passenger's belongings, surreptitiously or with friendly permission, is to impose requirements so seldom met that a "passenger's property" rule would dramatically reduce the ability to find and seize contraband and evidence of crime. . . . But once a "passenger's property" exception to car searches became widely known, one would expect passenger-confederates to claim everything as their own. And one would anticipate a bog of litigation—in the form of both civil lawsuits and motions to suppress in criminal trials—involving such questions as whether the officer should have believed a passenger's claim of ownership. . . . When balancing the competing interests, our determinations of "reasonableness" under the Fourth Amendment must take account of these practical realities. We think they militate in favor of the needs of law enforcement, and against a personal-privacy interest that is ordinarily weak.

* * *

We hold that police officers with probable cause to search a car may inspect passengers' belongings found in the car that are capable of concealing the object of the search. The judgment of the Wyoming Supreme Court is reversed.

It is so ordered.

FLORIDA
v.
JIMENO

500 U.S. 248, 111 S. Ct. 1801, 114 L. Ed. 2d 297 (1991)

[Footnotes and citations omitted.]

[Officer Trujillo, believing that Jimeno might be involved in illegal drug trafficking, followed Jimeno's car until he made a right turn at a red light without stopping, at which point he pulled Jimeno over to the side of the road, issued a traffic citation, and then asked for permission to search his car, stating that he had reason to believe that Jimeno was carrying narcotics in his car. Jimeno gave permission. Officer Trujillo then went to the passenger side, opened the door, and saw a folded, brown paper bag on the floorboard. He picked up the bag, opened it, and found a kilogram of cocaine inside. Jimeno was charged with possession with intent to distribute cocaine. Before trial, he moved to suppress the cocaine found in the bag on the ground that his consent to search the car did not extend to the closed paper bag inside of the car. The trial court granted the motion.]

Chief Justice REHNQUIST delivered the opinion of the Court.

In this case we decide whether a criminal suspect's Fourth Amendment right to be free from unreasonable searches is violated when, after he gives a police officer permission to search his automobile, the officer opens a closed container found within the car that might reasonably hold the object of the search. We find that it is not. The Fourth Amendment is satisfied when, under the circumstances, it is objectively reasonable for the officer to believe that the scope of the suspect's consent permitted him to open a particular container within the automobile.

* * *

The touchstone of the Fourth Amendment is reasonableness. The Fourth Amendment does not proscribe all state-initiated searches and seizures; it merely proscribes those which are unreasonable. Thus, we have long approved consensual searches because it is no doubt reasonable for the police to conduct a search once they have been permitted to do so. The standard for measuring the scope of a suspect's consent under the Fourth Amendment is that of "objective" reasonableness—what would the typical reasonable person have understood by the exchange between the officer and the suspect? The question before us, then, is whether it is reasonable for an officer to consider a suspect's general consent to a search of his car to include consent to examine a paper bag lying on the floor of the car. We think that it is.

The scope of a search is generally defined by its expressed object. In this case, the terms of the search's authorization were simple. Respondent granted Officer Trujillo permission to search his car, and did not place any explicit limitation on the scope of the search. Trujillo had informed respondent that he believed respondent was carrying narcotics, and that he would be looking for narcotics in the car. We think that it was objectively reasonable for the police to conclude that the general consent to search respondent's car included consent to search containers within that car which might bear drugs. A reasonable person may be expected to know that narcotics are generally carried in some form of container. Contraband goods rarely are strewn across the trunk or floor of a car. The authorization to search in this case, therefore, extended beyond the surfaces of the car's interior to the paper bag lying on the car's floor.

The facts of this case are therefore different from those in *State v. Wells*, on which the Supreme Court of Florida relied in affirming the suppression order on this case. There the Supreme Court of Florida held that consent to search the trunk of a car did not include authorization to pry open a locked briefcase found inside the trunk. It is very likely unreasonable to think that a suspect, by consenting to the search of his trunk, has agreed to the breaking open of a locked briefcase within the trunk, but it is otherwise with respect to a closed paper bag.

Respondent argues, and the Florida trial court agreed with him, that if the police wish to search closed containers within a car they must separately request permission to search each container. But we see no basis for adding this sort of superstructure to the Fourth Amendment's basic test of objective reasonableness. A suspect may of course delimit as he chooses the scope of the search to which he consents. But if his consent would reasonably be understood to extend to a particular container, the Fourth Amendment provides no grounds for requiring a more explicit authorization. "[T]he community has a real interest in encouraging consent, for the resulting search may yield necessary evidence for the solution and prosecution of crime, evidence that may ensure that a wholly innocent person is not wrongly charged with a criminal offense."

The judgment of the Supreme Court of Florida is accordingly reversed, and the case remanded for further proceedings not inconsistent with this opinion.

It is so ordered.

ARIZONA
v.
HICKS

480 U.S. 321, 107 S. Ct. 1149, 94 L. Ed. 2d 347 (1987)

[Citations and footnotes omitted.]

[A bullet was fired through the floor of respondent's apartment, striking and injuring a man in the apartment below. The police arrived and entered respondent's apartment to search for the shooter and the weapon. They found and seized three weapons, including a sawed-off rifle. While on the premises, one of the officers noticed some very expensive stereo equipment, which seemed out of place. Suspecting that the equipment was stolen, he turned the stereo around so he could read out the serial numbers to the radio operator. The operator checked the numbers and informed him that the equipment was stolen. The defendant was indicted and convicted of theft. The Arizona Court of Appeals, while conceding that the warrantless entry was justified by the exigent circumstances of the shooting, ruled that turning the stereo around to read the serial numbers resulted in an additional search, unrelated to the exigency, in violation of the Fourth Amendment, requiring that the fruits of this search be suppressed.]

Justice SCALIA delivered the opinion of the Court.

In *Coolidge v. New Hampshire*, we said that in certain circumstances a warrantless seizure by police of an item that comes within plain view during their lawful search of a private area may be reasonable under the Fourth Amendment. We granted certiorari in the present case to decide whether this "plain view" doctrine may be invoked when the police have less than probable cause to believe that the item in question is evidence of a crime or is contraband.

* * *

As an initial matter, the State argues that Officer Nelson's actions constituted neither a "search" nor a "seizure" within the meaning of the Fourth Amendment. We agree that the mere recording of the serial numbers did not constitute a seizure. ... [I]t did not "meaningfully interfere" with respondent's possessory interest in either the serial numbers or the equipment, and therefore did not amount to a seizure.

Officer Nelson's moving of the equipment, however, did constitute a "search" separate and apart from the search for the shooter, victims, and weapons that was the lawful objective of his entry into the apartment. Merely inspecting those parts of the turntable that came into view during the latter search would not have constituted an independent search, because it would have produced no additional invasion of respondent's privacy interest. But taking action, unrelated to the objectives of the authorized intrusion, which exposed to view concealed portions of the apartment or its contents, did produce a new invasion of respondent's privacy unjustified by the exigent circumstance that validated the entry. This is why, contrary to Justice POWELL's suggestion, the "distinction between 'looking' at a suspicious object in plain view and 'moving' it even a few inches" is much more than trivial for purposes of the Fourth Amendment. It matters not that the search uncovered nothing of any great personal value to the respondent—serial numbers rather than (what might conceivably have been hidden behind or under the equipment) letters or photographs. A search is a search, even if it happens to disclose nothing but the bottom of a turntable.

The remaining question is whether the search was "reasonable" under the Fourth Amendment.

* * *

... "It is well established that under certain circumstances the police may seize evidence in plain view without a warrant. Those circumstances include situations "[w]here the initial intrusion that brings the police within plain view of such [evidence] is supported ... by one of the recognized exceptions to the warrant requirement," such as the exigent-circumstances intrusion here. It would be absurd to say that an object could lawfully be seized and taken from the premises, but could not be moved for closer examination. It is clear, therefore, that the search here was valid if the "plain view" doctrine would have sustained a seizure of the equipment.

There is no doubt it would have done so if Officer Nelson had probable cause to believe that the equipment was stolen. The State has conceded, however, that he had only a "reasonable suspicion," by which it means something less than probable cause. . . . We have not ruled on the question whether probable cause is required in order to invoke the "plain view" doctrine ... We now hold that probable cause is required. To say otherwise would be to cut the "plain view" doctrine loose from its theoretical and practical moorings. The theory of that doctrine consists of extending to nonpublic places such as the home, where searches and seizures without a warrant are presumptively unreasonable, the

police's longstanding authority to make warrantless seizures in public places of such objects as weapons and contraband. And the practical justification for that extension is the desirability of sparing police, whose viewing of the object in the course of a lawful search is as legitimate as it would have been in a public place, the inconvenience and the risk—to themselves or to preservation of the evidence—of going to obtain a warrant. Dispensing with the need for a warrant is worlds apart from permitting a lesser standard of cause for the seizure than a warrant would require, i.e., the standard of probable cause. No reason is apparent why an object should routinely be seizable on lesser grounds, during an unrelated search and seizure, than would have been needed to obtain a warrant for that same object if it had been known to be on the premises.

We do not say, of course, that a seizure can never be justified on less than probable cause. We have held that it can—where, for example, the seizure is minimally intrusive and operational necessities render it the only practicable means of detecting certain types of crime. . . . No special operational necessities are relied on here, however—but rather the mere fact that the items in question came lawfully within the officer's plain view. That alone cannot supplant the requirement of probable cause.

The same considerations preclude us from holding that, even though probable cause would have been necessary for a seizure, the search of objects in plain view that occurred here could be sustained on lesser grounds. A dwelling-place search, no less than a dwelling-place seizure, requires probable cause, and there is no reason in theory or practicality why application of the plain-view doctrine would supplant that requirement. Although the interest protected by the Fourth Amendment injunction against unreasonable searches is quite different from that protected by its injunction against unreasonable seizures, neither the one nor the other is of inferior worth or necessarily requires only lesser protection. We have not elsewhere drawn a categorical distinction between the two insofar as concerns the degree of justification needed to establish the reasonableness of police action, and we see no reason for a distinction in the particular circumstances before us here. Indeed, to treat searches more liberally would especially erode the plurality's warning in Coolidge that "the 'plain view' doctrine to be used to extend a general exploratory search from one object to another until something incriminating at last emerges." In short, whether legal authority to move the equipment could be found only as an inevitable concomitant of the authority to seize it, or also as a consequence of some independent power to search certain objects in plain view, probable cause to believe the equipment was stolen was required.

Justice O'CONNOR's dissent suggests that we uphold the action here on the ground that it was a "cursory inspection" rather than a "full-blown search," and could therefore be justified by reasonable suspicion instead of probable cause. As already noted, a truly cursory inspection—one that involves merely looking at what is already exposed to view, without disturbing it—is not a "search" for Fourth Amendment purposes, and therefore does not even require reasonable suspicion. We are unwilling to send police and judges into a new thicket of Fourth Amendment law, to seek a creature of uncertain description that is neither a plain-view inspection nor yet a "full-blown search." Nothing in the prior opinions of this Court supports such a distinction . . .

Justice POWELL's dissent reasonably asks what it is we would have had Officer Nelson do in these circumstances. . . . The answer depends, of course, upon whether he had probable cause to conduct a search, a question that was not preserved in this case. If he had, then he should have done precisely what he did. If not, then he should have followed up his suspicions, if possible, by means other than a search—just as he would have had to do if, while walking along the street, he had noticed the same suspicious stereo equipment sitting inside a house a few feet away from him, beneath an open window. It may well be that, in such circumstances, no effective means short of a search exist. But there is nothing new in the realization that the Constitution sometimes insulates the criminality of a few in order to protect the privacy of us all. Our disagreement with the dissenters pertains to where the proper balance should be struck; we choose to adhere to the textual and traditional standard of probable cause.

The State contends that, even if Officer Nelson's search violated the Fourth Amendment, the court below should have admitted the evidence thus obtained under the "good faith" exception to the exclusionary rule. That was not the question on which certiorari was granted, and we decline to consider it.

For the reasons stated, the judgment of the Court of Appeals of Arizona is

Affirmed.

The concurring and dissenting opinions are not included.

UNITED STATES
v.
WEINBENDER

109 F.3d 1327 (8th Cir. 1997)

[Citations and footnotes omitted.]

[Police obtained a search warrant for Ralph Weinbender's home, listing items including: a bluish-gray windbreaker jacket; a dark pair of shorts, pockets in the front, one pocket in the rear; tannish Reebok shoes; and a ball hat with logo. Before the warrant was executed, the officers were advised that the defendant had several "hiding places" in his attic and basement in which the items listed in the warrant might be located. While executing the warrant, one of the officers entered a basement closet, removed a picture hanging on a wall and found a loose piece cut in the drywall. Upon removing the piece and shining a flashlight in, the officer discovered a homemade silencer sitting on an I-beam which the officer seized even though it was not listed in the warrant. Weinbender was prosecuted for unlawful possession of the silencer. After the trial court denied his motion to suppress the silencer, Weinbender entered a conditional plea of guilty and was sentence to a term of imprisonment of 24 months. This appeal followed.]

MONTGOMERY, District Judge.

* * *

A lawful search extends to all areas and containers in which the object of the search may be found. However, "[t]he manner in which a warrant is executed is always subject to judicial review to ensure that it does not traverse the general Fourth Amendment proscription against unreasonableness."

In this case, the search warrant authorized officers to search the entirety of Weinbender's home for the specified items. Moreover, the officers had been informed that "hiding places," including under the basement stairs, were utilized by Weinbender. The space along the I-beam was sufficiently large to permit any of the listed items to be stored there. . . .

* * *

In light of the information possessed by the searching officers, the relative ease with which the officer removed the drywall and the reasonable probability of finding the sought-for items hidden behind the drywall, the actions of Officer Schmit were reasonable.

Weinbender also argues that the seizure of the homemade silencer was not justified under the plain view doctrine. The plain view doctrine permits law enforcement officers to "seize evidence without a warrant when (1) 'the officer did not violate the Fourth Amendment in arriving at the place from which the evidence could be plainly viewed,' (2) the object's incriminating character is immediately apparent, and (3) the officer has 'a lawful right of access to the object itself.' "

In this case, the law enforcement officers gained access to Weinbender's residence under a properly issued warrant. As indicated [above], since the items listed in the warrant could have been concealed along the I-beam, the officers did not violate the Fourth Amendment by visually searching that location. In addition, to properly observe the items secreted along the I-beam and to ensure that no additional items were present there, each item had to be removed. Thus, Officer Schmit did not violate the Fourth Amendment in removing the items from their secret storage place along the I-beam.

When Officer Schmit pulled the first metal object from its resting spot along the I-beam, he believed that it was a pipe bomb. He later learned the object was part of a homemade silencer. "The 'immediately apparent' requirement means that

officers must have 'probable cause to associate the property with criminal activity.' " "Probable cause demands not that an officer be 'sure' or 'certain' but only that the facts available to a reasonably cautious man would warrant a belief 'that certain items may be contraband or stolen property or useful as evidence of a crime.' "

Here, the incriminating character of the object was immediately apparent to Officer Schmit. The possession of either a pipe bomb or a homemade silencer is illegal. The fact that the item turned out to be the silencer, instead of a pipe bomb, did not vitiate the probable cause. Thus, the seizure of the homemade silencer was justified under the plain view doctrine.

. . . Accordingly, we affirm the judgment of the district court.

STATE
v.
WILSON

112 N.C. App. 777,
437 S.E.2d 387 (1993)

[Citations and footnotes omitted.]

[Officer Faulkenberry, after receiving an anonymous tip that drugs were being sold out of an apartment building in a known drug area, went to that location. When his squad car pulled up, the defendant started running. Officer Faulkenberry stopped the defendant and performed a protective weapons frisk. While doing this, he felt a lump in the defendant's breast pocket that he immediately believed to be crack cocaine. Upon retrieving a bag from the pocket, Faulkenberry discovered crack, as he had suspected.]

LEWIS, Judge

* * *

There are two separate issues before this Court: (I) Whether Officer Faulkenberry had a reasonable suspicion to justify his stop of defendant, and (II) Whether Officer Faulkenberry's frisk of defendant was more intrusive than necessary.

* * *

As to the first issue defendant argues that the facts of this case are identical to those in *State v. Fleming*, where this Court held that reasonable suspicion did not exist. We do not agree. In Fleming this Court stated that: "... A brief investigative stop of an individual must be based on specific and articulable facts as well as inferences from those facts, viewing the circumstances surrounding the seizure through the eyes of a reasonable cautious police officer on the scene, guided by his experience and training." This Court further held that there was no reasonable suspicion because the officers seized a defendant who had merely been standing in an open area between two apartment buildings and then chose to walk in a direction away from the officers. The Fleming Court determined that the officers had only a generalized suspicion based on the time, place and the fact that defendant was unfamiliar to the area, and that if a generalized suspicion was enough then innocent citizens could be subjected to unreasonable searches at an officer's whim.

In the present case we find that Officer Faulkenberry had much more than a generalized suspicion. Officer Faulkenberry was in the area because the police had received an anonymous phone call that individuals were dealing drugs at the apartment complex. Further, when the squad car pulled into the parking lot, defendant and several other individuals attempted to flee the scene. Officer Faulkenberry also testified that as a seven-year veteran of the force, it was his experience that weapons were frequently involved in drug transactions. We find that when these factors are considered as a whole and from the point of view of a reasonably cautious officer present on the scene, Officer Faulkenberry had reasonable suspicion to seize defendant and to perform a pat down search.

We next address the question of whether or not Officer Faulkenberry's search of defendant was more intrusive than was necessary to assure himself that defendant was not dangerous. Since the filing of the briefs in this case, the United States Supreme Court decided the factually similar case of *Minnesota v. Dickerson*. In *Dickerson*, a police officer stopped a suspect and performed a routine pat down search. Although the search revealed no weapons, the officer became curious about a small lump in the front pocket of the defendant's jacket.

The officer testified "I examined it with my fingers and it slid and it felt to be a lump of crack cocaine in cellophane." Believing the lump to be cocaine the officer reached into defendant's pocket and retrieved a small cellophane bag, confirming his suspicion.

On appeal, the Supreme Court addressed the narrow question of whether or not an officer may seize nonthreatening contraband detected during a pat down search. The Supreme Court held that such was permissible as long as the officer's search was within the bounds established by *Terry v. Ohio*. Supplying the rationale for its decision, the Supreme Court stated that:

> [i]f a police officer lawfully pats down a suspect's outer clothing and feels an object whose contour or mass makes its identity immediately apparent, there has been no invasion of the suspect's privacy beyond that already authorized by the officer's search for weapons; if the object is contraband, its warrantless seizure would be justified by the same practical considerations that inhere in the plain view context.

Applying this "plain feel" exception to the facts before it, the Supreme Court held that the officer's search was not authorized by Terry because the incriminating character of the lump in defendant's pocket was not immediately apparent because the officer had to slide it through his fingers and otherwise manipulate the lump to determine its incriminating character.

In the present matter Officer Faulkenberry testified that while performing his pat down search he felt a package or a lump in defendant's pocket and that he could tell there were smaller pieces within the lump. At first blush, the present matter appears indistinguishable from *Dickerson*. However, upon closer examination there are several critical differences between the case at bar and *Dickerson*. In both *Dickerson* and the case at bar, the officer testified that he felt a lump and opined that it was cocaine. However, in *Dickerson* there was additional testimony that the officer manipulated the contents of the defendant's pocket to form his opinion that the substance was cocaine, thus refuting any notion that the character of the contraband was immediately apparent to the officer. In the case at bar there is no such additional testimony that Officer Faulkenberry manipulated the contents of defendant's pocket or that he performed a search that was not permitted under Terry. The extent of Officer Faulkenberry's testimony was:

As I was conducting the pat-down, I . . . started down the front and in his left breast pocket I felt a package or felt a lump. I could tell that there were small individual pieces inside of that lump and based on my past experience, I believed it to be a Controlled Substance, more than likely Crack.

Though Officer Faulkenberry's testimony sufficiently distinguishes this case from *Dickerson*, it still does not answer the ultimate question of whether the incriminating character of the lump in defendant's pocket was "immediately apparent." The resolution of this question is made difficult because the Supreme Court failed, for whatever reason, to provide a definition or a test for the phrase "immediately apparent." In fact, it has been suggested by one court that the "immediately apparent" test confuses "knowledge" and "suspicion" because an officer cannot truly verify the illegal character of a contraband substance without looking at it, and perhaps even testing it.

Since *Dickerson* was decided in June of this year, there have been several cases construing it. In *Ross*, the Southern District Court of Alabama held that the incriminating character of a matchbox found in the defendant's crotch during a lawful pat down was not immediately apparent because a matchbox is not contraband and it was irrelevant that the officer thought it contained cocaine. Similarly, in *United States v. Winter*, the Massachusetts District Court held that the "plain feel" rationale of *Dickerson* did not apply where the arresting officer repeatedly testified that he did not know the incriminating character of the contraband until he removed it. In contrast, the Wisconsin Court of Appeals upheld a trial court's denial of a motion to suppress in light of *Dickerson* when the arresting officer testified that he immediately recognized the incriminating character of a plastic bag found in defendant's waistband during a pat down search. The court reasoned that "given what the officer knew about the storage of cocaine, his conclusions about the character of the plastic baggie [were] reasonable." These cases clearly establish that the item seized must be contraband itself and that the officer must be aware of the incriminating character of the contraband before seizing such.

* * *

. . . [T]he above cases offer little more than case by case guidance and fall short of definitively answering the ultimate question of what is "immediately apparent." In resolving this question we are guided by search and seizure cases decided under the "plain view" exception to the Fourth Amendment, because the "immediately apparent" requirement is common to both the "plain view" exception and the "plain feel" exception. In *State v. White*, our Supreme Court held that in the context of the "plain view" exception the term "immediately apparent" is "satisfied if the police have probable cause to believe that what they have come upon is evidence of criminal conduct." Given this statement we need only determine whether Officer Faulkenberry had probable cause to believe that the contraband he felt during his pat down search was cocaine. "Probable cause is a 'common sense, practical question' based on 'the factual and practical considerations of everyday life on which reasonable and prudent men, not legal technicians, act.' " "The standard to be met when considering whether probable cause exists is the totality of the circumstances." Based upon the fact that Officer Faulkenberry was called to the scene to investigate alleged drug dealings and because he had made prior drug arrests in his seven years of service, we find that upon using his tactile senses, he had probable cause to believe that the contraband in defendant's pocket was cocaine. We hold that Officer Faulkenberry's search was no more intrusive than necessary because the incriminating character of the contraband substance was "immediately apparent" to him. We also distinguish this case from *Dickerson* because Officer Faulkenberry was in the midst of a weapons search when he felt the contraband, whereas in *Dickerson* the officer had already convinced himself that defendant's pocket did not contain a weapon. We find that the facts of this case are distinguishable from those in *Dickerson* and affirm the trial court's denial of defendant's motion to suppress.

Affirmed.

UNITED STATES
v.
DUNN

480 U.S. 294, 107 S. Ct. 1134,
94 L. Ed. 2d 326 (1987)

[Citations and footnotes omitted.]

[Dunn owned a 198 acres ranch, situated a half mile from a public road. The ranch was completely encircled by a perimeter fence and had several barbed wire interior fences. A fence also encircled the residence and a nearby small greenhouse. Two barns were located approximately 50 yards from this fence.

On the evening of November 5, 1980, a DEA agent accompanied by an officer from the Houston Police Department made a warrantless entry onto Dunn's property, crossing over the perimeter fence and one interior fence. Standing approximately midway between the residence and the barns, the DEA agent smelled what he believed to be the odor of phenylacetic acid, coming from the direction of the barns. The two officers crossed over a barbed wire fence and approached the smaller barn. They look inside, without entering. and observed only empty boxes. They then proceeded to the larger barn. Using a flashlight to peer inside, they observed a phenylacetone laboratory. They then departed.

The District Court denied Dunn's motion to suppress evidence seized under a subsequently issued search warrant and he was convicted.]

Justice WHITE delivered the opinion of the Court.

We granted the Government's petition for certiorari to decide whether the area near a barn, located approximately 50 yards from a fence surrounding a ranch house, is, for Fourth Amendment purposes, within the curtilage of the house . . .

* * *

The curtilage concept originated at common law to extend to the area immediately surrounding a dwelling house the same protection under the law of burglary as was afforded the house itself. The concept plays a part, however, in interpreting the reach of the Fourth Amendment. *Hester v. United States* held that the Fourth Amendment's protection accorded "persons, houses, papers, and effects" did not extend to the open fields, the Court observing that the distinction between a person's house and open fields "is as old as the common law."

We reaffirmed the holding of *Hester* in *Oliver v. United States*. There, we recognized that the Fourth Amendment protects the curtilage of a house and that the extent of the curtilage is determined by factors that bear upon whether an individual reasonably may expect that the area in question should be treated as the home itself. We identified the central component of this inquiry as whether the area harbors the "intimate activity associated with the 'sanctity of a man's home and the privacies of life.' "

Drawing upon the Court's own cases and the cumulative experience of the lower courts that have grappled with the task of defining the extent of a home's curtilage, we believe that curtilage questions should be resolved with particular reference to four factors: the proximity of the area claimed to be curtilage to the home, whether the area is included within an enclosure surrounding the home, the nature of the uses to which the area is put, and the steps taken by the resident to protect the area from observation by people passing by. We do not suggest that combining these factors produces a finely tuned formula that, when mechanically applied, yields a "correct" answer to all extent-of-curtilage questions. Rather, these factors are useful analytical tools only to the degree that, in any given case, they bear upon the centrally relevant consideration-whether the area in question is so intimately tied to the home itself that it should be placed under the home's "umbrella" of Fourth Amendment protection. Applying these factors to respondent's barn and to the area immediately surrounding it, we have little difficulty in concluding that this area lay outside the curtilage of the ranch house.

First. The record discloses that the barn was located 50 yards from the fence surrounding the house and 60 yards from the house itself. Standing in isolation, this substantial distance supports no inference that the barn should be treated as an adjunct of the house.

Second. It is also significant that respondent's barn did not lie within the area surrounding the house that was enclosed by a fence. We noted in *Oliver*, supra, that "for most homes, the boundaries of the curtilage will be clearly marked; and the conception defining the curtilage-as the area around the home to which the activity of home life extends-is a familiar one easily understood from our daily experience." Viewing the physical layout of respondent's ranch in its entirety, it is plain that the fence surrounding the residence serves to demark a specific area of land immediately adjacent to the house that is readily identifiable as part and parcel of the house. Conversely, the barn-the front portion itself enclosed by a fence-and the area immediately surrounding it, stands out as a distinct portion of respondent's ranch, quite separate from the residence.

Third. It is especially significant that the law enforcement officials possessed objective data indicating that the barn was not being used for intimate activities of the home. The aerial photographs showed that the truck Carpenter had been driving that contained the container of phenylacetic acid was backed up to the barn, "apparently," in the words of the Court of Appeals, "for the unloading of its contents." When on respondent's property, the officers' suspicion was further directed toward the barn because of "a very strong odor" of phenylacetic acid. As the DEA agent approached the barn, he "could hear a motor running, like a pump motor of some sort . . ." Furthermore, the officers detected an "extremely strong" odor of phenylacetic acid coming from a small crack in the wall of the barn. . . . When considered together, the above facts indicated to the officers that the use to which the barn was being put could not fairly be characterized as so associated with the activities and privacies of domestic life that the officers should have deemed the barn as part of respondent's home.

Fourth. Respondent did little to protect the barn area from observation by those standing in the open fields. Nothing in the record suggests that the various interior fences on respondent's property had any function other than that of the typical ranch fence; the fences were designed and constructed to corral livestock, not to prevent persons from observing what lay inside the enclosed areas.

Respondent submits an alternative basis for affirming the judgment below, one that was presented to but ultimately not relied upon by the Court of Appeals. Respondent asserts that he possessed an expectation of privacy, independent from his home's curtilage, in the barn and its contents, because the barn is an essential part of his business. Respondent overlooks the significance of *Oliver v. United States*.

We may accept, for the sake of argument, respondent's submission that his barn enjoyed Fourth Amendment protection and could not be entered and its contents seized without a warrant. But it does not follow on the record before us that the officers' conduct and the ensuing search and seizure violated the Constitution. *Oliver* reaffirmed the precept, established in *Hester*, that an open field is neither a "house" nor an "effect," and, therefore, "the government's intrusion upon the open fields is not one of those 'unreasonable searches' proscribed by the text of the Fourth Amendment." The Court expressly rejected the argument that the erection of fences on an open field-at least of the variety involved in those cases and in the present case-creates a constitutionally protected privacy interest. "[T]he term 'open fields' may include any unoccupied or undeveloped area outside of the curtilage. An open field need be neither 'open' nor a 'field' as those terms are used in common speech." It follows that no constitutional violation occurred here when the officers crossed over respondent's ranch-style perimeter fence, and over several similarly constructed interior fences, prior to stopping at the locked front gate of the barn. As previously mentioned, the officers never entered the barn, nor did they enter any other structure on respondent's premises. Once at their vantage point, they merely stood, outside the curtilage of the house and in the open fields upon which the barn was constructed, and peered into the barn's open front. And, standing as they were in the open fields, the Constitution did not forbid them to observe the phenylacetone laboratory located in respondent's barn. This conclusion flows naturally from our previous decisions.

Under *Oliver* and *Hester*, there is no constitutional difference between police observations conducted while in a public place and while standing in the open fields. Similarly, the fact that the objects observed by the officers lay within an area that we have assumed, but not decided, was protected by the Fourth Amendment does not affect our conclusion. Last Term, in *California v. Ciraolo* we held that warrantless naked-eye aerial observation of a home's curtilage did not violate the Fourth Amendment. We based our holding on the premise that the Fourth Amendment "has never been extended to require law enforcement officers to shield their eyes when passing by a home on public thoroughfares." Importantly, we deemed it irrelevant that the police observation at issue was directed specifically at the identification of marijuana plants growing on an area protected by the Fourth Amendment. Finally, the plurality opinion in *Texas v. Brown* notes that it is "beyond dispute" that the action of a police officer in shining his flashlight to illuminate the interior of a car, without probable cause to search the car, "trenched upon no right secured . . . by the Fourth Amendment." The holding in *United States v. Lee* is of similar import. Here, the officers' use of the beam of a flashlight, directed through the essentially open front of respondent's barn, did not transform their observations into an unreasonable search within the meaning of the Fourth Amendment.

The officers lawfully viewed the interior of respondent's barn, and their observations were properly considered by the Magistrate in issuing a search warrant for respondent's premises. Accordingly, the judgment of the Court of Appeals is reversed.

It is so ordered.

BRIGHAM CITY, UTAH
v.
STUART

547 U.S. 398, 126 S. Ct. 1943, 164 L. Ed. 2d 650 (2006)

[Citations and footnotes omitted.]

Chief Justice ROBERTS delivered the opinion of the Court.

In this case we consider whether police may enter a home without a warrant when they have an objectively reasonable basis for believing that an occupant is seriously injured or imminently threatened with such injury. We conclude that they may.

This case arises out of a melee that occurred in a Brigham City, Utah, home in the early morning hours of July 23, 2000. At about 3 a.m., four police officers responded to a call regarding a loud party at a residence. Upon arriving at the house, they heard shouting from inside, and proceeded down the driveway to investigate. There, they observed two juveniles drinking beer in the backyard. They entered the backyard, and saw-through a screen door and windows-an altercation taking place in the kitchen of the home. According to the testimony of one of the officers, four adults were attempting, with some difficulty, to restrain a juvenile. The juvenile eventually "broke free, swung a fist and struck one of the adults in the face." The officer testified that he observed the victim of the blow spitting blood into a nearby sink. The other adults continued to try to restrain the juvenile, pressing him up against a refrigerator with such force that the refrigerator began moving across the floor. At this point, an officer opened the screen door and announced the officers' presence. Amid the tumult, nobody noticed. The officer entered the kitchen and again cried out, and as the occupants slowly became aware that the police were on the scene, the altercation ceased.

The officers subsequently arrested respondents and charged them with contributing to the delinquency of a minor, disorderly conduct, and intoxication. In the trial court, respondents filed a motion to suppress all evidence obtained after the officers entered the home, arguing that the warrantless entry violated the Fourth Amendment. The court granted the motion, and the Utah Court of Appeals affirmed.

* * *

We granted certiorari in light of differences among state courts and the Courts of Appeals concerning the appropriate Fourth Amendment standard governing warrantless entry by law enforcement in an emergency.

It is a " 'basic principle of Fourth Amendment law that searches and seizures inside a home without a warrant are presumptively unreasonable.' " Nevertheless, because the ultimate touchstone of the Fourth Amendment is "reasonableness," the warrant requirement is subject to certain exceptions. We have held, for example, that law enforcement officers may make a warrantless entry onto private property to fight a fire and investigate its cause, to prevent the imminent destruction of evidence, or to engage in "hot pursuit" of a fleeing suspect. "[W]arrants are generally required to search a person's home or his person unless 'the exigencies of the situation' make the needs of law enforcement so compelling that the warrantless search is objectively reasonable under the Fourth Amendment."

One exigency obviating the requirement of a warrant is the need to assist persons who are seriously injured or threatened with such injury. "'The need to protect or preserve life or avoid serious injury is justification for what would be otherwise illegal absent an exigency or emergency.' " Accordingly, law enforcement officers may enter a home without a warrant to render emergency assistance to an injured occupant or to protect an occupant from imminent injury.

Respondents do not take issue with these principles, but instead advance two reasons why the officers' entry here was unreasonable. First, they argue that the officers were more interested in making arrests than quelling violence. They urge us to consider, in assessing the reasonableness of the entry, whether the officers were "indeed motivated primarily by a desire to save lives and property. . . .

Our cases have repeatedly rejected this approach. An action is "reasonable" under the Fourth Amendment, regardless of the individual officer's state of mind, "as long as the circumstances, viewed objectively, justify [the] action." The officer's subjective motivation is irrelevant. It therefore does not matter here-even if their subjective motives could be so neatly unraveled-whether the officers entered the kitchen to arrest respondents and gather evidence against them or to assist the injured and prevent further violence.

As respondents note, we have held in the context of programmatic searches conducted without individualized suspicion-such as checkpoints to combat drunk driving or drug trafficking-that "an inquiry into programmatic purpose" is sometimes appropriate. But this inquiry is directed at ensuring that the purpose behind the program is not "ultimately indistinguishable from the general interest in crime control." It has nothing to do with

discerning what is in the mind of the individual officer conducting the search.

Respondents further contend that their conduct was not serious enough to justify the officers' intrusion into the home. They rely on *Welsh v. Wisconsin*, in which we held that "an important factor to be considered when determining whether any exigency exists is the gravity of the underlying offense for which the arrest is being made." This contention, too, is misplaced. *Welsh* involved a warrantless entry by officers to arrest a suspect for driving while intoxicated. There, the "only potential emergency" confronting the officers was the need to preserve evidence (i.e., the suspect's blood-alcohol level)-an exigency that we held insufficient under the circumstances to justify entry into the suspect's home. Here, the officers were confronted with ongoing violence occurring within the home. *Welsh* did not address such a situation.

We think the officers' entry here was plainly reasonable under the circumstances. The officers were responding, at 3 o'clock in the morning, to complaints about a loud party. As they approached the house, they could hear from within "an altercation occurring, some kind of a fight." "It was loud and it was tumultuous." The officers heard "thumping and crashing" and people yelling "stop, stop" and "get off me." As the trial court found, "it was obvious that . . . knocking on the front door" would have been futile. The noise seemed to be coming from the back of the house; after looking in the front window and seeing nothing, the officers proceeded around back to investigate further. They found two juveniles drinking beer in the backyard. From there, they could see that a fracas was taking place inside the kitchen. A juvenile, fists clenched, was being held back by several adults. As the officers watch, he breaks free and strikes one of the adults in the face, sending the adult to the sink spitting blood.

In these circumstances, the officers had an objectively reasonable basis for believing both that the injured adult might need help and that the violence in the kitchen was just beginning. Nothing in the Fourth Amendment required them to wait until another blow rendered someone "unconscious" or "semi-conscious" or worse before entering. The role of a peace officer includes preventing violence and restoring order, not simply rendering first aid to casualties; an officer is not like a boxing (or hockey) referee, poised to stop a bout only if it becomes too one-sided.

The manner of the officers' entry was also reasonable. After witnessing the punch, one of the officers opened the screen door and "yelled in police." When nobody heard him, he stepped into the kitchen and announced himself again. Only then did the tumult subside. The officer's announcement of his presence was at least equivalent to a knock on the screen door. Indeed, it was probably the only option that had even a chance of rising above the din. Under these circumstances, there was no violation of the Fourth Amendment's knock-and-announce rule. Furthermore, once the announcement was made, the officers were free to enter; it would serve no purpose to require them to stand dumbly at the door awaiting a response while those within brawled on, oblivious to their presence.

Accordingly, we reverse the judgment of the Supreme Court of Utah, and remand the case for further proceedings not inconsistent with this opinion.

It is so ordered.

KENTUCKY
v.
KING

– U.S. –, 131 S. Ct. 1849,
179 L. Ed. 2d 865 (2011)

[Citations and footnotes omitted]

[Police followed a suspected drug dealer into an apartment building after observing him make a controlled sale of crack cocaine to a police informant. They heard a door slam, but were uncertain whether the suspect entered the apartment on the left or on the right. They picked the apartment on the left because they smelled a strong order of burnt marijuana outside the door. The officers pounded on the door and shouted "Police!" Immediately afterwards, they heard activity inside the apartment that they interpreted as an attempt to destroy evidence. The officers kicked in the door but did not find the initial suspect (who had entered the apartment on the right). Instead, they found Hollis King and a companion who was smoking marijuana, along with evidence of drug trafficking. The trial court denied King's motion to suppress the evidence, finding that the police were justified in entering his apartment to prevent destruction of evidence. The state supreme court reversed, holding that the exigent circumstances exception did not apply the police created the exigent circumstances by pounding on the door and announcing their presence.]

Justice ALITO delivered the opinion of the Court.

It is well established that exigent circumstances, including the need to prevent the destruction of evidence, permit police officers to conduct an otherwise permissible search without first obtaining a warrant. In this case, we consider whether this rule applies when police, by knocking on the door of a residence and announcing their presence, cause the occupants to attempt to destroy evidence. The Kentucky Supreme Court held that the exigent circumstances rule does not apply in the case at hand because the police should have foreseen that their conduct would prompt the occupants to attempt to destroy evidence. We reject this interpretation of the exigent circumstances rule. The conduct of the police prior to their entry into the apartment was entirely lawful. They did not violate the Fourth Amendment or threaten to do so. In such a situation, the exigent circumstances rule applies.

* * *

This Court has identified several exigencies that may justify a warrantless search of a home. Under the emergency aid exception, for example, officers may enter a home without a warrant to render emergency assistance to an injured occupant or to protect an occupant from imminent injury. Police officers may enter premises without a warrant when they are in hot pursuit of a fleeing suspect. And what is relevant here the need to prevent the imminent destruction of evidence has long been recognized as a sufficient justification for a warrantless search.

Over the years, lower courts have developed an exception to the exigent circumstances rule, the so-called "police-created exigency" doctrine. Under this doctrine, police may not rely on the need to prevent destruction of evidence when that exigency was "created" or "manufactured" by the conduct of the police.

In applying this exception for the "creation" or "manufacturing" of an exigency by the police, courts require something more than mere proof that fear of detection by the police caused the destruction of evidence. An additional showing is obviously needed because, as the Eighth Circuit has recognized, "in some sense the police always create the exigent circumstances." That is to say, in the vast majority of cases in which evidence is destroyed by persons who are engaged in illegal conduct, the reason for the destruction is fear that the evidence will fall into the hands of law enforcement. Destruction of evidence issues probably occur most frequently in drug cases because drugs may be easily destroyed by flushing them down a toilet or rinsing them down a drain. Persons in possession of valuable drugs are unlikely to destroy them unless they fear discovery by the police. Consequently, a rule that precludes the police from making a warrantless entry to prevent the destruction of evidence whenever their conduct causes the exigency would unreasonably shrink the reach of this well-established exception to the warrant requirement.

Presumably for the purpose of avoiding such a result, the lower courts have held that the police-created exigency doctrine requires more than simple causation, but the lower courts have not agreed on the test to be applied. Indeed, the petition in this case maintains that "[t]here are currently five different tests being used by the United States Courts of Appeals."

Despite the welter of tests devised by the lower courts, the answer to the question presented in this case follows directly and clearly from the principle that permits warrantless searches in the first place. As previously noted, warrantless searches are allowed when the circumstances make it reasonable, within the meaning of the Fourth Amendment, to dispense with the warrant requirement. Therefore, the answer to the question before us is that the exigent circumstances rule justifies a warrantless search when the conduct of the police preceding the exigency is reasonable in the same sense. Where, as here, the police did not create the exigency by engaging or threatening to engage in conduct that violates the Fourth Amendment, warrantless entry to prevent the destruction of evidence is reasonable and thus allowed.

We have taken a similar approach in other cases involving warrantless searches. For example, we have held that law enforcement officers may seize evidence in plain view, provided that they have not violated the Fourth Amendment in arriving at the spot from which the observation of the evidence is made. As we put it in *Horton*, "[i]t is . . . an essential predicate to any valid warrantless seizure of incriminating evidence that the officer did not violate the Fourth Amendment in arriving at the place from which the evidence could be plainly viewed." So long as this prerequisite is satisfied, however, it does not matter that the officer who makes the observation may have gone to the spot from which the evidence was seen with the hope of being able to view and seize the evidence.

Similarly, officers may seek consent-based encounters if they are lawfully present in the place where the consensual encounter occurs. If consent is freely given, it makes no difference that an officer may have approached the person with the hope or expectation of obtaining consent.

* * *

. . . Respondent contends that law enforcement officers impermissibly create an exigency when they engage in conduct that would cause a reasonable person to believe that entry is imminent and inevitable. In respondent's view, relevant factors include the officers' tone of voice in announcing their presence and the forcefulness of their knocks. But the ability of law enforcement officers to respond to an exigency cannot turn on such subtleties.

Police officers may have a very good reason to announce their presence loudly and to knock on the door with some force. A forceful knock may be necessary to alert the occupants that someone is at the door. Furthermore, unless police officers identify themselves loudly enough, occupants may not know who is at their doorstep. Officers are permitted indeed, encouraged to identify themselves to citizens, and in many circumstances this is cause for assurance, not discomfort. Citizens who are startled by an unexpected knock on the door or by the sight of unknown persons in plain clothes on their doorstep may be relieved to learn that these persons are police officers. Others may appreciate the opportunity to make an informed decision about whether to answer the door to the police.

If respondent's test were adopted, it would be extremely difficult for police officers to know how loudly they may announce their presence or how forcefully they may knock on a door without running afoul of the police-created exigency rule. And in most cases, it would be nearly impossible for a court to determine whether that threshold had been passed. The Fourth Amendment does not require the nebulous and impractical test that respondent proposes.

For these reasons, we conclude that the exigent circumstances rule applies when the police do not gain entry to premises by means of an actual or threatened violation of the Fourth Amendment. This holding provides ample protection for the privacy rights that the Amendment protects.

When law enforcement officers who are not armed with a warrant knock on a door, they do no more than any private citizen might do. And whether the person who knocks on the door and requests the opportunity to speak is a police officer or a private citizen, the occupant has no obligation to open the door or to speak. And even if an occupant chooses to open the door and speak with the officers, the occupant need not allow the officers to enter the premises and may refuse to answer any questions at any time.

Occupants who choose not to stand on their constitutional rights but instead elect to attempt to destroy evidence have only themselves to blame for the warrantless exigent-circumstances search that may ensue.

We now apply our interpretation of the police-created exigency doctrine to the facts of this case.

* * *

In this case, we see no evidence that the officers either violated the Fourth Amendment or threatened to do so prior to the point when they entered the apartment. Officer Cobb testified without contradiction that the "officers banged on the door as loud as [they] could and announced either 'Police, police, police' or 'This is the police.'" This conduct was entirely consistent with the Fourth Amendment, and we are aware of no other evidence that might show that the officers either violated the Fourth Amendment or threatened to do so (for example, by announcing that they would break down the door if the occupants did not open the door voluntarily).

Respondent argues that the officers demanded entry to the apartment, but he has not pointed to any evidence in the record that supports this assertion. . . . There is no evidence of a demand of any sort, much less a demand that amounts to a threat

to violate the Fourth Amendment. If there is contradictory evidence that has not been brought to our attention, the state court may elect to address that matter on remand.

Finally, respondent claims that the officers "explained to [the occupants that the officers] were going to make entry inside the apartment," but the record is clear that the officers did not make this statement until after the exigency arose. As Officer Cobb testified, the officers "knew that there was possibly something that was going to be destroyed inside the apartment," and "[a]t that point, . . . [they] explained . . . [that they] were going to make entry." (emphasis added). Given that this announcement was made after the exigency arose, it could not have created the exigency.

* * *

. . . Because the officers in this case did not violate or threaten to violate the Fourth Amendment prior to the exigency, we hold that the exigency justified the warrantless search of the apartment.

The judgment of the Kentucky Supreme Court is reversed, and the case is remanded for further proceedings not inconsistent with this opinion.

It is so ordered.

HERRING
v.
UNITED STATES

355 U.S. 135, 129 S. Ct. 695, 172 L. Ed. 2d 496 (2009)

[Citations and footnotes omitted]

[On July 7, 2004, Investigator Mark Anderson learned that Bennie Herring had driven to the Coffee County Sheriff's Department to retrieve something from his impounded truck. Since Herring had a criminal record, Anderson asked the Coffee County warrant clerk to check whether there were any outstanding warrants for his arrest. When she found none, he asked her to check with her counterpart in neighboring Dade County. Her counterpart initially reported the existence of an outstanding warrant for Herring's arrest, but moments later, called back to say that the initial report was inaccurate. The warrant had been recalled five months earlier but the police department database had not been updated to reflect this fact. By this time, Herring had already been arrested, searched, and methamphetamine had been found in his possession. He was indicted for illegal possession of drugs which he moved to suppress as the fruits of an illegal arrest. The trial judge denied the motion under the good faith exception to the exclusionary rule.]

Chief Justice ROBERTS delivered the opinion of the Court.

* * *

The Fourth Amendment forbids unreasonable searches and seizures, and this usually requires the police to have probable cause or a warrant before making an arrest. What if an officer reasonably believes there is an outstanding arrest warrant, but that belief turns out to be wrong because of a negligent bookkeeping error by another police employee? The parties here agree that the ensuing arrest is still a violation of the Fourth Amendment, but dispute whether contraband found during a search incident to that arrest must be excluded in a later prosecution.

* * *

[T]he exclusionary rule is not an individual right and applies only where it "'result[s] in appreciable deterrence.' ". We have repeatedly rejected the argument that exclusion is a necessary consequence of a Fourth Amendment violation. Instead we have focused on the efficacy of the rule in deterring Fourth Amendment violations in the future.

In addition, the benefits of deterrence must outweigh the costs."We have never suggested that the exclusionary rule must apply in every circumstance in which it might provide marginal deterrence." "[T]o the extent that application of the exclusionary rule could provide some incremental deterrent, that possible benefit must be weighed against [its] substantial social costs." The principal cost of applying the rule is, of course, letting guilty and possibly dangerous defendants go free—something that "offends basic concepts of the criminal justice system." "[T]he rule's costly toll upon truth-seeking and law enforcement objectives presents a high obstacle for those urging [its] application."

* * *

The extent to which the exclusionary rule is justified by these deterrence principles varies with the culpability of the law enforcement conduct. As we said in *Leon*,"an assessment of the flagrancy of the police misconduct constitutes an important step in the calculus" of applying the exclusionary rule. Similarly, in *Krull* we elaborated that "evidence should be suppressed "only if it can be said that the law enforcement officer had knowledge, or may properly be charged with knowledge, that the search was unconstitutional under the Fourth Amendment"

* * *

Indeed, the abuses that gave rise to the exclusionary rule featured intentional conduct that was patently unconstitutional. In *Weeks,* a foundational exclusionary rule case, the officers had broken into the defendant's home (using a key shown to them by a neighbor), confiscated incriminating papers, then returned again with a U.S. Marshal to confiscate even more. Not only did they have no search warrant, which the Court held was required, but they could not have gotten one had they tried. They were so lacking in sworn and particularized information that "not even an order of court would have justified such procedure."...

Equally flagrant conduct was at issue in *Mapp v. Ohio* which overruled *Wolf v. Colorado* and extended the exclusionary rule to the States. Officers forced open a door to Ms. Mapp's house, kept her lawyer from entering, brandished what the court concluded was a false warrant, then forced her into handcuffs and canvassed the house for obscenity. An error that arises from nonrecurring and attenuated negligence is thus far removed from the core concerns that led us to adopt the rule in the first place. And in fact since *Leon,* we have never applied the rule to exclude evidence obtained in violation of the Fourth Amendment, where the police conduct was no more intentional or culpable than this.

To trigger the exclusionary rule, police conduct must be sufficiently deliberate that exclusion can meaningfully deter it, and sufficiently culpable that such deterrence is worth the price paid by the justice system. As laid out in our cases, the exclusionary rule serves to deter deliberate, reckless, or grossly negligent conduct, or in some circumstances recurring or systemic negligence. The error in this case does not rise to that level.

* * *

Petitioner's claim that police negligence automatically triggers suppression cannot be squared with the principles underlying the exclusionary rule, as they have been explained in our cases. In light of our repeated holdings that the deterrent effect of suppression must be substantial and outweigh any harm to the justice system, we concludethat when police mistakes are the result of negligence such as that described here, rather than systemic error or reckless disregard of constitutional requirements, any marginal deterrence does not "pay its way." In such a case, the criminal should not "go free because the constable has blundered."

It is so ordered.

Cases Relating to Chapter 5

Laws Governing Police Surveillance

OLMSTEAD
v.
UNITED STATES

277 U.S. 438, 48 S. Ct. 564,
72 L. Ed. 944 (1928)

[Citations and footnotes omitted.]

[Olmstead was convicted of conspiring to violate the National Prohibition Act, based on evidence of private telephone conversations between him and others, intercepted by tapping his telephone line from a junction box located on a public street. The insertion was made without trespassing upon any property of the defendant. The wiretapping, which continued for many months, was conducted without probable cause or a warrant and in violation of local statutes. The trial court refused to suppress the conversations as the fruits of an illegal search. Olmstead was convicted and appealed the trial court's decision to admit the evidence.]

Mr. Chief Justice TAFT delivered the opinion of the Court.

* * *

The Fourth Amendment provides:

The right of the people to be secure in their persons, houses, papers, and effects, against unreasonable searches and seizures, shall not be violated, and no warrants shall issue, but upon probable cause, supported by oath or affirmation, and particularly describing the place to be searched, and the persons or things to be seized.

* * *

"The amendment itself shows that the search is to be of material things—the person, the house, his papers, or his effects. The description of the warrant necessary to make the proceeding lawful is that it must specify the place to be searched and the person or things to be seized."

* * *

[In *Ex parte Jackson*, we held that the protection of the Fourth Amendment was applicable to sealed letters and packages in the mail, and that, consistently with it, such matter could only be opened and examined upon warrants issued on oath or affirmation particularly describing the thing to be seized.]

* * *

It is urged that the language of Mr. Justice Field in *Ex parte Jackson* . . . offers an analogy to the interpretation of the Fourth Amendment in respect of wire tapping. But the analogy fails. . . . It is plainly within the words of the amendment to say that the unlawful rifling by a government agent of a sealed letter is a search and seizure of the sender's papers or effects. The letter is a paper, an effect, and in the custody of a government that forbids carriage, except under its protection.

. . . The amendment does not forbid what was done here. There was no searching. There was no seizure. The evidence was secured by the use of the sense of hearing and that only. There was no entry of the houses or offices of the defendants. By the invention of the telephone 50 years ago, and its application for the purpose of extending communications, one can talk with another at a far distant place.

The language of the amendment cannot be extended and expanded to include telephone wires, reaching to the whole world from the defendant's house or office. The intervening wires are not part of his house or office, any more than are the highways along which they are stretched.

* * *

Congress may, of course, protect the secrecy of telephone messages by making them, when intercepted, inadmissible in evidence in federal criminal trials, by direct legislation, and thus depart from the common law of evidence. But the courts may not adopt such a policy by attributing an enlarged and unusual meaning to the Fourth Amendment. The reasonable view is that one who installs in his house a telephone instrument with connecting wires intends to project his voice to those quite outside, and that the wires beyond his house, and messages while passing over them, are not within the protection of the Fourth Amendment. Here those who intercepted the projected voices were not in the house of either party to the conversation.

Neither the cases we have cited nor any of the many federal decisions brought to our attention hold the Fourth Amendment to have been violated as against a defendant, unless there has been an official search and seizure of his person or such a seizure of his papers or his tangible material effects or an actual physical invasion of his house 'or curtilage' for the purpose of making a seizure.

We think, therefore, that the wire tapping here disclosed did not amount to a search or seizure within the meaning of the Fourth Amendment.

What has been said disposes of the only question that comes within the terms of our order granting certiorari in these cases. But some of our number, departing from that order, have concluded that there is merit in the twofold objection, overruled in both courts below, that evidence obtained through intercepting of telephone messages by a government agent was inadmissible, because the mode of obtaining it was unethical and a misdemeanor under the law of Washington. . . .

* * *

Nor can we, without the sanction of congressional enactment, subscribe to the suggestion that the courts have a discretion to exclude evidence, the admission of which is not unconstitutional, because unethically secured. This would be at variance with the common-law doctrine generally supported by authority. There is no case that sustains, nor any recognized text-book that gives color to, such a view. Our general experience shows that much evidence has always been receivable, although not obtained by conformity to the highest ethics. The history of criminal trials shows numerous cases of prosecutions of oathbound conspiracies for murder, robbery, and other crimes, where officers of the law have disguised themselves and joined the organizations, taken the oaths, and given themselves every appearance of active members engaged in the promotion of crime for the purpose of securing evidence. Evidence secured by such means has always been received.

A standard which would forbid the reception of evidence, if obtained by other than nice ethical conduct by government officials, would make society suffer and give criminals greater immunity than has been known heretofore. In the absence of controlling legislation by Congress, those who realize the difficulties in bringing offenders to justice may well deem it wise that the exclusion of evidence should be confined to cases where rights under the Constitution would be violated by admitting it.

The statute of Washington, adopted in 1909, provides that:

Every person . . . who shall intercept, read or in any manner interrupt or delay the sending of a message over any telegraph or telephone line . . . shall be guilty of a misdemeanor.

This statute does not declare that evidence obtained by such interception shall be inadmissible, and by the common law, already referred to, it would not be. Whether the state of Washington may prosecute and punish federal officers violating this law, and those whose messages were intercepted may sue them civilly, is not before us. But clearly a statute, passed 20 years after the admission of the state into the Union, cannot affect the rules of evidence applicable in courts of the United States. . . .

* * *

AFFIRMED.

Mr. Justice BRANDEIS (dissenting).

. . . By objections seasonably made and persistently renewed, the defendants objected to the admission of the evidence obtained by wire tapping, on the ground that the government's wire tapping constituted an unreasonable search and seizure, in violation of the Fourth Amendment . . .

* * *

The government makes no attempt to defend the methods employed by its officers. Indeed, it concedes that, if wire tapping can be deemed a search and seizure within the Fourth Amendment, such wire tapping as was practiced in the case at bar was an unreasonable search and seizure, and that the evidence thus obtained was inadmissible. But it relies on the language of the amendment, and it claims that the protection given thereby cannot properly be held to include a telephone conversation.

* * *

When the Fourth and Fifth Amendments were adopted, 'the form that evil had theretofore taken' had been necessarily simple.... It could secure possession of his papers and other articles incident to his private life—a seizure effected, if need be, by breaking and entry. Protection against such invasion of 'the sanctities of a man's home and the privacies of life' was provided in the Fourth and Fifth Amendments by specific language. But 'time works changes, brings into existence new conditions and purposes.' Subtler and more far-reaching means of invading privacy have become available to the government. Discovery and invention have made it possible for the government, by means far more effective than stretching upon the rack, to obtain disclosure in court of what is whispered in the closet.

Moreover, 'in the application of a Constitution, our contemplation cannot be only of what has been, but of what may be.' The progress of science in furnishing the government with means of espionage is not likely to stop with wire tapping. Ways may some day be developed by which the government, without removing papers from secret drawers, can reproduce them in court, and by which it will be enabled to expose to a jury the most intimate occurrences of the home. Advances in the psychic and related sciences may bring means of exploring unexpressed beliefs, thoughts and emotions. 'That places the liberty of every man in the hands of every petty officer' was said by James Otis of much lesser intrusions than these. To Lord Camden a far slighter intrusion seemed 'subversive of all the comforts of society.' Can it be that the Constitution affords no protection against such invasions of individual security?

A sufficient answer is found in *Boyd v. United States*, a case that will be remembered as long as civil liberty lives in the United States. This court there reviewed the history that lay behind the Fourth and Fifth Amendments. We said with reference to Lord Camden's judgment in *Entick v. Carrington:*

'The principles laid down in this opinion affect the very essence of constitutional liberty and security. They reach farther than the concrete form of the case there before the court, with its adventitious circumstances; they apply to all invasions on the part of the government and its employee of the sanctities of a man's home and the privacies of life. It is not the breaking of his doors, and the rummaging of his drawers, that constitutes the essence of the offense; but it is the invasion of his indefeasible right of personal security, personal liberty and private property, where that right has never been forfeited by his conviction of some public offense—it is the invasion of this sacred right which underlies and constitutes the essence of Lord Camden's judgment. Breaking into a house and opening boxes and drawers are circumstances of aggravation; but any forcible and compulsory extortion of a man's own testimony or of his private papers to be used as evidence of a crime or to forfeit his goods, is within the condemnation of that judgment. In this regard the Fourth and Fifth Amendments run almost into each other.'

In *Ex parte Jackson*, it was held that a sealed letter intrusted to the mail is protected by the amendments. The mail is a public service furnished by the government. The telephone is a public service furnished by its authority. There is, in essence, no difference between the sealed letter and the private telephone message. As Judge Rudkin said below:

True, the one is visible, the other invisible; the one is tangible, the other intangible; the one is sealed, and the other unsealed; but these are distinctions without a difference.

The evil incident to invasion of the privacy of the telephone is far greater than that involved in tampering with the mails. Whenever a telephone line is tapped, the privacy of the persons at both ends of the line is invaded, and all conversations between them upon any subject, and although proper, confidential, and privileged, may be overheard. Moreover, the tapping of one man's telephone line involves the tapping of the telephone of every other person whom he may call, or who may call him. As a means of espionage, writs of assistance and general warrants are but puny instruments of tyranny and oppression when compared with wire tapping.

* * *

... The makers of our Constitution undertook to secure conditions favorable to the pursuit of happiness. They recognized the significance of man's spiritual nature, of his feelings and of his intellect. They knew that only a part of the pain, pleasure and satisfactions of life are to be found in material things. They sought to protect Americans in their beliefs, their thoughts, their emotions and their sensations. They conferred, as against the government, the right to be let alone—the most comprehensive of rights and the right most valued by civilized men. To protect, that right, every unjustifiable intrusion by the government upon the privacy of the individual, whatever the means employed, must be deemed a violation of the Fourth Amendment. And the use, as evidence in a criminal proceeding, of facts ascertained by such intrusion must be deemed a violation of the Fifth.

Applying to the Fourth and Fifth Amendments the established rule of construction, the defendants' objections to the evidence obtained by wire tapping must, in my opinion, be sustained. It is, of course, immaterial where the physical connection with the telephone wires leading into the defendants' premises was made. And it is also immaterial that the intrusion was in aid of law enforcement. Experience should teach us to be most on our guard to protect liberty when the government's purposes are beneficent. Men born to freedom are naturally alert to repel invasion of their liberty by evil-minded rulers. The greatest dangers to liberty lurk in insidious encroachment by men of zeal, well-meaning but without understanding.

Independently of the constitutional question, I am of opinion that the judgment should be reversed. By the laws of Washington, wire tapping is a crime. To prove its case, the government was obliged to lay bare the crimes committed by its officers on its behalf. A federal court should not permit such a prosecution to continue.

* * *

When these unlawful acts were committed they were crimes only of the officers individually. The

government was innocent, in legal contemplation; for no federal official is authorized to commit a crime on its behalf. When the government, having full knowledge, sought, through the Department of Justice, to avail itself of the fruits of these acts in order to accomplish its own ends, it assumed moral responsibility for the officers' crimes.... [A]nd if this court should permit the government, by means of its officers' crimes, to effect its purpose of punishing the defendants, there would seem to be present all the elements of a ratification. If so, the government itself would become a lawbreaker.

* * *

Decency, security, and liberty alike demand that government officials shall be subjected to the same rules of conduct that are commands to the citizen. In a government of laws, existence of the government will be imperiled if it fails to observe the law scrupulously. Our government is the potent, the omnipresent teacher. For good or for ill, it teaches the whole people by its example. Crime is contagious. If the government becomes a lawbreaker, it breeds contempt for law; it invites every man to become a law unto himself; it invites anarchy. To declare that in the administration of the criminal law the end justifies the means—to declare that the government may commit crimes in order to secure the conviction of a private criminal—would bring terrible retribution. Against that pernicious doctrine this court should resolutely set its face.

* * *

KATZ
v.
UNITED STATES

389 U.S. 347, 88 S. Ct. 507, 19 L. Ed. 2d 576 (1967)

[Citations and footnotes omitted.]

[Katz, a bookie, was convicted of transmitting wagering information, based on evidence overheard by FBI agents who had attached a recording device to the exterior of a public telephone booth from which Katz habitually made his business calls. The agents were able to overhear Katz's portion of a telephone conversation without physically intruding into the booth. The conversation proved incriminating and the defendant was convicted of illegal wagering.]

MR. JUSTICE STEWART delivered the opinion of the Court.

* * *

Because of the misleading way the issues have been formulated, the parties have attached great significance to the characterization of the telephone booth from which the petitioner placed his calls. The petitioner has strenuously argued that the booth was a "constitutionally protected area." The Government has maintained with equal vigor that it was not. But this effort to decide whether or not a given "area," viewed in the abstract, is "constitutionally protected" deflects attention from the problem presented by this case. For the Fourth Amendment protects people, not places. What a person knowingly exposes to the public, even in his own home or office, is not a subject of Fourth Amendment protection. But what he seeks to preserve as private, even in an area accessible to the public, may be constitutionally protected.

The Government stresses the fact that the telephone booth from which the petitioner made his calls was constructed partly of glass, so that he was as visible after he entered it as he would have been if he had remained outside. But what he sought to exclude when he entered the booth was not the intruding eye—it was the uninvited ear. He did not shed his right to do so simply because he made his calls from a place where he might be seen. No less than an individual in a business office, in a friend's apartment, or in a taxicab, a person in a telephone booth may rely upon the protection of the Fourth Amendment. One who occupies it, shuts the door behind him, and pays the toll that permits him to place a call is surely entitled to assume that the words he utters into the mouthpiece will not be broadcast to the world. To read the Constitution more narrowly is to ignore the vital role that the public telephone has come to play in private communication.

The Government contends, however, that the activities of its agents in this case should not be tested by Fourth Amendment requirements, for the surveillance technique they employed involved no physical penetration of the telephone booth from which the petitioner placed his calls. It is true that the absence of such penetration was at one time thought to foreclose further Fourth Amendment inquiry for that Amendment was thought to limit only searches and seizures of tangible property. But "[t]he premise that property interests control the right of the Government to search and seize has been discredited." Thus, although a closely divided Court supposed in *Olmstead* that surveillance without any trespass and without the seizure of any material object fell outside the ambit of the Constitution, we have since departed from the narrow view on which that decision rested. Indeed, we have expressly held that the Fourth Amendment governs not only the seizure of tangible items, but extends as well to the recording of oral statements, over-heard without any "technical trespass under . . . local property law." Once this much is acknowledged, and once it is recognized that the Fourth Amendment protects people—and not simply "areas"—against unreasonable searches and seizures, it becomes clear that the reach of that Amendment cannot turn upon the presence or absence of a physical intrusion into any given enclosure.

We conclude that the underpinnings of *Olmstead* and *Goldman* have been so eroded by our subsequent decisions that the "trespass" doctrine there enunciated can no longer be regarded as controlling. The Government's activities in electronically listening to and recording the petitioner's words violated the privacy upon which he justifiably relied while using the telephone booth and thus constituted a "search and seizure" within the meaning of the Fourth Amendment. The fact that the electronic device employed to achieve that end did not happen to penetrate the wall of the booth can have no constitutional significance.

The question remaining for decision, then, is whether the search and seizure conducted in this case complied with constitutional standards. In that regard, the Government's position is that its agents acted in an entirely defensible manner: They did not begin their electronic surveillance until investigation of the petitioner's activities had established a strong probability that he was using the telephone in question to transmit gambling information to persons in other States, in violation of federal law. Moreover, the surveillance was limited, both in scope and in duration, to the specific purpose of establishing the contents of the petitioner's unlawful telephonic communications. The agents confined their surveillance to the brief periods during which he used the telephone booth, and they took great care to overhear only the conversations of the petitioner himself.

Accepting this account of the Government's actions as accurate, it is clear that this surveillance was so narrowly circumscribed that a duly authorized magistrate, properly notified of the need for such investigation, specifically informed of the basis on which it was to proceed, and clearly apprised of the precise intrusion it would entail, could constitutionally have authorized, with appropriate safeguards, the very limited search and seizure that the Government asserts in fact took place. Only last Term we sustained the validity of such an authorization, holding that, under sufficiently "precise and discriminate circumstances," a federal court may em-power government agents to employ a concealed electronic device "for the narrow and particularized purpose of ascertaining the truth of the . . . allegations" of a "detailed factual affidavit alleging the commission of a specific criminal offense." Discussing that holding, the Court in *Berger v. New York*, said that "the order authorizing the use of the electronic device" in *Osborn* "afforded similar protections to those . . . of conventional warrants authorizing the seizure of tangible evidence." Through those protections, "no greater invasion of privacy was permitted than was necessary under the circumstances." Here, too, a similar judicial order could have accommodated "the legitimate needs of law enforcement" by authorizing the carefully limited use of electronic surveillance.

* * *

. . . Wherever a man may be, he is entitled to know that he will remain free from unreasonable searches and seizures. The government agents here ignored "the procedure of antecedent justification . . . that is central to the Fourth Amendment," a procedure that we hold to be a constitutional precondition of the kind of electronic surveillance involved in this case. Because the surveillance here failed to meet that condition, and because it led to the petitioner's conviction, the judgment must be reversed.

It is so ordered.

[Concurring and dissenting opinions omitted.]

UNITED STATES, PETITIONER
v.
ANTOINE JONES

– S. Ct., 2012 WL 171117 (U.S. 2012)

[Citations and footnotes omitted]

[The Government, as part of a drug investigation, installed a GPS tracking device on the undercarriage of Jones' vehicle, without a warrant, and used it to monitor his movements twenty-four hours a day for four weeks. Jones was indicted and convicted of conspacy to distribute cocaine based on the evidence obtained through the GPS device. The Supreme Court agreed to address two isssues: (1) whether the Government's installation of a GPS device to the undercarriage of Jones' vehicle, without a warrant or consent, constituted a search under the Fourth Amendment, and (2) whether the Government's continuous, long-term surveillance of the public movements of his vehicle, without a warrant, obtaining huge quantities of personal information, violated the Fourth Amendment. The Court addressed the first question, but not the second because its answer to the first question made consideration of the second one unnecessary.]

JUSTICE SCALIA delivered the opinion of the Court.

We decide whether the attachment of a Global-Positioning-System (GPS) tracking device to an individual's vehicle, and subsequent use of that device to monitor the vehicle's movements on public streets, constitutes a search or seizure within the meaning of the Fourth Amendment.

* * *

The Fourth Amendment provides in relevant part that "[t]he right of the people to be secure in their persons, houses, papers, and effects, against unreasonable searches and seizures, shall not be violated." It is beyond dispute that a vehicle is an "effect" as that term is used in the Amendment. We hold that the Government's installation of a GPS device on a target's vehicle, and its use of that device to monitor the vehicle's movements, constitutes a "search."

It is important to be clear about what occurred in this case: The Government physically occupied private property for the purpose of obtaining information. We have no doubt that such a physical intrusion would have been considered a "search" within the meaning of the Fourth Amendment when it was adopted. . . .

The text of the Fourth Amendment reflects its close connection to property, since otherwise it would have referred simply to "the right of the people to be secure against unreasonable searches and seizures"; the phrase "in their persons, houses, papers, and effects" would have been superfluous.

Consistent with this understanding, our Fourth Amendment jurisprudence was tied to common-law trespass, at least until the latter half of the 20th century. Thus, in *Olmstead* v. *United States*, we held that wiretaps attached to telephone wires on the public streets did not constitute a Fourth Amendment search because "[t]here was no entry of the houses or offices of the defendants."

* * *

The Government contends that . . . no search occurred here, since Jones had no "reasonable expectation of privacy" in the area of the Jeep accessed by Government agents (its underbody) and in the locations of the Jeep on the public roads, which were visible to all. But we need not address the Government's contentions, because Jones's Fourth Amendment rights do not rise or fall with the *Katz* formulation. At bottom, we must "assur[e] preservation of that degree of privacy against government that existed when the Fourth Amendment was adopted." As explained, for most of our history the Fourth Amendment was understood to embody a particular concern for government trespass upon the areas ("persons, houses, papers, and effects") it enumerates. *Katz* did not repudiate that understanding. Less than two years later the Court upheld defendants' contention that the Government could not introduce against them conversations between *other* people obtained by warrantless placement of electronic surveillance devices in their homes. The opinion rejected the dissent's contention that there was no Fourth Amendment violation "unless the conversational privacy of the homeowner himself is invaded." "[W]e [do not] believe that *Katz*, by holding that the Fourth Amendment protects persons and their private conversations, was intended to withdraw any of the protection which the Amendment extends to the home . . . ."

* * *

The Government contends that several of our post-*Katz* cases foreclose the conclusion that what occurred here constituted a search. It relies principally on two cases in which we rejected Fourth Amendment challenges to "beepers," electronic tracking devices that represent another form of electronic monitoring. The first case, *Knotts*, upheld against Fourth Amendment challenge the use of a "beeper" that had been placed in a container of chloroform, allowing law enforcement to monitor the location of the container. We said that there had been no infringement of Knotts' reasonable expectation of privacy since the information obtained—the location of the automobile carrying the container on public roads, and the location of the off-loaded container in open fields near Knotts' cabin—had been voluntarily conveyed to the public. But as we have discussed, the *Katz* reasonable-expectation-of-privacy test has been *added to*, not *substituted for*, the common-law trespassory test. The holding in *Knotts* addressed only the former, since the latter was not at issue. The beeper had been placed in the container before it came into Knotts' possession, with the consent of the then-owner. Knotts did not challenge that installation, and we specifically declined to consider its effect on the Fourth Amendment analysis. . . .

The Government also points to our exposition in *New York* v. *Class* that "[t]he exterior of a car . . . is thrust into the public eye, and thus to examine it does not constitute a 'search.'" That statement is of marginal relevance here since, as the Government acknowledges, "the officers in this case did *more* than conduct a visual inspection of respondent's vehicle." By attaching the device to the Jeep, officers encroached on a protected area. In *Class* itself we suggested that this would make a difference, for we concluded that an officer's momentary reaching into the interior of a vehicle did constitute a search.

* * *

. . . This Court has to date not deviated from the understanding that mere visual observation does not constitute a search. We accordingly held in *Knotts* that "[a] person traveling in an automobile on public thoroughfares has no reasonable expectation of privacy in his movements from one place to another." Thus, even assuming that the concurrence is correct to say that "[t]raditional surveillance" of Jones for a 4-week period "would have required a large team of agents, multiple vehicles, and perhaps aerial assistance," our cases suggest that such visual observation is constitutionally permissible. It may be that achieving the same result through electronic means, without an accompanying trespass, is an unconstitutional invasion of privacy, but the present case does not require us to answer that question.

* * *

The judgment of the Court of Appeals for the D. C. Circuit is affirmed.

It is so ordered.

UNITED STATES
v.
LEE

359 F.3d 194 (3d Cir. 2004)

[Citations and footnotes omitted.]

[Lee was a cofounder and president of the International Boxing Foundation (IBF), an organization that crowns international boxing champions and publishes monthly ratings of boxers within different weight divisions, used is to determine which boxers will fight in upcoming IBF championship bouts. In May 1996, the Federal Bureau of Investigation received information that boxing promoters were paying certain IBF officials in order to receive more favorable IBF ratings for their boxers. F.B.I. investigators questioned Don "Bill" Beavers, chairman of the IBF Executive Committee who agreed to co-operate.

With Beavers' cooperation, the FBI made audio and video recordings of three meetings between Beavers and Lee that took place in a hotel suite rented for Lee. The meetings were electronically monitored and recorded using equipment installed in the living room of Lee's suite by the FBI before Lee's arrival. The equipment consisted of a concealed camera and microphone that transmitted video and audio signals to a monitor and recorder located in an adjacent room. The FBI did not obtain a warrant authorizing the installation or use of the equipment, but instead relied on Beavers' consent. The government agents located in the room next to Lee's suite were instructed to monitor activity in the corridor to determine whether or not Beavers had entered Lee's rooms. The agents were further instructed to switch the monitor and recorder on only when Beavers was in the suite and that, at all other times, keep the monitor and recorder switched off. During one of the meetings, Lee was captured on tape accepting cash from Beavers that had originated as a bribe paid by a Colombian boxing promoter.

Lee was indicted and convicted on 6 counts of taking bribes from boxing promoters. He appealed.]

ALITO, Circuit Judge

* * *

Lee challenges the District Court's admission into evidence of tapes of meetings in his hotel suite. Lee contends that the monitoring and recording of these meetings violated his Fourth Amendment rights because the government did not obtain a warrant. Lee's argument, however, is inconsistent with well-established Fourth Amendment precedent concerning the electronic monitoring of conversations with the consent of a participant.

In *Hoffa v. United States*, a confidential government informant named Partin met with the defendant in the defendant's hotel suite and elsewhere and testified about those conversations at trial. The defendant argued that Partin had conducted an illegal search for verbal evidence and that, because the defendant was unaware of Partin's role as an informant, the defendant had not validly consented to his entry into the suite. The Supreme Court rejected this argument, holding that the defendant had "no interest legitimately protected by the Fourth Amendment." The Court concluded that the Fourth Amendment does not protect "a wrongdoer's misplaced belief that a person to whom he voluntarily confides his wrongdoing will not reveal it."

Although *Hoffa* involved testimony about conversations and not electronic recordings of conversations, the Supreme Court in later cases drew no distinction between the two situations. As the Court in *Caceres* put it, "Concededly a police agent who conceals his police connections may write down for official use his conversations with a defendant and testify concerning them, without a warrant authorizing his encounters with the defendant and without otherwise violating the latter's Fourth Amendment rights. For constitutional purposes, no different result is required if the agent instead of immediately reporting and transcribing his conversations with defendant, either (1) simultaneously records them with electronic equipment which he is carrying on his person; (2) or carries radio equipment which simultaneously transmits the conversations either to recording equipment located elsewhere or to other agents monitoring the transmitting frequency ..." The Court added that it had "repudiated any suggestion that [a] defendant had a 'constitutional right to rely on possible flaws in the agent's memory, or to challenge the agent's credibility without being beset by corroborating evidence that is not susceptible of impeachment.' " In short, the Court adopted the principle that, if a person consents to the presence at a meeting of another person who is willing to reveal what occurred, the Fourth Amendment permits the government to obtain and use the best available proof of what the latter person could have testified about. This principle appears to doom Lee's argument here.

Lee argues, however, that neither the Supreme Court nor our court has extended this principle to the circumstances present in this case. He points to three factors: (1) the agents used video rather than audio equipment; (2) the recording occurred in Lee's hotel room, a place where a person has a heightened expectation of privacy; and (3) the monitoring equipment remained in the room when Beavers was not present.

In making this argument, Lee relies on the First Circuit's decision in *United States v. Padilla*, which held that the defendant's Fourth Amendment rights were violated when agents placed an audio recording device in the defendant's hotel room and recorded conversations between the defendant and another person who consented to the recordings. In reaching this conclusion, the First Circuit expressed concern that if law enforcement officers were permitted to leave a monitoring or recording device in a hotel for a lengthy period of time the officers would be tempted to monitor or record conversations that occurred when no consenting participant was present. As the Court put it, [t]he government's position would turn on its head the carefully tailored [consenting party] exception to . . . one's expectation of privacy. Electronic devices could be installed for lengthy periods of time without antecedent authority, so long as only a suspect's conversations with police agents were offered in evidence and the enforcement officials alleged that nothing else was recorded. Under this approach a room or an entire hotel could be bugged permanently with impunity and with the hope that some usable conversations with agents would occur.

In contrast to the First Circuit, the Second and Eleventh Circuits have held that the Fourth Amendment is not violated by the use of a fixed electronic device to record a meeting between a defendant and a person who consents to the recording. In *Myers*, a defendant was videotaped during a meeting with a government informant at a townhouse maintained by the FBI. Rejecting the defendant's Fourth Amendment argument, the Court stated that the defendant's "conversations with undercover agents in whom he chose to confide were not privileged, and mechanical recordings of the sights and sounds to which the agents could have testified were proper evidence."

In *Yonn*, the Eleventh Circuit likewise held that the Fourth Amendment was not violated when agents placed a microphone in a motel room and monitored and recorded the defendant's conversations when a person who consented to the surveillance was present. The Court held that "[t]he location of the electronic equipment does not alter the irrefutable fact that Yonn had no justifiable expectation of privacy in his conversation with [the person who consented]." The Court also specifically rejected the reasoning of Padilla, stating that it saw "no reason to suppress the recording of a clearly unprotected conversation merely because the monitoring technique employed poses a hypothetical risk that protected conversations may be intercepted."

We have considered the concern expressed by the *Padilla* Court, but we remain convinced that the present case is governed by the well-established principle that a person has no legitimate expectation of privacy in conversations with a person who consents to the recording of the conversations. None of the three factors on which Lee relies appears to us to be sufficient to take this case beyond the reach of this principle.

First, we cannot distinguish this case on the ground that the recorded meetings occurred in a hotel suite. What is significant is not the type of room in which the surveillance occurred but Lee's action in admitting Beavers to the room. Although Lee had an expectation of privacy in the hotel suite so long as he was alone there, when Lee allowed Beavers to enter, any expectation of privacy vis-a-vis Beavers vanished. We note that in *Hoffa* many of the conversations also occurred in a hotel suite, but the Court nevertheless held that the case did not involve any legitimate Fourth Amendment interest.

Second, we cannot draw a constitutional distinction between consensual audio and video surveillance. The principle underlying the governing Supreme Court cases is that if a defendant consents to the presence of a person who could testify about a meeting and is willing to reveal what occurs, the defendant relinquishes any legitimate expectation of privacy with respect to anything that the testimony could cover. Thus, just as Lee gave up any expectation of privacy in the things that he allowed Beavers to hear, Lee also gave up any expectation of privacy in the things that he allowed Beavers to see. Although video surveillance may involve a greater intrusion on privacy than audio surveillance, the difference is not nearly as great as the difference between testimony about a conversation and audio recordings of conversations. As noted, however, the Supreme Court has not drawn any distinction between those two types of evidence, and we similarly see no constitutionally relevant distinction between audio and video surveillance in the present context.

Finally, we do not agree with the First Circuit that it is appropriate to suppress recordings of meetings between a defendant and a cooperating individual simply because the recording device was placed in the room rather than on the cooperating individual's person. To be sure, there are three circumstances in which this distinction would matter for Fourth Amendment purposes. First, if the defendant had an expectation of privacy in the premises at the time when the device was installed, the entry to install the device would constitute a search. Second, the cases involving consensual monitoring do not apply if recordings are made when the cooperating individual is not present. Third, the logic of those cases is likewise inapplicable if the placement of the recording device permits it to pick up evidence that the cooperating individual could not have heard or seen while in the room. Unless one of these circumstances is present, however, it does not matter for Fourth Amendment purposes whether the device is placed in the room or carried on the person of the cooperating individual. In either event, the recording will not gather any evidence other than that about which the cooperating witness could have testified.

As the government argues, the decision in *Padilla* appears to be based, not on the conclusion that the recordings in that case had been obtained in violation of the Fourth Amendment, but on a prophylactic rule designed to stamp out a law enforcement technique that the Court viewed as creating an unacceptable risk of abuse. Even assuming for the sake of argument that we have the authority to adopt such a rule, however, we would not do so. Although *Padilla* was decided more than a quarter century ago and has not been followed in any other circuit, we are not aware of evidence that the installation of recording devices to monitor meetings attended by a cooperating individual has led to the sort of abuse that the *Padilla* Court feared. Nor is it intuitively obvious that there is much risk of such abuse. As noted, the *Padilla* Court feared that law enforcement agents would install electronic devices in a hotel rooms and monitor what occurred "in the hope that some usable conversations with agents would occur." However, there are numerous reasons to doubt whether law enforcement is likely to find this an alluring strategy.

First, a person who illegally intercepts wire, oral, or electronic communicates is subject to criminal and civil penalties, and a federal agent who violates the Fourth Amendment may be sued under *Bivens v. Six Unknown Fed. Narcotics Agents*. Second, in order to install a monitoring device, law enforcement authorities or a person cooperating with them must acquire a right to enter the premises, such as by obtaining a warrant or renting the premises in which the device is to be installed. Thus, the *Padilla* Court's fear that agents might bug "an entire hotel," and the fear of the District Court in *Shabazz* that devices could be placed in a person's home seem misplaced. Third, it is not clear that law enforcement would have much to gain from monitoring conversations that occur when a cooperating individual is not present. A video tape of a conversation generally reveals whether a cooperating individual is present, and without proof of the presence of the cooperating individual, the tape is inadmissible. We do not go so far as to say that there is no risk of the type of abuse that worried that Padilla Court, but the risk is not great enough to justify the holding of the *Padilla* Court.

In the present case, there was no violation of Lee's Fourth Amendment rights. The monitoring devices were installed in the suite's living room at a time when Lee had no expectation of privacy in the premises. There is no evidence that conversations were monitored when Beavers was absent from the room, and Beavers was plainly there at the time of the incriminating meetings shown on the tapes that were introduced at Lee's trial. We are satisfied that the tapes do not depict anything material that Beavers himself was not in a position to hear or see while in the room. Finally, we reject Lee's suggestion that the government was required, before resorting to video surveillance, to demonstrate that less intrusive investigative techniques were unlikely to succeed. Although this requirement applies to monitoring governed by the federal wiretapping statute, that statute does not apply to electronic surveillance conducted with the prior consent of a party to the communication. Similarly, judicial decisions considering a similar requirement in cases involving silent video surveillance conducted without a participant's consent are inapplicable in this context. We therefore reject Lee's argument that the tapes should have been suppressed.

* * *

For the reasons explained above, we affirm the judgment of the District Court.

UNITED STATES
v.
HARTWELL

436 F.3d 174 (3d Cir. 2006)

[Citations and footnotes omitted.]

ALITO, Circuit Judge.

Christian Hartwell set off a metal detector at a security checkpoint in an airport. Transportation Security Administration ("TSA") agents then used a magnetic wand to pinpoint any metal on his person. They detected something in Hartwell's pocket and asked to see it. Ultimately, they discovered that the object was crack cocaine and placed Hartwell under arrest. Hartwell argues that the drugs should have been suppressed because the search offended the Fourth Amendment. We hold that it did not.

* * *

Hartwell's search at the airport checkpoint was justified by the administrative search doctrine. "A search or seizure is ordinarily unreasonable in the absence of individualized suspicion of wrongdoing. While such suspicion is not an 'irreducible' component of reasonableness, [the Supreme Court has] recognized only limited circumstances in which the usual rule does not apply." These circumstances typically involve administrative searches of "closely regulated" businesses, other so-called "special needs" cases, and suspicionless "checkpoint" searches.

Suspicionless checkpoint searches are permissible under the Fourth Amendment when a court finds a favorable balance between "the gravity of the public concerns served by the seizure, the degree to which the seizure advances the public interest, and the severity of the interference with individual liberty."

Michigan Dept. of State Police v. Sitz provides illustrative example of a permissible suspicionless checkpoint procedure. In that case, Michigan established a sobriety checkpoint along a state road, stopping every vehicle that passed by in order to question the driver and look for signs of intoxication. If the police observed indicia of impairment, they would pull drivers aside to conduct additional tests. Applying the *Brown* balancing test, the Court found the system permissible because "the balance of the State's interest in preventing drunken driving, the extent to which this system can reasonably be said to advance that interest, and the degree of intrusion upon individual motorists who are briefly stopped, weighs in favor of the state program." As to the State's interest, the Court wrote that "[n]o one can seriously dispute the magnitude of the drunken driving problem or the States' interest in eradicating it." The stop was deemed effective because some quantum of evidence showed that it furthered the purpose for which it was created. "Conversely," the Court stated, "the weight bearing on the other scale-the measure of the intrusion on motorists stopped briefly at sobriety checkpoints-is slight," because the stop lasted for only a short time and the investigation was of minimal intensity.

In this case, the airport checkpoint passes the *Brown* test. First, there can be no doubt that preventing terrorist attacks on airplanes is of paramount importance. Second, airport checkpoints also "advance[ ] the public interest," as *Brown* requires. As this Court has held, "absent a search, there is no effective means of detecting which airline passengers are reasonably likely to hijack an airplane." Additionally, it is apparent that airport checkpoints have been effective. of, and a responsibility for, limited public resources, including a finite number of police officers."

Third, the procedures involved in Hartwell's search were minimally intrusive. They were well-tailored to protect personal privacy, escalating in invasiveness only after a lower level of screening disclosed a reason to conduct a more probing search. The search began when Hartwell simply passed through a magnetometer and had his bag x-rayed, two screenings that involved no physical touching. Only after Hartwell set off the metal detector was he screened with a wand-yet another less intrusive substitute for a physical pat-down. And only after the wand detected something solid on his person, and after repeated requests that he produce the item, did the TSA agents (according to Hartwell) reach into his pocket.

In addition to being tailored to protect personal privacy, other factors make airport screening procedures minimally intrusive in comparison to other kinds of searches. Since every air passenger is subjected to a search, there is virtually no "stigma attached to being subjected to search at a known, designated airport search point." Moreover, the possibility for abuse is minimized by the public nature of the search. "Unlike searches conducted on dark and lonely streets at night where often the officer and the subject are the only witnesses, these searches are made under supervision and not far from the scrutiny of the traveling public." And the airlines themselves have a strong interest in

protecting passengers from unnecessary annoyance and harassment.

Lastly, the entire procedure is rendered less offensive-if not less intrusive-because air passengers are on notice that they will be searched. Air passengers choose to fly, and screening procedures of this kind have existed in every airport in the country since at least 1974. The events of September 11, 2001, have only increased their prominence in the public's consciousness. It is inconceivable that Hartwell was unaware that he had to be searched before he could board a plane. Indeed, he admitted that he had previously been searched before flying.

In conclusion, Hartwell's search does not offend the Fourth Amendment even though it was initiated without individualized suspicion and was conducted without a warrant. It is permissible under the administrative search doctrine because the State has an overwhelming interest in preserving air travel safety, and the procedure is tailored to advance that interest while proving to be only minimally invasive, as that term is understood in Brown.

KYLLO
v.
UNITED STATES

533 U.S. 527, 121 S. Ct. 2038, 150 L. Ed. 2d 94 (2001)

[Citations and footnotes omitted.]

JUSTICE SCALIA delivered the opinion of the Court.

This case presents the question whether the use of a thermal-imaging device aimed at a private home from a public street to detect relative amounts of heat within the home constitutes a 'search' within the meaning of the Fourth Amendment.

In 1991 Agent William Elliott of the United States Department of the Interior came to suspect that marijuana was being grown in the home belonging to petitioner Danny Kyllo, part of a triplex on Rhododendron Drive in Florence, Oregon. Indoor marijuana growth typically requires high-intensity lamps. In order to determine whether an amount of heat was emanating from petitioner's home consistent with the use of such lamps, at 3:20 A.M. on January 16, 1992, Agent Elliott and Dan Haas used an Agema Thermovision 210 thermal imager to scan the triplex. Thermal imagers detect infrared radiation, which virtually all objects emit but which is not visible to the naked eye. The imager converts radiation into images based on relative warmth—black is cool, white is hot, shades of gray connote relative differences; in that respect, it operates somewhat like a video camera showing heat images. The scan of Kyllo's home took only a few minutes and was performed from the passenger seat of Agent Elliott's vehicle across the street from the front of the house and also from the street in back of the house. The scan showed that the roof over the garage and a side wall of petitioner's home were relatively hot compared to the rest of the home and substantially warmer than neighboring homes in the triplex. Agent Elliott concluded that petitioner was using halide lights to grow marijuana in his house, which indeed he was. Based on tips from informants, utility bills, and the thermal imaging, a Federal Magistrate Judge issued a warrant authorizing a search of petitioner's home, and the agents found an indoor growing operation involving more than 100 plants. Petitioner was indicted on one count of manufacturing marijuana, in violation of 21 U.S.C. §841(a)(1). He unsuccessfully moved to suppress the evidence seized from his home and then entered a conditional guilty plea.

* * *

The present case involves officers on a public street engaged in more than naked-eye surveillance of a home. We have previously reserved judgment as to how much technological enhancement of ordinary perception from such a vantage point, if any, is too much. While we upheld enhanced aerial photography of an industrial complex in *Dow Chemical*, we noted that we found it important that this is not an area immediately adjacent to a private home, where privacy expectations are most heightened.

It would be foolish to contend that the degree of privacy secured to citizens by the Fourth Amendment has been entirely unaffected by the advance of technology. For example, as the cases discussed above make clear, the technology

enabling human flight has exposed to public view (and hence, we have said, to official observation) uncovered portions of the house and its curtilage that once were private. The question we confront today is what limits there are upon this power of technology to shrink the realm of guaranteed privacy.

The *Katz* test—whether the individual has an expectation of privacy that society is prepared to recognize as reasonable—has often been criticized as circular, and hence subjective and unpredictable. While it may be difficult to refine *Katz* when the search of areas such as telephone booths, automobiles, or even the curtilage and uncovered portions of residences are at issue, in the case of the search of the interior of homes—the prototypical and hence most commonly litigated area of protected privacy—there is a ready criterion, with roots deep in the common law, of the minimal expectation of privacy that exists, and that is acknowledged to be reasonable. To withdraw protection of this minimum expectation would be to permit police technology to erode the privacy guaranteed by the Fourth Amendment. We think that obtaining by sense-enhancing technology any information regarding the interior of the home that could not otherwise have been obtained without physical "intrusion into a constitutionally protected area," constitutes a search—at least where (as here) the technology in question is not in general public use. This assures preservation of that degree of privacy against government that existed when the Fourth Amendment was adopted. On the basis of this criterion, the information obtained by the thermal imager in this case was the product of a search.

The Government maintains, however, that the thermal imaging must be upheld because it detected "only heat radiating from the external surface of the house." The dissent makes this its leading point, contending that there is a fundamental difference between what it calls "off-the-wall" observations and "through-the-wall surveillance." But just as a thermal imager captures only heat emanating from a house, so also a powerful directional microphone picks up only sound emanating from a house—and a satellite capable of scanning from many miles away would pick up only visible light emanating from a house. We rejected such a mechanical interpretation of the

Fourth Amendment in *Katz*, where the eavesdropping device picked up only sound waves that reached the exterior of the phone booth. Reversing that approach would leave the homeowner at the mercy of advancing technology—including imaging technology that could discern all human activity in the home. While the technology used in the present case was relatively crude, the rule we adopt must take account of more sophisticated systems that are already in use or in development . . . .

The Government also contends that the thermal imaging was constitutional because it did not "detect private activities occurring in private areas." It points out that in *Dow Chemical* we observed that the enhanced aerial photography did not reveal any "intimate details." *Dow Chemical*, however, involved enhanced aerial photography of an industrial complex, which does not share the Fourth Amendment sanctity of the home. The Fourth Amendment's protection of the home has never been tied to measurement of the quality or quantity of information obtained. In *Silverman*, for example, we made clear that any physical invasion of the structure of the home, "by even a fraction of an inch," was too much, and there is certainly no exception to the warrant requirement for the officer who barely cracks open the front door and sees nothing but the nonintimate rug on the vestibule floor. In the home, our cases show, all details are intimate details, because the entire area is held safe from prying government eyes. Thus, in *Karo*, the only thing detected was a can of ether in the home; and in *Arizona v. Hicks*, the only thing detected by a physical search that went beyond what officers lawfully present could observe in "plain view" was the registration number of a phonograph turntable. These were intimate details because they were details of the home, just as was the detail of how warm—or even how relatively warm—*Kyllo* was heating his residence.

Limiting the prohibition of thermal imaging to "intimate details" would not only be wrong in principle; it would be impractical in application, failing to provide "a workable accommodation between the needs of law enforcement and the interests protected by the Fourth Amendment." To begin with, there is no necessary connection between the sophistication of the surveillance equipment and the "intimacy" of the details that it observes—which means that one cannot say (and the police cannot be assured) that use of the relatively crude equipment at issue here will always be lawful. The Agema Thermovision 210 might disclose, for example, at what hour each night the lady of the house takes her daily sauna and bath—a detail that many would consider "intimate"; and a much more sophisticated system might detect nothing more intimate than the fact that someone left a closet light on. We could not, in other words, develop a rule approving only that through-the-wall surveillance which identifies objects no smaller than 36 by 36 inches, but would have to develop a jurisprudence specifying which home activities are "intimate" and which are not. And even when (if ever) that jurisprudence were fully developed, no police officer would be able to know in advance whether his through-the-wall surveillance picks up "intimate" details—and thus would be unable to know in advance whether it is constitutional.

* * *

We have said that the Fourth Amendment draws "a firm line at the entrance to the house." That line, we think, must be not only firm but also bright—which requires clear specification of those methods of surveillance that require a warrant. While it is certainly possible to conclude from the videotape of the thermal imaging that occurred in this case that no "significant" compromise of the homeowner's privacy has occurred, we must take the long view, from the original meaning of the Fourth Amendment forward. "The Fourth Amendment is to be construed in the light of what was deemed an unreasonable search and seizure when it was adopted, and in a manner which will conserve public interests as well as the interests and rights of individual citizens." Where, as here, the Government uses a device that is not in general public use, to explore details of the home that would previously have been unknowable without physical intrusion, the surveillance is a "search" and is presumptively unreasonable without a warrant.

Since we hold the Thermovision imaging to have been an unlawful search, it will remain for the District Court to determine whether, without the evidence it provided, the search warrant issued in this case was supported by probable cause—and if not, whether there is any other basis for supporting admission of the evidence that the search pursuant to the warrant produced.

The judgment of the Court of Appeals is reversed; the case is remanded for further proceedings consistent with this opinion.

It is so ordered.

UNITED STATES
v.
MCINTYRE

582 F.2d 1221 (9th Cir. 1978)

[Citations and footnotes omitted.]

GOODWIN, Circuit Judge:

McIntyre and VanBuskirk appeal their convictions for violating and conspiring to violate 18 U.S.C. § 2511(1)(a) and (b). VanBuskirk was Chief of Police of Globe, Arizona, and McIntyre was a Lieutenant in that department. The Assistant Chief of Police was Robert McGann. VanBuskirk and McIntyre suspected McGann of leaking damaging information to political enemies of VanBuskirk. McIntyre also suspected McGann of narcotics trafficking.

On several occasions, McIntyre met with Officers Johnson and Ambos to discuss ways of confirming his suspicions concerning McGann. The three agreed that electronic surveillance of McGann's office would best serve that purpose. McIntyre and Johnson also met with VanBuskirk in a city park near the police station. During this meeting VanBuskirk approved of the plan to "bug" McGann's office if it "could be done legally".

Several days after the meeting in the park, Officer Johnson placed a microphone and transmitter in a briefcase in McGann's office. Johnson and Ambos attempted to monitor McGann's conversations. They were able to overhear only a brief exchange between McGann and Sergeant Gary Stucker. Johnson returned to McGann's office after 45 minutes and removed the briefcase, ending the surveillance. At no time did any of the

participants seek a court order or McGann's consent for the surveillance.

* * *

Title III prohibits the interception of "wire" and "oral communications". For purposes of §§ 2511 et seq., § 2510(2) defines "oral communication" as "any oral communication uttered by a person exhibiting an expectation that such communication is not subject to interception under circumstances justifying such expectation".

The legislative history behind § 2510(2) reflects Congress's intent that *Katz v. United States* serve as a guide to define communications that are uttered under circumstances justifying an expectation of privacy. Guided by *Katz*, our inquiry is whether the communications overheard by Johnson and Ambos were uttered by a person (1) who has a subjective expectation of privacy, and (2) whose expectation was objectively reasonable.

There is no question that McGann had a subjective expectation of privacy. At trial McGann testified that he believed that normal conversations in his office could not be overheard, even when the doors to his office were open.

Defendants contend, however, that McGann's expectation of privacy was objectively unreasonable. First, they say that McGann could not reasonably expect to be free from "administrative internal affairs investigations". Second, they say that the architecture of McGann's office made his expectation of privacy unreasonable. Both contentions must fail.

A police officer is not, by virtue of his profession, deprived of the protection of the Constitution. This protection extends to warrantless eavesdropping to overhear conversation from an official's desk and office.

An established regulatory scheme or specific office practice may, under some circumstances, diminish an employee's reasonable expectation of privacy. But defendants here have failed to show a regulatory scheme or specific office practice which would have alerted McGann to expect random monitoring of his conversations. Evidence that other, unconsented, "bugging" may have occurred within the Globe Police Department does not alter our conclusion. Sporadic illegal eavesdropping does not create a regulatory scheme or a specific office practice. In any event, the "bugging" here cannot be termed an "administrative" search.

Neither can the "bugging" be justified as an "internal affairs investigation". An employer may search the work area of an employee for misplaced property or, in some circumstances, to supervise work performance. But defendants' purpose in "bugging" McGann was, at least in part, to confirm their suspicion that he was involved in external crime (narcotics). Therefore, the "bugging" was not an "internal affairs investigation," but part of a criminal investigation, the area of activity for which [the Wiretap Act] was written.

Defendants next argue that the physical characteristics of McGann's office made his expectation of privacy unreasonable. At trial defendants introduced evidence to show that at the time of the "bugging" McGann's office doors were open, and that a records clerk worked fifteen feet away in an adjacent room.

We cannot accept the argument that an open door made McGann's expectation of privacy unreasonable. Johnson testified that conversations in McGann's office were difficult to overhear even with the office doors open. As noted previously, McGann believed his office conversations to be private. A business office need not be sealed to offer its occupant a reasonable degree of privacy. The evidence supported a finding that McGann had a reasonable expectation of privacy in his office. It follows that the conversation attempted to be overheard by Johnson and Ambos between McGann and Sergeant Stucker was an "oral communication" within the meaning of 18 U.S.C. § 2510(2).

* * *

Affirmed.

UNITED STATES
v.
TURNER

209 F.3d 1198 (10th Cir. 2000)

[Citations and footnotes omitted.]

STEPHEN H. ANDERSON, Circuit Judge.

* * *

On November 7, 1998, Wyoming Highway Patrolman Joe Ryle stopped Turner's car on state highway 85 because he observed a severe crack in the windshield and front end damage affecting a headlight. Upon request, Turner produced a driver's license and registration, but not proof of insurance. Ryle asked Turner to accompany him to the patrol car to discuss the reason for the stop. While in the front seat of the patrol car, Turner told Ryle that he was currently on parole.

Ryle returned Turner's documents and issued Turner a citation for not having proof of insurance. He asked Turner if he had any drugs, guns, or large amounts of cash in the car. Turner replied, "no." R. Ryle then asked for and received Turner's consent to search his car. Ryle asked Turner to sit in the back of the patrol car "for safety reasons," while Ryle conducted the search. Ryle went back to Turner's car, asked the passenger, Crystal Grooms, to exit the vehicle, and received her consent to search the car. Ryle told her that she could remain outside, "but it was safer if she sat in the [patrol] vehicle." Grooms then joined Turner in the back of the patrol car, leaving the door slightly open. Unknown to them, Ryle had activated a tape recorder with a microphone installed between the patrol car's roll bar and roof. The microphone recorded the conversation between Turner and Grooms while Ryle made a cursory search of Turner's car.

Following the search, Ryle asked Turner and Grooms to return to their car. He then retrieved and played back the recording of their conversation. Ryle testified that on the recording, "I heard Ms. Grooms state that he's going to find the guns; and I heard Mr. Turner say . . . no, he's not; he's not going to spend the time looking through all of that stuff [in the car]." Turner testified that Ryle accurately described the conversation. About this time, dispatch informed Ryle that Turner was on parole for aggravated robbery. Ryle called for backup since, as a felon, Turner could not lawfully possess a gun. When another officer arrived, Ryle handcuffed Turner and told him that he was being detained. Ryle took Turner and his car to the sheriff's office, where a search of the car revealed four firearms and a small quantity of marijuana. Ryle arrested and Mirandized Turner, at which time Turner admitted he owned the guns.

The district court held a hearing on February 24, 1999, to consider Turner's motion to suppress his statements and the physical evidence seized from the vehicle. On March 1, 1999, the district court denied the motion.

* * *

Turner argues that the recording of his conversation in the patrol car violated Title III of the Omnibus Crime Control and Safe Streets Act of 1968, 18 U.S.C. §§ 2510–2522 ("Title III"). Title III governs the interception by the government and private parties of wire, electronic, and oral communications. A court may not admit as evidence any protected oral communications intercepted in violation of Title III.

Title III protects oral communications "uttered by a person exhibiting an expectation that such communication is not subject to interception under circumstances justifying such expectation." The legislative history ... shows that Congress intended this definition to parallel the "reasonable expectation of privacy test" articulated by the Supreme Court in *Katz v. United States*. In *Longoria*, we stated that "for [the Wiretap Act] to apply, the court must conclude: (1) the defendant had an actual, subjective expectation of privacy—i.e., that his communications were not subject to interception; and (2) the defendant's expectation is one society would objectively consider reasonable."

Because the government stipulated that Turner had a subjective expectation of privacy, we need only address the second, objective prong: whether society would consider Turner's expectation of privacy to be reasonable. We conclude that under Title III or the Fourth Amendment society is not prepared to recognize an expectation that communications in a patrol car, under facts presented here, are not subject to interception.

Turner argues that his expectation of privacy is reasonable because of the circumstances: he was not in custody or being threatened with arrest, and the officer deliberately represented the car as a safe haven. We are not persuaded that either consideration is controlling. A police car is an official vehicle, used here for law enforcement purposes. We agree with the Eleventh Circuit in McKinnon that whether an individual is in custody does not materially affect an expectation of privacy in a police car. Furthermore, in addition to the status of the police vehicle, the practical realities of the situation should be apparent to occupants. Patrol cars bristle with electronics, including microphones to a dispatcher, possible video recording with audio pickup, and other electronic and recording devices.

As to his next argument, Turner contends that Officer Ryle's statements to him and Grooms that they should sit in the car for their safety created an expectation of a safe haven. Turner argues that a police car may be used as an ambulance, a roadblock, or for other purposes, and in those varied functions, occupants would be entitled to an expectation of privacy. We need not address those hypotheticals. Here, Ryle was directly involved in a law enforcement function. He made a legitimate law enforcement traffic stop and conducted a proper search. . . .

For the foregoing reasons, we AFFIRM the district court's denial of Turner's motion to suppress.

UNITED STATES
v.
WILLOUGHBY

860 F.2d 15 (2d Cir. 1988)

[Citations and footnotes omitted.]

[Quintin was convicted of armed bank robbery. The present prosecution arises out of his efforts, with Willoughby, to prevent certain witnesses from testifying at their trial. While he was an inmate in the New York Metropolitan Correctional Center ("MCC"), waiting trial on the bank robbery charges, Quintin called Willoughby at his home, using a correctional facility telephone that was available to inmates. Pursuant to MCC policy, all inmate calls made from correctional institutional telephones, except properly placed calls to attorneys, were automatically recorded. Quintin's call to Willoughby was thus recorded. During the conversation, Quintin and Willoughby discussed having a hit man kill a certain witness to prevent him from testifying. Quintin told Willoughby he would call back the next day and give him the hit man's telephone number. He urged Willoughby to make arrangements quickly, stating that "we gotta do it this week."

On the basis of these events, Quinton and Willoughby were indicted for obstruction of justice and conspiracy to tamper with witnesses. They moved to suppress the tape of their telephone conversation on the grounds that the taping violated the Wiretap Act ("Title III").]

KEARSE, Circuit Judge:

* * *

Title III generally prohibits the intentional interception of wire communications, including telephone conversations, in the absence of authorization by court order. The prohibition against interception does not apply, however, when "one of the parties to the communication has given prior consent to such interception." Such consent may be express or implied. In the prison setting, when the institution has advised inmates that their telephone calls will be monitored and has prominently posted a notice that their "use of institutional telephones constitutes consent to this monitoring," the inmates' use of those telephones constitutes implied consent to the monitoring within the meaning of Title III.

In the present case, the record established that MCC had a policy and practice of automatically recording and randomly monitoring all inmate calls, other than those properly placed to an attorney, made on institutional telephones. Inmates received ample notice of this practice. First, they were advised of the practice at orientation lectures upon their arrival at MCC; Quintin attended such a lecture in March 1987. In addition, MCC posted above each telephone available to inmates a bilingual sign, the English version of which read:

NOTICE

The Bureau of Prisons reserves the authority to monitor conversations on this telephone. Your use of institutional telephones constitutes consent to this monitoring. A properly placed telephone call to an attorney is not monitored.

In these circumstances the district court could properly find that Quintin impliedly consented to the monitoring and taping of his call to Willoughby.

Finally, Quintin was given a form that stated as follows:

The Bureau of Prisons reserve es the authority to monitor (this includes recording) conversations on any telephone located within its institutions, said monitoring to be done to preserve the security and orderly management of the institution and to protect the public. An inmate's use of institutional telephones constitutes consent to this monitoring.

Just above a line for the signature of the inmate, the form included the statement, "I understand that telephone calls I make from institution telephones may be monitored and recorded." Quintin signed the form on March 5, 1987. This sufficed to support a finding that Quintin expressly consented to the taping. We conclude that the court properly rejected Quintin's Title III contention.

The court also properly rejected the Title III arguments made on behalf of Willoughby. Whether or not Willoughby himself consented to the interception, the consent of Quintin alone, as a party to the conversation, sufficed to avoid the prohibitions of Title III. 18 U.S.C. § 2511(2)(c) (interception not prohibited when "one" of the parties to the communication has consented).

* * *

CONCLUSION

The judgments of conviction are affirmed.

UNITED STATES CODE ANNOTATED TITLE 18. CRIMES AND CRIMINAL PROCEDURE

PART I.   CRIMES

Chapter 121.   Stored Wire and Electronic Communications and Transactional Records Access

§ 2703. Required disclosure of customer communications or records

(a) Contents of wire or electronic communications in electronic storage. A governmental entity may require the disclosure by a provider of electronic communication service of the contents of a wire or electronic communication, that is in electronic storage in an electronic communications system for one hundred and eighty days or less, only pursuant to a warrant issued using the procedures described in the Federal Rules of Criminal Procedure by a court with jurisdiction over the offense under investigation or equivalent State warrant. A governmental entity may require the disclosure by a provider of electronic communications services of the contents of a wire or electronic communication that has been in electronic storage in an electronic communications system for more than one hundred and eighty days by the means available under subsection (b) of this section.

(b) Contents of wire or electronic communications in a remote computing service. (1) A governmental entity may require a provider of remote computing service to disclose the contents of any wire or electronic communication to which this paragraph is made applicable by paragraph (2) of this subsection

(A) without required notice to the subscriber or customer, if the governmental entity obtains a warrant issued using the procedures described in the Federal Rules of Criminal Procedure by a court with jurisdiction over the offense under investigation or equivalent State warrant; or

(B) with prior notice from the governmental entity to the subscriber or customer if the governmental entity–

(i) uses an administrative subpoena authorized by a Federal or State statute or a Federal or State grand jury or trial subpoena; or

(ii) obtains a court order for such disclosure under subsection (d) of this section; except that delayed notice may be given pursuant to section 2705 of this title.

(2) Paragraph (1) is applicable with respect to any wire or electronic communication that is held or maintained on that service

(A) on behalf of, and received by means of electronic transmission from (or created by means of computer processing of communications received by means of electronic transmission from), a subscriber or customer of such remote computing service; and

(B) solely for the purpose of providing storage or computer processing services to such subscriber or customer, if the provider is not authorized to access the contents of any such communications for purposes of providing any services other than storage or computer processing.

(c) Records concerning electronic communication service or remote computing service. (1) A governmental entity may require a provider of

electronic communication service or remote computing service to disclose a record or other information pertaining to a subscriber to or customer of such service (not including the contents of communications) only when the governmental entity

(A) obtains a warrant issued using the procedures described in the Federal Rules of Criminal Procedure by a court with jurisdiction over the offense under investigation or equivalent State warrant;

(B) obtains a court order for such disclosure under subsection (d) of this section;

(C) has the consent of the subscriber or customer to such disclosure;

(D) submits a formal written request relevant to a law enforcement investigation concerning telemarketing fraud for the name, address, and place of business of a subscriber or customer of such provider, which subscriber or customer is engaged in telemarketing (as such term is defined in section 2325 of this title); or

(E) seeks information under paragraph (2).

(2) A provider of electronic communication service or remote computing service shall disclose to a governmental entity the

(A) name;

(B) address;

(C) local and long distance telephone connection records, or records of session times and durations;

(D) length of service (including start date) and types of service utilized;

(E) telephone or instrument number or other subscriber number or identity, including any temporarily assigned network address; and

(F) means and source of payment for such service (including any credit card or bank account number), of a subscriber to or customer of such service when the governmental entity uses an administrative subpoena authorized by a Federal or State statute or a Federal or State grand jury or trial subpoena or any means available under paragraph (1).

(3) A governmental entity receiving records or information under this subsection is not required to provide notice to a subscriber or customer.

(d) Requirements for court order. A court order for disclosure under subsection (b) or (c) may be issued by any court that is a court of competent jurisdiction and shall issue only if the governmental entity offers specific and articulable facts showing that there are reasonable grounds to believe that the contents of a wire or electronic communication, or the records or other information sought, are relevant and material to an ongoing criminal investigation. In the case of a State governmental authority, such a court order shall not issue if prohibited by the law of such State. A court issuing an order pursuant to this section, on a motion made promptly by the service provider, may quash or modify such order, if the information or records requested are unusually voluminous in nature or compliance with such order otherwise would cause an undue burden on such provider.

(e) No cause of action against a provider disclosing information under this chapter. No cause of action shall lie in any court against any provider of wire or electronic communication service, its officers, employees, agents, or other specified persons for providing information, facilities, or assistance in accordance with the terms of a court order, warrant, subpoena, statutory authorization, or certification under this chapter.

(f) Requirement to preserve evidence.

(1) In general. A provider of wire or electronic communication services or a remote computing service, upon the request of a governmental entity, shall take all necessary steps to preserve records and other evidence in its possession pending the issuance of a court order or other process.

(2) Period of retention. Records referred to in paragraph (1) shall be retained for a period of 90 days, which shall be extended for an additional 90- day period upon a renewed request by the governmental entity.

(g) Presence of officer not required. Notwithstanding section 3105 of this title, the presence of an officer shall not be required for service or execution of a search warrant issued in accordance with this chapter requiring disclosure by a provider of electronic communications service or remote computing service of the contents of communications or records or other information pertaining to a subscriber to or customer of such service.

Cases Relating to Chapter 6

Interrogations and Confessions

ARIZONA
v.
FULMINANTE

499 U.S. 279, 111 S. Ct. 1246,
113 L. Ed. 2d 302 (1991)

[Fulminante was suspected of molesting and murdering a child in Arizona. While he was imprisoned in Florida on an unrelated offense, he shared a cell with Sarivola, who unbeknownst to him was an FBI informant. Sarivola made repeated attempts to influence the defendant to confess to the murder, but the defendant repeatedly denied involvement. Word of the heinous murder spread within the jail community and other inmates began to threaten Fulminante. Sarivola told Fulminante that he could protect the him, but that Fulminante would first have to tell him the truth about the murder. Fulminante then admitted to killing the child. Arizona tried Fulminante for murder and the confession was offered into evidence.]

Justice White delivered the opinion of the court.

* * *

We deal first with the State's contention that the court below erred in holding Fulminante's confession to have been coerced. . . . [T]he Arizona Supreme Court stated that a "determination regarding the voluntariness of a confession . . . must be viewed in a totality of the circumstances," and under that standard plainly found that Fulminante's statement to Sarivola had been coerced.

In applying the totality of the circumstances test to determine that the confession to Sarivola was

coerced, the Arizona Supreme Court focused on a number of relevant facts. First, the court noted that "because [Fulminante] was an alleged child murderer, he was in danger of physical harm at the hands of other inmates." In addition, Sarivola was aware that Fulminante had been receiving " 'rough treatment from the guys.' " Using his knowledge of these threats, Sarivola offered to protect Fulminante in exchange for a confession to Jeneane's murder, and "[i]n response to Sarivola's offer of protection, [Fulminante] confessed." Agreeing with Fulminante that "Sarivola's promise was 'extremely coercive,' " the Arizona court declared: "[T]he confession was obtained as a direct result of extreme coercion and was tendered in the belief that the defendant's life was in jeopardy if he did not confess. This is a true coerced confession in every sense of the word."

* * *

Although the question is a close one, we agree with the Arizona Supreme Court's conclusion that Fulminante's confession was coerced. The Arizona Supreme Court found a credible threat of physical violence unless Fulminante confessed. Our cases have made clear that a finding of coercion need not depend upon actual violence by a government agent; a credible threat is sufficient. As we have said, "coercion can be mental as well as physical, and . . . the blood of the accused is not the only hallmark of an unconstitutional inquisition." As in *Payne*, where the Court found that a confession was coerced because the interrogating police officer had promised that if the accused confessed, the officer would protect the accused from an angry mob outside the jailhouse door, so too here, the Arizona Supreme Court found that it was fear of physical violence, absent protection from his friend (and Government agent) Sarivola, which motivated Fulminante to confess. Accepting the Arizona court's finding, permissible on this record, that there was a credible threat of physical violence, we agree with its conclusion that Fulminante's will was overborne in such a way as to render his confession the product of coercion.

KAUPP
v.
TEXAS

539 U.S. 623, 123 S. Ct. 1843, 155 L. Ed. 2d 814 (2003)

PER CURIAM.

This case turns on the Fourth Amendment rule that a confession "obtained by exploitation of an illegal arrest" may not be used against a criminal defendant. After a 14-year-old girl disappeared in January 1999, the Harris County Sheriff's Department learned she had had a sexual relationship with her 19-year-old half brother, who had been in the company of petitioner Robert Kaupp, then 17 years old, on the day of the girl's disappearance. On January 26th, deputy sheriffs questioned the brother and Kaupp at headquarters; Kaupp was cooperative and was permitted to leave, but the brother failed a polygraph examination (his third such failure). Eventually he confessed that he had fatally stabbed his half sister and placed her body in a drainage ditch. He implicated Kaupp in the crime.

Detectives immediately tried but failed to obtain a warrant to question Kaupp. Detective Gregory Pinkins nevertheless decided (in his words) to "get [Kaupp] in and confront him with what [the brother] had said." In the company of two other plainclothes detectives and three uniformed officers, Pinkins went to Kaupp's house at approximately 3 a.m. on January 27th. After Kaupp's father let them in, Pinkins, with at least two other officers, went to Kaupp's bedroom, awakened him with a flashlight, identified himself, and said, "'we need to go and talk.' "Kaupp said "'Okay.' "The two officers then handcuffed Kaupp and led him, shoeless and dressed only in boxer shorts and a T-shirt, out of his house and into a patrol car. The State points to nothing in the record

indicating Kaupp was told that he was free to decline to go with the officers.

They stopped for 5 or 10 minutes where the victim's body had just been found, in anticipation of confronting Kaupp with the brother's confession, and then went on to the sheriff's headquarters. There, they took Kaupp to an interview room, removed his handcuffs, and advised him of his rights under *Miranda v. Arizona*. Kaupp first denied any involvement in the victim's disappearance, but 10 or 15 minutes into the interrogation, told of the brother's confession, he admitted having some part in the crime. He did not, however, acknowledge causing the fatal wound or confess to murder, for which he was later indicted.

* * *

A seizure of the person within the meaning of the Fourth and Fourteenth Amendments occurs when, "taking into account all of the circumstances surrounding the encounter, the police conduct would 'have communicated to a reasonable person that he was not at liberty to ignore the police presence and go about his business.' This test is derived from Justice Stewart's opinion in *United States v. Mendenhall* which gave several "[e]xamples of circumstances that might indicate a seizure, even where the person did not attempt to leave," including "the threatening presence of several officers, the display of a weapon by an officer, some physical touching of the person of the citizen, or the use of language or tone of voice indicating that compliance with the officer's request might be compelled."

Although certain seizures may be justified on something less than probable cause, we have never "sustained against Fourth Amendment challenge the involuntary removal of a suspect from his home to a police station and his detention there for investigative purposes ... absent probable cause or judicial authorization." Such involuntary transport to a police station for questioning is "sufficiently like arres[t] to invoke the traditional rule that arrests may constitutionally be made only on probable cause."

The State does not claim to have had probable cause here, and a straightforward application of the test just mentioned shows beyond cavil that Kaupp was arrested within the meaning of the Fourth Amendment, there being evidence of every one of the probative circumstances mentioned by Justice Stewart in *Mendenhall*. A 17-year-old boy was awakened in his bedroom at three in the morning by at least three police officers, one of whom stated " 'we need to go and talk.' "He was taken out in handcuffs, without shoes, dressed only in his underwear in January, placed in a patrol car, driven to the scene of a crime and then to the sheriff's offices, where he was taken into an interrogation room and questioned. This evidence points to arrest even more starkly than the facts in *Dunaway v. New York*. . . .

Since Kaupp was arrested before he was questioned, and because the State does not even claim that the sheriff's department had probable cause to detain him at that point, well-established precedent requires suppression of the confession unless that confession was "an act of free will [sufficient] to purge the primary taint of the unlawful invasion." Demonstrating such purgation is, of course, a function of circumstantial evidence, with the burden of persuasion on the State. Relevant considerations include observance of *Miranda*, "[t]he temporal proximity of the arrest and the confession, the presence of intervening circumstances, and, particularly, the purpose and flagrancy of the official misconduct."

The record before us shows that only one of these considerations, the giving of *Miranda* warnings, supports the State, and we held in *Brown* that "*Miranda* warnings, alone and per se, cannot always . . . break, for Fourth Amendment purposes, the causal connection between the illegality and the confession." All other factors point the opposite way. There is no indication from the record that any substantial time passed between Kaupp's removal from his home in handcuffs and his confession after only 10 or 15 minutes of interrogation. In the interim, he remained in his partially clothed state in the physical custody of a number of officers, some of whom, at least, were conscious that they lacked probable cause to arrest. In fact, the State has not even alleged "any meaningful intervening event" between the illegal arrest and Kaupp's confession. Unless, on remand, the State can point to testimony undisclosed on the record before us, and weighty enough to carry the State's burden despite the clear force of the evidence shown here, the confession must be suppressed.

The judgment of the State Court of Appeals is vacated, and the case is remanded for further proceedings not inconsistent with this opinion.

TITLE 18. CRIMES AND CRIMINAL PROCEDURE

§ 3501. Admissibility of confessions

(a) In any criminal prosecution brought by the United States or by the District of Columbia, a confession, as defined in subsection (e) hereof, shall be admissible in evidence if it is voluntarily given. Before such confession is received in evidence, the trial judge shall, out of the presence of the jury, determine any issue as to voluntariness. If the trial judge determines that the confession was voluntarily made it shall be admitted in evidence and the trial judge shall permit the jury to hear relevant evidence on the issue of voluntariness and shall instruct the jury to give such weight to the confession as the jury feels it deserves under all the circumstances.

(b) The trial judge in determining the issue of voluntariness shall take into consideration all the circumstances surrounding the giving of the confession, including
(1) the time elapsing between arrest and arraignment of the defendant making the confession, if it was made after arrest and before arraignment,
(2) whether such defendant knew the nature of the offense with which he was charged or of which he was suspected at the time of making the confession,
(3) whether or not such defendant was advised or knew that he was not required to make any statement and that any such statement could be used against him,
(4) whether or not such defendant had been advised prior to questioning of his right to the assistance of counsel; and
(5) whether or not such defendant was without the assistance of counsel when questioned and when giving such confession.
The presence or absence of any of the above-mentioned factors to be taken into consideration by the judge need not be conclusive on the issue of voluntariness of the confession.

(c) In any criminal prosecution by the United States or by the District of Columbia, a confession made or given by a person who is a defendant therein, while such person was under arrest or other detention in the custody of any law-enforcement officer or law-enforcement agency, shall not be inadmissible solely because of delay in bringing such person before a magistrate or other officer empowered to commit persons charged with offenses against the laws of the United States or of the District of Columbia if such confession is found by the trial judge to have been made voluntarily and if the weight to be given the confession is left to the jury and if such confession was made or given by such person within six hours immediately following his arrest or other detention: Provided, That the time limitation contained in this subsection shall not apply in any case in which the delay in bringing such person before such magistrate or other officer beyond such six-hour period is found by the trial judge to be reasonable considering the means of transportation and the distance to be traveled to the nearest available such magistrate or other officer.

MIRANDA
v.
ARIZONA

384 U.S. 436, 86 S. Ct. 1602, 16 L. Ed. 2d 694 (1966)

[On March 13, 1963, Ernesto Miranda was arrested at his home and taken in custody to a Phoenix police station. He was there identified by the complaining witness. The police then took him to "Interrogation Room No. 2" of the detective bureau, where he was questioned by two police officers. The officers admitted at trial that Miranda was not advised that he had a right to have an attorney present. Two hours later, the officers emerged from the interrogation room with a written confession signed by Miranda. At the top of the statement was a typed paragraph stating that the confession was made voluntarily, without threats or promises of immunity and "with full knowledge of my legal rights, understanding any statement I make may be used against me."

At his trial before a jury, the written confession was admitted into evidence over the objection of defense counsel, and the officers testified to the prior oral confession made by Miranda during the interrogation. Miranda was found guilty of kidnapping and rape. He was sentenced to 20 to 30 years' imprisonment on each count, the sentences to run concurrently. On appeal, the Supreme Court of Arizona held that Miranda's constitutional rights were not violated in obtaining the confession and affirmed the conviction. In reaching its decision, the court emphasized heavily the fact that Miranda did not specifically request counsel.]

MR. CHIEF JUSTICE WARREN delivered the opinion of the Court.

The cases before us raise questions which go to the roots of our concepts of American criminal jurisprudence: the restraints society must observe consistent with the Federal Constitution in prosecuting individuals for crime. More specifically, we deal with the admissibility of statements obtained from an individual who is subjected to custodial police interrogation and the necessity for procedures which assure that the individual is accorded his privilege under the Fifth Amendment to the Constitution not to be compelled to incriminate himself. We dealt with certain phases of this problem recently in *Escobedo v. Illinois*. . . .

* * *

We start here, as we did in *Escobedo*, with the premise that our holding is not an innovation in our jurisprudence, but an application of principles long recognized and applied in other settings. We have undertaken a thorough re-examination of the Escobedo decision and the principles it announced, and we reaffirm it. That case was but an explication of basic rights that are enshrined in our Constitution—that "No person ... shall be compelled in any criminal case to be a witness against himself," and that "the accused shall ... have the Assistance of Counsel"—rights which were put in jeopardy in this case through official overbearing. These precious rights were fixed in our Constitution only after centuries of persecution and struggle. And in the words of Chief Justice Marshall, they were secured "for ages to come, and designed to approach immortality as nearly as human institutions can approach it."

* * *

Our holding will be spelled out with some specificity in the pages which follow but briefly stated it is this: the prosecution may not use statements, whether exculpatory or inculpatory, stemming from custodial interrogation of the defendant unless it demonstrates the use of procedural safeguards effective to secure the privilege against self-incrimination. By custodial interrogation, we mean questioning initiated by law enforcement officers after a person has been taken into custody or otherwise deprived of his freedom of action in any significant way. As for the procedural safeguards to be employed, unless other fully effective means are devised to inform accused persons of their right of silence and to assure a continuous opportunity to exercise it, the following measures are required. Prior to any questioning, the person must be warned that he has a right to remain silent, that any statement he does make may be used as evidence against him, and that he has a right to the presence of an attorney, either retained or appointed. The defendant may waive effectuation of these rights, provided the waiver is made voluntarily, knowingly and intelligently. If, however, he indicates in any manner and at any stage of the process that he wishes to consult with an attorney before speaking there can be no questioning. Likewise, if the individual is alone and indicates in any manner that he does not wish to be interrogated, the police may not question him. The mere fact that he may have answered some questions or volunteered some statements on his own does not deprive him of the right to refrain from answering any further inquiries until he has consulted with an attorney and thereafter consents to be questioned.

* * *

An understanding of the nature and setting of this in-custody interrogation is essential to our decisions today. The difficulty in depicting what transpires at such interrogations stems from the fact that in this country they have largely taken place incommunicado. From extensive factual studies undertaken in the early 1930's, including the famous Wickersham Report to Congress by a Presidential Commission, it is clear that police violence and the "third degree" flourished at that time. In a series of cases decided by this Court long

after these studies, the police resorted to physical brutality—beating, hanging, whipping—and to sustained and protracted questioning incommunicado in order to extort confessions. . . .

* * *

Again, we stress that the modern practice of in-custody interrogation is psychologically rather than physically oriented. As we have stated before. "Since *Chambers v. Florida*, this Court has recognized that coercion can be mental as well as physical, and that the blood of the accused is not the only hallmark of an unconstitutional inquisition." Interrogation still takes place in privacy. Privacy results in secrecy and this in turn results in a gap in our knowledge as to what in fact goes on in the interrogation rooms. A valuable source of information about present police practices, however, may be found in various police manuals and texts which document procedures employed with success in the past, and which recommend various other effective tactics. These texts are used by law enforcement agencies themselves as guides. It should be noted that these texts professedly present the most enlightened and effective means presently used to obtain statements through custodial interrogation. By considering these texts and other data, it is possible to describe procedures observed and noted around the country.

* * *

To highlight the isolation and unfamiliar surroundings, the manuals instruct the police to display an air of confidence in the suspect's guilt and from outward appearance to maintain only an interest in confirming certain details. The guilt of the subject is to be posited as a fact. The interrogator should direct his comments toward the reasons why the subject committed the act, rather than court failure by asking the subject whether he did it. Like other men, perhaps the subject has had a bad family life, had an unhappy childhood, had too much to drink, had an unrequited desire for women. The officers are instructed to minimize the moral seriousness of the offense, to cast blame on the victim or on society. These tactics are designed to put the subject in a psychological state where his story is but an elaboration of what the police purport to know already—that he is guilty. Explanations to the contrary are dismissed and discouraged.

The texts thus stress that the major qualities an interrogator should possess are patience and perseverance. One writer describes the efficacy of these characteristics in this manner:

"In the preceding paragraphs emphasis has been placed on kindness and stratagems. The investigator will, however, encounter many situations where the sheer weight of his personality will be the deciding factor. Where emotional appeals and tricks are employed to no avail, he must rely on an oppressive atmosphere of dogged persistence. He must interrogate steadily and without relent, leaving the subject no prospect of surcease. He must dominate his subject and overwhelm him with his inexorable will to obtain the truth. He should interrogate for a spell of several hours pausing only for the subject's necessities in acknowledgment of the need to avoid a charge of duress that can be technically substantiated. In a serious case, the interrogation may continue for days, with the required intervals for food and sleep, but with no respite from the atmosphere of domination. It is possible in this way to induce the subject to talk without resorting to duress or coercion. The method should be used only when the guilt of the subject appears highly probable."

The manuals suggest that the suspect be offered legal excuses for his actions in order to obtain an initial admission of guilt. Where there is a suspected revenge-killing, for example, the interrogator may say:

"Joe, you probably didn't go out looking for this fellow with the purpose of shooting him. My guess is, however, that you expected something from him and that's why you carried a gun—for your own protection. You knew him for what he was, no good. Then when you met him he probably started using foul, abusive language and he gave some indication that he was about to pull a gun on you, and that's when you had to act to save your own life. That's about it, isn't it, Joe?"

Having then obtained the admission of shooting, the interrogator is advised to refer to circumstantial evidence which negates the self-defense explanation. This should enable him to secure the entire story. One text notes that "Even if he fails to do so, the inconsistency between the subject's original denial of the shooting and his present admission of at least doing the shooting will serve to deprive him of a self-defense 'out' at the time of trial."

When the techniques described above prove unavailing, the texts recommend they be alternated with a show of some hostility. One ploy often used has been termed the "friendly-unfriendly" or the "Mutt and Jeff" act:

". . . In this technique, two agents are employed. Mutt, the relentless investigator, who knows the subject is guilty and is not going to waste any time. He's sent a dozen men away for this crime and he's going to send the subject away for the full term. Jeff, on the other hand, is obviously a kindhearted man. He has a family himself. He has a brother who was involved in a little scrape like this. He disapproves of Mutt and his tactics and will arrange to get him off the case if the subject will cooperate. He can't hold Mutt off for very long. The subject would be wise to make a quick decision. The technique is applied by having both investigators present while Mutt acts out his role. Jeff may stand by quietly and demur at some of Mutt's tactics. When Jeff makes his plea for cooperation, Mutt is not present in the room."

The interrogators sometimes are instructed to induce a confession out of trickery. The technique here is quite effective in crimes which require identification or which run in series. In the identification situation, the interrogator may take a break in his questioning to place the subject among a group of men in a line-up. "The witness or complainant (previously coached, if necessary) studies the line-up and confidently points out the subject as the guilty party." Then the questioning resumes "as though there were now no doubt about the guilt of the subject." . . .

The manuals also contain instructions for police on how to handle the individual who refuses to discuss the matter entirely, or who asks for an attorney or relatives. The examiner is to concede him the right to remain silent. "This usually has a very undermining effect. First of all, he is disappointed in his expectation of an unfavorable reaction on the part of the interrogator. Secondly, a concession of this right to remain silent impresses the subject with the apparent fairness of his interrogator." After this psychological conditioning, however, the officer is told to point out the incriminating significance of the suspect's refusal to talk: "Joe, you have a right to remain silent. That's your privilege and I'm the last person in the world who'll try to take it away from you. If that's the way you want to leave this, O.K. But let me ask you this. Suppose you were in my shoes and I were in yours and you called me in to ask me about this and I told you, 'I don't want to answer any of your questions.' You'd think I had something to hide, and you'd probably be right in thinking that. That's exactly what I'll have to think about you, and so will everybody else. So let's sit here and talk this whole thing over."

Few will persist in their initial refusal to talk, it is said, if this monologue is employed correctly.

In the event that the subject wishes to speak to a relative or an attorney, the following advice is tendered: "(T)he interrogator should respond by suggesting that the subject first tell the truth to the interrogator himself rather than get anyone else involved in the matter. If the request is for an attorney, the interrogator may suggest that the subject save himself or his family the expense of any such professional service, particularly if he is innocent of the offense under investigation. The interrogator may also add, 'Joe, I'm only looking for the truth, and if you're telling the truth, that's it. You can handle this by yourself.' "

From these representative samples of interrogation techniques, the setting prescribed by the manuals and observed in practice becomes clear. In essence, it is this: "To be alone with the subject is essential to prevent distraction and to deprive him of any outside support. The aura of confidence in his guilt undermines his will to resist. He merely confirms the preconceived story the police seek to have him describe. Patience and persistence, at times relentless questioning, are employed. To obtain a confession, the interrogator must 'patiently maneuver himself or his quarry into a position from which the desired objective may be attained.'" When normal procedures fail to produce the needed result, the police may resort to deceptive stratagems such as giving false legal advice. It is important to keep the subject off balance, for example, by trading on his insecurity about himself or his surroundings. The police then persuade, trick, or cajole him out of exercising his constitutional rights.

* * *

In the cases before us today, given this background, we concern ourselves primarily with this interrogation atmosphere and the evils it can bring.

In No. 759, *Miranda v. Arizona*, the police arrested the defendant and took him to a special interrogation room where they secured a confession. . . .

In these cases, we might not find the defendants' statements to have been involuntary in traditional terms. Our concern for adequate safeguards to protect precious Fifth Amendment rights is, of course, not lessened in the slightest. In each of the cases, the defendant was thrust into an unfamiliar atmosphere and run through menacing police interrogation procedures. The potentiality for compulsion is forcefully apparent, for example, in *Miranda*, where the indigent Mexican defendant was a seriously disturbed individual with pronounced sexual fantasies. . . . To be sure, the records do not evince overt physical coercion or patent psychological ploys. The fact remains that in none of these cases did the officers undertake to afford appropriate safeguards at the outset of the interrogation to insure that the statements were truly the product of free choice.

It is obvious that such an interrogation environment is created for no purpose other than to subjugate the individual to the will of his examiner. This atmosphere carries its own badge of intimidation. To be sure, this is not physical intimidation, but it is equally destructive of human dignity. The current practice of incommunicado interrogation is at odds with one of our Nation's most cherished principles—that the individual may not be compelled to incriminate himself. Unless adequate protective devices are employed to dispel the compulsion inherent in custodial surroundings, no statement obtained from the defendant can truly be the product of his free choice.

* * *

Today, . . . there can be no doubt that the Fifth Amendment privilege is available outside of criminal court proceedings and serves to protect persons in all settings in which their freedom of action is curtailed in any significant way from being compelled to incriminate themselves. We have concluded that without proper safeguards the process of in-custody interrogation of persons suspected or accused of crime contains inherently compelling pressures which work to undermine the individual's will to resist and to compel him to speak where he would not otherwise do so freely. In order to combat these pressures and to permit a full opportunity to exercise the privilege against self-incrimination, the accused must be adequately and effectively apprised of his rights and the exercise of those rights must be fully honored.

... We encourage Congress and the States to continue their laudable search for increasingly effective ways of protecting the rights of the individual while promoting efficient enforcement of our criminal laws. However, unless we are shown other procedures which are at least as effective in apprising accused persons of their right of silence and in assuring a continuous opportunity to exercise it, the following safeguards must be observed.

At the outset, if a person in custody is to be subjected to interrogation, he must first be informed in clear and unequivocal terms that he has the right to remain silent. For those unaware of the privilege, the warning is needed simply to make them aware of it—the threshold requirement for an intelligent decision as to its exercise. More important, such a warning is an absolute prerequisite in overcoming the inherent pressures of the interrogation atmosphere. It is not just the subnormal or woefully ignorant who succumb to an interrogator's imprecations, whether implied or expressly stated, that the interrogation will continue until a confession is obtained or that silence in the face of accusation is itself damning and will bode ill when presented to a jury. Further, the warning will show the individual that his interrogators are prepared to recognize his privilege should he choose to exercise it.

The Fifth Amendment privilege is so fundamental to our system of constitutional rule and the expedient of giving an adequate warning as to the availability of the privilege so simple, we will not pause to inquire in individual cases whether the defendant was aware of his rights without a warning being given. Assessments of the knowledge the defendant possessed, based on information as to his age, education, intelligence, or prior contact with authorities, can never be more than speculation; a warning is a clear-cut fact. More important, whatever the background of the person interrogated, a warning at the time of the interrogation is indispensable to overcome its pressures and to insure that the individual knows he is free to exercise the privilege at that point in time.

The warning of the right to remain silent must be accompanied by the explanation that anything said can and will be used against the individual in court. This warning is needed in order to make him aware not only of the privilege, but also of the consequences of forgoing it. It is only through an awareness of these consequences that there can be any assurance of real understanding and intelligent exercise of the privilege. Moreover, this warning may serve to make the individual more acutely aware that he is faced with a phase of the adversary system that he is not in the presence of persons acting solely in his interest.

The circumstances surrounding in-custody interrogation can operate very quickly to overbear the will of one merely made aware of his privilege by his interrogators. Therefore, the right to have counsel present at the interrogation is indispensable to the protection of the Fifth Amendment privilege under the system we delineate today. Our aim is to assure that the individual's right to choose between silence and speech remains unfettered throughout the interrogation process. A once-stated warning, delivered by those who will conduct the interrogation, cannot itself suffice to that end among those who most require knowledge of their rights. A mere warning given by the interrogators is not alone sufficient to accomplish that end. Prosecutors themselves claim that the admonishment of the right to remain silent without more "will benefit only the recidivist and the professional." Even preliminary advice given to the accused by his own attorney can be swiftly overcome by the secret interrogation process. Thus, the need for counsel to protect the Fifth Amendment privilege comprehends not merely a right to consult with counsel prior to questioning, but also to have counsel present during any questioning if the defendant so desires.

The presence of counsel at the interrogation may serve several significant subsidiary functions as well. If the accused decides to talk to his interrogators, the assistance of counsel can mitigate the dangers of untrustworthiness. With a lawyer present the likelihood that the police will practice coercion is reduced, and if coercion is nevertheless exercised the lawyer can testify to it in court. The presence of a lawyer can also help to guarantee that the accused gives a fully accurate statement to the police and that the statement is rightly reported by the prosecution at trial.

An individual need not make a pre-interrogation request for a lawyer. While such request affirmatively secures his right to have one, his failure to ask for a lawyer does not constitute a waiver. No effective waiver of the right to counsel during interrogation can be recognized unless specifically made after the warnings we here delineate have been given. The accused who does not know his rights and therefore does not make a request may be the person who most needs counsel. . . .

* * *

Accordingly we hold that an individual held for interrogation must be clearly informed that he has the right to consult with a lawyer and to have the lawyer with him during interrogation under the system for protecting the privilege we delineate today. As with the warnings of the right to remain silent and that anything stated can be used in evidence against him, this warning is an absolute prerequisite to interrogation. No amount of circumstantial evidence that the person may have been aware of this right will suffice to stand in its stead. Only through such a warning is there ascertainable assurance that the accused was aware of this right.

If an individual indicates that he wishes the assistance of counsel before any interrogation occurs, the authorities cannot rationally ignore or deny his request on the basis that the individual does not have or cannot afford a retained attorney. The financial ability of the individual has no relationship to the scope of the rights involved here. The privilege against self-incrimination secured by the Constitution applies to all individuals. The need for counsel in order to protect the privilege exists for the indigent as well as the affluent. In fact, were we to limit these constitutional rights to those who can retain an attorney, our decisions today would be of little significance. The cases before us as well as the vast majority of confession cases with which we have dealt in the past involve those unable to retain counsel. While authorities are not required to relieve the accused of his poverty, they have the obligation not to take advantage of indigence in the administration of justice. Denial of counsel to the indigent at the time of interrogation while allowing an attorney to those who can afford one would be no more supportable by reason or logic than the similar situation at trial and on appeal struck down in *Gideon v. Wainwright.*

In order fully to apprise a person interrogated of the extent of his rights under this system then, it is necessary to warn him not only that he has the right to consult with an attorney, but also that if he is indigent a lawyer will be appointed to represent him. Without this additional warning, the admonition of the right to consult with counsel would often be understood as meaning only that he can consult with a lawyer if he has one or has the funds to obtain one. The warning of a right to counsel would be hollow if not couched in terms that would convey to the indigent—the person most often subjected to interrogation—the knowledge that he too has a right to have counsel present. As with the warnings of the right to remain silent and of the general right to counsel, only by effective and express explanation to the indigent of this right can there be assurance that he was truly in a position to exercise it.

Once warnings have been given, the subsequent procedure is clear. If the individual indicates in any manner, at any time prior to or during questioning, that he wishes to remain silent, the interrogation must cease. At this point he has shown that he intends to exercise his Fifth Amendment privilege; any statement taken after the person invokes his privilege cannot be other than the product of compulsion, subtle or otherwise. Without the right to cut off questioning, the setting of in-custody interrogation operates on the individual to overcome free choice in producing a statement after the privilege has been once invoked. If the individual states that he wants an attorney, the interrogation must cease until an attorney is present. At that time, the individual must have an opportunity to confer with the attorney and to have him present during any subsequent questioning. If the individual cannot obtain an attorney and he indicates that he wants one before speaking to police, they must respect his decision to remain silent. This does not mean, as some have suggested, that each police station must have a "station house lawyer" present at all times to advise prisoners. It does mean, however, that if police propose to interrogate a person they must make known to him that he is entitled to a lawyer and that if he cannot afford one, a lawyer will be provided for him prior to any interrogation. If authorities conclude that they will not provide counsel during a reasonable period of time in which investigation in the field is carried out, they may refrain from doing so without violating the person's Fifth Amendment privilege so long as they do not question him during that time.

If the interrogation continues without the presence of an attorney and a statement is taken, a heavy burden rests on the government to demonstrate that the defendant knowingly and intelligently waived his privilege against self-incrimination and his right to retained or appointed counsel. This Court has always set high standards of proof for the waiver of constitutional rights, and we reassert these standards as applied to in-custody interrogation. Since the State is responsible for establishing the isolated circumstances under which the interrogation takes place and has the only means of making available corroborated evidence of warnings given during incommunicado interrogation, the burden is rightly on its shoulders.

An express statement that the individual is willing to make a statement and does not want an attorney followed closely by a statement could constitute a waiver. But a valid waiver will not be presumed simply from the silence of the accused after warnings are given or simply from the fact that a confession was in fact eventually obtained. A statement we made in *Carnley v. Cochran*, is applicable here: "Presuming waiver from a silent record is impermissible. The record must show, or there must be an allegation and evidence which show, that an accused was offered counsel but intelligently and understandingly rejected the offer. Anything less is not waiver." Moreover, where in-custody interrogation is involved, there is no room for the contention that the privilege is waived if the individual answers some questions or gives some information on his own prior to invoking his right to remain silent when interrogated.

Whatever the testimony of the authorities as to waiver of rights by an accused, the fact of lengthy interrogation or incommunicado incarceration before a statement is made is strong evidence that the accused did not validly waive his rights. In these circumstances the fact that the individual eventually made a statement is consistent with the conclusion that the compelling influence of the interrogation finally forced him to do so. It is inconsistent with any notion of a voluntary relinquishment of the privilege. Moreover, any evidence that the accused was threatened, tricked, or cajoled into a waiver will, of course, show that the defendant did not voluntarily waive his privilege. The requirement of warnings and waiver of rights is a fundamental with respect to the Fifth Amendment privilege and not simply a preliminary ritual to existing methods of interrogation.

The warnings required and the waiver necessary in accordance with our opinion today are, in the absence of a fully effective equivalent, prerequisites to the admissibility of any statement made by a defendant. No distinction can be drawn between statements which are direct confessions and statements which amount to "admissions" of part or all of an offense. The privilege against self-incrimination protects the individual from being compelled to incriminate himself in any manner; it does not distinguish degrees of incrimination. Similarly, for precisely the same reason, no distinction may be drawn between inculpatory statements and statements alleged to be merely "exculpatory." If a statement made were in fact truly exculpatory it would, of course, never be used by the prosecution. In fact, statements merely intended to be exculpatory by the defendant are often used to impeach his testimony at trial or to demonstrate untruths in the statement given under interrogation and thus to prove guilt by implication. These statements are incriminating in any meaningful sense of the word and may not be used without the full warnings and effective waiver required for any other statement. In *Escobedo* itself, the defendant fully intended his accusation of another as the slayer to be exculpatory as to himself.

The principles announced today deal with the protection which must be given to the privilege against self-incrimination when the individual is first subjected to police interrogation while in custody at the station or otherwise deprived of his freedom of action in any significant way. It is at this point that our adversary system of criminal proceedings commences, distinguishing itself at the outset from the inquisitorial system recognized in some countries. Under the system of warnings we delineate today or under any other system which may be devised and found effective, the safeguards to be erected about the privilege must come into play at this point.

Our decision is not intended to hamper the traditional function of police officers in investigating crime. When an individual is in custody on probable cause, the police may, of course, seek out evidence in the field to be used at trial against him.

Such investigation may include inquiry of persons not under restraint. General on-the-scene questioning as to facts surrounding a crime or other general questioning of citizens in the fact-finding process is not affected by our holding. It is an act of responsible citizenship for individuals to give whatever information they may have to aid in law enforcement. In such situations the compelling atmosphere inherent in the process of in-custody interrogation is not necessarily present.

In dealing with statements obtained through interrogation, we do not purport to find all confessions inadmissible. Confessions remain a proper element in law enforcement. Any statement given freely and voluntarily without any compelling influences is, of course, admissible in evidence. The fundamental import of the privilege while an individual is in custody is not whether he is allowed to talk to the police without the benefit of warnings and counsel, but whether he can be interrogated. There is no requirement that police stop a person who enters a police station and states that he wishes to confess to a crime, or a person who calls the police to offer a confession or any other statement he desires to make. Volunteered statements of any kind are not barred by the Fifth Amendment and their admissibility is not affected by our holding today.

To summarize, we hold that when an individual is taken into custody or otherwise deprived of his freedom by the authorities in any significant way and is subjected to questioning, the privilege against self-incrimination is jeopardized. Procedural safeguards must be employed to protect the privilege and unless other fully effective means are adopted to notify the person of his right of silence and to assure that the exercise of the right will be scrupulously honored, the following measures are required. He must be warned prior to any questioning that he has the right to remain silent, that anything he says can be used against him in a court of law, that he has the right to the presence of an attorney, and that if he cannot afford an attorney one will be appointed for him prior to any questioning if he so desires. Opportunity to exercise these rights must be afforded to him throughout the interrogation. After such warnings have been given, and such opportunity afforded him, the individual may knowingly and intelligently waive these rights and agree to answer questions or make a statement. But unless and until such warnings and waiver are demonstrated by the prosecution at trial, no evidence obtained as a result of interrogation can be used against him.

* * *

We turn now to these facts to consider the application to these cases of the constitutional principles discussed above. . . .

* * *

. . . From the testimony of the officers and by the admission of respondent, it is clear that Miranda was not in any way apprised of his right to consult with an attorney and to have one present during the interrogation, nor was his right not to be compelled to incriminate himself effectively protected in any other manner. Without these warnings the statements were inadmissible. The mere fact that he signed a statement which contained a typed-in clause stating that he had "full knowledge" of his "legal rights" does not approach the knowing and intelligent waiver required to relinquish constitutional rights.

* * *

Therefore, in accordance with the foregoing, the judgments of the Supreme Court of Arizona in No. 759, of the New York Court of Appeals in No. 760, and of the Court of Appeals for the Ninth Circuit in No. 761 are reversed. . . .

It is so ordered.

BERKEMER
v.
McCARTY

468 U.S. 420, 104 S. Ct. 3138, 82 L. Ed. 2d 317 (1985)

[Citations and footnotes omitted.]

[Trooper Williams pulled respondent's car over after observing him weaving in and out of traffic on an interstate highway. He asked respondent to get out of the car. Upon noticing that respondent was having difficulty standing, Trooper Williams decided to take him into custody, but did not inform him of this fact until after asking him whether he had been using intoxicants. Respondent replied that "he had consumed two beers and had smoked several joints of marijuana a short time before." Williams thereupon formally placed respondent under arrest and transported him in the patrol car to the Franklin County Jail. At no time did Williams administer Miranda warnings.]

JUSTICE MARSHALL delivered the opinion of the Court.

. . . [D]oes the roadside questioning of a motorist detained pursuant to a traffic stop constitute custodial interrogation for the purposes of the doctrine enunciated in Miranda?

* * *

. . . Respondent urges that it should, on the ground that *Miranda* by its terms applies whenever "a person has been taken into custody or otherwise deprived of his freedom of action in any significant way." Petitioner contends that a holding that every detained motorist must be advised of his rights before being questioned would constitute an unwarranted extension of the *Miranda* doctrine.

It must be acknowledged at the outset that a traffic stop significantly curtails the "freedom of action" of the driver and the passengers, if any, of the detained vehicle. Under the law of most States, it is a crime either to ignore a policeman's signal to stop one's car or, once having stopped, to drive away without permission. Certainly few motorists would feel free either to disobey a directive to pull over or to leave the scene of a traffic stop without being told they might do so. Partly for these reasons, we have long acknowledged that "stopping an automobile and detaining its occupants constitute a 'seizure' within the meaning of [the Fourth] Amendmen[t], even though the purpose of the stop is limited and the resulting detention quite brief."

However, we decline to accord talismanic power to the phrase in the *Miranda* opinion emphasized by respondent. Fidelity to the doctrine announced in *Miranda* requires that it be enforced strictly, but only in those types of situations in which the concerns that powered the decision are implicated. Thus, we must decide whether a traffic stop exerts upon a detained person pressures that sufficiently impair his free exercise of his privilege against self-incrimination to require that he be warned of his constitutional rights.

Two features of an ordinary traffic stop mitigate the danger that a person questioned will be induced "to speak where he would not otherwise do so freely," First, detention of a motorist pursuant to a traffic stop is presumptively temporary and brief. The vast majority of roadside detentions last only a few minutes. A motorist's expectations, when he sees a policeman's light flashing behind him, are that he will be obliged to spend a short period of time answering questions and waiting while the officer checks his license and registration, that he may then be given a citation, but that in the end he most likely will be allowed to continue on his way. In this respect, questioning incident to an ordinary traffic stop is quite different from stationhouse interrogation, which frequently is prolonged, and in which the detainee often is aware that questioning will continue until he provides his interrogators the answers they seek.

Second, circumstances associated with the typical traffic stop are not such that the motorist feels completely at the mercy of the police. To be sure, the aura of authority surrounding an armed, uniformed officer and the knowledge that the officer has some discretion in deciding whether to issue a citation, in combination, exert some pressure on the detainee to respond to questions. But other aspects of the situation substantially offset these forces. Perhaps most importantly, the typical traffic stop is public, at least to some degree. Passersby, on foot or in other cars, witness the interaction of officer and motorist. This exposure to public view both reduces the ability of an unscrupulous policeman to use illegitimate means to elicit self-incriminating statements and diminishes the motorist's fear that, if he does not cooperate, he will be subjected to abuse. The fact that the detained motorist typically is confronted by only one or at most two policemen further mutes his sense of vulnerability. In short, the atmosphere surrounding an ordinary traffic stop is substantially less "police dominated" than that surrounding the kinds of interrogation at issue in *Miranda* itself.

In both of these respects, the usual traffic stop is more analogous to a so-called "*Terry* stop," than to a formal arrest. Under the Fourth Amendment, we have held, a policeman who lacks probable cause but whose "observations lead him reasonably to suspect" that a particular person has committed, is committing, or is about to commit a crime, may detain that person briefly in order to "investigate the circumstances that provoke suspicion." "[T]he stop and inquiry must be 'reasonably related in scope to the justification for their initiation.' " Typically, this means that the officer may ask the detainee a moderate number of questions to determine his identity and to try to obtain information confirming or dispelling the officer's suspicions. But the detainee is not obliged to respond. And, unless the detainee's answers provide the officer with probable cause to arrest him, he must then be released. The comparatively non-threatening character of detentions of this sort explains the absence of any suggestion in our opinions that *Terry* stops are subject to the dictates of *Miranda*. The similarly noncoercive aspect of ordinary traffic stops prompts us to hold that persons temporarily detained pursuant to such stops are not "in custody" for the purposes of *Miranda*.

Respondent contends that to "exempt" traffic stops from the coverage of *Miranda* will open the way to widespread abuse. Policemen will simply delay formally arresting detained motorists, and will subject them to sustained and intimidating interrogation at the scene of their initial detention. . . .

We are confident that the state of affairs projected by respondent will not come to pass. It is settled that the safeguards prescribed by *Miranda* become applicable as soon as a suspect's freedom of action is curtailed to a "degree associated with formal arrest." If a motorist who has been detained pursuant to a traffic stop thereafter is subjected to treatment that renders him "in custody" for practical purposes, he will be entitled to the full panoply of protections prescribed by *Miranda*.

Admittedly, our adherence to the doctrine just recounted will mean that the police and lower courts will continue occasionally to have difficulty deciding exactly when a suspect has been taken into custody. Either a rule that *Miranda* applies to all traffic stops or a rule that a suspect need not be advised of his rights until he is formally placed under arrest would provide a clearer, more easily administered line. However, each of these two alternatives has drawbacks that make it unacceptable. The first would substantially impede the enforcement of the Nation's traffic laws—by compelling the police either to take the time to warn all detained motorists of their constitutional rights or to forgo use of self-incriminating statements made by those motorists—while doing little to protect citizens' Fifth Amendment rights. The second would enable the police to circumvent the constraints on custodial interrogations established by *Miranda*.

Turning to the case before us, we find nothing in the record that indicates that respondent should have been given *Miranda* warnings at any point prior to the time Trooper Williams placed him under arrest. For the reasons indicated above, we reject the contention that the initial stop of respondent's car, by itself, rendered him "in custody." And respondent has failed to demonstrate that, at any time between the initial stop and the arrest, he was subjected to restraints comparable to those associated with a formal arrest. Only a short period of time elapsed between the stop and the arrest. At no point during that interval was respondent informed that his detention would not be temporary. Although Trooper Williams apparently decided as soon as respondent stepped out of his car that respondent would be taken into custody and charged with a traffic offense, Williams never communicated his intention to respondent. A policeman's unarticulated plan has no bearing on the question whether a suspect was "in custody" at a particular time; the only relevant inquiry is how a reasonable man in the suspect's position would have understood his situation. Nor do other aspects of the interaction of Williams and respondent support the contention that respondent was exposed to "custodial interrogation" at the scene of the stop. From aught that appears in the stipulation of facts, a single police officer asked respondent a modest number of questions and requested him to perform a simple balancing test at a location visible to passing motorists. Treatment of this sort cannot fairly be characterized as the functional equivalent of formal arrest.

* * *

Accordingly, the judgment of the Court of Appeals is

Affirmed.
[Concurring opinion omitted.]

RHODE ISLAND
v.
INNIS

446 U.S. 291, 100 S. Ct. 1682, 64 L. Ed. 2d 297 (1980)

[Citations and footnotes omitted.]

[A taxicab driver who was robbed by a man with a sawed-off shotgun identified Innis from a picture shown him by police. Shortly thereafter, a patrolman spotted Innis on the street, arrested him, and advised him of his *Miranda* rights. Innis stated that he understood his rights and wanted to speak with a lawyer. He was then placed in a squad car to be driven to the police station, accompanied by three officers who were instructed not to question him. While en route to the station, two of the officers engaged in a conversation between themselves concerning the missing shotgun. One of the officers stated that there were "a lot of handicapped children running around in this area" because a school for such children was located nearby, and "God forbid one of them might find a weapon with shells and they might hurt themselves." Innis interrupted the conversation, stating that the officers should turn the car around so he could show them where the gun was located. Upon returning to the scene of the arrest, Innis was again advised of his *Miranda* rights, replied that he understood his rights, but that he "wanted to get the gun out of the way because of the kids in the area in the school." He then led the police to the shotgun. The shotgun was used as evidence at his trial which resulted in a conviction.]

MR. JUSTICE STEWART delivered the opinion of the Court.

In *Miranda v. Arizona*, the Court held that, once a defendant in custody asks to speak with a lawyer, all interrogation must cease until a lawyer is present. . . .

In the present case, the parties are in agreement that Innis was fully informed of his *Miranda* rights and that he invoked his *Miranda* right to counsel when he told Captain Leyden that he wished to consult with a lawyer. It is also uncontested that Innis was "in custody" while being transported to the police station.

The issue, therefore, is whether the respondent was "interrogated" by the police officers in violation of the respondent's undisputed right under Miranda to remain silent until he had consulted with a lawyer. In resolving this issue, we first define the term "interrogation" under *Miranda* before turning to a consideration of the facts of this case.

The starting point for defining "interrogation" in this context is, of course, the Court's *Miranda* opinion. There the Court observed that "[b]y custodial interrogation, we mean questioning initiated by law enforcement officers after a person has been taken into custody or otherwise deprived of his freedom of action in any significant way." This passage and other references throughout the opinion to "questioning" might suggest that the *Miranda* rules were to apply only to those police interrogation practices that involve express questioning of a defendant while in custody.

We do not, however, construe the *Miranda* opinion so narrowly. The concern of the Court in *Miranda* was that the "interrogation environment" created by the interplay of interrogation and custody would "subjugate the individual to the will of his examiner" and thereby undermine the privilege against compulsory self-incrimination. The police practices that evoked this concern included several that did not involve express questioning. For example, one of the practices discussed in *Miranda* was the use of line-ups in which a coached witness would pick the defendant as the perpetrator. This was designed to establish that the defendant was in fact guilty as a predicate for further interrogation. . . . The Court in *Miranda* also included in its survey of interrogation practices the use of psychological ploys, such as to "posi[t]" "the guilt of the subject," to "minimize the moral seriousness of the offense," and "to cast blame on the victim or on the society." It is clear that these techniques of persuasion, no less than express questioning, were thought, in a custodial setting, to amount to interrogation.

This is not to say, however, that all statements obtained by the police after a person has been taken into custody are to be considered the product of interrogation. As the Court in *Miranda* noted:

> Confessions remain a proper element in law enforcement. Any statement given freely and voluntarily without any compelling influences is, of course, admissible in evidence. The fundamental import of the privilege while an

individual is in custody is not whether he is allowed to talk to the police without the benefit of warnings and counsel, but whether he can be interrogated. . . . Volunteered statements of any kind are not barred by the Fifth Amendment and their admissibility is not affected by our holding today.

It is clear therefore that the special procedural safeguards outlined in *Miranda* are required not where a suspect is simply taken into custody, but rather where a suspect in custody is subjected to interrogation. "Interrogation," as conceptualized in the *Miranda* opinion, must reflect a measure of compulsion above and beyond that inherent in custody itself.

We conclude that the *Miranda* safeguards come into play whenever a person in custody is subjected to either express questioning or its functional equivalent. That is to say, the term "interrogation" under *Miranda* refers not only to express questioning, but also to any words or actions on the part of the police (other than those normally attendant to arrest and custody) that the police should know are reasonably likely to elicit an incriminating response from the suspect. The latter portion of this definition focuses primarily upon the perceptions of the suspect, rather than the intent of the police. This focus reflects the fact that the *Miranda* safeguards were designed to vest a suspect in custody with an added measure of protection against coercive police practices, without regard to objective proof of the underlying intent of the police. A practice that the police should know is reasonably likely to evoke an incriminating response from a suspect thus amounts to interrogation. But, since the police surely cannot be held accountable for the unforeseeable results of their words or actions, the definition of interrogation can extend only to words or actions on the part of police officers that they should have known were reasonably likely to elicit an incriminating response.

Turning to the facts of the present case, we conclude that the respondent was not "interrogated" within the meaning of *Miranda*. It is undisputed that the first prong of the definition of "interrogation" was not satisfied, for the conversation between Patrolmen Gleckman and McKenna included no express questioning of the respondent. Rather, that conversation was, at least in form, nothing more than a dialogue between the two officers to which no response from the respondent was invited.

Moreover, it cannot be fairly concluded that the respondent was subjected to the "functional equivalent" of questioning. It cannot be said, in short, that Patrolmen Gleckman and McKenna should have known that their conversation was reasonably likely to elicit an incriminating response from the respondent. There is nothing in the record to suggest that the officers were aware that the respondent was peculiarly susceptible to an appeal to his conscience concerning the safety of handicapped children. Nor is there anything in the record to suggest that the police knew that the respondent was unusually disoriented or upset at the time of his arrest.

The case thus boils down to whether, in the context of a brief conversation, the officers should have known that the respondent would suddenly be moved to make a self-incriminating response. Given the fact that the entire conversation appears to have consisted of no more than a few offhand remarks, we cannot say that the officers should have known that it was reasonably likely that Innis would so respond. This is not a case where the police carried on a lengthy harangue in the presence of the suspect. Nor does the record support the respondent's contention that, under the circumstances, the officers' comments were particularly "evocative." It is our view, therefore, that the respondent was not subjected by the police to words or actions that the police should have known were reasonably likely to elicit an incriminating response from him.

The Rhode Island Supreme Court erred, in short, in equating "subtle compulsion" with interrogation. That the officers' comments struck a responsive chord is readily apparent. Thus, it may be said, as the Rhode Island Supreme Court did say, that the respondent was subjected to "subtle compulsion." But that is not the end of the inquiry. It must also be established that a suspect's incriminating response was the product of words or actions on the part of the police that they should have known were reasonably likely to elicit an incriminating response. This was not established in the present case.

For the reasons stated, the judgment of the Supreme Court of Rhode Island is vacated, and the case is remanded to that court for further proceedings not inconsistent with this opinion.

It is so ordered.

[Concurring and dissenting opinions omitted.]

BENSON
v.
STATE

698 So. 2d 333 (Fla. Dist. Ct. App. 1997)

[Citations and footnotes omitted.]

[When making an arrest for crack cocaine, police observed Benson place something in his mouth and start chewing. Believing Benson had swallowed the cocaine, and knowing that swallowing too much crack can be lethal, one of the officers asked Benson how much crack he had eaten. Benson replied that he had eaten one rock. Benson had not been Mirandized prior to this admission.]

PARIENTE, J.

The issue we address in this appeal is one of first impression in Florida: whether an exception to the *Miranda* rule may arise where a suspect is questioned by police in order to address a life-threatening medical emergency. The question in this case stemmed from the officer's objectively reasonable concern, based on his personal observations, over an immediate threat to defendant's health. Under these narrow circumstances, we find that the failure to administer *Miranda* warnings before asking defendant how much crack cocaine he had swallowed did not require suppression of defendant's inculpatory response. Accordingly, we affirm the trial court's denial of the motion to suppress.

* * *

The state, while conceding that *Miranda* would otherwise apply, argues that the response should not be suppressed because the circumstances fall within the "public safety" exception to the *Miranda* rule set forth in *New York v. Quarles.* In *Quarles,* the defendant was arrested in a supermarket. Police believed that just before the arrest the defendant had discarded a loaded firearm inside the supermarket in a place where a third party could gain access. Without first administering the *Miranda* warnings, police questioned the defendant about the location of the gun. The defendant responded with an inculpatory statement.

The Supreme Court concluded that the statement need not be suppressed:

We believe that this case presents a situation where concern for public safety must be paramount to adherence to the literal language of the prophylactic rules enunciated in Miranda.

* * *

Recognizing that emergencies require split-second decisions, the Supreme Court declined to place officers ... in the untenable position of having to consider, often in a matter of seconds, whether it best serves society for them to ask the necessary questions without the *Miranda* warnings and render whatever probative evidence they uncover inadmissible, or for them to give the warnings in order to preserve the admissibility of evidence they might uncover but possibly damage or destroy their ability to ... neutralize the volatile situation confronting them. [The Court ruled that when a life-threatening emergency arises, the need for answers to questions in a situation posing a threat to the public safety outweighs the need for the prophylactic rule protecting the Fifth Amendment's privilege against self-incrimination.]

... Since *Quarles,* however, several state and federal courts have addressed and applied the "public safety" exception to *Miranda* in a variety of circumstances, including concern for the safety of victims and police officers. ... [T]he ninth circuit upheld the admission of the defendant's incriminating response because the "[officer's] question stemmed from an objectively reasonable need to protect himself from immediate danger."

* * *

An analogous exception to the *Miranda* rule pertinent to the facts of this case is the rescue doctrine. ...

* * *

In *State v. Stevenson,* ... a deputy observed the defendant place something in his mouth and also saw a rock of cocaine drop to the ground. After arresting the defendant, the deputy observed a white residue in the defendant's mouth. It appeared to the deputy that the defendant had chewed up rock cocaine.

Concerned with a possible overdose, the deputy immediately transported the defendant to a local hospital. The emergency room doctor stated that the defendant was at risk of acute myocardial infarction and hemorrhagic stroke. In response to questioning by the officer, the defendant initially denied ingesting any narcotics. However, when told about the risk of ingesting any controlled substances, "appellant reluctantly admitted he had swallowed six to eight pieces of rock cocaine."

The *Stevenson* court found that the deputy had a reasonable belief that the defendant had consumed cocaine because the deputy saw the defendant place his hand to his mouth, recovered the rock of cocaine that dropped as the defendant's hand went to his mouth, and observed white residue in his mouth. The deputy, aware that cardiac arrest and death can result from a cocaine overdose, testified he felt an "obligation and responsibility" to make sure that the defendant received treatment if he had consumed a dangerous amount of narcotics.

* * *

The questioning in this case stemmed from an objectively reasonable concern over an immediate threat to defendant's health. The officers witnessed the defendant swallowing the contents of a film canister, which the officers reasonably believed contained cocaine. They did not know how much cocaine defendant swallowed, but if he had ingested too much, he could have overdosed. Detective Raulerson asked the question in response to an emergency situation which unfolded before his eyes. Objectively, it appears that his motive was to ascertain what defendant swallowed, not what he possessed.

Officers in such an emergency situation should not be placed in the untenable position of having to choose between having the response and any "fruits" of the response excluded and potentially saving the defendant's life. Neither defendants nor society would benefit from the application of an inflexible rule under these narrow circumstances.

* * *

... Most citizens would consider the police to be derelict in their duties if they administered the Miranda warnings before addressing a life-threatening situation. The right to remain silent would be of little practical value to a defendant who becomes comatose from a drug overdose while being read his *Miranda* rights.

BERGHUIS
v.
THOMPKINS

— U.S. —, 130 S. Ct. 2250, 176 L. Ed. 2d 1098 (2010)

[Citation and footnotes omitted].

[Thompkins was arrested for a shooting incident in which the victim died. At the beginning of the interrogation, Officer Helgert presented Thompkins with a form derived from the *Miranda* rule. To ensure that Thompkins was able to read and understand English, Officer Helgert asked him to read the fifth warning out loud. Thompkins complied. Helgert then read the other four *Miranda* warnings to Thompkins and asked him to sign the form to demonstrate that he understood his rights. Thompkins declined, but Helgert began the interrogation anyway. At no point during the interrogation did Thompkins say that he wanted to remain silent, that he did not want to talk with the police or that he wanted an attorney. Thompkins was largely silent during the interrogation, which lasted about three hours.

About 2 hours and 45 minutes into the interrogation, Helgert asked Thompkins, "Do you believe in God?" Thompkins made eye contact with Helgert and said "Yes," as his eyes welled up with tears. Helgert asked, "Do you pray to God?" Thompkins said "Yes." Helgert asked, "Do you pray to God to forgive you for shooting that boy down?" Thompkins answered "Yes" and looked away. Thompkins refused to make a written confession, and the interrogation ended about 15 minutes later.

Thompkins was charged with firs-degree murder, assault with intent to commit murder, and certain firearms-related offenses. He moved to suppress the statements made during the interrogation. He argued that he had invoked his Fifth Amendment right to remain silent, requiring police to end the interrogation at once, that he had not waived his right to remain silent, and that his inculpatory statements were involuntary. The trial court denied the motion. He was found guilty and sentenced to life in prison without parole.]

Justice KENNEDY delivered the opinion of the Court.

The *Miranda* Court formulated a warning that must be given to suspects before they can be subjected to custodial interrogation. The substance of the warning still must be given to suspects today. A suspect in custody must be advised as follows:

He must be warned prior to any questioning that he has the right to remain silent, that anything he says can be used against him in a court of law, that he has the right to the presence of an attorney, and that if he cannot afford an attorney one will be appointed for him prior to any questioning if he so desires.

All concede that the warning given in this case was in full compliance with these requirements. The dispute centers on the response - or nonresponse - from the suspect.

Thompkins makes various arguments that his answers to questions from the detectives were inadmissible. He first contends that he invoke[d] his privilege to remain silent by not saying anything for a sufficient period of time, so the interrogation should have cease[d] before he made his inculpatory statements.

This argument is unpersuasive. In the context of invoking the *Miranda* right to counsel, the Court in *Davis v. United States,* held that a suspect must do so unambiguously. If an accused makes a statement concerning the right to counsel that is ambiguous or equivocal or makes no statement, the police are not required to end the interrogation or ask questions to clarify whether the accused wants to invoke his or her *Miranda* rights.

The Court has not yet stated whether an invocation of the right to remain silent can be ambiguous or equivocal, but there is no principled reason to adopt different standards for determining when an accused has invoked the *Miranda* right to remain silent and the *Miranda* right to counsel at issue in *Davis*. Both protect the privilege against compulsory self-incrimination by requiring an interrogation to cease when either right is invoked.

There is good reason to require an accused who wants to invoke his or her right to remain silent to do so unambiguously. A requirement of an unambiguous invocation of *Miranda* rights results in an objective inquiry that avoid[s] difficulties of proof and . . . provide[s] guidance to officers on how to proceed in the face of ambiguity. If an ambiguous act, omission, or statement could require police to end the interrogation, police would be required to make difficult decisions about an accused's unclear intent and face the consequence of suppression if they guess wrong. Suppression of a voluntary confession in these circumstances would place a significant burden on society's interest in prosecuting criminal activity. Treating an ambiguous or equivocal act, omission, or statement as an invocation of *Miranda* rights might add marginally to *Miranda*'s goal of dispelling the compulsion inherent in custodial interrogation. But as *Miranda* holds, full comprehension of the rights to remain silent and request an attorney are sufficient to dispel whatever coercion is inherent in the interrogation process.

Thompkins did not say that he wanted to remain silent or that he did not want to talk with the police. Had he made either of these simple, unambiguous statements, he would have invoked his right to cut off questioning. Here he did neither, so he did not invoke his right to remain silent.

We next consider whether Thompkins waived his right to remain silent. Even absent the accused's invocation of the right to remain silent, the accused's statement during a custodial interrogation is inadmissible at trial unless the prosecution can establish that the accused in fact knowingly and voluntarily waived *[Miranda]* rights when making the statement. The waiver inquiry has two distinct dimensions: waiver must be voluntary in the sense that it was the product of a free and deliberate choice rather than intimidation, coercion, or deception, and made with a full awareness of both the nature of the right being abandoned and the consequences of the decision to abandon.

* * *

The prosecution . . . does not need to show that a waiver of *Miranda* rights was express. An implicit waiver of the right to remain silent is sufficient to admit a suspect's statement into evidence. . . . [A] waiver of *Miranda* rights may be implied through "the defendant's silence, coupled with an understanding of his rights and a course of conduct indicating waiver. . . .

If the State establishes that a *Miranda* warning was given and the accused made an uncoerced statement, this showing, standing alone, is insufficient to demonstrate a valid waiver of *Miranda* rights. The prosecution must make the additional showing that the accused understood these rights. Where the prosecution shows that a *Miranda* warning was given and that it was understood by the accused, an accused's uncoerced statement establishes an implied waiver of the right to remain silent.

Although *Miranda* imposes on the police a rule that is both formalistic and practical when it prevents them from interrogating suspects without first providing them with a *Miranda* warning, it does not impose a formalistic waiver procedure that a suspect must follow to relinquish those rights. As a general proposition, the law can presume that an individual who, with full understanding of his or her rights, acts in a manner inconsistent with their exercise has made a deliberate choice to relinquish the protection those rights afford. . . .

The record in this case shows that Thompkins waived his right to remain silent. There is no basis in this case to conclude that he did not understand his rights; and on these facts it follows that he chose not to invoke or rely on those rights when he did speak. First, there is no contention that Thompkins did not understand his rights; and from this it follows that he knew what he gave up when he spoke. There was more than enough evidence in the record to conclude that Thompkins understood his *Miranda* rights. Thompkins received a written copy of the *Miranda* warnings; Detective Helgert determined that Thompkins could read and understand English; and Thompkins was given time to read the warnings. Thompkins, furthermore, read aloud the fifth warning, which stated that you have the right to decide at any time before or during questioning to use your right to remain silent and your right to talk with a lawyer while you are being questioned. He was thus aware that his right to remain silent would not dissipate after a certain amount of time and that police would have to honor his right to be silent and his right to counsel during the whole course of interrogation. Those rights, the warning made clear, could be asserted at any time. Helgert, moreover, read the warnings aloud.

Second, Thompkins's answer to Detective Helgert's question about whether Thompkins prayed to God for forgiveness for shooting the victim is a course of conduct indicating waiver of the right to remain silent. If Thompkins wanted to remain silent, he could have said nothing in response to Helgert's questions, or he could have unambiguously invoked his *Miranda* rights and ended the interrogation. The fact that Thompkins made a statement about three hours after receiving a *Miranda* warning does not overcome the fact that he engaged in a course of conduct indicating waiver. Police are not required to rewarn suspects from time to time. Thompkins's answer to Helgert's question about praying to God for forgiveness for shooting the victim was sufficient to show a course of conduct indicating waiver. This is confirmed by the fact that before then Thompkins had given sporadic answers to questions throughout the interrogation.

* * *

Thompkins next argues that, even if his answer to Detective Helgert could constitute a waiver of his right to remain silent, the police were not allowed to question him until they obtained a waiver first. *Butler* forecloses this argument. The *Butler* Court held that courts can infer a waiver of *Miranda* rights from the actions and words of the person interrogated. The *Butler* Court thus rejected the rule proposed by the *Butler* dissent, which would have requir[ed] the police to obtain an express waiver of [*Miranda* rights] before proceeding with interrogation. This holding also makes sense given that the primary protection afforded suspects subject[ed] to custodial interrogation is the *Miranda* warnings themselves. The *Miranda* rule and its requirements are met if a suspect receives adequate *Miranda* warnings, understands them, and has an opportunity to invoke the rights before giving any answers or admissions. Any waiver, express or implied, may be contradicted by an invocation at any time. If the right to counsel or the right to remain silent is invoked at any point during questioning, further interrogation must cease.

* * *

In order for an accused's statement to be admissible at trial, police must have given the accused a *Miranda* warning. If that condition is established, the court can proceed to consider whether there has been an express or implied waiver of *Miranda* rights. In making its ruling on the admissibility of a statement made during custodial questioning, the trial court, of course, considers whether there is evidence to support the conclusion that, from the whole course of questioning, an express or implied waiver has been established. Thus, after giving a *Miranda* warning, police may interrogate a suspect who has neither invoked nor waived his or her *Miranda* rights. On these premises, it follows the police were not required to obtain [an express] waiver of Thompkins's *Miranda* rights before commencing the interrogation.

* * *

In sum, a suspect who has received and understood the *Miranda* warnings, and has not invoked his *Miranda* rights, waives the right to remain silent by making an uncoerced statement to the police. Thompkins did not invoke his right to remain silent and stop the questioning. Understanding his rights in full, he waived his right to remain silent by making a voluntary statement to the police. The police, moreover, were not required to obtain a waiver of Thompkins's right to remain silent before interrogating him. . . .

* * *

The judgment of the Court of Appeals is reversed, and the case is remanded with instructions to deny the petition.

It is so ordered.

DAVIS
v.
UNITED STATES

512 U.S. 452, 114 S. Ct. 2350,
129 L. Ed. 2d 362 (1994)

[Citations and footnotes omitted.]

[On October 3, 1988, the body of a sailor, beaten to death with a pool cue, was found at the Charleston Naval Base. The investigation gradually focused on Davis. A month later, Davis was interviewed by the Naval Investigative Service. The agents advised Davis that he was a suspect in the killing, that he was not required to make a statement, that any statement could be used against him at a trial by court-martial, and that he was entitled to speak with an attorney and have an attorney present during questioning. Davis waived his rights to remain silent and to counsel, both orally and in writing. About an hour and a half into the interview, Davis said, "Maybe I should talk to a lawyer." When the agents inquired whether he wanted a lawyer, he responded that he did not. The interview continued for another hour, at which point Davis said, "I think I want a lawyer before I say anything else," at which point questioning ceased. A military judge denied Davis's motion to suppress statements made at the interview, holding that his mention of a lawyer during the interrogation was not a request for counsel. He was convicted of murder, and, ultimately, the Court of Military Appeals affirmed.]

JUSTICE O'CONNOR delivered the opinion of the Court.

In *Edwards v. Arizona*, we held that law enforcement officers must immediately cease questioning a suspect who has clearly asserted his right to have counsel present during custodial interrogation. In this case, we decide how law enforcement officers should respond when a suspect makes a reference to counsel that is insufficiently clear to invoke the Edwards prohibition on further questioning.

* * *

The right to counsel recognized in *Miranda* is sufficiently important to suspects in criminal investigations, we have held, that it "requir[es] the special protection of the knowing and intelligent waiver standard." If the suspect effectively waives his right to counsel after receiving the *Miranda* warnings, law enforcement officers are free to question him. But if a suspect requests counsel at any time during the interview, he is not subject to further questioning until a lawyer has been made available or the suspect himself reinitiates conversation. This "second layer of prophylaxis for the *Miranda* right to counsel," is "designed to prevent police from badgering a defendant into waiving his previously asserted *Miranda* rights," To that end, we have held that a suspect who has invoked the right to counsel cannot be questioned regarding any offense unless an attorney is actually present. "It remains clear, however, that this prohibition on further questioning—like other aspects of *Miranda*—is not itself required by the Fifth Amendment's prohibition on coerced confessions, but is instead justified only by reference to its prophylactic purpose."

The applicability of the " 'rigid' prophylactic rule" of *Edwards* requires courts to "determine whether the accused actually invoked his right to counsel." To avoid difficulties of proof and to provide guidance to officers conducting interrogations, this is an objective inquiry. Invocation of the *Miranda* right to counsel "requires at a minimum, some statement that can reasonably be construed to be an expression of a desire for the assistance of an attorney." But if a suspect makes a reference to an attorney that is ambiguous or equivocal in that a reasonable officer, in light of the circumstances, would have understood only that the suspect might be invoking the right to counsel, our precedents do not require the cessation of questioning. ("The likelihood that a suspect would wish counsel to be present is not the test for applicability of Edwards").

Rather, the suspect must unambiguously request counsel. As we have observed, "a statement either is such an assertion of the right to counsel or it is not." Although a suspect need not "speak with the discrimination of an Oxford don," he must articulate his desire to have counsel present sufficiently clearly that a reasonable police officer, in the circumstances, would understand the statement to be a request for an attorney. If the statement fails to meet the requisite level of clarity, *Edwards* does not require that the officers stop questioning the suspect.

We decline petitioner's invitation to extend *Edwards* and require law enforcement officers to cease questioning immediately upon the making of an ambiguous or equivocal reference to an attorney. The rationale underlying *Edwards* is that the police must respect a suspect's wishes regarding his right to have an attorney present during custodial interrogation. But when the officers conducting the questioning reasonably do not know whether or not the suspect wants a lawyer, a rule requiring the immediate cessation of questioning "would transform the *Miranda* safeguards into wholly irrational obstacles to legitimate police investigative activity," because it would needlessly prevent the police from questioning a suspect in the absence of counsel even if the suspect did not wish to have a lawyer present. . . .

* * *

. . . The *Edwards* rule—questioning must cease if the suspect asks for a lawyer—provides a bright line that can be applied by officers in the real world of investigation and interrogation without unduly hampering the gathering of information. But if we were to require questioning to cease if a suspect makes a statement that might be a request for an attorney, this clarity and ease of application would be lost. Police officers would be forced to make difficult judgment calls about whether the suspect in fact wants a lawyer even though he hasn't said so, with the threat of suppression if they guess wrong. We therefore hold that, after a knowing and voluntary waiver of the *Miranda* rights, law enforcement officers may continue questioning until and unless the suspect clearly requests an attorney.

Of course, when a suspect makes an ambiguous or equivocal statement, it will often be good police practice for the interviewing officers to clarify whether or not he actually wants an attorney. That was the procedure followed by the NIS agents in this case. Clarifying questions help protect the rights of the suspect by ensuring that he gets an attorney if he wants one, and will minimize the chance of a confession being suppressed due to subsequent judicial second-guessing as to the meaning of the suspect's statement regarding counsel. But we decline to adopt a rule requiring officers to ask clarifying questions. If the suspect's statement is not an unambiguous or unequivocal request for counsel, the officers have no obligation to stop questioning him.

* * *

The courts below found that petitioner's remark to the NIS agents—"Maybe I should talk to a lawyer"—was not a request for counsel, and we see no reason to disturb that conclusion. The NIS agents therefore were not required to stop questioning petitioner, though it was entirely proper for them to clarify whether petitioner in fact wanted a lawyer. Because there is no ground for suppression of petitioner's statements, the judgment of the Court of Military Appeals is

Affirmed.

[Concurring opinions omitted.]

MARYLAND
v.
SHATZER

__ U.S.__, 130 S. Ct. 1213,
175 L. Ed. 2d 1045 (2010)

[Citations and footnotes omitted]

Justice SCALIA delivered the opinion of the Court.

We consider whether a break in custody ends the presumption of involuntariness established in *Edwards v. Arizona.*

In August 2003, a social worker assigned to the Child Advocacy Center in the Criminal Investigation Division of the Hagerstown Police Department referred to the department allegations that respondent Michael Shatzer, Sr., had sexually abused his 3-year-old son. At that time, Shatzer was incarcerated at the Maryland Correctional Institution-Hagerstown, serving a sentence for an unrelated child-sexual-abuse offense. Detective Shane Blankenship was assigned to the investigation and interviewed Shatzer at the correctional institution on August 7, 2003. Before asking any questions, Blankenship reviewed Shatzer's *Miranda* rights with him, and obtained a written waiver of those rights. When Blankenship explained that he was there to question Shatzer about sexually abusing his son, Shatzer expressed confusion - he had thought Blankenship was an attorney there to discuss the prior crime for which he was incarcerated. Blankenship clarified the purpose of his visit, and Shatzer declined to speak without an attorney. Accordingly, Blankenship ended the interview, and Shatzer was released back into the general prison population. Shortly thereafter, Blankenship closed the investigation.

Two years and six months later, the same social worker referred more specific allegations to the department about the same incident involving Shatzer. Detective Paul Hoover, from the same division, was assigned to the investigation. He and the social worker interviewed the victim, then eight years old, who described the incident in more detail. With this new information in hand, on March 2, 2006, they went to the Roxbury Correctional Institute, to which Shatzer had since been transferred, and interviewed Shatzer in a maintenance room outfitted with a desk and three chairs. Hoover explained that he wanted to ask Shatzer about the alleged incident involving Shatzer's son. Shatzer was surprised because he thought that the investigation had been closed, but Hoover explained they had opened a new file. Hoover then read Shatzer his *Miranda* rights and obtained a written waiver on a standard department form.

Hoover interrogated Shatzer about the incident for approximately 30 minutes. Shatzer denied ordering his son to perform fellatio on him, but admitted to masturbating in front of his son from a distance of less than three feet. Before the interview ended, Shatzer agreed to Hoover's request that he submit to a polygraph examination. At no point during the interrogation did Shatzer request to speak with an attorney or refer to his prior refusal to answer questions without one.

Five days later, on March 7, 2006, Hoover and another detective met with Shatzer at the correctional facility to administer the polygraph examination. After reading Shatzer his *Miranda* rights and obtaining a written waiver, the other detective administered the test and concluded that Shatzer had failed. When the detectives then questioned Shatzer, he became upset, started to cry, and incriminated himself by saying, I didn't force him. I didn't force him. After making this inculpatory statement, Shatzer requested an attorney, and Hoover promptly ended the interrogation.

The State's Attorney for Washington County charged Shatzer with second-degree sexual offense, sexual child abuse, second-degree assault, and contributing to conditions rendering a child in need of assistance. Shatzer moved to suppress his March 2006 statements pursuant to *Edwards.* The trial court held a suppression hearing and later denied Shatzer's motion. The *Edwards* protections did not apply, it reasoned, because Shatzer had experienced a break in custody for *Miranda* purposes between the 2003 and 2006 interrogations. Shatzer pleaded not guilty, waived his right to a jury trial, and proceeded to a bench trial based on an agreed statement of facts. In accordance with the agreement, the State described the interview with the victim and Shatzer's 2006 statements to the detectives. Based on the proffered testimony of the victim and the admission of the defendant as to the act of masturbation, the trial court found Shatzer guilty of sexual child abuse of his son.

The Fifth Amendment, which applies to the States by virtue of the Fourteenth Amendment provides that [n]o person . . . shall be compelled in any criminal case to be a witness against himself. In *Miranda v. Arizona*, the Court adopted a set of prophylactic measures to protect a suspect's Fifth Amendment right from the _inherently compelling pressures of custodial interrogation. The Court observed that incommunicado interrogation in an unfamiliar, police-dominated atmosphere, involves psychological pressures which work to undermine the individual's will to resist and to compel him to speak where he would not otherwise do so freely. Consequently, it reasoned, [u]nless adequate protective devices are employed to dispel the compulsion inherent in custodial surroundings, no statement obtained from the defendant can truly be the product of his free choice.

To counteract the coercive pressure, *Miranda* announced that police officers must warn a suspect prior to questioning that he has a right to remain silent, and a right to the presence of an attorney. After the warnings are given, if the suspect indicates that he wishes to remain silent, the interrogation must cease. Similarly, if the suspect states that he wants an attorney, the interrogation must cease until an attorney is present. Critically, however, a suspect can waive these rights. . . .

In *Edwards*, the Court determined that [the] traditional standard for waiver was not sufficient to protect a suspect's right to have counsel present at a subsequent interrogation if he had previously requested counsel; additional safeguards were necessary. The Court therefore superimposed a second layer of prophylaxis held:

> [W]hen an accused has invoked his right to have counsel present during custodial interrogation, a valid waiver of that right cannot be established by showing only that he responded to further police-initiated custodial interrogation even if he has been advised of his rights.... [He] is not subject to further interrogation by the authorities until counsel has been made available to him, unless the accused himself initiates further

communication, exchanges, or conversations with the police.

The rationale of *Edwards* is that once a suspect indicates that he is not capable of undergoing [custodial] questioning without advice of counsel, any subsequent waiver that has come at the authorities' behest, and not at the suspect's own instigation, is itself the product of the inherently compelling pressures' and not the purely voluntary choice of the suspect. Under this rule, a voluntary *Miranda* waiver is sufficient at the time of an initial attempted interrogation to protect a suspect's right to have counsel present, but it is not sufficient at the time of subsequent attempts if the suspect initially requested the presence of counsel. The implicit assumption, of course, is that the subsequent requests for interrogation pose a significantly greater risk of coercion. That increased risk results not only from the police's persistence in trying to get the suspect to talk, but also from the continued pressure that begins when the individual is taken into custody as a suspect and sought to be interrogated - pressure likely to increase as custody is prolonged. The *Edwards* presumption of involuntariness ensures that police will not take advantage of the mounting coercive pressures of prolonged police custody by repeatedly attempting to question a suspect who previously requested counsel until the suspect is badgered into submission.

* * *

It is easy to believe that a suspect may be coerced or badgered into abandoning his earlier refusal to be questioned without counsel in the paradigm *Edwards* case. That is a case in which the suspect has been arrested for a particular crime and is held in uninterrupted pretrial custody while that crime is being actively investigated. After the initial interrogation, and up to and including the second one, he remains cut off from his normal life and companions, thrust into and isolated in an unfamiliar, police-dominated atmosphere where his captors appear to control [his] fate That was the situation confronted by the suspects in *Edwards*, *Roberson*, and *Minnick*, the three cases in which we have held the *Edwards* rule applicable. Edwards was arrested pursuant to a warrant and taken to a police station, where he was interrogated until he requested counsel. The officer ended the interrogation and took him to the county jail, but at 9:15 the next morning, two of the officer's colleagues reinterrogated Edwards at the jail. Roberson was arrested at the scene of a just-completed burglary and interrogated there until he requested a lawyer. A different officer interrogated him three days later while he was still in custody pursuant to the arrest. Minnick was arrested by local police and taken to the San Diego jail, where two FBI agents interrogated him the next morning until he requested counsel. Two days later a Mississippi Deputy Sheriff reinterrogated him at the jail. None of these suspects regained a sense of control or normalcy after they were initially taken into custody for the crime under investigation.

When, unlike what happened in these three cases, a suspect has been released from his pretrial custody and has returned to his normal life for some time before the later attempted interrogation, there is little reason to think that his change of heart regarding interrogation without counsel has been coerced. He has no longer been isolated. He has likely been able to seek advice from an attorney, family members, and friends. And he knows from his earlier experience that he need only demand counsel to bring the interrogation to a halt; and that investigative custody does not last indefinitely. In these circumstances, it is far fetched to think that a police officer's asking the suspect whether he would like to waive his *Miranda* rights will any more wear down the accused, than did the first such request at the original attempted interrogation - which is of course not deemed coercive. His change of heart is less likely attributable to badgering than it is to the fact that further deliberation in familiar surroundings has caused him to believe (rightly or wrongly) that cooperating with the investigation is in his interest. Uncritical extension of *Edwards* to this situation would not significantly increase the number of genuinely coerced confessions excluded. The justification for a conclusive presumption disappears when application of the presumption will not reach the correct result most of the time.

* * *

We conclude that such an extension of *Edwards* is not justified. . . . The protections offered by *Miranda*, which we have deemed sufficient to ensure that the police respect the suspect's desire to have an attorney present the first time police interrogate him, adequately ensure that result when a suspect who initially requested counsel is reinterrogated after a break in custody that is of sufficient duration to dissipate its coercive effects

If Shatzer's return to the general prison population qualified as a break in custody . . . , there is no doubt that it lasted long enough (2 1/2 years) to meet that durational requirement. But what about a break that has lasted only one year? Or only one week? It is impractical to leave the answer to that question for clarification in future case-by-case adjudication; law enforcement officers need to know, with certainty and beforehand, when renewed interrogation is lawful. . . .

. . . We think it appropriate to specify a period of time to avoid the consequence that continuation of the *Edwards* presumption will not reach the correct result most of the time. It seems to us that period is 14 days. That provides plenty of time for the suspect to get reacclimated to his normal life, to consult with friends and counsel, and to shake off any residual coercive effects of his prior custody.

* * *

The facts of this case present an additional issue. No one questions that Shatzer was in custody for *Miranda* purposes during the interviews with Detective Blankenship in 2003 and Detective Hoover in 2006. Likewise, no one questions that Shatzer triggered the *Edwards* protections when, according to Detective Blankenship's notes of the 2003 interview, he stated that he would not talk about this case without having an attorney present. After the 2003 interview, Shatzer was released back into the general prison population where he was serving an unrelated sentence. The issue is whether that constitutes a break in *Miranda* custody.

* * *

Interrogated suspects who have previously been convicted of crime live in prison. When they are released back into the general prison population, they return to their accustomed surroundings and daily routine - they regain the degree of control they had over their lives prior to the interrogation.

Sentenced prisoners, in contrast to the *Miranda* paradigm, are not isolated with their accusers. They live among other inmates, guards, and workers, and often can receive visitors and communicate with people on the outside by mail or telephone.

Their detention, moreover, is relatively disconnected from their prior unwillingness to cooperate in an investigation. The former interrogator has no power to increase the duration of incarceration, which was determined at sentencing. And even where the possibility of parole exists, the former interrogator has no apparent power to decrease the time served. This is in stark contrast to the circumstances faced by the defendants in *Edwards, Roberson, and Minnick*, whose continued detention as suspects rested with those controlling their interrogation, and who confronted the uncertainties of what final charges they would face, whether they would be convicted, and what sentence they would receive.

Shatzer's experience illustrates the vast differences between *Miranda* custody and incarceration pursuant to conviction. At the time of the 2003 attempted interrogation, Shatzer was already serving a sentence for a prior conviction. After that, he returned to the general prison population in the Maryland Correctional Institution-Hagerstown and was later transferred, for unrelated reasons, down the street to the Roxbury Correctional Institute. His continued detention after the 2003 interrogation did not depend on what he said (or did not say) to Detective Blankenship, and he has not alleged that he was placed in a higher level of security or faced any continuing restraints as a result of the 2003 interrogation. The inherently compelling pressures of custodial interrogation ended when he returned to his normal life.

* * *

Because Shatzer experienced a break in *Miranda* custody lasting more than two weeks between the first and second attempts at interrogation, *Edwards* does not mandate suppression of his March 2006 statements. Accordingly, we reverse the judgment of the Court of Appeals of Maryland, and remand the case for further proceedings not inconsistent with this opinion.

It is so ordered.

MONTEJO
v.
LOUISIANA

___ U.S ___ , 129 S. Ct. 2079,
173 L. Ed. 2d 955 (2009)

[Citations and footnotes omitted]

[Montejo was arrested in connection with a robbery and murder. At his arraignment, the court appointed a public defender to represent him without his request. This was in accordance with Louisiana law which required automatic appointment of counsel for indigent defendants. Later that day, two detectives visited him, and read him his *Miranda* rights. He waived his rights and agreed to accompany them on a trip to locate the murder weapon. During the excursion, Montejo wrote an inculpatory letter of apology to the widow of the murder victim. At his trial, the letter of apology letter was admitted over a defense objection based on *Michigan v. Jackson*, which held that a defendant who requests appointment of counsel at his arraignment cannot validly waive his Sixth Amendment during a police initiated interrogation. The jury convicted him of murder and he was sentenced to death.

The Louisiana Supreme Court ruled that the letter was not subject to suppression under *Michigan v. Jackson* because Montejo never affirmatively requested appointment of counsel which, in the court's view, was necessary for the case to apply.]

Justice Scalia delivered the opinion of the Court.

* * *

[The rule applied by the Louisiana Supreme Court would work] well enough in States that require the indigent defendant formally to request counsel before any appointment is made, which usually occurs after the court has informed him that he will receive counsel if he asks for it. That is how the system works in Michigan, for example, whose scheme produced the factual background for this Court's decision in *Michigan v. Jackson*. Jackson, like all other represented indigent defendants in the State, had requested counsel in accordance with the applicable state law.

But many States follow other practices. In some two dozen, the appointment of counsel is automatic upon a finding of indigency. . . . Nothing in our *Jackson* opinion indicates whether we were then aware that not all States require that a defendant affirmatively request counsel before one is appointed; and of course we had no occasion there to decide how the rule we announced would apply to these other States.

* * *

. . . Defendants in states that automatically appoint counsel would have no opportunity to invoke their rights and trigger *Jackson,* while those in other States, effectively instructed by the court to request counsel, would be lucky winners. That sort of hollow formalism is out of place in a doctrine that purports to serve as a practical safeguard for defendants' rights.

* * *

Our precedents . . . place beyond doubt that the Sixth Amendment right to counsel may be waived by a defendant, so long as relinquishment of the right is voluntary, knowing, and intelligent. The defendant may waive the right whether or not he is already represented by counsel; the decision to waive need not itself be counseled. And when a defendant is read his *Miranda* rights (which include the right to have counsel present during interrogation) and agrees to waive those rights, that typically does the trick, even though the *Miranda* rights purportedly have their source in the *Fifth* Amendment: "As a general matter . . . an accused who is admonished with the warnings prescribed by this Court in *Miranda* . . . has been sufficiently apprised of the nature of his Sixth Amendment rights, and of the consequences of abandoning those rights, so that his waiver on this basis will be considered a knowing and intelligent one."

* * *

The *only* question raised by this case, and the only one addressed by the *Jackson* rule, is whether courts must *presume* that such a waiver is invalid under certain circumstances. We created such a presumption in *Jackson* by analogy to a similar prophylactic rule established to protect the Fifth Amendment based *Miranda* right to have counsel present at any custodial interrogation. *Edwards v. Arizona* decided that once "an accused has invoked his right to have counsel present during custodial interrogation . . . [he] is not subject to further interrogation by the authorities until counsel has been made available," unless he initiates the contact.

* * *

Jackson represented a "wholesale importation of the *Edwards* rule into the Sixth Amendment." The *Jackson* Court decided that a request for counsel at an arraignment should be treated as an invocation of the Sixth Amendment right to counsel "at every critical stage of the prosecution." . . . [A]ny subsequent waiver would thus be "insufficient to justify police-initiated interrogation." In other words, we presume such waivers involuntary "based on the supposition that suspects who assert their right to counsel are unlikely to waive that right voluntarily" in subsequent interactions with police.

* * *

With this understanding of what *Jackson* stands for and whence it came, it should be clear that Montejo's interpretation of that decision—that no *represented* defendant can ever be approached by the State and asked to consent to interrogation-is off the mark. When a court appoints counsel for an indigent defendant in the absence of any request on his part, there is no basis for a presumption that any subsequent waiver of the right to counsel will be involuntary. There is no "*initial* election" to exercise the right that must be preserved through a prophylactic rule against later waivers. No reason exists to assume that a defendant like Montejo, who has done *nothing at all* to express his intentions with respect to his Sixth Amendment rights, would not be perfectly amenable to speaking with the police without having counsel present. And no reason exists to prohibit the police from inquiring. *Edwards* and *Jackson* are meant to prevent police from badgering defendants into changing their minds about their rights, but a defendant who never asked for counsel has not yet made up his mind in the first instance.

* * *

So on the one hand, requiring an initial "invocation" of the right to counsel in order to trigger the *Jackson* presumption is consistent with the theory of that decision, but would be unworkable in more than half the States of the Union. On the other hand, eliminating the invocation requirement would render the rule easy to apply but depart fundamentally from the *Jackson* rationale.

We do not think that *stare decisis* requires us to expand significantly the holding of a prior decision—fundamentally revising its theoretical basis in the process—in order to cure its practical deficiencies. To the contrary, the fact that a decision has proved "unworkable" is a traditional ground for overruling it. . . .

* * *

. . . Under *Miranda*'s prophylactic protection of the right against compelled self-incrimination, any suspect subject to custodial interrogation has the right to have a lawyer present if he so requests, and to be advised of that right. Under *Edwards* 'prophylactic protection of the *Miranda* right, once such a defendant "has invoked his right to have counsel present," interrogation must stop. And under *Minnick*'s prophylactic protection of the *Edwards* right, no subsequent interrogation may take place until counsel is present, "whether or not the accused has consulted with his attorney."

These three layers of prophylaxis are sufficient. Under the *Miranda-Edwards-Minnick* line of cases (which is not in doubt), a defendant who does not want to speak to the police without counsel present need only say as much when he is first approached and given the *Miranda* warnings. At that point, not only must the immediate contact end, but "badgering" by later requests is prohibited. If that regime suffices to protect the integrity of "a suspect's voluntary choice not to speak outside his lawyer's presence" before his arraignment, it is hard to see why it would not also suffice to protect that same choice after arraignment, when Sixth Amendment rights have attached. And if so, then *Jackson* is simply superfluous.

It is true, as Montejo points out in his supplemental brief, that the doctrine established by *Miranda* and *Edwards* is designed to protect Fifth Amendment, not Sixth Amendment, rights. But that is irrelevant. What matters is that these cases, like *Jackson,* protect the right to have counsel during custodial interrogation—which right happens to be guaranteed (once the adversary judicial process has begun) by *two* sources of law. Since the right under both sources is waived using the same procedure, doctrines ensuring voluntariness of the Fifth Amendment waiver simultaneously ensure the voluntariness of the Sixth Amendment waiver.

* * *

On the other side of the equation are the costs of adding the bright-line *Jackson* rule on top of *Edwards* and other extant protections. The principal cost of applying any exclusionary rule "is, of course, letting guilty and possibly dangerous criminals go free . . ." *Jackson* not only "operates to invalidate a confession given by the free choice of suspects who have received proper advice of their *Miranda* rights but waived them nonetheless," but also deters law enforcement officers from even trying to obtain voluntary confessions. The "ready ability to obtain uncoerced confessions is not an evil but an unmitigated good." Without these confessions, crimes go unsolved and criminals unpunished. These are not negligible costs, and in our view the *Jackson* Court gave them too short shrift.

* * *

In sum, when the marginal benefits of the *Jackson* rule are weighed against its substantial costs to the truth-seeking process and the criminal justice system, we readily conclude that the rule does not "pay its way" *Michigan v. Jackson* should be and now is overruled.

* * *

The judgment of the Louisiana Supreme Court is vacated, and the case is remanded for further proceedings not inconsistent with this opinion.

KUHLMANN
v.
WILSON

477 U.S. 436, 106 S. Ct. 2616, 91 L. Ed. 2d 364 (1986)

[Citations and footnotes omitted.]

[After his arraignment on charges arising from a robbery and murder, the defendant was confined in a cell with a prisoner named Benny Lee, who had previously agreed to act as a police informant. Lee was instructed not to solicit any admissions, but simply to "keep his ears open." The defendant told Lee the same story he had told the police that he had fled from the scene to avoid being held responsible for crimes he did not commit. Lee advised him that his story "didn't sound too good" and that he should come up with a better one.

After receiving a disturbing visit from his brother who reported that the family believed he was involved in the murder, the defendant confessed his crimes to Lee who passed the information on to the authorities. The defendant was convicted and subsequently brought a petition for habeas corpus relief, asserting that his statement to Lee was obtained in violation of his Sixth Amendment right to counsel. The District Court denied the petition, but the Court of Appeals reversed.]

JUSTICE POWELL announced the judgment of the Court.

* * *

. . . In *Maine v. Moulton*, the defendant made incriminating statements in a meeting with his accomplice, who had agreed to cooperate with the police. During that meeting, the accomplice, who wore a wire transmitter to record the conversation, discussed with the defendant the charges pending against him, repeatedly asked the defendant to remind him of the details of the crime, and encouraged the defendant to describe his plan for killing witnesses. The Court concluded that these investigatory techniques denied the defendant his right to counsel on the pending charges. Significantly, the Court emphasized that, because of the relationship between the defendant and the informant, the informant's engaging the defendant "in active conversation about their upcoming trial was certain to elicit" incriminating statements from the defendant. Thus, the informant's participation "in this conversation was 'the functional equivalent of interrogation.' "

As our recent examination of this Sixth Amendment issue in Moulton makes clear, the primary concern of the Massiah[1] line of decisions is secret interrogation by investigatory techniques that are the equivalent of direct police interrogation. Since "the Sixth Amendment is not violated whenever—by luck or happenstance—the State obtains incriminating statements from the accused after the right to counsel has attached," a defendant does not make out a violation of that right simply by showing that an informant, either through prior arrangement or

voluntarily, reported his incriminating statements to the police. Rather, the defendant must demonstrate that the police and their informant took some action, beyond merely listening, that was designed deliberately to elicit incriminating remarks.

* * *

The state court found that Officer Cullen had instructed Lee only to listen to respondent. . . . The court further found that Lee followed those instructions, that he "at no time asked any questions" of respondent concerning the pending charges, and that he "only listened" to respondent's "spontaneous" and "unsolicited" statements. The only remark made by Lee that has any support in this record was his comment that respondent's initial version of his participation in the crimes "didn't sound too good." . . . [T]he Court of Appeals focused on that one remark and gave a description of Lee's interaction with respondent that is completely at odds with the facts found by the trial court. . . .

* * *

The judgment of the Court of Appeals is reversed, and the case is remanded for further proceedings consistent with this opinion.

It is so ordered.

MISSOURI
v.
SEIBERT

542 U.S. 600, 124 S. Ct. 2601,
159 L. Ed. 2d 643 (2004)

[Citations and footnotes omitted.]

Respondent Seibert feared charges of neglect when her son, afflicted with cerebral palsy, died in his sleep. She was present when two of her sons and their friends discussed burning her family's mobile home to conceal the circumstances of her son's death. Donald, an unrelated mentally ill 18-year-old living with the family, was left to die in the fire, in order to avoid the appearance that Seibert's son had been unattended. Five days later, the police arrested Seibert, but did not read her her rights under *Miranda v. Arizona*. At the police station, Officer Hanrahan questioned her for 30 to 40 minutes, obtaining a confession that the plan was

---

[1]   [Author's note] Massiah v. United States, 377 U. S. 201, 84 S. Ct. 119, 12 L. Ed. 246 (1964) is discussed in § 6.9 (C).

for Donald to die in the fire. He then gave her a 20-minute break, returned to give her *Miranda* warnings, and obtained a signed waiver. He resumed questioning, confronting Seibert with her prewarning statements and getting her to repeat the information. Seibert moved to suppress both her prewarning and postwarning statements. Hanrahan testified that he made a conscious decision to withhold *Miranda* warnings, question first, then give the warnings, and then repeat the question until he got the answer previously given. The District Court suppressed the prewarning statement but admitted the postwarning one, and Seibert was convicted of second-degree murder. . . .

SOUTER, J., announced the judgment of Court and delivered an opinion, in which STEVENS, GINSBURG, and BREYER, JJ., joined.

This case tests a police protocol for custodial interrogation that calls for giving no warnings of the rights to silence and counsel until interrogation has produced a confession. Although such a statement is generally inadmissible, since taken in violation of *Miranda v. Arizona*, the interrogating officer follows it with *Miranda* warnings and then leads the suspect to cover the same ground a second time. The question here is the admissibility of the repeated statement. Because this midstream recitation of warnings after interrogation and unwarned confession could not effectively comply with *Miranda's* constitutional requirement, we hold that a statement repeated after a warning in such circumstances is inadmissible.

* * *

The technique of interrogating in successive, unwarned and warned phases raises a new challenge to *Miranda*. Although we have no statistics on the frequency of this practice, it is not confined to Rolla, Missouri. An officer of that police department testified that the strategy of withholding *Miranda* warnings until after interrogating and drawing out a confession was promoted not only by his own department, but by a national police training organization and other departments in which he had worked. . . .

When a confession so obtained is offered and challenged, attention must be paid to the conflicting objects of *Miranda* and question-first. *Miranda* addressed "interrogation practices . . . likely . . . to disable [an individual] from making

a free and rational choice" about speaking and held that a suspect must be "adequately and effectively" advised of the choice the Constitution guarantees. The object of question-first is to render *Miranda* warnings ineffective by waiting for a particularly opportune time to give them, after the suspect has already confessed.

Just as "no talismanic incantation [is] required to satisfy [*Miranda's*] strictures," it would be absurd to think that mere recitation of the litany suffices to satisfy *Miranda* in every conceivable circumstance. "The inquiry is simply whether the warnings reasonably 'conve[y] to [a suspect] his rights as required by *Miranda*.' " The threshold issue when interrogators question first and warn later is thus whether it would be reasonable to find that in these circumstances the warnings could function "effectively" as *Miranda* requires. Could the warnings effectively advise the suspect that he had a real choice about giving an admissible statement at that juncture? Could they reasonably convey that he could choose to stop talking even if he had talked earlier? For unless the warnings could place a suspect who has just been interrogated in a position to make such an informed choice, there is no practical justification for accepting the formal warnings as compliance with *Miranda*, or for treating the second stage of interrogation as distinct from the first, unwarned and inadmissible segment.

There is no doubt about the answer that proponents of question-first give to this question about the effectiveness of warnings given only after successful interrogation, and we think their answer is correct. By any objective measure, applied to circumstances exemplified here, it is likely that if the interrogators employ the technique of withholding warnings until after interrogation succeeds in eliciting a confession, the warnings will be ineffective in preparing the suspect for successive interrogation, close in time and similar in content. After all, the reason that question-first is catching on is as obvious as its manifest purpose, which is to get a confession the suspect would not make if he understood his rights at the outset; the sensible underlying assumption is that with one confession in hand before the warnings, the interrogator can count on getting its duplicate, with trifling additional trouble. Upon hearing warnings only in the aftermath of interrogation and just after making a confession, a suspect would hardly think he had a genuine right to remain silent, let alone persist in so believing once the police began to lead him over the same ground again. . . .

Missouri argues that a confession repeated at the end of an interrogation sequence envisioned in a question-first strategy is admissible on the authority of *Oregon v. Elstad*, but the argument disfigures that case. In *Elstad*, the police went to the young suspect's house to take him into custody on a charge of burglary. Before the arrest, one officer spoke with the suspect's mother, while the other one joined the suspect in a "brief stop in the living room," where the officer said he "felt" the young man was involved in a burglary. The suspect acknowledged he had been at the scene. This Court noted that the pause in the living room "was not to interrogate the suspect but to notify his mother of the reason for his arrest," and described the incident as having "none of the earmarks of coercion," The Court, indeed, took care to mention that the officer's initial failure to warn was an "oversight" that "may have been the result of confusion as to whether the brief exchange qualified as 'custodial interrogation' or . . . may simply have reflected . . . reluctance to initiate an alarming police procedure before [an officer] had spoken with respondent's mother." At the outset of a later and systematic station house interrogation going well beyond the scope of the laconic prior admission, the suspect was given *Miranda* warnings and made a full confession. In holding the second statement admissible and voluntary, *Elstad* rejected the "cat out of the bag" theory that any short, earlier admission, obtained in arguably innocent neglect of *Miranda*, determined the character of the later, warned confession; on the facts of that case, the Court thought any causal connection between the first and second responses to the police was "speculative and attenuated." Although the *Elstad* Court expressed no explicit conclusion about either officer's state of mind, it is fair to read *Elstad* as treating the living room conversation as a good-faith *Miranda* mistake, not only open to correction by careful warnings before systematic questioning in that particular case, but posing no threat to warn-first practice generally.

* * *

At the opposite extreme are the facts here, which by any objective measure reveal a police strategy adapted to undermine the *Miranda* warnings. The unwarned interrogation was conducted in the station house, and the questioning was systematic, exhaustive, and managed with psychological skill. When the police were finished there was little, if anything, of incriminating potential left unsaid. The warned phase of questioning proceeded after a pause of only 15 to 20 minutes, in the same place as the unwarned segment. When the same officer who had conducted the first phase recited the *Miranda* warnings, he said nothing to counter the probable misimpression that the advice that anything Seibert said could be used against her also applied to the details of the inculpatory statement previously elicited. In particular, the police did not advise that her prior statement could not be used. Nothing was said or done to dispel the oddity of warning about legal rights to silence and counsel right after the police had led her through a systematic interrogation, and any uncertainty on her part about a right to stop talking about matters previously discussed would only have been aggravated by the way Officer Hanrahan set the scene by saying "we've been talking for a little while about what happened on Wednesday the twelfth, haven't we?" The impression that the further questioning was a mere continuation of the earlier questions and responses was fostered by references back to the confession already given. It would have been reasonable to regard the two sessions as parts of a continuum, in which it would have been unnatural to refuse to repeat at the second stage what had been said before. These circumstances must be seen as challenging the comprehensibility and efficacy of the *Miranda* warnings to the point that a reasonable person in the suspect's shoes would not have understood them to convey a message that she retained a choice about continuing to talk.

. . . Because the question-first tactic effectively threatens to thwart *Miranda's* purpose of reducing the risk that a coerced confession would be admitted, and because the facts here do not reasonably support a conclusion that the warnings given could have served their purpose, Seibert's postwarning statements are inadmissible. . . .

Cases Relating to Chapter 7

Compulsory Self-Incrimination

UNITED STATES
v.
HUBBELL

530 U.S. 27, 120 S. Ct. 2037,
147 L. Ed. 2d 24 (2000)

[Citations and footnotes omitted.]

[As part of a grand jury investigation, Hubbell was served with a subpoena duces tecum calling for the production of 11 categories of documents. On November 19, he appeared before the grand jury and invoked his Fifth Amendment privilege against self-incrimination. In response to questioning by the prosecutor, respondent initially refused "to state whether there are documents within my possession, custody, or control responsive to the Subpoena." Thereafter, the prosecutor obained a court order, directing him to respond to the subpoena and granting him immunity "to the extent allowed by law." Respondent then produced 13,120 pages of documents and records and responded to a series of questions that established that those were all of the documents in his custody or control that were responsive to the commands in the subpoena, with the exception of a few documents he claimed were shielded by the attorney-client and attorney work-product privileges.

The contents of the documents produced by respondent provided the Independent Counsel with the information that led to this prosecution. On April 30, 1998, a grand jury in the District of Columbia returned a 10-count indictment charging respondent with various tax-related crimes and mail and wire fraud. . . .]

Justice STEVENS delivered the opinion of the Court.

* * *

It is useful to preface our analysis of the constitutional issue with a restatement of certain propositions that are not in dispute. The term "privilege against self-incrimination" is not an entirely accurate description of a person's constitutional protection against being "compelled in any criminal case to be a witness against himself."

The word "witness" in the constitutional text limits the relevant category of compelled incriminating communications to those that are "testimonial" in character. As Justice Holmes observed, there is a significant difference between the use of compulsion to extort communications from a defendant and compelling a person to engage in conduct that may be incriminating. Thus, even though the act may provide incriminating evidence, a criminal suspect may be compelled to put on a shirt, to provide a blood sample or handwriting exemplar, or to make a recording of his voice. The act of exhibiting such physical characteristics is not the same as a sworn communication by a witness that relates either express or implied assertions of fact or belief. Similarly, the fact that incriminating evidence may be the byproduct of obedience to a regulatory requirement, such as filing an income tax return, maintaining required records, or reporting an accident, does not clothe such required conduct with the testimonial privilege.

More relevant to this case is the settled proposition that a person may be required to produce specific documents even though they contain incriminating assertions of fact or belief because the creation of those documents was not "compelled" within the meaning of the privilege. Our decision in *Fisher v. United States* dealt with summonses issued by the Internal Revenue Service (IRS) seeking working papers used in the preparation of tax returns. Because the papers had been voluntarily prepared prior to the issuance of the summonses, they could not be "said to contain compelled testimonial evidence, either of the taxpayers or of anyone else." Accordingly, the taxpayer could not "avoid compliance with the subpoena merely by asserting that the item of evidence which he is required to produce contains incriminating writing, whether his own or that of someone else." It is clear, therefore, that respondent Hubbell could not avoid compliance with the subpoena served on him merely because the demanded documents contained incriminating evidence, whether written by others or voluntarily prepared by himself.

On the other hand, we have also made it clear that the act of producing documents in response to a subpoena may have a compelled testimonial aspect. We have held that "the act of production" itself may implicitly communicate "statements of fact." By "producing documents in compliance with a subpoena, the witness would admit that the papers existed, were in his possession or control, and were authentic." Moreover, as was true in this case, when the custodian of documents responds to a subpoena, he may be compelled to take the witness stand and answer questions designed to determine whether he has produced everything demanded by the subpoena. The answers to those questions, as well as the act of production itself, may certainly communicate information about the existence, custody, and authenticity of the documents. Whether the constitutional privilege protects the answers to such questions, or protects the act of production itself, is a question that is distinct from the question whether the unprotected contents of the documents themselves are incriminating.

Finally, the phrase "in any criminal case" in the text of the Fifth Amendment might have been read to limit its coverage to compelled testimony that is used against the defendant in the trial itself. It has, however, long been settled that its protection encompasses compelled statements that lead to the discovery of incriminating evidence even though the statements themselves are not incriminating and are not introduced into evidence. Thus, a half-century ago we held that a trial judge had erroneously rejected a defendant's claim of privilege on the ground that his answer to the pending question would not itself constitute evidence of the charged offense. As we explained: "The privilege afforded not only extends to answers that would in themselves support a conviction under a federal criminal statute but likewise embraces those which would furnish a link in the chain of evidence needed to prosecute the claimant for a federal crime." Compelled testimony that communicates information that may "lead to incriminating evidence" is privileged even if the information itself is not inculpatory. It is the Fifth Amendment's protection against the prosecutor's use of incriminating information derived directly or indirectly from the compelled testimony of the respondent that is of primary relevance in this case.

Acting pursuant to 18 U.S.C. § 6002, the District Court entered an order compelling respondent to produce "any and all documents" described in the grand jury subpoena and granting him "immunity to the extent allowed by law." . . .

* * *

The "compelled testimony" that is relevant in this case is not to be found in the contents of the documents produced in response to the subpoena. It is, rather, the testimony inherent in the act of producing those documents. The disagreement between the parties focuses entirely on the significance of that testimonial aspect.

* * *

It is apparent from the text of the subpoena itself that the prosecutor needed respondent's assistance both to identify potential sources of information and to produce those sources. Given the breadth of the description of the 11 categories of documents called for by the subpoena, the collection and production of the materials demanded was tantamount to answering a series of interrogatories asking a witness to disclose the existence and location of particular documents fitting certain broad descriptions. The assembly of literally hundreds of pages of material in response to a request for "any and all documents reflecting, referring, or relating to any direct or indirect sources of money or other things of value received by or provided to" an individual or members of his family during a 3-year period is the functional equivalent of the preparation of an answer to either a detailed written interrogatory or a series of oral questions at a discovery deposition. Entirely apart from the contents of the 13,120 pages of materials that respondent produced in this case, it is undeniable that providing a catalog of existing documents fitting within any of the 11 broadly worded subpoena categories could provide a prosecutor with a "lead to incriminating evidence," or "a link in the chain of evidence needed to prosecute."

... It is abundantly clear that the testimonial aspect of respondent's act of producing subpoenaed documents was the first step in a chain of evidence that led to this prosecution. The documents did not magically appear in the prosecutor's office like "manna from heaven." They arrived there only after respondent asserted his constitutional privilege, received a grant of immunity, and—under the compulsion of the District Court's order—took the mental and physical steps necessary to provide the prosecutor with an accurate inventory of the many sources of potentially incriminating evidence sought by the subpoena. It was only through respondent's truthful reply to the subpoena that the Government received the incriminating documents of which it made "substantial use ... in the investigation that led to the indictment."

For these reasons, we cannot accept the Government's submission that respondent's immunity did not preclude its derivative use of the produced documents because its "possession of the documents [was] the fruit only of a simple physical act—the act of producing the documents." It was unquestionably necessary for respondent to make extensive use of "the contents of his own mind" in identifying the hundreds of documents responsive to the requests in the subpoena. The assembly of those documents was like telling an inquisitor the combination to a wall safe, not like being forced to surrender the key to a strongbox. The Government's anemic view of respondent's act of production as a mere physical act that is principally non-testimonial in character and can be entirely divorced from its "implicit" testimonial aspect so as to constitute a "legitimate, wholly independent source" (as required by Kastigar) for the documents produced simply fails to account for these realities.

In sum, we have no doubt that the constitutional privilege against self-incrimination protects the target of a grand jury investigation from being compelled to answer questions designed to elicit information about the existence of sources of potentially incriminating evidence. That constitutional privilege has the same application to the testimonial aspect of a response to a subpoena seeking discovery of those sources. . . .

* * *

Given our conclusion that respondent's act of production had a testimonial aspect, at least with respect to the existence and location of the documents sought by the Government's subpoena, respondent could not be compelled to produce those documents without first receiving a grant of immunity under § 6003. As we construed § 6002 in Kastigar, such immunity is co-extensive with the constitutional privilege. Kastigar requires that respondent's motion to dismiss the indictment on immunity grounds be granted unless the Government proves that the evidence it used in obtaining the indictment and proposed to use at trial was derived from legitimate sources "wholly independent" of the testimonial aspect of respondent's immunized conduct in assembling and producing the documents described in the subpoena. . . .

Accordingly, the indictment against respondent must be dismissed. The judgment of the Court of Appeals is affirmed.

It is so ordered.

SCHMERBER
v.
CALIFORNIA

384 U.S. 757, 86 S. Ct. 1826, 16 L. Ed. 2d 908 (1966)

[Police arrested Schmerber at the scene of an automobile accident for driving under the influence of intoxicating liquor (DUI). While he was at a hospital being treated for injuries sustained in the accident, one of the officers instructed a physician to withdraw a blood sample. Schmerber refused to consent, but a sample was taken anyway. The sample revealed a blood alcohol content in excess of the state's maximum for DUI. Schmerber moved to suppress the test results on several grounds, including that withdrawal of his blood and admission of the test results into evidence violated his Fifth Amendment privilege against self-incrimination and his Fourth Amendment right not to be subjected to unreasonable searches and seizures. Schmerber's motion to suppress was denied and he was convicted.]

MR. JUSTICE BRENNAN delivered the opinion of the Court.

* * *

The Privilege Against
Self-Incrimination Claim

It could not be denied that in requiring petitioner to submit to the withdrawal and chemical analysis of his blood the State compelled him to submit to an attempt to discover evidence that might be used to prosecute him for a criminal offense. He submitted only after the police officer rejected his objection and directed the physician to proceed. The officer's direction to the physician to administer the test over petitioner's objection constituted compulsion for the purposes of the privilege. The critical question, then, is whether petitioner was thus compelled 'to be a witness against himself.'

* * *

It is clear that the protection of the privilege reaches an accused's communications, whatever form they might take, and the compulsion of responses which are also communications, for example, compliance with a subpoena to produce one's papers. On the other hand, both federal and state courts have usually held that it offers no protection against compulsion to submit to fingerprinting, photographing, or measurements, to write or speak for identification, to appear in court, to stand, to assume a stance, to walk, or to make a particular gesture. The distinction which has emerged, often expressed in different ways, is that the privilege is a bar against compelling 'communications' or 'testimony,' but that compulsion which makes a suspect or accused the source of 'real or physical evidence' does not violate it.

* * *

... Not even a shadow of testimonial compulsion upon or enforced communication by the accused was involved either in the extraction or in the chemical analysis. Petitioner's testimonial capacities were in no way implicated; indeed, his

participation, except as a donor, was irrelevant to the results of the test, which depend on chemical analysis and on that alone. Since the blood test evidence, although an incriminating product of compulsion, was neither petitioner's testimony nor evidence relating to some communicative act or writing by the petitioner, it was not inadmissible on privilege grounds.

* * *

The Search and Seizure Claim

In *Breithaupt*, as here, it was also contended that the chemical analysis should be excluded from evidence as the product of an unlawful search and seizure in violation of the Fourth and Fourteenth Amendments. The Court did not decide whether the extraction of blood in that case was unlawful, but rejected the claim on the basis of *Wolf v. People of State of Colorado*. That case had held that the Constitution did not require, in state prosecutions for state crimes, the exclusion of evidence obtained in violation of the Fourth Amendment's provisions. We have since overruled Wolf in that respect, holding in *Mapp v. Ohio* that the exclusionary rule adopted for federal prosecutions in *Weeks v. United States* must also be applied in criminal prosecutions in state courts. The question is squarely presented therefore, whether the chemical analysis introduced in evidence in this case should have been excluded as the product of an unconstitutional search and seizure.

The overriding function of the Fourth Amendment is to protect personal privacy and dignity against unwarranted intrusion by the State. In Wolf we recognized "(t)he security of one's privacy against arbitrary intrusion by the police" as being "at the core of the Fourth Amendment" and "basic to a free society." We reaffirmed that broad view of the Amendment's purpose in applying the federal exclusionary rule to the *States* in *Mapp*.

... But if compulsory administration of a blood test does not implicate the Fifth Amendment, it plainly involves the broadly conceived reach of a search and seizure under the Fourth Amendment. That Amendment expressly provides that "(t)he right of the people to be secure in their persons, houses, papers, and effects, against unreasonable searches and seizures, shall not be violated...." (Emphasis added.) It could not reasonably be argued, and indeed respondent does not argue, that the administration of the blood test in this case was free of the constraints of the Fourth Amendment. Such testing procedures plainly constitute searches of "persons," and depend antecedently upon seizures of "persons," within the meaning of that Amendment.

Because we are dealing with intrusions into the human body rather than with state interferences with property relationships or private papers—"houses, papers, and effects"—we write on a clean slate. Limitations on the kinds of property which may be seized under warrant, as distinct from the procedures for search and the permissible scope of search, are not instructive in this context. We begin with the assumption that once the privilege against self-incrimination has been found not to bar compelled intrusions into the body for blood to be analyzed for alcohol content, the Fourth Amendment's proper function is to constrain, not against all intrusions as such, but against intrusions which are not justified in the circumstances, or which are made in an improper manner. In other words, the questions we must decide in this case are whether the police were justified in requiring petitioner to submit to the blood test, and whether the means and procedures employed in taking his blood respected relevant Fourth Amendment standards of reasonableness.

In this case, as will often be true when charges of driving under the influence of alcohol are pressed, these questions arise in the context of an arrest made by an officer without a warrant. Here, there was plainly probable cause for the officer to arrest petitioner and charge him with driving an automobile while under the influence of intoxicating liquor. The police officer who arrived at the scene shortly after the accident smelled liquor on petitioner's breath, and testified that petitioner's eyes were "bloodshot, watery, sort of a glassy appearance." The officer saw petitioner again at the hospital, within two hours of the accident. There he noticed similar symptoms of drunkenness. He thereupon informed petitioner "that he was under arrest and that he was entitled to the services of an attorney, and that he could remain silent, and that anything that he told me would be used against him in evidence."

While early cases suggest that there is an unrestricted "right on the part of the government always recognized under English and American law, to search the person of the accused when legally arrested, to discover and seize the fruits or evidences of crime," the mere fact of a lawful arrest does not end our inquiry. The suggestion of these cases apparently rests on two factors—first, there may be more immediate danger of concealed weapons or of destruction of evidence under the direct control of the accused; second, once a search of the arrested person for weapons is permitted, it would be both impractical and unnecessary to enforcement of the Fourth Amendment's purpose to attempt to confine the search to those objects alone. Whatever the validity of these considerations in general, they have little applicability with respect to searches involving intrusions beyond the body's surface. The interests in human dignity and privacy which the Fourth Amendment protects forbid any such intrusions on the mere chance that desired evidence might be obtained. In the absence of a clear indication that in fact such evidence will be found, these fundamental human interests require law officers to suffer the risk that such evidence may disappear unless there is an immediate search.

Although the facts which established probable cause to arrest in this case also suggested the required relevance and likely success of a test of petitioner's blood for alcohol, the question remains whether the arresting officer was permitted to draw these inferences himself, or was required instead to procure a warrant before proceeding with the test. Search warrants are ordinarily required for searches of dwellings, and absent an emergency, no less could be required where intrusions into the human body are concerned. The requirement that a warrant be obtained is a requirement that inferences to support the search "be drawn by a neutral and detached magistrate instead of being judged by the officer engaged in the often competitive enterprise of ferreting out crime." The importance of informed, detached and deliberate determinations of the issue whether or not to invade another's body in search of evidence of guilt is indisputable and great.

The officer in the present case, however, might reasonably have believed that he was confronted with an emergency, in which the delay necessary to obtain a warrant, under the circumstances, threatened "the destruction of evidence." We are told that the percentage of alcohol in the blood begins to diminish shortly after drinking stops, as the body functions to eliminate it from the system.

Particularly in a case such as this, where time had to be taken to bring the accused to a hospital and to investigate the scene of the accident, there was no time to seek out a magistrate and secure a warrant. Given these special facts, we conclude that the attempt to secure evidence of blood-alcohol content in this case was an appropriate incident to petitioner's arrest.

Similarly, we are satisfied that the test chosen to measure petitioner's blood-alcohol level was a reasonable one. Extraction of blood samples for testing is a highly effective means of determining the degree to which a person is under the influence of alcohol. Such tests are commonplace in these days of periodic physical examination and experience with them teaches that the quantity of blood extracted is minimal, and that for most people the procedure involves virtually no risk, trauma, or pain. Petitioner is not one of the few who on grounds of fear, concern for health, or religious scruple might prefer some other means of testing, such as the "Breathalyzer" test petitioner refused, see n. 9, supra. We need not decide whether such wishes would have to be respected.

Finally, the record shows that the test was performed in a reasonable manner. Petitioner's blood was taken by a physician in a hospital environment according to accepted medical practices. We are thus not presented with the serious questions which would arise if a search involving use of a medical technique, even of the most rudimentary sort, were made by other than medical personnel or in other than a medical environment—for example, if it were administered by police in the privacy of the stationhouse. To tolerate searches under these conditions might be to invite an unjustified element of personal risk of infection and pain.

We thus conclude that the present record shows no violation of petitioner's right under the Fourth and Fourteenth Amendments to be free of unreasonable searches and seizures. It bears repeating, however, that we reach this judgment only on the facts of the present record. The integrity of an individual's person is a cherished value of our society. That we today told that the Constitution does not forbid the States minor intrusions into an individual's body under stringently limited conditions in no way indicates that it permits more substantial intrusions, or intrusions under other conditions.

Affirmed.

PENNSYLVANIA
v.
MUNIZ

496 U.S. 582, 110 S. Ct. 2638, 110 L. Ed. 2d 528 (1990)

[Citations and footnotes omitted.]

[A patrol officer, spotting Muniz's parked car on the shoulder of a highway, inquired whether he needed assistance, Muniz replied that he had stopped the car so he could urinate. The officer smelled alcohol on Muniz's breath and observed that Muniz's eyes were glazed and bloodshot and his face was flushed. The officer then directed Muniz to remain parked until his condition improved, and Muniz gave assurances that he would do so, but immediately drove off. After pursuing Muniz down the highway and pulling him over, the officer, without advising Muniz of his *Miranda* rights, asked him to perform two standard field sobriety tests: a "walk and turn" test and a "one leg stand" test. Muniz performed these tests poorly and informed the officer that he had failed the tests because he had been drinking. Muniz was taken to a booking center where, as was the routine practice, he was told that his actions and voice would be videotaped. He then answered seven questions regarding his name, address, height, weight, eye color, date of birth, and current age, stumbling over two responses. The officer then asked Muniz to take a Breathalyzer test and explained that under the law his refusal to take the test would result in automatic suspension of his driver's license for one year. Muniz asked a number of questions about the law and then, commenting about his inebriated state, refused to take the breath test. At this point, Muniz was for the first time advised of his *Miranda* rights. The video and audio portions of the tape were admitted at trial over Muniz's objection that this evidence was procured in violation of his Fifth Amendment privilege against self-incrimination. Muniz was convicted and appealed.]

JUSTICE BRENNAN delivered the opinion of the Court.

We must decide in this case whether various incriminating utterances of a drunken-driving suspect, made while performing a series of sobriety tests, constitute testimonial responses to custodial interrogation for purposes of the Self-Incrimination Clause of the Fifth Amendment.

* * *

The Self-Incrimination Clause of the Fifth Amendment provides that no "person . . . shall be compelled in any criminal case to be a witness against himself." Although the text does not delineate the ways in which a person might be made a "witness against himself, we have long held that the privilege does not protect a suspect from being compelled by the State to produce "real or physical evidence." Rather, the privilege "protects an accused only from being compelled to testify against himself, or otherwise provide the State with evidence of a testimonial or communicative nature." "[I]n order to be testimonial, an accused's communication must itself, explicitly or implicitly, relate a factual assertion or disclose information. Only then is a person compelled to be a 'witness' against himself."

* * *

Because Muniz was not advised of his *Miranda* rights until after the videotaped proceedings at the booking center were completed, any verbal statements that were both testimonial in nature and elicited during custodial interrogation should have been suppressed. We focus first on Muniz's responses to the initial informational questions . . .

In the initial phase of the recorded proceedings, Officer Hosterman asked Muniz his name, address, height, weight, eye color, date of birth, current age, and the date of his sixth birthday. Both the delivery and content of Muniz's answers were incriminating. As the state court found, "Muniz's videotaped responses . . . certainly led the finder of fact to infer that his confusion and failure to speak clearly indicated a state of drunkenness that prohibited him from safely operating his vehicle." The Commonwealth argues, however, that admission of Muniz's answers to these questions does not contravene Fifth Amendment principles because Muniz's statement regarding his sixth birthday was not "testimonial" and his answers to the prior questions were not elicited by custodial interrogation. We consider these arguments in turn.

We agree with the Commonwealth's contention that Muniz's answers are not rendered inadmissible by *Miranda* merely because the slurred nature of his speech was incriminating. The physical inability to articulate words in a clear manner due to "the lack of muscular coordination of his tongue and mouth," is not itself a testimonial component of Muniz's responses to Officer Hosterman's introductory questions. *In Schmerber v. California*, we drew a distinction between "testimonial" and "real or physical evidence" for purposes of the privilege against self-incrimination. We noted that in *Holt v. United States*, Justice Holmes had written for the Court that " '[t]he prohibition of compelling a man in a criminal court to be witness against himself is a prohibition of the use of physical or moral compulsion to extort communications from him, not an exclusion of his body as evidence when it may be material.' " We also acknowledged that "both federal and state courts have usually held that it offers no protection against compulsion to submit to fingerprinting, photographing, or measurements, to write or speak for identification, to appear in court, to stand, to assume a stance, to walk, or to make a particular gesture." Embracing this view of the privilege's contours, we held that "the privilege is a bar against compelling 'communications' or 'testimony,' but that compulsion which makes a suspect or accused the source of 'real or physical evidence' does not violate it." Using this "helpful framework for analysis," we held that a person suspected of driving while intoxicated could be forced to provide a blood sample, because that sample was "real or physical evidence" outside the scope of the privilege and the sample was obtained in a manner by which "[p]etitioner's testimonial capacities were in no way implicated."

* * *

We have since applied the distinction between "real or physical" and "testimonial" evidence in other contexts where the evidence could be produced only through some volitional act on the part of the suspect. In *United States v. Wade*, we held that a suspect could be compelled to participate in a lineup and to repeat a phrase provided by the police so that witnesses could view him and listen to his voice. We explained that requiring his presence and speech at a lineup reflected "compulsion of the accused to exhibit his physical characteristics, not compulsion to disclose any knowledge he might have." In *Gilbert v. California*, we held that a suspect could be compelled to provide a handwriting exemplar, explaining that such an exemplar, "in contrast to the content of what is written, like the voice or body itself, is an identifying physical characteristic outside [the privilege's] protection." And in *United*

States v. Dionisio, we held that suspects could be compelled to read a transcript in order to provide a voice exemplar, explaining that the "voice recordings were to be used solely to measure the physical properties of the witnesses' voices, not for the testimonial or communicative content of what was to be said."

Under *Schmerber* and its progeny, we agree with the Commonwealth that any slurring of speech and other evidence of lack of muscular coordination revealed by Muniz's responses to Officer Hosterman's direct questions constitute nontestimonial components of those responses. Requiring a suspect to reveal the physical manner in which he articulates words, like requiring him to reveal the physical properties of the sound produced by his voice, does not, without more, compel him to provide a "testimonial" response for purposes of the privilege.

* * *

We disagree with the Commonwealth's contention that Officer Hosterman's first seven questions regarding Muniz's name, address, height, weight, eye color, date of birth, and current age do not qualify as custodial interrogation as we defined the term in Innis, merely because the questions were not intended to elicit information for investigatory purposes. As explained above, the Innis test focuses primarily upon "the perspective of the suspect." We agree . . . however, that Muniz's answers to these first seven questions are nonetheless admissible because the questions fall within a "routine booking question" exception which exempts from *Miranda's* coverage questions to secure the " 'biographical data necessary to complete booking or pretrial services.' " The state court found that the first seven questions were "requested for record-keeping purposes only," and therefore the questions appear reasonably related to the police's administrative concerns. In this context, therefore, the first seven questions asked at the booking center fall outside the protections of *Miranda* and the answers thereto need not be suppressed.

* * *

. . . [W]e conclude that *Miranda* does not require suppression of the statements Muniz made when asked to submit to a Breathalyzer examination. Officer Deyo read Muniz a prepared script explaining how the test worked, the nature of Pennsylvania's Implied Consent Law, and the legal consequences that would ensue should he refuse. Officer Deyo then asked Muniz whether he understood the nature of the test and the law and whether he would like to submit to the test. Muniz asked Officer Deyo several questions concerning the legal consequences of refusal, which Deyo answered directly, and Muniz then commented upon his state of inebriation. After offering to take the test only after waiting a couple of hours or drinking some water, Muniz ultimately refused.

We believe that Muniz's statements were not prompted by an interrogation within the meaning of *Miranda*, and therefore the absence of *Miranda* warnings does not require suppression of these statements at trial. As did Officer Hosterman when administering the three physical sobriety tests, Officer Deyo carefully limited her role to providing Muniz with relevant information about the Breathalyzer test and the Implied Consent Law. She questioned Muniz only as to whether he understood her instructions and wished to submit to the test. These limited and focused inquiries were necessarily "attendant to" the legitimate police procedure, and were not likely to be perceived as calling for any incriminating response.

. . . Accordingly, the court's judgment reversing Muniz's conviction is vacated, and the case is remanded for further proceedings not inconsistent with this opinion.

It is so ordered.

[Concurring and dissenting opinions omitted.]

STATE
v.
TAPP

353 So. 2d 265 (La. 1977)

[Citations and footnotes omitted.]

[Police officers were executing a search warrant for narcotics at a house on Lowerline Street in New Orleans, Louisiana. All they uncovered was some heroin residue on a syringe found in the refrigerator. While they were inside the house, Tapp, the defendant, entered the door. When he saw the police, the defendant placed a small, cellophane-wrapped packet into his mouth. Three officers set upon him and attempted to force the packet out of his mouth. The ensuing fight rolled onto the front porch, down the steps, and into the yard where two other officers joined the fight. One officer held his hands around defendant's throat in an effort to prevent him from swallowing the evidence. According to the officers, they pummeled defendant in the face and head with their fists, and called on defendant to "Spit it out!" According to defendant's uncontradicted testimony one officer eventually held defendant's nose in an effort to cut off his breathing. The officers estimated that the fight, which one of them described as "one hell of a fight," lasted 15 to 20 minutes. Eventually the five officers successfully caused defendant to spit up the packet, which was then apparently lodged near or at the top of his esophagus, and they arrested him for heroin possession. A search warrant issued for a second house based in part on that evidence. Within they discovered a large amount of heroin. Based on the search of the second house, the defendant was charged with possession with intent to distribute. The trial court refused to suppress the evidence and the defendant was convicted.]

CALOGERO, Justice

* * *

We assume for our present purposes that the officers reasonably believed that defendant was attempting to swallow contraband, and that they had a reasonable basis on which to arrest him for its possession. That finding does not end the matter, however, for we must still decide whether the force with which the officers garnered the questioned evidence constituted an unreasonable search and seizure under the fourth amendment, and whether the manner of seizure fell short of civilized standards of decency and fair play in derogation of the due process clause of the fifth and fourteenth amendments.

The seminal case articulating the standards for police use of force to extract physical evidence from the body of a nonconsenting suspect is *Rochin v. California*. In *Rochin*, police officers, following an anonymous tip, burst into defendant's apartment. Defendant picked up two capsules from a night stand and swallowed them. The Court described the events in this way: "A struggle ensued, in the course of which the three officers " 'jumped upon him' and attempted to extract the capsules." When this effort failed, the officers took Rochin to a hospital where, against

his will, his stomach was pumped. The two capsules were vomited up and defendant was convicted of their possession. The high court held, on due process grounds, that the evidence seized should have been excluded at trial:

> [W]e are compelled to conclude that the proceedings by which this conviction was obtained do more than offend some fastidious squeamishness or private sentimentalism about combating crime too energetically. This is conduct that shocks the conscience. Illegally breaking into the privacy of the petitioner, the struggle to open his mouth and remove what was there, the forcible extraction of his stomach's contents this course of proceeding by agents of government to obtain evidence is bound to offend even hardened sensibilities. They are methods too close to the rack and the screw to permit of constitutional differentiation."

* * *

The decision in *Rochin*, which as indicated earlier was based entirely on due process grounds, can be compared to the same court's contrary result under the fourth amendment in *Schmerber v. California*. In that case, police arrested defendant at a hospital where he had been taken for treatment after an automobile accident. At police request, medical personnel took a blood sample from the defendant, without his consent and without a warrant. In approving this procedure, the court noted specifically that the officers proceeded in an accepted medical procedure and that the operation was performed in a reasonable manner without trauma or pain. Moreover, the court found an "emergency situation" in the highly evanescent nature of the evidence: "We are told that the percentage of alcohol in the blood begins to diminish shortly after drinking stops, as the body functions to eliminate it from the system. . . . [T]here was no time to seek out a magistrate and secure a warrant." The court emphasized that:

> [W]e reach this judgment only on the facts of the present record. The integrity of an individual's person is a cherished value of our society. That we today hold that the Constitution does not forbid the States minor intrusions into an individual's body under stringently limited conditions in no way indicates that it permits more substantial intrusions, or intrusions under other conditions.

We find that the forcible seizure of the evidence here is far closer to the facts in *Rochin* than those in *Schmerber*. The beating and choking of defendant Tapp is reminiscent of, if not more excessive than, the beating officers gave to defendant *Rochin*. The prolonged and brutal struggle to cause Tapp to disgorge the packet was excessive under the circumstances and thereby abused common conceptions of decency and civilized conduct. Although policemen can use reasonable force to attempt to prevent the swallowing of evidence, particularly when a search for evidence is underway pursuant to a warrant, police officers may not constitutionally beat and choke suspects in order to gain that evidence. In so doing, these officers used unreasonable force to recover the evidence, thus offending the fifth amendment guarantee of due process and causing the evidence so recovered to be inadmissible at defendant's trial.

The state urges us to adopt a rule it alleges is prevalent in some jurisdictions which would allow the choking of a suspect so as to recover physical evidence.

We do not find the legal principles in those cases different from those we here adopt. Those opinions recognize that the application of unreasonable force in the recovery of physical evidence offends due process, but find, on the facts there presented, that the force used was reasonable. In none of those cases was a suspect beaten at all, much less with the intensity of the beating administered to defendant Tapp.

In addition to the due process violation heretofore described, we also find that the search and seizure offended the fourth amendment. Unlike the situation in *Schmerber*, the extraction of this evidence was not the result of painless, medically approved procedures. Nor was there the need for speed in the gaining of evidence which the *Schmerber* court found persuasive. We see no evidence in the record (and indeed, the state does not so argue) that this material, if swallowed, would not have traveled through defendant's body without destruction of the evidence or harm to defendant. We hold that this was not the "minor intrusion into an individual's body under stringently limited conditions" approved in *Schmerber*, but rather a grievous, dangerous, painful and unjustifiable assault upon a human being in an effort to get physical evidence from inside his body. The evidence against him so obtained should not have been admitted at the trial because it was gained in violation of the fourth amendment.

We find therefore that the seizure of the packet of heroin from defendant Tapp's throat exceeded the constitutional limitations of the fourth amendment requirement that safeguards the right to be free from unreasonable searches and seizures, and of the fifth and fourteenth amendments which assure individuals fair and humane treatment by law enforcement officers. Thus, the packet of heroin extracted from defendant's person should not have been admitted into evidence against him.

* * *

For these reasons, defendant's convictions and sentences are reversed and the case remanded to the district court.

REVERSED AND REMANDED.

[Concurring opinion omitted.]

SANDERS, Chief Justice (dissenting).

In my opinion, the majority erroneously interprets the struggle between the officers and the defendant as one in which the officers' only goal was to extract the heroin from the defendant's mouth. The record clearly indicates that the police action was aimed at both preventing the defendant from effectuating his escape and seizing the contraband. As the police had two objectives, their action must be allocated between these objectives.

When the officers attempted to place the defendant under arrest, he immediately ran, placing the cellophane packet in his mouth. An officer attempted to grab him from the rear, but the defendant resisted. Other officers joined in the struggle. The defendant continued to resist, fighting and kicking the officers. In a stipulation by the State and defense, the officers admitted that they hit the defendant three times before he was subdued.

Louisiana Code of Criminal Procedure Article 220 provides:

A person shall submit peaceably to a lawful arrest. The person making a lawful arrest may use reasonable force to effect the arrest and detention, and also to overcome any resistance or threatened resistance of the person being arrested or detained.

Under this codal provision, I believe the officers' action in using force to effectuate the arrest justified.

Whether police action in extracting contraband from the defendant's person is unreasonable, uncivilized, or shocking depends upon the totality of the circumstances.

As I construe the record, the only police action that may be directly attributed to the seizure of the evidence is the police's choking the defendant and their order to expel the packet. The issue then becomes: is the choking and the command unreasonable, uncivilized, or shocking. I think not.

* * *

It is common knowledge that narcotic offenders often try to swallow narcotics to defeat the law enforcement process. Law enforcement officers, of course, may adopt reasonable measures to retrieve the contraband. In the present case, the officers used a spoon to remove the particles of marijuana from the defendant's tongue. Under the circumstances, the action of the officers was neither cruel nor bizarre. As the United States Supreme Court observed in Schmerber v. California, the officers were confronted with an emergency that threatened the destruction of evidence.

Several courts in other jurisdictions have upheld similar seizures. *State v. Young*, (the officer "placed his hands on his throat, constricting his ability to swallow" and another officer pinched his nose to make the defendant breathe through his mouth and spit out the evidence); *United States v. Harrison*, (the officer grabbed the defendant by the throat and made him expel the evidence); *State v. Santos*, (the officers grabbed the defendant by the throat and tried to pry his mouth open); *Espinoza v. United States*, (the officers choked the defendant and attempted "to pry open his mouth by placing pressure against his jaw and nose"); *State v. O'Shea*, (the officers struggled with the defendant and "forced him to disgorge the papers he was attempting to swallow").

Considering the facts of this case and the cited jurisprudence, I conclude that the record supports the trial court's ruling that the evidence was reasonably seized. Thus, I would affirm the denial of the motion to suppress.

For the reasons assigned, I respectfully dissent.

Cases Relating to Chapter 8

Right to Counsel

GIDEON
v.
WAINWRIGHT

372 U.S. 335, 83 S. Ct. 792,
9 L. Ed. 2d 799 (1963)

[Gideon was charged in a Florida state court with having broken and entered a poolroom, an offense that was a felony under Florida law. Appearing in court without funds and without a lawyer, he asked the court to appoint counsel for him. The judge denied Gideon's request, advising him that under Florida law appointment of counsel was available only for defendants charged with a capital offense. Placed on trial before a jury, Gideon conducted his defense about as well as could be expected from a layperson. He made an opening statement to the jury, cross-examined the State's witnesses, presented witnesses in his own defense, declined to testify himself, and made a short closing argument emphasizing his innocence. The jury returned a verdict of guilty, and sentenced Gideon to serve five years in the state prison. The Florida Supreme Court denied Gideon's habeas corpus petition attacking his conviction and sentence on the ground that the trial court's refusal to appoint counsel for him denied him his constitutional rights.]

MR. JUSTICE BLACK delivered the opinion of the Court.

. . .Since 1942, when *Betts v. Brady* was decided by a divided Court, the problem of a defendant's federal constitutional right to counsel in a state court has been a continuing source of controversy and litigation in both state and federal courts. To give this problem another review here, we granted certiorari. Since Gideon was proceeding in forma pauperis, we appointed counsel to represent him and requested both sides to discuss in their briefs and oral arguments the following: "Should this Court's holding in *Betts v. Brady* be reconsidered?"

The facts upon which Betts claimed that he had been unconstitutionally denied the right to have counsel appointed to assist him are strikingly like the facts upon which Gideon here bases his federal constitutional claim. Betts was indicted for robbery in a Maryland state court. On arraignment, he told the trial judge of his lack of funds to hire a lawyer and asked the court to appoint one for him. Betts was advised that it was not the practice in that county to appoint counsel for indigent defendants except in murder and rape cases. He then pleaded not guilty, had witnesses summoned, cross-examined the State's witnesses, examined his own, and chose not to testify himself. He was found guilty by the judge, sitting without a jury, and sentenced to eight years in prison. Like Gideon, Betts sought release by habeas corpus, alleging that he had been denied the right to assistance of counsel in violation of the Fourteenth Amendment. Betts was denied any relief, and on review this Court affirmed. It was held that a refusal to appoint counsel for an indigent defendant charged with a felony did not necessarily violate the Due Process Clause of the Fourteenth Amendment, which for reasons given the Court deemed to be the only applicable federal constitutional provision. The Court said:

> Asserted denial [of due process] is to be tested by an appraisal of the totality of facts in a given case. That which may, in one setting, constitute a denial of fundamental fairness, shocking to the universal sense of justice, may, in other circumstances, and in the light of other considerations, fall short of such denial.

Treating due process as "a concept less rigid and more fluid than those envisaged in other specific and particular provisions of the Bill of Rights," the Court held that refusal to appoint counsel under the particular facts and circumstances in the *Betts* case was not so "offensive to the common and fundamental ideas of fairness" as to amount to a denial of due process. Since the facts and circumstances of the two cases are so nearly indistinguishable, we think the *Betts v. Brady* holding if left standing would require us to reject Gideon's claim that the Constitution guarantees him the assistance of counsel. Upon full reconsideration we conclude that *Betts v. Brady* should be overruled.

The Sixth Amendment provides, "In all criminal prosecutions, the accused shall enjoy the right ... to have the Assistance of Counsel for his defence." We have construed this to mean that in federal courts counsel must be provided for defendants unable to employ counsel unless the right is competently and intelligently waived. Betts argued that this right is extended to indigent defendants in state courts by the Fourteenth Amendment. In response the Court stated that, while the Sixth Amendment laid down "no rule for the conduct of the States, the question recurs whether the constraint laid by the Amendment upon the national courts expresses a rule so fundamental and essential to a fair trial, and so, to due process of law, that it is made obligatory upon the States by the Fourteenth Amendment." In order to decide whether the Sixth Amendment's guarantee of counsel is of this fundamental nature, the Court in *Betts* set out and considered "relevant data on the subject ... afforded by constitutional and statutory provisions subsisting in the colonies and the States prior to the inclusion of the Bill of Rights in the national Constitution, and in the constitutional, legislative, and judicial history of the States to the present date." On the basis of this historical data the Court concluded that "appointment

of counsel is not a fundamental right, essential to a fair trial." It was for this reason the *Betts* Court refused to accept the contention that the Sixth Amendment's guarantee of counsel for indigent federal defendants was extended to or, in the words of that Court, "made obligatory upon the States by the Fourteenth Amendment." ...

* * *

We accept *Betts v. Brady's* assumption, based as it was on our prior cases, that a provision of the Bill of Rights which is "fundamental and essential to a fair trial" is made obligatory upon the States by the Fourteenth Amendment. We think the Court in *Betts* was wrong, however, in concluding that the Sixth Amendment's guarantee of counsel is not one of these fundamental rights. Ten years before *Betts v. Brady*, this Court, after full consideration of all the historical data examined in Betts, had unequivocally declared that "the right to the aid of counsel is of this fundamental character." While the Court at the close of its Powell opinion did by its language, as this Court frequently does, limit its holding to the particular facts and circumstances of that case, its conclusions about the fundamental nature of the right to counsel are unmistakable. Several years later, in 1936, the Court reemphasized what it had said about the fundamental nature of the right to counsel in this language:

> We concluded that certain fundamental rights, safeguarded by the first eight amendments against federal action, were also safeguarded against state action by the due process of law clause of the Fourteenth Amendment, and among them the fundamental right of the accused to the aid of counsel in a criminal prosecution.

And again in 1938 this Court said:

> "[The assistance of counsel] is one of the safeguards of the Sixth Amendment deemed necessary to insure fundamental human rights of life and liberty.... The Sixth Amendment stands as a constant admonition that if the constitutional safeguards it provides be lost, justice will not "still be done."

In light of these and many other prior decisions of this Court, it is not surprising that the Betts Court, when faced with the contention that "one charged with crime, who is unable to obtain counsel, must be furnished counsel by the State," conceded that "expressions in the opinions of this court lend color to the argument ..." The fact is that in deciding as it did—that "appointment of counsel is not a fundamental right, essential to a fair trial"—the Court in *Betts v. Brady* made an abrupt break with its own well-considered precedents. In returning to these old precedents, sounder we believe than the new, we but restore constitutional principles established to achieve a fair system of justice. Not only these precedents but also reason and reflection require us to recognize that in our adversary system of criminal justice, any person haled into court, who is too poor to hire a lawyer, cannot be assured a fair trial unless counsel is provided for him. This seems to us to be an obvious truth. Governments, both state and federal, quite properly spend vast sums of money to establish machinery to try defendants accused of crime. Lawyers to prosecute are everywhere deemed essential to protect the public's interest in an orderly society. Similarly, there are few defendants charged with crime, few indeed, who fail to hire the best lawyers they can get to prepare and present their defenses. That government hires lawyers to prosecute and defendants who have the money hire lawyers to defend are the strongest indications of the widespread belief that lawyers in criminal courts are necessities, not luxuries. The right of one charged with crime to counsel may not be deemed fundamental and essential to fair trials in some countries, but it is in ours. From the very beginning, our state and national constitutions and laws have laid great emphasis on procedural and substantive safeguards designed to assure fair trials before impartial tribunals in which every defendant stands equal before the law. This noble ideal cannot be realized if the poor man charged with crime has to face his accusers without a lawyer to assist him. A defendant's need for a lawyer is nowhere better stated than in the moving words of Mr. Justice Sutherland in *Powell v. Alabama*:

> The right to be heard would be, in many cases, of little avail if it did not comprehend the right to be heard by counsel. Even the intelligent and educated layman has small and sometimes no skill in the science of law. If charged with crime, he is incapable, generally, of determining for himself whether the indictment is good or bad. He is unfamiliar with the rules of evidence. Left without the aid of counsel he may be put on trial without a proper charge, and convicted upon incompetent evidence, or evidence irrelevant to the issue or otherwise inadmissible. He lacks both the skill and knowledge adequately to prepare his defense, even though he have a perfect one. He requires the guiding hand of counsel at every step in the proceedings against him. Without it, though he be not guilty, he faces the danger of conviction because he does not know how to establish his innocence.

The Court in *Betts v. Brady* departed from the sound wisdom upon which the Court's holding in *Powell v. Alabama* rested. Florida, supported by two other States, has asked that *Betts v. Brady* be left intact. Twenty-two States, as friends of the Court, argue that *Betts* was "an anachronism when handed down" and that it should now be overruled. We agree.

The judgment is reversed and the cause is remanded to the Supreme Court of Florida for further action not inconsistent with this opinion.

Reversed.

ROTHGERY
v.
GILLESPIE COUNTY, TEXAS

554 U.S. 191, 128 S. Ct. 2578, 171 L. Ed. 2d 366 (2008)

[Citations and footnotes omitted]

[Walter Allen Rothgery was arrested without a warrant and charged with being a felon in possession of a firearm. He was brought before a local magistrate, advised of the charges against him, a probable cause determination was made, and he was released on bond. Between the hearing and the indictment he made several requests for appointed counsel, but his request went unheeded. At his arraignment on the indictment, his bail was increased. When he could not post it, he was put in jail where he remained for several weeks until counsel was appointed. Appointed counsel quickly assembled paperwork establishing that Rothgery had never been convicted of a felony and the indictment was dismissed. Following his release, Rothgery sued, claiming that if the county had provided him with a lawyer within a reasonable time after his initial appearance, he would not have been indicted, rearrested, or jailed, and that its failure to do so violated his Sixth Amendment right to counsel.]

Justice SOUTER delivered the opinion of the Court.

* * *

The Sixth Amendment right of the "accused" to assistance of counsel in "all criminal prosecutions" is limited by its terms: "it does not attach until a prosecution is commenced." We have, for purposes of the right to counsel, pegged commencement to " 'the initiation of adversary judicial criminal proceedings—whether by way of formal charge, preliminary hearing, indictment, information, or arraignment,' " The rule is not a "mere formalism." but a recognition of the point at which the government has committed itself to prosecute," 'the adverse positions of government and defendant have solidified,' and the accused 'finds himself faced with the prosecutorial forces of organized society, and immersed in the intricacies of substantive and procedural criminal law.' " The issue is whether Texas's article 15.17 hearing marks that point, with the consequent state obligation to appoint counsel within a reasonable time once a request for assistance is made.

* * *

... [W]e have twice held that the right to counsel attaches at the initial appearance before a judicial officer. This first time before a court, also known as the "preliminary arraignment"; or "arraignment on the complaint," is generally the hearing at which "the magistrate informs the defendant of the charge in the complaint, and of various rights in further proceedings," and "determine[s] the conditions for pretrial release." Texas's article 15.17 hearing is an initial appearance: Rothgery was taken before a magistrate judge, informed of the formal accusation against him, and sent to jail until he posted bail.

* * *

... [By] the time a defendant is brought before a judicial officer, is informed of a formally lodged accusation, and has restrictions imposed on his liberty in aid of the prosecution, the State's relationship with the defendant has become solidly adversarial. And that is just as true when the proceeding comes before

the indictment (in the case of the initial arraignment on a formal complaint) as when it comes after it (at an arraignment on an indictment).

* * *

Our holding is narrow. We do not decide whether the 6-month delay in appointment of counsel resulted in prejudice to Rothgery's Sixth Amendment rights, and have no occasion to consider what standards should apply in deciding this. We merely reaffirm what we have held before and what an overwhelming majority of American jurisdictions understand in practice: a criminal defendant's initial appearance before a judicial officer, where he learns the charge against him and his liberty is subject to restriction, marks the start of adversary judicial proceedings that trigger attachment of the Sixth Amendment right to counsel. Because the Fifth Circuit came to a different conclusion on this threshold issue, its judgment is vacated, and the case is remanded for further proceedings consistent with this opinion.

It is so ordered.

STATE
v.
QUATTLEBAUM

338 S. C. 441, 527 S.E.2d 105 (2001)

[Appellant voluntarily went to the sheriff's office for questioning concerning his involvement in an armed robbery and murder and agreed to take a polygraph examination. After the exam was administered, he was left alone in the polygraph room where he was joined by his attorney. Unbeknownst to either of them, their conversation was audio and videotaped by detectives in the presence of a deputy solicitor. This fact was not revealed to appellant or his attorneys for two years. The deputy solicitor who participated in the eavesdropping was an active participant in appellant's trial and gave the closing argument in the guilt phase. The jury convicted appellant and recommended a sentence of death. This appeal followed.]

BURNETT, Justice:

* * *

Appellant argues his Sixth Amendment right to counsel was violated and the solicitor's office should have been disqualified as a result. We agree.

The Sixth Amendment right to counsel protects the integrity of the adversarial system of criminal justice by ensuring that all persons accused of crimes have access to effective assistance of counsel for their defense. The right is grounded in "the presumed inability of a defendant to make informed choices about the preparation and conduct of his defense." Although the Sixth Amendment right to counsel is distinguishable from the attorney-client privilege, the two concepts overlap in many ways. The right to counsel would be meaningless without the protection of free and open communication between client and counsel. The United States Supreme Court has noted that "conferences between counsel and accused ... sometimes partake of the inviolable character of the confessional."

* * *

This is, fortunately, a case of first impression in South Carolina. Never before have we addressed a case involving deliberate prosecutorial intrusion into a privileged conversation between a criminal defendant and his attorney. Federal jurisprudence in this area is decidedly ambiguous, and we have found no precedent dealing with a prosecutor deliberately eavesdropping on an accused and his attorney.

In the 1950s and 1960s, when first faced with cases involving government eavesdropping on attorney-client conversations, federal courts refused to examine either the government's motives or the degree of prejudice to the defendant. Over time, the rule that began to emerge would have required either a showing of deliberate prosecutorial misconduct or prejudice, but not both.

In 1977, the United States Supreme Court appeared to alter this standard in *Weatherford v. Bursey.* Weatherford involved an informant/codefendant who attended meetings between Bursey and his attorney. The Supreme Court found no Sixth Amendment violation where there was no tainted evidence, no communication of defense strategy to the prosecution, and no purposeful intrusion by the government. The Court held that establishing a violation of a defendant's Sixth Amendment right to counsel requires a showing of "at least a realistic possibility" of prejudice.

Because the government interceptions in *Weatherford* were "unintended and undisclosed," the Court did not address whether the rule would be different in a case involving deliberate misconduct by the government. Nor did the Court decide who bears the burden of proving prejudice. . . .

Weatherford is inapplicable to the case sub judice, where a member of the prosecution team intentionally eavesdropped on a confidential defense conversation. We conclude, consistent with existing federal precedent, that a defendant must show either deliberate prosecutorial misconduct or prejudice to make out a violation of the Sixth Amendment, but not both. Deliberate prosecutorial misconduct raises an irrebuttable presumption of prejudice. The content of the protected communication is not relevant. The focus must be on the misconduct. In cases involving unintentional intrusions into the attorney-client relationship, the defendant must make a prima facie showing of prejudice to shift the burden to the prosecution to prove the defendant was not prejudiced.

Because a deputy solicitor of the Eleventh Circuit Solicitor's Office eavesdropped on a privileged conversation between appellant and his attorney, we reverse appellant's conviction and disqualify the Eleventh Circuit Solicitor's office from prosecuting appellant at his new trial.

Although we have disqualified the Eleventh Circuit Solicitor's Office from prosecuting appellant, we address appellant's second assertion because of its importance to judges, attorneys, criminal defendants, and indeed all citizens of this state. Every South Carolinian has a vital interest in the fair administration of justice. This Court bears the ultimate responsibility for maintaining judicial integrity and high standards of professional conduct among the members of the bar, and for protecting and defending the constitutional rights of the accused.

The integrity of the entire judicial system is called into question by conduct such as that engaged in by the deputy solicitor and investigating officers in this case. Prosecutors are ministers of justice and not merely advocates. A prosecutor has special responsibilities to do justice and is held to the highest standards of professional ethics. The participation at trial of a prosecutor who has eavesdropped on the accused and his attorney tarnishes us all. We will not tolerate deliberate prosecutorial misconduct which threatens rights fundamental to liberty and justice.

REVERSED

UNITED STATES
v.
DOWNS

230 F.3d 272 (7th Cir. 2000)

DIANE P. WOOD, Circuit Judge.

* * *

On March 31, 1999, a white male wearing sunglasses and a blue hat resembling those issued by the LaPrairie Mutual Insurance Company approached Denise Brown, the walk-up teller at Heritage Bank. He told Brown to remove all of the money from the drawer, but then, speaking in a low voice, he altered his instructions and indicated that he wanted only bundles and no $1 bills. Brown later said that she paid close attention to his mouth and lower face, because she was concerned that the robber might become agitated if she had difficulty understanding him. In the 50-some seconds she had to observe him, she also formed the impression that he was lightly unshaven, between 5'6" and 5'8" tall, about 150 pounds, and between 35 and 45 years old. The other teller on duty, Karen Jones, was serving drive-up customers and thus caught only a glimpse of the robber; her description of him was similar to Brown's.

The next day, someone gave Peoria police officers and FBI agents a tip that a woman named Kim Salzman could help them. Salzman was cooperative. She told the officers that the person in the surveillance video from the bank strongly resembled her brother, Randy Downs. Her statement, along with her account that Downs's gambling problems had led him to break into her printing business and steal a compressor in order to pawn it, increased the suspicions of the investigators. They decided to assemble a photo array and show it to both Brown and Jones. They did so, but neither was able positively to identify Downs as the robber from the pictures. Brown suggested that it would be more helpful to see people wearing hats and sunglasses.

Later that day, the officers interviewed Downs himself, first on a gambling boat and then later in a security office. The next day, they talked to Richard Downs, his father. The elder Mr. Downs told the officers that he had given Randy a hat from LaPrairie Mutual Insurance very similar to the one that appeared on the video. He also volunteered that when he had refused to loan Randy $2,000, Randy had responded "you leave me little choice." After this, the officers searched Randy's apartment, with his consent; they found nothing there.

On April 5, the officers held the line-up that is the focus of this appeal. On that day, they had finally arrested Downs and brought him to the police station. One officer telephoned Jones and asked her to come to the station, and he informed Jones that they had arrested someone. Another officer called Brown and asked her to come, but it is unclear whether or not she was told there had been an arrest. For the line-up, each person was given a LaPrairie Mutual hat and a pair of sunglasses. They entered the room seriatim; each man stepped in, walked around, and said "No, put the money in the envelope, hurry." Downs was the second to walk in. As the exhibits Downs later introduced make crystal clear, the other four all sported heavy moustaches; only Downs had no facial hair at all. Otherwise (but it is a big "otherwise"), they were similar in body build.

At the line-up, both Brown and Jones identified Downs as the robber. Jones was not very confident in her choice, describing her certainty as a seven out of ten, if ten meant absolutely sure. Brown, in contrast, jumped behind one of the detectives the minute she saw Downs enter the room, and exclaimed "Oh my God, that's him." She was crying and trembling, according to the testimony of another officer. Brown then viewed the last three line-up participants, and at the end reiterated that she was "positive" the robber was Downs, based on "the lower half of his face" and his "stocky upper body."

On July 1, 1999, the district court heard testimony on Downs's motion to suppress both the line-up and any in-court identification the government might want to elicit from Brown or Jones. The court concluded that the line-up was indeed too suggestive. It then decided that the Jones testimony would be so unreliable that both her line-up identification should be suppressed and she should be prevented from offering an in-court identification. With respect to Brown, the oral rulings and written record became somewhat confused. Orally, the court first indicated that the circumstances as a whole made Brown's identification reliable and thus admissible. Then, in response to a question from the prosecutor, the judge said that both women's line-up identifications would be suppressed. Later, however, in a written order the court ruled that Brown could be questioned about her line-up identification (and could give an in-court statement).

* * *

A ruling on a motion to suppress an identification, like many other matters in a criminal trial, presents the kind of mixed question of constitutional law and fact that the Supreme Court has instructed us to review de novo, but with due deference to findings of historical fact made by the district court.

On the merits, we conduct a two-step inquiry when we assess the admissibility of a line-up identification. First, we ask whether the line-up was unduly suggestive. If it was, then we look more closely to see if the totality of the circumstances nevertheless shows that the testimony was reliable. In this case, although the government has made a token effort to argue that the line-up was not unduly suggestive, we agree entirely with the district court that it was. Even a glance at the photographs of the men in the line-up, which appear as exhibits in the record, is enough to see why Downs jumps out from the others because of his lack of facial hair. We therefore turn immediately to the second question, whether Brown's testimony was reliable notwithstanding the problems with the line-up.

The reliability inquiry touches on five factors: (1) the opportunity of the witness to view the criminal at the time of the crime, (2) the witness's degree of attention, (3) the accuracy of the witness's prior description, (4) the level of certainty demonstrated by the witness at the confrontation, and (5) the length of time between the crime and the confrontation. All of these, in one way or another, support the reliability of Brown's identification. She could see the lower half of the robber's face, and this was the basis of her identification. At the time of the crime, she was very close to the robber, and she stated firmly that she was paying strict attention to what she saw. Although 50 seconds may not sound like much, under conditions of great stress they can pass quite slowly. The physical descriptions Brown had given of the robber were reasonably detailed and close to Brown's actual appearance. Brown's dramatic reaction when Downs walked into the room showed clearly that she was quite certain that Downs was the robber. Finally, five days between the incident and the line-up is not such a long span of time that memory lapses would be a problem.

Last is a point not mentioned in this particular five-factor test, but it gives us the opportunity both to note that these tests are principally useful as a guide to the inquiry at hand and that they are not intended to be straitjackets. Given the way this line-up was conducted, Brown had seen only one man (who had a moustache) before she saw Downs and emphatically identified him. She did not know then that the other three men would also have moustaches (or indeed that they would either resemble Downs or stand apart from him in any other way). This as well as the other evidence convinces us that Brown knew what she was talking about; her identification of Downs at the line-up was sufficiently reliable that the jury was entitled to learn about it, and there was no error in allowing her to identify him at trial.

In light of our conclusion that the flaws in the line-up did not require the suppression of Brown's testimony, we need not reach the government's alternative argument that any error in this respect was harmless. The judgment of the district court is

AFFIRMED.

Cases Relating to Chapter 9

Trial and Punishment

AMERICAN BAR ASSOCIATION STANDARDS FOR CRIMINAL JUSTICE (3RD. ED. 1992)

Chapter 8 FAIR TRIAL and FREE PRESS

STANDARD 8-1.1. EXTRAJUDICIAL STATEMENTS BY ATTORNEYS

(a) A lawyer should not make or authorize the making of an extrajudicial statement that a reasonable person would expect to be disseminated by means of public communication if the lawyer knows or reasonably should know that it will have a substantial likelihood of prejudicing a criminal proceeding.

(b) Statements relating to the following matters are ordinarily likely to have a substantial likelihood of prejudicing a criminal proceeding:

(1) the prior criminal record (including arrests, indictments, or other charges of crime) of a suspect or defendant;

(2) the character or reputation of a suspect or defendant;

(3) the opinion of the lawyer on the guilt of the defendant, the merits of the case or the merits of the evidence in the case;

(4) the existence or contents of any confession, admission, or statement given by the accused, or the refusal or failure of the accused to make a statement;

(5) the performance of any examinations or tests, or the accused's refusal or failure to submit to an examination or test, or the identity or nature of physical evidence expected to presented.

(6) the identity, expected testimony, criminal record or credibility of prospective witnesses;

(7) the possibility of a plea of guilty to the offense charged, or other disposition; and

(8) information which the lawyer knows or has reason to know would be inadmissible as evidence in a trial.

(c) Notwithstanding paragraphs (a) and (b), statements relating to the following matters may be made:

(1) the general nature of the charges against the accused, provided that there is included therein a statement explaining that the charge is merely an accusation and the defendant is presumed innocent until and unless proven guilty;

(2) the general nature of the defense to the charges or to other public accusations against the accused, including that the accused has no prior criminal record;

(3) the name, age, residence, occupation and family status of the accused;

(4) information necessary to aid in the apprehension of the accused or to warn the public of any dangers that may exist.

(5) a request for assistance in obtaining evidence;

(6) the existence of an investigation in progress, including the general length and scope of the investigation, the charge or defense involved, and the identity of the investigating officer or agency;

(7) the facts and circumstances of an arrest, including the time and place, and the identity of the arresting officer or agency;

(8) the identity of the victim, where the release of that information is not otherwise prohibited by law or would not be harmful to the victim;

(9) information contained within a public record, without further comment; and

(10) the scheduling or result of any stage in the judicial process;

(d) Nothing in this standard is intended to preclude the formulation or application of more restrictive rules relating to the release of information about juvenile offenders, to preclude the holding of hearings or the lawful issuance of reports by legislative, administrative, or investigative bodies, to preclude any lawyer from replying to charges of misconduct that are publicly made against him or her, or to preclude or inhibit any lawyer from making an otherwise permissible statement which serves to educate or inform the public concerning the operations of the criminal justice system.

STANDARD 8-2.1. RELEASE OF INFORMATION BY LAW ENFORCEMENT AGENCIES

(a) The provisions of Standard 1.1 should be applicable to the release of information to the public by law enforcement officers and agencies.

(b) Law enforcement officers and agencies should not exercise their custodial authority over an accused individual in a manner that is likely to result in either: (1) the deliberate exposure of a person in custody for the purpose of photographing or televising by representatives of the news media, or (2) the interviewing by representatives of the news media of a person in custody except upon request or consent by that person to an interview after being informed adequately of the right to consult with counsel and of the right to refuse to grant an interview.

(c) Nothing in this standard is intended to preclude any law enforcement officer or agency from replying to charges of misconduct that are publicly made against him or her from participating in any legislative, administrative, or investigative hearing, nor is the standard intended to supersede more restrictive rules governing the release of information concerning juvenile offenders.

KYLES
v.
WHITLEY

514 U.S. 419, 115 S. Ct. 1555, 131 L. Ed. 2d 490 (1995)

[Citations and footnotes omitted.]

[An elderly woman was shot in the head and killed in a grocery store parking lot. The killer took her keys and drove away in her car. Since the police believed the killer might have driven his own car to the lot and left it there when he drove off in the victim's car, they recorded the license numbers of the cars remaining in the parking lots around the store. Kyles's car was not among these listed. Police also took descriptions from six eyewitnesses. Their descriptions of the killer's height, age, weight, build, and hair length differed significantly from each other and most bore little resemblance to Kyles.

The investigation did not focus on Kyles until an informant known as Beanie, who resembled the descriptions given by the witnesses, told police that the Kyles committed the crime. Kyles was indicted for first-degree murder. Before trial, Kyles's attorney filed a motion for disclosure by the prosecutor of any exculpatory or impeachment evidence. The prosecutor responded that there was none. The prosecutor, however, was unaware of the following items in the hands of the police because the prosecutor was never informed of these items: (1) contemporaneous descriptions given by the six eyewitnesses; (2) the computer print-out of license numbers of cars parked in the grocery store parking lot on the night of the murder; and (3) evidence linking Beanie to other crimes committed in the same parking lot, including an unrelated murder.

Kyles's first trial ended in a hung jury. At the second trial, the prosecution offered a blown-up photograph taken at the crime scene soon after the murder and argued that a poorly-discernible vehicle in the background belonged to Kyles. Kyles maintained his innocence. The defense's theory was that Kyles had been framed by Beanie. Kyles was convicted and sentenced to death.]

JUSTICE SOUTER delivered the opinion of the Court.

* * *

The prosecution's affirmative duty to disclose evidence favorable to a defendant can trace its origins to early 20th-century strictures against misrepresentation and is of course most prominently associated with this Court's decision in *Brady v. Maryland*. *Brady* held "that the suppression by the prosecution of evidence favorable to an accused upon request violates due process where the evidence is material either to guilt or to punishment, irrespective of the good faith or bad faith of the prosecution.". . .

. . . [F]avorable evidence is material, and constitutional error results from its suppression by the government, "if there is a reasonable probability that, had the evidence been disclosed to the defense, the result of the proceeding would have been different."

* * *

While the definition of *Bagley* materiality in terms of the cumulative effect of suppression must accordingly be seen as leaving the government with a degree of discretion, it must also be understood as imposing a corresponding burden. On the one side, showing that the prosecution knew of an item of favorable evidence unknown to the defense does not amount to a *Brady* violation, without more. But the prosecution, which alone can know what is undisclosed, must be assigned the consequent responsibility to gauge the likely net effect of all such evidence and make disclosure when the point of "reasonable probability" is reached. This in turn means that the individual prosecutor has a duty to learn of any favorable evidence known to the others acting on the government's behalf in the case, including the police. But whether the prosecutor succeeds or fails in meeting this obligation (whether, that is, a failure to disclose is in good faith or bad faith), the prosecution's responsibility for failing to disclose known, favorable evidence rising to a material level of importance is inescapable.

The State of Louisiana would prefer an even more lenient rule. It pleads that some of the favorable evidence in issue here was not disclosed even to the prosecutor until after trial, and it suggested below that it should not be held accountable under *Bagley and Brady* for evidence known only to police investigators and not to the prosecutor. To accommodate the State in this manner would, however, amount to a serious change of course

from the *Brady* line of cases. In the State's favor it may be said that no one doubts that police investigators sometimes fail to inform a prosecutor of all they know. But neither is there any serious doubt that "procedures and regulations can be established to carry [the prosecutor's] burden and to insure communication of all relevant information on each case to every lawyer who deals with it." Since, then, the prosecutor has the means to discharge the government's *Brady* responsibility if he will, any argument for excusing a prosecutor from disclosing what he does not happen to know about boils down to a plea to substitute the police for the prosecutor, and even for the courts themselves, as the final arbiters of the government's obligation to ensure fair trials.

* * *

In this case, disclosure of the suppressed evidence to competent counsel would have made a different result reasonably probable.

As the District Court put it, "the essence of the State's case" was the testimony of eyewitnesses, who identified Kyles as Dye's killer. Disclosure of their statements would have resulted in a markedly weaker case for the prosecution and a markedly stronger one for the defense. To begin with, the value of two of those witnesses would have been substantially reduced or destroyed.

* * *

Next to be considered is the prosecution's list of the cars in the Schwegmann's parking lot at mid-evening after the murder. . . . [I]t would have had some value as exculpation and impeachment, and it counts accordingly in determining whether *Bagley*'s standard of materiality is satisfied. On the police's assumption, argued to the jury, that the killer drove to the lot and left his car there during the heat of the investigation, the list without Kyles's registration would obviously have helped Kyles and would have had some value in countering an argument by the prosecution that a grainy enlargement of a photograph of the crime scene showed Kyles's car in the background. The list would also have shown that the police either knew that it was inconsistent with their informant's second and third statements (in which Beanie described retrieving Kyles's car after the time the list was compiled) or never even bothered to check the informant's story against known fact. Either way, the defense would have had further support for arguing that the police were irresponsible in relying on Beanie to tip them off to the location of evidence damaging to Kyles.

* * *

[The State's obligation under *Brady* to disclose evidence favorable to the defense turns on the cumulative effect of all such evidence suppressed by the government. We hold that the prosecutor remains responsible for gauging that effect, regardless of any failure by the police to bring favorable evidence to the prosecutor's attention. Because the net effect of the evidence withheld by the State in this case raises a reasonable probability that its disclosure would have produced a different result, Kyles is entitled to a new trial.]

The judgment of the Court of Appeals is reversed, and the case is remanded for further proceedings consistent with this opinion.

It is so ordered.

[Concurring and dissenting opinions omitted.]

PEOPLE
v.
WRIGHT

658 N.E.2d 1009,
635 N.Y.S.2d 136 (N.Y. Ct. App. 1995)

[Citations and footnotes omitted.]

[Defendant was charged with assaulting a man named Washington. Her defense was that she was trying to fend off an attempted rape. According to the defendant, the two of them had met at a bar and as she prepared to leave the bar she noticed that her jacket was missing. Washington told her that his friend had it and offered to call him, but not from the bar. Defendant agreed to let Washington call from her apartment. At her apartment, she showed Washington the phone in the living room, and went to the bedroom to hide her purse. While she was in the bedroom Washington entered naked and announced his intention to have sex with her. Fearing for her safety, she took a knife and injured him. According to Washington, the defendant invited him back to her apartment, allowed him to undress in her bedroom and then took out a knife and attacked him.

After the altercation, the defendant called police to her home. Investigating officer Walczak stated in his police report that he recovered a pair of boxer shorts, a shoe and a hat from defendant's apartment that night, and that these articles were located outside the bedroom, facts that substantiated the defendant's account. At trial, however, he testified that the shoe and boxer shorts were found inside the bedroom, and that the hat was discovered at the threshold to the bedroom, which supported Washington's account. Detective Keane, who took Washington's statement, recorded that Washington stated he undressed outside the bedroom, but at trial testified that he could not remember whether Washington had said this.

The defendant was convicted and eventually moved to set aside her conviction after learning that Washington was an occasional informant for the police department. Defendant argued that the state's failure to disclose this information to the defense required a new trial because, among other reasons, the state should have disclosed the victim's status as a police informant.]

Chief Judge Kaye.

This case presents the question whether the People's failure to inform the defendant that the complainant had previously operated as an informant for the local police department violated defendant's right to due process. We conclude that the People were required to disclose this information pursuant to *Brady v. Maryland* and therefore reverse defendant's conviction.

* * *

In *Brady v. Maryland*, the Supreme Court held that the prosecution has an affirmative duty to disclose to the defense evidence in its possession that is both favorable to the defense and material to guilt or punishment. . . . [T]he failure to disclose *Brady* material violates a defendant's constitutional right to due process.

* * *

Manifestly, Washington's status as a police informant was evidence favorable to the defense here. Specifically, the reports prepared by Detective Keane and Officer Walczak confirmed defendant's claim that Washington was already undressed when he entered her bedroom. Nevertheless, at trial both officers supported Washington's version of events—Walczak contradicted his report and testified that Washington's boxer shorts and shoe were discovered inside defendant's bedroom, and Keane could no longer recall whether Washington had stated that he entered defendant's bedroom without any clothing. Had defendant been armed with the knowledge that Washington was an informant for the same police department that employed Keane and Walczak, she could have presented the jury with a motive for them to favor Washington. Like evidence tending to affect credibility, evidence establishing such a motive for prosecution witnesses to corroborate the complainant falls within the ambit of the Brady rule. Additionally, that Washington had previously operated as a police informant would have provided the defense with an explanation for the decision by the police to disbelieve, and subsequently to arrest, defendant—who promptly notified 911 following the incident—as opposed to Washington.

The People's failure to disclose this favorable evidence to the defense requires reversal, however, only if the evidence was material. . . . [T]he undisclosed evidence must be deemed material because there is a reasonable probability that, had the evidence been disclosed to the defense, the result of the proceeding would have been different.

The outcome of this case turned on whether the jury believed Washington's account of an unprovoked attack or defendant's claim that Washington entered the bedroom naked planning to rape her. Whether Washington undressed inside or outside the bedroom constituted a critical issue in this close credibility contest. Washington's status as a police informant provided the defense with an explanation for Keane's and Walczak's switch to a version of the facts that supported Washington's contention that he undressed inside the bedroom. Tellingly, during deliberations the jury focused on this aspect of Walczak's trial testimony—it asked for a readback of his testimony regarding where Washington's clothing was discovered.

Also of central importance to the defense in this case was the argument that Washington's reluctance to go to the hospital or the police after he was allegedly brutally victimized by defendant evidenced his consciousness of guilt and undermined his credibility. In summation, the prosecutor explained Washington's behavior by arguing that, because of his criminal record, Washington did not "expect justice from the system":

[M]aybe [Fred Washington] didn't want to go to the hospital because he's thinking the cops are going to think I did something wrong, this looks bad. You know, I didn't do anything but hey, the cops know me and maybe once a criminal, always a criminal, and you know, I didn't do anything, but hey, I've done things in the past. . . . You know, I've been on the other side of the criminal justice system. I've been arrested and the cops aren't my friends (emphasis added).

Evidence that Washington had, in fact, provided the police with information on prior occasions would have effectively refuted the prosecutor's proffered justification for Washington's behavior. Indeed, had the jury been aware that Washington had a relationship with the local police, his efforts to circumvent police discovery might have appeared even more suspicious.

Under these circumstances, Washington's history as a police informant was both favorable and material to the defense, and the People's failure to disclose this information to the defense violated defendant's constitutional right to due process. The People's reliance in their opposition papers on the trial prosecutor's lack of personal knowledge regarding any instances in which Washington had operated as an informant is unavailing. The mandate of Brady extends beyond any particular prosecutor's actual knowledge. Furthermore, "the individual prosecutor has a duty to learn of any favorable evidence known to the others acting on the government's behalf in the case, including the police." The People therefore were not relieved of their obligation to turn over Brady material by the trial prosecutor's failure to discover that the police were in possession of exculpatory information.

In light of our conclusion that the People's nondisclosure of Washington's status as a police informant violated defendant's right to due process, we need not reach defendant's remaining contentions.

Accordingly, the order of the Appellate Division should be reversed and the indictment dismissed without prejudice to an application by the People for leave to resubmit the charge of assault in the second degree.

Order reversed, etc.

ARIZONA
v.
YOUNGBLOOD

488 U.S. 51, 109 S. Ct. 333, 102 L. Ed.2d 281 (1988)

[Citations and footnotes omitted.]

[The victim, a 10-year-old boy, was abducted, molested, and sodomized by a middle-aged man. After the assault, he was taken to a hospital where a physician used a swab from a "sexual assault kit" to collect samples of the perpetrator's semen. The sample taken was insufficient for adequate testing. The police failed to refrigerate the boy's clothing, which also contained semen. As a result, police criminologists were unable to obtain information about the identity of the boy's assailant. The boy identified the respondent. Defense experts testified at the trial that respondent might have been completely exonerated by timely performance of tests on properly preserved semen samples. Respondent was convicted of child molestation, sexual assault, and kidnapping. The Arizona Court of Appeals reversed the conviction on the ground that the State had breached a constitutional duty to preserve the semen samples from the victim's body and clothing.]

Chief Justice REHNQUIST delivered the opinion of the Court.

* * *

Decision of this case requires us to again consider "what might loosely be called the area of constitutionally-guaranteed access to evidence." In *Brady v. Maryland* we held "that the suppression by the prosecution of evidence favorable to the accused upon request violates due process where the evidence is material either to guilt or to punishment, irrespective of the good faith or bad faith of the prosecution." In *United States v. Agurs*, we held that the prosecution had a duty to disclose some evidence of this description even though no requests were made for it, but at the same time we rejected the notion that a "prosecutor has a constitutional duty routinely to deliver his entire file to defense counsel."

There is no question but that the State complied with *Brady* and *Agurs* here. The State disclosed relevant police reports to respondent, which contained information about the existence of the swab and the clothing, and the boy's examination at the hospital. The State provided respondent's expert with the laboratory reports and notes prepared by the police criminologist, and respondent's expert had access to the swab and to the clothing.

If respondent is to prevail on federal constitutional grounds, then, it must be because of some constitutional duty over and above that imposed by cases such as *Brady* and *Agurs*. Our most recent decision in this area of the law, *California v. Trombetta*, arose out of a drunk driving prosecution in which the State had introduced test results indicating the concentration of alcohol in the blood of two motorists. The defendants sought to suppress the test results on the ground that the State had failed to preserve the breath samples used in the test. We rejected this argument for several reasons: first, "the officers here were acting in 'good faith and in accord with their normal practice' "; second, in the light of the procedures actually used the chances that preserved samples would have exculpated the defendants were slim; and, third, even if the samples might have shown inaccuracy in the tests, the defendants had "alternative means of demonstrating their innocence." In the present case, the likelihood that the preserved materials would have enabled the defendant to exonerate himself appears to be greater than it was in *Trombetta*, but here, unlike in *Trombetta*, the State did not attempt to make any use of the materials in its own case in chief.

* * *

The Due Process Clause of the Fourteenth Amendment, as interpreted in *Brady*, makes the good or bad faith of the State irrelevant when the State fails to disclose to the defendant material exculpatory evidence. But we think the Due Process Clause requires a different result when we deal with the failure of the State to preserve evidentiary material of which no more can be said than that it could have been subjected to tests, the results of which might have exonerated the defendant. Part of the reason for the difference in treatment is found in the observation made by the Court in *Trombetta* that "[w]henever potentially exculpatory evidence is permanently lost, courts face the treacherous task of divining the import of materials whose contents are unknown and, very often, disputed." Part of it stems from our unwillingness to read the "fundamental fairness" requirement of the Due Process Clause as imposing on the police an undifferentiated and absolute duty to retain and to preserve all material that might be of conceivable evidentiary significance in a particular prosecution. We think that requiring a defendant to show bad faith on the part of the police both limits the extent of the police's obligation to preserve evidence to reasonable bounds and confines it to that class of cases where the interests of justice most clearly require it, i.e., those cases in which the police themselves by their conduct indicate that the evidence could form a basis for exonerating the defendant. We therefore hold that unless a criminal defendant can show bad faith on the part of the police, failure to preserve potentially useful evidence does not constitute a denial of due process of law.

In this case, the police collected the rectal swab and clothing on the night of the crime: respondent was not taken into custody until six weeks later. The failure of the police to refrigerate the clothing and to perform tests on the semen samples can at worst be described as negligent. None of this information was concealed from respondent at trial, and the evidence—such as it was—was made available to respondent's expert who declined to perform any tests on the samples. The Arizona Court of Appeals noted in its opinion—and we agree—that there was no suggestion of bad faith on the part of the police. It follows, therefore, from what we have said, that there was no violation of the Due Process Clause.

The Arizona Court of Appeals also referred somewhat obliquely to the State's "inability to quantitatively test" certain semen samples with the newer P-30 test. If the court meant by this statement that the Due Process Clause is violated when the police fail to use a particular investigatory tool, we strongly disagree. The situation here is no different than a prosecution for drunk driving that rests on police observation alone; the defendant is free to argue to the finder of fact that a breathalyzer test might have been exculpatory, but the police do not have a constitutional duty to perform any particular tests.

The judgment of the Arizona Court of Appeals is reversed and the case remanded for further proceedings not inconsistent with this opinion.

Reversed.

COKER
v.
GEORGIA

433 U.S. 584, 97 S. Ct. 2861, 53 L. Ed. 2d 982 (1977)

[Citations and footnotes omitted.]

[Coker was convicted of rape and sentenced to death by a Georgia jury. His conviction and sentence were affirmed by the Georgia Supreme Court. Coker appealed, claiming that the punishment of death for the crime of rape violates the Eighth Amendment, which prohibits "cruel and unusual punishments."]

MR. JUSTICE WHITE announced the judgment of the Court

* * *

Furman v. Georgia, and the Court's decisions last Term in *Gregg v. Georgia* and others, make unnecessary the recanvassing of certain critical aspects of the controversy about the constitutionality of capital punishment. It is now settled that the death penalty is not invariably cruel and unusual punishment within the meaning of the Eighth Amendment; it is not inherently barbaric or an unacceptable mode of punishment for crime; neither is it always disproportionate to the crime for which it is imposed. It is also established that imposing capital punishment, at least for murder, in accordance with the procedures provided under the Georgia statutes saves the sentence from the infirmities which led the Court to invalidate the prior Georgia capital punishment statute in *Furman v. Georgia*.

In sustaining the imposition of the death penalty in *Gregg*, however, the Court firmly embraced the holdings and dicta from prior cases, *Furman v. Georgia*, *Robinson v. California*, *Trop v. Dulles*, and *Weems v. United States*, to the effect that the Eighth Amendment bars not only those punishments that are "barbaric" but also those that are "excessive" in relation to the crime committed. Under *Gregg*, a punishment is "excessive" and unconstitutional if it (1) makes no measurable contribution to acceptable goals of punishment and hence is nothing more than the purposeless and needless imposition of pain and suffering; or (2) is grossly out of proportion to the severity of the crime. A punishment might fail the test on either ground. Furthermore, these Eighth Amendment judgments should not be, or appear to be, merely the subjective views of individual Justices; judgment should be informed by objective factors to the maximum possible extent. To this end, attention must be given to the public attitudes concerning a particular sentence history and precedent, legislative attitudes, and the response of juries reflected in their sentencing decisions are to be consulted. In *Gregg*, after giving due regard to such sources, the Court's judgment was that the death penalty for deliberate murder was neither the purposeless imposition of severe punishment nor a punishment grossly disproportionate to the crime. But the Court reserved the question of the constitutionality of the death penalty when imposed for other crimes.

That question, with respect to rape of an adult woman, is now before us. We have concluded that a sentence of death is grossly disproportionate and excessive punishment for the crime of rape and is therefore forbidden by the Eighth Amendment as cruel and unusual punishment.

As advised by recent cases, we seek guidance in history and from the objective evidence of the country's present judgment concerning the acceptability of death as a penalty for rape of an adult woman. At no time in the last 50 years have a majority of the States authorized death as a punishment for rape. In 1925, 18 States, the District of Columbia, and the Federal Government authorized capital punishment for the rape of an adult female. By 1971 just prior to the decision in *Furman v. Georgia*, that number had declined, but not substantially, to 16 States plus the Federal Government. *Furman* then invalidated most of the capital punishment statutes in this country, including the rape statutes, because, among other reasons, of the manner in which the death penalty was imposed and utilized under those laws.

With their death penalty statutes for the most part invalidated, the States were faced with the choice of enacting modified capital punishment laws in an attempt to satisfy the requirements of *Furman* or of being satisfied with life imprisonment as the ultimate punishment for any offense. Thirty-five States immediately reinstituted the death penalty for at least limited kinds of crime.

This public judgment as to the acceptability of capital punishment, evidenced by the immediate, post-*Furman* legislative reaction in a large majority of the States, heavily influenced the Court to sustain the death penalty for murder in *Gregg v. Georgia*.

But if "the most marked indication of society's endorsement of the death penalty for murder is the legislative response to *Furman*," it should also be a telling datum that the public judgment with respect to rape, as reflected in the statutes providing the punishment for that crime, has been dramatically different. In reviving death penalty laws to satisfy *Furman's* mandate, none of the States that had not previously authorized death for rape chose to include rape among capital felonies. Of the 16 States in which rape had been a capital offense, only three provided the death penalty for rape of an adult woman in their revised statutes—Georgia, North Carolina, and Louisiana. In the latter two States, the death penalty was mandatory for those found guilty, and those laws were invalidated by *Woodson* and *Roberts*. When Louisiana and North Carolina, responding to those decisions, again revised their capital punishment laws, they re-enacted the death penalty for murder but not for rape; none of the seven other legislatures that to our knowledge have amended or replaced their death penalty statutes since July 2, 1976, including four States (in addition to Louisiana and North Carolina) that had authorized the death sentence for rape prior to 1972 and had reacted to *Furman* with mandatory statutes, included rape among the crimes for which death was an authorized punishment.

* * *

It should be noted that Florida, Mississippi, and Tennessee also authorized the death penalty in some rape cases, but only where the victim was a child and the rapist an adult. The Tennessee statute has since been invalidated because the death sentence was mandatory. The upshot is that Georgia is the sole jurisdiction in the United States at the present time that authorizes a sentence of death when the rape victim is an adult woman, and only two other jurisdictions provide capital punishment when the victim is a child.

The current judgment with respect to the death penalty for rape is not wholly unanimous among state legislatures, but it obviously weighs very heavily on the side of rejecting capital punishment as a suitable penalty for raping an adult woman.

* * *

These recent events evidencing the attitude of state legislatures ... do not wholly determine this controversy, for the Constitution contemplates that in the end our own judgment will be brought to bear on the question of the acceptability of the death penalty under the Eighth Amendment. Nevertheless, the legislative rejection of capital punishment for rape strongly confirms our own judgment, which is that death is indeed a disproportionate penalty for the crime of raping an adult woman.

We do not discount the seriousness of rape as a crime. It is highly reprehensible, both in a moral sense and in its almost total contempt for the personal integrity and autonomy of the female victim and for the latter's privilege of choosing those with whom intimate relationships are to be established. Short of homicide, it is the "ultimate violation of self." ...

* * *

Rape is without doubt deserving of serious punishment; but in terms of moral depravity and of the injury to the person and to the public, it does not compare with murder, which does involve the unjustified taking of human life. Although it may be accompanied by another crime, rape by definition does not include the death of or even the serious injury to another person. The murderer kills; the rapist, if no more than that, does not. Life is over for the victim of the murderer; for the rape victim, life may not be nearly so happy as it was, but it is not over and normally is not beyond repair. We have the abiding conviction that the death penalty, which is "unique in its severity and irrevocability," is an excessive penalty for the rapist who, as such, does not take human life.

* * *

... The judgment of the Georgia Supreme Court upholding the death sentence is reversed, and the case is remanded to that court for further proceedings not inconsistent with this opinion. So ordered.

[Concurring opinions omitted.]

Cases Relating to Chapter 10

Constitutional Rights and Liabilities in the Workplace

GARCETTI
v.
CEBALLOS

547 U.S. __, 126 S. Ct. 1951, 164 L. Ed. 2d 689 (2006)

[Citations and footnotes omitted.]

[Richard Ceballos was a supervising prosecutor in the Los Angeles County District Attorney's Office. His job responsibilities included reviewing pending cases and making recommendations for their disposition. In February 2000, he was contacted by a defense attorney who informed him that an affidavit used to obtain a critical search warrant in a pending prosecution contained serious misrepresentations and asked him to review the case. Requests like this were not uncommon. After examining the affidavit and conducting his own investigation, Ceballos concluded that the defense attorney was right. He submitted a memorandum to his supervisors, explaining his concerns and recommending dismissal of the case. His supervisors disregarded his advice and went ahead with the prosecution. Ceballos was subsequently transferred to a less desirable position and denied a promotion. He sued, claiming that these actions were in retaliation for his memorandum and violated his rights under the First Amendment.]

Justice KENNEDY delivered the opinion of the Court.

* * *

... [F]or many years "the unchallenged dogma was that a public employee had no right to object to conditions placed upon the terms of employment–including those which restricted the exercise of constitutional rights." That dogma has been qualified in important respects.

The Court has made clear that public employees do not surrender all their First Amendment rights by reason of their employment. Rather, the First Amendment protects a public employee's right, in certain circumstances, to speak as a citizen addressing matters of public concern.

Pickering provides a useful starting point in explaining the Court's doctrine. There the relevant speech was a teacher's letter to a local newspaper addressing issues including the funding policies of his school board. "The problem in any case," the Court stated, "is to arrive at a balance between the interests of the teacher, as a citizen, in commenting upon matters of public concern and the interest of the State, as an employer, in promoting the efficiency of the public services it performs through its employees." ... The Court found the teacher's speech "neither [was] shown nor can be presumed to have in any way either impeded the teacher's proper performance of his daily duties in the classroom or to have interfered with the regular operation of the schools generally." Thus, the Court concluded that "the interest of the school administration in limiting teachers' opportunities to contribute to public debate is not significantly greater than its interest in limiting a similar contribution by any member of the general public."

Pickering and the cases decided in its wake identify two inquiries to guide interpretation of the constitutional protections accorded to public employee speech. The first requires determining whether the employee spoke as a citizen on a matter of public concern. If the answer is no, the employee has no First Amendment cause of action based on his or her employer's reaction to the speech. If the answer is yes, then the possibility of a First Amendment claim arises. The question becomes whether the relevant government entity had an adequate justification for treating the employee differently from any other member of the general public. This consideration reflects the importance of the relationship between the speaker's expressions and employment. A government entity has broader discretion to restrict speech when it acts in its role as employer, but the restrictions it imposes must be directed at speech that has some potential to affect the entity's operations.

* * *

When a citizen enters government service, the citizen by necessity must accept certain limitations on his or her freedom. Government employers, like private employers, need a significant degree of control over their employees' words and actions; without it, there would be little chance for the efficient provision of public services. Public employees, moreover, often occupy trusted positions in society. When they speak out, they can express views that contravene governmental policies or impair the proper performance of governmental functions.

At the same time, the Court has recognized that a citizen who works for the government is nonetheless a citizen. The First Amendment limits the ability of a public employer to leverage the employment relationship to restrict, incidentally or intentionally, the liberties employees enjoy in their capacities as private citizens. So long as employees are speaking as citizens about matters of public concern, they must face only those speech restrictions that are necessary for their employers to operate efficiently and effectively.

The Court's employee-speech jurisprudence protects, of course, the constitutional rights of public employees. Yet the First Amendment interests at stake extend beyond the individual speaker. The Court has acknowledged the importance of promoting the public's interest in receiving the well-informed views of government employees engaging in civic discussion. *Pickering* again provides an instructive example. The Court characterized its holding as rejecting the attempt of school administrators to "limi[t] teachers' opportunities to contribute to public debate." It also noted that teachers are "the members of a community most likely to have informed and definite opinions" about school expenditures. The Court's approach acknowledged the necessity for informed, vibrant dialogue in a democratic society. It suggested, in addition, that widespread costs may arise when dialogue is repressed... The Court's decisions, then, have sought both to promote the individual and societal interests that are served when employees speak as citizens on matters of public concern and to respect the needs of government employers attempting to perform their important public functions. Underlying our cases has been the premise that while the First Amendment invests public employees with certain rights, it does not empower them to "constitutionalize the employee grievance."

With these principles in mind we turn to the instant case. Respondent Ceballos believed the affidavit used to obtain a search warrant contained serious misrepresentations. He conveyed his opinion and recommendation in a memo to his supervisor. That Ceballos expressed his views inside his office, rather than publicly, is not dispositive. Employees in some cases may receive First Amendment protection for expressions made at work. Many citizens do much of their talking inside their respective workplaces, and it would not serve the goal of treating public employees like "any member of the general public," to hold that all speech within the office is automatically exposed to restriction.

The memo concerned the subject matter of Ceballos' employment, but this, too, is nondispositive. The First Amendment protects some expressions related to the speaker's job. As the Court noted in *Pickering*: "Teachers are, as a class, the members of a community most likely to have informed and definite opinions as to how funds allotted to the operation of the schools should be spent. Accordingly, it is essential that they be able to speak out freely on such questions without fear of retaliatory dismissal." The same is true of many other categories of public employees.

The controlling factor in Ceballos' case is that his expressions were made pursuant to his duties as a calendar deputy. That consideration–the fact that Ceballos spoke as a prosecutor fulfilling a responsibility to advise his supervisor about how best to proceed with a pending case–distinguishes Ceballos' case from those in which the First Amendment provides protection against discipline. We hold that when public employees make statements pursuant to their official duties, the employees are not speaking as citizens for First Amendment purposes, and the Constitution does not insulate their communications from employer discipline.

Ceballos wrote his disposition memo because that is part of what he, as a calendar deputy, was employed to do.... Restricting speech that owes its existence to a public employee's professional responsibilities does not infringe any liberties the employee might have enjoyed as a private citizen. It simply reflects the exercise of employer control over what the employer itself has commissioned or created....

Ceballos did not act as a citizen when he went about conducting his daily professional activities, such as supervising attorneys, investigating charges, and preparing filings. In the same way he did not speak as a citizen by writing a memo that addressed the proper disposition of a pending criminal case. When he went to work and performed the tasks he was paid to perform, Ceballos acted as a government employee. The fact that his duties sometimes required him to speak or write does not mean his supervisors were prohibited from evaluating his performance.

This result is consistent with our precedents' attention to the potential societal value of employee speech. Refusing to recognize First Amendment claims based on government employees' work product does not prevent them from participating in public debate. The employees retain the prospect of constitutional protection for their contributions to the civic discourse. This prospect of protection, however, does not invest them with a right to perform their jobs however they see fit.

Our holding likewise is supported by the emphasis of our precedents on affording government employers sufficient discretion to manage their operations. Employers have heightened interests in controlling speech made by an employee in his or her professional capacity. Official communications have official consequences, creating a need for substantive consistency and clarity. Supervisors must ensure that their employees' official communications are accurate, demonstrate sound judgment, and promote the employer's mission. Ceballos' memo is illustrative. It demanded the attention of his supervisors and led to a heated meeting with employees from the sheriff's department. If Ceballos' superiors thought his memo was inflammatory or misguided, they had the authority to take proper corrective action.

Ceballos' proposed contrary rule, adopted by the Court of Appeals, would commit state and federal courts to a new, permanent, and intrusive role, mandating judicial oversight of communications between and among government employees and their superiors in the course of official business. This displacement of managerial discretion by judicial supervision finds no support in our precedents. When an employee speaks as a citizen addressing a matter of public concern, the First Amendment requires a delicate balancing of the competing interests surrounding the speech and its consequences. When, however, the employee is simply performing his or her job duties, there is no warrant for a similar degree of scrutiny. To hold otherwise would be to demand permanent judicial intervention in the conduct of governmental operations to a degree inconsistent with sound principles of federalism and the separation of powers.

* * *

Proper application of our precedents thus leads to the conclusion that the First Amendment does not prohibit managerial discipline based on an employee's expressions made pursuant to official responsibilities. Because Ceballos' memo falls into this category, his allegation of unconstitutional retaliation must fail.

Two final points warrant mentioning. First, as indicated above, the parties in this case do not dispute that Ceballos wrote his disposition memo pursuant to his employment duties. We thus have no occasion to articulate a comprehensive framework for defining the scope of an employee's duties in cases where there is room for serious debate. We reject, however, the suggestion that employers can restrict employees' rights by creating excessively broad job descriptions. The proper inquiry is a practical one. Formal job descriptions often bear little resemblance to the duties an employee actually is expected to perform, and the listing of a given task in an employee's written job description is neither necessary nor sufficient to demonstrate that conducting the task is within the scope of the employee's professional duties for First Amendment purposes.

Second, Justice SOUTER suggests today's decision may have important ramifications for academic freedom, at least as a constitutional value. There is some argument that expression related to academic scholarship or classroom instruction implicates additional constitutional interests that are not fully accounted for by this Court's customary employee-speech jurisprudence. We need not, and for that reason do not, decide whether the analysis we conduct today would apply in the same manner to a case involving speech related to scholarship or teaching.

* * *

We reject, however, the notion that the First Amendment shields from discipline the expressions employees make pursuant to their professional duties. Our precedents do not support the existence of a constitutional cause of action behind every statement a public employee makes in the course of doing his or her job.

The judgment of the Court of Appeals is reversed, and the case is remanded for proceedings consistent with this opinion.

It is so ordered.

VOSE
v.
KLIMENT

506 F.3d 565 (7th Cir. 2007)

[Citations and footnotes omitted]

BAUER, Circuit Judge.

In 2004, Vose was a police sergeant in the narcotics unit of the City of Springfield Police Department and had been with the Department for more than 26 years, including over 13 years in the narcotics unit. At that time, Donald Kliment was the Chief of Police of the City of Springfield, and William Rouse was the Deputy Chief of Police in charge of the investigations unit. As a sergeant in the narcotics unit, Vose supervised the narcotics unit and reported directly to Lieutenant David Dodson, who in turn reported to Rouse.

While working in the narcotics unit, Vose learned that detectives in the major case unit were using alleged drug investigations as a means to gather evidence by searching garbage from specific residences or locations in order to have a lawful basis to obtain search warrants for those locations. This search technique is called a "trash rip." Vose was worried that the trash rips could compromise ongoing drug investigations being conducted by his unit, and he was also concerned with the lack of coordination between the narcotics unit and the major case unit. Vose reviewed various applications for search warrants made by the major case unit and discovered that the major case unit detectives were not following City of Springfield Police Department procedures for obtaining search warrants, that the detectives were violating laws applicable to the search warrant process, and that the detectives filed false or misleading affidavits with the courts in support of the search warrants. Vose also learned that search warrants were being obtained by major case unit detectives by claiming that the warrants were for the purposes of obtaining information on drug investigations; in fact, no such drug investigations were undertaken by the narcotics unit. Vose brought these concerns to the attention of his supervisors, including Rouse and Kliment during the summer or early fall of 2004. Vose also voiced his concerns about the detectives' apparent misconduct at Department meetings during the fall of 2004. To Vose's knowledge, neither Kliment nor Rouse had taken any action on his complaints.

* * *

On April 12, 2005, Vose met with Kliment, Rouse, and two other police officers. Kliment told Vose to either "get along" with the detectives and supervisors about whom Vose had voiced concern or to request a transfer out of the narcotics unit to the patrol division. Vose was apparently instructed to make that decision and to report it to Kliment on Friday, April 15, 2005. . . .

* * *

Three days after Vose delivered his decision to involuntarily transfer to the patrol division to Kliment, Vose found two empty boxes with his name on them outside his office, insinuating that Vose was to be "sent packing." After Vose transferred to the patrol division, a command officer advised other Springfield police officers that Vose's "career in [the criminal investigation division] is history" and that Vose had "burned his bridges." Vose felt forced to resign from the Springfield Police Department, and did so on January 19, 2006.

On February 1, 2006, Vose filed a complaint in the district court alleging violations of his constitutional rights. Specifically, Vose alleged that his First Amendment rights were violated when Kliment and Rouse retaliated against him for voicing his concerns about the conduct of the major case unit detectives. . . .

* * *

We begin our inquiry with whether Kliment and Rouse violated Vose's constitutional right to free speech. Kliment and Rouse argue that Vose's speech was not constitutionally protected because Vose was speaking pursuant to his official duties as the supervisor of the narcotics unit, and not as a citizen. Vose argues that he spoke as a citizen in reporting the alleged misconduct to Kliment and Rouse, because he discovered the alleged misconduct in an independent investigation that was not part of his duties, and that the detectives were not under his supervision and were in a separate police unit.

* * *

Vose's initial statements regarding the alleged misconduct of the detectives in the major case unit were pursuant to his official duties as supervisor of the narcotics unit. Vose's complaint states that Vose learned of the major case unit detectives' trash rips when he was working in the narcotics unit, and that based on learning of the trash rips, he reviewed various applications for search warrants made by the major case unit detectives because he was concerned about "the possibility of these trash rips [compromising] ongoing investigations being conducted by his unit" and "the lack of coordination between the activities of the major case unit and the narcotics unit."

While Vose contends that his official duties as supervisor of the narcotics unit did not include responsibility for investigating potential misconduct of officers in another unit, this argument fails to consider his own admitted interests in the investigation: that the alleged misconduct could directly affect his narcotics unit. As a supervisor of the narcotics unit, it can hardly be said that Vose did not have a duty to make sure his unit's investigations were not compromised by some outside influence, or that Vose did not have a duty to coordinate his unit's work with other related units in the police department. Vose may have gone above and beyond his routine duties by investigating and reporting suspected misconduct in another police unit, but that does not mean that he spoke as a citizen and not as a public employee. "Th[e] focus on 'core' job functions is too narrow after *Garcetti,* which asked only whether an "employee's expressions [were] made pursuant to official responsibilities." Because Vose was responsible for the operations of the narcotics unit, his speech regarding alleged misconduct that may affect his unit was made pursuant to his official responsibilities, and not as a private citizen, despite not having explicit responsibility for the detectives involved or the search warrants at issue.

* * *

. . . Vose argues that his case is distinguishable from *Spiegla v. Hull.* In *Spiegla,* a corrections officer responsible for maintaining prison security reported a breach of a prison security policy by another prison employee to her superior. The *Spiegla* Court held that the corrections officer was speaking pursuant to her official duties—not as a citizen—when she reported the security policy breach because ensuring compliance with prison security policy was part of what she was employed to do.

Vose asserts that *Spiegla* differs because the corrections officer was responsible for prison security, which is what her speech addressed, but Vose was not responsible for policing the major case unit detectives. This distinction fails as well, since Vose was employed to oversee the narcotics unit's investigations, which Vose himself stated could have been compromised by the alleged misconduct of the major case unit detectives. Like the corrections officer, Vose was merely doing his job when he reported to his superiors his suspicions of the detectives' misconduct. A public employee's more general responsibilities are not beyond the scope of official duties for First Amendment purposes.

Finally, Vose attempts to distinguish *Sigsworth v. City of Aurora, Sigsworth* involved a police investigator working on a multi-jurisdictional task force investigating gang and drug activity. Sigsworth, the police investigator, suspected that certain task force members were tipping off the targets in a task force drug raid, and reported this concern to his supervisors.. This Court found that Sigsworth "was merely doing what was expected of him" as a member of the task force with supervisory responsibilities and pursuant to task force policy, and therefore his speech was not entitled to First Amendment protection.

Vose claims that the voluntary and independent nature of his investigation into the suspected wrongdoings of the major case unit detectives was not expected of him as a supervisor in the narcotics unit, which distinguishes him from Sigsworth. Again, Vose ignores his own statements that his independent investigation stemmed from his concerns about how the detectives' misconduct might affect his work in the narcotics unit. Ensuring the lawful operations of narcotics investigations was clearly expected of Vose.

In his final argument, Vose asserts that *Garcetti* was a narrow decision limited to the facts of the case. Vose asks us to interpret the holding in *Garcetti* to mean that only speech pursuant to a public employee's ordinary daily job duties are unprotected by the First Amendment. Such a reading, Vose claims, will foster the free flow of ideas as constitutionally guaranteed by the First Amendment. We decline to read beyond the text of *Garcetti* since we consider the *Garcetti* standard of "official duties" to be clear enough. While Vose may have gone beyond his ordinary *daily* job duties in reporting the suspected misconduct outside his unit, it was not beyond his official duty as a sergeant of the narcotics unit to ensure the security and propriety of the narcotics unit's operations.

For the reasons stated, we find that Vose's speech, albeit an honorable attempt to correct alleged wrongdoing, was not protected by the First Amendment.... Because no constitutional right was violated, Vose's complaint fails to state a claim under § 1983.

CONNICK
v.
MYERS

461 U.S. 138, 103 S. Ct. 1684, 75 L. Ed. 2d 708 (1983)

[Citations and footnotes omitted.]

[Sheila Myers was employed as an Assistant District Attorney in New Orleans for five and one-half years. She served at the pleasure of petitioner Harry Connick, the District Attorney for Orleans Parish. During this period, Myers competently performed her responsibilities of trying criminal cases.

In the early part of October, 1980, Myers was informed that she would be transferred to prosecute cases in a different section of the criminal court. Myers was strongly opposed to the proposed transfer and expressed her view to several of her supervisors, including Connick. Despite her objections, on October 6, Myers was notified that she was being transferred. That night Myers prepared a questionnaire soliciting the views of her fellow staff members concerning office transfer policy, office morale, the need for a grievance committee, the level of confidence in supervisors, and whether employees felt pressured to work in political campaigns. The following morning, Myers distributed the questionnaire to 15 assistant district attorneys. Shortly after noon, Connick was told that Myers was creating a "mini-insurrection" within the office and informed Myers that she was being terminated for refusal to accept the transfer. She was also told that her distribution of the questionnaire was considered an act of insubordination.

Myers sued, claiming that her discharge for circulating a questionnaire to co-workers violated her First Amendment rights. The issue before the Supreme Court was whether the First Amendment protects a government employee from discharge for circulating a questionnaire to co-workers enlisting their opinions about an internal office affair that had affected her.]

JUSTICE WHITE delivered the opinion of the Court.

* * *

... We hold only that when a public employee speaks not as a citizen upon matters of public concern, but instead as an employee upon matters only of personal interest, absent the most unusual circumstances, a federal court is not the appropriate forum in which to review the wisdom of a personnel decision taken by a public agency allegedly in reaction to the employee's behavior. Our responsibility is to ensure that citizens are not deprived of fundamental rights by virtue of working for the government; this does not require a grant of immunity for employee grievances not afforded by the First Amendment to those who do not work for the State.

Whether an employee's speech addresses a matter of public concern must be determined by the content, form, and context of a given statement, as revealed by the whole record. In this case, with but one exception, the questions posed by Myers to her co-workers do not fall under the rubric of matters of "public concern." We view the questions pertaining to the confidence and trust that Myers' co-workers possess in various supervisors, the level of office morale, and the need for a grievance committee as mere extensions of Myers' dispute over her transfer to another section of the criminal court.... Myers did not seek to inform the public that the District Attorney's Office was not discharging its governmental responsibilities in the investigation and prosecution of criminal cases. Nor did Myers seek to bring to light actual or potential wrongdoing or breach of public trust on the part of Connick and others.... While discipline and morale in the workplace are related to an agency's efficient performance of its duties, the focus of Myers' questions is not to evaluate the performance of the office but rather to gather ammunition for another round of controversy with her superiors. These questions reflect one employee's dissatisfaction with a transfer and an attempt to turn that displeasure into a cause celebre.

To presume that all matters which transpire within a government office are of public concern would mean that virtually every remark—and certainly every criticism directed at a public official—would plant the seed of a constitutional case. While as a matter of good judgment, public officials should be receptive to constructive criticism offered by their employees, the First Amendment does not require a public office to be run as a roundtable for employee complaints over internal office affairs.

* * *

... When a government employee personally confronts his immediate superior, the employing agency's institutional efficiency may be threatened not only by the content of the employee's message but also by the manner, time, and place in which it is delivered. Here the questionnaire was prepared and distributed at the office; the manner of distribution required not only Myers to leave her work but others to do the same in order that the questionnaire be completed....

* * *

Myers' questionnaire ... is most accurately characterized as an employee grievance concerning internal office policy. The limited First Amendment interest involved here does not require that Connick tolerate action which he reasonably believed would disrupt the office, undermine his authority, and destroy close working relationships. Myers' discharge therefore did not offend the First Amendment....

Our holding today is grounded in our longstanding recognition that the First Amendment's primary aim is the full protection of speech upon issues of public concern, as well as the practical realities involved in the administration of a government office. Although today the balance is struck for the government, this is no defeat for the First Amendment. For it would indeed be a Pyrrhic victory for the great principles of free expression if the Amendment's safeguarding of a public employee's right, as a citizen, to participate in discussions concerning public affairs were confused with the attempt to constitutionalize the employee grievance that we see presented here. The judgment of the Court of Appeals is

Reversed.

[Dissenting opinion omitted.]

LOCURTO
v.
GIULIANI

447 F.3d 159 (2d Cir. 2006)

[Citations and footnotes omitted.]

[The plaintiffs were formerly New York City police officers and firefighters. All three lived in Broad Channel, a small, predominantly white community in southeast Queens. Each year, Broad Channel hosts a loosely organized Labor Day parade. The parade features, among other things, floats with varying themes and of varying degrees of sophistication. Local politicians award prizes to floats designated, for example, "prettiest," "most original," and "funniest."

For the September 7, 1998 Labor Day parade, the plaintiffs, decided to enter a float called "Black to the Future-Broad Channel 2098." The float theme, a play on the 1985 time-travel film Back to the Future, depicted how Broad Channel would look in 2098 when, presumably, the community would be more integrated than it was in 1998. Each of the float participants, including the plaintiffs, covered their faces in black lipstick, donned Afro wigs, and accompanied the float along the procession in attire ranging from overalls with no T-shirt underneath, to cut-off jeans and ratty T-shirts, to athletic pants and sweatshirts. The float itself featured two buckets of Kentucky Fried Chicken on the hood of a flatbed truck. The float participants ate a watermelon and at one point threw the remains into the crowd, engaged in various chants, and simulated "break dancing."

The next evening, a local news broadcast aired amateur video footage of the float in a piece entitled "Racist Float." Extensive press coverage followed immediately, with the New York Times reporting three days later on the front of its Metro section that, according to "city officials," New York City police officers and firefighters had taken part in the float. The paper quoted Mayor Giuliani as saying, in a statement, " 'I've spoken to Commissioners Safir and Von Essen and we all agree that any police officer, firefighter or other city employee involved in this disgusting display of racism should be removed from positions of responsibility immediately. . . . They will be fired.' "

Shortly thereafter, the NYPD charged Locurto with "conduct prejudicial to the good order, efficiency and discipline of the Department" by participating in a Labor Day parade float "which depicted African-Americans in a demeaning and offensive manner." A hearing was held. After listening to testimony, the hearing officer concluded that the float did not express an opinion on "a matter of public concern," but rather "was designed to

mimic and mock a racial group for the amusement of the participants and spectators," and that "[i]n light of the egregiousness of [Locurto's] misconduct and the overwhelmingly negative notoriety this has wrought upon [the] Department . . .," the appropriate discipline was to dismiss Locurto from the police force.]

CALIBRASI, Circuit Judge.

* * *

Under our cases, the first step in the . . . inquiry is to determine whether an employee is speaking on a matter of public concern. The question of whether a public employee's First Amendment activity relates to a matter of public concern "is ordinarily a question of law decided on the whole record by taking into account the content, form, and context of a given statement." Thus, in the Supreme Court case of Rankin v. McPherson, a data entry employee in a county constable's office who said of an attempt on President Reagan's life, "[I]f they go for him again, I hope they get him," was speaking on a matter of public concern because her comments were "made in the course of a conversation addressing the policies of the President's administration." The Court made clear that "[t]he inappropriate or controversial character of a statement is irrelevant to the question [of] whether it deals with a matter of public concern."

* * *

Some courts, including both our Court and the Supreme Court, have questioned the extent to which the public concern test applies to off-duty speech on topics unrelated to employment. The Supreme Court noted in Roe that, under its previous decision in Treasury Union, "when government employees speak or write on their own time on topics unrelated to their employment, the speech can have First Amendment protection, absent some governmental justification 'far stronger than mere speculation' in regulating it." . . .

* * *

It is more sensible . . . to treat off-duty, non-work-related speech as presumptively entitled to First Amendment protection regardless of whether, as a threshold matter, it may be characterized as speech on a matter of public concern. . . .

But we need not today decide and hence do not resolve whether it was necessary for the plaintiffs to satisfy the public concern test as a threshold matter. This is because, given our resolution of the ... balancing test, we can assume arguendo that the plaintiffs' speech in this case did in fact relate to a matter of public concern....

* * *

We ... find that the defendants' interest in maintaining a relationship of trust between the police and fire departments and the communities they serve outweighed the plaintiffs' expressive interests in this case. If the NYPD and FDNY have any greater interests than these, they are few. And the speech at issue in this case was not merely of passing interest to members of the African-American community; rather, they were the very objects of the plaintiffs' derision. The First Amendment does not require a Government employer to sit idly by while its employees insult those they are hired to serve and protect. Under the circumstances, "an individual police officer's [or firefighter's] right to express his personal opinions must yield to the public good."

* * *

CONCLUSION

We do not today endorse Justice Holmes's widely discredited dictum that one has "a constitutional right to talk politics, but ... has no constitutional right to be a policeman." One does, of course, have a First Amendment right not to be terminated from public employment in retaliation for engaging in protected speech. But one's right to be a police officer or firefighter who publicly ridicules those he is commissioned to protect and serve is far from absolute. Rather, it is tempered by the reasonable judgment of his employer as to the potential disruptive effects of the employee's conduct on the public mission of the police and fire departments. We find, in this case, that the judgment of the defendants was reasonable, that it was the clear motive for the plaintiffs' dismissals, and that it outweighed the plaintiffs' individual First Amendment interests in participating in the "Black to the Future" float.

The judgment of the district court is therefore reversed and the case is remanded with instructions to enter judgment in favor of the defendants...

CITY OF ONTARIO, CALIFORNIA v. QUON

– US –, 130 S. Ct. 2619, 177 L. Ed. 2d 216 (2010) (2010)

[Citations and footnotes omitted.]

[Jeffrey Quon, a member of the Ontario Police Department SWAT team, was issued a pager for official use on the job. Under the City's contract with Arch Wireless, each pager was allotted 25,000 characters per month, after which the City was required to pay an overage charge. The City had a Computer, Internet and E-mail Use policy, warning employees that their use of City-owned computers for personal benefit was a violation of City policy, that the City reserved the right to monitor all network activity, with or without notice, and that users should not expect privacy when using these resources. While this policy did not, on its face, apply to text messaging, Quon was informed, both personally and in writing, that text messages were subject to the same policy and that the Department reserved the right to audit them. However, he was informally told by the lieutenant in charge of administering the pager program, that his text messages would not be audited for billing purposes so long as he paid for the usage above his monthly allotment. Quon regularly exceeded his monthly allotment, but paid for the overage. The lieutenant in charge of the pager program eventually tired of this arrangement, and told the chief that Quon habitually exceeded his monthly character limit. The chief obtained transcripts of Quon's messages for a two-month period from Arch Wireless and ordered an audit to determine whether the 25,000 monthly character limit was high enough to cover department business or whether Quon's overage charges were due to personal use. Quon's off-duty messages were redacted from the transcript. The audit revealed that only a small part of Quon's on-duty messages related to police business, and that many of his personal messages were salacious. The matter was referred to internal affairs and Quon was disciplined. He sued, claiming that the police department's auditing of his text messages violated his Fourth Amendment right.]

Justice KENNEDY delivered the opinion of the Court.

This case involves the assertion by a government employer of the right, in circumstances to be described, to read text messages sent and received on a pager the employer owned and issued to an employee. The employee contends that the privacy of the messages is protected by the ban on unreasonable searches and seizures found in the Fourth Amendment. . . .

* * *

The Fourth Amendment states: The right of the people to be secure in their persons, houses, papers, and effects, against unreasonable searches and seizures, shall not be violated .... It is well settled that the Fourth Amendment's protection extends beyond the sphere of criminal investigations. The Amendment guarantees the privacy, dignity, and security of persons against certain arbitrary and invasive acts by officers of the Government, without regard to whether the government actor is investigating crime or performing another function. The Fourth Amendment applies as well when the Government acts in its capacity as an employer.

The Court discussed this principle in *O'Connor [v. Ortega]*. There a physician employed by a state hospital alleged that hospital officials investigating workplace misconduct had violated his Fourth Amendment rights by searching his office and seizing personal items from his desk and filing cabinet. All Members of the Court agreed with the general principle that individuals do not lose Fourth Amendment rights merely because they work for the government instead of a private employer. A majority of the Court further agreed that special needs, beyond the normal need for law enforcement, make the warrant and probable-cause requirement impracticable for government employers.

The *O'Connor* Court did not disagree on the proper analytical framework for Fourth Amendment claims against government employers. A four-Justice plurality concluded that the correct analysis has two steps. First, because some government offices may be so open to fellow employees or the public that no expectation of privacy is reasonable, a court must consider [t]he operational realities of the workplace in order to determine whether an employee's Fourth Amendment rights are implicated. On this view, the question whether an employee has a reasonable expectation of privacy must be addressed on a case-by-case basis. Next, where an employee has a legitimate privacy expectation, an employer's intrusion on that expectation for noninvestigatory, work-related purposes, as well as for investigations of work-related misconduct, should be judged by the standard of reasonableness under all the circumstances.

* * *

. . . In the two decades since *O'Connor*, however, the threshold test for determining the scope of an employee's Fourth Amendment rights has not been clarified further. . . . . .

* * *

Even if Quon had a reasonable expectation of privacy in his text messages, petitioners did not necessarily violate the Fourth Amendment by obtaining and reviewing the transcripts. Although as a general matter, warrantless searches are per se unreasonable under the Fourth Amendment, there are a few specifically established and well-delineated exceptions to that general rule. The Court has held that the special needs' of the workplace justify one such exception.

Under the approach of the *O'Connor* plurality, when conducted for a noninvestigatory, work-related purpos[e] . . . a government employer's warrantless search is reasonable if it is "'justified at its inception and if the measures adopted are reasonably related to the objectives of the search and not excessively intrusive in light of the circumstances giving rise to the search. The search here satisfied the standard of the O'Connor plurality and was reasonable under that approach.

The search was justified at its inception because there were reasonable grounds for suspecting that the search [was] necessary for a noninvestigatory work-related purpose. As a jury found, Chief Scharf ordered the search in order to determine whether the character limit on the City's contract with Arch Wireless was sufficient to meet the City's needs. This was, as the Ninth Circuit noted, a legitimate work-related rationale. The City and OPD had a legitimate interest in ensuring that employees were not being forced to pay out of their own pockets for work-related expenses, or on the other hand that the City was not paying for extensive personal communications.

As for the scope of the search, reviewing the transcripts was reasonable because it was an efficient and expedient way to determine whether Quon's overages were the result of work-related messaging or personal use. The review was also not excessively intrusive. Although Quon had gone over his monthly allotment a number of times, OPD requested transcripts for only the months of August and September 2002. While it may have been reasonable as well for OPD to review transcripts of all the months in which Quon exceeded his allowance, it was certainly reasonable for OPD to review messages for just two months in order to obtain a large enough sample to decide whether the character limits were efficacious. And it is worth noting that during his internal affairs investigation, McMahon redacted all messages Quon sent while off duty, a measure which reduced the intrusiveness of any further review of the transcripts.

* * *

Because the search was motivated by a legitimate work-related purpose, and because it was not excessive in scope, the search was reasonable under the approach of the *O'Connor* plurality. For these same reasons-that the employer had a legitimate reason for the search, and that the search was not excessively intrusive in light of that justification-the Court also concludes that the search would be regarded as reasonable and normal in the private-employer context and would satisfy the approach of Justice SCALIA's concurrence. The search was reasonable, and the Court of Appeals erred by holding to the contrary. Petitioners did not violate Quon's Fourth Amendment rights.

* * *

It is so ordered.

LINGLER
v.
FECHKO

312 F.3d 237 (6th Cir. 2002)

DAVID A. NELSON, Circuit Judge

* * *

On what must have been a slow day for crime in Seven Hills, Ohio, police officers James Lingler and Jeffrey Gezymalla, the plaintiffs in this civil rights action, decided to tidy up the station house. In the course of their housekeeping efforts the officers removed an old couch and some dilapidated chairs from a training room. The furniture was placed in a dumpster behind the building.

The chief of police, defendant John R. Fechko, had not authorized any such property disposal. When he found that the furniture was not in its usual place, he ordered a "full investigation." Suspicion soon fell on Officers Lingler and Gezymalla, whose daily activity logs made reference to "station cleanup."

Chief Fechko called Officer Gezymalla into his office and asked him to explain the log entry. The officer detailed his efforts to clean up the station house, including the discarding of the old furniture. Whether in earnest or in an attempt to "impress upon Officer Gezymalla the gravity of his actions," Chief Fechko observed that the disposal of the furniture could be considered theft of city property. In this connection the chief spoke of reading the officer his rights.

Chief Fechko next met with Officer Lingler, who responded in the negative to a question about knowledge of "possible theft, missing city property." When asked about the "station cleanup" entry on his activity log, Officer Lingler replied "oh, you mean the junk furniture." During this interview Officer Lingler said he wanted to have an attorney present if the investigation were criminal in nature.

Following these meetings, Chief Fechko ordered the officers to prepare detailed written statements concerning the station cleanup. The officers objected, and Officer Lingler again stated that he wanted a lawyer. Chief Fechko said that the matter was not criminal, and he ordered the men to turn in their statements by the end of their work shift.

The officers did so, producing statements that described the cleanup efforts generally but made no reference to the furniture. Because of what he viewed as a failure to comply with his order, the chief then initiated disciplinary proceedings against the officers. After consulting counsel, the officers submitted statements with detailed accounts of the station house cleanup and the removal of the furniture. At no stage, as far as the record discloses, was either officer required to waive his constitutional privilege against self-incrimination.

Although Chief Fechko recommended that the mayor suspend the officers for 30 days, no punishment of any kind was imposed. We are told that the chief also recommended the initiation of criminal proceedings, but that this recommendation was rejected as well. The officers were never prosecuted.

In due course the officers sued the chief in an Ohio court. The complaint asserted a claim under 42 U.S. C. § 1983 for violation of the constitutional privilege against self-incrimination. . . . The case was removed to the United States District Court for the Northern District of Ohio, where the chief moved for summary judgment. The district court granted the motion. . . . A final judgment thus having been entered, the officers perfected the present appeal.

To prevail on their first claim the officers would have to prove that the chief, while acting under color of state law, subjected them to the deprivation of a right secured by the Constitution or laws of the United States. See 42 U.S.C. § 1983. The right of which the officers contend they were deprived is one arising from the Fifth Amendment prohibition (made applicable to the states by the Fourteenth Amendment) against any person being "compelled in any criminal case to be a witness against himself." We agree with the district court that the chief did not violate this right.

By its terms, the Fifth Amendment does not prohibit the act of compelling a self-incriminating statement other than for use in a criminal case. See . . . *Mahoney v. Kesery*, ("the Fifth Amendment does not forbid the forcible extraction of information but only the use of information so extracted as evidence in a criminal case . . .").

The statements given by Officers Lingler and Gezymalla were not used against them in any criminal case. Indeed, under *Garrity v. New Jersey*, the statements could not have been so used. See *Garrity* (holding that the constitutional protection against coerced statements "prohibits use in subsequent criminal proceedings of statements obtained under threat of removal from office, and . . . it extends to all, whether they are policemen or other members of our body politic").

* * *

. . . There is an important distinction . . . between plaintiffs not on the public payroll—"private citizens who may claim a generalized right to be free from compelled interrogation by the government"—and plaintiffs who are public employees. Plaintiffs who wear the uniforms of

police officers "can make no tenable claim that a Fifth Amendment violation occurred when the Police Department merely exercised its legitimate right, as an employer, to question them about matters narrowly relating to their job performance."

AFFIRMED.

RICCI
v.
DeSTEFANO

557 U.S. _____, 129 S. Ct. 2658, 174 L. Ed. 2d 490 (2009)

[Citations and footnotes omitted]

[The process for promotion to the rank of lieutenant or captain in the New Haven, Connecticut Fire Department involves both written and oral exams, with the written exam counting for sixty percent of the total score. After each examination, the civil service board certifies a rank-order list of candidates who passed. When filing vacancies, the fire department must choose one of the three candidates with the highest exam scores.

The City of New Haven hired an outside consulting firm to prepare the 2003 exams for promotion to the rank of lieutenant and captain. The consulting firm performed job analyses to identify the tasks, knowledge, skills, and abilities essential for each position. Representatives interviewed incumbent captains and lieutenants and their supervisors. They rode with and observed other on-duty officers. Using information from those interviews and ride-alongs, they prepared job-analysis questionnaires and administered them to most of the incumbent battalion chiefs, captains, and lieutenants in the Department. The job-analysis information was used to develop multiple-choice examination questions designed to measure the candidates' job-related knowledge. The consulting firm compiled a list of training manuals, Department procedures, and other materials that were used as sources for the test questions. After the examinations were prepared, the City opened a 3-month study period. It gave candidates a list that identified the source material for the questions, including the specific chapters from which the questions were taken.

More than 100 New Haven firefighters took the exams. Many studied for months, at considerable personal and financial cost. The exam results exhibited a significant racial disparity. The pass rate of white candidates was nearly twice that of minority candidates. There were 8 lieutenant and 7 captain positions vacant at the time of the exam. Based on how the passing candidates ranked and an application of the "rule of three," certifying the examination would have meant that the City could not have considered black candidates for any of the then-vacant lieutenant or captain positions. A rancorous public debate ensued. Some firefighters argued that the tests should be discarded because the results showed the tests to be discriminatory. They threatened a discrimination lawsuit if the City made promotions based on the tests. Other firefighters said the exams were neutral and fair. And they, in turn, threatened a discrimination lawsuit if the City, relying on the statistical racial disparity, ignored the test results and denied promotions to the candidates who had performed best. Caught in the middle, the City sided with those who protested the test results and threw out the examinations. White and Hispanic firefighters who passed the exams but were denied a chance at promotions by the City's refusal to certify the test results, sued the City, alleging that discarding the test results discriminated against them based on their race in violation of Title VII of the Civil Rights Act of 1964.]

Justice KENNEDY delivered the opinion of the Court.

Title VII of the Civil Rights Act of 1964, 42 U.S. C. § 2000e *et seq.,* as amended, prohibits employment discrimination on the basis of race, color, religion, sex, or national origin. Title VII prohibits both intentional discrimination (known as "disparate treatment") as well as . . . practices that are not intended to discriminate but in fact have a disproportionately adverse effect on minorities (known as "disparate impact").

* * *

Our analysis begins with this premise: The City's actions would violate the disparate-treatment

prohibition of Title VII absent some valid defense. All the evidence demonstrates that the City chose not to certify the examination results because of the statistical disparity based on race—i.e., how minority candidates had performed when compared to white candidates. As the District Court put it, the City rejected the test results because "too many whites and not enough minorities would be promoted were the lists to be certified." Without some other justification, this express, race-based decisionmaking violates Title VII's command that employers cannot take adverse employment actions because of an individual's race.

* * *

. . . [R]espondents and the Government assert that an employer's good-faith belief that its actions are necessary to comply with Title VII's disparate-impact provision should be enough to justify race-conscious conduct. But the original, foundational prohibition of Title VII bars employers from taking adverse action "because of . . . race." And when Congress codified the disparate-impact provision in 1991, it made no exception to disparate-treatment liability for actions taken in a good-faith effort to comply with the new, disparate-impact provision. . . . Allowing employers to violate the disparate-treatment prohibition based on a mere good-faith fear of disparate-impact liability would encourage race-based action at the slightest hint of disparate impact. A minimal standard could cause employers to discard the results of lawful and beneficial promotional examinations even where there is little if any evidence of disparate-impact discrimination. That would amount to a *de facto* quota system, in which a "focus on statistics . . . could put undue pressure on employers to adopt inappropriate prophylactic measures." . . .

In searching for a standard that strikes a more appropriate balance, we note that this Court has considered cases similar to this one, albeit in the context of the Equal Protection Clause of the Fourteenth Amendment. The Court has held that certain government actions to remedy past racial discrimination-actions that are themselves based on race-are constitutional only where there is a "strong basis in evidence" that the remedial actions were necessary. . .

The same interests are at work in the interplay between the disparate-treatment and disparate-impact provisions of Title VII. Congress has imposed liability on employers for unintentional discrimination in order to rid the workplace of "practices that are fair in form, but discriminatory in operation." But it has also prohibited employers from taking adverse employment actions "because of" race. Applying the strong-basis-in-evidence standard to Title VII gives effect to both the disparate-treatment and disparate-impact provisions, allowing violations of one in the name of compliance with the other only in certain, narrow circumstances. The standard leaves ample room for employers' voluntary compliance efforts, which are essential to the statutory scheme and to Congress's efforts to eradicate workplace discrimination. And the standard appropriately constrains employers' discretion in making race-based decisions: It limits that discretion to cases in which there is a strong basis in evidence of disparate-impact liability, but it is not so restrictive that it allows employers to act only when there is a provable, actual violation.

* * *

The City argues that, even under the strong-basis-in-evidence standard, its decision to discard the examination results was permissible under Title VII. That is incorrect. Even if respondents were motivated as a subjective matter by a desire to avoid committing disparate-impact discrimination, the record makes clear there is no support for the conclusion that respondents had an objective, strong basis in evidence to find the tests inadequate, with some consequent disparate-impact liability in violation of Title VII.

* * *

The racial adverse impact here was significant, and petitioners do not dispute that the City was faced with a prima facie case of disparate-impact liability. On the captain exam, the pass rate for white candidates was 64 percent but was 37.5 percent for both black and Hispanic candidates. On the lieutenant exam, the pass rate for white candidates was 58.1 percent; for black candidates, 31.6 percent; and for Hispanic candidates, 20 percent. The pass rates of minorities, which were approximately one-half the pass rates for white candidates, fall well below the 80-percent standard set by the EEOC to implement the disparate-impact provision of Title VII. Based on how the passing candidates ranked and an application of the "rule

of three," certifying the examinations would have meant that the City could not have considered black candidates for any of the then-vacant lieutenant or captain positions.

* * *

Based on the degree of adverse impact reflected in the results, respondents were compelled to take a hard look at the examinations to determine whether certifying the results would have had an impermissible disparate impact. The problem for respondents is that a prima facie case of disparate-impact liability-essentially, a threshold showing of a significant statistical disparity, and nothing more-is far from a strong basis in evidence that the City would have been liable under Title VII had it certified the results. That is because the City could be liable for disparate-impact discrimination only if the examinations were not job related and consistent with business necessity, or if there existed an equally valid, less-discriminatory alternative that served the City's needs but that the City refused to adopt. We conclude there is no strong basis in evidence to establish that the test was deficient in either of these respects. . . .

* * *

There is no genuine dispute that the examinations were job-related and consistent with business necessity. The City's assertions to the contrary are "blatantly contradicted by the record." The CSB heard statements from Chad Legel (the IOS vice president) as well as city officials outlining the detailed steps IOS took to develop and administer the examinations. IOS devised the written examinations, which were the focus of the CSB's inquiry, after painstaking analyses of the captain and lieutenant positions-analyses in which IOS made sure that minorities were overrepresented. And IOS drew the questions from source material approved by the Department. Of the outside witnesses who appeared before the CSB, only one, Vincent Lewis, had reviewed the examinations in any detail, and he was the only one with any firefighting experience. Lewis stated that the "questions were relevant for both exams." . . .

* * *

On the record before us, there is no genuine dispute that the City lacked a strong basis in evidence to believe it would face disparate-impact liability if it certified the examination results. In other words, there is no evidence—let alone the required strong basis in evidence—that the tests were flawed because they were not job-related or because other, equally valid and less discriminatory tests were available to the City. Fear of litigation alone cannot justify an employer's reliance on race to the detriment of individuals who passed the examinations and qualified for promotions. The City's discarding the test results was impermissible under Title VII, and summary judgment is appropriate for petitioners on their disparate-treatment claim.

* * *

The record in this litigation documents a process that, at the outset, had the potential to produce a testing procedure that was true to the promise of Title VII: No individual should face workplace discrimination based on race. Respondents thought about promotion qualifications and relevant experience in neutral ways. They were careful to ensure broad racial participation in the design of the test itself and its administration. As we have discussed at length, the process was open and fair.

The problem, of course, is that after the tests were completed, the raw racial results became the predominant rationale for the City's refusal to certify the results. The injury arises in part from the high, and justified, expectations of the candidates who had participated in the testing process on the terms the City had established for the promotional process. Many of the candidates had studied for months, at considerable personal and financial expense, and thus the injury caused by the City's reliance on raw racial statistics at the end of the process was all the more severe. Confronted with arguments both for and against certifying the test results—and threats of a lawsuit either way—the City was required to make a difficult inquiry. But its hearings produced no strong evidence of a disparate-impact violation, and the City was not entitled to disregard the tests based solely on the racial disparity in the results.

* * *

Petitioners are entitled to summary judgment on their Title VII claim. . . The judgment of the Court of Appeals is reversed, and the cases are remanded for further proceedings consistent with this opinion.

It is so ordered.

DOTHARD
v.
RAWLINSON

433 U.S. 321, 97 S. Ct. 2720, 53 L. Ed. 2d 786 (1977)

[Citations and footnotes omitted.]

[Dianne Rawlinson, a 22-year-old college graduate with a major in correctional psychology, sought employment with the Alabama Board of Corrections as a prison guard, called in Alabama a "correctional counselor." A correctional counselor's primary duty was to maintain security and control of the inmates by continually supervising and observing their activities. To be eligible for consideration, an applicant had to possess a valid Alabama driver's license, a high school education or its equivalent, be free from physical defects, be between the ages of 20 years and 45 years at the time of appointment, and fall between the minimum height and weight requirements of 5 feet 2 inches and 120 pounds, and the maximum of 6 feet 10 inches, and 300 pounds. Rawlinson was refused employment because she failed to meet the minimum 120-pound weight requirement. She filed suit challenging the statutory height and weight minima as violative of Title VII. She also challenged Regulation 204, which established gender criteria for "contact positions" in maximum-security institutions that required continual close physical proximity to inmates.]

MR. JUSTICE STEWART delivered the opinion of the Court.

* * *

In enacting Title VII, Congress required "the removal of artificial, arbitrary, and unnecessary barriers to employment when the barriers operate invidiously to discriminate on the basis of racial or other impermissible classification." The District Court found that the minimum statutory height and weight requirements that applicants for employment as correctional counselors must meet constitute the sort of arbitrary barrier to equal employment opportunity that Title VII forbids. The appellants assert that the District Court erred both in finding that the height and weight standards discriminate against women, and in its refusal to find that, even if they do, these standards are justified as "job related."

The gist of the claim that the statutory height and weight requirements discriminate against women does not involve an assertion of purposeful discriminatory motive. It is asserted, rather, that these facially neutral qualification standards work in fact disproportionately to exclude women from eligibility for employment by the Alabama Board of Corrections. We dealt in *Griggs v. Duke Power Co.* and *Albemarle Paper Co. v. Moody* with similar allegations that facially neutral employment standards disproportionately excluded Negroes from employment, and those cases guide our approach here.

Those cases make clear that to establish a prima facie case of discrimination, a plaintiff need only show that the facially neutral standards in question select applicants for hire in a significantly discriminatory pattern. Once it is thus shown that the employment standards are discriminatory in effect, the employer must meet "the burden of showing that any given requirement [has] . . . a manifest relationship to the employment in question." If the employer proves that the challenged requirements are job related, the plaintiff may then show that other selection devices without a similar discriminatory effect would also "serve the employer's legitimate interest in 'efficient and trustworthy workmanship.' "

* * *

Although women 14 years of age or older compose 52.75% of the Alabama population and 36.89% of its total labor force, they hold only 12.9% of its correctional counselor positions. In considering the effect of the minimum height and weight standards on this disparity in rate of hiring between the sexes, the District Court found that the 5'2" requirement would operate to exclude 33.29% of the women in the United States between the ages of 18-79, while excluding only 1.28% of men between the same ages. The 120-pound weight restriction would exclude 22.29% of the women and 2.35% of the men in this age group. When the height and weight restrictions are combined, Alabama's statutory standards would exclude 41.13% of the female population while excluding less than 1% of the male population. Accordingly, the District Court found that

Rawlinson had made out a prima facie case of unlawful sex discrimination.

* * *

. . . [W]e cannot say that the District Court was wrong in holding that the statutory height and weight standards had a discriminatory impact on women applicants. . . .

We turn, therefore, to the appellants' argument that they have rebutted the prima facie case of discrimination by showing that the height and weight requirements are job related. These requirements, they say, have a relationship to strength, a sufficient but unspecified amount of which is essential to effective job performance as a correctional counselor. In the District Court, however, the appellants produced no evidence correlating the height and weight requirements with the requisite amount of strength thought essential to good job performance. Indeed, they failed to offer evidence of any kind in specific justification of the statutory standards.

If the job-related quality that the appellants identify is bona fide, their purpose could be achieved by adopting and validating a test for applicants that measures strength directly. Such a test, fairly administered, would fully satisfy the standards of Title VII because it would be one that "measure[s] the person for the job and not the person in the abstract." But nothing in the present record even approaches such a measurement.

For the reasons we have discussed, the District Court was not in error in holding that Title VII of the Civil Rights Act of 1964, as amended, prohibits application of the statutory height and weight requirements to Rawlinson and the class she represents.

III

Unlike the statutory height and weight requirements, Regulation 204 explicitly discriminates against women on the basis of their sex. In defense of this overt discrimination, the appellants rely on § 703 (e) of Title VII, 42 U.S.C. § 2000e-2 (e), which permits sex-based discrimination "in those certain instances where . . . sex . . . is a bona fide occupational qualification reasonably necessary to the normal operation of that particular business or enterprise."

* * *

We are persuaded—by the restrictive language of § 703 (e), the relevant legislative history, and the consistent interpretation of the Equal Employment Opportunity Commission—that the bfoq exception was in fact meant to be an extremely narrow exception to the general prohibition of discrimination on the basis of sex. In the particular factual circumstances of this case, however, we conclude that the District Court erred in rejecting the State's contention that Regulation 204 falls within the narrow ambit of the bfoq exception.

The environment in Alabama's penitentiaries is a peculiarly inhospitable one for human beings of whatever sex. Indeed, a Federal District Court has held that the conditions of confinement in the prisons of the State, characterized by "rampant violence" and a "jungle atmosphere," are constitutionally intolerable. The record in the present case shows that because of inadequate staff and facilities, no attempt is made in the four maximum-security male penitentiaries to classify or segregate inmates according to their offense or level of dangerousness—a procedure that, according to expert testimony, is essential to effective penological administration. Consequently, the estimated 20% of the male prisoners who are sex offenders are scattered throughout the penitentiaries' dormitory facilities.

In this environment of violence and disorganization, it would be an oversimplification to characterize Regulation 204 as an exercise in "romantic paternalism." In the usual case, the argument that a particular job is too dangerous for women may appropriately be met by the rejoinder that it is the purpose of Title VII to allow the individual woman to make that choice for herself. More is at stake in this case, however, than an individual woman's decision to weigh and accept the risks of employment in a "contact" position in a maximum-security male prison.

The essence of a correctional counselor's job is to maintain prison security. A woman's relative ability to maintain order in a male, maximum-security, unclassified penitentiary of the type Alabama now runs could be directly reduced by her womanhood. There is a basis in fact for expecting that sex offenders who have criminally assaulted women in the past would be moved to do so again if access to women were established within the prison. There would also be a real risk that other inmates, deprived of a normal heterosexual environment, would assault women guards because they were women. In a prison system where violence is the order of the day, where inmate access to guards is facilitated by dormitory living arrangements, where every institution is understaffed, and where a substantial portion of the inmate population is composed of sex offenders mixed at random with other prisoners, there are few visible deterrents to inmate assaults on women custodians.

Appellee Rawlinson's own expert testified that dormitory housing for aggressive inmates poses a greater security problem than single-cell lockups, and further testified that it would be unwise to use women as guards in a prison where even 10% of the inmates had been convicted of sex crimes and were not segregated from the other prisoners. The likelihood that inmates would assault a woman because she was a woman would pose a real threat not only to the victim of the assault but also to the basic control of the penitentiary and protection of its inmates and the other security personnel. The employee's very womanhood would thus directly undermine her capacity to provide the security that is the essence of a correctional counselor's responsibility.

There was substantial testimony from experts on both sides of this litigation that the use of women as guards in "contact" positions under the existing conditions in Alabama maximum-security male penitentiaries would pose a substantial security problem, directly linked to the sex of the prison guard. On the basis of that evidence, we conclude that the District Court was in error in ruling that being male is not a bona fide occupational qualification for the job of correctional counselor in a "contact" position in an Alabama male maximum-security penitentiary.

The judgment is accordingly affirmed in part and reversed in part, and the case is remanded to the District Court for further proceedings consistent with this opinion.

It is so ordered.

[Concurring opinions have been omitted.]

ROGERS
v.
CITY OF LITTLE ROCK, ARK.

152 F.3d 790 (8th Cir. 1998)

[Citations and footnotes omitted.]

MURPHY, Circuit Judge.

Vivian Ann Rogers brought this action under 42 U.S.C. § 1983 against former Little Rock police officer Vincent Morgan. . ., alleging that her constitutional rights were violated when Morgan raped her while he was on duty. After a bench trial the district court found Morgan liable in his individual capacity and awarded Rogers $100,000 in damages. . . . We affirm.

Little Rock police officer Vincent Morgan stopped Rogers for a broken tail light on August 27, 1994, and asked her for proof she carried automobile insurance. She indicated that she did not have the necessary papers with her, and Morgan called for a tow truck which was standard procedure in such a situation. He later decided to cancel the tow, however, and he followed her home in his patrol car and went into her house. Rogers was unable to locate the papers, and Morgan told her he would let her off but that she owed him one. He then started touching and kissing her and led her into the bedroom where he told her to take off her clothes. Although she began to undress, she stopped when Morgan said she did not have to have sex with him. When he nevertheless repeated his demand that she disrobe, Rogers finished removing her clothes. Morgan then pushed her onto the bed and had sexual intercourse with her. Rogers said that she yelled because it hurt, but Morgan told her to be quiet and covered the microphone on his uniform.

* * *

Both Rogers and Morgan testified at trial, and the court found Rogers the more credible witness, accepted her version of the encounter, and made findings that Rogers was afraid of Morgan and what might happen if she didn't cooperate with a police officer and that he coerced her into sexual intercourse. The court also made specific findings leading to its conclusion that Morgan was acting under color of state law at the time. The court concluded that Morgan was liable under § 1983

because he had violated Rogers' due process right to be free from physical abuse. It rejected Morgan's defense of qualified immunity because it concluded that he would have known that his actions were clearly contrary to law. . . . The court also found that Rogers was damaged in the amount of $100,000 for emotional distress and physical pain caused by Morgan's acts.

* * *

. . . The evidence in this case supports the district court's conclusion that Rogers suffered a violation of her right to intimate bodily integrity that was conscience shocking. This case involves an egregious, nonconsensual entry into the body which was an exercise of power without any legitimate governmental objective. It therefore violated Rogers' substantive due process right. Morgan's rape was an intentional act that produced constitutional injury and that was an "arbitrary exercise of the powers of government. . . ." The rape falls at the extreme end of the scale of egregious conduct by a state actor and was "unjustifiable by any government interest." The district court did not err in analyzing the case under the due process clause or in its conclusion that the violation of Rogers' due process rights was shocking to the conscience.

* * *

Morgan argues that the district court erred in finding that he was acting under color of state law. He contends that not towing Rogers' car when she did not have proof of insurance, going to her home, and then having sex with her were all substantial departures from his duties as a Little Rock police officer which means he was not acting under color of law. An official acts under color of state law even if he "abuses the position given him by the State . . . while acting in his official capacity or while exercising his responsibilities pursuant to state law." The issue depends on "the nature and circumstances of the officer's conduct and the relationship of that conduct to the performance of his official duties." There were facts produced to show that Morgan relied on his authority as a police officer to facilitate the assault. He stopped Rogers for a broken tail light, raised the prospect of towing her car when she did not have the insurance papers, and later after going to her home said that she owed him a favor in exchange for letting her go. He remained in uniform, and Rogers testified that she felt she had to cooperate with his demands because he was a police officer.

Morgan thus abused his power while carrying out the official duties entrusted to him by the state, and the district court did not err in finding that he acted under color of state law.

Morgan claims that he was entitled to qualified immunity, which protects an official when his conduct "does not violate clearly established statutory or constitutional rights of which a reasonable person would have known." The court properly denied immunity, however, since Morgan's sexual assault violated the clearly established due process right to be free of physical abuse by public officials, and a reasonable officer would have known of this right.

* * *

Since we conclude that the evidence at trial supports the findings and conclusions of the district court ..., we affirm the final judgment in all respects.

VANN
v.
CITY OF NEW YORK

72 F.3d 1040 (2d Cir. 1995)

[Citations and footnotes omitted.]

[Walter Vann, while driving a bus on his regular route, collided with Officer Raul Morrison's personal vehicle. Morrison, who was then off-duty and out-of-uniform, got out of his car, identified himself as a police officer, drew his service revolver, and told Vann, "I should shoot you nigger and make sure you never drive a bus." Morrison proceeded to hit Vann in the head and face several times, threw him against a wall and against the bus several times, and handcuffed him. Morrison placed Vann under arrest and took him to the police station, where the precinct commander voided the arrest. As a result of Morrison's use of force, Vann was treated at a hospital for injuries to the head, face, and body. The injuries forced Vann to miss work for some seven weeks.

Prior to this incident, numerous complaints of violent behavior had been lodged against Morrison, both by civilians and by colleagues. Morrison had been disciplined several times, received a negative psychological evaluation, and had been placed on restricted duty. Approximately 21 months before this incident, Morrison was returned to active duty, following which he was involved in several additional incidents before assaulting Vann. These incidents included injuring a civilian by ramming him in the stomach with a nightstick, threatening to "beat the shit out" of another civilian, and assaulting and pointing his gun at a motorist while off-duty.

After his reinstatement, Morrison was not monitored by Psychological Services Unit ("PSU"), the unit responsible for evaluating employees who were experiencing psychological problems. The three new civilian complaints against Morrison were not communicated to PSU.

Vann sued the police department on the theory that its policy of failing to monitor violence-prone police officers after they were restored to full-duty status caused the violation of his constitutional rights.]

KEARSE, Circuit Judge:

* * *

In order to establish the liability of a municipality in an action under § 1983 for unconstitutional acts by a municipal employee below the policy-making level, a plaintiff must establish that the violation of his constitutional rights resulted from a municipal custom or policy. This does not mean that the plaintiff must show that the municipality had an explicitly stated rule or regulation. A § 1983 plaintiff injured by a police officer may establish the pertinent custom or policy by showing that the municipality, alerted to the possible use of excessive force by its police officers, exhibited deliberate indifference.

* * *

In the present case, Vann presented evidence of the Department's general methods of dealing with problem policemen and of its responses to past incidents involving Morrison. Taken in the light most favorable to Vann, the evidence of the Department's system for dealing with problem officers in the earlier stages of their difficulties highlights the paucity of its monitoring system after such officers were reinstated. The deposition testimony indicated that, after a problem officer was restored to full-duty status, the Department's supervisory units paid virtually no attention to the filing of new complaints against such officers even though such filings should have been red-flag warnings of possibly renewed and future misconduct. DAO (Department Advocate's Office), which monitored officers who were on disciplinary probation, was typically not informed by CPI, by precinct commanders, or by the CCRB as to the filing of civilian complaints. In any event, DAO, woefully understaffed for any significant monitoring function, was not concerned that officers they monitored were the subject of new civilian complaints. And the director of PSU, who acknowledged that the receipt of new complaints was significant for the evaluation of the likelihood that the problem officer would engage in future wrongful conduct, also testified that she "typically" did not tell the commanders to alert DAO or PSU to the receipt of such complaints.

With respect to Morrison in particular, PSU psychologists had early noted Morrison's personality disorder; they had noted thereafter that he did not respond productively to counseling and that he altered his attitude and behavior only in response to administrative discipline; they foresaw that if restored to full duty his problems might recur; and they suggested that if he engaged in further misconduct, he should be dismissed. Yet even while Morrison was on disciplinary probation, there was no mechanism for ensuring that DAO or PSU was alerted that within two months of his restoration to full-duty service the Department had begun to receive new complaints of his physical abuse of civilians. . . .

. . . [T]he three post-reinstatement complaints indicated that Morrison was acting in accordance with his established, and departmentally well known, tendency to escalate confrontations, inappropriately, to the point where he used force. In light of the Department's "systemic failure" to alert the supervisory units of the filing of new complaints against problem officers, and in the absence of any significant administrative response to Morrison's resumption of his abusive misconduct upon reinstatement, it was entirely foreseeable that Morrison would engage in misconduct yet again.

In sum, a rational jury could find that, where an officer had been identified by the police department as a "violence-prone" individual who had a personality disorder manifested by frequent quick-tempered demands for "respect," escalating into physical confrontations for which he always disavowed responsibility, the need to be alert for new civilian complaints filed after his reinstatement to full-duty status was obvious. The jury

could also rationally find that the Department's election to staff DAO with the equivalent of just 11/4 employees to monitor 200 problem officers, together with the systematic lack of communication to the supervisory divisions of information with regard to new civilian complaints, including PSU's routine failure, despite its expertise, to instruct commanders to relay that information reflected a deliberate indifference on the part of the municipal defendants to the dangers posed by problem policemen who had been restored to full-duty service.

* * *

CONCLUSION

We have considered all of the municipal defendants' arguments in support of the judgment in their favor and have found them to be without merit. For the foregoing reasons, the judgment of the district court is vacated and the case is remanded.

YANG
v.
HARDIN

37 F.3d 282 (7th Cir. 1994)

[Citations and footnotes omitted.]

[On January 8, 1991, at approximately 11:00 P.M., Mike Yang, co-owner of a south-side shoe store, received a call from his alarm company notifying him that the store had been burglarized. Yang called his brother, Myung, and an employee, Bob. The defendants, uniformed police officers employed by the Chicago Police Department, had already arrived at the store when Yang got there. While Yang and his employee and brother busied themselves with repairing the shattered front display window, Officer Hardin prepared a police report by the front door of the store, adjacent to the broken window. Officer Brown entered the store to investigate. While inside the store looking for a board to repair the window, employee Bob noticed that Officer Brown was perusing the store in the manner of a shoplifter. Bob alerted Yang to this. As Officers Brown and Hardin began to leave,

Yang noticed a bulge in Officer Brown's jacket. Believing that Officer Brown had stolen some merchandise, Yang approached the officer and requested that the merchandise be returned. At first, Officer Brown denied that he had taken any merchandise. But after a discussion that escalated into an argument, Officer Brown reached into his jacket and pulled out a pair of "L.A. Raiders" shorts and threw them at Yang. Officers Brown and Hardin then proceeded to enter their police car to drive away. When Yang followed, Officer Brown shoved Yang. Throughout the confrontation, Officer Hardin stood by the passenger door of the squad car. He did not speak or intervene in any manner despite Yang's repeated requests for Officer Hardin to call the police sergeant.

In an attempt to prevent Officer Brown from leaving, Yang held onto the driver's side door of the squad car to keep it open so that Officer Brown could not drive off. However, Officer Brown drove anyway, with the driver's side door ajar and Yang hanging onto the car. Officer Brown drove fast and recklessly in a zig-zagging pattern, braking and accelerating, in an attempt to throw Yang off. Officer Brown also repeatedly struck Yang in the ribs with his left elbow. Yang asserts that he was unable to let go of the car without being run over. Throughout the drive, Officer Hardin sat in the passenger seat. Officer Hardin did not say anything or in any way attempt to intervene. The squad car traveled, with Yang hanging on, more than two full city blocks until two men on the sidewalk saw what was happening and ran out to the street to stop the police car. Yang let go when the car stopped. Officer Brown then got out of the car and punched Yang in the face, knocking him to the ground. Officers Brown then got back in the police car and drove away.

Yang pressed criminal charges and both officers were convicted of felonies. He then sued both officers 42 U.S.C. § 1983. The trial judge found against Brown and ordered him to pay $229,658.10 in damages. However, the judge ruled that Officer Hardin was not liable for violating § 1983. Yang appealed.]

BAUER, Circuit Judge.

* * *

Liability under § 1983 requires proof of two essential elements: that the conduct complained of

(1) "was committed by a person acting under color of state law" and (2) "deprived a person of rights, privileges, or immunities secured by the Constitution or laws of the United States." In the present case there is no dispute that Yang has proved the first element. The district court found that both Officers Brown and Hardin acted under color of state law. They were on duty, wearing Chicago police uniforms, driving a marked squad car and were investigating a crime when the incident occurred. The crux of this case is whether Officer Hardin's failure to intervene deprived Yang of his liberty rights under the Due Process Clause of the Fourteenth Amendment and his rights under the Fourth Amendment to be free from unreasonable seizure.

* * *

Byrd v. Brishke remains the seminal case in this circuit on the duty of an officer to intervene to prevent summary punishment. In *Brishke*, this court held that "one who is given a badge of authority of a police officer may not ignore the duty imposed by his office and fail to stop other officers who summarily punish a third person in his presence or otherwise within his knowledge." This responsibility to intervene applies equally to supervisory and nonsupervisory officers. An officer who is present and fails to intervene to prevent other law enforcement officers from infringing the constitutional rights of citizens is liable under § 1983 if that officer had reason to know: (1) that excessive force was being used, (2) that a citizen has been unjustifiably arrested, or (3) that any constitutional violation has been committed by a law enforcement official; and the officer had a realistic opportunity to intervene to prevent the harm from occurring.

The district court orally ruled in favor of Officer Hardin. The court found that the facts alleged by Yang did not demonstrate the availability of a reasonable time for Officer Hardin to intervene, or a reasonable likelihood of successful intervention. This finding is clearly erroneous. Although Yang's complaint fails to explicitly specify the existence of an opportunity for Officer Hardin to have intervened, the facts demonstrate several opportunities during which Hardin could have acted. At a minimum Officer Hardin could have called for a backup, called for help, or at least cautioned Officer Brown to stop. In fact, Officer Hardin should have arrested Officer Brown. . . .

Glossary

Absolute immunity (from prosecution): Court order compelling a witness who has invoked the Fifth Amendment privilege against self-incrimination to testify, but granting the witness immunity from prosecution for crimes revealed.

Accused: A person against whom formal charges have been lodged.

Affidavit: A written statement of facts, signed and sworn to before a person having authority to administer an oath.

Aggravating circumstances: Factors that must be present before the death penalty may be imposed on a defendant convicted of a capital crime. Also called aggravating factors.

Anticipatory search warrant: A warrant that authorizes police to search for evidence that is not currently at the specified location, but is expected to be there at the time of the search.

Apparent authority: A search is valid based on apparent authority when police at the time of the search reasonably, but mistakenly, believe that the person giving consent possesses common authority over the premises.

Appearance evidence: Physical evidence derived from body characteristics that are routinely displayed to the public, such as one's physical appearance, voice, handwriting, and fingerprints.

Appointed counsel: An attorney provided by the government free of charge to an indigent person.

Arraignment: The defendant's initial appearance before a committing magistrate. During this appearance, the defendant is read the charges, informed of his or her right to counsel, and given an opportunity to request appointment of counsel. See **formal charges**.

Arrest: A seizure performed with the announced intent of making a formal arrest or one that lasts too long or is too invasive to be treated as an investigatory stop. See **investigatory detention**, **investigatory stop**, **seizure**, and *Terry* **stop**.

Arrest warrant: A written order of a court, made on behalf of the government, directing an officer to arrest a person and bring him or her before a magistrate.

Bodily evidence: Physical evidence derived from: (1) searching parts of a suspect's body not normally exposed to the public, (2) seizing biological materials, or (3) seizing foreign substances on or inside the body.

Child pornography: Works that visually depict real children engaged in sexual acts.

Commercial speech: Speech designed to arouse interest in a commercial transaction.

Common law: A body of legal principles that derives its authority from the decisions of courts rather than statutes; unwritten law.

Confrontation: Any pretrial event in which the prosecution or the police engage the accused for the purpose of gathering evidence or advancing the prosecution.

Container: Any receptacle that is capable of holding another object, such as luggage, boxes, bags, purses, briefcases, automobile glove compartments, etc.

Contempt (of court): Willful disobedience of court procedures or orders. Contempt of court is punishable by fines or imprisonment.

Contraband: Any property that it is unlawful to possess, such as illegal drugs, illegal weapons, and stolen property. See **seizable evidence**.

Corpus delicti: The requirement that the prosecution put on proof, independent of a confession, that the crime charged was in fact committed by someone, before a confession may be introduced in evidence.

Critical stage: The accused is entitled to counsel during all critical stages in a criminal proceeding. To be considered a critical stage, the event must occur after the initiation of a prosecution and involve a confrontation between the accused and the government in which the lack of counsel may have a prejudicial effect on the outcome of the case (i.e., rights may be lost, defenses waived, or privileges not claimed).

Curtilage: The grounds and outbuildings immediately surrounding a dwelling, which are regularly used for domestic and family purposes, such as the yard and garage.

Custodial interrogation: Questioning initiated by law enforcement officers after a person has been taken into custody or otherwise deprived of his freedom of action in any significant way. See **custody** and **investigative questioning**.

Custody: The restraint of a suspect's liberty to the degree associated with a formal arrest. This determination is made from the point of view of a reasonable person in the suspect's position.

De facto **arrest:** An arrest that occurs by operation of law when an investigatory detention lasts too long or is too invasive to be treated as an investigatory detention, resulting in a violation of the Fourth Amendment unless probable cause is present.

De minimis: Trivial; of no real consequence.

Derivative evidence: Evidence that is inadmissible because it derives from an illegal confession or other illegally obtained evidence.

Detention: A temporary, limited seizure made for the purpose of investigating suspicious circumstances; also called an investigatory stop or a *Terry* stop. See **arrest**, **investigatory stop**, **seizure**, and *Terry* **stop**.

Device: Any apparatus used to monitor or record an oral, wire, or electronic communication.

Disparate impact discrimination: A Title VII violation committed when an employer uses selection criteria that disproportionately eliminate members of a protected class without being valid predictors of the knowledge, skills, or traits necessary for successful performance of the job.

Disparate treatment discrimination: A Title VII violation committed when a person is deliberately treated unequally in employment matters because of race, sex, religion, color, or national origin.

Eavesdropping: Listening with the unaided ear to the conversations of others.

Electronic communications: Transmissions of matters other than the human voice, such as written words, signs, signals, symbols, images, or other data transmitted over a wide range of mediums, including wire, radio, electromagnetic, and photo-optical.

Elements (of a crime): The acts, accompanying mental state, and consequences that constitute the statutory components of a crime.

Exigent circumstances: A situation that requires swift action to protect lives or safety, or to prevent destruction of evidence or escape.

Expressive conduct: Conduct that communicates a message — such as picketing, marching, distributing handbills, soliciting funds, using a bullhorn, or engaging in symbolic speech.

Facially valid warrant: A search warrant that appears regular on its face. To be regular on its face, the warrant must describe with particularity the place to be searched and the items to be seized.

Felony: A crime punishable by death or imprisonment for a term of one year or more. See **misdemeanor**.

Fighting words: Personally abusive and derogatory words spoken to another in a face-to-face encounter under circumstances that, as a matter of common knowledge, are inherently likely to provoke the other person into making an immediate violent response.

Foreign intelligence information: Information that relates to actual or potential attacks by foreign governments or their agents, foreign spying activity inside the United States, domestic activity of international terrorist organizations, and the national defense and security of the United States.

Formal charges: Depending on local procedures, formal charges may be initiated by an arraignment, preliminary hearing, indictment, or information. See **arraignment**, **indictment**, and **information**.

Fresh pursuit: The right of police officers to cross jurisdictional lines when they are in immediate, uninterrupted pursuit of a fleeing suspect.

Frisk: A limited weapons search conducted by patting down a suspect's outer clothing.

Fruits (of a crime): Tangible objects derived through or in consequence of the commission of a crime, such as stolen money or property or funds obtained from the sale of stolen property. See **seizable evidence**.

Fruits (of an unconstitutional search or seizure): Evidence uncovered during an unconstitutional search or seizure, plus any further evidence that is later derived from or discovered as a result of that evidence.

Full search: Search conducted to discover incriminating evidence.

Grand jury: A grand jury is a jury of inquiry empaneled to hear evidence presented by the prosecutor and decide whether the evidence is sufficient to hold the person for trial. If the evidence is deemed sufficient, the grand jury will return an indictment. See **formal charges** and **indictment**.

Hate speech: Speech that offends, denigrates, or belittles others because of their race, creed, color, religion, sexual orientation, or other personal characteristic that makes them vulnerable.

Hostile work environment sexual harassment: A Title VII violation that is committed by unwelcome verbal or physical conduct of a sexual nature, so severe or pervasive that it alters the conditions of the victim's employment and creates an intimidating, hostile, abusive, or offensive work environment.

Hot pursuit: The right of police officers to make a warrantless entry into a private residence or other protected area when they are in immediate, uninterrupted pursuit of a fleeing felon.

Impoundment: Occurs when police take custody of a person's property for reasons other than use as evidence. Examples include taking custody of an arrestee's belongings incident to jailing, towing an abandoned or illegally parked car to a police lot, etc.

Indictment: A formal written accusation made by a grand jury. See **formal charges** and **information**.

Information: A formal accusation or complaint, filed by the prosecutor, charging a person with a designated crime. It is used as a substitute for an indictment in certain classes of criminal cases. See **formal charges** and **indictment**.

Inventory search: A search conducted to make an inventory of property that police have taken into custody.

Instrumentalities (of a crime): Tools, vehicles, etc., used to commit a crime. See **seizable evidence**.

Intensity of a search: The thoroughness of the search activity that is permitted. Depending on the grounds for search authority, the permissible intensity can vary from a cursory inspection to a microscopic examination. The intensity of a search may be no greater than necessary to discover the items for which police have search authority.

Interception: Use of a device to monitor or record the contents of an oral, wire, or electronic communication.

Interrogation: Questioning that is designed to elicit an incriminating response. Interrogation also includes actions that are the functional equivalent of a question, such as telling the suspect that an eyewitness has identified him or her. See **custody**, **custodial interrogation**, and **investigative questioning**.

Investigative questioning: Questioning of a suspect who is not in custody or charged with the crime to which the questions relate.

Investigatory detention: Temporary, limited seizure made for the purpose of investigating suspicious circumstances; also called an investigatory stop or a *Terry* stop. See **arrest**, **investigatory stop**, **seizure**, and *Terry* **stop**.

Investigatory stop: Temporary, limited seizure made for the purpose of investigating suspicious circumstances; also called an investigatory detention or a *Terry* stop. See **arrest**, **investigatory detention**, **seizure**, and *Terry* **stop**.

Jury Pool: Entire group.

Jury venire: Group of potential jurors from which the trial jury is selected; also called "jury pool."

Limited weapons search: A search conducted to disarm a suspect and remove weapons so that an officer can conduct a traffic stop, *Terry* investigation, execute a search warrant, etc., without fear for personal safety. See **frisk**, **pat down**, and **protective sweep**.

Lineup: A police identification procedure in which a group of individuals with similar characteristics are exhibited, to determine whether the victim or an eyewitness can make an identification.

Manual body cavity search: A search of rectal or genital cavities that includes touching or probing.

Mere evidence: Evidence that links a suspect to a crime, other than the fruits or instrumentalities of the crime or contraband. Clothing worn during the crime is an example. See **seizable evidence**.

Misdemeanor: A crime less serious than a felony, punishable by a fine or a jail sentence, generally for a term of less than one year. See **felony**.

Mitigating circumstances: Factors that permit the sentencer to show mercy and withhold the death penalty for a crime for which the death penalty is authorized. Also called **mitigating factors**.

Nonpublic forum: Government facilities reserved for the government's business uses.

Obscenity: Movies, books, literature, magazines, and other similar materials that appeal to the prurient interest, depict hard-core sexual acts in a patently offensive way, and lack serious literary, artistic, political, scientific, or other value.

Open field: Outdoor spaces surrounding a home that lie beyond the curtilage; open fields are not protected by the Fourth Amendment.

Open view: Anything a police officer is able to detect through the use of one or more of his senses from a vantage point where the officer is lawfully present is said to be in "open view." Observation of matters in open view is not a search.

Oral communications: Human voice communications that travel through the air by sound waves. Face-to-face conversations are the most common example. The communication must be spoken under circumstances that create a reasonable expectation of freedom from interception in order to be protected by the Wiretap Act.

Panhandling: Begging in a public place.

Pat down: A weapons frisk that is performed by patting down the person's outer clothing; reasonable suspicion that the person is armed or may be dangerous is necessary to perform a pat-down search.

Per se: Necessarily; as a matter of course; in all cases.

Peremptory challenge: The right to challenge and strike a potential juror without being required to give a reason. In most jurisdictions, each side has a specified number of peremptory challenges and, after using them, must establish cause, such as bias, for further challenges to witnesses.

Petit jury: A jury empaneled to decide whether an accused is guilty; also called a "trial jury."

Photographic identification: A pretrial identification procedure in which a group of photographs is shown to the victim or a witness to determine whether an identification can be made.

Physical evidence: Tangible evidence of a crime. Physical evidence includes everything except testimony.

Plain view doctrine: An exception to the warrant requirement that allows police to seize articles without a search warrant describing them if the officer comes across the article while conducting a lawful search and its incriminating nature is immediately apparent to the officer.

Prejudicial error: An error committed during trial that is sufficiently serious that it furnishes grounds for a new trial, or for reversal on appeal. Also called reversible error.

Pretextual traffic stop: A stop made for a traffic violation in which the officer's real motive is to check a hunch about unrelated criminal activity.

Privilege (evidentiary): The right to withhold evidence that the government could otherwise compel.

Probable cause (to arrest): The degree of factual certainty needed to justify an arrest. Probable cause exists when an officer is aware of facts and circumstances sufficient to warrant a reasonable person in believing a crime has been committed and the person to be arrested committed it. Probable cause is sometimes referred to as reasonable grounds. See **reasonable grounds**.

Probable cause (to search): The degree of factual certainty needed for the issuance of a search warrant. Probable cause exists if a prudent person would conclude that specific objects linked to a crime will be found at a particular location.

Probable cause (to seize): The degree of factual certainty needed to seize an object as evidence. Probable cause to seize exists if a prudent person would conclude that the object in question is associated with criminal activity.

Protective sweep: Cursory visual inspection of closets and other spaces immediately adjoining the place of arrest in which persons posing a danger to the officer could be hiding; permitted whenever the police arrest someone inside a dwelling.

Public forums by designation: Property the government has deliberately set aside for speech uses by members of the public.

Qualified immunity: Immunity from liability for unconstitutional acts that a reasonable police officer would have believed was lawful.

***Quid pro quo* sexual harassment:** A Title VII violation committed when the victim's submission to a supervisor's unwelcome sexual advances is explicitly or implicitly made a condition of receiving tangible job benefits or not suffering tangible job detriments.

Racial profiling: Police interventions that are based on racial or ethnic stereotypes and that have the effect of treating members of minority groups differently from other members of the public. It includes decisions as to whom to stop for investigation or for a traffic violation, actions taken during the stop, such as ordering the occupants to step out of the vehicle, questioning them about drugs, etc.; decisions as to whom to frisk, search, or request consent to search; summoning a drug detection dog to the scene, etc. Racial profiling violates the equal protection clause of the Fourteenth Amendment.

Reasonable expectation of privacy: Factor that determines whether police activity constitutes a search or an interception. See **search**.

Reasonable grounds: An alternative expression for probable cause. See **probable cause**.

Reasonable suspicion: The level of suspicion needed for an investigatory stop. Reasonable suspicion exists when an officer can articulate and point to facts that, together with rational inferences that flow from them, would warrant a reasonable police officer in suspecting the person detained of committing, having committed, or being about to commit a crime. See **probable cause** and **reasonable grounds**.

Retained counsel: An attorney hired and paid for by the accused.

"Same elements" test: The test used in the federal courts and a majority of state courts to determine when prosecutions brought under different sections of the penal code represent the same offense. This test treats crimes defined under different sections of the penal code as distinct offenses for double jeopardy purposes so long as each statute requires proof of at least one distinct element.

"Same transaction" test: Test used in a minority of state courts to determine when prosecutions brought under different sections of the penal code represent the same offense for purposes of double jeopardy. This test treats all crimes committed as part of the same underlying transaction as a single offense for double jeopardy purposes.

Scope (of a search): Areas police have the authority to search. In searches under the authority of a search warrant, the scope of the search is determined by the warrant's description of the place to be searched.

Search: A search occurs when the police perform acts that intrude on a suspect's "reasonable expectation of privacy." A search can occur either by: (1) physically intruding into a constitutionally protected location or (2) technological invasions of privacy.

Search warrant: A written order, issued by a justice or magistrate, in the name of the state, authorizing an officer to search a specified location for described objects that constitute evidence of a crime or contraband.

Seizable evidence: Objects that police have probable cause to believe are connected to a crime. There are four categories: (1) the fruits of a crime, (2) instrumentalities used in its commission, (3) contraband, and (4) mere evidence.

Seizure (of a person): A seizure occurs when a suspect submits to a police officer's show of legal authority or the officer gains physical control over him or her. Seizures are separated into two classes — investigative stops and arrests — based on their scope and duration. See **arrest**, **investigatory detention**, **investigatory stop**, **show of legal authority**, and *Terry* **stop**.

Seizure (of things): A seizure occurs when police commit a meaningful interference with a suspect's possessory rights in property.

Self-incrimination: Declarations and declaratory acts, furnished or performed under government compulsion, that implicate a person in a crime.

Sequester (a jury): To isolate jurors from contact with the public during the course of a trial.

Show of legal authority: Police words or conduct that would induce a reasonable person to believe that he or she was not free to leave. See **seizure**.

Showup: An identification procedure in which police bring the suspect to the victim or a witness for identification.

Sovereign: The government of an independent nation or state.

Statute of limitations: A law prescribing the period following a crime during which the government must either bring charges or lose the right to prosecute.

Strip search: Strip search in a Fourth Amendment sense refers to any forced exposure or observation of a portion of a person's body where the person has a "reasonable expectation of privacy." Complete disrobing is not necessary.

Subpoena *ad testificatum*: Command by a court or legislative body to appear at a certain time and date and give testimony.

Subpoena *duces tecum*: Command by a court or legislative body to produce designated documents, books, papers, records, or other things.

Suspect: Person whom the government believes committed a crime, but who has not yet been formally charged.

Symbolic speech: Mute conduct performed for the sake of communicating a message that is likely to be understood by those who view it.

***Terry* stop:** Temporary, limited seizure of a person made for the sake of investigating suspicious circumstances; also called an investigatory stop or investigatory detention. See **arrest**, **investigatory stop**, **investigatory detention**, and **seizure**.

Testimony/testimonial evidence: Statements elicited from a witness.

Traditional public forums: Used in First Amendment analysis to refer to streets, sidewalks, and parks.

Tribunal: The factfinder at a trial; the petit jury functions as the factfinder in a jury trial and the judge functions as the factfinder in a bench trial.

"Under color of" state law: The misuse of power, possessed by virtue of state law, and made possible only because the wrongdoer is clothed with the authority of state law.

Use immunity/derivative use immunity: Court order compelling a witness who has invoked the Fifth Amendment privilege against self-incrimination to testify, but barring the government from using the testimony and evidence derived from it against the witness in a subsequent criminal prosecution.

Voir dire: A preliminary examination of a prospective juror, conducted by the court or counsel, to determine the prospective juror's qualifications and suitability for jury service.

Voluntary encounter: An investigative encounter in which a suspect's cooperation is voluntary.

Vulgar speech: Speech that is crude, coarse, profane, ribald, or patently offensive.

Wire communication: Communications containing the human voice that travel through wires at some point in their transmission.

Wiretap order: A judicial order, similar to a search warrant, which authorizes interception of a communication.

Witness: A person who is called to testify before a court or to provide answers to official questions.

Whistle-blower speech: Speech that exposes fraud, corruption, mismanagement, abuse of power, waste, etc., by government officials.

Appendix

The Constitution of the United States of America

We the People of the United States, in Order to form a more perfect Union, establish Justice, insure domestic Tranquillity, provide for the common defence, promote the general Welfare, and secure the Blessings of Liberty to ourselves and our Posterity, do ordain and establish this Constitution for the United States of America.

Article I.

Section 1. All legislative Powers herein granted shall be vested in a Congress of the United States, which shall consist of a Senate and House of Representatives.

Section 2. The House of Representatives shall be composed of Members chosen every second Year by the People of the several States, and the Electors in each State shall have the Qualifications requisite for Electors of the most numerous Branch of the State Legislature.

No Person shall be a Representative who shall not have attained to the age of twenty five Years, and been seven Years a Citizen of the United States, and who shall not, when elected, be an Inhabitant of that State in which he shall be chosen.

Representatives and direct Taxes shall be apportioned among the several States which may be included within this Union, according to their respective Numbers, which shall be determined by adding to the whole Number of free Persons, including those bound to Service for a Term of Years, and excluding Indians not taxed, three fifths of all other Persons. The actual Enumeration shall be made within three Years after the first Meeting of the Congress of the United States, and within every subsequent Term of ten Years, in such Manner as they shall by Law direct. The Number of Representatives shall not exceed one for every thirty Thousand, but each State shall have at Least one Representative; and until such enumeration shall be made, the State of New Hampshire shall be entitled to chuse three, Massachusetts eight, Rhode-Island and Providence Plantations one, Connecticut five, New-York six, New Jersey four, Pennsylvania eight, Delaware one, Maryland six, Virginia ten, North Carolina five, South Carolina five, and Georgia three.

When vacancies happen in the Representation from any State, the Executive Authority thereof shall issue Writs of Election to fill such Vacancies.

The House of Representatives shall chuse their Speaker and other Officers; and shall have the sole Power of Impeachment.

Section 3. The Senate of the United States shall be composed of two Senators from each State, chosen by the Legislature thereof, for six Years; and each Senator shall have one Vote.

Immediately after they shall be assembled in Consequence of the first Election, they shall be divided as equally as may be into three Classes. The Seats of the Senators of the first Class shall be vacated at the Expiration of the second Year, of the second Class at the Expiration of the fourth Year, and of the third Class at the Expiration of the sixth Year, so that one third may be chosen every second Year; and if Vacancies happen by Resignation, or otherwise, during the Recess of the Legislature of any State, the Executive thereof may make temporary Appointments until the next Meeting of the Legislature, which shall then fill such Vacancies.

No Person shall be a Senator who shall not have attained to the Age of thirty Years, and been nine Years a Citizen of the United States, and who shall not, when elected, be an Inhabitant of that State for which he shall be chosen.

The Vice President of the United States shall be President of the Senate but shall have no Vote, unless they be equally divided.

The Senate shall chuse their other Officers, and also a President pro tempore, in the Absence of the Vice President, or when he shall exercise the Office of President of the United States.

The Senate shall have the sole Power to try all Impeachments. When sitting for that Purpose, they shall be on Oath or Affirmation. When the President of the United States is tried, the Chief Justice shall preside: And no Person shall be convicted without the Concurrence of two thirds of the Members present.

Judgment in Cases of Impeachment shall not extend further than to removal from Office, and disqualification to hold and enjoy any Office of honor, Trust or Profit under the United States: but the Party convicted shall nevertheless be liable and subject to Indictment, Trial, Judgment and Punishment, according to Law.

Section 4. The Times, Places and Manner of holding Elections for Senators and Representatives, shall be prescribed in each State by the Legislature thereof; but the Congress may at any time by Law make or alter such Regulations, except as to the Places of chusing Senators.

The Congress shall assemble at least once in every Year, and such Meeting shall be on the first Monday in December, unless they shall by Law appoint a different Day.

Section 5. Each House shall be the Judge of the Elections, Returns and Qualifications of its own Members, and a Majority of each shall constitute a Quorum to do Business; but a smaller Number may adjourn from day to day, and may be authorized to compel the Attendance of absent Members, in such Manner, and under such Penalties as each House may provide.

Each House may determine the Rules of its Proceedings, punish its Members for disorderly Behaviour, and, with the Concurrence of two thirds, expel a Member.

Each House shall keep a Journal of its Proceedings, and from time to time publish the same, excepting such Parts as may in their Judgment require Secrecy; and the Yeas and Nays of the Members of either House on any question shall, at the Desire of one fifth of those Present, be entered on the Journal.

Neither House, during the Session of Congress, shall, without the Consent of the other, adjourn for more than three days, nor to any other Place than that in which the two Houses shall be sitting.

Section 6. The Senators and Representatives shall receive a Compensation for their Services, to be ascertained by Law, and paid out of the Treasury of the United States. They shall in all Cases, except Treason, Felony and Breach of the Peace, be privileged from Arrest during their Attendance at the Session of their respective Houses, and in going to and returning from the same; and for any Speech or Debate in either House, they shall not be questioned in any other Place.

No Senator or Representative shall, during the Time for which he was elected, be appointed to any civil Office under the Authority of the United States, which shall have been created, or the Emoluments whereof shall have been encreased during such time; and no Person holding any Office under the United States, shall be a Member of either House during his Continuance in Office.

Section 7. All Bills for raising Revenue shall originate in the House of Representatives; but the Senate may propose or concur with amendments as on other Bills.

Every Bill which shall have passed the House of Representatives and the Senate, shall, before it become a law, be presented to the President of the United States: If he approve he shall sign it, but if not he shall return it, with his Objections to that House in which it shall have originated, who shall enter the Objections at large on their Journal, and proceed to reconsider it. If after such Reconsideration two thirds of that House shall agree to pass the Bill, it shall be sent, together with the Objections, to the other House, by which it shall likewise be reconsidered, and if approved by two thirds of that House, it shall become a Law. But in all such Cases the Votes of both Houses shall be determined by Yeas and Nays, and the Names of the Persons voting for and against the Bill shall be entered on the Journal of each House respectively. If any Bill shall not be returned by the President within ten Days (Sundays excepted) after it shall have been presented to him, the Same shall be a Law, in like Manner as if he had signed it, unless the Congress by their Adjournment prevent its Return, in which Case it shall not be a Law.

Every Order, Resolution, or Vote to which the Concurrence of the Senate and House of Representatives may be necessary (except on a question of Adjournment) shall be presented to the President of the United States; and before the Same shall take Effect, shall be approved by him, or being disapproved by him, shall be repassed by two thirds of the Senate and House of Representatives, according to the Rules and Limitations prescribed in the Case of a Bill.

Section 8. The Congress shall have Power To lay and collect Taxes, Duties, Imposts and Excises, to pay the Debts and provide for the common Defence and general Welfare of the United States; but all Duties, Imposts and Excises shall be uniform throughout the United States;

To borrow Money on the credit of the United States;

To regulate Commerce with foreign Nations, and among the several States, and with the Indian Tribes;

To establish an uniform Rule of Naturalization, and uniform Laws on the subject of Bankruptcies throughout the United States;

To coin Money, regulate the Value thereof, and of foreign Coin, and fix the Standard of Weights and Measures;

To provide for the Punishment of counterfeiting the Securities and current Coin of the United States;

To establish Post Offices and post Roads;

To promote the Progress of Science and useful Arts, by securing for limited Times to Authors and Inventors the exclusive Right to their respective Writings and Discoveries;

To constitute Tribunals inferior to the Supreme Court;

To define and punish Piracies and Felonies committed on the high Seas, and Offences against the Law of Nations;

To declare War, grant Letters of Marque and Reprisal, and make Rules concerning Captures on Land and Water;

To raise and support Armies, but no Appropriation of Money to that Use shall be for a longer Term than two Years;

To provide and maintain a Navy;

To make Rules for the Government and Regulation of the land and naval Forces;

To provide for calling forth the Militia to execute the Laws of the Union, suppress Insurrections and repeal Invasions;

To provide for organizing, arming, and disciplining, the Militia, and for governing such Part of them as may be employed in the Service of the United States, reserving to the States respectively, the Appointment of the Officers, and the Authority of training the Militia according to the discipline prescribed by Congress;

To exercise exclusive Legislation in all Cascs whatsoever, over such District (not exceeding ten Miles square) as may, by Cession of Particular States, and the Acceptance of Congress, become the Seat of the Government of the United States, and to exercise like Authority over all Places purchased by the Consent of the Legislature of the State in which the Same shall be, for the Erection of Forts, Magazines, Arsenals, dock-Yards and other needful Buildings; — And

To make all Laws which shall be necessary and proper for carrying into Execution the foregoing Powers and all other Powers vested by this Constitution in the Government of the United States, or in any Department or Officer thereof.

Section 9. The Migration or Importation of such Persons as any of the States now existing shall think proper to admit, shall not be prohibited by the Congress prior to the Year one thousand eight hundred and eight, but a Tax or duty may be imposed on such Importation, not exceeding ten dollars for each Person.

The Privilege of the Writ of Habeas Corpus shall not be suspended, unless when in Cases of Rebellion or Invasion the public Safety may require it.

No Bill of Attainder or ex post facto Law shall be passed.

No Capitation, or other direct, Tax shall be laid, unless in Proportion to the Census of Enumeration herein before directed to be taken.

No Tax or Duty shall be laid on Articles exported from any State.

No Preference shall be given by any Regulation of Commerce or Revenue to the Ports of one State over those of another: nor shall Vessels bound to, or from, one State, be obliged to enter, clear or pay Duties in another.

No Money shall be drawn from the Treasury, but in Consequence of Appropriations made by Law; and a regular Statement and Account of the Receipts and Expenditures of all public Money shall be published from time to time.

No Title of Nobility shall be granted by the United States: And no Person holding any Office of Profit or Trust under them, shall, without the Consent of the Congress, accept of any present, Emolument, Office, or Title, of any kind whatever, from any King, Prince or foreign State.

Section 10. No State shall enter into any Treaty, Alliance, or Confederation; grant Letters of Marque and Reprisal; coin Money; emit Bills of Credit; make any Thing but gold and silver Coin a Tender in Payment of Debts; pass any Bill of Attainder, ex post facto Law, or Law impairing the Obligation of Contracts, or grant any Title of Nobility.

No State shall, without the Consent of the Congress, lay any Imposts or Duties on Imports or Exports, except what may be absolutely necessary for executing it's inspection Laws: and the net Produce of all Duties and Imposts, laid by any State on Imports or Exports, shall be for the Use of the Treasury of the United States; and all such Laws shall be subject to the Revision and Control of the Congress.

No State shall, without the Consent of Congress, lay any Duty of Tonnage, keep Troops, or Ships of War in time of Peace, enter into any Agreement or Compact with another State, or with a foreign Power, or engage in War, unless actually invaded, or in such imminent Danger as will not admit of delay.

Article II.

Section 1. The executive Power shall be vested in a President of the United States of America. He shall hold his Office during the Term of four Years, and, together with the Vice President, chosen for the same Term, be elected, as follows:

Each State shall appoint, in such Manner as the Legislature thereof may direct, a Number of Electors, equal to the whole Number of Senators and Representatives to which the State may be entitled in the Congress: but no Senator or Representative, or Person holding an Office of Trust or Profit under the United States, shall be appointed an Elector.

The Electors shall meet in their respective States, and vote by Ballot for two Persons, of whom one at least shall not be an Inhabitant of the same State with themselves. And they shall make a List of all the Persons voted for, and of the Number of Votes for each; which List they shall sign and certify, and transmit sealed to the Seat of the Government of the United States, directed to the President of the Senate. The President of the Senate shall, in the Presence of the Senate and House of Representatives, open all the Certificates, and the Votes shall then be counted. The Person having the greatest Number of Votes shall be the President, if such Number be a Majority of the whole Number of Electors appointed; and if there be more than one who have such Majority, and have an equal Number of Votes, then the House of Representatives shall immediately chuse by Ballot one of them for President; and if no Person have a Majority, then from the five highest on the List the said House shall in like Manner chuse the President. But in chusing the President, the Votes shall be taken by States, the Representatives from each State having one Vote; a quorum for this Purpose shall consist of a Member or Members from two thirds of the States, and a Majority of all the States shall be necessary to a Choice. In every Case, after the Choice of the President, the Person having the greatest Number of Votes of the Electors shall be the Vice President. But if there should remain two or more who have equal Votes, the Senate shall chuse from them by Ballot the Vice President.

The Congress may determine the Time of chusing the Electors, and the Day on which they shall give their Votes; which Day shall be the same throughout the United States.

No Person except a natural born Citizen, or a Citizen of the United States, at the time of the Adoption of this Constitution, shall be eligible to the Office of President; neither shall any person be eligible to that Office who shall not have attained to the Age of thirty five Years, and been fourteen Years a Resident within the United States.

In Case of the Removal of the President from Office, or of his Death, Resignation, or Inability to discharge the Powers and Duties of the said Office, the Same shall devolve on the Vice President, and the Congress may by Law provide for the Case of Removal, Death, Resignation or Inability, both of the President and Vice President, declaring what Officer shall then act as President, and such Officer shall act accordingly, until the Disability be removed, or a President shall be elected.

The President shall, at stated Times, receive for his Services, a Compensation, which shall neither be encreased nor diminished during the Period for which he shall have been elected, and he shall not receive within that Period any other Emolument from the United States, or any of them.

Before he enter on the Execution of his Office, he shall take the following Oath or Affirmation: — "I do solemnly swear (or affirm) that I will faithfully execute the Office of President of the United States, and will to the best of my Ability, preserve, protect and defend the Constitution of the United States."

Section 2. The President shall be Commander in Chief of the Army and Navy of the United States, and of the Militia of the several States, when called into the actual Service of the United States; he may require the Opinion, in writing, of the principal Officer in each of the executive Departments, upon any Subject relating to the Duties of their respective Offices, and he shall have Power to Grant Reprieves and Pardons for Offences against the United States, except in Cases of Impeachment.

He shall have Power, by and with the Advice and Consent of the Senate, to make Treaties, provided two thirds of the Senators present concur; and he shall nominate, and by and with the Advice and Consent of the Senate, shall appoint Ambassadors, other public Ministers and Consuls, Judges of the supreme Court, and all other Officers of the United States, whose Appointments are not herein otherwise provided for, and which shall be established by Law: but the Congress may by Law vest the Appointment of such inferior Officers, as they think proper, in the President alone, in the Courts of Law, or in the Heads of Departments.

The President shall have Power to fill up all Vacancies that may happen during the Recess of the Senate, by granting Commissions which shall expire at the End of their next Session.

Section 3. He shall from time to time give to the Congress Information on the State of the Union, and recommend to their Consideration such Measures as he shall judge necessary and expedient; he may, on extraordinary Occasions, convene both Houses, or either of them, and in Case of Disagreement between them, with Respect to the Time of Adjournment, he may adjourn them to such Time as he shall think proper; he shall receive Ambassadors and other public Ministers; he shall take Care that the Laws be faithfully executed, and shall Commission all the Officers of the United States.

Section 4. The President, Vice President and all Civil Officers of the United States, shall be removed from Office on Impeachment for and Conviction of, Treason, Bribery, or other high Crimes and Misdemeanors.

Article III.

Section 1. The judicial Power of the United States, shall be vested in one supreme Court, and in such inferior Courts as the Congress may from time to time ordain and establish. The Judges, both of the supreme and inferior Courts, shall hold their Offices during good Behaviour, and shall, at stated Times, receive for their Services, a Compensation, which shall not be diminished during their Continuance in Office.

Section 2. The judicial Power shall extend to all Cases, in Law and Equity, arising under this Constitution, the Laws of the United States, and Treaties made, or which shall be made, under their Authority; — to all Cases affecting Ambassadors, other public ministers and Consuls; — to all Cases of admiralty and maritime Jurisdiction; — to Controversies to which the United States shall be a Party; — to Controversies between two or more States; — between a State and Citizens of another State; — between Citizens of different States; — between Citizens of the same State claiming Lands under Grants of different States, and between a State, or the Citizens thereof, and foreign States, Citizens or Subjects.

In all Cases affecting Ambassadors, other public Ministers and Consuls, and those in which a State shall be Party, the supreme Court shall have original Jurisdiction. In all the other Cases before mentioned, the supreme Court shall have appellate Jurisdiction, both as to Law and Fact, with such Exceptions, and under such Regulations as the Congress shall make.

The Trial of all Crimes, except in Cases of Impeachment, shall be by Jury; and such Trial shall be held in the State where the said Crimes shall have been committed; but when not committed within any State, the Trial shall be at such Place or Places as the Congress may by Law have directed.

Section 3. Treason against the United States, shall consist only in levying War against them, or in adhering to their Enemies, giving them Aid and Comfort. No Person shall be convicted of Treason unless on the Testimony of two Witnesses to the same overt Act, or on Confession in open Court.

The Congress shall have Power to declare the Punishment of Treason, but no Attainder of Treason shall work Corruption of Blood, or Forfeiture except during the Life of the Person attainted.

Article IV.

Section 1. Full Faith and Credit shall be given in each State to the public Acts, Records, and judicial Proceedings of every other State. And the Congress may by general Laws prescribe the Manner in which such Acts, Records and Proceedings shall be proved, and the Effect thereof.

Section 2. The Citizens of each State shall be entitled to all Privileges and Immunities of Citizens in the several States.

A Person charged in any State with Treason, Felony, or other Crime, who shall flee from Justice, and be found in another State, shall on Demand of the executive Authority of the State from which he fled, be delivered up, to be removed to the State having Jurisdiction of the Crime.

No Person held to Service or Labour in one State, under the Laws thereof, escaping into another, shall, in Consequence of any Law or Regulation therein, be discharged from such Service or Labour, but shall be delivered up on Claim of the Party to whom such Service or Labour may be due.

Section 3. New States may be admitted by the Congress into this Union; but no new State shall be formed or erected within the Jurisdiction of any other State; nor any State be formed by the Junction of two or more States, or Parts of States, without the Consent of the Legislatures of the States concerned as well as of the Congress.

The Congress shall have Power to dispose of and make all needful Rules and Regulations respecting the Territory or other Property belonging to the United States; and nothing in this Constitution shall be so construed as to Prejudice any Claims of the United States, or of any particular State.

Section 4. The United States shall guarantee to every State in this Union a Republican Form of Government, and shall protect each of them against Invasion; and on Application of the Legislature, or of the Executive (when the Legislature cannot be convened) against domestic Violence.

Article V.

The Congress, whenever two thirds of both Houses shall deem it necessary, shall propose Amendments to this Constitution, or, on the Application of the Legislatures of two thirds of the several States, shall call a Convention for proposing Amendments, which, in either Case, shall be valid to all Intents and Purposes, as Part of this Constitution, when ratified by the Legislatures of three fourths of the several States, or by Conventions in three fourths thereof, as the one or the other Mode of Ratification may be proposed by the Congress; Provided that no Amendment which may be made prior to the Year One thousand eight hundred and eight shall in any Manner affect the first and fourth Clauses in the Ninth Section of the first Article; and that no State, without its Consent, shall be deprived of its equal Suffrage in the Senate.

Article VI.

All Debts contracted and Engagements entered into, before the Adoption of this Constitution, shall be as valid against the United States under this Constitution, as under the Confederation.

This Constitution, and the Laws of the United States which shall be made in Pursuance thereof; and all Treaties made, or which shall be made, under the Authority of the United States, shall be the supreme Law of the Land; and the Judges in every State shall be bound thereby, any Thing in the Constitution or Laws of any state to the Contrary notwithstanding.

The Senators and Representatives before mentioned, and the Members of the several State Legislatures, and all executive and judicial Officers, both of the United States and of the several States, shall be bound by Oath or Affirmation, to support this Constitution; but no religious Test shall ever be required as a Qualification to any Office or public Trust under the United States.

Article VII.

The Ratification of the Conventions of nine States, shall be sufficient for the Establishment of this Constitution between the States so ratifying the same.

Done in Convention by the Unanimous Consent of the States present the Seventeenth Day of September in the Year of our Lord one thousand seven hundred and Eighty seven and of the Independence of the United States of America the Twelfth. In witness whereof We have hereunto subscribed our Names.

Go. WASHINGTON—Presid't. and deputy from Virginia

New Hampshire	JOHN LANGDON NICHOLAS GILMAN	Delaware	GEO: READ GUNNING BEDFORD JUN JOHN DICKINSON RICHARD BASSETT JACO: BROOM
Massachusetts	NATHANIEL GORHAM RUFUS KING	Maryland	JAMES MCHENRY DAN OF ST THOS JENIFER DAN'L CARROLL
Connecticut	WM. SAML. JOHNSON ROGER SHERMAN		
New York	ALEXANDER HAMILTON	Virginia	JOHN BLAIR JAMES MADISON, JR.
New Jersey	WIL: LIVINGSTON DAVID BREARLEY WM. PATTERSON JONA: DAYTON	North Carolina	WM. BLOUNT RICHD DOBBS SPAIGHT HU WILLIAMSON J. RUTLEDGE

Pennsylvania	B FRANKLIN	South	J. RUTLEDGE
	THOMAS MIFFLIN	Carolina	CHARLES
	ROB'T MORRIS		COTESWORTH
	GEO. CLYMER		PINCKNEY
	THOS. FITZSIMONS		CHARLES PINCKNEY
	JARED INGERSOL		PIERCE BUTLER
	JAMES WILSON		
	GOUV MORRIS		
		Georgia	WILLIAM FEW
			ABR BALDWIN

Articles in addition to, and amendment of, the Constitution of the United States of America, proposed by Congress, and ratified by the several states, pursuant to the Fifth Article of the original Constitution

Amendment I

Congress shall make no law respecting an establishment of religion, or prohibiting the free exercise thereof; or abridging the freedom of speech, or of the press; or the right of the people peaceably to assemble, and to petition the Government for a redress of grievances.

Amendment II

A well regulated Militia, being necessary to the security of a free State, the right of the people to keep and bear Arms, shall not be infringed.

Amendment III

No Soldier shall, in time of peace be quartered in any house, without the consent of the Owner, nor in time of war, but in a manner to be prescribed by law.

Amendment IV

The right of the people to be secure in their persons, houses, papers, and effects, against unreasonable searches and seizures, shall not be violated, and no Warrants shall issue, but upon probable cause, supported by Oath or affirmation, and particularly describing the place to be searched, and the persons or things to be seized.

Amendment V

No person shall be held to answer for a capital, or otherwise infamous crime, unless on a presentment or indictment of a Grand Jury, except in cases arising in the land or naval forces, or in the Militia, when in actual service in time of War or public danger; nor shall any person be subject for the same offence to be twice put in jeopardy of life or limb; nor shall be compelled in any criminal case to be a witness against himself, nor be deprived of life, liberty, or property, without due process of law; nor shall private property be taken for public use, without just compensation.

Amendment VI

In all criminal prosecutions, the accused shall enjoy the right to a speedy and public trial, by an impartial jury of the State and district wherein the crime shall have been committed, which district shall have been previously ascertained by law, and to be informed of the nature and cause of the accusation; to be confronted with the witnesses against him; to have compulsory process for obtaining witnesses in his favor, and to have the Assistance of Counsel for his defence.

Amendment VII

In Suits at common law, where the value in controversy shall exceed twenty dollars, the right of trial by jury shall be preserved, and no fact tried by a jury, shall be otherwise re-examined in any Court of the United States, than according to the rules of the common law.

Amendment VIII

Excessive bail shall not be required, nor excessive fines imposed, nor cruel and unusual punishments inflicted.

Amendment IX

The enumeration in the Constitution, of certain rights, shall not be construed to deny or disparage others retained by the people.

Amendment X

The powers not delegated to the United States by the Constitution, nor prohibited by it to the States, are reserved to the States respectively, or to the people.

Amendment XI

The Judicial power of the United States shall not be construed to extend to any suit in law or equity, commenced or prosecuted against one of the United States by Citizens of another State, or by Citizens or Subjects of any Foreign State.

Amendment XII

The Electors shall meet in their respective states and vote by ballot for President and Vice-President, one of whom, at least, shall not be an inhabitant of the same state with themselves; they shall name in their ballots the person voted for as President, and in distinct ballots the person voted for as Vice-President, and they shall make distinct lists of all persons voted for as President, and of all persons voted for as Vice-President, and of the number of votes for each, which lists they shall sign and certify, and transmit sealed to the seat of the government of the United States, directed to the President of the Senate; — The President of the Senate shall, in the presence of the Senate and House of Representatives, open all the certificates and the votes shall then be counted; — The person having the greatest Number of votes for President, shall be the President, if such number be a majority of the whole number of Electors appointed; and if no person have such majority, then from the persons having the highest numbers not exceeding three on the list of those voted for as President, the House of Representatives shall choose immediately, by ballot, the President. But in choosing the President, the votes shall be taken by states, the representation from each state having one vote; a quorum for this purpose shall consist of a member or members from two-thirds of the states, and a majority of all the states shall be necessary to a choice. And if the House of Representatives shall not choose a President whenever the right of choice shall devolve upon them, before the fourth day of March next following, then the Vice-President shall act as President, as in the case of the death or other constitutional disability of the President. — The person having the greatest number of votes as Vice-President, shall be the Vice-President, if such number be a majority of the whole number of Electors appointed, and if no person have a majority, then from the two highest numbers on the list, the Senate shall choose the Vice-President; a quorum for the purpose shall consist of two-thirds of the whole number of Senators, and a majority of the whole number shall be necessary to a choice. But no person constitutionally ineligible to the office of President shall be eligible to that of Vice-President of the United States.

Amendment XIII

Section 1. Neither slavery nor involuntary servitude, except as a punishment for crime whereof the party shall have been duly convicted, shall exist within the United States, or any place subject to their jurisdiction.

Section 2. Congress shall have power to enforce this article by appropriate legislation.

Amendment XIV

Section 1. All persons born or naturalized in the United States and subject to the jurisdiction thereof, are citizens of the United States and of the State wherein they reside. No State shall make or enforce any law which shall abridge the privileges or immunities of citizens of the United States; nor shall any State deprive any person of life, liberty, or property, without due process of law; nor deny to any person within its jurisdiction the equal protection of the laws.

Section 2. Representatives shall be apportioned among the several States according to their respective numbers, counting the whole number of persons in each State, excluding Indians not taxed. But when the right to vote at any election for the choice of electors for President and Vice President of the United States, Representatives in Congress, the Executive and Judicial officers of a State, or the members of the Legislature thereof, is denied to any of the male inhabitants of such State, being twenty-one years of age, and citizens of the United States, or in any way abridged, except for participation in rebellion, or other crime, the basis of representation therein shall be reduced in the proportion which the number of such male citizens shall bear to the whole number of male citizens twenty-one years of age in such State.

Section 3. No person shall be a Senator or Representative in Congress, or elector of President and Vice President, or hold any office, civil or military, under the United States, or under any State, who, having previously taken an oath, as a member of Congress, or as an officer of the United States, or as a member of any State legislature, or as an executive or judicial officer of any State, to support the Constitution of the United States, shall have engaged in insurrection or rebellion against the same, or given aid or comfort to the enemies thereof. But Congress may by a vote of two thirds of each House, remove such disability.

Section 4. The validity of the public debt of the United States, authorized by law, including debts incurred for payment of pensions and bounties for services in suppressing insurrection or rebellion, shall not be questioned. But neither the United States nor any State shall assume or pay any debt or obligation incurred in aid of insurrection or rebellion against the United States, or any claim for the loss or emancipation of any slave; but all such debts, obligations and claims shall be held illegal and void.

Section 5. The Congress shall have power to enforce, by appropriate legislation, the provisions of this article.

Amendment XV

Section 1. The right of citizens of the United States to vote shall not be denied or abridged by the United States or by any State on account of race, color, or previous condition of servitude.

Section 2. The Congress shall have power to enforce this article by appropriate legislation.

Amendment XVI

The Congress shall have power to lay and collect taxes on incomes, from whatever source derived, without apportionment among the several States, and without regard to any census or enumeration.

Amendment XVII

The Senate of the United States shall be composed of two Senators from each State, elected by the people thereof, for six years; and each Senator shall have one vote. The electors in each State shall have the qualifications requisite for electors of the most numerous branch of the State legislatures.

When vacancies happen in the representation of any State in the Senate, the executive authority of such State shall issue writs of election to fill such vacancies: Provided, That the legislature of any State may empower the executive thereof to make temporary appointments until the people fill the vacancies by election as the legislature may direct.

This amendment shall not be so construed as to affect the election or term of any Senator chosen before it becomes valid as part of the Constitution.

Amendment XVIII

Section 1. After one year from the ratification of this article the manufacture, sale, or transportation of intoxicating liquors within, the importation thereof into, or the exportation thereof from the United States and all territory subject to the jurisdiction thereof for beverage purposes is hereby prohibited.

Section 2. The Congress and the several States shall have concurrent power to enforce this article by appropriate legislation.

Section 3. This article shall be inoperative unless it shall have been ratified as an amendment to the Constitution by the legislatures of the several States, as provided in the Constitution, within seven years from the date of the submission hereof to the States by the Congress.

Amendment XIX

The right of citizens of the United States to vote shall not be denied or abridged by the United States or by any State on account of sex.

Congress shall have power to enforce this article by appropriate legislation.

Amendment XX

Section 1. The terms of the President and Vice President shall end at noon on the 20th day of January, and the terms of Senators and Representatives at noon on the 3d day of January, of the years in which such terms would have ended if this article had not been ratified; and the terms of their successors shall then begin.

Section 2. The Congress shall assemble at least once in every year, and such meeting shall begin at noon on the 3d day of January, unless they shall by law appoint a different day.

Section 3. If, at the time fixed for the beginning of the term of the President, the President elect shall have died, the Vice President elect shall become President. If a President shall not have been chosen before the time fixed for the beginning of his term, or if the President elect shall have failed to qualify, then the Vice President elect shall act as President until a President shall have qualified; and the Congress may by law provide for the case wherein neither a President elect nor a Vice President shall have qualified, declaring who shall then act as President, or the manner in which one who is to act shall be selected, and such person shall act accordingly until a President or Vice President shall have qualified.

Section 4. The Congress may by law provide for the case of the death of any of the persons from whom the House of Representatives may choose a President whenever the right of choice shall have devolved upon them, and for the case of the death of any of the persons from whom the Senate may choose a Vice President whenever the right of choice shall have devolved upon them.

Section 5. Sections 1 and 2 shall take effect on the 15th day of October following the ratification of this article.

Section 6. This article shall be inoperative unless it shall have been ratified as an amendment to the Constitution by the legislatures of three fourths of the several States within seven years from the date of its submission.

Amendment XXI

Section 1. The eighteenth article of amendment to the Constitution of the United States is hereby repealed.

Section 2. The transportation or importation into any State, Territory, or Possession of the United States for delivery or use therein of intoxicating liquors, in violation of the laws thereof, is hereby prohibited.

Section 3. This article shall be inoperative unless it shall have been ratified as an amendment to the Constitution by conventions in the several States, as provided in the Constitution, within seven years from the date of the submission hereof to the States by the Congress.

Amendment XXII

Section 1. No person shall be elected to the office of the President more than twice, and no person who has held the office of President, or acted as President, for more than two years of a term to which some other person was elected President shall be elected to the office of the President more than once. But this Article shall not apply to any person holding the office of President, when this Article was proposed by the Congress, and shall not prevent any person who may be holding the office of President, or acting as President, during the term within which this Article becomes operative from holding the office of President or acting as President during the remainder of such term.

Section 2. This article shall be inoperative unless it shall have been ratified as an amendment to the Constitution by the legislatures of three-fourths of the several States within seven years from the date of its submission to the States by the Congress.

Amendment XXIII

Section 1. The District constituting the seat of Government of the United States shall appoint in such manner as Congress may direct:

A number of electors of President and Vice President equal to the whole number of Senators and Representatives in Congress to which the District would be entitled if it were a State, but in no event more than the least populous State; they shall be in addition to those appointed by the States, but they shall be considered, for the purposes of the election of President and Vice President, to be electors appointed by a State; and they shall meet in the District and perform such duties as provided by the twelfth article of amendment.

Section 2. The Congress shall have power to enforce this article by appropriate legislation.

Amendment XXIV

Section 1. The right of citizens of the United States to vote in any primary or other election for President or Vice President, for electors for President or Vice President, or for Senator or Representative in Congress, shall not be denied or abridged by the United States or any State by reason of failure to pay any poll tax or other tax.

Section 2. The Congress shall have power to enforce this article by appropriate legislation.

Amendment XXV

Section 1. In case of the removal of the President from office or of his death or resignation, the Vice President shall become President.

Section 2. Whenever there is a vacancy in the office of the Vice President, the President shall nominate a Vice President who shall take office upon confirmation by a majority vote of both Houses of Congress.

Section 3. Whenever the President transmits to the President pro tempore of the Senate and the Speaker of the House of Representatives his written declaration that he is unable to discharge the powers and duties of his office, and until he transmits to them a written declaration to the contrary, such powers and duties shall be discharged by the Vice President as Acting President.

Section 4. Whenever the Vice President and a majority of either the principal officers of the executive departments or of such other body as Congress may by law provide, transmit to the President pro tempore of the Senate and the Speaker of the House of Representatives their written declaration that the President is unable to discharge the powers and duties of his office, the Vice President shall immediately assume the powers and duties of the office as Acting President.

Thereafter, when the President transmits to the President pro tempore of the Senate and the Speaker of the House of Representatives has written declaration that no inability exists, he shall resume the powers and duties of his office unless the Vice President and a majority of either the principal officers of the executive department or of such other body as Congress may by law provide, transmit within four days to the President pro tempore of the Senate and the Speaker of the House of Representatives their written declaration that the President is unable to discharge the powers and duties of his office. Thereupon Congress shall decide the issue, assembling within forty-eight hours for that purpose if not in session. If the Congress, within twenty-one days after receipt of the latter written declaration, or, if Congress is not in session, within twenty-one days after Congress is required to assemble, determines by two thirds vote of both Houses that the President is unable to discharge the powers and duties of his office, the Vice President shall continue to discharge the same as Acting President; otherwise, the President shall resume the powers and duties of his office.

Amendment XXVI

Section 1. The right of citizens of the United States, who are eighteen years of age or older, to vote shall not be denied or abridged by the United States or by any State on account of age.

Section 2. The Congress shall have power to enforce this article by appropriate legislation.

Amendment XXVII

No law, varying the compensation for the services of the Senators and Representatives, shall take effect, until an election of Representatives shall have intervened.

Index of Cases

Note: Page numbers followed by *np* indicate footnotes.

Gros v. The Port Washington Police Dist., 944 F. Supp. 1072 (E.D.N.Y. 1996), 482*np*

Grow v. City of Milwaukee, 84 F. Supp. 2d 990 (E.D. Wis. 2000), 492*np*

Grusendorf v. City of Oklahoma City, 816 F.2d 539 (10th Cir. 1987), 499*np*

Grutter v. Bolinger, supra note 138, 510*np*

Grutter v. Bolinger, 539 U.S. 306, 123 S. Ct. 2325, 156 L. Ed. 2d 304 (2003), 510*np*

H

Hague v. C.I.O., 307 U.S. 496, 59 S. Ct. 954, 83 L. Ed. 1423 (1939), 69*np*, 78*np*

Halbert v. Michigan, 545 U.S. 605, 125 S. Ct. 2582, 162 L. Ed. 2d 552 (2005), 402*np*

Hamilton v. Alabama, 368 U.S. 52, 82 S. Ct. 157, 7 L. Ed. 2d 114 (1961), 402*np*

Hanlon v. Berger, 526 U.S. 808, 119 S. Ct 1706, 143 L. Ed. 2d 978 (1999), 203*np*

Harbin v. City of Alexandria, 712 F. Supp. 67 (E.D. Va. 1989), 106*np*

Hardister v. State, 849 N.E.2d 563 (Ind. 2006), 236*np*

Harlow v. Fitzgerald, 457 U.S. 800, 102 S. Ct. 2727, 73 L. Ed. 2d 396 (1982), 514*np*

Harmelin v. Michigan, 501 U.S. 957, 111 S. Ct. 268, 115 L. Ed. 2d 836 (1991), 461*np*

Harrison v. Oakland County, 612 F. Supp. 2d 848 (E.D. Mich. 2009), 479*np*

Harris v. City of Canton, 489 U.S. 378, 109 S. Ct. 1197, 103 L. Ed. 3d 412 (1989), 514*np*

Harris v. Forklift Sys., Inc., *supra* note 121, 507*np*

Harris v. Forklift Sys., Inc., 510 U.S. 17, 114 S. Ct. 367, 126 L. Ed. 2d 295 (1993), 507*np*

Harris v. New York, supra note 139, 354*np*

Harris v. New York, 401 U.S. 222, 91 S. Ct. 643, 28 L. Ed. 2d 1 (1971), 353*np*

Harris v. Roderick, 126 F.3d 1189 (9th Cir. 1997), 155*np*

Hayes v. Civil Service Comm'n, 348 Ill. App. 346, 108 N.E.2d 505 (1952), 499*np*

Hayes v. Florida, supra note 62, 380*np*, 381*np*

Hayes v. Florida, supra note 119, 121*np*, 122*np*

Hayes v. Florida, 470 U.S. 811, 105 S. Ct. 1643, 84 L. Ed. 2d 705 (1985), 379*np*, 411*np*, 563–564

Hayes v. Florida, 470 U.S. 811, 817, 105 S. Ct. 1643, 1647, 84 L. Ed. 2d 705 (1985), 118*np*

Haynes v. City of Circleville, Ohio, 474 F.3d 357 (6th Cir. 2007), 477*np*

Haynes v. City of Circleville, Ohio, *supra* note 4, 479*np*

Haynes v. United States, 390 U.S. 85, 88 S. Ct. 722, 19 L. Ed. 2d 923 (1968), 376*np*

Haywood v. Ball, 586 F.2d 996 (4th Cir. 1978), 30*np*

Hazelwood School District v. Kuhlmeier, 484 U.S. 260, 108 S. Ct. 562, 98 L. Ed. 2d 592 (1988), 66*np*

Heart of Atlanta Motel, Inc. v. United States, 379 U.S. 241, 85 S. Ct. 348, 13 L. Ed. 2d 258 (1964), 14*np*

Heath v. Alabama, 474 U.S. 82, 106 S. Ct. 433, 88 L. Ed. 2d 387 (1985), 430*np*

Heller v. Doe, 509 U.S. 312, 113 S. Ct. 2637, 125 L. Ed. 2d 257 (1993), 33*np*

Heller v. New York, supra note 55, 56*np*

Heller v. New York, 413 U.S. 483, 93 S. Ct. 2789, 37 L. Ed. 2d 745 (1973), 55*np*

Helling v. McKinney, 509 U.S. 25, 113 S. Ct. 2475, 125 L. Ed. 2d 22 (1993), 469*np*

Hendrix v. State, 843 So. 2d 1003 (Fla. Dist. Ct. App. 2003), 387*np*

Henry v. United States, 361 U.S. 98, 100, 80 S. Ct. 168, 170, 4 L. Ed. 2d 134 (1959), 90*np*

Hernandez v. New York, 500 U.S. 352, 111 S. Ct. 1859, 114 L. Ed. 2d 395 (1991), 453*np*

Hernandez v. Robles, 7 N.Y.3d 338, 855 N.E.2d 1 (N.Y. 2006), 34*np*

Hernandez v. Robles, supra note 117, 34*np*

Herring v. United States (2009), 256*np*

Herring v. United States, supra note 363, 255*np*

Herring v. United States, 355 U.S. 135, 129 S. Ct. 695, 172 L. Ed. 2d 496 (2009), 251*np*, 604–606

Hess v. Indiana, 414 U.S. 105, 94 S. Ct. 326, 8 L. Ed. 2d 303 (1973), 541–542

Hess v. Indiana, 414 U.S. 105, 94 S. Ct. 326, 38 L. Ed. 2d 303 (1973), 61*np*

Hiibel v. Sixth Judicial Dist. Court, 542 U.S. 177, 124 S. Ct. 2451, 159 L. Ed. 2d 292 (2004), 117*np*

Hiller v. County of Suffolk, 977 F. Supp. 202 (E. D. N. Y. 1997), 510*np*

Hill v. California, 401 U.S. 797, 91 S. Ct. 1106, 28 L. Ed. 2d 484 (1971), 146*np*, 220*np*

Hill v. Colorado, 530 U.S. 730, 120 S. Ct. 240, 147 L. Ed. 2d 597 (2000), 75*np*

Hoffa v. United States, supra note 19, 274*np*

United States v. Jacobsen, supra note 27 (postal package), 177*np*

United States v. Jacobsen, supra note 78, 286*np*

United States v. Jacobsen, 466 U.S. 109, 104 S. Ct. 1652, 80 L. Ed. 2d 85 (1984), 175*np*, 286*np*

United States v. Janis, 428 U.S. 433, 96 S. Ct. 3021, 49 L. Ed. 2d 1046 (1976), 258*np*

United States v. Jarrett, 338 F.3d 339 (4th Cir. 2003), 175*np*

United States v. Jeffers, 342 U.S. 48, 72 S. Ct. 93, 96 L. Ed. 59 (1951), 182*np*, 183*np*

United States v. Jerez, 108 F.3d 684 (7th Cir. 1997), 98*np*

United States v. J.H.H., 22 F.3d 821 (8th Cir. 1994), 59*np*

United States v. Jimenez, 419 F.3d 34 (1st Cir. 2005), 183*np*

United States v. Johnson, 467 F.2d 630 (2d Cir. 1972), 328*np*

United States v. Johnson, 990 F.2d 1129 (9th Cir. 1993), 189*np*

United States v. Johnson, 64 F.3d 1120, 1126 (8th Cir. 1995), cert. denied, 516 U.S. 1139, 116 S. Ct. 971, 133 L. Ed. 2d 891 (1996), 334*np*

United States v. Johnson, 42 Fed. Appx. 959 (9th Cir. 2002), 290*np*

United States v. Johnson, 196 F. Supp. 2d 795 (N.D. Iowa 2002), 355*np*

United States v. Johns, 469 U.S. 478, 105 S. Ct. 881, 83 L. Ed. 2d 890 (1985), 227*np*

United States v. Jones, 234 F.3d 234 (5th Cir. 2000), 129*np*

United States v. Jones, 524 F.2d 834 (D.C. Cir. 1975), 435*np*

United States v. Jones, 543 F.2d 627 (8th Cir.), cert. denied, 429 U.S. 1051, 97 S. Ct. 763, 50 L. Ed. 2d 767 (1976), 199*np*

United States v. Jones, 364 F. Supp. 2d 1303 (D. Utah 2005), 307*np*

United States v. Jones, 451 F. Supp. 2d 71 (D.D.C. 2006), 294*np*, 306*np*

United States v. Jones, supra note 123, 297*np*

United States v. Jones, supra note 177, 129*np*

United States v. Kahn, 415 U.S. 143, 94 S. Ct. 977, 39 L. Ed. 2d 225 (1974) (10th Cir. 2002), 296*np*

United States v. Karo, supra note 25, 273*np*

United States v. Karo, 468 U.S. 705, 104 S. Ct. 3296, 82 L. Ed. 2d 530 (1984), 272*np*

United States v. Khounsavanh, 113 F.3d 279 (1st Cir. 1997), 242*np*

United States v. Khoury, 901 F.2d 948 (11th Cir. 1990), 215*np*

United States v. Kimes, 246 F.3d 800 (6th Cir. 2001), 232*np*

United States v. Kim, 292 F.3d 969 (9th Cir. 2002), 334*np*

United States v. Kimoana, 383 F.3d 1215 (10th Cir. 2004), 182*np*

United States v. King, 227 F.3d 732 (6th Cir. 2000), 145*np*, 200*np*, 571–574

United States v. Knotts, 460 U.S. 276, 103 S. Ct. 1081, 75 L. Ed. 2d 55 (1983), 174*np*, 272*np*

United States v. Kobli, 172 F.2d 919 (3d Cir. 1949), 437*np*

United States v. Kokinda, supra note 117, 69*np*, 70*np*, 76*np*

United States v. Kokinda, 497 U.S. 720, 110 S. Ct. 3115, 111 L. Ed. 2d 571 (1990), 68*np*

United States v. Koon, 34 F.3d 1416 (9th Cir. 1994), 494*np*

United States v. Lane, 909 F. 2d 895 (6th Cir. 1990), 119*np*

United States v. Langley, 848 F.2d 152 (11th Cir. 1988), 349*np*

United States v. Lanier, 520 U.S. 259, 117 S. Ct. 1219, 137 L. Ed. 2d 432 (1997), 31*np*

United States v. Lanza, supra note 12, 430*np*

United States v. Lanza, 260 U.S. 377, 43 S. Ct. 141, 67 L. Ed. 314 (1922), 425*np*

United States v. LeBrun, 306 F.3d 545 (8th Cir. 2002), 321*np*

United States v. Lee, 359 F.3d 194 (3d Cir. 2004), 274*np*, 283*np*, 614–617

United States v. Lee, supra note 63, 283*np*

United States v. Leon, supra note 139, 251*np*

United States v. Leon, supra note 372, 254*np*

United States v. Leon, 468 U.S. 897, 104 S. Ct. 3405, 82 L. Ed. 2d 677 (1984), 201*np*, 254*np*

United States v. Leon, 468 U.S. 897, 906, 104 S. Ct. 3405, 3411, 82 L. Ed. 2d 677 (1984), 325*np*

United States v. Leon, 468 U.S. 897, 914, 104 S. Ct. 3405, 3416, 82 L. Ed. 2d 677 (1984), 143*np*

United States v. Leshuk, 65 F. 3d 1105 (4th Cir. 1995), 190*np*

Index

Note: Page numbers followed by *b* indicate boxes, *f* indicate figures.